GATE PREP SERIES

GATE

Graduate Aptitude Test in Engineering

2021

Topic-wise
Previous Solved Papers

31 Years'
Solved Papers

Computer Science & Information Technology

G. K. PUBLICATIONS (P) LTD.

CL MEDIA (P) LTD.

Edition : 2021

ISBN : 978-93-89718-69-0

Typeset by : *CL Media DTP Unit*

Administrative and Production Offices

Published by : CL Media (P) Ltd.

A-45, Mohan Cooperative Industrial Area,
Near Mohan Estate Metro Station,
New Delhi - 110044

Marketed by : G.K. Publications (P) Ltd.

A-45, Mohan Cooperative Industrial Area,
Near Mohan Estate Metro Station,
New Delhi - 110044

For product information :

Visit ***www.gkpublications.com*** or email to ***gkp@gkpublications.com***

GATE
Computer Science &
Information Technology

Contents

Solved Papers (Topic-Wise)

Unit VI Algorithms

GATE

Graduate Aptitude Test in Engineering

IIT Institutes

GATE 2021 will be conducted by
Indian Institute of Technology, Mumbai

Indian Institute of Technology, Kharagpur

GATE 2020 conducted by
Indian Institute of Technology, Delhi

Indian Institute of Technology, Chennai

Indian Institute of Technology, Guwahati

Indian Institute of Technology, Roorkee

Indian Institute of Technology, Kanpur

Preface

Whether you want to work with esteemed PSUs including the Maharatna and Navratna companies or do your Masters from IITs and IISc, GATE is your entry to career and academic avenues post your graduation. Thousands of students write the GATE paper annually. The level of competition is fierce, owing to the increasing competition every year for a limited number of seats. If you are a serious aspirant, it is advisable to start preparing for GATE from the second year of your Graduation with the right books.

GK Publications has been the guiding force for GATE aspirants for the last 3 decades. Better known as the **"Publisher of Choice"** to students preparing for GATE and other technical test prep examinations in the country, we published the first set of books in 1994 when GATE exam, both objective and conventional, was conducted in the paper and pencil environment and used as a checkpoint for entry to postgraduate courses in IITs and IISCs. At that time, students had little access to technology and relied mainly on instructor-led learning followed by practice with books available for these examinations.

A lot has changed since then!

Today, GATE is conducted in an online-only mode with multiple choice and numerical based questions.The exam pattern too has evolved over the years. Instead of theory, the questions today test a student's basic understanding and his capacity to put fundamentals to practical applications.The exam only rewards those with a concrete foundational clarity of basics.

We, at GKP, have also embraced change. Today, our preparatory manuals are not mere books but torchbearers in your GATE preparation journey. We understand that tackling the syllabus one chapter at a time is not only easy but also allows students to cope with the looming exam pressure. A major game changer is the habit to practice and solve previous year questions and this is why, our **GATE 2021 Topic-wise Solved Papers of Computer Science and Information Technology** is your best bet to be GATE READY by 2021!

The entire book has been divided into 11 units covering 30 years' GATE papers from 1990 to 2020 to facilitate your practice and subsequent learning. These units are divided into chapters which are further segmented into topics and eventually, the break-up is in a year-wise format. The questions carry detailed answers, supported by in-depth explanations and diagrams.

Each chapter carries detailed analysis of 5 previous years' solved papers (all sets) so that you are well-versed with the latest exam pattern and how it has evolved over time. Both MCQs and Numerical have been explained in a lucid and detailed fashion, so that you take your preparation forward - one question at a time.

With each question, its marks' weightage has also been given so that you can gauge the level of question and make judicious use of your time.

Today's students have easy access to technology and the concept of a monologue within the classroom has changed to dialogue where students come prepared with concepts and then discuss topics. We have launched a web portal and mobile app to help you take your preparation on the go - so that you learn, revise and practice mock tests online.

The mobile app provides access to video lectures, short tests and provides regular updates about the exam. The web portal in addition to what is available on the app provides full-length mock tests to mimic the actual exam to help you gauge your level of preparedness. The combination of practice content in print, video lectures, and short and full-length tests on mobile and web make this product complete courseware for GATE preparation.

We also know that improvement is a never-ending process and hence we welcome your suggestions and feedback or spelling and technical errors if any. Please write to us at gkp@gkpublications.com

We hope that our small effort will help you prepare well for the examination.

We wish you all the best!

Team GKP

About GATE

The Graduate Aptitude Test in Engineering (GATE) conducted by IISc and IITs has emerged as one of the bench mark tests for engineering and science aptitude in facilitating admissions for higher education (M.Tech./Ph.D.) in IITs, IISc and various other Institutes/Universities/ Laboratories in India. With the standard and high quality of the GATE examination in 23 disciplines of engineering and science subjects, it identifies the candidate's understanding of a subject and aptitude and eligibility for higher studies. During the last few years, GATE score is also being used as one of the criteria for recruitment in Government Organizations such as Cabinet Secretariat, and National/State Public Sector Undertakings in India. Because of the importance of the GATE examination, the number of candidates taking up GATE exams has increased tremendously. GATE exams are conducted by the IITs and IISc as a computer based test having multiple choice questions and numerical answer type questions. The questions are mostly fundamental, concept based and thought provoking. From 2017 onwards GATE Exam is being held in Bangladesh, Ethiopia, Nepal, Singapore, Sri Lanka and United Arab Emirates. An Institute with various nationalities in its campus widens the horizons of an academic environment. A foreign student brings with him/her a great diversity, culture and wisdom to share. Many GATE qualified candidates are paid scholarships/assistantship, especially funded by Ministry of Human Resources Development, Government of India and by other Ministries. Indian Institute of Technology Bombay is the Organizing Institute for GATE 2021.

Why GATE?

Admission to Post Graduate and Doctoral Programmes

Admission to postgraduate programmes with MHRD and some other government scholarships/ assistantships in engineering colleges/institutes is open to those who qualify through GATE. GATE qualified candidates with Bachelor's degree in Engineering/Technology/Architecture or Master's degree in any branch of Science/Mathematics/Statistics/Computer Applications are eligible for admission to Master/Doctoral programmes in Engineering/Technology/Architecture as well as for Doctoral programmes in relevant branches of Science with MHRD or other government scholarships/assistantships. Candidates with Master's degree in Engineering/ Technology/Architecture may seek admission to relevant Ph.D programmes with scholarship/ assistantship without appearing in the GATE examination.

Financial Assistance

A valid GATE score is essential for obtaining financial assistance during Master's programs and direct Doctoral programs in Engineering/Technology/Architecture, and Doctoral programs in relevant branches of Science in Institutes supported by the MHRD or other Government agencies. As per the directives of the MHRD, the following procedure is to be adopted for admission to the post-graduate programs (Master's and Doctoral) with MHRD scholarship/ assistantship. Depending upon the norms adopted by a specific institute or department of the Institute, a candidate may be admitted directly into a course based on his/her performance in GATE only **or** based on his/her performance in GATE **and** an admission test/interview conducted by the department to which he/she has applied **and/or** the candidate's academic record. If the candidate is to be selected through test/interview for post-graduate programs, a minimum of

70% weightage will be given to the performance in GATE and the remaining 30% weightage will be given to the candidate's performance in test/interview and/or academic record, as per MHRD guidelines. The admitting institutes could however prescribe a minimum passing percentage of marks in the test/interview. Some colleges/institutes specify GATE qualification as the mandatory requirement even for admission without MHRD scholarship/assistantship. To avail of the financial assistance (scholarship), the candidate must first secure admission to a program in these Institutes, by a procedure that could vary from institute to institute. Qualification in GATE is also a minimum requirement to apply for various fellowships awarded by many Government organizations. Candidates are advised to seek complete details of admission procedures and availability of MHRD scholarship/assistantship from the concerned admitting institution. The criteria for postgraduate admission with scholarship/assistantship could be different for different institutions. The management of the post-graduate scholarship/ assistantship is also the responsibility of the admitting institution. Similarly, reservation of seats under different categories is as per the policies and norms prevailing at the admitting institution and Government of India rules. *GATE offices will usually not entertain any enquiry about admission, reservation of seats and/or award of scholarship/assistantship.*

PSU Recruitments

As many as 37 PSUs are using GATE score for recruitment. It is likely that more number of PSUs may start doing so by next year. Below is the list of PSUs:

MDL, BPCL, GAIL, NLC LTD, CEL, Indian Oil, HPCL, NBPC, NECC, BHEL, WBSEDCL, NTPC, ONGC, Oil India, Power Grid, Cabinet Secretariat, Govt. of India, BAARC, NFL, IPR, PSPCL, PSTCL, DRDO, OPGC Ltd., THDC India Ltd., BBNL, RITES, IRCON, GHECL, NHAI, KRIBHCO, Mumbai Railway Vikas Corporation Ltd. (MRVC Ltd.), National Textile Corporation, Coal India Ltd., BNPM, AAI, NALCO, EdCIL India.

Important :

1. Admissions in IITs/IISc or other Institutes for M.Tech./Ph.D. through GATE scores shall be advertised separately by the Institutes and GATE does not take the responsibility of admissions.
2. Cabinet Secretariat has decided to recruit officers for the post of Senior Field Officer (Tele) (From GATE papers of EC, CS, PH), Senior Research Officer (Crypto) (From GATE papers of EC, CS, MA), Senior Research Officer (S&T) (From GATE papers EC, CS, CY, PH, AE, BT) in the Telecommunication Cadre, Cryptographic Cadre and Science & Technology Unit respectively of Cabinet Secretariat. The details of the scheme of recruitment shall be published in National Newspaper/Employment News by the concerned authority.
3. Some PSUs in India have expressed their interest to utilize GATE scores for their recruitment purpose. The Organizations who intend to utilize GATE scores shall make separate advertisement for this purpose in Newspapers etc.

Who Can Appear for GATE?

Eligibility for GATE

Before starting the application process, the candidate must ensure that he/she meets the eligibility criteria of GATE given in Table.

Eligibility Criteria for GATE 2021

Qualifying Degree	Qualifying Degree/Examination (Descriptive)	Description of Eligible Candidates	Year of qualification cannot be later than
B.E./B.Tech./ B.Pharm.	Bachelor's degree holders in Engineering/ Technology (4 years after 10+2 or 3 years after B.Sc./Diploma in Engineering/ Technology)	Currently in the final year or already completed	2021
B. Arch.	Bachelor's degree holders of Architecture (Five years course)	Currently in the final year or already completed	2021
B.Sc. (Research)/ B.S.	Bachelor's degree in Science (Post-Diploma/4 years after 10+2)	Currently in the 4th year or already completed	2021
M. Sc./ M.A./MCA or equivalent	Master's degree in any branch of Science/Mathematics / Statistics / Computer Applications or equivalent	Currently in the final year or already completed	2021
Int. M.E. / M.Tech. (Post-B.Sc.)	Integrated Master's degree programs in Engineering / Technology (Four year program)	Currently in the 2nd/3rd/4th year or already completed	2023
Int. M.E./ M.Tech. or Dual Degree(after Diploma or 10+2)	Integrated Master's degree program or Dual Degree program in Engineering / Technology (Five year program)	Currently in the 4th/5th year or already completed	2022
Int. M.Sc./ Int. B.S.-M.S.	Integrated M.Sc. or Five year integrated B.S.-M.S. program	Currently in the final year or already completed	2021
Professional Society Examinations (equivalent to B.E./B.Tech./B.Arch.)	B.E./B.Tech./B.Arch. equivalent examinations, of Professional Societies, recognized by MHRD/UPSC/AICTE (e.g., AMIE by Institution of Engineers-India, AMICE by the Institute of Civil Engineers-India)	Completed section A or equivalent of such professional courses	NA

In case a candidate has passed one of the qualifying examinations as mentioned above in 2020 or earlier, the candidate has to submit the degree certificate / provisional certificate / course completion certificate / professional certificate / membership certificate issued by the society or institute. In case, the candidate is expected to complete one of the qualifying criteria in 2021 or later as mentioned above, he/she has to submit a certificate from Principal or a copy of marks card for section A of AMIE.

Certificate From Principal

Candidates who have to submit a certificate from their college Principal have to obtain one from his/her institution beforehand and upload the same during the online submission of the application form.

Candidates With Backlogs

Candidates, who have appeared in the final semester/year exam in 2021, but with a backlog (arrears/failed subjects) in any of the papers in their qualifying degree should upload a copy of any one of the mark sheets of the final year,

OR

obtain a declaration from their Principal along with the signature and seal beforehand and upload the same during the online submission of the application form.

GATE Structure

Structure of GATE

For the GATE examination, a candidate can apply for only one of the 25 papers listed in Tables below. The syllabus for each of the papers is given separately. Making a choice of the appropriate paper during GATE application is the responsibility of the candidate. Some guidelines in this respect are suggested below.

The candidate is expected to appear in a paper appropriate to the discipline of his/her qualifying degree. However, the candidate can choose any paper according to his/her admission plan, keeping in mind the eligibility criteria of the institutions in which he/she wishes to seek admission. For more details regarding the admission criteria in any particular institute, the candidate is advised to refer to the website of that institute.

List of GATE Papers and Corresponding Codes

Paper	Code	Paper	Code
Aerospace Engineering	AE	Geology and Geophysics	GG
Agricultural Engineering	AG	Instrumentation Engineering	IN
Architecture and Planning	AR	Mathematics	MA
Biomedical Engineering	BM	Mechanical Engineering	ME
Biotechnology	BT	Mining Engineering	MN
Civil Engineering	CE	Metallurgical Engineering	MT
Chemical Engineering	CH	Petroleum Engineering	PE
Computer Science and Information Technology	CS	Physics	PH
Chemistry	CY	Production and Industrial Engineering	PI
Electronics and Communication Engineering	EC	Statistics	ST
Electrical Engineering	EE	Textile Engineering and Fibre Science	TF
Ecology and Evolution	EY	Engineering Sciences	XE*
		Life Sciences	XL**

*XE Paper Sections	Code	**XL Paper Sections	Code
Engineering Mathematics (Compulsory)	A	Chemistry (Compulsory)	P
Fluid Mechanics	B	Biochemistry	Q
Materials Science	C	Botany	R
Solid Mechanics	D	Microbiology	S
Thermodynamics	E	Zoology	T
Polymer Science and Engineering	F	Food Technology	U
Food Technology	G		
Atmospheric and Oceanic Sciences	H		

*XE (Engineering Sciences) and **XL (Life Sciences) papers are of general nature and will comprise of Sections listed in the above table. More detailed explanation is given as following pages.

General Aptitude Questions

All the papers will have a few questions that test the General Aptitude (Language and Analytical Skills), apart from the core subject of the paper.

XE Paper

A candidate appearing in the XE paper has to answer the following

1. Section A – Engineering Mathematics
2. GA – General Aptitude
3. Any two of XE sections B to H

The choice of two sections from B to H can be made during the examination after viewing the questions. Only two optional sections can be answered at a time. A candidate wishing to change midway of the examination to another optional section must first choose to deselect one of the previously chosen optional sections (B to H).

XL Paper

A candidate appearing in the XL paper has to answer the following

1. Section P – Chemistry

2. GA – General Aptitude

3. Any two of XL sections Q to U

The choice of two sections from Q to U can be made during the examination after viewing the questions. Only two optional sections can be answered at a time. A candidate wishing to change midway of the examination to another optional section must first choose to deselect one of the previously chosen optional sections (Q to U).

Duration and Examination Type

The GATE examination consists of a single paper of **3-hour** duration that contains **65** questions carrying a maximum of **100 marks**. The question paper will consist of both multiple choice questions (MCQ) and numerical answer type (NAT) questions. The pattern of question papers is discussed in following paragraphs.

The examination for all the papers will be carried out in an ONLINE Computer Based Test (CBT) mode where the candidates will be shown the questions in a random sequence on a computer screen. The candidates are required to either select the answer (for MCQ type) or enter the answer for numerical answer type question using a mouse on a virtual keyboard (keyboard of the computer will be disabled). Each candidate will be provided with a scribble pad for rough work. The scribble pad has to be returned after the examination. At the end of the 3-hour window, the computer will automatically close the screen from further actions.

Pattern of Question Papers

In all the papers, there will be a total of 65 questions carrying 100 marks, out of which 10 questions carrying a total of 15 marks will be on General Aptitude (GA).

In the papers bearing the codes AE, AG, BT, CE, CH, CS, EC, EE, IN, ME, MN, MT, PE, PI, TF and XE, the Engineering Mathematics will carry around **15% of the total marks**, the General Aptitude section will carry **15% of the total marks** and the **remaining 70% of the total marks** is devoted to the subject of the paper.

In the papers bearing the codes AR, CY, EY, GG, MA, PH and XL, the General Aptitude section will carry **15% of the total marks** and the **remaining 85% of the total marks** is devoted to the subject of the paper.

GATE 2020 would contain questions of two different types in various papers:

(*i*) **Multiple Choice Questions (MCQ)** carrying 1 or 2 marks each in all papers and sections. These questions are objective in nature, and each will have a choice of four answers, out of which the candidate has to mark the correct answer(s).

(*ii*) **Numerical Answer Questions** of 1 or 2 marks each in all papers and sections. For these questions the answer is a real number, to be entered by the candidate using the virtual keypad. No choices will be shown for this type of questions.

Marking Scheme

For **1-mark** multiple-choice questions, **1/3** mark will be deducted for a wrong answer. Likewise, for **2-mark** multiple-choice questions, **2/3** mark will be deducted for a wrong answer. **There is NO negative marking for numerical answer type questions.**

Consult syllabus before proceeding

General Aptitude (GA) Questions

In all papers, GA questions carry a total of **15 marks**. The GA section includes 5 questions carrying **1-mark** each (sub-total **5 marks**) and 5 questions carrying **2-marks** each (sub-total **10 marks**).

Question Papers other than GG, XE and XL

These papers would contain **25** questions carrying **1-mark** each (sub-total **25 marks**) and **30** questions carrying **2-marks** each (sub-total **60 marks**). The question paper will consist of questions of multiple choice and numerical answer type. For numerical answer questions, choices will not be given. Candidates have to enter the answer (which will be a real number, signed or unsigned, e.g., 25.06, – 25.06, 25, – 25 etc.) using a virtual keypad. An appropriate range will be considered while evaluating the numerical answer type questions so that the candidate is not penalized due to the usual round-off errors.

GG (Geology and Geophysics) Paper

Apart from the General Aptitude (GA) section, the GG question paper consists of two parts: Part A and Part B. Part A is common for all candidates. Part B contains two sections: Section 1 (Geology) and Section 2 (Geo-physics). Candidates will have to attempt questions in Part A and either Section 1 or Section 2 in Part B.

Part A consists of **25** multiple-choice questions carrying **1-mark** each (sub-total **25 marks** and some of these may be numerical answer type questions). Each section in Part B (Section 1 and Section 2) consists of **30** multiple choice questions carrying **2-marks** each (sub-total **60 marks** and some of these may be numerical answer type questions).

XE Paper (Engineering Sciences)

In XE paper, Engineering Mathematics section (Section A) is **compulsory**. This section contains **11** questions carrying a total of **15 marks**: 7 questions carrying **1-mark** each (sub-total **7 marks**), and 4 questions carrying **2-marks** each (sub-total **8 marks**). Some questions may be of numerical answer type questions.

Each of the other sections of the XE paper (Sections B through H) contains 22 questions carrying a total of **35 marks**: 9 questions carrying **1-mark** each (sub-total **9 marks**) and 13 questions carrying **2-marks** each (sub-total **26 marks**). Some questions may be of numerical answer type.

XL Paper (Life Sciences)

In XL paper, Chemistry section (Section P) is **compulsory**. This section contains **15** questions carrying a total of **25 marks**: 5 questions carrying **1-mark** each (sub-total **5 marks**) and 10 questions carrying **2-marks** each (sub-total **20 marks**). Some questions may be of numerical answer type.

Each of the other sections of the XL paper (Sections Q through U) contains 20 questions carrying a total of **30 marks**: 10 questions carrying **1-mark** each (sub-total **10 marks**) and 10 questions carrying **2-marks** each (sub-total **20 marks**). Some questions may be of numerical answer type.

Note on Negative Marking for Wrong Answers

For a wrong answer chosen for the **multiple choice questions** (MCQs), there would be negative marking. For **1-mark** multiple choice questions, **1/3** mark will be deducted for a wrong answer. Likewise, for **2-mark** multiple choice questions, **2/3** mark will be deducted for a wrong answer. However, there is **NO negative marking for a wrong answer in numerical answer type questions**.

GATE Score

After the evaluation of the answers, the raw marks obtained by a candidate will be converted to a normalized GATE Score.

The GATE score will be computed using the formula given below.

Calculation of Normalized Marks for CE, CS, EC, EE and ME papers (multi-session papers)

In GATE, examination for some papers may be conducted in multi-sessions. Hence, for these papers, a suitable normalization is applied to take into account any variation in the difficulty levels of the question papers across different sessions. The normalization is done based on the fundamental assumption that "in all multi-session GATE papers, the distribution of abilities of candidates is the same across all the sessions". This assumption is justified since the number of candidates appearing in multi-session papers in GATE is large and the procedure of allocation of session to candidates is random. Further it is also ensured that for the same multi-session paper, the number of candidates allotted in each session is of the same order of magnitude.

Based on the above, and considering various normalization methods, the committee arrived at the following formula for calculating the normalized marks for the multi-session papers.

Normalization mark of jth candidate in the ith session $\widehat{M_{ij}}$ is given by

$$\widehat{M_{ij}} = \frac{\bar{M}_t^g - M_q^g}{\bar{M}_{ti} - M_{iq}}(M_{ij} - M_{iq}) + M_q^g$$

where

M_{ij} : is the actual marks obtained by the jth candidate in i^{th} session

$\bar{M}_t^g$: is the average marks of the top 0.1% of the candidates considering all sessions

M_q^g : is the sum of mean and standard deviation marks of the candidates in the paper considering all sessions

$\bar{M}_{ti}$: is the average marks of the top 0.1% of the candidates in the ith session

M_{iq} : is the sum of the mean marks and standard deviation of the ith session

After evaluation of the answers, normalized marks based on the above formula will be calculated corresponding to the raw marks obtained by a candidate and the GATE Score will be calculated based on the normalized marks.

For all papers for which there is only one session, actual marks obtained will be used for calculating the GATE Score.

Calculation of GATE Score For All Papers

GATE 2020 score will be calculated using the formula

$$\text{GATE Score} = S_q + (S_t - S_q)\frac{(M - M_q)}{(\bar{M}_t - M_q)}$$

In the above formulae

M : marks obtained by the candidate (actual marks for single session papers and normalized marks for multi-session papers)

M_q : is the qualifying marks for general category candidate in the paper

$\bar{M}_t$: is the mean of marks of top 0.1% or top 10 (whichever is larger) of the candidates who appeared in the paper (in case of multi-session papers including all sessions)

S_q : 350, is the score assigned to M_q

S_t : 900, is the score assigned to $\bar{M}_t$

In the GATE 2020 score formula, M_q is usually 25 marks (out of 100) or + s, whichever is larger. Here μ is the mean and s is the standard deviation of marks of all the candidates who appeared in the paper.

After the declaration of results, GATE Scorecards can be downloaded by

(a) All SC/ST/PwD candidates whose marks are greater than or equal to the qualifying mark of SC/ST/PwD candidates in their respective papers, and

(b) All other candidates whose marks are greater than or equal to the qualifying mark of OBC (NCL) candidates in their respective papers.

There is no provision for the issue of hard copies of the GATE Scorecards

The GATE Committee has the authority to decide the qualifying mark/score for each GATE paper. In case any claim or dispute arises in respect of GATE, the Courts and Tribunals in Bangalore alone shall have the exclusive jurisdiction to entertain and settle any such dispute or claim.

candidates appearing in multi-session papers in GATE is large and the procedure of allocation of session to candidates is random. Further it is also ensured that for the same multi-session paper, the number of candidates allotted in each session is of the same order of magnitude.

Based on the above, and considering various normalization methods, the committee arrived at the following formula for calculating the normalized marks for the multi-session papers.

Normalization mark of j-th candidate in the i-th session $\hat{M}_{ij}$ is given by

$$\hat{M}_{ij} = \frac{\bar{M}_t^g - M_q^g}{\bar{M}_{ti} - M_{iq}}\left(M_{ij} - M_{iq}\right) + M_q^g$$

where,

M_{ij} is the actual marks obtained by the j-th candidate in i-th session

$\bar{M}_t^g$ is the average marks of the top 0.1% of the candidates considering all sessions

M_q^g is the sum of mean and standard deviation marks of the candidates in the paper considering all sessions

$\bar{M}_{ti}$ is the average marks of the top 0.1% of the candidates in the i-th session

M_{iq} is the sum of the mean marks and standard deviation of the i-th session

After evaluation of the answers, normalized marks based on the above formula will be calculated corresponding to the raw marks obtained by a candidate and the GATE Score will be calculated based on the normalized marks.

For all papers for which there is only one session, actual marks obtained will be used for calculating the GATE Score.

Calculation of GATE Score for All Papers

GATE 2020 score will be calculated using the formula

$$\text{GATE Score} = S_q + (S_t - S_q)\frac{(M - M_q)}{(\bar{M}_t - M_q)}$$

In the above formula,

M = marks obtained by the candidate (actual marks for single session papers and normalized marks for multi-session papers)

M_q = is the qualifying marks for general category candidate in the paper

$\bar{M}_t$ = is the mean of marks of top 0.1% or top 10 (whichever is larger) of the candidates who appeared in the paper (in case of multi-session papers including all sessions)

S_q = 350, is the score assigned to M_q

S_t = 900, is the score assigned to $\bar{M}_t$

In the GATE 2020 score formula, M_q is usually 25 marks (out of 100) or $\mu + \sigma$, whichever is larger. Here μ is the mean and σ is the standard deviation of marks of all the candidates who appeared in the paper.

After the declaration of results, GATE Scorecards can be downloaded by

(a) All SC/ST/PwD candidates whose marks are greater than or equal to the qualifying mark of SC/ST/PwD candidates in their respective papers, and

(b) All other candidates whose marks are greater than or equal to the qualifying mark of OBC (NCL) candidates in their respective papers.

There is no provision for the issue of hard copies of the GATE Scorecards.

The GATE Committee has the authority to decide the qualifying mark/score for each GATE paper. In case any claim or dispute arises in respect of GATE, the Courts and Tribunals in Bangalore alone shall have the exclusive jurisdiction to entertain and settle any such dispute or claim.

GATE Syllabus

Section 1: Engineering Mathematics

Discrete Mathematics

Propositional and first order logic. Sets, relations, functions, partial orders and lattices. Groups. Graphs: connectivity, matching, coloring. Combinatorics: counting, recurrence relations, generating functions.

Linear Algebra

Matrices, determinants, system of linear equations, eigenvalues and eigenvectors, LU decomposition.

Calculus

Limits, continuity and differentiability. Maxima and minima. Mean value theorem. Integration.

Probability

Random variables. Uniform, normal, exponential, poisson and binomial distributions. Mean, median, mode and standard deviation. Conditional probability and Bayes theorem.

Section 2: Digital Logic

Boolean algebra. Combinational and sequential circuits. Minimization. Number representations and computer arithmetic (fixed and floating point).

Section 3: Computer Organization and Architecture

Machine instructions and addressing modes. ALU, data-path and control unit. Instruction pipelining. Memory hierarchy: cache, main memory and secondary storage; I/O interface (interrupt and DMA mode).

Section 4: Programming and Data Structures

Programming in C. Recursion. Arrays, stacks, queues, linked lists, trees, binary search trees, binary heaps, graphs.

Section 5: Algorithms

Searching, sorting, hashing. Asymptotic worst case time and space complexity. Algorithm design techniques: greedy, dynamic programming and divide - and - conquer. Graph search, minimum spanning trees, shortest paths.

Section 6: Theory of Computation

Regular expressions and finite automata. Context-free grammars and push-down automata. Regular and contex-free languages, pumping lemma. Turing machines and undecidability.

Section 7: Compiler Design

Lexical analysis, parsing, syntax-directed translation. Runtime environments. Intermediate code generation.

Section 8: Operating System

Processes, threads, inter-process communication, concurrency and synchronization. Deadlock. CPU scheduling. Memory management and virtual memory. File systems.

Section 9: Databases

ER-model. Relational model: relational algebra, tuple calculus, SQL. Integrity constraints, normal forms. File organization, indexing (e.g., B and B+ trees). Transactions and concurrency control.

Section 10: Computer Networks

Concept of layering. LAN technologies (Ethernet). Flow and error control techniques, switching. IPv4/IPv6, routers and routing algorithms (distance vector, link state). TCP/UDP and sockets, congestion control. Application layer protocols (DNS, SMTP, POP, FTP, HTTP). Basics of Wi-Fi. Network security: authentication, basics of public key and private key cryptography, digital signatures and certificates, firewalls.

SOLVED PAPER - 2020

INSTRUCTIONS

1. Total of 65 questions carrying 100 marks, out of which 10 questions carrying a total of 15 marks are in General Aptitude (GA)
2. The Engineering Mathematics will carry around **15% of the total marks,** the General Aptitude section will carry **15% of the total marks** and the **remaining 70% of the total marks.**
3. **Types of Questions**
   (*a*) **Multiple Choice Questions (MCQ)** carrying 1 or 2 marks each in all papers and sections. These questions are objective in nature, and each will have a choice of four options, out of which the candidate has to mark the correct answer(s).
   (*b*) **Numerical Answer Questions** of 1 or 2 marks each in all papers and sections. For these questions the answer is a real number, to be entered by the candidate using the virtual keypad. No choices will be shown for these type of questions.
4. For **1-mark** multiple-choice questions, **1/3 marks** will be deducted for a wrong answer. Likewise, for **2-marks** multiple-choice questions, **2/3** marks will be deducted for a wrong answer. There is no negative marking for numerical answer type questions.

Chapter-Wise Analysis

#	Chapters	Marks		
		1	2	Total
1	General Aptitude	5	5	15
2	Engineering Mathematics	3	8	19
3	Theory of Computation	1	1	3
4	Digital Logic	2	2	4
5	Computer Organization & Architecture	4	5	14
6	Programming & Data Structures	3	3	9
7	Algorithm	2	2	6

#	Chapters	Marks		
		1	2	Total
8	Compiler Design	4	2	8
9	Operating System	2	4	10
10	Data Bases	2	3	8
11	Computer Networks	2	1	4
12	* Software Engineering	0	0	0
13	* Web Technology	0	0	0

GENERAL APTITUDE (GA)

Q. 1 to Q. 5 : Carry One Mark Each.

1. Raman is confident of speaking English _______ six months as he has been practising regularly _______ the last three weeks.

(a) during, for (b) for, since

(c) for, in (d) within, for

2. His knowledge of the subject was excellent but his classroom performance was _______.

(a) extremely poor (b) good

(c) desirable (d) praiseworthy

3. Select the word that fits the analogy:

Cook : Cook :: Fly : _______

(a) Flyer (b) Flying

(c) Flew (d) Flighter

4. The dawn of the 21st century witnessed the melting glaciers oscillating between giving too much and too little to billions of people who depend on them for fresh water. The UN climate report estimates that without deep cuts to man-made emissions, at least 30% of the northern hemisphere's surface permafrost could melt by the end of the century. Given this situation of imminent global exodus of billions of people displaced by rising seas, nation-states need to rethink their carbon footprint for political concerns, if not for environmental ones.

Which one of the following statements can be inferred from the given passage?

(a) Nation-states do not have environmental concerns.

(b) Nation-states are responsible for providing fresh water to billions of people.

(c) Billions of people are responsible for man-made emissions.

(d) Billions of people are affected by melting glaciers.

5. There are multiple routes to reach from node 1 to node 2, as shown in the network.

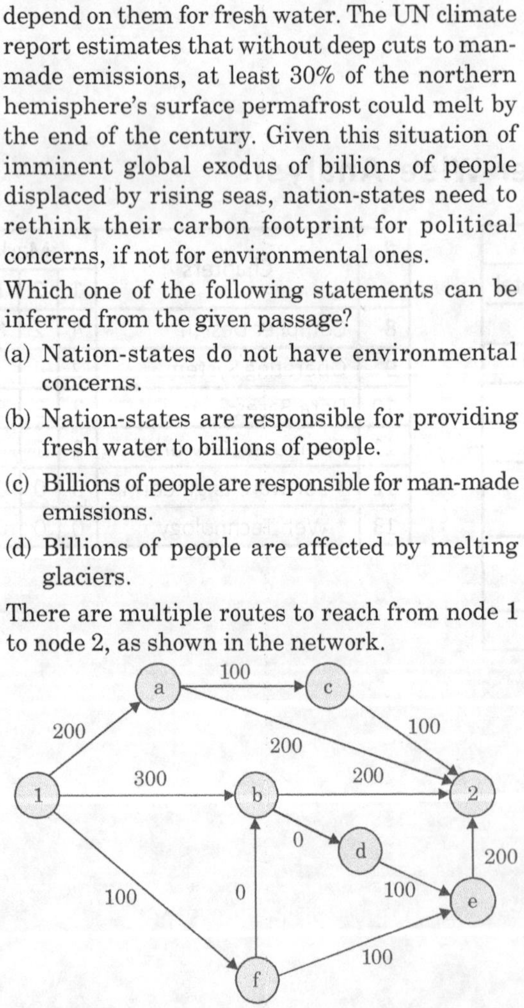

The cost of travel on an edge between two nodes is given in rupees. Nodes 'a', 'b', 'c', 'd', 'e' and 'f' are toll booths. The toll price at toll booths marked 'a' and 'e' is Rs. 200 and is Rs. 100 for the other toll booths. Which is the cheapest route from node 1 to node 2?

(a) 1-a-c-2 (b) 1-f-b-2

(c) 1-b-2 (d) 1-f-e-2

Q. 6 to Q. 10 : Carry Two Marks Each.

6. Goods and Services Tax (GST) is an indirect tax introduced in India in 2017 that is imposed on the supply of goods and services, and it subsumes all indirect taxes except few. It is a destination-based tax imposed on goods and services used, and it is not imposed at the point of origin from where goods come. GST also has a few components specific to state governments, central government and Union Territories (UTs).

Which one of the following statements can be inferred from the given passage?

(a) GST is imposed on the production of goods and services.

(b) GST includes all indirect taxes.

(c) GST does not have a component specific to UT.

(d) GST is imposed at the point of usage of goods and services.

7. If P = 3, R = 27, T = 243, then Q + S = _______.

(a) 40 (b) 80

(c) 90 (d) 110

8. The figure below shows an annular ring with outer and inner radii as b and a, respectively. The annular space has been painted in the form of blue colour circles touching the outer and inner periphery of annular space. If maximum n number of circles can be painted, then the unpainted area available in annular space is _____.

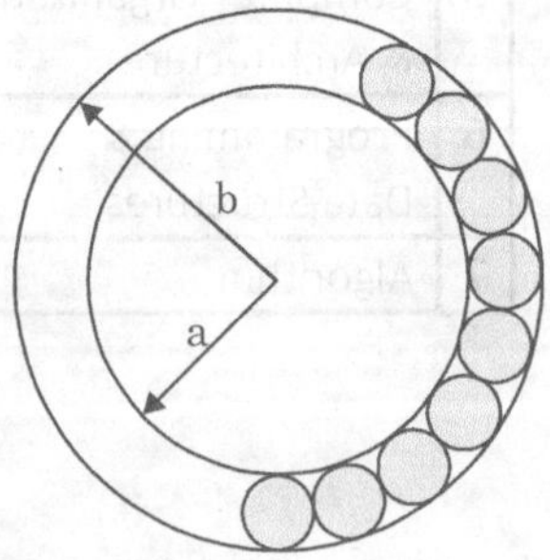

(a) $\pi\left[(b^2 - a^2) - \frac{n}{4}(b - a)^2\right]$

(b) $\pi\ [(b^2 - a^2) - n\,(b - a)^2]$

(c) $\pi\left[(b^2 - a^2) + \frac{n}{4}(b - a)^2\right]$

(d) $\pi[(b^2 - a^2) + n(b - a)^2]$

9. Two straight lines are drawn perpendicular to each other in X-Y plane. If α and β are the acute angles the straight lines make with the X-axis, then $\alpha + \beta$ is ________.

(a) 60° (b) 90°
(c) 120° (d) 180°

10. The total revenue of a company during 2014-2018 is shown in the bar graph. If the total expenditure of the company in each year is 500 million rupees, then the aggregate profit or loss (in percentage) on the total expenditure of the company during 2014-2018 is ________.

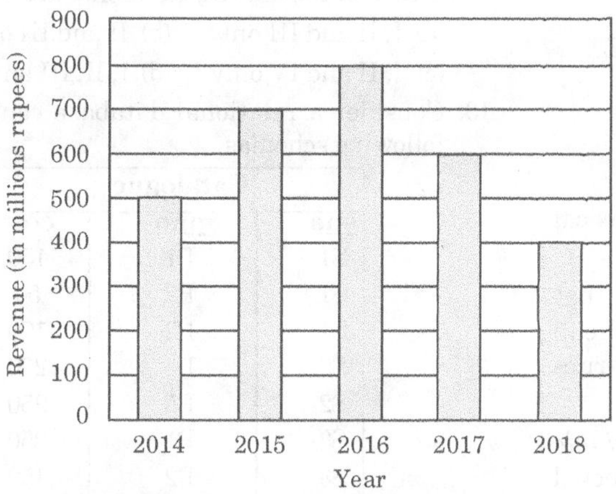

(a) 16.67% profit (b) 16.67% loss
(c) 20% profit (d) 20% loss

COMPUTER SCIENCE & IT

Q. 1 to Q. 25 : Carry One Mark Each.

1. Consider the functions:

I. e^{-x}

II. $x^2 - \sin x$

III. $\sqrt{x^3 + 1}$

Which of the above functions is/are increasing everywhere in [0, 1]?

(a) III only (b) II only
(c) II and III only (d) I and III only

2. For parameters a and b, both of which are $\omega(1)$, $T(n) = T(n^{1/a}) + 1$, and $T(b) = 1$. Then T (n) is

(a) $\Theta(\log_a \log_b n)$ (b) $\Theta(\log_{ab} n)$
(c) $\Theta(\log_b \log_a n)$ (d) $\Theta(\log_2 \log_2 n)$

3. Consider the following statements:

I. Daisy chaining is used to assign priorities in attending interrupts.

II. When a device raises a vectored interrupt, the CPU does polling to identify the source of interrupt.

III. In polling, the CPU periodically checks the status bits to know if any device needs its attention.

IV. During DMA, both the CPU and DMA controller can be bus masters at the same time.

Which of the above statements is/are TRUE?

(a) I and II only
(b) I and IV only
(c) I and III only
(d) III only

4. Consider the following data path diagram.

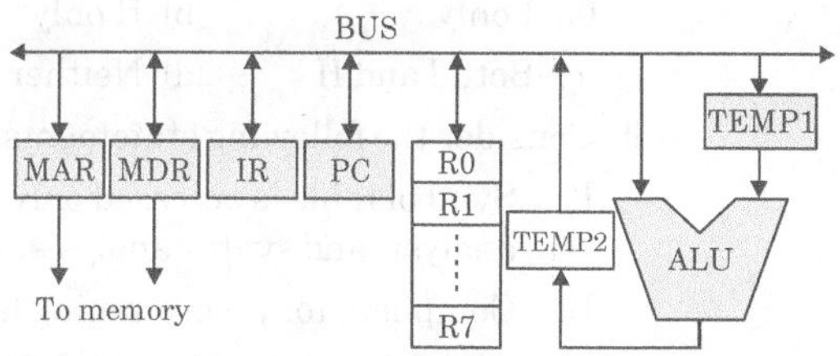

Consider an instruction: R0 ← R1 + R2. The following steps are used to execute it over the given data path. Assume that PC is incremented appropriately. The subscripts r and w indicate read and write operations, respectively.

1. $R2_r$, $TEMP1_r$, ALU_{add}, $TEMP2_w$
2. $R1_r$, $TEMP1_w$
3. PC_r, MAR_w, MEM_r
4. $TEMP2_r$, $R0_w$
5. MDR_r, IR_w

Which one of the following is the correct order of execution of the above steps?

(a) 2, 1, 4, 5, 3 (b) 1, 2, 4, 3, 5
(c) 3, 5, 2, 1, 4 (d) 3, 5, 1, 2, 4

5. The preorder traversal of a binary search tree is 15, 10, 12, 11, 20, 18, 16, 19.

Which one of the following is the postorder traversal of the tree?

(a) 10, 11, 12, 15, 16, 18, 19, 20
(b) 11, 12, 10, 16, 19, 18, 20, 15
(c) 20, 19, 18, 16, 15, 12, 11, 10
(d) 19, 16, 18, 20, 11, 12, 10, 15

6. What is the worst case time complexity of inserting n^2 elements into an AVL-tree with n elements initially?

(a) $\Theta(n^4)$ (b) $\Theta(n^2)$
(c) $\Theta(n^2 \log n)$ (d) $\Theta(n^3)$

7. Which one of the following regular expressions represents the set of all binary strings with an odd number of 1's?

(a) ((0 + 1)* 1(0 + 1)*1)*10*

(b) (0*10*10*)*0*1

(c) 10* (0*10*10*)*

(d) (0*10*10*)*10*

8. Consider the following statements.

I. If $L_1 \cup L_2$ is regular, then both L_1 and L_2 must be regular.

II. The class of regular languages is closed under infinite union.

Which of the above statements is/are TRUE?

(a) I only (b) II only

(c) Both I and II (d) Neither I nor II

9. Consider the following statements.

I. Symbol table is accessed only during lexical analysis and syntax analysis.

II. Compilers for programming languages that support recursion necessarily need heap storage for memory allocation in the run-time environment.

III. Errors violating the condition *'any variable must be declared before its use'* are detected during syntax analysis.

Which of the above statements is/are TRUE?

(a) I only (b) I and III only

(c) II only (d) None of I, II and III

10. Consider the language $L = \{a^n \mid n \geq 0\} \cup \{a^nb^n \mid n \geq 0\}$ and the following statements.

I. L is deterministic context-free.

II. L is context-free but not deterministic context-free.

III. L is not LL(k)for any k.

Which of the above statements is/are TRUE?

(a) I only (b) II only

(c) I and III only (d) III only

11. Consider allocation of memory to a new process. Assume that none of the existing holes in the memory will exactly fit the process's memory requirement. Hence, a new hole of smaller size will be created if allocation is made in any of the existing holes. Which one of the following statements is TRUE?

(a) The hole created by first fit is always larger than the hole created by next fit.

(b) The hole created by worst fit is always larger than the hole created by first fit.

(c) The hole created by best fit is never larger than the hole created by first fit.

(d) The hole created by next fit is never larger than the hole created by best fit.

12. Consider the following statements about process state transitions for a system using preemptive scheduling.

I. A running process can move to ready state.

II. A ready process can move to running state.

III. A blocked process can move to running state.

IV. A blocked process can move to ready state.

Which of the above statements are TRUE?

(a) I, II and III only (b) II and III only

(c) I, II and IV only (d) I, II, III and IV

13. Consider a relational database containing the following schemas.

Catalogue

sno	pno	cost
S1	P1	150
S1	P2	50
S1	P3	100
S2	P4	200
S2	P5	250
S3	P1	250
S3	P2	150
S3	P5	300
S3	P4	250

Suppliers

sno	sname	location
S1	M/s Royal furniture	Delhi
S1	M/s Balaji furniture	Bangalore
S3	M/s Premium furniture	Chennai

Parts

pno	sname	part_spec
P1	Table	Wood
P2	Chair	Wood
P3	Table	Steel
P4	Almirah	Steel
P5	Almirah	Wood

The primary key of each table is indicated by underlining the constituent fields.

```
SELECT    s.sno, s.sname
FROM      Suppliers s,   Catalogue c
WHERE     s.no = c.sno AND
          cost> (SELECT AVG (cost)
                FROM Catalogue
                WHERE pno =  `P4´
                GROUP BY pno);
```

The number of rows returned by the above SQL query is

(a) 4 (b) 5

(c) 0 (d) 2

14. Which one of the following is used to represent the supporting many-one relationships of a weak entity set in an entity-relationship diagram?

(a) Diamonds with double/bold border

(b) Rectangles with double/bold border

(c) Ovals with double/bold border

(d) Ovals that contain underlined identifiers

15. Consider the following statements about the functionality of an IP based router.

I. A router does not modify the IP packets during forwarding.

II. It is not necessary for a router to implement any routing protocol.

III. A router should reassemble IP fragments if the MTU of the outgoing link is larger than the size of the incoming IP packet.

Which of the above statements is/are TRUE?

(a) I and II only (b) I only

(c) II and III only (d) II only

16. What is the worst case time complexity of inserting n elements into an empty linked list, if the linked list needs to be maintained in sorted order?

(a) $\Theta(n)$ (b) $\Theta(n \log n)$

(c) $\Theta(n^2)$ (d) $\Theta(1)$

17. Let R be the set of all binary relations on the set {1,2,3}. Suppose a relation is chosen from R at random. The probability that the chosen relation is reflexive(round off to 3 decimal places) is _____.

18. Let G be a group of 35 elements. Then the largest possible size of a subgroup of G other than G itself is ________.

19. A multiplexer is placed between a group of 32 registers and an accumulator to regulate data movement such that at any given point in time the content of only one register will move to the accumulator, The minimum number of select lines needed for the multiplexer is ________.

20. If there are m input lines and n output lines for a decoder that is used to uniquely address a byte addressable 1 KB RAM, then the minimum value of m + n is _______.

21. A direct mapped cache memory of 1 MB has a block size of 256 bytes. The cache has an access time of 3 ns and a hit rate of 94%. During a cache miss, it takes 20 ns to bring the first word of a block from the main memory, while each subsequent word takes 5 ns. The word size is 64 bits. The average memory access time in ns (round off to 1 decimal place) is _______.

22. Consider the following C program:

```
#include <stdio.h>
int main( )   {
    int a[4][5] ={{1, 2, 3, 4, 5},
                  {6, 7, 8, 9, 10},
                  {11, 12, 13, 14, 15},
                  {16, 17, 18, 19, 20}};
printf("%d\n",*(*(a+**a+2)+3));
return(0);
}
```

The output of the program is ________.

23. Consider a double hashing scheme in which the primary hash function is $h_1(k) = k \bmod 23$ and the secondary hash function is $h_2(k) = 1 + (k \bmod 19)$. Assume that the table size is 23. Then the address returned by probe 1 in the probe sequence (assume that the probe sequence begins at probe 0) for key value k = 90 is _______.

24. Consider the following grammar.

$S \rightarrow aSB \mid d$

$B \rightarrow b$

The number of reduction steps taken by a bottom-up parser while accepting the string aaadbbb is _______.

25. Assume that you have made a request for a web page through your web browser to a web server. Initially the browser cache is empty. Further, the browser is configured to send HTTP requests in non-persistent mode. The web page contains text and five very small images. The minimum number of TCP connections required to display the web page completely in your browser is ________.

Q. 26 to Q. 55 : Carry Two Marks Each.

26. Which of the following languages are undecidable? Note that $\langle M \rangle$ indicates encoding of the Turing machine M.

$L_1 = \{\langle M \rangle \mid L(M) = \phi\}$

$L_2 = \{\langle M \rangle\ w, q\rangle \mid$ M on input w reaches state q in exactly 100 steps}

$L_3 = \{\langle M \rangle \mid L(M)$ is not recursive)

$L_4 = \{\langle M \rangle \mid L(M)$ contains at least 21 members}

(a) L_1, L_3 and L_4 only

(b) L_1 and L_3 only

(c) L_2 and L_3 only

(d) L_1, L_3 and L_4 only

27. Let A and B be two n × n matrices over real numbers. Let rank(M) and det(M) denote the rank and determinant of a matrix M, respectively. Consider the following statements:

I. rank (AB) = rank(A) rank(B)

II. det(AB) = det(A) det(B)

III. rank(A + B) ≤ rank(A) + rank(B)

IV. det(A + B) ≤ det(A) + det(B)

Which of the above statements are TRUE?

(a) I and II only (b) I and IV only

(c) II and III only (d) III and IV only

28. Consider the Boolean function z(a, b, c).

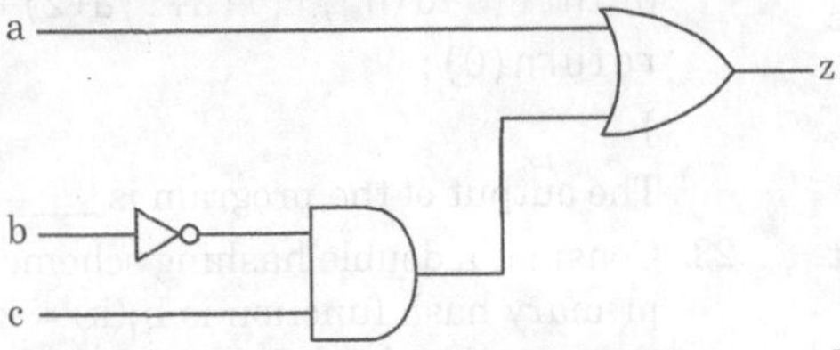

Which one of the following minterm lists represents the circuit given above?

(a) z = Σ(0, 1, 3, 7) (b) z = Σ(1, 4, 5, 6, 7)

(c) z = Σ(2, 4, 5, 6, 7) (d) z = Σ(2, 3, 5)

29. Consider three registers R1, R2, and R3 that store numbers in IEEE-754 single precision floating point format. Assume that R1 and R2 contain the values(in hexadecimal notation) 0x42200000 and 0xC1200000, respectively.

If $R3 = \frac{R1}{R2}$, what is the value stored in R3?

(a) 0x40800000 (b) 0xC0800000

(c) 0x83400000 (d) 0xC8500000

30. A computer system with a word length of 32 bits has a 16 MB byte-addressable main memory and a 64 KB, 4-way set associative cache memory with a block size of 256 bytes. Consider the following four physical addresses represented in hexadecimal notation.

A1 = 0×42C8A4, A2 = 0×546888, A3 = 0×6A289C, A4 = 0×5E4880

Which one of the following is TRUE?

(a) A1 and A4 are mapped to different cache sets.

(b) A2 and A3 are mapped to the same cache set.

(c) A3 and A4 are mapped to the same cache set.

(d) A1 and A3 are mapped to the same cache set.

31. Let G = (V, E) be a weighted undirected graph and let T be a Minimum Spanning Tree (MST) of G maintained using adjacency lists. Suppose a new weighted edge (u, v) ∈ V × V is added to G. The worst case time complexity of determining if T is still an MST of the resultant graph is

(a) $\Theta(|E| + |V|)$ (b) $\Theta(|E|\,|V|)$

(c) $\Theta(|E| \log |V|)$ (d) $\Theta(|V|)$

32. Consider the following languages.

$L_1 = \{w\,x\,yx \mid w, x, y \in (0 + 1)^+\}$

$L_2 = \{xy \mid x, y \in (a + b)^*, |x| = |y|, x \neq y\}$

Which one of the following is TRUE?

(a) L_1 is regular and L_2 is context-free.

(b) L_1 is context-free but not regular and L_2 is context-free.

(c) Neither L_1 nor L_2 is context-free.

(d) L_1 is context-free but L_2 is not context-free.

33. Consider the productions A → PQ and A → XY. Each of the five non-terminals A, P, Q, X and Y has two attributes: s is a synthesized attribute, and *i* is an inherited attribute. Consider the following rules.

Rule 1: P.i = A.i + 2, Q.i = P.i + A.i and A.s = P.s + Q.s

Rule 2: X.i = A.i + Y.s and Y.i = X.s + A.i

Which one of the following is TRUE?

(a) Both Rule 1 and Rule 2 are L-attributed.

(b) Only Rule 1 is L-attributed.

(c) Only Rule 2 is L-attributed.

(d) Neither Rule 1 nor Rule 2 is L-attributed.

34. Each of a set of n processes executes the following code using two semaphores a and b initialized to 1 and 0, respectively. Assume that count is a shared variable initialized to 0 and not used in CODE SECTION P.

CODE SECTION P

```
wait(a); count=count+1;
if (count==n)signal(b);
signal(a); wait(b); signal(b);
```

CODE SECTION Q

What does the code achieve?

(a) It ensures that no process executes CODE SECTION Q before every process has finished CODE SECTION P.

(b) It ensures that at most two processes are in CODE SECTION Q at any time.

(c) It ensures that all processes execute CODE SECTION P mutually exclusively.

(d) It ensures that at most n – 1 processes are in CODE SECTION P at any time.

35. Consider the following five disk access requests of the form (request id, cylinder number) that are present in the disk scheduler queue at a given time.

(P, 155), (Q, 85), (R, 110), (S, 30), (T, 115)

Assume the head is positioned at cylinder 100. The scheduler follows Shortest Seek Time First scheduling to service the requests.

Which one of the following statements is FALSE?

(a) T is serviced before P.

(b) Q is serviced after S, but before T.

(c) The head reverses its direction of movement between servicing of Q and P.

(d) R is serviced before P.

36. Consider a relational table R that is in 3NF, but not in BCNF. Which one of the following statements is TRUE?

(a) R has a non-trivial functional dependency $X \to A$, where X is not a superkey and A is a prime attribute.

(b) R has a non-trivial functional dependency $X \to A$, where X is not a superkey and A is a non-prime attribute and X is not a proper subset of any key.

(c) R has a non-trivial functional dependency $X \to A$, where X is not a superkey and A is a non-prime attribute and X is a proper subset of some key.

(d) A cell in R holds a set instead of an atomic value.

37. Consider a schedule of transactions T_1 and T_2:

T_1	RA			RC		WD		WD	Commit	
T_2		RB	WB		RD		WC			Commit

Here, RX stands for "Read(X)" and WX stands for "Write(X)"". Which one of the following schedules is conflict equivalent to the above schedule?

(a)

T_1				RA	RC	WD	WB		Commit	
T_2	RB	WB	RD					WC		Commit

(b)

T_1	RA	RC	WD	WB					Commit	
T_2					RB	WB	RD	WC		Commit

(c)

T_1	RA	RC	WD				WB		Commit	
T_2				RB	WB	RD		WC		Commit

(d)

T_1					RA	RC	WD	WB	Commit	
T_2	RB	WB	RD	WC						Commit

38. An organization requires a range of IP addresses to assign one to each of its 1500 computers. The organization has approached an Internet Service Provider (ISP) for this task. The ISP uses CIDR and serves the requests from the available IP address space 202.61.0.0/17. The ISP wants to assign an address space to the organization which will minimize the number of routing entries in the ISP's router using route aggregation.

Which of the following address spaces are potential candidates from which the ISP can allot any one to the organization?

I. 202.61.84.0/21 II. 202.61.104.0/21

III. 202.61.64.0/21 IV. 202.61.144.0/21

(a) I and II only (b) II and III only

(c) III and IV only (d) I and IV only

39. Which one of the following predicate formulae is NOT logically valid?

Note that W is a predicate formula without any free occurrence of x.

(a) $\forall x(p(x) \vee W) \equiv \forall x\, p(x) \vee W$

(b) $\exists x(p(x) \wedge W) \equiv \exists x\, p(x) \wedge W$

(c) $\forall x(p(x) \to W) \equiv \forall x\, p(x) \to W$

(d) $\exists x(p(x) \to W) \equiv \forall x\, p(x) \to W$

40. Let G = (V, E)be a directed, weighted graph with weight function $w : E \to R$. For some function $f : V \to R$, for each edge$(u, v) \in E$, define $w'(u, v)$ as $w(u, v) + f(u) - f(v)$. Which one of the options completes the following sentence so that it is TRUE?

"The shortest paths in G under w are shortest paths under w′ too, ________".

(a) for every $f : V \to R$

(b) if and only if $\forall u \in V$, f (u) is positive

(c) if and only if $\forall u \in V$, f (u) is negative

(d) if and only if f (u) is the distance from s to u in the graph obtained by adding a new vertex s to G and edges of zero weight from s to every vertex of G

41. In a balanced binary search tree with n elements, what is the worst case time complexity of reporting all elements in range [a, b]? Assume that the number of reported elements is k.

(a) $\Theta(\log n)$ (b) $\Theta(\log n + k)$

(c) $\Theta(k \log n)$ (d) $\Theta(n \log k)$

42. The number of permutations of the characters in LILAC so that no character appears in its original position, if the two L's are in distinguishable, is ________.

43. Consider a non-pipelined processor operating at 2.5 GHz. It takes 5 clock cycles to complete an instruction. You are going to make a 5-stage pipeline out of this processor. Overheads associated with pipelining force you to operate the pipelined processor at 2 GHz. In a given program, assume that 30% are memory instructions. 60% are ALU instructions and the rest are branch instructions. 5% of the memory instructions cause stalls of 50 clock cycles each due to cache misses and 50% of the branch instructions cause stalls of 2 cycles each. Assume that there are no stalls associated with the execution of ALU instructions. For this program, the speedup achieved by the pipelined processor over the non-pipelined processor (round off to 2 decimal places) is ________.

44. A processor has 64 registers and uses 16-bit instruction format. It has two types of instructions: I-type and R-type. Each I-type instruction contains an opcode, a register name, and a 4-bit immediate value. Each R-type instruction contains an opcode and two register names. If there are 8 distinct I-type opcodes, then the maximum number of distinct R-type opcodes is ______.

45. For n > 2, let $a \in \{0,1\}^n$ be a non-zero vector. Suppose that x is chosen uniformly at random from $\{0, 1\}^n$. Then, the probability that $\sum_{i=1}^{n} a_i x_i$ is an odd number is ______.

46. Consider the following C functions:

```
int fun1 (int n) {
    static int i = 0;
    if (n > 0) {
        ++i;
        fun1 (n – 1);
    }
    return (i);
}
int fun2 (int n) {
    static int i = 0;
    if (n > 0) {
        i = i + (fun1(n);
        fun2 (n–1);
    }
    return (i);
}
```

The return value of fun2 (5) is ______.

47. Consider the array representation of a binary min-heap containing 1023 elements. The minimum number of comparisons required to find the maximum in the heap is ______.

48. Consider the following C functions:

```
int tob (int b, int* arr) {
    int i;
    for (i=0, b>0; i++) {
    if (b%2)  arr [i] = 1;
    else  arr[i]=0;
    b=b/2;
    }
    return (i);
}

int pp(int a, int b) {
    int arr[20];
    int i, tot=1, ex, len;
    ex=a;
    len=tob (b,arr);
    for(i=0; i<len; i++) {
        if (arr[i]==1)
        tot=tot * ex;
        ex = ex * ex;
    }
    return (tot);
}
```

The value returned by pp (3,4) is ______.

49. Consider a graph G = (V, E), where V = $\{v_1, v_2, ..., v_{100}\}$, E = $\{(v_i, v_j) \mid 1 \le i < j \le 100\}$, and weight of the edge (v_i, v_j) is $|i - j|$. The weight of minimum spanning tree of G is ______.

50. Consider the following set of processes, assumed to have arrived at time 0. Consider the CPU scheduling algorithms Shortest Job First (SJF) and Round Robin (RR). For RR, assume that the processes are scheduled in the order P_1, P_2, P_3, P_4.

Processes	P_1	P_2	P_3	P_4
Burst time (in ms)	8	7	2	4

If the time quantum for RR is 4 ms, then the absolute value of the difference between the average turnaround times (in ms) of SJF and RR (round off to 2 decimal places) is ______.

51. Consider the following language.

L = $\{x \in \{a, b\}^* \mid$ number of a's in x is divisible by 2 but not divisible by 3$\}$

The minimum number of states in a DFA that accepts L is ______.

52. Graph G is obtained by adding vertex s to $K_{3,4}$ and making s adjacent to every vertex of $K_{3,4}$. The minimum number of colours required to edge-colour G is ______.

53. Consider a paging system that uses 1-level page table residing in main memory and a TLB for address translation. Each main memory access takes 100 ns and TLB lookup takes 20 ns. Each page transfer to/from the disk takes 5000 ns. Assume that the TLB hit ratio is 95%, page fault rate is 10%. Assume that for 20% of the total page faults, a dirty page has to be written back to disk before the required page is read in from disk. TLB update time is negligible. The average memory access time in ns (round off to 1 decimal places) is ______.

54. Consider a database implemented using B+ tree for file indexing and installed on a disk drive with block size of 4 KB. The size of search key is 12 bytes and the size of tree/disk pointer is 8 bytes. Assume that the database has one million records. Also assume that no node of the B+ tree and no records are present initially in main memory. Consider that each record fits into one disk block. The minimum number of disk accesses required to retrieve any record in the database is ________.

55. Consider a TCP connection between a client and a server with the following specifications: the round trip time is 6 ms, the size of the receiver advertised window is 50 KB, slowstart threshold at the client is 32 KB, and the maximum segment size is 2 KB. The connection is established at time t = 0. Assume that there are no timeouts and errors during transmission. Then the size of the congestion window (in KB) at time t + 60 ms after all acknowledgments are processed is ________.

ANSWERS

General Aptitude (GA)

1. (d)	**2.** (a)	**3.** (a)	**4.** (d)	**5.** (b)	**6.** (d)	**7.** (c)	**8.** (a)
9. (b)	**10.** (c)						

Computer Science & IT

1. (a)	**2.** (a)	**3.** (c)	**4.** (c)	**5.** (b)	**6.** (c)	**7.** (d)	**8.** (d)
9. (d)	**10.** (c)	**11.** (c)	**12.** (c)	**13.** (a)	**14.** (a)	**15.** (d)	**16.** (c)
17. (0.125)	**18.** (7)	**19.** (5)	**20.** (1034)	**21.** (13.5)	**22.** (19)	**23.** (13)	**24.** (7)
25. (6)	**26.** (a)	**27.** (c)	**28.** (b)	**29.** (b)	**30.** (b)	**31.** (d)	**32.** (a)
33. (b)	**34.** (a)	**35.** (b)	**36.** (a)	**37.** (a)	**38.** (b)	**39.** (c)	**40.** (a)
41. (b)	**42.** (12)	**43.** (2.15 to 2.18)	**44.** (14)	**45.** (0.5)	**46.** (55)	**47.** (511)	**48.** (81)
49. (99)	**50.** (5.25)	**51.** (6)	**52.** (7)	**53.** (154.5 to 155.5)		**54.** (4)	**55.** (44)

EXPLANATIONS

GENERAL APTITUDE

1. "Within" Preposition that is used to express something that occurs inside a particular period of time.
Here, because Sentance is in 'present perfect continuous tense' "For is"used when we talk about a period of time.
2. Here, we have to note that the confunction used is 'but'. 'But' is used for introducing an idea which contrasts with the statement that has been already said.
3. (i) Flyer : Relation is Verb : Noun
(ii) One who cooks is a cook, and one who flies any aircraft is a flyer.
5. • Cost of 1-a-C-2 : 200 + 200 + 100 + 100 + 100 = 700
• Cost of 1-f-e-2 : 100 + 100 + 100 + 200 + 200 = 700
• Cost of 1-b-2 : 300 + 100 + 200 = 600
• Cost of 1-f-b-2 : 100 + 100 + 100 +200 = 500
Hence, 1-f-b-2 is having minimum cost.
6. According to given passage GST is imposed on the usage or supply of goods and services hence, option (d) is correct.
7. As given that
$P = 3^1, Q = 9 = 3^2, R = 27 = 3^3, S = 81 = 3^4,$
$T = 243 = 3^5$
Hence, Q + S = 9 + 81 = 90.
8. Unpainted area = Area of annular ring – Area of n blue color circles
Area of annular ring = $\pi b^2 - \pi a^2$
i.e. $\pi(b^2 - a^2)$
$$\text{Area of 1 blue circle} = \pi\left(\frac{b-a}{2}\right)^2$$
$$\text{Hence, area of n blue circles} = n\pi\left(\frac{b-a}{2}\right)^2$$
$$\Rightarrow \text{Unpainted area} = \pi\left[(b^2 - a^2) - \frac{\pi}{4}(b-a)^2\right]$$
9. Since, α and β are acute angles hence it will form the interior angles of straight lines $\alpha + \beta = 180° - 90° = 90°$
10. As given that,
Total expenditure = 2500 million
Total revenue = 3000 million
Total profit = 3000 – 2500 = 500
$$\text{So,} \quad \text{profit \%} = \frac{500}{2500} \times 100 = 20\%$$

COMPUTER SCIENCE & IT

1. If, $f(x) = \sqrt{x^3 + 1}$
$$f'(x) = \frac{1}{\sqrt{x^3+1}} \cdot 3x^2 \geq 0$$
Here, for all points in [0, 1]
∴ Therefore, it is increasing function.
4. The correct order is as fallowing steps:
Step 1:Send the address to memory via MAR.
Step 2:Read the opcode into R from the memory via MBR.
Step 3:Send the first operand to Temp 1(ALU).
Step 4:Read the second operand directly from the R2 and process the data in ALU and store the result into TEMP2.
Step 5: Store the result into R0.
5. **Inorder:** 10, 11, 12, (15), 16, 18, 19, 20
(10, 11, 12 = LST; 16, 18, 19, 20 = RST)

Preorder: (15), 10, 12, 11, 20, 18, 16, 19
(15 → 1st root)

→ The BST, we can make usign preorder and inorder.

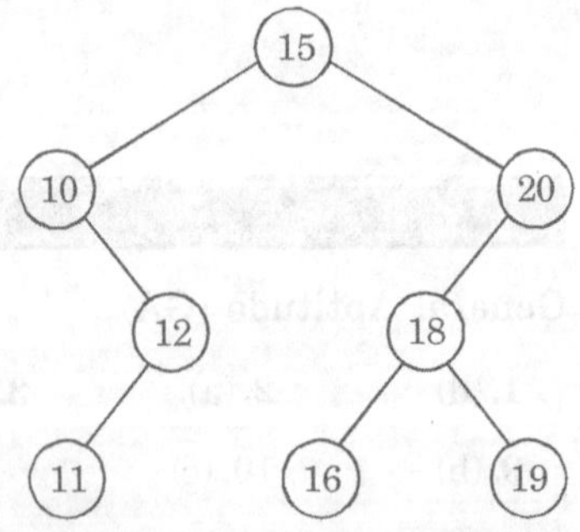

So, postorder : 11, 12, 10, 16, 19, 18, 20, 15
6. AVL with n element : [height balanced [–1, 0, + 1] BST]
log n level due to balanced BST.
(i) Every insertion of element:
log n: Find place to insert.
long n: If properly no satisfied do rotation.
(ii) n^2 element insertion :
For 1 element ≡ 2 log n
So, for (upper bound function) n^2 element ≡ $\theta(\log(n)^{n2})$ $\theta(n^2 \log n)$

7. Try to find counter example to show expression incomplete.

(a) is incorrect because it force to end "10".

(b) is incorrect because it forces the string to start with "1" and hence cannot generate a string like "01", which has odd number of ones.

(c) is same as (0 + 1)* 10* which will generate some wrong string like "110" which has even number of 1's. It is a superset and hence not correct.

(d) is same as (0* 1 0* 1 0*)* 1 0* which is most suitable answer for the given problem according to given options.

8. If $L_1 U L_2$ is Regular, then L_1 and L_2 are also regular languages: false, since $\{a^nb^n\} \cup \{a^nb^n\} = \Sigma^*$ which is regular, but $\{a^nb^n\}$ not regular.

Infinite union of regular languages are also regular: false, since may infinite language can be broken into invidual strings which will be infinite union of finite languages. So if regular is closed under infinite union, then all infinite language will become regular, which is untrue. Hence, II is also false.

9. Symbal table can be accessed only in Lexical analysis and syntex analys is.

None of the given statements are correct.

10. $L = \{a^n | n \geq 0\} \cup R\, a^nb^n \mid n \geq 0\}$

$L = \{\varepsilon, a, aa, aaa, b, bb, ab, aabb \ldots\ldots\ldots\}$

$L = \{a^nb^n \mid n \geq 0\}$ is a well known DCFL.

$\{a^n b^n \mid n \geq 0\}$ is a well known regular language.

So, L = DCFL ∪ Regular = DCFL by closure properly.

DCFL is the strongest correct answer.

11. The hole created by best fit is never larger than the hole created by first fit.

Best fit always allocates the request that provided minimum hole sizes. Thus, best fit will never produce hales that are greater than the holes created by first fit.

12. From the process state diagram, we can see that there cannot be a transition from the waiting/blocked state to the running state. Hence, statement I, II and IV are correct.

13. SELECT S.sno, S. sname

From Supplier S, catalog C

WHERE S. sno = C.sno AND

cost > (SELECT AVG (cost)

FROM Catalog

WHERE pno = 'P4' GroupBy pno);

Catalog

sno	pno	cost
S1	P1	150
S1	P2	50
S1	P3	100
S2	P4	200
S2	P5	250
S3	P1	250
S3	P2	150
S3	P5	300
S3	P4	250

AVG cost
225

sno	pno	cost
S2	P4	200
S4	P4	250

Results

sno	sname
S1	RF
S2	BF
S3	PF
S2	PF

$$\left[\because \text{Avg cost} = \left[\frac{200 + 250}{2}\right]\right] = 225$$

Here, the outer query will return S_{no} and S_{name} of supliers having cost > 225. So the total number of tuples returned by the query is 4.

14.

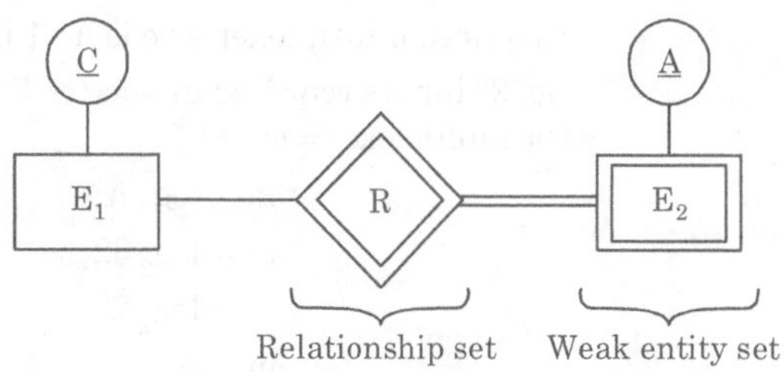

In this the identification relationship represented by a Diamond shape with double line bold borders

15. I. A router modifies the IP packets during forwarding because TTL is changing.

II. A router can also be used in LAN network routers are configured with routing algorithms so, it does not require routing protocol at that time.

III. Packet fragmentation is done if packet size is more than MTU.

16. Insert element at the beginning of empty linked list, take Θ (1)

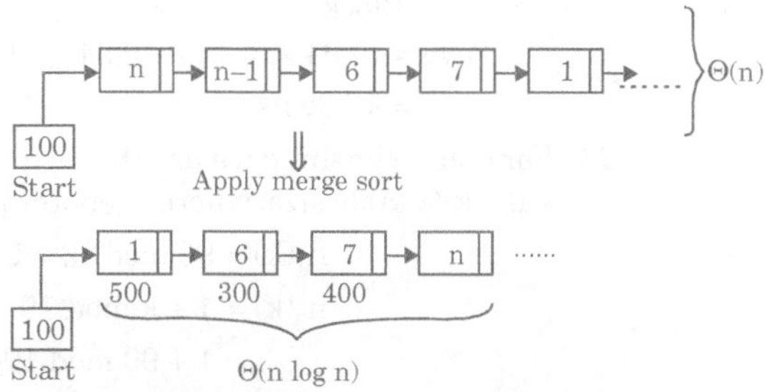

⇒ Θ(nlogn) + Θ(n)

= Θ(nlogn)

17. As given that,

$A = \{1, 2, 3\}$

$n = |A| = 3$

Number of relations on A = $2^{n^2} = 2^{3^2} = 29$

Number of reflexive relations on A = $2^{n^2-n} = 2^{3^2}$ $- 3 = 2^6$

$$P[\text{reflexive}] = \frac{2^{n^2-n}}{2^{n^2}} = \frac{2^6}{2^9} = \frac{1}{8} = 0.125$$

18. The order of a subgroup always divides the order of groups.

Size of group = O(G) = 35

Let H be subgroup of G

$\therefore$ O(H) | O(G)

Possible orders of H are 1,5,7,35

So, size of largest possible proper subgroup of G other than G itself would be = 7.

19. Number of registers = n = 32

Required multiplexer size is n : 1 i.e. 32 : 1

So, 2^n inputs required m selected lines required to the multiplexer = m

$$\therefore \quad m = \log_2 n$$
$$m = \log_2 32$$
$$= \log_2 2^5$$
$$m = 5$$

20. We need 10 input lines and 1024 outputs lines to map 1 KB RAM.

For this we need 10×2^{10} decoder.

Here, M = 10 and N = 2^{10} = 1024

Therefore, M + N = 1034

21. As given that

Hit ratio = 94%

Word length or size = 64 bit = 8B

Block size = 256 B

$$\therefore \frac{\text{Number of words}}{\text{Block}} = \frac{256}{8} = 2^5(32)$$

$$T_{avg} = (0.94 \times 3) + (1 - 0.94)\,[20 + (31 \times 5)]$$
$$= 13.32 \text{ ns}$$

23. For double hashing we use the formula as (h_1(k) + ih_2(k)% table size, where i denotes probe value.

$$h_1(k) = 90 \bmod 23 = 21$$
$$h_2(k) = 1 + k \bmod 19$$
$$= 1 + 90 \bmod 19 = 15$$

For probe 1 the value of i = 1 so, (21 + 15) mod 23 = 13

24. S → aSB

→ aaSBB [S → aSB]

→ aaaSBBB [S → aSB]

→ aaadBBB [S → d]

→ aaabBB [B → b]

→ aaadbbB [B → b]

→ aaadbbb [B → b]

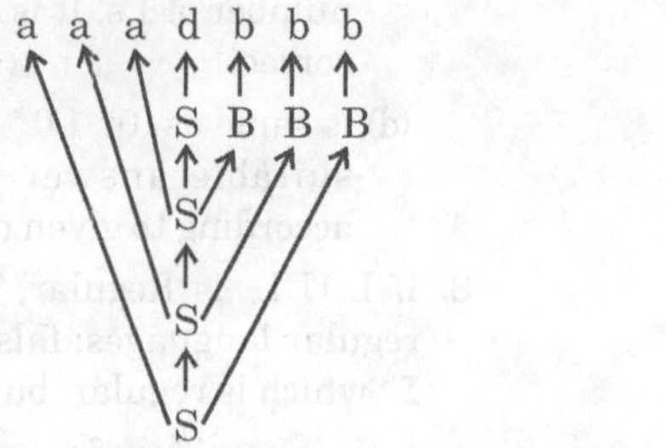

So, Total number of steps/reductions in the derivation is: 7 required.

25. In non persistent HTTP for every objects there is a TCP connection required. So, 1 TCP connection for text and 5 TCP connections for images required.

1 Text + 5 images = 6 objects

So total 6 connections are required.

26. (i) L_1 = {<M> | M is a TM with L(M) = ϕ } is emptiness problem of TM, which is undecidable, by Rice's theorem since it is a non-trival problem.

(ii) L_2 = {<M, w, q> | M on input-w reaches state q in exactly 100 steps} Decidable after 100 steps. It is non-recursive and non-trivbal problem, since some TM can accept non-recursive language and some may not, so by Rice's theorem it is undecidable.

(iii) L_3 = {M>/M is not recursive} Rice's theorem applied and hence L_3 is undecidable.

(iv) L_4 = {M>/M contains at least, 21 members} Membership problems with UTM we can check it M accept string by 100 steps. So L_4 decidable L_1, L_2 and L_3 are undecidable.

27. (i) When two (3 × 3) non-singular matrices each having rank is 3. Then the product of these two non-singular matrices also has rank (A.B) = 3.

(ii) The properties of the determinant |AB| = |A| · |B|

Statement 2 and 3 are correct statements.

28. The given functions:

$$\therefore \quad z(a,b,c) = a + \bar{b}c$$

K-map of the output z is

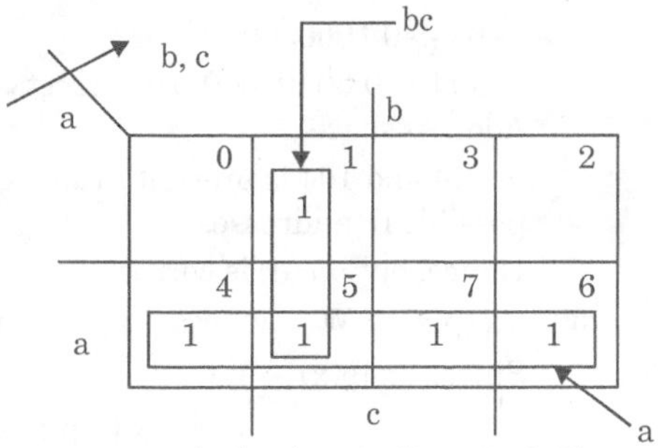

$\therefore$ $z(a, b, c) = \Sigma m(1, 4, 5, 6, 7)$

Therefore, the minterm $\sum(1, 4, 5, 6, 7)$ represents the function $Z = a + b'c$

29. R1 : 0×42200000

R2 : 0×C1200000

32 bit format

	S	BE	M
R1 :	0	100000100	010000········

32 bit format

	S	BE	M
R21 :	0	10000010	010000········

Step 1: Subtract the exponents i.e. divisor exponent from the divided exponent.

```
        2
  10000100          AE :    111111
                            00000010
  10000010          Bias :  01111111  (+ 127)
AE : 00000010       AE :    10000001
```

Step 2: Divide the mantissa i.e.

R1 M : 1.010...

R2 M : 1.010... (Divide)

Result : 1

Step 3: Sign (opposite sign division result sing is –ve)

32 bit formate

R3 :	1	100000001	000000········

C 0 8 00000

30. As given that,

Word length = 32 bit, MM size = 16 MB

Physical address = 24 bit, CM size = 64 KB

4-way set associative

Block size = 256 Blocks

Cache size or number of lines (N)

$$= \frac{64\text{ K}}{256} \Rightarrow \frac{2^{16}}{2^8} = 2^8$$

= 256 Blocks

4-way set associative cache:

$$\text{Number of sets index (S)} = \frac{N}{\text{P-way}} \Rightarrow \frac{2^8}{4} = 2^6$$

= 64 = 6 bits

Address format:

TAG	No. of set	Word offset
10	6	8
10 bit	$\log_2 2^6$	$\log_2 2^8$

← 24 bit →

A1 : $(42C8A4)_H$

4211	001000	A4

= 8th set (Set offset)

A2 : $(546888)_H$

5401	001000	88

= 40th set (Set offset)

A3 : $(6A289C)_H$

6A00	001000	9C

(Set offset)

A2 and A3 are in same set

A4 : $(5E4880)_H$

5E01	001000	80

(Set offset)

A1 and A4 are in same set = 8th set

Hence, option (b) is correct choice.

32. L1 is regular and L2 is CFL.

In L1 putting x as 0 and 1 we get a subset

$$w0y0 + w1y1 = (0 + 1)^+ 0 (0 + 1)^+ 0 + (0 + 1)^+ 1(0 + 1)^+ 1$$

Now by putting x as 00, 01, 10, 11 we can show that above minimal regular expression covers all such things and hence above expression is not a subset but is equal to given language.

$S \rightarrow AB/BA$

$A \rightarrow XAX \mid 0$

$B \rightarrow XBX \mid 1$

$X \rightarrow 0/1$

Since we wrote regular expression for L1, it is regular.

33. Rule 1 : $P \cdot i = A \cdot i + 2$, $Q \cdot i = P \cdot i + A \cdot i$

$As = P \cdot s + Q \cdot s$

It is L-attributed by definition.

Rule 2 : It is not L-attributed because this expression $(X \cdot i = X \cdot i + Y \cdot s)$ and $(Y \cdot i = X \cdot S + A) \cdot i$ fails to satisfy the definition of L-attributed.

34. All the processes running the given code will remain block due to wait(b) until the value of count becomes n.

When the value of count will become equals to n, value of b changes to 1 which will subsequently allow a process to go into section Q.

So, no process can go to section Q until all the process executes code section P.

36. R(A, B, C, D, E)

key : <u>ABC</u>, <u>BCD</u>

$$FD : \underbrace{BC}_{x} \to \underbrace{D}_{A} :$$

Thus, for a non-trivial dependency X-> A

'x' should not super key and 'A' is prime attribute in order to satisfy 3NF and not BCNF.

37.

T_1	T_2
$r_1(A)$	
	$r_2(B)$
	$w_2(B)$
$r_1(C)$	
	$r_2(D)$
$w_1(D)$	
	$w_2(c)$
$w_1(B)$	
Commit	
	Commit

$\Longrightarrow$ conflict equal

T_1	T_2
	$r_2(B)$
	$w_2(B)$
	$r_2(D)$
$r_1(A)$	
$r_1(C)$	
$w_1(D)$	
$w_1(B)$	
	$w_2(c)$
Commit	
	Commit

Conflicting operations are:

$R_1(C) \to W_2(C)$, $R_2(B) \to W_1(B)$, $W_2(B) \to W_1(B)$, $R_2(D) \to W_1(D)$

Now, check, all the given options then we get option (b) had equivalent conflicting.

38. $/17 \Rightarrow$ 11111111 11111111
10000000 00000000
$\Rightarrow$ 255.255.128.0

$1500 \simeq 2048 = 2^{11} = 2^3 \times 2^8$

$= 2^{32-21} = 2^{11} = /21$

$/17 \Rightarrow$ 202.61.0.0/17

<u>00000000.00000000</u>
<u>00000111.11111111</u> } (0.0 – 7.255)

0.0 ⇒ <u>00001000.00000000</u>
<u>00001111.11111111</u> } (8.0 – 15.255)

<u>00010000.00000000</u>
<u>00010111.11111111</u> } (16.0 – 23.255)

Sequence is 0, 8, 16, 24, 32, 40, 48, 56, 64, 72, 80, 96, 104, 112, 120.

By Analyze the third octet:

Total of 17 net bits, 4 subnet bits, 11 host bits

→ 84 -> 0 **1010** 100 → Incorrect ↓ (host bit contains 1)

→ 104 -> 0 **1101** 000

→ 64 -> 0 **1000,** 000

→ 144 -> 0 **0010,** 000 → Incorrect ↓ (Not belong to Address space)

So, 64 and 104 is present in sequence so it is the possible IP addresses.

Hence, option (d) is correct.

39. $\forall x\,(p(x) \to W) \equiv \forall x\,p(x) \to W$ is wrong

Since, $\forall x\,[p(x) \to W]$

$\equiv \forall x\,[\neg\,p(x) \vee W]$

$\equiv \forall x(\neg\,p(x) \vee W$

$\equiv \neg\,(\exists x\,p(x)) \vee W$

$\forall x\,[\,p(x) \to W] \equiv \exists x\,p(x) = \to W$

Hence, LHS and RHS are not equivalent.

So, If is not valid.

40. As given that:

w(u, v) = (u, v) edge weight

$$w(u,v) = w(u, v) + \underbrace{f(u) - f(v)}_{0}$$

= w(u, v)

Hence, option (a) correct.

41.

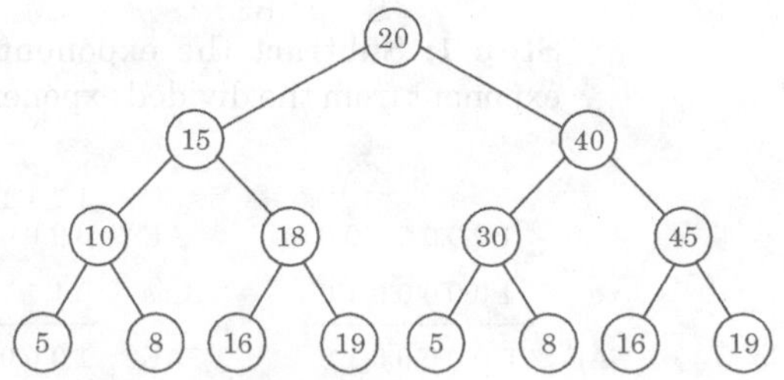

We need first find the indices of (a) & (b).

Let a = 16, b = 42

16 : Find the '16' element in the BST = O(log n)

42 : Find the '42' element in the BST = O(log n)

[16, 42]: Inorder sorted element between 16 to 42

[16, 18, 19, 20, 25, 30, 35, 40, 42] ⇒ requires O(k) time for k element. As 'K' can significantly larger than log n.

Hence, total time: ≡ O(log n + k)

42. Number of derangement

Since both L's are indistinguishable.

First L's can be arranged remaining 3 positions in $^3C_2$ ways.

[i.e., = _ <u>L</u> _ <u>L</u> _ or _ <u>L</u> _ <u>L</u> _ or _ <u>L</u> _ _ <u>L</u>]

For each of these cases remaining 3 letters can be deranged in 2 × 2! ways = 4 ways

[i.e., _ <u>L</u> _ <u>L</u> _ C can lake only 1 or 3 positions 2 → ways. For each of this IA can be arranged in remaining 2 positions in 2 ways].

Number of derangements = ${}^3C_2 \times 2 \times 2! = 12$
They are:
CLILA, ILCLA, ALCIL, CLAIL, ILACL, ALICL, CAILL, ACILL, ICALL, IACLL, ALCLI, CLALI.

43. Non-pipeline:
Clock frequency = 2.5 GHz

$$\text{Cycle time} = \frac{1}{2.5\,\text{GHz}} = 0.4\ \text{ns}$$

$$\text{CPI} = 5$$

So, time for the non-pipelined processor

$$ET_{\text{non-pipe}} = \text{CPI} \times \text{Cycle time}$$
$$= 5 \times 0.4\ \text{ns} = 2\ \text{ns}$$

Pipeline:
Clock frequency = 2.5 GHz

$$\text{Cycle time} = \frac{1}{2\,\text{GHz}} = 0.5\ \text{ns}$$

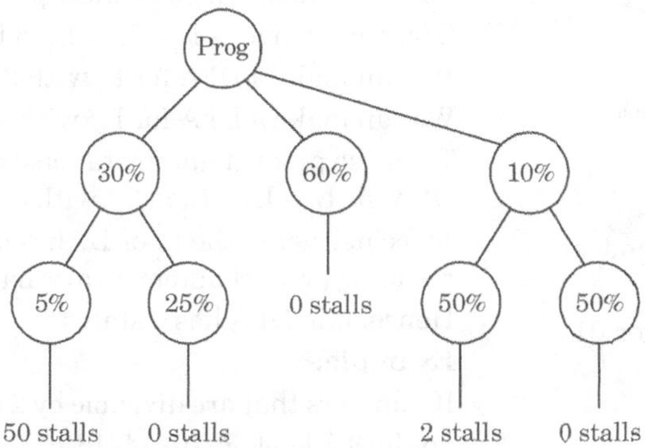

Number of stalls cycle/instruction
$= 0.3(0.05 \times 50) + 0.1(0.5 \times 2)$
$= 0.75 + 0.1 = 0.85$
Time for pipelined processor is:

$$ET_{\text{pipe}} = (1 + \text{Number of stalls/instruction}) \times \text{Cycle time}$$
$$= (1 + 0.85) \times 0.5\ \text{ns} = 0.925\ \text{ns}$$

$$\text{Speed up: (S)} = \frac{ET_{\text{non-pipe}}}{ET_{\text{pipe}}}$$

$$= \frac{2}{0.925}$$
$$= 2.16$$

44. As given that, 16 bit instruction and 64 registers
I-type:
It contans opcode Register name 4-bit immediate data.

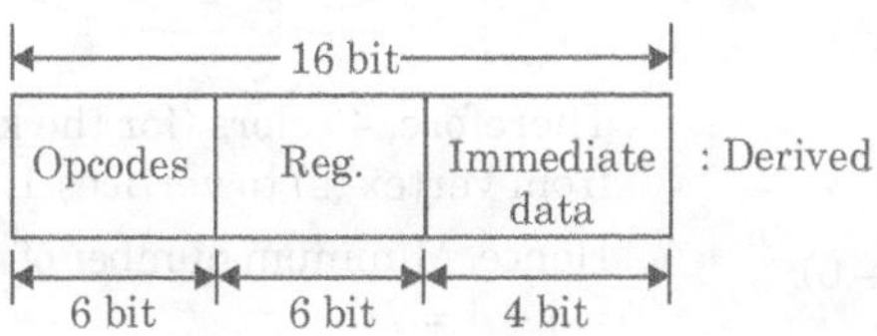

R-type: It contains opcode, Register name 1, Register name 2.

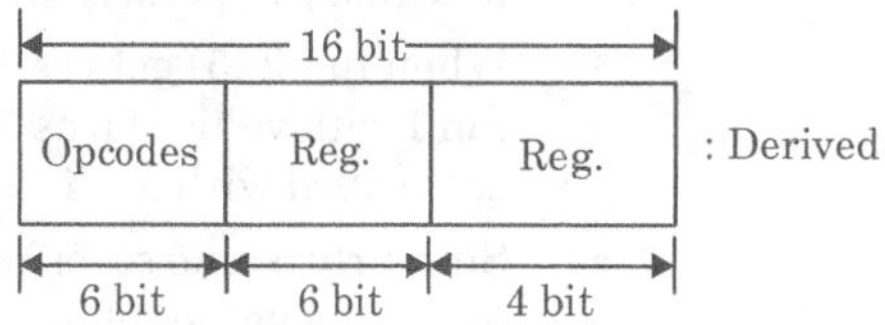

1. Primitive instruction
R-type:

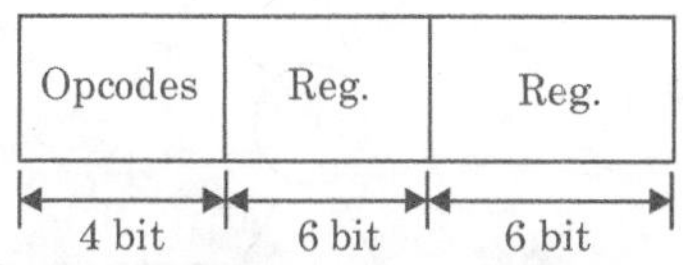

2. Number of operation possible = $2^4 = 16$
3. Number of tree opcodes = $(16 - R)$
Assume x is number of R-type instruction existed.
4. Number of I-type instruction possible = $(16 - R) \times 2^2$

$$8 = 64 - 4R$$
$$4R = 64 - 8 = 56$$
$$R = \frac{56}{4} \Rightarrow 14$$

Hence, possible R-type instructore are 14.

45. $a = \begin{bmatrix} a_1 \\ a_2 \\ \vdots \\ a_n \end{bmatrix}, x = \begin{bmatrix} x_1 \\ x_2 \\ \vdots \\ x_n \end{bmatrix}$

Fixed non-zero
$a_i = 0$ or 1
$x_i = 0$ or 1

$\sum_{i=1}^{n} a_i x_i$ as an odd and even number that value lies between 0 to n.
Total number cases = 2n

$a_i x_i$	0	1	2	……	n
fav	${}^nC_0$	${}^nC_1$	${}^nC_2$	……	${}^nC_n$

$$P\left[\sum_{i=1}^{n} a_i x_i \text{ is odd}\right] = \frac{{}^nC_1 + {}^nC_3}{2^n}$$

$$= \frac{2^{n-1}}{2^n} = \frac{1}{2}$$
$$= 0.5$$

Hence, the over all the probability (that the result is odd) = 0.5.

46. According to the given program:

- Variable i is static in both the functions thus its value will persist throught the program.
- When fun 2 (5) gets called, it will first call fun 1 with value of n as 5 and then fun 2 will gets called with n = 4.
- Similarly, same steps are taken for all the upcoming values of n.

47.

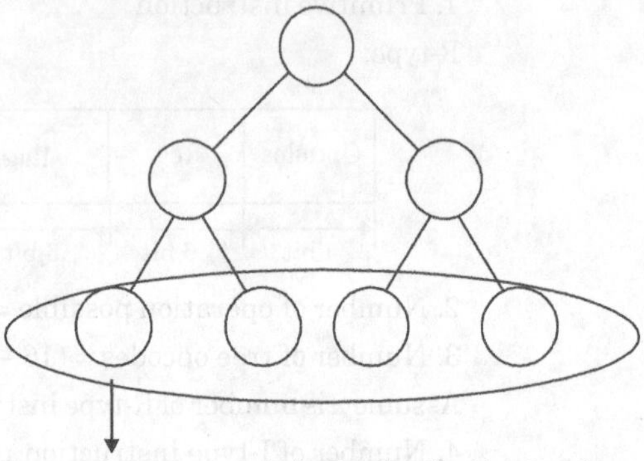

Maximum element can only be found at leaf level nodes

Number of element = $\left\lceil \frac{1023}{2} \right\rceil = 512$

To get the maximum value of these leaf nodes we requires 511 comparisons.

48. After executing the given C program integer 81 is returned.

49. Consider small instance of 4-vertices

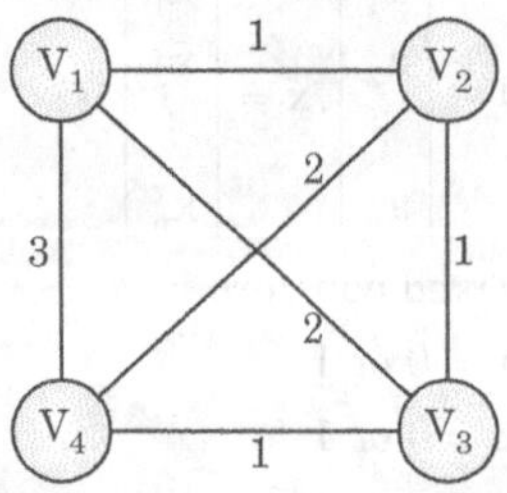

Clearly,

would be a MST with cost 3.

The number of edges of the MST is $|V| - 1$, in case of the given question $|V| = 100$, now the cost for this is $= |V| - 1 = 99$.

Hence, for 100 vertices, 99 will the weight of minumum spanning tree.

50. STF:

P_3	P_4	P_2	P_1

0 2 6 13 21

So, Turn Around Time (TAT) = (21 – 0) + (13 – 0) + (2 – 0) + (6 – 0)

Average TAT = $\frac{42}{4} = 10.5$

RR :

P_1	P_2	P_3	P_4	P_1	P_2

0 4 8 10 14 18 21

Turn Arount Time (TAT)

= (18 – 0) + (21 – 0) + (10 – 0) + (14 – 0)

= 18 + 21 + 10 + 14 = 63

Average TAT = $\frac{63}{4} = 15.75$

Hence, Absolute difference

= | SJE (TAT) – RR(TAT) |

= | 10.5 – 15.75 |

= 5.25 units

51. $L = \{w \in \{a, b\}^* \mid n_a(w) = \text{multiple of 2 but not 3}\}$

Let $L_1 = \{w \in \{a, b\}^* \mid n_a(w) = \text{multiple of 2}\}$

$L_2 = \{w \in \{a, b\}^* \mid n_a(w) = \text{multiple of 3}\}$

Given language is $L_1 - L_2 = L_1 \cap L_2^c$

We can make a DFA for L_1 with 2 states.

We can make a DFA for L_2^c with 3 states.

Then use product automata construction to get a DFA for $L_1 - L_2 = L_1 \cap L_2^c$ with 6 sates.

Since neither of the L_1 or L_2^c has a trap state, so resulting product automata also has no trap state.

Hence, min DFA has 6 states.

Example:-

If numbers that are divisible by 2 but not by 3 = {2, 4, 8, 10, 14, 16, ...}

= {aaa, aaaa, aaaaaaaa, ...}

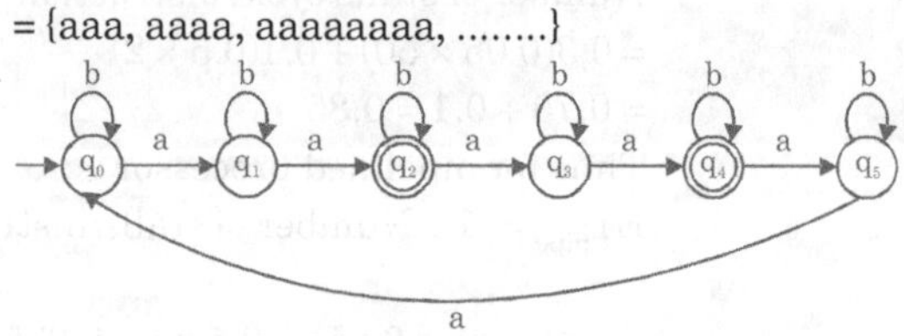

52.

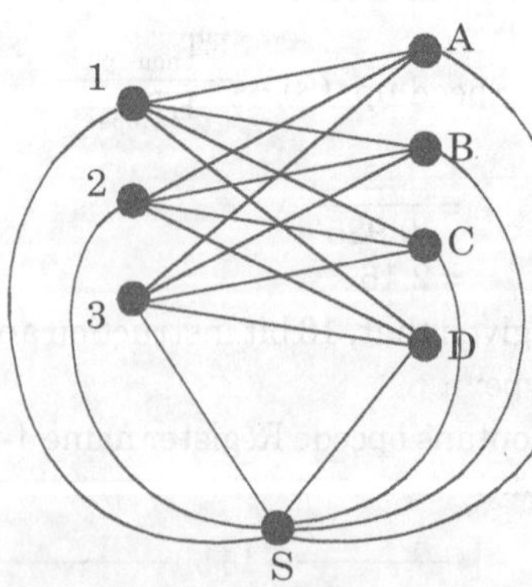

Therefore, 4 colors (for the k3, 4) + 3 new colors from vertex (s) to vertices 1, 2, 3.

Hence, Minimum number of edge-colors required = 3 + 4 = 7.

53. $EMAT = 0.95 \times (20 + 100)\ 0.05 \times (20 + 0.10 \times (0.80 \times 5000 + 0.20 \times 10000))$

(0.95: TLB hit ratio; 20: TLB time; 100: MMAT; 0.05: TLB miss; 20: TLB time; 0.10: Pare fault rate; 0.80: Not a dirty page fault rate; 5000: PFST; 0.20: Dirty page fault rate; 10000: PFST 2 times)

= 725 ns

54. As given that,

Block size = 4 KB

Search key = 12 bytes

Tree pointer = 8 bytes

DB records 1 million = 1000000

As we know that,

B+ tree index each record fits into one block

⇒ Keys given to find levels of B+ tree : Bulk loading B + tree design we can use

⇒ Order or B tree nodes $P \times B_p + (P - 1)$ keys $\le$ Block size

$$P \times 8 + (P - 1)\ 12 \le 4096$$

$$20P \le 4108$$

$$P = \left\lfloor \frac{4108}{20} \right\rfloor = 205$$

⇒ Minimum levels and index : Max fill factor of each node.

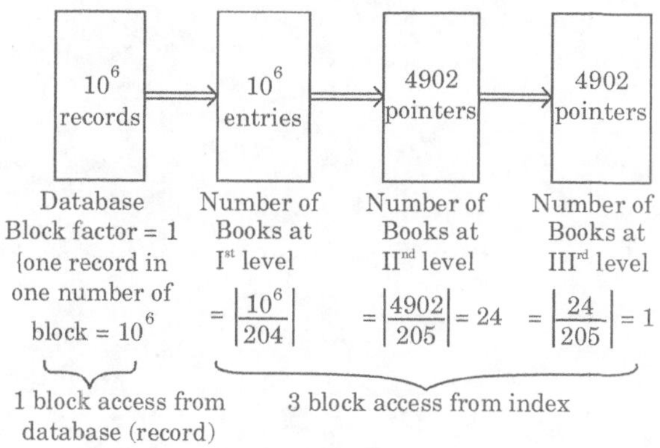

Thus, the total block access for a search is 3 + 1

So, Minimum 4 block access required to access record.

55. At time t = 0 there are not timeouts

Threshold = 32 KB

MSS = 2 KB

So,

	(Window size) time(t)
(1) First transmission :	2KB → 6ms
(2) Second transmission :	2KB → 6ms
(3) Third transmission :	2KB → 6ms
(4) Fourth transmission :	2KB → 6ms
(5) Fifth transmission :	2KB → 6ms
(6) Six transmission :	2KB → 6ms
(7) Seventh transmission :	2KB → 6ms
(8) Eighth transmission :	2KB → 6ms
(9) Nineth transmission :	2KB → 6ms
(10)Tenth transmission :	2KB → 6ms

After 10 ms completion, total time = 6 × 10 = 60 ms

At 11th transmission time t + 60, then window size = 44

Unit - I

Engineering Mathematics

Syllabus

Discrete Mathematics

Propositional and first order logic. Sets, relations, functions, partial orders and lattices. Groups. Graphs: connectivity, matching, coloring. Combinatorics: counting, recurrence relations, generating functions.

Linear Algebra

Matrices, determinants, system of linear equations, eigenvalues and eigenvectors, LU decomposition.

Calculus

Limits, continuity and differentiability. Maxima and minima. Mean value theorem. Integration.

Probability

Random variables. Uniform, normal, exponential, poisson and binomial distributions. Mean, median, mode and standard deviation. Conditional probability and Bayes theorem.

Contents

1 CHAPTER

Engineering Mathematics

Analysis of Previous GATE Papers											
Units	Year → Topics ↓		2019	2018	2017 Set 1	2017 Set 2	2016 Set 1	2016 Set 2	2015 Set 1	2015 Set 2	2015 Set 3
MATHEMATICAL LOGIC	1 Mark	MCQ Type	1		2	1			1	1	1
		Numerical Type	1				1	1			
	2 Marks	MCQ Type		1	1			1	1	1	
		Numerical Type									
	Total		2	2	4	1	1	3	3	3	1
SET THEORY AND ALGEBRA	1 Mark	MCQ Type	1						2	1	2
		Numerical Type		1	1	1				1	
	2 Marks	MCQ Type	1	1				2	1		1
		Numerical Type									1
	Total		3	3	1	1		4	4	2	6
COMBINATORICS	1 Mark	MCQ Type					1				
		Numerical Type									1
	2 Marks	MCQ Type							1		
		Numerical Type		1		1	2				
	Total			2		2	5		2		1
GRAPH THEORY	1 Mark	MCQ Type	1	1							
		Numerical Type				1	1	1			1
	2 Marks	MCQ Type	1							2	
		Numerical Type		1							1
	Total		3	3		1	1	1		4	3
PROBABILITY	1 Mark	MCQ Type									
		Numerical Type		1	1		1	1			
	2 Marks	MCQ Type				2					
		Numerical Type	1	1		1	1				1
	Total		2	3	1	6	3	1			2
LINEAR ALGEBRA	1 Mark	MCQ Type	1		1			1			1
		Numerical Type		1		2	1	1	1	1	
	2 Marks	MCQ Type		1	1				1		1
		Numerical Type	1							1	
	Total		3	3	3	2	1	2	3	3	3
CALCULUS	1 Mark	MCQ Type	1		1	1			1		1
		Numerical Type		1		1	1	1			
	2 Marks	MCQ Type								1	1
		Numerical Type							1		
	Total		1	1	1	2	1	1	3	2	3

MATHEMATICAL LOGIC

1. Indicate which of the following well formed formula are valid
   (a) $((P\to Q)\wedge(Q\to R))\to(P\to R)$
   (b) $(P\to Q)\to(\neg P\to\neg Q)$
   (c) $(P\wedge(\neg P V \neg Q))\to Q$
   (d) $((P\to R)\vee(Q\to R))\to((P\vee Q))\to R)$

[1990 : 2 Marks]

2. Which of the following predicate calculus statements is/are valid
   (a) $(\forall x)P(x)\vee(\forall x)Q(x)\to(\forall x)\{P(x)\vee Q(x)\}$
   (b) $(\exists x)P(x)\wedge(\exists x)Q(x)\to(\exists x)\{P(x)\wedge Q(x)\}$
   (c) $(\exists x)\{P(x)\vee Q(x)\}\to(\forall x)P(x)\vee(\forall x)Q(x)$
   (d) $(\exists x)\{P(x)\vee Q(x)\}\to\sim(\forall x)$

[1992 : 1 Mark]

3. Which of the following is/are tautology:
   (a) $(a\vee b)\to(b\wedge c)$ (b) $(a\wedge b)\to(b\vee c)$
   (c) $(a\vee b)\to(b\to c)$ (d) $(a\to b)\to(b\to c)$

[1992 : 1 Mark]

4. The proposition $p\wedge(\sim p\vee q)$ is
   (a) A tautology (b) $\Leftrightarrow(p\wedge q)$
   (c) $\Leftrightarrow(p\vee q)$ (d) A contradiction

[1993 : 1 Mark]

5. Let p and q be propositions. Using only the truth table decide whether $p\leftrightarrow q$ does not imply $p\to\neg q$ is true or false.

[1994 : 2 Marks]

6. If the proposition $\neg p\leftrightarrow q$ is true, then the truth value of the proposition $\neg p\vee(p\to q)$, where $\neg$ is negation 'V' is inclusive or and '$\Rightarrow$' is implication, is
   (a) True (b) Multiple valued
   (c) False (d) Cannot be detemind

[1995 : 2 Marks]

7. Which one of the following is false? Read $\wedge$ as AND, $\vee$ as OR, ~ as NOT, $\to$ as one way implication and $\leftrightarrow$ as two way implication.
   (a) $((x\to y)\wedge x)\to y$
   (b) $((\sim x\to y)\wedge(\sim x\to\sim y))\to x$
   (c) $(x\to(x\vee y))$
   (d) $((x\vee y)\leftrightarrow(\sim x\to\sim y))$

[1996 : 2 Marks]

8. Let a, b c d be propositions, Assumes that the equivalence $a\leftrightarrow(b\vee\neg b)$ and $b\leftrightarrow c$ hold. Then the truth-value of the formula $(a\wedge b)\to(a\wedge c)\vee d$ is always
   (a) True
   (b) False
   (c) Same as the truth-value of b
   (d) Same as the truth-value of d

[2000 : 2 Marks]

9. What is the converse of the following assertion? I stay only if you go
   (a) I stay if you go
   (b) If I stay then you go
   (c) If you do not go then I do not stay
   (d) If I do not stay then you go

[2001 : 1 Mark]

10. Consider two well formed formulas in propositional logic:
    $F_1: P\Rightarrow\neg P$
    $F_2: (P\Rightarrow\neg P)\vee(\neg P\Rightarrow P)$
    Which of the following statements is correct?
    (a) F_1 is satisfiable, F_2 is valid
    (b) F_1 is unsatisfiable, F_2 is satisfiable
    (c) F_1 is unsatisfiable, F_2 is valid
    (d) F_1 and F_2 are both satisfiable

[2001 : 1 Mark]

11. "If X then Y unless Z" is represented by which of the following formulas in propostional logic? ("$\neg$") is negation, "$\wedge$" is conjuction, and "$\to$" is implication)
    (a) $(X\wedge\neg Z)\to Y$
    (b) $(X\wedge Y)\to\neg Z$
    (c) $X\to(Y\wedge\neg Z)$
    (d) $(X\to Y)\wedge\neg Z$

[2002 : 1 Mark]

12. Which of the following is a valid first order formula? (Here α and β are first order formulae with x as their as their only free variable)
    (a) $((\forall x)[\alpha]\to(\forall x)[\beta])\to(\forall x)[\alpha\to\beta]$
    (b) $(\forall x)[\alpha]\to(\exists x)[\alpha\wedge\beta]$
    (c) $(\forall x)[\alpha\wedge\beta]\to(\exists x)[\alpha]\to(\forall x)[\alpha]$
    (d) $(\forall x)[\alpha\to\beta]\to((\forall x)[\alpha]\to(\forall x)[\beta])$

[2003 : 2 Marks]

13. Consider the following formula α and its two interpretations I_1 and I_2

$\alpha : (\forall x)[P_x \Leftrightarrow (\forall y)[Q_{xy} \Leftrightarrow \neg Q_{yy}]]$

$\Rightarrow (\forall x)[\neg P_x]$

I_1 : Same as I_1 except that P_x = 'x is a composite number.'

P_2 = 'x is a prime number'

Q_{xy} = 'y divides x'

I_2 : Same as I_1 except that P_x = 'x is a composite number.

Which of the following statements is true?

(a) I_1 satisfies α, I_2 does not

(b) I_2 satisfies α, I_1 does not

(c) Naither I_2 nor I_1 satisfy α

(d) Both I_1 nor I_2 satisfy α

[2003 : 2 Marks]

14. The following resolution rule is used in logic programming: Drive clause $(P \vee Q)$ from clauses $(P \vee R), (Q \vee \neg R)$

Which of the following statements related to this rule is FALSE?

(a) $(P \vee R) \wedge (Q \vee \neg R) \rightarrow (P \vee Q)$ is logically valid

(b) $(P \vee Q) \rightarrow (P \vee R) \wedge (Q \vee \neg R)$ is logically valid

(c) $(P \vee Q)$ is satisfiable if and only if $(P \vee R) \wedge (Q \vee \neg R)$ is satisfiable

(d) $(P \vee Q) \Rightarrow$ FALSE if and only if both P and Q are uusatisfiable

[2003 : 2 Marks]

15. Identify the correct translation into logical notation of the following assertion. Some boys in the class are taller then all the girls

Note: Taller (x, y)is true if x is taller then y.

(a) $(\exists x)(\text{boy}(x) \rightarrow (\forall y)(\text{girl}(y) \wedge \text{taller}(x,y)))$

(b) $(\exists x)(\text{boy}(x) \wedge (\forall y)(\text{girl}(y) \wedge \text{taller}(x,y)))$

(c) $(\exists x)(\text{boy}(x) \rightarrow (\forall y)(\text{girl}(y) \rightarrow \text{taller}(x,y)))$

(d) $(\exists x)(\text{boy}(x) \wedge (\forall y)(\text{girl}(y) \rightarrow \text{taller}(x,y)))$

[IT-2004 : 1 Mark]

16. Let a(x,y), b(x,y)and c(x,y) be three statementys with variable *x* and *y* chosen from some universe. Consider the following statemet:

$$(\exists x)(\forall y)[(a(x,y) \wedge b(x,y)) \wedge \neg c(x,y)]$$

Which one of the following is its equivalent?

(a) $(\forall x)(\exists y)[(a(x,y) \vee b(x,y)) \rightarrow c(x,y)]$

(b) $(\exists x)(\forall y)[(a(x,y) \vee b(x,y)) \wedge \neg c(x,y)]$

(c) $\neg(\forall x)(\exists y)[(a(x,y) \wedge b(x,y)) \rightarrow c(x,y)]$

(d) $\neg(\forall x)(\exists y)[(a(x,y) \vee b(x,y)) \rightarrow c(x,y)]$

[IT-2004 : 1 Mark]

17. Let *p*,*q*, *r* and *s* be four primitive statements. Consider the following arguments:

P: $[(\neg p \vee q) \wedge (r \rightarrow s) \wedge (p \vee r)] \rightarrow (\neg s \rightarrow q)$

Q: $[(\neg p \vee q) \wedge [q \rightarrow (p \rightarrow r)]] \rightarrow \neg r$

R: $[[(q \wedge r) \rightarrow p] \wedge (\neg q \vee p)] \rightarrow r$

S: $[p \wedge (p \rightarrow r) \wedge (q \vee \neg r)] \rightarrow q$

Which of the above arguments are valid

(a) P and Q only
(b) P and R only
(c) P and S only
(d) P, Q, R and S

[2004 : 2 Marks]

18. The following propositional statementis

$$(P \rightarrow (Q \vee R)) \rightarrow ((P \wedge Q) \rightarrow R)$$

(a) Satisfiable but not valid

(b) Valid

(c) A contradictiction

(d) None of the above

[2004 : 2 Marks]

19. Let P, Q and R be three atomic propositional assertions. Let X denote $(P \vee Q) \rightarrow$ R and Y denote $(P \rightarrow R) \vee (Q \rightarrow R)$. Which one of the following is a taulology?

(a) $X \equiv Y$
(b) $X \rightarrow Y$
(c) $Y \rightarrow X$
(d) $\neg Y \rightarrow X$

[2005 : 2 Marks]

20. What is the first order predicate calculus statement equivalent to the following? Every teacher is liked by some student

(a) $\forall(x)[teacher(x) \rightarrow \exists(y)[\text{student}(y) \rightarrow \text{likes}(y,x)]]$

(b) $\forall(x)[teacher(x) \rightarrow \exists(y)[student(y) \wedge likes(y,x)]]$

(c) $\exists(y)\forall(x)[teacher(x) \rightarrow [student(y) \wedge likes(y,x)]]$

(d) $\forall(x)[teacher(x) \wedge \exists(y)[student(y) \rightarrow likes(y,x)]]$

[2005 : 2 Marks]

21. Let P(x) and Q(x) be arbitrary predicates. Which of the following statements is always TRUE?

(a) $(\forall x(P(x) \vee Q(x))) \Rightarrow ((\forall xP(x)) \vee (\forall xQ(x)))$

(b) $(\forall x(P(x) \Rightarrow Q(x))) \Rightarrow ((\forall xP(x)) \Rightarrow (\forall xQ(x)))$

(c) $(\forall x(P(x) \Rightarrow (\forall xQ(x)))) \Rightarrow (\forall x(P(x) \Rightarrow Q(x)))$

(d) $((\forall x(P(x)) \Leftrightarrow (\forall xQ(x))) \Rightarrow (\forall x(P(x) \Leftrightarrow Q(x)))$

[IT-2005 : 2 Marks]

22. Consider the following first order logic formula in which R is a binary relation symbol.

$\forall x \forall y(R(x, y) \Rightarrow R(y, x))$

The formula is

(a) Satisfiable and valid

(b) Satisfiable and so is its nagation

(c) Unsatisfiable but its negation is valid

(d) Satisfiable but its negation is unsatisfiable

[IT-2006 : 2 Marks]

23. Which one of the first order predicate calculus statements given below correctly expresses the following English statement?

Tigers and lions attack if they are hungry or threatened.

(a) $\forall x[(\text{tiger}(x) \wedge \text{lion}(x)) \rightarrow \{(\text{hungry}(x) \vee \text{threatened}(x)) \rightarrow \text{attacks}(x)\}]$

(b) $\forall x[(\text{tiger}(x) \vee \text{lion}(x)) \rightarrow \{(\text{hungry}(x) \vee \text{threatened}(x)) \wedge \text{attacks}(x)\}]$

(c) $\forall x[(\text{tiger}(x) \vee \text{lion}(x)) \rightarrow \{(\text{attacks}(x) \rightarrow (\text{hungry}(x) \vee \text{threatened}(x))\}]$

(d) $\forall x[(\text{tiger}(x) \vee \text{lion}(x)) \rightarrow \{(\text{hungry}(x) \vee \text{threatened}(x)) \rightarrow \text{attacks}(x)\}]$

[2006 : 2 Marks]

24. Consider the following propositional statements:

$P_1 : ((A \wedge B) \rightarrow C)) \equiv ((A \rightarrow C) \wedge (B \rightarrow C))$

$P_2 : ((A \vee B) \rightarrow C)) \equiv ((A \rightarrow C) \vee (B \rightarrow C))$

Which one of the following is true?

(a) P_1 is tautology, but not P_2

(b) P_2 is a tautology, but not P_1

(c) P_1 and P_2 are both tautologies

(d) Both P_1 and P_2 are not tautologies

[2006 : 2 Marks]

25. A logical binary relation ⊙, is defined as follows:

A	B	A⊙B
True	True	True
True	False	True
False	True	False
False	False	True

Let ~ be the unary negation (NOT) operator, with higher precedence, than ⊙. Which one of the following is equivalent to $A \wedge B$?

(a) (–A⊙B) (b) ~(A⊙~B)

(c) ~(~A⊙~B) (d) ~(~A⊙B)

[2006 : 2 Marks]

26. Let Grabh (x) be a predicate which denotes that x is a graph. Let connected (x) be a predicate which denotes that x is connected. Which of the following first order logic sentences DOES NOT represent the statement; "Not every grabh is connected"?

(a) $\neg \forall x(\text{Graph}(x) \Rightarrow \text{Connected}(x))$

(b) $\exists x(\text{Graph}(x) \wedge \neg\text{Connected}(x))$

(c) $\neg \forall x(\neg\text{Graph}(x) \vee \text{Connected}(x))$

(d) $\forall x(\text{Graph}(x) \Rightarrow \neg\text{Connected}(x))$

[2007 : 2 Marks]

27. Which of the following is TRUE about formulae in Conjuctive Normal Form?

(a) For any formula, there is a truth assignment for which at least half the clauses evaluate to true.

(b) For any formula, there is a truth assignment for a which all the clauses evaluate to true.

(c) There is a formula such that for each truth assignment at most one-fourth of the clauses evaluate to true.

(d) None of the above **[2007 : 2 Marks]**

28. Which one of these first-order logic formulae is valid?

(a) $\forall x(P(x) \Rightarrow Q(x)) \Rightarrow ((\forall xP(x)) \Rightarrow (\forall xQ(x)))$

(b) $\exists x(P(x) \vee Q(x)) \Rightarrow ((\exists xP(x)) \Rightarrow (\exists xQ(x)))$

(c) $\exists x(P(x) \wedge Q(x)) \Leftrightarrow ((\exists xP(x)) \wedge (\exists xQ(x)))$

(d) $\forall x \exists y\ P(x, y) \Rightarrow \exists y \forall x P(x,y)$

[IT-2007 : 2 Marks]

29. Let *fsa* and *pda* be two predicates such that *fsa(x)* means x is a finite state automaton, and *pda(y)* means, that y is a pushdown automaton. Let equivalent be another predicate such that equivalent (a, b) means a and b are equivalent. Which of the following first order logic statement represents the following:

Each finite state automaton has an equivalent pushdown automaton.

(a) $(\forall x\, fsa(x) \Rightarrow (\exists y\, pda(y) \wedge equivalent(x, y))$

(b) $\sim \forall y(\exists x\, fsa(x) \Rightarrow pda(y) \wedge equivalent(x,y))$

(c) $\forall x \exists y(fsa(x) \wedge pda(y) \wedge equivalent(x, y))$

(d) $\forall x \exists y(fsa(y) \wedge pda(x) \wedge equivalent(x, y))$

[2008 : 1 Mark]

30. Which of the following first order formulae is logically valid? Here $a(x)$ is a first order formula with x as a free variable, and β is a first order formula with no free variable.

(a) $[\beta \rightarrow (\exists x, \alpha(x))] \rightarrow [\forall x, \beta \rightarrow \alpha(x)]$

(b) $[\exists x, \beta \rightarrow \alpha(x)] \rightarrow [\beta \rightarrow (\forall x, \alpha(x))]$

(c) $[(\exists x, \alpha(x)) \rightarrow \beta] \rightarrow [\forall x, \alpha(x) \rightarrow \beta]$

(d) $[(\forall x, \alpha(x)) \rightarrow \beta] \rightarrow [\forall x, \alpha(x) \rightarrow \beta]$

[IT-2008 : 2 Marks]

31. Which of the following is the negation of

$[(\forall x, \alpha \rightarrow (\exists y, \beta \rightarrow (\forall u, \exists v, \gamma))]$

(a) $[\exists x, \alpha \rightarrow (\forall y, \beta \rightarrow (\exists u, \forall v, \gamma))]$

(b) $[\exists x, \alpha \rightarrow (\forall y, \beta \rightarrow (\exists u, \forall v, \neg\gamma))]$

(c) $[\forall x, \neg\alpha \rightarrow (\exists y, \neg\beta \rightarrow (\forall u, \exists v, \neg\gamma))]$

(d) $[\forall x, \alpha \wedge (\exists y, \beta \wedge (\exists u, \forall v, \neg\gamma))]$

[IT-2008 : 2 Marks]

32. P and Q are two propositions. which of the following logical expressions are equivalent?

1. $P \vee \sim Q$

2. $\sim(\sim P \wedge Q)$

3. $(P \wedge Q) \vee (P \wedge \sim Q) \vee (\sim P \wedge \sim Q)$

4. $(P \wedge Q) \vee (P \wedge \sim Q) \vee (\sim P \wedge \sim Q)$

(a) Only 1 and 2
(b) Only 1, 2 and 3
(c) Only 1, 2 and 4
(d) All of these

[2008 : 2 Marks]

33. Which one of the following is the most appropriate logical formula to represent the statement:

"Gold and silver ornaments are precious"

The following notations are used:

G(x): x is a gold ornament

S(x): x is a silver ornament

P(x): x is precious

(a) $\forall x(P(x) \rightarrow (G(x) \wedge S(x)))$

(b) $\forall x(G(x) \wedge (S(x) \rightarrow P(x)))$

(c) $\exists x((G(x) \wedge S(x)) \rightarrow P(x))$

(d) $\forall x((G(x) \vee S(x)) \rightarrow P(x))$ **[2009 : 2 Marks]**

34. The binary operation □ is defined as follows:

P	Q	P□Q
T	T	T
T	F	T
F	T	F
F	F	T

Which one of the following is equivalent to $P \vee Q$?

(a) ¬Q□¬P
(b) P□¬Q
(c) ¬P□Q
(d) ¬P□¬Q

[2009 : 2 Marks]

35. Consider the following well-formed formulae:

I. $\neg\forall x(P(x))$
II. $\neg\exists x(P(x))$
III. $\neg\exists x(\neg P(x))$
IV. $\exists x(\neg P(x))$

Which of the above are equivalent?

(a) I and II
(b) I and IV
(c) II and III
(d) II and IV

[2009 : 2 Marks]

36. Suppose the predicate F(x, y, t) is used to represent the statement that person x can fool person y at time t. Which one of the statements below expresses best the meaning of the formula $\forall x \exists y \exists t(\neg F(x, y, t))$?

(a) Everyone can fool some person at some time

(b) No one can fool everyone all the time

(c) Everyone cannot fool some person all the time

(d) No one can fool some person at some time

[2010 : 2 Marks]

37. Which one of the following options is CORRECT given three positive integers x, y and z, and a predicate

$$P(x) = \neg(x=1) \wedge \forall y(\exists z(x = y * z) \Rightarrow (y = x) \vee (y = 1)$$

(a) P(x) being true means that x is a prime number

(b) P(x) being true means that x is a number other that 1

(c) P(x) is always true irrespective of the value of x

(d) P(x) being true means that x has exactly two factors other than 1 and x

[2011 : 2 Marks]

38. Consider the following logical inferences.

I_1: If it rains then the cricket match will not be played.

The cricket match was played.

Inference: There was no rain.

I_2: If it rains then the cricket match will not be played.

It did not rain.

Infernce: The cricket match was played. Which of the following is TRUE?

(a) Both I_1 and I_2 are correct inferences

(b) I_1 is correct but I_2 is not a correct inference

(c) I_1 is not correct but I_2 is a correct inference

(d) Both I_1 and I_2 are not correct inferences

[2012 : 1 Mark]

39. What is the correct translation of the following statement into mathematical logic?

"Some real numbers are rational"

(a) $\exists x(real(x) \vee rational(x))$

(b) $\forall x(real(x) \rightarrow rational(x))$

(c) $\exists x(real(x) \wedge rational(x))$

(d) $\exists x(rational(x) \rightarrow real(x))$ **[2012 : 1 Mark]**

40. What is the logical translation of the following statements?

"None of my friends are perfect"

(a) $\exists x(F(x) \wedge \neg P(x))$ (b) $\exists x(\neg F(x) \wedge P(x))$

(c) $\exists x(\neg F(x) \wedge \neg P(x))$ (d) $\neg \exists x(F(x) \wedge P(x))$

[2013 : 2 Marks]

41. Which one of the following it NOT logically equivalent to $\neg \exists x(\forall y(\alpha) \wedge \forall z(\beta))$

(a) $\forall x(\exists z(\neg \beta) \rightarrow \forall y(\alpha))$

(b) $\forall x(\forall z(\beta) \rightarrow \exists y(\neg \alpha))$

(c) $\forall x(\forall y(\alpha) \rightarrow \exists z(\neg \beta))$

(d) $\forall x(\exists y(\neg \alpha) \vee \exists z(\neg \beta))$ **[2013 : 2 Marks]**

42. Consider the statement:

"Not all that glitters is gold"

Predicate glitters (x) is true if x glitters and predicate gold (x) is true if x is gold. Which one of the following logical formulae represents the above statement?

(a) $\forall x: glitters(x) \Rightarrow \neg gold(x)$

(b) $\forall x: gold(x) \Rightarrow glitters(x)$

(c) $\exists x: gold(x) \wedge \neg glitters(x)$

(d) $\exists x: glitters(x) \wedge \neg gold(x)$

[2014 (Set-1) : 1 Mark]

43. Which one of the following propositional logic formulas is TRUE when exactly two of p, q, and r are TRUE?

(a) $((p \leftrightarrow q) \wedge r) \vee (p \wedge q \wedge \sim r)$

(b) $(\sim(p \leftrightarrow q) \wedge r) \vee (p \wedge q \wedge \sim r)$

(c) $((p \rightarrow q) \wedge r) \vee (p \wedge q \wedge \sim r)$

(d) $(\sim(p \leftrightarrow q) \wedge r) \wedge (p \wedge q \wedge \sim r)$

[2014 (Set-1) : 2 Marks]

44. Which one of the following Boolean expressions is NOT a tautology?

(a) $((a \rightarrow b) \wedge (b \rightarrow c)) \rightarrow (a \rightarrow c)$

(b) $(a \leftrightarrow c) \rightarrow (\sim b \rightarrow (a \wedge c))$

(c) $(a \wedge b \wedge c) \rightarrow (c \vee a)$

(d) $a \rightarrow (b \rightarrow a)$

[2014(Set-2) : 2 Marks]

45. Consider the following statements:

P: Good mobile phones are not cheap

Q: Cheap mobile phones are not good

L: P implies Q

M: Q implies P

N: P is equivalent to Q

Which one of the following about L, M and N is CORRECT?

(a) Only L is TRUE (b) Only M is TRUE

(c) Only N is TRUE (d) L, M and N are TRUE.

[2014 (Set-3) : 1 Mark]

46. The CORRECT formula for the sentence, "not all rainy days are cold" is

(a) $\forall d(Rainy(d) \wedge \sim Cold(d))$

(b) $\forall d(\sim Rainy(d) \rightarrow Cold(d))$

(c) $\exists d(\sim Rainy(d) \rightarrow Cold(d))$

(d) $\exists d(Rainy(d) \wedge \sim Cold(d))$

[2014 (Set-3) : 2 Marks]

47. Which one of the following is Not equivalent to $p \leftrightarrow q$?

(a) $(\neg p \vee q) \wedge (p \vee \neg q)$ (b) $(\neg p \vee q) \wedge (q \rightarrow p)$

(c) $(\neg p \wedge q) \vee (p \vee \neg q)$ (d) $(\neg p \wedge \neg q) \vee (p \vee q)$

[2015 (Set-1 : 1 Mark]

48. The binary operator $\neq$ is defined by the following truth table.

p	q	$p \neq q$
0	0	0
0	1	1
1	0	1
1	1	0

Which one of the following is true about the binary operator $\neq$?

(a) Both commutative and associative

(b) Commutative but not associative

(c) Not commutative but associative

(d) Neither commutative nor associative

[2015 (Set-1) : 2 Marks]

49. Consider the following two statement:

S_1: If a condidate is known to be corrupt, then he will not be elected.

S_2: If a condidate is kind, he will be elected.

Which one of the following statements follows from S_1 and S_2 as per sound inference rules of logic?

(a) If a person is known to be corrupt, he is kind

(b) If a person is not known to be corrupt, he is not kind

(c) If a person is kind,he is not known to be corrupt

(d) If a person is not kind, he is not known to be corrupt

[2015 (Set-2) : 1 Mark]

50. Which one of the following well formed formulae is a tautology?

(a) $\forall x\, \exists y\; R(x,y) \leftrightarrow \exists y\, \forall x\, R(x,y)$

(b) $(\forall x[\exists y\; R(x,y) \rightarrow S(x,y)]) \rightarrow \forall x\, \exists y\, S(x,y)$

(c) $[\forall x \exists y (P(x,y) \rightarrow R(x,y))] \leftrightarrow [\forall x \exists y (\neg P(x,y) \vee R(x,y))]$

(d) $\forall x\, \forall y\, P(x,y) \rightarrow \forall x\, \forall y\, P(y,x)$

[2015 (Set-2) : 2 Marks]

51. In a room there are only two types of people, namely Type 1 and Type 2. Type 1 people always tell the truth and Type 2 people always lie. You give a fair coin to a person in that room, without knowing which type he is from and tell him to toss it and hide the result from you till you ask for it. Upon asking, the person replies the following:

"The result of the toss is head if and only if I am telling the truth."

Which of the following options is correct?

(a) The result is head

(b) The result is tail

(c) If the person is of Type 2, then the result is tail

(d) If the person is of Type 1, then the result is tail

[2015 (Set-3) : 1 Mark]

52. Let p, q, r, s represent the following propositions.

p: $x \in \{8, 9, 10, 11, 12\}$

q: x is a composite number

r: x is a perfect square

s: x is a prime number

The integer $x \geq 2$ which satisfies $\neg((p \Rightarrow q) \wedge (\neg r \vee \neg s))$ is ___.

[2016 (Set-1) : 1 Mark]

53. Consider the following expressions:

(i) False (ii) Q

(iii) True (iv) $P \vee Q$

(v) $\neg Q \vee P$

The number of expressions given above that are logically implied by $P \vee (P \Rightarrow Q)$ is ___.

[2016 (Set-2) : 1 Mark]

54. Which one of the following well-formed formulae in predicate calculus is **NOT** valid?

(a) $(\forall x\, p(x) \Rightarrow \forall x q(x)) \Rightarrow (\exists x \neg p(x) \vee \forall x\, q(x))$

(b) $(\exists x\, p(x) \vee \exists x\, q(x)) \Rightarrow \exists x (p(x) \vee q(x))$

(c) $\exists x (p(x) \wedge q(x)) \Rightarrow (\exists x\, p(x) \wedge \exists x\, q(x))$

(d) $\forall x (p(x) \vee q(x)) \Rightarrow (\forall x\, p(x) \vee \forall x\, q(x))$

[2016 (Set-2 : 2 Marks]

55. Consider the first-order logic sentence $F : \forall x (\exists y\, R(x,y))$. Assuming non-emply logical domains, which of the sentences below are implied by F?

I. $\exists y (\exists x\, R(x,y))$ II. $\exists y (\forall x\, R(x,y))$

III. $\forall y (\exists x\, R(x,y))$ IV. $\neg \exists x (\forall y \neg R(x,y))$

(a) IV only (b) I and IV only

(c) II only (d) II and III only

[2017 (Set-1) : 1 Mark]

56. The statement is $(\neg p) \Rightarrow (\neg q)$ logically equivalent to which of the statements below?

I. $p \Rightarrow q$ II. $q \Rightarrow p$

III. $(\neg q) \vee p$ IV. $(\neg p) \vee q$

(a) I only (b) I and IV only

(c) II only (d) II and III only

[2017 (Set-1) : 1 Mark]

57. Let p, q and r be propositions and the expression $(p \rightarrow q) \rightarrow r$ be a contradiction. Then, the expression $(r \rightarrow p) \rightarrow q$ is

(a) A tautology

(b) A contradiction

(c) Always TRUE when p is FALSE

(d) Always TRUE when q is TRUE

[2017 (Set-1) : 2 Marks]

58. Let p, q, r denote the statements "It is raining", "It is cold", and "It is pleasant", respectively. Then the statement "It is not raining and it is pleasant, and it is not pleasant only if it is raining and it is cold" is represented by

(a) $(\neg p \wedge r) \wedge (\neg r \rightarrow (p \wedge q))$

(b) $(\neg p \wedge r) \wedge ((p \wedge q) \rightarrow \neg r)$

(c) $(\neg p \wedge r) \vee ((p \wedge q) \rightarrow \neg r)$

(d) $(\neg p \wedge r) \vee (r \rightarrow (p \wedge q))$

[2017 (Set-2) : 1 Mark]

59. Consider the first order logic sentence:

$$\varphi \equiv \exists s \exists t \exists u \forall v \forall w \forall x \forall y \psi(s,t,u,v,w,x,y)$$

where ψ (s, t, u, v, w, x, y) is a quantifier-free first-order logic formula using only predicate symbols and possibly equality, but no function symbols. Suppose φ has a model with a universe containing 7 elements.

Which one of the following statements is necessary true?

(a) There exists at least one model of φ with universe of size less than or equal to 3.

(b) There existsno model of φ with universe of size less than or equal to 3.

(c) There exists no model of φ with universe of size greater than 7.

(d) Every model of φ has a universe of size equal to 7. **[2018 : 2 Marks]**

60. The value of 3^{51} mod 5 is ______. **[2019 : 1 Mark]**

61. Let G be an arbitrary group. Consider the following relations on G:

R_1: ∀ a, b ∈ G, a R_1 b if and only if ∃ g ∈ G such that $a = g^{-1}bg$

R_2: ∀ a, b ∈ G, aR_2b if and only if $a = b^{-1}$

Which of the above is/are equivalence relation/relations?

(a) Neither R_1 nor R_2 (b) R_2 only

(c) R_1 only (d) R_1 and R_2 **[2019 : 1 Mark]**

SET THEORY AND ALGEBRA

1. State whether the following statement are TRUE or FALSE :

The union of two equivalence relations is also an equivalence relation. **[1987 : 1 Mark]**

2. (a) How many binary relations are there on a set A with n elements?

(b) How many one-to-one functions are there from a set A with n elements onto itself. **[1987 : 1 Mark]**

3. The complements(s)of the element 'a' in the lattice shown in figure is (are).........

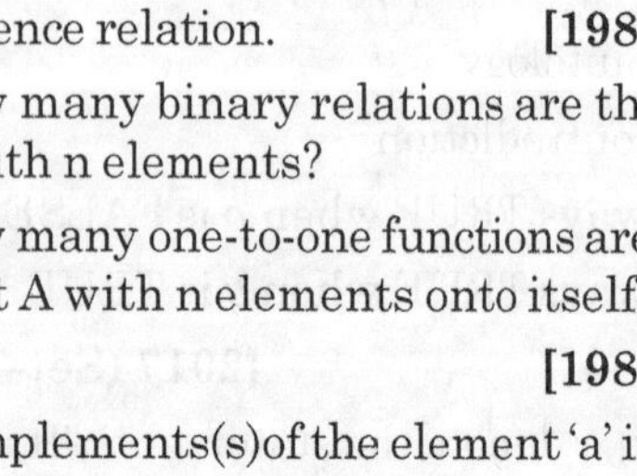

[1988 : 2 Mark]

4. The transitive closure of the relation {(1, 2), (2, 3) (3, 4)(5, 4)} on the set A = {1, 2, 3, 4, 5} is .... **[1989 : 2 Mark]**

5. Let S be an infinite set and S1, S2, ...Sn be sets such that $S_1 \cup S_2 \cup ..... \cup S_n = S$. Then

(a) At least one of the sets S_i is a finite set

(b) Not more than one of the sets S_i can be finite

(c) At least one of set Si is infinite

(d) Not more than one the set Si is an a infinite set. **[1993 : 1 Mark]**

6. Let A be a finite set of size n. The number of elements in the power set of A × A is

(a) 2^{2^n} (b) 2^{n^2}

(c) 2n (d) 2^n **[1993 : 1 Mark]**

7. Some group (G, o)is known to be abelian. Then, which one of the following is true for G?

(a) $g = g^{-1}$ for every g ∈ G

(b) $g = g^2$ for every g ∈ G

(c) $(goh)^2 = g^2 o h^2$ for every g, h ∈ G

(d) G is finite order **[1994 : 2 Marks]**

8. Let R be a symmetric and transitive relation on a set A. Then

(a) R is reflexive and hence an equivalence relation

(b) R is reflexive and hence a partial order

(c) R is reflexive and hence not an equivalence relation

(d) None of the above **[1995 : 1 Mark]**

9. The number of elements in the power set P(S) of the set S = {(ϕ), 1, (2, 3)} is :

(a) 2 (b) 4

(c) 8 (d) None of these **[1995 : 1 Mark]**

10. Let A be the set of all nonsingular matrices over real numbers and let * be the matrix multiplication operator. Then

(a) A is closed under * but (A, *) is not a semigroup

(b) (A, *) is a semigroup but not a monoid.

(c) (A, *) is monoid but not a group.

(d) (A, *) is a group but not an abelian group **[1995 : 2 Marks]**

11. Let A and B be sets and let A^c and B^c denote the complements of the sets A and B. The set $(A - B) \cup (B - A) \cup (A \cap B)$ is equal to

(a) $A \cup B$ (b) $A^c \cup B^c$

(c) $A \cap B$ (d) $A^c \cap B^c$ **[1996 : 1 Mark]**

12. Let X = {2, 3, 6, 12, 24}. Let ≤ be the partial order defined by x ≤ y if x divides y. The number of edges in the Hasse diagram of (X, ≤) is

(a) 3 (b) 4

(c) 9 (d) None of these

[1996 : 1 Mark]

13. Suppose X and Y are sets and |X| and |Y| are their respective cardinalities. It is given that there are exactly 97 functions from X to Y. From this one can conclude that

(a) |X| = 1, |Y| = 97 (b) |X| = 97, |Y| = 1

(c) |X| = 97, |Y| = 97 (d) None of the above

[1996 : 1 Mark]

14. Which of the following statements is false?

(a) The set of rational numbers is an abelian group under addition

(b) The set of integers in an abelian group under addition

(c) The set of rational numbers form an abelian group under multiplication

(d) The set of real numbers excluding zero in an abelian group under multiplication

[1996 : 1 Mark]

15. Let R denote the set of seal numbers. Let f : R × R → R × R be a bijective function defined by f(x, y) = (x + y, x – y). The inverse function of f is given by

(a) $f^{-1}(x, y) = \left(\frac{1}{x+y}, \frac{1}{x-y}\right)$

(b) $f^{-1}(x, y) = (x - y, x + y)$

(c) $f^{-1}(x, y) = \left(\frac{x+y}{2}, \frac{x-y}{2}\right)$

(d) $f^{-1}(x, y) = 2(x - y), 2(x + y)$

[1996 : 2 Marks]

16. Let R be a non-empty relation on a collection of sets defined by ARB if and only if $A \cap B = \phi$. Then, (pick the true stateent)

(a) R is reflexive and transitive

(b) R is symmetric and not transitive

(c) R is an equivalence relation

(d) R is not reflexive and not symmetric.

[1996 : 2 Marks]

17. Which one of the following is false?

(a) The set of all bijective functions on a finite set forms a group under function composition.

(b) The set {1, 2, ..., p – 1) forms a group under multiplication mod p where p is a prime number.

(c) The set of all strings over a finite alphabet Σ forms a group under concatenation.

(d) A subset $s \neq \phi$ of G is a subgroup of the group (G, *) if and only if for any pair of elements a, $b \in s, a * b^{-1} \in s$.

[1996 : 2 Marks]

18. The number of equivalence relations on the set {1, 2, 3, 4} is

(a) 15 (b) 16

(c) 24 (d)

[1997 : 1 Mark]

19. Suppose A is a finite set with n elements. The number of elements in the Largest equivalence relation of A is

(a) n (b) n^2

(c) 1 (d) n + 1

[1998 : 1 Mark]

20. Let R_1 and R_2 be two equivalence relations on a set. Consider the following assertions :

(i) $R_1 \cup R_2$ is an equivalence relation

(ii) $R_1 \cap R_2$ is an equivalence relation

Which of the following is correct?

(a) both assertions are true

(b) assertion (i) is true but assertion (ii) is not true

(c) assertion (ii) is true but assertion (i) is not true

(d) neither (i) nor (ii)is true **[1998 : 1 Mark]**

21. The number of functions from m element set to an n element set is

(a) m + n (b) m^n

(c) n^m (d) m * n

[1998 : 1 Mark]

22. The binary relation R = {(1, 1), (2, 1), (2, 2), (2, 3), (2, 4), (3, 1), (3, 2), (3, 3), (3, 4)} on the set A = {1, 2, 3, 4} is

(a) Reflexive, symmetric and transitive

(b) Neither reflexive, nor irreflexive but transitive

(c) Irreflexive, symmetric and transitive

(d) Irreflexive and antisymmetric

[1998 : 2 Marks]

23. Suppose A = {a, b, c, d} and Π is the following partition of A

$$\Pi_1 = \{\{a, b, c\}, \{d\}\}$$

(a) List the ordered pairs of the equivalence relations induced by Π_1

(b) Draw the graph of the above equivalence relation

[1998 : 2 Marks]

24. Let (A, *) be a semigroup. Furthermore, for every a and b in A, if $a \neq b$, then $a * b \neq b * a$.

(a) Show that for every a in A
$a * a = a$

(b) Show that for every a, b in A
$a * b * a = a$

(c) Show that for every a, b, c in A
$a * b * c = a * c$

[1998 : 2 Marks]

25. The number of binary relations on a set with n elements is

(a) n^2 (b) 2n

(c) 2^{n^2} (d) None of these

[1999 : 1 Mark]

26. (a) Mr. X claims the following : If a relation R is both symmetric and transitive, then R is reflexive. For this, Mr. X offers the following proof.

"From xRy, using symmetry we get yRx. Now because R is transitive, xRy and yRx together imply xRx. Therefore, R is reflexive."

(b) Give an example of a relation R which is symmetric and transitive but not reflexive.

[1999 : 2 Marks]

27. A relation R is defined on the set of integers as xRy iff (x + y)is even. Which of the following statements is true ?

(a) R is not an equivalence relation

(b) R is an equivalence relation having 1 equivalence class

(c) R is an equivalence relation having 2 equivalence classes

(d) R is an equivalence relation having 3 equivalence classes **[2000 : 2 Marks]**

28. Let P(S)denote the power set of a set S. Which of the following is always true ?

(a) $P(P(S)) = P(S)$ (b) $P(S) \cap P(P(S)) = \{\varnothing\}$

(c) $P(S) \cap S = P(S)$ (d) $S \notin P(S)$

[2000 : 2 Marks]

29. Consider the following relations

R_1 (a, b) iff (a + b)is even over the set of integers

R_2 (a, b) iff (a + b)is odd over the set of integers

R_1 (a, b) iff a.b > 0 over the set of non-zero rational numbers.

R_4(a, b) iff $|a - b| < 2$ over the set of natural numbers

Which of the following statements is correct?

(a) R_1 and R_2 are equivalence relations, R_3 and R_4 are not

(b) R_1 and R_3 are equivalence relations, R_2 and R_4 are not

(c) R_1 and R_4 are equivalence relations, R_2 and R_4 are not

(d) R_1, R_2 R_3 and R_4 are all equivalence relations

[2001 : 1 Mark]

30. Consider the following statements :

S_1 : There exist infinite sets A, B, C such that $A \cap (B \cap C)$ is finite.

S_2 : There exist two irrational numbers x and y such that (x + y)is rational.

Which of the following is true about S_1 and S_2?

(a) Only S_1 is correct

(b) Only S_2 is correct

(c) Both S_1 and S_2 are correct

(d) None of S_1 and S_2 is correct

[2001 : 2 Marks]

31. Let $f : A \to B$ be a function, and let E and f be subsets of A. Consider the following statements about images.

$S_1 : f(E \cup F) = f(E) \cup f(F)$

$S_2 : f(E \cap F) = f(E) \cap f(F)$

(a) Only S_1 is correct

(b) Only S_2 is correct

(c) Both S_1 and S_2 are correct

(d) None of S_1 and S_2 is correct

[2001 : 2 Mark]

32. The binary relation S = f(empty set)on set A = {1, 2, 3} is

(a) Neither reflexive nor symmetric

(b) Symmetric and reflexive

(c) Transitive and reflexive

(d) Transitive and symmetric

[2002 : 2 Mark]

33. Consider the set Σ^* of all strings over the alphabet $\Sigma = \{0,1\}$. Σ^* with the concatenation operator for strings

(a) does not form a group

(b) forms a non-commutative group

(c) does not have a right identity element

(d) forms a group if the empty string is removed from Σ^*

[2003 : 1 Mark]

34. Let (S, $\leq$) be a partial order with two minimal elements a and b, and a maximum element c. Let Let P : S $\rightarrow$ {True, False) be a predicate defined on S. Suppose that P(a)= True, P(b) = False and P(x) $\Rightarrow$ P(y)for all x, y $\in$ S satisfying x $\leq$ y, where $\Rightarrow$ stands for logical implication. Which of the following statements CANNOT be true?

(a) P(x) = True for all x $\in$ S such that x $\neq$ b

(b) P(x) = False for all x $\in$ S such that x $\neq$ a and x $\neq$ c

(c) P(x) = False for all x $\in$ S such that b $\leq$ x such that x $\neq$ c

(d) P(x) = False for all x $\in$ S such that a $\leq$ x and b $\neq$ x

[2003 : 2 Marks]

35. Consider the set {a, b, c} with binary operators + and × defined as follows :

+	a	b	c
a	b	a	c
b	a	b	c
c	a	c	b

×	a	b	c
a	a	b	c
b	b	c	a
c	c	c	b

For example, a + c = c = c + a = a, c × b = c and b × c = a.

Given the following set of equations :

(a × x) + (a × y) = c

(b × x) + (c × y) = c

The number of solution (s) (i.e., pair (s) (x, y)that satisfies the equations) is

(a) 0 (b) 1

(c) 2 (d) 3

[2003 : 2 Marks]

36. Consider the binary relation :

S = {(x, y) | y = x + 1 and x, y $\in$ {0, 1, 2, ...}}

The reflexive transitive closure of S is

(a) {(x, y) | y > x and x, y $\in$ {0, 1, 2, ...}}

(b) {(x, y) | y $\geq$ x and x, y $\in$ {0, 1, 2, ...}}

(c) {(x, y) | y < x and x, y $\in$ {0, 1, 2, ...}}

(d) {(x, y) | y $\leq$ x and x, y $\in$ {0, 1, 2, ...}}

[2004 : 1 Mark]

37. The number of different n × n symmetric matrices with each element being either 0 or 1 is : (Note : power (2, x) is same as 2^x)

(a) power (2, n)

(b) power (2, n^2)

(c) power (2, (n^2 + n)/2

(d) power (2, (n^2 – n)/2)

[2004 : 1 Mark]

38. In a class of 200 students, 125 students have taken programming Language course, 85 students have taken Data Structures course, 65 students have taken Computer Organization course; 50 students have taken both Programming Language and Data Structure 35 students have taken both Data Structures and Computer Organization; 30 students have taken both Data Structures and Computer Organization, 15 students have taken all the three courses. How many students have not taken any of the three courses?

(a) 15 (b) 20

(c) 25 (d) 30

[IT-2004 : 1 Mark]

39. Let R_1 be a relation from A = {1, 3, 5, 7} to B = {2, 4, 6, 8} and R_2 be another relation from B to C = {1, 2, 3, 4} as defined below :

(i) An elements x in A is related to an element y in B (under R_1)if x + y is divisible by 3.

(ii) An elements x in B is related to an element y in C (under R_2)if x + y is even but not divisible by 3.

Which is the composite relation R_1R_2 from A to C?

(a) R_1R_2 = {(1, 2), (1, 4)(3, 3), (5, 4), (7, 3)}

(b) R_1R_2 = {(1, 2), (1, 3)(3, 2), (5, 2), (7, 3)}

(c) R_1R_2 = {(1, 2), (3, 2)(3, 4), (5, 4), (7, 2)}

(d) R_1R_2 = {(3, 2), (3, 4)(5, 1), (5, 3), (7, 1)}

[IT-2004 : 1 Mark]

40. The following is the incomplete operation table of a 4-element group.

*	e	a	b	c
e	e	a	b	c
a	a	b	c	e
b				
c				

The last row of the table is

(a) c a e b (b) c b a e

(c) c b e a (d) c e a b

[2004 : 2 Marks]

41. The inclusion of which of the following sets into S = {{1, 2}, {1, 2, 3}, {1, 3, 5}, {1, 2, 4}, {1, 2, 3, 4, 5}} is necessary and sufficient to make S a complete lattice under the partial order defined by set containment?

(a) {1}

(b) {1}, {2, 3}

(c) {1}, {1, 3}

(d) {1}, {1, 3}, {1, 2, 3, 4}, {1, 2, 3, 5}

[2004 : 2 Marks]

42. Let A, B and C be non-empty sets and let X = (A – B) – C and Y = (A – C)– (B – C)
Which one of the following is TRUE :
(a) X = Y (b) $X \subset Y$
(c) $Y \subset X$ (d) None of these
[2005 : 1 Mark]

43. The following is the Hasses diagram of the poset [{a, b, c, d, e} $\le$]

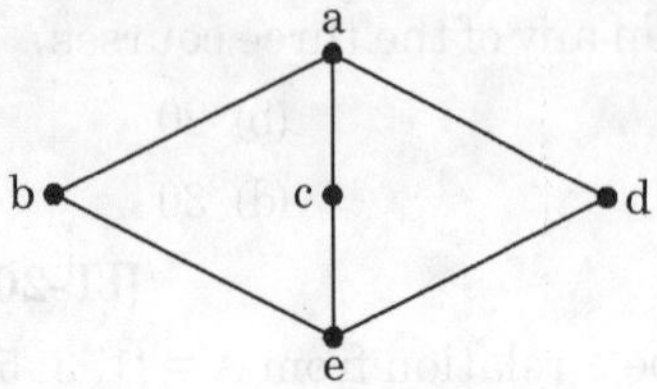

The poset is
(a) not a lattice
(b) a lattice but not a distributive lattice
(c) a distributive lattice but not a Boolean algebra
(d) a Boolean algebra
[2005 : 1 Mark]

44. The set {1, 2, 4, 7, 8, 11, 13, 14} is a group under multiplication modulo 15. The inverses of 4 and 7 are respectively
(a) 3 and 13 (b) 2 and 11
(c) 4 and 13 (d) 8 and 14
[2005 : 1 Mark]

45. Let R and S be any two equivalence relations on a non-empty set A. Which one of the following statements is TRUE?
(a) $R \cap S$, $R \cup S$ are both equivalence relations
(b) $R \cup S$ is an equivalence relation
(c) $R \cap S$ is an equivalence relation
(d) Neither $R \cup S$ nor $R \cap S$ is an equivalence relation
[2005 : 2 Marks]

46. Let $f : B \to C$ and $g : A \to B$ be two functions and let h = f o g. Given that h is an onto function.
(a) f and g should both be onto functions
(b) f should be onto but g need not be onto
(c) g should be onto but f not be onto
(d) both f and g need not be onto
[2005 : 2 Marks]

47. Consider the set H of all 3 × 3 matrices of the type

$$\begin{bmatrix} a & f & e \\ 0 & b & d \\ 0 & 0 & c \end{bmatrix}$$

where a, b, c, d, e and f are real numbers and abc $\neq$ 0. Under the matrix multiplication operation, the set H is
(a) a group
(b) a monoid but not group
(c) a semigroup but not a monoid
(d) neither a group nor a semigroup
[2005 : 2 Marks]

48. Let f be a function from a set A to a set B, g a function from B to C, and h a function from A to C, such that h(a) = g(f(a)) for all a $\in$ A. Which of the following statements is always true for all such functions f and g?
(a) g is onto $\Rightarrow$ h is onto
(b) h is onto $\Rightarrow$ f is onto
(c) h is onto $\Rightarrow$ f is onto
(d) h is onto $\Rightarrow$ f and g are onto
[IT-2005 : 2 Marks]

49. Let A be a set with n elements. Let C be a collection of distinct subsets of A such that for any two subsets S_1 and S_2 in C, either $S_1 \subset S_2$ or $S_2 \subset S_1$. What is the maximum cardinality of C?
(a) n (b) n + 1
(c) $2^{n-1} + 1$ (d) n!
[IT-2006 : 1 Mark]

50. For the set N of natural numbers and a binary operation f : N × N $\to$ N, an element n N is called an identity for f, if f(a, z)= a = f(z, a), for all a N. Which of the following binary operations have a identity?
I. f(x, y) = x + y – 3 II. f(x, y) = max (x, y)
III. f(x, y) = x^y
(a) I and II only (b) II and III only
(c) I and III only (d) None of these
[2006 : 1 Mark]

51. Let, X, Y, Z be sets of sizes x, y and z respectively. Let W = X × Y and E be the set of all subsets of W. The number of functions from Z to E is
(a) z (b) z × 2^{xy}
(c) 2^z (d) 2^{xyz}
[2006 : 1 Mark]

52. The set {1, 2, 3, 5, 7, 8, 9} under multiplication modulo 10 is not a group. Given below are four possible reasons. Which one of them is false?
(a) It is not closed
(b) 2 does not have an inverse
(c) 3 does not have an inverse
(d) 8 does not have an inverse
[2006 : 1 Mark]

53. A relation R is defined on ordered pairs of integers as follows : (x, y) R (u, v) if x < u and y > v. Then R is

(a) Neither a Partial Order nor an Equivalence Relation
(b) A Partial Order but not a Total Order
(c) A Total Order
(d) An Equivalenc Relation **[2006 : 1 Mark]**

54. Let E, F and G be finite sets :

Let $X = (E \cap F) - (F \cap G)$ and

$Y = (E - (E \cap G) - (E \cap F)$

Which one of the following is true ?

(a) $X \subset Y$ (b) $X \supset Y$
(c) $X = Y$ (d) $X - Y \neq \varnothing$ and $Y - X \neq \varnothing$

[2006 : 2 Marks]

55. Let S = {1, 2, 3, ..., m}, m > 3. Let X_1, X_2, ... Xn be subsets of S each of size 3. Define a function f from S to the set of natural numbers as, f(i) is the number of sets X that contains the element i. That is $f(i) = |\{j \mid i \in X_j\}|$.

Then $\sum_{i=1}^{m} f(i)$ is

(a) 3m (b) 3n
(c) 2m + 1 (d) 2n + 1

[2006 : 2 Marks]

56. Let P, Q and R be sets let Δ denote the symmetric difference operator defined as $P \Delta Q = (P \cup Q) - (P \cap Q)$. Using Venn diagrams, determine which of the following is/are TRUE ?

I. $P \Delta (Q \cap R) = (P \Delta Q) \cap (P \Delta R)$.

II. $P \cap (Q \Delta R) = (P \cap Q) \Delta (P \cap R)$

(a) I only (b) II only
(c) Neither I nor II (d) Both I and II

[IT-2006 : 2 Marks]

57. What is the cardinality of the set of integers X defined below? X = {n | 1 ≤ n ≤ 123, n is not divisible by 2, 3 or 5}

(a) 28 (b) 33
(c) 37 (d) 44

[IT-2006 : 2 Marks]

58. Let S be a set of n elements. The number of ordered pairs in the largest and the smallest equivalence relations on S are

(a) n and n (b) n^2 and n
(c) n^2 and 0 (d) n and 1

[2007 : 1 Mark]

59. Consider the set S = {a, b, c, d}. Consider the following 4 partitions $\pi_1, \pi_2, \pi_3, \pi_4$, on

S : $\pi_1 = \{\overline{abcd}\}$, $\pi_2\{\overline{ab}, \overline{cd}\}$,

$\pi_3 = \{\overline{abc}, \overline{d}\}$, $\pi_4 = \{\overline{a}, \overline{b}, \overline{c}, \overline{d}\}$

Let ≺ be the partial order on the set of partitions $S' = (\pi_1, \pi_2, \pi_3, \pi_4)$ defined as follows $\pi_i \prec \pi_j$ if and only if π_i refines π_j. The poset diagram for (S', ≺) is

(a) 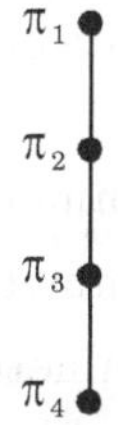

(b) 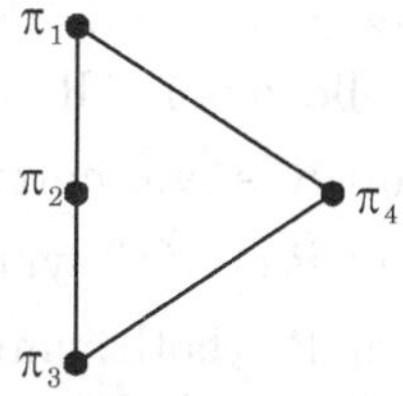

(c) 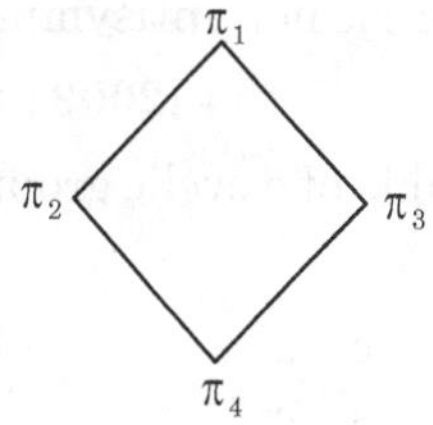

(d) 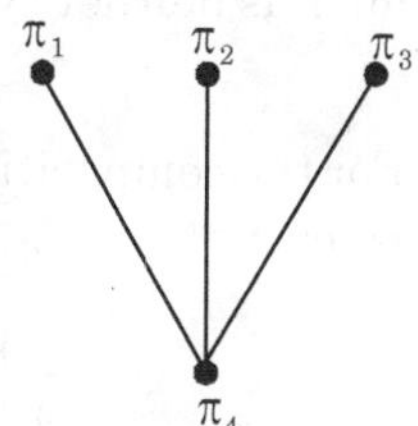

[2007 : 2 Marks]

60. Apartial order P is defined on the set of natural numbers as follows. Here x/y denotes integer division.

(i) (0, 0) ∈ P.

(ii) (a, b) ∈ P if and only if a % 10 ≤ b % 10 and (a/10, b/10) ∈ P.

Consider the following ordered pairs :

(i) (101, 22) (ii) (22, 101)
(iii) (145, 265) (iv) (0, 153)

Which of these ordered pairs of natural numbers are contained in P?

(a) (i) and (iii) (b) (ii) and (iv)
(c) (i) and (iv) (d) (iii) and (iv)

[IT-2007 : 2 Marks]

61. If P, Q, R are subset of the universal set U, then $(P \cap Q \cap R) \cup (P^c \cap Q \cap R) \cup Q^c \cup R^c$ is

(a) $Q^c \cup R^c$ (b) $P \cup Q^c \cup R^c$
(c) $P^c \cup Q^c \cup R^c$ (d) U **[2008 : 1 Mark]**

62. Consider the following Hasse diagrams.

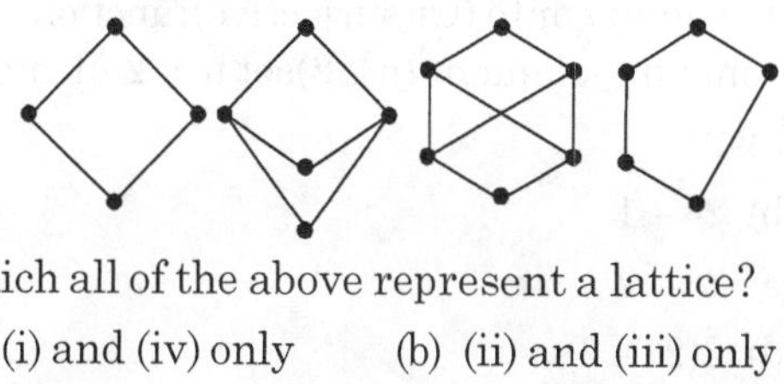

Which all of the above represent a lattice?

(a) (i) and (iv) only (b) (ii) and (iii) only
(c) (iii) only (d) (i), (ii) and (iv) only

[IT-2008 : 2 Marks]

63. Which one of the following is NOT necessarily a property of a Group?
(a) Commutativity
(b) Associativity
(c) Existence of inverse for every element
(d) Existence of identity

[2009 : 1 Mark]

64. Consider the binary relation : R = {(x, y), (x, z), (z, x), (z, y)} on the set {x, y, z}. Which one of the following is TRUE ?
(a) R is symmetric but NOT antisymmetric
(b) R is NOT symmetric but antisymmetric
(c) R is both symmetric and antisymmetric
(d) R is neither symmetric nor antisymmetric

[2009 : 1 Mark]

65. For the composition table of a cyclic group shown below :

*	a	b	c	d
a	a	b	c	d
b	b	a	d	e
c	c	d	b	a
d	d	c	a	b

Which one of the following choices is correct?
(a) a, b are generators
(b) b, c are generators
(c) c, d are generators
(d) d, a are generators **[2009 : 2 Marks]**

66. What is the possible number of reflexive relations on a set of 5 elements ?
(a) 2^{10} (b) 2^{15}
(c) 2^{20} (d) 2^{25}

[2010 : 1 Mark]

67. Consider the set S = {1, ω, ω²}, where ω and ω² are cube roots of unity. If * denotes are multiplication operation, the structure {S, *} forms
(a) a group (b) a ring
(c) an integral domain (d) a field

[2010 : 1 Mark]

68. How many onto (Or surjective)functions are there from an n-element ($n \geq 2$)set to a 2-element set?
(a) 2^n
(b) $2^n - 1$
(c) $2^n - 2$
(d) $2(2^n - 2)$

[2012 : 2 Marks]

69. A binary operation ⊕ on a set of integers is defined as $x \oplus y = x^2 + y^2$. Which one of the following statements is TRUE about ⊕ ?
(a) Commutative but not associative
(b) Both commutative and associative
(c) Associative but not commutative
(d) Neither commutative nor associative

[2013 : 1 Mark]

70. Let S denote the set of all functions $f:\{0,1\}^4 \to \{0,1\}$. Denote by N the number of functions from S to the set {0, 1}. The value of $\log_2$ $\log_2 N$ is ....

[2014 (Set-1) : 2 Marks]

71. Consider the following relation on subsets of the set S of integers between 1 and 2014. For two distinct subsets U and V of S we say U < V if the minimum element in the symmetric difference of the two sets is in U.
Consider the following two statements :
S_1 : There is a subset of S that is larger than every other subset.
S_2 : There is a subset of S that is smaller than every other subset.
Which one of the following is CORRECT?
(a) Both S_1 and S_2 are true
(b) S_1 is true and S_2 is false
(c) S_2 is true and S_1 is false
(d) Neither S_1 nor S_2 is true

[2014 (Set-2) : 2 Marks]

72. Let X and Y be finite sets and f : X → Y be a function. Which one of the following statements is TRUE?
(a) For any subsets A and B of X.
$$|f(A \cup B)| = |f(A)| + |f(B)|$$
(b) For any subsets A and B of X.
$$f(A \cap B) = f(A) \cap f(B)$$
(c) For any subsets A and B of X.
$$|f(A \cap B)| = \min\{|f(A)|, |f(B)|\}$$
(d) For any subsets S and T of Y.
$$f^{-1}(S \cap T) = f^{-1}(S) \cap f^{-1}(T)$$

[2014 (Set-3) : 1 Mark]

73. Let G be a group with 15 elements. Let L be a subgroup of G. It is known that L ≠ G and that the size of L is at least 4. The size of L is ....

[2014 (Set-3) : 1 Mark]

74. Consider the set of all functions f : {0, 1, ...,2014} → {0, 1, ...,2014} such that f(f(i) = i, for all $0 \le i \le 2014$. Consider the following statements :

P : For each such function it must be the case that for every i, f(i) = i.

Q : For each such function it must be the case that for every i, f(i) = i.

R : Each such function must be onto.

Which one of the following is CORRECT?

(a) P, Q and R are true

(b) Only Q and R are true

(c) Only P and Q are true

(d) Only R is true

[2014 (Set-3) : 2 Marks]

75. There are two elements x, y in a group (G, *) such that every element in the group can be written as a product of some number of x's and y's in some rde. It is known that

x*x = y*y = x*y*x*y = y*x*y*x = e

where e is the identity element. The maximum number of elements in such a group is ....

[2014 (Set-3) : 2 Marks]

76. If g(x) = 1 – x and h(x) = $\frac{x}{x-1}$, then $\frac{g(h(x))}{h(g(x))}$ is

(a) $\frac{h(x)}{g(x)}$

(b) $\frac{-1}{x}$

(c) $\frac{g(x)}{h(x)}$

(d) $\frac{x}{(1-x)^2}$

[2015 (Set-1) : 1 Mark]

77. For a set A, the power set of A is denoted by 2^A. If A = {5}, {6}, {7}}, which of the following options are True ?

1. $\varnothing \in 2^A$

2. $\varnothing \subseteq 2^A$

3. {5, {6}} ∈ 2A

4. {5, {6}} ⊆ 2^A

(a) 1 and 3 only

(b) 2 and 3 only

(c) 1, 2 and 3 only

(d) 1, 2 and 4 only

[2015 (Set-1) : 1 Mark]

78. Suppose $\mathcal{L}$ = {p, q, r, s, t} is a lattice represented by the following Hasse diagram :

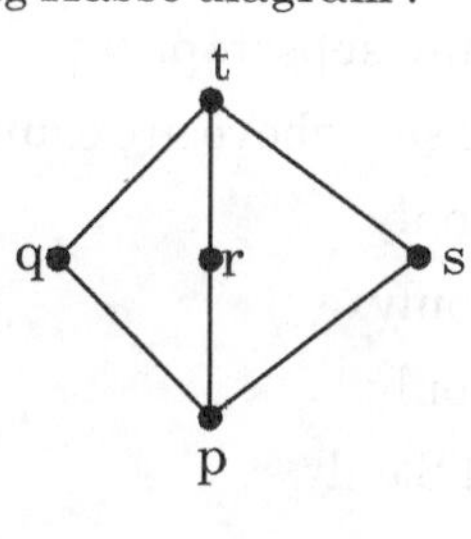

For any xy ∈ $\mathcal{L}$, not necessarily distinct, x ∨ y and x ∧ y are join and meet of x, y respectively. Let $\mathcal{L}^3$ = {(x, y, z): x, y, z∈ $\mathcal{L}$} be the set of all ordered triplets of the elements of $\mathcal{L}$. Let p_r be the probability that an element (x, y, z) ∈ $\mathcal{L}^3$ chosen euiprobably satisfies x(y ∧ z) = (x ∨ y) ∧ (x ∨ z). Then

(a) $p_r = 0$

(b) $p_r = 1$

(c) $0 < p_r \le \frac{1}{5}$

(d) $\frac{1}{5} < p_r < 1$

[2015 (Set-1) : 2 Marks]

79. Let R be the relation on the set of positive integers such that aRb if and only if a and b are distinct and have a common divisor other than 1. Which one of the following statements about R is True?

(a) R is symmetric and reflexive but not transitive

(b) R is reflexive but not symmetric and not transitive

(c) R is transitive but not reflexive and not symmetric

(d) R is symmetric but not reflexive and not transitive

[2015 (Set-2) : 1 Mark]

80. The cardinality of the power set of {9, 1, 2,...,10} is ....

[2015 (Set-2) : 1 Mark]

81. The number of onto functions (surjective functions) from set X = {1, 2, 3, 4} to set Y = {a, b, c} is ....

[2015 (Set-2) : 2 Marks]

82. Let X and Y denote the sets containing 2 and 20 distinct objects respectively and F denote the set of all possible functions defined from X and Y. Let f be randomly chosen from F. The probability of f being one-to-one is ....

83. Let # be a binary operator defined as X # Y = X′ + Y′ where X and Y are Boolean variables. Consider the following two statements :

S_1 : (P # Q)# R = P # (Q # R)

S2 : Q # R = R # Q

Which of the following is/are true for the Boolean variables P, Q and R?

(a) Only S_1 is true

(b) Only S_2 is True

(c) Both S_1 and S_2 are True

(d) Neither S_1 nor S_2 are True

[2015 (Set-3) : 1 Mark]

84. Suppose U is the power set of the set S = {1, 2, 3, 4, 5, 6}. For any T ∈ U, let | T | denote the number of elements in T and T' denote the complement of T. For any T, R ∈ U, let T\R be the set of all elements in T which are not in R. Which one of the following is true?

(a) $\forall X \in U(|X| = |X'|)$

(b) $\exists X \in U \exists Y \in U(|X| = 5, |Y| = 5 \text{ and } X \cap Y = \varnothing)$

(c) $\forall X \in U \forall Y \in U(|X| = 2, |Y| = 3 \text{ and } X \setminus Y = \varnothing)$

(d) $\forall X \in U \forall Y \in U(X \setminus Y = Y' \setminus X')$

[2015 (Set-3) : 1 Mark]

85. Let R be a relation on the set of ordered pairs of positive integers such that ((p, q), (r, s)) R if and only if p – s = q – r. Which one of the following is true about R?

(a) Both reflexive and symmetric

(b) Reflexive but not symmetric

(c) Not reflexive but symmetric

(d) Neither reflexive nor symmetric

[2015 (Set-3) : 2 Mark]

86. A function $f: N^+ \to N^+$ defined on the set of positive integers N^+, satisfies the following properties :

f(n) = f(n/2) if n is even

f(n) = f(n + 5) if n is odd

Let $R = \{i \mid \exists j : f(j) = i\}$ be the set of distinct values that f takes. The maximum size of R is ....

[2015 (Set-3) : 2 Marks]

87. A binary relation R on N × N is defined as follows: (a, b) R (c, d) if $a \le c \text{ or } b \le d$. Consider the following propositions :

P : R is reflexive

Q : R is transitive

Which one of the following statements is TRUE ?

(a) Both P and Q are true

(b) P is true and Q are false

(c) P is false and Q are true

(d) Both P and Q are false

[2016 (Set-2) : 2 Marks]

88. Consider a set U of 23 different compound in a Chemistry lab. There is a subset S of U of 9 compounds, each of which reacts with exactly 3 compounds of U. Consider the following statements:

I. Each compound in U\S reacts with an odd number of compounds.

II. At least one compound in U\S reacts with an odd number of compounds.

III. Each compound in U\S reacts with an even number of compounds

Which one of the above statements is ALWAYS TRUE?

(a) Only I (b) Only II

(c) Only III (d) None of these

[2016 (Set-2) : 2 Marks]

89. Consider the set X = {a, b, c, d, e} under the partial ordering :

R = {(a, a), (a, b), (a, c), (a, d), (a, e), (b, b), (b, c), (b, e), (c, c), (c, e), (d, d), (d, e), (e, e)}.

The Hasse diagram of the partial order (X, R) is shown below :

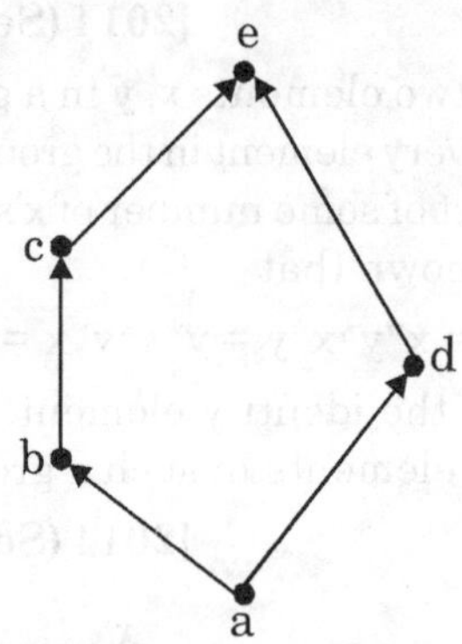

The minimum number of ordered pairs that need to be added to R to make (X, R) a lattice is ....

[2017 (Set-2) : 1 Mark]

90. The number of integers between 1 and 500 (both inclusive)that are divisible by 3 or 5 or 7 is ....

[2017 (Set-1) : 1 Mark]

91. Let G be a finite group on 84 elements. The size of a largest possible proper subgroup of G is ....

[2018 : 1 Mark]

92. Let N be the set of natural numbers. Consider the following sets :

P. Set of Rational numbers (positive and negative)

Q. Set of functions from {0, 1} to N.

R. Set of functions from N to {0, 1}.

S. Set of finite subsets of N.

Which of the sets above are countable ?

(a) Q and S only

(b) P and S only

(c) P and R only

(d) P, Q and S only

[2018 : 2 Marks]

93. Let U = {1, 2, ..., n}. Let A = {(x, X | x ∈ X, X ⊆ U }. Consider the following two statements on |A|.

I. $|A| = n2^{n-1}$

II. $|A| = \sum_{k=1}^{n} k\binom{n}{k}$

Which of the above statements is/are TRUE?

(a) Neither I nor II (b) Only I

(c) Only II (d) Both I and II

[2019 : 1 Mark]

94. Consider the first order predicate formula φ :

$\forall x\ [(\forall z\ z \mid x \Rightarrow ((z = x) \vee (z = 1)))$

$\Rightarrow \exists w\ (w > x) \wedge (\forall z\ z \mid w \Rightarrow (w = z) \vee (z = 1)))]$

Here 'a/b' denotes that 'a divides b', where a and b are integers. Consider the following sets:

S1. {1,2,3, ··· 100}

S2. Set of all positive integers

S3. Set of all integers

Which of the above sets satisfy φ ?

(a) S2 and S3 (b) S1 and S2

(c) S1 and S3 (d) S1, S2 and S3

[2019 : 2 Marks]

COMBINATORICS

1. (a) Solve the recurrence equations :

$T(n) = T(n-1) + n$

$T(1) = 1$

(b) What is the generating function G(z) for the sequence of Fibronacci numbers?

[1987 : 2 Mark]

2. Solve the recurrence equations :

$T(n) = T\left(\frac{n}{2}\right) + 1$

$T(1) = 1$ **[1988 : 2 Mark]**

3. How many substrings can be formed from a character string of length n? **[1989 : 2 Mark]**

4. The number of binary strings of n zeros and k ones that no two ones are adjacent is

(a) $^{n+1}C_k$ (b) $^{n}C_k$

(c) $^{n}C_{k+1}$ (d) None of these

[1990 : 2 Mark]

5. The number of substrings (of all lengths inclusive) that can be formed from a character string of length n is

(a) n (b) n^2

(c) $\frac{n(n-1)}{2}$ (d) $\frac{n(n+1)}{2}$

[1994 : 2 Mark]

6. In a room containing 28 people, there are 18 people who speak English, 15 people who speak Hindi and 22 people who speak Kannada. 9 persons speak both English and Hindi, 11 person speak both Hindi and Kannada whereas 13 persons speak both Kannada and English. How many people speak all three languages?

(a) 9 (b) 8

(c) 7 (d) 6

[1998 : 2 Mark]

7. Solve the following recurrence relation

$x_n = 2x_{n-1} - 1, n > 1$

$x_1 = 2$ **[1998 : 2 Mark]**

8. Two girls have picked 10 roses, 15 sunflowers and 14 daffodils. What is the number of ways they can divide the flowers among themselves?

(a) 1638

(b) 2100

(c) 2640

(d) None of these

[1999 : 2 Mark]

9. The minimum number of cards to be dealt from an arbitrarily shuffled deck of 52 cards to guarantee that three cards are from some same suit is

(a) 3 (b) 8

(c) 9 (d) 12

[2000 : 1 Mark]

10. How many 4 digit even numbers have all 4 digits distinct?

(a) 2240 (b) 2296

(c) 2620 (d) 4536

[2001 : 2 Mark]

11. The solution to the recurrence equation $T(2^k) = 3T(2^{k-1}) + 1$, T(1) = 1 is

(a) 2^k (b) $\frac{(3^{k+1}-1)}{2}$

(c) $3^{\log_2 k}$ (d) $2^{\log_3 k}$

[2002 : 1 Mark]

12. The minimum number of colours required to colour the vertices of a cycle with n nodes in such a way that no two adjacent nodes have the same colour is

(a) 2 (b) 3

(c) 4 (d) $n - 2\left\lfloor\frac{n}{2}\right\rfloor + 2$

[2002 : 1 Mark]

13. Let A be a sequence of 8 distinct integers sorted in ascending order. How many distinct pairs of sequences, B and C are there such that (i) each is sorted in ascending order, (ii)B has 5 and C has 3 elements, and (iii)the result of merging B and C gives A?

(a) 2 (b) 30
(c) 56 (d) 256

[2003 : 1 Mark]

14. n couples are invited to a party with the condition that every husband should be accompanied by his wife. However, a wife need not be accompanied by her husband. The number of different gatherings possible at the party is

(a) $\binom{2n}{n} * 2^n$ (b) 3^n
(c) $\frac{(2n)!}{2^n}$ (d) $\binom{2n}{n}$

[2003 : 1 Mark]

15. Mala has a colouring book in which each English letter is drawn two times. She wants to paint each of these 52 prints with one of k colours, such that the colour-pairs used to colour any two letters are different. Both prints of a letter can also be coloured with the same colour. What is the minimum value of k that satisfies this requirements?

(a) 9 (b) 8
(c) 7 (d) 6 **[2004 : 2 Mark]**

16. In how many ways can we distribute 5 distinct balls, $B_1, B_2, ..., B_5$ in 5 distinct cells, $C_1, C_2, ... C_5$ such that Ball B_i is not in cell C_i, $\forall_i = 1, 2, ..., 5$ and each cell contains exactly one ball?

(a) 44 (b) 96
(c) 120 (d) 3125

[IT-2004 : 2 Mark]

17. Let $n = p^2q$, where p and q are distinct prime numbers. How many numbers m satisfy $1 \leq m \leq n$ and gcd (m, n)= 1? Note that gcd (m, n) is the greatest common divisor of m and n.

(a) $p(q-1)$ (b) pq
(c) $(p^2-1)(q-1)$ (d) $p(p-1)(q-1)$

[IT-2005 : 2 Mark]

18. What is the minimum number of ordered pairs of non-negative numbers that should be chosen to ensure that there are are two pairs (a, b) and (c, d) in the chosen set such that a = c mod 3 and b = d mod 5

(a) 4 (b) 6
(c) 16 (d) 24 **[2005 : 2 Marks]**

19. Let $G(x)= 1/(1-x)^2 = \sum_{i=0}^{\infty} g(i)x^i$ where $|x| < 1$. What is g(i) ?

(a) i (b) i + 1
(c) 2i (d) 2^i **[2005 : 2 Marks]**

20. For each element in a set of size 2n, an unbiased coin is tossed. The 2n coin tossed are independent. An element is chosen if the corresponding coin toss were head. The probability that exactly n elements are chosen is

(a) $\binom{2n}{n} \Big/ 4^n$ (b) $\binom{2n}{n} \Big/ 2^n$
(c) $1 \Big/ \binom{2n}{n}$ (d) $\frac{1}{2}$

[2006 : 2 Marks]

Common Data for Q. 21 & 22

Suppose that a robot is placed on the Cartesian plane. At each step it is allowed to move either one unit up or one unit right, i.e., if it is at (i, j) then it can move to either (i + 1, j) or (i, j + 1).

21. How many distinct paths are there for the robot to reach the point (10, 10)starting from the initial position (0, 0)?

(a) $\binom{20}{10}$ (b) 2^{20}
(c) 2^{10} (d) None of these

[2007 : 2 Marks]

22. Suppose that the robot is not allowed to traverse the line segment from (4, 4) to (5, 4). With this constraint, how many distinct paths are there for the robot to reach (10, 10)starting from (0, 0)?

(a) 2^9 (b) 2^{19}
(c) $\binom{8}{4} \times \binom{11}{5}$ (d) $\binom{20}{10} - \binom{8}{4} \times \binom{11}{5}$

[2007 : 2 Marks]

23. Let, $P = \sum_{\substack{1 \leq i \leq 2k \\ i\ odd}} i$ and $Q = \sum_{\substack{1 \leq i \leq 2k \\ i\ even}} i$

where k is positive integer. Then

(a) P = Q – k (b) P = Q + k
(c) P = Q (d) P = Q + 2k

[2008 : 2 Marks]

Common Data for Q. 24 & 25

24. Which of the following recurrences does x_n satisfy?

(a) $x_n = 2x_{n-1}$ (b) $x_n = x_{[n/2]} + 1$
(c) $x_n = x_{[n/2]} + n$ (d) $x_n = x_{n-1} + x_{n-2}$

[2008 : 2 Marks]

25. The value of x_5 is

(a) 5 (b) 7

(c) 8 (d) 13 **[2008 : 2 Marks]**

26. The exponent of 11 in the prime factorization of 300! is

(a) 27 (b) 28

(c) 29 (d) 30

[IT-2008 : 2 Mark]

27. In how many ways can *b* blue balls and *r* red balls be distributed in n distinct boxes?

(a) $\frac{(n+b-1)!(n+r-1)!}{(n-1)!b!(n-1)!r!}$

(b) $\frac{(n+(b+r)-1)!}{(n-1)!(n-1)!(b+r)!}$

(c) $\frac{n!}{b!r!}$

(d) (n + (b + r) −1)! /n! (b + r − 1)

[2008 : 2 Mark]

28. A penant is a sequence of numbers, each number being 1 or 2. An n-pennant is a sequence of numbers with sum equal to n. For example, (1,1,2) is a 4-pennants. The set of all possible 1-pennant is {(1)}, the set of all possible 2-pennants is {(2), (1,1) and the set of all 3-pennants is P(2, 1), (1,1,1), (1, 2)}. Note that the pennant (1, 2) is not the same as the pennant (2, 1). The number of 10-pennants is ....

[2014 (Set-1) : 2 Marks]

29. Each of the nine words in the sentence

"The quick brown fox jumps over the lazy dog"

is written on a separate piece of paper. These nine pieces of paper are kept in a box. One of the pieces is drawn at random from the box. the expected length of the word drawn is .... (The answer should be rounded to one decimal piece).

[2014 (Set-2) : 1 Mark]

30. The number of distinct positive integral factors of 2014 is ....

[2014 (Set-2) : 2 Marks]

31. $\sum_{x=11}^{99} \frac{1}{x(x+1)} =$ ....

[2014 (Set-1) : 2 Marks]

32. Let a_n represent the number of bit stgrings of length n containing two consecutive 1s. What is the recurrence relation for a_n?

(a) $a_{n-2} + a_{n-1} + 2^{n-2}$ (b) $a_{n-2} + 2a_{n-1} + 2^{n-2}$

(c) $2a_{n-2} + a_{n-1} + 2^{n-2}$ (d) $2a_{n-2} + 2a_{n-1} + 2^{n-2}$

[2015 (Set-1) : 2 Marks]

33. The number of divisors of 2100 is ....

[2014 (Set-2) : 2 Marks]

34. The number of 4 digit numbers having their digits in non-decreasing order (from left to right) constructed by using the digits belonging to the set {1, 2, 3} is .... **[2015 (Set-3) : 1 Mark]**

35. Let a_n be the number of n-bit strings that do NOT contain two consecutive 1's. Which one of the following is the recurrence relation for a_n?

(a) $a_n = a_{n-1} + 2a_{n-2}$ (b) $a_n = a_{n-1} + a_{n-2}$

(c) $a_n = 2a_{n-1} + a_{n-2}$ (b) $a_n = 2a_{n-1} + 2a_{n-2}$

[2016 (Set-1) : 1 Mark]

36. The coefficient of x^{12} in $(x^3 + x^4 + x^5 + x^6 + ...)^3$ is ....

[2016 (Set-1) : 2 Marks]

37. Consider the recurrence relation $a_1 = 8$, $a_n = 6n^2 + 2n + a_{n-1}$. Let $a_{99} = K \times 10^4$. The value of K is ....

[2016 (Set-1) : 2 Marks]

38. If the ordinary generating function of a sequence $\{a_n\}_{n=0}^{\infty}$ is $\frac{1+z}{(1-z)^3}$ then $a_3 - a_0$ is equal to ....

[2017 (Set-2) : 2 Marks]

39. Which one of the following is a closed form expression for the generating function of the sequence $\{a_n\}$, where $a_n = 2n + 3$ for all n = 0, 1, 2, ...?

(a) $\frac{3}{(1-x)^2}$ (b) $\frac{3x}{(1-x)^2}$

(c) $\frac{2-x}{(1-x)^2}$ (d) $\frac{3-x}{(1-x)^2}$

[2018 : 2 Marks]

GRAPH THEORY

1. Which of the following graphs is/are planar? (see Figure)

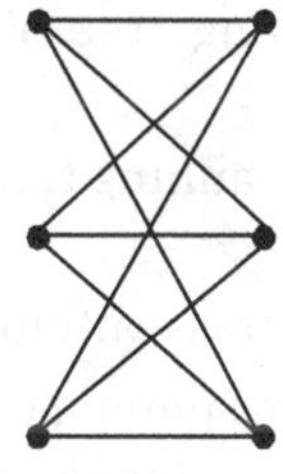

G1

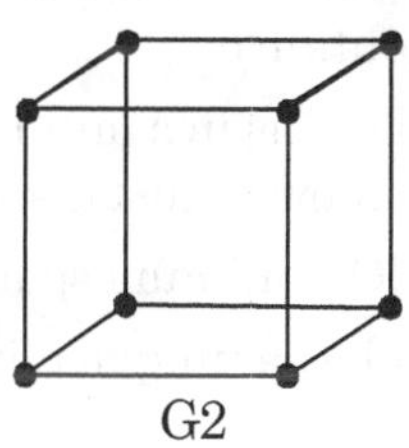

G2

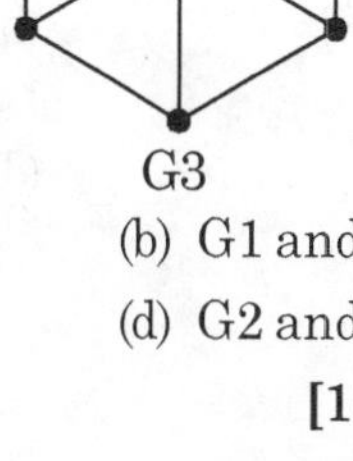

G3

(a) G1 only (b) G1 and G2

(c) G2 only (d) G2 and G3

[1989 : 2 Marks]

2. A graph is planar if and only if,

(a) If does not contain subgraphs homeomorphic to K_5 and $K_{3,3}$.

(b) It does not contain subgraphs isomorphic to K_5 or $K_{3,3}$.

(c) It does not contain subgraphs isomorphic to K_5 and $K_{3,3}$.

(d) It does not contain subgraphs homeomorphic to K_5 or $K_{3,3}$.

[1990 : 2 Marks]

3. The maximum number of possible edges in an undirected graph with 'a' vertices and 'k' components is ____.

[1991 : 2 Marks]

4. A non-planar graph with minimum number of vertices has

(a) 9 edges, 6 vertices

(b) 6 edges, 4 vertices

(c) 10 edges, 5 vertices

(d) 9 edges, 5 vertices **[1992 : 2 Marks]**

5. Maximum number of edges in a planar graph with n vertices is____ **[1992 : 2 Marks]**

6. The number of distinct simple graphs with upto three nodes is

(a) 15 (b) 10

(c) 7 (d) 9 **[1994 : 1 Mark]**

7. Prove that in a finite graph, the number of vertices of odd degree is always even. **[1995 : 2 Marks]**

8. Let G be an undirected connected graph with distinct edge weights. Let e_{max} be the edge with maximum weight and e_{min} be the edge with minimum weight. Which of the following statements is false?

(a) Every minimum spanning tree of G must contain e_{min}

(b) If e_{max} is in a minimum spanning tree, then its removal must disconnect G

(c) NO minimum spanning tree contains e_{max}

(d) G has a unique minimum spannig tree

[2000 : 2 Marks]

9. How many undirected graphs (not necessary connected can be constructed out of a given set V = {v_1, v_2, ...v_n} of n vertices?

(a) $\frac{n(n-1)}{2}$ (b) 2^n

(c) n! (d) $2^{\frac{n(n-1)}{2}}$

[2001 : 2 Marks]

10. Maximum number or edges in a n-node undirected graph without self loops is

(a) n^2 (b) n(n-1)/2

(c) n–1 (d) (n+1)(n)/2

[2002 : 1 Mark]

11. Let G be an arbitrary graph with n nodes and k components. It a vertex is removed from G, the number of components in the resultant graph must necessarily lie between.

(a) k and n (b) k–1 and k + 1

(c) k–1 and n–1 (d) k+1 and n–k

[2003 : 1 Mark]

12. How many perfect matchings are there in a complete graph of 6 vertices?

(a) 15 (b) 24

(c) 30 (d) 60

[2003 : 2 Marks]

13. A Graph G = (V, E) satisfies $|E| \le 3|V| - 6$. The min-degree of G is defined as $\min_{v \in V}$ {degree (v)}. Therefore, min-degree of G connot be

(a) 3 (b) 4

(c) 5 (d) 6

[2003 : 2 Marks]

14. The Minimum number of colours required to colour the following graph, such that no two adjacent vertices are assigned the same colour, is

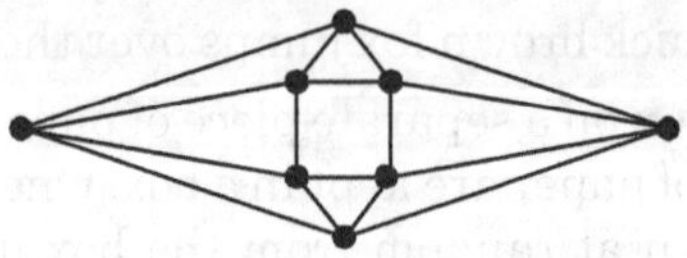

(a) 2 (b) 3

(c) 4 (d) 5 **[2004 : 2 Marks]**

15. How many graphs on n labeled vertices exist which have at least $(n^2\text{-}3n)/2$ edges?

(a) ${}^{(n^2-n)/2}C_{(n^2-3n)/2}$

(b) $\sum_{k=0}^{(n^2-3n)/2} {}^{(n^2-n)/2}C_k$

(c) ${}^{(n^2-n)/2}C_n$

(d) $\sum_{k=0}^{n} {}^{(n^2-n)/2}C_k$

[2004 : 2 Marks]

16. What is the maximum number of edges in an acyclin undirected graph with n vertices?

(a) n – 1 (b) n
(c) n + 1 (d) 2n – 1

[IT-2004 : 1 Mark]

17. What is the number of vertices in an undirected connected graph with 27 edges, 6 vertices of degree 2, 3 vertices of degree 4 and remaining of degree 3?

(a) 10 (b) 11
(c) 18 (d) 19

[IT-2004 : 2 Marks]

18. Let G be a simple connected planar graph with 13 vertices and 19 edges. Then, the number of faces in the planar embedding of the graph is

(a) 0 (b) 8
(c) 9 (d) 13 **[2005 : 1 Mark]**

19. Which one of the following graphs is NOT plannar?

(a) G_1: 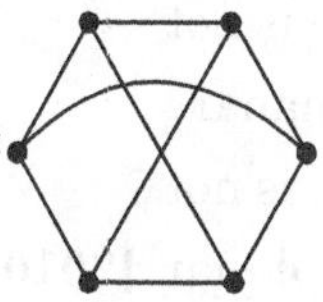

(b) G_2: 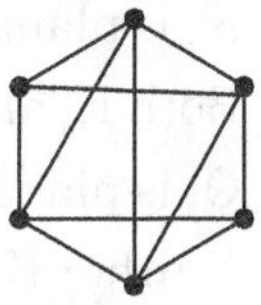

(c) G_3: 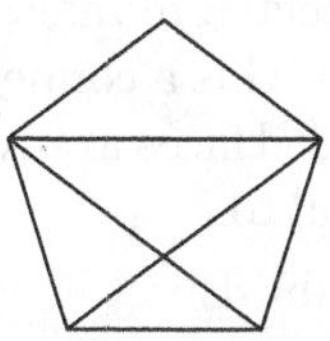

(d) G_4: 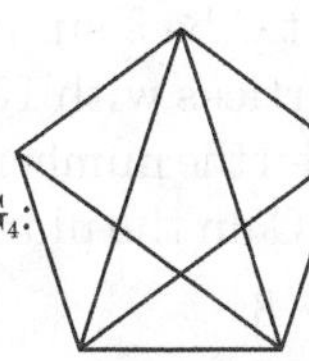

[2005 : 2 Marks]

20. If all the edge weights of an undirected graph are positive, then any subset of edges that connects all the vertices and has minimum total weight is a

(a) Hamiltonian cycle (b) Grid
(c) Hypercube (d) Tree

[IT-2006 : 1 Mark]

21. Consider the undirected graph G defined as follows. The vertices of G are bit strings of length n. We have an edge between vertex u and vertex v if and only if u and v differ in exactly one bit position (in other words, v can be obtained from u by flipping a single bit). The ratio of the chromatic number of G to the diameter of G is

(a) $1/(2^{n-1})$
(b) 1/n
(c) 2/n
(d) 3/n

[IT-2006 : 2 Marks]

Common Data for Q. 22 to 24

The 2^n vertices of graph G correspond to all subsets of a set of size n, for $n \geq 6$. Two vertices of G are adjacent if and only if the corresponding sets intersect in exactly two elements.

22. The number of vertices of degree zero in G is

(a) 1 (b) n
(c) n + 1 (d) 2^n

[2006 : 2 Marks]

23. The maximu degree of a vertex in G is

(a) $\binom{n/2}{2} 2^{n/2}$ (b) 2^{n-2}
(c) $2^{n-3} \times 3$ (d) 2^{n-1}

[2006 : 2 Marks]

24. The number of connectd components in G is

(a) n (b) n + 2
(c) $2^{n/2}$ (d) $2^n/n$

[2006 : 2 Marks]

25. Let G be the non-planar graph with the minimum possible number of edges. Then G has

(a) 9 edges and 5 vertices
(b) 9 edges and 6 vertices
(c) 10 edges and 5 vertices
(d) 10 edges and 6 vertices **[2007 : 1 Mark]**

26. Consider the DAG with V = {1, 2, 3, 4, 5, 6}, shown below:

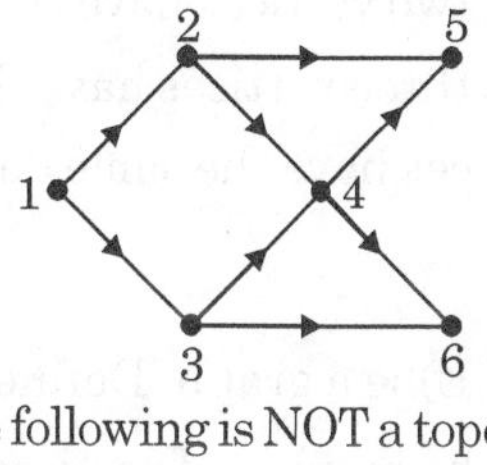

Which of the following is NOT a topological ordering?

(a) 1 2 3 4 5 6 (b) 1 3 2 4 6 5
(c) 1 3 2 4 5 6 (d) 3 2 4 1 6 5

[2007 : 1 Mark]

27. Which of the following graphs has an Eulerian circuit?

(a) Any k-regular graph where k is an even number
(b) A complete graph on 90 vertices
(c) The complement of a cycle on 25 vertices
(d) None of the above **[2007 : 2 Marks]**

28. What is the size of the smallest MIS (Maximal Independent Set)of a chain of nine nodes?

(a) 5 (b) 4
(c) 3 (d) 2 **[IT-2008 : 1 Mark]**

29. What is the chromatic number of the following graph?

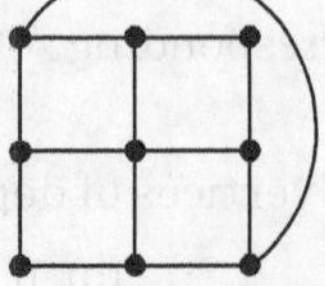

(a) 2 (b) 3
(c) 4 (d) 5

[IT-2008 : 1 Mark]

30. G is a simple, connected, undirected graph. Some vertices of G are of odd degree. Add a node v to G and make it adjacent to each odd degree vertex of G. The resultant graph is sure to be

(a) Regular (b) Complete
(c) Hamiltonian (d) Euler

[IT-2008 : 2 Marks]

31. What is the chromatic number of an n-vertex simple connected graph which does not contain any odd length cycle? Assume $n \geq 2$.

(a) 2 (b) 3
(c) n-1 (d) n

[2009 : 1 Mark]

32. Which one of the following is TRUE for any simple connected undirected graph with more than 2 vertices?

(a) No two vertices have the same degree
(b) At least two vertices have the same degree
(c) At least three vertices have the same degree
(d) All vertices have the same degree

[2009 : 1 Mark]

33. Let, G = (V,E) be a graph. Define $\xi(G) = \sum_d i_d \times d$, where i_d is the number of vertices of degree d in G. If S and T are two different trees with $\xi(S) = \xi(T)$, then

(a) $|S| = 2|T|$ (b) $|S| = |T| - 1$
(c) $|S| = |T|$ (d) $|S| = |T| + 1$

[2010 : 1 Mark]

34. In a binary tree with n nodes, every node has an odd number of descendants. Every node is considered to be its own descendant. What is the number of nodes in the tree that have exactly one child?

(a) 0 (b) 1
(c) (n–1)/2 (d) n–1 **[2010 : 1 Mark]**

35. The degree sequence of a simple graph is the sequence of the degrees of the nodes in the graph in decreasing order. Which of the following sequences can not be the degree sequence of any graph?

I. 7,6,5,4,4,3,2,1 II. 6,6,6,6,3,3,2,2
III. 7,6,6,4,4,3,2,2 IV. 8,7,7,6,4,2,1,1

(a) I and II (b) III and IV
(c) IV only (d) II and IV

[2010 : 2 Marks]

36. K_4 and Q_3 are graphs with the following structures:

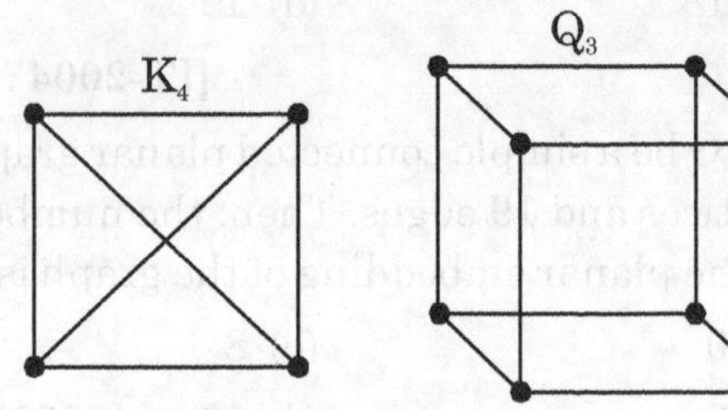

Which one of the following statement is TRUE in relation to these graphs?

(a) K_4 is planar while Q_3 is not
(b) Both K_4 and Q_3 are planar
(c) Q_3 is planar while K_3 is not
(d) Neither K_4 nor Q_3 is planar **[2010 : 2 Marks]**

37. Let G be a simple undirected planar graph on 10 vertices with 15 edges. If G is a connected graph, then the number of bounded faces in any embedding of G on the plane is equal to

(a) 3 (b) 4
(c) 5 (d) 6 **[2012 : 1 Mark]**

38. Which of the following graphs is isomorphic to

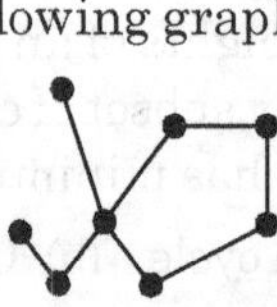

(a) 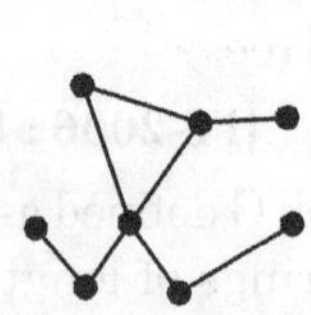 (b) 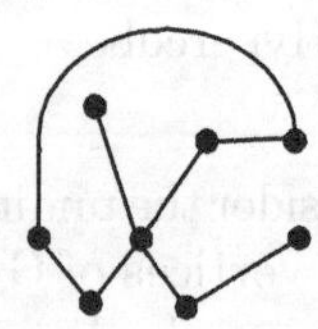

(c) 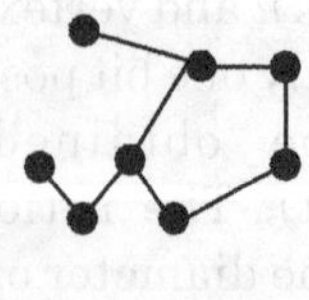 (d) 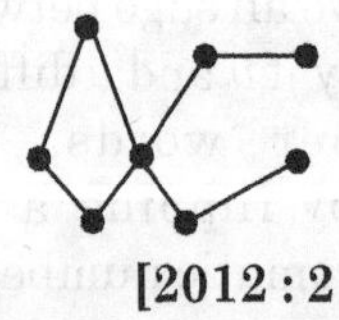

[2012 : 2 Marks]

39. Let G be a complete undirected graph on 6 vertices. If vertices of G are labeled, then the number of distinct cycles of length 4 in G is equal to

(a) 15 (b) 30
(c) 90 (d) 360

[2012 : 2 Marks]

40. Consider an undirected random graph of eight vertices. The probability that there is an edge between a pair of vertices is $\frac{1}{2}$. What is the expected numbers of unordered cycles of length three?

(a) $\frac{1}{8}$ (b) 1

(c) 7 (d) 8

[2013 : 1 Mark]

41. Which of the following statements is/are TRUE for undirected graph?

P: Number of odd degree vertices is even.

Q: Sum of degrees of all vertices is even.

(a) P only (b) Q only

(c) Both P and Q (d) Neither P nor Q

[2013 : 1 Mark]

42. Let G = (V, E)be a directed graph where V is theset of vertices and E the set of edges. Then which one of the following graphs has the same strongly connected components as G?

(a) $G_1 = (V,E_1)$where $E_1 = \{(u,v) \mid (u,v) \notin E\}$

(b) $G_2 = (V,E_2)$where $E_2 = \{(u,v) \mid (v,u) \in E\}$

(c) $G_3 = (V,E_3)$where $E_3 = \{(u,v) \mid$ there is a path of length ≤ 2 from u to v in E}

(d) $G_4 = (V_4,E)$where V_4 is the set of vertices in G which are not isolated

[2014 (Set-1) : 1 Mark]

43. Consider an undirected graph G where self-loops are not allowed. The vertex set of G is $\{(i,j)$: $1 \leq i \leq 12, 1 \leq j \leq 12\}$. There is an edge between (a,b) and (c,d)if $|a-c| \leq 1$ and $|b-d| \leq 1$.

The number of edges in this graph is____.

[2014 (Set-1) : 2 Marks]

44. An ordered *n-tuple* $(d_1, d_2 ..., d_n)$ with $d_1 \geq d_2 \geq ... \geq d_n$ is called graphic if there exists a simple undirected graph with n vertices having degrees $d_1, d_2, ..., d_n$ respectively. Which of the following 6-tuples is NOT graphic?

(a) (1,,1,1,1,1,1)

(b) 2,2,2,2,2,2)

(c) (3,3,3,1,0,0

) (d) (3,2,1,1,1,0)

[2014 (Set-1) : 2 Marks]

45. The maximum number of edges in a bipartite graph on 12 vertices is___.

[2014 (Set-2) : 1 Mark]

46. A cycle on n vertices is isomorphic to its complement. The value of n *is*____.

[2014 (Set-2) : 2 Marks]

47. The number of distinct minimum spanning trees for the weighted graph below is___.

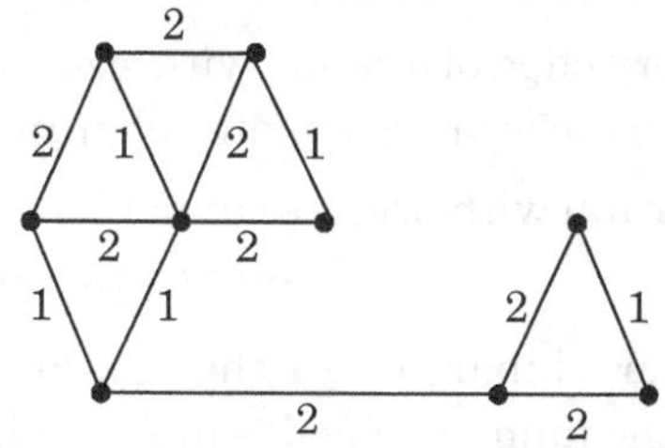

[2014 (Set-2) : 2 Marks]

48. If G is a forest with n-vertices and k connected components, how many edges does G have?

(a) $\lfloor n/k \rfloor$

(b) $\lceil n/k \rceil$

(c) $n-k$

(d) $n-k+1$

[2014 (Set-3) : 2 Marks]

49. Let δ denote the minimum degree of a vertex in a graph. For all planar graphs on n vertices with $\delta \geq 3$ which one of the following is **TRUE**?

(a) In any planar embedding the number of faces is at least $\frac{n}{2}+2$

(b) In any planar embedding, the number of faces is less than $\frac{n}{2}+2$

(c) There is a planar embedding in which the number of faces is less than $\frac{n}{2}+2$

(d) There is planar embedding in which the number of faces is at most $\frac{n}{\delta+1}$

[2014 (Set-3 : 2 Marks]

50. Let G be a connected planar graph with 10 vertices. If the number of edges on each face is three, then the number of edges in G is___.

[2014 (Set-5) : 2 Marks]

51. A graph is self-complementary if it is isomorphic to its complement. For all self-complementary graphs on n vertices, n is

(a) A multiple of 4

(b) Even

(c) Odd

(d) Congruent to 0 mod 4,or 1 mod4

[2015 (Set-2) : 2 Marks]

52. In a connected graph,a bridge is an edge whose removal disconnects a graph. Which one of the following statements is True?

(a) A tree has no bridges

(b) A bridge cannot be part of a simple cycle

(c) Every edge of a clique with size ≥ 3 is a bridge (A clique is any complete subgraph of a graph)

(d) A graph with bridges cannot have a cycle

[2015 (Set-2) : 2 Marks]

53. Consider a binary tree *T* that has 200 leaf nodes. Then, the number of nodes in *T* that have exactly two children are ___.

[2015 (Set-3) : 1 Mark]

54. Let *G* be connected undirected graph of 100 vertices and 300 edges. The weight of a minimum spanning tree of G is 500. When the weight of each edge of G is increased by five, the weight of a minimum spanning tree becomes___.

[2015 (Set-3) : 2 Marks]

55. The minimum number of colour that is sufficient to vertex-colour any planar graph is___.

[2016 (Set-2) : 1 Mark]

56. Let *T* be a tree with 10 vertices. The sum of the degree of all the vertices in *T* is____.

[2016 (Set-1) : 1 Mark]

57. G is an undirected graph with *n* vertices and 25 edges such that each vertex of G has degree at least 3. Then the maximum possible value of *n* is___. **[2017 (Set-2) : 1 Mark]**

58. The chromatic number of the following graph is____.

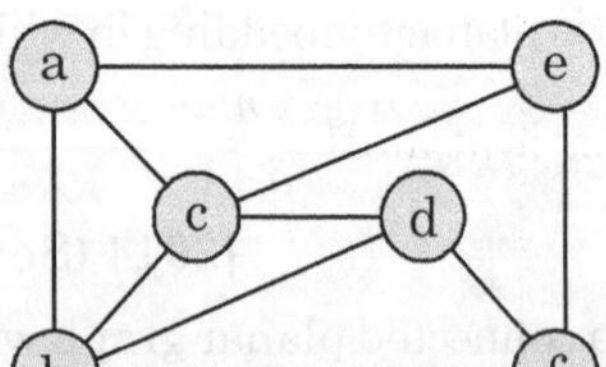

[2018 : 1 Mark]

59. Let G be a graph with 100! vertices,with each vertex labelled by a distinct permutation of the numbers 1,2, ... 100. There is an edge between vertices *u* and *v* if and only if the label of *u* can be obtained by swapping two adjacent numbers in the label of *v*. Let *y* denote the degree of a vertex in *G* and *z* denote the number of connected components in *G*. Then, *y* + 10z = ____.

[2018 : 2 Marks]

60. Let G be an undirected complete graph on n vertices, where n > 2. Then, the number of different Hamiltonian cycles in G is equal to

(a) n! (b) $\frac{(n-1)!}{2}$

(c) 1 (d) (n – 1)!

[2019 : 1 Mark]

61. Let G be any connected weighted undirected graph.

I. G has a unique minimum spanning tree, if no two edges of G have the same weight.

II. G has a unique minimum spanning tree, if, for every cut of G, there is a unique minimum-weight edge crossing the cut.

Which of the above two statements is/are TRUE?

(a) Both I and II

(b) I only

(c) Neither I nor II

(d) II only

[2019 : 2 Marks]

PROBABILITY

1. Let A and B be any two arbitrary events, then, which one of the following is true ?

(a) $P(A \cap B) = P(A) + P(B)$

(B) $P(A \cup B) = P(A) + P(B)$

(C) $P(A \mid B) = P(A \cap B) / P(B)$

(D) $P(A \cup B) < P(A) + P(B)$

[1994 : 1 Mark]

2. A bag contains 10 white balls and 15 black balls. Two balls are drawn in succession. The probability that one of them is black and the other is white is

(a) $\frac{2}{3}$ (b) $\frac{4}{5}$

(c) $\frac{1}{2}$ (d) $\frac{1}{3}$ **[1995 : 2 Mark]**

3. Two dice are thrown simultaneously. The probability that at least one of them will have 6 facing up is

(a) $\frac{1}{36}$ (b) $\frac{1}{3}$

(c) $\frac{25}{36}$ (d) $\frac{11}{36}$ **[1996 : 1 Mark]**

4. The probability that top and bottom cards of a randomly shuffled deck are both aces is

(a) $\frac{4}{52}\times\frac{4}{52}$ (b) $\frac{4}{52}\times\frac{3}{52}$

(c) $\frac{4}{52}\times\frac{3}{51}$ (d) $\frac{4}{52}\times\frac{4}{51}$

[1996 : 2 Mark]

5. The probability that it will rain today is 0.5. The probability that it will rain tomorrow is 0.6. The probability that it will rain either today or tomorrow is 0.7. What is the probability that it will rain today and tomorrow?

(a) 0.3 (b) 0.25

(c) 0.35 (d) 0.4

[1997 : 1 Mark]

6. A die is rolled three times. The probability that exactly one odd number turns up among the three outcomes is

(a) $\frac{1}{6}$ (b) $\frac{3}{8}$

(c) $\frac{1}{8}$ (d) $\frac{1}{2}$

[1998 : 1 Mark]

7. Suppose that the expectation of a random variable X is 5. Which of the following statements is true?

(a) There is a sample point at which X has the value 5.

(b) There is a sample point at which X has value greater than 5.

(c) There is a sample point at which X has a value greater than or equal to 5.

(d) None of the above

[1999 : 1 Mark]

8. Consider two events E_1 and E_2 such that probability of E_1, Pr $[E_1] = \frac{1}{2}$, probability of E_2, $Pr[E_2] = \frac{1}{3}$, and probability of E_1 and E_2, $Pr[E_1 \text{ and } E_2] = \frac{1}{5}$. Which of the following statements is/are true ?

(a) $Pr[E_1 \text{ or } E_2]$ is $\frac{2}{3}$

(b) Events E_1 and E_2 are independent

(c) Events E_1 and E_2 are not independent

(d) $Pr\left[\frac{E_1}{E_2}\right] = \frac{4}{5}$

[1999 : 2 Marks]

9. E1 and E2 are events in a probability space satisfying the following constraints :

Pr(E1) = Pr(E2)

$Pr(E1 \cup E2] = 1$

E1 and E2 are independent

The value of Pr(E1), the probability of the event E1, is

(a) 0 (b) $\frac{1}{4}$

(c) $\frac{1}{2}$ (d) 1

[2000 : 2 Marks]

10. Seven (distinct)car accidents occurred in a week. What is the probability that they all occurred on the same day?

(a) $\frac{1}{7^7}$ (b) $\frac{1}{7^6}$

(c) $\frac{1}{2^7}$ (d) $\frac{7}{2^7}$

[2001 : 2 Marks]

11. Four fair coins are tossed simultaneously. The probability that at least one head and one tail turn up is

(a) $\frac{1}{16}$ (b) $\frac{1}{8}$

(c) $\frac{7}{8}$ (d) $\frac{15}{16}$

[2002 : 2 Marks]

12. Let P(E)denote the probability of the event E. Given P(A) = 1, P(B)= 1/2, and A and B are independent, the values of P(A | B)and P(B | A) respectively are

(a) $\frac{1}{4},\frac{1}{2}$ (b) $\frac{1}{2},\frac{1}{4}$

(c) $\frac{1}{2},1$ (d) $1,\frac{1}{2}$

[2003 : 1 Marks]

13. A program consists of two modulus executed sequentially. Let $f_1(t)$ and $f_2(t)$ respectively denote the probability density functions of time taken to execute the two modulues. The probability density function of the overall time taken to execute the program is given by

(a) $f_1(t) + f_2(t)$ (b) $\int_0^t f_1(x)f_2(x)dx$

(c) $\int_0^t f_1(x)f_2(t-x)dx$ (d) max $\{f_1(t), f_2(t)\}$

[2003 : 2 Marks]

14. If a fair coin is tossed four times. What is the probability that two heads and two tailss will result?

(a) $\frac{3}{8}$ (b) $\frac{1}{2}$

(c) $\frac{5}{8}$ (d) $\frac{3}{4}$ **[2004 : 1 Marks]**

15. In a population of N families, 50% of the families have three children, 30% of the families have two children and the remaining families have one child. What is the probability that a randomly picked child belongs to a family with two children?

(a) $\frac{3}{23}$ (b) $\frac{6}{23}$

(c) $\frac{3}{10}$ (d) $\frac{3}{5}$ **[2004 : 1 Mark]**

16. Let X and Y be two exponentially distributed and independent random variables with mean α and β, respectively. If $Z = \min(X, Y)$, then the mean of Z is given by

(a) $(1/(\alpha + \beta))$ (b) $\min(\alpha, \beta)$

(c) $(\alpha\beta/(\alpha + \beta))$ (d) $\alpha + \beta$

[2004 : 2 Marks]

17. An examination paper has 150 multiple-choice questions of one mark each, with each question havinig four choices. Each incorrect answer fetches – 0.25 mark. Suppose 1000 students choose all their answers randomly with uniform probability. The sum total of he expected marks obtained by all these students is

(a) 0 (b) 2550

(c) 7525 (d) 9375

[2004 : 2 Marks]

18. Two n bit binary strings, S_1 and S_2 are chosen randomly with uniform probability. The probability that the Hamming distance between these strings (the number of bit positions where the two strings differ) is equal to d is

(a) ${}^nC_d / 2^n$ (b) ${}^nC_d / 2^d$

(c) $d/2^n$ (d) $1/2^d$

[2004 : 2 Marks]

19. A point is randomly selected with uniform probability in the X-Y. Plane within the rectangle with corners at (0, 0), (1, 0), (1, 2)and (0, 2). If p is the length of the position vector of the point, the expected value of p^2 is

(a) $\frac{2}{3}$ (b) 1

(c) $\frac{4}{3}$ (d) $\frac{5}{3}$ **[2004 : 2 Marks]**

20. Let f(x)be the continuous probability density function of a random variable X. The probability that $a < X \le b$, is

(a) $f(b - a)$ (b) $f(b) - f(a)$

(c) $\int_a^b f(x)\,dx$ (d) $\int_a^b x f(x)\,dx$

[2005 : 1 Mark]

21. A bag contains 10 blue marbles, 20 green marbles and 30 red marbles. A marble is drawn from the bag, its colour recorded and it is put back in the bag. This process is repeated 3 times. The probability that no two of the marbles drawn have the same colour is

(a) $\frac{1}{36}$ (b) $\frac{1}{6}$

(c) $\frac{1}{4}$ (d) $\frac{1}{3}$

[IT-2005 : 1 Mark]

22. An unbiased coin is tossed repeatedly until the outcome of two successive tosses is the same. Assuming that the trials are independent, the expected number of tosses is

(a) 3 (b) 4

(c) 5 (d) 6

[IT-2005 : 2 Marks]

23. In a certain town, the probability that it will rain in the afternoon is known to be 0.6. Moreover, meterological data indicates that if the temperature at noon is less than or equal to 25°C, the probability that it will rain in the afternoon is 0.4. The temperature at noon is equally likely to be above 25°C, or at/below 25°C.

What is the probability that it will rain in the afternoon on a day when the temperature at noon is above 25°C?

(a) 0.4 (b) 0.6

(c) 0.8 (d) 0.9

[IT-2005 : 1 Mark]

24. When a coin is tossed, the probability of getting a Head is p, $0 < p < 1$. Let N be the random variable denoting the number of tosses till the first Head appears, including the toss where the Head appears. Assuming that successive tosses are independent, the expected value of N is

(a) $1/p$

(b) $1/(1 - p)$

(c) $1/p^2$

(d) $1/(1 - p^2)$ **[IT-2006 : 2 Marks]**

25. Suppose there are two coins. The first coin gives heads with probability $\frac{5}{8}$ when tossed, while the second coin gives heads with probability $\frac{1}{4}$. One of the two coins is picked up at random with equal probability and tossed. What is the probability of obtaining heads?

(a) $\frac{7}{8}$ (b) $\frac{1}{2}$

(c) $\frac{7}{16}$ (d) $\frac{5}{32}$

[IT-2007 : 1 Mark]

26. Suppose we uniformly and randomly select a permutation from the 20! permutations of 1, 2, 3, ..., 20. What is the probability that 2 appears at an earlier position that any other even number in the selected permutation?

(a) $\frac{1}{2}$ (b) $\frac{1}{10}$

(c) $\frac{9!}{20!}$ (d) None of these

[2007 : 2 Marks]

27. In a multi-user operating system on an average, 20 requests are made to use a particular resource per hour. The arrival of requests follows a Poisson distribution. The probability that either one three or five requests are made in 45 minutes is given by :

(a) $6.9 \times 10^6 \times e^{-20}$ (b) $1.02 \times 10^6 \times e^{-20}$

(c) $6.9 \times 10^3 \times e^{-20}$ (b) $1.02 \times 10^3 \times e^{-20}$

[IT-2007 : 2 Marks]

28. A sample space has two events A and B such that probabilities

$P(A \cap B) = 1/2, P(\overline{A}) = 1/3, P(\overline{B}) = 1/3.$

What is $P(A \cup B)$

(a) $\frac{11}{12}$ (b) $\frac{10}{12}$

(c) $\frac{9}{12}$ (d) $\frac{8}{12}$

[IT-2008 : 1 Mark]

29. What is the probability that in a randomly chosen group of r people at least there people have the same birthday.

(a) $1-\frac{365.364...(365-r+1)}{365^r}$

(b) $1-\frac{365.364...(365-r+1)}{365^r}+$

$^rC_2.365.\frac{364.363...(364-(r-2)+1)}{364^{r-2}}$

(c) $1-\frac{365.364...(365-r+1)}{365^r}-$

$^rC_2.365.\frac{364.363...(364-(r-2)+1)}{364^{r-2}}$

(d) $\frac{365.364...(365-r+1)}{365^r}$

[IT-2008 : 2 Marks]

30. Aishwarya studies either computer science or mathematics everyday. If she studies computer science on a day, then the probability that she studies mathematics the next day is 0.6. If she studies mathematics on a day, then the probability that she studies computer science the next day is 0.4. Given that Aishwarya studies computer science on Monday, what is the probability that she studies computer science on Wednesday?

(a) 0.24 (b) 0.36

(c) 0.4 (d) 0.6

[2008 : 2 Marks]

31. Let X be a random variable following normal distribution with mean +1 and variance 4. Let Y be another normal variable with mean –1 and variance unknown. If $P(X \le -1) = P(Y \ge 2)$ the standard deviation of Y is

(a) 3 (b) 2

(c) $\sqrt{2}$ (d) 1

[2008 : 2 Marks]

32. An unbalanced dice (with 6 faces, numbered from 1 to 6)is thrown. The probability that the face value is odd is 90% of the probability that the face value is even. The probability of getting any even numbered face is the same.

If the probability that the face is even given that it is greater than 3 is 0.75, which one of the following options is closet to the probability that the face value exceeds 3?

(a) 0.453 (b) 0.468

(c) 0.485 (d) 0.492

[2009 : 2 Marks]

33. Consider a company that assembles computers. The probability of a faulty assembly of any computer is p. The company therefore subjects each computer to a testing process. This testing process gives the correct result for any computer with a probability of q. What is the probability of a computer being declared faulty?

(a) $pq + (1-p)(1-q)$ (b) $(1-q)p$

(c) $(1-p)q$ (d) pq

[2010 : 2 Marks]

34. What is the probability that a divisor of 10^{99} is a multiple of 10^{96}?

(a) $\frac{1}{625}$ (b) $\frac{4}{625}$

(c) $\frac{12}{625}$ (d) $\frac{16}{625}$

[2010 : 2 Marks]

35. If two fair coins are flipped and at least one of the outcomes is known to be a head, what is the probability that both outcomes are heads?

(a) $\frac{1}{3}$ (b) $\frac{1}{4}$

(c) $\frac{1}{2}$ (d) $\frac{2}{3}$

[2011 : 2 Marks]

36. If the difference between the expectation of the square of a random variable ($E[x^2]$ and the square of the expectation of the random variable $(E[x])^2$ is denoted by R, then

(a) $R = 0$ (b) $R < 0$

(c) $R \geq 0$ (d) $R > 0$

[2010 : 2 Marks]

37. Consider the finite sequence of random values $X = [x_1, x_2, ..., x_n]$. Let μ_x be the mean and σ_x be the standard deviation of X. Let another finite sequence Y of equal length be derived from this as $y_i = a * x_i + b$, where a and b are positive constant. Let μ_y be the mean and σ_y be the standard deviation of this sequence. Which one of the following statements INCORRECT?

(a) Index position of mode X in X is the same as the index position of mode of Y in Y.

(b) Index position of median of X in X is the same as the index position of median of Y in Y

(c) $\mu_y = a\mu_x + b$

(d) $\sigma_y = a\sigma_x + b$

[2011 : 2 Marks]

38. A deck of 5 cards (each carrying a distinct number from 1 to 5)is shuffled thoroughly. Two cards are then removed one at a time from the deck. What is the probability that the two cards are selected with the number on the first card being one higher than the number on the second card?

(a) $\frac{1}{5}$ (b) $\frac{4}{25}$

(c) $\frac{1}{4}$ (d) $\frac{2}{5}$

[2011 : 2 Marks]

39. Consider a random variable X that takes values +1 and –1 with probability 0.5 each. The values of the cumulative distribution function F(x) at x = –1 and +1 are

(a) 0 and 0.5 (b) 0 and 1

(c) 0.5 and 1 (d) 0.25 and 0.75

[2012 : 1 Mark]

40. Suppose a fair six-sided die is rolled once. If the value on the die is 1, 2 or 3 then die is rolled a second time. What is the probability that the sum total of valves that turn up is at least 6?

(a) $\frac{10}{21}$ (b) $\frac{5}{12}$

(c) $\frac{2}{3}$ (d) $\frac{1}{6}$

[2012 : 2 Marks]

41. Suppose p is the number of cars per minute passing through a certain road junction between 5 PM, and p has Poisson distribution with mean 3. What is the probability of observing fewer than 3 cars during any given minute in this interval?

(a) $8/(2e^3)$

(b) $9/(2e^3)$

(c) $17/(2e^3)$

(d) $26/(2e^3)$

[2013 : 1 Mark]

42. Suppose you break a stick of unit length at a point chosen uniformly at random. Then the expected length of the shorter stick is ....

[2014 (Set-1) : 1 Mark]

43. Four fair six-sided dice are rolled. The probability that the sum of the results being 22 is $\frac{x}{1296}$. The value of x is ....

[2014 (Set-1) : 2 Marks]

44. The security system at an IT office is composed of 10 computers of which exactly four are working. To check whether the system is functional, the officials inspect four of the computers picked at random (without replacement). The system is deemed functional if at least three of the four computers inspected are working. Let the probability that the system is deemed functional be denoted by p.

Then 100p = ...

[2014 (Set-2) : 2 Mark]

45. The probability that a given positive integer lying between 1 and 100 (both inclusive) is NOT divisible by 2, 3 or 5 is ....

[2014 (Set-2) : 2 Marks]

46. Let S be a sample space and two mutually exclusive events A and B be such that $A \cup B = S$. If P(.) denotes the probability of the event, the maximum value of P(A) P(B) is ....

[2014 (Set-3) : 2 Marks]

47. Suppose X_i for i = 1, 2, 3 are independent and identically distributed random variables whose probability mass functions are

$Pr[X_i = 0] = Pr[X_i = 1] = 1/2$ for i = 1, 2, 3

Define another random variable

$Y = X_1X_2 \oplus X_3$, where $\oplus$ denotes XOR.

Then $Pr[Y = 0 \mid [X_3 = 0] =$ ....

[2015 (Set-3) : 2 Marks]

48. A probability density function on the interval [a, 1] is given by $1/x^2$ and outside this interval the value of the function is zero. The value of a is ....

[2016 (Set-1) : 1 Mark]

49. Consider the following experiment.

Step 1. Flip a fair coin twice.

Step 2. If the outcomes are (TAILS, HEADS)then output Y and stop.

Step 3. If the outcomes are either (HEADS, HEADS)or (HEADS, TAILS), then output N and stop.

Step 4. If the outcomes are (TAILS, TAILS), then go to Step 1.

The probability that the output of the experiment is Y is .... (up to two decimal places).

[2016 (Set-1) : 2 Marks]

50. Suppose that a shop has an equal number of LED bulbs of two different types. The probability of an LED bulb lasting more than 100 hours given that it is of Type 1 is 0.7, and given that it is of Type 2 is 0.4. The probability that an LED bulb chosen uniformly at random lasts more than 100 hours is .... **[2016 (Set-2) : 1 Mark]**

51. Let X be a Gaussian random variable with mean 0 and variance σ^2. Let Y = max (X, 0) where max (a, b)is the maximum of a and b. The median of Y is .... **[2017 (Set-1) : 1 Mark]**

52. P and Q are considering to apply for a job. The probability that P applies for the job is $\frac{1}{4}$, the probability that P applies for the job given that Q applies for the job is $\frac{1}{2}$, and the probability that Q applies for the job given that P applies for the job is $\frac{1}{3}$. Then the probability that P does not apply for the jon given that Q does not apply for the job is

(a) $\frac{4}{5}$ (b) $\frac{5}{6}$

(c) $\frac{7}{8}$ (d) $\frac{11}{12}$

[2017 (Set-2) : 2 Marks]

53. For any discrete random variable X, with probability mass function $P(X = j) = p_j, p_j \geq 0$, $j \in \{0, ..., N\}$, and $\sum_{j=0}^{N} p_j = 1$, define the polynomial function $g_x(z) = \sum_{j=0}^{N} p_j z^j$. For a certain discrete random variable Y, there exists a scalar $\beta \in [0, 1]$ such that $g_Y(z) = (1 - \beta + \beta z)^N$. The expectation of Y is

(a) $N\beta (1 - \beta)$

(b) $N\beta$

(c) $N (1 - \beta)$

(d) Not expressible in terms of N and β alone

[2017 (Set-2) : 2 Mark]

54. If a random variable X has a poisson distribution with mean 5, then the expectation $E(X + 2)^2]$ equals ....

[2017 (Set-2) : 2 Mark]

55. Two people P and Q, decide to independently roll two identical dice, each with 6 faces, numbered 1 to 6. The person with the lower number wins. In case of a tie, they roll the dice repeatedly until there is no tie. Define a trial as a throw of the dice by P and Q. Assume that all 6 numbers on each dice are equi-probable and that all trials are independent. The probability (rounded to 3 decimal places)that one of them wins on the third trial is .... **[2018 : 1 Mark]**

56. Consider Guwahati (G) and Delhi (D) whose temperatures can be classified as high (H), medium (M)and low (L). Let $P(H_G)$denote the probability that Guwahati has high temperature. Similarly, $P(M_G)$ and $P(L_G)$ denotes the probability of Guwahati having medium and low temperatures respectively. Similarly, we use $P(H_D)$, $P(M_D)$ and $P(L_D)$ for Delhi.

The following table gives the conditional probabilites for Delhi's temperature given Guwahati's temperature.

	H_D	M_D	L_D
H_G	0.40	0.48	0.12
M_G	0.10	0.65	0.25
L_G	0.01	0.50	0.49

Consider the first row in the table given. The first entry denotes that if Guwahati has high temperature (H_G) then the probability of Delhi also having a high temperature (H_D) is 0.40; i.e., $P(H_D \mid H_G) = 0.40$. Similarly, the next two entries are $P(M_D \mid H_G) = 0.48$ and $P(L_D \mid Hg) = 0.12$. Similarly for the other rows.

If it is known that $P(H_G) = 0.2$, $P(M_G) = 0.5$ and $P(L_G) = 0.3$, then the probability (correct to two decimal places) that Guwahati has high temperature given that Delhi has high temperature is .... **[2018 : 2 Marks]**

57. Suppose Y is distributed uniformly in the open interval (1, 6). The probability that the polynomial $3x^2 + 6xY + 3Y + 6$ has only real roots is (rounded off to 1 decimal place)______.

[2019 : 2 Marks]

LINEAR ALGEBRA

1. If a, b and c are constants, which of the following is a linear inequality?

(a) $ax + bcy = 0$ (b) $ax^2 + cy = 21$

(c) $abx + a^2y \geq 15$ (d) $xy + ax \geq 20$

[1987 : 2 Marks]

2. A square matrix is signular whenever :

(a) The rows are linearly independent

(b) The columns are linearly independent

(c) The rows are linearly dependent

(d) None of the above

[1987 : 2 Marks]

3. If A and B are real symmetric matrices of size n × n. Then, which one of the following is true ?

(a) $AA^T = I$ (b) $A = A^{-1}$

(c) $AB = BA$ (d) $(AB)^T = BA$

[1994 : 2 Marks]

4. The rank of the following (n + 1) × (n + 1) matrix, where is a real number is

$$\begin{bmatrix} 1 & a & a^2 & . & . & . & a^n \\ 1 & a & a^2 & . & . & . & a^n \\ . & . & . & & & & . \\ . & . & . & & & & . \\ . & . & . & & & & . \\ 1 & a & a^2 & . & . & . & a^n \end{bmatrix}$$

(a) 1

(b) 2

(c) n

(d) Depends on the value of a

[1995 : 1 Mark]

5. Let AX = B be a system of linear equations where A is an m × n matrix and b is a m × 1 column vector and X is a n × 1 column vector of unknown. Which of the following is false?

(a) The system has a solution if and only if, both A and the augmented matrix [A, B] have the same rank.

(b) If m < n and B is the zero vector, then the system has infinitely many solutions.

(c) If m = n and B is non-zero vector, then the system has a unique solution.

(d) The system will have only a trivial solution when m = n, B is the zero vector and rank (A) = n.

[1996 : 1 Mark]

6. The matrices $\begin{bmatrix} \cos\theta & -\sin\theta \\ \sin\theta & \cos\theta \end{bmatrix}$ and $\begin{bmatrix} a & 0 \\ 0 & b \end{bmatrix}$ commute under multiplication

(a) if a = b or $\theta = n\pi$, n is an integer

(b) always

(c) never

(d) if $a \cos\theta \neq b \sin\theta$ **[1996 : 2 Marks]**

7. The determinant of the matrix

$$\begin{bmatrix} 6 & -8 & 1 & 1 \\ 0 & 2 & 4 & 6 \\ 0 & 0 & 4 & 8 \\ 0 & 0 & 0 & -1 \end{bmatrix}$$ is

(a) 11 (b) –48

(c) 0 (d) –24 **[1997 : 1 Mark]**

8. Let $a = (a_{ij})$ be an n-rowed square matrix and I_{12} be the matrix obtained by interchanging the first and second rows of the n-rowed Identity matrix. Then AI_{12} is such that its first

(a) row the same that as its first

(b) row is the same as the second row of A

(c) column is the same as the second column A

(d) row is all zero **[1997 : 2 Marks]**

9. Consider the following set of equations

$$x + 2y = 5$$
$$4x + 8y = 12$$
$$3x + 6y + 3z = 15$$

This set

(a) has a unique solution

(b) has no solution

(c) has finite number of solutions

(d) has infinite number of solutions

[1998 : 1 Mark]

10. The rank of the matrix given below is

$$\begin{bmatrix} 1 & 4 & 8 & 7 \\ 0 & 0 & 3 & 0 \\ 4 & 2 & 3 & 1 \\ 3 & 12 & 24 & 21 \end{bmatrix}$$

(a) 3 (b) 1

(c) 2 (d) 4

[1998 : 2 Marks]

11. Consider the following determinant

$$\Delta = \begin{vmatrix} 1 & a & bc \\ 1 & b & ca \\ 1 & c & ab \end{vmatrix}$$

Which of the following is a factor of Δ?

(a) $a + b$ (b) $a - b$

(c) $a + b + c$ (d) abc

[1998 : 2 Marks]

12. An $n \times n$ array v is defined as follows :

$v[i, j] = i - j$ for all $i, j, 1 \leq i \leq n, 1 \leq j \leq n$

The sum of the elements of the array v is

(a) 0 (b) $n - 1$

(c) $n^2 - 3n + 2$ (d) $n^2 \dfrac{(n+1)}{2}$

[2000 : 1 Mark]

13. The determinant of the matrix $\begin{bmatrix} 2 & 0 & 0 & 0 \\ 8 & 1 & 7 & 2 \\ 2 & 0 & 2 & 0 \\ 9 & 0 & 6 & 1 \end{bmatrix}$ is

(a) 4 (b) 0

(c) 15 (d) 20 **[2001 : 1 Mark]**

14. Consider the following statements :

S1 :The sum of two singular $n \times n$ matrices may be non-singular

S2 :The sum of two $n \times n$ non-singular matrices may be singular

Which of the following statements is correct?

(a) S_1 and S_2 are both true

(b) S_1 is true S_2 is false

(c) S_1 is false, S_2 is true

(d) S_1 and S_2 are both false **[2002 : 1 Mark]**

15. The rank of the matrix $\begin{bmatrix} 1 & 1 \\ 0 & 0 \end{bmatrix}$ is

(a) 4 (b) 2

(c) 1 (d) 0

[2002 : 1 Mark]

16. Obtain the eigen values of the matrix

$$A = \begin{bmatrix} 1 & 2 & 34 & 49 \\ 0 & 2 & 43 & 94 \\ 0 & 0 & -2 & 104 \\ 0 & 0 & 0 & -1 \end{bmatrix}$$

[2002 : 2 Marks]

17. Consider the following system of linear equations

$$\begin{bmatrix} 2 & 1 & -4 \\ 4 & 3 & -12 \\ 1 & 2 & -8 \end{bmatrix} \begin{bmatrix} x \\ y \\ z \end{bmatrix} = \begin{bmatrix} \alpha \\ 5 \\ 7 \end{bmatrix}$$

Notice that the second and third columns of the coefficient matrix are linearly dependent. For how many values of α, does this sytem of equations have infinitely many solutions?

(a) 0 (b) 1

(c) 2 (d) infinitely many

[2003 : 2 Marks]

18. Let A, B, C, D be $n \times n$ matrices, each with non-zero determinant, If $ABCD = I$, then B^{-1} is

(a) $D^{-1} C^{-1} A^{-1}$

(b) CDA

(c) ADC

(d) does not necessarily exist

[2004 : 1 Mark]

19. What values of x, y and z satisfy the following system of linear equations ?

$$\begin{bmatrix} 1 & 2 & 3 \\ 1 & 3 & 4 \\ 2 & 2 & 3 \end{bmatrix} \begin{bmatrix} x \\ y \\ z \end{bmatrix} = \begin{bmatrix} 6 \\ 8 \\ 12 \end{bmatrix}$$

(a) $x = 6, y = 3, z = 2$

(b) $x = 12, y = 3, z = -4$

(c) $x = 6, y = 6, z = -4$

(d) $x = 12, y = -3, z = 0$

[IT-2004 : 1 Mark]

20. Let A be an $n \times n$ matrix of the following form.

$$A = \begin{bmatrix} 3 & 1 & 0 & 0 & 0 & \cdots & 0 & 0 & 0 \\ 1 & 3 & 1 & 0 & 0 & \cdots & 0 & 0 & 0 \\ 0 & 1 & 3 & 1 & 0 & \cdots & 0 & 0 & 0 \\ 0 & 0 & 1 & 3 & 1 & \cdots & 0 & 0 & 0 \\ \cdots \\ \cdots \\ 0 & 0 & 0 & 0 & 0 & \cdots & 1 & 3 & 1 \\ 0 & 0 & 0 & 0 & 0 & \cdots & 0 & 1 & 3 \end{bmatrix}_{n \times n}$$

What is the value of the determinant of A?

(a) $\left(\frac{5+\sqrt{3}}{2}\right)^{n-1}\left(\frac{5\sqrt{3}+7}{2\sqrt{3}}\right)+\left(\frac{5-\sqrt{3}}{2}\right)^{n-1}\left(\frac{5\sqrt{3}-7}{2\sqrt{3}}\right)$

(b) $\left(\frac{7+\sqrt{5}}{2}\right)^{n-1}\left(\frac{7\sqrt{5}+3}{2\sqrt{5}}\right)+\left(\frac{7-\sqrt{5}}{2}\right)^{n-1}\left(\frac{7\sqrt{5}-3}{2\sqrt{5}}\right)$

(c) $\left(\frac{3+\sqrt{7}}{2}\right)^{n-1}\left(\frac{3\sqrt{7}+5}{2\sqrt{7}}\right)+\left(\frac{3-\sqrt{7}}{2}\right)^{n-1}\left(\frac{3\sqrt{7}-5}{2\sqrt{7}}\right)$

(d) $\left(\frac{3+\sqrt{5}}{2}\right)^{n-1}\left(\frac{3\sqrt{5}+7}{2\sqrt{5}}\right)+\left(\frac{3-\sqrt{5}}{2}\right)^{n-1}\left(\frac{3\sqrt{5}-7}{2\sqrt{5}}\right)$

[IT-2004 : 2 Marks]

21. If matrix $X=\begin{bmatrix} a & 1 \\ -a^2+a-1 & 1-a \end{bmatrix}$ and $X^2-X+I=O$ (I is the identity matrix and O is the zero matrix), then the inverse of X is

(a) $\begin{bmatrix} 1-a & -1 \\ a^2 & a \end{bmatrix}$ (b) $\begin{bmatrix} 1-a & -1 \\ a^2-a+1 & a \end{bmatrix}$

(c) $\begin{bmatrix} -a & 1 \\ -a^2+a-1 & 1-a \end{bmatrix}$ (d) $\begin{bmatrix} a^2-a+1 & a \\ 1 & 1-a \end{bmatrix}$

[IT-2004 : 2 Marks]

22. How many solutions does the following system of linear equations have ?

$-x+5y=-1$

$x-y=2$

$x+3y=3$

(a) infinitely many (b) two distinct solutions

(c) unique (d) none of these

[2004 : 2 Marks]

23. The determinant of the matrix given below is

$$\begin{bmatrix} 0 & 1 & 0 & 2 \\ -1 & 1 & 1 & 3 \\ 0 & 0 & 0 & 1 \\ 1 & -2 & 0 & 1 \end{bmatrix}$$

(a) –1 (b) 0

(c) 1 (d) 2 **[IT-2005 : 1 Mark]**

24. Consider the following system of equations in three real variables x_1, x_2 and x_3

$2x_1-x_2+3x_3=1$

$3x_1-2x_2+5x_3=2$

$-x_1-4x_2+x_3=3$

This system of equations has

(a) no solution

(b) a unique solution

(c) more than one but a finite number of solutions

(d) an infinite number of solutions

[2005 : 2 Marks]

25. What are the eigenvalues of the following 2 × 2 matrix?

$$\begin{bmatrix} 2 & -1 \\ -4 & 5 \end{bmatrix}$$

(a) –1 and 1 (b) 1 and 6

(c) 2 and 5 (d) 4 and –1

[2005 : 2 Marks]

26. F is an n × n real matrix, b is an n × 1 real vector. Suppose there are two n × 1 vectors, u and v such that u ≠ v, and Fu = b, Fv = b.

Which one of the following statements is false?

(a) Determine of F is zero

(b) There are an infinite number of solutions to Fx = b

(c) There is an x = 0 such that Fx = 0

(d) F must have two identical rows

[2006 : 2 Marks]

27. What are the eigenvalues of the matrix P given below

$$P=\begin{pmatrix} a & 1 & 0 \\ 1 & a & 1 \\ 0 & 1 & a \end{pmatrix}$$

(a) $a, a-\sqrt{2}, a+\sqrt{2}$ (b) a, a, a

(c) 0, a, 2a (d) –a, 2a, 2a

[IT-2006 : 2 Marks]

28. Let A be the matrix $\begin{bmatrix} 3 & 1 \\ 1 & 2 \end{bmatrix}$. What is the maximum value of $x^T Ax$ where the maximum is taken over all x that are the unit eigenvectors of A?

(a) 3

(b) $(5+\sqrt{5})/2$

(c) 3

(d) $(5-\sqrt{5})/2$

[IT-2007 : 1 Mark]

29. Consider the set of (column) vectors defined by $X=\{x \in R^3 \mid x_1+x_2+x_3=0,$ where $X^T=[x_1, x_2, x_3]^T\}$. Which of the following is TRUE ?

(a) $\{[1,-1,0]^T, [1,0,-1]^T\}$ is a basis of the subspace X.

(b) $\{[1,-1,0]^T, [1,0,-1]^T\}$ is a linearly independent set, but it does not span X and therefore is not a basis of X

(c) X is not a subspace for R^3

(d) None of the above **[2007 : 2 Marks]**

30. The following system of equations

$$x_1 + x_2 + 2x_3 = 1$$
$$x_1 + 2x_3 + 3x_3 = 2$$
$$x_1 + 4x_2 + ax_3 = 4$$

has a unique solution. The only possible value(s) for a is/are

(a) 0

(b) either 0 or 1

(c) one of 0, 1 or –1

(d) any real number other than 5

[2008 : 1 Mark]

31. How many of the following matrices have an eigenvalue 1 ?

$$\begin{bmatrix}1 & 0\\ 0 & 0\end{bmatrix}, \begin{bmatrix}0 & 1\\ 0 & 0\end{bmatrix}, \begin{bmatrix}1 & -1\\ 1 & 1\end{bmatrix} \text{ and } \begin{bmatrix}-1 & 0\\ 1 & -1\end{bmatrix}$$

(a) one (b) two

(c) three (d) four

[2008 : 2 Marks]

32. If M is a square matrix with a zero determinant, which of the following assertion (s) is (are) correct ?

S1 : Each row of M can be represented as a linear combination of the other rows

S2 :Each column of M can be represented as a linear combination of the other columns

S3 : MX = 0 has a nontrivial solution

S4 : M has an inverse

(a) S3 and S2 (b) S1 and S4

(c) S1 and S3 (d) S1, S2 and S3

[IT-2008 : 2 Marks]

33. Consider the following matrix.

$$A = \begin{bmatrix}2 & 3\\ x & y\end{bmatrix}$$

If the eigenvalues of A are 4 and 8, then

(a) x = 4, y = 10 (b) x = 5, y = 8

(c) x = –3, y = 9 (d) x = –4, y = 10

[2010 : 2 Marks]

34. Consider the matrix as given below :

$$\begin{bmatrix}1 & 2 & 3\\ 0 & 4 & 7\\ 0 & 0 & 3\end{bmatrix}$$

Which one of the following options provides the CORRECT values of the eigenvalues of the matrix ?

(a) 1, 4, 3 (b) 3, 7, 3

(c) 7, 3, 2 (d) 1, 2, 3

[2011 : 2 Marks]

35. Let A be the 2 × 2 matrix with elements $a_{11} = a_{12} = a_{21} = +1$ and $a_{22} = -1$.

Then the eigenvalues of the matrix A^{19} are

(a) 1024 and –1024

(b) $1024\sqrt{2}$ and $-1024\sqrt{2}$

(c) $4\sqrt{2}$ and $-4\sqrt{2}$

(d) $512\sqrt{2}$ and $-512\sqrt{2}$

[2012 : 1 Mark]

36. Which one of the following does NOT equal

$$\begin{vmatrix}1 & x & x^2\\ 1 & y & y^2\\ 1 & z & z^2\end{vmatrix} ?$$

(a) $\begin{vmatrix}1 & x(x+1) & x+1\\ 1 & y(y+1) & y+1\\ 1 & z(z+1) & z+1\end{vmatrix}$ (b) $\begin{vmatrix}1 & x+1 & x^2+1\\ 1 & y+1 & y^2+1\\ 1 & z+1 & z^2+1\end{vmatrix}$

(c) $\begin{vmatrix}0 & x-y & x^2-y^2\\ 0 & y-z & y^2-z^2\\ 1 & z & z^2\end{vmatrix}$ (d) $\begin{vmatrix}0 & x+y & x^2+y^2\\ 0 & y+z & y^2+z^2\\ 1 & z & z^2\end{vmatrix}$

[2013 : 1 Mark]

37. Consider the following system of equations :

$$3x + 2y = 1$$
$$4x + 7z = 1$$
$$x + y + z = 3$$
$$x - 2y + 7z = 0$$

The number of solutions for this system is ....

[2014 (Set-1) : 1 Mark]

38. The value of the dot product of the eigenvectors corresponding to any pair of different eigen values of a 4-by-4 symmetric positive definite matrix is ....

[2014 (Set-1) : 1 Mark]

39. If the matrix A is such that

$$A\begin{bmatrix}2\\ -4\\ 7\end{bmatrix}\begin{bmatrix}1 & 9 & 5\end{bmatrix}$$

then the determinant of A is equal to ....

[2014 (Set-2) : 1 Mark]

40. The product of the non-zero eigenvalues of the matrix

$$\begin{bmatrix}1 & 0 & 0 & 0 & 1\\ 0 & 1 & 1 & 1 & 0\\ 0 & 1 & 1 & 1 & 0\\ 0 & 1 & 1 & 1 & 0\\ 1 & 0 & 0 & 0 & 1\end{bmatrix}$$

is ....

[2014 (Set-2) : 2 Marks]

41. Which one of the following statements is TRUE about every $n \times n$ matrix with only real eigenvalues ?

(a) If the trace of the matrix is positive and the determinant of the matrix is negative, at least one of its eigenvalues is negative.

(b) If the trace of the matrix is positive, all its eigenvalues are positive.

(c) If the determinant of the matrix is positive, all its eigenvalues are positive.

(d) If the product of the trace and determinant of the matrix is positive, all its eigenvalues are positive.

[2014 (Set-3) : 1 Mark]

42. If V_1 and V_2 are 4-dimensional subspaces of a 6-dimensional vector space V, then the smallest possible dimension of $V_1 \cap V_2$ is ....

[2014 (Set-3) : 1 Mark]

43. The minimum number of arithmetic operations required to evaluate the polynomial $P(X) = X^5 + 4X^3 + 6X + 5$ for a given value of X, using only one temporary variable is ....

[2014 (Set-3) : 1 Mark]

44. Consider the following 2 × 2 matrix A where two elements are unknown and are marked by 'a' and 'b'. The eigenvalues of this matrix are –1 and 7. What are the values of 'a' and 'b'?

$$A = \begin{pmatrix} 1 & 4 \\ b & a \end{pmatrix}$$

(a) a = 6, b = 4

(b) a = 4, b = 6

(c) a = 3, b = 5

(d) a = 5, b = 3

[2015 (Set-1) : 2 Marks]

45. The larger of the two eigenvalues of the matrix $\begin{bmatrix} 4 & 5 \\ 2 & 1 \end{bmatrix}$ is ....

[2015 (Set-2) : 1 Mark]

46. Perform the following operations on the matrix

$$\begin{bmatrix} 3 & 4 & 45 \\ 7 & 9 & 105 \\ 13 & 2 & 195 \end{bmatrix}.$$

1. Add the third row to the second law.

2. Subtract the third column from the first column.

The determinant of the resultant matrix is ....

[2015 (Set-2) : 2 Marks]

47. In the given matrix $\begin{bmatrix} 1 & -1 & 2 \\ 0 & 1 & 0 \\ 1 & 2 & 1 \end{bmatrix}$, one of the eigenvalues is 1. The eigenvectors corresponding to the eigenvalue 1 are

(a) $\{\alpha(4,2,1) \mid a \neq 0, \alpha \in R\}$

(b) $\{\alpha(-4,2,1) \mid a \neq 0, \alpha \in R\}$

(c) $\{\alpha(\sqrt{2},0,1) \mid a \neq 0, \alpha \in R\}$

(d) $\{\alpha(-\sqrt{2},0,1) \mid a \neq 0, \alpha \in R\}$

[2015 (Set-3) : 1 Mark]

48. In the LU decomposition of the matrix $\begin{bmatrix} 2 & 2 \\ 4 & 9 \end{bmatrix}$, if the diagonal elements of U are both 1, then the lower diagonal entry l_{22} of L is ....

[2015 (Set-1) : 1 Mark]

49. If the following system has non-trivial solution,

$$px + qy + rz = 0$$
$$qx + ry + pz = 0$$
$$rx + py + qz = 0$$

then which one of the following options is TRUE ?

(a) $p - q + r = 0$ or $p = q = -r$

(b) $p + q - r = 0$ or $p = q = r$

(c) $p + q + r = 0$ or $p = q = r$

(d) $p - q + r = 0$ or $p = -q = -r$

[2015 (Set-3) : 2 Mark]

50. Two eigenvalues of a 3 × 3 real matrix P are $(2 + \sqrt{-1})$ and 3. The determinant of P is ....

[2016 (Set-1) : 1 Mark]

51. Consider the systems, each following of m linear equations in n variables.

I. If m < n, then all such systems have a solution.

II. If m > n, then none of these systems has a solution.

III. If m = n, then there exists a system which has a solution

Which one of the following is CORRECT ?

(a) I, II and III are true

(b) Only II and III are true

(c) Only III is true

(d) None of them is true

[2016 (Set-2) : 1 Mark]

52. Suppose that the eigenvalues of matrix A are 1, 2, 4. The determinant of $(A^{-1})^T$ is ....

[2016 (Set-2) : 1 Mark]

53. Let $c_1, ..., c_n$ be scalars, not all zero, such that $\sum_{i=1}^{n} c_i a_i = 0$ where a_i are column vectors in R^n.

Consider the set of linear equations

$$Ax = b$$

where $A = [a_1, ..., a_n]$ and $b = \sum_{i=1}^{n} a_i$. The set of equations has

(a) a unique solution at $x = J_n$ where J_n denotes a n-dimensional vector of all 1

(b) no solution

(c) infinitely many solutions

(d) finitely many solutions

[2017 (Set-1) : 1 Mark]

54. Let A be n × n real valued square symmetric matrix of rank 2 with $\sum_{i=1}^{n}\sum_{j=1}^{n} A_{ij}^2 = 50$. Consider the following statements.

I. One eigenvalue must be in [–5, 5]

II. The eigenvalue with the largest magnitude must be strictly greater than 5.

Which of the above statements about eigenvalues of A/is are necessarily CORRECT ?

(a) Both I and II (b) I only

(c) II only (d) Neither I nor II

[2017 (Set-1) : 2 Marks]

55. Let $P = \begin{bmatrix} 1 & 1 & -1 \\ 2 & -3 & 4 \\ 3 & -2 & 3 \end{bmatrix}$ and $Q = \begin{bmatrix} -1 & -2 & 1 \\ 6 & 12 & 6 \\ 5 & 10 & 5 \end{bmatrix}$ be two matrices. Then the rank of P + Q is ....

[2017 (Set-2) : 1 Mark]

56. If the characteristic polynomial of a 3 × 3 matrix M over R (the set of real numbers) is $\lambda^3 - 4\lambda^2 + a\lambda + 30$, $a \in R$ and one eigenvalue of M is 2, then the largest among the absolute values of the eigenvalues of M is ....

[2017 (Set-2) : 1 Mark]

57. Consider a matrix $A = uv^T$ where $u = \begin{pmatrix} 1 \\ 2 \end{pmatrix}$, $v = \begin{pmatrix} 1 \\ 1 \end{pmatrix}$.

Note that v^T denotes the transpose of v. The largest eigenvalue of A is ....

[2018 : 1 Mark]

58. Consider a matrix P whose only eigenvectors are the multiples of $\begin{bmatrix} 1 \\ 4 \end{bmatrix}$.

Consider the following statements.

I. P does not have an inverse.

II. P has a repeated eigenvalue.

III. P cannot be diagonalized.

Which one of the following options is correct ?

(a) Only I and III are necessarily true

(b) Only II is necessarily true

(c) Only I and II are necessarily true

(d) Only II and III are necessarily true

[2018 : 2 Mark]

59. Let X be a square matrix. Consider the following two statements on X.

I. X is invertible

II. Determinant of X is non-zero

Which one of the following is TRUE?

(a) I and II are equivalent statements.

(b) I implies II; II does not imply I.

(c) I does not imply II; II does not imply I.

(d) II implies I; I does not imply II.

[2019 : 1 Mark]

60. Consider the following matrix:

$$R = \begin{bmatrix} 1 & 2 & 4 & 8 \\ 1 & 3 & 9 & 27 \\ 1 & 4 & 16 & 64 \\ 1 & 5 & 25 & 125 \end{bmatrix}$$

The absolute value of the product of Eigen values of R is ______.

[2019 : 2 Marks]

CALCULUS

1. If at every point of a certain curve, the slope of the tangent equals $\frac{-2x}{y}$ the curve is

(a) A straight line (b) A parabola

(c) A circle (d) An ellipse

[1995 : 1 Mark]

2. The formula used to compute an approximation for the second derivative of a function f at a point x_0 is

(a) $\frac{f(x_0 + h) + f(x_0 - h)}{2}$

(b) $\frac{f(x_0 + h) + f(x_0 - h)}{2h}$

(c) $\frac{f(x_0 + h) + 2(x_0) + f(x_0 - h)}{h^2}$

(d) $\frac{f(x_0 + h) - 2f(x_0) + f(x_0 - h)}{h^2}$

[1996 : 1 Mark]

3. What is the maximum value of the function f(x) = $2x^2 - 2x + 6$ in the interval [0, 2]?

(a) 6 (b) 10

(c) 12 (d) 5.5

[1997 : 2 Marks]

4. Consider the function y = | x | in the interval [–1, 1]. In this interval, the function is

(a) continuous and differentiable

(b) continuous but not differentiable

(c) differentiable but not continuous

(d) neither continuous not differentiable

[1998 : 1 Mark]

5. What is the value of $\int_0^{2\pi} (x-\pi)^3 (\cos x)dx$

(a) –1 (b) 0

(c) 1 (d) π

[IT-2005 : 2 Marks]

6. The following definite integral evaluates to

$$\int_{-\infty}^{0} e^{-\left(\frac{x^2}{2}\right)} dx$$

(a) $\frac{1}{2}$ (b) $\pi\sqrt{10}$

(c) $\sqrt{\pi/2}$ (d) π

[IT-2006 : 2 Marks]

7. If f(x) is defined as follows, what is the minimum value of f(x) for $x \in (0,2]$?

$$f(x) = \begin{cases} \frac{25}{8x} & \text{when } x \le \frac{3}{2} \\ x + \frac{1}{x} & \text{otherwise} \end{cases}$$

(a) 2 (b) $2\left(\frac{1}{12}\right)$

(c) $2\left(\frac{1}{6}\right)$ (d) $2\left(\frac{1}{2}\right)$

[IT-2008 : 2 Marks]

8. Consider the following two statements about the function f(x) = | x |

P : f(x) is continuous for all real values of x

Q : f(x) is differentiable for all real values of x

Which of the folliwng is TRUE?

(a) P is true and Q is false

(b) P is false and Q is true

(c) Both P and Q are true

(d) Both P and Q are false

[2007 : 1 Mark]

9. $\lim_{x\to\infty} \frac{x - \sin x}{x + \cos x}$ equals

(a) 1 (b) –1

(c) ∞ (d) $-\infty$ **[2008 : 1 Mark]**

10. A point on a curve is said to be an extermum if it is a local minimum or a local maximum. The number of distinct extrema for the curve $3x^4 - 16x^3 + 4x^2 + 37$ is

(a) 0 (b) 1

(c) 2 (d) 3 **2008 : 2 Marks]**

11. $\int_0^{\pi/4} (1 - \tan x)/(1 + \tan x)\, dx$ evaluates to

(a) 0 (b) 1

(c) ln2 (d) $\frac{1}{2}\ln 2$

[2009 : 2 Marks]

12. What is the value of $\lim_{n\to\infty}\left(1-\frac{1}{n}\right)^{2n}$?

(a) 0 (b) e^{-2}

(c) $e^{-1/2}$ (d) 1 **[2010 : 1 Mark]**

13. Given $i = \sqrt{-1}$, what will be the evaluation of the definite integral $\int_0^{\pi/2} \frac{\cos x + i\sin x}{\cos x - i\sin x} dx$?

(a) 0 (b) 2

(c) –i (d) i **[2011 : 2 Marks]**

14. Consider the function f(x) = sin(x) in the interval $x \in [\pi/4, 7\pi/4]$. The number and location(s) of the local minima of this function are

(a) One, at $\pi/2$

(b) One, at $3\pi/2$

(c) Two, at $\pi/2$ and $3\pi/2$

(d) Two, at $\pi/4$ and $3\pi/2$ **[2012 : 1 Mark]**

15. Which one of the following functions is continuous at x = 3?

(a) $f(x) = \begin{cases} 2, & \text{if } x = 3 \\ x-1, & \text{of } x > 3 \\ \frac{x+3}{3}, & \text{of } x < 3 \end{cases}$

(b) $f(x) = \begin{cases} 4, & \text{if } x = 3 \\ 8-x & \text{if } x \ne 3 \end{cases}$

(c) $f(x) = \begin{cases} x+3 & \text{if } x \le 3 \\ x-4 & \text{if } x > 3 \end{cases}$

(d) $f(x) = \frac{1}{x^3 - 27}$, if $x \ne 3$

[2013 : 1 Mark]

16. Let the function

$$f(q) = \begin{vmatrix} \sin\theta & \cos\theta & \tan\theta \\ \sin(\pi/6) & \cos(\pi/6) & \tan(\pi/6) \\ \sin(\pi/3) & \cos(\pi/3) & \tan(\pi/3) \end{vmatrix}$$

where $\theta \in \left[\frac{\pi}{6}, \frac{\pi}{3}\right]$ and $f'(\theta)$ denote the derivative of f with respect to θ. Which of the following statements is/are TRUE?

I : There exists $\theta \in \left[\frac{\pi}{6}, \frac{\pi}{3}\right]$ such that $f'(\theta) = 0$.

II : There exists $\theta \in \left[\frac{\pi}{6}, \frac{\pi}{3}\right]$ such that $f'(\theta) \neq 0$.

(a) I only (b) II only
(c) Both I and II (d) Neither I nor II

[2014 (Set-1) : 1 Mark]

17. The function f(x) = x sin x satisfies the following equation : $f''(x) + f(x) + t\cos x = 0$. The value of t is ....

[2014 (Set-1) : 2 Marks]

18. A function f(x) is continuous in the interval [0, 2]. It is known that f(0) = f(2) = –1 and f(1) = 1. Which one of the following statements must be true?

(a) There exists a y in the interval (0, 1) such that f(y) = f(y + 1)
(b) For every y in the interal (0, 1), f(y) = f(2 – y)
(c) The maximum value of the function in the interval (0, 2) is 1
(d) There exists a y in the interval (0, 1) such that f(y) = –f(2 – y)

[2014 (Set-1) : 2 Marks]

19. A non-zero polynomial f(x) of degree 3 has roots at x = 1, x = 2 and x = 3. Which one of the following must be TRUE ?

(a) f(0) f(4) < 0 (b) f(0) f(4) > 0
(c) f(0) + f(4) > 0 (d) f(0) + f(4) < 0

[2014 (Set-2) : 1 Mark]

20. If $\int_0^{2\pi} |x\sin x|\, dx = k\pi$, then the value of k is equal to ....

[2014 (Set-3) : 1 Mark]

21. The value of the integral given below is

$\int_0^{\pi} x^2 \cos x dx$

(a) –2π (b) π
(c) –π (d) 2π

[2014 (Set-3) : 2 Marks]

22. $\lim_{x\to\infty} x^{1/x}$ is

(a) ∞ (b) 0
(c) 1 (d) Not defined

[2015 (Set-1) : 1 Mark]

23. $\int_{1/\pi}^{2/\pi} \frac{\cos(1/x)}{x^2} dx =$ ....

[2015 (Set-1) : 2 Marks]

24. Let $f(x) = x^{-(1/3)}$ and A denote the area of the region bounded by f(x) and the X-axis, when x varies from –1 to 1.Which of the following statements is/are True ?

1. f is continuous in [–1, 1]
2. f is not bounded in [–1, 1]
3. A is nonzero and finite

(a) 2 only (b) 3 only
(c) 2 and 3 only (d) 1, 2 and 3

[2015 (Set-2) : 2 Marks]

25. The value of $\lim_{x\to\infty}(1 + x^2)^{e^{-x}}$ is

(a) 0 (b) $\frac{1}{2}$
(c) 1 (d) ∞

[2015 (Set-3) : 1 Mark]

26. If for non-zero x, $af(x) + bf\left(\frac{1}{x}\right) = \frac{1}{x} - 25$ where $a \neq b$ then $\int_1^2 f(x)dx$ is

(a) $\frac{1}{a^2 - b^2}\left[a(\ln 2 - 25) + \frac{47b}{2}\right]$

(b) $\frac{1}{a^2 - b^2}\left[a(\ln 2 - 25) + \frac{47b}{2}\right]$

(c) $\frac{1}{a^2 - b^2}\left[a(21n2 - 25) + \frac{47b}{2}\right]$

(d) $\frac{1}{a^2 - b^2}\left[a(\ln 2 - 25) - \frac{47b}{2}\right]$

[2015 (Set-3) : 2 Marks]

27. $\lim_{x\to 4} \frac{\sin(x-4)}{x-4} =$ ....

[2016 (Set-1) : 1 Mark]

28. Let f(x) be a polynomial and g(x) = f'(x) be its derivative. If the degree of (f(x) + f(–x) is 10, then the degree of (g(x) – g(–x) is ....

[2016 (Set-2) : 1 Mark]

29. The value of $\lim_{x\to 1}\frac{x^7-2x^5+1}{x^3-3x^2+2}$

(a) is 0
(b) is –1
(c) is 1
(d) does not exist

[2017 (Set-1) : 1 Mark]

30. Consider a quadratic equation $x^2 - 13x + 36 = 0$ with coefficients in a base 'b'. The solutions of this equation in the same base 'b' are x = 5 and x = 6. Then b = ...

[2017 (Set-2) : 1 Mark]

31. If $f(x) = R\sin\left(\frac{\pi x}{2}\right) + S, f'\left(\frac{1}{2}\right) = \sqrt{2}$ and $\int_0^1 fx(dx) = \frac{2R}{\pi}$, then the constants R and S are, respectively

(a) $\frac{2}{\pi}$ and $\frac{16}{\pi}$ (b) $\frac{2}{\pi}$ and 0
(c) $\frac{4}{\pi}$ and 0 (d) $\frac{4}{\pi}$ and $\frac{16}{\pi}$

[2017 (Set-2) : 1 Mark]

32. The value of $\int_0^{\pi/4} x\cos(x^2)dx$ correct to three decimal places (assuming that p = 3.14) is ....

[2018 : 1 Mark]

33. Compute $\lim_{x\to 3}\frac{x^4-81}{2x^2-5x-3}$

(a) 53/12
(b) 1
(c) Limit does not exist
(d) 108/7

[2019 : 1 Mark]

ANSWERS

MATHEMATICAL LOGIC

1. (1)	**2.** (a)	**3.** (b)	**4.** (b)	**5.** (False)	**6.** (d)	**7.** (d)	**8.** (a)	**9.** (a)	**10.** (a)
11. (a)	**12.** (d)	**13.** (d)	**14.** (b)	**15.** (d)	**16.** (c)	**17.** (c)	**18.** (a)	**19.** (b)	**20.** (b)
21. (b)	**22.** (b)	**23.** (d)	**24.** (d)	**25.** (d)	**26.** (d)	**27.** (a)	**28.** (a)	**29.** (a)	**30.** (c)
31. (d)	**32.** (b)	**33.** (d)	**34.** (b)	**35.** (b)	**36.** (b)	**37.** (a)	**38.** (b)	**39.** (c)	**40.** (d)
41. (a)	**42.** (d)	**43.** (a)	**44.** (b)	**45.** (d)	**46.** (d)	**47.** (c)	**48.** (*)	**49.** (c)	**50.** (c)
51. (a)	**52.** (11)	**53.** (b)	**54.** (d)	**55.** (b)	**56.** (d)	**57.** (d)	**58.** (a)	**59.** (a)	**60.** (2)
61. (c)									

SET THEORY AND ALGEBRA

1. (False)	**2.** (a)	**3.** (4)	**4.** (*)	**5.** (c)	**6.** (b)	**7.** (c)	**8.** (d)	**9.** (c)	**10.** (d)
11. (a)	**12.** (b)	**13.** (a)	**14.** (c)	**15.** (c)	**16.** (a)	**17.** (c)	**18.** (a)	**19.** (b)	**20.** (c)
21. (c)	**22.** (b)	**23.** (a)	**24.** (*)	**25.** (c)	**26.** (a)	**27.** (c)	**28.** (b)	**29.** (b)	**30.** (d)
31. (*)	**32.** (d)	**33.** (a)	**34.** (d)	**35.** (c)	**36.** (b)	**37.** (c)	**38.** (c)	**39.** (c)	**40.** (d)
41. (a)	**42.** (a)	**43.** (b)	**44.** (c)	**45.** (c)	**46.** (b)	**47.** (a)	**48.** (c)	**49.** (b)	**50.** (a)
51. (d)	**52.** (c)	**53.** (a)	**54.** (c)	**55.** (b)	**56.** (b)	**57.** (b)	**58.** (b)	**59.** (c)	**60.** (d)
61. (d)	**62.** (a)	**63.** (a)	**64.** (d)	**65.** (c)	**66.** (c)	**67.** (a)	**68.** (c)	**69.** (a)	**70.** (16)
71. (a)	**72.** (d)	**73.** (5)	**74.** (b)	**75.** (4)	**76.** (a)	**77.** (c)	**78.** (d)	**79.** (d)	**80.** (2048)
81. (36)	**82.** (0.95)	**83.** (b)	**84.** (d)	**85.** (c)	**86.** (3)	**87.** (a)	**88.** (b)	**89.** (0)	**90.** (271)
91. (42)	**92.** (d)	**93.** (d)	**94.** (a)						

COMBINATORICS

1. (a) **2.** (*) **3.** (*) **4.** (a) **5.** (d) **6.** (d) **7.** (*) **8.** (c) **9.** (c) **10.** (b)

11. (b) **12.** (d) **13.** (c) **14.** (b) **15.** (d) **16.** (a) **17.** (d) **18.** (c) **19.** (b) **20.** (a)

21. (a) **22.** (d) **23.** (a) **24.** (d) **25.** (c) **26.** (c) **27.** (a) **28.** (89) **29.** (3.8 to 3.9)

30. (8) **31.** (0.99) **32.** (a) **33.** (36) **34.** (15) **35.** (b) **36.** (10) **37.** (198) **38.** (15) **39.** (d)

GRAPH THEORY

1. (c) **2.** (d) **3.** (*) **4.** (c) **5.** (*) **6.** (c) **7.** (*) **8.** (c) **9.** (d) **10.** (b)

11. (c) **12.** (a) **13.** (d) **14.** (d) **15.** (d) **16.** (a) **17.** (d) **18.** (b) **19.** (a) **20.** (d)

21. (c) **22.** (c) **23.** (c) **24.** (b) **25.** (b) **26.** (d) **27.** (c) **28.** (b) **29.** (b) **30.** (d)

31. (a) **32.** (b) **33.** (c) **34.** (a) **35.** (d) **36.** (b) **37.** (d) **38.** (b) **39.** (c) **40.** (c)

41. (c) **42.** (b) **43.** (506) **44.** (c) **45.** (36) **46.** (5) **47.** (6) **48.** (c) **49.** (a) **50.** (24)

51. (d) **52.** (d) **53.** (199) **54.** (995) **55.** (4) **56.** (18) **57.** (16) **58.** (3) **59.** (109) **60.** (b)

61. (a)

PROBABILITY

1. (c) **2.** (c) **3.** (d) **4.** (c) **5.** (d) **6.** (b) **7.** (c) **8.** (d) **9.** (d) **10.** (b)

11. (c) **12.** (d) **13.** (c) **14.** (a) **15.** (b) **16.** (c) **17.** (d) **18.** (a) **19.** (d) **20.** (c)

21. (b) **22.** (a) **23.** (c) **24.** (a) **25.** (c) **26.** (d) **27.** (b) **28.** (b) **29.** (c) **30.** (c)

31. (a) **32.** (b) **33.** (b) **34.** (a) **35.** (a) **36.** (c) **37.** (d) **36.** (a) **39.** (c) **40.** (*)

41. (c) **42.** (0.25) **43.** (10) **44.** (11.85 to 11.95) **45.** (0.259 to 0.261) **46.** (0.25) **47.** (*) **48.** (0.5)

49. (0.33) **50.** (0.55) **51.** (0) **52.** (a) **53.** (b) **54.** (54) **55.** 0.023 **56.** 0.60 **57.** (0.8)

LINEAR ALGEBRA

1. (c) **2.** (*) **3.** (d) **4.** (a) **5.** (c) **6.** (a) **7.** (b) **8.** () **9.** (b) **10.** (a)

11. (b) **12.** (a) **13.** (a) **14.** (a) **15.** (c) **16.** (*) **17.** (b) **18.** (b) **19.** (c) **20.** (d)

21. (b) **22.** (c) **23.** (c) **24.** (b) **25.** (b) **26.** (d) **27.** (a) **28.** (b) **29.** (b) **30.** (d)

31. (a) **32.** (d) **33.** (d) **34.** (a) **35.** (d) **36.** (a) **37.** (1) **38.** (0) **39.** (0 to 0)

40. (6 to 6) **41.** (a) **42.** (2) **43.** (7) **44.** (d) **45.** (6) **46.** 0 **47.** (b) **48.** (5) **49.** (c)

50. (15) **51.** (c) **52.** (0.125) **53.** (c) **54.** (d) **55.** (2) **56.** (5) **57.** (3) **58.** (d) **59.** (a)

60. 12

CALCULUS

1. (d) **2.** (d) **3.** (b) **4.** (b) **5.** (b) **6.** (c) **7.** (b) **8.** (a) **9.** (a) **10.** (b)

11. (d) **12.** (b) **13.** (d) **14.** (b) **15.** (a) **16.** (c) **17.** (2) **18.** (a) **19.** (a) **20.** (4)

21. (a) **22.** (c) **23.** (1) **24.** (c) **25.** (c) **26.** (a) **27.** (1) **28.** (9) **29.** (c) **30.** (8)

31. (c) **32.** (0.289) **33.** (d)

EXPLANATIONS

MATHEMATICAL LOGIC

1. $(P \rightarrow Q) \wedge (Q \rightarrow R) \rightarrow (P \rightarrow R)$

is a hypothetical syllogism.

It is well formed formula.

2. According to distributive properties.

$\forall x(P(x) \wedge Q(x)) \leftrightarrow \forall x P(x) \wedge \forall x Q(x)$

$\forall x(P(x) \vee \forall x Q(x) \rightarrow \forall x(P(x) \vee Q(x)$

3. $(a \wedge b) \rightarrow (b \vee c)$

a	b	c	(1) a ^ b	(2) bvc	(a ^ b) → (bvc)
T	T	T	T	T	T
T	T	F	T	T	T
T	F	T	F	T	T
T	F	F	F	F	T
F	T	T	F	T	T
F	T	F	F	T	T
F	F	T	F	T	T
F	F	F	F	F	T

(1) → (2) is a tautology.

4. The proposition $p \wedge (\sim p \vee q)$

$\equiv (p \wedge \sim p) \vee (p \wedge q)$

$\equiv F \wedge (p \vee q)$

$\equiv (p \wedge q)$

5. $p \leftrightarrow q$ is equivalent to

$p \rightarrow \sim q$ iff

$(p \leftrightarrow q) \leftrightarrow (p \rightarrow \sim q)$ is not a tautology (using truth table).

Hence statment is false.

6. $(\sim p \rightarrow q)$ is true then

$\sim p \wedge (p \rightarrow q)$ is true or not?

We can't determine with the help of given information.

7. $(x \vee y) \leftrightarrow (\sim x \rightarrow \sim y)$

is false using truth table

x	y	(1) x ∨ y	~x	~y	(2) ~x→ ~y	(1) ↔ (2)
T	T	T	F	F	T	T
T	F	T	F	T	T	T
F	T	T	T	F	F	F
F	F	F	T	T	T	F

(1) ↔ (2) is not a tautology

Hence statment is false.

8. $a \leftrightarrow (b \vee \sim b)$

$a \leftrightarrow$ True

So a is true i.e. $a = 1$

$b \leftrightarrow c$ i.e. $b = c$

Now, the given expression is

$(a \wedge b) \rightarrow (a \wedge c) \vee d \equiv ab \rightarrow ac + d$

Put $a = 1$

$\Rightarrow 1.\, b \rightarrow 1.c + d$

$\Rightarrow b \rightarrow c + d$

$\Rightarrow b' + c + d$

$\Rightarrow c' + c + d \equiv 1 + d \equiv 1.$ $\quad [\because b = c]$

So the expression is always true.

9. Assume

P = I stay

Q = you go

Given expression is

"I stay only if you go"

is same as $P \rightarrow Q$

Converse of $P \rightarrow Q$ is $Q \rightarrow P$

Now, option (a) I stay if you go is zame as $Q \rightarrow P$

Hence (1) is true.

10. F_1: $P \rightarrow \sim P \equiv P' + P' \equiv P'$

So F_1 is always false. Hence

It is satisfiable but not valid.

$F_2 : (P \rightarrow \sim P) \wedge (\sim P \rightarrow P)$

Is valid because result is always true i.e. tautology.

11. "if X then Y unless Z" means "if X is true and Z is false then Y is true"

So $(X \wedge \sim Z) \rightarrow Y$

12. $(\forall x)\ (\alpha \rightarrow \beta) \rightarrow ((\forall(x)\alpha \rightarrow \forall(x)\beta)$

is logical equivalence so it is valid.

13. $\alpha : (\forall x)\left[P_x \leftrightarrow \forall y\left[Q_{xy} \leftrightarrow \sim Q_{yy}\right]\right]$

$\rightarrow \forall x\left[\sim P_x\right]$

I_1: P_x = 'x is a Prime Number'

O_{xy} = 'y divides x'

α: (∀ x is a prime numbr iff ∀ y) y does not divide x)) → (∀ x) x is not prime.

i.e. x is prime number iff no number divides x implies that no number is prime.

So the above statment satisfy the definition of prime number. Similary I_2 also statisy α.

14. (P ∨ Q) → (P ∨ R) ∧ (Q ∨ ~ R) is may or may not be true.

Hence it is false.

15. The statment is "Some boys in the class are taller then all the girls."

(∃x) (boy (x) ∧ (∀ y) (girl (y) → taller (x, y)))

16. From option (c)

~(∀ x) (∃ y) [(a(x, y) ∧ b(x, y)) → c(x, y)]

⇒ (∃ x) (∀ y) [a(x, y) ∧ b(x, y) ∨ ~ c(x, y)]

17. P : ((~p ∧ q) ∧ (r → s) ∧ (p ∨ r) → (~s → q)

≡ [(p → q) ∨ (r → s) ∧ (p ∧ r)] → (q ∧ s)

it is rule of inference

So it is valid.

S : [p ∧ (p → r) ∧ (q ∨ ~ r)] → q

Using truth table

(1)			(2)	(3)		(4)	(5)	
p	q	r	p → r	(1) ^ (2)	~r	qv ~ r	(3)^(4)	(5)→(q)
T	T	T	T	T	F	T	T	T
T	T	F	F	F	T	T	F	T
T	F	T	T	T	F	F	F	T
T	F	F	F	F	T	T	F	T
F	T	T	T	F	F	T	F	T
F	T	F	T	F	T	T	F	T
F	F	T	T	F	F	F	F	T
F	F	F	T	F	T	T	F	T

(5) → q is tautology, hence S is also valid.

18. (P → (Q ∧ R)) → ((P ∧ Q) → R)

			(1)	(3)	(2)	(4)	
P	Q	R	Q∨R	P→(1)	P ^Q	(2)→ R	(3)→ (4)
T	T	T	T	T	T	T.	T
T	T	F	T	T	T	F	F
T	F	T	T	T	F	T	T
T	F	F	F	F	F	T	T
F	T	T	T	T	F	T	T
F	T	F	T	T	F	T	T
F	F	T	T	T	F	T	T
F	F	F	F	T	F	T	T

(3) → (4) is contingency i.e. it is satisfiable but not valid.

19. X = (P ∧ Q) → R

Y = (P → R) ∨ (Q → R)

X → Y is a tautology.

20. "Every teacher is liked by some Student"

∀ (x) [teacher (x) → ∃ (y) [Student (y) ∧ likes (y,x)]]

21. By Rule, option (b) is true.

22. ∀ x ∀ y (R(x, y) → R(y, x))

A binary Relation may or may not be Symmetric. So it is not valid but is satisfiable and regation of negation statment is also satisfiable.

23. Given statement can be interpreted as follows :

If x is lion or tiger, if it is hungry or it is threatened, x will attack.

P (x) = lion (x) v tiger (x)

Q (x) = hungry (x) v threatened (x)

R (x) = attacks (x)

P (x) → (Q (x) → R (x))

Expanding, ∀ x [tiger (x) ∨ (lion (x)) → {(hungry (x) ∨ threatened (x)) → attacks (x)}]

24.

A	B	C	A∨B	A∧B	(A∨B)→C	(A∧B)→C	A→C	B→C
T	T	T	T	T	T	T	T	T
T	T	F	T	T	F	F	F	F
T	F	T	T	F	T	T	T	T
T	F	F	T	F	F	T	F	T
F	T	T	T	F	T	T	T	T
F	T	F	T	F	F	T	T	F
F	F	T	F	F	T	T	T	T
F	F	F	F	F	T	T	T	T

(A → C) ∧ (B → C)	(A → C) ∨ (B → C)
T	T
F	F
T	T
F	T
T	T
F	T
T	T
T	T

It is apparent from the truth table that P_1 and P_2 are not tautologies.

25.

A	B	A⊙B	~(~A⊙B)	A∧B
T	T	T	~ F = T	T
T	F	T	~ T = F	F
F	T	F	~T = F	F
F	F	T	~T =F	F

26. $\forall_x$ [Graph (x) ⇒ ~ connected (x)] represents "for every x if x is a graph then it is not connected"

27. In conjective normal form for any formula, there is a truth assignment for which at least half the clauses evaluate to true.

28. ∀ x (P(x) → Q(x) → (∀ x P(x) → ∀ xQ(x))

29. "For x which is an fsa, there exists a y which is a pda and which is equivalent to x."

(∀ x fsa (x)) ⇒ (∃y pda (y) ∧ equivalent (x, y)) is the logical representation.

30. Option (c) is true by identify rule.

31. Given Predicate is

$[\forall x, \alpha \rightarrow (\exists y, \beta \rightarrow (\forall u, \exists v, \gamma)]$

The negation of this predicate is

$\equiv \sim (\forall x, \alpha \rightarrow (\exists y, \beta \rightarrow (\forall u, \exists v, \gamma))]$

$\equiv \sim (\forall x, \alpha \rightarrow (\forall y \sim \beta \vee \forall u, \exists v, \gamma))]$

$\equiv \sim (\exists x, \sim \alpha \vee (\forall y \sim \beta \vee \forall u, \exists v, \gamma))]$

$\equiv \sim (\forall x \ \alpha \wedge \exists y \beta \wedge \exists u \ \forall v \sim]$

32. (i) $P \vee \sim Q \equiv P + Q'$

(ii) $\sim (\sim P \wedge Q) \equiv (P' \cdot Q)' \equiv (P + Q')$

(iii) $(P \wedge Q) \vee (P \wedge \sim Q) \vee (\sim P \wedge \sim Q)$

$\equiv (PQ + PQ' + P'Q')$

$\equiv (P(Q + Q') + P' \ Q')$

$\equiv P + P' \ Q' \qquad (\because Q + Q' = 1)$

$\equiv (P + P') \cdot (P + Q')$

$\equiv 1 \cdot (P + Q') \equiv (P + Q')$

Hence 1, 2, 3 are equivivalent.

33. Given : gold and silver ornament are precious.

We use

gold and silver — gold $\vee$ silver

$\forall ((G(x) \vee S(x)))$

gold and silver $\rightarrow$ precious

$\forall x((G(x) \vee S(x)) \rightarrow P(x)$

Alternately:

"Gold and silver ornaments are precious"

Gold ornaments are alone precious.

Silver ornaments are also alone precious.

Gold and silver ornaments are also precious

$\forall x((G(x) \vee S(x)) \rightarrow P(x))$

34. Truth table of P ☐ Q is given so accordingly.

		(1)		(2)
P	Q	P ∨ Q	~ Q	P☐ ~ Q
T	T	T	F	T
T	F	F	T	T
F	T	T	F	T
F	F	F	T	F

(1) ≡ (2) Hence (b) is true.

35. Universal qualification of $P(x)$ is denoted $\forall x P(x)$.

The symbol $\forall$ is called *universal quantifier.*

The existential qualification of predicate $P(x)$ is statement, there exist a value of x for which $P(x)$ is true. The existential qualification of $P(x)$ is denoted by $\exists(x)$ $P(x)$. The symbol $\exists$ is called *existential quantifier.*

$\therefore \qquad \neg \forall x P(x) = \exists x(\neg P(x))$

$\neg$ sign is for not

36. Given : $F(x, y, t)$ a predicate

$\forall x \exists y \exists t (\neg F(x, y, t))$

Since $\forall x \exists y \exists t (\neg F(x, y, t))$

$\Rightarrow \ \forall x \neg (\forall y \forall t (F(x, y, t))$

So, we can say no one can fool everyone all the time.

37. $P(x) = \sim (x = 1) \vee \forall y (\exists z (x = y \times z) \rightarrow (y = x) \vee (y = 1)$

The above predicate gives P(x) true if x is not equal to one and for all y there exist some z such that x has two factor either y = x or y = 1.

i.e. x is prime number.

38. Assume

P = It rains

Q = Cricket match will not be played.

$I_1 : \ P \rightarrow Q$

$\sim Q$

$\sim P$

I_2 is like $(P \rightarrow Q \wedge \sim P) \rightarrow \sim Q$

I_2 is not a tautology

So I_2 is false.

39. $\exists x$ (real (x) $\wedge$ rational (x))

i.e. Some x are real as well as rational

So we can say that

Some real numbers are rational.

40. $\exists x (f(x) \wedge P(x)$ says.

Some of my friends are perfect.

Negation of above statment that means some of my friends are prefect is false.

i.e. None of my friends are perfect.

41. $\sim \exists x (\forall y (\alpha) \wedge \forall z (\beta))$

$\equiv \forall x (\exists y (\sim) \vee \exists z (\sim \beta)$

$\equiv \forall x (\forall y (\alpha) \rightarrow \exists z (\sim \beta))$

$\equiv \forall x (\forall z (\beta) \rightarrow \exists y (\sim \alpha))$

42. It means "It is false that every glitter is gold" or "some glitters are not gold". Then we can say "atleast one glitter object is not gold".

43. **(a)** The given truth table is for $p'q + pq' \equiv p \oplus q$ which '$\oplus$' is commutative as well as associative.

44.

a	b	c	$a\leftrightarrow c$	$\sim b$	$a\wedge c$	$\sim b\rightarrow (a\wedge c)$	$(a\leftrightarrow c)\rightarrow (\sim b\rightarrow (a\wedge c))$
F	F	F	T	T	F	T	T
F	F	T	F	T	F	T	F
F	T	F	T	F	F	T	T
F	T	T	F	F	F	T	F
T	F	F	F	T	F	T	F
T	F	T	T	T	T	T	T
T	T	F	F	F	F	F	T
T	T	T	T	F	T	F	T

Hence $(a\leftrightarrow c)\rightarrow(\sim b\rightarrow(a\wedge c))$ is not Tautology.

45. g : mobile is good

c : mobile is cheap

P : Good mobile phones are not cheap

$$\cong g\rightarrow\neg c\cong(\neg g\vee\neg c)$$

$$[\because a\rightarrow b\equiv\neg a\vee b]$$

Q : Cheap mobile phones are not good

$$\cong c\rightarrow\neg g\cong(\neg c\vee\neg g)$$

$\therefore$ Both P and Q are equivalent which means P and Q imply each other.

46. Given statement is

$$\sim\forall d\left[r(d)\rightarrow c(d)\right]$$

$$\equiv\sim\forall d\left[\sim r(d)\vee c(d)\right]$$

$$\equiv\exists d\left[r(d)\wedge\sim c(d)\right]$$

Since $p\rightarrow q\equiv\sim p\vee q$ and let $r(d)$ be rainy day, $c(d)$ be cold day).

47. Option (a) $(\sim p \vee q)\wedge(p\vee\sim q)$

$$\equiv(p\rightarrow q)\wedge(q\rightarrow p)$$

$$\equiv(p\leftrightarrow q)$$

Option (b) $(\sim p\vee q)\wedge(q\rightarrow p)$

$$\equiv(p\leftrightarrow q)\wedge(q\rightarrow p)$$

$$\equiv(p\leftrightarrow q)$$

Option (d) $(\sim p\wedge\sim q)\vee(p\wedge q)$

$$\equiv p'\,Q'+PQ$$

$$\equiv P\leftrightarrow Q$$

49. If the person is kind, he is not known to be corrupt

50. For option (c)

$P(x, y) = A(x)$

$R(x, y) = B(x)$

$\forall x)\ \exists y$ is same for both the side

$(A(x)\rightarrow B(x)\leftrightarrow(\sim A(x)\vee B(x))$

is tautology.

51. According to the given conditions correct option is (a) only.

52. $\sim((P\rightarrow q)\vee(\sim r\vee\sim s))$ is

$P\rightarrow q$ gives value 8, 9, 10, 12

$\sim r$ gives {8, 10, 12, 11}

$\sim s$ gives (8, 0, 10, 12)

$(\sim r\vee\sim s)$ gives (8, 9, 10, 11, 12)

$(P\rightarrow q)\wedge(\sim r\wedge\sim s)$ gives {8, 0, 10, 12}

So negation of above statment gives result 11.

53. Let us denote the problem by a non directed graph with 23 vertices (compounds). If two compounds in chemistry lab react with each other, then there exists an edge between the corresponding vertices. In the graph, we have 9 vertices with degree 3 (i.e. odd degree). By sum of degrees of vertices theorem atleast one of the remaining vertices should have odd degree.

55. (I) $\forall x\ \exists y\ R(x\cdot y)\rightarrow(\exists y\ R(x, y))$ is true.

because $\exists y\ (\exists x\ R(x, y)\equiv\exists x\ (\exists y\ R(x, y))$

(II) $\forall x\ \exists y\ R(x, y)\rightarrow\ \exists y\ (\forall x\ R(x, y))$ is false.

(III) $\forall x\ \exists y\ R(x, y)\rightarrow\ \forall y\ \exists x\ R(x, y)$

is false because R(x, y) may or may not be symmetric

(IV) $\forall x\ \exists y\ R(x, y)\rightarrow\sim\exists x\ R(\forall y\sim R(x, y))$

is true.

Hence option (b) is correct.

56. $\sim p\rightarrow\sim q\equiv p'\rightarrow q'\equiv p+q'$

(I) $p\rightarrow q\equiv p'+q$

(II) $q\rightarrow p\equiv q'+p$

(III) $(\sim q \vee p) \equiv q' + p$

(IV) $(\sim p \vee q) \equiv p' + q$

So II & IV is equivivalent of expression given in question.

57. Given $(p \rightarrow q) \rightarrow r$ = false.

$\equiv \sim(\sim p \vee q) \vee r$ = false

above statment is only possible if

$\sim (\sim p \vee q)$ is false

or r is false.

$\sim(\sim p \vee q) \equiv p \vee \sim q$

So $p \wedge \sim q$ is false iff

p is false or ~q is false.

So finally we can say that

r = false and (p = false or q' = false)

Now $(r \rightarrow p) \rightarrow q$

$\equiv \sim(\sim r \vee p) \vee q$

$\equiv (r \wedge \sim p) \vee q$

According to previous condition r = false

So, $r \wedge \sim p$ = false

So $(r \rightarrow p) \rightarrow q \equiv (r \wedge \sim p) \vee q$

$\equiv$ false $\vee\, q \equiv q$

So the given expression $(r \rightarrow p) \rightarrow q$ is equivalent to q i.e. it is true when q is true.

58. The given statement is equivalent to

$(\sim p \wedge r) \wedge (\sim r \rightarrow (p \wedge q))$

59. Let us see

$\forall$ are always true & $\exists$ are always false for empty sets. So there exists at least one model with universe of size 3 (or less then). So option (a) Should be true.

60. By Fermat's theorem

$3^{(5-1)}$ mod 5 = 1

$\therefore\ 3^4$ mod 5 = 1

Now 3^{51} mod 5 = $(3^4)^{12}$. 3^3 mod 5 = 3^3 mod 5 = 2

61. $R_1 : \forall\ a, b \in G, a R_1 b$ if and only if $\exists g \in G$ such that $a = g^{-1}bg$

Reflexive: $a = g^{-1}$

ag can be satisfied by putting g = e, identity "e" always exists in a group.

So reflexive

Symmetric: aRb $\Rightarrow a = g^{-1}$ bg for some g

$\Rightarrow b = gag^{-1} = (g^{-1})^{-1} ag^{-1}$

g^{-1} always exists for every $g \in G$.

So symmetric

Transitive: aRb and bRc

$\Rightarrow a = g_1^{-1} bg_1$ and $b = g_2^{-1} cg_2$ for some $g_1 g_2 \in G$.

Now $a = g_1^{-1}g_2^{-1}cg_2g_1 = (g_2g_1)^{-1} cg_2g_1$

$g_1 \in G$ and $g_2 \in G \Rightarrow g_2g_1 \in G$ since group is closed so aRb and aRb $\Rightarrow$ aRc hence transitive

Clearly R_1 is equivalence relation.

R_2 is not equivalence it need not even be reflexive, since $aR_2 a \Rightarrow a = a^{-1}\ \forall$ a which not be true in a group.

R_1 is equivalence relation is the correct answer.

SET THEORY AND ALGEBRA

1. Union of two equivalence relation is not equivalence because equivalence relation satisfy 3 properties.

(1) Reflexive (2) Symmetric (3) Transitive

So union of two reflexive and union of two symmetric relations are reflexive and symmetric but union of two transitive may or may not be transitive. Therefore union of two equivalence may or may not be equivalence.

Example: $R_1\{(1, 2)\}$ on set A = {1, 2, 3}

R2 = {(2, 1)} on set A = {1, 2, 3}

Both R_1 & R_2 are transitive

But

$R_1 \cup R_2$ = ({1, 2} {2, 1}) is not transitive because (1, 1,) is not present.

2. (a) If set A = {$a_1, a_2, \ldots\ldots a_n$} then total number of binary relation on set

$$\boxed{A = 2^{n^2}}$$

(b) Number of one to one function from set A with n elements on to itself is

$^nP_n = n!$

3.

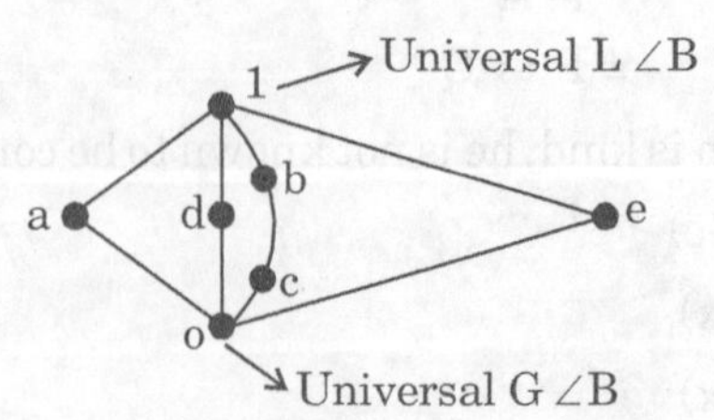

x is complement of y if ∠UB and G∠B between x & y is universal ∠UB & G∠B respectively.

So complement of a is = {b, c, d, e}

4. A = {1, 2, 3, 4, 5}

Transitive closure of relation

{(1, 2), (2, 3), (3, 4), (5, 4)}

is {(1, 2) (2, 3), (1, 3), (3, 4), (5, 4), (1, 4) (2, 4)}

5. $S_1 \cup S_2 \cup S_3 \cup ..... \cup S_n = S$

At least one set in ($S_1, S_2 ..... S_n$) must be infinite to generate infinite set S.

6. No of elements in A × A = n^2

So power set of (A × A) = P(A × A)

$= 2^{n^2}$

7. Abelian group follow both commutative and associative properties.

$(go\ h)^2 = g^2 0\ h^2$

⇒ (goh) 0 (goh)

⇒ go(hog) o h

⇒ go (go h) oh

⇒ (gog) o (hoh)

⇒ g^2 o h^2

8. If relation is symmetric and transitive then it may be not reflexive.

Example R = { } not reflexive but symmetric & transitive.

9. S = {ϕ}′, (2, 3)

S contain 3 element so power set of S contains 2^3 = 8 elements.

10. Matrix multiplication is group but not abelian because, matrix multiplication does not follow commutative property

If A & B two Matrices

then AB ≠ BA.

11. (A – B) ∪ (B – A) ∪ (A ∩ B)

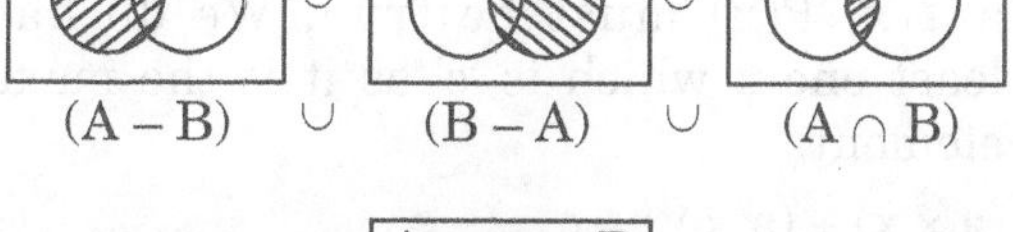

(A – B) ∪ (B – A) ∪ (A ∩ B)

⇒ (A ∩ B)

12. X = {2, 3, 6, 12, 24}

minimal elements are 2 and 3.

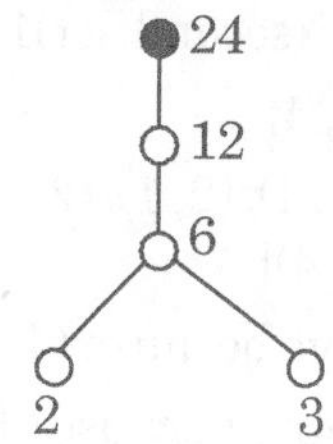

So total 4 edge.

13. Function : X → Y

total function = Y^X

97 = Y^X

So. |Y| = 97

|X| = 1

14. There is not any inverse for rational number "O" under multiplication.

15. F(x, y) = (x + y, x – y)

$$\text{So. } F\left(\frac{x+y}{2}, \frac{x-y}{2}\right) = \left(\frac{x+y+x-y}{2}, \frac{x+y-x+y}{2}\right)$$

$$\left(\frac{x+y}{2}, \frac{x-y}{2}\right) = (x,\ y)$$

Now inverse of F is $F^{-1}(x, y) = \left(\dfrac{x+y}{2}, \dfrac{x-y}{2}\right)$

16. A R B iff A ∩ B = ϕ

So. For reflexive A Ç A ≠ ϕ so it is not reflexive.

and For symmetric if A ∩ B = ϕ then B ∩ A = ϕ (True)

(3) For tansistive if A ∩ B = ϕ and B ∩ C = ϕ then A ∩ C = ϕ (not always true)

So R is only symmetric.

17. The set of all strings over a finite alphabet forms a monoid but not group. Under concatenation because inverse of strings does not exist.

18. By using Bell's traingle, total relation (Equivalence) for set of 4 element is 15.

1

1 2

2 3 5

5 7 10 15

19. Largest equivalence relation contain all elements of A × A = (n^2)

n^2

20. Intersection of two equivalence relation is always equivalence. But union of two equivalence may or may not equivalence. Because intersection of two transitive need not be transitive.

21. 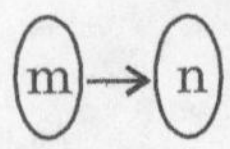

total function = (second set)1st set = $(n)^m$

22. Set A = {1, 2, 3, 4}

Relation R = {(1, 1), (2, 1), (2, 2), (2, 3), (2, 4), (3, 1), (3, 2), (3, 3), (3, 4)}.

R is not reflexive because (4, 4) not exist.

R is not symmetric because (4, 2), (1, 3), (4, 3) not exists.

R is not irreflexive because (1, 1), (2, 2) and (3, 3) are exist.

So. Only option 'b' is correct.

23. (a) Orderd pairs of Equivalence relation by π_1 is

$R = (a, b, c) \times (a, b, c) \cup (d) \times (d)$

R = {(a, a), (a, b), (a, c), (b, b), (b, a), (b, c), (c, a), (c, b), (c, c), (d, d)}

(b) 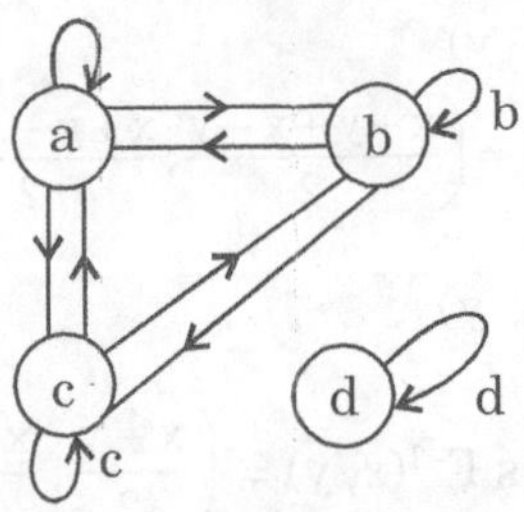

24. If $a \neq b$ then $a \times b \neq b \times a$

Means $a \times b = b \times a$ then $a = b$.

(a) By associative law

$a \times (a \times a) = (a \times a) \times a.$

$\therefore \quad a = a \times a.$

(b) $a \times b \times a = a$

$\Rightarrow (a \times b \times a) \times a = a \times b \times (a \times a)$

$\Rightarrow a \times b \times a$

$\therefore (a \times b \times a) \times a = a \times (a \times b \times a)$

(c) $(a \times b \times c) \times (a \times c) = a \times b \times (c \times a \times c)$

$= a \times b \times c$

$= (a \times c) \times (a \times b \times c) = (a \times c \times a) \times b \times c$

$= a \times b \times c$

So $(a \times b \times c) \times (a \times c) = (a \times c) \times (a \times b \times c)$

Hence $a \times b \times c = a \times c$.

25. If set A = n elements.

then Binry relation is on $(A \times A) \Rightarrow n^2$.

So. total possible passible Binary relation is 2^{n2}.

26. (a) Empty relation ϕ is both symmetric and transitive. However ϕ is not reflexive.

(b) Set A = {a, b, c}

R = {(a, b) (b, a), (a, a)}

R is symmetric & transitive but not reflexive.

27. A relation R on set of integers defined as x R y iff (x + y) is even

(1) Reflexive : x R x

$x + x = 2x \Rightarrow$ even. So reflexive.

(2) Symmetric : x R y then y R x.

x + y = even then y + x is also even.

(3) Transitive : if x R y and y R z then x R z.

x + y is even

y + z is even

then x + z is also even.

So relation R is equivalence and there are 2 Equivalence class one on set of even number and other on set of odd number.

28. $P(s) \cap P(p(s)) = \phi$ only ϕ is common in Both set.

29. R is equivalence because sum of two even no is always even.

R_2 is not eauivalence because sum of two odd no is not odd.

R_3 is equivalence because product of two non-zero rational no is always greater then zero if both are positve or both are negative.

R_4 is not equivalence because not satisfy transitive properties.

Example a = 2, b = 3, c = 4

$|a - b| = |2 - 3| = 1 < 2$ true

$|b - c| = |3 - 4| = 1 < 2$ true

$|a - c| = |2 - 4| = 2 < 2$ false

32. Empty relation satisfy all properties except reflexive so option "d" is correct.

33. $\Sigma = \{0, 1\}$

$S^* = \{0, 1\}^*$

= {λ, 0, 1, 00, 01, 10, ... All combination of 0 & 1}

Here identity element is λ (null)

Because concatenation of any string with λ always generate that string.

E.g. $\lambda \cdot 1 = 1 = 1 \cdot 1$

But there is not any "inverse" of any String, because concetenation of two string is not null.

So it is not group.

34. Option d is false, P(a) = true, ∀ x such that $a \leq x$, P(x) must be true, We do have at least one x which is 'c' as it is the maximum element.

35. $(a \times x) + (a \times y) = c$

$(b \times x) + (x \times y) = c$

Only two pairs (b, c) and (c, b) will satisfy both the equation Simultaneausly.

dor $\Rightarrow x = b, y = c$.

$(a \times b) + (a \times c)$ Equation 1st

$b + c = c$ true.

For $x = c, y = b$

$(a \times c) + (a \times b)$ Equation 1st

$c + b \Rightarrow c$ true

Similarly equation 2nd also satisfy both pair (b, c) and (c, b).

36. $S = \{(x, y) / y = x + 1$ and $x, y \in \{0, 1, 2 ...\}\}$

reflexive transitive closure of s is

If $s = \{(0, 1) (1, 2)\}$

Then reflexive closure of S is

$= \{(0, 0), (0, 1), (1, 2), (1, 1), (2, 2)\}$

and transitive closure of above relation is

$= \{(0, 0), (0, 1) (1, 2) (0, 2) (1, 1), (2, 2)\}$

So it satisfy by option "B"

37. Total number of Symmetric matrices is

$\boxed{2^{(n^2+n)/2}}$

38. Total = 200

Programining language (P) = 125

Datastructure (D) = 85

Computer organization (c) = 65

P and D = 50

P and C = 35

D and C = 30

P, D and C = 15

$$|P \cup D \cup C| = |P| + |D| + |C| - |P \cap D| - |P \cap C| + |D \cap C| + |P \cap D \cap C|$$

$= 125 + 85 + 65 - 50 - 35 - 30 + 15 = 175$

No of student who have not taken any of 3 courses is

$200 - 175 = 25$

39. $R_1 R_2$ from A to C is

$R_1 R_2 = \{(1, 2), (3, 2), (3, 4), (5, 4), (7, 2)\}$

40. By given table it is clear that e is and identify element and inverse of a is c because $a \times c = e$. is given in table, so by this inverse of 'c' must be 'a'

So $c \times a$ must be "e" that is given only in option "d"

41. Hasse diagram of given set by using set containment rule is

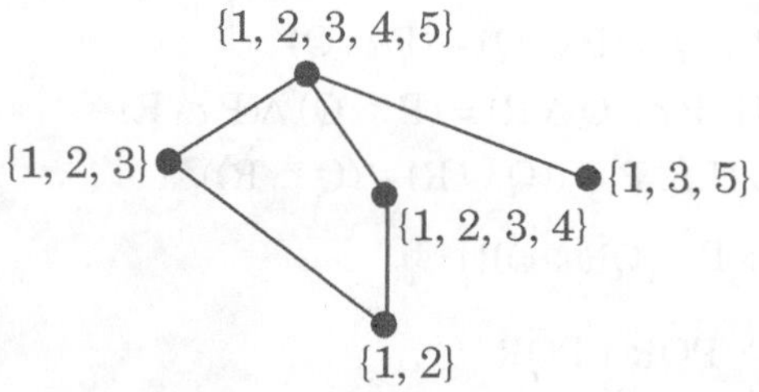

Now to make complete lotlice {1} is necessary & sufficent.

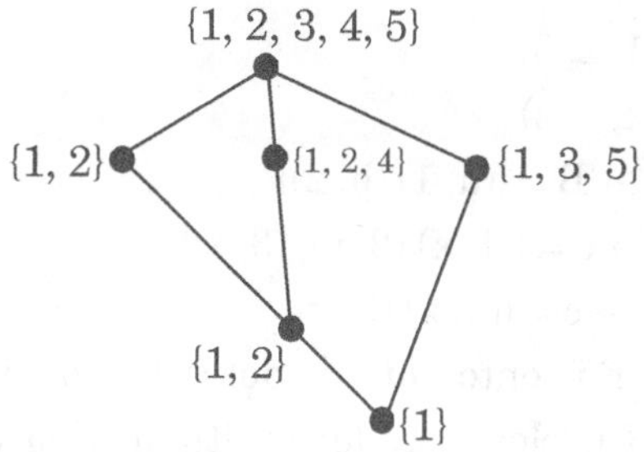

42. $X = (A - B) - C, y = (A - C) - (B - C)$

By using venn diagram.

X =

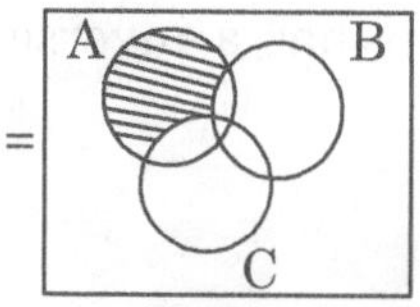

(A–B)–C

Y =

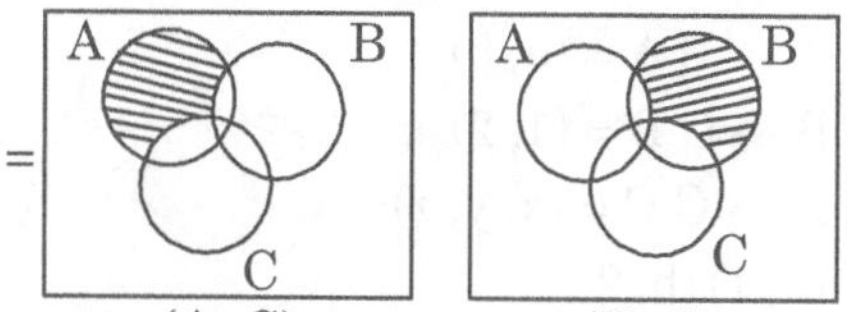

(A–C) (B–C)

So (A – C) – (B – C) is

$\Rightarrow$

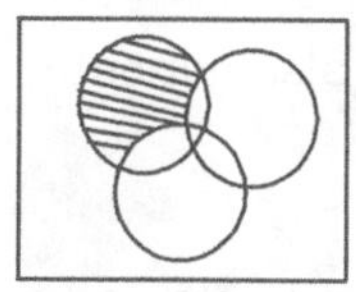

So X = Y

43.

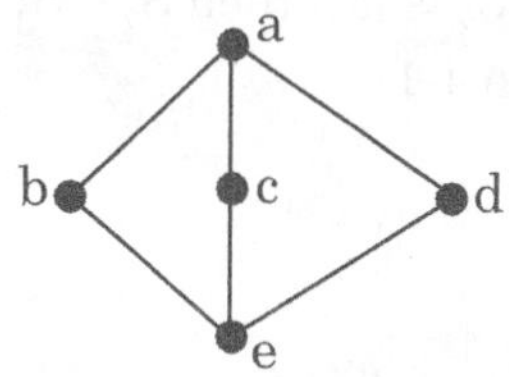

The given Hasse diagram is lattice because all pair of element has exactly and LUB and GLB.

But not distributine Latice because all triplets of element does not satisfy distributive properties of meet ($\wedge$) and Join ($\vee$)

Example $b \wedge (c \vee d) \Rightarrow b \wedge a \Rightarrow b$

But $(b \wedge c) \vee (b \wedge d) \Rightarrow e \vee e \Rightarrow e$. not equal

44. Set = {1, 2, 4, 7, 8, 11, 13, 14}

identity element = 1.

inverse of 4 is 4.

as $(4 \times 4) \bmod 15 = 1$ (identity)

inverse of 7 is 13.

as $(7 \times 13) \bmod 15 = 1$ (identity)

45. Intersection of two equivalence is always equivalence, but it is not true for union.

46. F should be onto but "g" need not be

Example: A = (a, b)

B = (1, 2, 3)

C = (x, y, z)

g : A → B = {(a, 1) (b, 2)}

f : B → c = {(1, x) (2, y), (3, z)}

h : A → c = {(a, x) (b, y)}

Here F is onto but g is not onto, so y is onto.

47. Set H is closed under multiplication will result always in upper traingular matrix.

Matrix multiplication is associative always.

Every matrix has a inverse because identify matrix is

$$\begin{bmatrix} 1 & 0 & 0 \\ 0 & 1 & 0 \\ 0 & 0 & 1 \end{bmatrix}$$

48. f : A → B A = (a, b)

g : B → C B = (1, 2)

h : A → C C = (x, y, z)

f : ((a, 1) (b, 2))

g : ((1, x) (2, y))

h : ((a, x) (b, 4))

Here g is not onto so h is also not onto.

So h is onot if g is onto.

49. $A = \{a, a_2....a_n\}$

$C = \{\phi, \{a\}, \{a_1, a_2\}, \{a_1, a_2, a_3\}.... \{a_1, a_2, a_3...a_n\}\}$

So if S_1 is $\{a_1, a_2\}$ and S_2 is $\{a_1\}$ then $S_2 < S_1$

So cardinality of c is (n + 1)

50. F : N × N → N.

(i) f(x, y) = x + y – 3

x + I – 3 = x

So I = 3 (identity)

(ii) F(x, y) = max (x, y)

For F(x, I) = max (x, I) = x.

at I = 1 (identity)

(iii) $f(x) = x^y$

For $x^I = x = I^x$

not any value of I satisfy above condition

51. Number of functions from a set A to a set B where

$|A| = m$

and $|B| = n$ is n^m

$W = X \times Y$

∴ $|W| = xy$

$|E| = 2^{xy}$

$|Z| = z$

Hence number of functions from Z to E

$= (2^{xy})^z = 2^{xyz}$

52. Binary operation multiplication modul 10 is defined as follows

$$aob = (a \times b)\ \%\ 10$$

The identity element for the given set is 1.

For closure property, 2 o 7 = 4 ∉ set

∴ Set is not closed.

2 and 8 do not have an inverse, 3o7 = 1

∴ 7 is the inverse of 3.

Hence (*c*) is false

53. Reflexive property is an essential condition for partial order, Total order as well as Equivalence relation.

Given set is not reflexive as ∀ *x*, *y* ∈ I, (*x*, *y*) is not related to (*x*, *y*)

54. X = (E ∩ F) – (F ∩ G)

Y = (E – E ∩ G) – (E ∩ F)

By using venn diagram

For X

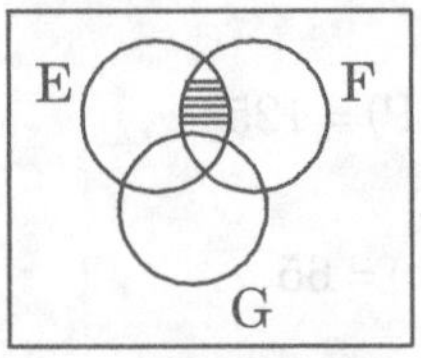

(E ∩ F) – (F ∩ G)

For Y

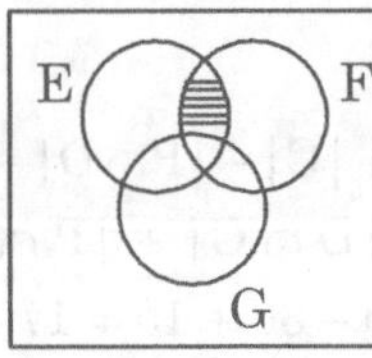

(E ∩ F ∩ G) – (E ∩ F)

55. S = {1, 2, 3....m}

Number of subsets of s of size 3 is m_{c_3}

So n = m_{c_3}

Now numbr of subsets in which a particular element 'i' appears $(m-1)_{c_2}$

{For select remaining 2 element}

So $\sum_{i=1}^{m} F(i) = m \times m-1_{c_2} = 3 \times m_{c_3} = 3m$

56. P Δ Q = (P ∪ Q) – (P ∩ Q)

(II) P ∩ (Q Δ R) = (P ∩ Q) Δ(P ∩ R)

L.H.S. P Ç ((Q ∪ R) – (Q ∩ R))

$\Rightarrow P \cdot (Q\bar{R} + \bar{Q}R)$

$\Rightarrow PQ\bar{R} + P\bar{Q}R$

R.H.S

$(P \cap Q) \Delta (P \cap R)$

$\Rightarrow (PQ) \Delta (PR)$

$\Rightarrow PQ(\overline{PR}) + \overline{PQ}\,PR$

$\Rightarrow PQ(\bar{P} + \bar{R}) + (\bar{P} + \bar{Q})PR$

$\Rightarrow PQ\bar{P} + PQ\bar{R} + \bar{P}PR + \bar{Q}PR$

$\Rightarrow PQ\bar{R} + \bar{Q}PR$

So LHS = RHS

57. No's divisible by 2 in X = $\left[\frac{123}{2}\right] = 61$

No's divisible by 3 in x = $\left[\frac{123}{3}\right] = 41$

Numbers divisible by 5 is = $\left[\frac{123}{5}\right] = 24$

No's divisible by 2 & 3 = $\left[\frac{123}{2 \times 3}\right] = 20$

2 & 5 = 12

3 & 5 = 8

2 & 3, 5 = 4

2 or 3 or 5 = $n(A \cup B \cup C)$

$n(A \cup B \cup C) = n(A) + n(B) + n(C) - n(A \cap B)$
$- n(B \cap C) - n(A \cap C) + n(A \cap B \cap C)$

$= 61 + 41 + 24 - 20 - 12 - 8 + 4 = 90$

So For not divisible by 2, 3, 5 is

$123 - 90 = 33$

58. S = {1, 2, 3, ... n}

Smallest equivalence relation an S

Contains all self pair so cardinality is n

Largest Equivalence relation on S is S × S, so cardinality is $n \times n = n^2$

59. S = {a, b, c, d}

Partition of S is

$\pi_1 = \{\overline{abcd}\}$, $\pi_2 = \{\overline{ab}, \overline{cd}\}$

$\pi_3 = \{\overline{abc}, \bar{d}\}$, $\pi_4 = \{\bar{a}, \bar{b}, \bar{c}, \bar{d}\}$

Option c correctly satisfy because.

π_4 is refinement of π_2, π_3 & π_1

π_2 and π_3 are refinements of π_1 and π_2 and π_3 are not comparable.

So

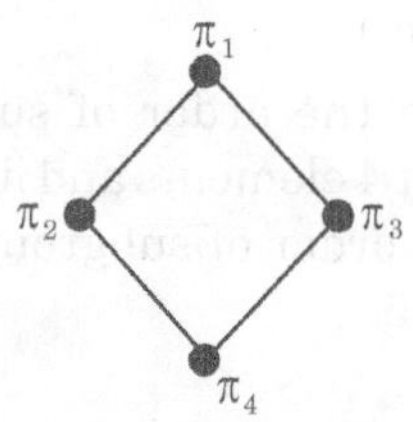

60. Partial order P is defined on set of Natural No. Condition is

(i) $(0, 0) \in P$

(ii) $(a, b) \in P$ iff $a\% 10 \le b\% 10$, $\left(\frac{1}{10}, \frac{b}{10}\right) \in p$

pair (iii) and (iv) satisfy above condition.

(iii) $(145, 265) \in P$

if $(145\% 10) \le (265\% 10) \Rightarrow 5 \le 5$ (true).

and $\left(\frac{145}{10}, \frac{265}{10}\right) = (14, 26) \in P$.

if $(14\% 10) \le (26\% 10) \Rightarrow 4 \le 6$ (true)

and $\left(\frac{14}{10}, \frac{26}{10}\right) = (1, 2) \in P$

if $(1\% 10) \le (2\% 10) \Rightarrow 1 \le 2$ (true).

and $\left(\frac{1}{10}, \frac{2}{10}\right) = (0, 0) \in P$

Similarly (iv) $(0, 153) \in P$

61. $(P \cap Q \cap R) \cup (\bar{Q} \cap Q \cap R) \cup \bar{Q} \cup \bar{R}$

$\Rightarrow PQR + \bar{P}QR + \bar{Q} + \bar{R}$

$= QR(P + \bar{P}) + \bar{Q} + \bar{R}$

$= QR + \bar{Q} + \bar{R}$ $\{\because (P + \bar{P}) = 1\}$

$\Rightarrow (Q + \bar{Q}) \cdot (R + \bar{Q}) + \bar{R}$ {∵ distributive law}

$\Rightarrow R + \bar{Q} + \bar{R}$

$\Rightarrow 1 + \bar{Q}$

$\Rightarrow 1 \Rightarrow U$

62. 1st and 4th Hasse diagram is lattice because every pair of vertices in both diagram have exactly one least upper bound and Greatest Lower bound.

63. Group have a properties f

(a) closure

(b) Associativity

(c) Existance of identiy

(d) Existance of inverse.

64. R = {(x, y), (x, z), (z, x), (z, y)}

R is not symmetric because (y, z) and (y, z) pairs are not exist.

R is not antisymmetric beacuse (x, z) and (z, x) both are exist.

65.

*	a	b	c	d
a	a	b	c	d
b	b	a	d	c
c	c	d	b	a
d	d	c	a	b

Hence c, d is generator

Alternately:

Every element in Cyclic Group can be represented in the power of any generator.

From given table

$$a^*a = a$$
$$b^*b = a$$
$$c^*c = c^2 = b$$
$$c^3 = c^*c^2 = c^*b = d$$
$$c^4 = c^*c^3 = c^*d = a$$
$$d^*d = d^2 = b$$
$$d^3 = d^*d^2 = d^*b = c$$
$$d^4 = d^*d^3 = d^*c = a$$

66. Total number of reflexive relations in set of n elements

$$= 2^{n^2-n}$$
$$= 2^{5^2-5} \quad \text{.....(since } n = 5)$$
$$= 2^{20}$$

67. *A group should satisfy following relations :*

(*i*) Closure (*ii*) Inverse

(*iii*) Identity (*iv*) Associative

in $(1, \omega, \omega^2)$

We can say

$1 * \omega = \omega$ all are elements

$\omega * \omega^2 = 1$ of group than

$\omega^2 * 1 = \omega^2$ it is closure

Hence, we think about inverse, then this should satisfy

$$a * e = a$$

where e is identity element means $\exists\ e \in$ G have identity element 1

means $1 * \omega = \omega,\ 1 * 1 = 1$ identities

$1 * \omega^2 = \omega^2$

Hence it should be inverse

means $a * b = 3$

means b is the inverse element a, b, e 64

here $1 * 1 = 1,\ \omega * \omega^2 = 1,\ \omega^2 * \omega = 1$ } inverse

So, it also hold Associative for this

$$a * (b * c) = (a * b) * c$$

means $1 * (\omega * \omega^2) = (1 * \omega) * \omega^2$ } Associative

means $(1, \omega, \omega^2)$ is a group.

68. Total number of functions is 2^n, out of which there will be exactly two functions where all elements map to exactly one element, so total number of onto functions is $2^n - 2$

69.
$$x \oplus y = x^2 + y^2$$
$$y \oplus x = y^2 + x^2$$
$$= x^2 + y^2 \quad \text{(Q addition is cumulative)}$$
$$= x \oplus y$$

$\therefore\ \oplus$ is cumulative

$$(x \oplus y) \oplus z = (x^2 + y^2)^2 + z^2$$
$$x \oplus (y \oplus z) = 2 \oplus (y^2 + z^2)^2$$
$$= x^2 + (y^2 + z^2)^2$$

Clearly, $(x \oplus y) \oplus z\ ^1\ x \oplus (y \oplus z)$

$\therefore\ \oplus$ is not associative

70. The number of functions from A to B where size of A = $|A|$ and size of B = $|B|$ is $|B|^{|A|}$

$$\{0,1\}^4 = \{0,1\}\ X\{0,1\}X\{0,1\}\ X\{0,1\} = 16$$
$$|S| = 2^{16}$$
$$N = 2^{|S|}$$

loglog N = log log $2^{|S|}$ = log$|S|$ = log 2^{16} = 16

71. Let U = {1, 2, ... 1008}

V = {1009, ... 2014}

Since subset S_1 will be greater than every other subset *i.e.* V & subset S_2 will be less than every other subset *i.e.* U, So both statements will be true.

72. f: X → Y defined by $f(a) = 1$, $f(b) = 1$, $f(c) = 2$ where

$X = \{a, b, c\}\ Y = \{1,2\}$

Let $A = \{a, c\}$, $B = \{b, c\}$ be subsets of X

then $|f(A \cup B)| = 2;\ |f(A)| = 2;\ |f(B)| = 2$

$f(A \cap B) = \{2\};\ f(A) = \{1,2\};\ f(B) = \{1,2\}$

$f(A) \cap f(B) = \{1,2\}$

$|f(A \cap B)| = 1$

$\therefore$ Option (*a*), (*b*), (*c*) are not true

Hence, Option (*d*) is true

73. Order of subgroup divides order of group (Lagrange's theorem).

3, 5 and 15 can be the order of subgroup. As subgroup has atleast 4 elements and it is not equal to the given group, order of subgroup can't be 3 and 15. Hence it is 5.

74. Let us consider a function (counter example) as

$f(0) = 1,\ f(1) = 0,\ f(2) = 3,\ f(3) = 2, \ldots\ldots,$
$f(2012) = 2013,$

$f(2013) = 2012$ and $f(2014) = 2014$

Clearly $f(f(i)) = i$ for $0 \le i \le 2014$

Here $f(i) \ne i$ for every i and $f(i) = i$ for some i

Also f is onto

Hence, only Q and R are true

75. $x \times x = e \Rightarrow x$ is its own inverse

$y \times y = e \Rightarrow y$ is its own inverse

$(x \times y) \times (x \times y) = e \Rightarrow (x \times y)$ is its own inverse

$(y \times x) \times (y \times x) = e \Rightarrow (y \times x)$ is its own inverse

also $x \times x \times e = e \times e$ can be rewritten as follows

$x \times y \times y \times x = e \times y \times y \times e = e$ [$\because y \times y = e$]

$(x \times y) \times (y \times x) = e$ shows that $(x \times y)$ and $(y \times x)$ Are each other's inverse and we already know that

$(x \times y)$ and $(y \times x)$ are inverse of its own.

As per (G,*) to be group any element should have only one inverse element (unique)

This process $x \times y = y \times x$ (is one element)

So the elements of such group are 4 which are $\{x, y, e, x \times y\}$

76. $g(x) = 1 - x$ and $h(x) = \dfrac{x}{x-1}$

$$\text{Now } g(h(x)) = g\left(\frac{x}{x-1}\right) = 1 - \frac{x}{x-1}$$

$$= \frac{x-1-x}{x-1} = \frac{-1}{x-1}$$

$$\text{and } h(g(x)) = h(1-x) = \frac{1-x}{1-x-1} = \frac{1-x}{-x}$$

$$\text{Now } \frac{g(h(x))}{h(g(x))} = \frac{-1}{x-1} \times \frac{(-x)}{1-x} = \frac{-x}{(x-1)^2}$$

Now from option (*a*),

$$\frac{h(x)}{g(x)} = \frac{x}{x-1} \times \frac{1}{1-x}$$

$$= \frac{-x}{(x-1)^2}$$

$\therefore$ Option (*a*) is correct.

77. $A = \{5, \{6\}, \{7\}\}$

Power Set of A, $(2^A) = \{\phi, 5, \{6\}, \{7\}, \{5, \{6\}\}, \{5, \{7\}\}, \{\{6\}, \{7\}\}, \{5, \{6\}, \{7\}\}\}$

Options I, II and III are satisfied.

$\therefore$ Option (*c*) is correct.

78. $\dfrac{1}{5} < P_r < 1$

79. R is not Reflexive because and b are differe in a R b.

R is symmetric because if a R b then b R a is also true because common divisor is not change.

R is not transitive

Example $(2, 4) \in R$ and $(4, 2) \in R$.

but $(2, 2) \notin R$.

80. Cordinality of power set

$\{0, 1, 2, \ldots\ldots, 10\} = 2^{11} = 2048$

81. Number of anto function from X to Y.

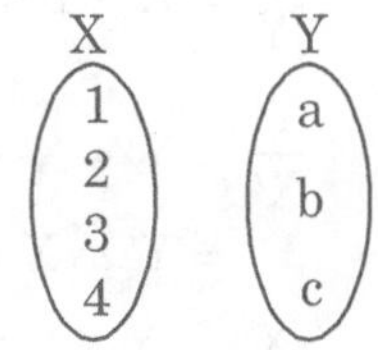

By using formula

$\Rightarrow n^m - n_{c1}(n-1)^m + n_{c_2}(n-2)^m + \ldots + (-1)^{n-1} n_{c_{n-1}} 1^m$

$\Rightarrow$ Here m = 4 and n = 3.

$\Rightarrow 3^4 - 3c_1(3-1)^4 + 3c_2(3-2)^4$

$\Rightarrow 81 - 48 + 3 = 36$

82. $|x| = 2$

and $|y| = 20$

Total number of function from set x to set y is

$20^2 = 400$

and total number of one-one function from set x to set y is

$$^{20}P_2 = \frac{20!}{(20-2)!} = \frac{20!}{18!} \qquad \left(\because {}^nP_r = \frac{n!}{(n-r)!}\right)$$

$= 20 \times 19 = 380$

$\therefore$ Probabiltiy the F chosen to be one-one function

$$= \frac{380}{400} = \frac{38}{40} = \frac{19}{20} = 0.95$$

83. $X \ne Y = \bar{X} + \bar{Y}$

So $Y \ne X = \bar{Y} + \bar{X}$ also true.

because given operation follow commutative but not associative so S_2 is true.

84. Counter example :

(A) Let $X = \{1\}$

$\Rightarrow$ $X' = S - X = \{2, 3, 4, 5, 6\}$

$\Rightarrow$ $|X| = |X'|$

(B) Since $|S| = 6$

and $|X| = 5 = |Y|$

$\therefore$ Atleast 4 elements common in X and Y

$\Rightarrow$ $X \cap Y = \phi$ is false

(C) Counter Example :

Let $X = \{1, 2\}$

and $Y = \{2, 3, 4\}$

then $\frac{X}{Y} = \{1\} = \phi$

(D) $\frac{X}{Y} = X - Y = X \cap Y'$

and $\frac{Y'}{X'} = Y' - X' = Y' \cap (X')$

$= Y' \cap X = X \cap Y'$

$\therefore$ $\frac{X}{Y} = \frac{Y'}{X'}, \forall X, Y \in U$

85. Since $p - q \neq q - p$

$\therefore$ $(p, q)\ R\ (p, q)$

$\Rightarrow$ R is not reflective

Let $(p, q)\ R\ (r, s)$

then $p - s = q - r$

$\Rightarrow$ $r - q = s - p$

$\Rightarrow$ $(r, s)\ R\ (p, q)$

$\Rightarrow$ R is symmetric

86. Maximum number of distinct values f takes is only 3.

$1^{st} \Rightarrow f(1) = f(2) = f(3) = f(4) = f(8)$

$2^{nd} \Rightarrow f(5) = f(10)$

$3^{rd} \Rightarrow f(6) = f(7) = f(9)$

Remaining all other n values will provide only one of these three values.

87. A binary relation R on N × N is defined as (a, b) R(C, d)

Reflexive: (a, a) R(a, a)

Since $a \leq a$, and $a \leq a$

Transitive: (a, b) R (c, d) and (c, d) R(m, n) then (a, b) R(m, n)

Suppose (a, b) R(c, d)

$\Rightarrow$ $a \leq c$ and $b \leq d$

and (c, d) R(m, n)

$\Rightarrow$ $c \leq m$, $d \leq n$

Since $a \leq c$, and $c \leq m$ so $a \leq m$

$b \leq d$ and $d \leq n$, so $b \leq n$

$\therefore$ (a, b) R(m, n)

(OR)

P. we have $a \leq a$ and $b \leq b$

$\Rightarrow$ (a, b) R(a, b)

$\Rightarrow$ R is reflexive

$\therefore$ P is true

Q. Let (a, b) R(c, d) and (c, d) R (e, f)

$\Rightarrow$ $\{a \leq c$ and $b \leq d\}$ and $\{c \leq e$ and $d \leq f\}$

$\Rightarrow$ $\{a \leq e$ and $b \leq f\}$

$\Rightarrow$ (a, b) R (e, f)

$\Rightarrow$ R is transitive

Hence both the statements P and Q are true.

88. Let us denote the problem by a non directed graph with 23 vertices (compounds). If two compounds in chemistry lab react with each other, then there exists an edge between the corresponding vertices. In the graph, we have 9 vertices with degree 3 (i.e. odd degree). By sum of degrees of vertices theorem atleast one of the remaining vertices should have odd degree.

89. R = {(a, a), (a, b), (a, c), (a, d), (a, c), (b, b), (b, c), (b, e), (c, c), (d, d), (d, e), (e, e)}

The given set is already a partiar order set and the given.

Hasse diagram is also a Lattice.

90. $(A \cup B \cup C) = A + B + C - (A \cap B) - (A \cap C) - (B \cap C) + (A \cap B \cap C)$

Here A = 3, B = 5 and C = 7

$$\Rightarrow \frac{500}{3} + \frac{500}{5} + \frac{500}{7} - \frac{500}{3 \times 5} - \frac{500}{3 \times 7} - \frac{500}{5 \times 7} + \frac{500}{3 \times 7 \times 5}$$

$\Rightarrow 271$

91. Order of subgroup always divides the order of group. So the passible subgroup of group an 84 elements are

1, 2, 3, 4, 6, 7, 12, 14, 21, 28, 42, 84

Laogest Proper Subgroup = 42 elements.

92. P : Set of rational number → countable

Q : Set of functions from {0, 1} to N → N

0 1

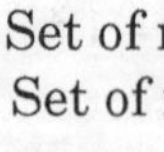

$N \times N$

0 can be assigned in N ways

1 can be assigned in N ways

There are N × N functions, cross product of countable set in countable.

R : Set of functions from N to {0, 1}

1 2 3 4 5 6

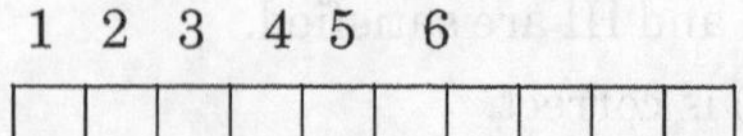

Each of thus boxes can be assigned to 0 or 1 so each such function is a binary number with infinite number of bits.

Example: 0000 ..... is the binary number corresponding to 0 is assigned to all boxes and so on.

Since each such binary number represents a subset of N (the set of natural numbers) by characteristic function method, therefore, the set of such function is same as power set of N which is uncountable due to Cantor's theorem, which says that power set of a countably infinite set is always uncountably infinite.

S : Set of finite subsets of N $\rightarrow$ countably infinite since we are counting only finite subsets.

So, P, Q and S are countable.

93. $A = \{(x, X), x \in X \text{ and } X \subseteq U\}$

The number of k element subsets of a set U with n elements = ^nC_k.

The number of possible ordered pairs (x, X) where $x \in X$ is $k \cdot {}^nC_k$ $1 \le k \le n$ 1 to n.

So total number of ordered pairs in A is given

$$= |A| = \sum_{k=1}^{n} k \cdot {}^nC_k = \sum_{k=1}^{n} k \cdot \binom{n}{k}$$

So II is correct.

But by the combinational identity

$$\sum_{k=1}^{n} k \cdot \binom{n}{k} = n \cdot 2^{n-1}$$

So I is also correct.

So both I and II are correct.

COMBINATORICS

1. (a) $T(n) = T(n - 1) + n$

$T(1) = 1$

$T(n) = T(n - 1) + n$

$= T(n - 2) + (n - 1) + n$

$= T(n - 3) + (n - 2) + (n - 1) + n$

$= T(n - k) + \ldots\ldots\ldots (n - 2) + (n - 1) + n$

Assume $n - k = 1$

$k = n - 1$

$= T(1) + \ldots\ldots (n - 2) + (n - 1) + n$

$= 1 + 2 + \ldots\ldots. + (n - 2) + (n - 1) + n$

$$\boxed{T(n) = \frac{n(n+1)}{2}}$$

(b) Fibonacci numbers generating function

$$G(z) = \frac{1}{1 - z - z^2}$$

2. $T(n) = T\left(\frac{n}{2}\right) + 1$

$= T\left(\frac{n}{2^2}\right) + 1 + 1$

$= T\left(\frac{n}{2^3}\right) + 1 + 1 + 1$

$= T\left(\frac{n}{2^k}\right) + k$

Put $n = 2^k$ there $= T(1) + \log_2 n$

$$\boxed{T(n) = 1 + \log_2 n}$$

3. The number of substrings from the character of length n is

$$\frac{n(n+1)}{2} + 1$$

{Note: ablition of 1 because of $\in$ string}

4. The number of binary strings of n zeros & k ones that no two cones are adjacent is $^{n+1}C_k$.

5. here does say all length inclusive means minimum length should start with 1.

So total substrings possible is $\frac{n(n+1)}{2}$.

6. E = Persons Speaks English

H = Persons Speaks Hindi

K = Persons Speaks Kannada

Given that $n(E \cup H \cup K) = 28$

$n(E) = 18$

$n(K) = 22$

$n(H) = 15$

$n(E \cap K) = 13$

$n(K \cap H) = 11$

$n(E \cap H) = 9$

$n(K \cap H \cap E) \Rightarrow ?$

By theorm

$n(E \cup H \cup K) = n(E) + n(H) + n(K)$

$- n(E \cap H) - n(H \cap K)$

$- n(K \cap E) + n(K \cap E \cap H)$

$28 = 18 + 15 + 22 - 9 - 11 - 13 + n(K \cap E \cap H)$

So $n(K \cap E \cap H) = 6$

7. $x_n = 2x_n - 1, n > 1$

$x_1 = 2$

Put $x_n = T(n)$

So, $T(n) = 2\,T(n-1) - 1, n < 1$

$T(1) = 2$

By iteration method.

$$T(n) = 2T(n-1) + 1$$
$$= 2[2T(n-2) + 1] + 1$$
$$= 2^2\, T(n-2) + 2 + 1$$
$$= 2^2[2T\,(n-2) + 1] + 2 + 1$$
$$= 2^3\, T(n-3) + 2^2 + 2 + 1$$
$$= 2^k\, T(n-k) + 2^{k-1} \,....\, + 2^2 + 2 + 1$$

Put $n - k = 1$

$$= 2^{n-1}\, T(1) + 2^{n-2} + ...\, 2^2 + 2 + 1$$
$$= 2^{n-1} \times 2 + 2^{n-2} + ...\, 2^2 + 2 + 1$$
$$= 2^{n-1} + \underbrace{2^{n-1} + 2^{n-2} + ...2^2 + 2 + 1}_{\text{Using G.P.}}$$
$$= 2^{n-1} + \frac{1(2^n - 1)}{2 - 1} = 2^{n-1} + 2^n - 1$$

8. The number of ways for distributing 10 roses among the two girls $= {}^{(n-1+r)}C_r = {}^{2-1+10}C_{10} = 11$

Similary, the number of ways for distributing 15 sunflowers among two girls $= {}^{2-1+15}C_{15} = 16$

Similarly the numbr of ways for distributing 14 daffodils among the two girls.

$$= {}^{(2-1+14)}C_{14} = {}^{15}C_{14} = 15$$

$\therefore$ Total numbers of ways = 11 × 16 × 15 = 2640

9. Assume the number of cards to be dealt from an arbitratily shuffled deck of 52 cards be x.

Number of Suits = 4

Required number of cards from the Same Suit = 3

Using pigeonhole Principle

$$\left[\frac{x-1}{4}\right] + 1 = 3$$
$$\left[\frac{x-1}{4}\right] = 2$$
$$x \geq 9$$

10. If numbr is even then it should end with 0, 2, 4, 6, or 8. and number should be distinct 4 digit number then first digit cannot be 0.

So total 4 digit even number

= 4 digit even numbers Ending with 0 + 4 digit even number ending with 2, 4, 6, 8.

4 digit even numbers ending with 0

9 × 8 × 7 × 1

~~0~~			0

$\Rightarrow$ 504 ways.

4 digit even numbers ending with 2, 4, 6, 8

8 × 8 × 7 × 4 = 1792 ways

~~0~~			← Either 2, 4, 6, 8

= 504 + 1792 = 2296.

11. $T(2^k) = 3T(2^{k-1}) + 1$

$T(1) = 1$

For $K = 0$ $T(1) = 1$

$K = 1$ $T(2) = 3T(1) + 1 = 4$

$K = 2$ $T(4) = 3T(2) + 1 = 13$

Only option (b)

Statisty

Put $K = 0 \Rightarrow \dfrac{(3^{0+1} - 1)}{2} = 1$

$K = 1 \Rightarrow \dfrac{3^{1+1} - 1}{2} = 4$

$K = 2 \Rightarrow \dfrac{3^{2+1} - 1}{2} = 13$

12. Number of color required to clolor even length cycle = 2 and for odd length cycle = 3

So $n - 2\left(\dfrac{n}{2}\right) + 2$ gives 2

If n is even and gives 3 if n is odd.

13. Number of way are $= \dfrac{8!}{5! \times 3!} = 56$

14. According to the given conditions total number of possibilities are 3^n.

15. The given problem is to find how may distinct order color pairs (c_1, c_2) are possible with k colors.

Since C_1 & C_2 can be any of the K color. So total combinations are $K \times K = K^2$.

Now each pair of letters must be colored with diffrent color pair so at least 26 colour pair required.

So $K^2 \geq 26$.

i.e. to satisfy above equation the minimum value of K is 6.

16. $D_n = \sum_{r=2}^{n} (-1)^r \dfrac{n!}{r!}$

$$D_5 = \sum_{r=2}^{5} (-1)^r \frac{5!}{r!}$$
$$= \frac{5!}{2!} - \frac{5!}{3!} + \frac{5!}{4!} - \frac{5!}{5!}$$
$$= 44 \text{ ways.}$$

17. We know $n = p^2 q$

gcd (m, n) = 1

So the diffrent possible value of m is $p(p-1)(q-1)$.

Such that it satisfy given condition.

18. Total diffrent pairs are 3 × 5 = 15. So if we select 16 pair then at least two peir (a mod 3, b mod 5) is same.

19. $G(x) = \frac{1}{(1-x)^2} = \sum_{i=0}^{\infty} g(i)x^i$

Formula is

$$\frac{1}{(1-x)^n} = \sum_{r=0}^{\infty} {}^{n-1+r}C_r\, x^r$$

Put n = 2

$$\frac{1}{(1-x)^2} = \sum_{r=0}^{\infty} {}^{2-1+r}C_r\, x^r = \sum_{r=0}^{\infty} {}^{r+1}C_r\, x^r$$

$$= \sum_{r=0}^{\infty} {}^{(r+1)x^r} = \sum_{r=0}^{\infty} (i+1)x^r$$

[Assume r = i]

So $\boxed{g(i) = i+1}$

20. Required favourable cases

= Number of ways of selecting n elements out of the set of size $2n = \binom{2n}{n}$

Since each toss may result in either Head or Tail (2 possibilities), hence for $2n$ tosses,

total combinations = $2^{2n} = 4^n$

$\therefore$ Required probability = $\frac{\text{Favourable cases}}{\text{Total cases}}$

$$= \frac{\binom{2n}{n}}{4^n}$$

21. To reach (10, 10) from (0, 0) the available number of Paths are

$$\frac{20!}{10!\,10!} = {}^{20}C_{10}$$

22. No. of ways to reach (4, 4) from (0,0) is

$$\frac{8!}{4! \times 4!} = {}^{8}C_4$$

No of ways to reach (10, 10) from (5, 4) is

$$\frac{11!}{5! \times 6!} = {}^{11}C_5$$

NO. of ways robot can move from (0, 0) to (10, 10) without using (4, 4) to (5, 4) move is

${}^{20}C_{10} - {}^{8}C_4 \times {}^{11}C_5$ ways.

23. $P = \sum_{1 \le i \le 2k} i$

$Q = \sum_{1 \le i \le 2k} i$

i even

P = 1 + 3 + 5 + 7 .... (2k – 1)

Q = 2 + 4 + 6 + 8 ... 2k.

Apply A.P. on P & Q.

Formular for A.P.

$$\frac{n}{2} \times (2a + (n-1)d)$$

$$P = \frac{k}{2} \times (2 \times 1 + (k-1) \times 2)$$

$\boxed{P = k^2}$

$$Q = \frac{k}{2}(2 \times 2 + (k-1) \times 2) = \frac{k}{2}(2k+2)$$

$\boxed{Q = k^2 + k}$

So [P = Q – k]

24. Number of 0 bit binary String that do not contain consecutive o's,.

$\Rightarrow \{\in\}$ i.e. $x_0 = 1$

Number of 1 bit binary strings that do not contain consecutive o's.

$\Rightarrow \{0, 1\}$ i.e. $x_1 = 2$

Number of 2 bit binary strings that do not contain Consecutive o's.

$\Rightarrow \{01, 10, 11\}$ i.e $x_2 = 3$.

Cross verity

Put n = 2 in option (d).

$x_2 = x_1 + x_0$

$[x_2 = 2 + 1]$

So $x_2 = 3$

Hence option (d) is true

25. Using Previous Question Equation is

$x_n = xn{-}1 + x_{n-2}$.

$x_0 = 1$

$x_1 = 2$

$x_2 = 3$

$x_4 = 5$

$x_5 = 8$

26. 300! = 1 × 2 × 3 × ... 300

$$\left\lfloor \frac{300}{11} \right\rfloor = 27$$

i.e. there are 27 multiples of 11 from to 300.

So they will include 11 ars a prime factor atleast once.

Only 121 & 242. contain extra 17.

So 27 + 2 = 29

27. 'b' blue balls can be distribute into n diffrent boxes in

$$= \frac{(n-1+b)!}{(n-1)! \times b!}$$

'r' red ball can be distribute in

$$\frac{(n-1+r)!}{(n-1)!\times r!}$$

Since both are independent.

So by product rule

$$\text{No. of ways are} = \frac{(n-1+b)!\times(n-1+r)!}{(n-1)!\times b!\times(n-1)!\times r!}$$

28. In a 10-pennant let as assume that x ones and y twos.

So $x + 2y = 10$ ...(1)

Put $x = 0$ in equations (1)

then $y = 5$

So (0, 5) is solution i.e. a 10 pennant could have 0 ones and 5 twos.

The number of ordered permetations of 0 ones and 5 twos.

$$= \frac{5!}{5!} = 1$$

Put $x = 2$ there $y = 4$

So (2, 4) is a solution then the number of ordered permutations of 2 ones & 4 twos

$$= \frac{6!}{2!4!} = 15$$

Similarly (4, 3) (6, 2) (8, 1) and (10, 0) are possible solution.

$$\frac{7!}{4!\,3!} = 35, \frac{8!}{6!\,2!} = 28$$

$$\frac{9!}{8!\times 1!} = 9\ \frac{10!}{10!\,0!} = 1 = 1 + 15 + 35 + 28 + 9 + 1 = 89$$

29. Given words are

THE, QUICK, BROWN, FOX, JUMPS, OVER, THE, LAXY, DOG

LET X be the random variable such that X =length of the word

The Length of the words THE, FOX, THE, DOG is 3

The Length of the words OVER, LAXY is 4

The length of the words QUICK, BROWN, JUMPS, is 5

The corresponding probabilities are given below

x	3	4	5
P(X)	$\frac{4}{9}$	$\frac{2}{9}$	$\frac{3}{9}$

Expected length of the word

$$= \sum xp(x) = 3\left(\frac{4}{9}\right) + 4\left(\frac{2}{9}\right) + 5\left(\frac{3}{9}\right)$$

$$= 3.8889$$

30. Prime factor of 2014 is

$2^1 \times 19^1 \times 53^1$.

Use formula

if $n = n = P_1^{n_1} \times P_2^{n_2} \ldots P_k^{n_k}$ is the prime factor of n then the number of district factor of n is $(n_1 + 1)(n_2 + 1) \ldots (n_k + 1)$.

So $(1 + 1)(1 + 1)(1 + 1) = 8$.

31. $$\sum_{x=1}^{99} \frac{1}{x(x+1)} = \sum_{x=1}^{99}\left[\frac{1}{x} - \frac{1}{x+1}\right]$$

$$= \left[\frac{1}{1} - \frac{1}{2}\right] + \left[\frac{1}{2} - \frac{1}{3}\right] + \ldots \left[\frac{1}{99} - \frac{1}{100}\right]$$

$$= 1 - \frac{1}{100} = \frac{99}{100} = 0.99$$

32. Number of 0 bit binary string that contain two consecutive 1 is zero.

So $[9_0 = 0]$

Similary No. of 1 bit bianry String that contain two conseuetice 1 is 0.

$[9, = 0]$

Now 11 is only two bit binary string that contain two consecutive 1.

So $[a_2 = 1]$

Similary 3 bit strings one

{01, 110, 111} $[a_3 = 3]$

Cross check using option (a)

$a_n = a_{n-2} + a_{n-1} + 2^{n-2}$ $n = 3$

$a_3 = a_1 + a_2 + 2^{3-2} = 0 + 1 + 2^1 = 3$

33. Prime factor of 2100 are

$2100 = 2^2 \times 3^1 \times 5^2 \times 7^1$

factor of 2100 = (2 + 1) (1 + 1) (2 + 1) (1 + 1)

= 36 factors.

34. 1111, 1112, 1113, 1122, 1123, 1133, 1222, 1223, 1233, 1333, 2222, 2223, 2233, 2333, 3333

Total number of 4-digit numbers are 15.

35. Number of 0 bit binary string that do not contain two consecutive 1's is {∈} i.e. $[9_0 = 1]$

Number of 1 bit – 11

– 11 is {0, 1}

i.e. $[a_1 = 2]$

Number of 2 bit – 11

– 11 is {00, 01, 10}

i.e. $[a_2 = 3]$

So option (b) gives $a_2 = 3$.

36. $(x^3 + x^4 + x^5 + x^6 \ldots\ldots)^3$

$$\Rightarrow \left(\frac{x}{1-x} - x - x^2\right)^3$$

$$\Rightarrow \left(\frac{x - x(1-x) - x^2(1-x)}{(1-x)}\right)^3$$

$$\Rightarrow \left(\frac{x - x - x^2 + x^2 + x^3}{(1-x)}\right)^3$$

$$\Rightarrow \left(\frac{x^3}{1-x}\right)^3$$

$\Rightarrow$ Coefficient of x^{12} in $\left(\frac{x^3}{1-x}\right)^3$

$\Rightarrow$ Coefficient of x^3 in $\left(\frac{1}{1-x}\right)^3$

$\Rightarrow$ Coefficient of x^3 in $(1-x)^{-3}$

$$f(0) + xf'(0) + \frac{x^2}{2!} f''(0) + \frac{x^3}{3!} f'''(0)$$

$f(x) = (1-x)^{-3}$

$f'(x) = +3(1-x)^{-4}$

$f''(x) = +12(1-x)^{-5}$

$f'''(x) = +60(1-x)^{-6}$

Coefficient of x^3 in $(1-x)^{-3} = \frac{60}{3!} = 10$

37. $a_n = 6n^2 + 2n + a_{n-1}$, $a_1 = 8$.

$a_2 = 6 \times 2^2 + 2 \times 2 + a_1$

$a_3 = 6 \times 3^2 + 2 \times 3 + a_2$

$= 6 \times 3^2 + 2 \times 3 + 6 \times 2^2 + 2 \times 2 + a_1$

$\vdots$

$a_{99} = 6 \times 99^2 + 2 \times 99 + 6 \times 98^2 + 2 \times 98$

$+ \ldots + 6 \times 2^2 + 2 \times 2 + 8$

$= 6[1^2 + 2^2 + 3^2 + \ldots + 99^2] + 2[1 + 2 + \ldots 99]$

$$= 6.\frac{(99(99+1)(2\times 99+1))}{6} + 2\frac{(99(99+1))}{2}$$

$= 99 \times 100 \times 199 + 99 \times 100$

$= 100 \times 99\,(199 + 1)$

$= 2 \times 99 \times 10^4 = \boxed{198} \times 10^4$

$\Downarrow$ value of K

38. Then generating function $\{a_n\}_{n=0}^{\infty}$ is $\frac{1+z}{(1-z)^3}$

$$A(z) = \sum a_r z^r = \frac{1+z}{(1-z)^3}$$

We can replace z by x, we get

$$A(x) = \sum a_r x^r = \frac{1+x}{(1-x)^3} = \frac{1}{(1-x)^3} + \frac{x}{(1-x)^3}$$

$$= \sum_{r=0}^{\infty} {}^{3-1+r}C_r x^r + x\sum_{r=0}^{\infty} {}^{3-1+r}C_r x^r$$

$$= \sum_{r=0}^{\infty} {}^{r+2}C_2 x^r + \sum_{r=0}^{\infty} {}^{r+2}C_2 x^{r+1}$$

$${}^2C_2 x^0 + {}^3C_2 x^1 + {}^4C_2 r^2 + {}^5C_2 x^3 \ldots\ldots\ldots$$

$$+ {}^2C_2 x^1 + {}^3C_2 x^2 + {}^4C_2 x^3 + \ldots\ldots\ldots$$

Now we read to find a_0 and a_3 which are coefficient of x^0 and x^3 respectively.

a_0 = Coefficient $x^0 = {}^2C_2 = 1$

a_3 = Coefficient x^3

$= {}^5C_2 + {}^4C_2 = 16$

So, $a_3 - a_0 = 16 - 1 = 15$

39. Given, $a_n = 2n + 3$

Since generating function for 1 is $\frac{1}{1-x}$ and n is $\frac{x}{(1-x)^2}$, the generating function for a_n is

$$A(x) = \frac{2x}{(1-x)^2} + \frac{3}{1-x}$$

$$\frac{2x + 3(1-x)}{(1-x)^2} = \frac{3-x}{(1-x)^2}$$

which is option (d).

GRAPH THEORY

1. G_1 is K_{3}, 3 (bipentite) graph which is non-planer.

G_2, is planner because it can be colored in two color.

G_3 is isomorphic of K_3, 3 which is non-planner graph.

2. A graph is planner iff it does not contain sub- graph home morphic to K_S or K_3, 3

3. Maximum possible Edges in an Undirected graph with "a" rentices and K component is

$$\boxed{E_{max} = \frac{(a-k+1)(a-k)}{2}}$$

4. (c) It is know that upto K_4 all graph's are planner and from K_5 to on words all are non-planner.

So. In K_5 there are 5 Vetices and 10 edges.

5. Maximum no. of edges in planner graph with n vertices is = 3x – 6 "By Theorem"

6.

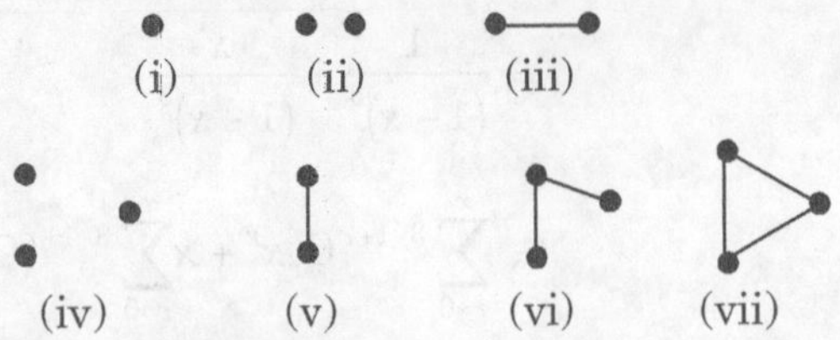

7. We know that the sum of degree of all vertices is always even and tocie of edges.

$$\boxed{\sum_{v=1}^{n} \deg(v) = 2e}$$

Sol. $\sum_{v=1}^{n} \deg(v) = \sum_{v=ve} \deg(v) + \sum_{v=vo} \deg(v)$

$\Rightarrow 2e$

So sum is always multiple of 2 that's why it is even.

8. Leg

G = 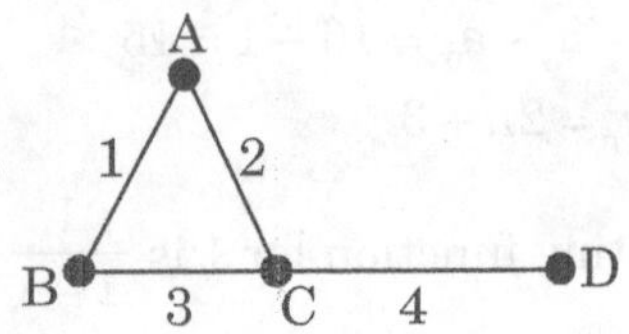

$E_{min} = 1$

$E_{max} = 4$

Minimum tree is Spanning

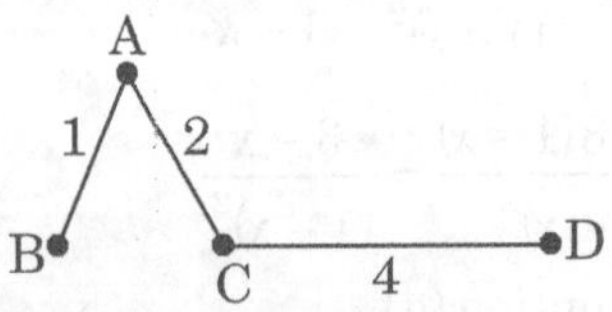

So option (c) is wrong

9. V = {$v_1, v_2 \ldots v_n$}

Maximum number of edges in graph with n vertices is

$$E = \frac{n(n-1)}{2}$$

Now there is two choise for each, that the edge either select or not select so total number of graph

is = $2^{\frac{n(n-1)}{2}}$

10. Number of edge in complete graph of n vertices (K_n) is

$$= \frac{n(n-1)}{2}$$

11. Let G ⇒ 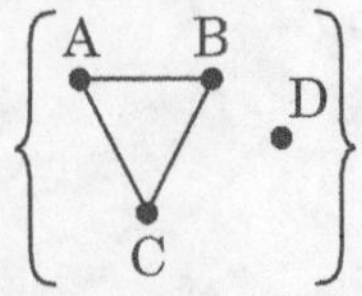

Here n = 4 and k = 2 is we remove vertex D then K = 1 (So minimum component is (k – 1))

Now Let G = 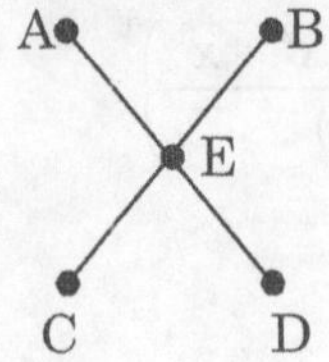

Here n = 5, k = 1

Now if we remove "E" then graph break into 4 component.

G = 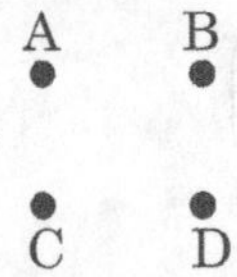

So $\boxed{K = (n-1)}$

So range is (k – 1) to (n – 1)

12. The no. of perfect matchings in complete graph of n verticies is

$$= \begin{cases} (n-1)\times(n-2)\times(n-5)\ldots\text{if } n = \text{even} \\ 0 \qquad\qquad \text{if } n = \text{odd.} \end{cases}$$

So. For n = 6

(n – 1) × (n – 3) × (n – 5)

(6 – 1) × (6 – 3) × (6 – 5)

5 × 3 × 1 = 15

13. $|E| \le 3|V| - 6$

Let d be the minimum degree of graph

So $d \le \frac{2|E|}{|V|}$

So $d \le \frac{2(3|v|-6)}{|v|}$

$d \le 6 - \frac{12}{|v|}$

So minimum degree is always less then 6.

14.

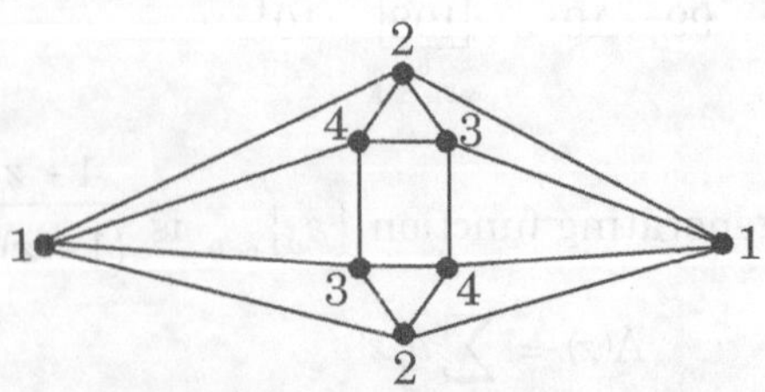

So total 3 colour are required.

15. The number of graphs on n labeled vertics with at least

$\frac{n^2 - 3n}{2}$ Edges is $\sum_{k=0}^{n} (n^2 - n)_2 C_k$

16. Maximum Number of edges in connected Acyclic (tree) graph contain n vertices is (n – 1)

17. $\sum_{v=1}^{n} \deg(v_i) = 2 \times$ no of edges.

$(6 \times 2) + (3 \times 4) + (x \times 3) = 2 \times 27$

$12 + 12 + 3x = 54$

$3x = 30$

$x = 10$

So total vertices = 6 + 3 + 10 = 19.

18. For simple plannar connectd graph

$|V| - |E| + |R| = 2$

$13 - 19 + R = 2$

$\boxed{R = 8}$

19. G_1 is not plannar, becuse there is not any isomorphic of G_1

Here G_1 is same as K_3, 3 which non-plannar graph.

20. Any subset of edges that connectos all vertices and has minimum total weight is always a tree.

21. The given graph is the defination of Hyper cube graph and the chromatic number of this graph is 2 and diameter is "n" so the ratio is 2/n.

22. $S = \{a_1, a_2 .... a_n\}$

So total 2^n subsets of set s are possible two substes are adjecent iff they are intersect in exectly two elements so for this each subset must centain atleast 2 elements.

So total vertices of zero degree is

$= \{\phi, \{a_1\}, \{a_2\}, \{a_3\}...\{a_n\}\}$

$\Rightarrow n + 1$

23. Maximum degree in this can be obtain by using following formula directly $\boxed{3 \times 2^{n-3}}$

24. There (n + 1) vertices of degree zero and remaining all vertices are connected as a single component so total number of connectal companent is n + 1 + 1 = n + 2

25. Kurtowsk is 3, 3 ($K_{3,\,3}$) is non–planer graph with minimum number of edges.

It has 9 edges and 6 vertices.

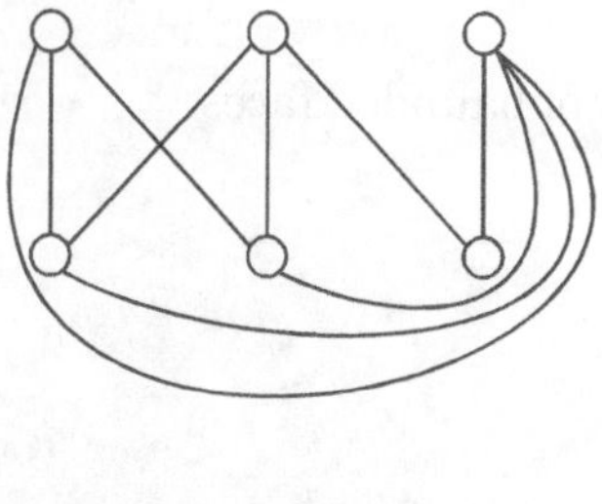

26. Here, INDEG(v) = In degree of verter v.

Since, INDEG(1) = 0

INDEG(2) = 1

INDEG(3) = 1

INDEG(4) = 2

INDEG(5) = 2m

INDEG(6) = 2

Node 1 is with zero indegree, so first node in ordering will always 1. Hence answer (d) is not a topological ordering.

27. The complement of cycle on 24 vertices is eulerian. In cycle of 25 vertices, all vertices have degree as 2. In complement graph, all vertices would have degree 22 and graph would be connected.

28.

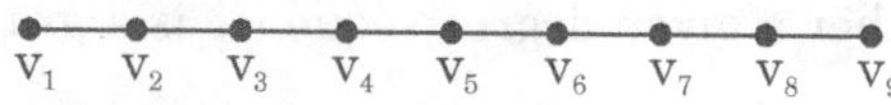

Maximal Independert set is:

$\{v_1, v_3, v_5, v_7, v_9\}$ and $\{v_2, v_4, v_6, v_8\}$

So smallest MIS Size = 4.

29.

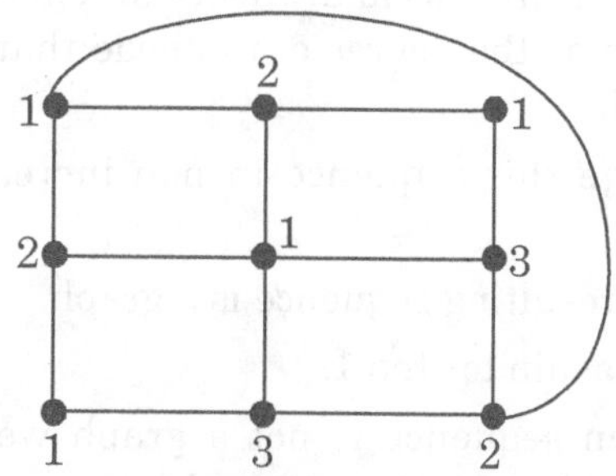

Chromatic Number = 3

30. The number of odd degree vertices in a graph is always even so when we, add a new node v then it make al vertices degree even. So the resultant graph is Euler.

31. Chromatic number of even length cycle graph is always 2.

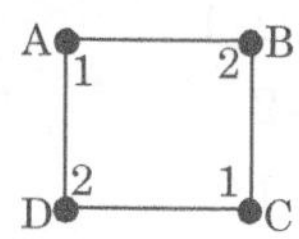

Chromatic No. = 2.

32. Atleast 2 vertices have the same degree.

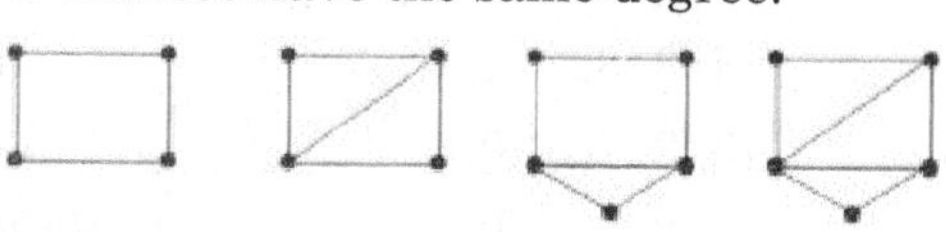

Alternately

For simple corrected graph with more than two vertices at least 2 vertices have the same degree

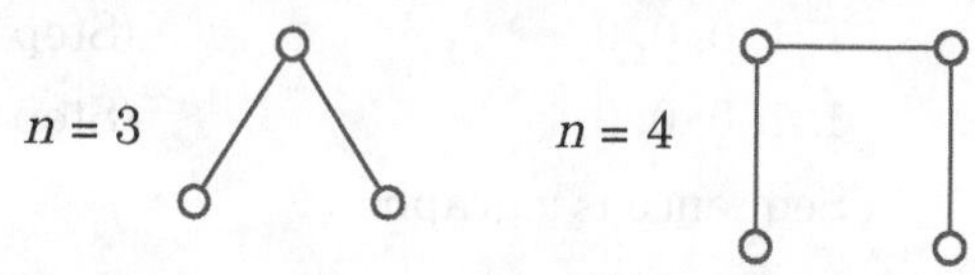

33. Since $\Sigma\partial(V) = 2e$

$\therefore \quad \xi(s) = \xi(T)$

$\Rightarrow \quad |S| = |T|$

34. Given that a node has odd number of descendants possible only when it is fully binary tree like.

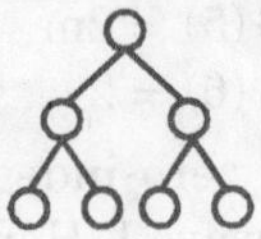

- So in fully binary tree, every node has two child or zero child (zero child when there is one node exactly)
- So, number of nodes in tree that type having exactly one child is zero = e]

35. Havell-Hakimi algorithm can be used to check whether a given degree sequence is a graph or not.

The algorithm is

1. remove top node of the sequence.
2. subtract "1" from as many nodes in remaining sequence as the degree of top node that was removed.
3. rearrange this sequence in non increasing order.
4. check if resulting sequence is a graph.
5. proceed again to step 1.

If the given sequence is not a graph we will see a voilation in step 4, such as presence of negative degrees in the sequence. Otherwise the algorithm will bottom out with a degree sequence consisting of only even no. of 1's and any number of 0's.

Now applying the algorithm to the degree sequence I, II, III and IV, one by one :

I. 7, 6, 5, 4, 3, 2, 1

6, 5, 4, 4, 3, 2, 1 (Step 1)
5, 4, 3, 3, 2, 1, 0 (Step 2)
5, 4, 3, 3, 2, 1, 0 (Step 3)
Sequence is a graph (Step 4)
4, 3, 3, 2, 1, 0 (Step 1)
3, 2, 2, 1, 0, 0 (Step 2)
3, 2, 2, 1, 0, 0 (Step 3)
Sequence is a graph (Step 4)
2, 2, 1, 0, 0 (Step 1)
1, 1, 0, 0, 0 (Step 2)
1, 1, 0, 0, 0 (Step 3)
Sequence is a graph

Now, the algorithm ends, since the sequence has only 0's and even number of 1's.

The final sequence corresponds to following valid greah.

Similarly for sequence II.

II. 6, 6, 6, 6, 3, 3, 2, 2

6, 6, 6, 3, 3, 2, 2 (Step 1)
5, 5, 5, 2, 2, 1, 2 (Step 2)
5, 5, 5, 2, 2, 2, 1 (Step 3)
Sequence is a graph (Step 4)
5, 5, 2, 2, 2, 1 (Step 1)
4, 4, 1, 1, 1, 1 (Step 2)
4, 4, 1, 1, 1, 1 (Step 3)
Sequence is a graph (Step 4)
4, 1, 1, 1, 1 (Step 1)
3, 0, 0, 0, 1 (Step 2)
3, 1, 0, 0, 0 (Step 3)
Sequence is a graph (Step 4)
1, 0, 0, 0 (Step 1)
0, – 1, – 1, 0 (Step 2)
0, 0, – 1, – 1 (Step 3)

The sequence is not a graph (Step 4), since negative degrees not possible in a valid graph. So, algorithm ends.

II is cannot be the degree sequence of any graph.

Similarly we can show that III is degree sequence of some graph and IV is not a degree sequence of any grpah.

So, correct answer is choice (d) II and IV.

36. Both are plannar graphs

K_4

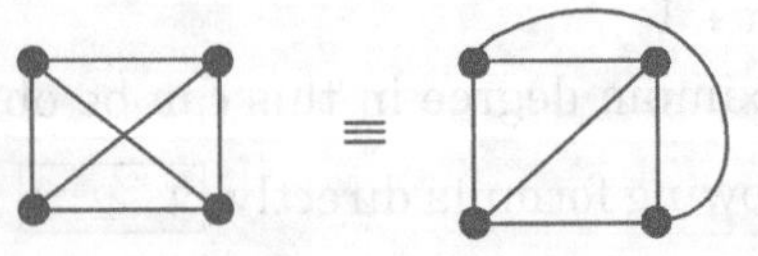

Q_3

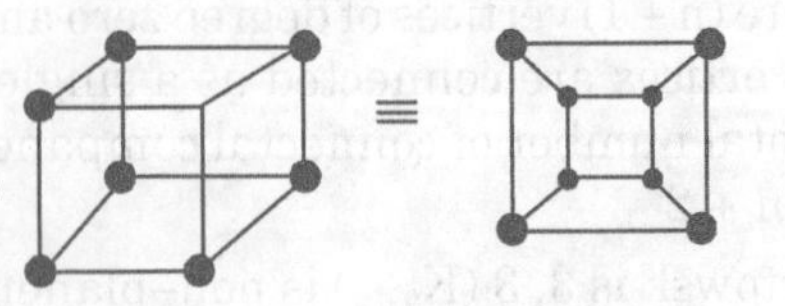

37. $V - E + R = 2$

$10 - 15 + R = 2$

$R = 7$

Number of baunded faces

$\Rightarrow R - 1$

$\Rightarrow 7 - 1$

$\Rightarrow 6$

38. Given graph is:

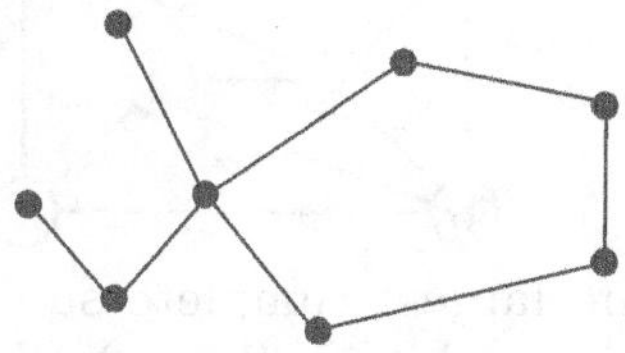

In given graph the number of vertices of degree 1 = 2.

No. of vertices of degree 2 = 5

There is one cycle of length 5

All this point are setisfy by option (b)

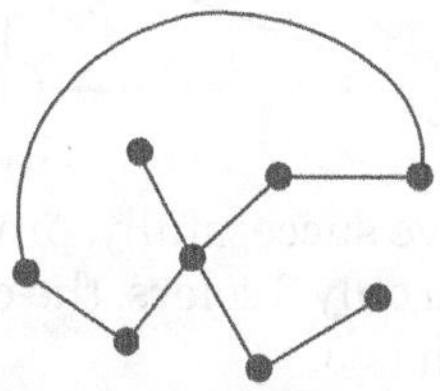

39. In complete undirected labeled graph of n vertices, total number of cycle of length r is

$= n_{cr} \times (r-1)!$

$= 6_{c4} \times 3! = 90$

40. Unorderal cycle of length or from n vertices is n_{cr} and probability of choosing any edge is 1/2.

So for 3 edges $\Rightarrow \frac{1}{2} \times \frac{1}{2} \times \frac{1}{2} = \frac{1}{8}$

No. of cycles $= 8_{c_3} \times \frac{1}{8} = 7$

41. Number of odd degree vertices is always even and sum of degrees of all vertices is also even.

42. G = (V, E) is directed graph

$G_2 = (V, E_2)$ where $E_2 = \{(4, v)/(v, 4) \in E\}$

Means G_2 and G has same strangly connected components only the difference is G_2 is that all edges of G have been reversed direction.

43. Accurding to given data.

(i) four corner vertices have each 3 degrees which gives 4 × 3 = 12 degrees.

(ii) The 40 side vertics have 5 degrees each contributing a total of 40 × 5 = 200 degree.

(iii) The 100 interior vertices each have 8 degree, 100 × 8 = 800 degree.

Total degree of graph = 2 × No of edges.

12 + 200 + 800 = 2 × E

$\boxed{E = 506}$

44. (c) = (3, 3, 3, 1, 0, 0)

$\Rightarrow$ (3, 3, 3, 1, 0, 0)

$\Rightarrow$ (2, 2, –1, 0, 0)

–1 contein so not graphical vertor.

45. From 12 vertices maximum number edge bipertite graph is $K_{6, 6} \Rightarrow 6 \times 6 = 36$

46. C_5 is self complementry graph because in self complemntry graph number of edges $= \frac{n(n-1)}{4}$

And in cycle graph – Edges = Vertices

So $n = \frac{n(n-1)}{4}$

$\Rightarrow \boxed{n = 5}$

47.

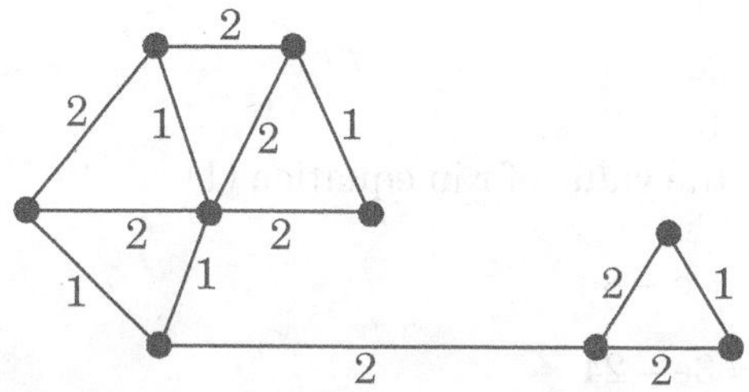

Spanning Tree

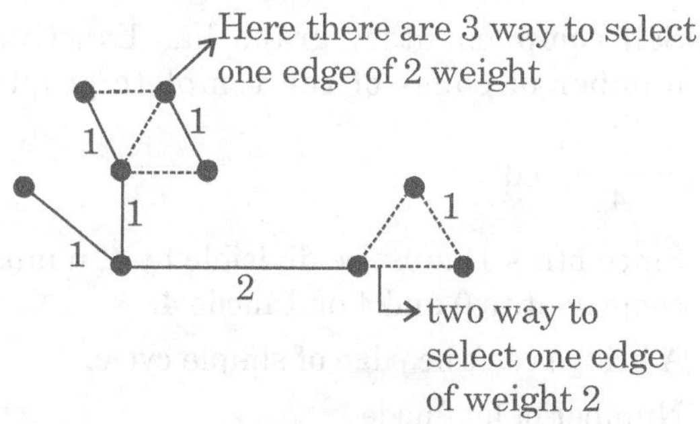

So total $3_{c_1} \times 2_{c_1} = 3 \times 2 = 6$

48. Number of edges in spanning forest with n vertices and k component is (n – k)

Example:

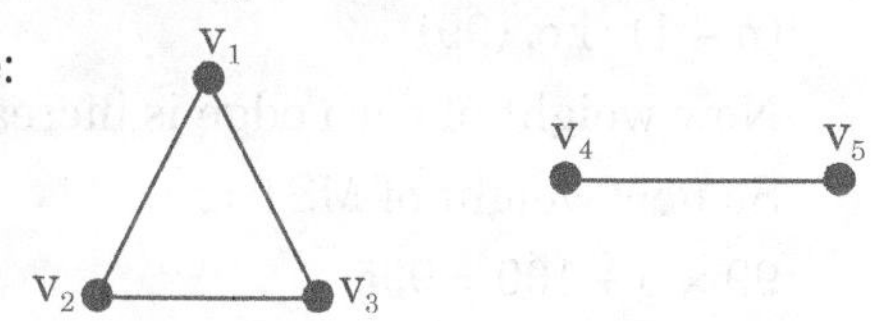

49. $\sum \deg = 2 \times E$

Given data

$\delta \geq 3$ also $\delta \leq 2E/n$

i.e. $e \geq n\delta/2$

$\Rightarrow e \geq 3n/2.$

Euler's formula

$|E| - |V| + 2 = r$

$\frac{3n}{2} - n + 2 = r$

$\frac{n}{2} + 2 = r$

So the no. of faces atleast $\frac{n}{2} + 2$.

50. Number of vertices = 10

degree of each region = 3

Euler's formula.

$r = |E| - |V| + 2$

$r = e - 10 + 2$

$r = e - 8$ ...(1)

We know that,

$\sum \text{degree region} = 2 \times E$

$3r = 2 \times e$

$r = \frac{2e}{3}$

Put the value of r in equation (1)

$\frac{2e}{3} = e - 8$

$2e = 3e - 24$

$e = 24$

51. Self complementary graph has Exactly half number of edges of the complete graph i.e.

$\frac{n(n-1)}{4}$ edges

Since n(n – 1) must be divisible by 4, n must be congruent to 0 and 4 or 1 mode 4.

52. A bridge can't be edge of simple cycle.

53. Number of leaf node

= Number of internal node with two child – 1

= 200 – 1 ⇒ 199

54. Number of edges in minimum spanning tree is (n – 1) · i.e. (99)

Now weight of each edge is increased by 5

So new weight of MST is

99 × 5 + 100 = 995

55. By 4 – color theorem, Every planar graph is 4 – colorable

56. $\sum d(v_i) = 2 \times |E|$

in tree $|E| = n - 1 = 10 - 1 = 9$

$\sum d(v_i) = 2 \times 9 = 18$

57. Number of Edges = 25

Now $\sum d(v_i) = 2 \times E$

$3n = 2 \times 25$

$n = \frac{50}{3}$

$\boxed{n = 16}$.

58.

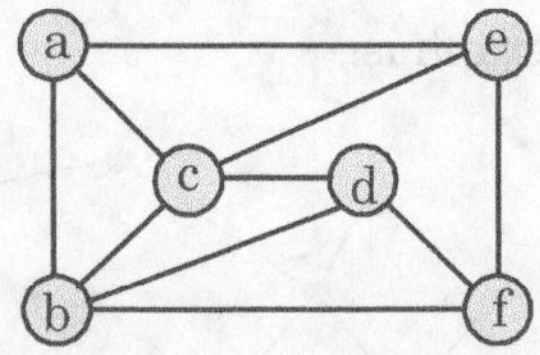

Since the largest complete sub graph is K_3, chromatic number is atleast 3. We can try for a chromatic number of 3 by using 3 colors, as follows:

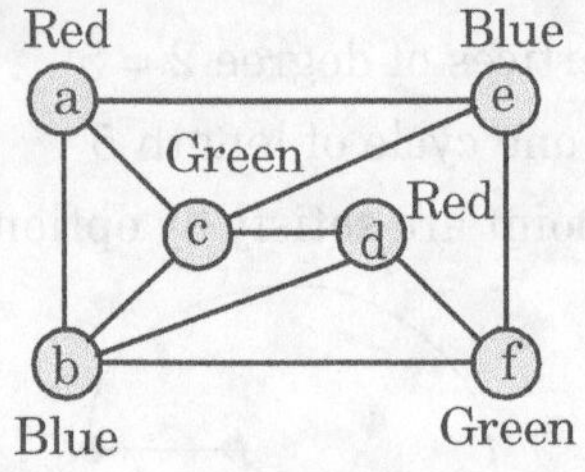

Since we have successfully, properly coloured all vertices with only 3 colors, the chromatic number of this graph is 3.

59. The graph has 100! vertices which each vertex labelled by one of the 100! permutation.

Let us find degree of each vertex.

Let us take a vertex whose labelling is say 1, 2, 3, 4,....100.

Now it will be connected to all vertices where exactly 2 of the adjacent numbers all swapped.

The two swapped numbers could be (1, 2), (2, 3), (3, 4) .... etc. upto (99, 100) which makes for 99 edges for each such vertex.

So the graph is a regular graph with each vertex connected to 99 other vertices.

So y = 99

The number of connected components = z = 1 since we can go from any vertex to any other vertex by only swapping 2 adjacent number at a time, many times i.e. there is a path from any vertex to any other vertex.

Graph is connected.

So z = 1

So y + 10z = 99 + 10 × 1 = 109

60. In a complete graph we can traverse the n vertices in any order and return to the starting vertex and form a Hamiltonian cycle. The number of such cycles required is n!

While for is circular rotations ignored. Since for example K_4 with vertices {1, 2, 3, 4}, the cycle 1-2-3-4 is same as 2-3-4-1 is same as 3-4-1-2 etc. we now get only (n – 1)! distinct Hamiltonian cycles. Further, the cycle 1-2-3-4 and 1-4-3-2 are also same (clockwise and anticlockwise).

∴ we get $\frac{(n-1)!}{2}$ distinct Hamiltonian cycles

61. If no two edges of G have same weight surely G will have unique spanning tree is true. So I is true

And if, for every cut of G, there is a unique minimum weight edge crossing the cut then G will have unique spanning tree is also true. So II is true

So both I and II are true.

Option (d) is correct.

PROBABILITY

1. $P\left(\frac{A}{B}\right) = \frac{P(A \cap B)}{P(B)}$

2. Bag contain 10 white & 15 black balls the probability to draw two balls (one black & other one white) is

$$\frac{{}^{10}C_1 \times {}^{15}C_1}{{}^{25}C_2} = \frac{10 \times 15}{\frac{25 \times 24}{2}} = \frac{1}{2}$$

3. P(a least one of dice will have 6 facing)

= 1 – P(noneof dice having 6 facing)

$= 1 - \frac{5}{6} \times \frac{5}{6} = \frac{11}{36}$

4. Probability of bottom card of deck is ace

$= \frac{4}{52}$ {∵ there are 4 ace out of 52 cards}

Praobability that top card is also ace

$= \frac{3}{51}$ {∵ because only 3 ace remain out of 4}

So required probability = $\frac{4}{52} \times \frac{3}{51}$

5. Given data

P(rain today) = 0.5

P(rain tomorrow) = 0.6

P(rain todfay ∪ rain tomorrow) = 0.7

P(rain today ∩ rain tomorrow) = ?

P(rain today ∪ rain tomorrow)

= P(Rain today) + P(rain tomorrow)

– P(rain today ∩ rain tomorrow)

0.7 = 0.5 + 0.6 + x

$\boxed{x = 0.4}$

6. Probability of getting an odd number in rolling of a die = $\frac{3}{6} = \frac{1}{2}$

Now using binomial distribution.

P (Exactly one odd number among three outcomes)

$$= {}^3C_1\left(\frac{1}{2}\right)^1\left(\frac{1}{2}\right)^2 = 3 \times \left(\frac{1}{2}\right)^3 = \frac{3}{8}.$$

7. Option (c) is true only.

8. Option (d) $P\left(\frac{E_1}{E_2}\right) = \frac{4}{5}$

Now, $P\left(\frac{E_1}{E_2}\right) = \frac{P(E_1 \cap E_2)}{P(E_2)} = \frac{3}{5}$

Hence (d) is false.

9. Given data

(i) $P_r(E_1) = P_r(E_2) = 9$

(ii) $P_r(E_1 \cup E_2) = 1$

$P_r(E_1 \cap E_2) = P_r(E_1)\, P_r(E_2)$ because E_1 & E_2 are independent.

$P_r(E_1 \cap E_2) = a \times 9 = a^2$

Now we know that

$P_r(E_1 \cup E_2) = P_r(E_1) + P_r(E_2) - P_r(E_1 \cap E_2)$

$1 = a + a - a^2$

$a^2 - 2a + 1 = 0$

$(a - 1)^2 = 0$

$a = 1$

i.e. $P_r(E_1) = P_r(E_2) = a = 1$

10. Probatrility is $\frac{7}{7^7} = \frac{1}{7^6}$

11. P_r(atleast one head and one tail)

= 1 – P_r(no head ∪ no tail)

= 1 – [P_r (no head) + P_r(no tail)

– P_r(no head ∩ no tail)]

$$= 1 - \left[\frac{1}{2^4} + \frac{1}{2^4} - 0\right] = 1 - \frac{2}{16} = \frac{7}{8}$$

12. Given data P(a) = 1, P(b) = $\frac{1}{2}$

We know that both events are independent there

$P\left(\frac{A}{B}\right) = P(A) = 1$

$P\left(\frac{B}{A}\right) = P(B) = \frac{1}{2}$

13. The formula is $\int_0^t f_1(x)\ f_2(t - x)dx$

14. Given data

$P(H) = \frac{1}{2},\ P(T) = \frac{1}{2}$

Apply Bernoull's theorm

$$P(X = 2) = {}^4C_2\left(\frac{1}{2}\right)^2\left(1 - \frac{1}{2}\right)^{4-2} = \frac{{}^4C_2}{2^4} = \frac{3}{8}$$

15. **(b)** Assume 100 families are there out of which 50 has 3 child, 30 has 2 child & 20 has 1 child.

So total childs are

$= 50 \times 3 + 30 \times 2 + 20 \times 1 = 230$

The numbr of child who come from 2 child families are $30 \times 2 = 60$

So Probability is $= \frac{60}{230} = \frac{6}{23}$

16. Mean of $z = \frac{1}{\frac{1}{\alpha}+\frac{1}{\beta}} = \frac{\alpha\beta}{\alpha+\beta}$

17. Marks obtain per qustion = X.

Probatrity :

X	1	– 0.25
P(x)	1/4	3/4

Expected Marks Per Question

$= E(x) = \sum X\,P(X)$

$= 1 \times \frac{1}{4} + (-0.25) \times \frac{3}{4}$

$= \frac{1}{16}$ Marks

Total maks for 150 questions.

$= \frac{1}{16} \times 150 = \frac{75}{8}$ marks per student.

Total expected marks of 1000 students.

$= \frac{75}{8} \times 1000 = 9375$ marks.

18. So this is a binomial distribution with n trials and d successes and probability of success

$P = \frac{2}{4} = \frac{1}{2}$

So $P(X = d) = {}^nC_d \left(\frac{1}{2}\right)^d \left(\frac{1}{2}\right)^{n-d} = \frac{{}^nC_d}{2^n}$

19. Answer is $\frac{5}{3}$

20. If f(x) is the continuous probability density function of a random variable X there,

$P(a < x \le b) = P(a \le x \le b) = \int_a^b f(x)dx$

21. Probability of getting a blue first green second and red third.

$= \frac{10}{60} \times \frac{20}{60} \times \frac{30}{60}$

Required Probability

$= 6 \times \frac{10}{60} \times \frac{20}{60} \times \frac{30}{60} = \frac{1}{6}$

22. **(a)**

23. Let x = Rain in the afternoon

$T > 25$ = temperature more than 25°C

Let the desired probabity

$T\left(\frac{x}{T \le 25}\right) = a$

Given $P(x) = 0.6$

Total probabity

$P(x) = \frac{1}{2} \times 0.4 + \frac{1}{2} \times x$

$0.6 = 0.2 + 0.5x$

$x = 0.8$

24. The expected value in geometric distributor

$E(x) = \frac{1}{p}$

Where p is the probability of success in any one attempt.

25. $P(H) = \frac{1}{2} \times \frac{5}{8} + \frac{1}{2} \times \frac{1}{4} = \frac{7}{16}$

26. Number of permutations with '2' in the first position = 19!

Number of permutations with '2' in the second position = 10 × 18!

(fill the first space with any of the 10 odd numbers and the 18 spaces after the 2 with 18 of the remaining numbers in 18! ways)

Number of permutations with '2' in 3rd position = 10 × 9 × 17!

(fill the first 2 places with 2 of the 10 odd numbers and then the remaining 17 places with remaining 17 numbers) and so on until '2' is in 11th place. After that it is not possible to satisfy the given condition, since there are only 10 odd numbers available to fill before the '2'. So the desired number of permu-tations which satisfied the given condition is

$19! + 10 \times 18! + 10 \times 9 \times 17! + 10 \times 9 \times 8 \times 16! + \ldots + 10! \times 9!$

Now the probability of this happenning is given by

$\frac{19! + 10 \times 18! + 10 \times 9 \times 17! \ldots + 10! \times 9!}{20!}$

Which is clearly not choices (*a*), (*b*) or (*c*)

∴ Answer is (*d*)

27. $\Delta T = 45 \text{ minutes} = \frac{45}{60} = \frac{3}{4}$ hr

$\alpha = 20$ request / hr

Poission distribution

$\lambda = \propto \Delta T = 20 \times \frac{3}{4} = 15$

The requirerd probability

$= P(x = 1) + P(x = 3) + P(x = 5)$

$= \frac{e^{-15}15}{1!} + \frac{e^{-15}15^3}{3!} + \frac{e^{-15}15^5}{5!}$

$= 1002 \times 10^6 \times e^{-20}$

28. $P(A \cup B) = P(A) + P(B) - P(A \cap B)$

$= \left(1-\frac{1}{3}\right) + \left(1-\frac{1}{3}\right) - \frac{1}{2}$

$= \frac{4}{3} + \frac{1}{2} = \frac{10}{12}.$

29. The probability that in a randomly chosen group of r people at least there people have the same birthday is

$= 1 - \frac{365 \times 364 ...(365 - r + 1)}{365^r}$

${}^rC_2 \times 365 \times \frac{364 \times 363 - (364 - (r-2) + 1)}{364^{r-2}}$

30. Combinations are CMC, CMM, CCC, CCM.

Probability of

CMC= $0.6 \times 0.4 = 0.24$ — Favourable

CMM= $0.6 \times 0.6 = 0.36$

CCC= $0.4 \times 0.4 = 0.16$ — Favourable

CCM= $0.4 \times 0.6 = 0.24$

Total probability = 1

Favourable= $0.24 + 0.16 = 0.4$

$\therefore$ $P = 0.4/1$

31. Here standard deviation is 3.

32. Given : P(ODD) = 0.9*P(EVEN) $\neq$ P(2) = P(4) = P(6) $\neq$ P(EVEN | Exceeds 3) = 0.75

Now we know

P(ODD) = 1 – P (EVEN)

or 0.9*P (EVEN) = 1 – P (EVEN)

{Given P(ODD) = 0.9*P(EVEN)}

or P(EVEN) = 1/1.9

Because of independent events

P(2) = P(4) = P(6) = P(2 $\cup$ 4 $\cup$ 6)/3

= P(EVEN)/3 = 1/(3*1.9)

Now, P(EVEN | Exceeds 3)

= P(EVEN $\cap$ Exceeds 3)/P(Exceeds 3)

P(Exceeds 3) = P(EVEN $\cap$ Exceeds 3)/P(EVEN | Exceeds 3)

P(Exceeds 3) = P(4 $\cup$ 6)/0.75

P(Exceeds 3) = (P(4) + P(6))/0.75

P(Exceeds 3) = (1/3*1.9) + 1/(1.9 * 3))/0.75

P(Exceeds 3) = 0.468

33. Probability of faulty declared

= (already faulty) $\times$ (declared faulty after testing)

Let probability of already faulty = p

Probability that after testing it declares faulty

$= (1 - q)$

$\therefore$ Required probability = $(1 - q)\, p$

34. Total number of divisors of $10^{99} = 2^{99} \times 5^{99} = 2 \times 5$

and that are most direct of 10^{96}

$\equiv (99 + 1)(991 + 1)\, 10^{96} \times 10^3$

$\Rightarrow 10^{96}, 2 \times 10^{96}, 4 \times 10^{96}, 9 \times 10^{96}, 8 \times 10^{96}$

$\left|\frac{1000}{n}\right| = 0$

$\Rightarrow 10 \times 10^{96}, 20 \times 10^{96}, 29 \times 10^{96}, 40 \times 10^{96}, 50 \times 10^{96}$

$n = 1—100$ $125 \times 10^{96}, 250 \times 10^{96}, 500 \times 10^{96}, 100 \times 10^{96}, 100 \times 10^{96}, 200 \times 10^{96}$

= total 16

$\therefore$ Required probability = $\frac{10}{10000} = \frac{1}{625}$

35. Sample space = {HH,HT, TH}

Required probability = $\frac{1}{3}$

36. $V(x) = E(x^2) - [E(x)]^2 = R$

Since variance is σ_x^2 and hence it should be positive i.e. $R \geq 0$.

37. Standard deviation is affected by scale but not by shift of origin.

So $y_i = ax_i + b$; $\sigma_y = a\sigma_x$

if a could be negative then $\sigma_y = |a|\,\sigma_x$ is more correct since standard deviation can't be negative

So $\sigma_y = a\,\sigma_x + b$ is false.

38. (2, 1), (3, 2), (4, 3), (5, 4)

Required probability = $\frac{4}{5 \times 4} = \frac{4}{20} = \frac{1}{5}$

39. The probability distribution of the radom variable is

X	–1	+1
P(x)	0.5	0.5

The cumulative distribution function is

X	–1	+1
F(x)	0.5	1.0

40.

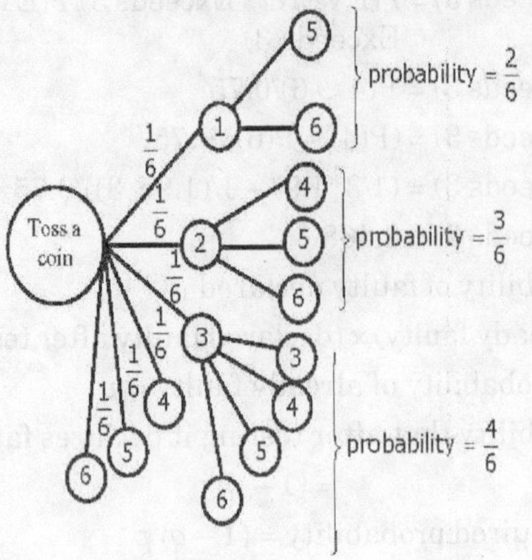

$\therefore$ Required probability

$$= \frac{1}{6}\times\frac{2}{6}+\frac{1}{6}\times\frac{3}{6}+\frac{1}{6}\times\frac{4}{6}+\frac{1}{6}=\frac{15}{36}=\frac{5}{12}$$

41. **Given:** P # of cars passing every minute

P is a random variable following Poisson's Distribution

$$\therefore \quad \frac{\text{Prob. } (P = K) = \dfrac{\lambda^k e^{-\lambda}}{K!}}{\text{Mean} = E[P] = 1}$$

$\therefore \quad \lambda = 3$

Probability of observing fewer than 3 cars

= Prob. (P = 0) + Prob (P = 1) + Prob (P = 2)

$$= \frac{3^0.e^{-3}}{0!}+\frac{3^1.e^{-3}}{1!}+\frac{3^2.e^{-3}}{2!} = \frac{1}{e^3}\left[1+3+\frac{9}{2}\right] = \boxed{\frac{17}{2e^3}}$$

42. The smaller sticks, therefore, will range in length from almost 0 meters up to a maximum of 0.5 meters, with each length equally possible. Thus, the average length will be about 0.25 meters, or about a quarter of the stick.

43. 22 occurred in following ways

6	6	6	4	$\rightarrow$ 4 ways
6	6	5	5	$\rightarrow$ 6 ways

$$\text{Required probability} = \frac{6+4}{2296} = \frac{10}{2296}$$

$\Rightarrow \quad x = 10$

44. p = P [at least three computers are working]

= P (3 or 4 computers working)

$$= \frac{(4_{C_3})\times(6_{C_1})}{10_{C_4}}+\frac{4_{C_4}}{10_{C_4}}$$

$$= \frac{5}{42}$$

$\Rightarrow$ 100 p = 11.9.

45. Positive number between 1 to 100 (inclusive) not divisible by 2, 3 or 5 are

{1, 7, 11, 13, 17, 19, 23, 29, 31, 37, 41, 43, 47, 49, 53, 59, 61, 67, 71, 73, 77, 79, 83, 89, 91, 97}

$$P(E) = \frac{26}{100} = 0.26$$

46. Given $A \cup B = S$

$\Rightarrow P(A \cup B) = P(S) = 1$

$\Rightarrow P(A) + P(B) = 1$

($\because$ A & B are mutually exclusive)

$\Rightarrow P(B) = 1 - P(A)$

Maximum value of P(A) P(B) = ?

Maximum value of P (A) [1 – P (A)] = ?

Let P(A) = X

Let $f(x) = x(1-x) = x - x^2$

for $f(x)$ maximum $\Rightarrow f'(x) = 0$

$\Rightarrow 1 - 2x = 0$

$\Rightarrow x = \frac{1}{2}$

$f''(x) = -2;\ f''\left(\frac{1}{2}\right) < 0$

$\therefore$ $f(x)$ has maximum

At $x = \frac{1}{2}$ and maximum value

$$= f\left(\frac{1}{2}\right) = \frac{1}{2}\left(1-\frac{1}{2}\right) = \frac{1}{2}.\frac{1}{2} = \frac{1}{4} = 0.25$$

47. ****

48. Given $f(x) = \frac{1}{x}\ \alpha \le x \le 1 = 0$ Else

So $\int_\alpha^1 f(x) = 1$

$$\int_\alpha^1 \frac{1}{x^2} = 1$$

$$\left[\frac{-1}{x}\right]_\alpha^1 = 1$$

$$-\left[\frac{1}{1}-\frac{1}{\alpha}\right] = 1$$

$$\frac{1}{\alpha} = 2$$

$\alpha = 0.5$

49. Probability $= \frac{1}{3} = 0.33$.

50. P(losts > 100 hr) = 0.5 × 0.7 + 0.5 × 0.4

= 0.35 + 0.2 = 0.55

51. As per given condition media of 4 is 0.

52. Given that

$$p(P) = \frac{1}{4} \quad ...(i)$$

$$p(P \mid Q) = \frac{1}{2} \quad ...(ii)$$

$$p(Q \mid P) = \frac{1}{3} \quad ...(iii)$$

$$p(\bar{P} \mid \bar{Q}) = ?$$

First solve for $p(Q)$ and $p(P \cap Q)$ from equation (*ii*) and (*iii*) as follows :

From equation (*ii*)

$$p(P \mid Q) = \frac{p(P \cap Q)}{p(Q)} = \frac{1}{2} \quad ...(iv)$$

From equation (*iii*) $p(Q \mid P) = \dfrac{p(P \cap Q)}{p(P)} = \dfrac{1}{3}$

$$\Rightarrow \quad p(P \cap Q) = \frac{1}{3} \times p(P)$$

$$= \frac{1}{3} \times \frac{1}{4} = \frac{1}{12}$$

Substitute in equation (*iv*) get

$$p(Q) = \frac{p(P \cap Q)}{1/2} = \frac{1/12}{1/2} = \frac{2}{12} = \frac{1}{6}$$

$$p(P) = \frac{1}{4}$$

$$p(Q) = \frac{1}{6}$$

and $\quad p(P \cap Q) = \dfrac{1}{12}$

we need to find

$$p(\bar{P} \mid \bar{Q}) = \frac{p(\bar{P} \cap \bar{Q})}{p(\bar{Q})}$$

$$= \frac{1 - (P \cup Q)}{1 - p(Q)}$$

$$= 1 - \frac{[p(P) + p(Q) - p(P \cap Q)]}{1 - p(Q)}$$

$$= \frac{1 - \left[\frac{1}{4} + \frac{1}{6} - \frac{1}{12}\right]}{1 - \frac{1}{6}} = \frac{\frac{2}{3}}{\frac{5}{6}} = \frac{4}{5}$$

$$p(\bar{P} \mid \bar{Q}) = \frac{4}{5}$$

53. $g_Y(z) = ((1 - \beta) + \beta z)^N$ Scalar $\beta \in [0,1]$

If $g_Y(z)$ is expanded, we would get a bionomial distribution with $n = N$ and $p = \beta$

So the $\quad E[Y] = np = N\beta$

54. We know that in Poisson distribution representation

$$E(X) = V(X) = \lambda$$

Given $\lambda = 5$

$$E(X) = V(X) = 5$$

We need $E[(X + 2)^2] = E(X^2 + 4x + 4)$

$$= E(X^2) + 4E(X + 4)$$

To find $E(X^2)$ we write,

$$V(X) = E(X^2) - (E(X))^2$$

$$5 = E(X^2) - 5^2$$

So, $\quad E(X^2) = 5^2 + 5 = 30$

$$\text{required value} = 30 + 4 \times 5 + 4 = 54$$

55. P(one of them wins in 3rd trial)

= P(1st trial is Tie) × P (IInd trial is Tie) × P(one of them wins 3rd trial)

P(Tie in any trial)

= P(P = 1 and Q = 1) + P(P = 2 and Q = 2) + ... + P(P = 6 and Q = 6)

$$= \frac{6}{36} = \frac{1}{6}$$

∴ P(one of them wins) = 1 – P(Tie)

$$= 1 - \frac{1}{6} = \frac{5}{6}$$

So, required probability

$$= \frac{1}{6} \times \frac{1}{6} \times \frac{5}{6} = \frac{5}{216} = 0.023$$

(rounded to 3 decimal places)

56. The condition probability table given is

	H_D	M_D	L_D
M_G	0.40	0.48	0.12
M_G	0.10	0.65	0.25
L_G	0.01	0.50	0.49

$P(H_G) = 0.2$

$P(M_G) = 0.5$

$P(L_G) = 0.3$

Drawing the tree diagram for HD we get.

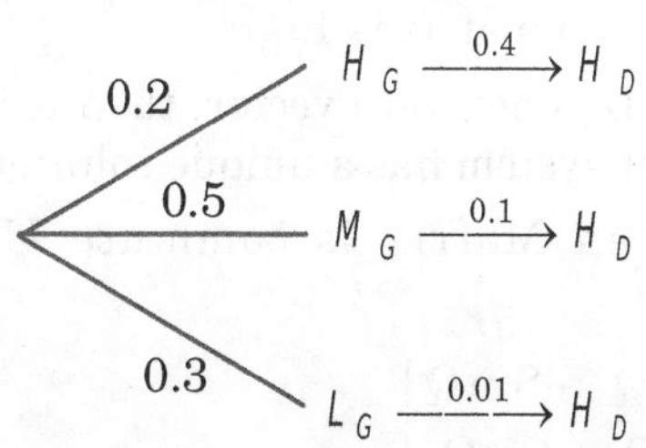

$$P(H_G \mid H_D) = \frac{P(H_G \cap H_D)}{P(H_D)}$$

From diagram,

$$P(H_G \cap H_D) = 0.2 \times 0.4$$

$$P(H_D) = 0.2 \times 0.4 + 0.5 \times 0.1 + 0.3 \times 0.01 = 0.133$$

Required probability, $P(H_G \mid H_D)$

$$= \frac{0.2 \times 0.4}{0.133} = 0.60$$

(rounding upto 2 decimal place)

57. Polynomial $3x^2 + 6xY + 3Y + 6$ has only real roots

$\therefore\ b^2 - 4ax \geq 0$

$(6Y)^2 - 4(3)(3Y + 6) \geq 0$

$Y^2 - Y + 2 \geq 0$

$Y \in (-\infty, -1] \cap [2, \infty)$

$\Rightarrow Y \in [2, 6)$

Now y is uniformly distributed in (1, 6)

Probability distribution function

$$f(Y) = \frac{1}{5} \qquad 1 < y < 6$$

$$\therefore\ p(2 \leq y < 6) = \int_2^6 f(Y)dy$$

$$\frac{1}{5}[Y]_2^6 = \frac{1}{5}(6-2) = \frac{4}{5} = 0.8$$

LINEAR ALGEBRA

1. In equation abx + a2y ≥ 15 both x and y is in its first degreee so it is linear in equality.

2. ****

3. The matrix M is said to be symmetric iff $M^T = M$

Now $(AB)T = B^T A^T = BA$.

4. In matrix all rows are same. So there exist only one independent row.

Now we know that

Rank of Matrix = Number of independent rows

So, Rank of given matrix is 1.

5. If m = n and B is non zero vector, then it is not necessary that system has a unique solution.

6. Ab = BA then Matrix is commute Under multiplication.

So $A = \begin{bmatrix} \text{Cos}Q & -\text{Sin}Q \\ \text{Sin}Q & \text{Cos}Q \end{bmatrix}$

$B = \begin{bmatrix} a & o \\ o & b \end{bmatrix}$

$AB = \begin{bmatrix} a\text{Cos}Q & -b\text{Sin}Q \\ a\text{Sin}Q & b\text{Cos}Q \end{bmatrix}$

$BA = \begin{bmatrix} a\text{Cos}Q & -a\text{Sin}Q \\ b\text{Sin}Q & b\text{Cos}Q \end{bmatrix}$

Simply we can say AB = BA iff a = b or $Q = \pm n\pi$

7. For upper triangular Matrix the determinant is product of principal diagonal elements.

So, Determinant of given Matrix is

$$= 6 \times 2 \times 4 \times 1 = -48$$

8. Assume $A = \begin{bmatrix} a & b \\ c & d \end{bmatrix}$

Given that I_{12} is the matrix obtained by inter– changing the first & Second row of indentily Martix

So, $I_{12} = \begin{bmatrix} 0 & 1 \\ 1 & 0 \end{bmatrix}$

Now $AI_2 = \begin{bmatrix} a & b \\ c & d \end{bmatrix}\begin{bmatrix} 0 & 1 \\ 1 & 0 \end{bmatrix} = \begin{bmatrix} b & a \\ d & c \end{bmatrix}$

AI_2 is matrix having first column same as the second column of A.

9. Given Equation is

$$x + 2y = 5$$
$$4x + 8y = 12$$
$$3x + 6y + 3z = 15$$

Now we can write above equations as

$$\begin{bmatrix} 1 & 2 & 0 \\ 4 & 8 & 0 \\ 3 & 6 & 3 \end{bmatrix}\begin{bmatrix} x \\ y \\ z \end{bmatrix} = \begin{bmatrix} 5 \\ 12 \\ 15 \end{bmatrix}$$

Augmented matrix [A: B] is given as

$$\begin{bmatrix} 1 & 2 & 0 & : & 5 \\ 4 & 8 & 0 & : & 12 \\ 3 & 6 & 3 & : & 15 \end{bmatrix}$$

Now perform

$R_2 = R_2 - 4R_1$

$R_3 = R_3 - 3R_1$

then

$$\begin{bmatrix} 1 & 2 & 0 & : & 5 \\ 0 & 0 & 0 & : & -8 \\ 0 & 0 & 3 & : & 0 \end{bmatrix}$$

So Rank of A = 2 and Rank [A : B] = 3

If Rank (A : B)> Rank (A) then System is inconsistent and has no solutions.

10. Given Matrix is

$$\begin{bmatrix} 1 & 4 & 8 & 7 \\ 0 & 0 & 3 & 0 \\ 4 & 2 & 3 & 1 \\ 3 & 12 & 24 & 21 \end{bmatrix}$$

$R_4 = R_4 - 3R_1$

$$\begin{bmatrix} 1 & 4 & 8 & 7 \\ 0 & 0 & 3 & 0 \\ 4 & 2 & 3 & 1 \\ 0 & 0 & 0 & 0 \end{bmatrix}$$

So Rank of Matrix is 3.

11. $$\Delta = \begin{bmatrix} 1 & a & bc \\ 1 & b & ca \\ 1 & c & ab \end{bmatrix}$$

$R_2 = R_2 - R_1$

$R_3 = R_3 - R_1$

$$= \begin{vmatrix} 1 & a & bc \\ 0 & (b-a) & -c(b-a) \\ 0 & (c-a) & -b(c-a) \end{vmatrix}$$

$$= \begin{vmatrix} (b-a) & -c(b-a) \\ (c-a) & -b(c-a) \end{vmatrix}$$

$$= (b-a)(c-a)\begin{vmatrix} 1 & -c \\ 1 & -b \end{vmatrix}$$

$= (b–a)\ (c–a)\ (–b + c)$

$= (a - b)\ (b - c)\ (c - a)$

So $(a - b)$ is factor of Δ.

12. Let V is 2 × 2 Matrix then

$$V = \begin{bmatrix} 0 & -1 \\ 1 & 0 \end{bmatrix}$$

Sum of all elements of array is 0.

13. Given Matrix is

$$\begin{bmatrix} 2 & 0 & 0 & 0 \\ 8 & 1 & 7 & 2 \\ 2 & 0 & 2 & 0 \\ 9 & 0 & 6 & 1 \end{bmatrix}$$

$$\text{Determinant} = 2 \times \begin{vmatrix} 1 & 7 & 2 \\ 0 & 2 & 0 \\ 0 & 6 & 1 \end{vmatrix}$$

$$= 2 \times 1 \times \begin{vmatrix} 2 & 0 \\ 6 & 1 \end{vmatrix} = 2 \times 1 \times 2 = 4$$

14. By properly of matrix.

[*] The sum of two singular matrix may be non singular.

[*] The sum of two non singular matrix may be singular.

15. $$M = \begin{vmatrix} 1 & 1 \\ 0 & 0 \end{vmatrix}$$

In above matrix only on independent row so Rank (M) = 1.

16. The eigen value of upper triangular Matrix one diagonal elements.

So 1, 2, –2, –1 are eigen values,

17. The augmented Matrix is

$$[A : B] = \begin{bmatrix} 2 & 1 & -4 & : & \propto \\ 4 & 3 & -12 & : & 5 \\ 1 & 2 & -8 & : & 7 \end{bmatrix}$$

Per form $R_2 = R_2 - R_1$

$R_3 = R_3 - 1/2R_1$

$$\begin{bmatrix} 2 & 1 & -4 & : & \propto \\ 0 & 1 & -4 & : & 5-2\propto \\ 0 & 3/2 & -6 & : & 7-\propto/2 \end{bmatrix}$$

Perform $R_3 = R_3 - \frac{3}{2}R_2$

$$\begin{bmatrix} 2 & 1 & -4 & : & \propto \\ 0 & 1 & -4 & : & 5-2\propto \\ 0 & 0 & 0 & : & \frac{5\propto -1}{2} \end{bmatrix}$$

Now for infinite many solution

$\frac{5\propto -1}{2}$ must be 0. So the value of $\propto$ is 1/5 i.e. there exist only one value of $\propto$ that gives infinite may solutions

18. Given that

$$\begin{aligned} ABCD &= I \\ ABCDD^{-1}C^{-1} &= D^{-1}C^{-1} \\ AB &= D–1\,C–1 \\ A^{-1}AB &= A^{-1}D^{-1}C^{-1} \\ B &= A^{-1}\,D^{-1}\,C^{-1} \\ B^{-1} &= (A^{-1}\,D^{-1}C^{-1})^{-1} \\ &= (C–1)^{-1}.\,(D–1)^{-1}.\,(A–1)^{-1} \\ &= CDA \end{aligned}$$

19. Equations are

$$\begin{aligned} x + 2y + 3Z &= 6 - (1) \\ x + 3y + 4Z &= 8 - (2) \\ 2x + 2y + 3Z &= 12 - (3) \end{aligned}$$

Put x = 6, y = 6, Z = –4 then all there equations are satisfies.

20. Matrix A can be expanded using first row as $|A_n| = 3*|A_{n-1}| + 1*|A_{n-2}|$ so the recurrence relation is

$T_n = 3T_{n-1} + T_{n-2}$

$Tn - 3T_{n-1} - T_{n-2} = 0$ –(1)

Equation (1) is homogenous system equation whose solution is

$$T_n = C_1\left(\frac{3+\sqrt{5}}{2}\right)^n + C_2\left(\frac{3-\sqrt{5}}{2}\right)^n$$

After putting the initial conditiar

$$T_1 = |3| = 3 \ \& \ T_2 = \begin{vmatrix} 3 & 1 \\ 1 & 3 \end{vmatrix} = 8$$

we get,

$$\left(\frac{3\sqrt{5}}{2}\right)^{n-1}\left(\frac{3\sqrt{5}+7}{2\sqrt{5}}\right) + \left(\frac{3-\sqrt{5}}{2}\right)^{n-1}\left(\frac{3\sqrt{5}-7}{2\sqrt{5}}\right)$$

21. Given $X = \begin{bmatrix} \propto & 1 \\ -\propto^2 + \propto - 1 & 1-\propto \end{bmatrix}$

and $X^2 - X + I = 0$

So $X - X^2 = I$

Multiply X^{-1} in both the side.

$X^{-1}(X - X^2) = X^{-1}$

$I - X = X^{-1}$

$$X^{-1} = \begin{bmatrix} 1 & 0 \\ 0 & 1 \end{bmatrix} - \begin{bmatrix} \propto & 1 \\ -\propto^2 + \propto + 1 & 1-\propto \end{bmatrix}$$

$$= \begin{bmatrix} 1-\propto & -1 \\ -\propto^2 - \propto + 1 & \propto \end{bmatrix}$$

22. The augmented Matrix is

$$[A : B] = \begin{bmatrix} -1 & 5 & : & -1 \\ 1 & -1 & : & 2 \\ 1 & 3 & : & 3 \end{bmatrix}$$

Perform $R_2 = R_2 + R_1$ and $R_3 = R_3 + R_1$

$$= \begin{bmatrix} -1 & 5 & : & -1 \\ 0 & 4 & : & 1 \\ 0 & 8 & : & 2 \end{bmatrix}$$

Perform $R_3 = R_3 - 2R_2$

$$= \begin{bmatrix} 1 & 5 & : & -1 \\ 0 & 4 & : & 1 \\ 0 & 0 & : & 0 \end{bmatrix}$$

Rank [A] = Rank [A:B] = 2 = Number of Variables.
So uniqul solution Exists.

23. $$A = \begin{bmatrix} 0 & 1 & 0 & 2 \\ -1 & 1 & 1 & 3 \\ 0 & 0 & 0 & 1 \\ 1 & -2 & 0 & 1 \end{bmatrix}$$

Expanding A by third row

$$A = -1\begin{vmatrix} 0 & 1 & 0 \\ -1 & 1 & 1 \\ 1 & -2 & 0 \end{vmatrix}$$

$$= -1 \times 1 \times \begin{vmatrix} -1 & 1 \\ 1 & 0 \end{vmatrix}$$

$= -1 \times 1 \times -1 = 1$

24. The augmented Martix is

$$\begin{bmatrix} 2 & -1 & 3 & : & 1 \\ 3 & -2 & 5 & : & 2 \\ -1 & -4 & 0 & : & 3 \end{bmatrix}$$

Perform $R_2 = R_2 - 3/2\, R_1$

$R_3 = R_3 + R\, 1/2$

$$\begin{bmatrix} 2 & -1 & 3 & : & 1 \\ 0 & -1/2 & 1/2 & : & 1/2 \\ 0 & -9/2 & 5/2 & : & 7/2 \end{bmatrix}$$

Per form $R_2 = R_2 - 9R_2$

$$\begin{bmatrix} 2 & -1 & 3 & : & 1 \\ 0 & -1/2 & 1/2 & : & 1/2 \\ 0 & 0 & -2 & : & -1 \end{bmatrix}$$

Rank (A/B) = 3 = R (A)

Number of Variables.

i.e. system has uniqul Solution

25. $A = \begin{bmatrix} 2 & -1 \\ -4 & 5 \end{bmatrix}$

The characteristic equation of this matrix is given by

$|A - \pi I| = 0$

$$\begin{vmatrix} 2-\pi & -1 \\ -4 & 5-\pi \end{vmatrix} = 0$$

on solving above

$\pi 2 - 7\pi + 6 = 0$

$\pi = 1, 6$

So two eigen values are there 1 and 6.

26. Eithere two identical rows or if there is two idential columns still determinate is zero.

27. Sum of eigen value = Trace (P)

Product of Eigen values = |P|

So Trace (P) = a + a + a = 3a

Product is $|P| = a(a^2 - 1) - a = a^3 - 2a$

28. Characteristic equation of A is

$$\begin{vmatrix} 3-\pi & 1 \\ 1 & 2-\pi \end{vmatrix} = 0$$

$$\pi^2 - 5\pi + 5 = 0$$

So eigen value are

$$\left\{\frac{5+\sqrt{5}}{2}, \frac{5-\sqrt{5}}{2}\right\}$$

The required answer is the maximum

Eigen Value of $A = \frac{5\sqrt{5}}{2}$

29. $X = \{x \in R^3 \mid x_1 + x_2 + x_3 = 0\}$

$X^T = [x_1, x_2, x_3]^T$ then

$\{[1, -1, 0]^T, [1, 0, -1]^T\}$ is a linearly independent set because one cannot be obtained from another by scalar multiplication. However $(1, -1, 0)$ and $(1, 0, -1)$ do not span X, since all such combinations (x_1, x_2, x_3) such that $x_1 + x_2 + x_3 = 0$ cannot be exp-ressed as linear combinations of $(1, -1, 0)$ $(1, 0, -1)$.

30. The augmented Matrix for above system is

$$[A : B] = \begin{bmatrix} 1 & 1 & 2 & : & 1 \\ 1 & 2 & 3 & : & 2 \\ 1 & 4 & a & : & 4 \end{bmatrix}$$

Perform $R_2 = R_2 - R_1$ and $R_3 = R_3 - R_1$

$$= \begin{bmatrix} 1 & 1 & 2 & : & 1 \\ 0 & 1 & 1 & : & 1 \\ 0 & 3 & a-2 & : & 3 \end{bmatrix}$$

Now $R_3 = 3R_2$

$$= \begin{bmatrix} 1 & 1 & 2 & : & 1 \\ 0 & 1 & 1 & : & 1 \\ 0 & 0 & a-5 & : & 0 \end{bmatrix}$$

Now as long as $a-5 \neq 0$, rank (A) = rank (A : B) = 3. So a can take any real value except 5.

31. (*i*) $\begin{bmatrix} 1 & 0 \\ 0 & 0 \end{bmatrix}$

$$\therefore \quad \begin{bmatrix} 1-\lambda & 0 \\ 0 & -\lambda \end{bmatrix} = 0$$

$$\Rightarrow \quad (1-\lambda)(-\lambda) = 0$$

Hence eigen values are

$$\lambda = 0, 1$$

(*ii*) $\begin{bmatrix} 0 & 1 \\ 0 & 0 \end{bmatrix}$

$$\therefore \quad \begin{bmatrix} 0-\lambda & 1 \\ 0 & -\lambda \end{bmatrix} = 0$$

$$\Rightarrow \quad (-\lambda)(-\lambda) = 0$$

Hence eigen values are $\lambda = 0, 0$

(*iii*) $\begin{bmatrix} 1 & -1 \\ 1 & 1 \end{bmatrix}$

$$\therefore \quad \begin{bmatrix} 1-\lambda & -1 \\ 1 & 1-\lambda \end{bmatrix} = 0$$

$$\Rightarrow \quad (1-\lambda)^2 + 1 = 0$$

$$\lambda^2 - 2\lambda + 2 = 0$$

$$\Rightarrow \quad \lambda \neq 1$$

(*iv*) $\begin{bmatrix} -1 & 0 \\ 1 & -1 \end{bmatrix}$

$$\therefore \quad \begin{bmatrix} -1-\lambda & 0 \\ 1 & -1-\lambda \end{bmatrix} = 0$$

$$\Rightarrow \quad (-1-\lambda)(-1-\lambda) - 1 = 0$$

$$\Rightarrow \quad (1+\lambda)^2 - 1 = 0$$

$$\Rightarrow \quad \lambda^2 + 2\lambda + = 0$$

Hence eigen values are $\lambda = 0, -2$

32. All statements are true.

33. Sum of eigen value = Trace (A)

So $\quad 2 + y = 12$

i.e = y = 10

Product of Eigen values = |A|

$$2y - 3x = 4 \times 8$$

$$2y - 3x = 32$$

Put y = 10 then x = – 4

34. The given Matrix is upper triangular so eigen values are 1,4 and 3.

35. From the matrix

$$A = \begin{bmatrix} 1 & 1 \\ 1 & -1 \end{bmatrix} \quad A^2 = 2\begin{bmatrix} 1 & 0 \\ 0 & 1 \end{bmatrix} = 2I$$

Where $\quad I = 2 \times 2$ unit matrix

So $\quad A^{19} = (A^2)^9 . A = (2I)^9 A = 2^9 A$

Now, to get Eigen values, we must solve the equation.

$$[\lambda I - A^{19}] = 0$$

$$\begin{vmatrix} \lambda - 2^9 & -2^9 \\ -2^9 & \lambda + 2^9 \end{vmatrix} = 0$$

$$\Rightarrow \quad \lambda^2 - 2^{18} - 2^{18} = 0$$

$$\Rightarrow \quad \lambda = \pm 512\sqrt{2}$$

36. Given :

$$\text{A matrix} \begin{vmatrix} 1 & x & x^2 \\ 1 & y & y^2 \\ 1 & z & z^2 \end{vmatrix}$$

To find: Which of the options are not equal to given matrix?

Analysis: Lets try to transform over the given matrix.

$$\begin{vmatrix} 1 & x & x^2 \\ 1 & y & y^2 \\ 1 & z & z^2 \end{vmatrix} \xrightarrow{C_2 \to C_2 + C_1} \begin{vmatrix} 1 & x+1 & x^2 \\ 1 & y+1 & y^2 \\ 1 & z+1 & z^2 \end{vmatrix}$$

$$\text{option } (b) : \to \begin{vmatrix} 1 & x+1 & x^2+1 \\ 1 & y+1 & y^2+1 \\ 1 & z+1 & z^2+1 \end{vmatrix} \; C_3 \to C_3 + C_1$$

$$\begin{vmatrix} 1 & x & x^2 \\ 1 & y & y^2 \\ 1 & z & z^2 \end{vmatrix} \xrightarrow[R_2 \to R_2 + R_3]{R_1 \to R_1 + R_2} \begin{vmatrix} 1 & x+y & x^2+y^2 \\ 1 & y+z & y^2+z^2 \\ 1 & z & z^2 \end{vmatrix}_{:\to \text{option (D)}}$$

$$\begin{vmatrix} 1 & x & x^2 \\ 1 & y & y^2 \\ 1 & z & z^2 \end{vmatrix} \xrightarrow[R_2 \to R_2 - R_3]{R_1 \to R_1 - R_2} \begin{vmatrix} 0 & x-y & x^2-y^2 \\ 0 & y-z & y^2-z^2 \\ 1 & z & z^2 \end{vmatrix}_{\text{option (C)}}$$

We are able to generate option B, C, and D from given matrix.

Hence, option a can be the possible solution, so lets try to operate on option A to see if we can prove it.

$$\begin{vmatrix} . & 0(y+1) & y+1 \\ 1 & z(z+1) & z+1 \end{vmatrix} \to C_3 \to C_3 - C_1$$

$$\begin{vmatrix} 1 & x^2 & x \\ 1 & y^2 & y \\ 1 & z^2 & z \end{vmatrix} \xleftarrow{C_2 \to C_2 - C_3} \begin{vmatrix} 1 & x^2+x & x \\ 1 & y^2+y & y \\ 1 & z^2+z & z \end{vmatrix}$$

We know, if we interchange any two columns of a matrix its determinan gets multiplied by '–1'.

Option (*a*) is formed from given matrix by interchanging column 2 and 3

$$\text{Hence} \begin{vmatrix} 1 & x & x^2 \\ 1 & y & y^2 \\ 1 & z & z^2 \end{vmatrix} = - \begin{vmatrix} 1 & x(x+1) & x+1 \\ 1 & y(y+1) & y+1 \\ 1 & z(z+1) & z+1 \end{vmatrix}$$

Hence (*a*) is the answer.

37. $3x + 2y = 1$

$4x + 7z = 1$

$x + y + z = 3$

$x - 2y + 7z = 0$

$$\text{Augmented matrix is} \begin{bmatrix} 3 & 2 & 0 & 1 \\ 4 & 0 & 7 & 1 \\ 1 & 1 & 1 & 3 \\ 1 & -2 & 7 & 0 \end{bmatrix}$$

$$R_1 \leftrightarrow R_3 \begin{bmatrix} 1 & 1 & 1 & 3 \\ 4 & 0 & 7 & 1 \\ 3 & 2 & 0 & 1 \\ 1 & -2 & 7 & 0 \end{bmatrix}$$

$R_2 \to R_2 - 4R_1$ $R_3 \to R_3 - 3R_1$, $R_4 \to R_4 - R_1$

$$\begin{bmatrix} 1 & 1 & 1 & 3 \\ 0 & -4 & 3 & -11 \\ 0 & -1 & -3 & -8 \\ 0 & -3 & 6 & -3 \end{bmatrix}$$

$$\begin{matrix} R_3 \to 4R_3 - R_2 \\ R_4 \to 4R_4 - 3R_2 \end{matrix} \begin{bmatrix} 1 & 1 & 1 & 3 \\ 0 & -4 & 3 & -11 \\ 0 & 0 & -15 & -21 \\ 0 & 0 & 15 & 21 \end{bmatrix}$$

$$R_4 \to R_4 + R_3 \begin{bmatrix} 1 & 1 & 1 & 3 \\ 0 & -4 & 3 & -11 \\ 0 & 0 & -15 & -21 \\ 0 & 0 & 0 & 0 \end{bmatrix}$$

$\rho(A : B) = \rho(A) = 3$ = no. of variables

$\therefore$ Unique solution exists

38. The eigen vectors corresponding to distinct eigen values of real symmetric matrix are orthogonal.

39. $A = \begin{bmatrix} 2 \\ -4 \\ 7 \end{bmatrix} [1\,9\,5]$

$$A = \begin{bmatrix} 2 & 18 & 10 \\ -4 & -36 & -20 \\ 7 & 63 & 35 \end{bmatrix}$$

$$|A| = 2(-36 \times 35 + 20 \times 63) - 18(-4 \times 35 + 140) + 10(-4 \times 63 + 36 \times 7)$$

$$= 2(-1260 + 1260) - 18(-140 + 140) + 10(-252 + 252) = 0$$

40. $A = \begin{bmatrix} 1 & 0 & 0 & 0 & 1 \\ 0 & 1 & 1 & 1 & 0 \\ 0 & 1 & 1 & 1 & 0 \\ 0 & 1 & 1 & 1 & 0 \\ 1 & 0 & 0 & 0 & 1 \end{bmatrix}$

$$\text{Let } X = \begin{bmatrix} x_1 \\ x_2 \\ x_3 \\ x_4 \\ x_5 \end{bmatrix}$$

$$Am = Xm \Rightarrow x_1 + x_5 = m\,x_1 = m\,x_5$$

$$\Rightarrow x_2 + x_3 + x_4 = m\,x_2 = m\,x_4$$

For $m \neq 0$

Say, $x_1 = x_5 = a$

$x_2 = x_3 = x_4 = b$

$\Rightarrow \quad x_1 + x_5 = m\,x_1$

$\Rightarrow \quad 2a = m\,a$

$\Rightarrow \quad m = 2$

$\Rightarrow \quad x_2 + x_3 + x_4 = m\,x_2$

$\therefore \quad 3b = mb$

$\therefore \quad m = 3$

For $m = 0 \Rightarrow$ eigenvalue $m = 0$

$\therefore$ There are 3 distinct eigen value = 0, 2, 3.

Product of non zero eigen value = $2 \times 3 = 6$.

41. If the trace of the matrix is positive and the determinant of the matrix is negative then atleast one of its eigen values is negative.

Since determinant = product of eigen values.

42. Let the basis of 6-dimensional vector space be {e1, e2, e3,e4, e5, e6}. In order for V1 ∩ V2 to have smallest possible dimension V1 and V2 could be, say, {e1, e2, e3,e4} and {e3, e4, e5, e6} respectively. The basis of V1 ∩ V2 would then be {e3, e4}. => Smallest possible dimension = 2.

43. $P(x) = x^5 + 4x^3 + 6x + 5$

$= x(x(x(x^2 + 4)) + 6) + 5$

So
```
t = x * x;
t = t + 4;
t = x * t;
t = x * t;
t = t + 6;
t = x * t;
t = t + 5;
```

So 7 Arithmetic operations needed.

44. Sum of Eigen values = Trace (matrix)

$6 = 1 + 9 \Rightarrow a = 5$

Product of eigen values = |Matrix|

$-7 = a\ \ 4b$

so $\boxed{b = 3}$

45. The given matrix is

$$A = \begin{bmatrix} 4 & 5 \\ 2 & 1 \end{bmatrix}$$

Inorder to find eigen values of above matrix

$|A - \lambda I| = 0$

$$\therefore \begin{vmatrix} 4-\lambda & 5 \\ 2 & 1-\lambda \end{vmatrix} = 0$$

$\therefore\ (4 - \lambda)(1 - \lambda) - 10 = 0$

$\therefore\ 4 - 5\lambda + \lambda^2 - 10 = 0$

$\therefore\ \lambda^2 - 5\lambda - 6 = 0$

$\therefore\ \lambda^2 - 6\lambda + 1\lambda - 6 = 0$

$\therefore\ \lambda(\lambda - 6) + 1(\lambda - 6) = 0$

$\therefore\ \lambda + 1 = 0$ or λ

$\therefore\ \lambda = -1$ or $\lambda = 6$

$\therefore$ Larger eigen value of matrix is 6

46. The given matrix is

$$A = \begin{bmatrix} 3 & 4 & 45 \\ 7 & 9 & 105 \\ 13 & 2 & 195 \end{bmatrix}$$

Now according to question

(*i*) $R_2 \to R_2 + R_3$ (Adding third row to the second row)

$$\therefore \quad B = \begin{bmatrix} 3 & 4 & 45 \\ 20 & 11 & 300 \\ 13 & 2 & 195 \end{bmatrix}$$

(*ii*) $C_1 \to C_1 - C_3$ (subtracting third column from first column)

$$\therefore \quad C = \begin{bmatrix} -42 & 4 & 45 \\ -280 & 11 & 300 \\ -182 & 2 & 195 \end{bmatrix}$$

Now $|C| = -42(2145 - 600) - 4(-54600 + 54600) + 45(-560 + 2002)$

$\therefore\ |C| = -42(1545) - 4(0) + 45(1442)$

$= -64890 + 64890 = 0$

47. $AX = \pi X$

Use vector given in optiomn (b)

$$\begin{bmatrix} 1 & -1 & 2 \\ 0 & 1 & 0 \\ 1 & 2 & 1 \end{bmatrix}\begin{bmatrix} 4 \\ 2 \\ 1 \end{bmatrix} = 1x\begin{bmatrix} -4 \\ 2 \\ 1 \end{bmatrix}$$

So the above equation is satisfied.

48. $$\begin{bmatrix} L11 & 0 \\ L21 & L22 \end{bmatrix}\begin{bmatrix} 1 & U_{12} \\ 0 & 1 \end{bmatrix} = \begin{bmatrix} 2 & 2 \\ 4 & 9 \end{bmatrix}$$

$$\begin{bmatrix} L11 & L11 \times U12 \\ L21 & L21 \times U12 + L22 \end{bmatrix} = \begin{bmatrix} 2 & 2 \\ 4 & 9 \end{bmatrix}$$

So $L_{11} = 2,\ L_{21} = 4$

$L_{11} \times U_{12} = 2$ i.e. $2\times U_{12} = 2 \Rightarrow [U_{12} = 1]$

$L_{21} \times U_{12} + L_{22} = 9$

$4\times 1 + L_{22} = 9$

$[L_{22} = 5]$

49. The system has non – trival solutions if $|A| = 0$

$$\text{So,} \begin{vmatrix} p & q & r \\ q & r & p \\ r & p & q \end{vmatrix} = 0$$

$R_1 = R_1 + R_2 + R_3$

Then $\begin{vmatrix} p+q+r & p+q+r & p+q+r \\ q & r & p \\ r & p & q \end{vmatrix}$

[i] if p+q+r = 0 then

$$\begin{vmatrix} 0 & 0 & 0 \\ q & r & p \\ r & p & q \end{vmatrix} = 0$$

[ii] if p = q = r then

$$\begin{vmatrix} 3p & 3p & 3p \\ p & p & p \\ p & p & p \end{vmatrix} \text{ So determinate ps 0.}$$

50. $(2 + i)$ is an eigenvalue

So $(2 - i)$ will be other.

So Determinant will be product of eigenvalues.

So $|A| = (2 + i)(2 - i) \times 3$

$(2^2 - i^2) \times 3 = 15$

51. Statement I

Consider 2 equations in three variables.

$x - y + z = 1$

$-x + y - z = 2$

This system has no solution (inconsistent)

x = 1 and y = 1

∴ Statement I is false

Statement II

Consider 3 equations in two variables.

$x + y = 2,$

$x - y = 0,$

$3x + y = 4$

This system has a unique solution

∴ Statement II is false.

Statement III

Consider a system with 2 equations and two variables

$x + y = 2$ and $x - y = 0$.

The system has a solution x = 1 and y = 1

∴ Statement III is true

52. Given the eigen values of matrix A is

$$\lambda = 1, 2, 4$$

$$|A| = 1 \times 2 \times 4 = 8$$

$$\Rightarrow \quad |A^{-1}| = \frac{1}{|A|} = \frac{1}{8}$$

$$\therefore \quad \left|\left(A^{-1}\right)^T\right| = |A^{-1}| = \frac{1}{8} = 0.125$$

So the determinant of $(A^{-1})^T$ is $\frac{1}{8}$ (i.e. 0.125).

53. The equation Ax = b becomes according to the given data is

$$[a1 \ldots\ldots an]\begin{bmatrix} x1 \\ xn \end{bmatrix} = a1 + a2 + \ldots\ldots an$$

Now given that $\sum ciai = 0$

it means n column vectors are not linearly independent. Hence rank (A) < n. So it has infinite many solutions.

54. Both statments are false.

55. By adding both P and Q

$$P + Q = \begin{bmatrix} 0 & -1 & -2 \\ 8 & 9 & 10 \\ 8 & 8 & 8 \end{bmatrix}$$

Magnitude of P & Q

$$|P+Q| = -16 + 16 = 0$$

So rank ≠ 3

rank < 3

Take the 2 × 2 minor $\begin{bmatrix} 0 & -1 \\ 8 & 9 \end{bmatrix} = 8 \neq 0$

So, rank of P + Q is 2

56. $f(\lambda) = \lambda^3 - 4\lambda^2 + a\lambda + 30 = 0$

Given $m = 2$ will be one root of polynomial

So, $\quad 2^3 - 4 \times 2^2 + a \times 2 + 30 = 0$

$\Rightarrow \quad 8 - 16 + 2a + 30 = 0$

$\Rightarrow \quad a = -11$ (satisfy the equation)

So, the equation is $\lambda^3 - 4\lambda^2 - 11\lambda + 30 = 0$

Divided polynomials by $(\lambda - 2)$

$$\frac{\lambda^3 - 4\lambda^2 - 11\lambda + 30}{\lambda - 2} = \lambda^2 - 2\lambda - 15$$

roots of $\lambda^2 - 2\lambda - 15 = 0$ are

$$\lambda = \frac{2 \pm \sqrt{4+60}}{2} = \frac{2+8}{2} = 5 \text{ and } -3$$

$\lambda_1 = 2$ $\lambda_2 = 5$ $\lambda_3 = 3$ the maximum absolute eigen value is 5.

57. $$u = \begin{pmatrix} 1 \\ 2 \end{pmatrix}, v = \begin{pmatrix} 1 \\ 1 \end{pmatrix}$$

$$A = uv^T = \begin{pmatrix} 1 \\ 2 \end{pmatrix}[1 \quad 1] = \begin{bmatrix} 1 & 1 \\ 2 & 2 \end{bmatrix}$$

Now $\quad |A - \lambda I| = 0$

$$\left|\begin{bmatrix} 1 & 1 \\ 2 & 2 \end{bmatrix} - \begin{bmatrix} \lambda & 0 \\ 0 & \lambda \end{bmatrix}\right| = 0$$

$$\begin{vmatrix} 1-\lambda & 1 \\ 2 & 2-\lambda \end{vmatrix} = 0$$

$\therefore \quad (1-\lambda)(2-\lambda)-2=0$

$$\lambda^2-3\lambda=0$$

$$\lambda(\lambda-3)=0$$

$$\lambda=0 \text{ or } \lambda=3$$

$\therefore$ The largest eigen value is 3.

58. Only Eigen vector is $\begin{bmatrix}1\\4\end{bmatrix}$ multiples means that eigen value is repeated since if eigen values were distinct we will get one more independent eigen vector. So, II P has repeated eigen values is true. I need not be true since $\begin{bmatrix}2&0\\0&2\end{bmatrix}$ has repeated eigen values and yet it is invertible. III is true since if matrix has repeated eigen values then it cannot be diagonalizable.

60. Product of eigen values is same as the determinant of a matrix.

$$\begin{bmatrix}1&2&2^2&2^3\\1&3&3^2&3^3\\1&4&4^2&4^3\\1&5&5^2&5^3\end{bmatrix}=\begin{bmatrix}1&2&2^2&2^3\\0&3-2&3^2-2^2&3^3-2^3\\0&4-2&4^2-2^2&4^3-2^3\\0&5-2&5^2-2^2&5^3-2^3\end{bmatrix}$$

$$=(3-2)(4-2)(5-2)\begin{bmatrix}1&5&19\\1&6&28\\1&7&39\end{bmatrix}$$

$$=1.2.3\begin{bmatrix}1&5&19\\0&1&9\\0&2&20\end{bmatrix}=1\times2\times3\times2=12$$

So the product of eigen value is 12.

CALCULUS

1. The slope of tongent $= -\dfrac{2x}{y}$

i.e. $\dfrac{dy}{dx}=-\dfrac{2x}{y}$

$ydy=-2x\,dx$

Integrating both the side

$\int ydy=\int -2ydx$

$$\frac{y^2}{2}=-2*\frac{x^2}{2}+C$$

$$\frac{y^2}{2}+x^2=C$$

it is in the form of $\dfrac{x^2}{a^2}+\dfrac{y^2}{b^2}=C$

So the curve is ellipse with

$a=1$ & $b=\sqrt{2}$

2. The formula for first derivation of a function f at a point x_0 is

$$f'(x_0)=\frac{f(x_0+h)-f(x_0)}{h}$$

So for second derivation it is

$$f''(x_0)=\frac{f'(x_0)-f'(x_0-h)}{h}$$

$$=\frac{\left[\dfrac{f(x_0+h)=f(x_0)}{h}-\dfrac{f(x_0)-f(x_0-h)}{h}\right]}{h}$$

$$=\frac{f(x_0+h)-2f(x_0)+f(x_0-h)}{h^2}$$

3. at x = 0 the value of f(x) is 6

at x = 2 the value of f (x) is 10

4. The function $y=|x|$ in internal [–1, 1] is

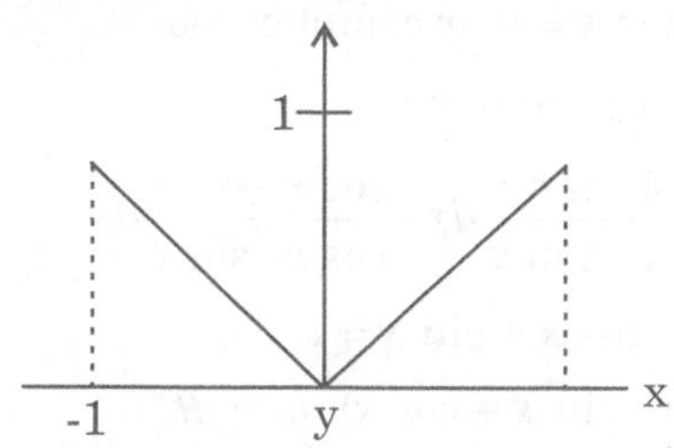

$|x|$ is continos and differentiable every where except at x = 0, where it is continuor but not differentiable.

5. $\int_0^{2\pi}(x-\pi)^3\cos x dx=0$

iff $f(2\pi-x)=-f(x)$

6. $\int_{-\infty}^{0} e^{-x2/2}dx$

Companing with area under the standard normal curve we get

$$\frac{1}{\sqrt{2\pi}}\int_{-\infty}^{0} e^{-x2/2}dx=0.5\Rightarrow\sqrt{\pi/2}$$

7. The minimum value is 2(1/12)

8. $f(x)=|x|$ is continuous for all values of x but it is not differentiable at x = 0

9.
$$\lim_{x\to\infty}\frac{x-\sin x}{x+\cos x}=\lim_{x\to\infty}\frac{x(1-\sin x/x)}{x(1+\cos x/x)}$$

$$=\lim_{x\to\infty}\frac{x1-\sin x/x}{x1+\cos x/x}$$

$$=\frac{1-\lim\limits_{x\to\infty}\dfrac{\sin x}{x}}{1+\lim\limits_{x\to\infty}\dfrac{\cos x}{x}}=\frac{1-0}{1+0}=1$$

10. Given : $y = 3x^4 - 16x^3 + 24x^2 + 37$

For maximum value or minimum

$$\frac{dy}{dx} = 12x^3 - 18x^2 + 43x = 0$$

$$\Rightarrow \quad x(x^2 - 4x + 4) = 0$$

$$\Rightarrow \quad x(x-2)^2 = 0$$

$$\Rightarrow \quad x = 0, 2, 2$$

$$\frac{d^2 y}{dx^2} = 36x^2 - 96x + 48$$

At $x = 0$, $\frac{d^2 y}{dx^2} = +48$

At $x = 2$, $\frac{d^2 y}{dx^2} = 36 \times 4 - 96 \times 2 + 48 = 0$

so only 1 local minima.

either $x = 0$ or complex root

so only value = 0

11. $$\frac{1-\tan x}{1+\tan x}dx = \frac{\cos x - \sin x}{\cos x + \sin x}dx$$

Let $\cos x + \sin x = t$

$\Rightarrow (-\sin x + \cos x)\, dx = dt$

$$\therefore \int \left(\frac{1}{t}\right) dt = \ln t$$

$$= \ln(\sin x + \cos x)$$

$$= \ln\left(\sin\frac{\pi}{4} + \cos\frac{\pi}{4}\right)$$

$$= \ln\left(\frac{1}{\sqrt{2}} + \frac{1}{\sqrt{2}}\right) = \frac{1}{2}\ln 2$$

12. $$\lim_{n\to\infty}\left(1-\frac{1}{n}\right)^{2n} = \left(\lim_{n\to\infty}\left(1-\frac{1}{n}\right)^{-n}\right)^{2}$$

$$= (e)^{-2} = e^{-2}$$

$$\left[\text{because } \lim_{n\to\infty}\left(1-\frac{1}{f(x)}\right)^{-f(x)}\right.$$

13. $$\int_0^{\pi/2}\frac{\text{Cosx} + i\sin x}{\text{Cosx} - i\sin x} = \int_0^{\pi/2}\frac{e^{ix}}{e^{-ix}}$$

{bydemoivre's theorm}

$$= \int_0^{\pi} e^{2in} dx \Rightarrow \left[\frac{e^{2ix}}{2i}\right]_0^{\pi\backslash 2}$$

$$= \frac{1}{2i}\left[e^{i\pi} - e^{o}\right] \Rightarrow \frac{1}{2i}[-1-1] = i$$

14.

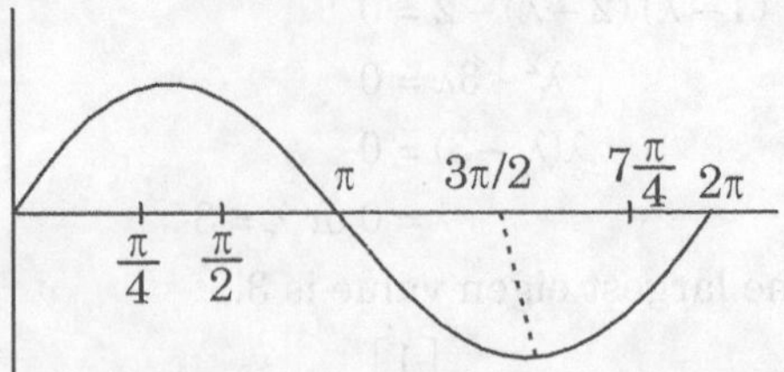

From the above graph we can easily see that in the range [π/4, 7π/4] , there is only one local minimam, at 3π/2.

15. Continuous at $x = 3$?

(a) $$f(x) = \begin{cases} 2 & \text{if } x = 3 \\ x-1 & \text{if } x > 3 \\ \frac{x+3}{3} & \text{if } x < 3 \end{cases}$$

$$\underset{x\to 3-}{\text{Lt}} f(x) = \underset{x\to 3-}{\text{Lt}} \frac{x+3}{3} = 2$$

$$\underset{x\to 3+}{\text{Lt}} f(x) = \underset{x\to 3+}{\text{Lt}} x - 1 = 2$$

$$\therefore \underset{x\to 3-}{\text{Lt}} f(x) = f(x)\big|_{x=3} = \underset{x\to 3+}{\text{Lt}} f(x)$$

$\Rightarrow$ This is continuous at $x = 3$

(b) $$f(x) = \begin{cases} 4 & \text{if } x = 3 \\ 8-x & \text{if } x \neq 3 \end{cases}$$

Option (*b*) is false

$$\underset{x\to 3^-}{\text{Lt}} = \underset{x\to 3^-}{\text{Lt}} 8 - x$$

$$= 5 \neq f(x)\big|_{x=3}$$

(c) $$f(x) = \begin{cases} x+3 & \text{if } x \le 3 \\ x-4 & x > 3 \end{cases}$$

$$\underset{x\to 3^+}{\text{Lt}} f(x) = \underset{x\to 3^+}{\text{Lt}} x - 4$$

$$f(x)\big|_{x=3} = 3 + 3 = 6 = -1$$

$$\underset{x\to 3^+}{\text{Lt}} f(x) \neq f(x)\big|_{x=3}$$

Option (*c*) is false

(d) $$f(x) = \frac{1}{x^3 - 27} \text{ if } x \neq 3$$

16. By Mean value theorem.

17. f(x) = x sin x

f'(x) = x cos x + sin x

f" (x) = (–x sin x + cos x) + cos x

f" (x) + f (x)+ t cos x = 0

⇒ –x sinx + cos x + cos x + x sin x + t cos x = 0

⇒ [t = – 2]

18. There exists a y in the interval (0,1) such that f(y) = f (y+1).

19. Given that polynomials are continuoay and since there is a 3 roots in the interval (0,1) by intermediate value theorm, surely f (o) f (4) < 0°.

20. $\int_0^{2\pi} |x\sin x| dx = K\pi$

$\Rightarrow \int_0^{\pi} x\sin x\, dx + \int_{\pi}^{2\pi} -(x\sin x)\, dx = K\pi$

$\left[\because |\sin x| = -\sin x \quad \pi < x < 2\pi\right]$

$\Rightarrow \quad x(-\cos x) - 1(-\sin x)\Big|_0^{\pi} - (-x\cos x + \sin x)\Big|_{\pi}^{2\pi} = K\pi$

$\Rightarrow \quad (-\pi\cos\pi + \sin\pi) - 0 - \left[(-2\pi\cos 2\pi + \sin 2\pi)\right.$

$\left. - (-\pi\cos\pi + \sin\pi)\right] = K\pi$

$\Rightarrow \pi + 0 - \left[-2\pi + 0 - (\pi + 0)\right] = K\pi$

$\Rightarrow \quad 4\pi = K\pi$

$\Rightarrow \quad K = 4$

21. $\int_0^{\pi} x^2 \text{wsx}dx = \left[x^2 \sin x\right]_0^{\pi} - 2\int_0^{\pi} x\sin x\, dx$

$= o - \int_0^{\pi} x\sin xdx = -\int_O^{\pi} x\sin xdx$

$= -2\pi$

22. $\lim_{x\to\infty} x^{1/x} = (\infty)^0 = 1$

$\therefore$ Option (*c*) is correct.

23. $\int_{1/\pi}^{2/\pi} \frac{\text{Cos}(1/x)}{x^2} dx = (-1)\int_{1/\pi}^{2/\pi} \frac{-1}{x^2} \text{Cos}\left(\frac{1}{x}\right)$

Let $\frac{1}{x} = t \Rightarrow dt = -1/x^2$

So, $\quad -1\int_{\pi}^{\pi/2} \text{Cost}\, dt \Rightarrow \int_{\pi/2}^{\pi} \text{Cost}\, dt$

$\Rightarrow [\text{Sint}]_{\pi/2}^{\pi} \Rightarrow [0 - 1] \Rightarrow -1$

24. (2) f is not bounded in [–1,1]. since at x = 0 it goes to – ∞ and –∞ the function is not bounded.

(3) A is non zero and finile

$A = \left|\int_{-1}^{0} x^{-1/3} dx\right| + \left|\int_0^1 x^{-1/3} dx\right|$

$= \frac{3}{2} + \frac{3}{2} = 3$

25. $y = \lim_{x\to\infty} \left(1 + x^2\right)e^{-x}$

Apply log both the side

$\log y = \lim_{x\to\infty} \log\left(1 + x^2\right)e^{-x} = \lim_{x\to\infty} \frac{\log\left(1 + x^2\right)}{e^{+x}}$

Apply L hospital rule

$\Rightarrow \log y = \lim_{x\to\infty} \frac{\frac{1}{1+x^2}(2x)}{e^x}$

$\log y = \lim_{x\to\infty} \frac{2x}{\left(1 + x^2\right)e^x}$

Again apply L hospital's rule

$\log y = \lim_{x\to\infty} \frac{2}{\left(1 + x^2\right)e^x + e^x.2x}$

$\log y = \frac{2}{\infty} = 0$

$y = 1$

26. $af(x) + b.f\left(\frac{1}{x}\right) = \frac{1}{x} - 25 \qquad ...(1)$

$\Rightarrow \quad af\left(\frac{1}{x}\right) + b.f(x) = x - 25 \qquad ...(2)$

Solving, we get

$f(x) = \frac{1}{a^2 - b^2}\left[a\left(\frac{1}{x} - 25\right) - b(x - 25)\right]$

$\therefore \int_1^2 f(x)dx = \frac{1}{a^2 - b^2}\left[a\{\ln x - 25x\}_1^2 - b\left\{\frac{x^2}{2} - 25x\right\}_1^2\right]$

$= \frac{1}{a^2 - b^2}\left[a\{\ln 2 - 25\} - b\left\{\frac{3}{2} - 25\right\}\right]$

$= \frac{1}{a^2 - b^2}\left[a\{\ln 2 - 25\} + \frac{47}{2}b\right]$

27. $\lim_{x\to y} \frac{\text{Sin}(x - 4)}{(x - 4)}$

Let x–4 = t

$\lim_{t\to 0} \frac{\text{Sint}}{t} = 1$

28. From the given question

If f(x) is a polynomial of degree 'n'

Then f′(x) is a polynomial of degree (n – 1)

f(x) + f(–x) is a polynomial of degree 10

$\therefore$ g(x) – g(–x) is a polynomial of degree 9

: 10 : SET-2 Afternoon Session

(OR)

If degree of {f(x) + f(x)} = 10, then the largest even exponent of x in f(x) = 10.

Now, the largest odd exponent of x in g(x) = 9

$\therefore$ degree of {g(x) – g(–x)} = 9

29. $\lim_{t\to 1} \frac{x^7 - 2x^5 + 1}{x^3 - 3x^2 + 2} = \frac{0}{0}$ form

Apply L hospital's rule

$= \lim_{t\to 1} \frac{7x^6 - 10x^4}{3x^3 - 3x} = \frac{7 - 10}{3 - 6} = \frac{-3}{-3} = 1$

30. $x^2 - 13x + 36 = 0$

In base b $\quad 13 = 1 \times b^1 + 3 \times b^0 = b + 3$

In base b $\quad 36 = 3 \times b^1 + 6 \times b^0$

$= 3b + 6$

So the equation becomes

$$x^2 - (b+3)x + (3b+6) = 0$$

Now since it is given that x = 5 is a solution , so

$$5^2 - (b+3)\,5 + (3b+6) = 0$$

$$\Rightarrow \quad -2b + 16 = 0$$

$$\Rightarrow \quad b = 8$$

Same can be obtained by putting $x = 6$ also.

31. Given,

$$f(x) = \mathrm{R}\sin\left(\frac{\pi x}{2}\right) + \mathrm{S}, \quad ...(1)$$

Given $\quad f'\left(\frac{1}{2}\right) = \sqrt{2} \quad ...(2)$

$$\int_0^1 f(x)\,dx = \frac{2\mathrm{R}}{\pi} \quad ...(3)$$

Now we need to find R and S.

$$f'(x) = \mathrm{R}\cos\left(\frac{\pi x}{2}\right)\frac{\pi}{2}$$

$$f'\left(\frac{1}{2}\right) = \mathrm{R}\cos\left(\frac{\pi}{4}\right) \times \frac{\pi}{2} = \sqrt{2}$$

$$\Rightarrow \quad \frac{\mathrm{R}}{\sqrt{2}} \times \frac{\pi}{2} = \sqrt{2}$$

$$\Rightarrow \quad \mathrm{R} = \frac{4}{\pi}$$

Now, $\quad \int f(x)\,dx = \int \mathrm{R}\sin\frac{\pi x}{2} + \mathrm{S}$

Putting $\quad \mathrm{R} = \frac{4}{\pi}$ we get

$$\int f(x)\,dx = \int \frac{4}{\pi}\sin\left(\frac{\pi x}{2}\right)dx + \int \mathrm{S}\,dx$$

$$= \frac{4}{\pi} \times -\frac{\cos\left(\frac{\pi x}{2}\right)}{\frac{\pi}{2}} + \mathrm{S}x$$

$$= \frac{-8}{\pi^2}\cos\left(\frac{\pi x}{2}\right) + \mathrm{S}x$$

Putting limit 0 and 1

$$\int_0^1 f(x)\,dx = \frac{-8}{\pi^2}\left(\cos\frac{\pi}{2} - \cos(0)\right) + \mathrm{S}(1-0)$$

$$= \frac{2\mathrm{R}}{\pi}$$

$$\Rightarrow \quad \frac{-8}{\pi^2}(0-1) + \mathrm{S} = \frac{2\mathrm{R}}{\pi}$$

Put $\mathrm{R} = \frac{4}{\pi}$ and solve for S

$$\Rightarrow \quad \mathrm{S} = 0$$

So, $\mathrm{R} = \frac{4}{\pi}$ and S = 0 is answer.

32. $\int_0^{\pi/4} x\cos\left(x^2\right)\,dx$

Let, $\quad t = x^2$

$$\therefore \quad \frac{dt}{dx} = 2x$$

$$dt = 2x\,dx$$

$$\Rightarrow \quad xdx = xdx = \frac{dt}{2}$$

when $x = 0 \Rightarrow t = 0$ and when $x = \frac{\pi}{4} \Rightarrow t = \left(\frac{\pi}{4}\right)^2$

So required integral reduce to

$$\int_0^{(\pi/4)^2} \cos t\,dt = [\sin t]_0^{(\pi/4)^2}$$

$$= \sin\left(\frac{\pi}{4}\right)^2 - \sin(0)$$

$$= \sin\left(\frac{\pi}{4}\right)^2 = 0.28898$$

$$\simeq 0.289$$

(rounded to 3 decimal places)

33. $\lim\limits_{x\to3}\frac{x^4 - 81}{2x^2 - 5x - 3}\left(\frac{0}{0}\text{form}\right)$

Now applying L′ Hospital rule we get

$$= \lim_{x\to3}\frac{4x^3}{4x-5} = \frac{108}{7}$$

Unit - II

Theory of Computation

Syllabus

Regular expressions and finite automata. Context-free grammars and push-down automata. Regular and contex-free languages, pumping lemma. Turing machines and undecidability.

Contents

1 CHAPTER Introduction and Finite Automata

Analysis of Previous GATE Papers											
Units	**Year → Topics ↓**		**2019**	**2018**	**2017 Set 1**	**2017 Set 2**	**2016 Set 1**	**2016 Set 2**	**2015 Set 1**	**2015 Set 2**	**2015 Set 3**
STRTING & LANGUAGES	**1 Mark**	MCQ Type									
		Numerical Type									
	2 Marks	MCQ Type									
		Numerical Type									
	Total										
ALPHABET	**1 Mark**	MCQ Type									
		Numerical Type									
	2 Marks	MCQ Type									
		Numerical Type									
	Total										
DFA	**1 Mark**	MCQ Type									
		Numerical Type			1	1		1			
	2 Marks	MCQ Type									
		Numerical Type	1						1	1	
	Total		2		1	1		1	2	2	
NFA	**1 Mark**	MCQ Type		1							
		Numerical Type									
	2 Marks	MCQ Type				1					
		Numerical Type									
	Total			1		2					
AUTOMATA & GRAMMAR	**1 Mark**	MCQ Type					1				
		Numerical Type									
	2 Marks	MCQ Type			1					1	
		Numerical Type									
	Total				2		1			2	

STRTING & LANGUAGES

1. How many substrings (of all lengths inclusive) can be formed from a character string of length n? Assume all characters to be distinct. Prove your answer. **[1989 : 2 Marks]**

2. The number of substrings (of all lengths inclusive) that can be formed from a characted string of length n is

   (a) n (b) n^2

   (c) $\frac{n(n-1)}{2}$ (d) $\frac{n(n+1)}{2}+1$

   [1994 : 2 Marks]

3. Which of the following definitions below generates the same language as L

   Where $L = \{x^n y^n \mid n \geq 1 \mid$

   (i) $E \rightarrow xEy \mid xy$

   (ii) $xy \mid (x^+xyy^+)$

   (iii) x^+y^+

   (a) (i) only (b) (i) and (ii)

   (c) (ii) and (iii) (d) (ii) only

   [1995 : 2 Marks]

4. Given $\Sigma = \{a, b\}$, which one of the following sets is not countable?

   (a) Set of the strings over Σ

   (b) Set of all language over Σ

   (c) Set of all regular languages over Σ

   (d) Set of all languages over Σ accepted by Turing Machines **[1997 : 1 Mark]**

5. The string 1101 does not belong to the set represented by

   (a) 110*(0+1) (b) 1(0+1)*0101

   (c) (10)*(01)*(00+11)* (d) (00+(11)*0)*

   [1998 : 1 Mark]

6. How many substrings of different lengths (non-zoro) can be formed from a character string of length n?

   (a) n (b) n^2

   (c) 2^n (d) $\frac{n(n+1)}{2}$

   [1998 : 1 Mark]

7. Consider the following languages:

   $L_1 = \{ww \mid w \in \{a,b\}^*\}$

   $L_2 = \{ww^R \mid w \in \{a, b\}^*, w^R$ is the reverse of w$\}$

   $L_3 = \{0^{2i} \mid$ i is an interger$\}$

   $L_4 = \{0^{i^2} \mid$ i is an integer$\}$

   Which of the languages are regular?

   (a) Only L_1 and L_2

   (b) Only L_2, L_3 and L_4

   (c) Only L_3 and L_4

   (d) Only L_3

   [2001 : 2 Marks]

8. If s is a string over (0+1)*, then let $n_0(s)$ denote the number of 0's in s and $n_1(s)$ the number of 1's in s. Which one of the following languages is not regular?

   (a) $L = \{s \in (0+1)^* \mid n_0(s)$ is a 3-digit prime$\}$

   (b) $L = \{s \in (0+1)^* \mid$ for every prefix s' of s, $|n_0(s') - n_1(s')| \leq 2\}$

   (c) $L = \{s \in (0+1)^* \mid |n_0(s) - n_1(s)| \leq 4\}$

   (d) $L = \{s \in (0+1)^* \mid n_0(s) \bmod 7 = n_1(s) \bmod 5 = 0\}$

   [IT-2006 : 2 Marks]

9. Given the language L = {ab, aa, baa}, which of the following strings are in L*?

   1. abaabaaabaa

   2. aaaabaaaa

   3. baaaaabaaaab

   4. baaaaabaa

   (a) 1, 2 and 3

   (b) 2, 3 and 4

   (c) 1, 2 and 4

   (d) 1, 3 and 4

   [2012 : 1 Mark]

10. The length of the shortest string NOT in the language (over $\Sigma = \{a, b\}$ of the following regular expression is ______.

    a*b*(ba)*a*

    [2014 (Set-3) : 1 Mark]

11. The C language is

    (a) A context free language

    (b) A context sensitive language

    (c) A regular language

    (d) Parsable fully only by a Turing machines

    [2002 : 2 Marks]

ALPHABET

12. Let R_1 and R_2 be regular sets defined over the alphabet then

    (a) $R_1 \cap R_2$ is not regular

    (b) $R_1 \cup R_2$ is not regular

    (c) $\Sigma^* - R_1$ is regular

    (d) $R_1{}^*$ is not regular **[1990 : 2 Marks]**

13. The two grammars given below generate a language over the alphabet {x, y, z}

G1: $S \to x \mid z \mid xS \mid zS \mid yB$

$B \to y \mid z \mid yB \mid zB \mid$

G2: $S \to y \mid z \mid yS \mid zS \mid xB$

$B \to y \mid yS$

Which one of the following choice describes the properties satisfied by the strings in these languages?

(a) G1 : No y appears before any x
G2 : Every x is following by at least one y

(b) G1 : No y appears before any x
G2 : No x appears before any y

(c) G1 : No y appears after any x
G2 : Every x is following by at least one y

(d) G1 : No y appears after any x
G2 : Every y is following by at least one x

[IT-2007 : 2 Marks]

14. Let Σbe a finite non-empty alphabet and let 2^{Σ^*} be the power set of Σ^*. Which one of the following is TRUE ?

(a) Both 2^{Σ^*} and Σ^* are countable

(b) 2^{Σ^*} is countable and Σ^* is uncountable

(c) 2^{Σ^*} is uncountable and Σ^* is countable

(d) Both 2^{Σ^*} and Σ^* are uncountable

[2014 (Set-3) : 1 Mark]

DFA

15. Which of the following set can be recognized by a Deterministic Finite state Automaton?

(a) The numbers 1, 2, 4, 8, ... 2^n, ... written in binary

(b) The numbers 1, 2, 4, ... 2^n, ... written in unary

(c) The set of binary string in which the number of zeros is the same as the number of ones,

(d) The set {1, 101, 11011, 1110111, ...}

[1998 : 1 Mark]

16. Let L be the set of all binary strings whose last two symbols are the same. The number of states in the minimum state deterministic finite state automaton accepting L is

(a) 2 (b) 5

(c) 8 (d) 3 **[1998 : 2 Marks]**

17. Consider a DFA over $\Sigma = \{a, b\}$ accepting all strings which have number of a's divisible by 6 and number of b's divisible by 8. What is the minimum number of state that the DFA will have?

(a) 8 (b) 14

(c) 15 (d) 48 **[2001 : 2 Marks]**

18. Consider the following deterministic finite state automaton M.

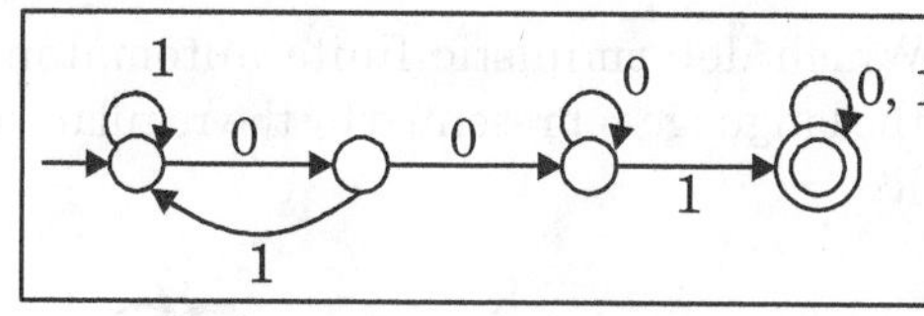

Let S denote the set of seven bit binary strings in which the first, the fourth, and the last bits are 1. The number of strings is S that are accepted by M is

(a) 1 (b) 5

(c) 7 (d) 8

[2003 : 2 Mark]

19. Consider the regular language L = (111+11111)*. The minimum number of states in any DFA accepting this language is

(a) 3 (b) 5

(c) 8 (d) 9

[IT-2006 : 2 Marks]

20. A minimum state deterministic finite automation accepting the language $L = \{w \mid w \in (0, 1)^*$, number of 0s & 1s in w are divisible by 3 and 5, respectively} has

(a) 15 states (b) 11 states

(c) 10 states (d) 9 states

[2007 : 2 Marks]

21. Consider the following DFA in which s_0 is the start state and s_1, s_3 are the final states.

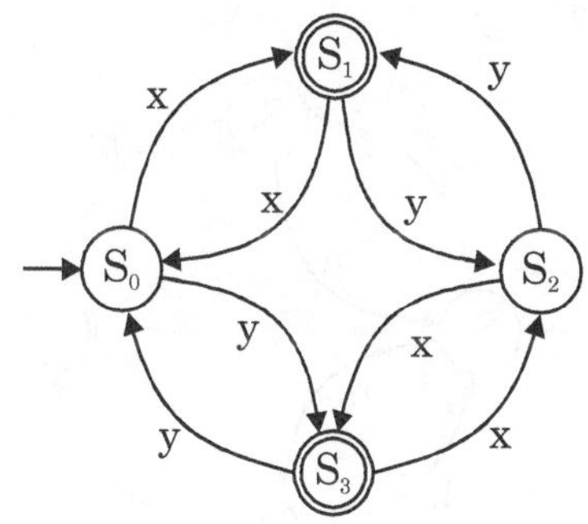

What language does this DFA recognize?

(a) All strings of x and y

(b) All strings of x and y which have either even number of x and even number of y or odd number or x and odd number of y

(c) All strings of x and y which have equal number of x and y

(d) All strings of x and y with either even number of x and odd number of y or odd number of x and even number of y

[IT-2007 : 2 Marks]

22. Consider the regular expression:

$R = (a+b)^* (aa+bb) (a+b)^*$

Which deterministic finite automaton accepts the language represented by the regular expression R?

(a) 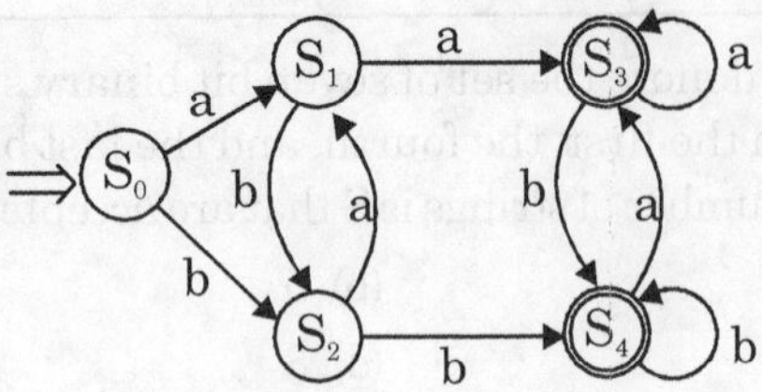

(b) 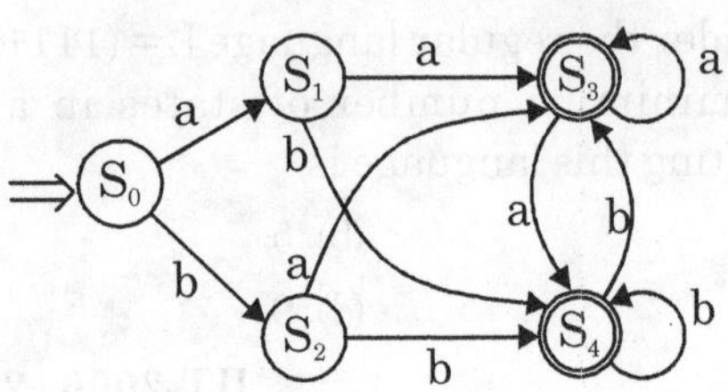

(c) 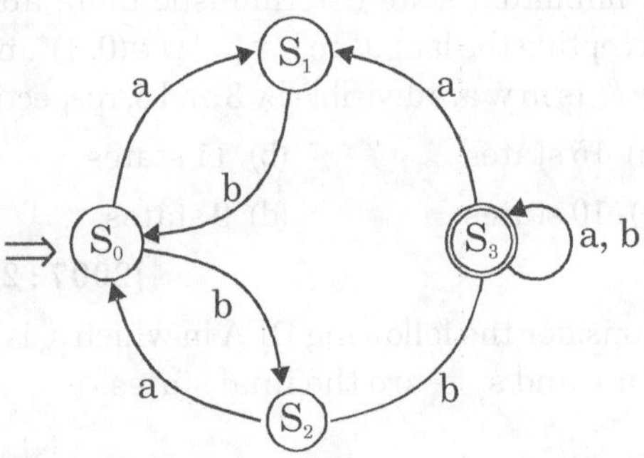

(d) 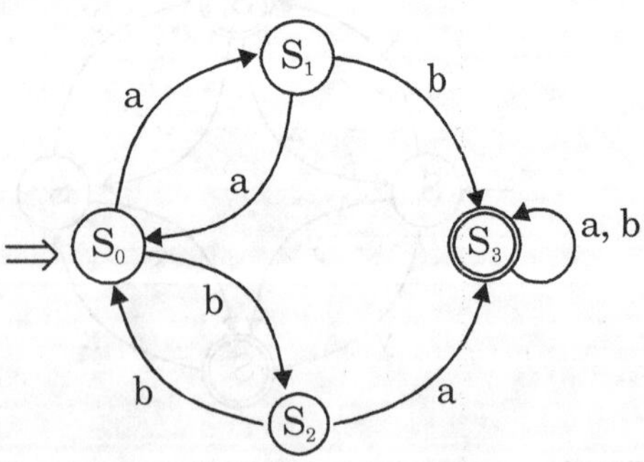

[IT-2007 : 2 Marks]

23. If the final states and non-final states in the DFA below are interchanged, then which of the following languages over the alphabet {a, b} will be accepted the the new DFA?

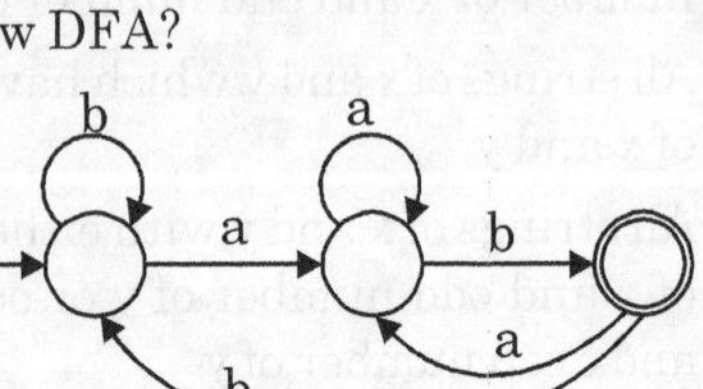

(a) Set of all strings that do not end with ab

(b) Set of all strings that begin with either an a or ab

(c) Set of all strings that do not contain the substring ab,

(d) The set described by the regular expression $b^*aa^*(ba)^*b^*$

[IT-2008 : 2 Marks]

24. The following DFA accepts the set of all strings over {0, 1} that

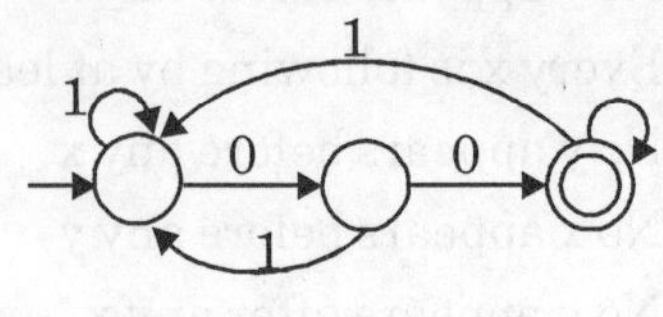

(a) begin either with 0 or 1

(b) end with 0

(c) end with 00

(d) contain the substring 00

[2010 : 2 Marks]

25. Definition of a language L with albhabet {a} is given as follows:

$L = \{a^{nk} \mid K > 0$, and n is a positive integer constant}.

What is the minimum number of states needed in a dfa to recognize L?

(a) k + 1
(b) n +1
(c) 2^{n+1}
(d) $^{2k+1}$

[2011 : 2 Marks]

26. A deterministic finite automaton (DFA) D with alphabe $\Sigma = \{a, b\}$ is given below:

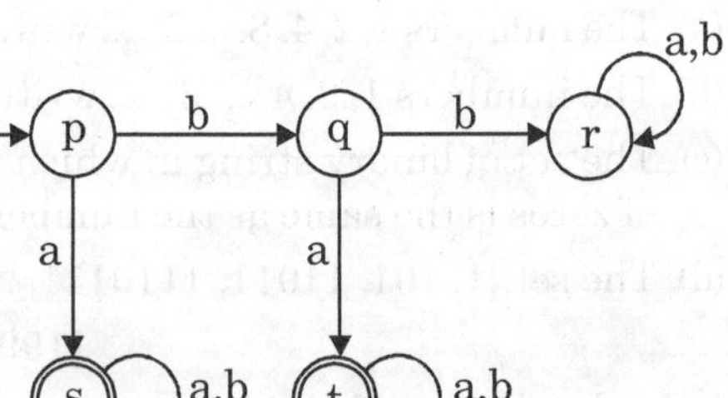

Which of the following finite state machines is a valid minimal DFA which accepts the same language as D?

(a) 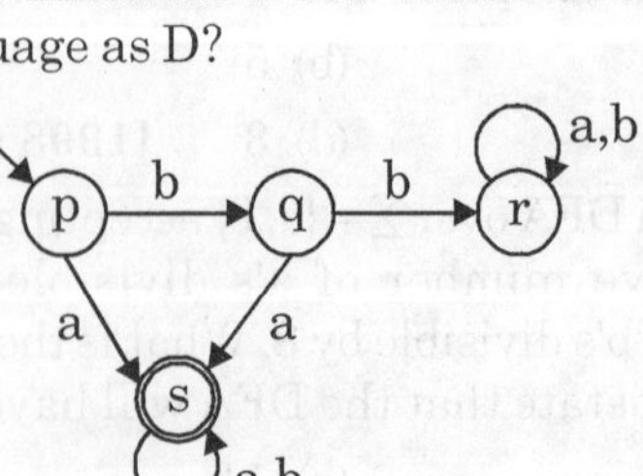

(b)

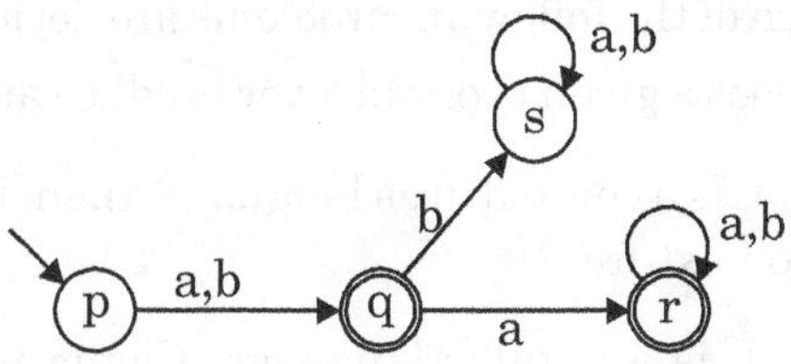

(c)

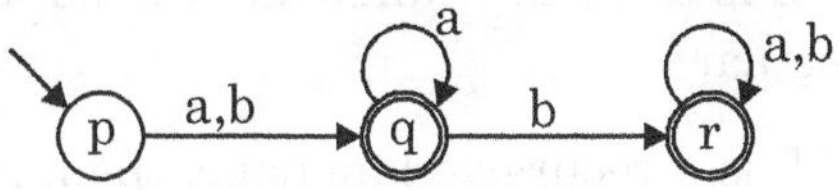

(d)

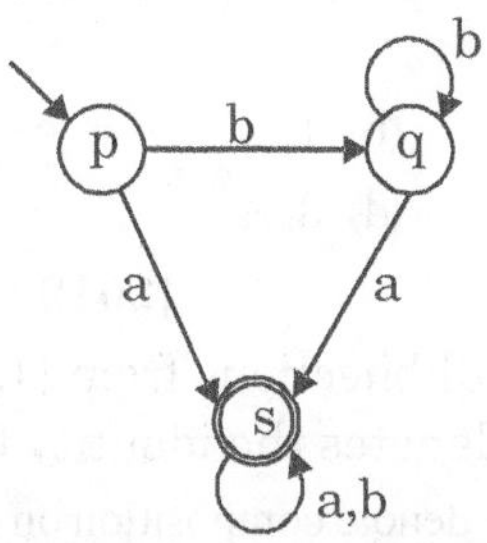

[2011 : 2 Marks]

27. Consider the set of strings on {0, 1} in which, every substring of 3 symbols has at most two zeros. For example. 001110 and 011001 are in the language, but 100010 ia not. All strings of length less than 3 are also in the language. A partially complete DFA that accepts this language is shown below.

The missing arcs in the DFA are

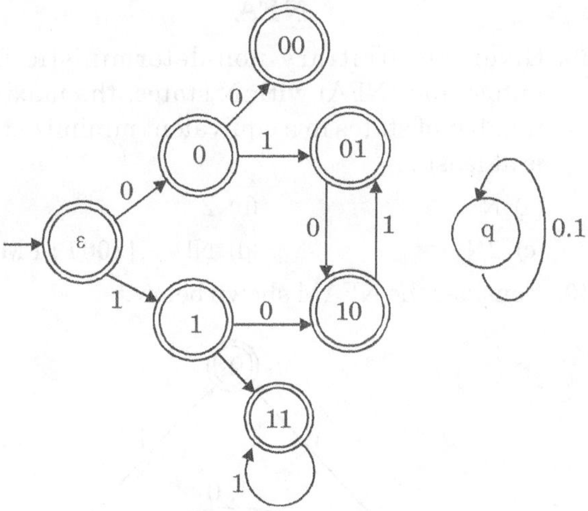

(a)

	00	01	10	11	q
00	1	0			
01				1	
10	0				
11			0		

(b)

	00	01	10	11	q
00		0			1
01		1			
10				0	
11		0			

(c)

	00	01	10	11	q
00		1			0
01		1			
10			0		
11		0			

(d)

	00	01	10	11	q
00		1			0
01				1	
10	0				
11			0		

[2012 : 2 Marks]

28. Consider the DFA A is given below:

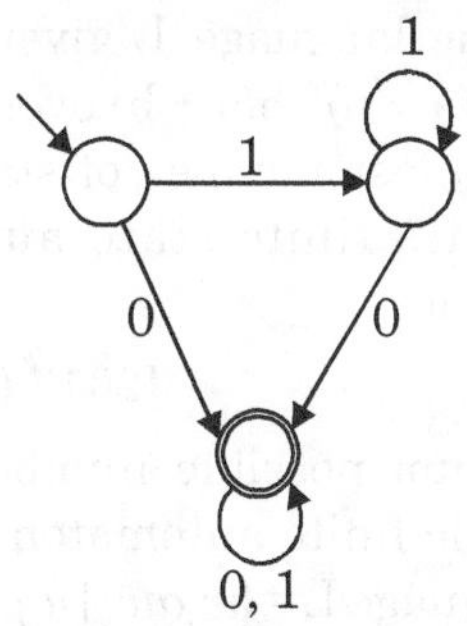

Which of the following are False?

1. Complement of L(A) is context-free.
2. L(A) = L(11 *0+0) (0 + 1)*0*1*)
3. For the language accepted by A, A is the minimal DFA.
4. A accepts all strings over {0, 1} of length at least 2.

(a) 1 and 3 only (b) 2 and 4 only
(c) 2 and 3 only (d) 3 and 4 only

[2013 : 2 Marks]

29. Which of the regular expression given below represent the following DFA?

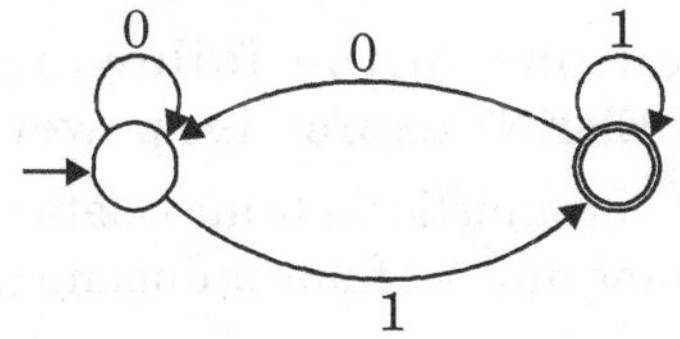

I. 0*1 (1 + 00* 1)* II. 0*1*1 + 11* 0* 1
III. (0 + 1)* 1

(a) I and II only
(b) I and III only
(c) II and III only
(d) I, II and III

[2014 (Set-1) : 2 Marks]

30. 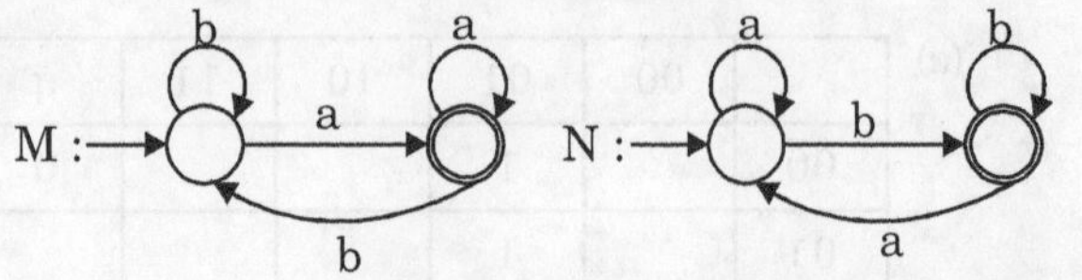

Consider the DFAs M and N given above. The number of states in minimal DFA that accepts the language L(M) ∩ L(N) is _____.

[2015 (Set-1 : 2 Marks]

31. The number of states in the minimal deterministic finite automaton corresponding to the regular expression (0+1)*(10) is ____.

[2015 (Set-2) : 2 Marks]

32. The number of states in the minimum sized DFA that accepts the language defined by the regular expression (0+1)* (0+1) (0+1)* is___.

[2016 (Set-2) : 1 Mark]

33. Consider the language L given by the regular expression (a + b)* b(a + b) over the alphabet {a, b}. The smallest number of states needed in a deterministic finite-state automaton (DFA) accepting L is _____.

[2017 (Set-1) : 1 Mark]

34. The minimum possible number of states of a deterministic finite automaton that accepts the regular language $L = \{w_1 a w_2 \mid w_1, w_2 \in \{a, b\}^*, |w_1| = 2, |w_2| \geq 3\}$ is ____.

[2017 (Set-2) : 1 Mark]

35. For s ∈ (0 + 1)* let d(s) denote the decimal value of s (e.g. d (101) = 5).

Let L = {s ∈ (0 + 1)* | d(s) mod 5 = 2 and d(s) mod 7 ≠ 4}

Which one of the following statements is true ?

(a) L is recursively enumerable, but not recursive
(b) L is recursive, but not context-free
(c) L is context-free, but not regular
(d) L is regular

[2006 : 2 Marks]

36. Which one of the following pairs have DIFFERENT expressive power

(a) Deterministic finite automata (DFA) and Non-deterministic finite automata (NFA).
(b) Determinstic push down automata (DPDA) and Non-deterministic push down automata (NPDA)
(c) Deterministic single-tape Turing machine and Non-deterministic single-tape Turing machine
(d) Single-tape Turing machine and multi-tape Turing machine

[2011 : 1 Mark]

37. Which of the following problems are decidable?

1. Does a given program ever produce an output?
2. If L is a context-free language, then, is $\bar{L}$ also context-free?
3. If L is a regular language, thenm is $\bar{L}$ also regular
4. If L is a recursive language, then, is $\bar{L}$ also recursive?

(a) 1, 2, 3, 4 (b) 1, 2
(c) 2, 3, 4 (d) 3, 4

[2012 : 1 Mark]

38. Let Σ be the set of all bijections from {1, ..., 5} to {1, ..., 5}, where id denotes the identity function, i.e. id(j) = j, ∀ j. Let ∘ denote composition on functions.

For a string $x = x_1x_2....x_n \in \Sigma^n, n \geq 0$,

let $\pi(x) = x_1 \circ x_2 \circ ... \circ x_n$.

Consider the language $L = \{\in \Sigma^* \mid \pi(x) = id\}$. The minimum number of states in any DFA accepting L is ____.

[2019: 2 Marks]

NFA

39. Given an arbitrary non-deterministic finite automaton (NFA) with N states, the maximum number of states in a equivalent minimized DFA is at least

(a) N^2 (b) 2^N
(c) 2N (d) N! **[2001 : 1 Mark]**

40. Consider the NFAM shown below.

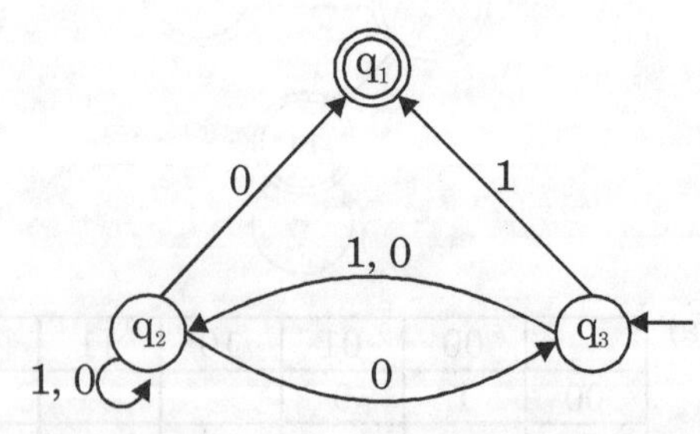

Let the language accepted by M be L. Let L_1 be the language accepted by the NFAM$_1$, obtained by changing the accepting state of M to a non-accepting state and by changing the non-accepting state of M to accepting states. Which of the following statemets is true?

(a) L_1 = {0, 1}*-L (b) L_1 = {0, 1}*
(c) $L_1 \subseteq L$ (d) $L_1 = L$

[2003 : 2 Marks]

41. Consider the non-deterministic finite automaton (NFA) shown in the figure.

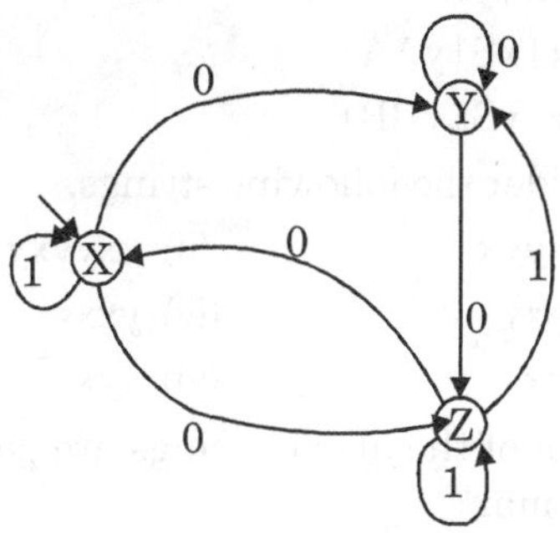

State X is the starting state of the automaton. Let the language accepted by the NFA with Y as the only accepting state be L1. Similarly, let the language accepted by the NFA with Z as the only accepting state be L2. Which of the following statements about L1 and L2 is TRUE?

(a) l1 = L2 (b) $L1 \subset L2$

(c) $L2 \subset L1$ (d) None of these

[IT-2005 : 2 Marks]

42. Consider the regular expression:

R = (a+b)* (aa+bb) (a+b)*

Which of the following non-deterministic finite automata recognizes the language defined by the regular expression R? Edges labeled λ denote transitions on the empty strings

(a) ⇒ 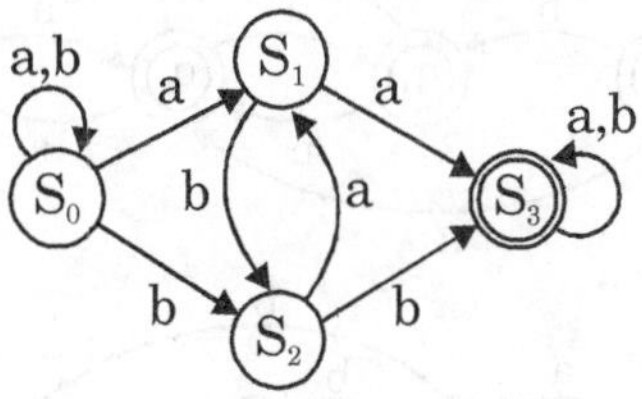

(b) ⇒ 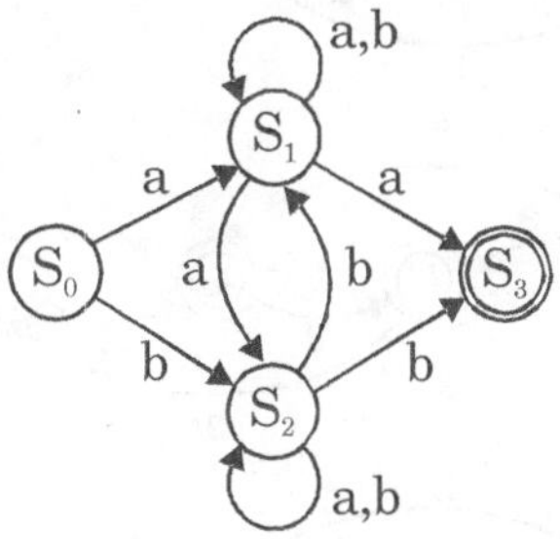

(c) ⇒ 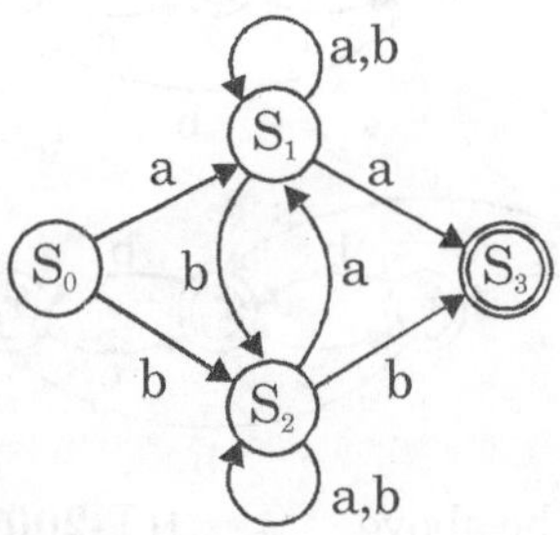

(d) ⇒ 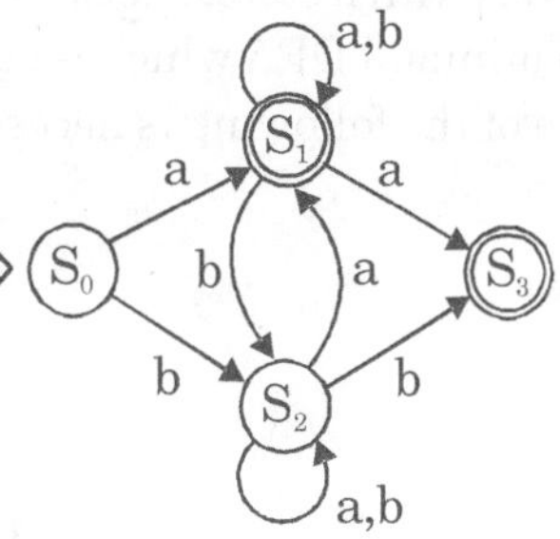

[IT-2007 : 2 Marks]

43. Let N be an NFA with n states and let M be the minimized DFA with m states recogniz-ing the same language. Which of the following in necessarily true?

(a) $m \leq 2^n$

(b) $n \leq m$

(c) M has one accept state

(d) $m = 2^n$

[IT-2008 : 1 Mark]

44. Let ω be any string of length n in {0, 1}*, Let L be the set of all substrings of ω. What is the minimum number of states in a non-deterministic finite automata that accepts L?

(a) n - 1 (b) n

(c) n + 1 (d) 2^{n+1}

[2010 : 2 Marks]

45. What is the complement of the language accepted by the NFA shown below? Assume $\Sigma = \{a\}$ and ε is the empty string.

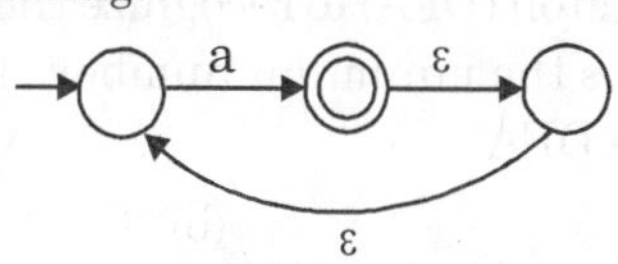

(a) ∅ (b) {ε}

(c) a* (d) {a, ε} **[2012 : 1 Mark]**

46. Let δ denote the transition function and $\hat{\delta}$ denote the extended transition function of the ε-NFA whose transition table is given below:

δ	∈	a	b
→ q_0	$\{q_2\}$	$\{q_1\}$	$\{q_0\}$
q_1	$\{q_2\}$	$\{q_2\}$	$\{q_3\}$
q_2	$\{q_0\}$	ϕ	ϕ
q_3	ϕ	ϕ	$\{q_2\}$

The $\hat{\delta}$ (q_2, aba) is

(a) ϕ (b) $\{q_0, q_1, q_3\}$

(c) $\{q_0, q_1, q_2\}$ (d) $\{q_0, q_2, q_3\}$

[2017 (Set-2) : 2 Marks]

47. Let N be an NFA with n states. Let k be the number of states of a minimal DFA which is equivalent to N. Which one of the following is necessarily true?

(a) $k \geq 2^n$

(b) $k \geq n$

(c) $k \leq n^2$

(d) $k \leq 2^n$

[2018 : 1 Mark]

AUTOMATA & GRAMMAR

48. Let L denotes the languate the language generated by the grammar $S \rightarrow 0S0 \mid 00$. Which of the following is true?

(a) $L = 0^+$

(b) L is regular but not 0^+

(c) L is context free but not regular

(d) L is not context free

[2000 : 1 Mark]

49. Consider the regular grammar:

$S \rightarrow Xa \mid Ya$

$X \rightarrow Za$

$Z \rightarrow Sa \mid \varepsilon$

$Y \rightarrow Wa$

$W \rightarrow Sa$

where S is the starting symbol, the set of terminals is {a} and the set of non-terminals is {S, W, X, Y, Z}. We wish to construct a deterministic finite automaton (DFA) to recognize the same language. What is the minimum number of states required for the DFA?

(a) 2 (b) 3

(c) 4 (d) 5

[IT-2005 : 2 Marks]

50. Conside the regular grammar below:

$S \rightarrow bS \mid aA \mid \varepsilon$

$A \rightarrow aS \mid bA$

The Myhill-Nerode equivalence classes for the language generated by the grammar are

(a) $\{w \in (a+b)^* \mid \#_a(w) \text{ is even}\}$ and $\{w \in (a+b)^* \mid \#_a(w) \text{ is odd}\}$

(b) $\{w \in (a+b)^* \mid \#_b(w) \text{ is even}\}$ and $\{w \in (a+b)^* \mid \#_b(w) \text{ is odd}\}$

(c) $\{w \in (a+b)^* \mid \#_a(w) = \#_b(w)\}$ and $\{w \in (a+b)^* \mid \#_a(w) \neq \#_b(w)\}$

(d) $\{\varepsilon\}$, $\{wa \mid w \in (a+b)^*\}$ and $\{wb \mid w \in (a+b)^*\}$

[IT-2006 : 2 Marks]

51. Consider the grammar given below:

$S \rightarrow xB \mid yA$

$A \rightarrow x \mid xS \mid yAA$

$B \rightarrow y \mid yS \mid yBB \mid$

Consider the following strings.

(i) xxyyx (ii) xxyyxy

(iii) xyxy (iv) yxxy

(v) yxx (vi) xyx

Which of the above strings are generated by the grammar?

(a) (i), (ii), and (iii) (b) (ii), (v), and (vi)

(c) (iii) and (iv) (d) (i), (ii), and (iv)

[IT-2007 : 2 Marks]

52. Consider the following finite automata P and Q over the alphabet {a, b, c}. The start states are indicated by a double arrow and final states are indicated by a double circle. Let the languages recognized by them be denoted by L(P) and (Q) respectively.

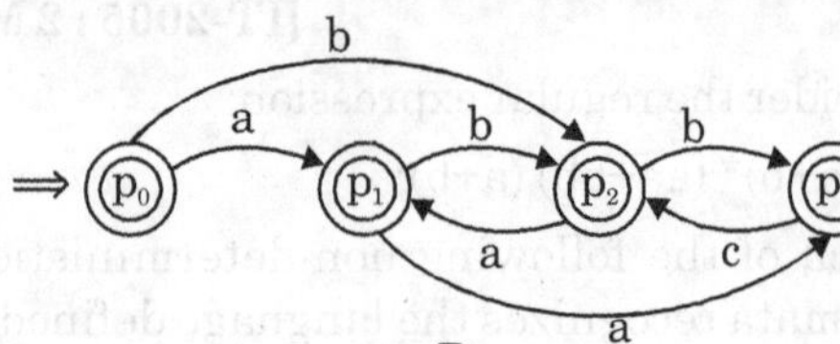

P

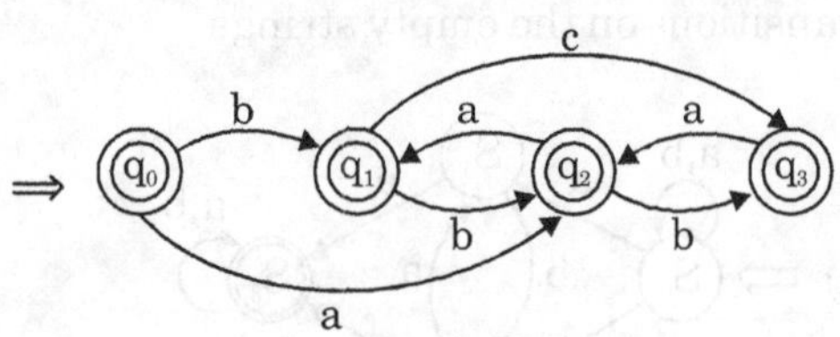

(a) 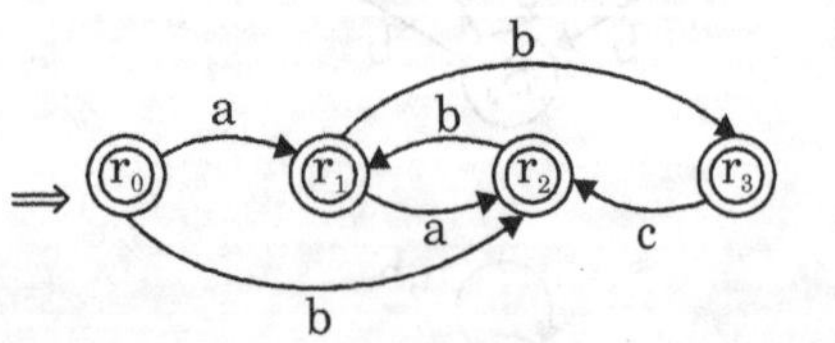

(b) 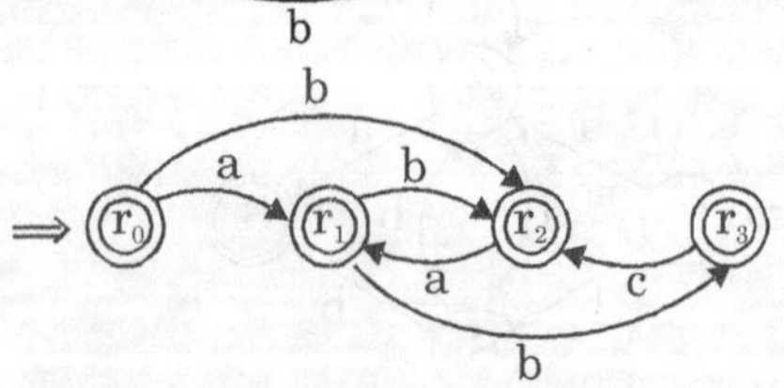

(c) 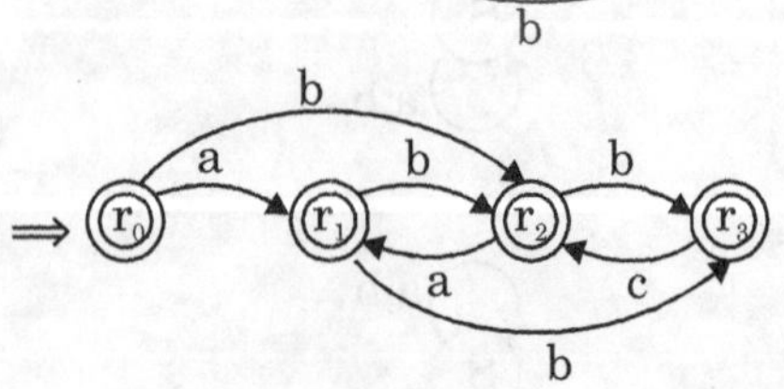

(d) 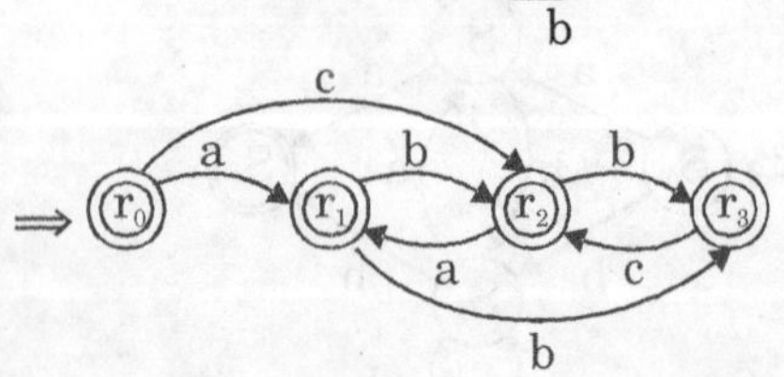

(e) None of the above

[IT-2007 : 2 Marks]

53. The lexical analysis for a modern computer language such as Java needs the power of which one of the following machine models in a necessary and sufficient sense?

(a) Finite state automata
(b) Deterministic pushdown automata
(c) Non-deterministic pushdown automata
(d) Turing machine

[2011 : 1 Mark]

54. Consider alphabe $\Sigma = \{0, 1\}$, the null/empty string λ and the sets of strings X_0, X_1 and X_2 generated by the corresponding non-terminals of a regular grammar. X_0, X_1 and X_2 are related as follows:

$X_0 = 1X_1$
$X_1 = 0X_1 + 1X_2$
$X_2 = 0X_1 + \{\lambda\}$

Which one of the following choices precisely represents the strings in X_2?

(a) 10(0*+(10)*)1
(b) 10(0*+(10)*)*1
(c) 1(0+10)*1
(d) 10(0+10)*1+110(0+10)*1

[2015 (Set-2) : 2 Marks]

55. Which of the following language is generated by the given grammar?

$$S \rightarrow aS \mid bS \mid \varepsilon$$

(a) $\{a^n b^m \mid n, m \geq 0\}$
(b) $\{w \in \{a,b\}^* \mid w$ has equal number of a's and b's$\}$
(c) $\{a^n \mid n \geq 0\} \cup \{b^n \mid n \geq 0\} \cup \{a^n b^n \mid n \geq 0\}$
(d) $\{a, b\}^*$

[2016 (Set-1) : 1 Mark]

56. If G is a grammar with productions

$$S \rightarrow SaS \mid aSb \mid bSa \mid SS \mid \epsilon$$

where S is the start variable, then which one of the following strings is not generated by G?

(a) *abab* (b) *aaab*
(c) *abbaa* (d) *babba*

[2017 (Set-1) : 2 Marks]

57. $S \rightarrow aSa \mid bSb \mid a \mid b$

The language generated by the above grammar over the alphabet {a, b} is the set of

(a) all palindromes
(b) all odd length palndromes
(c) strings that begin and end with the same symbol
(d) all even length palindromes

[2009 : 1 Mark]

ANSWERS

1. (*)	**2.** (*d*)	**3.** (*a*)	**4.** (*b*)	**5.** (*c*)	**6.** (*d*)	**7.** (*d*)	**8.** (*c*)	**9.** (*c*)	**10.** (3)
11. (*b*)	**12.** (c)	**13.** (*a*)	**14.** (*c*)	**15.** (*a*)	**16.** (*b*)	**17.** (*d*)	**18.** (*c*)	**19.** (*d*)	**20.** (*a*)
21. (*d*)	**22.** (*a*)	**23.** (*a*)	**24.** (*c*)	**25.** (*b*)	**26.** (*a*)	**27.** (*d*)	**28.** (*d*)	**29.** (*b*)	**30.** (1)
31. (3)	**32.** (2)	**33.** (4)	**34.** (8)	**35.** (*d*)	**36.** (*b*)	**37.** (*d*)	**38.** (120)	**39.** (*b*)	**40.** (*b*)
41. (*d*)	**42.** (*a*)	**43.** (*a*)	**44.** (*c*)	**45.** (*b*)	**46.** (*c*)	**47.** (*d*)	**48.** (*b*)	**49.** (*b*)	**50.** (*a*)
51. (*c*)	**52.** (*e*)	**53.** (*a*)	**54.** (*c*)	**55.** (*d*)	**56.** (*a*)	**57.** (*b*)			

EXPLANATIONS

1. Number of substrings (All lengths inclusive) can be formed from a character string of length n is determine by using the following formula.

$$\frac{n(n+1)}{2}+1$$

Example : If n = 3 and string is → abc

No. of substrings of 'O' length is 1 → λ (null)

No. of substring of 1 length is 3 → (a, b, c)

No. of subtring of 2 length is 2 → (ab, bc)

No. of subtring of 3 length is 1 → (abc)

So total No. of substrings is

$1 + 3 + 2 + 1 = 7$

So $\frac{n(n+1)}{2}+1 \Rightarrow \frac{3\times 4}{2}+1 = 7$

2. $\frac{n(n+1)}{2}+1$

By using this formula we can calculate the number of substrings (of all length inclusive)

for n = 3 total 7 strings are possible.

string = abc

substrings = {λ, a, b, c, ab, bc, abc}

3. $E \Rightarrow XEY \mid XY$

$$\begin{aligned} E &\Rightarrow XEY \\ &\Rightarrow XXEYY \\ &\Rightarrow XXXYYY \\ &\Rightarrow X^n\overline{Y}^n \end{aligned}$$

4. Set of all languages over Σ is incountable infinite set.

5. (*a*) 110* (0 + 1) = 1100, 1101

(*b*) 1 (0 + 1)* 101 = 10* 1* 101
= 101101

(*c*) (10)* (01) * (00 + 01)*
= (10)* (01)* (00)* (01)*
= 10 01 0001

(*d*) (00 + (11)* 0)*
= (00)* (11)* 0)*
= (00)* (110)*
= 00 110110

From above calculation (*c*) does not belong to 1101.

6. Total non-zero substring of different lengths from string of length n is

$$\frac{n(n+1)}{2}$$

Example n = 3, "abc"

substrings ⇒ {a, b, c, ab, bc, abc}

7. * 0^{2i} will regular when $i \geq 1$ [integer → 0 – *n*]
   * 0^{i2} will not regular when $i \geq 1$
   * {WWR (*a*, *b*)*, WR is the reverse of W} not regular.
   * (*a*, *b*) * (*b*, *a*)* not is regular.

[0^{i^2}, 0^{i^3}, 0^{2^n}, is not regular]

8. Choice (*a*) is regular since it is finite.

Choice (*b*) is regular since although comparison is made between 0's and 1's, it is for all prefixes and this can be done by dfa.

Note : $|n_0(s') - n_1(s')| \leq 2$ is same as $n_0(s') - n_1(s') \geq 2$ or $n_1(s') - n_0(s') \geq 2$.

Choice (*c*) involves comparison of number of 0's and 1's, but for the string as a whole, and this cannot be done by a dfa, since it has finite memory and has no stack for counting upto infinity. Therefore, choice (*c*) is not regular.

Choice (*d*) is regular since $n_0(s) \bmod 7 = n_1(s) \bmod 5 = 0$ means number of 0's is divisible by 7 and number of 1's is divisible by 5 and this can be accepted by a dfa with 7 × 5 = 35 states.

A dfa that will accept the language of choice (*b*) is shown below :

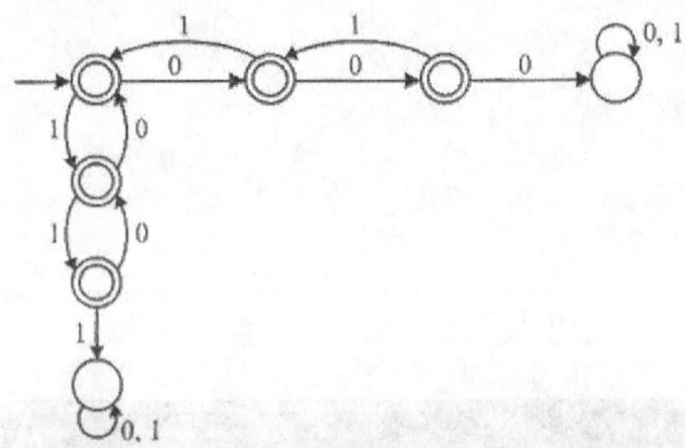

9. String 1, 2 and 4 are generate by language l*, L = {ab, aa, baa}.

10. R.E = a*b* (ba) *a*

Length 0 is present as it accepts ∈ all length 1 strings are present (a,b) also aa, ab, ba, bb are present, But 'bab ' is not present. So it is 3.

11. All morden languages are CSL.

12. Regular language (Regular sets) are closed under intersection (⋂), union (⋃), Kleene star (*) so option a, b, and d are wrong.

in option (c)

$\Sigma^* - R_1$ is Regular

$\Rightarrow \Sigma^* \cap \overline{R}_1$ (We can change "–" to intersection)

$\Rightarrow \Sigma^* \cap$ Regular {complement of regular is also regular)

$\Rightarrow$ Regular {inter section of two regular is also regular).

13. $G1 : S \rightarrow x \mid z \mid xS \mid yB$

$B \rightarrow y \mid z \mid yB \mid zB$

(In which No 'y' is appear before any x)

$G2 : S \rightarrow y \mid z \mid yS \mid zS \mid xB$

$B \rightarrow y \mid yS$

(In which every x is following by at least one y).

14. 2^{ε^*} is the power set of ε^*

ε^* is countabily infinite

The power set of countabily infinite set is uncountable.

So 2^{ε^*} is uncountable, and ε^* is countable.

15.

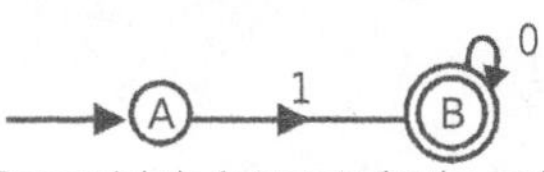

Deterministic Automata for the series

16.

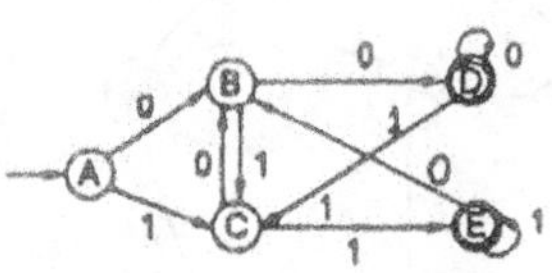

A to D $\rightarrow$ <u>00</u>, 1<u>00</u>, 11<u>00</u>, 011<u>00</u>

A to E $\rightarrow$ <u>11</u>, 0<u>11</u>, 00<u>11</u>, 100<u>11</u>

From above example we see A to D end with 00 and A to E end with 11.

So, number of state for deterministic finite state automation accepting L is **A, B, C, D, E** means 5.

17. For DFA over S {a, b}, If No. of a is divisible by "m" and no. of b is divisible by "n" then total minimum number of state is:-

$(m \times n)$

so for given question

$$6 * 8 = 48$$

18. Total 7 strings are possible

1 ------1 ----- 1

1001001

1001011

1001101

1001111

1011001

1101001

1111001

19. L(111 + 11111)*

DFA is

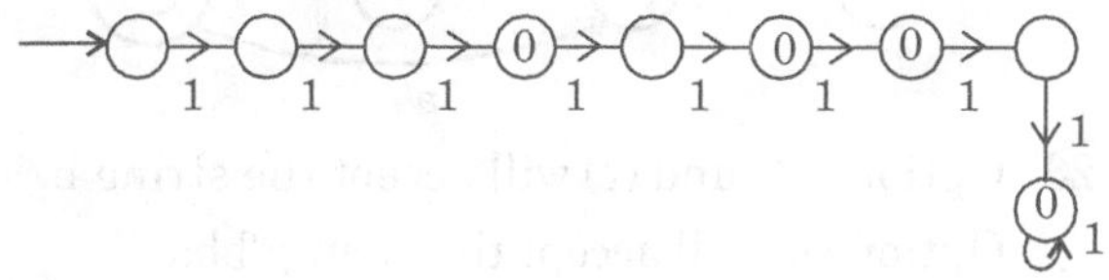

Total 9 state.

20. The minimum state deterministic finite automata accepting specified language will have 15 states.

21.

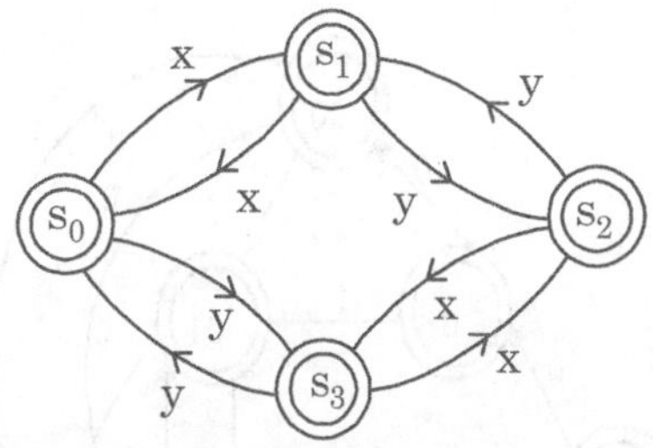

Here S_1 accept all string of x & y where No. of x is odd and y is even and S_2 accept all string where no. of x is even and y is odd.

22. R = (a + b)* (aa + bb) (a + b)*

DFA for R is

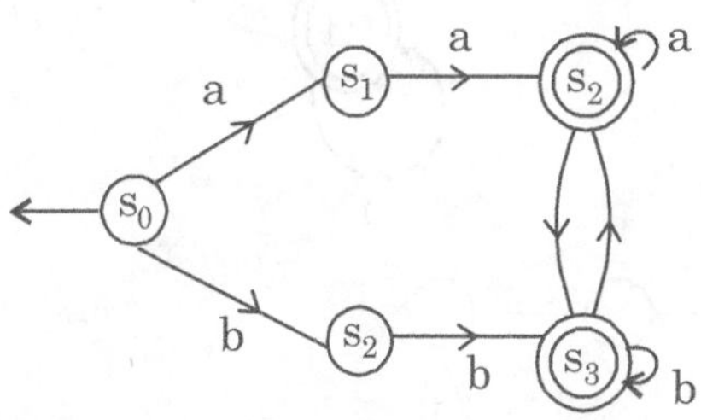

23. DFA

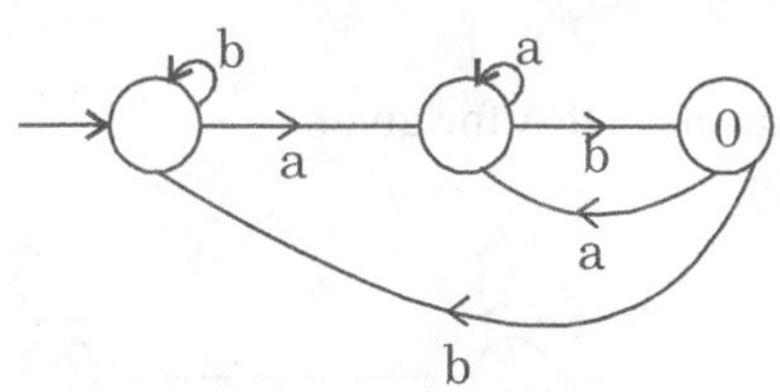

(Accept all strings end with ab)

Complemented DFA

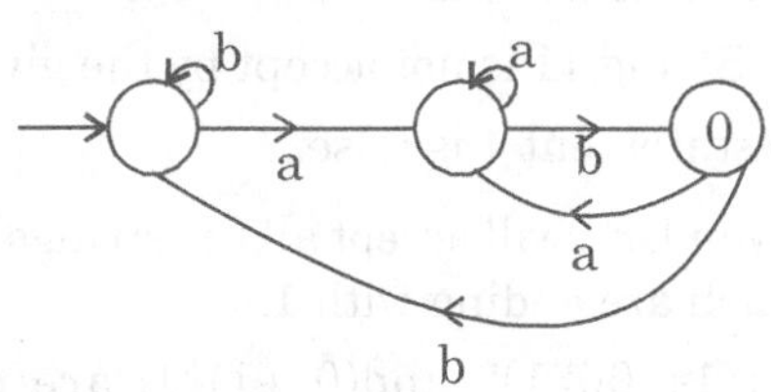

(It accepts all strings that do not end with ab)

24.

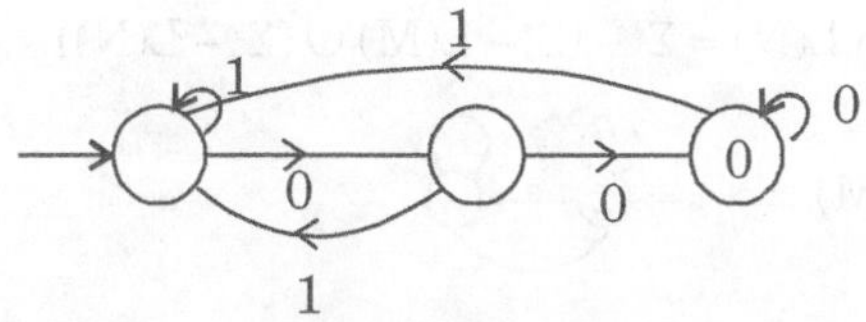

Accepts all strings end with 00.

25. Let $n = 3$ and $k = 1$

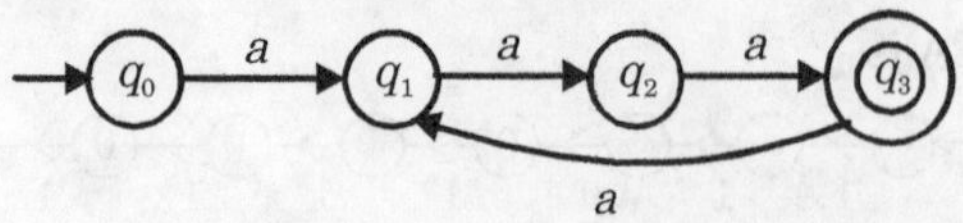

26. Options (*b*) and (*c*) will accept the string b

Option (*d*) will accept the string "bba"

Both are invalid strings.

So minimized DFA is option *a*

27. The complete DFA is

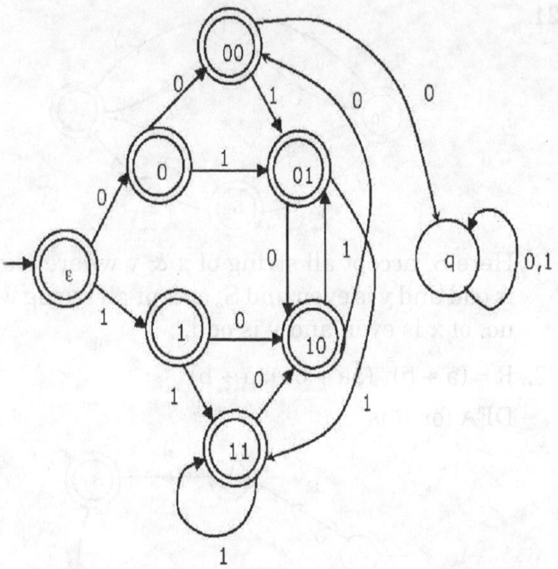

28.

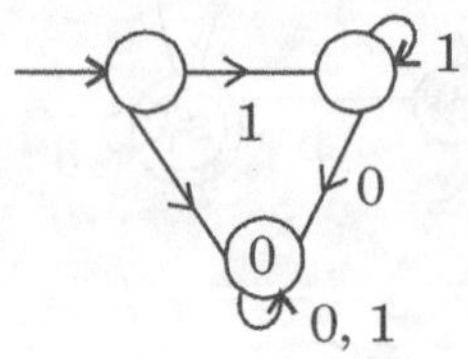

Minimal DFA for given.

DFA

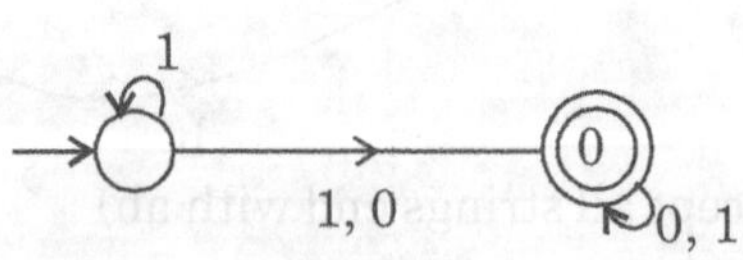

So statement 3 is false

* String 11 is not accept by the given DFA

So statement 4 is false.

29. Given DFA will accept all the strings over ε ={0,1} which are ending with 1.

0*1(1+ 00*1)* and(0 +1)*1, are the regular expressions for ending with 1.

30. $L(M) \cap L(N) = \Sigma^* - (\Sigma^* - L(M) \cup (\Sigma^* - L(N))$

$\Sigma^* - L(M) \Rightarrow$ 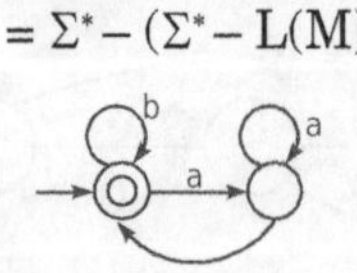

$\Sigma^* - L(N) \Rightarrow$ 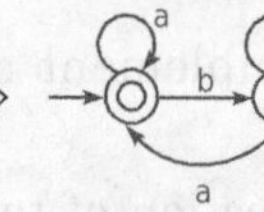

M accept all string end with a and N accept all string end with *b.* The intersection of both will accept empty language.

Hence

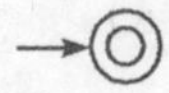

Then no. of state is 1.

31.

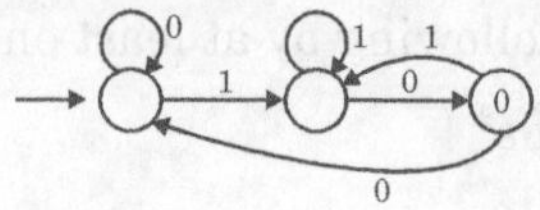

Ans = 3

32.

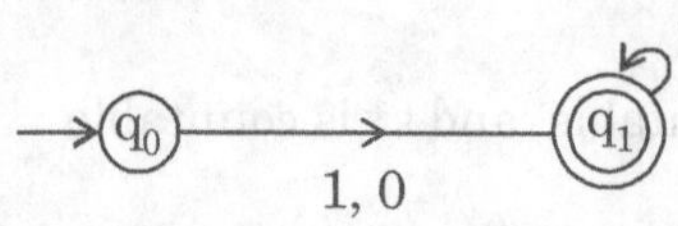

33. The Minimal DFA is

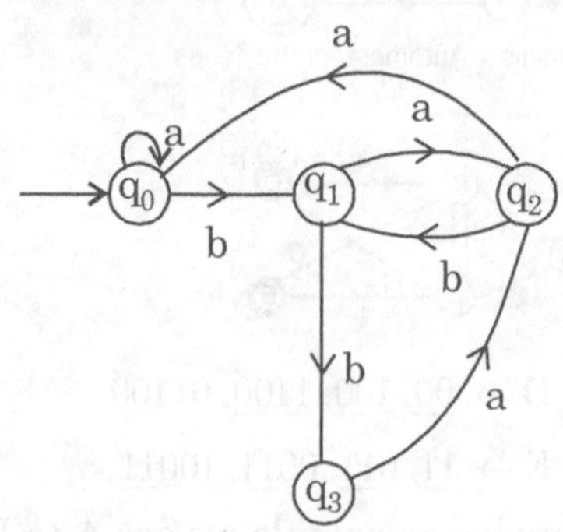

34. Given the regular language is :

Min DFA for L

$$= \left\{ w_1 a w_2 \,\middle|\, w_1, w_2 \in \{a, b\}^*, |w_1| = 2, |w_2| \geq 3 \right\}$$

Hence the regular expression for L is

$(a + b)\,(a + b)\,a\,(a + b)\,(a + b)(a + b)\,(a + b)^*$

The minimal DFA is

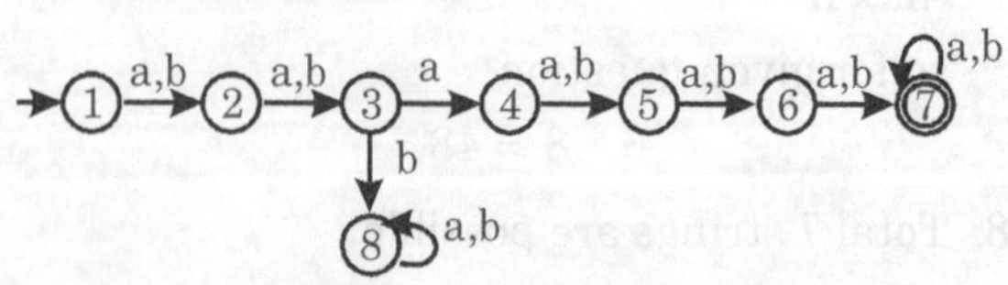

Hence the minimum possible number of states of DFA is 8.

35. $L_1 = d(s) \bmod 5 = 2$ is regular with 5 states.

$L_2 = d(s) \bmod 7 = 4$ is regular with 7 states.

$L_1 \cap L_2{}'$ is also regular with 35 states.

36. NPDA is more powerful than DPDA.

Hence answer is (*b*)

37. Regular and recuesive language are closed under complement operation. Hence they both are decidable.

38. The DFA for accepting L will have 5! = 120 states, since we need one state for every possible permutation function on 5 elements. The starting state will be "id" state, name as $\begin{pmatrix}12345\\12345\end{pmatrix}$ and from there n! arrows will go the n! states each named with a distinct permutation of the set {1, 2, 3, 4, 5}. Since composition of permutation function is closed every arrow has to go to some permutation and hence some state.

Since the language only has those strings where π(x) = id only the starting ("id" state) will be the final state. Sample machine with only 2 states is shown below

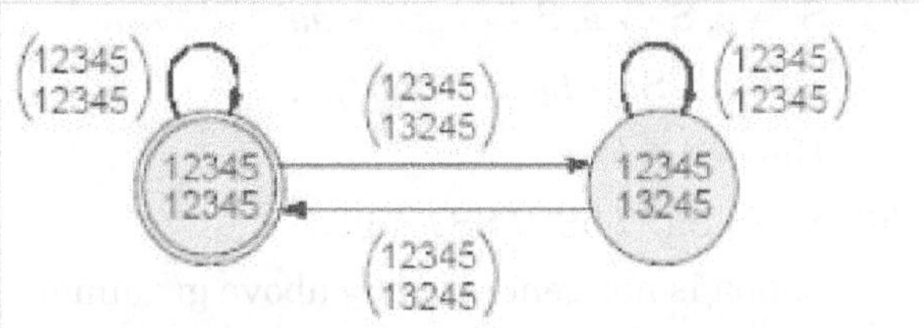

39. If NFA has n states then DFA has maximum 2^n states.

40. L_1 accepts all strings over input 0, So L_1 is (0 + 1)*.

41. L_1 can have 00 string while L_2 can't. L_2 can have 01 while L_1 can't. None of them can be either equal or proper subset of each other. So answer is D.

42. [*] "baa" is not accepted by B so B eliminated.

[*] "a" is accepted by D but "a" is not in regular expression

[*] option c accept extra expression.

43. A states in DFA is a proper subset of states of NFA.

Set of states of NFA = n

So, number of subset = 2^n

[m < = 2^n].

44. w be any string of length n in {0, 1} * and L is substring of L

means if **101** is the w

Then L = 01, 10, 01, 11

Then

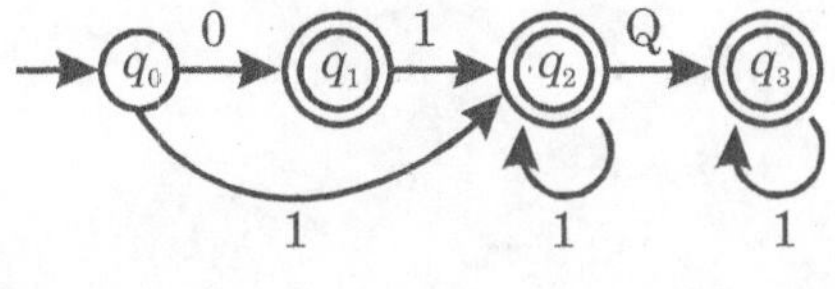

Then it should be $n + 1$, where n is length of the string.

Alternately

Let $w = 101$

∴ sub strings = 1, 0, 10, 11, 01, 101

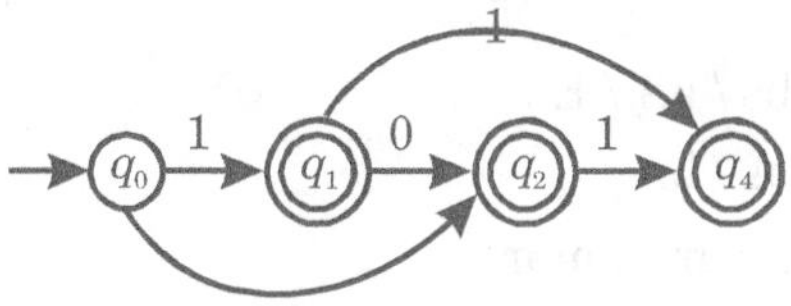

It requires 4 states.

If a string is of 'n' length, it requires $n + 1$ states

45. Language accepted by NFA is a^+, so complement of this language is {ε}

46. Draw the table from state diagram, we get,

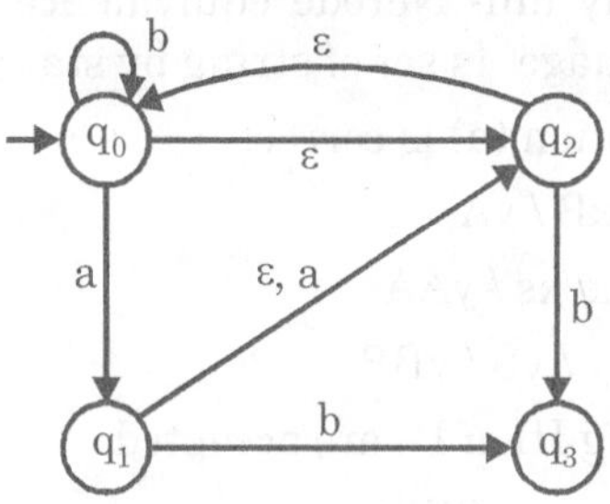

$\hat{\delta}(q_2, aba)$ = All states reachable from q_2 by "aba"

If aba is broken as ε.a.ε.ε.b.a. Then from q_2 we can reach q_1 and from there by null transition we can reach state q_2 as well as q_0.

$$\hat{\delta}(q_2, aba) = (q_0, q_1, q_2\}$$

47. n is number of states of given nfa (may not be minimal) k is number of states of equivalent min dfa. First we convert nfa to dfa using subset construction algorithm and we get an equivalent dfa which will have almost 2^n states. Then we can convert this dfa to a minimal dfa and get a minimal dfa with k states where $k \le 2^n$.

48. S → oso / oo

Language generated by grammar is $(oo)^+$ which is regular but not o^+

49. S → xa / ya

x → za

z → sa / e

y → wa

w → sa

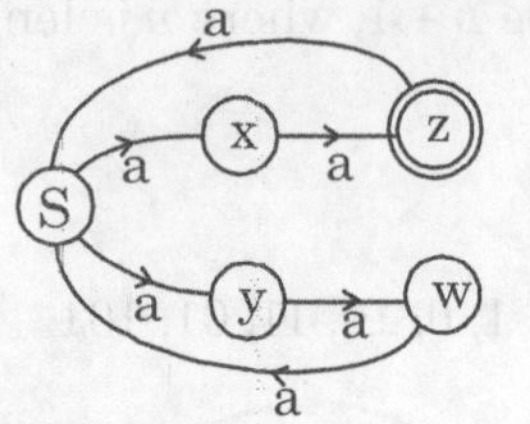

	a
→ s	xy
xy	zw
zw	s

50. S → bs / aA / E

A → as / bA

DFA of grammar is

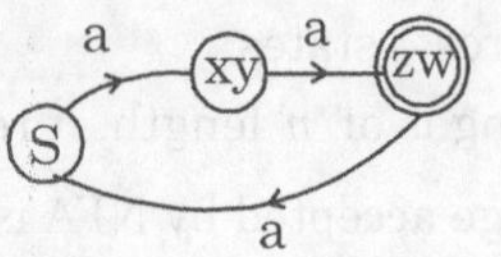

It accept all strings over {a,b}, having even No. Of a's

So my hill- Nerode equivalence classes for the language. Is set of string by state S and A

so option (a) is correct.

51. S → xB / yA

A → x/ xs / yAA

B → y / yS / yBB

String III & IV are accepted.

(iii) xyxy (IV) yxxy

S → xB	S → yA
→ xyS	S → yxS
→ xyxB	S → yxxS
→xyxy	S → yxxy

52. Actual Question is intersection of L (p) and so if we find L(p) ∩ L(o) intersection then intersection must accept "aa" because "aa" accept by both P,Q autometa but none of any option satisfy "aa" so option is (e).

53. Lexical Analysis is implemented by finite automata

54.

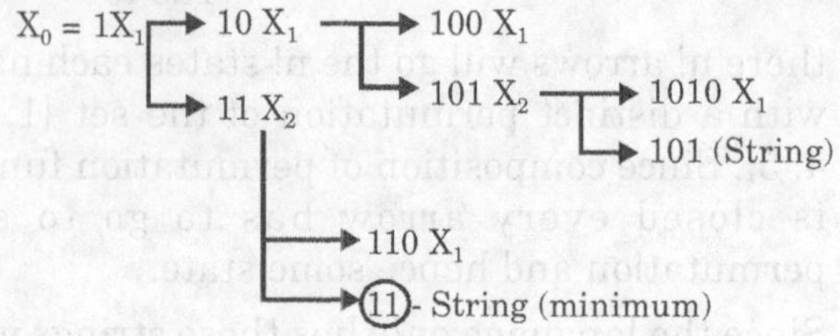

All string are starting with 1 with min string 11. which can be generated by 1(0* + 10)*1.

55. S → *a*S | *b*S |

S → ε, S → *a*, S → *b*, S → *aa*

S → *ab*, S → *ba*, S → *bb* ......

Hence {*a*, *b*}*.

56. S ---> SaS / bSa / SS / null

babba is not generated by above grammar.

57. S – > aSa | bSb | a | b

will generate all odd length palindromes

e.g. S = > aSa = > abSba = > abbSbba = > abbabba

2
CHAPTER

Regular Language & Regular Expression

Analysis of Previous GATE Papers											
Units	**Year → Topics ↓**		**2019**	**2018**	**2017 Set 1**	**2017 Set 2**	**2016 Set 1**	**2016 Set 2**	**2015 Set 1**	**2015 Set 2**	**2015 Set 3**
REGULAR EXPRESSION	**1 Mark**	MCQ Type									
		Numerical Type									
	2 Marks	MCQ Type									
		Numerical Type									
	Total										
FINI TE AUTOMATON	**1 Mark**	MCQ Type									
		Numerical Type									
	2 Marks	MCQ Type									
		Numerical Type									
	Total										
RE WI TH FA	**1 Mark**	MCQ Type									
		Numerical Type									
	2 Marks	MCQ Type									
		Numerical Type									
	Total										
REGULAR LANGUAGE	**1 Mark**	MCQ Type	2								
		Numerical Type									
	2 Marks	MCQ Type				1		1		1	
		Numerical Type		1							
	Total		2	2		2		2		2	

REGULAR EXPRESSION

1. Let r =(1+ 0)*, s = 11*0 and t = 1*0 be three regular expressions. Which one of the following is true?
 (a) $L(s) \subseteq L(r)$ and $L(s) \subseteq L(t)$
 (b) $L(r) \subseteq L(s)$ and $L(s) \subseteq L(t)$
 (c) $L(s) \subseteq L(t)$ and $L(s) \subseteq L(r)$
 (d) $L(t) \subseteq L(s)$ and $L(s) \subseteq L(r)$ **[1991 : 2 Marks]**

2. Which of the following regular expression identifies are true?
 (a) r(*) = r*   (b) (r* s*)* = (r + s)*
 (c) (r + s)* = r* + s*   (d) r* s* = r* + s*
 [1992 : 2 Marks]

3. Which two of the following four regular expressions are equivalent?
 (i) (00)* (ε+0)   (ii) (00)*
 (iii) 0 *   (iv) 0(00)*
 (a) (i) and (ii)   (b) (ii) and (iii)
 (c) (i) and (iii)   (d) (iii) and (iv)
 [1996 : 1 Mark]

4. Let $L \subseteq \Sigma^*$ where $\Sigma = \{a, b\}$, which of the following is true?
 (a) L = {x | x has an equal number of a's and b's is regular
 (b) $L = \{a^n b^n \mid n \geq 1\}$ is regular
 (c) L = {x | x has more a's is regular
 (d) $L = \{a^m b^n \mid m \geq, n \geq 1\}$ is regular
 [1996 : 1 Mark]

5. Which one of the following regular expressions over {0, 1} denotes the set of all strings not containg 100 as substrings?
 (a) 0*(1+0)*   (b) 0*1010*
 (c) 0*1*01*   (d) 0*(10+1)*
 [1997 : 2 Marks]

6. If the regular set A represented by A = (01+1)* and the regular set 'B' is represented by B = (((01)*1*)* which of the following is true?
 (a) $A \subset B$
 (b) $B \subset A$
 (c) A and B are incomparable
 (d) A = B **[1998 : 1 Mark]**

7. Let S and T be language over Σ = {a, b} represented by the regular expressions (a+b*)* and (a+b)*, respectively. Which of the following is true?
 (a) $S \subset T$ (b) $T \subset S$
 (c) S = T   (d) $S \cap T = \phi$
 [2000 : 1 Mark]

8. Which one of the following regular expressions is NOT equivalent to the regular expression (a+b+c)*?
 (a) (a* + b* + c*)*
 (b) (a*b*c*)*
 (c) ((ab)* + c*)*
 (d) (a*b* + c*)*
 [IT-2004 : 1 Mark]

9. Which of the following statement is TRUE about the regular expression 01*0?
 (a) It represents a finite set of finite strings.
 (b) It represents an infinite set of finite strings.
 (c) It represent a finite set of infinite strings.
 (d) It represents an infinite set of infinite strings.
 [IT-2005 : 1 Mark]

10. Which regular expression best describes the language accepted by the non-deterministic automaton below?

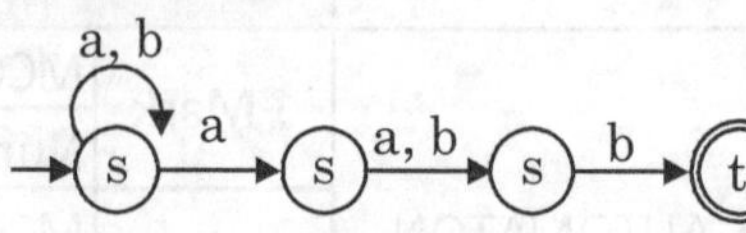

 (a) (a+b)* a(a+b)b
 (b) (abb)*
 (c) (a+b)* a(a+b) *b(a+b)*
 (d) (a+b)* **[IT-2006 : 1 Mark]**

11. Which of the following statements about regular languages is NOT true?
 (a) Every language has a regular superset
 (b) Every language has a regular subset
 (c) Every subset of a regular language is regular
 (d) Every subset of a finite language is regular
 [IT-2006 : 2 Marks]

Directions for Q.12 to Q.13:

Let L be a regular language. Consider the constructions on L below:

I. repeat (L) = {ww | w $\in$ L)
II. prefix (L) = {u | $\exists$v : uv $\in$ L)
III. suffix (L) = {v | $\exists$u : uv $\in$ L)
IV. half (L) = {u | v : | $\exists$v | = | u | and uv $\in$ L)

12. Which of the constructions could lead to a non-regular language?
 (a) Both I and IV
 (b) Only I
 (c) Only IV
 (d) Both II and II
 [IT-2006 : 2 Marks]

13. Which choice of L is best suited to support your answer above?

(a) (a+b)* (b) {ε, a, ab, bab}

(c) (ab)* (d) $\{a_n b_n \mid n \geq 0\}$

[IT-2006 : 2 Marks]

14. Which of the following is TRUE?

(a) Every subset of the regular set is regular

(b) Every finite subset of a non-regular set is regular

(c) The union of two non-regular sets is not regular

(d) Infinite union of finite sets is regular

[IT-2007 : 1 Mark]

15. Consider the regular expression:

R = (a+b)* (aa+bb) (a+b)*

Which one of the regular expressions given below defines the same language as defined by the regular expression R?

(a) (a(ba)* + b(ab)*) $(a+b)^+$

(b) (a(ba)* + b(ab)*)*(a+b)*

(c) (a(ba)* (a+bb) + b(ab)* (b+aa))(a+b)*

(d) (a(ba)* (a+bb) + b(ab*(b+aa))$(a+b)^+$

[IT-2007 : 2 Marks]

16. Which of the following regular expressions describes the language over {0, 1} consisting of strings that contain exactly two 1's?

(a) (0 + 1)* 11(0 + 1)*

(b) 0* 110*

(c) 0* 10* 10*

(d) (0 + 1)* 1(0 + 1)* 1(0 + 1)*

[IT-2008 : 1 Mark]

17. Math List-1 with List-II and select the correct answer using the codes given below the lists:

List-I

A.
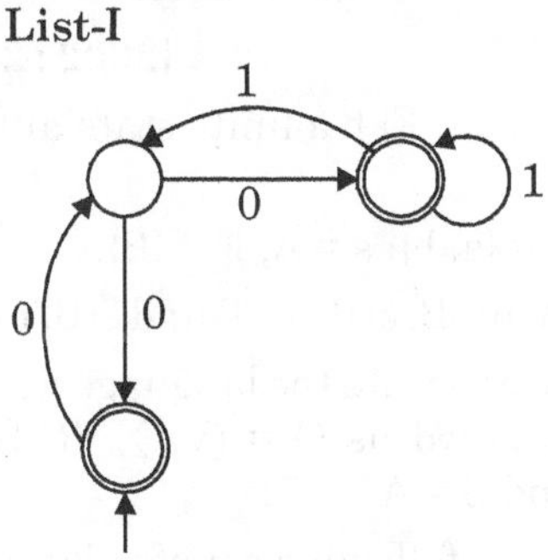

B.
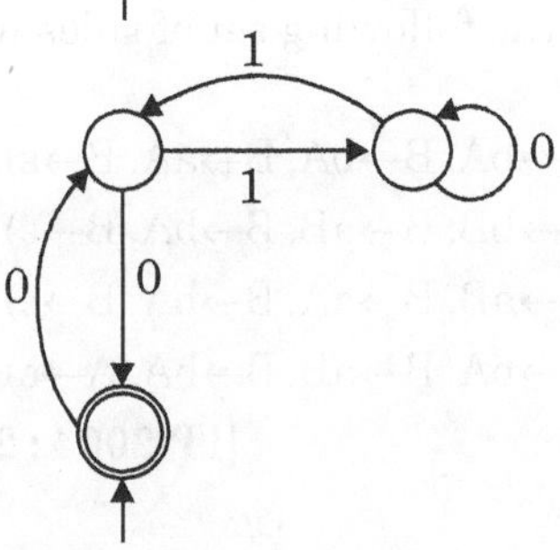

C.
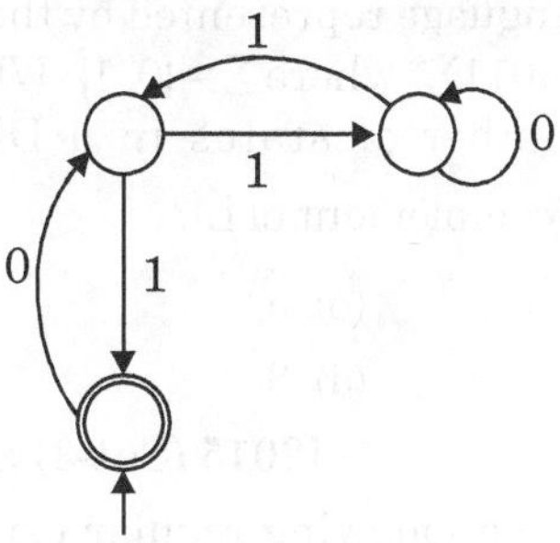

D.
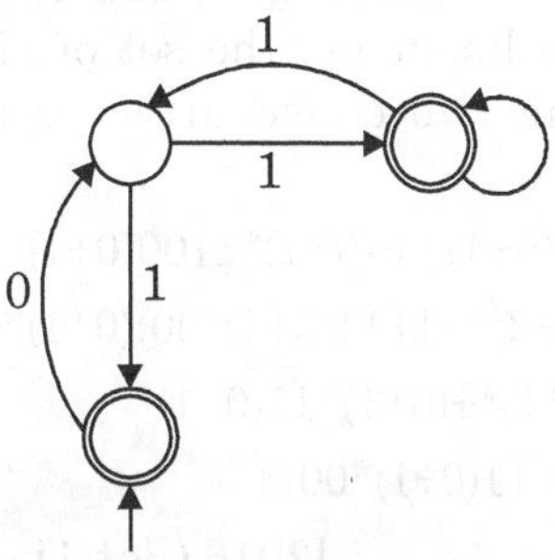

List-II

1. ε + 0(01*1+00)*01*
2. ε + 0(10*1+00)*0
3. ε + 0(10*1+10)*1
4. ε + 0(10*1+10)*10*

Codes:

	A	B	C	D
(a)	2	1	3	4
(b)	1	3	2	4
(c)	1	2	3	4
(d)	3	2	1	4

[2008 : 2 Marks]

18. Which one of the following language over the alphabet {0, 1) is described by the regular expression: (0 + 1)*0(0 + 1)*(0 + 1)*?

(a) The set of all strings containing the substring 00

(b) The set of all strings containing at most two 0's

(c) The set of all strings containing at least two 0's

(d) The set of strings that begin and end with either 0 or 1

[2009 : 1 Mark]

19. Let L = {ω∈ (0+1)* | ω has even number of 1s}, i.e. L is the set of all bit strings with even number of 1s. Which one of the regular expression below represents L?

(a) (0*10*1)*

(b) 0*(10*10*)*

(c) 0*(10*1)*0*

(d) 0*1(10*1)*10*

[2010 : 2 Marks]

20. Let L be the language represented by the regular expression $\Sigma^*0011\Sigma^*$ where $\Sigma = \{0, 1\}$. What is the minimum number of states in a DFA that recognizes $\overline{L}$ (complement of L)?

(a) 4 (b) 5

(c) 6 (d) 8

[2015 (Set-3) : 1 Mark]

21. Which one of the following regular expressions represents the language: the set of all binary strings having two consecutive 0s and two consecutive 1s?

(a) $(0+1)^*0011(0+1)^* + (0+1)^*1100(0+1)^*$

(b) $(0+1)^*(00(0+1)^*11+11(0+1)^*00)(0+1)^*$

(c) $(0+1)^*00(0+1)^*+(0+1)^*11(0+1)^*$

(d) $00(0+1)^*11+11(0+1)^*00$

[2016 (Set-1) : 1 Mark]

22. Match List-I with List-II and select the correct answer using the codes given below the lists :

List -I

A. Checking that identifies are declared before their use

B. Number of formal parameters in the declaration of a function agrees with the number of actual parameters in a use of that function

C. Arithmetic expression with matched pairs of parentheses

D. Palindromes

List-II

1. $L = \{a^n b^m c^n d^m \mid n \geq 1, m \geq 1\}$
2. $X \rightarrow X b X \mid X c X \mid d X f \mid g$
3. $L = \{wcw \mid w \in (a \mid b)^*\}$
4. $X \rightarrow b X b \mid c X c \mid \varepsilon$

Codes:

	A	B	C	D
(a)	1	3	2	4
(b)	3	1	4	2
(c)	3	1	2	4
(d)	1	3	4	2

[2008 : 2 Marks]

FINITE AUTOMATON

23. State True of False with one line explanation. A FSM (Finite State Machine) can be designed to add two integers of any arbitrary length (arbitrary number of digits).

[1994 : 1 Mark]

24. A finite state machine with the follows state table has a sngle input X and a single output Z.

present state	next state, z	next state, z
	x = 1	x = 0
A	D, 0	B, 0
B	B, 1	C, 1
C	B, 0	D, 1
D	B, 1	C, 0

It the initial state is unknown, then the shortest input sequence to reach the final state C is

(a) 01 (b) 10

(c) 101 (d) 110

[1995 : 2 Marks]

25. The finite state machine described by the following state diagram with A as starting state, where an arc lable is x/y and x stands for 1-bit input and y stands for 2-bit output

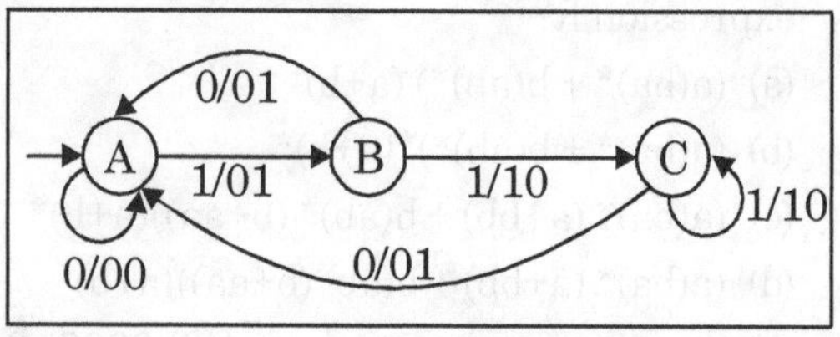

(a) Output the sum of the present and the previous bits of the input

(b) Outputs 01 whenever the input sequence contains 11

(c) Output 00 whenever the input sequence contains 10

(d) None of the above

[2002 : 2 Marks]

26. The smallest finite automation which accepts the language L = {x | length of x is divisible by 3} has

(a) 2 states (b) 3 states

(c) 4 states (d) 5 states

[2002 : 2 Marks]

27. Let M = (K, Σ, δ, s, F} b a finite state automaton, where

K = {A, B}, Σ = {a, b}, s = A, F = {B},

δ(A, a)=A, δ(A, b)=B, δ(B, a)=B and δ(B, b)=A

A grammar to generate the language accepted by M can be specified as G = (V, Σ, R, S),Where V = K ∪ Σ, and S = A

Which one of the following set of rules will make L(G) = L(M)?

(a) {A→aB, A→bA, B→bA, B→aA, B→ε)

(b) {A→aA, A→bB, B→aB, B→bA, B→ε)

(c) {A→bB, A→aB, B→aA, B→bA, B→ε)

(d) {A→aA, A→bA, B→aB, B→bA, A→ε)

[IT-2004 : 2 Marks]

28. The following finite state machine acepts all those binary strings in which the number of 1's and 0's are respectively

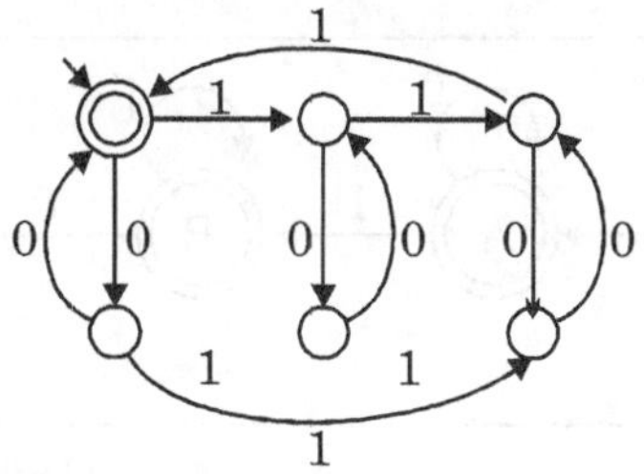

(a) divisible by 3 & 2

(b) odd and even

(c) even and odd

(d) divisible by 2 & 3

[2004 : 2 Marks]

29. Consider the machine M

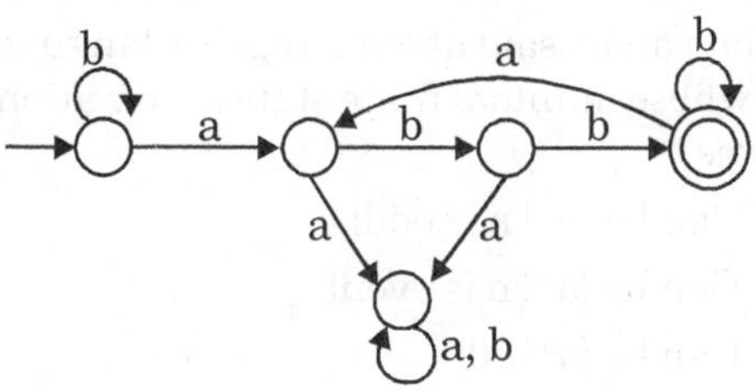

The language recogninzed by M is

(a) {w∈{a, b}* | every a in w is following by exactly two b's}

(b) {w∈{a, b}* every a in w is following by at least two b's}

(c) {w∈{a, b}* w containts the substring 'abb'

(d) {w∈{a, b}* w does not contain 'aa' as a substring}

[2005 : 2 Marks]

30. The following diagram represents a finite state machine which takes as input a binary number from the least significant bit

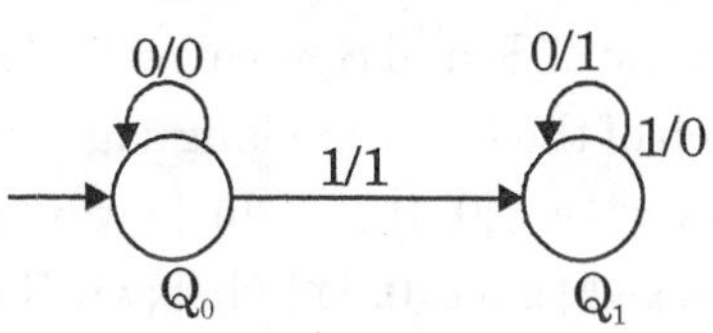

Which one the following is TRUE?

(a) It computes 1's complement fo the input number

(b) It computes 2's complement of the input nujmber

(c) It increments the input number

(d) It decrements the input number

[2005 : 2 Marks]

31. In the automaton below, s is the start state and t is the only final state.

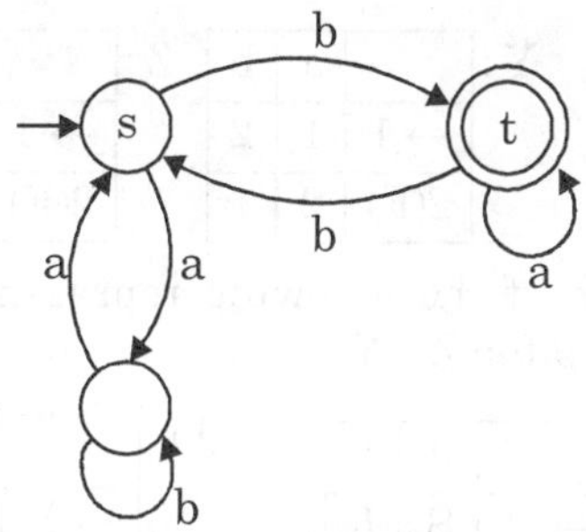

Consider the strings u = abbaba, v = bab, and w = aabb. Which of the following statements is true?

(a) The automaton accepts u and v but not w

(b) The automaton accepts each of u, v, and w

(c) The automaton rejects each of u, v, and w

(d) The automaton accepts u but rejects v and w

[IT-2006 : 1 Mark]

Common Data for Q. 32 & 33

Consider the following Finite State Automation

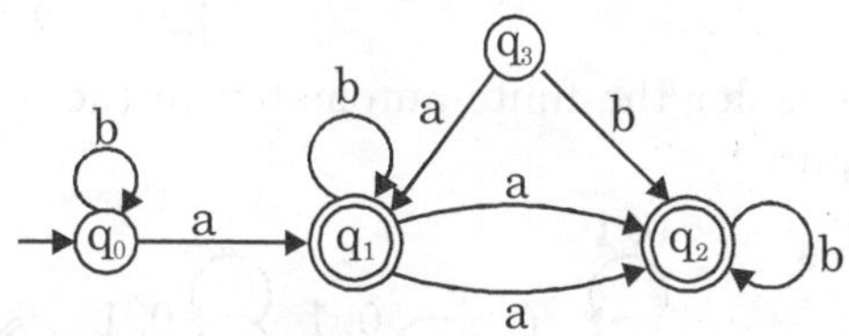

32. The language accepted by this automaton is given by the regular expression

(a) b * ab* ab* ab*

(b) (a + b)*

(c) b* a(a + b)*

(d) b* ab* ab*

[2007 : 2 Marks]

33. The minimum state automaton equivalent to the above FSA has the following number of states

(a) 1 (b) 2

(c) 3 (d) 4 **[2007 : 2 Marks]**

34. Consider the following two finite automata. M_1 accepts L_1 and M_2 accepts L_2. Which one of the following is TRUE?

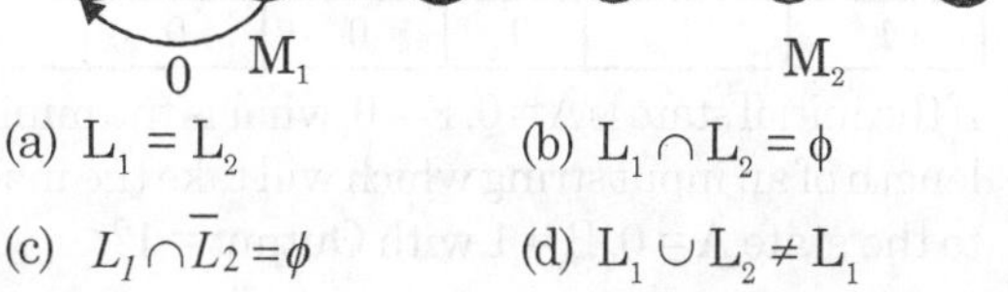

(a) $L_1 = L_2$ (b) $L_1 \cap L_2 = \phi$

(c) $L_1 \cap \bar{L}_2 = \phi$ (d) $L_1 \cup L_2 \neq L_1$

[IT-2008 : 2 Marks]

35. Given below are two finite state automata (→ indicates the start and F indicates a final state)

Y:

	a	b
→1	1	2
2(F)	2	1

Z:

	a	b
→1	2	2
2(F)	1	1

Which of the following represents the product automaton Z × Y?

(a)

	a	b
→P	S	R
Q	R	S
R(F)	Q	P
S	P	Q

(b)

	a	b
→P	Q	S
Q	R	S
R(F)	Q	P
S	Q	P

(c)

	a	b
→P	S	Q
Q	R	S
R(F)	Q	P
S	P	Q

(d)

	a	b
→P	S	Q
Q	S	R
R(F)	Q	P
S	Q	P

[2008 : 2 Marks]

36. Consider the finite automaton in the following figure.

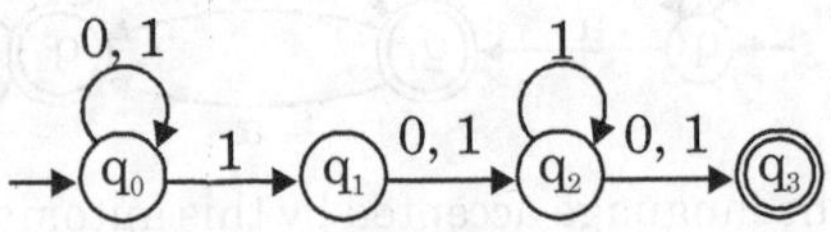

What is the set of reachable states for the input string 0011?

(a) $\{q_0, q_1, q_2\}$ (b) $\{q_0, q_1\}$

(c) $\{q_0, q_1, q_2, q_3\}$ (d) $\{q_3\}$

[2014 (Set-1 : 1 Mark]

37. Given the following state table of an FSM with two states A and B, one input and one output :

Present State A	Present State B	Input	Next State A	Next State B	Output
0	0	0	0	0	1
0	1	0	1	0	0
1	0	0	0	1	0
1	1	0	1	0	0
0	0	1	0	1	0
0	1	1	0	0	1
1	0	1	0	1	1
1	1	1	0	0	1

If the initial state is A = 0, B = 0, what is the minimum length of an input string which will take the machine to the state A = 0, B = 1 with Output = 1?

(a) 3 (b) 4

(c) 5 (d) 6

[2009 : 2 Marks]

RE WITH FA

38. The regular expession for the language recognized by the finite state automation

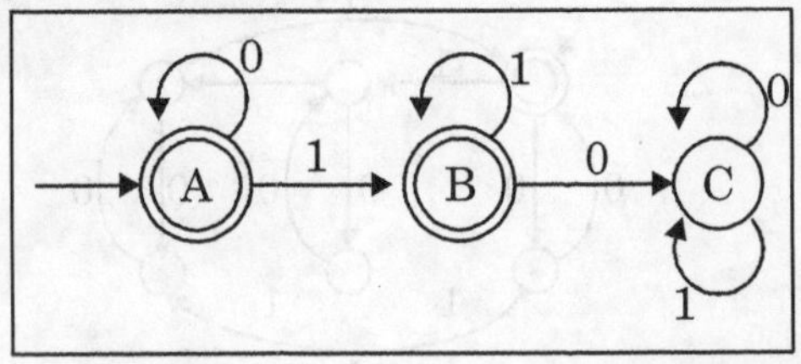

[1994 : 2 Marks]

39. Consider the regular expression (0+1)(0+1)...n times. The minimum state finite automation that recognizes the language represented by this regular expression contains

(a) n states (b) n+1 states

(c) n+2 states (d) None of these

[1999 : 1 Mark]

40. What can be said about a regular language L over {a} whose minimal finite state automation has two states?

(a) Can be $\{a^n \mid n \text{ is odd}\}$

(b) Can be $\{a^n \mid n \text{ is even}\}$

(c) Can be $\{a^n \mid \geq 0\}$

(d) Either L can be $\{a^n \mid n \text{ is odd}\}$ or L can be $\{a^n \mid n \text{ is even}\}$

[2000 : 2 Marks]

REGULAR LANGUAGE

41. Consider the following statements:

S1: $\{0^{2n} \mid n \geq 1\}$ is a regular language

S2: $\{0^m 1^n 0^{m+n} \mid m \geq 1 \text{ and } n \geq 1\}$ is a regular language

Which of the following is true about S_1 and S_2?

(a) Only S_1 is correct

(b) Only S_2 is correct

(c) Both S_1 and S_2 are correct

(d) None of S_1 and S_2 is correct **[2001 : 1 Mark]**

42. Which of the following language is regular?

(a) $\{ww^R \mid w \in \{0, 1\}^+\}$ (b) $\{ww^R x \mid x, w \in (0, 1)^+\}$

(c) $\{wxw^R \mid x, w \in (0, 1)^+\}$ (d) $\{xww^R \mid x, w \in \{0, 1\}^+\}$

[2007 : 2 Marks]

43. Which of the following languages is (are) non-regular?

$L_1 = \{0^m 1^n \mid 0 \leq m \leq n \leq 10000\}$

L_2 = {w | w reads the same forward and backward}

$L_3 = \{w \in \{0, 1\}^* \mid$ w contains an even number of 0's and an even number of 1's$\}$

(a) L_2 and L_3 only (b) L_1 and L_2 only

(c) L_3 only (d) L_2 only

[IT-2008 : 2 Marks]

44. Which of the following are regular sets?

1. $\{a^nb^{2m} \mid n \geq 0, m \geq 0\}$ 2. $\{a^nb^m \mid n = 2m\}$
3. $\{a^nb^m \mid n \neq m\}$ 4. $\{xcy \mid x, y \in \{a, b\}^*\}$

(a) 1 and 4 only (b) 1 and 3 only
(c) 1 only (d) 4 only

[2008 : 2 Marks]

45. Consider the language $L_1 = \phi$ and $L_2 = \{a\}$. Which one of the following represents $L_1L_2^* \cup L_1^*$?

(a) $\{\varepsilon\}$ (b) ϕ
(c) a^* (d) $\{\varepsilon, a\}$

[2013 : 1 Mark]

46. Which one of the following is TRUE?

(a) The language $L = \{a^nb^n \mid n \geq 0\}$ is regular.
(b) The language $L = \{a^n \mid n \text{ is prime}\}$ is regular.
(c) The language $L = \{w \mid w \text{ has } 3k + 1 \text{ b's for some } k \in N \text{ with } \Sigma = \{a, b\}\}$
(d) The language $L = \{ww \mid w \in \Sigma^* \text{ with } \Sigma = \{0, 1\}\}$ is regular.

[2014 (Set-1) : 1 Mark]

47. If $L_1 = \{a^n \mid n \geq 0\}$ and $L_2 = \{b^n \mid n \geq 0\}$, consider

I. $L_1 . L_2$ is a regular language
II. $L_1 . L_2$ $\{a^nb^n \mid n \geq 0\}$

Which one of the following is CORRECT?

(a) Only I (b) Only II
(c) Both I and II (d) Neither I nor Ii

[2014 (Set-2) : 1 Mark]

48. Let $L_1 = \{w \in \{0,1\}^* \mid w$ has at least as many occurrences of (110)'s as (011)'s$\}$. Let $L_2 = \{w \in \{0,1\}^* \mid w$ has at least as many occurrence of (000)'s as (111)'s$\}$. Which one of the following is TRUE?

(a) L_1 is regular but not L_2
(b) L_2 is regular but not L_1
(c) Both L_1 and L_2 are regular
(d) Neither L_1 not L_2 are regular

[2014 (Set-2) : 2 Marks]

49. Which of the following language is/are regular?

L_1: $\{wxw^R \mid w,x \in \{a,b\}^* \text{ and } |w|, |x| > 0\}$ w^R is the reverse of string w

L_2: $\{a^nb^m \mid m \neq n \text{ and } m, n \geq 0\}$

L_3: $\{a^pb^qc^r \mid p, q, r \geq 0$

(a) L_1 and L_3 only
(b) L_2 only
(c) L_2 and L_3 only
(d) L_3 only

[2015 (Set-2) : 2 Marks]

50. Consider the following two statements:

I. If all states of an NFA are accepting states then the language accepted by the NFA is Σ^*.
II. There exists a regular language A such that for all languages B, $A \cap B$ is regular.

Which one of the following is **CORRECT**?

(a) Only I is true
(b) Only II is true
(c) Both I and II are true
(d) Both I and II are false

[2016 (Set-2) : 2 Marks]

51. Given a language L, define L^i as follows:

$L^0 = \{\epsilon\}$

$L^i = L^{i-1}$. L fore $i > 0$

The order of a language L is defined as the smallest k such that $L^k = L^{k+1}$.

Consider the language L_1 (over alphabet 0) accepted by the following automaton.

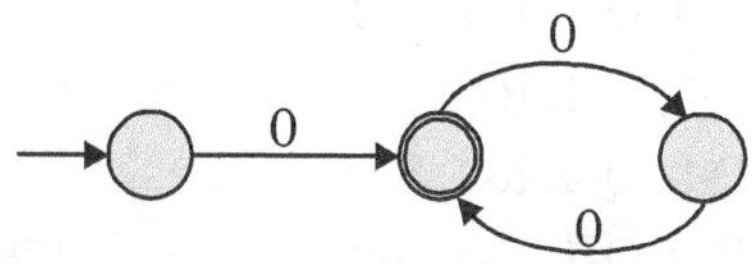

The order of L1 is ______. **[2018 : 2 Marks]**

52. Fortran is

(a) regular language
(b) context free language
(c) context sensitive language
(d) None of the above **[1987 : 2 Marks]**

53. Which of the following statement is false?

(a) Every finite subset of a non-regular set is regular
(b) Every subset of a regular set is regular
(c) Every finite subset of a regular set is regular
(d) The intersection of two regular sets is regular

[1998 : 2 Marks]

54. Let L be a regular language and M be a context-free language, both over the alphabet . Let L^c and M^c denote the complements of L and M respectively. Which of the following statements about the language $L^c \cup M^c$ is TRUE ?

(a) It is necessarily regular but not necessarily context-free.
(b) It is necessarily context-free.
(c) It is necessarily non-regular.
(d) None of the above

[IT-2005 : 1 Mark]

55. Which of the following statements is false?
   (a) Every NFA can be converted to an equivalent DFA.
   (b) Every o-deterministic Turing machine can be converted to an equivalent deterministic Turing machine
   (c) Every regular language is also a context-free language
   (d) Every subset of a recursively enumerable set is recursive

[2008 : 2 Marks]

56. Match all items in Group I with correct options from those given in Group 2

	Group 1		Group 2
P.	Regular expression	1.	Syntax analysis
Q.	Pushdown automata	2.	Code generation
R.	Dataflow analysis	3.	Lexical analysis
S.	Register allocation	4.	Code Optimization

   (a) P-4, Q-1, R-2, S-3
   (b) P-3, Q-1, R-4, S-2
   (c) P-3, Q-4, R-1, S-2
   (d) P-2, Q-1, R-4, S-2

[2009 : 1 Mark]

57. Which one of the following is the strongest correct statement about a finite language over some fiite alphabet Σ?
   (a) It could be undecidable
   (b) It is turing-machine recognizable
   (c) It is a regular language
   (d) It is a context-sensitive language

[1991 : 2 Marks]

58. Let L(R) be the language represented by regular expression r. Let L(G) be the language generated by a context free grammar G. Let L(M) be the language accepted by a Turing machine M.

Which of the following decision problems are undecidable?
   I. Given a regular expression R and a string w, is $\omega \in L(R)$?
   II. Given a context-free grammar G, is $L(G) = \phi$?
   III. Given a context-free grammar G, is $L(G) = \Sigma^*$ for some alphabet Σ ?
   IV. Given a Turing machine M and a string w, is $\omega \in L(M)$?

   (a) I and IV only
   (b) II and III only
   (c) II, III and IV only
   (d) III and IV only

[2017 (Set-2) : 2 Marks]

59. If L is a regular language over $\Sigma = \{a, b\}$, which one of the following language is NOT regular?
   (a) $L \cdot L^R = \{xy \mid x \in L, y^R \in L\}$
   (b) $\{ww^R \mid \omega \in L\}$
   (c) $\text{Suffix}(L) = \{y \in \Sigma^* \mid \exists x \in \Sigma^* \text{ such that } xy \in L\}$
   (d) $\text{Prefix}(L) = \{x \in \Sigma^* \mid \exists y \in \Sigma^* \text{ such that } xy \in L\}$

[2019 : 1 Mark]

60. For $\Sigma = \{a, b\}$, let us consider the regular language $L = \{x \mid x = a^{2+3k} \text{ or } x = b^{10+12k}, k \geq 0\}$. Which one of the following can be a pumping length (the constant guaranted by the pumping lemma) for L?
   (a) 9
   (b) 5
   (c) 3
   (d) 24

[2019 : 1 Mark]

ANSWERS

1. (a,c)	2. (b)	3. (c)	4. (d)	5. (d)	6. (d)	7. (c)	8. (*)	9. (b)	10. (a)
11. (c)	12. (b)	13. (a)	14. (b)	15. (c)	16. (c)	17. (c)	18. (c)	19. (b)	20. (b)
21. (b)	22. (a)	23. (*)	24. (b)	25. (a)	26. (b)	27. (b)	28. (a)	29. (b)	30. (b)
31. (d)	32. (c)	33. (b)	34. (a)	35. (a)	36. (a)	37. (a)	38. (*)	39. (b)	40. (d)
41. (a)	42. (c)	43. (d)	44. (a)	45. (a)	46. (c)	47. (a)	48. (a)	49. (a)	50. (b)
51. (2)	52. (b)	53. (b)	54. (d)	55. (d)	56. (b)	57. (c)	58. (d)	59. (b)	60. (d)

EXPLANATIONS

1. Here $r = (1 + 10)^*$
   $\Rightarrow$ (set of All strings of 0 & 1)
   $$S = (11^* 0) \Rightarrow 1^+ 0$$
   $$t = 1^* 0 \Rightarrow 1^* 0$$
   Set r are include all strings of s and t and 't' is superset of "s".
   So $L(s) \leq L(r)$
   $L(s) \leq L(t)$

2. According to regular expression rule
   $$(r^* s^*) = (r + s)^*$$

3. From options given, we see that $(00)^* (\in + 0)$ and 0^* is equivalent.

4. $L \leq \Sigma^*$ where $\Sigma = \{a, b\}$
   It is function of regular function,
   $$\Sigma^* = (a, b)^*$$
   or we write $a^m b^n$, $m > 1$, $n > 1$

5. Option 'a' and' 'b' generate 100 string as substring directly
   Option 'c' and 'd' both are not generate 100 substring directly
   But option c does not accept λ(null).
   But null is a string which does not contain 100 as a substring.
   So option 'd' is correct.

6. $$A = (01 + 1)^*$$
   $$B = ((01^*)1^*)^*$$
   So Both are equal according to identity rules.
   $$(R1 + R2)^* = (R1^* R2^*)^*$$
   Option (d) is correct.

7. $(a + b^*)$ and $(a + b)^*$ Both are equal according to identity rules.
   $$(R_1 + R_2)^* = (R_1 + R_2^*)^* = (R_1^* + R_2)^*$$

8. In option C $\Rightarrow ((ab)^* + c^*)^*$ we can not generate string a and b separately. But in given expression $(a + b + c)^*$ we can generate string a and b separately.

9. The Regular expression represents infinite set of finite strings.
   (string is always finite in length).

10. 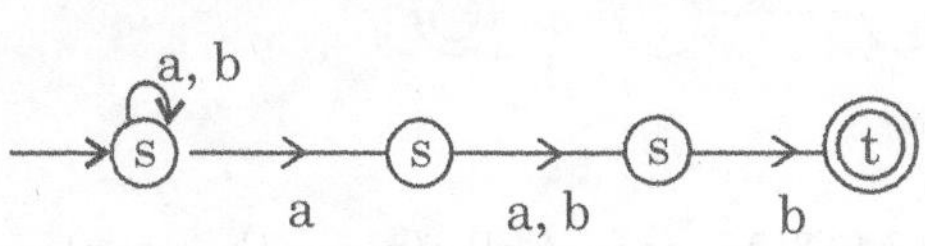

   option 'b' and 'd' generate λ(null) string which is not accepted by given automata option 'C' generate minimum length string "ab" which is not accepted given Automata.
   So option "a" is correct which generate all strings accepted by given automata.

11. Every subset of a Regular language is not always regular
    Example $L = a^* b^*$ is a Regular.
    But $L1 = a^n b^n$ is not Regular but $\boxed{L_1 \leq L}$ Not Regular.

12. Prefix; suffix and half of any regular language is also regular, according to properties of regular. But repeat (L) is not regular language.

13. $L = (a + b)^*$ then Repeat of L is
    Repeat (L) = $\{ww \mid w \in \{a, b\}^*\}$ is
    Clearly not Regular.

14. Every finite subset of a non – regular set is regular.

15. $R = (a + b)^* (aa + bb) (a + b)^*$
    By option "a" ® $(a(ba)^* + b(ab)^*) (a + b)^+$ we can generate string "ab" which is not accept by R.
    By option "b" ® $(a(ab)^* + b(ab)^*) (a + b)^*$ we can generate "λ" (null) which is not accept by R
    By option "d" $(a(ba)^* (a + bb) + b(ab^* (b + aa)) (a + b)^+$ we can not generate the string of length two, but R can be generate.

16. $0^*10^*10^*$ generate exactly two one's but not consecutive.
    (b) 0^*110^* generate two consecutive one's.

17. A is same as 1
    B is same as 2
    C is same as 3
    D is same as 4

18. R.E. = $(0+1)^*0(0+1)^*0(0+1)^*$
    Accepting Language will be
    L = {00, 000, 100, 001, 010, 0000, 0001, 1000, 1001, 0100, 1100, 0010, 0011, 0110, 0101, 1010, ...}
    atleast two zeros.

19. Every string should contain even number of 1's min string are
    $$\in, 0, 11, 101, 1010, 0101, 0110, \ldots$$
    We can't get it by
    $$0^* (10^* 1) 0^* \text{ and } 0^* 1 (10^* 1)^* 10^*$$
    because these don't give $\in$ and 0 string.

20. $L = \Sigma^* \, 0011 \, \Sigma^*$

Minimized DFA for L

L = 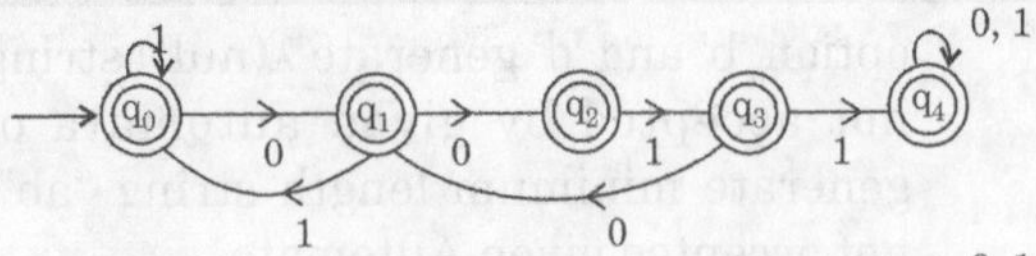

$\overline{L}$ = 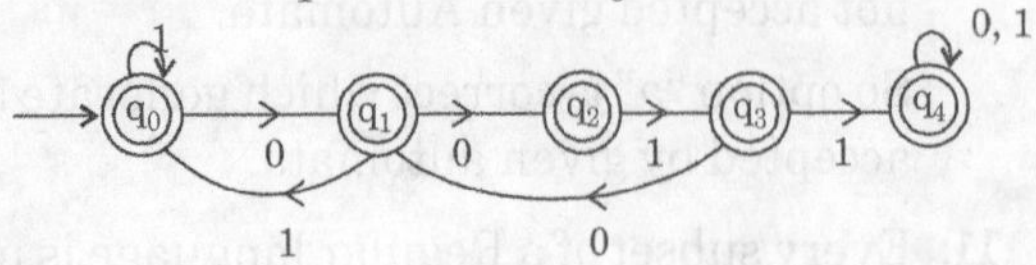

5 state

21. $(0 + 1)^* \, (00(0 + 1)^* \, 11 + 11(0 + 1)^*00) \, (0 + 1)^*$

22. Here $X \rightarrow b \; x \; b \,|\, c \; x \; c \,|\, \varepsilon$ surely repesent palindrome and $x \rightarrow x \; b \; x \,|\,|\, x \; c \; x \,|\, d \; x \; f \,|\, g$ Arithmetic expressions with match pair are simple & L = {wcw/wε (a/b)*}checking that identifier are declared before their use.

23. "false" - statement is false because FSM have finite memory and can not be store integers of any arbitrary length.

24.

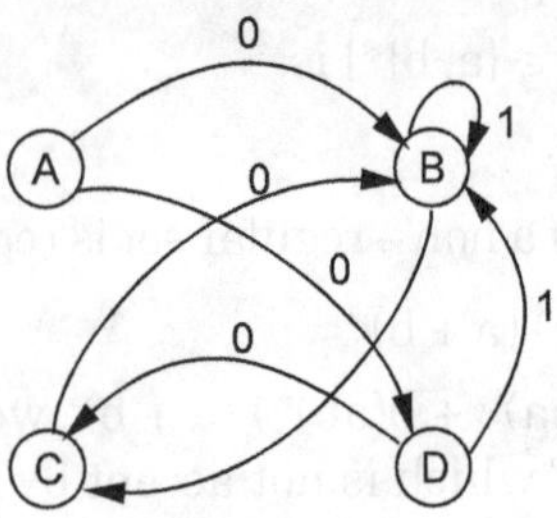

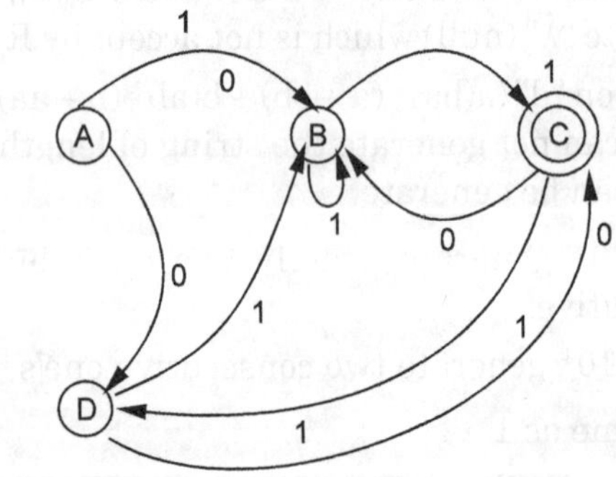

25. Start from A, B, C, we get output at A is 00 and input is sequence of 10.

A to A → input = 10, output = 00

B to A → input = 10, output = 00

C to A → input = 10, output = 00

26. 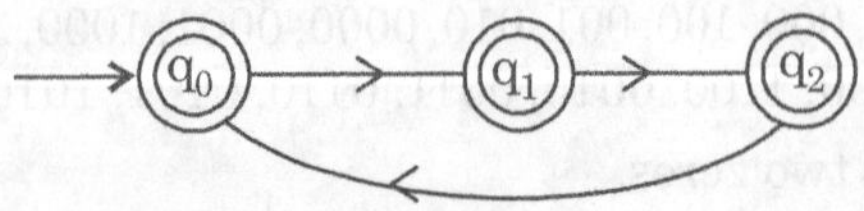

27. δ(A, a) = ⇒ A → aA

δ(A, b) = A ⇒ A → bB

δ(B, a) = B ⇒ B → aB

δ(B, b) = B ⇒ B → bA

B is final state, so we need to put B → ∈ So option b is correct

28. This automata accept 10 11 11 0 1 and checking for other input it is clear that it accept number divisible by 3 and 2.

29. (*a*) and (*d*) are two possible solutions but best is (*b*).

Why (a) is wrong : Run this string on DFA

a b b b : is stop in final stage while it have three b.

Why not (c) : As **a b b a a** have substring **'a b b'** but, don't stop at final state.

30. 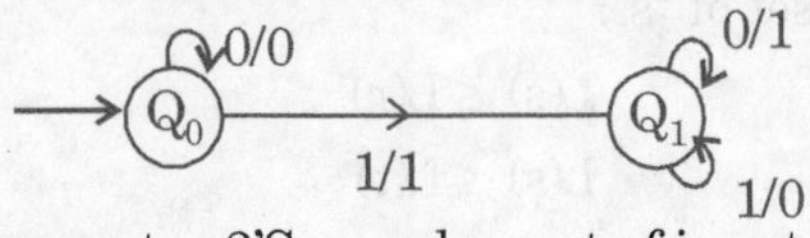

It computes 2'S complement of input Number

Example N = 001100

O/P ⇒ 110100.

31. Automata accept u but reject v and w

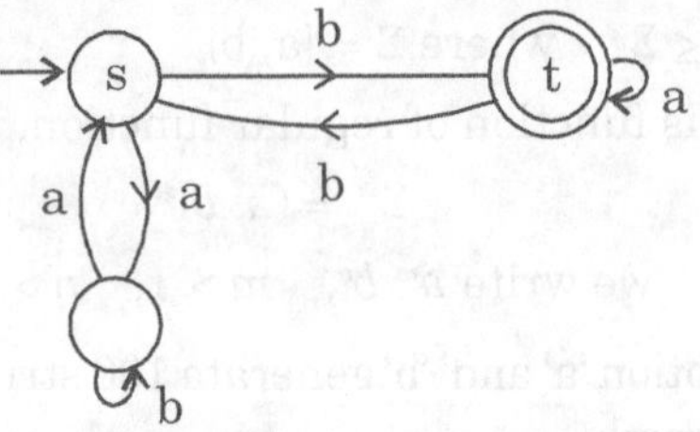

u = abbaba; v = bab; w = aabb

32. 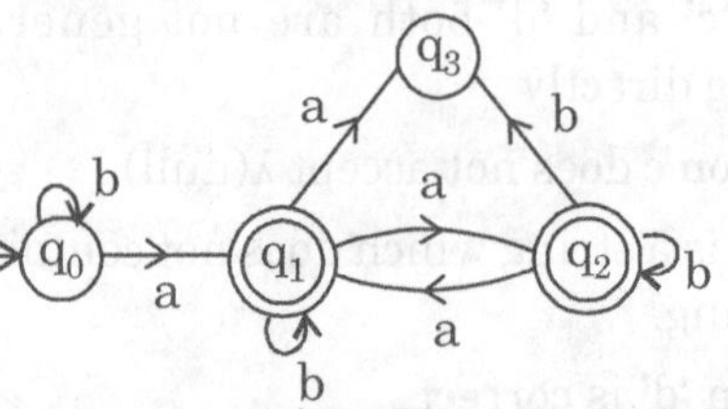

Language generated by automata is accepted by expression b* a(a + b)*

33. 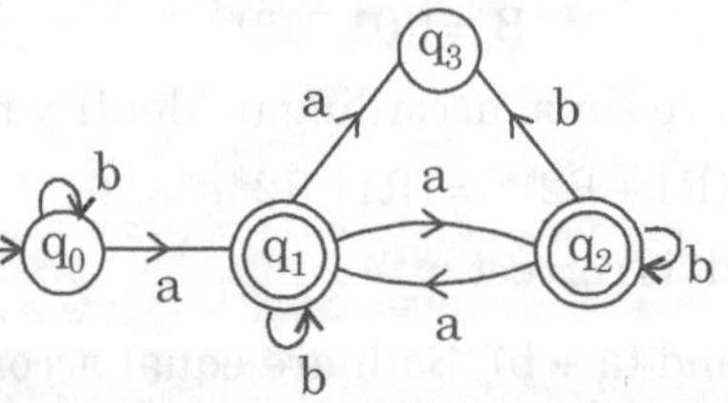

Here q3 is dead state so directly remove and a_1 & q_2 both final state are merge in minimized DfA

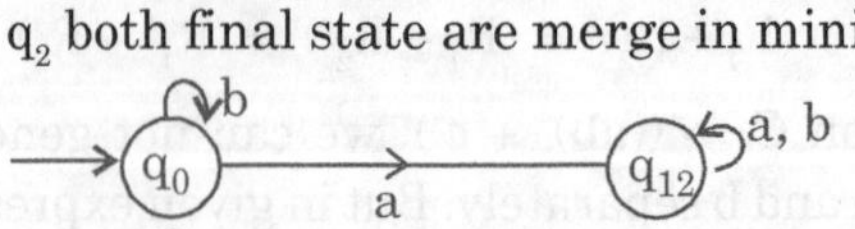 (2 state)

34. 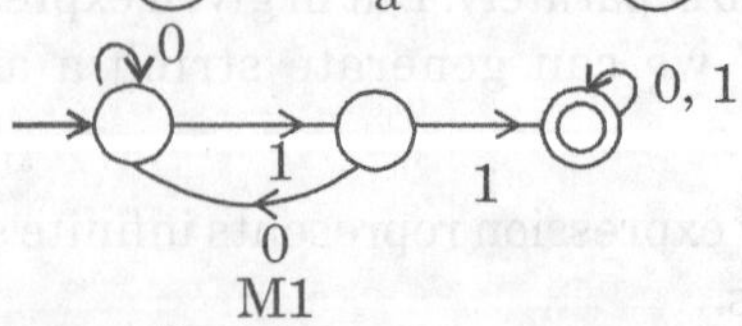

M1

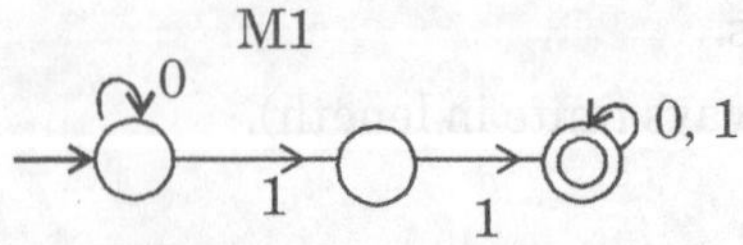

M2

Both M_1 & M_2 accept all strings that contain two consecutive 1'S.

35. y

	a	b
→1	1	2
2(f)	2	1

z

	a	b
→1	2	2
2(f)	1	1

= xy is

	a	b
→(1,1)	(2,1)	(2,2)
(1,2)	(2,2)	(2,1)
(2,1)	(1,1)	(1,2)
(F)(2,2)	(1,2)	(1,1)

So for input b on initial state (1, 1) we get final state (2, 2), which is present only in option (a).

36.
$$\delta(q_0, 0011) = \delta(q_0, 011)$$
$$= \delta(q_0, 11)$$
$$= \delta(\{q_0, q_1\}, 1)$$
$$= \delta(q_0, 1) \cup \delta(q_1, 1)$$
$$= \{q_0, q_1\} \cup \{q_2\} = \{q_0, q_1, q_2\}$$

37.

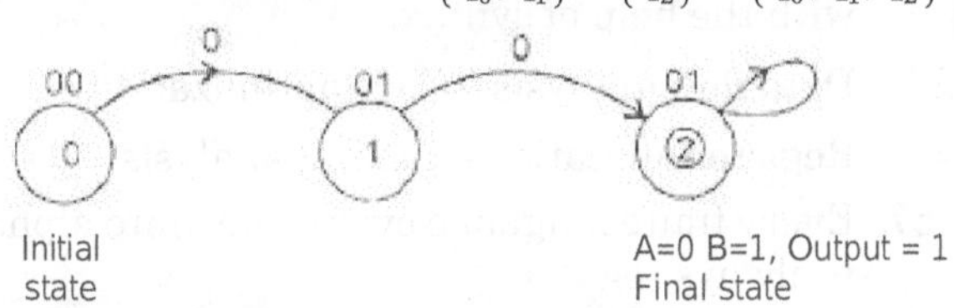

Hence length of input string is 3.

Alternately

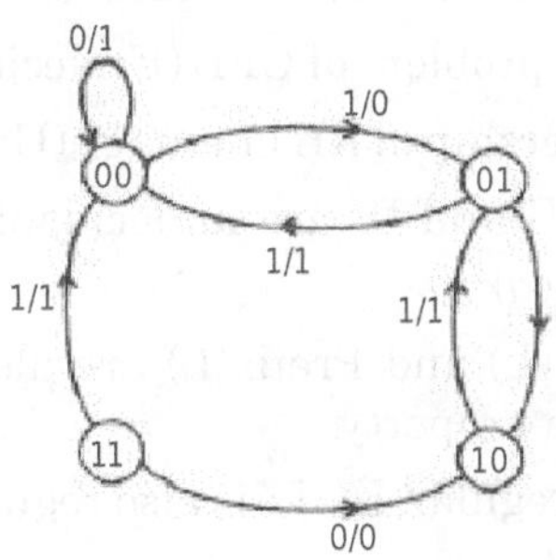

Fom state 00 to 01 with output 1 required minimum 3 length of string i.e. 101.

38.

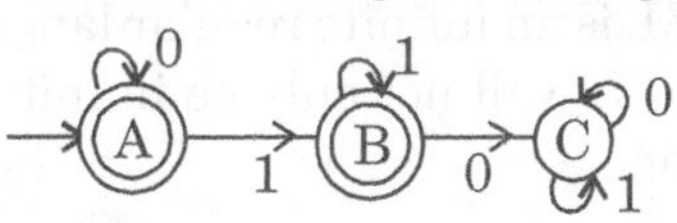

Here two final state A & B

So Regular expression = R.E. of state 'A' + R.E. of state B

= O* + O* 1 1*

= O* (λ + 11*)

= O* 1* {∵ (λ + 11*) = 1* But identify Rule)

39. For n length string we require (n + 1) state in finite automater

for n = 2

(0 + 1) (0 + 1)

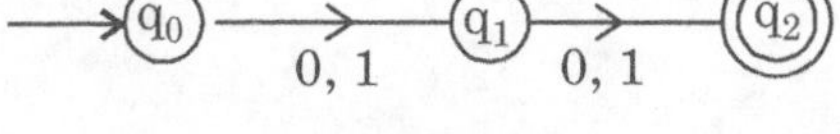

3 state

40. For both

$L_1 = \{a^n \mid n \text{ is odd}\}$

$L_2 = \{a^n \mid n \text{ is even}\}$

minimum state finite automater contain} 2 state

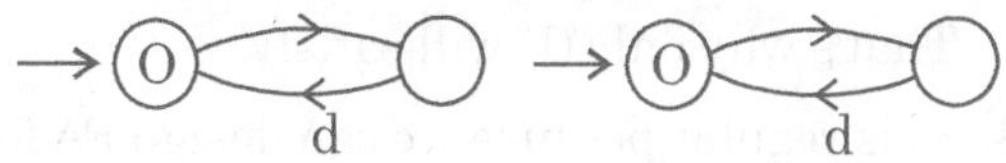

n is even n is odd

41.
$$S = \{0^{2n} | n \geq 1\} \text{ is a regular language}$$
$$= 00,\ 0000,\ 000000,\ \ldots\ldots\ldots\ldots$$
regular language
$$S_2 = \{0^m 1^n 0^{m+n} | mZ_1 \ and nZ_1\}$$
$$= 0100, 00110000, 000111000000$$

42. language $L = \{wxw^R \mid x_1\ w \in \{0, 1\}^+\}$ is a regular language.

43. L_3 is non regular because it generate set of Polynomial

$L_2 = \{w \mid w = w^R\}$

44. Only $\{a^n b^{2m} \mid n \geq 0, m \geq 0\}$

& $\{x_{cy}$, x, y ε (a, b)*} are regular sets.

Alternately

In a regular language, counting of numbers is not possible but counting that a input is repeated even times or odd times is possible; to get the number (even / odd say 4/7) is not possible.

I can be written as a*(bb)*

IV can be (a+b)* c (a+b)*

while for other regular expressions is not possible as they need the counting as number of times.

45. $L_1 = \phi$, $L_2 = \{a\}$

$L_1\ L_2^*$, UL_1^*

$\phi.\ \{a\}^* \cup \{\phi\}^*$

$\phi \cup \lambda\ = \lambda.$

46. (*a*) $L = \{a^n b^n | n \geq 0\}$ is a CFL but not regular, it requires memory for the representation.

(*b*) $L = \{a^n | n \text{ is prime}\}$ is neither regular nor CFL

(*c*) $L = \{w | w \text{ has } 3K + 1\ b\text{'s for some } k \in N \text{ with}\}$

$\Sigma = \{a, b\}$

is a regular language, since the total count of b's are multiple of 3 plus one. The regular expression is $a^*\ ba^*(a^*ba^*ba^*\ ba^*)^*$

$+ (a^*\ ba^*\ ba^*\ ba^*)^* a^*\ ba^*$

(*d*) $L = \{ww | w \in \Sigma^* \text{with } \Sigma = \{0,1\}\}$ is neither regular nor CFL

47. $L_1 . L_2$ will be regular language, concatenation of two regular language is language.

It will be like $L_1 . L_2 \neq \{a^n b^n \mid n \geq 0\}$

It will be like $L_1 . L_2 = \{a^n b^m \mid n, m \geq 0\}$

That's why only (I) will satisfy.

48. L_1 is regular because we can design FA for L_1 but we can not design FA for L_2. Hence L_1 is regular but not L_2.

49. $L_1 = \{W \times W^R \mid W, x \in (a, b)^*, |W|, |X| > 0\}$

W^R is reverse of string of W

It can not be regular, because we can not compare W is regular expression.

$L_2 = \{a^n b^m \mid m \neq n, \text{and } m, n \geq 0\}$ is also not regular due to comparision in a and b

$L_3 = \{a^p b^q c^r \mid p, q, r \geq 0\}$

Here a, b, c are independent and regular exp is $a^* b^* c^*$. Hence L_3 is regular.

50. II Statement is true, if we use $\{\phi\}$ as regular language.

i.e. $A = \{\phi\}$

then $A \cap B = \phi$ which is regular.

51. We need to find smallest value of k which satisfies

$$L_1^{\,k} = L_1^{\,k+1}$$

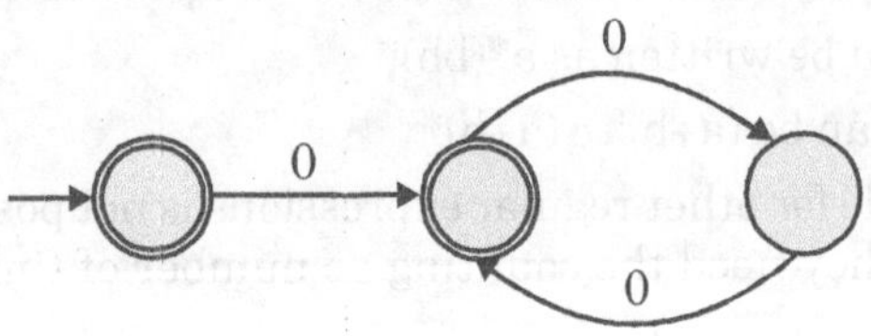

$$L_1 = \in (00)^*$$

Try $k = 0$ $\quad L_1^{\,0} = L_1^{\,1}$

$\Rightarrow$ $\quad \in = L_1$ which is false.

So order is not 0.

Try $k = 1$: $\quad L_1^{\,1} = L_1^{\,2}$

$\Rightarrow$ $\quad L_1^{\,2} = L_1$

Now, $\quad L_1^{\,2} = (\in +0(00)^*)(\in +0(00)^*)$

$\quad = \in +0(00)^* + 00(00)^* = 0^*$

Clearly $\quad L_1^{\,2} \neq L_1$

So order is not 1.

Try $k = 2$: $\quad L_1^{\,2} = L_1^{\,3}$

Now, $\quad L_1^{\,3} = L_1^{\,2} . L_1$

$\quad = 0^*(\in +0(00)^*) = 0^*$

Clearly $\quad L_1^{\,3} = L_1^{\,2} = 0^*$

(So order of L_1 is 2)

52. Fortran is context free language.

53. Not every subset of regular set is regular

Example

$L = a^* b^*$

$L_1 = a^n b^n$.

$L_1 \leq L$ but not regular.

54. All statement are wrong.

55. I, II and III are true

Instead true statement is, "every recursive set is recursively enumerable".

56. Regular expression denote structure of data specially text string-lexical analyser break input text into logical unit such as identifiers.

Push down automater- Syntax analysis. Study with the help of syntax.

Data flow analysis – Code optimization

Register allocation – Lexical analysis

57. Every finite language over some dinte alphabets is always regular.

58. I. Membership of regular language (Decidable)

II. Emptiness of CFL (Decidable)

III. $L = E^*$ problem of CFL (Undecidable)

IV. Membership of RE language (Undecidable)

So, only III and IV are undecidable. So correct answer is (d).

59.
- Suffix (L) and Prefix(L) are also regular by closure property.
- If L is regular, $L \cdot L^R$ is also regular by closure property.

However option(d) $\{ww^R \mid w \in L\}$ need not be regular since if L is an infinite regular language, then $\{ww^R \mid w \in L\}$ will not only be infinite, but also non-regular.

60. $L = \{a^{2+3k} \text{ or } b^{10+12k}\}$ for $k \geq 0$

$= a^2 (a^3)^* \text{ or } b^{10} (b^{12})^*$

$= \{a^2, a^5, a^7, \ldots, b^{10}, b^{22}, b^{34} \ldots\}$

The smallest string which can be pumped is a^5

$$a^5 = \underset{x}{a^2} \underset{y}{(a^3)} \underset{z}{\in}$$

So minimum pumping length = 5

3 CHAPTER

Context Free Language and Push Down Automata

Analysis of Previous GATE Papers

Units	Year → Topics ↓		2019	2018	2017 Set 1	2017 Set 2	2016 Set 1	2016 Set 2	2016 Set 3	2015 Set 1	2015 Set 2	2015 Set 3
CFG	1 Mark	MCQ Type			3							
		Numerical Type										
	2 Marks	MCQ Type						2	1			
		Numerical Type										
	Total				3			4	2			
CFL	1 Mark	MCQ Type				1						
		Numerical Type										
	2 Marks	MCQ Type	1	1	1	1	1					1
		Numerical Type										
	Total		2	2	2	3	2					2
PDA	1 Mark	MCQ Type										
		Numerical Type										
	2 Marks	MCQ Type										
		Numerical Type										
	Total											
NPDA	1 Mark	MCQ Type										
		Numerical Type										
	2 Marks	MCQ Type										
		Numerical Type										
	Total											
DPDA	1 Mark	MCQ Type										
		Numerical Type										
	2 Marks	MCQ Type										
		Numerical Type										
	Total											

CFG

1. The language $\{0^n 1^n 2^n \mid 1 \le n \le 10^6\}$ is
   (a) Regular
   (b) Context-free but not regular.
   (c) Context-free but its complement is not context-free.
   (d) Not context-free. **[IT-2005 : 1 Mark]**

2. A language L satisfies the Pumping Lemma for regular languages, and also the Pumping Lemma for contex-free language. Which of the following statements about L is TRUE?
   (a) L is necessarily a regular language.
   (b) L is necessarily a context-free language, but not necessarily a regular language.
   (c) L is necessarily a non-regular language.
   (d) None of the above. **[IT-2005 : 2 Marks]**

3. Consider the context-free grammars over the alphabet {*a, b, c,*} given below, *S* and *T* are non-terminals.
   $G_1 : S \to aSb \mid T,\ T \to cT \mid \in$
   $G_2 : S \to bSa \mid T,\ T \to cT \mid \in$
   The language $L(G_2) \cap L(G_2)$ is
   (a) Finite
   (b) Not finite but regualr
   (c) Context-free but not regular
   (d) Recursive but not context-free
   [2017 (Set-1) : 1 Mark]

4. A context-free grammar is ambiguous if
   (a) the grammar contains useless non-terminals
   (b) it produces more than one parse tree for some sentence
   (c) some production has two non-terminals side by side on the right-hand side
   (d) None of the above
   [1987 : 2 Marks]

5. If G is a context-free grammar and w is a string of length n in L(G), how long is a derivation of w in G, if G is Chomsky normal form ?
   (a) 2n (b) 2n + 1
   (c) 2n – 1 (d) n
   [1992 : 2 Marks]

6. Which of the following features cannot be captured by context-free grammar ?
   (a) Syntax of if-then-else statements
   (b) Syntax of recursive procedures
   (c) Whether a variable has been declared before its use
   (d) Variable names of arbitrary length.
   [1994 : 2 Marks]

7. Consider the grammar with the following productions.
   $S \to a\,\alpha\,b \mid b\,\alpha\,c \mid ab$
   $S \to \alpha\,S \mid b$
   $S \to \alpha\,bb \mid ab$
   $S\alpha \to bdb \mid bd$
   the above grammar is
   (a) context free grammar
   (b) regular grammar
   (c) context sensitive grammar
   (d) LR(k) **[1995 : 1 Mark]**

8. Let G be a context free grammar with productions given below.
   $S \to ABAC$
   $A \to aA \mid \varepsilon$
   $B \to bB \mid \varepsilon$
   $C \to d$
   Transform the grammar G to an equivalent form G' that has no ε productions and no unit productions. **[1996 : 2 Marks]**

9. If L_1 is a context free language and L_2 is a regular language which of the following is are false ?
   (a) $L_1 - L_2$ is not context free
   (b) $L_1 \cap L_2$ is not context free
   (c) $\sim L_1$ is context free
   (d) $\sim L_2$ is regular **[1999 : 2 Marks]**

10. Let G = ({S}, {a, b}, R, S) ne a context free grammar where the rule set R is
    $S \to a\,S\,b \mid S\,S \mid \varepsilon$
    Which of the following statements is true ?
    (a) G is not ambiguous
    (b) There exist x, $y \in L(G)$ such that $xy \notin L(G)$
    (c) There is a deterministic pushdown automation that accepts L(G)
    (d) We can find a determintic finite state automation that accepts L(G) **[2003 : 2 Marks]**

11. Consider the following grammar C
    $S \to bS \mid aA \mid b$
    $A \to bA \mid aB$
    $B \to bB \mid aS \mid a$
    Let N_a (w) and N_b(w) denote the number of a's and b's in a string w respectively. The language L(G) $\subseteq \{a, b\}^+$ generated by G is
    (a) $\{w \mid N_a(w) > 3N_b(w)\}$
    (b) $\{w \mid N_b(w) > 3N_a(w)\}$
    (c) $\{w \mid N_a(w) = 3k, k \in \{0, 1, 2, ...\}\}$
    (d) $\{w \mid N_b(w) = 3k, k \in \{0, 1, 2, ...\}\}$
    [2004 : 2 Marks]

12. In the context-free grammar below, S is the start symbol, a and b are terminals, and denotes the empty string

S aSa | bSb| a |b|

Which of the following strings is NOT generated by the grammar ?

(a) aaaa (b) baba
(c) abba (d) babaaabab

[IT-2006 : 1 Mark]

13. In the context free grammar below, S is the start symbol, a and b are terminals, and denotes the empty string.

$S \rightarrow aSAb \mid \varepsilon$

$A \rightarrow bA \mid \varepsilon$

The grammar generates the language

(a) $((a + b)^* b)^*$ (b) $\{a^m b^n \mid m \leq n\}$
(c) $\{a^m b^n \mid m = n\}$ (d) $a^* b^*$

[IT-2006 : 2 Marks]

14. Consider the following statements about the context-free grammar,

$G = \{S \rightarrow SS, S \rightarrow ab, S \rightarrow ba, S \rightarrow \varepsilon\}$

1. G is ambiguous.
2. G produces all strings with equal number of a's and b's.
3. G can be accepted by a deterministic PDA.

Which combination below expresses all the true statements about G?

(a) 1 only (2) 1 and 3 only
(c) 2 and 3 only (4) 1, 2 and 3

[2006 : 2 Marks]

15. Consider an ambiguous grammar G and its disambiguated version D. Let the language recognized by the two grammars be denoted by L(G) and L(D) respectively. Which one of the following is true ?

(a) $L(D) \subset L(G)$ (b) $L(D) \supset L(G)$
(c) $L(D) = L(G)$ (d) L(D) is empty

[2007 : 1 Mark]

16. Consider the following gramamrs. Names representing terminals have been specified in capital letters.

G1 : stmnt → WHILE (expr) stmnt
stmnt → OTHER
expr → ID

G2 : stmnt → WHILE (expr) stmnt
stmnt → OTHER
expr → expr + expr
expr → expr * expr
expr → ID

Which one of the following statements is true?

(a) G1 is context-free but not regular and G2 is regular
(b) G2 is context-free but not regular and G1 is regular
(c) Both G1 and G2 are regular
(d) Both G1 and G2 are context-free but neither of them is regular

[IT-2007 : 2 Marks]

17. Which of the following statements are true ?

1. Every left-recursive grammar can be converted to a right-recursive grammar and vice-versa
2. All ε-productions can be removed from any context-free grammar by suitable tranformations
3. The language generated by a context-free grammar all of whose productions are of the form $X \rightarrow w$ or $X \rightarrow wY$ (where, w is a string of terminals and Y is a non-terminal), is always regular
4. The derivation trees of strings generated by a context-free grammar in Chomsky Normal Form are always binary trees

(a) 1, 2, 3 and 4 (b) 2, 3 and 4 only
(c) 1, 3 and 4 only (d) 1, 2 and 4 only

[2008 : 2 Marks]

18. Consider a CFG with the following productions.

$S \rightarrow AA \mid B$

$A \rightarrow 0A \mid A0 \mid 1$

$B \rightarrow 0B00 \mid 1$

S is the start symbol, A and B are non-terminals and 0 and 1 are the terminals. The language generated by this grammar is

(a) $\{0^n 10^{2n} \mid n \geq 1\}$
(b) $\{0^i 10^j 10^k \mid i, j, k \geq 0\} \cup \{0^n 10^{2n} \mid n \geq 0\}$
(c) $\{0^i 10^j \mid i, j \geq 0\} \cup \{0^n 10^{2n} \mid n \geq 1\}$
(d) The set of all strings over {0, 1} containing at least two 0's

[IT-2008 : 2 Marks]

Directions for Question 19 to 20 :

A CFG G is given with the following productions where S is the start symbol, A is a non-terminal and a and b are terminals.

$S \rightarrow aS \mid A$

$A \rightarrow aAb \mid bAa \mid \varepsilon$

19. Which of the following strings is generated by the grammar above?

(a) aabbaba (b) aabaaba
(c) abababb (d) aabbaab

[IT-2008 : 2 Marks]

20. For the correct answer in above Question, how many steps are required to derive the string and how many parse trees are there?

(a) 6 and 1 (b) 6 and 2
(c) 7 and 2 (d) 4 and 2

[IT-2008 : 2 Marks]

21. Consider the following context-free grammars:

$G_1 : S \to aS \mid B,\ B \to b \mid bB$

$G_2 : S \to aA \mid bB,\ A \to aA \mid B \mid \varepsilon,\ B \to bB \mid \varepsilon$

Which of the following pairs of languages is generated by G1 and G2, respectively?

(a) $\{a^m b^n \mid m > 0 \text{ or } n > 0\}$ and $\{a^m b^n \mid m > 0 \text{ and } n > 0$
(b) $\{a^m b^n \mid m > 0 \text{ or } n > 0\}$ and $\{a^m b^n \mid m > 0 \text{ and } n \geq 0$
(c) $\{a^m b^n \mid m \geq 0 \text{ or } n > 0\}$ and $\{a^m b^n \mid m > 0 \text{ and } n > 0$
(d) $\{a^m b^n \mid m \geq 0 \text{ or } n > 0\}$ and $\{a^m b^n \mid m > 0 \text{ and } n > 0$

[2016 (Set-3) : 2 Marks]

22. Language L_1 is defined by the grammar:

$S_1 \to aS_1b \mid \varepsilon$

Language L_2 is defined by the grammar:

$S_2 \to abS_2/\in.$

Consider the following statements:

P : L_1 is regular
Q : L_2 is regular

Which one of the following is TRUE ?

(a) Both P and Q are true
(b) P is true and Q is false
(c) P is false and Q is true
(d) Both P and Q are false

[2016 (Set-2) : 2 Marks]

23. Which one of the following grammars is free from left recursion ?

$S \to AB\ S \to Ab \mid Bb \mid c$

(a) $A \to Aa \mid b$, $B \to c$, $S \to Aa \mid B$
(b) $A \to Bd \mid \varepsilon$, $B \to e$, $S \to Aa \mid Bb \mid c$
(c) $A \to Bb \mid Sc \mid \varepsilon$, $B \to d$
(d) $A \to Bd \mid \varepsilon$, $B \to Ae \mid \varepsilon$

[2016 (Set-2) : 2 Marks]

24. Consider the following context-free grammar over the alphabet = {a, b, c} with S as the start symbol:

$S \to abScT \mid abcT$
$T \to bT \mid b$

Which one of the following represents the language generated by the above grammar?

(a) $\{(ab)^n (cb)^n \mid n \geq 1\}$
(b) $\{(ab)^n\ cb^{m_1}\ cb^{m_2} \ldots cb^{m_n} \mid n, m_1, m_2, \ldots, m_n \geq 1\}$
(c) $\{(ab)^n (cb^m)^n \mid m, n \geq 1\}$
(d) $\{(ab)^n (cb^n)^m \mid m, n \geq 1\}$ **[2017 (Set-1) : 1 Mark]**

25. Identify the language generated by the following grammar, where S is the start variable.

$S \to XY$
$X \to aX \mid a$
$Y \to aYb \mid \in$

(a) $\{a^m b^n \mid m \geq n, n > 0\}$ (b) $\{a^m b^n \mid m \geq n, n \geq 0\}$
(c) $\{a^m b^n \mid m > n, n \geq 0\}$ (d) $\{a^m b^n \mid m > n, n > 0\}$

[2017 (Set-1) : 1 Mark]

CFL

26. Let P be a regular language and Q be a context-free language such that $Q \subseteq P$. (For example, let P be the language represented by the regular expression p^*q^* and Q be $\{p^nq^n \mid n \in N\}$. Then which of the following is ALWAYS regular?

(a) $P \cap Q$ (b) P - Q
(c) Σ^* - P (d) Σ^* - Q

[2011 : 1 Mark]

27. Context tree languages and regular languages both are closed under the operation (s) of

(a) union (b) interecection
(c) concatenation (d) complement

[1989 : 2 Marks]

28. Context free languages are

(a) closed under union
(b) closed under complementation
(c) closed under intersection
(d) closed under Kleene closure

[1992 : 2 Marks]

29. If L1 and L2 are context free languages and R a regular set, one of the languages below is not necessarily a context free languages. Which one?

(a) L_1L_2 (b) $L_1 \cap L_2$
(c) $L_1 \cap R$ (d) $L_1 \cup L_2$

[1996 : 2 Marks]

30. Context free languages are closed under

(a) union, intersection
(b) union, kleene closure
(c) intersection, complement
(d) complement, kleene clousre **[1999 : 1 Mark]**

31. Which of the following statement is true ?

(a) if a language is context free is can always be accepted by a deterministic push-down automation
(b) the union of two context free languages is context free
(c) the intersection of two context free languages is context free
(d) the complement of a context free languages is context free **[2001 : 1 Mark]**

32. Which of the following statements is FALSE?

(a) There exist context free languages such that all the context free grammars generating them are ambiguous

(b) An unambiguous context-free grammar always has a unique parse tree for each string of the language generated by it

(c) Both determinstic and non-deterministic pushdown automata always accept the same set of languages

(d) A finite set of strings from some alphabet is always a regular language **[IT-2004 : 1 Mark]**

33. The language $\{a^m b^n c^{m+n} \mid m, n \geq 1\}$ is

(a) regular

(b) context-free but not regular

(c) context sensitive but not context free

(d) type-0 but not context sensitive

[2004 : 2 Marks]

34. Consider the languages

$L_1 = \{a^n b^n c^m \mid n, m > 0\}$ and $L_2 = \{a^n b^m c^m \mid n, m > 0\}$

Which one of the following statements is FALSE?

(a) $L_1 \cap L_2$ is a context-free language

(b) $L_1 \cup L_2$ is a context-free language

(c) L_1 and L_2 are context-free language

(d) $L_1 \cap L_2$ is a context sensitive language

[2005 : 2 Marks]

35. Consider the languages

$L_1 = \{ww^R \mid w \in \{0, 1\}^*\}$

$L_2 = \{w\#w^R \mid w \in \{0, 1)^*\}$, where # is a special symbol

$L_3 = \{ww \mid w \in \{0, 1\}^*\}$

Which one of the following is TRUE ?

(a) L_1 is a deterministic CFL

(b) L_2 is a deterministic CFL

(c) L_3 is a CFL, but not a determistic CFL

(d) L_3 is a deterministic CFL **[2005 : 2 Marks]**

36. Let $L_1 = \{0^{n+m} 1^n 0^m \mid n, m \geq 0\}$,

$L_2 = \{0^{n+m} 1^{n+m} 0^m \mid n, m \geq 0\}$, and

$L_3 = \{0^{n+m} 1^{n+m} 0^{n+m} \mid n, m \geq 0\}$.

Which of these languages are NOT context free ?

(a) L_1 only (b) L_3 only

(c) L_1 and L_2 (d) L_2 and L_3

[2006 : 1 Mark]

37. Let L be a context-free language and M a regular language. Then the language $L \cap M$ is

(a) always regular

(b) never regular

(c) always a deteministic context-free language

(d) always a context-free language

[IT-2006 : 2 Marks]

38. The language $L = \{0^i 21^i \mid i \geq 0\}$ over the alphabet {0, 1, 2) is

(a) not recursive

(b) is recursive and is a deterministic CFL

(c) is a regular language

(d) is not a deterministic CFL but a CFL

[IT-2007 : 2 Marks]

39. Let $L = L_1 \cap L_2$, where L_1 and L_2 are language as defined below :

$L_1 = \{a^m b^m c a^n b^n \mid m, n \geq 0\}$

$L_2 = \{a^i b^j c^k \mid i, j, k \geq 0\}$

Then L is

(a) not recursive

(b) regular

(c) context-free but not regular

(d) recursively enumerable but not context-free

[2009 : 2 Marks]

40. Consider the language $L1 = \{0^i1^j \mid i = j\}$, $L2 = \{0^i1^j \mid i = j\}$, $L3 = (0^i1^j \mid i = 2j + 1\}$, $L4 = \{0^i1^j \mid i \neq 2j\}$.

Which one of the following statements is true?

(a) Only L2 is context free

(b) Only L2 and L3 are context free

(c) Only L1 and L2 are context free

(d) All are context free **[2010 : 2 Marks]**

41. Which of the following languages are context-free?

$L_1 = \{a^m b^n a^n b^m \mid m, n \geq 1\}$

$L_2 = \{a^m b^n a^m b^n \mid m, n \geq 1\}$

$L_3 = \{a^m b^n \mid m = 2n + 1\}$

(a) L_1 and L_2 only (b) L_1 and L_3 only

(c) L_2 and L_3 only (d) L_3 only

[2015 (Set-3) : 2 Marks]

42. Consider the transition diagram of a PDA given below with input alphabet = {a, b} and stack alphabet l = {X, Z}. Z is the initial stack symbol. Let L denote the language accepted by the PDA.

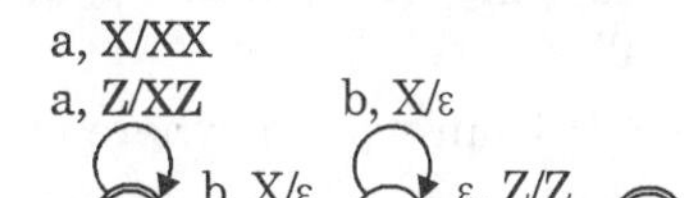

Which one of the following is TRUE ?

(a) $L = \{a^n b^n \mid n \geq 0\}$ and is not accepted by any finite automata

(b) $L = \{a^n \mid n \geq 0\} \cup \{a^n b^n \mid n \geq 0\}$ and is not accepted by any deterministic PDA

(c) L is not accepted by any Turning machine that halts on every input

(d) $L = \{a^n \mid n \geq 0\} \cup \{a^n b^n \mid n \geq 0\}$ and is deterministic context-free

[2016 (Set-1) : 2 Marks]

43. Consider the following language are the alphabet = {a,b,c}

Let $L_1 = \{a^n b^n c^m | m, n \geq 0\}$ and $L_2 = \{a^m b^n c^n \; m, n \geq 0\}$

Which of the following are context free languages?

I. $L_1 \cup L_2$ II. $L_1 \cap L_2$

(a) I only (b) II only

(c) Both (d) None of these.

[2017 (Set-1) : 2 Marks]

44. Let L1, L2 be any two context-free languages and R be any regular language. Then which of the following is/are CORRECT?

I. $L_1 \cup L_2$ is context-free. II. $\overline{L_1}$ is context-free.

III. $L_1 - R$ is context-free. IV. $L_1 \cap L_2$ is context-free.

(a) I, II and IV only (b) I and III only

(c) II and IV only (d) I only

[2017 (Set-2) : 1 Mark]

45. Consider the following languages :

$L_1 = \{a^p \mid p \text{ is a prime number}\}$

$L_2 = \{a^n b^m c^{2m} \mid n \geq 0, m \geq 0\}$

$L_3 = \{a^n b^n c^{2n} \mid n \geq 0\}$

$L_4 = \{a^n b^n \mid n \geq 1\}$

Which of the following are CORRECT?

I. L_1 is context-free but not regular.

II. L_2 is not context-free.

III. L_3 is not context-free but recursive.

IV. L_4 is deterministic context-free.

(a) I, II and IV only (b) II and III only

(c) I and IV only (d) III and IV only

[2017 (Set-2) : 2 Marks]

46. Consider the following languages :

I. $\{a^m b^n c^p d^q \mid m + p = n + q, \text{ where } m, n, p, q \geq 0\}$

II. $\{a^m b^n c^p d^q \mid m = n \text{ and } p = q, \text{ where } m, n, p, q \geq 0\}$

III. $\{a^m b^n c^p d^q \mid m = n = p \text{ and } p = q, \text{ where } m, n, p, q \geq 0\}$

IV. $\{a^m b^n c^p d^q \mid mn = p + q, \text{ where } m, n, p, q \geq 0\}$

Which of the language above are context-free?

(a) I and IV only (b) I and II only

(c) II and III only (d) II and IV only

[2018 : 2 Marks]

47. Let L be a language and $\overline{L}$ be its complement. Which one of the following is NOT a viable possibility?

(a) Neither L nor is recursively enumerable (r.e.).

(b) One of L and $\overline{L}$ is r.e. but not recursive, the other is not r.e.

(c) Both L and $\overline{L}$ are r.e. but not recursive.

(d) Both L and $\overline{L}$ are recursive.

[2014 (Set-1) : 2 Marks]

48. Which one of the following languages over $\Sigma = \{a, b\}$ is NOT context-free?

(1) $\{wa^n w^R b^n \mid w \in \{a,b\}^*, n \geq 0\}$

(2) $\{a^n b^i \mid i \in \{n, 3n, 5n\}, n \geq 0\}$

(3) $\{ww^R \mid w \in \{a, b\}^*\}$

(4) $\{wa^n b^n w^R \mid w \in \{a, b\}^*, n \geq 0\}$ **[2019 : 2 Marks]**

PDA

49. Which of the following language over {a, b, c} is accepted by a deterministic push down automata?

(a) $\{wcw^R \mid w \in \{a, b\}^*\}$

(b) $\{ww^R \mid w \in \{a, b, c\}^*\}$

(c) $\{a^n b^n c^n \mid n \geq 0\}$

(d) {W | W is a palindrome over {a, b, c}}

[1997 : 2 Marks]

50. Let L_D be the set of all language accepted by a PDA by final state and L_E the set of all languages accepted by empty stack. Which of the following is true ?

(a) $L_D = L_E$ (b) $L_D \supset L_E$

(c) $L_D \subset L_E$ (d) None of the above

[1999 : 1 Mark]

51. The language accepted by a Pushdown Automation in which the stack is limited to 10 items is best described as

(a) context free

(b) regular

(c) deterministic context free

(d) recursive **[2002 : 1 Mark]**

52. Let $M = (K, \Sigma, \Gamma, \Delta, s, F)$ be a pushdown automaton, where

$K = (s, f)$, $F = \{f\}$, $\Sigma = \{a, b\}$, $\Gamma = \{a\}$ and

$\Delta = \{((s, a, \varepsilon), (s, a)), ((s, b, \varepsilon), (s, a)), ((s, a, \varepsilon), (f, \varepsilon)), ((f, a, a), (f, \varepsilon)), ((f, b, a), (f, \varepsilon))\}$

Which one of the following strings is not a member of L(M)?

(a) aaa (b) aabab

(c) baaba (d) bab

[IT-2004 : 2 Marks]

53. Consider the pushdown automaton (PDA) below which runs over the input alphabet (a, b, c). It has the stack alphabet $\{Z_0, X\}$ where Z_0 is the bottom of stack marker. The set of states of the PDA is {s, t, u, f} where is the start state and f is the final state. The PDA accepts by final state. The transitions of the PDA given below are depicted in a standard manner. For example, the transition (s, b, X) → (t, XZ_0) means that if the PDA is in state s and the symbol on the top of the stack is X, then it can read b from the input and move to state t after popping the top of stack and pushing the symbols Z_0 and X_0 and X (in that order) on the stack.

$(s, a, Z_0) \rightarrow (s, XYZ_0)$
$(s, \varepsilon, Z_0) \rightarrow (f, \varepsilon)$
$(s, a, X) \rightarrow (s, XXX)$
$(s, b, X) \rightarrow (t, \varepsilon)$
$(t, b, X) \rightarrow (t, \varepsilon)$
$(t, c, X) \rightarrow (f, \varepsilon)$
$(u, c, X) \rightarrow (t, \varepsilon)$
$(u, \varepsilon, Z_0) \rightarrow (f, \varepsilon)$

The language accepted by the PDA is

(a) $\{a^l b^m c^n \mid l = m = n\}$
(b) $\{a^l b^m c^n \mid l = m\}$
(c) $\{a^l b^m c^n \mid 2l = m + n\}$
(d) $\{a^l b^m c^n \mid m = n\}$ **[IT-2006 : 2 Marks]**

54. Which one of the following is FALSE ?

(a) There is a unique minimal DFA for every regular language
(b) Every NFA can be converted to an equivalent PDA
(c) Complement of every context-free language is recursive
(d) Every nondeterministic PDA can be converted to an equivalent deterministic PDA

[2009 : 1 Mark]

55. Consider the language L1, L2 and L3 are given below :

$L1 = \{0^p 1^q \mid p, q \in N\}$,
$L2 = \{0^p 1^q \mid p, q \in N \text{ and } p = q\}$ and
$L3 = \{0^p 1^q 0^r \mid p, q, r \in N \text{ and } p = q = r\}$

Which of the following statements is NOT TRUE?

(a) Push Down Automata (PDA) can be used to recognize L1 and L2
(b) L1 is a regular language
(c) All the three languages are context free
(d) Turing machines can be used to recognize all the languages

[2011 : 2 Marks]

56. Consider the following languages

$L1 = \{0^p 1^q 0^r \mid p, q, r \geq 0\}$
$L2 = \{0^p 1^q 0^r \mid p, q, r \geq 0, p = r\}$

Which one of the following statements is FALSE?

(a) L_2 is context free
(b) $L_1 \cap L_2$ is context free
(c) Complement of L_2 is recursive
(d) Complement of L_1 is context-free but not regular

[2013 : 2 Marks]

57. Consider the following languages over the alphabet = {0, 1, c} :

$L_1 = \{0^n 1^n \mid n 0\}$
$L_2 = \{wcw^r \mid w \in \{0, 1\}^*\}$
$L_3 = \{ww^r \mid w \in \{0, 1\}^*\}$

Here, w^r is the reverse of the string w. Which of these languages are determinstic Context-free languages?

(a) None of the languages
(b) Only L_1
(c) Only L_1 and L_2
(d) All the three languages

[2014 (Set-3) : 2 Marks]

NPDA

58. Let P be a non-deterministic push-down automaton (NPDA) with exactly one state, q, and exactly one symbol, Z, in its stack alphabet. State q is both the starting as well as the accepting state of the PDA. The stack is intialized with one Z before the start of the operation of the PDA. Let the input alphabet of the PDA be Σ.

Let L(P) be the language accepted by the PDA by reading a string and reaching its accepting state. Let N(P) be the language accepted by the PDA by reading a string and emptying its stack. Which of the following statements is TRUE ?

(a) L(P) is necessarily Σ^* but N(P) is not necessarily Σ^*.
(b) N(P) is necessarily Σ^* but N(P) is not necessarily Σ^*.
(c) Both L(P) and N(P) is necessarily Σ^*.
(d) Neither L(P) nor N(P) are necessarily Σ^*.

[IT-2005 : 1 Mark]

59. Let N_f and N_p denote the classes of languages accepted by non-deterministic finite automata and non-deterministic push-down automata, respectively. Let D_f and D_p denote the classes of languages accepted by deterministic finite automata and deterministic push-down automata, respectively. Which one of the following is TRUE?

(a) $D_f \subset N_f$ and $D_p \subset N_p$
(b) $D_f \subset N_f$ and $D_p = N_p$
(c) $D_f = N_f$ and $D_p = N_p$
(d) $D_f = N_f$ and $D_p \subset N_p$

[2005 : 2 Marks]

60. Consider the NPDA $\langle Q = \{q_0, q_1, a_2\}, \Sigma = \{0, 1\}$ $\Gamma = \{0, 1, \perp\}$ δ, q_0, $\perp$, $F = \{q_2\}$, where (as per usual convention) Q is the set of states, Σ is the input alphabet, is stack alphabet, δ is the state transition function, q_0 is the initial state, $\perp$ is the initial stack symbol, and F is the set of accepting states, The state transition is as follows :

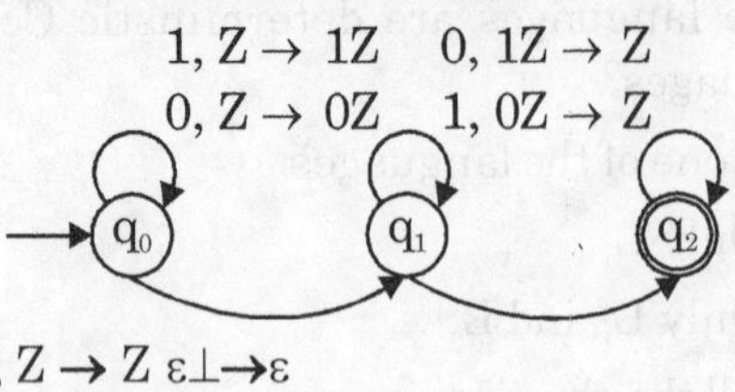

Which one of the following sequences must follow the string 101100 so that the overall string is accepted by the automation?

(a) 10110 (b) 10010
(c) 01010 (d) 01001

[2015 (Set-1) : 2 Marks]

61. In which of the cases stated below is the following statement true ?

"For every non-deterministic machine M_1 there exists an equivalent deterministic machine M_2 recognizing the same language".

(a) M_1 is non-deterministic finite automaton
(b) M_1 is a non-deterministic PDA
(c) M_1 is a non-deterministic Turing machine
(d) For no machine M1 use the above statement true **[1992 : 2 Marks]**

62. Which of the following conversions is not possible (algorithmically) ?

(a) Regular grammar to context free grammar
(b) Non-deterministic FSA to deterministic FSA
(c) Non-determinstic PDA to deterministic PDA
(d) Non-deterministic Turing machine to deterministic Turing machine

[1994 : 2 Marks]

63. Regarding the power of recognition of languages, which of the following statements is false?

(a) The non-deterministic finite-state automata are equivalent to deterministic finite-state automata
(b) Non-deterministic push-down automata are equivalent to deterministic push-down automata]
(c) Non-deterministic Turning machines are equivalent to deterministic Turning machines
(d) Multi-tape Turning machines are equivalent to Single-tape Turning machines.

[1998 : 1 Mark]

DPDA

64. Which of the following languages is accepted by a non-deterministic push down automaton (PDA) but NOT by a deterministic PDA?

(a) $\{a^n b^n c^n \mid n \geq 0\}$
(b) $\{a^l b^m c^n \mid l \neq m \text{ or } m \neq n\}$
(c) $\{a^n b^n \mid n \geq 0\}$
(d) $\{a^m b^n \mid m, n \geq 0\}$

[IT-2006 : 2 Marks]

65. Consider the following languages.

$L_1 = \{a^i b^j c^k \mid i = j, k \geq 1\}$

$L_2 = \{a^i b^j \mid j = 2i, i \geq 0\}$

Which of the following is true ?

(a) L_1 is not a CFL but L_2 is
(b) $L_1 \cap L_2$ = and ϕ L_1 is non-regular
(c) $L_1 \cup L_2$ is not a CFL but L_2 is
(d) There is a 4 state PDA that accept L_1, but there is no DPDA that accepts L_2

[IT-2008 : 2 Marks]

ANSWERS

1. (a)	2. (d)	3. (b)	4. (b)	5. (c)	6. (c)	7. (c)	8. (*)	9. (a, c)	10. (c)
11. (c)	12. (b)	13. (b)	14. (b)	15. (c)	16. (d)	17. (c)	18. (*)	19. (d)	20. (a)
21. (d)	22. (c)	23. (b)	24. (b)	25. (c)	26. (c)	27. (a,c)	28. (a,c)	29. (b)	30. (b)
31. (b)	32. (c)	33. (b)	34. (a)	35. (b)	36. (d)	37. (d)	38. (b)	39. (c)	40. (d)
41. (b)	42. (d)	43. (a)	44. (b)	45. (d)	46. (b)	47. (c)	48. (a)	49. (a)	50. (a)
51. (b)	52. (c)	53. (c)	54. (d)	55. (c)	56. (d)	57. (c)	58. (d)	59. (d)	60. (b)
61. (a, c)	62. (c)	63. (b)	64. (b)	65. (b)					

EXPLANATIONS

1. $L\{0^n1^n2^n | 1 \le n \le 10^6\}$ is finite language and every finite is regular language.
2. Pumping lemma is negative test. It is use to prove language is not regular as well as also use for to prove language is not CFL.
3. $L(G_1)\{a^nc^mb^n | n_1\ m \ge 0\}$

   $L(G_2)\{b^nc^mb^n | n_1\ m \ge 0\}$

   $L(G_1) \cap L(G_2)\{c^m | m \ge 0\}$

   It is regular.
4. If there exist more than one parse tree for a string then grammar is imbargoes.
5. If length of string is n the length of derivation is (2n – 1). If grammar is in CNF form.
6. Variable as been declared before its use or not we can't capture is by CFG.
7. $S \to \alpha S \to \alpha\alpha S \to \alpha\alpha\alpha bb$

   $S \to a\alpha b$

   $S \to \alpha S$

   $\to \alpha\alpha S$

   $\to \alpha\alpha ab$

   Some language cannot generated by any grammar.
8. Let us first eliminate $A \to \in$

   We get the following rules

   $S \to ABC \mid BAC \mid BC$

   $A \to a$

   By eliminating $B \to \in$ we get following rules

   $S \to AC \mid AAC \mid C$

   $B \to b$

   Hence, after eliminating $\in$, grammar becomes :

   $S \to ABAC \mid ABC \mid BAC \mid BC \mid AC \mid AAC \mid C$

   $A \to aA \mid a$

   $B \to bB \mid b$

   $C \to d$

   Now the eliminate unit production $S \to C$

   $S \to ABAC \mid ABC \mid BAC \mid BC \mid AC \mid AAC \mid d$

   $A \to aA \mid a$

   $B \to bB \mid b$

   $C \to d$
9. Intersection of a content free language and a regular language is context free. L1 – L2 is the same as L1 ∩ ~L2. Also ~L2 is regular, as complement of a regular language is regular. So L1 - L2 is context free. So (*a*) is false.

   The complement of a context free language need not be context free. So (*c*) is false.
10. $S \to asb \mid ss \mid \in$ is ambiguous grammar the language generated by grammar is NCFL
11. $S \to bs \mid a \mid b$

    $A \to bA \mid aB$

    $B \to bB \mid aS \mid a$

    This grammar will execute

    $\{w \mid Na(w) = 3k \quad k \in \{0, 1, 2, ...\}\}$.
12. $S \to asa \mid bsb \mid a \mid b$

    The grammar generate palindromes. baba is not a palindrome.
13. The language generated by grammar is

    $\{a^mb^n | m \le n\}$
14. String aabb can't produce by grammar G.
15. The language generated by ambiguous grammar and its unambiguous version is always same.
16. Let us assume that

    stmt = S

    while = S

    expr = E

    other = b

    ID = c

    then G_1 is

    $S \to a(E)\,S$

    $S \to b$

    $E \to c$

    Hence G_1 is CFG but not regular

    G2 =

    $S \to a(E)\,S$

    $S \to b$

    $E \to E + E$

    $E \to E * E$

    $E \to c$

    Hence G_2 is also CFG but not regular.
17. Statement III is false. In a context free grammar, right side of the productions should either have single terminal or one non-terminal followed by terminal or λ.
18. [Note: All options are false]

    [Key: - All are false]

    $A \to oA \mid Ao \mid 1$ gives $\{o^i \mid o^i \mid i, j \ge 0\}$

    $B \to oBoo \mid 1$ gives $\{o^n \mid o^{2n} \mid n \ge 0\}$

    $S \to AA \mid B$ concatenate A with A or gives B.

    Hence.

    $L\{o^i \mid o^i \mid o^k | i,j,k \ge o\} \cup \{o^n \mid o^{2n} | n \ge o\}$

    According to that no option is matched.

19. $S \Rightarrow as$

$S \Rightarrow aA$

$\Rightarrow aaAb$

$\Rightarrow aabAab$

$\Rightarrow aabbAaab$

$\Rightarrow aabbaab$

20. Total 6 steps required as shown in solution (19) and only one parse tree is there.

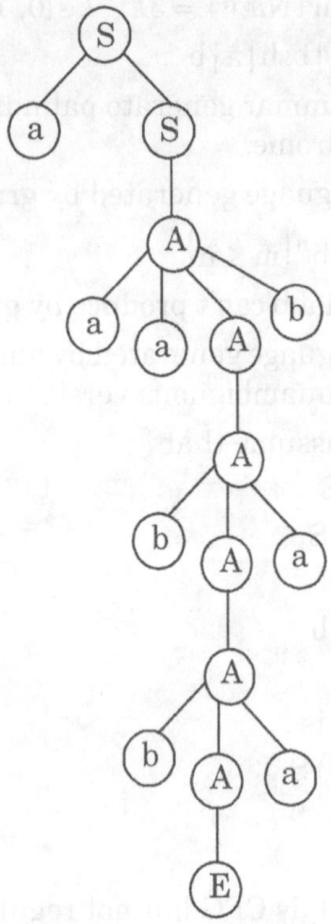

21. *a* can be 0.

b can't be 0.

22. $S_1 \to aS_1b/\in$.

$L = \{a^n b^n \mid n \geq 0\}$ is CFL

$S_2 \to abS_2/\in$.

$L = \{(ab)^n \mid n \geq 0\}$ is regular

23. From option (*b*)

$\left.\begin{array}{l} S \to Ab \mid Bb \mid \in \\ A \to Bd \mid \in \\ B \to e \end{array}\right\}$ Generates finite language

No Recursion at all

So, the given option (*b*) is free from left recursion.

24. ababab cbbbbcbcbb is a string generated by grammar as well as by language given in option (b).

25. X generates atleast one 'a' while y generates equal no of A's & b's (including Epsilon).

26. $\Sigma^* - P$ is the complement of P so it is always regular,

Since regular languages are closed under complementation

27. CFL & regular languages are closed under union and concatenation and complement but CFL is not closed.

28. Both CFL are closed under union and kleene closure operation and not closed under complement & intersection.

29. Intersection of few context free language is not necessary a context free language.

30. CFL are closed under union, kleene closure operation and not closed under intersection & complement

31. If language is CFL it may or may not be accepted by DPDA. Some CFL may be accepted by NPDA.

(*) CFL are not closed under intersection.

(*) CFL are not closed under complement.

32. Non deterministic Pushdown Automata is more powerful then deterministic Pushdown Automata. Hence the Set of languages may be different.

33. $L = \{a^m b^n c^{m+n} \mid m, n \geq 1\}$

The given language is context free but not regular language

34. $L_1 \cap L_2 = \{a^n b^n c^n \mid n \geq 0\}$

Here number of a, b and c are equal hence we can't design PDA for that language.

35. L_1 is CFL but not a DCFL, since accepting wwR necessarily involves finding the middle of the string, which involves non-determinism.

$\therefore$ (*a*) is false.

L_2 is a DCFL is true since "#" is a special symbol and middle of string can now be surely found by using "#", thereby eliminating the need for non-deterministic guessing. So (*b*) is true.

L_3 is a CSL and not a CFL. So (*c*) is false.

L_3 is not a DCFL either. So (*d*) is false.

36. In L_1, L_2 and L_3, only L_1 can be written as a context free language, the production for L_1 are

$$S \to 0\,S0 \mid 0A1 \mid \in$$

$$A \to 0A1 \mid \in$$

to generate $0^{n+m} \mid ^n 0^m$

i. e. $0^m 0^n 1^n 0^m$

first we apply, $S \to 0S0$, *m* times

So $S \xrightarrow{*} 0^m S\, 0^m$

Now we apply, $S \longrightarrow 0A1$

$S \xrightarrow{*} 0^m 0\, A\, 1\, 0^m$

Now apply, A → 0A1, $(n-1)$ times

$$S \xrightarrow{*} 0^m 0\, 0^{n-1} A\, 1^{n-1}\, 10^m$$

i.e. $S \xrightarrow{*} 0^m 0^n A\, 1^n 0^m$

Now $A \longrightarrow \in$

$$S \xrightarrow{*} 0^m 0^n 1^n 0^m$$

If $m = 0$ and $n \neq 0$

start from $S \rightarrow 0A1$

If $m \neq 0$ and $n = 0$

start from $S \rightarrow 0S0$ and never use $S \rightarrow 0A1$

If $m = n = 0$

use $S \rightarrow \in$

Hence G_1 can be written as a context free grammar and

$$L_1(G_1) = L_1\, \{0^{n+m} 1^n 0^m \mid n, m \geq 0\}$$

For L_2 and L_3 we can not generate a grammer that is context free like L_1,

37. Intersection of CFL and regular is always CFL.

38. Language $L = \{0^i 21^i \mid i \geq 0\}$ over alphabet {0, 1, 2} is recursive and is a deterministic CFL (every CFL is recursive)

39. $L1 = L1 = \{a^m b^m c\, a^n b^n \mid m, n \geq 0\}$

$L_2 = \{a^i b^j c^k \mid i, j \geq 0\}$

$L_1 \cap L_2 = \{a^n b^n c \mid m \geq 0\}$

Here no of a & b are equal hence it is CFL but not Regular.

40. Since L1, L2, L3, L4 can be recognised by push down automata, so these all are context-free grammer.

41. $a^m b^n a^n b^m \Rightarrow$ This one is CFL

$a^m b^n a^m b^n \Rightarrow$ by pumping lemma this one is not CFL.

$\{a^m b^n \mid m = 2n+1\}$ This is CFL.

42. The language accepted by PDA is

$\{a^n \mid n \geq 0\} \cup \{a^n b^n \mid n \geq 0\}$ and there exists DPDA for this language hence it is DCFL.

43. $L_1 \cap L_2 = \{a^i b^j c^k \mid i = j \text{ or } j = k\}$

it is CFL. $L_1 \cap L_2 = \{a^n b^n c^n \mid n \geq 0\}$

not CFL.

44. As given :

I. $L_1 \cup L_2$ is context- free = CFL ∪ CFL = CFL.

So True.

II. $\overline{L_1}$ is context-free = $\overline{\text{CFL}}$ = CSL but not CFL.

So False.

III. $L_1 - R$ is context-free = CFL ∩ $\overline{\text{Regular}}$ = CFL.

So,True

IV. $L_1 \cap L_2$ is context-free = CFL ∩ CFL = CSL.

So, False

45. $L_1 = \{a^p \mid p \text{ prime}\}$ is a CSL but not CFL (Prime number checking involve divsion)

$L_2 = \{a^n b^m c^{2m} \mid n \geq 0, m \geq 0\}$ is CFL (one comparision)

$L_3 = \{a^n b^n c^{2n} \mid n \geq 0\}$ is CSL (two comparision)

$L_4 = \{a^n b^n \mid n \geq 1\}$ is a DCFL

I. L_1 is CFL but not regular is false.

II. L_2 is not CFL is false.

III. L_3 is not CFL but recursive is true since every CSL is recursive.

IV. L_4 is DCFL is true.

Only III and IV are true and correct.

46. I. $\{a^m b^n c^p d^q \mid m + p = n + q\}$ is clearly CFL since, we can rearrange the equation as m – n + p – q = 0 which can be done by push, pop, push and pop and check if stack is empty at end.

II. $\{a^m b^n c^p d^q \mid m = n \text{ and } p = q\}$ is clearly CFL since, one comparison at a time can be done by pda.

III. $\{a^m b^n c^p d^q \mid m = n = p \text{ and } p \neq q\}$ is not CFL since m = n = p is a double comparison which cannot be done by PDA.

IV. $\{a^m b^n c^p d^q \mid mn = p + q\}$ is not a CFL, since mn involves multiplying number of a's and number b's which cannot be done by a PDA.

So, only I and II are CFL's.

47. Recursive languages are closed under complement. If a language L is recursive enumerable but not recursive then its complement is not a recursive enumerable, so both L and $\overline{L}$ are recursive enumerable but not recursive is not a viable possibility.

48. (a) $\{wa^n b^n w^R \mid w \in \{a,b\}^*, n \geq 0\}$ is a CFL, since we can first push w, then a's, b's pop with a's and w^R pops with the w. So PDA can accept the language.

(b) $\{ww^R \mid w \in \{a,b\}^*\}$ is a CFL

(c) $\{wa^n w^R b^n \mid w \in \{a,b\}^*, n \geq 0\}$ is a not CFL because after pushing w, we need to push a's into stack which will stop the w from being matched with w^R. If we don't push a's after w, than later we cannot match with b^n. So this language is not acceptable by a PDA and hence not a CFL.

(d) $\{a^n b^i \mid i \in \{n, 3n, 5n\}, n \geq 0\} = a^n b^n \cup a^n b^{3n} \cup a^n b^{5n}$ is CFL since each of the three parts is a CFL and closure under union guarantees that result also is a CFL.

49. Deterministic Push down Automata. DFA is special case of the NFA in which for each state there is a unique transition on each symbol.

(*a*) wCw^R means $w = w^R$

In DPA we used stack . If we take *a, b, c.* for input then w^R = *cba*, it matches. So, wCw^R accepted by DPA.

In case of ww^R, we have not information at which steps data be reversed.

50. Language accepted by PDA and empty stack is same.

51. If stack is limited to 10 then it accept all regular languages.

52. The given PDA is Non deterministic because there is more then one transition rule for given input symbol. We can parse spring aaa, aabab, bab with given PDA but baaba is not accepted by PDA.

53. $L = \{a^l b^m c^n \mid 2l = m + n\}$

Every a insert two × into the stack and each × is consumed by "b' or "c" only. So every string generated by option (c) is accepted by PDA.

54. (*a*) There is a unique minimal DFA for every regular language. TRUE

(*b*) Every NFA can be converted to an equivalent PDA. TRUE

(*c*) Complement of every context-free language is recursive. TRUE

Because context-free language is not closed under Complementation.

(*d*) Every nondeterministic PDA can be converted to an equivalent deterministic PDA. FALSE

Because ww^R can not be accepted by deterministic PDA but nondeterministic PDA can accept it. So there does not exist any equivalent deterministic PDA.

55. L1 :regular language

L2 : context free language

L3 : context sensitive language

56. $L_1 = \{o^p 1^q o^r \mid p, q, r \geq o\}$

is regular language.

Regular expression for L_1 is o* 1* o* and complement of regular language is always regular.

57. For the languages L_1 and L_2 we can have deterministic push down automata, so they are DCFL's, but for L_3 only non-deterministic PDA possible. So the language L_3 is not a deterministic CFL.

58. It is not necessary to L (P) or N (P) must be Σ^*.

59. There is a language ww^R which is N.C.F.L. but not D.C.F.L.

There is no language which is accepted by D.F.A. and not by N.D.F.A. or vice versa.

60. The overall string accepted by automata is 10010

61. (*) NFA and DFA is equivalent in power

(*) NTM and DTM is equivalent in power

(*) NPDA is more powerful then DPDA.

62. NPDA is more powerfull then DPDA. hence conversion from NPDA to DPDA is not possible.

63. (*) NPDA is more powerful then DPDA.

64. $L_1 = \{a^l b^m c^n \mid l \neq m \text{ or } m \neq n\}$

is union of two CFLS

$L_1 = \{a^l b^m c^n \mid l \neq m\}$

$L_2 = \{a^l b^m c^n \mid m \neq n\}$

L_1 & L_2 both having DPDA but when we take union of two DPDA it may be NPDA. So for this example resultant language L is NCFL.

65. $L_1 = \{a^i b^j c^k \mid i = j, k \geq 1\}$

$L_2 = \{a^i b^j \mid j = 2i, i \geq 0\}$

Here $L_1 \cap L_2 = \phi$ { Nothing is common between L_1 & L_2} and L1 is CFL but not regular language.

4

CHAPTER

Turing Machine and Recursive Functions

Analysis of Previous GATE Papers											
Units	**Year → Topics ↓**		**2019**	**2018**	**2017 Set 1**	**2017 Set 2**	**2016 Set 1**	**2016 Set 2**	**2015 Set 1**	**2015 Set 2**	**2015 Set 3**
UNDECIDABI LI TY	**1 Mark**	MCQ Type		1			1			1	
		Numerical Type									
	2 Marks	MCQ Type									
		Numerical Type									
	Total			**1**			**1**			**1**	
RECURSIVE & RECURSIVE	**1 Mark**	MCQ Type		1	1		1	1	1		
		Numerical Type									
	2 Marks	MCQ Type	1					1			
		Numerical Type									
	Total		**2**	**1**	**1**		**1**	**3**	**1**		
TM	**1 Mark**	MCQ Type									
		Numerical Type									
	2 Marks	MCQ Type									
		Numerical Type									
	Total										

UNDECIDABILITY

1. Which of the following decision problems are undecidable?

I. Given NFAs N_1 & N_2 is $L(N_1) \cap L(N_2) = \Phi$?

II. Given a CFG G = (N, Σ, P, S) and a string $x \in \Sigma^*$, does $x \in L(G)$?

III. Given CFGs G_1 and G_2, is $L(G_1) = L(G_2)$?

IV. Given a TM M, is $L(M) = \Phi$?

(a) I and IV only (b) II and III only
(c) III and IV only (d) II and IV only

[2016 (Set-1) : 1 Mark]

2. Which of the following problems are undecidable?

(a) Membership problem in context-free languages
(b) Whether a given context-free language is regular
(c) Whether a finite state automation halts on all inputs
(d) Membership problem for type 0 languages

[1989 : 2 Marks]

3. It is undecidable whether

(a) an arbitrary Turing machine halts within 10 steps
(b) a Turing machine prints a specific letter
(c) A Turing machine computes the product of two numbers
(d) None of the above

[1990 : 2 Marks]

4. Which of the following statements is false?

(a) The halting problem for Turing machine is undecidable
(b) Determining whether a context free grammar is ambiguous is undecidable
(c) Given two arbitrary context free grammars G_1 and G_2, it is undecidable whether $L(G_1) = L(G_2)$
(d) Given two regular grammars G_1 and G_2, it is undecidable whether $L(G_1) = L(G_2)$

[1996 : 1 Mark]

5. Which one of the following is not decidable ?

(a) Given a Turing machine M, a strings s and an integer k, M accepts a within k steps
(b) Equivalence of two Turing machines
(c) Language accepted by a given finite state machine is non empty
(d) Language accepted by a context free grammar is non empty

[1997 : 2 Marks]

6. Consider the following decision problems :

P_1 : Does a given finite state machine accept a given string

P_2 : Does a given context free grammar generate an infinite number of strings.

Which of the following statement is true ?

(a) P_1 and P_2 are decidable
(b) Neither P_1 nor P_2 are decidable
(c) Only P_1 is decidable
(d) Only P_2 is decidable

[2002 : 2 Marks]

7. Consider the following Problem X.

"Given a Turing machine M over the input alphabet Σ, any state q of M and a word Σ*, does the computation of M on w visit the state q"

Which of the following statements about X is correct?

(a) X is decidable
(b) X is undecidable but partially decidabe
(c) X is undecidable and not even partially decidable
(d) X is not a decision problem

[2002 : 2 Marks]

8. Consider three decision problems P_1, P_2 and P_3. It is known that P_1 is decidable and P_2 is undecidable. Which one of the following is TRUE?

(a) P_3 is decidable if P_1 is reducible to P_3
(b) P_3 is undecidable if P_3 is reducible to P_2
(c) P_3 is undecidable if P_2 is reducible to P_3
(d) P_3 is decidable if P_3 is reducible to P_2's complement

[2005 : 2 Marks]

9. Which one of the following problems is undecidable?

(a) Membership problem for CFGs
(b) Ambiguity problem for CFGs
(c) Finiteness problem for FSAs
(d) Equivalence problem for FSAs

[2007 : 1 Mark]

10. Which one of the following are decidable?

1. Whether the intersection of two regular languages is infinite
2. Whether a given context-free language is regular
3. Whether two push-down automata accept the same language
4. Whether a given grammar is context-free

(a) 1 and 2 (b) 1 and 4
(c) 2 and 3 (d) 2 and 4

[2008 : 1 Mark]

11. Which of the following is/are undecidable?
1. G is CFG. Is $L(G) = \phi$?
2. G is a CFG. Is $L(G) = \Sigma^*$?
3. M is a Turing machine. Is L(M) regular?
4. A is a DFA and N is an NFA. Is L(A) = L(N)?

(a) 3 only (b) 3 and 4 only
(c) 1, 2 and 3 only (d) 2 and 3 only

[2013 : 2 Marks]

12. Which one of the following problems is undeciable?
(a) Deciding if a given context-free grammar is ambiguous.
(b) Deciding if a given string is generated by a given context-free grammar.
(c) Deciding if the language generated by a given context-free grammar is empty.
(d) Deciding if the language generated by a given context-free grammar is finite.

[2014 (Set-3) : 2 Marks]

13. Consider the following statements :
1. The complement of every Turning decidable language is Turning decidable.
2. There exists some language which is in NP but is not Turing decidable.
3. If L is a language in NP, L is Turing decidable.

Which of the above statements is/are True?
(a) Only 2 (b) Only 3
(c) Only 1 and 2 (d) Only 1 and 3

[2015 (Set-2) : 1 Mark]

14. Consider the following problems L(G) denotes the language generated by a grammar G. L(M) denotes the language accepted by a machine M.
I. For an unrestricted grammar and G and a string w, whether $\omega \in L(G)$.
II. Given a Turing Machine M, whether L(M) is regular.
III. Given two grammars G1 and G2, whether L(G1) = L(G2).
IV. Given an NFA N, whether there is a determinstic PDA P such that N and P accept the same language.

Which one of the following statements is correct?
(a) Only I and II are undecidable
(b) Only III is undecidable
(c) Only II and IV are undecidable
(d) Only I, II and III are undeciable.

[2018 (Set-2) : 1 Marks]

RECURSIVE & RECURSIVE ENUMERABLE FUNCTION

15. Which of the following is true?
(a) The complement of a recursive language is recursive
(b) The complement of recursively enumerable language is recursively enumerable
(c) The complement of a recursively enumerable language is either recursive or recursively enumerable
(d) The complement of a context-free language is context-free

[2002 : 2 Marks]

16. Nobody knows yet if P = NP. Consider the language L defined as follows

$$L = \begin{cases} (0+1)^* \; if\ P = NP \\ \phi \; otherwise \end{cases}$$

Which of the following statements is true?
(a) L is recursive
(b) L is recursively enumerable but not recursive
(c) L is not recursively enumerable
(d) Whether L is recursive or not will be known after we find out if P = NP **[2003 : 1 Mark]**

17. If the strings of a language L can be effectively enumerated in lexicographic (i.e., alphabetic) order, which of the following statements is true?
(a) L is necessarily finite
(b) L is regular but not necessarily finite
(c) L is context free but not necessarily regular
(d) L is recursive but not necessarily context free

[2003 : 1 Mark]

18. Let L_1 be a recursive language, and let L_2 be a recursively enumerable but not a recursive language. Which one of the following is TRUE ?
(a) $\overline{L_1}$ is recursive and $\overline{L_2}$ is recursively enumerable.
(b) $\overline{L_1}$ is recursive and $\overline{L_2}$ is not recursively enumerable.
(c) $\overline{L_1}$ and $\overline{L_2}$ are recursively enumerable.
(d) $\overline{L_1}$ is recursively enumerable and $\overline{L_2}$ is recursive.

[2005 : 2 Marks]

19. Let L_1 be regular language, L_2 be a deterministic context-free language and L_3 a recursively enumerable, but not recursive, language. Which one of the following statements is false?
(a) $L_1 \cap L_2$ is a deterministic CFL
(b) $L_3 \cap L_1$ is recursive
(c) $L_1 \cup L_2$ is context-free.
(d) $L_1 \cap L_2 \cap L_3$ is recursively enumerable

[2006 : 2 Marks]

20. If L and $\overline{L}$ are recursively enumerable then L is
(a) regular (b) context-free
(c) context-sensitive (d) recursive
[2008 : 1 Mark]

21. Let L_1 be a recursive language. Let L_2 and L_3 be language that are recursively enumerable but not recursive. Which of the following statements is not necessarily true?
(a) $L_2 - L_1$ is recursive enumerable
(b) $L_1 - L_3$ is recursive enumerable
(c) $L_2 \cap L_3$ is recursive enumerable
(d) $L_2 \cup L_1$ is recursive enumerable
[2010 : 1 Mark]

22. Let $A \leq_m B$ denotes that language A is mapping reducible (also known as many-to-one reducible) to language B. Which one of the following is FALSE?
(a) If $A \leq_m B$ and B is recursive then A is recursive.
(b) If $A \leq_m B$ and a is undecidable then B is undecidable.
(c) If $A \leq_m B$ and B is recursively enumerable then A is recursively enumerable.
(d) If $A \leq_m B$ and B is not recursively enumerable then A is not recursively enumerable.
[2014 (Set-2) : 1 Marks]

23. For any two languages L_1 and L_2 such that L_1 is context free and L_2 is recursively enumerable but not recursive, which of the following is/are necessarily true?
1. $\overline{L_1}$ (complement of L_1) is recursive
2. $\overline{L_2}$ (complement of L_2) is recursive
3. $\overline{L_1}$ is context-free
4. $L_1 \cap L_2$ is recursively enumerable
(a) 1 only (b) 3 only
(c) 3 and 4 only (d) 1 and 4 only
[2015 (Set-1) : 1 Mark]

24. Let X be a recursive language and Y be a recursively enumerable but not recursive language. Let W and Z be two languages such that $\overline{Y}$ reduces to W, and Z reduces to $\overline{X}$ (reduction means the standard many-one reduction). Which one of the following statements is TRUE ?
(a) W can be recursively enumerable and Z is recursive
(b) W can be recursive and Z is recursively enumerable.
(c) W is not recursively enumerable and Z is recursive.
(d) W is not recursively enumerable and Z is not recursive.
[2016 (Set-1) : 1 Mark]

25. Consider the following types of languages L_1 : Regular L_2 : Context-free, L_3 : Recursive, L_4 : Recursively enumerable.
Which of the following is/are TRUE?
I. $\overline{L_3} \cup L_4$ is recursively enumerable.
II. $\overline{L_2} \cup L_3$ is recursive.
III. $L_1^* \cap L_2$ is context-free.
IV. $L_1 \cup \overline{L_2}$ is is context-free.
(a) I only (b) I and III only
(c) I and IV only (d) I, II, and III only
[2016 (Set-2) : 1 Mark]

26. Consider the following languages :
- $L_1 = \{\langle M \rangle \mid$ M takes at least 2016 steps on some input$\}$
- $L_2 = \{\langle M \rangle \mid$ M takes at least 2016 steps on all inputs$\}$ and
- $L_3 = \{\langle M \rangle \mid$ M accepts $\varepsilon\}$

where for each turning machine M, ⟨M⟩ denotes a specific encoding of M. Which one of the following is TRUE ?
(a) L_1 is recursive and L_2, L_3 are not recursive
(b) L_2 is recursive and L_1, L_3 are not recursive
(c) L_1, L_2 are recursive and L_3 is not recursive
(d) L_1, L_2, L_3 are recursive
[2016 (Set-2) : 2 Marks]

27. Let A and B be finite alphabets and let # be a symbol outside both A and B. Let f be a total function from A* to B*. We say f is computable if there exists a Turing machine M which given an input x in A*, always halts with f(x) on its tape. Let L_f denote the language $\{x\#f(x) \mid x \in A^*\}$. Which of the following statements is true :
(a) f is computable if and only if L_f is recursive.
(b) f is computable if and only if L_f is recursively enumerable
(c) If f is computable then L_f is recursive, but not convesely.
(d) If f is computable then L_f is recursively enumerable , but not conversely.
[2017 (Set-1) : 1 Mark]

28. The set of all recursively enumerable languages is
(a) closed under complementation
(b) closed under intersection
(c) a subset of the set of all recursive languages
(d) an uncountable set
[2018 (Set-1) : 1 Mark]

29. Consider the following sets:

S1. Set of all recursively enumerable languages over the alphabet {0, 1}

S2. Set of all syntactically valid C programs

S3. Set of all languages over the alphabet {0, 1}

S4. Set of all non-regular languages over the alphabet {0, 1}

Which of the above sets are uncountable?

(a) S2 and S3 (b) S1 and S2

(c) S1 and S4 (d) S3 and s4

[2019 : 2 Marks]

TM

30. A single tape Turing Machine M has two states q_0 and q_1, of which q_0 is the starting state. The tape alphabet of M is {0, 1, B} and its input alphabet is {0, 1}. The symbol B is the blank symbol used to indicate end of an inptu string. The transition function of M is described in the following table :

	0	0	B
q_0	q_1,1,R	q_1,1,R	Halt
q_1	q_1,1,R	q_0,1,L	q_0,B,L

The table is interpreted as illustrated below. The entry (q_1, 1, R) in row q_0 and column 1 signifies that if M is in state q_0 and reads 1 on the current tape square, then it writes 1 on the same tape tape square, then it writes 1 on the same tape square, moves its tape head one position to the right and transitions to state q_1. Which of the following statements is true about M?

(a) M does not halt on any string in $(0 + 1)^+$

(b) M does not halt on any string in $(00 + 1)^*$

(c) M halts on all string ending in a 0

(d) M halts on all string ending in a 1

[2003 : 2 Marks]

31. Which one of the following is true for the language $\{a^p \mid p \text{ is a prime}\}$?

(a) It is not accepted by a Turning Machine

(b) It is regular but not context free

(c) It is context-free but not regular

(d) It is neither regular nor context-free, but accepted by a Turing machine

[2008 : 1 Mark]

32. Which of the following statements is/are FALSE?

1. For every non-deterministic Turing machine, there exists an equivalent deterministic Turing machine.
2. Turing recognizable languages are closed under union and complementation.
3. Turing decidable languages are closed under intersection and complementation.
4. Turing recognizable languages are closed under union and intersection.

(a) 1 and 4 only (b) 1 and 3 only

(c) 2 only (d) 3 only

[2013 : 1 Mark]

33. Let <M> be the encoding of a Turing machine as a string over = {0, 1}. Let L = {<m >| M is a Turing machine that accepts a string of length 2014}. Then, L is

(a) decidable and recursively enumerable

(b) undecidable and recursively enumerable

(c) undecidable and not recursively enumerable

(d) decidable but not recursively enumerable

[2014 (Set-2) : 2 Marks]

ANSWERS

1. (c)	2. (b,d)	3. (b)	4. (d)	5. (a,b)	6. (a)	7. (b)	8. (c)	9. (b)	10. (b)
11. (d)	12. (a)	13. (d)	14. (d)	15. (a)	16. (a)	17. (d)	18. (b)	19. (b)	20. (d)
21. (b)	22. (d)	23. (d)	24. (c)	25. (d)	26. (c)	27. (a)	28. (b)	29. (d)	30. (a)
31. (d)	32. (c)	33. (b)							

EXPLANATIONS

1. $L[N_1] \cap L[N_2] \neq \phi$ – undecidable

   $x \in L(G)$ – decidable

   $L(G_1) = L(G_2)$ – decidable

   $L[M] = \phi$ is also undecidable.

2. (*) Regularity of CFL is undeadable.

   (*) Membership problem for Recessive Enumerable language is undeadable.

3. The Printing Problem of Turing Machine is Undecidable. This can be reduce to the nothing Problem can be reduce to the halting problem when the TM halts let it print something.

4. If $L(G_1) \leq L(G_2)$, then two regular grammars G_1 and G_2

   It is decidable whether $L(G_1) = L(G_2)$

5. (*) It is not possible for Turing Machine M accepts a string with in K steps because length of string is not given

   (*) Two TM is equivalent, is undecidable

6. (*) A finite state machine is always halt (either on final state or Non-final State).

   (*) We can check CFG generate finite strings or infinite strings using graph so it is so it is also decidable.

7. This problem is a state entry problem state entry problem can be reduced to halting problem. Like halting problm for recessive is decidable but for recessive enumerable language it is undecidable so we can say that it is partial decidable.

8. Note that in general if $L_1 \leq L_2$, L_2 decidable $\Rightarrow L_1$ decidable and L_1 undecidable $\Rightarrow L_2$ is undecidable.

   Given that P_1 is decidable and P_2 is undecidable.

   Consider (*a*) P_3 is decidable if P_1 is reducible to P_3

   i.e. $P_1 \leq_p P_3$

   and if P_1 is undecidable, then P_3 would be undecidable.

   But it is given that P_1 is decidable, therefore we cannot use this theorem.

   (*a*) is false.

   Consider (*b*) P_3 is undecidable if P_3 is reducible to P_2

   i.e. $P_3 \leq_p P_2$

   Now if P_3 is undecidable then P_2 is undecidable but nothing is given regarding P_3.

   Also if P_2 is decidable, then P_3 would be decidable, but it is given that P_2 is undecidable, so we can't use this.

   (*b*) is false.

   Consider (*c*) P_3 is undecidable if P_2 is reducible to P_3

   i.e. $P_2 \leq_p P_3$

   Now if P_2 is undecidable, this would mean P_3 is undecidable. Since it is given that P_2 is undecidable, therefore, surely P_3 is undecidable is correct.

   Choice (*c*) is correct.

9. As we know that Ambiguity problem for CFGs is undecidable.

10. Intersection of two regular languages can be determined by a given algorithm, it can be determined whether a given grammer is context free.

    Context free grammar should have all productions of the type

    $$A \to x$$

    where, $A \in V_N$ {set of varibale}

    $\alpha \in (V_N \, Uz)^*$ {z = set of terminal}

11. Which are/is undecidable

    1. G is CFG. Is $L(G) = \phi$?

       – Decidable

    2. G is a CFG. Is $L(G) = \Sigma^*$?

       – Undecidable

    3. M is a turing machine. Is L(M) regular?

       – Undecidable (Present in all options)

    4. A is a DFA and N is a NFA.

       Is L(A) = L(N)?

       – Decidable

    Ans. (*d*) 2 and 3 only.

    PS. Refer closere properties (wiki)

12. There were algorithms to find the membership of CFG (using CYK algorithm) and finiteness of CFG (using CNF graph) and emptiness. But there is no algorithm for ambiguity of CFG, so it is undecidable.

13. By property,

    Complement of every Turing decidable language is also turing decidable

    If L is in NP, L is Turing decidable.

14. The following are undecidable problems :-

    (*) String accepted by type 'o' grammar.

    (*) Regulation of Type's language.

    (*) Language generated by two different grammar is regular.

15. (*) Recursive languages are closed under complement operation.

(*) Recursive enumerable languages are not closed under complement.

(*) CFL are not closed under complement.

16. L is regular either P = NP or P≠NP. Every Regular language is recursive.

17. Let us take an example

$L = \{ a^i \mid p \text{ is prime number} \}$

Here L can be effectively enumerated in graphic order. And L is recursive but not CFL.

18. (*) Recursive language are closed under complement operation.

(*) Recursive enumerable languages are not closed under complement operation.

19. $L_3 \cap L_1$ is Recursive enumerable Hence option (b) is false.

20. If a language is recursively enumerable, and its complement is also, then the language is recursive.

21. L1 is recursive and L2, L3 are recursively enumerable. So L1∩L3 and L2∪L3 can recursively enumerable and also L2 – L1 can recursively enumerable. But we can't say that **L1-L3** is also **recursively enumerable.**

22. Since $A \leq_m B$ and since B is not enumerable recursively creates a situation for A to not to be recursively enumerable.

23. By the property.

If L_1 is context free, $\bar{L}_1$ is recursive.

If L_2 is recursively enumerable and $\bar{L}_1$ is recursive then union of recursive and recursively enumerable language is recursively enumerable.

II and III are false because complement of a context free language is not context free and complement of a recursively enumerable language is not recursive.

24. Since x is recursive & recursive language are closed under complement. So x' is also recursive. $Z \leq x'$ is recursive.

y is recursive enumerable not recursive so y' cannot be recursive enumerable. Since y' is reduces to W. So W is not recursive enumerable.

25. From the given question

L_1 : Regular

L_2 : CFL (Context-free)

L_3 : Recursive language

L_4 : REL (Recursively enumerable.)

(i) $\bar{L}_3$ is Recursive

$\bar{L}_3 \cup L_4$ is REL (Recursively enumerable)

(ii) $\bar{L}_2$ is recursive

$\bar{L}_3$ is recursive

$\Rightarrow \bar{L}_2 \cup L_3$ is also recursive

(iii) L_1^* is regular

L_2 is CFL (Context-free)

$\Rightarrow L_1^* \cup L_2$ is CFL

Since CFL is closed under the intersection with RL

∴ RL ∩ CFL is CFL

(iv) L_1 is RL

$\bar{L}_2$ is recursive

$\Rightarrow L_1 \cup \bar{L}_2$ is CFL is not possible

So, the statements (i), (ii) and (iii) are correct.

26. From the given language.

L_1 is Recursive

L_2 is Recursive

and L_3 is Not Recursive

27. The definition is given as halting problem of Turing machine. Every recursive language is computable but converse may not be true.

28. The set of RE languages is closed under intersection, not closed under complementation, is not subset of set of REC language and is a countable set.

29. S_1 : Infinite please remove from here hence it is countable corresponds with set of turing machines.

S_2 : Since syntactically valid C programs surely run on Turing machines, this set is also a subset of set of Turing machines, which is countable.

S_3 : Set of all languages = 2^{Σ^*} which is known to be uncountable. Σ* countably infinite ⇒ 2^{Σ^*} is uncountable.

S_4 : Set of all non-regular languages includes set $L_{NOT\,RE}$ which is uncountable infinite and hence is uncountable

So, S_3 and S_4 are uncountable.

30. M Halts only when input is empty string (E). Else it goes in infinite loop for every string in $(0+1)^+$.

31. L = {a^p is prime no}

L is neither regular nor CFL we can prove using pumping lemma but we can design TM for this language.

32. 1. TRUE. Non deterministic turing machine can be simulated by a Deterministic turing machine with exponential time.

2. Turing Recognizable languages are "not" closed under complementation. For any Toring recognizable language, the toring machine 'T' recognizing 'L', may not terminate on inputs $x \notin L$.

Hence this is FALSE

3. Toring Decidable languages are CLOSED under unioin and complementation. It is easy to construct a turing machine to decide $L_1 \cup L_2$, L'_1 if L_1, L_2 are turing decidable.

So, this is TRUE.

(*c*) is the only option which contains (2).

33. Turing machine accept the string of length 2014 if string belongs to language L but if string not belongs to language L then it may be halt or goes in infinite loop.

Unit - III

Digital Logic

Syllabus

Boolean algebra. Combinational and sequential circuits. Minimization. Number representations and computer arithmetic (fixed and floating point).

Contents

1

CHAPTER

Logic Function & Minimization

Analysis of Previous GATE Papers

Units	Year → Topics ↓		2019	2018	2017 Set 1	2017 Set 2	2016 Set 1	2016 Set 2	2015 Set 1	2015 Set 2	2015 Set 3
LOGIC REDUCTION	1 Mark	MCQ Type	1	1			1	1			
		Numerical Type									
	2 Marks	MCQ Type				1					
		Numerical Type								1	
	Total		1	1		2	1	1		2	
MAP REDUCTION	1 Mark	MCQ Type									
		Numerical Type			1						
	2 Marks	MCQ Type	1			1					1
		Numerical Type	1	1							1
	Total		4	2	1	2					4
NAND AND NOR IMPLEMENTATION	1 Mark	MCQ Type									
		Numerical Type									
	2 Marks	MCQ Type									
		Numerical Type									
	Total										

LOGIC REDUCTION

1. Let * be defined as $x*y = \bar{x} + y$. Let $z = x*y$ value of $z*x$ is

(a) $\bar{x} + y$ (b) x

(c) 0 (d) 1

[1997 : 1 Mark]

2. Let $f(x, y, z) = \bar{x} + \bar{y}z + xz$ be a switching function. Which one of the following is valid?

(a) $\bar{y}x$ is a prime implicant of f

(b) xz is a minterm of f

(c) xz is an implicant of f

(d) y is a prime implicant of f

[1997 : 2 Marks]

3. The simultaneous equations on the Boolean variables x, y, z and w,

$$x + y + z = 1$$
$$xy = 0$$
$$xz + w = 1$$
$$xy + \bar{z}\bar{w} = 0$$

have the following solution for x, y, z and w, respectively

(a) 0100 (b) 1101

(c) 1011 (d) 1000

[2000 : 2 Marks]

4. Consider the following logic circuit whose inputs are functions f_1, f_2, f_3 and output is f.

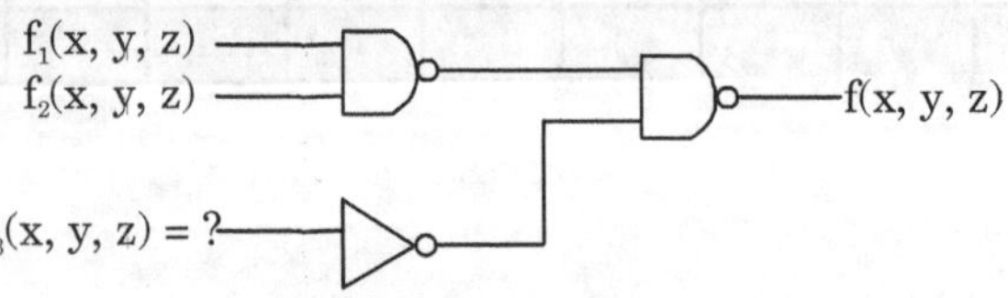

$f_1(x, y, z) = \Sigma(0, 1, 3, 5)$,

$f_2(x, y, z) = \Sigma(6, 5)$ and

$f(x, y, z) = \Sigma(1, 4, 5)$

f_3 is

(a) (1, 4, 5) (b) (6, 7)

(c) (0, 1, 3, 5) (d) None of these

[2002 : 2 Marks]

5. f(A, B) =A′ + B. Smplified expression for function f(f(x + y, y), z) is

(a) x′ + z

(b) xyz

(c) xy′ + z

(d) None of these

[2002 : 2 Marks]

6. Consider the following circuit composed of XOR gates and non-inberting buffers.

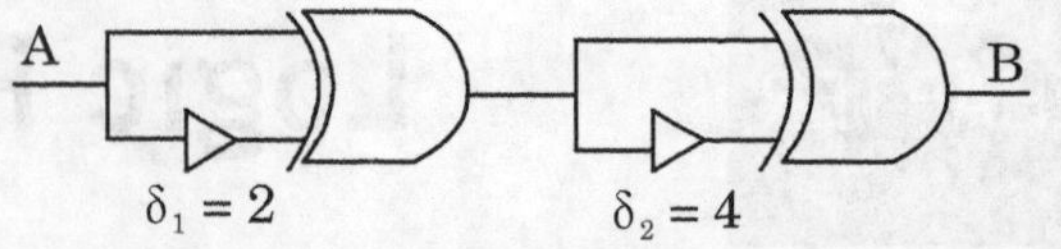

The non-inverting buffers have delays $\delta_1 = 2$ ns and $\delta_2 = 4$ ns as shown in the figure. Both XOR gates and all wires have zero delay. Asssume that all gate inputs, oututs and wires are stable at alogic leve 10 at time 0. If the following saveform is applied at input A, how many transition (s) (change of logic levels) occur(s) at B during the interval from 0 to 10 ns?

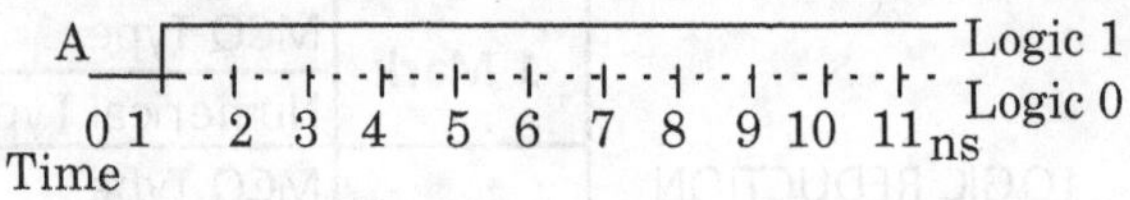

(a) 1 (b) 2

(c) 3 (4) 4

[2003 : 2 Marks]

7. The Boolean function x′y′ + xy + x′y is equivalent to

(a) x′ + y′ (b) x + y

(c) x + y′ (d) x′ + y

[2004 : 1 Mark]

8. Which of the following expressions is equivalent to $(A \oplus B) \oplus C$?

(a) $(A + B + C)(\bar{A} + \bar{B} + \bar{C})$

(b) $(A + B + C)(\bar{A} + \bar{B} + C)$

(c) $ABC + \bar{A}(B \oplus C) + \bar{B}(A \oplus C)$

(d) None of these

[2005 : 1 Mark]

9. A two-way switch has three terminals a, b and c. In ON position (logic value 1), a is connected to b, and in OFF position, a is connected to c. Two of these two-way switches S_1 and S_2 are connected to a bulb as shown below.

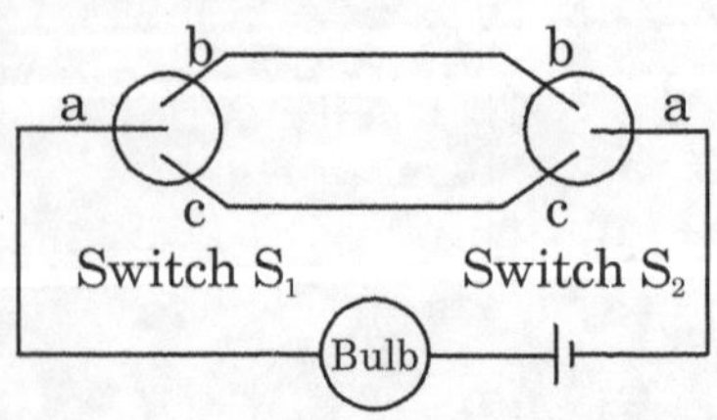

(a) $S1.\overline{S2}$

(b) S1 + S2

(c) $\overline{S1 \oplus s2}$

(d) $S1 \oplus S2$

[2005 : 1 Mark]

10. What is the maximum number of different Boolean functions involving in 'n' Boolean variables?

(a) n^2 (b) 2^n

(c) 2^{2^n} (d) 2^{n^2}

[2007 : 1 Mark]

11. Let f(w, x, y, z) = Σ(0, 4, 5, 7, 8, 9, 13, 15). Which of the following expressions are NOT equivalent to f?

(a) $x'y'z' + w'xy' + wy'z + xz$

(b) $w'y'z' + wx'y' + xz$

(c) $w'y'z' + wx'y' + xyz + xy'z$

(d) $x'y'z' + wx'y' + w'y$

[2007 : 2 Marks]

12. Define the connective * for the Boolean variable X and Y as : $X * Y = XY + X'Y'$

Let $Z = X * Y$. Consider the following expression P, Q and R.

$P : X = Y * Z$

$Q : Y = X * Z$

$R : X * Y * Z = 1$

Which of the following is TRUE

(a) Only P and Q are valid

(b) Only Q and R are valid

(c) Only P and R are valid

(d) All P, Q, R are valid

[2007 : 2 Marks]

13. For the given circuit f_1, f_3 and f are given below

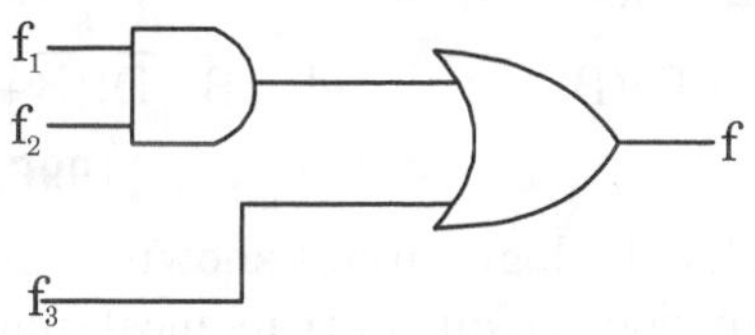

$f_1 = \Sigma m(4, 5, 6, 7, 8)$

$f_3 = \Sigma m(1, 6, 15)$

$f = \Sigma m(1, 6, 8, 15)$

Then f_2 is

(a) $\Sigma m(4, 6)$ (b) $\Sigma m(4, 8)$

(c) $\Sigma m(6, 8)$ (d) $\Sigma m(4, 6, 8)$

[2008 : 1 Mark]

14. If P, Q, R, are Boolean variables, then $(P + \bar{Q})(P.\bar{Q} + P.R)(\bar{P}\bar{R} + \bar{Q})$ simplifies to

(a) $P.\bar{Q}$ (b) $P.\bar{R}$

(c) $P.\bar{Q} + R$ (d) $P.\bar{R} + Q$

[2008 : 2 Marks]

15. The minterm expansion of

$f(P, Q, R) = PQ + Q\bar{R} + P\bar{R}$ is

(a) $m_2 + m_4 + m_6 + m_7$

(b) $m_0 + m_1 + m_3 + m_5$

(c) $m_0 + m_1 + m_6 + m_1$

(d) $m_2 + m_3 + m_4 + m_5$

[2010 : 1 Mark]

16. The simplified SOP (Sum of Product) form of the Boolean expression

$(P + \bar{Q} + \bar{R}).(P + \bar{Q} + R).(P + Q + \bar{R})$

(a) $(P + \bar{Q} + \bar{R})$

(b) $(P + \bar{Q}.\bar{R})$

(c) $(\bar{P}.Q + R)$

(d) $(P + Q + R)$

[2010 : 2 Marks]

17. Which one of the following circuits is NOT equivalent to a 2-input XNOR (exclusive NOR)

(a) 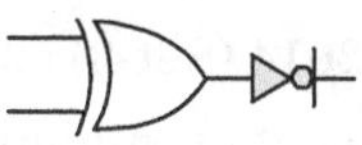

(b) 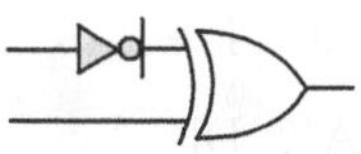

(c) 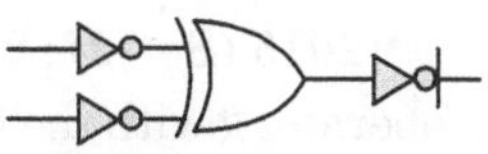

(d) 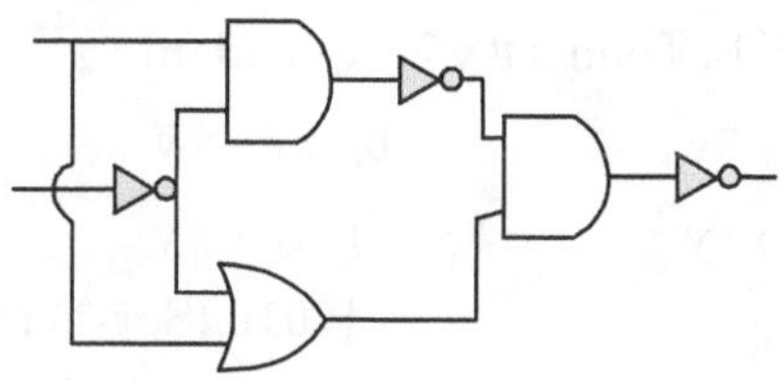

[2011 : 1 Mark]

18. The truth table

X	Y	f(X, Y)
0	0	0
0	1	0
1	0	1
1	1	1

represents the Boolean function

(a) X (b) X + Y

(c) $X \oplus Y$ (d) Y **[2012 : 1 Mark]**

19. Which one of the following expression does NOT represent exclusive NOR of x and y?

(a) $xy + x'y'$ (b) $x \oplus y'$

(c) $x' \oplus y$ (d) $x' \oplus y'$

[2013 : 1 Mark]

20. The dual of a Boolean function $F(x_1, x_2, ..., x_n, +,)$ written a F^D, is the same expression as that of F with + and swapped. F is said to be self-dual if $F = F^D$. The number of self-dual functions with n Boolean variables is

(a) 2n (b) 2^{n-1}

(c) 2^{2^n} (d) $2^{2^{n-1}}$

[2014 (Set-2) : 1 Mark]

21. Let ⊕ denote the Exclusive OR (XOR) operation. Let '1' and '0' denote the binary constants.

Consider the following Boolean expression for F over two variables P and Q.

$F(P,Q) = ((1 \oplus P) \oplus (P \oplus Q)) \oplus (P \oplus Q) \oplus (Q \oplus 0))$

The equivalent expression for F is

(a) $P + Q$ (b) $\overline{P+Q}$

(c) $P \oplus Q$ (d) $\overline{P \oplus Q}$

[2014 (Set-3) : 2 Marks]

22. The number of min-terms after minimizing the following Boolean expression is ....

[D'+AB'+A'C+AC'D+A'C'D]'

[2015 (Set-2) : 2 Marks]

23. Consider the Boolean operator # with the following properties : $x \# 0 = x$, $x \# 1 = \overline{x}$, $x \# x = 0$ and $x \# \overline{x} = 1$. Then $x \# y$ is equivalent to

(a) $x\overline{y} + \overline{x}y$ (b) $x\overline{y} + \overline{x}\,\overline{y}$

(c) $\overline{x}y + xy$ (d) $xy + \overline{x}\,\overline{y}$

[2016 (Set-1) : 1 Mark]

24. Let $x_1 \oplus x_2 \oplus x_3 \oplus x_4 = 0$ where x_1, x_2, x_3, x_4 are Boolean variables, and ⊕ is the XOR operator. Which one of the following must always be TRUE?

(a) $x_1 x_2 x_3 x_4 = 0$

(b) $x_1 x_3 + x_2 = 0$

(c) $\overline{x}_1 \oplus \overline{x}_3 = \overline{x}_2 \oplus \overline{x}_4$

(d) $x_1 + x_2 + x_3 + x_4 = 0$

[2016 (Set-2) : 1 Mark]

25. If w, x, y, z are Booleam variables, then which one of the following is INCORRECT?

(a) $wx + w(x + y) + x(x + y) = x + wy$

(b) $w\overline{x}(y+\overline{z}) + \overline{w}x = \overline{w} + x + \overline{y}z$

(c) $(w\overline{x}(y+x\overline{z}) + \overline{w}\,\overline{x})y = x\overline{y}$

(d) $(w + y)(wxy + wyz) = wxy + wyz$

[2017 (Set-2) : 2 Marks]

26. Let ⊕ and ⊙ denote the Exclusive OR and Exclusive NOR operations, respectively. Which one of the following is NOT CORRECT ?

(a) $\overline{P \oplus Q} = P \odot Q$

(b) $\overline{P} \oplus Q = P \odot Q$

(c) $\overline{P} \oplus \overline{Q} = P \oplus Q$

(d) $(P \oplus \overline{P}) \oplus Q = (P \odot \overline{P}) \odot \overline{Q}$

[2018 : 1 Mark]

27. Which one of the following is NOT a valid identity?

(a) $x \oplus y = x + y$, if $xy = 0$

(b) $x \oplus y = (xy + x'y')'$

(c) $(x + y) \oplus z = x \oplus (y + z)$

(d) $(x \oplus y) \oplus z = x \oplus (y \oplus z)$

[2019 : 1 Mark]

MAP REDUCTION

28. What is the equivalent Boolean expression in product-of-sums form for the Karnaugh map given in figure

CD \ AB	00	01	11	10
00		1	1	
01	1			1
11	1			1
10		1	1	

(a) $B\overline{D} + \overline{B}D$ (b) $(B+\overline{C}+D)(\overline{B}+C+\overline{D})$

(c) $(B+D)(\overline{B}+\overline{D})$ (d) $(B+\overline{D})(\overline{B}+D)$

[1996 : 2 Marks]

29. Consider the logic circuit shown in figure below. The function f_1, f_2 and f(in canonical sum of products form in decimal notation) are

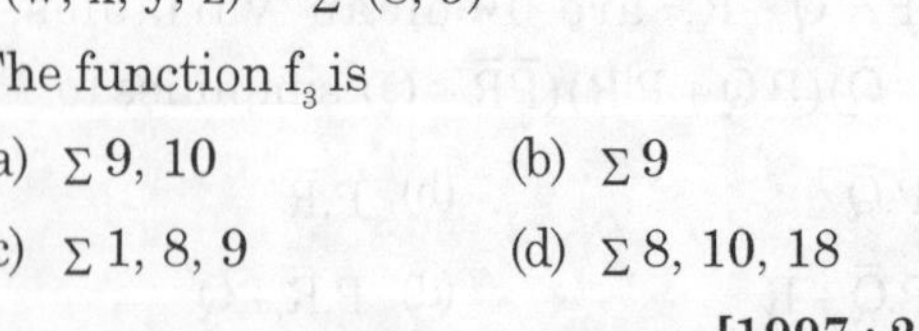

$f_1 (w, x, y, z) = \Sigma (8, 9, 10)$

$f_2 (w, x, y, z) = \Sigma (7, 8, 12, 13, 14, 15)$

$f (w, x, y, z) = \Sigma (8, 9)$

The function f_3 is

(a) Σ 9, 10 (b) Σ 9

(c) Σ 1, 8, 9 (d) Σ 8, 10, 18

[1997 : 2 Marks]

30. Which of the following functions implements the Karnaugh map shown below ?

AB\CD	00	01	11	10
00	0	0	1	0
01	X	X	1	X
11	0	1	1	0
10	0	1	1	0

(a) $\bar{A}B + CD$

(b) $D(C + A)$

(c) $AD + \bar{A}B$

(d) $(C + D)(\bar{C} + D)(A + B)$

[1991 : 1 Mark]

31. Which function does NOT implement the Karnaugh map given below ?

wz →	00	01	11	10
xy ↓				
00	0	×	0	0
01	0	×	1	1
11	1	1	1	1
10	0	×	0	0

(a) (w + x) y

(b) xy + yw

(c) (w + x) (w + y) (x + y)

(d) None of the above

[2000 : 2 Marks]

32. Given the following Karnaugh map, which one of the following represents the minimal Sum-of-Products of the map ?

yz \ wx	00	01	11	10
00	0	X	0	X
01	X	1	X	1
11	0	X	1	0
10	0	1	X	0

(a) xy + y'z

(b) wx'y' + xy + xz

(c) w'x + y'z + xy

(d) xz + y

[2001 : 1 Mark]

33. Minimum SOP for f(w, x, y, z) shown in Karnaugh-map below is

yz \ wx	00	01	11	10
00	0	1	1	0
01	x	0	0	1
11	x	0	0	1
10	0	1	1	0

(a) xz + y'z

(b) xz' + zx'

(c) x'y + zx'

(d) None of these

[2002 : 1 Mark]

34. The literal count of a boolean expression is the sum of the number of times each literal appears in the expression. For example, the literal count of (xy + xz) is 4. What are the minimum possible literal counts of the product-of-sum and sum-of-product representations respectively of the function given by the following Karnaugh map? Here, X denotes "don't care"

yz \ wx	00	01	11	10
00	X	1	0	1
01	0	1	X	0
11	1	X	X	0
10	X	0	0	X

(a) (11, 9)

(b) (9, 13)

(c) (9, 10)

(d) (11, 11)

[2003 : 2 Marks]

35. The function $AB'C + A'BC + ABC' + A'B'C + AB'C'$ is equivalent to

(a) $AC' + AB + A'C$

(b) $AB' + AC' + A'C$

(c) $A'B + AC' + AB'$

(d) $A'B + AC + AB'$

[2004 : 2 Marks]

36. Which of the essential prime implicants of the following Boolean function ?

f(a, b, c) = $a'c + ac' + b'c$

(a) a'c and ac'

(b) a'c and b'c

(c) a'c only

(d) ac' and bc'

[2004 : 2 Marks]

37. Consider the following circuit :

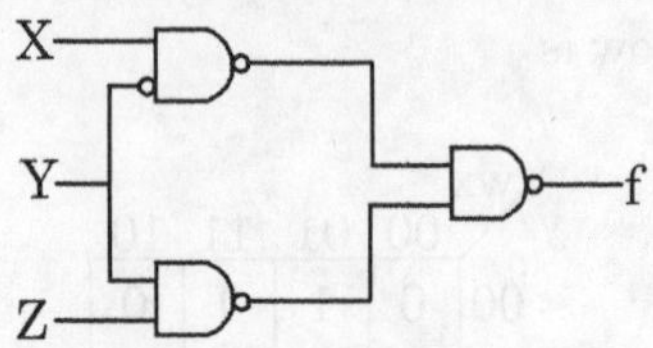

Which one of the following is TRUE ?

(a) f is independent of X

(b) f is independent of Y

(c) f is indendent of Z

(d) None of X, Y, Z is redundant

[2005 : 1 Mark]

38. The switching expression corresponding to f(A, B, C, D) = (1, 4, 5, 9, 11, 12) is

(a) BC'D'+ A'C'D + AB'D

(b) ABC'+ ACD + B'C'D

(c) ACD'+ A'B'C + AC'D'

(d) A'BD + ACD'+ BCD'

[2005 : 1 Mark]

39. Consider a boolean function f(w, x, y, z). Suppose that exactly one of its inputs is allowed to change at a time. If the function happens to be true for two input vectors $i_1 = < w_1, x_1, y_1, x_1 >$ and $i_2 = < w_2, x_2, y_2, z_2 >$, we would like the function to remain true as the input changes from i_1 to i_2 (i_1 and i_2 differ in exactly one bit position), without becoming false momentarily. Let f(w, x, y, z) = Σ(5, 7, 11, 12, 13, 15). Which of the following cube covers of f will ensure that the required cube covers of f will ensure that the required property is satisfied?

(a) $\bar{w}xz, wx\bar{y}, x\bar{y}z, xyz, wyz$

(b) $wxy, \bar{w}xz, wyz$

(c) $wx\overline{yz}, xz, w\bar{x}yz$

(d) $wyz, wxz, \bar{w}xz, x\bar{y}z, xyz$

[2006 : 2 Marks]

40. The boolean function for a combinational circuit with four inputs is represented by the following Karnaugh map.

RS \ PQ	00	01	11	10
00	1	0	0	1
01	0	0	1	1
11	1	1	1	0
10	1	0	0	1

Which of the product terms given below is an essential prime implicant of the function ?

(a) QRS

(b) PQS

(c) PQ'S'

(d) Q'S'

[2006 : 2 Marks]

41. Consider the following Boolean function of four variables

f(w, x, y, z) = (1, 3, 4, 6, 9, 11, 12, 14)

The function is

(a) independent of one variable

(b) independent of two variables

(c) independent of three variables

(d) dependent on all the variables

[2007 : 1 Mark]

Linked Answer Q. 42 & Q. 43 :

Consider the following expression : $a\bar{d} + \overline{ac} + b\bar{c}d$

42. Which of the following Karnaugh Maps correctly represents the expression ?

(a)

	$\bar{c}\bar{d}$	$\bar{c}d$	cd	$c\bar{d}$
$\bar{a}\bar{b}$	1	1		
$\bar{a}b$	1	1		
ab	1	1		1
$a\bar{b}$	1			1

(b)

	$\bar{c}\bar{d}$	$\bar{c}d$	cd	$c\bar{d}$
$\bar{a}\bar{b}$	1	1		
$\bar{a}b$	1			
ab	1	1		1
$a\bar{b}$	1	1		1

(c)

	$\bar{c}\,\bar{d}$	$\bar{c}\,d$	$c\,d$	$c\,\bar{d}$
$\bar{a}\,\bar{b}$	1	1		
$\bar{a}\,b$	1	1		1
$a\,b$	1	1		1
$\bar{a}\,\bar{b}$	1			1

(d)

	$\bar{c}\bar{d}$	$\bar{c}d$	cd	$c\bar{d}$
$\bar{a}\bar{b}$	1	1		
$\bar{a}b$	1	1		
ab	1	1		1
$a\bar{b}$	1		1	1

[2007 : 2 Marks]

43. Which of the following expressions does not correspond to the Karnaugh Map obtained in above question?

(a) $\bar{c}\bar{d} + a\bar{d} + ab\bar{c} + \overline{ac}d$

(b) $\overline{ac} + \bar{c}\bar{d} + a\bar{d} + ab\bar{c}d$

(c) $\overline{ac} + a\bar{d} + ab\bar{c} + \bar{c}d$

(d) $\bar{b}\bar{c}\bar{d} + ac\bar{d} + \overline{ac} + ab\bar{c}$ **[2007 : 2 Marks]**

44. In the Karnaugh map shown below, X denoted a don't care term. What is the minimal form ofthe function represented by the Karnaugh map

cd \ ab	00	01	11	10
00	1	1		1
01	x			
11	x			
10	1	1		x

(a) $\bar{b}.\bar{d} + \bar{a}.\bar{d}$ (b) $\bar{a}.\bar{b} + \bar{b}.\bar{d} + \bar{a}.b\bar{d}$

(c) $\bar{b}.\bar{d} + \bar{a}.b\bar{d}$ (d) $\bar{a}.\bar{b} + \bar{b}.\bar{d} + \bar{a}.\bar{d}$

[2008 : 1 Mark]

45. Consider the following Boolean function of four variables :

f(A, B, C, D) = (2, 3, 6, 7, 8, 9, 10, 11 12, 13)

The function is

(a) independent of one variable

(b) independent of two variables

(c) independent of three variable

(d) dependent on all the variables

[2008 : 1 Mark]

46. What is the minimal form of the Karnaugh map shown below? Assume that X denotes a don't care term.

cd \ ab	00	01	11	10
00	1	X	X	1
01	X			1
11				
10	1			X

(a) $\bar{b}\bar{d}$

(b) $\bar{b}\bar{d} + \bar{b}\bar{c}$

(c) $\bar{b}\bar{d} + a\bar{b}\bar{c}d$

(d) $\bar{b}\bar{d} + \bar{b}\bar{c} + \bar{c}\bar{d}$

[2012 : 2 Marks]

47. Consider the following Boolean expression for F :

$$F(P, Q, R, S) = PQ + \bar{P}QR + \bar{P}Q\bar{R}S$$

The minimal sum-of-products form of F is

(a) PQ + QR + QS

(b) P + Q + R + S

(c) $\bar{P} + \bar{Q} + \bar{R} + \bar{S}$

(d) $\bar{P}R + \bar{P}\bar{R}S + P$

[2014 (Set-1) : 1 Mark]

48. Consider the following minterm expression for F:

F(P, Q, R, S) = 0, 2, 5, 7, 8, 10, 13, 15

The minterms 2, 7, 8 and 13 are 'do not care' terms. The minimal sum-of-products form for F is

(a) $Q\bar{S} + \bar{Q}S$

(b) $\bar{Q}\bar{S} + QS$

(c) $\bar{Q}\bar{R}\bar{S} + \bar{Q}R\bar{S} + Q\bar{R}S + QRS$

(d) $\bar{P}\bar{Q}\bar{S} + \bar{P}QS + PQS + P\bar{Q}\bar{S}$

[2014 (Set-3) : 1 Mark]

49. The total number of prime implicants of the function f(w, x, y, z) = (0, 2, 4, 5, 6, 10) is ....

[2015 (Set-3) : 2 Marks]

50. Given the function F = P'+QR, where F is a function in three Boolean variables P, Q and R and P' = !P, consider the following statements.

S1 : F Σ(4, 5, 6)

S2 : F = Σ(0, 1, 2, 3, 7)

S2 : F = Π(4, 5, 6)

S4 : F = Π (0, 1, 2, 3, 7)

Which of the following is true ?

(a) S1-False, S2-True, S3-True, S4-False

(b) S1-True, S2-False, S3-False, S4-True

(c) S1-False, S2-False, S3-True, S4-True

(d) S1-True, S2-True, S3-False, S4-False

[2015 (Set-3) : 2 Marks]

51. Consider the Karnaugh map given below, where X represents "don't care" and blank represents 0.

dc \ ba	00	01	11	10
00		x	x	
01	1			x
11	1			1
10		x	x	

Assume for all inputs (a, b, c, d), the respective complements $(\overline{a}, \overline{b}, \overline{c}, \overline{d})$ are also available. The above logic is implemented using 2-input NOR gates only. The minimum number of gates required is ....

[2017 (Set-1) : 1 Mark]

52. Given f(w, x, y, z) = Σ_m(0, 1, 2, 3, 7, 8, 10) + d(5, 6, 11, 15), where d represents the don't-care condition in Karnaugh maps. Which of the following is a minimum product of sums (POS) form of f(w, x, y, z)?

(a) $f = (\overline{w}+\overline{z})(\overline{x}+z)$ (b) $f = (\overline{w}+z)(x+z)$

(c) $f = (w+z)(\overline{x}+z)$ (d) $f = (w+\overline{z})(\overline{x}+z)$

[2017 (Set-2) : 2 Marks]

53. Consider the minterm list form of a Boolean function F given below :

F(P, Q, R, S) = Σm(0, 2, 5, 7, 9, 11) + d(3, 8, 10, 12, 14)

Here, m denotes a minterm and d denotes a don't care term. The number of essential prime implicants of the function F is ....

[2018 : 2 Marks]

54. A circuit outputs a digit in the form of 4 bits. 0 is represented by 0000, 1 by 0001, ..., 9 by 1001. A combinational circuit is to be designed which takes these 4 bits as input and outputs 1 if the digit ≥ 5, and 0 otherwise. If only AND, OR and NOT gates may be used, what is the minimum number of gates required ?

(a) 2 (b) 3

(c) 4 (d) 5

[2004 : 2 Marks]

55. Consider three 4-variable functions f_1, f_2 and f_3, which are expressed in sum of-minterms as

f_1 = Σ(0, 2, 5, 8, 14),

f_2 = Σ(2, 3, 6, 8, 14, 15),

f_3 = Σ(2, 7, 11, 14)

For the following circuit with one AND gate and one XOR gate, the output function f can be expressed as:

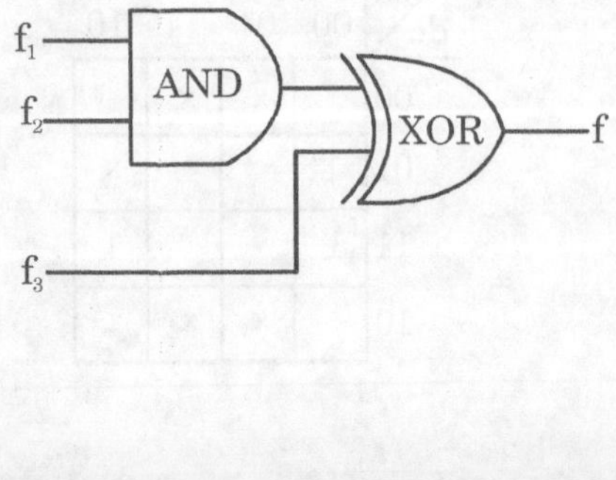

(a) Σ(2, 14)

(b) Σ(0, 2, 3, 5, 6, 7, 8, 11, 14, 15)

(c) Σ(2, 7, 8, 11, 14)

(d) Σ(7, 8, 11)

[2019 : 2 Marks]

56. What is the minimum number of 2-input NOR gates required to implement a 4-variable function expressed in sum-of-minterms form as f = Σ(0, 2, 5, 7, 8, 10, 13, 15)? Assume that all the inputs and their complements are available. Answer ______.

[2019 : 2 Marks]

NAND AND NOR IMPLEMENTATION

57. What is the minimum number of NAND gates required to implement a 2-input EXCLUSIVE- OR function without using any other logic gate?

(a) 3 (b) 4

(c) 5 (d) 6

[2004 : 1 Mark]

58. The following expression was to be realized using 2-input AND and OR gates. However, during the fabrication all 2-input AND gates were mistakenly substituted by 2-input NAND gates.

$$(a.b).c + (\overline{a}.c).d + (b.c).d + a.d$$

Which is the function finally realized ?

(a) 1 (b) $\overline{a}+\overline{b}+\overline{c}+\overline{d}$

(c) $\overline{a}+b+\overline{c}+\overline{d}$ (d) $\overline{a}+\overline{b}+c+\overline{d}$

[2007 : 2 Marks]

59. The line T in the following figure is permanently connected to the ground.

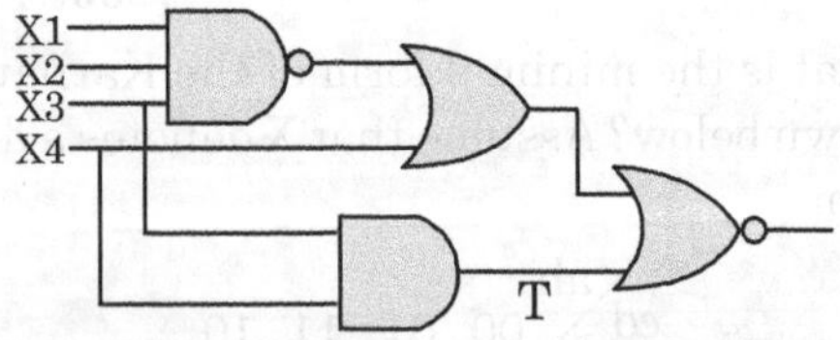

Which of the following inputs (X1 X2 X3 X4) will detect the fault?

(a) 0000 (b) 0111

(c) 1111 (d) None of these

[2007 : 2 Marks]

60. A set of Boolean connectives is functionally complete if all Boolean functions can be synthesized using those. Which of the following sets of connectives is NOT functionally complete?

(a) EX-NOR (b) Implication, negation

(c) Or, negation (d) NAND

[2008 : 1 Mark]

61. What is the minimum number of gates required to implement the Boolean function (AB + C) if we have to use only 2-input NOR gates ?

(a) 2 (b) 3

(c) 4 (d) 5

[2009 : 1 Mark]

62. What is the boolean expression for the output f of the combinational logic circuit of NOR gates given below ?

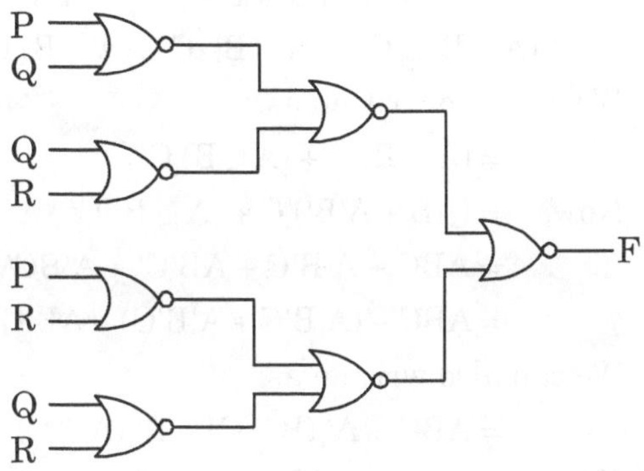

(a) $\overline{Q+R}$ (b) $\overline{P+Q}$

(c) $\overline{P+R}$ (d) $\overline{P+Q+R}$

[2010 : 2 Marks]

63. Transform the following logic circuit (without expressing its switching function) into an equivalent logic circuit that employs only 6 NAND gates each with 2-inputs.

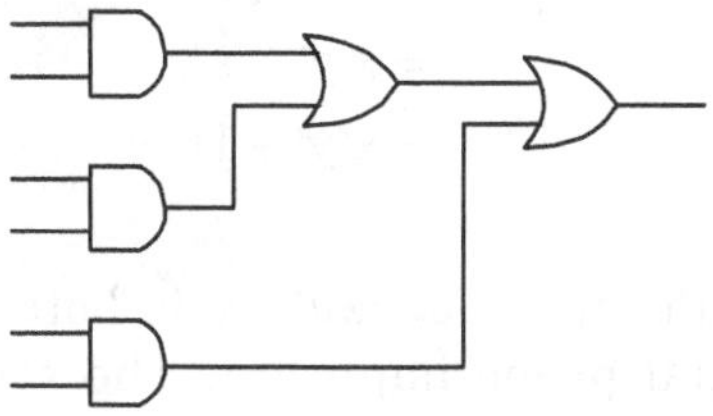

[2002 : 2 Marks]

ANSWERS

1. (*b*)	**2.** (*c*)	**3.** (*c*)	**4.** (*a*)	**5.** (*c*)	**6.** (*d*)	**7.** (*d*)	**8.** (*c*)	**9.** (*c*)	**10.** (*c*)
11. (*d*)	**12.** (*d*)	**13.** (*c*)	**14.** (*a*)	**15.** (*a*)	**16.** (*b*)	**17.** (*d*)	**18.** (*a*)	**19.** (*d*)	**20.** (*d*)
21. (*d*)	**22.** (1)	**23.** (*a*)	**24.** (*c*)	**25.** (*c*)	**26.** (*d*)	**27.** (*d*)	**28.** (*c*)	**29.** (*b*)	**30.** (*b*)
31. (*d*)	**32.** (*a*)	**33.** (*b*)	**34.** (*c*)	**35.** (*)	**36.** (*a*)	**37.** (*a*)	**38.** (*a*)	**39.** (*a*)	**40.** (*d*)
41. (*b*)	**42.** (*c*)	**43.** (*a*)	**44.** (*a*)	**45.** (*a*)	**46.** (*b*)	**47.** (*a*)	**48.** (*b*)	**49.** (3)	**50.** (*a*)
51. (1)	**52.** (*a*)	**53.** (3)	**54.** (*c*)	**55.** (*d*)	**56.** (3)	**57.** (*b*)	**58.** (*c*)	**59.** (*d*)	**60.** (*a*)
61. (*b*)	**62.** (*a*)	**63.** (*)							

EXPLANATIONS

1. Given

   x * y = x′ + y

   z = x * y

   Therefore z = x′ + y

   z * x = z′ + x

   = (x′ + y)′ + x

   = x.y′ + x

   = x(y′ + 1)

   = x

2. xz is an implicant and ¬y is both prime and essential prime implicant. The sop would be z + ¬x + ¬y.

3. Solve this question by options

   X + Y + Z =1

   XY = 0

   XZ + W = 1

   option (c) says X : 1 Y : 0 Z : 1 W : 1

   put these values in above it will satisfy.

4. 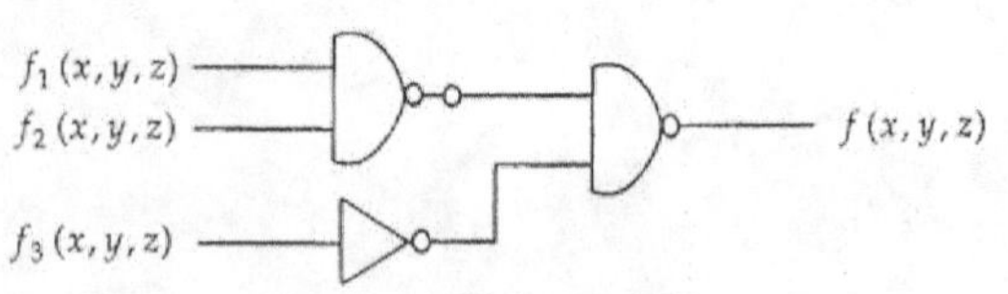

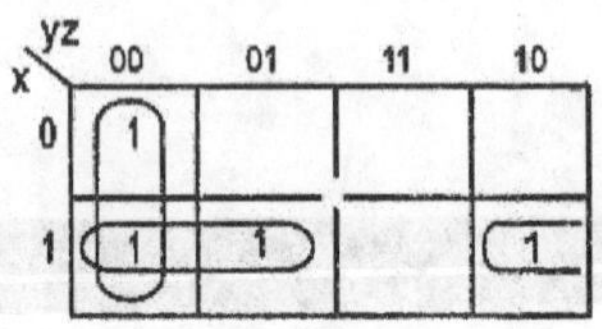

$f_1(x, y, z) = \bar{y}\,\bar{z} + x\,\bar{y} + x\,\bar{z}$

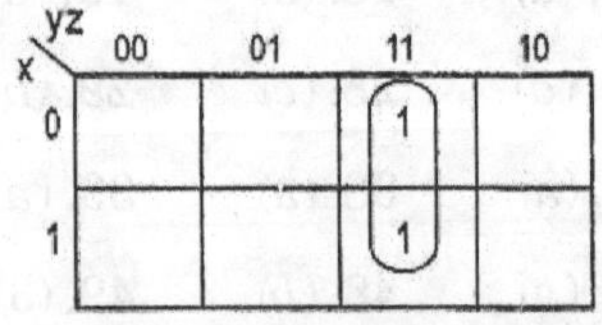

$f_2(x, y, z) = yz$

5. f(f (x + y, y), z) = f ((x + y)′ + y), z)

   = ((x + y)′ + y)′ + z

   = (x + y).y′ + z(∵ (a + b)′ = a′.b′)

   = xy′ + z

6. Note that, buffer is used for introducing delay. Output at 'P' is will be obtained at 2ns and at 'R' will be obtained 4ns after the change in their inputs.

   So, waveforms of 'P' and 'R' are shifted by 2ns and 4ns as compared to their inputs.

   Also, note that 'Q' and 'B' are plotted using their corresponding input waveforms.

   Finally, we can see that there are 4 changes in logic levels in the waveforms of 'B'.

7. $x'y' + xy + x'y$

   $= x'(y + y') + xy$

   $= x' + xy$

   $= (x' + x)(x' + y) = x' + y$

8. (A □ B) □ C = (A □ B)′ C + (A □ B) C′

   We can also written as:

   = (A □ B) C + (A □ B) C′

   Now, = (AB + A′B′) C + (A □ B) C′

   = ABC + A′B′C + AB′C′ + A′BC′

   = ABC + (A′B′C + A′B′C) + AB′C′ + A′BC′

   We can also written as:

   = ABC + A′ (B □ C) + B′ (A □ C)

9. If we draw truth table of the above circuit, it'll be

S1	S2	Bulb
0	0	on
0	1	off
1	0	off
1	1	on

   = (S1 □ S2)'

10. For n binary variables, we can obtain 2^n distinct minterm or maxterms.
    Since function can be either 1 or 0 for each minterm or maxterm, therefore we can form 2^{2^n} function from n variables.

11. Each of the functions P, Q and R includes same minterms which f includes, where S doesn't includes same minterms as f.

    $P = \Sigma(0, 4, 5, 7, 8, 9, 13, 15)$

    $= Q = R = f$

    whereas $S = \Sigma(0, 2, 3, 5, 7, 8, 9) \neq f$

12. Truth table for X, Y and Z

X	Y	Z = X * Y	Y * Z	X * Z	X * Y * Z
0	0	1	0	0	1
0	1	0	0	1	1
1	0	0	1	0	1
1	1	1	1	1	1

From above truth table we can say that all P, Q and R are valid.

13. f_1 and f_2 are connected with and gates, so when $f_2 = \Sigma m(6, 8)$ then f is true for Σm (1, 6, 8, 15)

14. (P + Q′) (PQ′ + PR) (P′R′ + Q′)

= (PQ′ + PR + PQ′ + PRQ′) (P′R′ + Q′)

= (PQ′ + PR + PRQ′) (P′R′ + Q′)

= (PQ′ + PR (1 + Q′)) (P′R′ + Q′)

= (PQ′ + PR) (P′R′ + Q′)

= PQ′ + PRQ′

= PQ′ (1 + R) = PQ′

15. Given : f(P, Q, R) = $PQ + Q\bar{R} + P\bar{R}$

By K-map

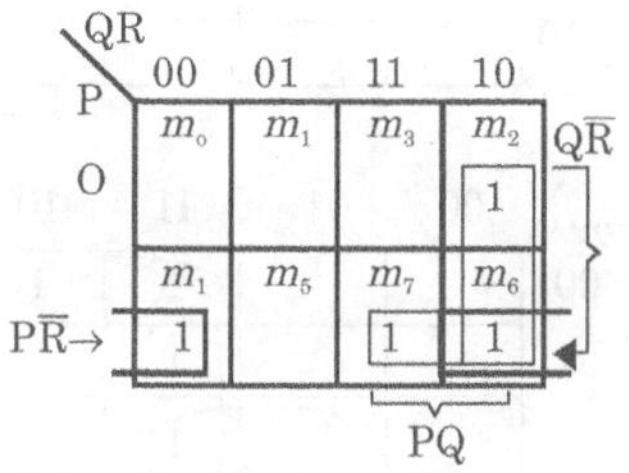

These are min terms means sum of products in k-map

Then answer is $\mathbf{PQ + Q\bar{R} + P\bar{R}}$

So answer is $\boldsymbol{m_2 + m_4 + m_6 + m_7}$ because all other answer conflict the requirment.

16. (P + Q′ + R′).(P + Q + R).(P + Q + R′)

(P + Q′ + R′).(P + (Q + R)(Q + R′))

(P + Q′ + R′).(P + Q)

(P + (Q′ + R′)Q)

P + QR′

Hence, option(B)P + QR′

17. All options except option ‘*d*’ gives EX-NOR gates

18. XY′ + XY = X(Y′+Y)

= X.1 = X

19. Exclusive NOR of x & y $\overline{x \oplus y}$

Truth table:

x	y	$2 \oplus y$	$\overline{x \oplus y}$
0	0	0	1
0	1	1	0
1	0	1	0
1	1	0	1

Option (A):

x	y	xy	$x'y'$	$xy + x'y'$
0	0	0	1	1
0	1	0	0	0
1	0	0	0	0
1	1	1	1	1

Same as $\overline{x \oplus y}$

Option (B):

x	y	y'	$x \oplus y'$
0	0	1	1
0	1	0	0
1	0	1	0
1	1	0	1

$\equiv \overline{x \oplus y}$

Option (C):

x	y	x'	$x' \oplus y$
0	0	1	1
0	1	1	0
1	0	0	0
1	1	0	1

$\equiv \overline{x \oplus y}$

Option (D):

x	y	x'	y'	$x' \oplus y'$
0	0	1	1	0
0	1	1	0	1
1	0	0	1	1
1	1	0	0	0

This is not equivalent to $\overline{x \oplus y}$ So, the answer is (*d*)

20. According to the passage, kaliningrad is a part of Russia despite it not being contiguous with the rest of Russia.

21. $F(P,Q) = \left((1 \oplus P) \oplus (P \oplus Q)\right) \oplus \left((P \oplus Q) \oplus (Q \oplus 0)\right)$

$= \left(\bar{P} \oplus \left(P\bar{Q} + \bar{P}Q\right)\right) \oplus \left(\left(P\bar{Q} + \bar{P}Q\right) \oplus Q\right)$

$= \left[\bar{P}\left(PQ + \bar{P}\bar{Q}\right) + P\left(P\bar{Q} + \bar{P}Q\right)\right]$

$\oplus \left[\left(PQ + \bar{P}\bar{Q}\right)Q + \left(P\bar{Q} + \bar{P}Q\right)\bar{Q}\right]$

$= \left(\bar{P}\bar{Q} + P\bar{Q}\right) \oplus \left(PQ + P\bar{Q}\right) = \bar{Q} \oplus P$

$= PQ + \bar{P}\bar{Q} = \overline{P \oplus Q}$

22.

AB \ CD	00	01	11	10
00	1	1	1	1
01	1	1	1	1
11	1	1	ⓧ	1
10	1	1	1	1

Ans = 1, ABCD

23. The function # basically represents XOR.
Following are true with XOR.
(1) XOR(x) with 0 is x itself.
(2) XOR(x) with 1 is complement of x.
(3) XOR(x) with x is 0.
(4) XOR(x) with x' is 1.
XOR is represented as x'y + y'x.

24. Take the value of x1 = x2 = x3 = x4 = 1.
Only option (c) is correct.

25. $$\left(w\bar{x}\left(y+\bar{x}z\right)+\overline{wx}\right)y=\bar{x}y$$

$$\left(w\bar{x}y+\overline{wx}\right)y$$

$$w\bar{x}y+\overline{wx}y$$

$$\bar{x}y\left(w+\bar{w}\right),\text{ since }\left(w+\bar{w}\right)\text{ evaluate to 1}$$

$$\bar{x}y \neq x\bar{y} \qquad \text{False}$$

26. (A) $\overline{P\oplus Q}=P\odot Q$ true
(B) $\bar{P}\oplus Q=P\odot Q$ true
(C) $\bar{P}\oplus\bar{Q}=P\oplus Q$ true
(D) $(P\oplus\bar{P})\oplus Q=(P\odot\bar{P})\odot\bar{Q}$ false
$(P\oplus\bar{P})\oplus Q=1\oplus Q=\bar{Q}$
$(P\odot\bar{P})\odot\bar{Q}=0\oplus\bar{Q}=Q$
$(P\oplus\bar{P})\oplus Q\neq(P\odot\bar{P})\odot\bar{Q}$

27. (a) $(x\oplus y)\oplus z=x\oplus(y\oplus z)$
Associativity is true on Ex-OR operator so it valid.

(b) $x\oplus y=(x+y)(\bar{x}+\bar{y})$
$=(x+y)\overline{xy}=(x+y)\bar{0}$
$=(x+y)$, so it is valid.

(c) $x\oplus y=(xy+x'y')'=(x\odot y)'$
$=x\oplus y$, it is valid.

(d) $(x+y)\oplus z=\overline{(x+y)}\cdot z+(x+y)\bar{z}$
$=\underset{1}{\bar{x}\bar{y}z}+\underset{4,6}{x\bar{Z}}+\underset{2,6}{y\bar{Z}}=\sum m(1, 2, 4, 6)$

$x\oplus(y+z)=\bar{x}(y+z)+x\overline{(y+z)}$
$=\underset{2,3}{\bar{x}y}+\underset{1,3}{\bar{x}z}+\underset{4}{x\bar{y}\bar{z}}=\sum m(1, 2, 3, 4)$
$(x+y)\oplus z\neq x\oplus(y+z)$
Hence it is invalid.

28. If all the empty cells are filled with '0' and then the POS expression is calculated as:
$$f=(D+B)(D'+B')$$

29. Given $f_1(w, x, y, z)=\Sigma\, 8, 9, 10$
$f_2(w, x, y, z)=\Sigma\, 7, 8, 12, 13, 14, 15$
$f(w, x, y, z)=\Sigma\, 8, 9$

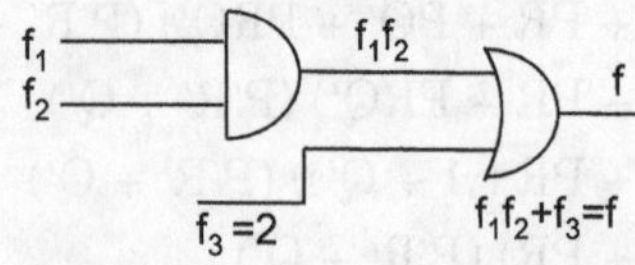

wx \ yz	00	01	11	10
00				1
01				1
11				1
10				

wx \ yz	00	01	11	10
00			1	1
01			1	
11		1	1	
10			1	

$$f_1 = y\bar{z}(\bar{w})+y\bar{z}(x)$$
$$= y\bar{z}(\bar{w}+x)$$
$$f_2 = yz+\bar{w}\bar{x}y+w\times z$$
$$f_1f_2 = y\bar{z}(\bar{w}+x)(y2+\bar{w}\,\bar{x}\,y+w\times z)$$
$$= (y\bar{z}\,\bar{w}+y\bar{z}x)(y2+\overline{wx}\,y+wxz)$$
$$= \bar{w}y\bar{z}\,\bar{x} = y\bar{z}\,\bar{w}\,\bar{x}$$

wx \ yz	00	01	11	10
00				1
01				1
11				
10				

$f=y\bar{z}\bar{w}$

From figure $f=f_1f_2+f_3$
$$y\bar{z}\bar{w} = y\bar{z}\bar{w}\,\bar{x}+f_3=y\bar{z}\bar{w}\bar{z}+y\bar{z}\bar{w}x$$
$$= y\bar{z}\bar{w}(x+\bar{x})$$

So, $f_3 = y\bar{z}\,\bar{w}\,x$

K map for f_3

wx \ yz	00	01	11	10
00				
01				1
11				
10				

$f_3=\bar{w}\,x\,y\bar{z}$
$f_3=\Sigma 9$

30. After solving K map equation is

$$= CD + AD$$
$$= D(C + A)$$

31. Option a and option b is same we can derive from the given Kmap. Option C is product of sum (POS) form. So answer is (d)

32.

yz \ wx	00	01	11	0
00	0	x	0	x
01	x	1	x	1
11	0	x	1	0
10	0	1	x	0

On solving above xy + y'z.

33. For taking minterm (SOP)

$$f = xz' = zx'$$

yz \ wx	00	01	11	10
00	0	1	1	0
01	x	0	0	1
11	x	0	0	1
10	0	1	1	x

34. Sum of product is = wy + w'y' + z'wx' + xyz'

total Literal count for SOP is 10

Product of Sum is (w' + z')(x' + y)(z + w + x)(z' + y')

Total Literal count for POS is 9

So, option (C) is correct.

36. K-map of given function is

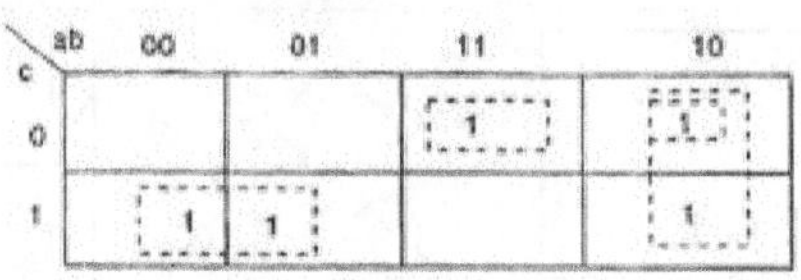

Essential prime implicant of this boolean function is

011, 011 and 110,100

which is a'c and ac' which is *(a)*.

37. $\overline{X\overline{Y}} \cdot YZ = F$

$$X\overline{Y} + \overline{YZ}$$
$$X\overline{Y} + \overline{Y} + \overline{Z}$$
$$\overline{Y} + \overline{Z}$$

38. Given : $f(A, B, C, D) = \Sigma(1, 4, 5, 9, 11, 12)$

$$= \overline{A}\,\overline{C}D + B\overline{C}\,\overline{D} + A\overline{B}D$$

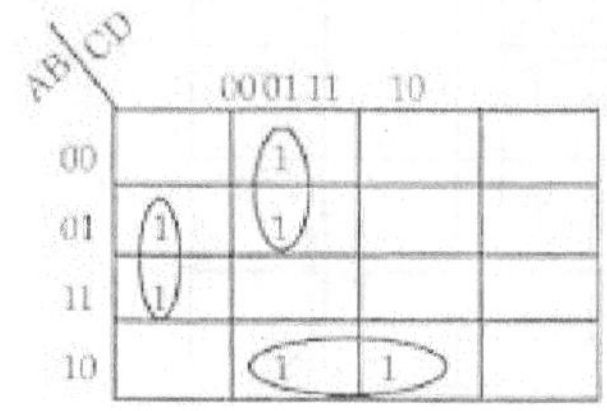

39.

wx \ yz	00	01	11	10
00	0	0	0	0
01	0	1	1	0
11	1	1	1	0
10	0	0	1	0

The cube covers of *(a)* contain following cells.

$\overline{w}\,xz$	0101, 0111
$wx\overline{y}$	1101, 1100
$x\overline{y}z$	0101,1101
xyz	0111, 1111
wyz	1011,1111

Atleast one member of a pair should satisfy the condition of differing by one bit by at least one member of each of other pairs. This is true regarding the above cubes.

40. Essential prime implicants are prime implicants that cover an output of the function that no combination of other prime implicants is able to cover. So option D is not cover in any other prime implicants.

41. Karnaugh map of given function will be as follows:

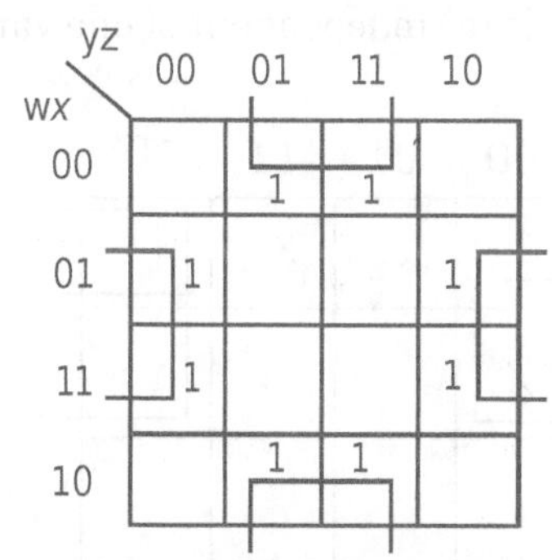

Simplified form of *f* will be

$$f = x'z + xz'$$

Therefore, it is independent of two variables.

42.

	$\bar{c}\bar{d}$	$\bar{c}d$	cd	$c\bar{d}$
$\bar{a}\bar{b}$	1	1		
$\bar{a}b$	1	1		1
ab	1	1		1
$\bar{a}\bar{b}$	1			1

$\Rightarrow a\bar{d} + \overline{ac} + b\bar{d} + b\bar{c}$

$\Rightarrow a\bar{d} + \overline{ac} + b\bar{c}d$

43. c′d′ + ad′ + abc′ + (ac)′d not genrated by K map

44.

cd \ ab	00	01	11	0
00	1	1		1
01	x			
11	x			
10	1	1		x

$f = \overline{b}\overline{d} + \overline{a}\overline{d}$

45. The Kmap for given function is

	A′B′	A′B	A B	A B′
A′B′			1	1
A′B			1	
A B	1	1		
A B′	1	1	1	1

A′ C + AC′ + B′ C

So Ans is (a) independent of one variable.

46.

cd \ ab	00	01	11	10
00	1	X	X	1
01	X			1
11				
10	1			X

Boolean express for K map is f = b′d′ + b′c′

47. $PQ + \overline{P}QR + \overline{P}QR\overline{S}$

$= PQ + \overline{P}Q(R + \overline{R}S)$

$= PQ + \overline{P}Q\left((R + \overline{R})(R+S)\right)$

$[\because A + BC = (A + B)(A + C)]$

$= PQ + \overline{P}Q(R + S)$ $\quad [\because R + \overline{R} = 1]$

$= Q\left(P + \overline{P}(R + S)\right)$

$= Q\left((P + \overline{P})(P + R + S)\right)$

$[\because A + BC = (A + B)(A + C)]$

$= Q(P + R + S)$ $\quad \because [P + \overline{P} = 1]$

$= PQ + QR + QS$

48.

PQ \ RS	$\overline{R}\overline{S}$	$\overline{R}S$	RS	$\overline{S}$
$\overline{P}\overline{Q}$	1			ϕ
$\overline{P}Q$		1	ϕ	
PQ		ϕ	1	
$P\overline{Q}$	ϕ			1

→ P_1 (corner group); → P_2 (centre group)

The K-map for the function F is as follows :

$P_1 = \overline{Q}\overline{S}$

and $P_2 = QS$

$\therefore F(P, Q, R, S) = P_1 + P_2$

$= \overline{Q}\overline{S} + QS$

49.

wx \ yz	00	01	11	10
00	*1	0	0	1
01	1	1*	0	1*
11	0	0	0	0
10	0	0	0	1*

There are three groups, and all the containing esential-1, so all are prime implicants as well as essential prime implicants also.

50. After drwaing KMAP of F = P′ + QR ,we can find out S2 and S3 are TRUE.

51.

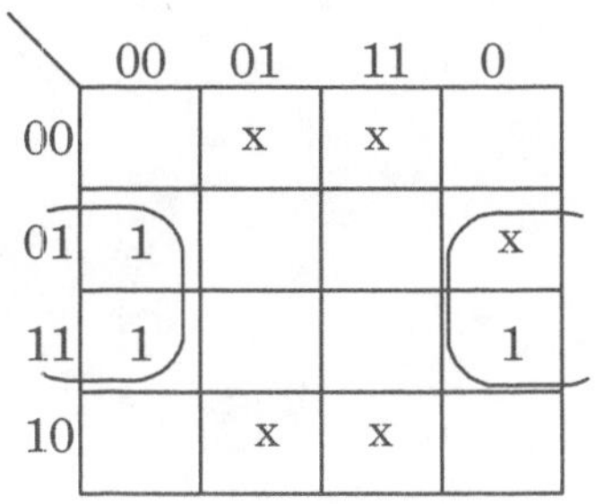

$f = a'c \Rightarrow ((a'c)')' = (a + c')'$

only one NOR Gate is Required.

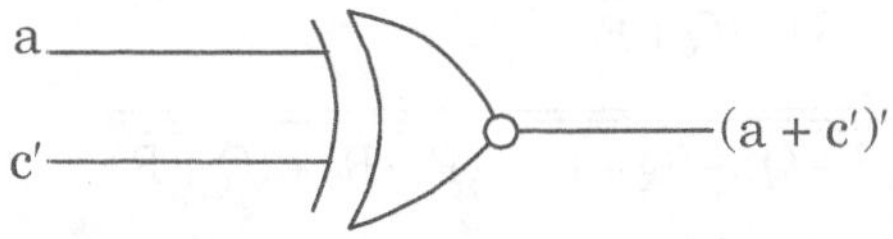

52. Given

$f(w, x, y, z) = \Sigma_m\{0, 1, 2, 3, 7, 8, 10) + d(5, 6, 11, 15)$

$= \pi_M \{4, 9, 12, 13, 14). d(5, 6, 11, 15)$

draw K-map

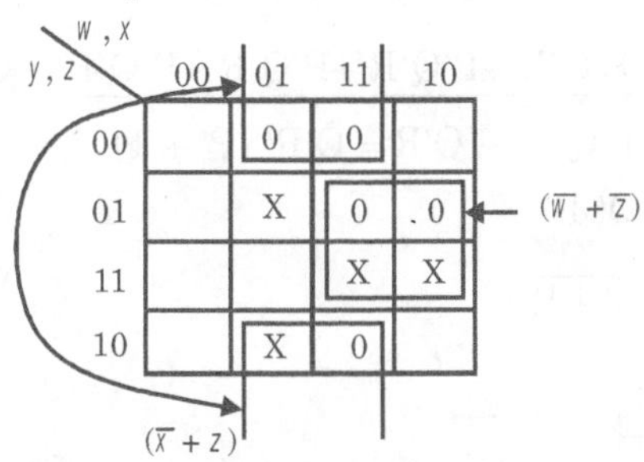

$f(w, x, y, z) = (\overline{w} + \overline{z})(\overline{x} + z)$]

This is minimum POS form of $f(w, x, y, z)$

53. F(P, Q, R, S) = Σm(0, 2, 5, 7, 9, 11) + d(3, 8, 10, 12, 14)

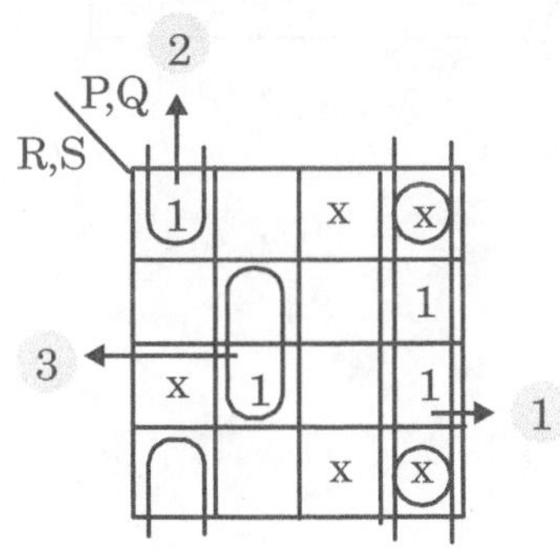

Number of EPI = 3

54. Output is form of 4 bit and output is 1 when input is greater than 5, So, output will be 1 in case of

0101 – 5

0110 – 6

0111 – 7

1000 – 8

1001 – 9

This can be implemented with the help of 3 logic gate of type AND OR and NOT.

55. $f_1.f_2 = \Sigma(2, 8, 14)$

$f_1 = f_3 \oplus (f_1.f_2)$

$= \Sigma(7, 8, 11)$

56. $f = \Sigma_m(0, 2, 5, 7, 8, 10, 13, 15)$

$f = \Pi_M(1, 3, 4, 6, 9, 11, 12, 14)$

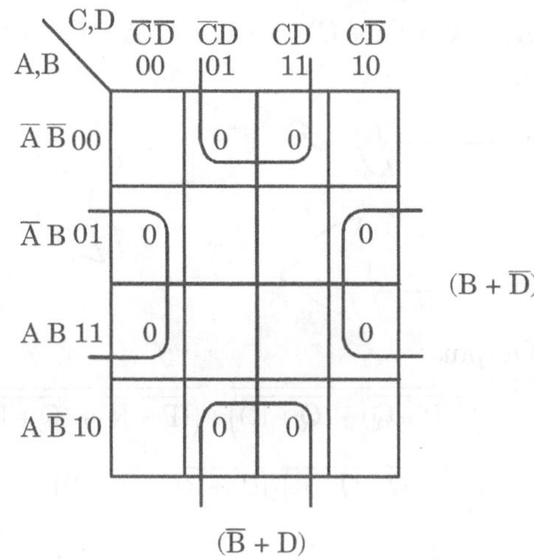

$$f = (\overline{B} + D)(B + \overline{D})$$

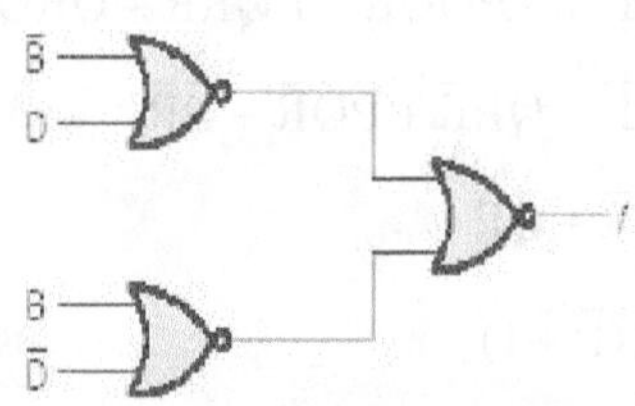

So 3 NOR gates is required to implement above function.

57.

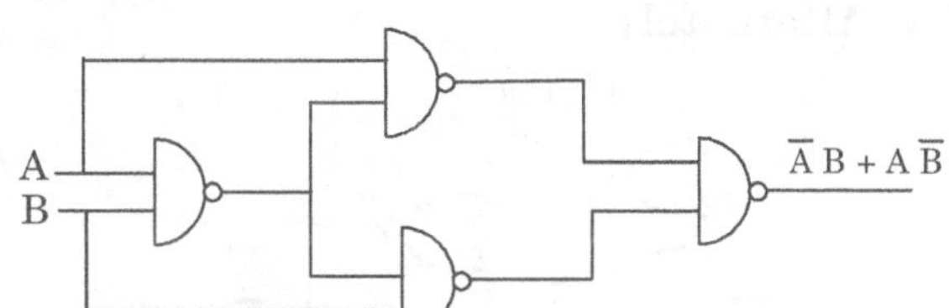

total 4 NAND Gate Required.1

58. $a' + c' + d' + a'c + ab + bc$

$= a'(c + 1) + c' + d' + ab + bc$

$= a' + c' + d' + ab + bc$

$= (a' + a)(a' + b) + (c' + c)(c' + b) + d'$

$= a' + b + c' + b + d'$

$= a' + b + c' + d'$

59. We can write equation for the circuit as

$(((x1.x2.x3)' + x4) + x3.x4)'$

$= ((x1.x2.x3)' + x4)'.(x3.x4)'$

$= x1.x2.x3.x'4.(x'3 + x'4)$

$= x1.x2.x3.x'4$

For the faulty circuit output will be

((x1.x2.x3)′ + x4)′ = x1.x2.x3.x′4

So, there is no effect of T being grounded here. Answer is D option.

60. The EX-NOR is not functionally complete because we cannot synthesize all Boolean functions using EX-NOR gate only.

61. AB + C = (A + C) (B + C) = ((A + C)′ + (B + C)′)′

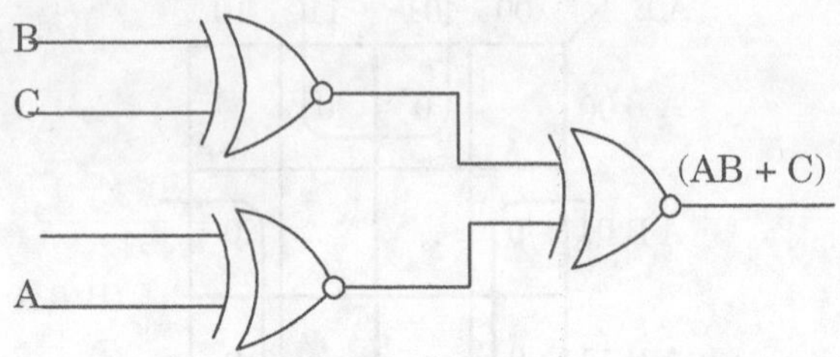

62. Output

$$= \overline{\left(\overline{P+Q}+\overline{Q+R}\right)}+\overline{\left(\overline{P+R}+\overline{Q+R}\right)}$$

$$= \left(\overline{P+Q}+\overline{Q+R}\right)\cdot\left(\overline{P+R}+\overline{Q+R}\right)$$

$$\left(\because \overline{A+B}=\bar{A}\,\bar{B}\right)$$

$$= \left(\bar{P}\bar{Q}+\bar{Q}\bar{R}\right)\left(\bar{P}\bar{R}+\bar{Q}\bar{R}\right)$$

$$= \bar{P}\bar{Q}\bar{P}\bar{R}+\bar{P}\bar{O}\bar{Q}\bar{R}+\bar{P}\bar{Q}\bar{R}\bar{R}+\bar{Q}\bar{R}\bar{Q}\bar{R}$$

$$= \bar{P}\bar{Q}\bar{R}+\bar{Q}\bar{P}\bar{R}+\bar{P}\bar{Q}\bar{R}+\bar{Q}\bar{R}$$

$$= \bar{P}\bar{Q}\bar{R}+\bar{Q}\bar{R}$$

$$= \bar{Q}\bar{R}(\bar{P}+1) \quad ..... \left[\text{since}\,(\bar{P}+1)=1\right]$$

$$= \overline{(Q+R)}$$

Alternately

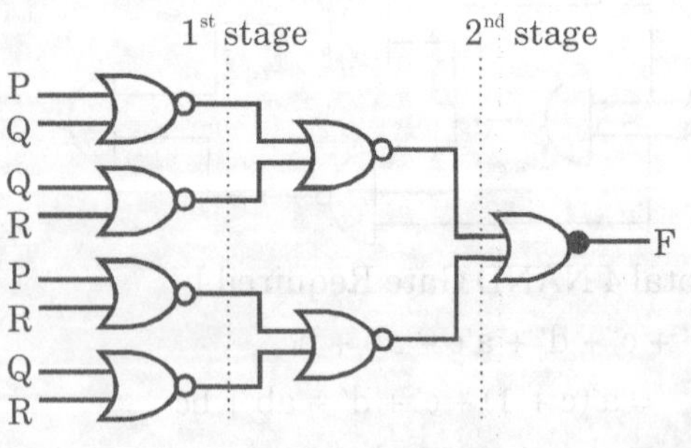

At first stage

- $\overline{(P+Q)}$
- $\overline{(Q+R)}$
- $\overline{(P+R)}$
- $\overline{(Q+R)}$

At second stage

- $\overline{\overline{(P+Q)}+\overline{(Q+R)}}$
- $\overline{\overline{(P+R)}+\overline{(Q+R)}}$

$$F = \overline{\overline{\overline{(P+Q)}+\overline{(Q+R)}}+\overline{\overline{(P+R)}+\overline{(Q+R)}}}$$

$$= \overline{\overline{\overline{(P+Q)}+\overline{(Q+R)}}}\cdot\overline{\overline{\overline{(P+R)}+\overline{(Q+R)}}}$$

$$= \left(\overline{(P+Q)}+\overline{(Q+R)}\right)\cdot\left(\overline{(P+R)}+\overline{(Q+R)}\right)$$

$$= (P'Q'+Q'R')\cdot(P'R'+Q'R')$$

$$= P'Q'R'+P'Q'R'+P'Q'R'+P'Q'R'+Q'R'$$

$$= P'Q'R' + Q'R' = Q'R'\,(P'+1)$$

$$= Q'\,R'$$

$$= \overline{Q+R}$$

63.

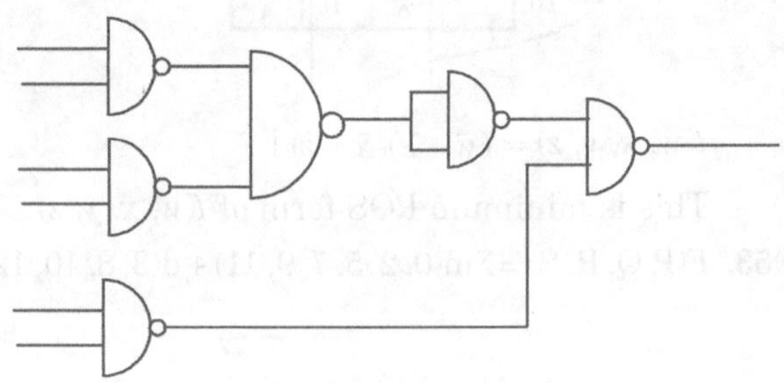

2

CHAPTER

Combination Circuit

Analysis of Previous GATE Papers											
Units	Year → Topics ↓		2019	2018	2017 Set 1	2017 Set 2	2016 Set 1	2016 Set 2	2015 Set 1	2015 Set 2	2015 Set 3
BINARY ADDER/SUBTRACTOR	1 Mark	MCQ Type			1						
		Numerical Type						1			
	2 Marks	MCQ Type					1				
		Numerical Type								1	
	Total				1		2	1		2	
COMBINATIONAL CIRCUIT ANALYSIS	1 Mark	MCQ Type	1								
		Numerical Type									
	2 Marks	MCQ Type									
		Numerical Type									
	Total		1								
MULTIPL EXER	1 Mark	MCQ Type									
		Numerical Type									
	2 Marks	MCQ Type					1				
		Numerical Type									
	Total						2				
DECODER	1 Mark	MCQ Type									
		Numerical Type									
	2 Marks	MCQ Type									
		Numerical Type									
	Total										
ENCODER	1 Mark	MCQ Type									
		Numerical Type									
	2 Marks	MCQ Type									
		Numerical Type									
	Total										

BINARY ADDER/SUBTRACTOR

1. Fill in the blanks

In the two bit full-adder/subtractor unit shown in figure, when the switch is in position 2 .... using .... arithmetic

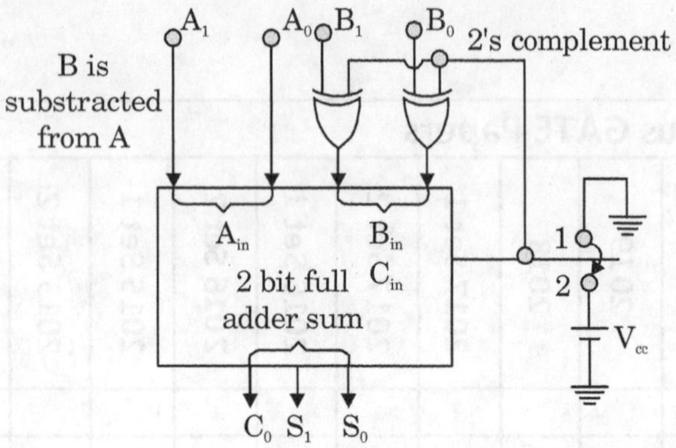

[1990 : 2 Marks]

2. Consider the circuits in figure which has a four bit binary number $b_3\ b_2\ b_1\ b_0$ as input and a five bit binary number $d_4\ d_3\ d_2\ d_1\ d_0$ as output. The circuit implements :

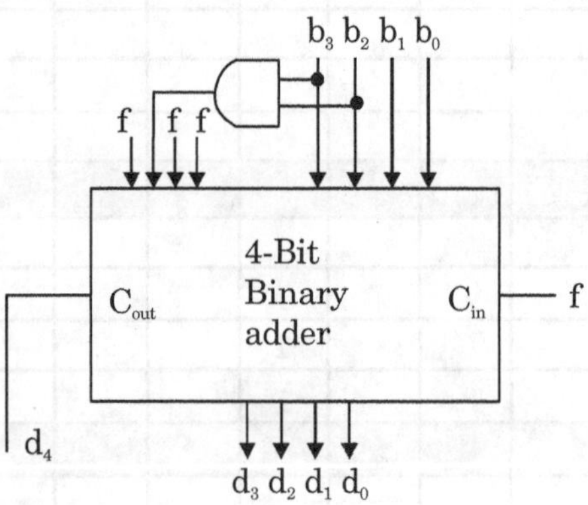

(a) Binary to Hex conversion

(b) Binary to BCD conversion

(c) Binary to grey code conversion

(d) Binary to radix-12 conversion

[1996 : 2 Marks]

3. Consider the ALU shown below :

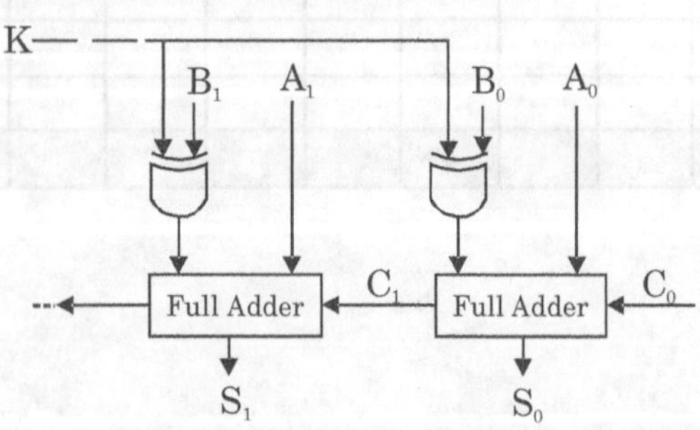

If the operands are in 2's complement representation, which of the following operations can be performed by suitably setting the control like K and C_0 only (+ and – denote addition and subtraction respectively)?

(a) A + B, and A – B, but not A + 1

(b) A + B, and A + 1, but not A – B

(c) A + B, but not A – B, or A + 1

(d) A + B, and A – B, and A + 1

[2003 : 2 Marks]

4. A 4-bit carry lookahead adder, which adds two 4-bit numbers, is designed using AND, OR NOT, NAND, NOR gates only. Assuming that all the inputs are available in both complemented and uncomplemented forms and the delay of each gate is one time unit, what is the overall propagation delay of the adder? Assume that the carry network has been implemented using two-level AND-OR logic.

(a) 4 time units (b) 6 time units

(c) 10 time units (d) 12 time units

[2004 : 2 Marks]

5. A half adder is implemented with XOR and AND gates. A full adder is implemented with two half adders and one OR ate. The propagation delay of an XOR gate is twice that of an AND/OR gate. The propagation delay of an AND/OR gate is 1.2 microseconds.

A 4-bit ripple-carry binary adder is implemented by using four full adders. The total propagation time of this 4-bit binary adder in microseconds is ....

[2015 (Set-2) : 2 Marks]

6. Consider a carry lookahead adder for adding two n-bit integers, built using gates of fan-in atmost two. The time to perform addition using this adder is

(a) $\Theta(1)$ (b) $\Theta(\log(n))$

(c) $\Theta(\sqrt{n})$ (d) $\Theta(n)$

[2016 (Set-1) : 2 Marks]

7. Consider an eight bit ripple-carry adder for computing the sum of A and B, where A and B are integers represented in 2's complement form. If the decimal value of A is one, the decimal value of B that leads to the longest latency for the sum to stabilize is ....

[2016 (Set-2) : 1 Mark]

8. When two 8-bit numbers $A_7 .....A_0$ and $B_7 .... B_0$ in 2's complement representation (with A_0 and B_0 as the least significant bits) are added using a ripple-carry adder, the sum bits obtained are S_7 .... S_0 and the carry bits are $C_7 .....C_0$. An overflow is said to have occured if

(a) the carry bit C_7 is 1

(b) all the carry bits (C_7, ..., C_0) are 1

(c) $\left(A_7 . B_7 . \bar{S}_7 + \bar{A}_7 . \bar{B}_7 . S_7\right)$ is 1

(d) $\left(A_0 . B_0 . \bar{S}_0 + \bar{A}_0 . \bar{B}_0 . S_0\right)$ is 1

[2017 (Set-1) : 1 Mark]

9. Given two 3-bit numbers $a_2a_1a_0$ and $b_2b_1b_0$ and c, the carry in, the function that represents the carry generate function when these two numbers are added is

(a) $a_2b_2 + a_2a_1b_1 + a_2a_1a_0b_0 + a_2a_0b_1b_0 + a_1b_2b_1 + a_1a_0b_2b_0 + a_0b_2b_1b_0$

(b) $a_2b_2 + a_2b_1b_0 + a_2a_1b_1b_0 + a_1a_0b_2b_1 + a_1a_0b_2 + a_1a_0b_2b_0 + a_2a_0b_1b_0$

(c) $a_2 + b_2 + (a_2 \oplus b_2)[a_1 + b_1 + (a_1 \oplus b_1)(a_0 + b_0)]$

(d) $a_2b_2 + \overline{a_2}\, a_1 b_1 + \overline{a_2 a_1}\, a_0 b_0 + \overline{a_2}\, a_0 \overline{b_1}\, b_0 + a_1 \overline{b_2} b_1 + \overline{a_1} a_0 \overline{b_2} b_0 + a_0 \overline{b_2 b_1} b_0$

[2006 : 2 Marks]

10. We consider the addition of two 2's complement numbers $b_{n-1}\, b_{n-2} \ldots b_0$ and $a_{n-1}\, a_{n-2} \ldots a_0$. A binary adder for adding unsigned binary numbers is used to add the two numbers. The sum is denoted by $c_{n-1}\, c_{n-2} \ldots c_0$ and the carryout by c_{out}.
Which one of the following options correctly identifies the overflow condition?

(a) $c_{out}\overline{(a_{n-1} \oplus b_{n-1})}$

(b) $a_{n-1}b_{n-1}\overline{c_{n-1}} + \overline{a_{n-1}b_{n-1}}\, c_{n-1}$

(c) $c_{out} \oplus c_{n-1}$

(d) $a_{n-1} \oplus b_{n-1} \oplus c_{n-1}$

[2006 : 2 Marks]

11. In a look-ahead carry generator, the carry generate function G_i and the carry propagate function P_i for inputs, A_i and B_i are given by

$$P_i = A_i \oplus B_i \text{ and } G_i = A_iB_i$$

The expression fo the sum bit S_i and carry bit C_{i+1} of the look-ahead carry adder are given by $S_i = P_i \oplus C_i$ and $C_{i+1} = G_i + P_iC_i$, where C_0 is the input carry.

Consider a two-level logic implementation of the look-ahead carry generator. Assume that all P_i and G_i are available for the carry generator circuit and that the AND and OR gages can have any number of inputs. The number of AND gates and OR gates needed to implement the look-ahead carry generator for a 4-bit adder with S_3, S_2, S_1, S_0 and C_4 as its outputs are respectively

(a) 6, 3
(b) 10, 4
(c) 6, 4
(d) 10, 5

[2007 : 2 Marks]

COMBINATIONAL CIRCUIT ANALYSIS

12. Which of the following sets of component(s) is/are sufficient to implement any arbitrary Boolean function ?

(a) XOR gates, NOT gates
(b) 2 to 1 multiplex
(c) AND gates, XOR gates
(d) Three-input gates that output (A . B) + C for the inputs A, B and C.

[1999 : 2 Marks]

13. The majority function is a Booleam function f(x, y, z) that takes the value 1 whenever a majority of the variables x, y, z and 1. In the circuit diagram for the majority function shown below, the logic gates for the boxes labeled P and Q are, respectively,

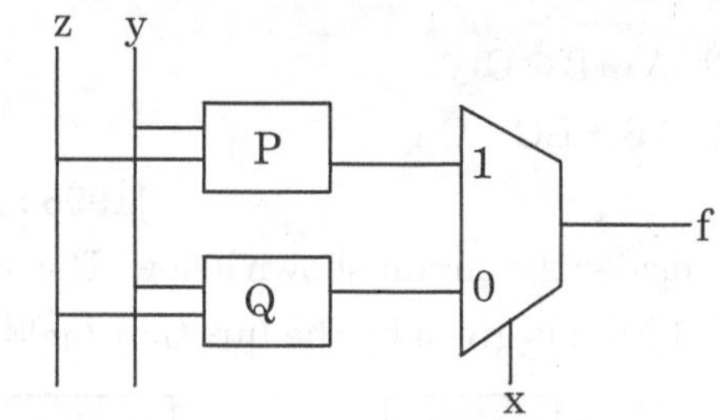

(a) XOR, AND
(b) XOR, XOR
(c) OR, OR
(d) OR, AND

[2006 : 2 Marks]

14. **Consider the operations**

$$f(X, Y, Z) = X'YZ + XY' + Y'Z' \text{ and}$$
$$g(X, Y, Z) = X'YZ + X'YZ' + XY$$

Which one of the following is correct.

(a) Both {f} and {g} are functionally complete
(b) Only {f} is functionally complete
(c) Only {g} is functioally complete
(d) Neither {f} nor {g} is functionally complete

[2015 (Set-1) : 2 Marks]

15. The chip select logic for a certain DRAM chip in a memory system design is shown below. Assume that the memory system has 16 address lines denoted by A_{15} to A_0. What is the range of addresses (in hexadecimal) of the memory system that can get enabled by the chip select (CS) signal?

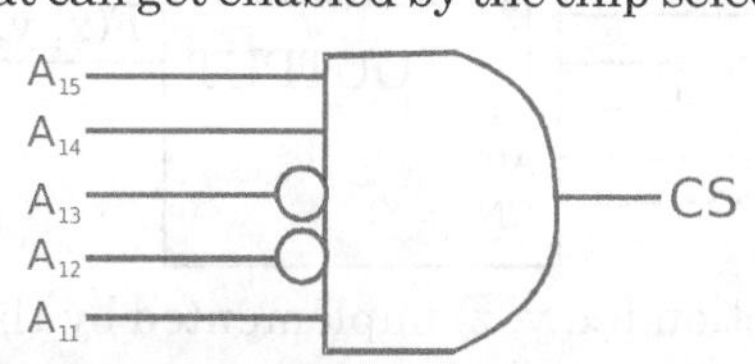

(a) CA00 to CAFF
(b) C800 to CFFF
(c) DA00 to DFFF
(d) C800 to C8FF

[2019 : 1 Mark]

MULTIPLEXER

16. Consider the circuit in figure shown. F implements

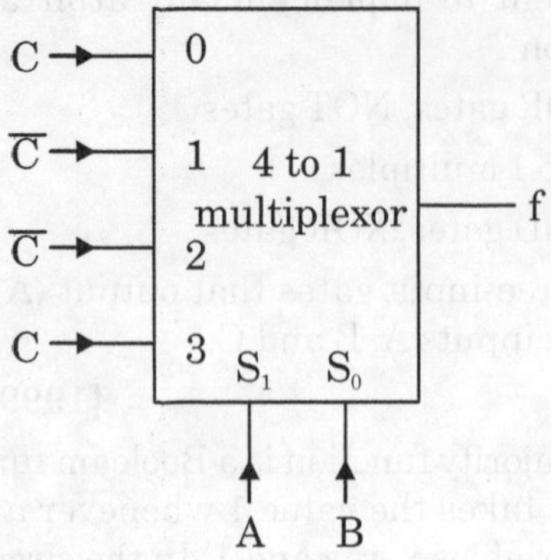

(a) $\bar{A}\bar{B}C + \bar{A}B\bar{C} + ABC$

(b) $A + B + C$

(c) $A \oplus B \oplus C$

(d) $AB + BC + CA$

[1996 : 2 Marks]

17. Consider the circuit shown below. The output of a 2 : 1 Mux is given by the function (ac'+ bc).

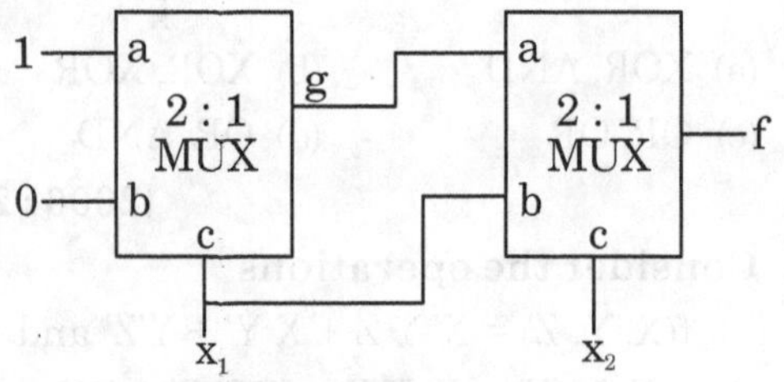

Which of the following is true ?

(a) $f = x_1' + x_2$ (b) $f = x_1 x_2 + x_1 x_2'$

(c) $f = x_1 x_2 + x_1' x_2'$ (d) $f = x_1 + x_2$

[2001 : 2 Marks]

18. Consider the following multiplexer where I0, I1, I2, I3 and four data input lines selected by two address line combinations A1A0 = 00, 01, 10, 11 respectively and f is the output of the multiplexer, EN is the Enable input.

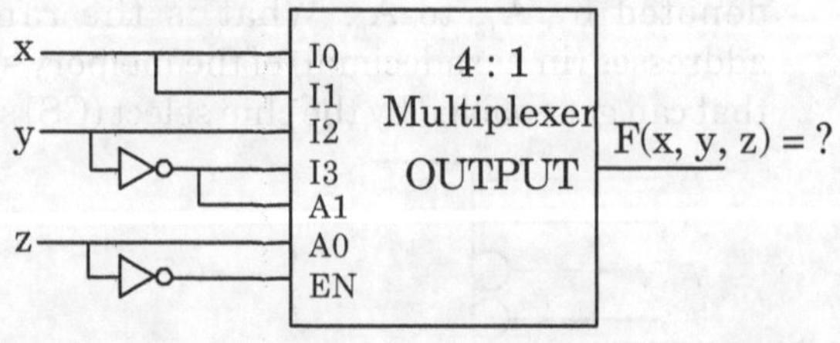

The function f(x, y, z) implemented by the above circuit is

(a) xyz′ (b) xyz

(c) x + y (d) None of these

[2002 : 2 Marks]

19. The circuit shown below implements a 2-input NOR gate using two 2 : 1 MUX (control signal 1 selects the upper input). What are the values of signals x, y and z ?

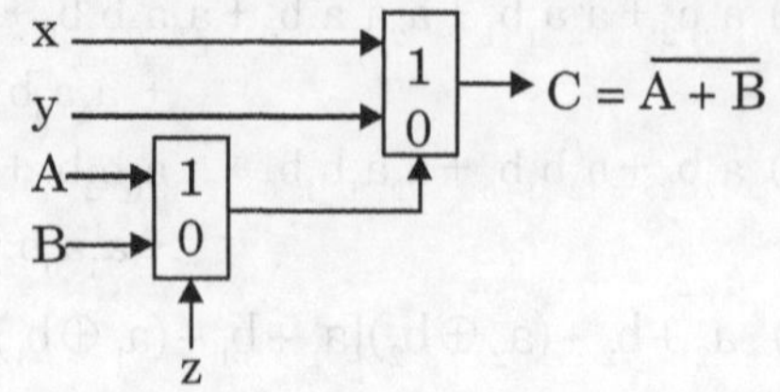

(a) 1, 0, B (b) 1, 0, A

(c) 0, 1, B (d) 0, 1, A

[2005 : 2 Marks]

20. Consider the circuit below. Which one of the following options correctly represents f(x, y, z)?

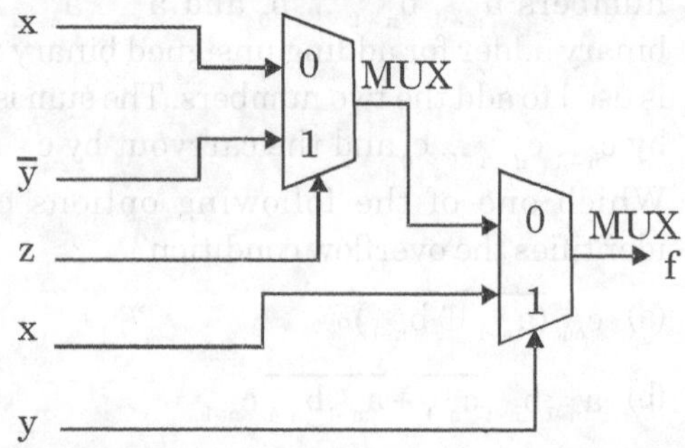

(a) $x\bar{z} + xy + \bar{y}z$ (b) $x\bar{z} + xy + \overline{yz}$

(c) $xz + xy + \overline{yz}$ (d) $xz + x\bar{y} + \bar{y}z$

[2006 : 2 Marks]

21. The following circuit implements a two-input AND gate using two 2-1 multiplexers.

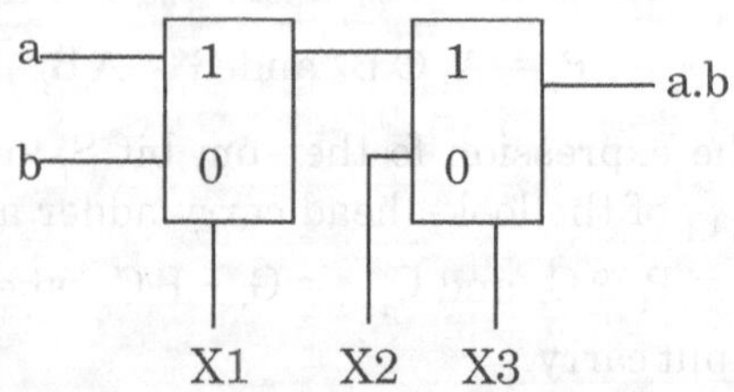

What are the values of X1, X2, X3?

(a) X1 = b, X2 = 0, X3 = a

(b) X1 = b, X2 = 1, X3 = b

(c) X1 = a, X2 = b, X3 = 1

(d) X1 = a, X2 = 0, X3 = b

[2007 : 1 Mark]

22. Suppose only one multiplexer and one inverter are allowed to be used to implement any Boolean function of n variables. What is the minimum size of the multiplexer needed?

(a) 2^n line to 1 line (b) 2^{n+1} line to 1 line

(c) 2^{n-1} line to 1 line (d) 2^{n-2} line to 1 line

[2007 : 2 Marks]

23. The Boolean expression for the output f of the multiplexer shown below is

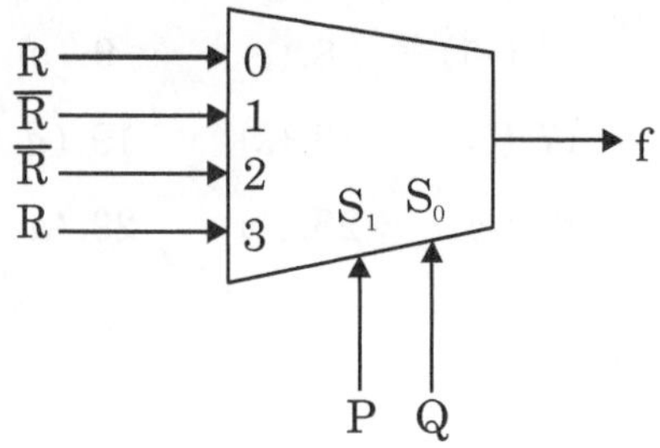

(a) $\overline{P \oplus Q \oplus R}$ (b) $P \oplus Q \oplus R$

(c) $P + Q + R$ (d) $\overline{P + Q + R}$

[2010 : 1 Mark]

24. Consider the 4 to 1 multiplexer with two select lines S_1 and S_0 given below :

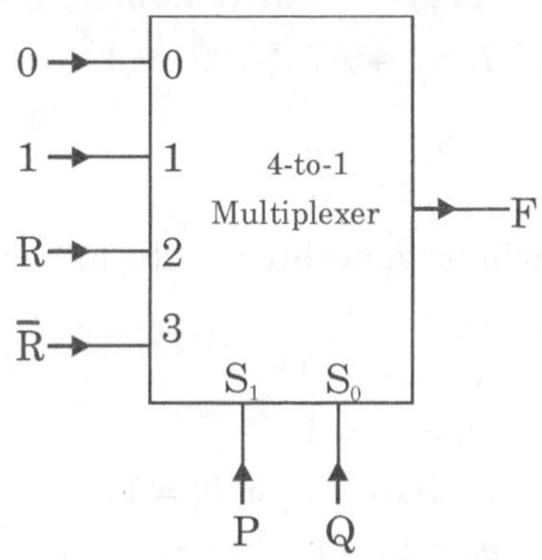

The minimal sum-of-products form of the Boolean expression for the output F of the multiplex is

(a) $\overline{P}Q + Q\overline{R} + P\overline{Q}R$

(b) $\overline{P}Q + \overline{P}Q\overline{R} + PQ\overline{R} + P\overline{Q}R$

(c) $\overline{P}QR + \overline{P}Q\overline{R} + Q\overline{R} + P\overline{Q}R$

(d) $PQ\overline{R}$

[2014 (Set-1) : 2 Marks]

25. Consider the following combinational function block involving four Boolean variables x, y, a, b where x, a, b are inputs and y is the output.

```
f (x, y, a, b)
{
    if (x is 1) y = a;
    else y = b;
}
```

Which one of the following digital logic blocks is the most suitable for implementing this function?

(a) Full adder (b) Priority encoder

(c) Multiplexer (d) Flip-flop

[2014 (Set-3) : 1 Mark]

26. Consider the two cascaded 2-to-1 multiplexer as shown in figure.

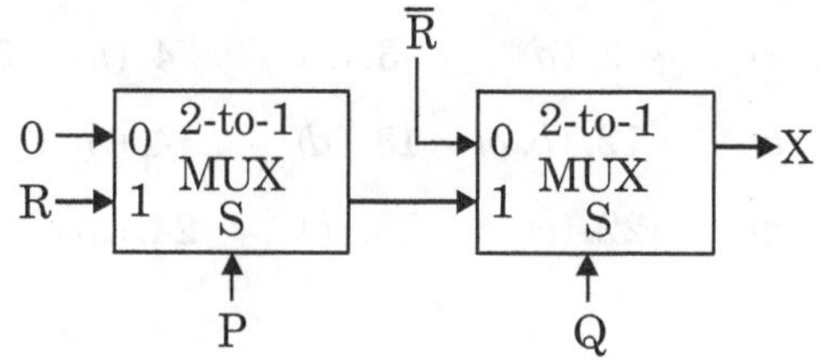

The minimal sum of products form of the output X is

(a) $\overline{P}\,\overline{Q} + PQR$ (b) $\overline{P}Q + QR$

(c) $PQ + \overline{P}\,\overline{Q}R$ (d) $\overline{Q}\,\overline{R} + PQR$

[2016 (Set-1) : 2 Marks]

DECODER

27. How many 3-to-8 line decoders with an enable input are needed to construct a 6-to-64 line decoder without using any other logic gates?

(a) 7 (b) 8

(c) 9 (d) 10

[2007 : 1 Mark]

28. What Boolean function does the circuit below realize?

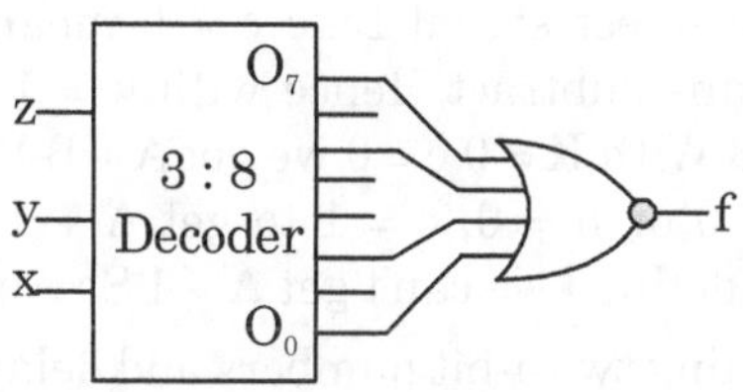

(a) $xz + \overline{x}\,\overline{z}$ (b) $x\overline{z} + \overline{x}z$

(c) $\overline{x}\,\overline{y} + yz$ (d) $xy + \overline{y}\,\overline{z}$

[2008 : 1 Mark]

ENCODER

29. In the following turth table, V = 1 if and only if the input is valid.

Inputs				Output		
D_0	D_1	D_2	D_3	X_0	X_1	V
0	0	0	0	X	X	0
1	0	0	0	0	0	1
X	1	0	0	0	1	1
X	X	1	0	1	0	1
X	X	X	1	1	1	1

What function does the truth table represent?

(a) Priority encoder (b) Decoder

(c) Multiplexer (d) Demultiplexer

[2013 : 1 Mark]

ANSWERS

1. (*)	2. (d)	3. (a)	4. (a)	5. (19.2)	6. (b)	7. (–1)	8. (c)	9. (a)	10. (c)
11. (b)	12. (b, c)	13. (d)	14. (b)	15. (b)	16. (c)	17. (c)	18. (a)	19. (d)	20. (a)
21. (a)	22. (c)	23. (b)	24. (a)	25. (c)	26. (d)	27. (c)	28. (b)	29. (a)	

EXPLANATIONS

1. Switch in position 2 : A – B (A+ 2's complement of B).

2. Binary to radix-12 conversion.

3. Set the value of k and c to 0 or 1

Two ways are there

1. If we take XOR of any number with 1 we get it in its complement form.
2. If we take XOR of any number with 0 we get that number itself.

So on setting k = 1 we can get –B and c will work like select signal Like c = 0 means add C = 1 means subtract Hence with k = 1 c = 1 we get A-B With K = 0 c = 0 we get A + B We need b = 1, c = 0 or b = 0, c = 1 to get A + 1 since b isn't predefined we can't get A + 1 So Ans is (A) part.

4. Adding two 4-bit numbers and delay of each gate is one time limit.

Delay of adder = {4 × delay in one gate}.

$$= 4 \times 1 = 4 \text{ time unit}$$

5. Propagation delay for AND/OR Gate

$$= 1 \times 2 \ \mu s$$

Propagation delay for XOR Gate

$$= 2 \times 1.2 = 2.4 \ \mu s$$

Propagation time for a half adder

$$= 1.2 + 2.4 = 3.6 \ \mu s$$

Propagation time for full adder

$$= 2 \times 3.6 + 1.2$$
$$= 7.2 + 1.2 = 8.4 \ \mu s$$

Total 4-adders are used in 4-bit binary adder

Hence 8.4 × 4 = **33.6 μs**

6. Time to perform addition using this adder is O(log *n*).

7. When all bits in 'B' register is '1', then it gives only the highest delay.

∴ '–1' in 8 bit notation of 2's complement is 1111 1111

8. It depends on S7 for overflow. when S7 is 0 while adding two negative numbers and when S7 is 1 while adding two positive numbers

$$A7.\ B7.\ S7' + A7'.B7'.S7 = 1$$

9.

$$\begin{matrix} a_2 & a_1 & a_0 \\ b_2 & b_1 & b_0 \end{matrix}$$

Carry will be generated in the following cases

$$a_2 = 1,\ b_2 = 1$$
$$a_2 \oplus b_2 = 1$$

and $a_1 = b_1 = 1$

$$a_2 \oplus b_2 = a_1 \oplus b_1 = 1$$

and $a_0 = b_0 = 1$

Considering options :

In option (*b*), second term is invalid

as if $a_2 = 1,\ b_2 = 0,\ b_1 = 1,\ b_0 = 1,\ c \neq 1$

In option (*c*), a_2 is invalid term

In option (*d*), $a_2\ a_1,\ b_1$, is invalid as, if

$$a_2 = 0,\ a_1 = b_1 = 1,\ b_2 = 0,\ c^1 \neq = 1$$

Hence only option (*a*) encompasses possibilities.

10.

$$B = b_{n-1}\ b_{n-2} \dots b_0$$
$$A = a_{n-1}\ a_{n-2} \dots a_0$$
$$S = c_{n-1}\ c_{n-2} \dots c_0$$

Over flow condition,

$$V = b'_{n-1}\ a'_{n-1}\ c_{n-2} + b_{n-1}\ a_{n-1}\ c'_{n-2}$$

c_{n-1} is c_{out}, so

$$V = c_{out} \oplus c_{n-1}$$

Hence over flow condition is

$$c_{out} \oplus c_{n-1}$$

11. A 4-bit adder with S_3, S_2, S_1, S_0 and C_4 as its output require 2-1 bit adder and a single one bit adder require 5 AND gates and 2 OR gates in two level logic. Hence required gate are 10 AND gate and 4 OR gates.

12. The XOR gate can be used to implement NOT by doing $A \oplus 1$. Using the AND gate and the NOT realization of XOR, we can get a NAND gate, which is a univeral gate. So, C is right.

    The 2 to 1 multiplexer gives the function AX + BX', where X is the selector input. It can be used to implement a NOT by making A = 0 and B = 1, thus we get X'. We can get an AND gate by putting B = 0 and thus getting A.X. Using NOT and AND we can get a NAND, which is a universal gate. So B, is wrong. We also can't implement a NOT gate using A. B. + C. So, D is wrong.

13.

Y	Z	XOR	OR	AND
0	0	0	0	0
0	1	1	1	0
1	0	1	1	0
1	1	0	1	1

So, 'OR' and 'AND' gives different output on (0, 0) 2 (1, 1)

So encoder decide output of the function according to X.

14. Both {f} and {g} are functionally complete

15.

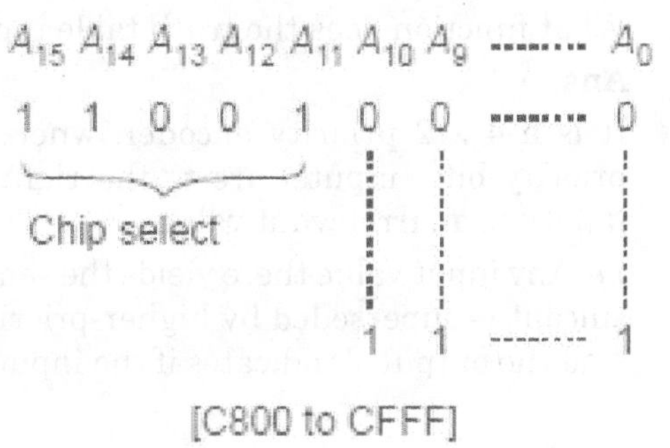

16.

A \ B	0	1
0	C	C
1	C	C

A	B	C
0	0	C
0	1	C
1	0	C
1	1	C

$$F = \overline{A}\,\overline{B}C + \overline{A}BC + A\overline{B}C + ABC$$

$$A \oplus (B\overline{C} + \overline{B}C) = \overline{A}(B\overline{C} + \overline{B}C) + A\,(\overline{B} + C)\,(B + \overline{C})$$

$$= \overline{A}B\overline{C} + \overline{A}\,\overline{B}C + A\overline{B}\,\overline{C} + ABC$$

17. g = (a and x1′) or (b and x1)

    g = (1 and x1′) or (0 and x1)

    g = x1′

    f = ac′ + bc

    f = (a and x2′) or (b and x2)

    f = (g and x2′) or (x1 and x2)

    f = x1′x2′ + x1x2

18. F = (XYZ′ + XYZ + Y′ZY + ZY′)Z′

    F = (XYZ′ + XYZ + ZY′(Y + 1))Z′

    F = (XYZ′ + XYZ + ZY′ * 1)Z′

    F = (XY(Z′ + Z) + ZY′)Z′

    F = (XY + ZY′)Z′

    F = XYZ′ + ZY′Z′

    F = XYZ′

19. For MUX1 g = Az + Bz′

    For MUX2 f = xg + yg′ = x(Az + Bz′) + y (Az + Bz′)′

    Function 'f' should be equal to (A + B)′.

    Using option (d) x = 0, y = 1 and z = A.

    f = 0(AA + BA′) + 1(AA + BA′)′

    f = (A + A′B)′

    f = (A + B)′

20. MUX1 output is => Z′X + ZY′

    MUX2 output is => Y′(Z′X + ZY′) + YX

    =>Y′Z + Y′Z′X + YX

    =>Y′Z + X(Y′Z′ + Y)

    =>Y′Z + X(Y + Z′) (use identity A + A′B = (A + B))

    =>Y′Z + XY + XZ′

21. The output equation for circuit is

    F = (bX1′ + aX1)X3 + X2X3′

    Using option (a) X1 = b, X2 = 0, X3 = a

    We will get F = ab.

22. Multiplexes of size 2^{n-1} to 1 will be needed.

23. Make the table

$P(S_1)$	$Q(S_0)$	Z	
0	0	R	0
0	1	$\overline{R}$	1
1	0	$\overline{R}$	2
1	1	R	3

} as given in figure

Add these all for result because output is the mixing of these signals.

$$\therefore\ \overline{P}\,\overline{Q}R + \overline{P}Q\overline{R} + P\overline{Q}\,\overline{R} + PQR$$

$$= \overline{P}\left(\overline{Q}R + Q\overline{R}\right) + P\left(Q\overline{R} + QR\right)$$

$$= \overline{P}(Q \oplus R) + P(Q \Theta R) = P \oplus Q \oplus R$$

Alternately

P and Q are lines out of which only one will enable at a time.

P	Q	F
0	0	R
0	1	$\overline{R}$
1	0	$\overline{R}$
1	1	R

$\therefore$ $P'Q'R + P'QR' + PQ'R' + PQR$

$= P'(Q'R + QR') + P(Q'R' + QR)$

$= P'(Q \oplus R) + P(Q \odot R)$

$= P'(Q \oplus R) + P(Q \oplus R)'$

$= P'Z + PZ'$ ....[take $(Q \oplus R) = Z$]

$= P \oplus Z$

$= P \oplus Q \oplus R$

24.

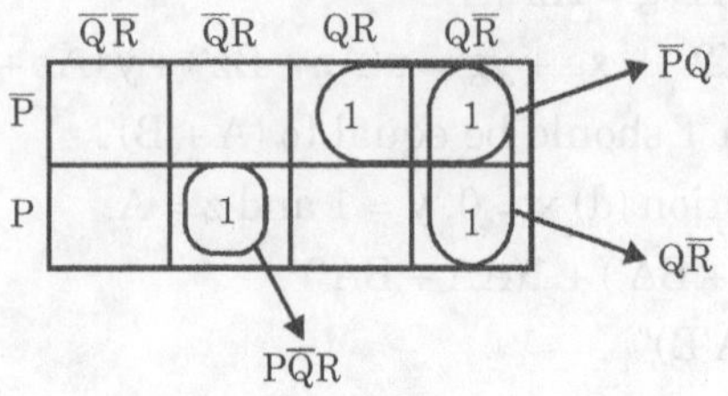

$\overline{P}\overline{Q}.O + \overline{P}Q.1 + P\overline{Q}.R + PQ\overline{R}$

$= \overline{P}Q + P\overline{Q}.R + PQ\overline{R}$

Hence the minimized expression is

$\overline{P}Q + Q\overline{R} + P\overline{Q}R$

25. Consider the given function as it having two inputs a, b and select signal x. The Output y will depend on the select signal x.

Function will be like (ax + bx'). So it will work as a Multiplexer.

26.

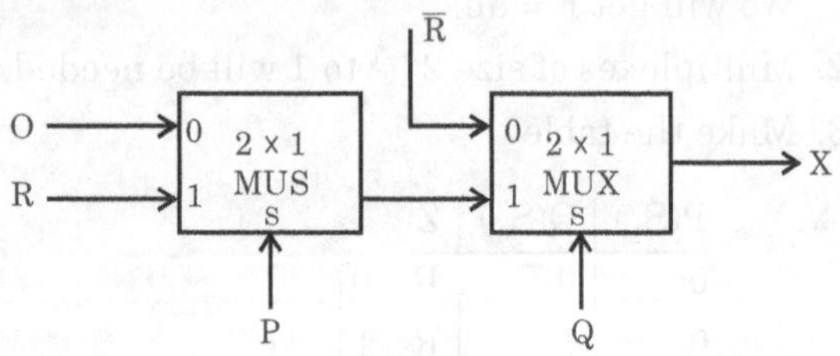

P′ then 0 ⇒ P′ 0 = 0

P then R ⇒ PR

Q′ then R ⇒ Q′R

Q then (0 + PR) ⇒ Q(0 + PR) = QPR.

$X = Q'R + PQR$

27. To get 6:64 we need 64 o/p

We have 3:8 decode with 8 o/p.

So, we need 64/8 = 8 decoders.

Now, to select any of this 8 decoder we need one more decoder.

Total = 8 + 1 = 9 decoder

28. Output of circuit is xz′ + x′z

29. In following truth table, $v = 1$ if and only if the input is valid

Inputs				Outputs		
D_0	D_1	D_2	D_3	X_0	X_1	V
0	0	0	0	X	X	0
1	0	0	0	0	0	1
X	1	0	0	0	1	1
X	X	1	0	1	0	1
X	X	X	1	1	1	1

What function does the truth table represent?

Ans. A

It is a 4 × 2 priority encoder, where highest priority bits (inputs) are to the right and "X" indicates an irrelevant value.

i.e. Any input value there yields the same output since it is superseded by higher-priority input. And the output V indicates if the input is valid.

3 CHAPTER

Sequential Logic Circuit and Memory

Analysis of Previous GATE Papers

Units	Year → / Topics ↓		2019	2018	2017 Set 1	2017 Set 2	2016 Set 1	2016 Set 2	2015 Set 1	2015 Set 2	2015 Set 3
PLA	1 Mark	MCQ Type									
		Numerical Type									
	2 Marks	MCQ Type									
		Numerical Type									
	Total										
FILP FLOP	1 Mark	MCQ Type									
		Numerical Type									
	2 Marks	MCQ Type									
		Numerical Type									
	Total										
SHIFT REGISTER	1 Mark	MCQ Type									
		Numerical Type									
	2 Marks	MCQ Type									
		Numerical Type									
	Total										
ASSWSMD	1 Mark	MCQ Type									
		Numerical Type									
	2 Marks	MCQ Type									
		Numerical Type									
	Total										
ACSSWSMD	1 Mark	MCQ Type									
		Numerical Type									
	2 Marks	MCQ Type									
		Numerical Type									
	Total										
LATCH	1 Mark	MCQ Type									
		Numerical Type									
	2 Marks	MCQ Type									
		Numerical Type									
	Total										
SYNCHORONOUS COUNTER	1 Mark	MCQ Type									
		Numerical Type									
	2 Marks	MCQ Type									
		Numerical Type									
	Total										
COUNTER	1 Mark	MCQ Type							1		
		Numerical Type					1				
	2 Marks	MCQ Type									
		Numerical Type								1	
	Total						1		1	2	

PLA

1. RAM is a combinational Circuit and PLA is a sequential circuit ? (T/F)

[1990 : 2 Marks]

FLIP FLOP

2. Find the maximum clock frequency at which the counter in figure, can be operated. Assume that the propagation delay through each flip-flop and AND gate is 10 ns. Also assume that the setup time for the JK inputs of the flip-flops is negligible.

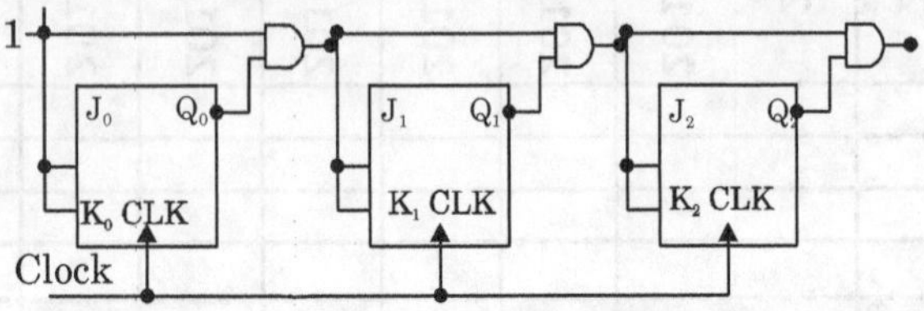

[1991 : 2 Marks]

3. The following arrangement of master-slave flip flops

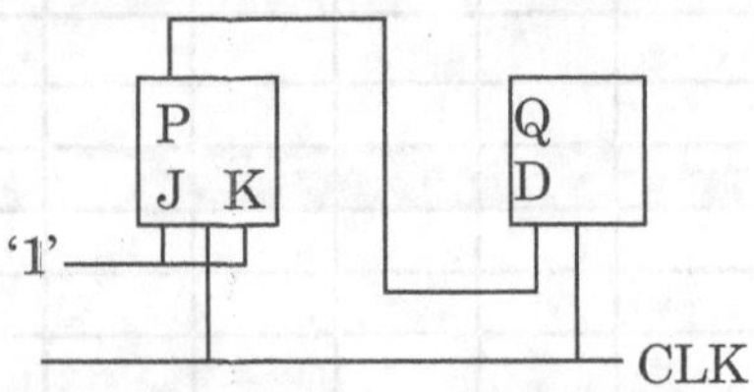

Has the initial state of P, Q as 0, 1 (respectively). After the clock cycles the output state P, Q is (respectively),

(a) 1, 0 (b) 1, 1

(c) 0, 0 (d) 0, 1

[2002 : 2 Marks]

4. Consider the following circuit with initial state $Q_0 = Q_1 = 0$. The D flip-flops are positive edged triggered and have set up time 20 ns and hold time is 0 ns.

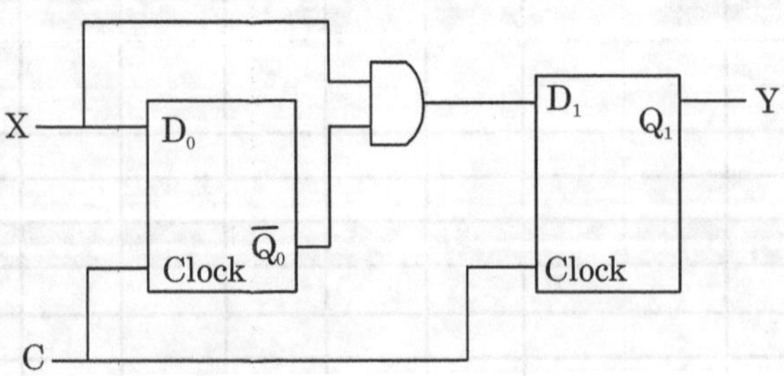

Consider the following timing diagrams of X and C; the clock period of C ≥ 40 nanosecond. Which one is the correct plot of Y?

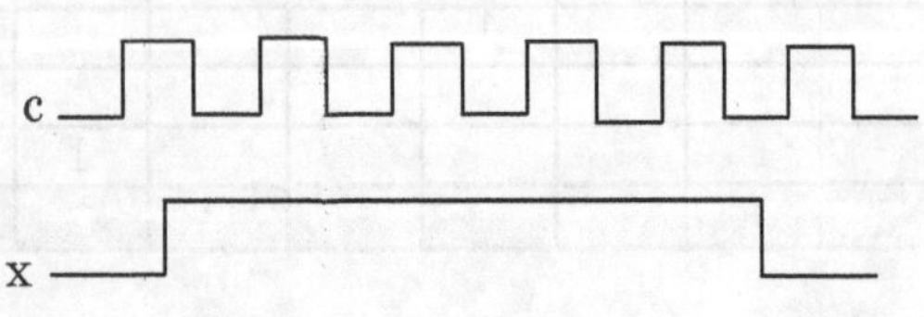

(a) 

(b) 

(c) 

(d) 

[2001 : 2 Marks]

5. Which of the following input sequences for a cross-coupled R-S flip-flop realized with two NAND gates may lead to an oscillation ?

(a) 11, 00 (b) 01, 10

(c) 10, 01 (d) 00, 11

[2006 : 1 Mark]

6. The minimum number of D flip-flops needed to design a mod-258 counter is

(a) 9

(b) 8

(c) 512

(d) 258

[2011 : 1 Mark]

SHIFT REGISTER

7. Consider the circuit given below with initial state $Q_0 = 1, Q_1 = Q_2 = 0$. The state of the circuit is given by the value $4Q_2 + 2Q_1 + Q_0$

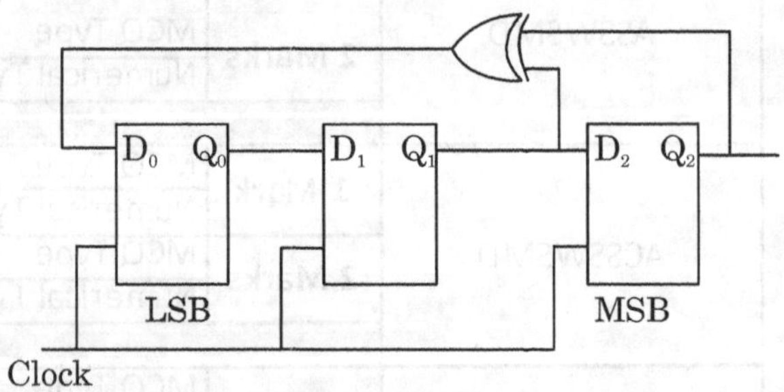

Which one of the following is the correct state sequence of the circuit

(a) 1, 3, 4, 6, 7, 5, 2 (b) 1, 2, 5, 3, 7, 6, 4

(c) 1, 2, 7, 3, 5, 6, 4 (d) 1, 6, 5, 7, 2, 3, 4

[2001 : 2 Marks]

8. What is the final value stored in the linear feedback shift register if the input is 101101?

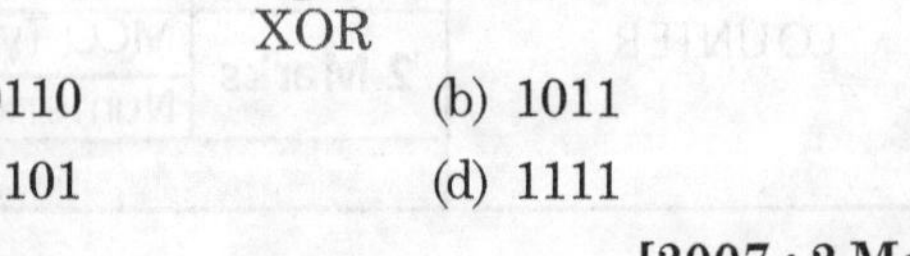

(a) 0110 (b) 1011

(c) 1101 (d) 1111

[2007 : 2 Marks]

9. Consider a combination of T and D flip-flops connected as shown below. The output of the D flip-flop is connected to the input of the T flip-flop and the output of the T flip-flop is connected to the input of the D flip-flop.

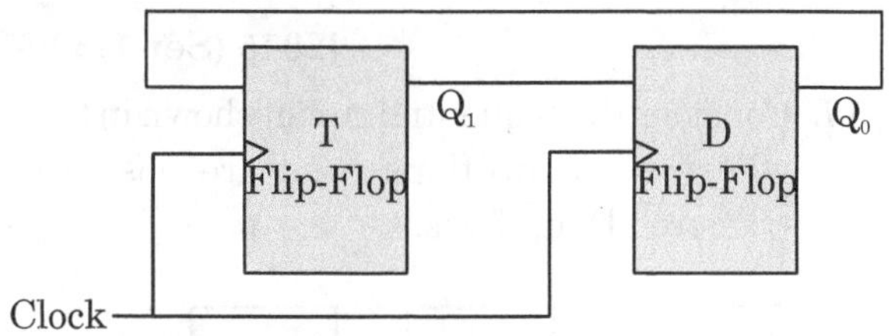

Initially, both Q0 and Q1 are set to 1 (before the 1st clock cycle). The outputs

(a) Q_1Q_0 after the 3rd cycle are 11 and after the 4th cycle are 00 respectively

(b) Q_1Q_0 after the 3rd cycle are 11 and after the 4th cycle are 01 respectively

(c) Q_1Q_0 after the 3rd cycle are 00 and after the 4th cycle are 11 respectively

(d) Q_1Q_0 after the 3rd cycle are 01 and after the 4th cycle are 01 respectively.

[2017 (Set-1) : 2 Marks]

ASSWSMD

10. A 1-input, 2-output synchronous sequential circuit behaves as follows :

Let z_k, n_k denote the number of 0's and 1's respectively in initial k bits of input ($z_k + n_k = k$). The circuit outputs 00 until one of the following conditions holds.

1. $z_k - n_k = 2$. In this case, the output at the k-th and all subsequently clock ticks is 10.
2. $n_k - z_k = 2$. In this case, the output at the k-th and all subsequent clock ticks is 01.

What in the minimum number of states required in the state transition graph of the above circuit?

(a) 5 (b) 6

(c) 7 (d) 8

[2003 : 2 Marks]

11. Which of the following input sequences will always generate a 1 at the output z at the end of the third cycle?

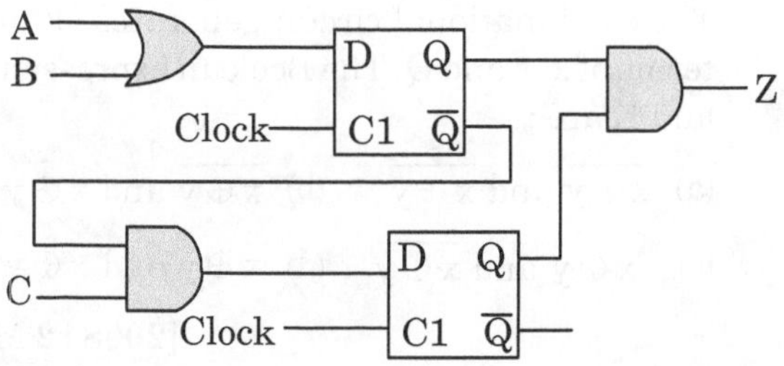

(a) A B C
0 0 0
1 0 1
1 1 1

(b) A B C
1 0 1
1 1 0
1 1 1

(c) A B C
0 1 1
1 0 1
1 1 1

(b) A B C
0 0 1
1 1 0
1 1 1

[2005 : 2 Marks]

12. Consider the following circuit involving a positive edge triggered D FF.

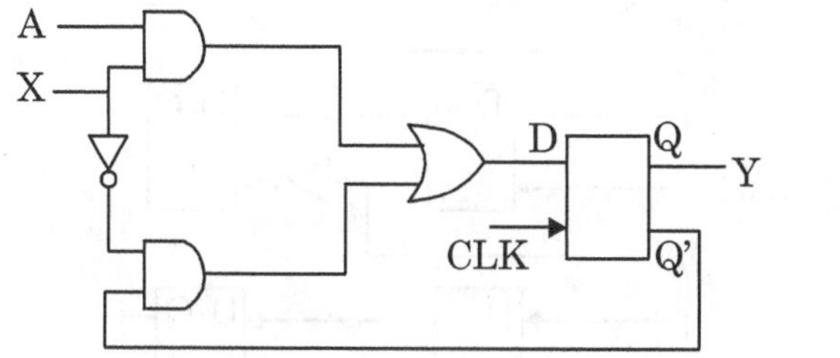

Consider the following timing diagram. Let A_i represent the logic level on the line A in the i-th clock period.

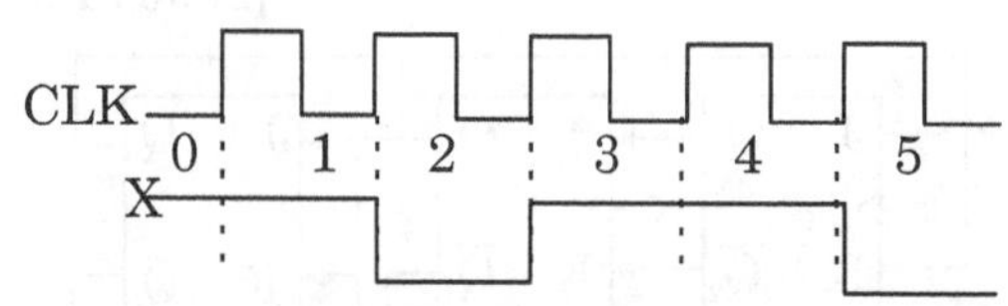

Let A' represent the complement of A. The correct output sequence on Y over the clock periods 1 through 5 is

(a) $A_0 A_1 A_1' A_3 A_4$ (b) $A_0 A_1 A_2' A_3 A_4$

(c) $A_1 A_2 A_2' A_3 A_4$ (d) $A_1 A_2' A_3 A_4 A_5'$

[2005 : 2 Marks]

13. Consider the following circuit

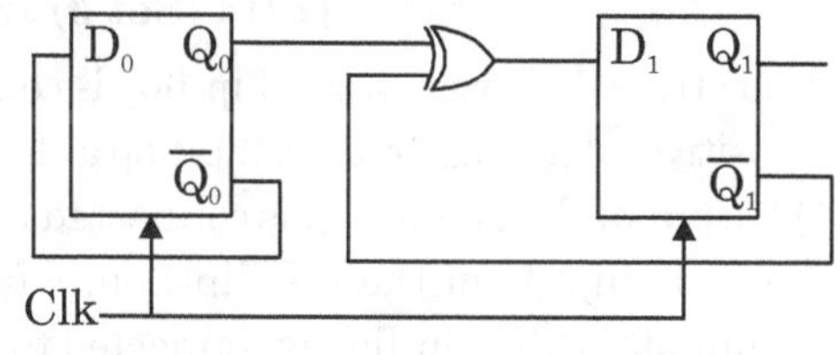

The flip-flops are positive edge triggered D FFs. Each state is designated as a two bit string Q_0Q_1. Let the initial state be 00. The state transition sequence is

(a) 00 → 11 → 01 (back to 00)

(b) 00 → 11 (back to 00)

(c) 00 → 10 → 01 → 11 (back to 00)

(d) 00 → 11 → 01 → 10 (back to 00)

[2005 : 2 Marks]

14. You are given a free running clock with a duty cycle of 50% and a digital waveform f which changes only at the negative edge of the clock.

Which one of the following circuits (using clocked D flip-flops) will delay the phase of by 180°?

(a)
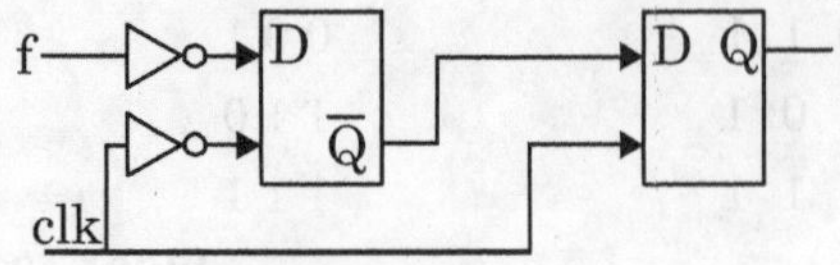

(b)
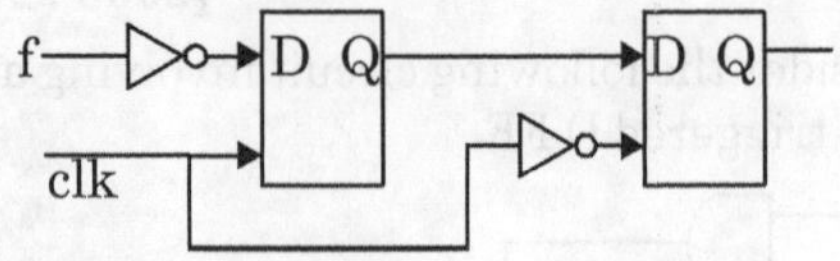

(c)
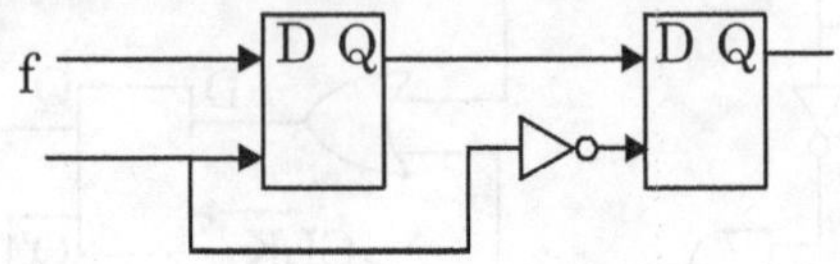

(d)
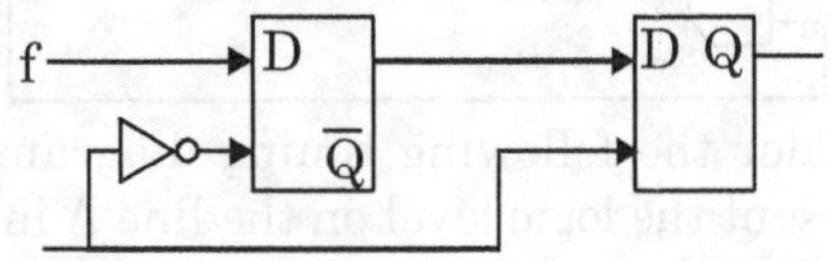

[2006 : 1 Mark]

15.
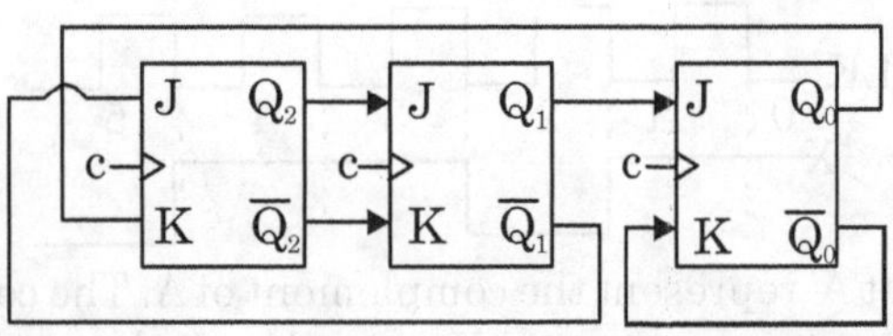

The above synchronous sequential circuit built using JK flip-flops is intialized with $Q_2Q_1Q_0 = 000$. The state sequence for this circuit for the next 3 clock cycles is

(a) 001, 010, 011 (b) 111, 110, 101

(c) 100, 110, 111 (d) 100, 011, 001

[2014 (Set-3) : 2 Marks]

16. A positive edge-triggered D flip-flop is connected to a positive edge-triggered JK flip-flop as follows. The Q output of the D flip-flop is connected to both the J and K inputs of the JK flip-flop, while the Q output of the JK flip-flop is connected to the input of the D flip-flop. Initially, the output of the D flip-flop is set to logic one and the output of the JK flip-flop is cleared.

Which one of the following is the bit sequence (including the initial state) generated at the Q output of the JK flip-flop when the flip-flops are connected to a free-running common clock? Assume that J = K = 1 is the toggle mode and J = K = 0 is the state-holding mode of JK flip-flop. Both the flip-flops have non-zero propagation delays.

(a) 0110110...

(b) 01001000...

(c) 011101110...

(d) 011001100

[2015 (Set-1) : 1 Mark]

17. Consider the sequential circuit shown in the figure, where both flip-flops used are positive edge-triggered D flip-flops.

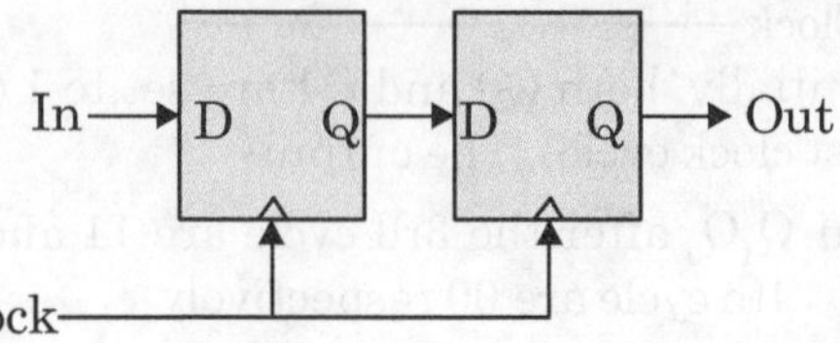

The number of states in the state transition diagram of the circuit that have a transition back to the same state on some value of "in" is ....

[2018 : 1 Marks]

ACSSWSMD

18. For a state machine with the following state diagram the expression for the next state S^+ in terms of the current state S and the input variables x and y is

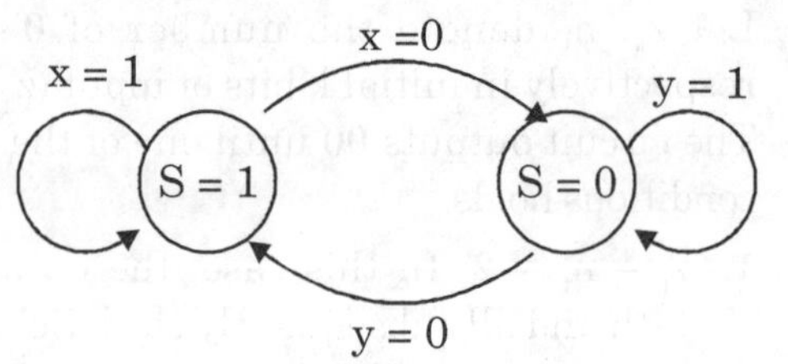

(a) $S^+ = S'.y' + S.x$ (b) $S^+ = S.x.y' + S'.y.x'$

(c) $S^+ = x.y'$ (d) $S^+ = S'.y + S.x'$

[2006 : 2 Marks]

19. Consider the following state diagram and its realization by a JK flip flop.

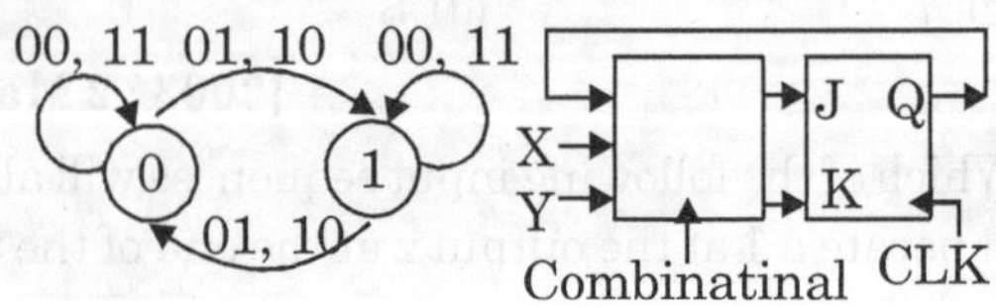

The combinational circuit generates. J and K in terms of x, y and Q. The Boolean expressions for J and K are :

(a) $\overline{x \oplus y}$ and $\overline{x \oplus y}$ (b) $\overline{x \oplus y}$ and $x \oplus y$

(c) $x \oplus y$ and $\overline{x \oplus y}$ (d) $x \oplus y$ and $x \oplus y$

[2008 : 2 Marks]

LATCH

20. In an SR latch made by cross-coupling two NAND gates, if both S and R inputs are set to 0, then it will result in

(a) Q = 0, Q' = 1 (b) Q = 1, Q' = 0

(c) Q = 1, Q' = 1 (d) Indeterminate states

[2004 : 1 Marks]

SYNCHORONOUS COUNTER

21. Consider the partial implementation of a 2-bit counter using T flip-flops following the sequence 0-2-3-1-0, as shown below :

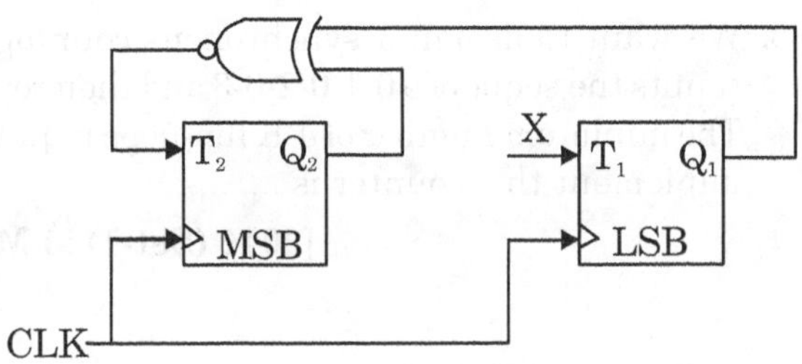

To complete the circuit, the input X should be

(a) Q_2' (b) Q2 + Q1

(c) $(Q_1 \oplus Q_2)'$ (d) $Q_1 \oplus Q_2$

[2004 : 2 Marks]

22. How many pulses are needed to change the contents of a 8-bit upcounter from 10101100 to 00100111 (rightmost bit is the LSB)?

(a) 134 (b) 133

(c) 124 (d) 123

[2005 : 1 Mark]

COUNTER

23. The control signal functions of 4-bit binary counter are given below (where X is "don't care")

Clear	Clock	Load	Count	Function
1	X	X	X	Clear to 0
0	X	0	0	No change
0	↑	1	x	Load input
0	↑	0	1	Count next

The counter is connected as follows

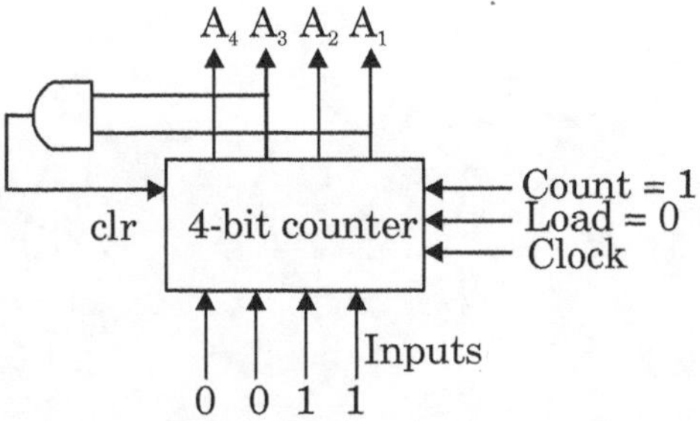

Assume that the counter and gate delays are negligible. If the counter starts at 0, then it cycles through the following sequence

(a) 0, 3, 4

(b) 0, 3, 4, 5

(c) 0, 1, 2, 3, 4

(d) 0, 1, 2, 3, 4, 5

[2007 : 2 Marks]

24. In the sequential circuit shown below, if the initial value of the output Q_1Q_0 is 00, what are the next four values of Q_1Q_0?

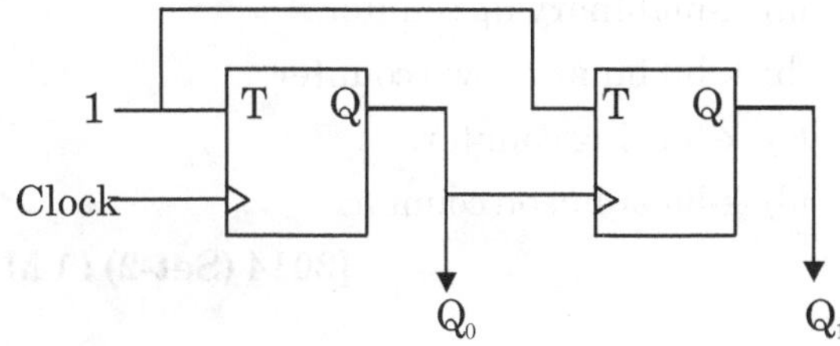

(a) 11, 10, 01, 00

(b) 10, 11, 01, 00

(c) 10, 00, 01, 11

(d) 11, 10, 00, 01

[2010 : 2 Marks]

Common Data Q. 25 & Q. 26

Consider the following circuit involving three D-type flip-flops used in a certain type of counter configuration

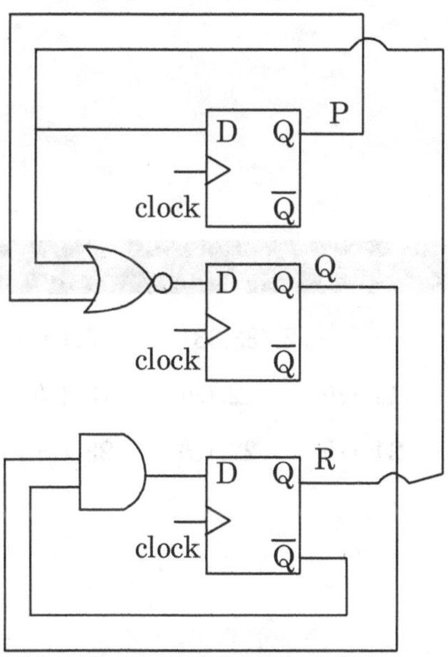

25. If at some instance prior to the occurrence of the clock edge, P, Q and R have a value 0, 1 and 0 respectivel, what shall be the value of PQR after the clock edge?

(a) 000 (b) 001

(c) 010 (d) 011

[2011 : 2 Marks]

26. If all the flip-flops were reset to 0 at power on, what is the total number of distinct outputs (states) represented by PQR generated by the counter?

(a) 3

(b) 4

(c) 5

(d) 6

[2011 : 2 Marks]

27. Let K = 2^n. A circuit is built by giving the output of an n-bit binary counter as input to an n-to-2^n bit decoder. This circuit is equivalent to a

(a) k-bit binary up counter

(b) k-bit binary down counter.

(c) k-bit ring counter.

(d) k-bit Johnson counter.

[2014 (Set-2) : 1 Mark]

28. Consider a 4 bit-Johnson counter with an initial value of 0000. The counting sequence of this counter is

(a) 0, 1, 3, 7, 15, 14, 12, 8, 0

(b) 0, 1, 3, 5, 7, 9, 11, 13, 15, 0

(c) 0, 2, 4, 6, 8, 10, 12, 14, 0

(d) 0, 8, 12, 14, 15, 7, 3, 1, 0

[2015 (Set-1) : 1 Mark]

29. The minimum number of JK flip-flops required to construct a synchronous counter with the count sequence (0, 0, 1, 1, 2, 2, 3, 3, 0, 0,...) is ....

[2015 (Set-2) : 2 Marks]

30. We want to design a synchronous counter that counts the sequence 0-1-0-2-0-3 and then repeats. The minimum number of J-K flip-flops required to implement this counter is ....

[2016 (Set-1) : 1 Mark]

ANSWERS

1. (False)	**2.** (33.33)	**3.** (*a*)	**4.** (*a*)	**5.** (*d*)	**6.** (*a*)	**7.** (*b*)	**8.** (*a*)	**9.** (*b*)
10. (*a*)	**11.** (*d*)	**12.** (*a*)	**13.** (*d*)	**14.** (*c*)	**15.** (*c*)	**16.** (*a*)	**17.** (2)	**18.** (*a*)	**19.** (*d*)
20. (*d*)	**21.** (*d*)	**22.** (*d*)	**23.** (*c*)	**24.** (*a*)	**25.** (*d*)	**26.** (*b*)	**27.** (*c*)	**28.** (*d*)	**29.** (2)
30. (4)									

EXPLANATIONS

1. False. PLA is a combinational circuit as ROM & RAM is Sequential logic circuit.

2. Time to get output from FF once input (and clock) is given = 10ns. (Propagation Delay)

   Time for inputs to reach FF1 = 0. (Zero AND gate)

   Time for inputs to reach FF2 = 10. (One AND gate)

   Time for inputs to reach FF3 = 20. (Two AND gates)

   So, minimum time period needed for clock is 10 + max(0,10,20) = 10 + 20 = 30ns

   Which would mean a maximum clock frequency of 1/30GHz = 33.33MHz

3. Given P = 0, J = 1 and k = 1
   - JK flipflop toggles the input in '11' state. Therefore, output of first flipflop at P is '1'.
   - Initial value of P is input for D flipflop. So, D = 0 .Therefore, output of second flipflop at Q is '0'.

4. Following two things are given

   (1) Set up time

   (2) hold time

   Just to ensure that edge triggering works properly.

   1. Since clock is positive edge triggered, so first positive edge trigger: X = 0, so output will be 0. Also, Q0 and Q0′ are 0 and 1 respectively.
   2. Now, in second II, Q0′ would be 1 because of setup time of flip-flop is 20 ns and clock-period is ≥ 40 ns.

      Therefore, second positive edge trigger: Because of X is 1 and Q0′ is 1, so output is 1.
   3. Now, Q0′ will became 0, but output Y won't change as the flip-flop is positive edge triggered.

      Third positive edge trigger: Because of X is 1 and Q0′ is 0, so output is 0.
   4. Now, output never changes back to 1 as Q0′ is always 0 and when Q0′ finally becomes 1, X is 0. aa.

5. RS flip flop using NAND gates. So, 00 input causes indeterminate state which MAY lead to oscillation.

6. $2^n \geq 258$

   $\Rightarrow n = 9$

7.

	Q0	Q1	Q2	2Q1+4Q2+Q0
clk	1	0	0	1
1	0	1	0	2
2	1	0	1	5
3	1	1	0	3
4	1	1	1	7
5	0	1	1	6
6	0	0	1	4

8. The linear feedback shift register makes use of XOR gate for tapping and providing feedback. It works by shifting and placing the feedback value. Feedback value is determined by last bit and second bit tapped and fed to XOR gate.

A	B	XOR
0	0	0
0	1	1
1	0	1
1	1	0

9.

Clock	T=Q1	D=Q0	T1=Q0	D0=Q1
	1	1	1	1
1	0	1	1	0
2	1	0	0	1
3	1	1	1	1
4	0	1		

It can be observed from the diagram that :

Q_1 Q_0 after the 3rd cycle are 11 and after the 4th cycle are 01

10. The answer must be 5 to this question as we just need to count the difference of the number of 0's and 1's in the first k bit of a number. And we just need to count till this count reaches 2 or –2 (negative when number of 0's is less than number of 1's) . So, the possibilities are –2, –1, 0, 1 and 2 which represents the five states of the state transition diagram.

    For state –2, the output of the circuit will be 01, for state 2, output will be 10 (both these states not having any outgoing transitions) and for other 3 states, output will be 00 as per the given description of the circuit.

11. Let's take cycles as 1,2,3.

There are two flip-flops, let's call them D1 and D2.

And Q1, Q2 to be the output for flip-flop D1, D2 respectively.

Here Q11 means output of D1 flip-flop for 1st cycle, similarly Q12 is the output of D1 flip-flop for 2nd Cycle.

A1, A2, A3 means input for A at cycles 1, 2, 3 respectively. Similarly for B and C.

Let's check for the option D where:

A1 = 0 A2 = 1 A3 = 1

B1 = 0 B2 = 1 B3 = 1

C1 = 1 C2 = 0 C3 = 1

Q11 = 0

Q12 = A1.B1 = 0.0 = 0

Q13 = A2.B2 = 1.1 = 1

~Q11 = 1

~Q12 = ~(A1.B1) = 1

~Q13 = ~(A2.B2) = 0

Q21 = 0

Q22 = C1.(~Q11) = 1.1 = 1

Q23 = C2.(~Q12) = 0.1 = 0

Z1 = 0

Z2 = Q12.Q21 = 0.0 = 0

Z3 = Q13.Q22 = 1.1 = 1

Hence, sequence given in option D is generating a 1 at the output z at the end of the third cycle (Z3).

12. $D = A \cdot X + \bar{X}\bar{Q}$

Consider for first two cases,

$\bar{X}\bar{Q} = 0$

because X = 1, so $0.\bar{Q} = 0$.

So, answer depend only on A . X

For first clock pulse '0'

$\Rightarrow \quad D = A_0$

For clock pulse '1'

$\Rightarrow$ output $= A_0$

$\Rightarrow \quad D =$ again A_1

For clock pulse '2'

$\Rightarrow$ output $= A_1$

$D = \overline{A_1}$

because $\quad$ A. X = 0 and X = 0

$\therefore \quad \bar{X} = 1$

$\bar{X}\bar{Q} = \bar{Q}$

13. Q_0 will toggle in every cycle because Q_0'(Q_0 complement) is fed as input to the D0 flip flop.

For the D_1 flip flop, $D_1 = Q_0$ □ Q1′, i.e., Q_0 XOR Q_1'.

Q0	Q1
0	0
1	1
0	1
1	0
0	0
.	.
.	.

14. Clock with duty cycle 50%. In choice (*c*), there are two D-Flip Flop if left most is activated or clock value 1 the clock value of right most 1 D flip-flop is 0, so it delay the phase *f* by 180°.

15.

P.S.			FFinputs						N.S.		
Q_2	Q_1	Q_0	J_2 $(\overline{Q}_1)$	K_2 (Q_0)	J_1 (Q_2)	K_1 $(\overline{Q}_2)$	J_0 (Q_1)	K_0 $(\overline{Q}_0)$	Q_2^+	Q_1^+	Q_0^+
0	0	0	1	0	0	1	0	1	1	0	0
1	0	0	1	0	1	0	0	1	1	1	0
1	1	0	0	0	1	0	1	1	1	1	1

16.

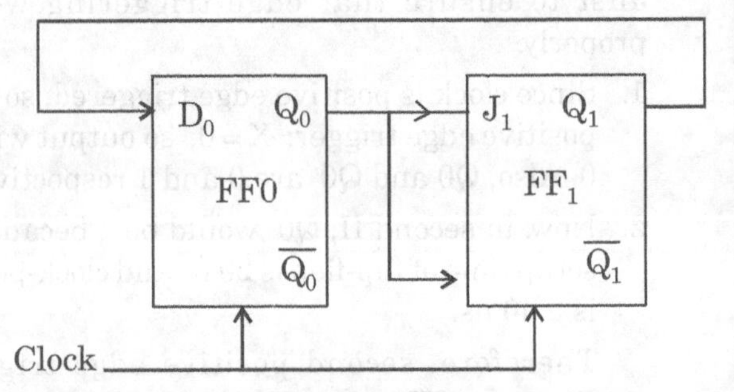

Clock	$Q_1 Q_0$	FF1 $J_1 = Q_0$	$K_1 = Q_0$	FF0 $Q_0 - Q_1$
Initial State →	0 1	1	1	0
1	1 0	0	0	1
2	1 1	1	1	1
3	0 1	1	1	0
4	1 0			

17.

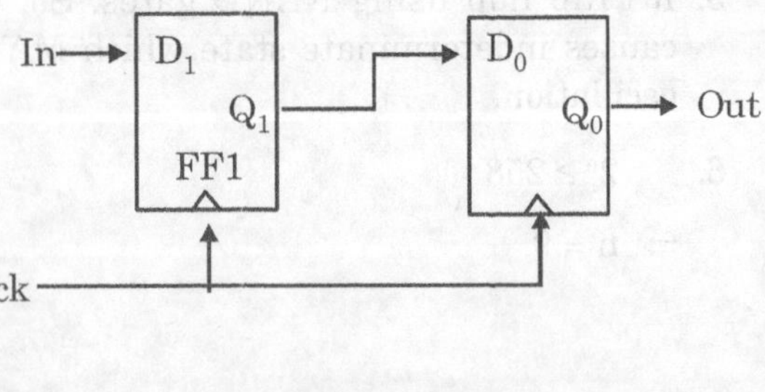

State Table:

P.S		Input	FF Inputs		N.S		
Q_1	Q_0	x	D_1=x	D_0=Q_1	Q_1	Q_0	Out = Q_0
0	0	0	0	0	0	0	0
0	0	1	1	0	1	0	0
0	1	0	0	0	0	0	0
0	1	1	1	0	1	0	0
1	0	0	0	1	0	1	1
1	0	1	1	1	1	1	1
1	1	0	0	1	0	1	1
1	1	1	1	1	1	1	1

State Transition Diagram:

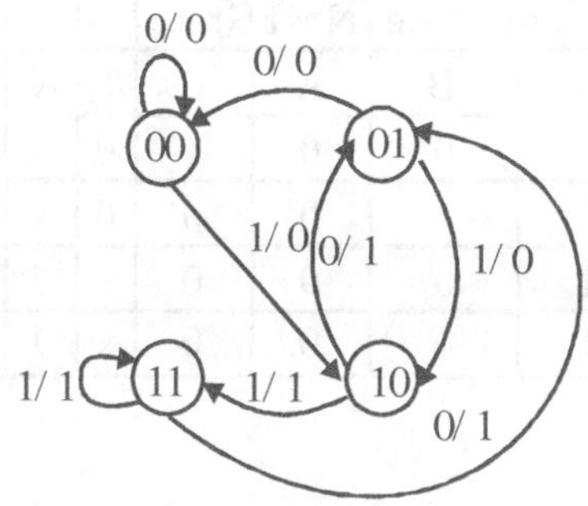

The question is the number of self loop states.

The number of self loop states are 00 and 11.

Hence answer is 2.

18.

Present state	input		Next State
S	x	y	S^+
0	X	0	1
0	X	1	0
1	0	X	0
1	1	X	1

So by the table

$\boxed{S^{-1} = S^1y^1 + S.x}$

19. (i) $xy = \sigma ff \Rightarrow j = x \oplus y = o$

$xy = 11 \Rightarrow k = x \oplus y = o$

gf jk = 00 retaine privious output

(ii) $xy = 01 \Rightarrow j = x \oplus y = 1$

$xy = 10 \Rightarrow k = xy = 1$

gf jk = 11 toggles the previous $\frac{O}{P}$

$j = x \oplus y, k = x \oplus y$

20.

Input		Output
S	R	
0	0	interminate
1	0	1
0	1	0
1	1	? ⟶ indeterminate

21.

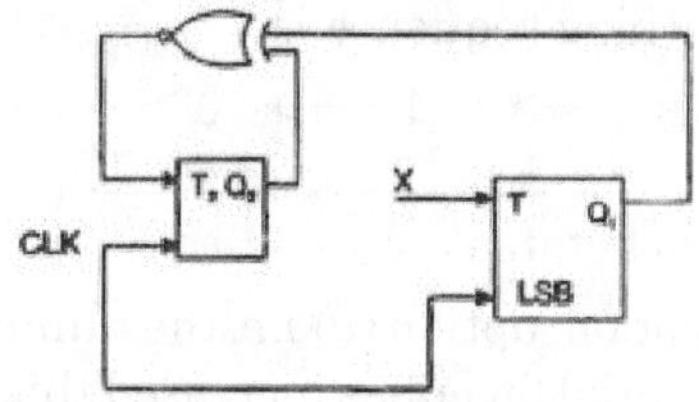

The flip - flop shown are T-type.

To implement this as a 2-bit counter, the input should be input of X - OR of two input Q_1 and Q_2 hence $Q_1 \oplus Q_2$.

22. 8 bit Counter range 0-255

To go from 10101100 (172) to 00100111 (39)

3. first counter will move from 172 to 255(255 − 172 = 83)
4. 255 to 0 = 1 pulse
5. and then 0 to 39(39 − 0 = 39).

Total = 83 + 1 + 39 = 123

23. Initially A1 A2 A3 A4 =0000

Clr = A1 and A3

So when A1 and A3 both are 1 it again goes to 0000

Hence 0000(init.) → 0001(A1 and A3 = 0) → 0010 (A1 and A3 = 0) → 0011(A1 and A3 = 0) → 0100 (A1 and A3 = 1)[clear condition satisfied] → 0000(init.) so it goes through 0 → 1 → 2 → 3→ 4

24. Initially Q_1 Q_0

0 0

Here T flip-flop

If T = 0 the next state is present state

If T = 1 next state is compliment of present

Since T = 1 initially, so outputs is compliment

Next second Q_1 remain 1 since Q_0 become 0 when TIP is 1 (compliment of present), so 2n second clock not present remains in same state.

So sequence is like 11, 10, 01, 00

25.

	P Q R	$D_P = R$	$D_O = \overline{P+R}$	$D_{R=O}\overline{R}$
Initial state	0 1 0	0	1	1
1	0 1 1			

26.

ClK	P Q R	$D_P = R$	$D_O = \overline{P+R}$	$D_R = O\overline{R}$
	0 0 0	0	1	0
1	0 0 0	0	1	1
2	0 1 0	1	0	0
3	1 0 0	0	0	0
4	0 0 0			

So counter swiching sequence is

→000 → 010 → 011 → 100 → (back to 000)

So No. of distinct states = 4.

27. Among given option, option (*d*) *i.e.* the number of people with malarial fever has increased this year do not contradic the conclusion.

28. The counting sequence for given 4-bit Johnson Counter with initial value 0000 is

0, 8, 12, 14, 15, 7, 3, 1, 0

29. The minimum number of flip-flop required is 2.

30. 2 J-K flip- flops for synchronous counter + 2 J-K flip-flop to make 2 bit counter.

Actually, when we are repeating again then after 3 we don't know that our Synchronous counter will go to which zero.

To make it work right, we need to move it to

1st zero after 3

2nd zero after 1

3rd zero after 2

i.e. $0 \rightarrow 1 \rightarrow 0 \rightarrow 2 \rightarrow 0 \rightarrow 3$ (from here it again go to 1st zero).

In order to decide which zero to move on we use counter from 1 to 3, I have attached truth table of normal 2 bit synchronous counter using JK flip flop.

Present State		Next State					
A	B	A	B	J_a	K_a	J_b	K_b
0	0	0	1	0	x	1	x
0	1	0	0	0	x	x	1
1	0	0	0	x	1	0	X
1	1	0	0	x	1	x	1

4

CHAPTER

Number System & Arithmetic

Analysis of Previous GATE Papers											
Units	Year → Topics ↓		2019	2018	2017 Set 1	2017 Set 2	2016 Set 1	2016 Set 2	2015 Set 1	2015 Set 2	2015 Set 3
NSA	1 Mark	MCQ Type									
		Numerical Type									
	2 Marks	MCQ Type									
		Numerical Type									
	Total										
SIGNED BINARY	1 Mark	MCQ Type	2								
		Numerical Type	1								
	2 Marks	MCQ Type									
		Numerical Type									
	Total		3								
MEMORY	1 Mark	MCQ Type									
		Numerical Type									
	2 Marks	MCQ Type									
		Numerical Type									
	Total										
BINARY MULTIPLICATION	1 Mark	MCQ Type									
		Numerical Type									
	2 Marks	MCQ Type									
		Numerical Type									
	Total										

NSA

1. Consider the number given by the decimal expression.

$$16^3 \times 9 + 16^2 \times 7 + 16 \times 5 + 3$$

The number of 1's in the unsigned binary representation of the number is ....

2. Using the 8087 arithmetic coprocessor with the 80186 CPU requires that the 8087 CPU is operated for ....

3. When two 4-bit binary number $A = a_3\ a_2\ a_1\ a_0$, $B = b_3\ b_2\ b_1\ b_0$ are multiplied, the digit c_1 of the product C is given by

4. Given $\sqrt{(224)_r} = (13)_r$. The value of the radix' r is

(a) 10 (b) 8
(c) 5 (d) 6 **[1997 : 2 Marks]**

5. The number 43 in 2's complement representation is

(a) 01010101 (b) 110110101
(c) 00101011 (d) 10101011

[2000 : 1 Mark]

6. Consider the values $A = 2.0 \times 10^{30}$, $B = -2.0 \times 10^{30}$, $C = 1.0$ and the sequence. What will be the values of X and Y if the following sequence of statements are carried out

X = A + B
Y : A + C
X : = X + C
Y : = Y + B

(a) X = 1.0, Y = 1.0 (b) X = 0.0. Y = 1.0
(c) X = 1.0, Y = 0.0 (d) X = 0.0, Y = 0.0

[2000 : 2 Marks]

7. The 2's complement representation of $(-539)_{10}$ in hexadecimal is

(a) ABE (b) DBC
(c) DE5 (d) 9E7

[2001 : 2 Marks]

8. The decimal value 0.25

(a) is equivalent to binary 0.1
(b) is equivalent to binary 0.01
(c) is equivalent to binary 0.00111
(d) can not be represented precisely in binary

[2002 : 1 Marks]

9. If 73_x (in base-x number system) is equal to 54_y, (in base-y number system), the possible values of x and y are

(a) 8, 16 (b) 10, 12
(c) 9, 13 (d) 8, 11

[2004 : 1 Mark]

10. The number $(123456)_8$ is equivalent to

(a) $(A72E)_{16}$ and $(22130232)_4$
(b) $(A72E)_{16}$ and $(22131122)_4$
(c) $(A72E)_{16}$ and $(22130232)_4$
(d) $(A62E)_{16}$ and $(22120232)_4$ **[2004 : 2 Marks]**

11. The hexadecimal representation of 657_8 is

(a) 1AF (b) D78
(c) D71 (d) 32F

[2005 : 1 Mark]

12. $(34.4)_8 \times (23.4)_8$ evaluates to

(a) (1053.6)8 (b) (1053.2)8
(c) (1024.2)8 (d) None of these

[2005 : 2 Marks]

13. The addition of 4-bit, two's complement, binary numbers 1101 and 0100 results in

(a) 0001 and an overflow
(b) 1001 and an overflow
(c) 0001 and no overflow
(d) 1001 and an overflow **[2006 : 1 Mark]**

14. Let a denote number system radix. The only value(s) of r that satisfy the equation $\sqrt{121} = 11$, is/are

(a) decimal 10 (b) decimal 11
(c) decimal 10 and 11 (d) any value > 2

[2008 : 1 Mark]

15. $(1217)_8$ is equivalent to

(a) $(1217)_{16}$
(a) $(028F)_{16}$
(c) $(2297)_{10}$
(d) $(0B17)_{16}$

[2009 : 1 Mark]

16. The base (or radix) of the number system such that the following equation holds is ....

$$\frac{312}{20} = 13.1$$

[2014 (Set-1) : 1 Mark]

SIGNED BINARY

17. A 32-bit floating-point number is represented by a 7-bit signed exponent, and a 24-bit fractional mantissa. The base of the scale factor is 16,

(a) the range of the exponent is ....
(b) the range of the exponent is .... if the scale factor is represented in excess-64 format.

[1990 : 2 Marks]

18. Consider the following floating point number representation.

31 24	23 0
Exponent	Mantissa

The exponent is in 2's complement representation and mantissa is in the sign magnitude representation. The range of the magnitude of the normalized numbers in this representation is

(a) 0 to 1 (b) 0.5 to 1

(c) 2^{-23} to 0.5 (d) 0.5 to $(1 - 2^{-23})$

[1996 : 1 Mark]

19. Zero has two representation in :

(a) Sign magnitude (b) 1's complement

(c) 2's complement (d) None of these

[1999 : 2 Marks]

20. The 2's complement representation of the decimal value –15 is

(a) 1111 (b) 11111

(c) 111111 (d) 10001

[2002 : 1 Mark]

21. Sign extension is the step in

(a) Floating point multiplication

(b) Signed 16 bit integer additioin

(c) Arithmtic left shift

(d) Converting a signed integer from one size to another

[2002 : 1 Mark]

22. Assuming all numbers are in 2's complement representation, which of the following numbers is divisible by 11111011?

(a) 11100111

(b) 11100100

(c) 11010111

(d) 11011011

[2003 : 1 Mark]

23. The following is a scheme for floating point number representation using 16 bits.

Bit position 15	14 ……… 9	8 ……… 0
s	e	m
Sign	Exponent	Mantissa

Let s, e, and m be the numbers represented in binary in the sign, exponent, and mantissa fields respectively. Then the floating point number represented is

$$\begin{cases} (-1)^8 (1 + m \times 2^{-9}) 2^{e.31}, \text{if the exponent} \# 111111 \\ 0 \text{ otherwise} \end{cases}$$

What is the maximum difference between two successive real numbers representable in this system ?

(a) 2^{-40} (b) 2^{-9}

(c) 2^{22} (d) 2^{31}

[2003 : 2 Marks]

24. What is the result of evaluating the following two expressions using three-digit floating point arithmetic with rounding?

(11.3. + –111.) + 7.51

11.3. + (–111.+ 7.51)

(a) 9.51 and 10.0 respectively

(b) 10.0 and 9.51 respectively

(c) 9.51 and 9.51 respectively

(d) 10.0 and 10.0 respectively

[2004 : 1 Mark]

25. Let A = 1111 1010 and B = 0000 1010 be two 8-bit 2's complement numbers. Their product in 2's complement is

(a) 1100 0100 (b) 1001 1100

(c) 1010 0101 (d) 1101 0101

[2004 : 2 Marks]

26. The range of integers that can be represented by an n bit 2's complement number system is

(a) -2^{n-1} to $(2^{n-1} - 1)$

(b) $-(2^{n-1} - 1)$ to $(2^{n-1} - 1)$

(c) -2^{n-1} to 2^{n-1}

(d) $-(2^{n-1} + 1)$ to $(2^{n-1} - 1)$

[2005 : 1 Mark]

Common Data Q. 27 to Q. 28

Consider the following floating point format

15	14 8	7 0
Sign bit	Excess-64 Exponent	Mantissa

Mantissa is a pure fraction is sign-magnitude form.

27. The decimal number 0.239×2^{13} has the following hexadecimal representation without normalization and rounding off

(a) 0D 24

(b) 0D 4D

(c) 4D 0D

(d) 4D 3D

[2005 : 2 Marks]

28. The normalized representation for the above format is specified as follows. The mantissa has an implicit 1 preceding the binary (radix) point. Assume that only 0's are padded in while shifting a field. The normalized representation of the above number (0.239×2^{13}) is

(a) 0A 20 (b) 11 34

(c) 4D D0 (d) 4A E8

[2005 : 2 Marks]

29. When multiplicant Y is multiplied by multiplier X = xn–1 xn–2, ..., x0 using bit-pair recoding in Booth's algorithm, partial products are generated according to the following table.

Row	X_{i+1}	x_i	X_{i-1}	Partial Product
1	0	0	0	0
2	0	0	1	Y
3	0	1	0	Y
4	0	1	1	2Y
5	1	0	0	?
6	1	0	1	-Y
7	1	1	0	-Y
8	1	1	1	?

The partial products for rows 5 and 8 are

(a) 2Y and Y (b) –2Y and 2Y

(c) –2Y and 0 (d) 0 and Y

[2006 : 2 Marks]

30. $(C012.25)_H - (10111001110.101)_B =$

(a) $(135103.412)_0$ (b) $(564411.412)_0$

(c) $(564411.205)_0$ (d) $(135103.205)_0$

[2007 : 2 Marks]

31. The following bit pattern represents a floating point number in 1EEE 754 single precision format :

1 10000011 10100000000000000000000

The value of the number in deciaml form is

(a) –10

(b) –13

(c) –26

(d) None of these

[2008 : 1 Mark]

32. In the 1EEE floating point representation the hexadecimal value 0x0000000 corresponds to

(a) the normalized value 2^{-127}

(b) the normalized value 2^{-126}

(c) the normalized value +0

(d) the special value + 0

[2008 : 1 Mark]

33. P is a 16-bit signed integer. The 2's complement representation of P is $(F87B)_{16}$. The 2's complement representation of 8*P is

(a) $(C3D8)_{16}$ (b) $(187B)_{16}$

(c) $(F878)_{16}$ (d) $(987B)_{16}$

[2010 : 1 Mark]

34. The decimal value 0.5 in 1EEE single precision floating point representation has

(a) fraction bits of 000 ... 000 and exponent value of 0

(b) fraction bits of 000 ... 000 and exponent value of –1

(c) fraction bits of 100 ... 000 and exponent value of 0

(d) no exact representation

[2012 : 1 Mark]

35. The smallest integer that can be represent by and 8-bit number in 2's complement form is

(a) – 256 (b) – 128

(c) – 127 (d) 0

[2013 : 1 Mark]

36. Consider Z = X – Y, where X, Y and Z are all in sign-magnitude form. X and Y are each represented in n bits. To avoid overflow, the representation of Z would require a minimum of:

(a) n + 2 bits (b) n + 1 bits

(c) n – 1 bits (d) n bits

[2019 : 1 Mark]

37. Two numbers are chosen independently and uniformly at random from the set {1, 2,..., 13}. The probability (rounded off to 3 decimal places) that their 4-bit (unsigned) binary representations have the same most significant bit is ______.

[2019 : 1 Mark]

38. In 16-bit 2's complement representation, the decimal number –28 is:

(a) 1111 1111 1110 0100

(b) 1111 1111 0001 1100

(c) 1000 0000 1110 0100

(d) 0000 0000 1110 0100

[2019 : 1 Mark]

MEMORY

39. A ROM is used to store the table for multiplication of two 8-bit unsigned integers. The size of ROM required is

(a) 256 × 16 (b) 64K × 8

(c) 4K × 16 (d) 64K × 16

[1996 : 1 Mark]

BINARY MULTIPLICATION

40. Booth's algorithm for integer multiplication gives worst performance when the multiplier pattern is

(a) 101010.....1010

(b) 100000...001

(c) 111111...1111

(d) 011111...1110

[1996 : 1 Mark]

41. Booth's coding in 8 bits for the decimal number –57 is

(a) 0 – 100 + 1000

(b) 0 – 100 + 100 – 1

(c) 0 – 1 + 100 – 10 + 1

(d) 00 – 10 + 100 – 1

[1999 : 1 Mark]

42. Using Booth's Algorithm for multiplication, the multiplier –57 will be recoded as

(a) 0 – 1 0 0 1 0 0 –1 (b) 1 1 0 0 0 1 1 1

(c) 0 –1 0 0 1 0 0 0 (d) 0 1 0 0 –1 0 0 1

[2005 : 1 Mark]

43. The two numbers given below are multiplied using the Booth's algorithm

Multiplicand : 0101 1010 1110 1110

Multiplier : 0111 0111 1011 1101

How many additions/Subtractions are required for the multiplication of the above two numbers?

(a) 6 (b) 8

(c) 20 (d) 12

[2008 : 2 Marks]

ANSWERS

1. (9)	**2.** (*)	**3.** (*)	**4.** (*c*)	**5.** (*c*)	**6.** (*c*)	**7.** (*c*)	**8.** (*b*)	**9.** (*d*)	**10.** (*a*)
11. (*a*)	**12.** (*a*)	**13.** (*c*)	**14.** (*d*)	**15.** (*b*)	**16.** (5)	**17.** (*)	**18.** (*d*)	**19.** (*a,b*)	**20.** (*d*)
21. (*d*)	**22.** (*a*)	**23.** (*c*)	**24.** (*a*)	**25.** (*a*)	**25.** (*a*)	**27.** (*d*)	**28.** (*d*)	**29.** (*c*)	**30.** (*d*)
31. (*c*)	**32.** (*d*)	**33.** (*a*)	**34.** (*b*)	**35.** (*b*)	**36.** (*b*)	**37.** 0.503	**38.** (*a*)	**39.** (*d*)	**40.** (*a*)
41. (*b*)	**42.** (*a*)	**43.** (*b*)							

EXPLANATIONS

1. Hexadecimal representation of given no. is $(9753)_{16}$
   Its binary representation is $(1001011101010011)_2$
   The no. of 1's is 9
2. Floating point representation
3. C1 = a1b0 + a0b1
4. $\sqrt{(224)_r} = (13)r$
   or $\sqrt{2r^2 + 2r + 4} = r + 3$
   or $2r^2 + 2r + 4 = r^{2+9+6r}$
   or $^2 - 4r - 5 = 0$
   or $(r-5)(r+1) = 0$
   or $r = 5$
5. 00101011
6. Given 32 bits representation. So, the maximum precision can be 32 bits.
   Therefore, A + C should make the 31st digit to 1, which is surely outside the precision level of A (it is 31st digit and not 31st bit). So, this addition will just return the value of A which will be assigned to Y.
   So, Y + B will return 0.0 while X + C will return 1.0.
7. + 53910 = 0010 0001 1011
   – 53910 = 1101 1110 0101(DE5)
8. 0.25 * 2 = 0.50   0 (whole part)
   0.50 * 2 = 1.00   1 (whole part)
   So, $0.25_{10} = 0.01_2$
9. $(73)_x = (54)_y$
   The possible value of x and y is 8 and 11 evaluated by putting the value alternative option.
10. $(123456)_8 = (001\ 010\ 011\ 100\ 101\ 110)_2$
    $= (A72E)_{16}$
    $= (22130232)_4$
11. Given : $(657)_8$
    First we find its decimal.
    $(6 \times 8^2 + 5 \times 8^1 + 7 \times 8^0)$
    $= 6 \times 64 + 5 \times 8 + 7 \times 1$
    $= 384 + 40 + 7 = 431$

256	128	64	32	16	8	4	2	1
0 001	1	0	1	0	1	1	1	1
I		A				F		

    Hence $(657)_8 = (IAF)_{16}$.
12. $(34.4)_8 = 011100.1$
    $= 16 + 8 + 4 + 0.5 = (28.5)_{10}$
    $(23.4)_8 = 010\ 011.1$
    $16 + 2 + 1 + 0.5 = (19.5)_{10}$
    $(28.5)_{10} \times (19.5)_{10} = (555.75)_{10} = (1053.6)_8$
13. In carry

```
 (1)
 1101
 0101
------
(1)0001
```

    out carry
14. $\sqrt{121_r} = (11)_r$
    So we till take base r any value that is greater than 2.
15. $(1217)_8 = 001\ 010\ 001\ 111$
    $0010\ 1000\ 1111 = (028F)_{16}$

    Alternately

    Given digit in octal 1217.

    Convert them in binary $\overline{001}\ \overline{010}\overline{001}\overline{111}$
    Now convert binary to hexa
    $\overline{0010}\ \overline{1000}\ \overline{1111} = (028F)_{16}$
    2   8   F
16. Let x (? 0) be the base of the given equation.
    We have,
    LHS = (3x2 + x + 2)/(2x) = (3x/2) + (1/2) + (1/x)
    RHS = x + 3 + (1/x)
    Now, for the equation to hold true, LHS = RHS
    (3x/2) + (1/2) + (1/x) = x + 3 + (1/x)
    ⇒ 3x + 1 = 2x + 6
    ⇒ x = 5
17. (a) As given exponent bits are 7 bits. So Minimum exponent is 0 and maximum exponent is 2^6-1 = 63
    (b) Minimum number = 0, maximum number = 127
18. The minimum value of mantisa is
    = 0.100 0000 0000 0000 0000 0000
    = 1 * 2 – 1
    = 0.5
    and maximum value of Mantissa ⇒
    = 0.111 1111 1111 1111 1111 1111
    $= [(223) - 1] * 2^{-23}$
    $= 1 - 2^{-23}$

19. Sign Magnitude

+ 0 = 0000

– 0 = 1000

1's complement

+ 0 = 0000

– 0 = 1111

20. Binary number of 15 = 1111

2's complemnt = 0000

$\underline{\quad 1}$

0001

So, we represent decimal value – 15 in 2's complemnt form as → 10001

21. Sign extension is a step in converting a signed integer from one size to another.

22. 2's complement → 00000101 = 5

2's complement of 11100111 is 00011001 = 25

23. 15 14.................9 8...................0

s	e	m
Sign	Exponent	Mantissa

s = signbit

e = exponent = 2^6 = 0 to 63

m = 2^8 = 0 to 255

Floating point representation is

$(-1)^s(1 + m \times 2^{-9})\, 2^{e-31}$ if the exponent ≠ 111111

$(-1)^s(1 + 2^9\, 2^{-9})\, 2^{e-31} = (-1)^s(1 + 2^{\circ})\, (2^{e-31})$

If exponent is 111110 or 111101

then e = 62

e_2 = 61

∴ Successine difference = 2^{22}.

24. (113. + – 111.) + 7.51

113. + (– 111. + 7.51)

The exponent value is 10.0.

The value evaluated by the expression is 9.51 and 10.0.

25. A = 11111010

$= -2^7 + 2^6 + 2^5 + 2^4 + 2^3 + 2^1$

= – 6 (since number. is stored in two's complement format)

B = $2^3 + 2^1$

= 8 + 2 = 10

∴ AB = – 60, which is 11000100

26. Negative numbers are represented by the forms

1. sign magnitude
2. one's complement
3. two's complement

For sign and one's complement representation, we have two zero's –ve and +ve, while in case of two's complement +ve is only one zero.

This additional code which is waste in top two representation is used to assign one more negative code.

27. Binary of 0.239 is 0. 00111101 *2^{13}

15 14 87 0

Sign	Exponent	Mantissa

Matissa = 00111101

exponent = 13 + 64 = 77 = 1001101

0	1 0 0 1 1 0 1	00 1111 0 1

4 D 3 D

28. 0.239 * 2^{13} = 0. 00111101 * 2^{13}

Normalized form = 1. 11101000 * 2^{10}

Mantissa form = 11101000

exponent = 10 + 64 = 74 = 1001010

0	1 0 0 1 0 1 0	1 1 1 0 1 0 0 0

4 D 3 D

29. Here partial product is calculated by bit pair recoding in booth's algorithm.

(–2 Xi + 1 + Xi + Xi –1)Y

30. $(C012.25)_H - (10111001110.101)_B$

= 1100 0000 0001 0010. 0010 0101

– 0000 0101 1100 1110. 1010 0000

= 1011 1010 0100 0011. 1000 0101

= 1 011 101 001 000 011 . 100 001 010 (make pairing of 3 to convert in octal)

= (135103.412)o

31. exponent bits are 10000011

The number is = 131 – 127 = 4

⇒ – 1.1010 * 2^4

⇒ – (11010) = -26

32. It represent the special value +0.

33. $(F87B)_{16} = \underbrace{1111}_{F}\,\underbrace{1000}_{8}\,\underbrace{0111}_{7}\,\underbrace{1011}_{B}$

But it is 2's complement of P

So for getting original numbers, take 2's complement of $(F87B)_{16}$

It is P = 0000 01111 0000101

$= (1925)_{10}$

Then $P * 8 = 1925 \times 8$

$= 15400$

$(15400)_{10} = 0011110000101000$

Now, 2's complement of this 15400 in binary

$= \underbrace{1100}_{C}\underbrace{0011}_{3}\underbrace{1101}_{D}\underbrace{1000}_{8} = (C3D8)_{16}$

34. $(0.5)_{10} = (1.0)_2 \times 2^{-1}$

So, exponent = – 1 and fraction is 000 - - - 000

35. Option (*a*) : 256 cannot be represented by 8-bit 2's complement no.

or 2'S complement representation, the general formula for n-bits is

$(-2^{n-1}$ to $2^{n-1}-1)$

for $n = 8$, the max negative number is -2^{8-1}

$= -2^7 = -128$

Hence answer is option (*b*).

36. For example:

Let,

$$\left.\begin{array}{l} X = +6, n = 4 \\ Y = -5, n = 4 \end{array}\right\} \Rightarrow (X - Y) = +11$$

So Z = 11 which required 5 bits which is (n + 1) bits

38. '28' in binary code is written as

+28 ⇒ 0000 0000 0001 1100

Now, (2's complement form)

–28 ⇒ 1111 1111 1110 0100

39. If we multiply two 8 bit numbers result my vary upto 16 bits.

So, 16 bits are requierd for each of the multiplication result.

Possible results are = 28 × 28 = 216 = 64 K as we need to store all possible results of multiplying two 8 bit numbers.

Hence answer is 64K × 16.

40. 10101010....10 pattern gives maximum number of addition and substraction.

41. 0–100 + 100–1 evaluates to 57 in Booth's coding as below

$(0*2^7) - (1*2^6) + (0*2^5) + (0*2^4) + (1*2^3) + (0*2^2) + (0*2^1) - (1*2^0) = -64 + 8 - 1 = -57$

42. Using option (a)

0 –1 0 0 1 0 0 –1

= 0 * (2^6) –1 * (2^6) + 0 * (2^5) + 0 * (2^4) + 1 * (2^3) + 0 * (2^2) + 0 * (2^1) –1 * (2^0)

= –2^6 + 2^3 – 2^0 = –64 + 8 – 1 = – 57

43. Both's recording of multiplier is

+1 0 0 –1 + 1 0 0 0 –1 +1 0 0 0 –1 +1 –1

Hence 4 addition (number of positive 1) and 4 subtraction (number of negative 1) is requierd.

Unit - IV

Computer Organization and Architecture

Syllabus

Machine instructions and addressing modes. ALU, data-path and control unit. Instruction pipelining. Memory hierarchy: cache, main memory and secondary storage; I/O interface (interrupt and DMA mode).

Contents

1 CHAPTER

Cache and Main Memory

Analysis of Previous GATE Papers											
Units	Year → Topics ↓		2019	2018	2017 Set 1	2017 Set 2	2016 Set 1	2016 Set 2	2015 Set 1	2015 Set 2	2015 Set 3
CACHE PERFORMANCE	1 Mark	MCQ Type									
		Numerical Type									
	2 Marks	MCQ Type									
		Numerical Type									
	Total										
ADDRESS MAPPING & REPLACEMENT	1 Mark	MCQ Type									1
		Numerical Type									
	2 Marks	MCQ Type									
		Numerical Type			2						
	Total				4						1
CACHE COCEPT	1 Mark	MCQ Type	1								
		Numerical Type									
	2 Marks	MCQ Type									
		Numerical Type	1								
	Total		3								
VIRTUAL MEMORY	1 Mark	MCQ Type									
		Numerical Type									
	2 Marks	MCQ Type									
		Numerical Type									
	Total										
MAIN MEMORY	1 Mark	MCQ Type									
		Numerical Type		1				1			
	2 Marks	MCQ Type									
		Numerical Type									
	Total			1				1			
DESIGN ISSUES & PERFORMANCE	1 Mark	MCQ Type									
		Numerical Type						1		1	
	2 Marks	MCQ Type				1					
		Numerical Type			2	1					
	Total				4	4		1		1	
CPU PERFORMANCE	1 Mark	MCQ Type									
		Numerical Type									
	2 Marks	MCQ Type									
		Numerical Type									
	Total										

CACHE PERFORMANCE

1. State whether the following statements are TRUE or FALSE with reason. Transferring data in blocks from the main memory to the cache memory enables an interleaved main memory bit to operate unit at its maximum speed.

[1990 : 2 Marks]

2. Consider a system with 2 level cache. Access times of Level 1 cache, Level 2 cache and main memory are 1 ns, 10 ns, and 500 ns, respectively. The hit rates of Level 1 and Level 2 caches are 0.8 and 0.9, respectively. What is the average access time of the system ignoring the search time within the cache?

(a) 13.0 ns (b) 12.8 ns
(c) 12.6 ns (d) 12.4 ns

[2004 : 1 Mark]

3. Consider a small two-way set-associative cache memory, consisting of four blocks. For choosing the block to be replaced, use the least recently used (LRU) scheme. The number of cache misses for the following sequence of block addresses is 8, 12, 0, 12, 8

(a) 2 (b) 3
(c) 4 (d) 5 **[2004 : 2 Marks]**

4. A cache line is 64 bytes. The main memory has latency 32ns and bandwidth 1 GB/s. The time required to fetch the entire cache line from the main memory is

(a) 32 ns (b) 64 ns
(c) 96 ns (d) 128 ns

[2006 : 2 Marks]

5. A CPU has a cache with block size 64 bytes. The main memory has k banks, each bank being c bytes wide. Consecutive c-byte chunks are mapped on consecutive banks with warp-around. All the k banks can be asscessed in parallel, but two accesses to the same bank must be serialized. A cache block access may involve multiple iterations of parallel bank accesses depending on the amount of data obtained by accessing all the k banks in parallel. Each iteration requires decoding the bank numbers to be accessed in parallel and this takes k/2 ns. The latency of one bank access is 80 ns. If c = 2 and k = 24, then latency of retrieving a cache block starting at address zero from main memory is

(a) 92 ns
(b) 104 ns
(c) 172 ns
(d) 184 ns

[2006 : 2 Marks]

Common Data for 6 & 7.

A CPU has a 32 KB direct mapped cache with 28-byte block size. Suppose A is a two dimensional tray of size 512 × 512 with elements that occupy 8-bytes each. Consider the following two C code segments P_1 and P_2.

```
P1 : for (i = 0, i < 512; i++) {
       for (j = 0, j < 512; j++) {
         x+ = A [i] [j];
       }
     }
P2 :  for (i = 0, i < 512; i++) {
       for (j = 0, j < 512; j++) {
         x+ = A [i] [j];
       }
     }
```

P1 and P2 are executed independently with the same initial state, namely, the array A is not in the cache and i, j, x are in registers. Let the number of cache misses experienced by P1 be M_1 and that for P2 be M_2.

6. The value of M_1 is

(a) 0 (b) 2048
(c) 16384 (d) 262144

[2006 : 2 Marks]

7. The value of the ratio M_1/M_2 is

(a) 0 (b) $\frac{1}{16}$
(c) $\frac{1}{8}$ (d) 16 **[2006 : 2 Marks]**

Common Date for Q. 8 & Q. 9

Consider a machine with a byte addressable main memory of 2^{16} bytes. Assume that a direct mapped data cache consisting of 32 lines of 64 bytes each is used in the system. A50 × 50 two-dimensional array of bytes is stored in the main memory starting from memory location 1100 H. Assume that the data cache is initially empty. The complete array is accessed twice. Assume that the contents of the data cache do not change in between the two acceses.

8. How many data cache misses will occur in total?

(a) 48 (b) 50
(c) 56 (d) 59

[2007 : 2 Marks]

9. Which of the following lines of the data cache will be replaced by new blocks in accessing the array

(a) line 4 to line 11 (b) line 4 to line 12
(c) line 0 to line 7 (d) line 0 to line 8

[2007 : 2 Marks]

ADDRESS MAPPING & REPLACEMENT

10. A block-set associative cache memory consists of 128 blocks divided into four blocks sets. The main memory consists of 16,384 blocks and each block contains 256 eight bit words.

(i) How many bits are required for addressing the main memory?

(ii) How many bits are needed to represent the TAG, SET and WORD fields?

[1990 : 2 Marks]

11. The main memory of a computer has 2 cm blocks while the cache has 2 c blocks. If the cache uses the set associative mapping scheme with 2 blocks per set, then block k of the main memory maps to the set

(a) (k mod m) of the cache

(b) (k mod c) of the cache

(c) (k mod 2c) of the cache

(d) (k mod 2 cm) of the cache

[1999 : 1 Mark]

12. Consider a direct mapped cache of size 32 KB with block size 32 bytes. The CPU generates 32 bit addresses. The number of bits needed for cache indexing and the number of tag bits are respectively

(a) 10, 17 (b) 10, 22

(c) 15, 17 (d) 5, 17

[2005 : 2 Marks]

13. A computer system has a level-1 instruction cache (1-cache), a level-1 data cache (D-cache) and a level-2 cache (L2-cache) with the following specifications :

	Capacity	Mapping method	Block size
1-cache	4K words	Direct mapping	4 Words
D-cache	4K words	2-way set-associative mapping	4 Words
1, 2-cache	64K words	2-way set-associative mapping	16 Words

Capacity Mapping method Block size 1-cache 4K words Direct mapping 4 Words D-cache 4K words 2-way set-associative mapping 4 Words L2 cache 64K words 4-way set-association mapping 16 Words The length of the physical address of a word in the main memory is 30 bits. The capacity of the tag memory in the 1-cache D-cache and L2-cache is, respectively,

(a) 1K × 18 bit, 1K × 19-bit, 4K × 16 bit

(b) 1K × 16 bit, 1K × 19-bit, 4K × 18 bit

(c) 1K × 16 bit, 512 × 18-bit, 1K × 16 bit

(d) 1K × 18 bit, 512 × 18-bit, 4K × 18 bit

[2006 : 2 Marks]

Common Data for 14 & 15

Consider two cache organizations : The first one is 32 KB 2-way set associative with 32-byte block size. The second one is of the same size but direct mapped. The size of an address is 32 bits in both cases. A 2-to-1 multiplexer has latency of 0.6 ns while a k-bit comparator has a latency of k/10 ns. The hit latency of the set associative organization is h_1 while that of the direct mapped one is h_2.

14. The value of h_1 is

(a) 2.4 ns (b) 2.3 ns

(c) 1.8 ns (d) 1.7 ns

[2006 : 2 Marks]

15. The value of h_2 is

(a) 2.4 ns (b) 2.3 ns

(c) 1.8 ns (d) 1.7 ns

[2006 : 2 Marks]

16. Consider a 4-way set associative cache consisting of 128 lines with a line size of 64 words. The CPU generates a 20-bit address of a word in main memory. The number of bits in the TAG, LINE and WORD fields are respectively

(a) 9, 6, 5 (b) 7, 7, 6

(c) 7, 5, 8 (d) 9, 5, 6

[2007 : 1 Mark]

Common Date for Q. 17 & Q. 18

Consider a computer with a 4-ways set-associative mapped cache of the following characteristics : a total of 1 MB of main memory, a word size of 1 byte, a block size of 128 words and a cache size of 8 KB.

17. The number of bits in the TAG, SET and WORD fields, respectively are :

(a) 7, 6, 7 (b) 8, 5, 7

(c) 8, 6, 6 (d) 9, 4, 7

[2008 : 2 Marks]

18. While accessing the memory location 0C795H by the CPU, the contents of the TAG field of the corresponding cache line is

(a) 000011000

(b) 110001111

(c) 00011000

(d) 110010101

[2008 : 2 Marks]

19. Consider a 4-way set associative cache (initially empty) with total 16 cache blocks. The main memory consists of 256 blocks and the request for memory blocks is in the following order:

0, 255, 1, 4, 3, 8, 133, 159, 216, 129, 63, 8, 48, 32, 73, 92, 155

Which of the following memory block will NOT be in the cache if LRU replacement policy is used?

(a) 3
(b) 8
(c) 129
(d) 216

[2009 : 2 Marks]

20. Consider a machine with a byte addressable main memory of 2^{20} bytes, block size of 16 bytes and a direct mapped cache having 2^{12} cache lines. Let the addresses of two consecutive bytes in main memory be $(E201F)_{16}$ and $(E2020)_{16}$. What are the tag and cache line address (in hex) for main memory address $(E201f)_{16}$?

(a) E, 201
(b) F, 201
(c) E, E20
(d) 2, 01F

[2015 (Set-3) : 1 Mark]

21. A cache memory unit with capacity of N words and block size of B words is to be designed. If it is designed as a direct mapped cache the length of the TAG field is 10 bits. If the cache unit is now designed as a 16-way set-associative cache, the length of the TAG field is .... bits.

[2017 (Set-1) : 2 Marks]

22. Consider a machine with a byte addressable main memory of 2^{32} divided into blocks of size 32 bytes. Assume that a direct mapped cache having 512 cache lines is used with this machine. The size of the tag field in bits is ....

[2017 (Set-1) : 2 Marks]

23. The size of the physical address space of a processor is 2^P bytes. The word length is 2^W bytes. The capacity of cache memory is 2^N bytes, the size of each cache block is 2^M words. For a K-way set-associative cache memory, the length (in number of bits) of the tag field is

(a) $P-N-\log_2 K$
(b) $P-N+\log_2 K$
(c) $P-N-M-W-\log_2 K$
(d) $P-N-M-W+\log_2 K$

CACHE COCEPT

24. The principle of locality justifies the use of

(a) Interrupts
(b) DMA
(c) Polling
(d) Cache Memory

[1995 : 1 Mark]

25. A graphics card has on board memory of 1 MB. Which of the following modes can be card not support?

(a) 1600 × 400 resolution with 256 colours on a 17 inch monitor
(b) 1600 × 400 resolution with 16 million colours on a 14 inch monitor
(c) 800 × 400 resolution with 16 million colours on a 17 inch monitor
(d) 800 × 800 resolution with 256 colours on a 14 inch monitor

[2000 : 2 Marks]

26. Which of the following requires a device driver?

(a) Register
(b) Cache
(c) Main memory
(d) Disk

[2001 : 1 Mark]

27. More than one word are put in one cache block to

(a) exploit the temporal locality of reference in a program
(b) exploit the spatial locality of reference in a program
(c) reduce the miss penalty
(d) None of the above

[2001 : 1 Mark]

28. For inclusion to hold between two cache level L1 and L2 in a multilevel cache hierarchy, which of the following are necessary?

1. L1 must be a write-through cache
2. 2 must be a write-through cache
3. The associativity of L2 must be greater that of L1
4. The L2 cahce must be at least as large as the L1 cache

(a) 4 only
(b) 1 and 2 only
(c) 1, 2 and 4 only
(d) 1, 2, 3 and 4

[2008 : 2 Marks]

29. In a k-way set associative cache, the cache is divided into v sets, each of which consists of k lines. The lines of a set are placed in sequence on afte another. The lines in set s are sequenced before the lines in set (s + 1). The main memory blocks are numbered 0 onwards. The main memory block numbered 'j' must be mapped to any one of the cache lines from

(a) (j mod v) * k to (j mod v) * k + (k – 1)

(b) (j mod v) * (j mod v) + (k – 1)

(c) (j mod k) to (j mod k) + (v – 1)

(d) (j mod k) * v (j mod k)* v + (v – 1)

[2013 : 1 Mark]

30. If the associativity of a processor cache is doubled while keeping the capacity and block size unchanged, which one of the following is guaranteed to be NOT affected?

(a) Width of tag comparator

(b) Width of set index decoder

(c) Width of way selection multiplexor

(d) Width of processor to main memory data bus

[2014 (Set-2) : 2 Marks]

31. A certain processor uses a fully associative cache of size 16 kB. The cache block size is 16 bytes. Assume that the main memory is byte addressable and uses a 32-bit address. How many bits are required for the Tag and the Index fields respectively in the addresses generated by the processor?

(a) 24 bits and 4 bits

(b) 28 bits and 4 bits

(c) 24 bits and 0 bits

(d) 28 bits and 0 bits

[2019 : 1 Mark]

32. A certain processor deploys a single-level cache. The cache block size is 8 words and the word size is 4 bytes. The memory system uses a 60-MHz clock. To service a cache miss, the memory controller first takes 1 cycle to accept the starting address of the block, it then takes 3 cycles to fetch all the eight words of the block, and finally transmits the words of the requested block at the rate of 1 word per cycle. The maximum bandwidth for the memory system when the program running on the processor issues a series of read operations is ________ $\times 10^6$ bytes/sec.

[2019 : 2 Marks]

VIRTUAL MEMORY

33. In a two-level virtual memory, the memory access time for main memory, $t_{A_1} = 10^{-8}$ sec, and the memory, tag = 10^{-3} sec. What must be the hit ratio, H such that the access efficiency is within 80 percent of its maximum value. **[1990 : 2 Marks]**

34. The total size of address space in a virtual memory systems limited by

(a) the length of MAR

(b) the available secondary storage

(c) the available main memory

(d) All of the above **[1991 : 2 Marks]**

35. Which of the following is/are advantage of virtual memory?

(a) Faster access to memory on an average.

(b) Processes can be given protected address spaces.

(c) Linker can assign addresses independent of where the program will be loaded in physical memory.

(d) Programs larger than the physical memory size can be run.

[1999 : 2 Marks]

36. Which of the following statements is false?

(a) Virtual memory implements the translation of a program's address space into physical memory address space

(b) Virtual memory allows such program to exceed the size of the primary memory

(c) Virtual memory increases the degree of multiprogramming

(d) Virtual memory reduces the context switching overhead **[2001 : 1 Mark]**

37. The total size of address space in a virtual memory system is limited by

(a) the length of MAR

(b) the available secondary storage

(c) the available main memory

(d) All of the above **[1991 : 2 Marks]**

MAIN MEMORY

38. A dynamic RAM has a memory cycle time of 64 nsec. It has to be refreshed 100 times per msec and each refresh takes 100 nsec. What percentage of the memory cycle time is used for refreshing?

(a) 10 (b) 6.4

(c) 1 (d) 0.64 **[2005 : 1 Mark]**

39. Increasing the RAM of a computer typically improves performance because

(a) Virtual memory increases

(b) Larger RAMs are faster

(c) Fewer page faults occur

(d) Fewer segmentation faults occur

[2005 : 1 Mark]

40. How many 32K × 1 RAM chips are needed to provide a memory capacity of 256 K-bytes?

(a) 8 (b) 32

(c) 64 (d) 128

[2009 : 1 Mark]

41. A main memory unit with a capacity 4 megabytes is built using 1M × 1-bit DRAM chips. Each DRAM chip has 1K rows of cells with 1K cells in each row. The time taken for a single refresh operation is 100 nanoseconds. The time required to perform one refresh operation on all the cells in the memory unit is

(a) 100 nanoseconds

(b) $100*2^{10}$ nanoseconds

(c) $100*2^{20}$ nanoseconds

(d) $3200*2^{20}$ nanoseconds **[2010 : 1 Mark]**

42. A RAM chip has capacity of 1024 words of 8 bits each (1K × 8). The number of 2 × 4 decoders with enable line needed to construct a 16 K × 16 RAM from 1K × 8 RAM is

(a) 4 (b) 5

(c) 6 (d) 7

[2013 : 2 Marks]

43. Consider a main memory system that consists of 8 memory modules attached to the system bus, which is one word wide. When a write request is made, the bus is occupied for 100 nanoseconds (ns) by the data, address, and control signals, During the same 100 ns, and for 500 ns thereafter, the addressed memory module executes one cycle accepting and storing the data. The (internal) operation of different memory modules may overlap in time, but only one request can be on the bus at any time.

The maximum number of stores (of one word each) that can be initiated in 1 millisecond is ....

[2014 (Set-2) : 2 Marks]

44. A processor can support a maximum memory of 4GB, where the memory is word-addressable (a word consists of two bytes). The size of the address bus of the processor is at least .... bits.

[2016 (Set-1) : 1 Mark]

45. A 32-bit wide main memory unit with a capacity of 1 GB is built using 256 M × 4-bit DRAM chips. The number of rows of memory cells in the DRAM chip is 2^{14}. The time taken to perform one refresh operation is 50 nanoseconds. The refresh period is 2 milliseconds. The percentage (rounded to the closest integer) of the time available for performing the memory read/write operations in the main memory unit is .... **[2018 : 1 Mark]**

46. What is the minimum size of ROM required to store the complete truth table of an 8-bit × 8 bit multiplier?

(a) 32 K × 16 bits (b) 64 K × 16 bits

(c) 16 K × 32 bits (d) 64 K × 32 bits

[2004 : 1 Mark]

47. The amount of ROM needed to implement at 4 bit multiplier is

(a) 64 bits (b) 128 bits

(c) 1 Kbit (d) 2 Kbits

[2012 : 1 Mark]

48. Transferring data in blocks from the main memory to the cache memory enables an interleaved main memory unit to operate unit at its maximum speed. **[1990 : 2 Marks]**

DESIGN ISSUES & PERFORMANCE

Common Data for Q. 49 to 50

Consider a machine a 2-way set associative data cache of size 64 Kbytes and block size 16 bytes. The cache is managed using 32 bit virtual addressed and the page size is 4 Kybytes. A program to be run on this machine begins as follows :

```
double APR {1024] [1024]
int i, j ;
/ * Initalize array APR to 0.0*/
for (i = 0; i < 1024; i ++)
    for (j = 0; j < 1024; j++
        APR [i] [j] = 0.0;
```

The size of double 8 bytes. Array APR is memory starting at the beginning of virtual page 0 × FF000 and stored in row major order. The cache is initially empty and no pre-fetching is done. The only data memory references made by the program are those to array APR.

49. The total size of the tags in the cache directory is

(a) 32 kbits (b) 34 kbits

(c) 64 kbits (d) 68 kbits

[2008 : 2 Marks]

50. Which of the following array elements has the same cache index as APR [0] [0] ?

(a) APR [0] [4] (b) APR [4] [0]

(c) APR [0] [5] (d) APR [5] [0]

[2008 : 2 Marks]

51. The cache hit ratio for this initialization loop is

(a) 0% (b) 25%

(c) 50% (d) 75%

[2008 : 2 Marks]

Common Data for Q. 52 & Q. 53

A computer system has an L1 and L2 cache, an L2 cache, and a main memory unit connected as shown below. The block size in L1 cache is 4 words. The block size in L2 cache is 16 words. The memory access times are 2 nanoseconds, 20 nanoseconds and 200 nanoseconds for L1 cache, L2 cache and main memory unit respectively.

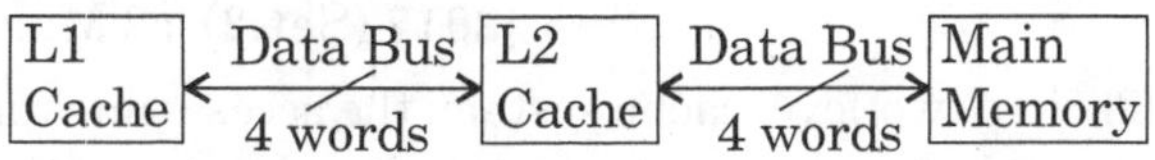

52. When there is a miss in L1 cache and a hit in L2 cache, a block is transferred from L2 cache to L1 cache. What is the time taken for this transfer?

(a) 2 nanoseconds (b) 20 nanoseconds

(c) 22 nanoseconds (d) 88 nanoseconds

[2010 : 2 Marks]

53. When there is a miss in both L1 cache and L2 cache, first a block is transferred from main memory to L2 cache, and then a block is transferred from L2 cache to L1 cache. What is the total time taken for these transfers?

(a) 222 nanoseconds (b) 888 nanoseconds

(c) 902 nanoseconds (d) 968 nanoseconds

[2010 : 2 Marks]

54. An 8KB direct-mapped write back cache is organized as multiple blocks, each of size 32 bytes. The processor generates 32 bit addresses. The cache controller maintains the tag information for each cache block comprising of the following.

1 Valid bit

1 Modified bit

As many bits as the minimum needed to identify the memory block mapped in the cache.

What is the total size of memory needed at the cache controller to store meta-data (tags) for the cache?

(a) 4864 bits (b) 6144 bits

(c) 6656 bits (d) 5376 bits

[2011 : 2 Marks]

Linked Answer Q. 55 & Q. 56

A computer has a 256 Kbytes, 4-way set associative, write back data cache with block size of 32 Bytes. The processor sends 32 bit addresses to the cache controller. Each cache tag directory entry contains, in addition to address tag, 2 valid bits, 1 modified bit and 1 replacement bit.

55. The number of bits in the tag field of an address is

(a) 11 (b) 14

(c) 16 (d) 27

[2012 : 2 Marks]

56. The size of the cache tag directory is

(a) 160 Kbits

(b) 136 Kbits

(c) 40 Kbits

(d) 32 Kbits

[2012 : 2 Marks]

57. An access sequence of cache block address of length N and contains n unique block addresses. The number of unique block addresses between two consecutive accesses to the same block address is bounded above by k. What is the miss ratio if the access sequence is passed through a cache of associativity A ≥ k exercising least-recently used replacement policy?

(a) $\frac{n}{N}$ (b) $\frac{1}{N}$

(c) $\frac{1}{A}$ (d) $\frac{k}{n}$

[2014 (Set-1) : 2 Marks]

58. A 4-ways set-associative cache memory unit with a capacity of 16 KB is built using a block size of 8 words. The word length is 32 bits. The size of the physical address space is 4 GB. The number of bits for the TAG field is ....

[2014 (Set-2) : 1 Marks]

59. In designing a computer's cache system, the cache block (or cache line) size is an important parameter. Which one of the following statements is correct in this context ?

(a) A smaller block size implies better spatial locality

(b) A smaller block size implies a smaller cache tag and hence lower cache tag overhead

(c) A smaller block size implies a larger cache tag and hence lower cache hit time

(d) A smaller block size incurs a lower cache miss penalty.

[2014 (Set-2) : 2 Marks]

60. The memory access time is 1 nanosecond for a read operation with a hit in cache, 5 nanoseconds for a read operation with a miss in cache, 2 nanoseconds for a write operation with a hit in cache and 10 nanoseconds for a write operation with a miss in cache. Execution of a sequence of instructions involves 100 instruction fetch operations, 60 memory operand read operations and 40 memory operand write operations. The cache hit-ratio is 0.9. The average memory access time (in nanoseconds) in executing the sequence of instructions is ....

[2014 (Set-3) : 2 Marks]

61. Assume that for a certain processor, a read request takes 50 nanoseconds on a cache miss and 5 nanoseconds on a cache hit. Suppose while running a program, it was observed that 80% of the processor's read requests result in a cache hit. The average read access time in nanoseconds is ....

[2015 (Set-2) : 1 Mark]

62. The width of the physical address on a machine is 40 bits. The width of the tag field in a 512 KB 8-way set associative cache is ________ bits.

[2016 (Set-1) : 1 Mark]

63. Consider a 2-way set associative cache with 256 blocks and uses LRU replacement. Initially the cache is empty. Conflict misses are those misses which occur due to contention of multiple blocks for the same cache set. Compulsory misses occur due to first time access to the block. The following sequence of accesses to memory blocks (0, 128, 256, 128, 0, 128, 256, 128, 1, 129, 257, 129, 1, 129, 257, 129) is repeated 10 times. The number of conflict misses experienced by the cache is ....

[2017 (Set-1) : 2 Marks]

64. Consider a two-level cache hierarchy with L1 and L2 caches, An application incurs 1.4 memory accesses per instruction oon average. For this application, the miss rate of L1 cache is 0.1; the L2 cache experiences, on average, 7 misses per 1000 instructions. The miss rate of L2 expressed correct to two decimal places is ....

[2017 (Set-1) : 2 Marks]

65. The read access tiems and the hit ratios for different caches in a memory hierarchy are as given below :

Code	Read access time (in nanoseconds)	HIt ratio
I-Cache	2	0.8
D-Cache	2	0.9
L2-Cache	8	0.9

The read access time of main memory is 90 nanoseconds. Assume that the caches use the referred word-first read policy and the write back policy. Assume that all the caches are direct mapped caches. Assume that the dirty bit is always 0 for all the blocks in the caches. In execution of a program, 60% of memory reads are for instruction fetch and 40% are for memory operand fetch. The average read access time in nanoseconds (upto 2 decimal places) is ....

[2017 (Set-2) : 2 Marks]

66. In a two-level cache system, the access times of L1 and L2 caches are 1 and 8 clock cycles, respectively. The miss penalty from the L2 cache to main memory is 18 clock cycles. The miss rate of L1 cache is twice that of L2. The average memory access time (AMAT) of this cache system is 2 cycles. The miss rates of L_1 and L_2 respectively are :

(a) 0.111 and 0.056
(b) 0.056 and 0.111
(c) 0.0892 and 0.1784
(d) 0.1784 and 0.0892

[2017 (Set-2) : 2 Marks]

CPU PERFORMANCE

67. In an enhancement of a design of a CPU, the speed of a floating point unit has been increased by 20% and the speed of a fixed point unit has been increased by 10%. What is the overall speedup achieved if the ratio of the number of floating point operations to the number of fixed point operations is 2 : 3 and the floating point operation used to take twice the time taken by the fixed point operation in the original design?

(a) 1.155
(b) 1.185
(c) 1.255
(d) 1.285

[2004 : 2 Marks]

ANSWERS

1. (true)	2. (*c*)	3. (*b*)	4. (*c*)	5. (*d*)	6. (*c*)	7. (*b*)	8. (*c*)	9. (*a*)	10. (*)
11. (*b*)	12. (*a*)	13. (*a*)	14. (*a*)	15. (*d*)	16. (*b*)	17. (*d*)	18. (*a*)	19. (*d*)	20. (*a*)
21. (14)	22. (18)	23. (*b*)	24. (*d*)	25. (*b*)	26. (*d*)	27. (*b*)	28. (*a*)	29. (*a*)	30. (*d*)
31. (*d*)	32. 160	33. (20%)	34. (*b*)	35. (*d*)	36. (*d*)	37. (*b*)	38. (*c*)	39. (c)	40. (*c*)
41. (*d*)	42. (*b*)	43. (10000 to 10000)	44. (31)	45. (59)	46. (*b*)	47. (*d*)	48. (*)	49. (*d*)	
50. (*b*)	51. (*c*)	52. (*d*)	53. (*d*)	54. (*d*)	55. (*c*)	56. (*a*)	57. (*a*)	58. (20 to 20)	
59. (*d*)	60. (1.68)	61. (14)	62. (24)	63. (76)	64. (0.05)	65. (4.72)	66. (*a*)	67. (*a*)	

EXPLANATIONS

1. Statement is true, main memory transfer the data in the form of block to cache and cache transfer the data in the form of words, so it enables the interleaved main memory unit to operate unit at maximum speed.

2. First, the system will look in cache 1. If it is not found in cache 1, then cache 2 and then further in main memory (if not in cache 2 also).

   The average access time would take into consideration success in cache 1, failure in cache 1 but success in cache 2, failure in both the caches and success in main memory.

   Average access time

   $$= [H_1 * T_1] + [(1 - H_1) * H_2 * T_2] + [(1 - H_1)(1 - H_2) * Hm * Tm]$$

   where,

   H_1 = Hit rate of level 1 cache = 0.8

   T_1 = Access time for level 1 cache = 1 ns

   H_2 = Hit rate of level 2 cache = 0.9

   T_2 = Access time for level 2 cache = 10 ns

   H_m = Hit rate of Main Memory = 1

   T_m = Access time for Main Memory = 500 ns

   So, Average Access Time

   $$= (0.8 * 1) + (0.2 * 0.9 * 10) + (0.2 * 0.1 * 1 * 500)$$
   $$= 0.8 + 1.8 + 10$$
   $$= 12.6 \text{ ns}$$

3. 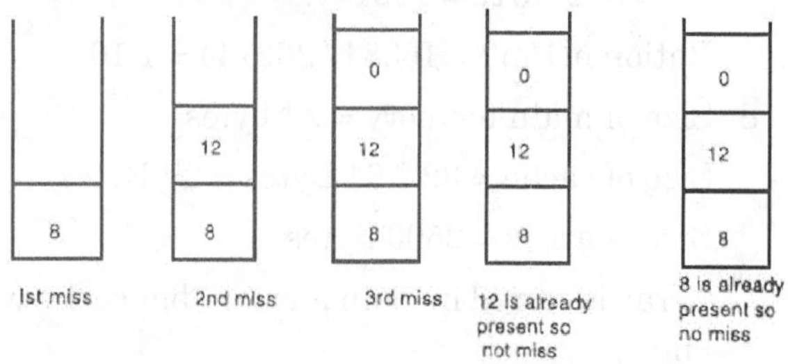

   So, total number of miss is (3).

4. For 1 GBps bandwidth ⇒ it takes 1 sec to load 109 bytes on line

   so, for 64 bytes it will take 64 * 1 /109 = 64 ns main memory latency given is 32

   so, total time required to place cache line is 64 + 32 = 96 ns

5. The main memory consists of 24 banks, each of 2 bytes. Since parallel accesses to all banks are possible, only two parallel accesses of all banks are needed to traverse the whole data.

   For one parallel access,

   $$\text{Total time} = \text{Decoding Time} + \text{Latency Time} = \frac{24}{2} + 80 = 92 \text{ ns}$$

   Hence, for 2 such accesses,

   $$\text{time} = 2 \times 92 = 184 \text{ ns}$$

6. [P2] runs the loops in a way that access elements of A in row major order and [P2] accesses elements in column major order.

No of cache blocks = Cache Size/Block Size

= 32KB / 128 Byte = 256

No. of array elements in Each Block

= Block Size/Element Size

= 128 Byte / 8 Byte = 16

Total Misses for [P1] = ArraySize * (No. of array elements in Each Block) / (No of cache blocks)

= 512 * 512 * 16/256

= 16384

7. Total Misses for [P1] = ArraySize * (No. of array elements in Each Block) / (No of cache blocks)

= 512 * 512 * 16 / 256 = 16384

Total Misses for [P2] = Total Number of elements in array (For every element, there would be a miss)

= 512 * 512 = 262144.

Ration m1/m2 = 16384 / 262144 = 1/16.

8. Size of main memory = 2^{16} bytes

Size of cache = 32 * 64 Bytes = 2^{11} Bytes

Size of array = 2500 Bytes

Array is stored in main memory but cache will be empty

Size of cache = 2048 Bytes

So number of page faults = 2500 – 2048

= 452

Complete array will be access twice

So for second access no. of total page faults

= 452 * 2

= 904

So total page faults = 452 + 904

= 1356

So data cache misses will be 56

9. Line 0 to Line 11.

10. No. of Block in cache = 128

$$\text{No. of set} = \frac{128}{4} = 32$$

Main Memory size = 16384 * 256 words

= $2^{14} * 2^{8}$ words

= 2^{22} words

(i) Number of bits required for addressing the main Memory is 22 bits.

(ii) Set associative Cache

← 22 bit →

Tag	Set No.	Word offset
← 9 bit →	← 5 bit →	← 8 bit →

No. of bits in word offset in 8 bits.

No. of set = 32 ⇒ 2^5 ⇒ 5 bits

No. of bits in Tag = 22 – (8 + 5) = 9 bits,

11. Since the cache has 2c blocks and there are 2 blocks per set, the cache thus has c sets. So, block *k* of the main memory would map to block (k mod c) of the cache.

12. Here, we have 32 bit virtual address space.

32 kB cache memory hence, we need 15 bit for occuring them (not all for indexing explained next).

So 17 used for tag.

But here cache are in block of 32 bytes. So, there actually 1 K (blocks) for a indexing 1 K location, we need 10 bits.

Remainder five are used for selecting byte

17 bit	10	5 bit
⇓	⇓	⇓
for tag	for cache index	for selecting byte within word (32 bytes)

13. 1. I-cache

Number of blocks in cache = 4K/4 = 2^{10} blocks.

Bits to represent blocks = 10

Number of words in a block = 4 = 2^2 words.

Bits to represent words = 2.

tag bits = 30 – (10 + 2) = 18.

Each block will have it's own tag bits.

So total tag bits =1K × 18 bits.

2. D-cache

Number of blocks in cache = 4K/4 = 2^{10} blocks.

Number of sets in cache = $2^{10}/2 = 2^9$ sets.

Bits to represent sets = 9.

Number of words in a block = 4 = 2^2 words.

Bits to represent words = 2

tag bits = 30 – (9 + 2) = 19

Each block will have it's own tag bits.

So total tag bits = 1K × 19 bits.

3. L2 cache

Number of blocks in cache = 64K/16 = 2^{12} blocks.

Number of sets in cache = $2^{12}/4$ = 1024 sets.

Bits to represent sets = 10

Number of words in cache = 16 = 2^4 words.

Bits to represent words = 4.

tag bits = 30 – (10 + 4) = 16

Each block will have it's own tag bits.

So total tag bits = 212 × 16-bits = 4K × 16-bits.

14. Block size = 32 byte = 25 byte

cache memory size = 32 KB

1st cache → 2-way set associative

Physical add res → 32bit

← 32 bit →

Tag	Set No.	Word offset
18	9	5

$$\text{No. of Block} = \frac{\text{Cache M. Size}}{\text{Block Size}} = \frac{32KB}{32B}$$

$= 2^{10}$ Blocks.

$$\text{No. of sets} = \frac{2^{10}}{2} = 2^9 \text{ sets}$$

$$h_1 = \frac{18}{10} + 0.6 \text{ ns}$$

$= 1.8 + 0.6 = 2.4$ ns

15. ← 32 bit →

17	10	5
Tag	Block No.	Offset

2nd cache Direct max

So $h_2 = \frac{17}{10}$ ns $= 1.7$ ns

16. For identifying each of 128 lines uniquely,

number of bits required = 7 bits.

Since each line is of size 64 words, so number of bits needed to identify each word uniquely = 6 bits.

Now, since there are 20 bits in address generated by CPU

∴ Bits needed for tag = 20 – (7 + 6) = 7 bits.

17. Size of main Memory = 1 MB = 2^{20} byte

Size of cache Memory = 8 KB

Block Size = 128 words ⇒ 2^7.

$$\text{No. of Block in Cache Memory} = \frac{8KB}{128} = 64$$

$$\text{No. of set's} = \frac{64}{4} = 16 \Rightarrow 2^4.$$

← 20 →

Tag	Set No.	Word offset
9	4	7

offset is from Block size ⇒ 2^7.

Tag = 20 – set no. – word offset

= 20 – 4 – 7

= 9

18.

Tag	Set No.	Word offset
9	4	7

Address = OC795H

in Binary = 000011000 (Tay) 1111 (Set No) 0010101 (offset)

Tag bit = 000011000

19.

Set	Block
Set 0	~~0~~ 48
	~~4~~ 32
	8
	~~216~~ 92
Set 1	1
	133
	129
	73
Set 2	
Set 3	~~255~~ 155
	3
	159
	63

20. Main Memor = 2^{20} byte

{∵ 20 bits for physical Add.}

Block size = 16 byte

cache lines = 2^{12}.

{∵ 12 bit for line number or block number)

← 20 bit →

Tag	Block No.	Offset
5	12	4

So for Main Memory Address $(E201F)_{16}$ dirst 4 dit is dor tag and next 12 bit for cache line

tag = E

Cache line = 201

Off set = F

21. Type of mapping is direct map; for this direct map, 10 bits are required in its Tag. It is updated to 16 way set Associative map then new tag field size = 10 + $\log_2 16$ = 14 bits, because for k way set associative map design, $\log_2 k$ bits are additionally required to the number of bits in tag field for Direct map design.

22. Total address space = 32 bit

offset bit (B) = 5 bit

No. of bit to represent line no (L) = 9.

Tag bit + B + L = 32

⇒ X + 5 + 9 = 32

⇒ X = 18

23. ← P bit →

Tag	Set No.	Offset

We can directly find the Tag bits if Main Memory size and cache memory size is give.

Main Memory size = 2^P byte.

cahce Memory size = 2^N byte

Set Associativity = K

tag = Main Memory bit – Cahce Memory bit + $\log_2$ (set Associate)

$$\boxed{tag = P - N + \log_2 K}$$

24. Cache memory is placed between main memory and CPU.

25. A disk driver is software which enables communication between internal hard disk (or drive) and computer.

It allows a specific disk drive to interact with the remainder of the computer.

26. Exploit the spatial locality of reference in a program as, if the next locality is addressed immediately, it will already be in the cache.

27. Statement I is not necessary because at the same point of time, data need not to be exactly same. Therefore, write back policy can also be used.

Statement II is not necessary when when discussing only about L1 and L2.

Statement III is not necessary because associativity can be equal.

Statement IV is necessary, The L2 cache must be at least as large as the L1 cache.

28. Number of sets in cache = v. So, main memory block j will be mapped to set (j mod v), which will be any one of the cache lines from (j mod v) * k to (j mod v) * k + (k – 1).

29. When associativity is doubled, then the set offset will be effected, accordingly, the number of bits used for TAG comparator be effected. Width of set index decoder also will be effected when set offset is changed. Width of wag selection multiplexer wil be effected when the block offset is changed. With of processor to main memory data bus is guaranteed to be NOT effected.

31. Cache memory size= 16 kB

Block size = 16 B

Main memory address = 32 bit

$$\text{Number of lines (N)} = \frac{16K}{16}$$

$$\Rightarrow \frac{2^{14}}{2^4} = 2^{10}$$

Fully associative cache memory (N-way)

$$\therefore \text{ number of sets (S)} = \frac{N}{\text{P-way}}$$

$$\therefore \frac{2^{10}}{2^{10}} = 1$$

32 bit

∴ Address format :

TAG	WO
28 bit	$\log_2 16$ = 4bit

∴ TAG = 28 bit

Index = 0 bit

32. Total time to transfer a cache block = 1 + 3 + 8
= 12 cycles
8 W ______ 12 cycles
8 × 4 bytes ______ 12 cycles
? B ______ 1 sec

$$= \frac{32B}{12 \times \left(\frac{1}{60} + 10^{-6}\right) \text{sec}}$$

= 160 × 10^6 bytes/sec

33. Main Memory access time = 10^{-8} sec ⇒ (ta_1)
Secondary Memo. access time = 10–3 sec ⇒ (ta_2)
Access efficiency (n) = 80% = 0.8
Average Access time

$$t_{avg} = n * ta_1 = 0.8 \times 10^{-3} \text{ sec}$$

for Hit ratio H

$$t_{avg} = H * ta_1 + (1 - H) * ta_2.$$

$$0.8 \times 10^{-3} = H * 10^{-8} + (1 - H) * 10^{-3}.$$

$$0.8 = H \times 10^{-5} + (1 - H)$$

$$H(1 - 10^{-5}) = 0.2$$

$$H = \frac{0.2}{(1 - 10^{-5})}$$

= 0.200002
= 20%

$\boxed{H = 20\%}$

34. Virtual memory concept is independent of size of main memory and depends only on the availability of the secondary storage.

35. Virtual memory is a concept which allows programs larger than the physical memory size to run.

36. Virtual memory increases the context switching overhead

37. Virtual memory concept is independent of size of main memory and depends only on the availability of the secondary storage.

38. Memory cycle time = 64 ns

Memory is refreshed 100 times per msec.

Number of refreshes in 1 memory cycle (i.e in 64 ns)

= (100 * 64 * 10 – 9)/10 – 3 = 64 * 10 – 4.

Time taken for each refresh = 100 ns

Time taken for 64 * 10 – 4 refreshes

= 64 * 10 – 4 * 100 * 10-9 sec

= 64 * 10 – 11 sec.

Percentage of the memory cycle time used for refreshing :

= (Time taken to refresh in 1 memory cycle/ Total time) * 100

= (64 * 10 – 11/64 * 10 – 9) * 100

= 1 %

39. As size increase, page frame increase. If we apply any replacement rule which is not cause 'blady anamoly' is always reduce page fault.

40. Number of chips required $= \frac{256 * 1024 * 8}{32 * 1024 * 1} = 64$

41. Main memory unit has capacity = 4 MB

Number of DRAM chips $= \frac{4\text{MB}}{1\text{M} \times 1\text{bit}} = 32$

1 DRAM chip has 1 K(2^{10}) rows and 1 K(2^{10}) cells

In each row = 32 × 2^{10} × 2^{10} = 32 × 2^{20}

Time taken in one refresh op^n = 100 ns

Time required to perform one refresh operation on all the cells in MM unit

= 32 × 2^{20} × 100 = 3200 × 2^{20} ns

42. RAM chip size = 1k × 8[1024 words of 8 bits each]

RAM to construct = 16k × 16

Number of chips required = (16k × 16)/(1k × 8)
= (16 × 2)

[16 chips vertically with each having 2 chips horizontally]

So to select one chip out of 16 vertical chips, we need 4 × 16 decoder.

Available decoder is 2 × 4 decoder

To be constructed is 4 × 16 decoder

Hence 4 + 1 = 5 decoders are required.

43. Each write request, the bus is occupied for 100 n.s

Storing of data requires 100 n.s.

In 100 n.s. – 1 store

$$\frac{100}{10^6} \text{ n.s.} = 1\text{store}$$

$$1 \text{ m.s.} = \frac{10^6}{100} \text{ stores}$$

= 10000 stores.

44. $\frac{2^{30+2}}{2} = 2^{31}$

So 31 bits required.

45. Given, total number of rows is 2^{14} and time taken to perform one refresh operation is 50 nanoseconds.

So, total time taken to perform refresh operation

$= 2^{14} * 50$ nanoseconds

= 819200 nanoseconds

= 0.819200 milliseconds.

But refresh period is 2 milliseconds.

So, time spent in refresh period in percentage

= (0.819200 milliseconds) / (2 milliseconds)

= 0.4096 = 40.96%

Hence, time spent in read/write operation

= 100% – 40.96% = 59.04% = 59

(in percentage and rounded to the closet integer).

46. Input to ROM – 2 lines, 8 bit each.

Possible combinations in ROM – (2^8) × (2^8)

Size of truth table = (2^8)*(2^8)

= 2^16 = 64 KB

Maximum output size = 16 bit

47. For a 4 bit multiplier there are $2^4 \times 2^4$

$= 2^8$

= 256 combinations.

Output will contain 8 bits.

So the amount of ROM needed is $2^8 \times$ 8bits = 2 Kbits.

48. Statement is true, main memory transfer the data in the form of block to cache and cache transfer the data in the form of words, so it enables the interleaved main memory unit to operate unit at maximum speed

49. Virtual Address = 32 bits

Cache address is divided into TAG, SET, BLOCK

For BLOCK of 16 bytes, we need 4 bits.

Total number of sets(each set containing 2 Blocks)

$= 64$ KB/(2 * 16) B $= 2^{11}$

So, Number of SET bits = 11

Number of TAG bits = 32 – (11 + 4) = 17

So, cache address = 17 |11| 4 (TAG |SET| BLOCK)

Tag memory size

= Number of tag bits * Total number of blocks

= 17 * 2 * 211 (Total Number of blocks

= 2 * Total number of sets)

= 68 KB

50. ARR[0][0] is located at virtual address 0xFF000000. Here FF000 is page address and 000 is page offset. So, index bits are 00000000000 Address of ARR[4][0] = 0xFF000 + 4 * 1024* size of (double) [since we use row major storage] = 0xFF000000 + 4096 * 8 = 0xFF000000 + 0x8000 = 0xFF008000 (index bits matches that of ARR[0][0] as both read 00000000000)

51. block size of cache = 16 bytes

element size = 8 bytes

During a memory access only the next element gets filled in the cache. i.e.; every alternative memory access is a cache miss giving a hit ratio of 50%.

52. A block to access in L2 cache requires 20 nanoseconds, and 2 seconds to place in L1-cache.

The block size in L1 cache is 4 words, and L2 block size is 16 words

So, total time = 4 * (time to access L2

+ time to place in L1)

= 4 * (20 + 2) = 88 ns.

53. Since the block size of L2 cache is 16 words and the bandwidth of main memory → L2 cache is 4 words, it requires a transfer of 4 words 4 times and then a transfer of required 16 words from L2 cache to L1 cache.

So total time is 4 * (200 + 20) + 4 * (20 + 2)

= 968 nano seconds.

54.

19 + 2	8	5
↓ TAG	↓ block offset	↓ Byte offset $=2^5$

$= \frac{2^{13}}{2^5} = 2^8$

Required answer = 256 × (19 + 2)

= 5376 bits

55. Number of blocks = Cache-Size/Block-Size

= 256 KB/32 Bytes

$= 2^{13}$

Number of Sets $= 2^{13}/4 = 2^{11}$

Tag no. + Set no. + offset = 32

Tag + 11 + 5 = 32

Tag = 16 bit

56. Tag is 16 bit, 2 bit valid, 1 modified, 1 replace

Total bits for tag entry = 16 + 2 + 1 + 1 = 20

Size of tag array = 20 × no. of blocks

= 160 K bits.

57. Miss ratio = (Cache miss)/(No. of request)

= n/N

58. Physical address size = 32 bits

Cache size = 16k bytes = 2^{14} Bytes

block size = 8 words = 8 × 4 Byte

= 32 Bytes

(where each word = b Bytes)

$$\text{No. of blocks} = \frac{2^{14}}{2^5} = 2^9$$

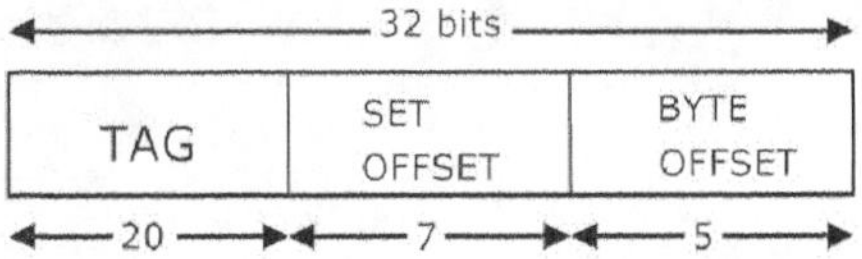

block offset = 9^{bits}

$$\text{No. of sets} = \frac{2^9}{4} = 2^7$$

set offset = 7 bits

Byte offset 8 × 4 Bytes = 32 Byte

= 2^5 = 5 bits

TAG = 32 – (7 + 5) = 20 bits.

59. When a cache block size is smaller, it could accommodate more number of blocks, it improves the hit ratio for cache, so the miss penalty for cache will be lowered.

60. Total instruction

$$= \frac{100\text{ instruction}}{\text{fetch operation}} + \begin{matrix}\text{60memory}\\ \text{operand read}\\ \text{operation}\end{matrix} + \frac{\text{40memory}}{\text{operand write op}}$$

= 200 instructions (operations)

Time taken for fetching 100 instructions (equivalent to read) = 90 * 1ns + 10*5ns =140ns

Memory operand Read operations

= 90% (60)* 1ns + 10% (60)× 5ns

= 54ns + 30 ns

= 84 ms

Memory operand write operation time = 90%(40)* 2ns + 10% (40)*10ns

= 72ns + 40 ns

= 112 ns

Total time taken for executing 200 instructions

= 140 + 84 + 112 = 336ns

$$\therefore \text{ Average memory access time} = \frac{336\text{ns}}{200} = 1.68 \text{ ns}$$

61. Average access time can be calculated as

0.8 × 5 + 0.2 × 50 = 14ns

62. Physical Address = Tag + Set + Offset

= 40 bits

Set = 8

Size of cache = 512 KB

line size is = 512 / 8 = 64 KB

So, Offset = 64/8 = 8 bits

Set + offset = 8 + 8 = 16 bits

so, Tag = 40 – 16 = 24 bits

63. In 1st iteration total 4 conflict Miss occur (for 0, 1, 127, 266)

The No of conflict Miss for second iteration is 8.

So for rest of all iteration it would be 8.

4 + 9 * 8 = 76.

64. As given, 1.4 memory accesses are required for one instruction execution.

So, for 1000 instructions, 1400 accesses are needed.

Number of misses occurred in cache L2 for 1000 instruction = 7/1400 = 0.005

Miss rate of L2 cache = misses occured in L2 cache / miss rate in L1 cache

= 0.005 / 0.1

= 0.05

65. Average Instruction fetch Time = L1 access time + L1 miss rate * L2 access time + L1 miss rate * L2 miss rate * Memory access time

= 2 + 0.2 × 8 + 0.2 × 0.1 × 90

= 5.4 ns

Average Data fetch Time = L1 access time + L1 miss rate * L2 access time + L1 miss rate * L2 miss rate * Memory access time

= 2 + 0.1 × 8 + 0.1 × 0.1 × 90

= 3.7 ns

So, average memory access time

= 0.6 × 5.4 + 0.4 × 3.7

= 4.72 ns

66. Given data

Hit time L_1 = 1 cycle

Hit time L_2 = 8 cycles

Miss penality L_2 = 18 cycles

Tavg = 2 ns

Miss rate $L_1 = 2x$

Miss rate $L_2 = x$

- Tavg = Hit time L_1 + (Miss rate L_1 × Miss penality L_1)

  T_{avg} = 2ns
- Miss penality L_1 = Hit time L_2 + (Miss rate L_2 × Miss penality L_2)
- Substitute the above data and verifying with respect to the given options.
- $L_1 = 0.111$ $L_2 = 0.056$

67. Time taken by the original design

= (2n * 2t) + (3n * t)

= 7nt

Time taken by enhanced design

= (2n * 2t /1.2) + (3n * t/1.1)

= 6.06 nt

Speed up = 7 nt/6.06 nt

= 1.155

2

CHAPTER

Instructions

Analysis of Previous GATE Papers

Units	Year → Topics ↓		2019	2018	2017 Set 1	2017 Set 2	2016 Set 1	2016 Set 2	2015 Set 1	2015 Set 2	2015 Set 3
INSTRUCTION	1 Mark	MCQ Type									
		Numerical Type									
	2 Marks	MCQ Type									
		Numerical Type		1	1		1				
	Total			2	2		2				
EXECUTION OF COMPLETE INSTRUCTION	1 Mark	MCQ Type									
		Numerical Type									
	2 Marks	MCQ Type									1
		Numerical Type		1				1			
	Total			2				2			2
MICROPROGRAM SEQUENCING	1 Mark	MCQ Type									
		Numerical Type									
	2 Marks	MCQ Type									
		Numerical Type								1	
	Total									2	
INS CYCLE & SUB-CYCLE	1 Mark	MCQ Type									
		Numerical Type									
	2 Marks	MCQ Type									
		Numerical Type									
	Total										
VERTICAL HORIZONTAL MICROPROG	1 Mark	MCQ Type									
		Numerical Type									
	2 Marks	MCQ Type									
		Numerical Type									
	Total										
HARDWIRED & MICROPROIGRAMMED CONTROL	1 Mark	MCQ Type									
		Numerical Type									
	2 Marks	MCQ Type									
		Numerical Type									
	Total										

INSTRUCTION

1. Which of the following is not a form of memory?
   (a) Instruction cache
   (b) Instruction Register
   (c) Instruction opcode
   (d) Translation look aside buffer

[2002 : 1 Mark]

2. For a pipelined CPU with a single ALU, consider the following situations
   1. The j + 1st instruction uses the result of the jth instruction as an operand
   2. The execution of a conditional jump instructioin
   3. The jth and j + 1st instructions require the ALU at the same time

   Which of the above can cause a hazard ?
   (a) 1 and 2 only
   (b) 2 and 3 only
   (c) 3 only
   (d) All the three **[2003 : 1 Mark]**

3. Which of the following statements about relative addressing mode is FALSE ?
   (a) It enables reduced instruction size
   (b) It allows indexing of array elements with same instruction
   (c) It enables easy relocation of data
   (d) It enables faster address calculations than absolute addressing

[2006 : 2 Marks]

4. Which of the following must be true for the RFE (Return from Exception) instruction on a general purpose processor.
   1. It must be a trap instruction
   2. It must be a privileged instruction
   3. An exception can not be allowed to occur during execution of an RFE instruction.

   (a) 1 only
   (b) 2 only
   (c) 1 and 2 only
   (d) 1, 2 and 3 only

[2008 : 2 Marks]

5. Consider two processors P1 and P2 executing the same instruction set. Assume that under identical conditions, for the same input, a program running on P2 takes 25% less time but incurs 20% more CPI (clock cycles er instruction) as compared to the program running on P1. If the clock frequency of P1 is 1GHz, then the clock frequency of P2 (in GHz) is .... **[2014 (Set-1) : 2 Marks]**

6. Suppose the functions F and G can be computed in 5 and 3 nanoseconds by functional units U_F and U_G, respectively. Given two instances of U_F and two instances of U_G, it is required to implement the computation $F(G(X_i)$ for $1 \le i \le 10$. Ignoring all other delays, the minimum time required to complete this computation is .... nanoseconds.

[2016 (Set-1) : 2 Marks]

7. **Consider** a RICS machine where each instruction is exactly 4 bytes long. Conditional and unconditional branch instructions use PC-relative addressing mode with Offset specified in bytes to the target location of the branch instruction. Further the Offset is always with respect to the address of the next instruction in the program sequence. Consider the following instruction sequence.

Instr. No	Instruction
i	add R2, R3, R4
i + 1	sub R5, R6, R7
i + 2	cmp R1, R9, R10
i + 3	beq R1, Offset

   If the target of the branch instruction is i, then the decimal value of the Offset is ....

[2017 (Set-1) : 2 Marks]

8. A processor has 16 integer registers (R0, R1, ..., R15) and 64 floating point registers (F0, F1, ..., F63). It uses a 2-byte instruction format. There are four categories of instructions : Type-1, Type-2, Type-3 and Type-4. Type-1 category consists of four instructions, each with 3 integer register operands (3 Rs.). Type 2-category consists of eight instructions, each with 2 floating point register operands (2Fs). Type-3 category consists of fourteen instructions, each with one integer register operand and one floating point register operand (1R + 1F). Type-4 category consists of N instructions, each with a floating point register operand (1F).

   The maximum value of N is .... **[2018 : 2 Marks]**

9. Arrange the following configuration for CPU in decreasing order of operating speeds : Hard wired control, vertical micro-programming, horizontal micro-programming.
   (a) Hard wired control, vertical micro-programming, horizontal micro-programming.
   (b) Hard wired control, horizontal micro-programming, vertical micro-programming.
   (c) Horizontal micro-programming, vertical micro-programming, Hard wired control.
   (d) Vertical micro-programming, horizontal micro-programming, hard wired control.

[1999 : 2 Marks]

10. The flags are affected when conditional CALL or JUMP instructions are executed.

[1990 : 2 Marks]

11. The microinstructions stored in the control memory of a processor have a width of 26 bits. Each microinstruction is divided into three fields: a micro-operation field of 13 bits, a next address field (X), and a MUX select field (Y).

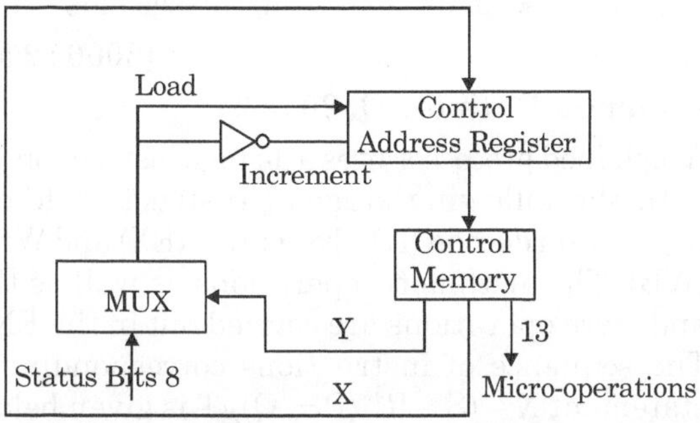

How many bits are there in the X and Y fields, and what is the size of the control memory in number of words ?

(a) 10, 3, 1024 (b) 8, 5, 256

(c) 5, 8, 2048 (d) 10, 3, 512

[2004 : 2 Marks]

EXECUTION OF COMPLETE INSTRUCTION

Common Date for Q. 12 to 13.

Consider the following assembly language program for a hypothetical processor. A, B and C are 8 bit registers. The meanings of various instructions are shown as comments.

```
    MOV B, #0 ;  B ← 0
    MOV C, #8 ;  C ← 8
Z : CMP C, #0 ;  Compare C with 0
    JZ  X     ;  Jump to X if 0 flag is set
    SUB C, #1 ;  C ← C – 1
    RRC A, #1 ;  Rotate right A through carry by
                 one bit
    JC  Y     ;  Jump to Y if any carry flag is set
    JMP Z     ;  Jump to Z
Y : ADD B, #1 ;  B ← B + 1
    JMP Z     ;  Jump to Z
X :
```

12. If the initial value of register A is A_0, the value of register B after the program execution will be

(a) the number of 0 bits in A_0

(b) the number of 1 bits in A_0

(c) A_0

(d) 8 **[2003 : 2 Marks]**

13. Which of the following instructions when inserted at location X will ensure that the value of register A after program execution is the same as its initial value?

(a) RRC A, # 1

(b) NOP; no operation

(c) LRC A, # 1; left rotate A through carry flag by one bit

(d) ADD A, # 1 **[2003 : 2 Marks]**

14. Consider the following program segment for a hypothetical CPU having three user registers R1, R2 and R3.

Instruction	Operation	Instruction Size (in words)
MOV R1,5000	; R1 ← Memory [5000]	2
MOV R2, (R1),	; R2 ← Memory [R1]	1
ADD R2, R3	; R2 ← R2 + R3	1
MOV 6000, R2	; Memory [6000] ← R2	2
HALT	; Machine halts	1

Let the clock cycles required for various operations be as follows :

Register to/from memory transfer.

3 clock cycles

ADD with both operands in register.

1 clock cycles

Instruction fetch and decode :

2 clock cycles per word

The total number of clock cycles required to execute the program is

(a) 29 (b) 24

(c) 23 (d) 20 **[2004 : 2 Marks]**

15. A 5 stage pipelined CPU has the following sequence of stages

IF - Instruction fetch from instruction memory.

RD - Instruction decode and register read,

EX - Execute : ALU operation for data and address computation.

MA - Data memory access – for write access the register read at RD stage it used,

WB - Register write back.

Consider the following sequence of instructions :

I_1 : L RO, Loc 1; RO ⇐ M[Loc1]

I_2 : A RO, RO; RO ⇐ RO + RO

I_3 : A R2, RO, R2 ⇐ R2 – RO

Let each stage take one clock cycle.

What is the number of clock cycles taken to complete the above sequence of instructions starting from the fetch of I1?

(a) 8 (b) 10

(c) 12 (d) 15 **[2005 : 2 Marks]**

Common Data for Q. 16 & 17

Consider the following data path of a CPU

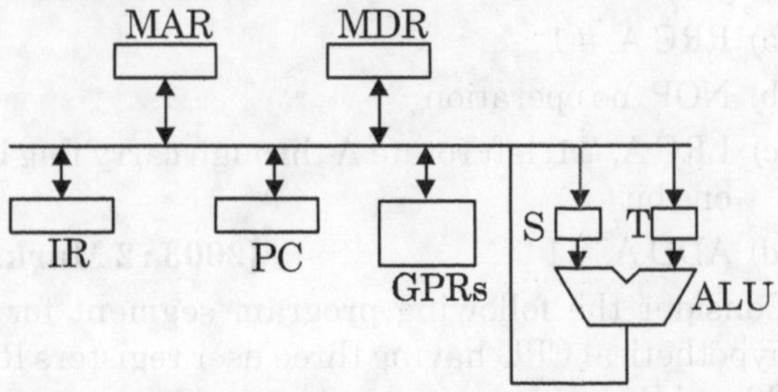

The, ALU, the bus and all the registers in the data path are of identical size. All operations including incrementation of the PC and the GPRs are to be carried out in the ALU. Two clock cylces are needed for memory read operation - the first one for loading address in the MAR and the next one for loading data from the memory but into the MDR.

16. The instruction "add R0, R1" has the register transfer interpretatio R0 < = R0 + R1. The minimum number of clock cycles needed for execution cycle of this instruction is

(a) 2 (b) 3

(c) 4 (d) 5 **[2005 : 2 Marks]**

17. The instruction "call Rn, sub" is a two word instruction. Assuming that PC is incremented during the fetch cycle of the first word of the instruction, its register transfer interpretation is

Rn ⇐ PC + 1;

PC ⇐M[PC];

The minimum number of CPU clock cycles needed during the execution cycle of this instruction is

(a) 2 (b) 3

(c) 4 (d) 5 **[2005 : 2 Marks]**

18. The memory locations 1000, 1001 and 1020 have data values 18, 1 and 16 respectively before the following program is executed.

MOVI	Rs. 1	Move immediate
LOAD	Rd, 1000(Rs)	Load from memmory
ADDI	Rd, 1000	Add immediate
STORE1	0(Rd), 20	Store immediate

Which of the following below is TRUE after the program is executed ?

(a) Memory location 1000 has value 20

(b) Memory location 1020 has value 20

(c) Memory location 1021 has value 20

(d) Memory location 1001 has value 20

[2006 : 2 Marks]

19. A CPU has five-stages pipeline and runs at 1 GHz frequency. Instruction fetch happens in the first stage of the pipeline. A conditional branch instruction computes the target address and evaluates the condition in the third stage of the pipeline. The processor stops fetching new instructions following a conditional branch until the branch outcome is known. A program executes 109 instructions out of which 20% are conditional branches. If each instruction takes only cycle to complete on average, then total execution time of the program is

(a) 1.0 second (b) 1.2 seconds

(c) 1.4 seconds (d) 1.6 seconds

[2006 : 2 Marks]

Common Data for Q. 20 & 21.

A pipelined processor uses a 4-stage instruction pipeline with the following stages : Instruction fetch (IF), Instruction decode (ID), Executive (EX) and Writeback (WB). The arithmetic operations as well as the load and store operations are carried out in the EX stage. The sequence of instructions corresponding to the statement X = (S – R* (P + Q))/T is given below. The values of variables P, Q, R, S and T are available in the registers R0, R1, R2, R3 and R4 respectively, before the execution of the instruction sequence.

ADD	R5, R0, R1	;	R5 → R0 + R1
MUL	R6, R2, R5	;	R6 → R2 * R5
SUB	R5, R3, R6	;	R5 → R3 – R6
DIV	R6, R5, R4	;	R6 → R5/R4
STORE	R6, X	;	X → R6

20. The number of Read-After-Write (RAW) dependencies, Write-After-Read (WAR) dependencies, and Write-After-Write (WAW) dependencies in the sequence of instructions are, respectively

(a) 2, 2, 4 (b) 3, 2, 3

(c) 4, 2, 2 (d) 3, 3, 2

[2006 : 2 Marks]

21. The IF, ID and WB stages take 1 clock cycle each. The EX stage takes 1 clock cycle each for the ADD, SUB and STORE operations, and 3 clock cycles each for MUL and DIV operations. Operand forwarding from the Ex stage to the ID stage is used. The number of clock cycles required to complete the sequence of instructions is

(a) 10 (b) 12

(c) 14 (d) 16

[2006 : 2 Marks]

22. A processor takes 12 cycles to complete an instruction 1. The corresponding pipelined processor uses 6 stages with the execution times of 3, 2, 5, 4, 6 and 2 cycles respectively. What is the asymptotic speedup assuming that a very large number of instructions are to be executed?

(a) 1.83 (b) 2

(c) 3 (d) 6

[2007 : 1 Marks]

23. Consider a pipelines processor with the following four stages

IF : Instruction Fetch

ID : Instruction Decode and Operand Fetch

Ex : Executive

WB : Write Back

The IF, ID and WB stages take one clock cycle each to complete the operation. The number of clock cycles for the EX stage depends on the instruction. The ADD and SUB instruction need 1 clock cycle and the MUL instruction need 3 clock cycles in the Ex stage. Operand forwarding is used in the pipelined processor. What is the number of clock cycles taken to complete the following sequence of instructions?

ADD	R2,	R1,	R0 $R2 \leftarrow R1 + R0$
MUL	R4,	R3,	R2 $R4 \leftarrow R3 * R2$
SUB	R6,	R5,	R4 $R6 \leftarrow R5 - R4$

(a) 7 (b) 8

(c) 10 (d) 14

[2007 : 2 Marks]

Common Data for Q,. 24 to 26

Consider the following program segment. Here R1, R2 and R3 are the general purpose registers.

Instruction	**Operation**	**Instruction size (no. of words)**
MOVI R1, (3000)	$R1 \leftarrow M[3000]$	2
LOOP :		
MOV R2, M [R3]	$R2 \leftarrow M[R3]$	1
ADD R2, R1	$R2 \leftarrow R1 + R2$	1
MOV (R3), R2	$M[R3] \leftarrow R2$	1
INC R3	$R3 \leftarrow R3 + 1$	1
DEC R1	$R1 \leftarrow R1 - 1$	1
BNZ LOOP	Branch on not zero	2
HALT	Stop	

Assume that the content of memory location 3000 is 10 and the content of the register R3 is 2000. The content of each of the memory locations from 2000 to 2010 is 100. The program is loaded from the memory location 1000. All the numbers are in decimal.

24. Assume that the memory is word addressable. The numebr of memory references for accessing the data in executing the program completely is

(a) 10 (b) 11

(c) 20 (d) 21

[2007 : 2 Marks]

25. Assume that the memory is word addressable. After the execution of this program, the content of memory location 2010 is

(a) 100 (b) 101

(c) 102 (d) 110

[2007 : 2 Marks]

26. Assume that the memory is byte addressable and the word size is 32 bits. If an interrupt occurs during the execution of the instruction "INC R3", what return address will be pushed on to the stack?

(a) 1005 (b) 1020

(c) 1024 (d) 1040 **[2007 : 2 Marks]**

27. A processor that has carry, overflow and sign flag bits as part of its program status word (PSW) performs addition of the following two 2's complement numbers 01001101 and 11101001. After the execution of this addition operation the status of the carry, overflow and sign flags, respectively will be :

(a) 1, 1, 0 (b) 1, 0, 0

(c) 0, 1, 0 (d) 1, 0, 1

[2008 : 1 Mark]

28. Consider the following code sequences having five instructions I1 to I5. Each of these instructions has the following format.

OP, Ri, Rj, Rk

where operation OP is performed on contents of registers Rj and Rk and the result the stored in register Ri.

I1 : ADD R1, R2, R3

I2: MUL R7, R1, R3

I3 : SUB R4, R1, R5

I4 : ADD R3, R2, R4

I5 : MUL R7, R8, R9

Consider the following three statements :

S1 : There is an anti-dependence between instructions I2 and I5.

S2 : There is an anti-dependence between instructions I2 and I4.

S3 : Within an instruction pipeline an anti-depenence always creates one or more stalls.

Which one of the above statements is/are correct?

(a) Only S1 is true

(b) Only S2 is true

(c) Only S1 and S3 are true

(d) Only S2 and S3 are true

[2015 (Set-3) : 2 Marks]

29. Consider a processor with 64 registers and an instruction set of size twelve. Each instruction has five distinct fields, namely, opcode, two source register identifies, one destination register identifer, and a twelve-bit immediate value. Each instruction must be stored in memory in a byte-aligned fashion. If a program has 100 instructions, the amount of memory (in bytes) consumed by the program text is ....

[2016 (Set-2) : 2 Marks]

30. The instruction pipeline of a RISC processor has the following stages. Instruction Fetch (IF), Instruction Decode (ID), Operand Fetch (OF), Perform Operation (PO) and Write back (WB). The IF, ID, OF and WB stages take 1 clock cycle each for every instruction. Consider a sequence of 100 instruments. In the PO stage, 4 instructions take 3 clock cycles each, 3 instructions take 2 clock cycles each, and the remaining 25 instructions take 1 clock cycle each. Assume that there are no data hazards and no control hazards.

The number of clock cycles required for completion of execution of the sequence of instructions is ....

[2018 : 2 Marks]

MICROPROGRAM SEQUENCING

31. If we use internal data forwarding to speed up the performance of A CPU (R1, R2 and R3 are registers and M[100] is a memory reference), then the sequence of operations

R1 → M[100]

M [100] → R2

M [100] → R3

can be replaced by

(a) R1 → R3
    R2 → M[100]

(b) M[100] → R2
    R1 → R2
    R1 → R3

(c) R1 → M[100]
    R2 → R3

(d) R1 → R2
    R1 → R3
    R1 → M[100]

[2004 : 2 Marks]

32. The data path shown in the figure computes the number of 1s in the 32-bit input word corresponding to an unsigned even integer stored in the shift register. The unsigned counter, intially zero, is incremented if the most significant bit of the shift register is 1.

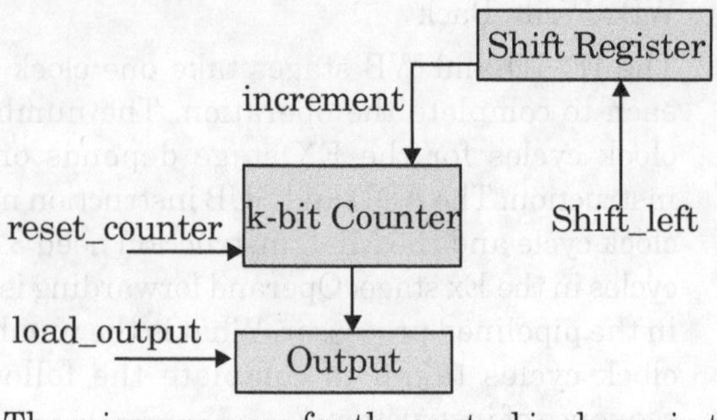

The microprogram for the control is shown in the table below with missing control words for microinstructions $I_1, I_2, ..., I_n$.

Micro-instruction	reset_counter	shift_left	load_output
BEGIN	1	0	0
I_1	?	?	?
:	:		:
I_n	?	?	?
END	0	0	1

The counter width (k), the number of missing microinstructions (n), and the control word for microinstructions I1, I2, ..., In are, respectively,

(a) 32, 5, 010
(b) 5, 32, 010
(c) 5, 31, 011
(d) 5, 31, 010

[2006 : 2 Marks]

33. Consider the following sequence of micro operations.

MBR ← PC

MAR ← X

PC ← Y

Memory ← MBR

Which one of the following is a possible operation performed by this sequence

(a) Instruction fetch
(b) Operand fetch
(c) Conditional branch
(d) Initiation of interrupt service **[2013 : 2 Marks]**

34. A micro program control unit is required to generate a total of 25 control signals. Assume that during any microinstruction at most two control signals are active. Minimum number of bits requuired in the control word to generate the required control signal

(a) 2
(b) 25
(c) 10
(d) 12 **[1996 : 2 Marks]**

INS CYCLE & SUB-CYCLE

Common Data for 35 to 36

Consider the following program segment for a hypothetical CPU having three user registers R1, R2 and R3.

Instruction	Operation	Instruction Size (in words)
MOV R1,5000	; R1 ← Memory [5000]	2
MOV R2, (R1),	; R2 ← Memory [R1]	1
ADD R2, R3	; R2 ← R2 + R3	1
MOV 6000, R2	; Memory [6000] ← R2	2
HALT	; Machine halts	1

35. Consider that the memory is byte addressable with size 32 bits, and the program has been loaded starting from memory location 1000 (decimal). If an interrupt occurs while the CPU has been halted after executing the HALT instruction, the return address (in decimal) saved in the stack will be

(a) 1007 (b) 1020

(c) 1024 (d) 1028

[2004 : 2 Marks]

36. Consider that the memory is word addressable with size 32 bits and the program has been loaded starting from memory location 1000 (decimal). If an interrupt occurs during the ADD instruction, what will be the return address pushed on to the stack.

(a) 1007 (b) 1004

(c) 1005 (d) 1016

[2004 : 2 Marks]

37. Consider a three word machine instruction ADD $A[R_0]$, @ B

The first operand (destination) "a [RO]" uses indexed addressing mode with RO as the index register. The second operand (source) "@B" uses indirect addressing mode. A and B are memory addresses residing at the second and the third words, respectively. The first word of the instruction specifies the opcode, the index register designation and the source and destination addressing modes. During execution of ADD instruction, the two operands are added and stored in the destination (first operand).

The number of memory cycles needed during the execution cycle of the instruction is

(a) 3 (b) 4

(c) 5 (d) 6

[2005 : 2 Marks]

38. Data forwarding techniques can be used to speed up the oeprations in presence of data dependencies. Consider the following replacements of LHS with RHS.

(i) R1 → Loc, Loc → R2 ≡ R1 → R2, R1 → Loc

(ii) R1 → Loc, Loc → R2 ≡ R1 → R2

(iii) R1 → Loc, R2 → Loc ≡ R1 → Loc

(iv) R1 → Loc, R2 → Loc ≡ R2 → Loc

In which of the following options, will be result of executing the RHS be the same as executing the LHS irrespective of the instructions that follow?

(a) (i) and (iii)

(b) (i) and (iv)

(c) (ii) and (iii)

(d) (ii) and (iv)

[2007 : 1 Marks]

39. Following table indicates the latencies of operations between the instruction producing the result and instruction using the result.

Instruction Production the result	Instruction using the result	Latency
ALU Operation	ALU Operation	2
ALU Operation	Store	2
Load	ALU Operation	1
Load	Store	0

Consider the following segment.

Load R1, Loc1;	Load R1 from memory location Loc1
Load R2, Loc2;	Load R2 from memory location Loc2
Add R1, R2, R1;	Add R1 and R2 and save result in R1
Dec R2;	Decrement R2
Dec R1;	Decrement R1
Mpy R1, R2, R3;	Multiply R1 and R2 and save result in R3
Store R3, Loc 3;	Store R3 in memory location Loc3

What is the number of cycles needed to executed the above code segment assuming each instruction takes one cycle to execute?

(a) 7

(b) 10

(c) 13

(d) 14

[2007 : 2 Marks]

40. Consider evaluating the following expressions tree on a machine with load-store architecture in which memory can be accessed only through load and store instructions. The variables a, b, c, d and e are initially stored in memory. The binary operators used in this expression tree can be evaluated by the machine only when the operands are in registers. The instructions produce result only in a register. If no intermediate results can be stored in memory, what is the minimum number of registers needed to evaluate this expression?

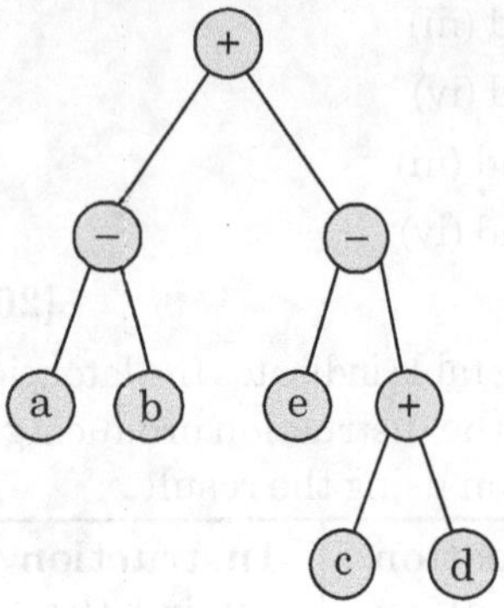

(a) 2 (b) 9
(c) 5 (d) 3 **[2011 : 2 Marks]**

41. Consider the sequence of machine instructions given below :

MUL	R5, R0, R1
DIV	R6, R2, R3
ADD	R7, R5, R6
SUB	R8, R7, R4

In the above sequence, R0 to R8 are general purpose registers. In the instructions shown, the first register stores the result of the operation performed on the second and the third registers. This sequence of instructions is to be executed in a pipelined instruction processor with the following 4 stags : (1) Instruction Fetch and Decode (IF), (2) Operand Fetch (OF), (3) Perform Operation (PO) and (4) Write back the Result (WB). The IF, OF and WB stages take 1 clock cycle each for any instruction. The PO stage takes 1 clock cycle for ADD or SUB instruction, 3 clock cycles for MUL instruction and 5 clock cycles for DIV instruction. The pipelined processor uses operand forwarding from the PO stage to the OF stage. The number of clock cycles taken for the execution of the above sequence of instructions is ....

[2015 (Set-2) : 2 Marks]

42. The use of multiple register windows with overlap causes a reduction in the number of memory accesses for

1. function locals and parameters
2. register saves and restores
3. instruction fetches

(a) 1 only
(b) 2 only
(c) 3 only
(d) 1, 2 and 3

[2008 : 2 Marks]

VERTICAL HORIZONTAL MICROPROG

43. Horizontal microprogramming

(a) does not require use of signal decoders
(b) results in larger sized microinstructions than vertical microprogramming
(c) uses one bit for each control signal
(d) All of the above

[2002 : 2 Marks]

44. An instruction set of a processor has 125 signals which can be divided into 5 groups of mutually exclusive signals as follows :

Group 1 : 20 signals, Group 2 : 70 signals, Group 3 : 2 signals, Group 4 : 10 signals, Group 5 : 23 signals.

How many bits of the control words can be saved by using vertical microprogramming over horizontal microprogramming ?

(a) 0 (b) 103
(c) 22 (d) 55

[2005 : 2 Marks]

45. Consider a CPU where all the instructions require 7 clock cycles to complete execution. There are 140 instructions in the instruction set. It is found that 125 control signals are needed to be generated by the control unit. While designing the horizontal micro-programmed control unit, single address field format is used for branch control logic. What is the minimum size of the control word and control address register?

(a) 125, 7
(b) 125, 10
(c) 135, 9
(d) 135, 10

[2008 : 2 Marks]

HARDWIRED & MICROPROIGRAMMED CONTROL

46. A CPU has only three instructions I1, I2 and I3, which use the following signals in time steps T1-T5.

I1 : T1 : Ain, Bout, Cin
T2 : PCout, Bin
T3 : Zout, Ain
T4: Pcin, BOut
T5 : End
I2 : T1 : Cin, Bout, Din
T2 : Aout, Ain
T3 : Zout, Ain
T4 : Bin, Cout
T5 : End
I3 : T1 : Din, Aout
T2 : Ain, Bout
T3 : Zout, Ain
T4 : Dout, Ain
T5 : End

Which of the following logic functions will generate the hardwired control for the signal Ain.

(a) T1.I1 + T2.I3 + T4.I3 + T3

(b) (T1 + T2 + T3) . I3 + T1. I1

(c) (T1 + T2) . I1+ (T2 + T4) . I3 + T3

(d) (T1 + T2) . I2+ (T1 + T3) . I1 + T3

[2004 : 2 Marks]

47. A hardwired CPU uses 10 control signals S1 to S10 in various time steps T1 to T5 to implement 4 instructions I1 to I4 as shown below.

	T1	T2	T3	T4	T5
I1	S1, S3, S5	S2, S4, S6	S1, S7	S10	S3, S8
I2	S1, S3, S5	S8, S9, S10	S4, S6, S7	S6	S10
I3	S1, S3, S5	S7, S8, S10	S2, S6, S9	S10	S1, S3
I4	S1, S3, S5	S2, S6, S7	S5, S10	S6, S9	S10

Which of the following pairs of expressions represent the circuit for generating control signals S5 and S10 respectively [(IJ + Ik) Tn indicates that the control signals should be generated in time step Tn if the instruction being executed is IJ or lk]?

(a) S5 = T1 + T2.T3 and
S10 = (I1 + I3).T4 + (I2 + I4).T5

(b) S5 = T1 + (I2 + I4).T3 and
S10 = (T1 + I3).T4 + (I2 + I4).T5

(c) S5 = T1 + (I2 + I4).T3 and
S10 = (I2 + I3 + I4).T2 + (I1 + I3).T4 + (I2 + I4).T5

(d) 5 = T1 + (I2 + I4).T3 and
s10 = (I2 + I3).T2 + I4.T3 + (I1 + I3).T4 + (I2 + I4).T5

[2005 : 2 Marks]

ANSWERS

1. (*c*)	**2.** (*d*)	**3.** (*d*)	**4.** (*d*)	**5.** (1.6)	**6.** (28)	**7.** (–16)	**8.** (32)	**9.** (*b*)	**10.** (false)
11. (*a*)	**12.** (*b*)	**13.** (*a*)	**14.** (*b*)	**15.** (*b*)	**16.** (*b*)	**17.** (*b*)	**18.** (*d*)	**19.** (*c*)	**20.** (*c*)
21. (*b*)	**22.** (*b*)	**23.** (*b*)	**24.** (*d*)	**25.** (*a*)	**26.** (*c*)	**27.** (*b*)	**28.** (*b*)	**29.** (500)	**30.** (219)
31. (*d*)	**32.** (*d*)	**33.** (*d*)	**34.** (*c*)	**35.** (*d*)	**36.** (*b*)	**37.** (*b*)	**38.** (None)	**39.** (*c*)	**40.** (*d*)
41. (13)	**42.** (*a*)	**43.** (*d*)	**44.** (*b*)	**45.** (*d*)	**46.** (*a*)	**47.** (*d*)			

EXPLANATIONS

1. Instruction opcode is not a memory.

2. (*i*) j + 1st instruction uses result of the jth instruction as an operand, then read-after-write (RAW) hazard occurs. It is a part of data dependency.

   (*ii*) Execution of a conditional jump instruction causes a flushing so conditional dependency occurs.

   (*iii*) jth and j + 1st instructions require the ALU at the same time causes write-after-read (WAR) hazard.

3. As relative address are calculated from absolute address, So relative addressing cannot be faster than absolute addressing.

4. For any exception, while executing RFE, no exception is alllowed (no interrupts). It is a priveleged instruction, as soon as exception occurs RFE is called (executed).

5. 1 cycle time for $p_1 = \frac{10^9}{1GH} = 1n.s$

   Assume p_1 takes 5 cycles for a program then p_2 takes 20% more, means, 6 cycles.

   p_2 Takes 25% less time, means, if p_1 takes 5 n.s, then p_2 takes 3.75 n.s.

   Assume p_2 clock frequency is x GHz.

   p_2 taken 6 cycles, so $\frac{6\times10^9}{xGH} = 3.75,\ x = 1.6$

6. There are two functional units each unit get 5 numbers of units to compute on. Suppose computation starts at time 0.

   which means G starts at 0 and F starts at 3rd second since G finishes computing first element at third second.

   Time at which F ends computing = 3 + 5 * 5 = 28

7.

Instruction	Butes
i	0 – 3
i + 1	4 – 7
i + 2	8 – 11
i + 3	12 – 15

Next Instruction ⇒ 16

Effective PC address = Next Address to offset

0 = 16 + offset

[offset = –16]

8. Instruction size = 16 bit

   Type I instruction design:

   16 bit

opcode	IR	IR	IR
4 bit	4 bit	4 bit	4 bit

   Number of operations = 2^4

   = 16

   ↓

   Face opcodes = 16 – 4 = 12

   Type II instruction design:

   16 bit

opcode	FR	FR
4 bit	6 bit	6 bit

   Face opcodes after type 1 instruction = 12

   Face opcodes after type 2 instruction = 12 – 8 = 4

   Type III instruction design:

   16 bit

opcode	IR	FR
6 bit	4 bit	4 bit

   Expand opcode size = 6 bit

   ↓

   Number of opcodes = $4 \times 2^2 = 16$

   ∴ Number of free opcodes after type 3 instruction

   = 16 – 14 = 2

   Type IV instruction design:

   16 bit

opcode	*FR*
10 bit	6 bit

   Expand opcodes size = 10 bit

   ↓

   Number of opcodes = $2 \times 2^4 = 2^5 = 32$

9. Hardwired control is the fastest. Since horizontal microprogramming involves lesser number of instructions, it is faster than vertical microprogramming.

10. False. Flags are tested during conditional call and jump not affected or changed.

11. Control memory processor has 26 bit microinstruction divided into three field microoperation field is 13.

    So, next address field (X) = 10

    MAX select field = 3

    Size of control = $2^{10} = 1024$

12. The value of B after execution of the program is number of 1 bits in A0 because Jump is occur only when carry flag is set to 1.

13. X : RRC A, # 1 then the value of A is same as its actual value.

14. OperationInstruction Required

	Size	Clock cycles
$R_1 \leftarrow$ Memory [500]	2	6 + 2 = 8
$R_2 \leftarrow$ Memory [(R_1)]	1	3 + 2 = 5
$R_2 \leftarrow (R_2 + R_3)$	1	1 = 1
Memory [6000] $\leftarrow R_2$	2	6 + 2 = 8
Machine Halt	1	1 + 1 = 2
	Total = 24	

15. Clock Cycles

	1	2	3	4	5	6	7	8	9	10
R_0 = M[Loc 1]	IF	RD	EX	MA	WB					
$R_0 = R_0 + R_0$			IF	RD	EX	MA	WB			
$R_2 = R_2 - R_0$						IF	RD	EX	MA	WB

So it requires 10 CPU clock cycles.

16. RTL $R_0 \Rightarrow R_0 + R_1$

Sequence of micro-instruction takes place in following cycles:

I cycle : R_{1out}, S_{in}

II cycle : R_{2out}, T_{in}

III cycle : S_{out}, T_{out}, ALU_{add}, R_{in}

Hence 3 cycles will be required to execute.

17. RTL R_n = PC + 1

P_c = M[Pc]

Sequence of micro-instrution take place in following cycles:

I cycle : PC_{out}, S_{in}, MAR_{in} (MAR can be loaded with PC_{out})

II cycle : S_{out}, $ALU_{increment}$, $R_{n\ in}$

III cycle : MDR_{out}, PC_{in} (MDR_{out} can be performed once MAR_{in} has been performed)

Hence 3 cycles will be required to execute.

18. Rs = 1

Rd = 1

Rd = 1001

M[1001] = 20

19. In the 3rd stage of pipeline, there will be 2 stall cycles i.e. 2 delay slots.

Total number of instructions = 109

= (0.2 * (2 + 1) + 0.8 * 1) * 10^9

= 1.4 sec

20. Read After Write:

1. ADD → MUL (beacuse of R5)
2. MUL → SUB (beacuse of R6)
3. SUB → DIV (beacuse of R5)
4. DIV → STORE (beacuse of R6)

Write After Read

1. MUL → SUB (beacuse of R5)
2. DIV → STORE (beacuse of R6)

Write After Write

1. ADD → SUB (beacuse of R5)
2. MUL – DIV (beacuse of R6)

21. (*) operand forwarding is used.

	IF	ID	Ex	WB
1	I_1			
2	I_2	I_1		
3	I_3	I_2	I_1	
4	I_4	I_3	I_2	I_1
5	I_5		I_2	
6			I_2	
7		I_4	I_3	I_2
8		I_5	I_4	I_3
9			I_4	
10			I_4	
11			I_5	I_4
12				I_5

(*) I_1 = ADD

I_2 = MUL

I_3 = SUB

I_4 = DIV

I_5 = Store

22.

$$\text{Speed up Ration} = \frac{\text{Non Pipeline Time}}{\text{Pipeline time}}$$

$$= \frac{t_n * n}{(K + n -) * tp}$$

$$= \frac{12 * n}{(6 + n - 1) * 6}$$

$$= \frac{12n}{(5 + n) * 6}$$

$$\lim_{n \to \infty} \frac{12n}{30 + 6n} \Rightarrow \frac{12}{6} = 2$$

23. For each of the three instruction four stages will be there. Since ,it is a pipelined processor, so one instruction may be fetched while other is being decoded or executed or written back action performed in each clock cycle may be represented as

Clock Cycle	ADD	MUL	SUB
1	IF		
2	ID	IF	
3	EX	ID	IF
4	WB	EX	ID
5		EX	
6		EX	
7		WB	EX
8			WB

Only, two instructions cannot be executed simulteneously.

24. Ist memory reference R1 ← M[3000] and then in the loop which runs for 10 times, because the content of memory location 3000 is 10 given in question and loop will run 10 times as

{
R2 ← M[R3]
M[R3] ← R2
}

So Two memory reference every iteration

$$10 * 2 = 20$$

$$\text{Total} = 20 + 1 = 21$$

25. The given program stores results from memory loacation 2000 to 2009.

It stores values like 110,109,108....100.

No change at loacation 2010 So at 2010 value is 100

26.

Introduction	word	location
Mov R_1, 3000	2	1000 to 1007
Mov R_2,R_1	1	1008 to 1011
Add R_2, R_1	1	1010 to 1015
Mov (R_3), R_2	1	1016 to 1019
Mov (R_3), R_2	1	1020 to 1023

Now Interupt occur during execution of "INC R_3", so CPU will complete execute of "INC R_3", So CPU will complete Execute the instruction "InC R_3" and return address to serve interrupt is 1024.

27.

  01001101
+ 11101001

100110110 (in 2's complemet ignore carry bit so ignore 1 at msb)

After carry bit is ignored the value at msb is 0 meanse number is positive so sign bit is 0.

Overflow flag is set only if the X-OR between the carry-into the sign bit and carry -out of the sign bit is 1.

Therefore,

carry flag = 1,

overflow flag = 0,

sign bit = 0

28. An antidependency also known as write-after-read (WAR) dependency.

S1 is False, I2 and I5 they both write R7. So, No WAR.

S2 is true, There is an anti-dependence between instructions I2 and I4.

I2 reads R3 and I4 writes it.

S3 is false.depends on how many instruction between the antidependence instructions.

29. According to question

One instruction needs 34 bits

So number of bytes needed = 5 (Since 1 byte = 8 bits)

∴ Program size = 100

∴ Size of the memory (in bytes) = 500

So the amount of memory consumed by the program text is 500 bytes.

30.

	IF	ID	OF	PO	WB
Type(I_1)	1	1	1	3	1
Type(I_2)	1	1	1	2	1
Type(I_3)	1	1	1	1	1

$I_1 : 1 + 1 + 1 + 3 + 1 = 7$

I_2 :, I_3 : } usually takes cycles each due to overlapping

but I_1(PO) takes 2 cycles to add "1" cycle extra (2 + 1)

$\Rightarrow 7 + 8 + 1 = 10$

	1	2	3	4	5	6	7	8	9	10
I_1	IF	ID	OF	PO	PO	PO	WB			
I_2		IF	ID	OF	OF	OF	PO	PO	WB	
I_3			IF	ID	ID	ID	OF	OF	PO	PO

	IF	ID	OF	PO	WB
I_1	1	1	1	3	1
I_2	1	1	1	3	1
I_3	1	1	1	2	1
I_4	1	1	1	2	1
I_5	1	1	1	1	1
I_6	1	1	1	1	1

If Type 1 – 2 instruction

Type 2 – 2 instruction

Type 3 – 2 instruction

$I_1 : 1 + 1 + 1 + 3 + 1 = 7$

I_2 : 1 + 2 extra cycles = 3

I_3 : 1 + 1 extra cycles = 2

I_4 : 1 + 1 extra cycles = 2

I_5 : 1 extra cycles = 1

I_6 : 1 extra cycles = 1 = 16

	1	2	3	4	5	6	7	8	9	10	11	12	13	14	15	16
I_1	IF	ID	OF	PO	PO	PO	WB									
I_2		IF	ID	OF	OF	OF	PO	PO	PO	WB						
I_3			IF	ID	ID	ID	OF	OF	OF	PO	PO	WB				
I4				IF	IF	IF	ID	ID	ID	OF	OF	PO	PO	WB		
I_5							IF	IF	IF	ID	ID	OF	OF	PO	WB	
I_6										IF	IF	ID	ID	OF	PO	WB

In this way, if we compute 100 instruction number of cycles required is

If ID OF PO WB

$\Rightarrow 1 + 1 + 1 + [(40 \times 3) + (35 \times 2)\ (25 \times 1)] + 1$

$\Rightarrow 219$

31. To achive speedup we can transfer directly like the code given below.

$R1 \rightarrow R2$

$R1 \rightarrow R3$

$R1 \rightarrow M[100]$

32. If number is even then LSB bit should be 0.

So total 31 1's for an unsigned EVEN integer.

And 31 left shifts are needed to determine number of 1's.

33. Given: A sequence of micro operations

MBR ← PC

MAR ← X

PC ← Y

Memory ← MBR

To find: What these micro operation represents?

Analysis: On converting these operations to normal english

1. First micro operation stores the value of PC into memory Base register (MBR)
2. Second micro operation stores value of X into Memory Address register (MAR)
3. Third micro operation stores value of Y into PC
4. Fourth micro operation stores value of MBR to memory.

So before execution of these instructions PC holds the value of next instruction to be executed. We first stores the value of PC to MBR and then through MBR to memory i.e. we are saving the value of PC in memory and then load PC with a new value. This can be done only in two types of operations conditional branch and interrupt service. As we are not checking here for any conditions so it is interrupt service.

35.

Instruction	Instruction size	Location (Decimal)
MOV R_1, 1000	2	1000 to 1007
MOV R_2, (R1)	1	1008 to 1011
ADD R_2, R_3	1	1012 to 1015
MOV 1005, R_2	2	1016 to 1023
Halt	1	1024 to 1027

If an interrupt occurs the CPU has been halted after executing the HALT instruction the return address 1028 saved in the stack

36. If memory is word addresable then 1st instruction requier two words space (1000 – 1001) 2nd instruction requiers only 1 word space (1002) and instruction 3rd requiers only 1 word space (1003) hence 3rd is add instruction and interrupt occurs during that so after executing that instruction CPU handles the interrupt so return address is 1004

37. In Indexed addressing mode, the base address is already in the instruction i.e A and to fetch the index data from R0 no memory access is required because it's a register So to fetch the operand only 1 memory cycle is required. Indirect Addressing mode requires 2 memory cycles only

38. Only (i) Is true, as both registers and location are updated.

39.

CC	Instruction
1	I_1
2	I_2
3	
4	I_3
5	I_4
6	
7	I_5
8	
9	
10	I_6
11	
12	
13	I_7

Total 13 clock cycle.

40. R1 ← c, R2 ← d, R2 ← R1 + R2, R1 ← e, R2 ← R1-R2

Now to calculate the rest of the expression we must load a and b into the registers but we need the content of R2 later. So we must use another Register.

R1 ← a, R3 ← b, R1 ← R1 – R3, R1 ← R1 + R2

41.

1	2	3	4	5	6	7	8	9	10	11	12	13
			IF	-	-	OF					PO	WB
		IF	-		OF					PO	WB	
	IF	OF	-	-	PO	PO	PO	PO	PO	WB		
IF	OF	PO	PO	PO	WB							

Total clock cycle require = 13

42. I is true as by using multiple register windows, we eliminate the need to access the variable values again and again from the memory. Rather, we store them in the registers.

43. All statements are true.

44. No. of bits for horizontal M.P. is = 125

No of bits for vertical M.P. is

Group	No of bits
1.	$\log_2(20) = 5$
2.	$\log_2(70) = 7$
3.	$\log_2(2) = 1$
4.	$\log_2(10) = 4$
5.	$\log_2(23) = 5$

So, 5 + 7 + 1 + 4 + 5 = 22 bits.

No. of bits saved = 125 – 22 103 bits.

45. As per question each instruction takes 7 cycles

= 140 instructions will take = 140 * 7 cycles

= 2m> = 980

= m> = 10

= 10 + 125 bits and 10 bits

46. T1.I1 + T2.I3 + T4.I3 + T3

47. s5 = T1 + (I2 + I4).T3 and

s10 = (I2 + I3).T2 + I4.T3 + (I1 + I3).T4 + (I2 + I4).T5

3 CHAPTER

Functionality of Digital System

Analysis of Previous GATE Papers											
Units	Year → Topics ↓		2019	2018	2017 Set 1	2017 Set 2	2016 Set 1	2016 Set 2	2015 Set 1	2015 Set 2	2015 Set 3
ADDRESSING MODE	1 Mark	MCQ Type							1		
		Numerical Type									
	2 Marks	MCQ Type			1				1		
		Numerical Type						1			
	Total				2			2	3		
NS	1 Mark	MCQ Type									
		Numerical Type									
	2 Marks	MCQ Type									
		Numerical Type									
	Total										
MEMORY BASICS	1 Mark	MCQ Type									
		Numerical Type									
	2 Marks	MCQ Type									
		Numerical Type									
	Total										

ADDRESSING MODE

1. The most appropriate matching for the following pairs

X. Indirect addressing	1. Loops
Y. Immediate addressing	2. Pointers
Z. Auto decrement	3. Constant

(a) X – 3 Y – 2 Z – 1

(b) X – 1 Y – 3 Z – 2

(c) X – 2 Y – 3 Z – 1

(d) X – 3 Y – 1 Z – 2

[2000 : 1 Mark]

2. In serial data transmission, every byte of data is padded with a '0' in the beginning and one or two '1' at the end of byte because

(a) Receiver is to be synchronized for byte reception

(b) Receiver recovers lost '0' and '1' s from these padded bits

(c) Padded bits are useful in parity computation

(d) None of the above

[2002 : 1 Mark]

3. Which of the following addressing modes are suitable for program relocation at run time?

1. Absolute addressing
2. Based addressing
3. Relative addressing
4. Indirect addressing

(a) 1 and 4

(b) 1 and 2

(c) 2 and 3

(d) 1, 2 and 4

[2004 : 1 Mark]

4. Match List-I with List-II and selected the correct answer using the codes given below the lists :

List-I	**List-II**
A. A[I] = B[J]	1. Indirect addressing
B. while [*A++]	2. Indexed addressing
C. int temp = *x;	3. Autoincrement

Codes :

	A	B	C
(a)	3	2	1
(b)	1	3	2
(c)	2	3	1
(d)	1	2	3

5. A CPU has 24-bit instructions. A program starts at address 300 (in decimal). Which one of the following is a legal program counter (all values in decimal)?

(a) 400 (b) 500

(c) 600 (d) 500

[2006 : 1 Mark]

6. Assume that EA = (X) + is the effective address equal to the contents of location X, with X incremented by one word length after the effective address is calculated; EA = –(X) is the effective address equal to the contents of location X, with x decremented by one word length before the effective address is calculated; EA = (X)– is the effective address equal to the contents of location X, with X decremented by one word length after the effective address is calculated. The format of the instruction is (opcode, source, destination), which means (destination ← source op destination). Using X as a stack pointer, which of the following instructions can pop the top two elements from the stack, perform the addition operation and push the result back to the stack.

(a) ADD (X)–, (X)

(b) ADD (X), (X)–

(c) ADD –(X), (X)+

(d) ADD –(X), (X)

[2008 : 2 Marks]

7. Th program below uses six temporary variable a, b, c, d, e, f.

a = 1
b = 10
c = 20
d = a + b
e = c + d
f = c + e
b = c + e
e = b + f
d = 5 + e
return d + f

Assuming that all operations take their operands from registers, what is the minimumb number of registers needed to execute this program without spilling ?

(a) 2 (b) 3

(c) 4 (d) 6

[2010 : 2 Marks]

8. Consider a hypothetical processor with a instruction of type LW R1, 20(R2), which during execution reads a 32-bit word from memory and stores it in a 32-bit register R1. The effective address of the memory location is obtained by the addition of a constant 20 and the contents of register R2. Which of the following best reflects the addressing mode implemented by this instruction for the operand in memory?

(a) Immediate Addressing

(b) Register

(c) Register-Indirect Scaled Addressing

(d) Base Indexed Addressing **[2011 : 1 Mark]**

9. A machine has a 32-bit architecture, with 1 word long instructions. It has 64 registers, each of which is 32 bits long. It needs to support 45 instructions, which have an immediate operand in addition to two register operands. Assuming that the immediate operand is an unsigned integer, the maximum value of the immediate operand is ....

[2014 (Set-1) : 1 Marks]

10. For computers based on three-address instruction formats, each address field can be used to specify which of the following :

S1 : A memory operand

S2 : A processor register

S3 : An implied accumulator register

(a) Either S1 or S2 (b) Either S2 or S3

(c) Only S2 and S3 (d) All of S1, S2 and S3

[2015 (Set-1) : 1 Mark]

11. Consider a processor with byte-addressable memory. Assume that all registers, including Program Counter (PC) and Program Status Word (PSW), are of size 2 bytes. A stack in the main memory is implemented from memory location $(0100)_{16}$ and it grows upward. The stack pointer (SP) points to the top element of the stack. The current value of SP is $(016E)_{16}$. The CALL instruction is of two words, the first word is the op-code and the second word is the starting address of the subroutine (one word = 2 bytes). The CALL instruction is implemented as follows:

Store the current value of PC i the stack.

Store the vale of PSW register i the stack.

Load the starting address of teh subroutine in PC.

the content of PC just before the fetch of a CALL instruction is $(5FAO)_{16}$. After execution of the CALL instruction, the value of the stack pointer is

(a) $(016A)_{16}$ (b) $(016C)_{16}$

(c) $(0170)_{16}$ (d) $(0172)_{16}$

[2015 (Set-2) : 2 Marks]

12. A processor has 40 distinct instructions and 24 general purpose registers. A 32-bit instruction word has an opcode, two register operands and an immediate operand. The number of bits available for the immediate operand field is ....

[2016 (Set-2) : 2 Marks]

13. Consider the C struct defined below :

```
Struct data {
    int marks [100];
    char grade;
    int cnumber;
};
struct data student;
```

The base address of student is available in register R1. The field student, grade can be accessed efficiently using

(a) Post-increment addressing mode, (R1) +

(b) Pre-decrement addressing mode, - (R1)

(c) Register direct addressing mode, R1

(d) Index addressing mode, X(R1). where X is an offset represented in 2's complement 16-bit representation.

[2017 (Set-1) : 2 Marks]

14. Which of the most appropriate match for the items in the first column with the items i the second column

List-I	List-II
X. Indirect Addressing	I. Array implementation
Y. Indexed Addressing	II. Writing re-locatable code
Z. Base Register Addressing	III. Passing array as parameter

(a) (X, III) (Y, I) (Z, II)

(b) (X, II), (Y, III) (Z, I)

(c) (X, III), (Y, II) (Z, I)

(d) (X, I), (Y, III) (Z, II)

15. The absolute addressing mode

(a) the operand is inside the instruction

(b) the address of the operand is inside the instruction

(c) the register containing the address of the operand is specified inside the instruction

(d) the location of the operand is implicit

[2002 : 1 Mark]

16. Which of the following is/are true of the auto increment addressing mode ?

1. It is useful in creating self relocating code
2. If it is included in an Instruction Set Architecture, then an additional ALU is required for effective address caculation
3. The amount of increment depends on the size of the data item accessed.

(a) 1 only (b) 2 only
(c) 3 only (d) 2 and 3 only

[2008 : 2 Marks]

NS

17. In 2's complement addition, overflow

(a) is flagged whenever there is carry from sign bit addition
(b) cannot occur when a +ve value is added to a –ve value
(c) is flagged when the carries from sign bit and previous bit match
(d) None of the above

[2002 : 1 Mark]

18. Using a 4-bit 2's complement arithmetic, which of the following additions will result in an overflow?

(i) 1100 + 1100 (ii) 0011 + 0111
(iii) 1111 + 0111

(a) (i) only (b) (ii) only
(c) (iii) only (d) (i) and (iii) only

[2004 : 2 Marks]

19. Consider an array multiplier for multiplying two n bit numbers. If each gate in the circuit has a unit delay, the total delay of the multiplier is

(a) $\Theta(1)$ (b) $\Theta(\log n)$
(c) $\Theta(n)$ (d) $\Theta(n^2)$ **[2003 : 1 Mark]**

MEMORY BASICS

20. RAID configurations of disks are used to provide

(a) fault-tolerance (b) high speed
(c) high data density (d) None of these

[1999 : 2 Marks]

21. The correct matching for the following pairs is

A. DMA I/O	1. High speed RAM
B. Cache	2. Disk
C. Interrupt	3. Printer
D. Condition code Register	4. ALU

Codes :

(a) A – 4, B – 3, C – 1, D – 2
(b) A – 2, B – 1, C – 3, D – 4
(c) A – 4, B – 3, C – 2, D – 1
(d) A – 2, B – 3, C – 4, D – 1 **[1997 : 1 Mark]**

22. Formatting of floppy disk refers to

(a) arranging the data on the disk in contiguous fashion
(b) writing the directory
(c) erasing the system area
(d) writing identification information on all tracks and sectors **[1998 : 2 Mark]**

23. A disk has 8 equidistant tracks. The diameters of the innermost and outermost tracks are 1 cm and 8 cm respectively. The innermost track has a storage capacity of 10 MB.

What is the total amount of data that can be stored on the disk if it is used with a drive that rotates it with (i) Constant Linear Velocity (ii) Constant Angular Velocity?

(a) (i) 80 MB (ii) 2040 MB
(b) (i) 2040 MB (ii) 80 MB
(c) (i) 80 MB (ii) 360 MB
(d) (i) 360 MB (ii) 80 MB

[2005 : 2 Marks]

24. For a magnetic disk with concentric circular tracks, the latency is not linearly proportional to the seek distance due to

(a) non-uniform distribution of requests
(b) arm starting and stopping inertia
(c) higher capacity of tracks on the periphery of the platter
(d) use of unfair arm scheduling policies.

[2008 : 2 Marks]

ANSWERS

1. (*c*)	**2.** (*a*)	**3.** (*c*)	**4.** (*c*)	**5.** (*c*)	**6.** (*a*)	**7.** (*b*)	**8.** (*d*)	**9.** (16383)	**10.** (*a*)
11. (*d*)	**12.** (16)	**13.** (*d*)	**14.** (*a*)	**15.** (*b*)	**16.** (*c*)	**17.** (*b*)	**18.** (*b*)	**19.** (*c*)	**20.** (*a, b*)
21. (*b*)	**22.** (*d*)	**23.** (*d*)	**24.** (*b*)						

EXPLANATIONS

1. In Indirect addressing mode the instruction does not have the address of the data to be operated on, but the instruction points where the address is stored.

   In immediate addressing mode the data is to be used is immediately given in instruction it self; so it deals with constant data.

   In Auto decrement addressing mode, Before determining the effective address, the value in the base register is decremented by the size of the data item which is to be accessed.

2. In serial data transmission, every byte of data is padded with a '0' in the beginning and one or two '1' at the end of byte because receiver is to be synchronized for byte reception.

3. For address reloaction we can use Based addressing , Relative addressing modes.

4. Correct matching:

1. A[1] = B[J]	Indexed Addressing Mode
2. While [*A++]	Autoincrement
3. int temp = *x;	Indirect Addressing Mode

5. Size of instruction = 24/8 = 3 bytes.

   So Program Counter shift 3 bytes at a time to jump to next instruction.According to that the given options must be divisible by 3. only 600 is satisfied.

6. ADD (X)–, (X)

7. $a = 1$

   b= 10 Let a is in Accumulator than for b and c we want

   c = 20 Register than **2 registers** want till now 1 for b and 1 for c

   $d = a + b$ Now $d = a + b$ can be stored in Accumulator because we don't want a again

   $e = c + d$. Now for f we wan't **next, one register** because we wan't ***c* & *e*** again

   $f = c + e$

   $b = c + e$. Now at $b = c + e$ we can store value in register b already, so we don't want another

   $e = b + f$. Now at $e = b + f$ we can store it in 0 register of ***b*** because we don't want another

   $d = 5 + e$ Now at $d = 5 + e$ we can store it in d because we don't want e again

   than we can say only 3 registers we want.

8. Here 20 will act as base and content of R_2 will be index

9. 1 Word = 32 bits

   Each instruction has 32 bits

   To support 45 instructions, opcode must contain 6-bits

   Register operand1 requires 6 bits, since the total registers are 64.

   Register operand 2 also requires 6 bits

← 6 →	← 6 →	← 6 →	← 14 →
opcode	Reg opd 1	Reg opd 2	immediate opnd

   ← 32 bits →

   14-bits are left over for immediate Operand Using 14-bits, we can give maximum 16383, Since 2^{14} =16384 from 0 to 16383.

10. In Three address instruction format, each operand specifies either a memory address or a register.

11. The current value of Stack pointer is $(016E)_{16}$

    The value of SP after following operations is asked in question

    (1) Store the current value of PC in the stack.

    This operation increments SP by 2 bytes as size of PC is given 2 bytes in question.

    So $(016E)_{16} + 2 = (0170)_{16}$

    (2) Store the value of PSW register in the stack.

    This operation also increments SP by 2 bytes as size of PSW is also given 2 bytes.

    So $(0170)_{16} + 2 = (0172)_{16}$

    (3) Load the starting address of the subroutine in PC.

    The Load operation doesn't change SP.

    So new value of SP is $(0172)_{16}$

12. ← 32 bits →

Operation	A_1	A_2	Operand
$\log_2^{40}$	$\log_2^{24}$	$\log_2^{24}$	
6	5	5	xxx

    ∴ 32 – 16 = 16

    So, the number of bits available for the immediate operand field is 16.

13. Index addressing mode, X(R1), where X is an offset represented in 2's complement 16-bit representation.

14. Indexed addressing is used for array implementation.

    Base register is used to relocatable code.

    Indirect addressing is done when array is passed as parameter.

15. Absolute addressing mode means address of operand is given in the instruction.

16. Auto increment add mode is basically used for incrementing a data. It depends on size of data.

17. In 2's complement addition, overflow cannot occur when a +ve value is added to a –ve value.

18. Overflow flag is set only if the X-OR between the carry-into the MSB and carry -out of the MSB is 1.

19. Number of gates used in 'n' bit array multiplier is (2n – 1)

    Each gate in the circuit has a unit delay. So total delay is 1 * (2n – 1) = O(2n – 1) = O(n).

20. Fault tolerance and High Speed

21. (*a*) DMA I/O → Date is transfer between disk and I/O without involving CPU.

    (*b*) Cache → Cache is fastest memory. It is situated between RAM and CPU. In cache, copy of data from main memory is stored in this cache memory for fastest execution.

    (*c*) Interrupt → Due to interrupt, I/O is affected, or due to I/O interrupt occur.

    (*d*) ALU is a part of condition code register.

22. The formatted disk capacity is always less than the "raw" unformatted capacity specified by the disk's manufacturer, because some portion of each track is used for sector identification and for gaps (empty spaces) between sectors and at the end of the track.

23. (i) Constant linear velcoity

    Data is linearly vary from inner track to outer track.

    So (10 + 20 + 30 + 40 + 50 + 60 + 70 + 80 MB) = 360 MB

    (ii) Constant Angular Velocity:-

    Data is equal on every track.

    So 8 × 10 MB = 80 MB.

24.

co-centric circular tracks

The seek latency is not linearly proportional to the seak distance due to arm starting and stoping inertia.

4 CHAPTER

CPU Control Design & Parallel Processing

Analysis of Previous GATE Papers

Units	Year → Topics ↓		2019	2018	2017 Set 1	2017 Set 2	2016 Set 1	2016 Set 2	2015 Set 1	2015 Set 2	2015 Set 3
PI PELINING	1 Mark	MCQ Type									
		Numerical Type									
	2 Marks	MCQ Type									
		Numerical Type			1		1	1	1		1
	Total				**2**		**2**	**2**	**2**		**2**
I NTERRUPTS	1 Mark	MCQ Type		1							
		Numerical Type									
	2 Marks	MCQ Type									
		Numerical Type									
	Total			**1**							
RISC & CISC	1 Mark	MCQ Type		1							
		Numerical Type									
	2 Marks	MCQ Type									
		Numerical Type									
	Total			**1**							
IO INITIATED	1 Mark	MCQ Type									
		Numerical Type									
	2 Marks	MCQ Type									
		Numerical Type									
	Total										
DISK SCHEDULING	1 Mark	MCQ Type									
		Numerical Type									
	2 Marks	MCQ Type									
		Numerical Type							1	1	
	Total								**2**	**2**	
DMA	1 Mark	MCQ Type									
		Numerical Type									
	2 Marks	MCQ Type									
		Numerical Type					1				
	Total						**2**				

PIPELINING

1. In an instruction execution pipeline, the earliest that the data TLB (Translation Look a side Buffer) can be acessed is
   (a) before effective address calculation has started
   (b) during effective address calculation
   (c) after effective address calculation has completed
   (d) after data cache lookup has completed

   [2008 : 2 Marks]

2. Comparing the time T1 taken for a single instruction on a pipelined CPU with time T2 taken on a non-pipelined but identical CPU, we can say that
   (a) $T1 \leq T2$
   (b) $T1 \leq T2$
   (c) $T1 < T2$
   (d) T1 plus T2 is the time taken for one instruction fetch cycle

   [2000 : 1 Mark]

3. The performance of a pipelined processor suffers if
   (a) the pipeline stages have different delays
   (b) consecutive instructions are dependent on each other
   (c) the pipeline stages share hardware resources
   (d) All of the above

   [2002 : 2 Marks]

4. Consider a pipelines processor with 4 stages S1 to S4. We want to execute the following loop : for (i = 1, i < = 1000; i++) {I1, I2, I3, I4} where the time taken (in ns) by instructions I1 to I4 for stages S1 to S4 are given below :

	S1	S2	S3	S4
I1 :	1	2	1	2
I2 :	2	1	2	1
I3 :	1	1	2	1
I4 :	2	1	2	1

   The output of I1 for i = 2 will be available after
   (a) 11 ns (b) 12 ns
   (c) 13 ns (d) 28 ns

   [2004 : 2 Marks]

5. a 4-stage pipleline has the stage delays as 150, 120, 160 and 140 nanoseconds respectively. Registers that are used between the stages have a delay of 5 nanoseconds each. Assuming constant clocking rate, the total time taken to process 1000 data items on this pipeline will be
   (a) 120.4 microseconds
   (b) 160.5 microseconds
   (c) 165.5 microseconds
   (d) 590.0 microseconds

   [2004 : 2 Marks]

6. We have two designs D1 and D2 for a synchronous pipeline processor. D1 has 5 pipeline stages with execution times of 3 nsec, 2 nsec, 4 nsec and 3 nsec while the design D2 has 8 pipeline stages each with 2 nsec execution time. How much time can be saved using design D2 over design D1 for executing 100 instructions?
   (a) 214 nsec (b) 202 nsec
   (c) 86 nsec (d) –200 nsec

   [2005 : 2 Marks]

7. A nonpipelined single cycle processor operating at 100 MHz is converted into a synchronous pipelined processor with five stages requiring 2.5 nsec, 1.5 nsec, 2 nsec, 1.5 nsec and 2.5 nsec, respetively. The delay of the latches is 0.5 nsec. The speedup of the pipeline processor for a large number of instructions is
   (a) 4.5 (b) 4.0
   (c) 3.33 (d) 3.0

   [2008 : 2 Marks]

8. Which of the following are NOT true in a pipelines processor?
   1. Bypassing can handle all Raw hazards.
   2. Register renaming can eliminate all register carried WAR hazards.
   3. Control hazard penalties can be eliminated by dynamic branch prediction.

   (a) 1 and 2 only (b) 1 and 3 only
   (c) 2 and 3 only (d) 1, 2 and 3

   [2008 : 2 Marks]

Common Data for Q. 9 & 10.

Delayed branching can help in the handling of control hazardous

9. For all delayed conditional branch instructions, irrespective of whether the condition evaluates to true or false, A
   (a) the instruction following the conditional branch instrucion in memory is executed
   (b) the first instruction in the fall through path is executed
   (c) the first instruction in the taken path is executed
   (d) the branch takes longer to execute than any other instruction **[2008 : 2 Marks]**

10. The following code is to run on a pipelines processor with one branch delay slot

I1 : ADDR2 ← R7 + R8

I2 : SIN R4 ← R5 – R6x

I3 : ADD R1 ← R2 + R3

I4 : STORE Memory [R4] ← R1

BRANCH to Label if R1 == 0

Which of the instruction 11, 12, 13 or 14 can legitimatly occupy the delay slot without any other program modification?

(a) 11 (b) 12

(c) 13 (d) 14 **[2008 : 2 Marks]**

11. Consider a 4 stage pipeline processor. The number of cycles needed by the four instructions 11, 12, 13, 14 in stage S1, S2, S3, S4 is shown below :

	S1	S2	S3	S4
I1	2	1	1	1
I2	1	3	2	2
I3	2	1	1	3
I4	1	2	2	2

What is the number of cycles needed to execute the following loop ?

for (i = 1 to 2) {I1; I2; I3; I4;}

(a) 16 (b) 23

(c) 28 (d) 30

[2008 : 2 Marks]

12. A 5-stage pipelines processor has Instruction Fetch (IF), Instruction Decode (ID), Operand Fetch (OF), Perform Operation (PO) and Write Operand (WO) stages. The IF, ID, OF and WO stages take 1 clock cycle each for any instruction. The PO stage takes 1 clock cycle for ADD and SUB instructions 3 clock cycles for MUL instruction, and 6 clock cycles for DIV instruction respectively. Operand forwarding is used in the pipeline. What is the number of clock cycles needed to execute the following sequence of instructions ?

Instruction Meaning of Instruction

I_0: MUL R_2, R_0, R_1 $R_2 \leftarrow R_0 * R_1$

I_1 : DIV R_5, R_3, R_4 $R_5 \leftarrow R_3/R_4$

I_2 : ADD R_2, R_5, R_2 $R_2 \leftarrow R_5 + R_2$

I_3 : SUB R_5, R_2, R_6 $R_5 \leftarrow R_2 - R_6$

(a) 13 (b) 15

(c) 17 (d) 19

[2010 : 2 Marks]

13. Consider an instruction pipeline with four stages (S1, S2, S3 and S4) each with combinational circuit only. The pipeline registers are required between each stage and at the end of the last stage. Delays for the stages and for the pipeline registers are as given in the figure.

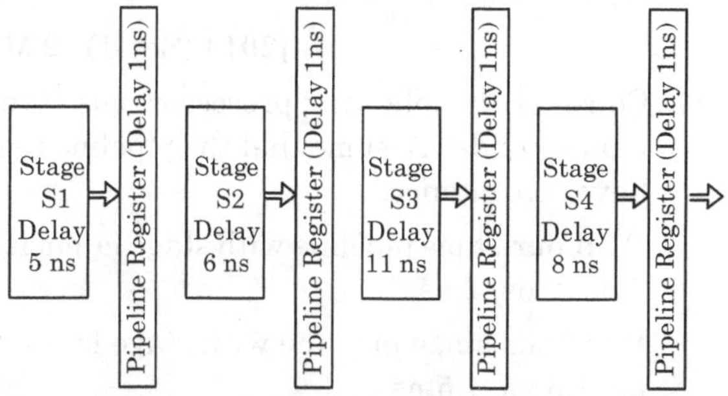

What is the approximate speed up of the pipeline in steady state under ideal conditions when compated to the corresponding non-pipeline implementation?

(a) 4.0 (b) 2.5

(c) 1.1 (d) 3.0

[2011 : 2 Marks]

14. Register renaming is done in pipelined processors

(a) as an alternative to register allocation at compile time

(b) for efficient access to function parameters and local variables

(c) to handle certain kinds of hazards

(d) as part of address translation

[2012 : 1 Marks]

15. Consider an instruction pipeline with five stages without any branch prediction : Fetch Instruction (FI), Decode Instruction (DI), Fetch Operand (FO), Execute Instruction (EI) and Write Operand (WO). The stage delays for FI, DI, FO, EI and WO are 5 ns, 7 ns, 10 ns, 8 ns and 6 ns, respectively. There are intermediate storage buffers after each stage and the delay of each buffer is 1 ns. A program consisting of 12 instruction I1, I2, I3, ... I12 is execute in the pipelined processor. Instruction I4 is the only branch instruction and its branch target is I9. If the branch is taken during the execution of this program, the time (in ns) needed to complete the program is

(a) 132 (b) 165

(c) 176 (d) 328

[2013 : 2 Marks]

16. Consider a 6-stage instruction pipeline, where all stages are perfectly balanced. Assume that there is no cycle-time overhead of pipelining. When an application is executing on this 6-stage pipeline the speedup achieved with respect to non-pipelined execution if 25% of the instructions incur 2 pipeline stall cycles is ......

[2014 (Set-1) : 2 Marks]

17. Consider the following processors (ns stands for nanoseconds). Assume that the pipeline registers have zero latency.

P1 :Four-stage pipeline with stage latencies 1 ns, 2 ns, 2 ns, 1 ns.

P2 : Four-stage pipeline with stage latencies 1.5 ns, 1.5 ns, 1.5 ns.

P3 : Five-stage pipeline with stage latencies 0.5 ns, 1 ns, 1 ns, 0.6 ns, 1 ns.

P4 : Five-stage pipeline with stage latencies 0.5 ns, 0.5 ns, 1 ns, 1 ns, 1.1 ns.

Which processor has the highest peak clock frequency?

(a) P1

(b) P2

(c) P3

(d) P4

[2014 (Set-3) : 1 Marks]

18. An instruction pipeline has five stages, namely, instruction fetch (IF), instruction decode and register fetch (ID/RF), instruction execution (EX), memory access (MEM), and register writeback (WB) with stage latencies 1 ns, 2.2 ns, 2 ns, 1 ns, and 0.75 ns, respectively (ns stands for nanoseconsd). To gain in terms of frequency, the designers have decided to split the ID/RF stage into three stages (ID, RF1, RF2) each of latency 2.2/3 ns. Also, the EX stage is split into two stages (EX1, EX2) each of latency 1 ns. The new design has a total of eight pipeline stages. A program has 20% branch instructions which execute in the EX stage and produce the next instruction pointer at the end of the EX stage in the old design and at the end of the EX2 stage i the new design. The IF stage stalls after fetching a branch instruction until the next instruction pointer is computed. All instructions other than the branch instruction have an average CPI of one in both the designs. The execution times of this program on the old and the new design are P and Q nanoseconds, respectively. The value of P/Q is ....

[2014 (Set-3) : 2 Marks]

19. Consider a non-pipelined processor with a clock rate of 2.5 gigahertz and average cycles per instruction of four. The same processor is upgraded to a pipelined processor with five stages; but due to the internal pipeline delay, the clcok speed is reduced to 2 gigahertz. Assume that there are no stalls in the pipeline. The speed up achieved in this pipelined processor is ....

[2015 (Set-1) : 2 Marks]

20. Consider the following reservation table for a pipeline having three stages S_1, S_2 and S_3.

	Time →				
	1	2	3	4	5
S_1	X				X
S_2		X		X	
S_3			X		

The minimum average latency (MAL) is ....

[2015 (Set-3) : 2 Marks]

21. The stage delays in a 4-stage pipeline are 800, 500, 400 and 300 picoseconds. The first stage (with delay 800 picoseconds) is replaced with a functionally equivalent design involving two stages with respective delays 600 and 350 picoseconds. The throughout increase of the pipeline is .... percent.

[2016 (Set-1) : 2 Marks]

22. Consider a 3 GHz (gigahertz) processor with a three-stage pipeline and stage latencies τ_1, τ_2, and τ_3 sch that $\tau_1 = 3\tau_2/4 = 2\tau_3$. If the longest pipeline stage is split into two pipeline stages of equal latency, the new frequency is .... GHz, ignoring delays in the pipeline registers.

[2016 (Set-2) : 2 Marks]

23. Instruction execution in a processor is divided into 5 stages. Instruction Fetch (IF), Instruction Decode (ID), Operand Fetch (OF), Execute (EX) and Write Back (WB). These stages take 5, 4, 20, 10 and 3 nanoseconds (ns) respectively. A pipelined implementation of the processor requires buffering between each pair of consecutive stages with a delay of 2 ns. Two pipelined implementations of the processor are contemplated :

(i) a naive pipeline implementation (NP) with 5 stages and

(ii) an efficient pipeline (EP) where the OF stage is divided into stages OF1 and OF2 with execution times of 12 ns and 8 ns respectively.

The speedup (correct to two decimal places) achieved by EP over NP in exdecuting 20 independent instructions with no hazards is ....

[2017 (Set-1) : 2 Marks]

24. Consider the following data path of a simple non-pipelined CPU. The registers A, B, A_1, A_2, MDR, the bus and the ALU are 8-bit wide. SP and MAR are 16-bit registers. The MUX is of size 8 × (2 : 1) and the DEMUX is of size 8 × (1 : 2). Each memory operation takes 2 CPU clock cycles and uses MAR (Memory Address Register) and MDR (Memory Data Register). SP can be decremented locally.

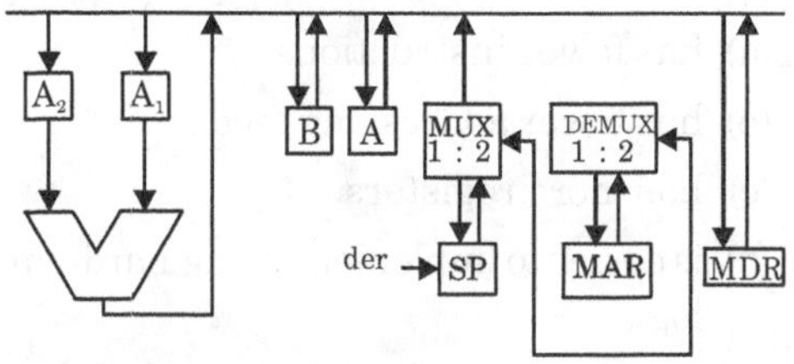

The CPU instruction "push r", where r = A or B, has the specification

M[SP] ← r

SP ← SP – 1

How many CPU clock cycles are needed to execute the 'push r" instruction?

(a) 2 (b) 3

(c) 4 (d) 5 **[2001 : 2 Marks]**

25. A line L in a circuit is said to have a stuck-at-0 fault if the line permanently has a logic value 0. Similarly a line L in a circuit is said to have a stuck-at-1 fault if the line permenently has a logic value 1. A circuit is said to have a multiple stuck-at fault if one or more lines have stuck at faults. The total number of distinct multiple stuck-at faults possible in a circuit with N lines is

(a) 3^N (b) $3^N - 1$

(c) $2^N - 1$ (d) 2^N **[2005 : 2 Marks]**

26. The floating point unit of a processor using a design D takes 2t cycles compared to t cycles taken by the fixed point unit. There are two more design suggestions D1 and D2. D1 uses 30% more cycles for fixed point but 30% less cycles for floating point unit as compared to design D. D2 uses 40% less cycles for fixed point unit but 10% more cycles for floating point unit as compared to design D. For a given program which has 80% fixed point operations and 20% floating point operations, which of the following ordering reflects the rlative performances of three designs? (Di > Dj denotes that Di is faster than Dj)

(a) D1 > D > D2

(b) D2 > D > D1

(c) D > D2 > D1

(d) D > D1 > D2

[2007 : 2 Marks]

27. Which of the following systems is a most likely candidate example of a pipe and filter architecture?

(a) Expert system

(b) DB repository

(c) Aircraft flight controller

(d) Signal processing **[2007 : 1 Mark]**

INTERRUPTS

28. The following are some events that occur after a device controller issues an interrupt while process L is under executon.

(P) The processor pushes the process status of L onto the control stack.

(Q) The processor finishes the execution of the current instruction.

(R) The processor executes the interrupt service routine.

(S) The processor pops the process status of L from the control stack.

(T) The processor loads the new PC value based on the interrupt.

Which one of the following is the correct order in which the events above occur?

(a) QPTRRS (b) PRTSQ

(c) TRPQS (d) QTPRS

[2018 : 1 Marks]

29. When an interrupt occurs, an operating system

(a) ignores the interrupt

(b) always changes state of interrupted process after processing the interrupt

(c) always resumes execution of interrupted process after processing the interrupt

(d) may change state of interrupted process to 'blocked' and schedule another process

[1997 : 1 Mark]

30. A processor needs software interrupt to

(a) test the interrupt system of the processor

(b) implement co-routines

(c) obtain system services which need execution of priviledged instructions

(d) return from subroutine

[2001 : 1 Mark]

31. A device employing INTR line for device interrupt puts the CALL instruction on the data bus while

(a) $\overline{\text{INTA}}$ is active (b) HOLD is active

(c) READY is active (d) None of these

[2002 : 1 Mark]

32. Which one of the following is true for a CPU having a single interrupt request line and a single interrupt grant line?

(a) Neither vectored interrupt nor multiple interrupting devices are possible

(b) Vectored interrupts are not possible but multiple interrupting devices are possible

(c) Vectored interrupts and multiple interrupting devices are both possible

(d) Vectored interrupt is possible but multiple interrupting devices are not possible.

[2005 : 1 Mark]

33. A CPU generally handles an interrupt by executing an interrupt service routine

(a) as soon as an interrupt is raised

(b) by checking the interrupt register at the end of fetch cycle

(c) by checking the interrupt register after finishing the execution of the current instruction

(d) by checking the interrupt register at fixed time intervals

[2009 : 1 Mark]

34. For the daisy chain scheme of connecting I/O devices, which of the following statements is true?

(a) It gives non-uniform priority to various devices

(b) It gives uniform priority to all devices

(c) It is only useful for connecting slow devices to a processor device

(d) It requires a separate interrupt pin on the processor for each device

[1996 : 1 Mark]

35. A device with data transfer rate 10 KB/sec is connected to a CPU. Data is transferred byte-wise. Let the interrupt overhead be 4 μsec. The byte transfer time between the device interface register and CPU or memory is negligble. What is the minimum performance gain of operating the device under interrupt mode over operating under program controlled mode?

(a) 15 (b) 25

(c) 35 (d) 45 **[2005 : 2 Marks]**

RISC & CISC

36. Consider the following processor design characteristics :

I. Register-to-register arithmetic operations only.

II. Fixed-length instruction format.

III. Hardwired control unit.

Which of the characteristics above are used in the design of a RISC processor ?

(a) I and II only (b) II and III only

(c) I and III only (d) I, II and III

[2018 : 1 Marks]

37. The main differences(s) between a CISC and A RISC processor is/are that a RISC processor typically

(a) has fewer instructions

(b) has fewer addressing modes

(c) has more registers

(d) is easier to implement using hard-wired control logic

[1998 : 2 Marks]

IO INITIATED

38. Normally user programs are prevented from handling I/O directly by I/O instructions in them. For CPUs having explicit I/O instructions, such I/O protection is ensured by having the I/O instructions privileged. In a CPU with memory mapped I/O, there is no explicit I/O instruction. Which one of the following is true for a CPU with memory mapped I/O ?

(a) I/O protection is ensured by operating system routine(s)

(b) I/O protection is ensured by a hardware trap

(c) I/O protection is ensured during system configuration

(d) I/O protection is not possible **[2005 : 1 Mark]**

39. The data transfer between memory and I/O devices using programmed I/O is faster than interrupt driven I/O. **[1990 : 2 Marks]**

40. I/O redirection

(a) implies changing the name of a file

(b) can be employed to use an existing file as input file for a program

(c) implies connection 2 programs through a pipe

(d) None of the above

[1997 : 1 Mark]

41. Which of the following DNA transfer modes and interrupt handling mechanisms will enable the highest I/O band-width?

(a) Transparent DMA and Polling interrupts

(b) Cycle-stealing and Vectored interrupts

(c) Block transfer and Vectored interrupts

(d) Block transfer and Polling interrupts

[2006 : 1 Mark]

DISK SCHEDULING

42. A certain moving arm disk storage, with one head, has the following specifications.

Number of tracks/recording surface = 200

Disk rotation speed = 2400 rpm

Track storage capacity = 62, 500 bits

The average latency of this device is P msec and the data transfer rate is Q bits/sec.

Write the value of P and Q.

[1991 : 2 Marks]

43. If teh disk is rotating at 3600 rpm, determine the effective data transfer rate which is defined as the number of bytes transferred per second between disk and memory. (Given size of track = 512 bytes)

[1995 : 2 Marks]

44. The storage area of a disk has innermost diameter of 10 cm and outermost diameter of 20 cm. The maximum storage density of the disk is 1400 bits/cm. The disk rotates at a speed of 4200 RPM. The main memory of a computer has 64-bit word length and 1 μs cycle time. If cycle stealing is used for data transfer from the disk, the percentage of memory cycles stolen for transferring one word is

(a) 0.5% (b) 1%

(c) 5% (d) 10%

[2004 : 2 Marks]

45. A disk has 8 equidistant tracks. The diameters of the innermost and outermost tracks are 1 cm and 8 cm respectively. The innermost track has a storage capacity of 10 MB.

If the disk has 20 sectors per track and is currently at the end of the 5th sector of the inner-most track and the head can move at a speed of 10 meters/sec and it is rotating at constant angular velocity of 6000 RPM, how much time will it take to read 1 MB contiguous data starting from the sector 4 of the outer-most track?

(a) 13.5 ms

(b) 10 ms

(c) 9.5 ms

(d) 20 ms

[2005 : 2 Marks]

46. What is the swap space in the disk used for?

(a) Saving temporary html pages

(b) Saving process data

(c) Storing the superblock

(d) Storing device drivers

[2005 : 1 Mark]

47. Consider a disk drive with the following specifications.

16 surfaces, 512 tracks/surface, 512 sectors/track, 1 KB/sector, rotation speed 3000 rpm. The disk is operated in cycle stealing mode whereby whenever one byte word is ready it is sent to memory; similarly, for writing, the disk interface reads a 4 byte word from the memory in each DMA cycle. Memory cycle time is 40 nsec. The maximum percentage of time that the CPU gets blocked during DMA operation is

(a) 10 (b) 25

(c) 40 (d) 50

[2005 : 2 Marks]

48. Consider a disk pack with 16 surfaces, 128 tracks per surface and 256 sectors per track. 512 bytes of data are stored in a bit serial manner in a sector. The capacity of the disk pack and the number of bits required to specify a particular sector in the disk are respectively

(a) 256 Mbyte, 19 bits (b) 256 Mbyte, 28 bits

(c) 512 Mbyte, 20 bits (d) 64 Gbyte, 28 bits

[2007 : 1 Mark]

49. A hard disk system has the following parameters:

Number of tracks = 500

Number of sectors/track = 100

Number of bytes/sector = 500

Time taken by the head to move from one track to adjacent track = 1 ms Rotation speed = 600 rpm. What is the average time taken for transferring 250 bytes from the disk?

(a) 300.5 ms (b) 255.5 ms

(c) 255 ms (d) 300 ms

[2007 : 2 Marks]

Common Data for 50 and 51.

A hard disk has 63 sectors per track, 10 platters each with 2 recording surfaces and 1000 cylinders. The address of a sector is given as a triple (c, h, s), where c is the cyclinder number, h is the surface number and s is the sector number. Thus, the 0th sector is addressed as (0, 0, 0), the 1st sector as (0, 0, 1), and so on.

50. The address (400, 16, 29) corresponds to sector number :

(a) 505035 (b) 505036

(c) 505037 (d) 505038

[2009 : 2 Marks]

51. The address of 1039th sector is

(a) (0, 15, 31) (b) (0, 16, 30)

(c) (0, 16, 31) (d) (0, 17, 31)

[2009 : 2 Marks]

52. An application loads 100 libraries at start-up. Loading each library requires exactly one disk access. The seek time of the disk to a random location is given as 10 ms. Rotational speed of disk is 6000 rpm. If all 100 libraries are loaded from random locations on the disk, how long does it take to load all libraries? (The time to transfer data from the disk block once the head has been positioned at the start of the block may be neglected.)

(a) 0.50 s (b) 1.50 s
(c) 1.25 s (d) 1.00 s

[2011 : 2 Marks]

53. Consider a hard disk with 16 recording surfaces (0-15) having 16384 cyclinders (0-16383) and each cylinder contain 64 sectors (0-63). Data storage capacity in each sector is 512 bytes. Data are organized cylinder-wise and addressing format is <cylinder no., surface no., sector no>. A file of size 42797 KB is stored in the disk and the starting location of the file is < 1200, 9, 40 >. What is the cylinder number of the last sector of the file, if it is stored in a contiguous manner?

(a) 1281 (b) 1282
(c) 1283 (d) 1284

[2013 : 2 Marks]

54. Consider a disk pack with a seek time of 4 milliseconds and rotational speed of 100000 rotations per minute (RPM). It has 600 sectors per track and each sector can store 512 bytes of data. Consider a file stored in the disk. The file contains 2000 sectors. Assume that every sector access necessitates a seek, and the average rotational latency for accessing each sector is half of the time for one complete rotation. The total time (in milliseconds) needed to read the entire file is ....

[2015 (Set-1) : 2 Marks]

55. Consider a typical disk that rotates at 15000 rotations per minute (RPM) and has a transfer rate of 50×10^6 bytes/sec. If the average seek time of the disk is twice the average rotational delay and the controller's transfer time is 10 times the disk transfer time, the average time (in milliseconds) to read or write a 512 byte sector of the disk is ....

[2015 (Set-2) : 2 Marks]

DMA

56. A hard disk with a transfer rate of 10 M bytes/second is constantly transferring data to memory using DMA. The processor runs at 600 MHz, and takes 300 and 900 clock cycles to initiate and complete DMA transfer respectively. If the size of the transfer is 20 Kbytes, what is the percentage of processor time consumed for the transfer operation?

(a) 5.0% (b) 1.0%
(c) 0.5% (d) 0.1%

[2004 : 2 Marks]

57. Consider a Direct Mapped Cache with 8 cache blocks (numbered 0-7). If the memory block requests are in the following order 3, 5, 2, 8, 0, 63, 9, 16, 20, 17, 25, 18, 30, 24, 2, 63, 5, 82, 17, 24. Which of the following memory blocks will not be in the cache at the end of the sequence?

(a) 3 (b) 18
(c) 20 (d) 30

[2007 : 2 Marks]

58. On a non-pipelined sequential processor, a program segment, which is a part of the interrupt service routine, is given to transfer 500 bytes from an I/O device to memory.

Initialize the address register
Initialize the count to 500
LOOP : Load a byte from device
Store in memory at address given by address register
Increment the address register
Decrement the court
If count ! = 0 go to LOOP

Assume that each statement in this program is equivalent to a machine instruction which takes one clock cycle to execute it it is a non-load/store instruction. The load-store instructions take two clock ccles to execute.

The designer of the system also has an alternate approach of using the DMA controller to implement the same transfer. The DM controller requires 20 clock cycles for initialization and other overhead. Each DMA transfer cycle takes two clock cycles to transfer one byte of data from interrupt driven program based input-output?

(a) 3.4 (b) 4.4
(c) 5.1 (d) 6.7

[2011 : 2 Marks]

59. The size of the data count register of a DMA controller is 16 bits. The processor needs to transfer a file of 29,154 kilobytes from disk to main memory. The memory is byte addressable. The minimum number of times the DMA controller needs to get the control of the system bus from the processor to transfer the file from the disk to main memory is ....

[2016 (Set-1) : 2 Marks]

ANSWERS

1. (*b*)	**2.** (*b*)	**3.** (*d*)	**4.** (*c*)	**5.** (*b*)	**6.** (*b*)	**7.** (*c*)	**8.** (*a*)	**9.** (*b*)	**10.** (*b*)
11. (*d*)	**12.** (*b*)	**13.** (*b*)	**14.** (*c*)	**15.** (165)	**16.** (4)	**17.** (*c*)	**18.** (1.54)	**19.** (3.2)	**20.** (3)
21. (33.28)	**22.** (4)	**23.** (1.50-1.51)	**24.** (*a*)	**25.** (*b*)	**26.** (*a*)	**27.** (*d*)	**28.** (*a*)	**29.** (*d*)	**30.** (*c*)
31. (*a*)	**32.** (*c*)	**33.** (*c*)	**34.** (*a*)	**35.** (*b*)	**36.** (*d*)	**37.** (*a, b, c, d*)	**38.** (*a*)	**39.** (False)	**40.** (*b*)
41. (*c*)	**42.** (*)	**43.** (30720)	**44.** (*c*)	**45.** (*a*)	**46.** (*b*)	**47.** (*b*)	**48.** (*a*)	**49.** (*d*)	**50.** (*c*)
51. (*c*)	**52.** (*b*)	**53.** (*d*)	**54.** (14020)	**55.** (6.1-6.2)		**56.** (*d*)	**57.** (*b*)	**58.** (*a*)	**59.** (456)

EXPLANATIONS

1. Translations Lookaside Buffer can be accessed during effective address calculations.

2. Pipelining does not increase the execution time of a single instruction. It increases the overall performance by executing instructions in multiple pipeline stages.

   For N=1

   Pipelined CPU :

   Total time (T1) = (K + (N – 1)) * T = KT

   Non-Pipelined CPU :

   Total time (T2) = KNT = KT

   Considering buffer delays in pipelined CPU,

   T1 > = T2

3. Pipelining is a method to execute a program breaking it in several independent sequence of stages.

   In that case pipeline stages can't have different delays, no dependency among consecutive instructions and sharing of hardware resources should not be there.

4.

S_1	S_2	S_3	S_4
I_1			
I_2	I_1		
I_3	I_1		
I_4	I_1	I_1	
I_4	I_3	I_2	I_1
I_1		I_2	I_1
	I_4	I_3	I_2
		I_4	
	I_1	I_4	I_3
	I_1	I_4	
		I_1	I_4
		I_1	I_4
			I_1

13 block cycle

5. Delay is 5 nanosecond/stage.

   Total delay in pipeline = 150 + 120 + 160 + 140

   = 570

   Delay due to stage delay = 15

   Total delay = 585

   $$\text{Total time taken} = \frac{1000(\text{data item size})}{585(\text{ns})}$$

   = 165.5 microsecond

6. Total execution time = (k + n – 1) * maximum clock cycle

   Where k = total number of stages and n = total number of instructions

   For D1 :

   k = 5 and n = 100

   Maximum clock cycle = 4ns

   Total execution time = (5 + 100 – 1) * 4 = 416

   For D2 :

   k = 8 and n = 100

   Each clock cycle = 2ns

   Total execution time = (8 + 100 – 1) * 2 = 214

   Thus, time saved using D2 over D1

   = 416 – 214

   = 202

7. For non pipelined system time required

   = 2.5 + 1.5 + 2.0 + 1.5 + 2.5 = 10

   for pipelined system

   = Max (stage delay) + Max(Latch delay)

   ⇒ 2.5 + 0.5 = 3.0

   speedup = time in non-pipelined system/time in pipelined system

   = 10/3 = 3.33

8. In pipelined processor bypassing can handle all RAW hazards and register remaining can eliminate all register carried WAR hazard.

9. For all delayed conditional branch instructions the first instruction in the fall through path is executed

10. In delay slot I2 will be there

11.

	S_1	S_2	S_3	S_4	No. of clock cycle
I_1	2	1	1	1	5
I_2	1	3	2	2	5
I_3	2	1	1	3	3
I_4	1	2	2	2	2
					15

1st time for loop required is cycle and again second time 15 cycle

So, total = 30 cycle

12. Clocks

	1	2	3	4	5	6	7	8	9	10	11	12	13	14	15	16
20	2F	2D	OF	PO	PO	PO	WO									
21		2F	2D	OF	Stall	Stall	PO	P[O	PO	PO	PO	PO	WO			
22			2F	2D	OF	-	-	-	-	-	-	-	PO	WO		
23				2F	2D	OF	-	-	-	-	-	-	-	PO	WO	

So total 15 cycles required.

Alternately

	1	2	3	4	5	6	7	8	9	10	11	12	13	14	15

I_0 IF ID OF PO PO PO WO

I_1 IF ID OF .... PO PO PO PO PO POWO

I_2 IF ID OF ... POWO

I_3 IF ID OF .... PO WO

So that 15 cycles required.

13. Pipeline registers overhead is not counted in normal time execution

So the total count will be

5 + 6 + 11 + 8 = 30 [without pipeline]

Now, for pipeline, each stage will be of 11 n-sec (+ 1 n-sec for overhead).

and, in steady state output is produced after every pipeline cycle. Here, in this case 11 n-sec. After adding 1n-sec overhead, We will get 12 n-sec of constant output producing cycle.

dividing 30/12 we get 2.5

14. Register renaming is done to eliminate WAR/WAW hazards.

15. **Given:** Five stage instruction pipeline Delays for FI, DI, FO, EI and wo are 5, 7, 10, 8, 6 ns resp.

To find: Time needed to execute 12 instruction prog.

Analysis: Since the max. time taken by any stage is 10 ns and additional 1 ns is required for delay of buffer. Therefore total time for an instruction to pass from one stage to another is 11ns Now instructions are executed as follows:

$$\xrightarrow[\text{execution with time}]{I_1, I_2, I_3, I_4, I_9, I_{10}, I_{11}, I_{12}}$$

Now when I_4 is in its executioin stage we detect the branch and when I_4 is in WO stage we fetch I_9 so time for execution of instructions from I_1 to I_4 is = 11 ∗ 5 + (4 – 1) ∗ 11 = 88 ns.

and time for execution of instructions from I_9 to I_{12} is

= 11 ∗ 5 + (4 – 1) ∗ 11 = 88 ns

But we have 11ns when fetching I_9. i.e. I_9 requires only 44 ns additional instead of 55 ns because time for fetching I_9 can be overlap with WO of I_4

Hence total time is = 88 + 88 – 11 = 165 ns

16. For 6 stages, non-pipelining takes 6 cycles

There were 2 stall cycles for pipelining for 25% of the instructions

$$\text{So pipe line time} = \left(1 + \frac{25}{100}2\right) = \frac{3}{2} = 1.5$$

$$\text{Speed up} = \frac{\text{Non–pipeline time}}{\text{Pipeline time}} = \frac{6}{1.5} = 4$$

17. Peak clock frequency = 1 / Maximum latency

Maximum of latencies is minimum in P3

i.e. P1 : f = 1/2 = 0.5 GHz

P2 : f = 1/1.5 = 0.67 GHz

P4 : f = 1/1.1 GHz

P3 : f = 1/1 GHz = 1

Thus P3 is be the right answer

18.

	No. of stage	Stall cycle	Stall Frequency	Clock period	Average access time
Old design	5	2	20%	2.2ns	P
New design	8	5	20%	1 ns	Q

$$P = \left[80\%(1\text{clock}) + 20\%\left(\underset{\text{Completion}}{1} + \underset{\text{stall clock}}{2}\right)\right] \times T_{c-p}$$

P = (.8 + .6) × 2.2ns = 3.08ns

$$Q = \left[80\%(1\text{clock}) + 20\%\left(\underset{\text{Completion}}{1} + \underset{\text{stall clock}}{5}\right)\right] \times T_{c-p}$$

P =(.8 +.12) × 1ns = 2ns

$$\text{So the value of } \frac{P}{Q} = \frac{3.08\text{ns}}{2\text{ ns}} = 1.54$$

19. Speedup = ExecutionTimeOld/Execution Time New

Execution Time Old = CPI_{Old} * Cycle $Time_{Old}$

[Here CPI is Cycles Per Instruction]

= CPIOld * CycleTimeOld

= 4 * 1/2.5 Nanoseconds

= 1.6 ns

Since there are no stalls, CPUnew can be assumed 1 on average.

Execution Time New = CPI_{new} * Cycle $Time_{new}$

= 1 * 1/2

= 0.5

Speedup = 1.6/0.5 = 3.2

20. Minimum average latency is 3

22. From question

Stage 1 (t_1)	Stage 2 (t_2)	Stage 3 (t_3)
$(3/4)t_2$	$1t_2$	$(3/8)t_2$

Old pipeline Clock frequency is 3GHz if time is t_2.

Stage 1 (t_1)	Stage 21(t_{21})	Stage 22(t_{22})	Stage 3(t_3)
$(3/4)t_2$	$(t_2/2)$	$(t_2/2)$	$(3/8)t_2$

Clock frequency of new pipeline with time

$(3/4)t_2 \rightarrow \frac{4}{3} \times 3$ GHz = 4 GHz

So, the new frequency is 4 GHz.

23. Number of stages(k) = 5

Clock time (Tp) = max {(stage delay+buffer delay)}

= {7, 6, 22, 12, 5} = 22 nsec

Execution time (Enp) = (k + n - 1) * Tp

= (5 + 20 – 1)*22

= 528 nsec

Number of stages(k) = 6 (delay with 20 nsec stage is divided into 12 nsec and 8 nsec)

Clock time (Tp) = max {(stage delay+buffer delay)}

= {7, 6, 14, 10, 14, 5} = 14 nsec

Execution time (Eep) = (k + n – 1) * Tp

= (6 + 20 – 1) * 14 = 350 nsec

Therefore,

Speedup = (Enp)/(Eep)

= 528/350 = 1.508

24. Push 'r' consist of following operations :

M[SP]!R

SP!SP-1

'r' is stored at memory at address stack pointer currently is, this take 2 clock cycles

SP is then decremented to point to next top of stack

25. In a line, there can be three possibilities :

1. Stuck-at 0 fault
2. Stuck-at 1 fault
3. No fault

Thus, total combinations = 3^N

It is mentioned that one or more lines have stuck at faults.

So, a case in which there is no fault in any line i.e. all lines are correct can not occur.

Total combinations = $3^N - 1$

26. 0.8 * (time taken in fixed point) + 0.2 (time taken in floating point) Say, t = 1

D = 0.8(1) + 0.2(2)

= 1.2

D1 = 0.8(1.3) + 0.2(1.4)

= 1.04 +.28 = 1.32

D2 = 0.8(1 – 0.04) + 0.2(2 – 2*0.1)

= 0.8 * 0.96 + 0.2 * 1.8

= 0.768 + 0.36 = 1.128

D1 > D > D2

27. In the pipes and filters pattern, components are filters and connectors are pipes.

Each filter takes input in some form and produces output in some other form,which may or may not be similar to the input form. Hopefully, each filter will add value to the output stream because of processing done inside the filter. Each filter is independent and is unaware of the up and down stream filters. Pipes are conduits of the data streams. Famous example of the pipes and filters architectural pattern are UNIX shells,signal processing systems and distributed systems

28. Processor required to handle the interrupt:

1. Processor finishes the execution of the current instruction.
2. Processor pushes the process status of L onto the control stack.
3. Processor loads the new PC value based on the interrupt.
4. Processor executes the interrupt service routine.
5. Processor pops the process status of "L" from the control stack.

29. It dependes on scheduler. It may decides that the interrupted process will complete execution or some other process will be executed.

30. A processor needs software interrupt to obtain system services which need execution of priviledged instructions.

31. A device employing INTR line for device interrupt puts the CALL instruction on the data bus while INTA is active

32. It depends on what kind of CPU.

33. A CPU generally handles an interrupt by executing ISR by checking the interrupt register after finishing execution of the current instruction.

34. Daisy Chain Scheme. When device A has a cable that plugs into device B has a cable that plugs into device C and device C plugs into a port on the computer, this arrangement is called a Daisy Chain. It usually operates as a bus.

35. If overhead of a single byte transfer with interface mode is 4 μ sec, then actual data transfer can be 250000.

Actually transfer take place at the rate → 10000

Now 25 is the minimum performance gain.

36. RISC processor characteristics:

1. It supports mode registers, so ALU operations are performed only on a register data.
2. It support fixed length instructions.
3. It uses hard-wired control unit.

37. All statments are true.

38. We have two regestion limit and base. So, when we refer memory location which is not in range provided by these two regestor is always cause OS to interface.

39. The data transfer between memory and I/O devices using interrupt driven I/O is faster than programmed I/O.

40. I/O redirection can be employed to use an existing file as input file for a program.

41. In block transfer the entire block of data is transfered then only CPU again becomes the bus master and in vectored Interrupts I/o device along with interrupts send vector address of Interrupt Service routine which guides CPU to execute for a specific I/O device.

42. RPM = 2400 means in 60s, the disk rotates 2400 times.

Average latency time is half of a rotation time

$= 0.5 \times 60/2400s = 3/240s = 12.5ms.$

In one full rotation, entire data in a track can be transferred. Track storage capacity = 62500 bits.

So, disk transfer rate = $62500 \times 2400/60s$

$= 2.5 \times 106$ bps.

$P = 12.5$

$Q = 2.5 \times 10^6$

43. RPM = 3600 means in 60 sec the disk rotates 3600 times

So 1 revolution time is 60/3600 sec

In one full rotation, entire data in a track can be transferred. Track storage capacity = 512 byte

So disk transfer rate is 512 bytes × 3600/60 sec

= 30720 bytes per sec

44. The capacity of each track

$= \pi * D = \text{Density}$

$= \pi * 10 * 1400$ bits

$= 14000\,\pi$ bits

RPM = 4200

So 1 revolution in $\frac{60}{4200}\text{sec} = \frac{1}{70}\text{sec}$ i.e. $\frac{1}{70}\text{sec}$

we can transfer 14000 π bits.

Now the data transfer is done by DMA controller which will be operated in memory cycle time i.e. 1 M sec and it has 64 bit word length.

So in 1 cycle it is able to transfer total 64 bits.

i.e. in 1 sec it can transfer 64×10^6 bits

in sec disk can Read $14000\,\pi * 70$

$= 3.08 * 10^6$ bits.

So total memory cycle stolen is

$$\frac{3.08 * 10^6}{(64 * 10^6)}\% = 5\%$$

45. Innermost track radius is 0.5 cm

Outermost track radius is 4 cm

Distance traversed by header

$= 4 - 0.5 = 3.5$ cm $= 3.5/100$ m $= 350$ m

Time taken by header = 350/10 = 3500 s = 3.5 ms (as given speed: 10 meters/sec)

Now, It is given that header at the end of the 5th sector of the innermost track. To start from front of 4th sector it must rotate upto 18 sector.

So, header does 6000 rotations in 60,000ms (60 seconds) and 1 rotation in 10 ms. So, to traverse sector 18 it takes 9 ms.

Storage capacity = 10 MB

So, 10 MB data is read in 10 ms.

1 MB can be read in 1 ms.

Total Time = Seek + Rotation + Transfer.

Total time taken to read 1 MB contiguous data

= 1 ms + 9 ms + 3.5 ms

= 13.5 ms

46. The swap space is basically used for saving process data. Consider CPU contains two process P_1 and P_2 if P_1 is running on the CPU then P_2 is swap out and all data (Pc for process, content etc) are saved in the disk, when CPU executes process P_2 then all data items of P_1 saved on a risk.

47. Round per minute (R.P.M.) = 3000

Round per sec = $\frac{3000}{60}$ = 50

In one round data read = 512 * 1kB = 512 KB

(Here in round)

We can read one track = $\frac{2^{19}}{4} = 2^{17}$

In one second = $2^{17} * 50$.

Hard disk interrupt = 6553600 C.P.U.

(DMA at most)

Each intruption take = 4 *n*sec

So, 6553600 Intrupts takes = 0.262144 s

∴ Percentage = $\frac{0.262144}{1} \times 100$

= 26.2144 (approx)

In case, we use 1 kB = 1000, then answer is 25.

48. Size of disk

= Number of surfaces × number of Tracks per surface × number of Sectors per track × capacity of each sector

= 16 × 128 × 256 × 512 bytes

= 256 Mega bytes (MB)

Since, total number of sector in disk

= 16 × 128 × 256 = 512 K = 2^{19} Sector

therefore, it requires 19 bits to specify a particular sector.

49. Average transfer time

= Avg. seek time + Avg. rotational delay + Data transfer time

Seek time is time taken to move from one track to one track

So, Avg Seek time = (0 + 1 + 2 + 3 + ... + 499)/500

= 249.5 ms

Avg Rotational Delay = half of revolution time 6000 RPM i.e. 1 revolution in 60/600 sec

= 1/10 sec = 0.1 sec

Avg Rotational Delay = 1/2(0.1sec) = 50 msec

Data Transfer Rate = In One 1 Rotation we can read data on one track = 100 * 500 = 50,000 B data is read in one rotation. 250 bytes → 0.1 * 250 / 50,000 = 0.5 ms

So total is 249.5 + 50 + 0.5 = 300 ms

50. Sector no = 400 × 20 × 63 + 16 × 63 + 29 = 505037.

51. For option

(a) sector no. = 0 * 20 * 63 + 15 * 63 + 31 = 976 sector.

(b) Sector no = 0 * 20 * 63 + 16 * 63 + 30 = 1038

(c) Sector no = 0 * 20 * 63 + 16 * 63 + 31

= 1039 sector

Hence answer is (c).

52. 6000 rotations ________ 60 sec

1 rotation ________ 10 ms

∴ Rotational latency = 5 ms

Time for one disk access = 15 ms

Time to load all libraries = 15 × 100

= 1500 ms = 1.5 sec

53. Since starting on disk starts from <1200, 9, 40> so no of sectors left on 9th surface is 24

so, on 9th surface total storage of "12288" B is possible Now, a part from 9th surface, on cylinder no. 1200 only 6 surface is left.

To storage possible on these 6 surface are

= $6 * 2^6 * 2^9$ → storage on each sector.

↓

No. of sectors on each surface

= 196608 B

So total on cylinder no. 1200, storage possible

⇒ 196608 + 12288 = 208896 B

So Since file size is 42797 kB and out of which 208896 B are stored on cylinder no. 1200. So we are left only with only 43615232 B.

Since in 1 cylinder, Storage Possible is

= $2^4 * 2^6 * 2^9$ B = 524288 B

So we need about = $\frac{43615232}{524288\,\text{B}}$ B

= 83.189 more cylinders.

Hence we'll need the **1284th Cylinder** to completely store the file. C_{02} after 1283rd cylinder we will left with data which will need .189

54. Given seek time = 4 ms and 10000 rotation per minute i.e. $\frac{60\,\text{sec}}{10000}$ = 1 rotation

⇒ 1 rotation = 6 ms rotation latency

= $\frac{1}{2} \times 6\,\text{ms}$ = 3 ms

No. of sector = 600 per track,

1 sector = $\frac{6\,\text{ms}}{600}$ = 0.01 ms

2000 sector = 2000 × 0.01 = 20 ms.

Total time required = (2000 × (4 + 3)) + 20

= 14020 ms

55. 15000 rotation in 1 minute

$$1 \text{ rotation} = \frac{1}{15000} \text{ or } \frac{60\,\text{sec}}{1500} = 4 \text{ ms.}$$

$$\text{rotational delay} = \frac{1}{2} \times 4 = 2 \text{ ms}$$

$$\text{Seek time} = 2 \times 2 = 4 \text{ ms}$$

$$\text{transfer time} = 0.1 \text{ ms.}$$

$$\text{Average time} = 4 + 2 + 0.1 = 6.1\text{ms}$$

56. Data transfer rate = 10M bytes/sec

$$= 10 \times 2^{10} \text{ k byte/sec}$$

Size of transfer = 20 k bytes

$$10 \times 2^{10} \times x\% = 20$$

$$10 \times 2^{10} \times \frac{x}{100} = 20 = \frac{20 \times 100}{10 \times 2^{10}} = \frac{200}{1024}$$

$$x = 0.19\%$$

$$x = 0.10\%$$

57. Index = M.M request MOD number of blocks in cache

0	0 16 24
1	9 17 25 17
2	2 18 2 82
3	3
4	20
5	5
6	30
7	63

{As per above cache 3, 20, 30 is in cache but 18 is not is cache.}

3 % 8 = 3
5 % 8 = 5
2 % 8 = 2
0 % 8 = 0
63 % 8 = 7
9 % 8 = 7
16 % 8 = 0
17 % 8 = 1
25 % 8 = 1
18 % 8 = 2
30 % 8 = 6
24 % 8 = 0
2 % 8 = 2
63 % 8 = 7 (Hit)
5 % 8 = 2
82 % 8 = 2
17 % 8 = 1
24 % 8 = 0 (Hit)

58. Interrrupt driven transfer time

$$= 1 + 1 + 500 \times (2 + 2 + 1 + 1 + 1) = 3502$$

DMA based transfer time = 20 + 500 * 2 = 1020

Speedup = 3502/1020 = 3.4(approx.)

59. Size of data count register is 16 bits

Data that can be transferred in one time

$$= 2^{16} \text{ bytes} = 64 \text{ kilobytes}$$

File size to be transferred = 29154 kilobytes

So, number of times the DMA controller needs to get the control is 29154/64 = 455.53 (take 456).

Unit - V

Programming and Data Structures

Syllabus

Programming in C. Recursion. Arrays, stacks, queues, linked lists, trees, binary search trees, binary heaps, graphs.

Contents

1

CHAPTER

Programming

Analysis of Previous GATE Papers

Units		Year → Topics ↓	2019	2018	2017 Set 1	2017 Set 2	2016 Set 1	2016 Set 2	2015 Set 1	2015 Set 2	2015 Set 3
C BASICS	1 Mark	MCQ Type									1
		Numerical Type									
	2 Marks	MCQ Type				1			1		
		Numerical Type				1					1
	Total					4			2		3
C POINTER	1 Mark	MCQ Type		1							
		Numerical Type	1	1			1	1			
	2 Marks	MCQ Type		1							
		Numerical Type	1		1	1					1
	Total		3	4	2	2	1	1			2
PASCAL	1 Mark	MCQ Type									
		Numerical Type									
	2 Marks	MCQ Type									
		Numerical Type									
	Total										
FORTRAN	1 Mark	MCQ Type									
		Numerical Type									
	2 Marks	MCQ Type									
		Numerical Type									
	Total										
STRUCTURE & UNION	1 Mark	MCQ Type									
		Numerical Type									
	2 Marks	MCQ Type									
		Numerical Type									
	Total										
C-FUNCTION	1 Mark	MCQ Type				1				1	
		Numerical Type	2	1			1		1	1	
	2 Marks	MCQ Type	2	1	2		2	1			1
		Numerical Type			1						1
	Total		6	3	6	1	5	2	1	2	4

C BASICS

1. Study the following program written in a block-structured language:

```
var x, y : integer;
procedure P(n:integer);
begin
x : = (n + 2) / (n — 3);
end;
procedure Q
var x, y : integer;
begin
x : = 3;
y : = 4;
P(y);
Write (x)                ...(1)
end;
begin
x : = 7;
y : = 8;
Q;
Write (x)                ...(2)
end
```

What will be printed by write statements marked (1) and (2) in the program if variables are statically scoped?

(a) 3, 6
(b) 6, 7
(c) 3, 7
(d) None of these

[1987 : 2 Marks]

2. Indicate all the true statements from the following:

(a) A programming language not supporting either recursion or pointer type does not need the support of dynamic memory allocation.
(b) Although C does not support call by name parameter passing, the effect can be correctly simulated in C.

[1991 : 1 Mark]

3. Match the pairs in the following:

List-I	List-II
A. Small talk	P. Logic programming
B. LISP	Q. Data flow programming
C. Prolog	R. Functional programming
D. VAL	S. Object-Oriented programming

[1993 : 2 Marks]

4. What does the following code do?

```
var a, b : integer;
begin
a:=a+b;
b:=a—b;
a:=a —b
end;
```

(a) exchanges (a) and (b)
(b) doubles (a) and stores in (b)
(c) doubles (b) and stores in (a)
(d) leaves (a) and (b) unchanged

[1993 : 2 Marks]

5. An unrestricted use of the "goto" statement is harmful because

(a) it makes it more difficult to verify programs
(b) it increases the running time of the programs
(c) it increases the memory required for the programs
(d) it results in the complier generating longer machine code

[1994 :1 Mark]

6. Given the programming constructs

(i) assignment
(ii) for loops where the loop parameter cannot be changed within the loop
(iii) if-then-else
(iv) forward go to
(v) arbitrary go to
(vi) non-recursive procedure call
(vii) recursive procedure/function call
(viii) repeat loop,

which constructs will you not include in a programming language such that it should be possible to program that terminates (i.e., halting) function in the same programming language.

(a) (ii), (iii), (iv) (b) (v), (vii), (viii)
(c) (vi), (vii), (viii) (d) (iii), (vii), (viii)

[1999: 2 Marks]

7. Consider the following C function definition

```
int Trial (int a, int b, int c)
{
    if ((a > = b) && (c < b) return b;
    else if (a > = b) return Trial (a,c,b);
    else return Trial (b,a,c);
}
```

The function Trial:

(a) Finds the maximum of a, b and c

(b) Finds the minimum of a, b and c

(c) Finds the middle number of a, b and c

(d) None of the above

[1999 : 2 Marks]

8. Aliasing in the context of programming languages refers to

(a) multiple variables having the same memory location

(b) multiple variables having the same value

(c) multiple variables having the same identifier

(d) multiple uses of the same variable

[2000 :1 Mark]

9. The goal of structured programming is to

(a) have well indented programs

(b) be able to infer the flow of control from the compiled code

(c) be able to infer the flow of control from the program text

(d) avoid the use of GOTO statements

[2004 :1 Mark]

10. Let x be an integer which can take a value of 0 or 1. The statement

```
if (x = = 0) x = 1;
else x = 0;
```

is equivalent to which one of the following?

(a) x = 1 + x; (b) x = 1 — x;

(c) x = x — 1; (d) x = 1% x;

[2004: 1 Mark]

11. Consider the following C program

```
main()
{
    int x, y, m, n;
    scanf ("%d %d", &x , &y);
    / * Assume x > 0 and y > 0* /
    m = x; n = y;
    while(m! = n)
    {
    if(m>n)
    m = m - n;
    else
    n = n — m;
    }
    printf ("% d", n);
}
```

The program computes

(a) x ÷ y, using repeated subtraction

(b) x mod y using repeated subtraction

(c) the greatest common divisor of x and y

(d) the least common multiple of x and y

[2004 : 2 Marks]

12. Choose the best matching between the programming styles in Group 1 and their characteristics in Group 2.

Group-I	Group-2
P. Functional	1. Command-based, procedural
Q. Logic	2. Imperative, abstract data types
R. Object-oriented	3. Side-effect free, declarative, expression evaluation
S. Imperative	4. Declarative, clausal represent, theorem proving

Codes:

(a) P-2, Q-3, R-4, S-1

(b) P-4, Q-3, R-2, S-1

(c) P-3, Q-4, R-1, S-2

(d) P-3, Q-4, R-2, S-1

13. Consider the following program fragment for reversing the digits in a given integer to obtain a new integer. Let $n = d_1d_2 \ldots d_m$.

```
int n, rev ;
rev = 0 ;
while (n > 0) {
rev = rev * 10 + n % 10 ;
n = n/10;
}
```

The loop invariant condition at the end of the ith iteration is

(a) $n = d_1\ d_2 \ldots d_{m-i}$ and $rev = d_m\ d_{m-1} \ldots d_{m-i+i}$

(b) $n = d_{m-i+1} \ldots d_{m-1}\ d_m$ or $rev = d_{m-i} \ldots d_2\ d_1$

(c) $n \neq rev$

(d) $n = d_1\ d_2 \ldots d_m$ or $rev = d_m \ldots d_2\ d_1$

[2004 : 2 Marks]

14. A common property of logic programming languages and functional languages is

(a) both are procedural language

(b) both are based on λ-calculus

(c) both are declarative

(d) all of the above

[2005 : 1 Mark]

15. Which of the following are essential features of an object-oriented programming languages?

1. Abstraction and encapsulation
2. Strictly-typedness
3. Type-safe property coupled with sub-type rule
4. Polymorphism in the presence of inheritance

(a) 1 and 2 only (b) 1 and 4 only
(c) 1, 2 and 4 only (d) 1, 3 and 4 only

[2005 : 1 Mark]

16. Match the following concepts and their best possible descriptions.

Concept	Description
(i) overloading	(a) allows to define a class to have properties of another class
(ii) friend	(b) defining a set of similar functions
(iii) constructor	(c) used in dereferencing
(iv) protected	(d) used to give a non-member function access to the private parts of an object
(v) this	(e) a function which is automatically called when an object is created
(vi) inheritance	(f) allows a derived class to have access to the private parts of the base class
	(g) a pointer to the object associated with the current function
	(h) used to obtain object persistence

(a) i-b, ii-d, iii-e, iv-f, v-g, vi-a
(b) i-c, ii-a, iii-e, iv-d, v-h, vi-f
(c) i-c, ii-f, iii-h, iv-a, v-g, vi-d
(d) i-b, ii-e, iii-c, iv-f, v-g, vi-s

[2006 : 2 Marks]

17. Consider this C code to swap two integers and these five statements : the code

```
void swap (int*px, int* py) {
    *px = *px  -  *py;
    *py = *px + *PY;
    *px =*py  -  *px;
}
```

S1 : will generate a compilation error

S2 : may generate a segmentation fault at runtime depending on the arguments passed

S3 : Correctly implements the swap procedure for all input pointers referring to integers stored in memory locations accessible to the process

S4 : implements the swap procedure correctly for some but not all valid input pointers

S5 : may add or subtract integers and pointers

(a) S1 (b) S2 and S3
(c) S2 and S4 (d) S2 and S5

[2006 : 2 Marks]

18. Consider the C program given below:

```
# include <stdio.h>
int main ()
{
int sum = 0, maxsum = 0, i, n = 6;
int a( ) = {2, –2, –1, 3, 4, 2};
for(i = 0; i < n; i++)
{
if(i = = 0 | | a[i] < 0 | | a[i] < a[i – 1])
{
if(sum > maxsum)
maxsum = sum;
sum = (a[i] > 0) ? a[i] : 0;
}
else sum + = a [i];
if(sum > maxsum) maxsum = sum;
printf ("%d\n", maxsum);
}
```

What is the value printed out when this program is executed?

(a) 9
(b) 8
(c) 7
(d) 6

[2007 : 2 Marks]

19. Early binding refers to a binding performed at compile time and late binding refers to a binding performed at execution time. Consider the following statements:

(i) Static scope facilitates wl bindings.
(ii) Dynamic scope requires w2 bindings.
(iii) Early bindings w3 execution efficiency.
(iv) Late bindings w4 execution efficiency.

The right choices of wl, w2, w3 and w4 (in that order) are

(a) Early, late, decrease, increase
(b) Late, early, increase, decrease
(c) Late, early, decrease, increase
(d) Early, late, increase, decrease

[2007 : 2 Marks]

20. Match the programming paradigms and languages given in the following table.

List-I (Paradigms)	List-II (Languages)
I. Imperative	A. Prolog
II. Object oriented	B. Lisp
III. Functional.	C. C, Fortran 77, pascal
IV. Logic	D. C++, Smalltalk, Java

Codes:

(a) I–C, II–D, III–B, IV–A

(b) I–A, II–D, III–C, IV–B

(c) I–D, II–C, III–B, IV–A

(d) I–C, II–D, III–A, IV–B

[2008: 1 Mark]

21. Which combination of the integer variables x, y and z makes the variable a get the value 4 in the following expression?

a = (x > y) ? ((x > z) ? x : z) : ((y>z) ? y : z)

(a) x = 3, y = 4, z = 2

(b) x = 6, y = 5, z = 3

(c) x = 6, y = 3, z = 5

(d) x = 5, y = 4, z = 5

[2008 :1 Mark]

22. Consider the following C program that attempts to locate an element x in an array Y[ ] using binary search. The program is erroneous.

```
f(int Y[10] , int x) {
int i, j, k;
i = 0; j = 9;
do {
k=(i+j)/ 2;
if (Y[K] < x) i = k; else j = k;
} while (( Y[k] ! = x) && ( i < j));
if (Y[k] = = x )
printf("x is in the array") ;
else
printf("x is not in the array");
}
```

On which of the following contents of Y and x does the program fail?

(a) Y is [1 2 3 4 5 6 7 8 9 10] and x < 10

(b) Y is [1 3 5 7 9 11 13 15 17 19] and x < 1

(c) Y is [2 2 2 2 2 2 2 2 2 2] and x > 2

(d) Y is [2 4 6 8 10 12 14 16 18 20] and 2 < x < 20 andxiseven

[2008 : 2 Marks]

23. The following program is to be tested for statement coverage:

```
begin
if (a = = b) {S1; exit;}
else if (c = = d) {S2;}
else {S3; exit;}
S4;
end
```

The test cases T1, T2, T3 and T4 given below are expressed in terms of the properties satisfied by the values of variables a, b, c and d. The exact values are not given.

T1 : a, b, c and d are all equal

T2 : a, b, c and d are all distinct

T3 : a = b and c != d

T4: a !=b and c = d

Which of the test suites given below ensures coverage of statements S1, S2, S3 and S4?

(a) T1, T2, T3 (b) T2, T4

(c) T3, T4 (d) T1, T2, T4

[2010 : 2 Marks]

24. Consider the following pseudo code. What is the total number of multiplications to be performed?

```
D = 2
for i = 1 to n do
for j = i to n do
for k = j + 1 to n do
D = D * 3
```

(a) Half of the product of the 3 consecutive integers.

(b) One-third of the product of the 3 consecutive integers.

(c) One-sixth of the product of the 3 consecutive integers.

(d) None of the above.

[2014 (Set-1): 2 Marks]

25. Suppose n and p are unsigned int variables in a *C*program. We wish to set p to ${}^nC_3$. If n is large, which one of the following statements is most likely to set p correctly?

(a) p = n*(n – 1)*(n – 2)/6;

(b) p = n*(n – 1)/2*(n – 2)/3;

(c) p = n*(n – 1)/3*(n – 2)/2;

(d) p = n*(n – 1)*(n – 2)/6.0;

[2014 (Set-2): 1 Mark]

26. Consider the following pseudo code, where x and y are positive integers.

```
begin
q:=0;
r :=x;
while r ≥ y do
begin r := r – y ; q := q + 1 ; end
end
```

The post condition that needs to be satisfied after the program terminates is

(a) $\{r = qx + y \wedge r < y\}$

(b) $\{x = qy + r \wedge r < y\}$

(c) $\{y = qx + r \wedge 0 < r < y\}$

(d) $\{q + 1 < r - y \wedge y > 0\}$

[2015 (Set-1): 2 Marks]

27. Consider the following C program segment.

```
# include <stdio.h>
int main() {
char s1[7] = "1234", *p;
p = s1 + 2;
*p = '0' ;
printf ("%s", s1);
}
```

What will be printed by the program?

(a) 12 (b) 120400

(c) 1204 (d) 1034

[2015 (Set-3) : 1 Mark]

28. Consider the following C program:

```
# include <stdio.h>
int main() {
int i, j, k = 0;
j = 2 * 3 / 4 + 2.0 / 5 + 8 / 5;
k – = – –j;
for(i = 0; i < 5; i++) {
switch(i + k)
{
case 1:
case 2: printf("\n%d", i + k);
case 3: printf("\n%d", i + k);
default: printf("\n%d", i + k); }
}
}
return 0;
}
```

The number of times printf statement is executed is ________.

[2015 (Set-3) : 2 Marks]

29. Consider the following C program

```
# include <stdio.h>
int main()
{
int m = 10;
int n, n1;
n = ++m;
n1 = m++;
n – –;
– – n1;
n – = n1;
printf("%d", n);
return 0;
}
```

The output of the program is ________.

[2017 (Set-2) : 2 Marks]

30. Consider the C program fragment below which is meant to divide x by y using repeated subtractions. The variables x, y, q and r are all unsigned int.

```
while
(r >= y)
{ r = r – y;
q = q + 1;
}
```

Which of the following conditions on the variables x, y, q and r before the execution of the fragment will ensure that the loop terminates in a state satisfying the condition x == (y x q + r)?

(a) (q == r) && (r == 0)

(b) (x > 0) && (r == x) && (y > 0)

(c) (q == 0) && (r == x) && (y > 0)

(d) (q == 0) && (y > 0)

[2017 (Set-2) : 2 Marks]

31. Consider the following C program

```
#include <stdio.h>
int main()(
float sum = 0.0, j = 1.0, i = 2.0;
while (i/j > 0.0625){
j = j + j;
sum = sum + i/j;
printf("%f\n", sum);
}
return 0;
}
```

The number of times the variable sum will be printed, when the above program is executed is ________.

C POINTER

32. In which of the following case(s) is it possible to obtain different results for call-by-reference and call-by-name parameter passing?

(a) Passing an expression as a parameter

(b) Passing an array as a parameter

(c) Passing a pointer as a parameter

(d) Passing an array element as a parameter

[1989 : 2 Marks]

33. In which one of the following cases is it possible to obtain different results for call-by reference and call-by-name parameter passing methods?

(a) Passing a constant value as a parameter

(b) Passing the address of an array as a parameter

(c) Passing an array element as a parameter

(d) Passing an array **[1994 : 2 Marks]**

34. Consider the following three C functions:

```
[P1] int *g (void)
     {
     int x = 10;
     return (&x);
     }
[P2] int*g (void)
     {
     int *px;
     *px = 10;
     return px;
     }
[P3] int *g(void)
     {
     int *px;
     px = (int *) malloc (size of (int));
     *px = 10;
     return px;
     }
```

Which of the above three functions are likely to cause problems with pointers?

(a) Only P3 (b) Only P1 and P3

(c) Only P1 and P2 (d) P1, P2 and P3

[2001 : 2 Marks]

35. The results returned by function under value-result and reference parameter passing return conventions

(a) Do not differ

(b) Differ in the presence of loops

(c) Differ in all cases int

(d) May differ in the presence of exception

[2002 : 1 Mark]

36. Consider the C program shown below.

```
# include <stdio.h>
# define print (x) printf ("%d", x)
int x;
void Q (int z) {
z + = x; print (z);
}
void p (int *y) {
int x = *y + 2;
Q (x); *y = x — 1;
print (x);
}
main (void) {
x = 5;
p (&x);
print(x);
}
```

The output of this program is

(a) 12 7 6 (b) 22 12 11

(c) 14 6 6 (d) 7 6 6

[2003 : 2 Marks]

37. Consider the following C program:

```
#include <stdio.h>
typedef struct
{
char *a;
char *b;
} t;
void fl(t s);
void f2(t *p);
main( )
{
static t s = {"A", "B"};
printf("%s %s \n", s.a, s.b);
fl (s);
printf("%s %s \n", s.a, s.b);
f2(&s);
}
void f1(t s)
{
s.a = "U";
s.b = "V"
printf(%s %s \n", s.a, s.b);
return;
}
void f2(t *p)
```

```
{
p → a = "V";
p → b = "W"
printf("%"s %s\n", p → a, p → b);
return;
}
```

What is the output generated by the program?

(a) A B
U V
V W
V W

(b) A B
U V
A B
V W

(c) A B
U V
U V
V W

(d) A B
U V
V W
U V

[2004 : 2 Marks]

38. What does the following C-statement declare?

int (*f) (int *);

(a) A function that takes an integer pointer as argument and returns an integer
(b) A function that takes an integer pointer as argument and returns an integer pointer
(c) A pointer to a function that takes an integer pointer as argument and returns an integer
(d) A function that takes an integer pointer as argument returns a function pointer

[2005: 1 Mark]

39. Which one of the choices given below would be printed when the following program is executed?

```
#include <stdio.h>
void swap (int *x, int *y)
{
static int *temp;
temp = x;
x = y;
y = temp;
}
void printab ( )
{
static int i, a = –3, b = – 6:
i = 0;
while (i < = 4)
{
if ((i ++)%2 = = 1) continue;
a = a + i;
b = b + i;
}
swap (&a, &b);
printf("a = %d, b = %d\n", a, b);
}
main ()
printab ();
printab ();
}
```

(a) a = 0, b = 3
a = 0, b = 3
(b) a = 3, b = 0
a = 12, b = 9
(c) a = 3, b = 6
a = 3, b = 6
(d) a = 6, b = 3
a = 15, b = 12

[2006 : 2 Marks]

40. What is printed by the following C program?

```
int f(int x, int *py, int ** ppz)
{ int y, z;
**ppz + = 1; z = **ppz;
*py += 2; y=*py;
x+ = 3;
return x + y + z;
}
void main( )
{   int c, *b, **a;
c = 4; b=&c;a=&b;
printf ("% d", f (c, b, a));
}
```

(a) 18
(b) 19
(c) 21
(d) 22

[2008 : 2 Marks]

41. Consider the program below:

```
# include <stdio.h>
int fun (int n, int *f_p) {
int t, f;
if (n < = 1) {
*f_p = 1 ;
return 1 ;
}
t = fun(n–1, f_p) ;
f = t + * f _p;
*f_p = t ;
return f ;
}
int main( )
{
int x = 15 ;
printf ("% d\n", fun (5, &x)) ;
return 0;
}
```

The value printed is

(a) 6
(b) 8
(c) 14
(d) 15

[2009 : 1 Mark]

42. What does the following program print?

```
#include < stdio.h>
void f(int *p, int *q)
{
p = q;
*p = 2;
}
int i = 0, j = 1;
int main( )
{
f(&i, &j);
printf ("%d %d\n", i, j);
return 0;
}
```

(a) 2 2 (b) 2 1
(c) 0 1 (d) 0 2

[2010 : 1 Mark]

43. What is the value printed by the following C program?

```
#include < stdio.h>
int f(int *a, int n)
{
if (n <= 0) return 0;
else if (*a % 2 == 0)
return *a + f(a + 1, n – 1);
else return *a – f(a + 1, n – 1);
}
int main ( )
{
int a [ = {12, 7, 13, 4, 11, 6};
printf("%d", f(a, 6));
return 0;
}
```

(a) –9 (b) 5
(c) 15 (d) 19

[2010 : 2 Marks]

44. What does the following fragment of C program print?

```
char c = "GATE2011";
char *p = c;
printf("%s", p + p[3] – p[1]);
```

(a) GATE 2011
(b) E2011
(c) 2011
(d) 011

[2011 : 1 Mark]

45. Consider the following program in C language:

```
#include <stdio.h>
main()
{
int i;
int *pi = &i;
scanf("%d",pi);
printf("%d\n", i+5);
}
```

Which one of the following statements is TRUE?

(a) Compilation fails.
(b) Execution results in a run-time error.
(c) On execution, the value printed is 5 more than the address of variable i.
(d) On execution, the value printed is 5 more than the integer value entered.

[2014 (Set-1) : 1 Mark]

46. Consider the following C program.

```
# include < stdio.h>
int main() {
static int a[ ] = {10, 20, 30, 40, 50};
static int *p[ ] = {a, a+3, a+4, a+1, a+2};
int **ptr = p; ptr++;
printf ("%d%d", prt-p, **ptr);
}
```

The output of the program is______.

[2015 (Set-3): 2 Marks]

47. Consider the following C program.

```
# include<stdio.h>
void mystery (int *ptra, int *ptrb)
{ int *temp;
temp = ptrb;
ptrb = ptra;
ptra = temp;
}
int main()
{ int a = 2016, b = 0, c = 4, d = 42;
mystery(&a, &b);
if(a<c)
mystery(&c, &a);
mystery(&a, &d);
printf("%d\n", a);
}
```

The output of the program is_____.

[2016 (Set-1): 1 Mark]

48. The value printed by the following program is_______.

```
void f(int* p, int m)
{ m = m + 5;
*p = *p + m;
return;
}
void main ()
{ int i = 5, j = 10;
f(& i, j);
print f("%d", i + j);
}
```

[2016 (Set-2): 1 Mark]

49. Consider the following C program.

```
#include <stdio.h>
#include <string.h>
void printlength (char *s, char *t)
{
unsigned int c = 0;
int len = ((strlen(s) – strlen(t)) > c) ? strlen(s):
strlen(t);
printf("%d\n", len);
}
void main ()
{
char *x = "abc";
char *y = "defgh";
printlength (x, y);
```

Recall that strlen is defined in string.h as returning a value of type size_t, which is an unsigned int. The output of the program is______.

[2017 (Set-1) : 2 Marks]

50. Consider the following C program.

```
# include <stdio.h>
# include <string.h>
int main()
{ char* c = "GATECSIT2017";
char* p = c;
printf("%d", (int) strlen (c+2[p] – 6[p]–1)); return 0;
}
```

The output of the program is__________.

[2017 (Set-2) : 2 Marks]

51. Consider the following C program:

```
#include <stdio.h>
struct ournode {
char x, y, z;
};
int main () {
struct ournode p = {'1', '0', 'a' + 2};
struct ournode *q = &p;
printf("%c, %c", *((char*) q + 1),
*((char*)q + 2));
return 0;
}
```

The output of this program is:

(a) 0, c (b) 0, a + 2
(c) '0', 'a + 2' (d) '0', 'c' **[2018:1 Mark]**

52. Consider the following C program:

```
#include <stdio.h>
int counter = 0;
int calc (int a, int b) {
int c;
counter ++;
if (b = = 3) return (a × a × a);
else{
c = calc (a, b/3);
return (c × c × c);
}
}
int main () {
calc(4, 81);
printf("%d", counter);
}
```

The output of this program is________.

[2018 : 1 Mark]

53. Consider the following C program:

```
#include <stdio.h>
void funl (char *sl, char *s2) {
char *tmp;
tmp = s1;
s1 = s2;
s2 = tmp;
}
void fun2 (char **sl, char **s2) {
char *tmp;
tmp = *sl;
*s1 = *s2;
*s2 = tmp;
}
int main () {
char *str1 = "Hi", *str2 = "Bye";
fun1 (strl, str2); printf("%s %s", str1, str2);
fun2 (&str1, &str2); printf("%s %s", str1, str2);
return 0;
}
```

The output of the program above is

(a) Hi Bye Bye Hi (b) Hi Bye Hi Bye
(c) Bye Hi Hi Bye (d) Bye Hi Bye Hi

[2018:2 Marks]

54. Consider the following C program :

```
#include <studio.h>
int main ( ) {
    int arr [ ] = {1, 2, 3, 4, 5, 6, 7, 8, 9, 0, 1, 2, 5},
    *ip=arr +4;
    print f("%d\n", ip[1]);
    return 0;
}
```

The number that will be displayed on execution of the program is ________.

[2019 : 1 Mark]

55. Consider the following C program

```
#include <stdio.h>
int main()
{
int a[] = {2, 4, 6, 8, 10};
int i, sum = 0, *b = a + 4;
for (i = 0; i < 5; i ++)
sum = sum + (*b – i) – *(b – i);
printf ("%d/n", sum);
return 0;
}
```

The output of the above C program is _____.

[2019 : 2 Marks]

PASCAL

Common Data Questions 56 & 57:

Consider the Pascal program shown in below.

```
program PARAM (input, output):
var m, n : integer;
procedure P(var x, y : integer);
var m : integer;
begin
m : = 1;
x : = y + 1;
end;
procedure Q (x : integer; var y : integer);
begin
x : = y + 1;
end;
begin
m : = 0; P(m, m); write (m);
n : = 0; Q (n*1, n) ; write (n)
end.
```

56. The value of m, output by the program PARAM is

(a) 1, because m is a local variable in P

(b) 0, because m is the actual parameter that corresponds to the formal parameter in p

(c) 0, because both x and y are just reference to m and y has the value 0

(d) 1, because both x and y are just references to m which gets modified in procedure P

[1993 : 2 Marks]

57. The value of n, output by the program PARAM is

(a) 0, because n is the actual parameter corresponding to x in procedure Q.

(b) 0, because n is the actual parameter to y in procedure Q.

(c) 1, because n is the actual parameter corresponding to x in procedure Q.

(d) 1, because n is the actual parameter corresponding to yin procedure Q.

(e) none of the above

[1993: 2 Marks]

58. What is the scope of m declared in the main program?

(a) PARAM, P, Q (c) PARAM, Q

(b) PARAM, P (d) P, Q

[1993 : 2 Marks]

59. What is the value of X printed by the following program?

```
program COMPUTE (input, output);
var X:integer;
procedure FIND (X:real);
begin X: = sqrt(X); end;
begin
X: = 2
Find(X)
Writeln(X)
end
```

(a) 1 (b) 2

(c) Run time error (d) None of these

[1995 : 2 Marks]

60. Given the following Pascal like program segment

```
Procedure A;
x, y:integer;
Procedure B;
x, z:real;
S1
end B;
Procedure C;
i:integer;
```

S2
end C;
end A;
The variables accessible in S1 and S2 are

(a) x of A, y, x of B and z in S1 and x of B, y and i in S2
(b) x of B, y and z in S1 and x of B, i and z in S2
(c) x of B, z and y in S1 and x of A, i and y in S2
(d) None of the above **[1997 : 2 Marks]**

61. Consider the following program in a language that has dynamic scoping:

```
var x: real;
procedure show:
begin print(x);end;
procedure small;
var x: real;
begin x: = 0.125;
show; end;
begin
x:=0.25;
show; small
end.
```

Then the output of the program is:

(a) 0.125 0.125 (b) 0.25 0.25
(c) 0.25 0.125 (d) 0.125 0.25

[1999: 2 Marks]

62. Consider the program given below, in a block-structured pseudo-language with lexical scoping and nesting of procedures permitted.

```
.Program main;
Var ...
Procedure Al;
Var...
Call A2;
EndAl
Procedure A2;
Var...
Procedure A21;
Var...
Call Al,
EndA21
Call A21;
EndA2
Call Al;
End main;
```

Consider the calling chain:
Main → A1 → A2 → A21 → A1

The correct set of activation records along with their access links is given by

(a)

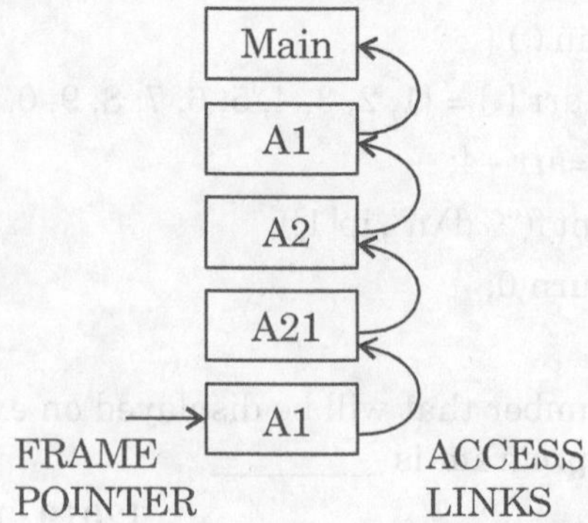

(b)

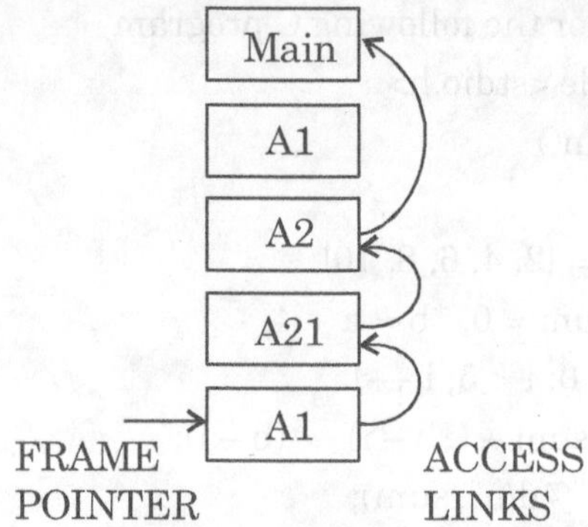

(c)

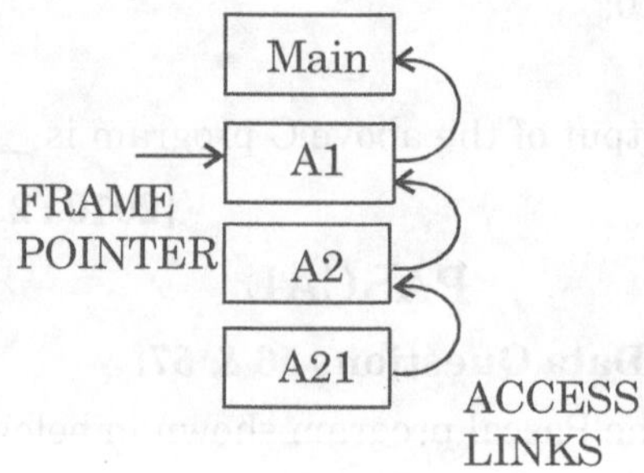

(d)

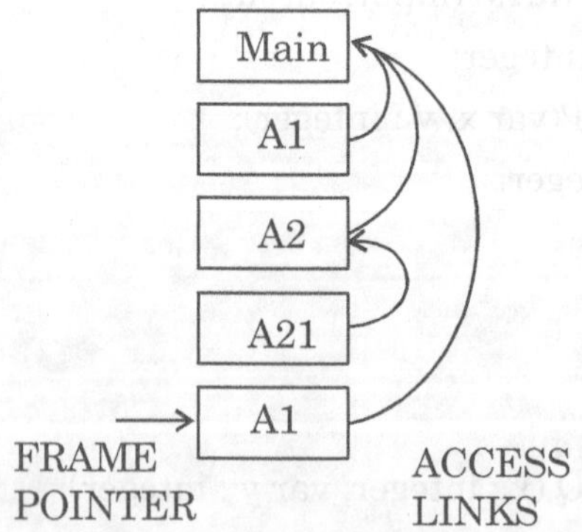

FORTRAN

63. FORTRAN implementation do not permit recursion because

(a) they use static allocation for variables
(b) they use dynamic allocation for variables
(c) stacks are not available on all machines
(d) it is not possible to implement recursion on all machines. **[1994 :1 Mark]**

STRUCTURE & UNION

64. The following C declarations

```
struct node{
int i:
float j;
};
struct node *s [10];
```

define s to be

(a) An array, each element of which is a pointer to a structure of type node
(b) A structure of 2 fields, each field being a pointer to an array of 10 elements
(c) A structure of 3 fields: an integer, a float, and an array of 10 elements
(d) An array, each element of which is a structure of type node **[2000 :1 Mark]**

65. Consider the following C declaration

```
struct {
short s[5];
union {
float y;
long z;
} u;
} t;
```

Assume that objects of the type short, float and long occupy 2 bytes, 4 bytes and 8 bytes, respectively. The memory requirement for variable t, ignoring alignment considerations, is

(a) 22 bytes (b) 14 bytes
(c) 18 bytes (d) 10 bytes

[2000 :1 Mark]

C-FUNCTION

66. What is printed by the print statements in the program P1 assuming call by reference parameter passing?

```
Program P1()
{
x=10;
y = 3;
funcl(y, x, x);
print x;
print y;
}
funcl(x, y, z)
{
y = y + 4;
z = x + y + z;
}
```

(a) 10, 3 (b) 31, 3
(c) 27, 7 (d) None of these

67. Consider the following program

```
Program P2
var n:int;
procedure W(var x:int)
begin
x = x + 1;
print x;
end
procedure D
begin
var n:int;
n = 3;
W(n);
end
begin //begin P2
n = 10;
D;
end
```

If the language has dynamic scoping and parameters are passed by reference, what will be printed by the program?

(a) 10 (b) 11
(c) 3 (d) None of these

[2001 : 2 Marks]

68. What is the output of the following program?

```
#include <stdio.h>
int funcf (int x);
int funcg (int y);
main( )
}
int x = 5, y = 10, count;
for(count = 1; count < = 2; ++count)
{
y + = funcf(x) + funcg(x);
print f("%d", y);
}
}
funcf(int x)
{
int y;
y = funcg(x);
return (y);
}
funcg (int x)
{
static int y = 10;
y + = 1;
return (y + x);
}
```

(a) 43 80 (b) 42 74
(c) 33 37 (d) 32 32

[2004 : 2 Marks]

69. Consider the following C function

```
int f (int n)
{   static int i = 1 ;
if (n > = 5) return n ;
n = n + i;
i++;
return f (n);
}
```

The value returned by f(1) is

(a) 5 (b) 6

(c) 7 (d) 8 **[2004 : 2 Marks]**

70. Consider the following C-program

```
double foo (double); /* Line 1*/
int main () {
double da, db;
// input da
db = foo (da);
}
double foo (double a){
return a;
}
```

The above code complied without any error or warning. If Line 1 is deleted, the above code will show

(a) no compile warning or error

(b) some complier-warning not leading to unitended results

(c) Some complier-warning due to type-mismatch eventually leading to unintended results

(d) Compiler errors **[2005 : 2 Marks]**

71. Consider the following C-program

```
void foo (int n, int sum) {
int k = 0, j = 0;
if (n = = 0) return;
k = n % 10;
j = n / 10;
sum = sum + k;
foo ( j, sum);
printf ("% d", k);
}
int main () {
int a = 2048, sum = 0;
foo (a, sum);
printf ("%d\n", sum);
}
```

What does the above program print?

(a) 8, 4, 0, 2, 14 (b) 8, 4, 0, 2, 0

(c) 2, 0, 4, 8, 14 (d) 2, 0, 4, 8, 0

[2005 : 2 Marks]

72. What is the output printed by the following program?

```
# include <stdio.h>
int f(int n, int k)
{
if (n = = 0) return 0;
else if (n% 2) return f(n/2, 2*k)+k;
else return f(n/2, 2*k) - k;
}
int main()
{
printf("%d", f(20, 1));
return 0;
}
```

(a) 5 (b) 8

(c) 9 (d) 20 **[2005 : 2 Marks]**

73. The following function computes the value of $\binom{m}{n}$ correctly for all legal values m and n ($m \geq 1$, $n \geq 0$ and $m > n$)

```
int func(int m, int n)
{
if (E) return 1;
else return(func(m –1, n) + func(m – 1, n–1));
}
```

In the above function, which of the following is the correct expression for E?

(a) (n = = 0) | |(m = =l)

(b) (n = = 0) && (m = = 1)

(c) (n = = 0) I I (m = = n)

(d) (n = = 0) && (m = = n) **[2006 : 2 Marks]**

74. Consider the following code written in a pass-by-reference language like FORTAN and these statements about the code.

```
Subroutine swap (ix,iy)
it = ix
L1 :                    ix = iy
L2:iy = it
end
ia = 3
ib = 8
call swap (ia, ib + 5)
print ia, ib
end
```

S1: The compiler will generate code to allocate a temporary nameless cell, initialize it to 13, and pass the address of the cell to swap

S2: On execution the code will generate a runtime error on line L1

S3: On execution the code will generate a runtime error on line L2

S4: The program will print 13 and 8

S5: The program will print 13 and -2

Exactly the following set of statement (s) is correct:

(a) S1 and S2 (b) S1 and S4

(c) S3 (d) S1 and S5

[2006 : 2 Marks]

75. Consider these two functions and two statements Si and S2 about them.

```
int workl (int* a, int i, int j)
{
    int x = a [i+2] ;
    a [j]=x+1;
    return a [i+2] – 3;
}
```

```
int work2 (int* a, int i, int j)
{
    int t1=i +2;
    int t2=a [tl];
    a [j] = t2 + 1;
    return t2-3;
}
```

S1 :The transformation from work1 to work2 is valid, i.e., for any program state and input arguments, work2 will compute the same output and have the same effect on program state as work1

S2: All the transformations applied to workl to get work2 will always improve the performance (i.e. reduce CPU time) of work2 compared to workl

(a) S1 is false and S2 is false

(b) S1 is false and S2 is true

(c) S1 is true and S2 is false

(d) S1 is true and S2 is true **[2006 : 2 Marks]**

76. Consider the following C function:

```
int f(int n)
{ static int r = 0;
if(n < = 0) return 1;
if(n > 3)
{
r = n;
return f(n – 2) + 2;
}
return f(n – 1) + r;
}
```

What is the value of f(5)?

(a) 5 (b) 7

(c) 9 (d) 18 **[2007 : 2 Marks]**

77. The function f is defined as follows:

```
int f(int n)
{
if (n < = 1)
return 1;
else if (n % 2 = = 0) return f(n/2);
else return f(3n – 1);
```

Assuming that arbitrarily large integers can be passed as a parameter to the function, consider the following statements.

(i) The function f terminates for finitely many different values of $n \geq 1$.

(ii) The function f terminates for infinitely many different values of $n \geq 1$.

(iii) The function f does not terminate for finitely many different values of $n \geq 1$.

(iv) The function f does not terminate for infinitely many different values of $n \geq 1$.

Which one of the following options is true of the above?

(a) (i) and (iii) (b) (i) and (iv)

(c) (ii) and (iii) (d) (ii)and(iv)

[2007 : 2 Marks]

78. Consider the program below in a hypothetical language which allows global variables and a choice of call by reference or call by value methods of parameter passing.

```
int i;
program main ( )
{   int j = 60;
i = 50;
call f(i, j);
print i, j;
}
procedure f(x, y)
{
i = 100;
x = 10;
y = y + i ;
}
```

Which one of the following options represents the correct output of the program for the two parameter passing mechanisms?

(a) Call by value : i = 70, j = 10; Call by reference : i = 60, j = 70

(b) Call by value : i = 50, j = 60; Call by reference : i = 50, j = 70

(c) Call by value : i = 10, j = 70; Call by reference : i = 100, j = 60

(d) Call by value : i = 100, j = 60; Call by reference : i = 10, j = 70 **[2007 : 2 Marks]**

79. Consider the program below in a hypothetical programming language which allows global variables and a choice of static or dynamic scoping.

```
int i ;
program main( )
{
i = 10;
call f( );
}
procedure f( )
{
int i = 20;
call g( );
}
procedure g( )
{
print i;
```

Let x be the value printed under static scoping and y be the value printed under dynamic scoping. The x and y are

(a) x = 10, y = 10 (b) x = 20, y = 10

(c) x = 10, y = 20 (d) x = 20, y = 20

[2007 : 2 Marks]

80. Consider the C program below. What does it print?

```
# include <stdio.h>
# define swapl (a,b) tmp = a; a = b; b =tmp; void
swap2 ( int a, int b)
{
int tmp;
tmp = a; a = b; b = tmp;
}
void swap3 (int*a, int*b)
{
int tmp;
tmp = *a; *a = *b; *b = tmp;
}
int main()
{
int numl = 5, num2 = 4, tmp;
if(numl > num2)
{ swapl (numl, num2);}
if (numl < num2)
{ swap2(numl + 1, num2); }
if (numl > = num2)
{ swap3 (&numl, &num2); }
printf ("%d, %d", numl, num2);
}
```

(a) 5, 5 (b) 5, 4

(c) 4, 5 (d) 4, 4

[2008 : 2 Marks]

Directions for Question 81 to 82:

Consider the code fragment written in C below:

```
void f(int n)
{
if(n ≤ 1 )
{
printf("%d", n);
}
else
{
f(n/2);
printf("%d", n%2);
}
}
```

81. What does f(173) print?

(a) 010110101 (b) 010101101

(b) 10110101 (d) 10101101

[2008: 2 Marks]

82. Which of the following implementations will produce the same output for f(173) as the one from above Question?

P1:	P2:
void f(int n)	void f(int n)
{	{
if(n/2)	if(n< = 1)
{	{
f(n/2);	printf("%d", n);}
}	else
printf("%d", n%2);	{printf("%d", n%2);
}	f(n/2);
	}

(a) Both PI and P2 (b) P2 only

(c) PI only (d) Neither P1 nor P2

[2008 : 2 Marks]

83. Choose the correct option to fill ?1 and ?2 so that the program below prints an input string in reverse order. Assume that the input string is terminated by a newline character.

```
void reverse (void) {
int c;
if (?1) reverse ();
?2
} main ( ) {
printf ("Enter Text") ; printf ("\n");
reverse ( ); printf ("\ n");
}
```

(a) ? 1 is (getchar ( ) ! = ' \n')
? 2 is getchar (c);

(b) ? 1 is (c = getchar ()) ! = '\n')
? 2 is getchar (c)

(c) ? 1 is (c ! = '\n')
? 2 is putchar (c);

(d) ? 1 is ((c = getchar ()) ! = '\n')
? 2 is putchar (c);

[2008 : 2 Marks]

84. Consider the following C program that attempts to locate an element x in an array Y[ ] using binary search. The program is erroneous.

```
1. f(int Y[10] , int x) {
2. int i, j, k;
3. i = 0; j = 9;
4. do {
5. k=(i+j)/ 2;
6. if (Y[K] < x) i = k; else j = k;
7. } while (( Y[k] ! = x) && ( i < j));
8. if (Y[k] = = x )
printf("x is in the array") ;
9. else
printf("x is not in the array");
10. }
```

The correction needed in the program to make it work properly is

(a) change line 6 to : if (Y[k] < x) i = k + 1; else j = k -1;
(b) change line 6 to : if (Y[k] < x) i = k -1; else j = k +1;
(c) change line 6 to : if (Y [k] < x) i = k; else j = k;
(d) change line 7 to : while ((Y [k] = = x) && (i < j));

[2008 : 2 Marks]

Common Data Question 85 and 86:

Consider the following recursive C function that takes two arguments.

```
unsigned int foo(unsigned int n, unsigned int r)
{
if(n>0) return ((n%r)+foo(n/r,r));
else return 0;
}
```

85. What is the return value of the function foo when it is called as foo(345, 10)?

(a) 345
(b) 12
(c) 5
(d) 3

[2011 : 2 Marks]

86. What is the return value of the function foo when it is called as foo(513, 2)?

(a) 9 (b) 8
(c) 5 (d) 2

[2011 : 2 Marks]

87. What will be the output of the following C program segment?

```
char inChar = 'A' ;
switch(inChar)
{
case 'A' : printf ("Choice A\ n") ;
case 'B' :
case 'C' : printf ("Choice B");
case 'D' :
case 'E' :
default : printf ("NO Choice") ;}
```

(a) No Choice
(b) Choice A
(c) Choice A
Choice B No Choice
(d) Program.gives no output as it is erroneous

[2012 : 1 Mark]

Common Data for Questions 88 and 89:

Consider the following C code segment.

```
int a, b, c = 0;
void prtFun (void);
main()
{static int a= 1;/* Line 1*/
prtFun();
a+=l;
prtFun();
printf("\n%d %" ',a,b);}
void prtFun(void)
{static int a = 2;/*Line 2*/
int b = 1;
a += ++b;
printf("\n%d %d", a,b);}
```

88. What output will be generated by the given code segment?

(a)			(b)		
	3	1		4	2
	4	1		6	1
	4	2		6	1
(c)	4	2	**(d)**	3	1
	6	2		5	2
	2	0		5	2

[2012 : 2 Marks]

89. What output will be generated by the given code segment if:

Line 1 is replaced by auto int a=l;

Line 2 is replaced by register int a=2;

(a) 3 1
4 1
4 2

(b) 4 2
6 1
6 1

(c) 4 2
6 2
2 0

(d) 4 2
4 2
2 0

[2012 : 2 Marks]

90. What is the return value of f(p, p), if the value of p is initialized to 5 before the call? Note that the first parameter is passed by reference, whereas the second parameter is passed by value.

```
int f (int &x, int c)
{ c = c – l;
if (c = = 0) return 1;
x = x + 1;
return f(x, c) * x; }
```

(a) 3024 (b) 6561
(c) 55440 (d) 161051

[2013 : 2 Marks]

91. Consider the function func shown below: int func(int num)

```
{ int count = 0;
while (num)
{ count++; num>>= 1;
}
return (count);
}
```

The value returned by function (435) is_____.

[2014 (Set-2): 1 Mark]

92. Consider the following function

```
double f(double x) {
if(abs(x*x- 3) < 0.01) return x;
else return f(x/2 + 1.5/x);
}
```

Give a value q (to 2 decimals) such that f(q) will return q :________.

[2014 (Set-2) : 2 Marks]

93. Consider the C function given below.

```
intf(intj) {
static int i = 50;
int k;
if (i == j) {
printf("something");
k = f(i);
return 0;
}
else return 0;
}
```

Which one of the following is TRUE?

(a) The function returns 0 for all values of j.

(b) The function prints the string something for all values of j.

(c) The function returns 0 when j = 50.

(d) The function will exhaust the runtime stack or run into an infinite loop when j = 50.

[2014 (Set-2) : 2 Marks]

94. The output of the following C program is_____.

```
void f 1 (int a, int b) {
int c;
c=a; a=b; b=c;
}
void f2 (int *a, int *b) {
int c;
c=*a; *a=*b; *b=c;
}
int main() {
int a=4, b=5, c=6;
fl(a,b);
f2(&b,&c);
printf("%d",c – a – b);
}
```

[2015 (Set-1): 1 Mark]

95. Consider the following C function.

```
int fun (int n) {
int x=l, k;
if (n==l) return x;
for (k=l; k<n; ++k)
x=x + fun (k) * fun (n - k);
return x;
}
```

The return value of fun (5) is_________.

[2015 (Set-2): 1 Mark]

96. Consider the following function written in the C programming language.

```
void foo (char *a) {
if(*a&&*a!=' ') {
foo (a+1);
putchar (*a);
}
}
```

The output of the above function on input "ABCDEFGH"is

(a) ABCDEFGH (b) ABCD
(c) HGFEDCBA (d) DCBA

[2015 (Set-2): 1 Mark]

97. Consider the following recursive C function.

```
void get (int n) {
if (n < 1) return;
get (n-1);
get (n-3);
printf ("%d", n);
}
```

If get(6) function is being called in main() then how many times will the get() function be invoked before returning to the main()?

(a) 15 (b) 25
(c) 35 (d) 45

[2015 (Set-3): 2 Marks]

98. Consider the following C program.

```
# include <stdio.h>
int fl (void);
int f2(void);
int f3(void);
int x = 10;
int main( )
{
int x = 1;
x +=fl( ) + f2( ) + f3( ) + f2( );
pirntf("%d", x);
return 0;
}
int fl( ) { int x = 25; x++; return x; }
int f2( ) { static int x = 50; x++; return x; }
int f3( ) { x *= 10; return x; }
```

The output of the program is__________.

[2015 (Set-3): 2 Marks]

99. Consider the following C program.

```
void f(int, short);
void main()
{
int i = 100;
short s = 12;
short *p = &s;
___________; // call to f( )
}
```

Which one of the following expressions, when placed in the blank above, will NOT result in a type checking error?

(a) f(s,*s) (b) i= f(i,s)
(c) f(i, *s) (d) f(i, *p)

[2016 (Set-1): 1 Mark]

100. What will be the output of the following C program?

```
void count(int n)
{ static int d= 1;
print/("%d", n);
print/("%d", d);
d++;
if (n > 1) count (n-1);
print f("%d", d);
}
void main()
{
count (3);
}
```

(a) 312213444 (b) 312111222
(c) 3 1 2 2 1 3 4 (d) 3 1 2 1 1 1 2

[2016 (Set-1): 2 Marks]

101. What will be the output of the following pseudo-code when parameters are passed by reference and dynamic scoping is assumed?

```
a = 3;
void n(x)
{
x = x * a; print(x);
}
void m(y)
{ a = 1; a = v – a; n(a);
print(a);
}
void main()
{
m(a);
}
```

(a) 6, 2 (b) 6, 6
(c) 4, 2 (d) 4, 4

[2016 (Set-1): 2 Marks]

102. The following function computes X^Y for positive integers X and Y.

```
int exp (int X, int Y)
{ int res = 1, a = X, b = Y;
while (b ! = 0)
{ if (b% 2 = = 0)
{ a = a*a; b = 6/2; }
else {res = res*a; b = b – 1;
}
}
return res;
}
```

Which one of the following conditions is TEUE befor every iteration of the loop?

(a) $X^Y=a^b$

(b) $(res * a)^Y = (res * X)^b$

(c) $X^Y = res * a^b$

(d) $X^Y = (res * a)^b$

[2016 (Set-2) : 2 Marks]

103. The output of executing the following C program is __________.

```
#include <stdio.h>
int total (int v)
{ static int count = 0;
while (v)
{ count+ = v & 1;
v >> = 1;
}
return count;
}
void main ( )
{ static int x = 0;
int i = 5;
for (; i > 0; i – –) {
x = x + total (i);
}
printf ("%d\n", x);
}
```

[2017 (Setr-1) : 2 Marks]

104. Consider the C functions foo and bar given below:

```
int foo (int val)
{
int x = 0;
while (val > 0)
{
x = x + foo (val – –);
}
return val;
}
int bar (int val)
{
int x = 0;
{
while (val > 0)
x = x + bar (val – 1);
}
return val;
}
```

Invocations of foo (3) and bar (3) will result in:

(a) Return of 6 and 6 respectively.

(b) Infinite loop and abnormal termination respectively.

(c) Abnormal termination and infinite loop respectively.

(d) Both terminating abnormally.

[2017 (Set-1) : 2 Marks]

105. Consider the following two functions:

```
void funl (int n)
{ if (n = = 0) return;
printf ("%d", n);
fun2 (n – 2);
printf ("%d", n);
}
void fun2 (int n)
{ if (n = = 0) return;
printf ("%d", n);
funl(++n);
printf ("%d", n);
}
```

The output printed when funl (5) is called is

(a) 53423122233445 (b) 53423120112233

(c) 53423122132435 (d) 53423120213243

[2017 (Set-1) : 2 Marks]

106. Consider the following function implemented in C:

```
void printxy (int x, int y)
{
int *ptr;
x = 0;
ptr = &x;
y = *ptr;
*ptr = 1;
printf ("%d, %d", x, y);
}
```

The output of invoking printxy (1, 1) is

(a) 0, 0 (b) 0, 1

(c) 1, 0 (d) 1, 1

[2017 (Set-2) : 1 Mark]

107. Consider the following program written in pseudo-code. Assume that x and y are integers:

```
Count (x, y) {
if (y ! = 1) {
if(x! = 1){
print ("*");
Count (x/2, y);
```

```
}
else {
y = y – 1;
Count (1024, y);
}
}
}
```

The number of times that the print statement is executed by the call Count (1024, 1024) is ____.

[2018:1 Marks]

108. Consider the following C code. Assume that unsigned long int type length is 64 bits. unsigned long int fun (unsigned long int n) {

```
unsigned long int i, j = 0, sum = 0;
for (i = n; i > 1; i = i/2) j++;
for (; j > 1; j = j/2) sum++;
return (sum);
   }
```

The value returned when we call fun with the input 2^{40} is

(a) 4 (b) 5

(c) 6 (d) 40

[2018: 2 Marks]

109. The following C program is executed on a Unix/Linux system:

```
#include <unistd.h>
int main()
{
int i;
for (i = 0; i < 10; i ++)
 if (i%2 == 0) fork();
return 0;
}
```

The total number of child processes created is ________.

[2019 : 1 Mark]

110. Consider the following C program:

```
#include <stdio.h>
intjumble(int x, int y){
    x = 2*x + y;
    return x;
}
int main(){
    int x = 2, y = 5;
    y = jumble (y, x);
    x = jumble(y, x);
    printf("%d /n", x);
    return 0;
}
```

The value printed by the program is ________.

[2019 : 1 Mark]

111. Consider the following C program:

```
#include <stdio.h>
int r () {
    static int num = 7;
    return nun --;
}
int main() {
    for (r(); r(); r())
        printf("%d",r());
    return 0;
}
```

Which one of the following values will be displayed on execution of the programs?

1. 41 2. 52

3. 630 4 63

[2019 : 2 Marks]

112. Consider the following C function.

```
void convert(int n){
        if (n<0)
            printf ("%d", n);
        else {
            convert(n/2);
            printf ("%d",n%2);
        }
}
```

Which one of the following will happen when the function convert is positive integer n as argument?

1. It will print the binary representation of n in the reverse order and terminate
2. It will print the binary representation of n but will not terminate
3. It will not print anything and will not terminate
4. It will print the binary representation of n and terminate

[2019 : 2 Marks]

ANSWERS

1. (a)	2. (a)	3. (*)	4. (a)	5. (a)	6. (b)	7. (c)	8. (a)	9. (c)	10. (b)
11. (c)	12. (d)	13. (a)	14. (c)	15. (b)	16. (a)	17. (c)	18. (c)	19. (d)	20. (a)
21. (a)	22. (c)	23. (d)	24. (c)	25. (b)	26. (b)	27. (c)	28. (10)	29. (a)	30. (c)
31. (5)	32. (b)	33. (c)	34. (c)	35. (d)	36. (a)	37. (b)	38. (c)	39. (d)	40. (b)
41. (b)	42. (d)	43. (c)	44. (c)	45. (d)	46. (140)	47. (2016)	48. (30)	49. (b)	50. (2)
51. (a)	52. (4)	53. (a)	54. (6)	55. (10)	56. (b)	57. (e)	58. (a)	59. (b)	60. (c)
61. (c)	62. (d)	63. (a)	64. (a)	65. (c)	66. (c)	67. (d)	68. (*)	69. (c)	70. (d)
71. (d)	72. (c)	73. (c)	74. (a)	75. (c)	76. (d)	77. (d)	78. (d)	79. (c)	80. (c)
81. (d)	82. (c)	83. (d)	84. (a)	85. (b)	86. (d)	87. (c)	88. (c)	89. (d)	90. (b)
91. (9)	92. (1.72 to 1.74)		93. (d)	94. (–5)	95. (51)	96. (d)	97. (b)	98. (230)	99. (d)
100. (a)	101. (d)	102. (c)	103. (23)	104. (c)	105. (a)	106. (c)	107. (10230)	108. (b)	109. (31)
110. (26)	111. (b)	112. (c)							

EXPLANATIONS

1. First, procedure Q is called from the main procedure. Q has local variables x and y with values 3 and 4 respectively. This local variable y (value 4) is being passed to procedure P during call, and received in local variable n inside procedure P. Now, as P does not have any local definition for variable x, it will assign the evaluated value of (n + 2)/(n – 3) i.e. (4 + 2)/(4 –3) = 6 to the global variable x, which was previously 7. After the call of procedure P, procedure Q writes the value of local variable x which is still 3. Lastly, the main procedure writes the value of global variable x which has been changed to 6 inside procedure P. So, the output will be 3, 6.
2. (a) False; (b) True
3. (a) Small talk (s) Object-oriented programming
   (b) LISP (r) Functional programming
   (c) Prolog (p) Logic programming
   (d) VAL (q) Data flow programming
4. The Given code exchange the value of a and b.
5. An unrestricted use of the "goto" statement is harmful because it makes it more difficult to verify programs.
6. An arbitrary goto can lead to infinite loops as follows

   Label1 : Goto Label2;

   Label2 : Goto Label1;

   Recursive procedure/functional calls may be non-terminating if the terminating condition is never satisfied.

   A repeat loop can also lead to infinite loops if the condition to exit the loop is never satisfied.
7. If the value of a = 1, b = 1, c = 1 then the final return statement is c < b, so this never returns.
8. Aliasing describes a situation in which a data location in memory can be accessed through different symbolic names in the program.
9. The goal of strecture programming is to determine the flow of control from program text (source program hence C is correct answer).
10. If X is o then result is 1 and if x is 1 then result is 0 so simply expression is x = 1 – x.
11. This program will evaluate the greatest common divisor of X and Y.
12. Simply match.
13. int *n*, rev ;

    rev = 0 ;

    while (*n* > 0)

    {

    rev = rev * 10 + *n*% 10 ;

    n = *n*/10 ;

    }

    If $n = d_1 \, d_2 \, d_3 -- d_{m-i}$

    then after intering into the loop

loop	n	rev
1	$d_1 \, d_2 \, ... \, d_{m-i-1}$	d_{m-i}
2	$d_1 \, d_2 \, .. \, d_{m-i-2} (d_{m-i})$	$(d_{m-i-1}) + (d_{m-i-1})$

    After executing *m* times within the loop, rev will be

    $$\text{rev} = d_m \, d_m \, d_{m-1} -- d_{in-i+1}.$$
14. A common property of logic programming languages and functional languages is both are declarative because we declare any statement before we will use it.

15. Object oriented programming language is Object based PL + Abstraction + Inheritance. The last wo are must for any L to be OOPL.

16. i-b, ii-d, iii-e, iv-f, v-g, vi-a

17. S2 and S4 are true.

18. (1) When i = 1

-> i==0 is false, but a[i] maxsum is true, since sum = 2 and maxsum = 0. So maxsum=2. sum = (a [i] > 0) ? a [i] : 0; , sum=0 since a[i]<0.

(2) When i=2

-> i==0 is false, a[i] maxsum is false, since sum=0 and maxsum=2. Since sum = (a [i] > 0) ? a [i] : 0; , sum=0 since a[i]<0.

(3) When i=3

-> i==0 is false , a[i]<0 is false and a [i] < a [i – 1] is false so condition (1) is false. Now sum += a [i] = 3.

(4) When i=4

-> i==0 is false , a[i]<0 is false and a [i] < a [i – 1] is false so condition (1) is false. Now sum += a [i] = 7.

(5) When i=5

-> i==0 is false , a[i]<0 is false and a [i] maxsum is true, since sum=7 and maxsum=2,so maxsum=7.Since sum =

(a [i] > 0) ? a [i] : 0, so sum = 2 since a[5]>0.

19. As we know that Static scoping can do early binding i.e. during compile time. Early binding increases efficiency and dynamic scoping requires late binding i.e. during execution time so late binding decreases efficiency as this binding needs to be done at runtime but it increases flexibility.

20. I–C, II–D, III–B, IV–A

21.

```
     3   4                          4      2
a = (x > y) ? ((x > z) ? x : z) : ((y > z ? y : z))
                                            4
```

x = 3, y = 4, z = 2 satisfy the values, so we get a value 4.

22. The program given in question doesn't work for the cases where element to be searched is the last element of array Y[] or maximum element in Y[]. For such cases, program goes in an infinite loop. Option C will goes in infinte loop.

23. begin

if (*a* = = *b*) {S1; exit;}

else if (*c* = = *d*) {S2 ;}

else {S3; exit;}

S4;

end

24. $i=1, j=1, k=2$ to $n \Rightarrow n-1$ times

$i=1, j=2, k=3$ to $n \Rightarrow n-2$ times

$i=1, j=3, k=4$ to $n \Rightarrow n-3$ times

:

$i=1, j=n-2, k=n-1$ to $n \Rightarrow 2$ times

$i=1, j=n-1, k=n$ to $n \Rightarrow 1$ time

$i=2, j=2, k=3$ to $n \Rightarrow n-2$ times

$i=2, j=3, k=4$ to $n \Rightarrow n-3$ times

: :

: :   } $\Sigma(n-1)$ times

$i=2, j=n-1, k=n$ to $n \Rightarrow 1$ time

:

:

$i=n-1, j=n-1, k=n$ to $n \Rightarrow 1$ time }Σ 1 times

$\therefore$ Total number of multiplications

$\Rightarrow \Sigma 1 + \Sigma 2 + \Sigma 3 + \ldots \Sigma(n-1)$

$$= \underset{S_1}{1} + \underset{S_2}{(1+2)} + \underset{S_3}{(1+2+3)} + \ldots + \underset{S_{n-1}}{(1+2+3+\ldots n-1)}$$

$$= \sum_{i=1}^{n-1} S_i = \sum \frac{n(n-1)}{2}$$

$$= \frac{1}{2}\sum n^2 - \frac{1}{2}\sum n$$

$$= \frac{1}{2}\frac{n(n+1)(2n+1)}{6} - \frac{1}{2}\frac{n(n+1)}{2}$$

$$= \frac{(n-1)(n)(n+1)}{6}$$

25. ${}^nC_3$ will stand for

$$= n * \frac{n-1}{2} \quad \ldots (i)$$

$$\frac{n-1}{3} \quad \ldots (ii)$$

Multiplying (*i*) by (*ii*), we get

$$\rho = n * \frac{(n-1)}{2} * \frac{(n-2)}{3}$$

27. 1204

S_1 is 1 2 3 4

1	2	3	4

$P = S_1 + 2$

P = 0

1	2	0	4

28. *j* and *k* will be evaluated to 2 and -1 respectively.

In for loop :

When $i = 0$; 1 time printed (– 1)

When $i = 1$; 1 time printed (0)

When $i = 2$; 3 times printed (1, 1, 1)

When $i = 3$; 3 times printed (2, 2, 2)

When $i = 4$; 2 times printed (3, 3)

$\therefore$ on the whole printf is executed 10 times

29. M =10;

n = ++m; (n = 11)

n1 = m++; (n1 = 11)

n--; (n = 10)

--n1;)n = 10)

n -= n1; (n = 0)

so final result is 0.

30. x == (y * q + r)

x = product, y = multiplicand, q = quotient, r = remainder

For loop to be terminated, the value of q should be 0 hence options C and D are left. if q = 0 then r = x so, only C is correct answer.

31. ****

32. Passing an array as a parameter will generate different result.

33. Passing an array as a parameter will generate different result.

34. In program segment P1, In g() the pointer variable x is a local variable. g() returns pointer to this variable. x may vanish after g() has returned as x exists on stack. So, &x may become invalid.

In P2, pointer variable px is being assigned a value without allocating memory to it. So it gives an error.

35. IN call by results, the results of formal parameter is updated to actual parameter at the time of function termination. In call by reference, any change in the variable reflects immediately.

36. $* \, y = \& \, x = 5$

$x = * \, y + 2 = 7$

$Q\,(x)$;

$z = x = 7$

$z = z + x = 12$

print (z) = 12

$* \, y = x - 1 = 6$

print (x) = 7

print (x) = 6

37. printf ("%s %s\n", s.a, s.b); // print local static values of a and b; A B

f1(s); give call to printf ("%s %s\n", s.a, s.b); // print local values of a and b; U V

print f ("%s %s\n", s.a, s.b);// print local static values of a and b;A B

f2(&s); ->print f("%s %s\n", p -> a, p -> b); // gives present contents at memory location i.e U V

38. int (**f*) (int*);

return type int, (**f*) is a pointer to a function the argumen is (int *) an integer pointer So int (**f*) (int*) means a pointer to a function that takes an integer pointer as argument and returns an integer.

39. (i) Here swap function just swaps addresses in local variables x and y. which is effectively nothing once swap function returns.

(ii) print ab() function adds 9 to static variables a and b. The number 9 comes from the fact that the while loop executes those arithmetic statements only when i = 1, 3, 5.

Hence, when print ab() is called for the first time, these are the local variable values: a = –3 + 9 and b = –6 + 9. On the second time, a = –3 + 9 + 9 and b = –6 + 9 + 9 are the desired values.

So correct answer is a = 6, b = 3; a = 15, b = 12.

40. **ppz += 1 (// it change value of c = 5 but x is unaffected)

z= **ppz; (// z = 5)

*py += 2; (// c = 7 but x is unchanged)

y = *py; (// y = 7)

x += 3; (// x is incremented by 3)

return x + y + z; (7 + 7 + 5)

41. *Stack Positions :*

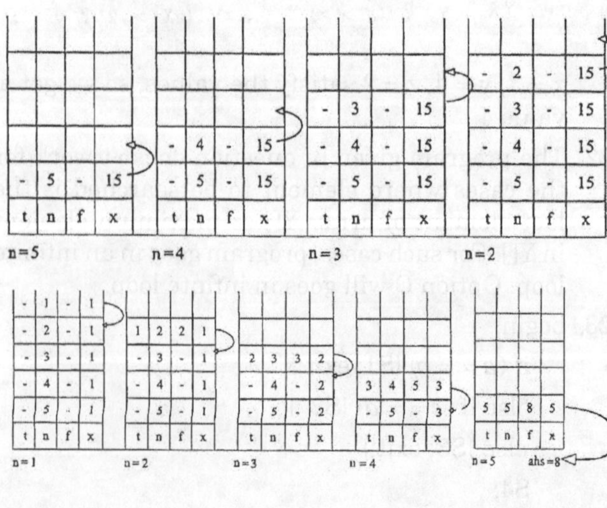

42. Given :

```
# include < stdio.h>
void f(int * p, int * q){
{ p = q;
 * p = 2;
}
int i = 0, j = 1;
int main() {
{ f (& i, & j); → Passing the address of i, j
print f("% d % n", i, j);
retur, 0;
}
```

Let address of *i* and *j* are 200, 400

means [*i* = 0] [*j* = 0]

200 400

in function *f pRq* are pointers that have address of *i*, *j* than by *p* = *q* copy address of *j* in *p*

means initially [200] [400]

p *q*

after *p* = *q* [400] [400]

p *q*

by * *p* it represent value of *j* now

then * *p* = 2 changes value of *j*

So after print *f* statement *i* = 0, *j* = 2.

43. Note : in the given question please replace this line

int a [= {12, 7, 13, 4, 11, 6};

by that line

int a [] = {12, 7, 13, 4, 11, 6};

44. p now has the base address string "GATE2011"

p[3] is 'E' and p[1] is 'A'.

p[3] – p[1] = ASCII value of 'E' – ASCII value of 'A' = 4

The expression p + p[3] – p[1] becomes p + 4 which is base address of string "2011".

45. pi contains the address of *i*. So scanf("%d",pi) places the value entered in console into variable i.e So printf("%d\n", *i* + 5),prints 5 more than the value entered in console.

46.

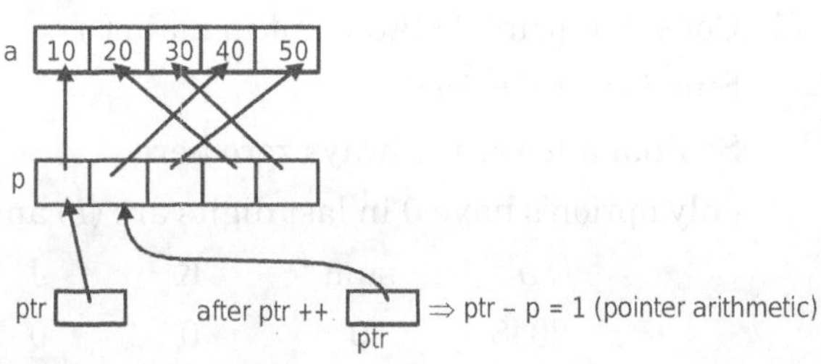

**ptr = 40

∴ printf(" %d%d", p + r – p, p + r) will print 140

47.

```
int main ( )
{
    int a = 2016, b = 0, c = 4, d = 42;
```

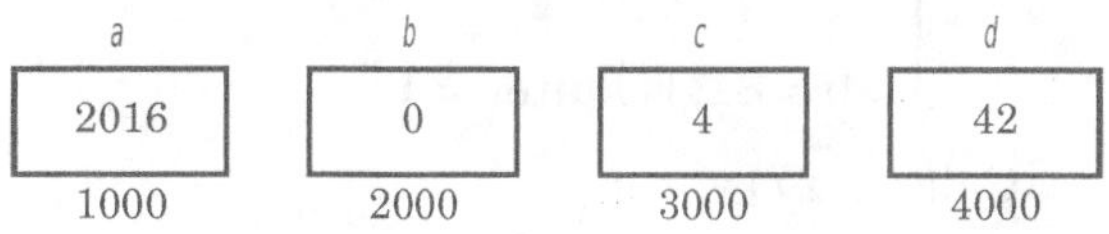


```
    mystery (&a, &b);
    if (a < c)
    mystery (&c, &a);
    mystery (&a, &d);
    printf("%d \ n", a);
}
void mystery (int * ptra, int * ptrb)
{
    int * temp;
    temp = ptrb;
    ptrb = ptra;
    ptra = temp;
}
```

Output → 2016.

48.

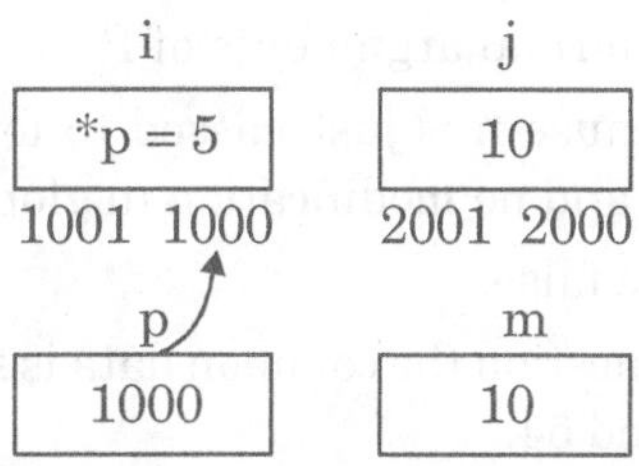

m = m + 5; // m = 15

*p = *p + m; // * p = *p + m = 5 + 15

*p = 20 (i.e., i = 20)

i + j = 20 + 10 = 30

So, the output of the given program is 30.

49. ((strlen(s) – strlen(t)) > c) ? strlen (s) : strlen (t)

= (3 – 5 > 0)

= (–2 > 0) unsigned comparision so result will be positive

So, out of these two, strlen (s) will be printed. Therefore, option B is correct.

50. c + 2[p] – 6[p] – 1

= c + p[2] – p[6] – 1

= c + T – I – 1

= c + 11 – 1

= c + 10

strlen (17) = 2

51. 'a' + 2 will be 'c', so p = {'1', '0', 'c'} and output will be 0, c.

52. Calc (4, 81)
a = 4
b = 81, Counter = 1
↓
Calc (4, 27)
a = 4
b = 2, Counter = 2
↓
Calc (4, 9)
b = 9
a = 4, Counter = 3
↓
Calc (4, 3)
a = 4
b = 3, Counter = 4
↓
return (4 × 4 × 4) = 64

53. The scope of fun1(char *s1, char *s2) is local, so the value changed here doesn't affect actual parameters. hence the output will be 'Hi Bye'.

In fun2(char **s1, char **s2) function value is pointer to pointer, so it changes pointer of the actual value. So output is 'Bye Hi'

56. Answer is 0, because global m is not modified, m is just passed to formal arguments of P.

57. Answer is 0, because n is just passed to formal parameters of Q and no modification in global n. So all options are false.

58. Note : for these question the common data is same as question 53 and 54.

Since m is defined global it is visible inside all the procedures.

59. As per call by value concept. X in the procedure FIND is a local variable. no change will be reflected in global var x.

60. From program we get, *x* of B, *z* and *y* in S_1 and *x* of A, *i* and *y* in S_2 are variables acceisble in S_1 and S_2.

61. When the procedure "show" is called from the main program, the value of the global variable *x* – 0.25 in this case- gets printed. When the same "show" is called from the procedure "small", the value of the local variable *x* – 0.125 in this case - gets printed.

62. The given Calling sequence is

Main → A1 → A2 → A21 → A1

Now A1 and A2 are defined under Main. So A1, A2 Access link are pointed to main A21 is Defined under A2 hence its Access link will point to A2.

63. Because they use static allocation for variables.

64. [] has higher precedence than * in C. So, s becomes an array of pointers.

65. Short s[5]; (total 10 byte) memory allocated for the union is equal to memory needed for the largest member of it, so allocate 8 byte.

Total memory allocation for Structure is

10 + 8 = 18 byte

66. y = y + 4 ⇒ y = 10 + 4 = 14

and z = x + y + z ⇒ z = 14 + 14 + 3 = 31

z will be returned to x. So, x = 31 and y will remain 3

67. In dynamic scoping or run-time scoping the free variables are referred as the variables in the most recent frame of function call stack.

69. The program is

```
int f(int n)
{
Static int i = 1
   if (n z= 5) return n          ......... (1)
   n = n + i ;
   i ++ ;
   return f(n) ;
}
```

as 1 not full fill the condition of if statement so excute next instruction, the iteration will be as

iteration	*n*	*i*
1	1 + 1 = 2	2
2	2 + 2 = 4	2 + 1 + 3
3	4 + 3 = 7	*i* = 4

as 7 is greater than 5 so it will return to the main program.

70. When we don't declare a function (specify the prototype), the default rules that the function (foo in our case) would have been assumed to be int, even though it really return a double. This will generates compiler warning and our program will have undefined behaviour is disastrous.

71. Consider 'print *f* statement in main ( )

Sum is initilize to 0

So final answer is always zero here

only option's have 0 in last digits are (*b*) and (*d*)

n	sum	K	J
2048	0	0	0
		8	204

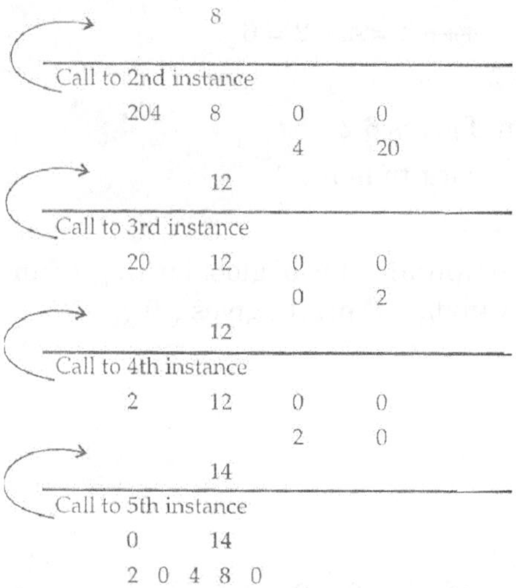

72. f(20, 1) calls f(10, 2) – 1 calls f(5, 4) – 2 calls f(2, 8) + 4 calls f(1, 16) – 8 calls f(0, 32) + 16.

f(20, 1) = 9.

f(10, 2) – 1 = 9

f(5, 4) - 2 = 10

f(2, 8) + 4 = 12

f(1, 16) – 8 = 8

f(0, 32) + 16 = 16

Answer is 9.

73. The program calculate value of C(m, n) so C(m, n) = 1 if (n = = 0) || (m = = n)

74. S1 is true S_4 and S5 are false as the program will print 3 and 8. The option left is (*a*).

75. Only an extra variable t 1 has been added in work 2 instead of directly computing the subscript as in work 1. The output will be the same. S1 is true. The addition of variables *t*1 and *t*2 will not improve the performance in any way. i.e. S2 is false.

76. *Calbing sequence will be*

Sequencereturns

f(5)   *f*(3) + 2 = 18

↓ ↑

f(3)   *f*(2) + 5 = 16

↓ ↑

f(2)   *f*(1) + 5 = 11

↓ ↑

f(1)   *f*(0) + 5 = 6

↓ ↑

f(0)   1 = 1

77. The function terminates for all values having a factor of 2. So, (i) is false and (ii) is TRUE.

Suppose n = 3, it will terminate in 2nd iteration.

Suppose n = 5, it will go like 5 – 14 – 7 – 20 – 10 – 5 – and now it will repeat.

And any number whose factor is 5 and 2, there are infinite recursions possible.

So, (iv) is TRUE and (iii) is false.

78. **Call by value:** A Value of actual parameter is copied to formal parameter at the time of function calling after then no relation between actual parameter and formal parameter.

Call by reference: Actual and formal parameter share same memory location.

79. In static Scoping :

```
int i ;
program main ()
{
i = 10;
call f();
}
procedure f()
{
int i = 20;
call g ();
}
procedure g ()
{
print i; //as i = 20 is scoped only within f() so it will point to global i} So, 10 is printed
```

In Dynamic scoping:

```
int i ;
program main ()
{
i = 10;
call f();
}
procedure f()
{
int i = 20;//here global scoped i is changed call g ();
}
procedure g ()
{
print i;//global value changed so, i=20 printed
}
```

80. "if (num1 > = num2) {swap3 (&num1, &num2);}" statement is true, so call by reference will be performed and output is 45.

81. Program perform decimal to binary conversion $(173)_2$ = 10101101

82. The given function f prints the binary representation of the number.

The function in P1 also prints the binary representation of the number.

The function in p2 prints the binary representation but in reverse order.

83. Whenever character input is not return key (in) it accept character input ? 1 (c = getchar()) = ! (in) ? 2 for bringing all character after reverse functions so ?2 is putchar (c).

Alternately

To print reverse of the input, this programme basically collects the input in buffer with the help of some f^n (i.e. f^n is getcher ()) and by using stack, then where ↵ is pressed stack is popped off and characters are printed in reverse order as that of the process call, i.e. last process call to reverse is processed first because of stack.

84. Change line 6 to: if (Y[k] < x) i = k + 1; else j = k –1;

85. The call foo(345, 10) returns sum of decimal digits (because r is 10) in the number n. Sum of digits for 345 is 3 + 4 + 5 = 12.

86. foo(513, 2) will return 1 + foo(256, 2). All subsequent recursive calls (including foo(256, 2)) will return 0 + foo(n/2, 2) except the last call foo(1, 2). The last call foo(1, 2) returns 1. So, the value returned by foo(513, 2) is 1 + 0 + 0...+ 0 + 1.

The function foo(n, 2) basically returns sum of bits (or count of set bits) in the number n.

87. In the given program no break statement with any of the case so it print value of all the cases Answer is

Choice A

Choice B No Choice

88. main

a = 1

prtFun()

a = 2

b = 1

a = a +++ b = 2 + 2 = 4

b = 2

print f gives 4 2

then back to main

a = a + 1 → 1 + 1 → 2 (local static a is taken)

prtFun()

a = 4 // previous value in the function is retained because of static

b = 1

a = a +++ b = 4 + 2 = 6

b = 2

print f gives 6 2

then back to main

a = 2

b = 0 (initial value of global b. in prtFun local b is only updated) print f gives 2 0

89. main

a = 1

prtFun()

a = 2

b = 1

a = a +++ b = 2 + 2 = 4

b = 2

print f gives 4 2

then back to main

a = a + 1 = 1 + 1 → 2

prtFun()

a = 1 //previous a is lost

b = 1

a = a +++ b = 2 + 2 = 4

b = 2

print f gives 4 2

then back to main

a = 2 b = 0 (initial value of global b. in prtFun local b is only updated)

printf gives 2 0

90. Since, reference of p is passed as '*x*'

Thus, any change in value of *x* in *f* would be reflected globally.

The recursion can be broken down as:

$f\begin{pmatrix}5 & 5\\ x, & c\end{pmatrix}$

$\quad\hookrightarrow x * f\begin{pmatrix}6 & 4\\ x, & c\end{pmatrix}$

$\qquad\hookrightarrow x * f\begin{pmatrix}7 & 3\\ x, & c\end{pmatrix}$

$\qquad\quad\hookrightarrow x * f\begin{pmatrix}8 & 2\\ x, & c\end{pmatrix}$

$\qquad\qquad\hookrightarrow x * f\begin{pmatrix}9 & 1\\ x, & c\end{pmatrix}$

$\qquad\qquad\hookrightarrow 1 \qquad [\because c = 0 \text{ in this code}]$

∴ Our answer = $x * x * x * x$

The final value of $x = 9$

∴ $9^4 = \boxed{6561}$

91. >> (right shift i.e. divide by 2)

If keep on dividing by 2, we get: 435, 217, 108, 54, 27, 13, 6, 3, 1.

So, the count is 9.

92. When we take the value from 1·72 to 1·74, we will see that else condition will be true *i.e.* return $f(x/2 + 1.5/x)$;

That's why value to $f(q)$ such that it returns q is 1·72 to 1·74.

93. When $f = 50$, the f^n will exhaust run time stack, because function will be called infinite times which results into an infinite loop at $j = 50$.

94. No changes by f1(a, b) as the values are passed by value.

The function call f2(&b, &c) swaps values of b and c. So b becomes 6 and c becomes 5. Value of c – a – b becomes 5 – 4 – 6 which is – 5.

95. fun(5) = 1 + fun(1) * fun(4) + fun(2) * fun(3) + fun(3) * fun(2) + fun(4) * fun(1)

= 1 + 2*[fun(1)*fun(4) + fun(2)*fun(3)]

Substituting fun(1) = 1

= 1 + 2*[fun(4) + fun(2)*fun(3)]

Calculating fun(2), fun(3) and fun(4)

fun(2) = 1 + fun(1)*fun(1) = 1 + 1*1 = 2

fun(3) = 1 + 2*fun(1)*fun(2) = 1 + 2*1*2 = 5

fun(4) = 1 + 2*fun(1)*fun(3) + fun(2)*fun(2)

= 1 + 2*1*5 + 2*2 = 15

Substituting values of fun(2), fun(3) and fun(4)

fun(5) = 1 + 2*[15 + 2*5] = 51

96. DCBA is the output

The condition will fail on encountering (' '-space), and printed character will be DCBA

97.

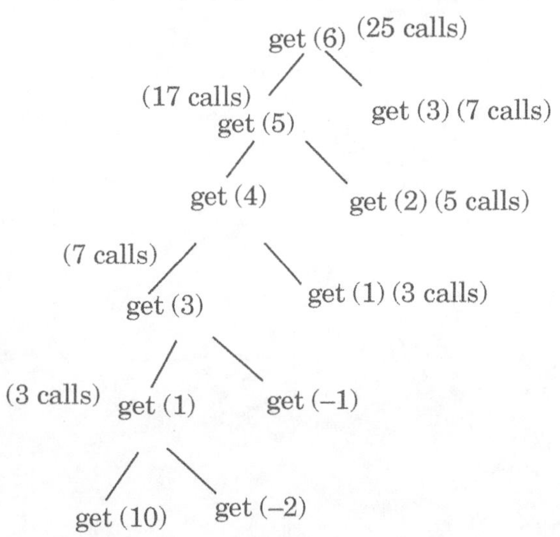

98. x + = f1() + f2() + f3() + f2();

x = x + f1() + f2() + f3() + f2();

f1() returns 26

f2() returns 51

f3() returns 100

second call to f2() returns 52 (As x is static in f2()]

x = 1 + 26 + 51 + 100 + 52 = 230

99. $f(i, * p)$

```
void f(int, short);
    void main( )
{
    int i = 100;
    short s = 12;
    short * p = &s;
    f(i, * p);
}
```

100.

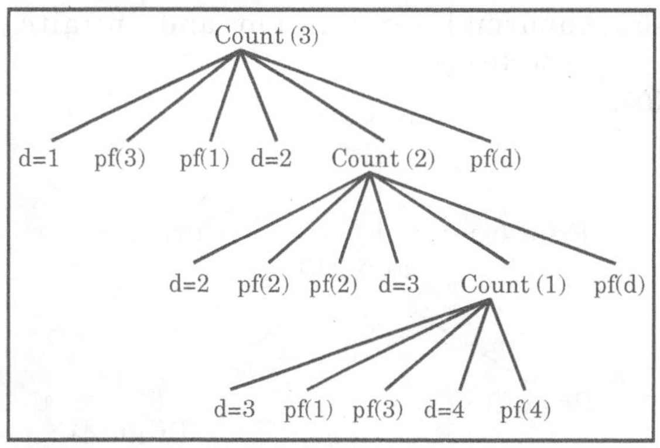

Output : 3 1 2 2 1 3 4 4 4

101. a = 3;

```
void main()
{
    // Calls m with 'a' being passed by reference
    // Since there is no local 'a', global 'a' is passed.
    m(a);
}
// y refers to global 'a' as main calls "m(a)"
void m(y)
{
    // A local 'a' is created with value 1.
    a = 1;
    // a = 3 – 1 = 2
    a = y – a;
    // Local 'a' with value 2 is passed by
    // reference to n()
    n(a);
    // Modified local 'a' is printed
    print(a);
}
```

```
// Local 'a' of m is passed here
void n(x)
{
// x = 2 * 2 [Note : again local 'a' is referred
            // because of dynamic scoping]
x = x * a;
// 4 is printed and local 'a' of m() is also
// changed to 4.
print(x);
}
```

102. X^y = res * a^b

103. Binary of digits : 5 = 0101, 4 = 0100, 3 = 0011, 2 = 0010, 1 = 0000

Count of 1s : 2, 3, 5, 6, 7

Total: 2 + 3 + 5 + 6 + 7 = 23

total(i) = 23

104. Abnormal termination and infinite loop respectively

105.

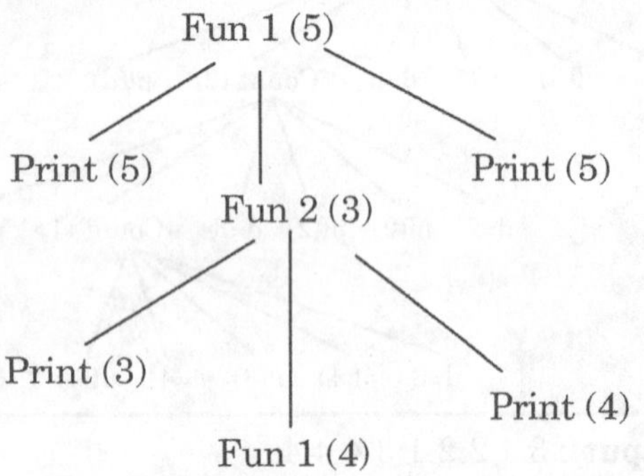

Simply string start with 52 ...... 45 (end with 45)

So only option (a) is correct.

106.
```
void main()
{
int x = 1, y = 1;
printxy(x,y);
}
void printxy(int x, int y)
{
    int *ptr;
    x = 0;
    // ptr point to variable of value 0
    ptr = &x;
    // y has value pointed by ptr -> x= 0;
    y = *ptr;
    // value pointed by ptr is set to 1 -> x= 1;
    *ptr = 1;
    //x be changed to 1 and y will remain 0
    print f("%d,%d", x, y);
}
```

107. Firstly, Count(1024, 1024) will be called and value of x will be deducted by x/2. 'x' will be printed 10 times. On count = 10, value of x will become 1.

Since x = 1, inner else loop will start executing. On each call value of y will be decreased by 1 and will be executed until value of y becomes 1 (which is on 1023th call).

Since count() is called recursively for every y = 1023 and count() is called 10times for each y. Therefore, 1023 × 10 = 10230

108. N = 2^40 then it return 5.

2

CHAPTER

Array

Analysis of Previous GATE Papers											
Units	Year → Topics ↓		2019	2018	2017 Set 1	2017 Set 2	2016 Set 1	2016 Set 2	2015 Set 1	2015 Set 2	2015 Set 3
ARRAY	1 Mark	MCQ Type									
		Numerical Type									
	2 Marks	MCQ Type	1								1
		Numerical Type								1	1
	Total		2							2	4
ARRAY POINTER	1 Mark	MCQ Type									
		Numerical Type									
	2 Marks	MCQ Type					1				
		Numerical Type						1			
	Total						2	2			
ARRAY MEMORY	1 Mark	MCQ Type									
		Numerical Type									
	2 Marks	MCQ Type									
		Numerical Type				1					
	Total					2					
ARRAY VAL	1 Mark	MCQ Type									
		Numerical Type									
	2 Marks	MCQ Type									
		Numerical Type									
	Total										
ASYMPTOTIC NOTATIONS	1 Mark	MCQ Type									
		Numerical Type									
	2 Marks	MCQ Type									
		Numerical Type									
	Total										
MULTIDIMENSION ARRAY	1 Mark	MCQ Type									
		Numerical Type									
	2 Marks	MCQ Type						1			
		Numerical Type									
	Total							2			

ARRAY

1. Faster access to non-local variables is achieved using an array of pointers to activation records called a
   (a) stack (b) heap
   (c) display (d) activation tree
   [1998: 2 Marks]

2. A Young tableau is a 2D array of integers increasing from left to right and from top to bottom. Any unfilled entries are marked with ∞, and hence there cannot be any entry to the right of, or below a ∞. The following Young tableau consists of unique entries.

1	2	5	14
3	4	6	23
10	12	18	25
31	∞	∞	∞

   When an element is removed from a Young tableau, other elements should be moved into its place so that the resulting table is still a Young tableau (unfilled entries may be filled in with a ∞). The minimum number of entries (other than 1) to be shifted, to remove 1 from the given Young tableau is_______. **[2015 (Set-2): 2 Marks]**

3. Consider the following C function in which size is the number of elements in the array E:

```
int MyX(int *E, unsigned int size) {
int Y = 0;
int Z;
int i, j, k;
for(i = 0; i < size; i++)
Y = Y + E[i];
for(i = 0; i < size; i++)
for(j = i; j < size; j++)
{
z = 0;
for(k = i; k <= j; k++)
Z = Z + E[k];
if (Z > Y)
Y = Z;
}
return Y;
}
```

   The value returned by the function MyX is the
   (a) maximum possible sum of elements in any sub-array of array E.
   (b) maximum element in any sub-array of array E.
   (c) sum of the maximum elements in all possible sub-arrays of array E.
   (d) the sum of all the elements in the array E.
   [2014 (Set-1) : 2 Marks]

4. Consider the following two C code segments. Y and X are one and two dimensional arrays of size n and n x n respectively, where $2 \le n \le 10$. Assume that in both code segments, elements of Y are initialized to 0 and each element X[i][j] of array X is initialized to i + j. Further assume that when stored in main memory all elements of X are in same main memory page frame.

   Code segment 1:

```
// initialize elements of Y to 0
// initialize elements X[i] [j] of X to i+j
for (i = 0; i < n; i++)
Y[i] + = X[0] [i];
```

   Code segment 2:

```
// initialize elements of Y to 0
// initialize elements X[i] [j] of X to i+j
for (i = 0; i < n; i++)
Y[i] + = X[i] [0];
```

   Which of the following statements is/are correct?
   S1: Final contents of array Y will be same in both code segments.
   S2: Elements of array X accessed inside the for loop shown in code segment 1 are contiguous in main memory.
   S3: Elements of array X accessed inside the for loop shown in code segment 2 are contiguous in main memory.
   (a) Only S2 is correct
   (b) Only S3 is correct
   (c) Only S1 and S2 are correct
   (d) Only S1 and S3 are correct
   [2015 (Set-3) : 2 Marks]

5. Suppose $c = \langle c[0],\ldots\ldots,c[k-1]\rangle$ is an array of length k, where all the entries are from the set {0, 1}. For any positive integers a and n, consider the following pseudocode.

```
DOSOMETHING (c, a, n)
z ← 1
for i ← 0 to k – 1
do z ← z² mod n
if c[i] = 1
then z ← (z × a) mod n
return z
```

   If k = 4, $c = \langle 1,0,1,1\rangle$, a = 2 and n = 8, then the output of DOSOMETHING (c, a, n) is ______.
   [2015 (Set-3) : 2 Marks]

6. There are n unsorted arrays: $A_1, A_2, ...A_n$. Assume that n is odd. Each of $A_1, A_2, ..., A_n$ contains n distinct elements. There are no common elements between any two arrays. The worst-case time complexity of computing the median of the medians of $A_1, A_2, ..., A_n$ is

(a) $O(n^2)$ (b) $\Omega(n^2 \log n)$

(c) $O(n \log n)$ (d) $O(n)$ **[2019 : 2 Marks]**

ARRAY POINTER

7. Assume the following C variable declaration int*A[10], B[10] [10];

Of the following expressions

1. A[2] 2. A[2] [3]

3. B[1] 4. B[2] [3]

Which will not give compile-time errors if used as left hand sides of assignment statements in a C program?

(a) 1, 2 and 4 only (b) 2, 3 and 4 only

(c) 2 and 4 only (d) 4 only **[2003 :1 Mark]**

8. In the following C program fragment j, k, n and TwoLog_n are integer variables, and A is an array of integers. The variable n is intialized to an integer ≥ 3, and TwoLog_n is initialized to the value of $2 * \lfloor \log_2(n) \rfloor$

```
for (k = 3; k < = n; k++)
A [k] = 0;
for (k = 2; k < = TwoLog_n; k++)
for (j = k + 1; j < = n; j++)
A [j] = A [j] | | (j%k);
for (j = 3; j < = n; j++)
if (!A[j]) print f ("%d", j);
```

The set of numbers printed by this program fragment is

(a) $\{m \mid m \leq n, (\exists i)\ [m = i!]\}$

(b) $\{m \mid m \leq n, (\exists i)\ [m = i^2]\}$

(c) $\{m \mid m \leq n, m \text{ is prime}\}$

(d) { } **[2003 : 2 Marks]**

9. Consider the following C program segment: char p [20] ;

```
char * s = "string" ;
int length = strlen (s) ;
for (i = 0 ; i < length; i++)
p[i] = s [length – i] ;
printf ("%s", p) ;
```

The output of the program is

(a) gnirts (b) string

(c) gnirt (d) no output is printed

[2004: 2 Marks]

10. The following C function takes two ASCII strings and determines whether one is an anagram of the other. An anagram of a string s is a string obtained by permuting the letters in s.

```
int anagram (char *a, char *b)
{
int count [128], j;
for (j = 0; j < 128; j++)
count[j] = 0;
j = 0;
while (a[j] && b[j])
{
A;
B;
}
for (j = 0; j < 128; j++)
if (count [j]) return 0;
return 1;
}
```

Choose the correct alternative for statements A and B.

(a) A : count [a[j]]++ and B : count[b[j]]— —

(b) A : count [a[j]]++ and B : count[b[j]]++

(c) A : count [a[j++]]++ and B : count[b[j]] – –

(d) A : count [a[j]]++ and B : count[b[j++]] – –

[2005 : 2 Marks]

11. Which one of the choices given below would be printed when the following program is executed?

```
#include <stdio.h>
struct test
{
int i;
char *c;
} st[ ] = {5, "become", 4, "better", 6, "jungle", 8,
"ancestor", 7, "brother"};
main( )
{
struct test *p = st;
p+ = 1;
++p → c;
printf("%s", p++ → c);
printf("%c", *++p → c);
printf("%d", p [0] .i);
printf("%s \n", p → c);
```

(a) jungle, n, 8, ncestor

(b) etter, u, 6, ungle

(c) cetter, k, 6, jungle

(d) etter, u, 8, ncestor **[2006 : 2 Marks]**

12. Which one of the choices given below would be printed when the following program is executed?

```
#include <stdio.h>
int a1 [ ] = {6, 7, 8, 18, 34, 67};
int a2[ ]= {23, 56, 28, 29};
int a3[ ] = {-12, 27, -31};
int *x[ ] = {al, a2, a3};
void print(int *a [ ])
{
printf("%d,", a[0][2]);
printf("%d,",*a[2]);
printf("%d,", *++a[0])
printf("%d,", *(++a)[0]);
printf("%d\n", a[-1][+1];
}
main( )
{
print(x);
}
```

(a) 8, –12, 7, 23, 8
(b) 8, 8, 7, 23, 7
(c) –12, –12, 27, –31, 23
(d) –12, –12, 27, –31, 56

[2006 : 2 Marks]

13. The following function computes the maximum value contained in an integer array p[ ] of size n(n > = 1).

```
int max(int *p, int n)
{ int a = 0, b = n – 1;
while (_________)
{
if(p[a]<=p[b])
{
a = a + 1;
} else
{
b = b – 1;
}
}
return p [a];
}
```

The missing loop condition is

(a) a ! = n (b) b ! = 0
(c) b > (a + 1) (d) b ! = a

[2016 (Set-1): 2 Marks]

14. Consider the following program:

```
int f(int *p, int n)
{ if (n < = 1) return 0;
else return max (f(p+1, n–1), p[0] – p[1]);
}
int main ()
{ int a[ ] = {3, 5, 2, 6, 4};
print f("%d", f(a, 5));
}
```

Note: max (x, y) returns the maximum of x and y.

The value printed by this program is______.

[2016 (Set-2) : 2 Marks]

ARRAY MEMORY

15. Consider the following C program which is supposed to compute the transpose of a given 4 × 4 matrix M. Note that, there is an X in the program which indicates some missing statements. Choose the correct option to replace X in the program.

```
#include <stdio.h>
#define ROW 4
#define COL 4
int M[ROW] [COL] = {1, 2, 3, 4, 5, 6, 7, 8, 9, 10, 11, 12, 13, 14, 15, 16};
main()
{
int i, j, t;
for (i = 0; i < 4; ++i)
{
X
}
for (i = 0; i < 4; ++i)
for (j = 0; j < 4; ++j)
printf ("%d", M [i] [j]);
}
```

(a)
```
for(j = 0; j < 4; ++j)
{
t = M[i][j];
M[i][j] = M[j] [i];
M[j] [i] = t;
}
```

(b)
```
for(j = 0; j < 4; ++j)
{
M[i] [j] = t;
t = M[j] [i];
M[j] [i] = M[i] [j];
}
```

(c)
```
for(j = i; j < 4; ++j)
{
t = M[j] [i];
M[i][j] = M[j] [i];
M[j] [i] = t;
}
```

(d)
```
for(j = i; j < 4; ++j)
{
M[i][j] = t;
t = M[j] [i];
M [j] [i] = M[i] [j];
}
```
[2004: 2 Marks]

Linked Answer Questions 16 & 17:

A sink in a directed graph is a vertex i such that there is an edge from every vertex j ≠ i to i and there is no edge from i to any other vertex. A directed graph G with n vertices is represented by its adjacency matrix A, where A[i] [j] = 1 if there is an edge directed from vertex i to j and 0 otherwise. The following algorithm determines whether there is a sink in the graph G.

```
i = 0;
do
{
j = i + 1;
while ((j < n) && E1) j++;
if (j < n) E2;
} while (i < n);
flag = 1;
for (j = 0; j < n; j++)
if ((j! = i) && E3) flag = 0;
if (flag) printf("Sink exists");
else printf ("Sink does not exist");
```

16. Choose the correct expressions for E_1 and E_2

(a) E_1 : A[i] [j] and E_2 : i = j;

(b) E_1 : !A[i][j] and E_2 : i = j + 1;

(c) E_1: !A[i][j] and E_2 : i = j;

(d) E_1 : A[i] [j] and E_2 : i = j + 1; **[2005 : 2 Marks]**

17. Choose the correct expression for E_3

(a) (A[i][j] && !A[j] [i]) (b) (!A[i] [j] && !A[j] [i])

(c) (!A[i] [j] | | A[j] [i]) (d) (A[i] [j] | | !A[j] [i])

[2005 : 2 Marks]

18. Consider the following C-function in which a [n] and b [m] are two sorted integer arrays and c [n+ m] be another integer array.

```
void xyz (int a[] , int b[] , int c[]) {
int i, j, k;
i = j = k = 0;
while ((i < n) && (j < m))
if (a [i] < b [j]) c[k++] = a[i ++];
else c[k ++] = b[j ++];
}
```

Which of the following condition (s) hold (s) after the termination of the while loop?

(i) j < m, k = n + j – 1, & a [n – 1] < b [j] if i = n

(ii) i < n, k = m + i – 1, & b [m – 1] ≤ a [i] if j = m

(a) only (i)

(b) only (ii)

(c) either (i) or (ii) but not both

(d) neither (i) nor (ii) **[2006 : 2 Marks]**

19. What is the output printed by the following C code?

```
# include <stdio.h>
int main( )
{
char a[6] = "world";
int i, j;
for (i = 0, j = 5; i < j; a[i++] = a [j – –]);
printf ("%s\n", a);
}
```

(a) dlrow (c) dlrld

(b) Null string (d) worow

[2008 : 2 Marks]

20. Consider the C program given below. What does it print?

```
# include <stdio.h>
int main( )
{
int i, j;
int a[8] = {1, 2, 3, 4, 5, 6, 7, 8};
for(i = 0; i < 3; i++)
{
a[i] = a[i]+1;
i++;
}
i – –;
for (j = 7; j > 4, j – –)
{
int i = j/2;
a[i] = a[i] – 1;
}
printf ("%d", %d", i, a [i]);
}
```

(a) 2, 3 (b) 2, 4

(c) 3, 2 (d) 3, 3

[2008: 2 Marks]

21. A C program is given below:

```
# include <stdio.h>
int main( )
{
int i, j;
char a[2] [3] = {{'a' 'b', 'c'}, {'d', 'e', 'f'}};
char b[3] [2];
char *p = *b;
for (i = 0; i < 2; i++)
```

```
{
for (j = 0; k < 3; j ++)
{
*(p + 2*j + i) = a [i] [j];
}
}
```

What should be the contents of the array b at the end of the program?

(a) a b
    c d
    e f

(b) a d
    b e
    c f

(c) a c
    e b
    d f

(d) a e
    d c
    b f

[2008 : 2 Marks]

22. Consider the following snippet of a C program. Assume that swap (&x, &y) exchanges the contents of x and y.

```
int main( )
{
int array[ ] = {3, 5, 1, 4, 6, 2};
int done = 0;
int i;
while (done = = 0)
{
done = 1;
for (i = 0; i <= 4; i++)
{
if (array [i] < array [i +1])
{ swap(&array[i], &array[i + 1]);
done = 0;
}
}
}
for (i = 5; i > = 1; i – –)
{
if (array [i] > array [i – 1])
{
swap(&array[i], &array[i – 1]);
done = 0;
}
}
printf("%d", array[3]);
}
```

The output of the program is________.

[2017 (Set-2) : 2 Marks]

23. In a compact single dimensional array representation for lower triangular matrices (i.e. all the elements above the diagonal are zero) of size n × n, non-zero elements (i.e. elements of the lower triangle) of each row are stored one after another, starting from the first row, the index of the (i, j)th element of the lower triangular matrix in this new representation is

(a) $i + j$ (b) $i + j - 1$

(c) $(j - 1) + \frac{i(i-1)}{2}$ (d) $i + \frac{j(j-1)}{2}$

[1994 : 2 Marks]

24. Let A be a two-dimensional array declared as follows:

A : array [1 ... 10] [1 ... 15] of integer; Assuming that each integer takes one memory location. The array is stored in row-major order and the first element of the array is stored at location 100, what is the address of the element A[i] [j]?

(a) $15i + j + 84$ (b) $15j + i + 84$

(c) $10i + j + 89$ (d) $10j + i + 89$

[1998 : 2 Marks]

25. A program P reads in 500 integers in the range (0, 100) representing the scores of 500 students. If prints the frequency of each score above 50, what would be the best way for P to store the frequencies?

(a) An array of 50 numbers

(b) An array of 100 numbers

(c) An array of 500 numbers

(d) A dynamically allocated array of 550 numbers

[2005 :1 Mark]

ARRAY VAL

26. An n × n array v is defined as follows:

v[i, j] = i – j for all i, j, 1≤ i ≤ n, 1 ≤ j ≤ n

The sum of the elements of the array v is

(a) 0 (b) $n - 1$

(c) $n^2 - 3n + 2$ (d) $n^2(n + 1)/2$

[2000 : 1 Mark]

27. Suppose you are given an array s [1...n] and a procedure reverse(s, i, j) which reverses the order of elements in between positions i and j (both inclusive). What does the following sequence do, where 1 ≤ k ≤ n:

reverse (s, 1, k);

reverse (s, k + 1, n);

reverse (s, 1, n);

(a) Rotates s left by k positions

(b) Leaves s unchanged

(c) Reverses all elements of s

(d) None of the above **[2000 : 1 Mark]**

28. Let a be an array containing n integers in increasing order. The following algorithm determines whether there are two distinct numbers in the array whose difference is a specified number S > 0.

```
i = 0; j = 1;
while (j < n)
if (E) j++;
else if (a[j] – a[i] = = S) break;
else i++;
}
if (j < n) printf("yes");
else printf ("no");
```

Choose the correct expression for E.

(a) a[j] – a [i] > S (b) a [j] – a [i] < S

(c) a[i] – a [j] < S (d) a[i] – a [j] > S

[2005 : 2 Marks]

29. Let a and b be two sorted arrays containing n integers each, in non-decreasing order. Let c be a sorted array containing 2n integers obtained by merging the two arrays a and b. Assuming the arrays are indexed starting from 0, consider the following four statements

I. $a[i] \geq b[i] \Rightarrow c[2i] \geq a[i]$

II. $a[i] \geq b[i] \Rightarrow c[2i] \geq b[i]$

III. $a[i] \geq b[i] \Rightarrow c[2i] \leq a[i]$

IV. $a[i] \geq b[i] \Rightarrow c[2i] \leq b[i]$

Which of the following is TRUE

(a) only I and II (b) only I and IV

(c) only II and III (d) only III and IV

[2005 : 2 Marks]

ASYMPTOTIC NOTATIONS

30. An array of integers of size n can be converted into a heap by adjusting the heaps rooted at each internal node of the complete binary tree starting at the node $\lfloor (n-1)/2 \rfloor$, and doing this adjustment up to the root node (root node is at index 0) in the order $\lfloor (n-1)/2 \rfloor$, $\lfloor (n-3)/2 \rfloor$,..., 0. The time required to construct a heap in this manner is

(a) O(log n) (b) O(n)

(c) O (n log log n) (d) O(n log n)

[2004 : 2 Marks]

MULTIDIMENSION ARRAY

31. Let A be a square matrix of size n × n. Consider the following pseudocode. What is the expected output?

```
C = 100;
for i=1 to n do
for j=1 to n do
{
Temp = A[i][j] + C;
A[i][j] = A[j] [i];
A[j] [i] = Temp - C;
}
for i=1 to n do
for j =1 to n do
output (A[i] [j]);
```

(a) The matrix A itself

(b) Transpose of the matrix A

(c) Adding 100 to the upper diagonal elements and subtracting 100 from lower diagonal elements of A

(d) None of the above

[2014 (Set-3) :1 Mark]

32. What is the output. of the following C code? Assume that the address of x is 2000 (in decimal) and an integer requires four bytes of memory.

```
int main( )
{   unsigned int x[4] [3] =
{{1, 2, 3}, {4, 5, 6}, {7, 8, 9}, {10, 11, 12}};
printf("%u,%u, %u", x+3, *(x+3),*(x+2)+3);
}
```

(a) 2036, 2036, 2036 (b) 2012, 4, 2204

(c) 2036, 10, 10 (d) 2012, 4, 6

[2015 (Set-1) : 2 Marks]

ANSWERS

1. (*d*)	**2.** (5)	**3.** (*a*)	**4.** (*c*)	**5.** (0)	**6.** (*a*)	**7.** (*a*)	**8.** (*b*)	**9.** (*a*)	**10.** (*d*)
11. (*b*)	**12.** (*a*)	**13.** (*d*)	**14.** (*c*)	**15.** (*c*)	**16.** (*c*)	**17.** (*d*)	**18.** (*c*)	**19.** (*b*)	**20.** (*c*)
21. (*b*)	**22.** (*c*)	**23.** (*c*)	**24.** (*a*)	**25.** (*a*)	**26.** (*a*)	**27.** (*a*)	**28.** (*b*)	**29.** (*c*)	**30.** (*b*)
31. (*a*)	**32.** (*a*)								

EXPLANATIONS

1. Faster access to non-locals than with links can be obtained using an array α of pointers to a activation record is called display.

2. Minimum No. of movement are 5 After shiting the tebleau is :-

2 ←	4 ↑	5	14
3	6 ←	18 ↖	23
10	12	25 ←	∞
∞	∞	∞	∞

3. int Myx (int*E, un sin ged int sixe)

```
{
    int Y= 0 ;
    int Z ;
    int i, j, k ;
    for (i = 0; i < size ; i++)
        Y = Y + E[i]
    for (i = 0; i < size ; i++)
    for (j = i; j < size ; j++)
    {
      Z = 0
      for (k = i; k <= j ; k++)
          Z = Z + E[k];
      if (Z >Y) → Checks whether sum of
                  elements of each subarry
      Y = Z ;     is greater than the sum of
                  elements of array if so, that
                  sum is assigned to Y, if not
                  'Y' will be the sum of
                  elements of complete array
      }
    return Y ;
    }
```

Ultimately returns the maximum possible sum of elements in any sub array of given array E.

4. S1 : Final contents of array Y will be same is both segments.

Y	0	1	2	3	4	5	6	7	8	----	n – 1
	0	1	2	3	4	5	6	7	8	----	n – 1

S2 : X contents are stored row wise in C-program Hence code segment row 'O' accessed Continuous memory

S3 : content of X are not accessed in continuous in code segment?.

5. If k = 4, c = {1, 0, 1, 1}, a = 2, 8 n = 8 for i = o, z =1 mod 8 = 1, since c [0] = 1, z = 1 * 2 mod 8 z = 2 for 1 = 1, z = 2 * 2 mod 8 = 1, since c [1] = 0, z = 4 for i = 2, z = 16 mod 8 = 0

6. ****

7. int * A [10], B [10] [10] ;

int * A [10] is an array of 10 pointer to integer So A [2] [3], A [2] both are possible in left Hand side and B [2] [3] is also possible.

8. If(!A[j]) condition

If(A[j] == 0)

Prints the value. But no zero is the array.

9. *Given program is*

```
Chav P [20] ;
Chav * S = "string" ;
int length = strlen(s) ;
for (i = 0 ; i< length ; i + +)
p [i] = S [length – i] ;
print f("% s", P) ;
```

After executing within the loop

P [0] = *g*

P [1] = *n*

P [2] = *i*

P [3] = *r*

P [4] = *t*

P [5] = *s*

length will be 6 from the statement

length = strlen (s) ;

so after that it will go not of the loop, then

P = gnirts

10. A = count [a[i]] + +

B = count [b[i + +]] –

11. etter, 4, 6, ungle

12. int *x[] = {a1, a2, a3}; line makes x[0] = a1 and likewise. Therefore whenever x[0] is referenced, internally a1 array is being looked upon.

a[0][2] = a1[2] = 8

*a[2] = *a3 = a3[0] = –12

*++a[0] = *(++a[0]) = a1[1] = 7 : a[0] is now pointing to second element of a1.

*(++a)[0] = *a2 = a2[0] = 23 : a is now pointing to array a2.

a[–1][+ 1] = *(a1 + 1 + 1) = a1[2] = 8 : *(a – 1) = a1 + 1 due to last two expressions.

Hence, correct answer would be 8, –12, 7, 23, 8.

13. b ! = a

14. From the given program, we have

	0	1	2	3	4
Q: 100	3	5	2	6	4
	100	102	104	106	108

main ()
↓↗ P
f(100, 5) [100]
↓↗
max (f(102, 4); –2)
↓↗
max (f(104, 3), 3)
↓↗
max (f(106, 2), –4)
↓↗
max (f(108, 1), 2)
↓↗
0

So, the value printed by the program is 3.

15. To compute transpose j needs to be started with i, so A and B are WRONG. In D, given statement is wrong as temporary variable t needs to be assigned some value and NOT vice versa

M[i][j] = t;

16. For vertex i to be a sink, there should be no edge from i to any other vertex.

A[i][j] should be 0 for all j

A[j][i] should be 1 for all j.

The above pseudo code checks every vertex i for sink, starting from i = 0. It basically checks every vertex j after i for being a sink. The trick in pseudo code is, it doesn't check for j smaller than i. The i picked by this loop may not be sink. It basically makes sure that we don't ignore a potential sink. The check whether i is actually a sink or not is done later after do while loop.

Vertex i is a potential sink while A[i][j] is zero

Thus, E1 : !A[i][j]

If the above condition is false, then i is not a sink. All j < i can also not be a sink because there is no edge from i to j.

Now, the next potential sink can be j.

So, E2 : i = j.

17. The following pseudo code basically checks if the potential sink picked by the code above is actually a sink or not.

```
flag = 1;
for (j = 0; j < n; j++)
    if ((j! = i) && E3)
        flag = 0;
```

flag equals to 0 means i is not a sink. The code sets the flag 0 as soon as it finds out that i is not a sink.

A node i is not a sink if either of the following two conditions become true for any j not equal to i.

A[i][j] is 1 for any j

OR

A[j][i] is 0 for any j

E3 : (A[i][j] | | !A[j][i])

18. (*i*) will occur, if $i = n$ occurs before $j = n$ so that the whilé loop terminates till that time j–1 elements of b and n elements of a would have been inserted in c. $i = n$ would have occured only if i would have been incremented i.e,

$a[i] < b[j]$ for the last i.

$\Rightarrow \quad a[n-1] < b[j]$

$\therefore \quad k = j - 1 + n$

19.

w	0	r	1	d	20
0	1	2	3	4	5

When Loop will execute 1st time

a [0] = a [5]

a [0] = '10'

print f (" % s", a)

string starting at address 'a' prints the string starting with '10' and it indicate the end of string, so it will print null string.

20. There are two variables named: i, with different scope.There are 2 main points to consider while solving this question. Scope of variable i and integer division.

First for loop will run for i = 0, 2 and 4 as i is incremented twice inside loop and resultant array will be a = 2, 2, 4, 4, 5, 6, 7, 8 (Loop will terminate at i = 4)

After that i value is 3 as there is a decrement operation after for loop.

Next for loop is running for j = 7, 6 and 5 and corresponding i values which is a local variable inside for loop will be 3 (7/2), 3 (6/2) and 2 (5/2). Array after this for loop will be

a = 2, 2, 3, 2, 5, 6, 7, 8

After the for loop, current i value is 3 and element at a[3] = 2.

21. *p = a[0][0]

*(p + 2) = a[0][1]

*(p + 4) = a[0][2]

*(p + 1) = a[1][0]

*(p + 3) = a[1][1]

*(p + 5) = a[1][2]

22. After the execution of the for loop, the content of array:

First time: 5 3 4 6 2 1

Second time: 6 5 4 3 2 1

Third time: 6 5 4 3 2 1

Now, when while loop execute again, done = 1 and first and second for loop if condition will not be satisfied .

Therefore, At the end, value of are [3] = 3

23. In array Row 1 is stored first, Row 2 next, Row 3 next, and so no.

Here Row 1 has one element. Row 2 has 2 elements. Row 3 has 3 elements, ..., Row $(i-1)$ has $(i-1)$ elements (non - zero).

Hence (i, j)th element present in the array only after presence of

1 element of row 1,

2 elements of row 2,

....

$(i-1)$ elements of row $(i-1)$ and

first $(i-1)$ elements of row i.

Hence the index of (i, j)th element in the array is

$$1 + 2 + 3 + \ldots\ldots + (i-1) + j$$

$$= \frac{(i-1)(i-1+1)}{2} + j = j + \frac{i(i-1)}{2}$$

Consider the following example,

$$\begin{array}{l} R_1 \\ \\ R_2 \\ \\ R_3 \\ \\ R\,(i-1) \end{array} \begin{bmatrix} \underbrace{2}_{1} & 0 & 0 & \ldots\ldots & 0 \\ \\ \underbrace{2 \quad 3}_{2} & & 0 & \ldots\ldots & 0 \\ \\ \underbrace{1 \quad 3 \quad 4}_{3} & & & \ldots\ldots & x \\ \\ \underbrace{x \quad x \quad x \quad \ldots\ldots \quad x}_{i-1} \end{bmatrix}$$

24. A $[i]$ $[j]$th location = Starting address + $(i - 1)$ × Number of columns × Size of one element + $(j - 1)$ × Size of one element.

$$= 100 + (i-1)\,15 + (j-1)$$

$$= 100 + 15i - 15 + j - 1 = 15i + j + 84$$

25. Apply concept of hashing where hash function return index where to increment corresponding entry

Index = (no. – 51)

(no. is given no.)

So mapping goes through 0 — 49

Hence, an array of 50 numbers

26. The sum of element of array is always zero

Example for 2 × 2 array $\begin{bmatrix} 0 & -1 \\ 1 & 0 \end{bmatrix} \Rightarrow \boxed{\text{Sum} = 0}$

27. Let array s = [1, 2, 3, 4, 5}

n = 5

Let k = 2

reverse (s, 1, 2) ⇒ [2, 1, 3, 4, 5]

reverse (s, 3, 5) ⇒ [2, 1, 5, 4, 3]

reverse (s, 1, 5) ⇒ [3, 4, 5, 1, 2]

so array is rotate left by k position

28. For same i if we find that difference of (A[j] – A[i] <s) we increment j to make this difference winder so that it becomes equal to s.

29. Since both a and b are sorted in the beginning, there are i elements smaller than or equal to a[i](i starts from 0), and similarly i elements smaller than or equal to b[i]. So, a[i] ≥ b[i] means there are 2i elements smaller than or equal to a[i], and hence in the merged array a[i] will come after these 2i elements (its index will be >2i). So, c[2i] ≤ a[i] (equality takes care of the "equal to" case which comes when array contains repeated elements).

Similarly, a[i] ≥ b[i] says for b that, there are not more than 2i elements smaller than b[i] in the sorted array (i elements from b, and maximum another i elements from a). So, b[i] ≤ c[2i]

So, II and III are correct is option (c).

30. Upper bound of time complexity is O(n)

31. In the computation of given pseudo code for each row and column of Matrix A, each upper triangular element will be interchanged by its mirror image in the lower triangular and after that the same lower triangular element will be again re-interchanged by its mirror image in the upper triangular, resulting the final computed Matrix A same as input Matrix A.

32. 2036, 2036, 2036,

It will return initial address for all three i.e 2036

3
CHAPTER

Stack

Analysis of Previous GATE Papers											
Units	Year → Topics ↓		2019	2018	2017 Set 1	2017 Set 2	2016 Set 1	2016 Set 2	2015 Set 1	2015 Set 2	2015 Set 3
STACK	1 Mark	MCQ Type									1
		Numerical Type									
	2 Marks	MCQ Type									
		Numerical Type								1	
		Total								2	1
QUEUE	1 Mark	MCQ Type									
		Numerical Type									
	2 Marks	MCQ Type									
		Numerical Type									
		Total									
CIRCULAR QUEUE	1 Mark	MCQ Type				1					
		Numerical Type									
	2 Marks	MCQ Type									
		Numerical Type									
		Total				1					
DOUBLY ENDED QUEUE	1 Mark	MCQ Type		1			1				
		Numerical Type									
	2 Marks	MCQ Type									
		Numerical Type					1				
		Total		1			3				
PRIORI TY QUEUE	1 Mark	MCQ Type									
		Numerical Type									
	2 Marks	MCQ Type									
		Numerical Type									
		Total									

STACK

1. Consider the following C program:

```
# include <stdio.h>
# define EOF – 1
void push (int); /* push the argument on the stack */
int pop (void); /* pop the top of the stack */
void flagError ( );
int main( );
{
int c, m, n, r;
while ((c = getchar ( )) ! = EOF)
{   if (isdigit (c)) push (c);
else if ((c = = '+') | | (c = = '*'))
{
m = pop ( );
n = pop ( );
r = (c = = '+') ? n + m : n*m;
push (r);
}
else if (c ! = ' ')
flagError ( );
}
printf("% c", pop ( ));
}
```

What is the output of the program for the following input?

5 2 * 3 3 2 + * +

(a) 15 (b) 25
(c) 30 (d) 150

[2007 : 2 Marks]

2. The following sequence of operations is performed on a stack:

PUSH (10), PUSH (20), POP, PUSH (10), PUSH (20), POP, POP, POP, PUSH (20), POP The sequence of values popped out is:

(a) 20, 10, 20, 10, 20
(b) 20, 20, 10,10, 20
(c) 10, 20, 20, 10, 20
(d) 20, 20, 10, 20, 10

[1991 : 2 Marks]

3. Which of the following permutations can be obtained in the output (in the same order) using a stack assuming that the input is the sequence 1, 2, 3, 4, 5 in that order?

(a) 3, 4, 5, 1, 2 (b) 3, 4, 5, 2, 1
(c) 1, 5, 2, 3, 4 (d) 5, 4, 3, 1, 2

[1994 : 2 Marks]

4. The postfix expression for the infix expression A + B * (C + D)/F + D*E is

(a) AB + CD + *F/D+ E* (b) ABCD + *F/+DE*++
(c) A *B + CD/F *DE++ (d) A *BCD/F* DE++

[1995 : 2 Marks]

5. Consider the following statements:

(i) First-in-first out types of computations are efficiently supported by STACKS.
(ii) Implementing LISTS on linked lists is more efficient than implementing LISTS on an array for almost all the basic LIST operations.
(iii) Implementing QUEUES on a circular array is more efficient than implementing QUEUES on a linear array with two indices.
(iv) Last-in-first-out type of computations are efficiency supported by QUEUES.

(a) (ii) & (iii) are true (b) (i) & (ii) are true
(c) (iii) & (iv) are true (d) (ii) & (iv) are true

[1996 : 1 Mark]

6. Which of the following is essential for converting an infix expression to the post fix form efficiently?

(a) An operator stack
(b) An operand stack
(c) An operand stack and an operator stack
(d) A parse tree

[1997 :1 Mark]

7. A priority queue Q is used to implement a stack that stores characters. PUSH (C) is implemented INSERT (Q, C, K) where K is an appropriate integer key chosen by the implementation. POP is implemented as DELETEMIN(Q). For a sequence of operations, the keys chosen are in

(a) non-increasing order
(b) non-decreasing order
(c) strictly increasing order
(d) strictly decreasing order **[1997 : 2 Marks]**

8. Compute the postfix equivalent of the following expression:

$3^* \log(x + 1) - \frac{a}{2}$

[1998 : 2 Marks]

9. What value would the following function return for the input x = 95?

Function fun (x:integer): integer;
Begin If x > 100 then fun = x –10
Else fun : = fun(fun (x + 11))
End;

(a) 89 (b) 90
(c) 91 (d) 92

[1998 : 2 Marks]

10. Let S be a stack of size n ≥ 1. Starting with the empty stack, suppose we push the first n natural numbers in sequence, and then perform n pop operations. Assume that Push and Pop operation take X seconds each, and Y seconds elapse between the end of one such stack operation and the start of the next operation. For m ≥ 1, define the stack-life of m is the time elapsed from the end of push(m) to the start of the pop operation that removes m from S. The average stack-life of an element of this stack is

(a) n (X + Y) (b) 3Y + 2X
(c) n (X + Y) – X (d) Y + 2X

[2003 : 2 Marks]

11. A single array A[1...MAXSIZE] is used to implement two stacks. The two stacks grow from opposite ends of the array. Variables top1 and top2 (topl < top2) point to the location of the topmost element in each of the stacks. If the space is to be used efficiently, the condition for "stack full"is

(a) (top1 = MAXSIZE/2) and (top2 = MAXSIZE/2 + 1)
(b) top 1 + top2 = MAXSIZE
(c) (top1 = MAXSIZE/2) or (top2 = MAXSIZE)
(d) top1 = top2 — 1

[2004 : 1 Mark]

12. The best data structure to check whether an arithmetic expression has balanced parentheses is a

(a) queue (b) stack
(c) tree (d) list

[2004 : 1 Mark]

13. Assume that the operators +, –, × are left associative and ^ is right associative. The order of precedence (from highest to lowest) is ^, x, +, –. The postfix expression corresponding to the infix expression a+ b × c – d ^ e ^ f is

(a) abc × + def ^ ^–
(b) abc × + de ^ f ^
(c) ab + c × d – e ^ f ^
(d) – + a × bc ^^ def

[2004 : 2 Marks]

14. A program attempts to generate as many permutations as possible of the string, 'abcd' by pushing the characters a, b, c, d in the same order onto a stack, but it may pop off the top character at any time. Which one of the following strings CANNOT be generated using this program?

(a) abed (b) dcba
(c) cbad (d) cabd

[2004 : 2 Marks]

15. A function f defined on stacks of integers satisfies the following properties. f(ϕ) = 0 and f(push (S, i)) = max (f(S), 0) + i for all stacks S and integers i. If a stack S contains the integers 2, – 3, 2, – 1, 2 in order from bottom to top, what is f(S)?

(a) 6 (b) 4
(c) 3 (d) 2

[2005 : 1 Mark]

16. The following postfix expression with single digit operands in evaluated using a stack

8 2 3 ^ / 2 3* + 5 1*–

Note that ^ is the exponentiation operator. The top two elements of the stack after the first* is evaluated are

(a) 6, 1 (b) 5, 7
(c) 3, 2 (d) 1,5 **[2007 : 2 Marks]**

17. Consider the C program below.

```
# include <stdio.h>
int *A, stkTop;
int stkFunc (int opcode, int val)
{
static int size=0, stkTop = 0;
switch (opcode)
{
case –1: size = val; break;
case 0: if (stkTop < size)
A[stkTop++] = val; break;
default: if (stkTop)
return A[-- stkTop];
}
return –1;
}
int main ()
{
int B[20]; A=B; stkTop = –1
stkFunc (–1, 10);
stkFunc (0, 5);
stkFunc (0, 10);
printf ("%d\n", stkFunc (1, 0)+stkFunc (1, 0));
}
```

The value printed by the above program is

[2015 (Set-2) : 2 Marks]

18. The result evaluating the postfix expression 10 5 + 60 6 / * 8 – is

(a) 284 (b) 213
(c) 142 (d) 71

[2015 (Set-3) :1 Mark]

QUEUE

19. An implementation of a queue Q, using two stacks S1 and S2, is given below

```
void insert(Q, x)
{
push(S1, x);
}
void delete(Q, x)
{
if(stack-empty(S2)) then
if(stack-empty(S1)) then
{
print("Q is empty");
return;
}
else while (! stack-empty(S1))
{
x = pop(S1);
push(S2, x);
}
x = pop(S2);
}
```

Let n insert and m (≤ n) delete operations be performed in an arbitrary order on an empty queue Q. Let x and y be the number of push and pop operations performed respectively in the processes. Which one of the following is true for all m and n?

(a) $n + m \le x \le 2n$ and $2m \le y \le n + m$

(b) $n + m \le x < 2n$ and $2m \le y \le 2n$

(c) $2m \le x < 2n$ and $2m \le y \le n + m$

(d) $2m \le x < 2n$ and $2m \le y \le 2n$

[2006 : 2 Marks]

20. Suppose you are given an implementation of a queue of integers. The operations that can be performed on the queue are:

(i) isEmpty (Q) : returns true if the queue is empty, false otherwise.

(ii) delete (Q) : deletes the element at the front of the queue and returns its value.

(iii) insert (Q, i) : inserts the integer i at the rear of the queue.

Consider the following function:

```
void f (queue Q)
{
int i;
if (! is Empty (Q))
{
i = delete (Q);
f(Q);
insert (Q, i);
}
}
```

What operation is performed by the above function f ?

(a) Leaves the queue Q unchanged

(b) Reverses the order of the elements in the queue Q

(c) Deletes the element at the front of the queue Q and inserts it at the rear keeping the other elements in the same order

(d) Empties the queue Q **[2007 : 2 Marks]**

21. Suppose a stack implementation supports an instruction REVERSE, which reverses the order of elements on the stack, in addition to the PUSH and POP instructions. Which one of the following statements is TRUE with respect to this modified stack?

(a) A queue cannot be implemented using this stack.

(b) A queue can be implemented where ENQUEUE takes a single instruction and DEQUEUE takes a sequence of two instructions.

(c) A queue can be implemented where ENQUEUE takes a sequence of three instructions and DEQUEUE takes a single instruction.

(d) A queue can be implemented where both ENQUEUE and DEQUEUE take a single instruction each. **[2014 (Set-2) : 2 Marks]**

CIRCULAR QUEUE

22. Suppose a circular queue of capacity (n – 1) elements is implemented with an array of n elements. Assume that the insertion and deletion operations are carried out using REAR and FRONT as array indeed variables, respectively. Initially, REAR = FRONT = 0. The conditions to detect queue full and queue empty are

(a) full : (REAR + 1) mod n == FRONT empty : REAR == FRONT

(b) full : (REAR + 1) mod n == FRONT empty : (FRONT + 1) mod n == REAR

(c) full : REAR == FRONT empty : (REAR + 1) mod n == FRONT

(d) full : (FRONT + 1) mod n == REAR empty : REAR == FRONT

[2012 : 2 Marks]

23. A circular queue has been implemented using a singly linked list where each node consists of a value and a single pointer pointing to the next node. We maintain exactly two external pointers **FRONT** and **REAR** pointing to the front node and the rear node of the queue, respectively. Which of the following statements is/are CORRECT for such a circular queue, so that insertion and deletion operations can be performed in O(1) time?

I. Next pointer of front node points to the rear node.

II. Next pointer of rear node points to the front node.

(a) I only (b) II only

(c) Both I and II (d) Neither I nor II

[2017 (Set-2) : 1 Mark]

DOUBLY ENDED QUEUE

24. Consider the following operation along with Enqueue and Dequeue operations on queues, where k is a global parameter.

```
Multi-Dequeue (Q) {
m = k;
while (Q is not empty) and (m > 0) {
Dequeue (Q);
m = m -1;
}
}
```

What is the worst case time complexity of a sequence of n queue operations on an initially empty queue?

(a) $\Theta(n)$ (b) $\Theta(n + k)$

(c) $\Theta(nk)$ (d) $\Theta(n^2)$

[2013 : 2 Marks]

25. A queue is implemented using an array such that ENQUEUE and DEQUEUE operations are performed efficiently. Which one of the following statements is CORRECT (n refers to the number of items in the queue)?

(a) Both operations, can be performed in O(1) time

(b) At most one operation can be performed in O(1) time but the worst case time for the other operation will be $\Omega(n)$

(c) The worst case time complexity for both operations will be $\Omega(n)$

(d) Worst case time complexity for both operations will be $\Omega(\log n)$

[2016 (Set-1) : 1 Mark]

26. Let Q denote a queue containing sixteen numbers and S be an empty stack. Head(Q) returns the element at the head of the queue Q without removing it from Q. Similarly Top(S) returns the element at the top of S without removing it from S. Consider the algorithm given below.

```
while Q is not Empty do
if S is Empty OR Top (S) ≤ Head(Q) then
x : = Dequeue (Q);
Push (S, x);
else
x : = Pop (S);
Enqueue (Q, x);
end
end
```

The maximum possible number of iterations of the while loop in the algorithm is ______ .

[2016 (Set-1) : 2 Marks]

27. A queue is implemented using a non-circular singly linked list. The queue has a head pointer and tail pointer, as shown in the figure. Let n denote of number of nodes in the queue. Let enqueue be implemented by inserting a new node at the head and dequeue be implemented by deletion of a node from the tail.

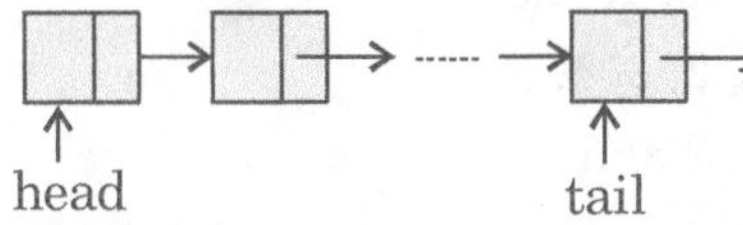

Which one of the following is the time complexity of the most time-efficient implementation of enqueue and dequeue, respectively, for this data structure?

(a) $\theta(1), \theta(1)$ (b) $\theta(1), \theta(n)$

(c) $\theta(n), \theta(1)$ (d) $\theta(n), \theta(n)$

[2018 : 1 Mark]

PRIORITY QUEUE

28. A priority-Queue is implemented as a Max-Heap. Initially, it has 5 elements. The level-order traversal of the heap is given below:

10, 8, 5, 3, 2

Two new elements '1' and '7' are inserted in the heap in that order. The level-order traversal of the heap after the insertion of the elements is

(a) 10, 8, 7, 5, 3, 2, 1 (b) 10, 8, 7, 2, 3, 1, 5

(c) 10, 8, 7, 1, 2, 3, 5 (d) 10, 8, 7, 3, 2, 1, 5

[2005 : 2 Marks]

ANSWERS

1. (*b*)	**2.** (*b*)	**3.** (*b*)	**4.** (*b*)	**5.** (*a*)	**6.** (*a*)	**7.** (*d*)	**8.** (*)	**9.** (*c*)	**10.** (*c*)
11. (*d*)	**12.** (*b*)	**13.** (*a*)	**14.** (*d*)	**15.** (*c*)	**16.** (*a*)	**17.** (15)	**18.** (*c*)	**19.** (*a*)	**20.** (*b*)
21. (*c*)	**22.** (*a*)	**23.** (*b*)	**24.** (*a*)	**25.** (*a*)	**26.** (256)	**27.** (*b*)	**28.** (*d*)		

EXPLANATIONS

1. Program is for the execution of postfix expression using stack

7/P = 5 2 * 3 3 2 + * +

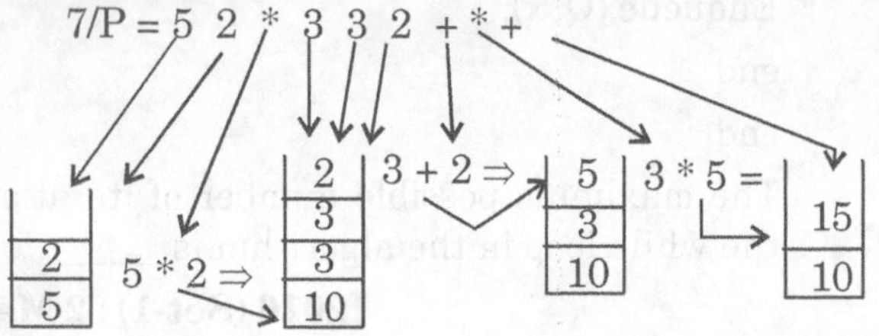

2.

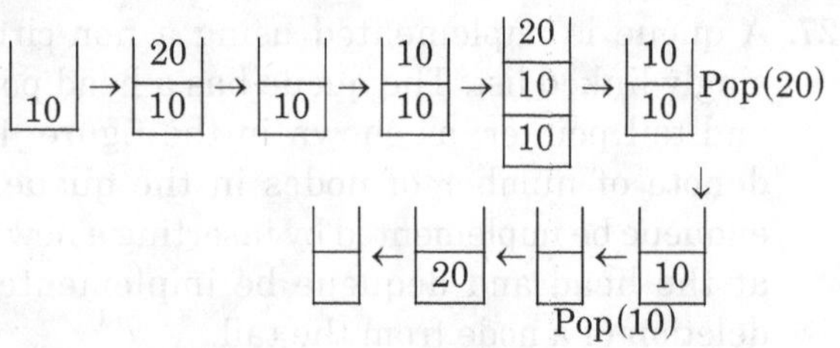

20, 20, 10, 10, 20

3. I/P = 1, 2, 3, 4, 5

Push 1, 2 and 3

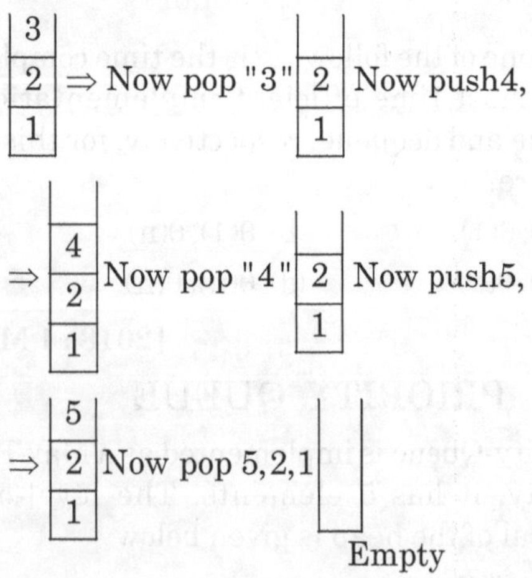

So O/P is ⇒ 3, 4, 5, 2, 1

4. A + B * (C + D)/F + D * E

⇒ A + B *(CD+)/F + D * E

⇒ A + B *(CD+) * F/DE*+

⇒ AB CD + * F/DE*++

5. LIFO is supported by stack so 1st statement is false

FIFO is supported by queue so 4th statement is false.

So II and III are true.

6. For infix to post fix conversion only operator stack is used.

7. Priority queue is used to implement stack, so according to properties of stack last element should delete first.

So that key element must be in strictly decreasing order.

8. $3*\log(x+1)-\frac{9}{2} = 3*(x+1)\log-\frac{a}{2}$

= 3 * x1 + log– a2 /–

= 3x 1 + log x – a2/–

= 3x 1 + log * a2/–

9. fun (95) = fun (fun (106))

= fun (96)

= fun (fun (107))

= fun (97)

= fun (fun (108))

= fun (98)

= (fun (fun (109))

= fun (99)

= fun (fun (140)),

= fun (100)

= fun (fun (111))

= fun (101) = 91.

10. If we consider n = 1 (single element) then after push and pop operation of 1, the life time of 1 is only "y" second (time elapse between two stack operation)

So if we put n = 1 in the options

So from option "c" we get "y"

⇒ n(x + y) – x

⇒ 1(x + y) – x = x + y – x = y

11.

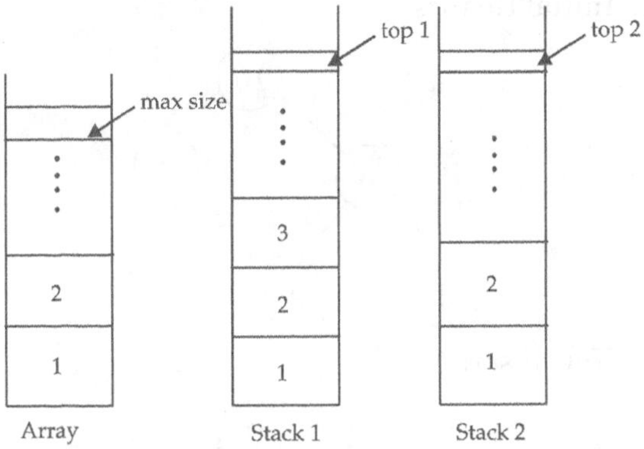

As insertion in stock starts from opposite end, then if A [1] is inserted into stock 1 and A [max size] is inserted into the other stock, stock 2 as all element of arrang are placed into stack

so, top + 1 = top 2

$\Rightarrow$ top 1 = top 2 – 1

12. Stock is used to check whether aur arithmetic expression has balanced parenthesis or not the algorither are as follow :

1. If opening parenthesis is encountered PUSH into the Stock
2. If closing parenthesis is encounter POP from the stock
3. Check wether Stack is empty or not
4. If stock is empty' then Parenthesis are balanced else parenthesis are not balanced.

13. Given expression are

$$\{(a + (b \quad c)) - (d\,^\wedge(e^\wedge f))\}^*$$

The parrenthesis are arranged in this way because $\wedge$ is right associative so converting into postfix stepwise

$$\{(a + (b \quad c)) - (d^\wedge\,(e^\wedge f))\}$$
$$= (a + (bc\ )) - (def^{\wedge\wedge})$$
$$= (abc+) - (def^{\wedge\wedge})$$
$$= abc\ + def^{\wedge\wedge} -$$

This is same as (*a*).

14. "Cabd" is not possible because a can not be popped before 'b' any how.

15.

f(s)	max(f(s),0)	i	f(s) = max
0	0	2	2
2	2	–3	–1
–1	0	2	2
2	2	–1	1
1	1	2	3

(f(s), 0) + i

option c is correct

16. Evaluation will proceed as

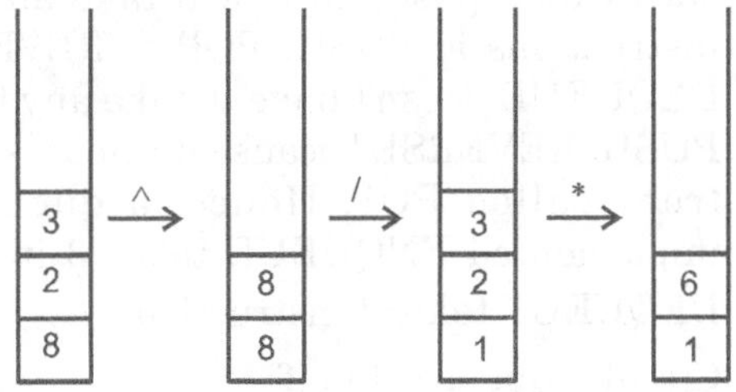

So after evaluation of first *top elements will be 6, 1.

17. StK func (–1, 10) $\Rightarrow$ size = 10, StKtop = 0

So [case - 1 executed]

StK func (0, 5) $\Rightarrow$ A[0] = 5 and StK Top = 1

So [case - 0 executed]

StK func (0, 10) $\Rightarrow$ A[1] = 10 and

StK top = 2 so [case 0 executed]

StKfunc (1, 0) $\Rightarrow$ returns 10 and

AtKop = 1 [default case]

StKfunc (1, 0) $\Rightarrow$ returns 5 and

AtKop = 0 [default case executed]

$\therefore$ Program prints 10 + 5 = 15

18.

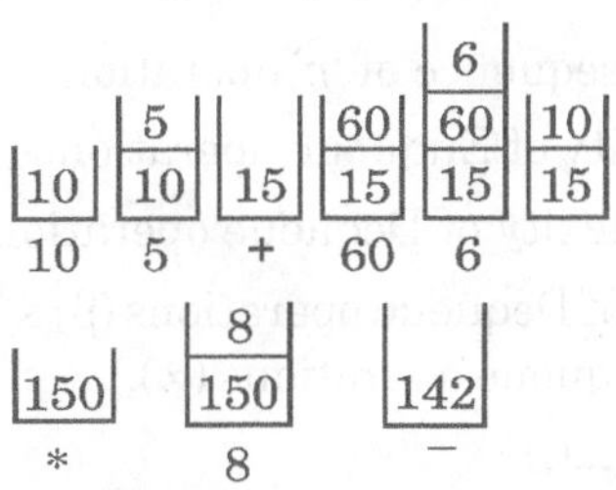

19. Number of push operations will be minimum when *m* alternate insert and delete *op* are performed with *n–m*, incerts in the end.

For each alternate insert and delete *op* 1 push is needed

$\therefore$ $2m$

Rest of the $n - m$ inserts need $n - m$ push

$\therefore$ Minimum push = $2m + n^{-n}$

$= m + n$

Number of *pop* operations will be maximum when *n* insertions are done consecutively and then *m* deletions are performed.

For the first deletion, first *n* element have to be popped from S_1, then all the *m* deletions can be performed each by a single pop.

$\therefore$ Maximum *pop* = $n + m$

20. [*] if queue is empty then no change would happen on queue.

[*] if queue is non empty then it delete all elements one by one from the queue then last deleted element insert at 1st position and so on. So finally we get reverse order of given input queue.

3.8 Stack

21. Since enqueue means to add an item from the back called push, So it will take all the three instructions ie PUSH, POP & REVERSE, but DEQUEUE doesn't have to take any thing from PUSH, REVERSE because it removes item from front called POP. Hence, a queue will be implemented ENQUEUE takes 3 instructions, DEQUEUE takes 1 instruction.

22. Circular queue is full if

Front = = (rear +1) mod n circular queue will be empty if front = = rear

23.

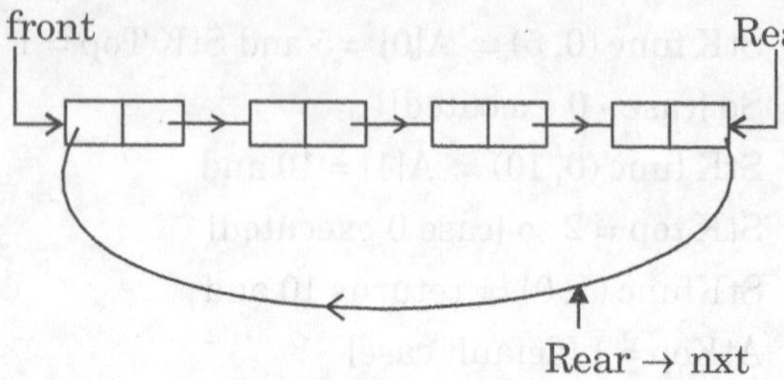

So if Rear → nxt points to the front then we can perform Equeue & Dequeue operation in Q(i) time.

24. Complexity of a sequence of '*n*' operations

= Total Complexity of Enqueue operations (∝)

+ Total complexity of Dequeue operations (β)

total complexity of Dequeue operations (β) ≤ Total complexity of Enqueue operations (∝).

$\beta \leq \propto \ldots(i)$

Total complexity of Enquence operations

$(\propto) \leq n \ldots(2)$

∴ Total complexity of n operations

$= \propto + \beta$

$\leq \propto + \propto$ (from (1))

$\leq n + n$ (from (2)) $\leq 2n$.

25. Equeue & Dequeue operation should perform in 0(i) time.

26. for $n = 16$.

Algorithm runs while loop $16 \times 16 = 256$.

27. Equeue can be perform in Q(1) because we need to update only two pointers i.e.

(i) Create node p

(ii) P → info = data

(iii) Head = P

for Dqueue time complexity is Q(n) because we need to put null to the next to second last node so, for that we need to traverse the link list.

28. Initial Heap is

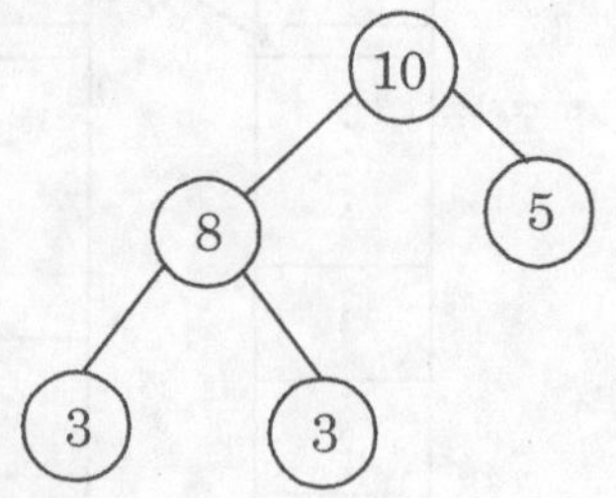

Now insert 1

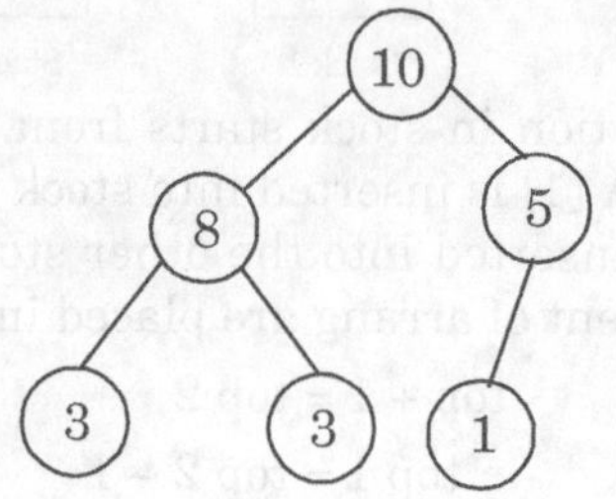

Now insert 7

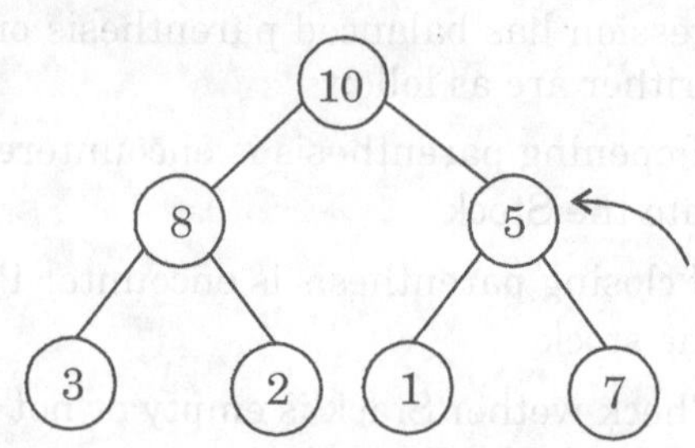

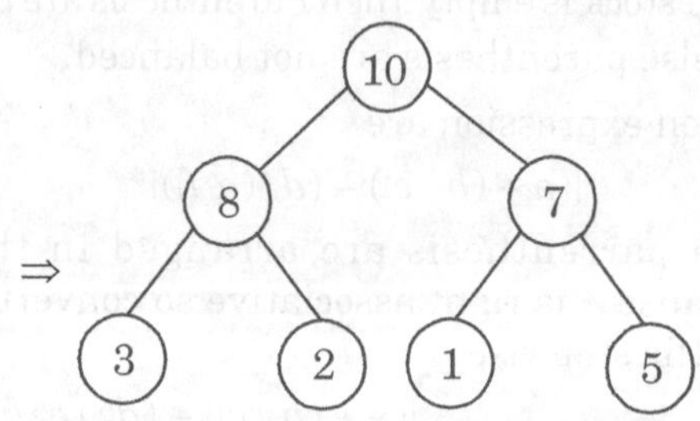

level order traversal of resultant tree is 10, 8, 7, 3, 2, 1, 5.

4 CHAPTER

Linked List

Analysis of Previous GATE Papers

Units	Year → Topics ↓		2019	2018	2017 Set 1	2017 Set 2	2016 Set 1	2016 Set 2	2015 Set 1	2015 Set 2	2015 Set 3
DOUBLY LINKED LIST	1 Mark	MCQ Type									
		Numerical Type									
	2 Marks	MCQ Type									
		Numerical Type									
	Total										
CIRCULAR ll	1 Mark	MCQ Type									
		Numerical Type									
	2 Marks	MCQ Type									
		Numerical Type									
	Total										
SINGLY ll	1 Mark	MCQ Type			1						
		Numerical Type									
	2 Marks	MCQ Type									
		Numerical Type									
	Total				**1**						

DOUBLY LINKED LIST

1. A circularly linked list is used to represent a Queue. A single variable p is used to access the Queue. To which node should p point such that both the operations enQueue and deQueue can be performed in constant time?

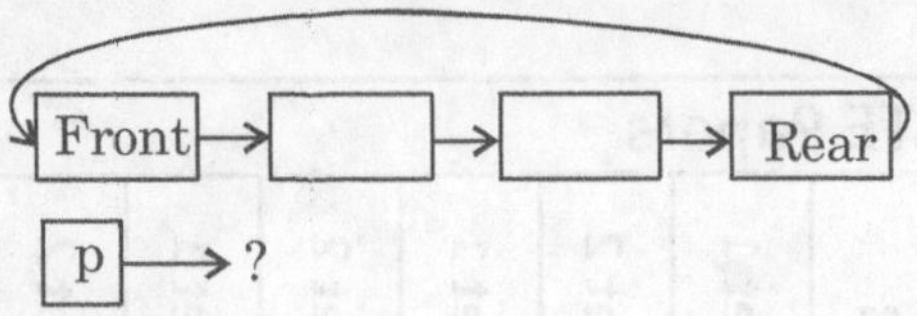

(a) rear node
(b) front node
(c) not possible with a single pointer
(d) node next to front **[2004 : 2 Marks]**

CIRCULAR LL

2. In a circular linked list organization, insertion of a record involves modification of

(a) One pointer (b) Two pointers
(c) Multiple pointers (d) No pointer

[1987 : 2 Marks]

3. The following C function takes a singly-linked list as input argument. It modified the list by moving the last element to the front of the list and returns the modified list. Some part of the code is left blank.

```
typed of struct node
{
int value;
struct node *next;
}Node;
Node *mode_to_front (Node *head)
{
Node *p, *q;
if ((head ==NULL) | |(head→ next ==
NULL))
return head;
q = NULL;
p = head;
while (p→ next! = NULL)
{
q = p;
p = p→ next;
}
________________
return head;
}
```

Choose the correct alternative to replace the blank line.

(a) q = NULL; p→ next = head; head = p;
(b) q→next = NULL; head = p; p→next = head;
(c) head = p; p→next = q; q→next = NULL;
(d) q→next = NULL; p→next = head; head = p;

[2010 : 2 Marks]

SINGLY LL

4. Linked lists are not suitable data structures of which one of the following problems?

(a) Insertion sort
(b) Binary search
(c) Radix sort
(d) Polynomial manipulation **[1994 : 2 Marks]**

5. In the worst case, the number of comparisons needed to search singly linked list of length n for a given element is

(a) $\log_2 n$ (b) n/2
(c) $\log_2 n - 1$ (d) n **[2002 : 1 Mark]**

6. Consider the function f defined below:

```
struct item
{
int data;
struct item* next;
};
int f(struct item *p)
{
return((p = = NULL) | |(p→ next = =NULL)| |
((p→data ⇐ p→next→data)&& f(p→next)));
}
```

For a given linked list p, the function f returns 1 if and only if

(a) the list is empty or has exactly one element
(b) the elements in the list are sorted in non-decreasing order of data value
(c) the elements in the list are sorted in non-increasing order of data value
(d) not all elements in the list have the same data value **[2003 : 2 Marks]**

7. Let P be a singly linked list. Let Q be the pointer to an intermediate node x in the list. What is the worst-case time complexity of the best-known algorithm to delete the node x from the list?

(a) O(n) (b) $O(\log^2 n)$
(c) O(log n) (d) O(1) **[2004 : 1 Mark]**

8. The following C function takes a singly-linked list of integers as a parameter and rearranges the elements of the list. The list is represented as pointer to a structure. The function is called with the list containing the integers 1, 2, 3, 4, 5, 6, 7 in the given order. What will be the contents of the list after the function completes execution?

```
struct node {int value; struct node *next;);
void rearrange (struct node *list)
{
struct node *p, *q;
int temp;
if (!list | | !list→ next) return;
p = list;
q = list→ next;
while (q)
{
temp = p→ value;
p →value = q→ value;
q→ value = temp;
p = q→ next;
q = p ? p → next : 0;
}
}
```

(a) 1, 2, 3, 4, 5, 6, 7 (b) 2, 1, 4, 3, 6, 5, 7

(c) 1, 3, 2, 5, 4, 7, 6 (d) 2, 3, 4, 5, 6, 7, 1

[2005 : 2 Marks]

9. The following C function takes a singly-linked list of integers as a parameter and rearranges the elements of the list. The function is called with the list containing the integers 1, 2, 3, 4, 5, 6, 7 in the given order. What will be the contents of the list after the function completes execution?

```
struct node {
int value;
struct node *next;
};
void rearrange (struct node *list){
Struct node *p, *q;
int temp;
if (!list | |! list→ next) return;
p = list; q = list→ next;
while (q) {
temp = p→ value;
p→ value = q→ value;
q→ value = temp; p = q→ next;
q = p? p→ next: 0;
}
}
```

(a) 1, 2, 3, 4, 5, 6, 7 (b) 2, 1, 4, 3, 6, 5, 7

(c) 1, 3, 2, 5, 4, 7, 6 (d) 2, 3, 4, 5, 6, 7, 1

[2008 : 2 Marks]

10. Consider the C code fragment given below.

```
typedef struct node
{ int data;
node* next;
}node;
void join (node* m, node* n)
{
node* p= n;
while (p→ next ! = NULL)
{
p = p→ next;
}
p→ next = m;
}
```

Assuming that m and n point to valid NULL-terminated linked lists, invocation of join will

(a) append list m to the end of list n for all inputs.

(b) either cause a null pointer dereference or append list m to the end of list n.

(c) cause a null pointer dereference for all inputs.

(d) append list n to the end of list m for all inputs.

[2017 (Set-1) : 1 Mark]

ANSWERS

1. (*c*) **2.** (*b*) **3.** (*d*) **4.** (*b*) **5.** (*d*) **6.** (*b*) **7.** (*a*) **8.** (*b*) **9.** (*b*) **10.** (*b*)

EXPLANATIONS

1. Single variable are used to access the queuce. So it is not possible to operate enqueue and deque operation with constant, as insertion and deletion takes from oposite end rear and front respectively.

2. Start

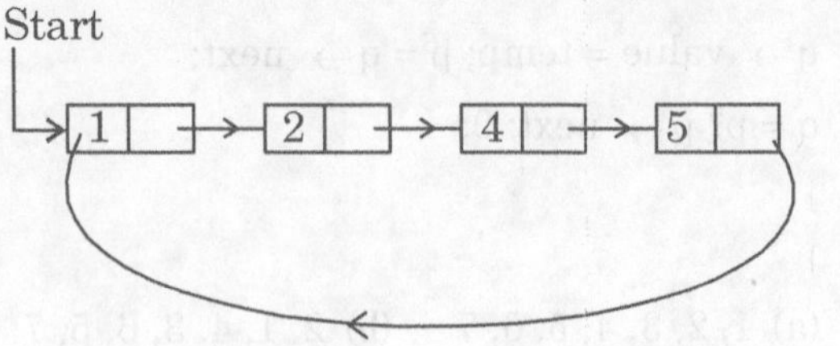

it we want to store node → 3 | x between 2 & 4 then.

Start

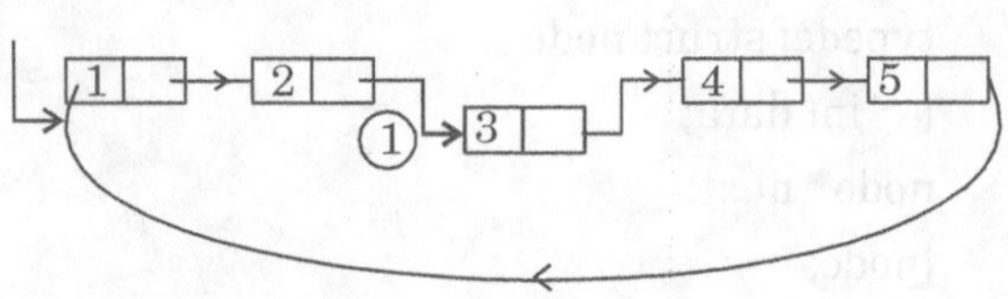

Two pointers are modified to insert node 3.

3. We assigned initial q = NULL, p = head

Now we checked 0 is there $p \to$ next ≠ NULL if it is then break means if we are at the end of linked-list.

Now we are at $p \to$ next = NULL and $q \to$ next = p and we are out of loop

Now we want p as a head and q is last node

Then we have to $p \to$ next = head means we assign first node as the next node of p and declare p = head means at head is p means **head = p**

Now it is ring because $q \to$ next = p till now

So declare $q \to$ next = NULL

then we have to write at blank line

$q \to$ next = NULL, $p \to$ next = head, head = p

Alternately

```
1.  typedef struct node
2.  {  int value;
3.  struct node * next;
4.  } Node;
5.  Node * move-to-front (Node * head)
6.  }
7.  Node * p, * q;
8.  if((head = = NULL) || (head→next = = NULL))
9.  return head
10. q = NULL;
11. p = head;
12. while (p → next ! = NULL)
13. {
14. q = p;
15. p = p → next;
16. }
17. q → next = NULL;
18. p → next = head
19. head = p ;
20. return head
21. }
```

Line 1-4 declare the structure

Line 5 function definition

Line 7 declare two pointer variable of type NODE

Line 8 check whether list is empty or contain only 1 node

Line 10-11 if condition at line 8 fails, then it set p and q

Line 12-16 iteration till node with NULL is fetched and each time p and q gets update

e.g.

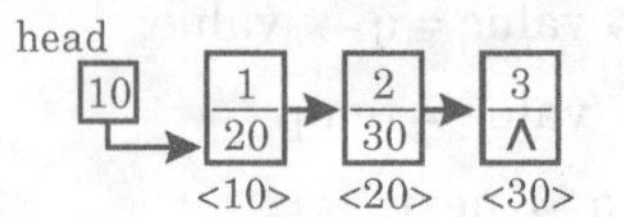

initially

q – NULL, 10, 20

p – 10, 20, 30 – loop terminate

Now, we have to move 3rd node at 1st place.

So,

Line 17 $q \to$ next = NULL

i.e. 20→ next = NULL

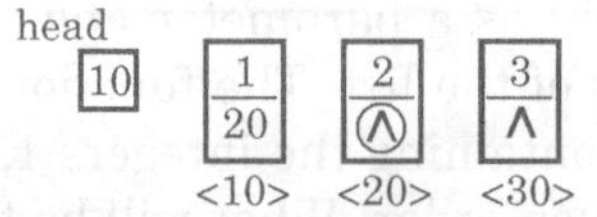

Line 18 $p \to$ next = head [∵ head = 10]

30 → next = 10

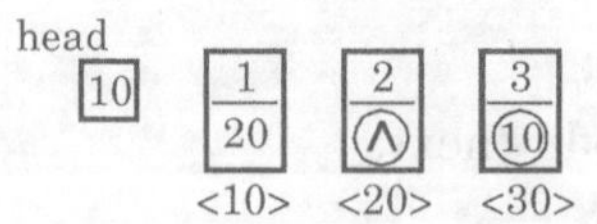

Line 19

head = p

head = 30

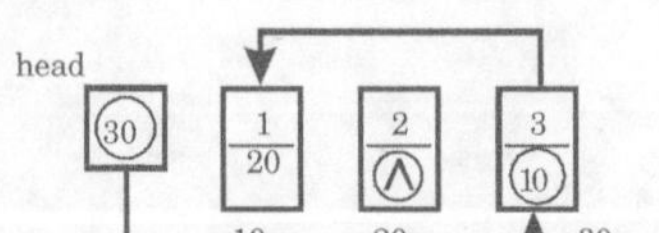

OR

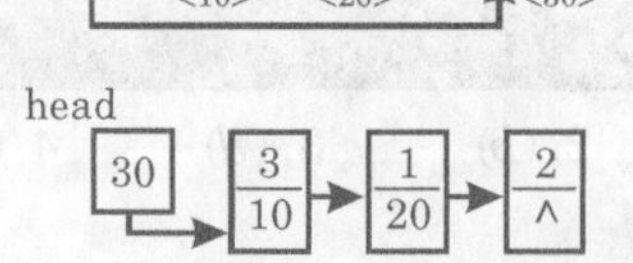

4. Using linked list binary search will take O(n) time so it is inefficient.
5. The maximum no. of comparisons is n to search any item from singly link list.
6. Function return 1 if (P = = NULL) or

   (P → next = = NULL)

   or (P → data < = (P → next → data)

   i.e. function & returns 1 iff data in the list are sorted in non-decreasing order of the data value.
7. To delete x we should find out address of Previous node of x, and to find that address we need to traverse the link list so in worst case it take o(n) time.
8. The given code interchange the value of two consecutive node of the list. So the Inpt sequence is

   1, 2, 3, 4, 5, 6, 7

   then output sequence will be

   2, 1, 4, 3, 6, 5, 7
9. In function rearrange the string of integer 1, 2, 3, 4, 5, 6, 7 converted in to 2, 1, 4, 3, 6, 5, 7 we can check this by execute this program.

   Alternately

   Initially

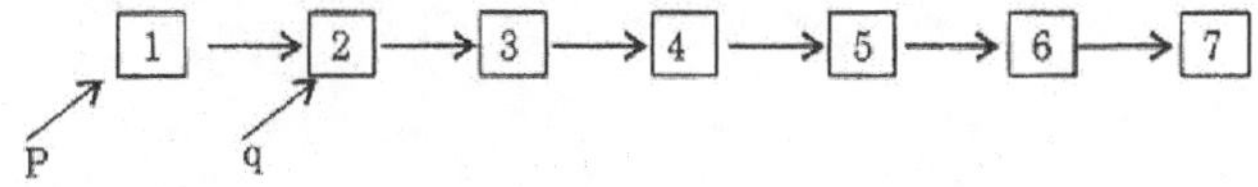

   1st iteration of while

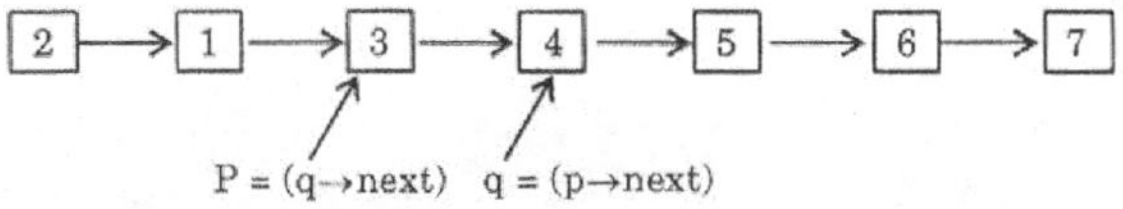

   2nd iteration

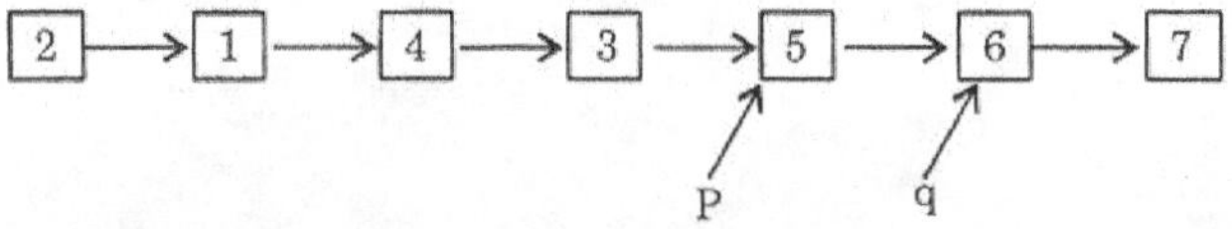

   3rd iteration

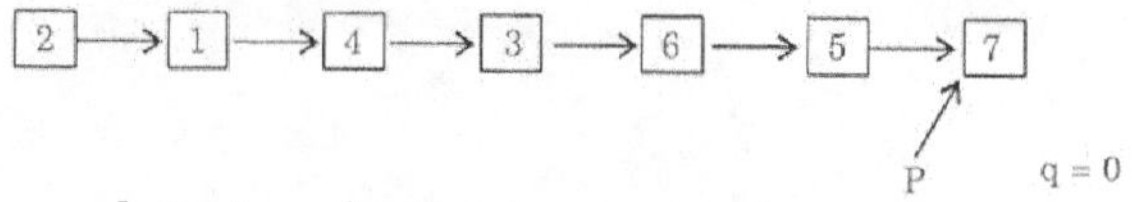

   so loop terminates
10. List m append to the end of list n but it may gives null pointer dereference if list m is empty.

5
CHAPTER

Tree

Analysis of Previous GATE Papers											
Units	**Year → Topics ↓**		**2019**	**2018**	**2017 Set 1**	**2017 Set 2**	**2016 Set 1**	**2016 Set 2**	**2015 Set 1**	**2015 Set 2**	**2015 Set 3**
BINARY TREE	1 Mark	MCQ Type							1		
		Numerical Type							1		
	2 Marks	MCQ Type									
		Numerical Type									
		Total							2		
TREE TRAVERSAL	1 Mark	MCQ Type									
		Numerical Type		1							
	2 Marks	MCQ Type				1					
		Numerical Type									
		Total		1		2					
BALANCED BINARY TREE	1 Mark	MCQ Type									
		Numerical Type									
	2 Marks	MCQ Type									
		Numerical Type									
		Total									
BINARY SEARCH TREE	1 Mark	MCQ Type			1				1		1
		Numerical Type									
	2 Marks	MCQ Type									
		Numerical Type						1			
		Total			1			2	1		1
COMPLETE BINARY TREE	1 Mark	MCQ Type									
		Numerical Type									
	2 Marks	MCQ Type									
		Numerical Type									
		Total									

BINARY TREE

1. Consider the following New-order stragety for traversing a binary tree:
   - Visit the root;
   - Visit the right subtree using New-order;
   - Visit the left subtree using New-order;

   The New-order traversal of the expression tree corresponding to the reverse polish expression 3 4 * 5 – 2 ^ 6 7 * 1 + – is given by
   (a) + – 1 6 7 * 2 ^ 5 – 3 4 *
   (b) – + 1 * 6 7 ^ 2 – 5 * 3 4
   (c) – + 1 * 7 6 ^ 2 – 5 * 4 3
   (d) 1 7 6 * + 2 5 4 3 * – ^ –
2. If the number of leaves in a tree is not a power of 2, then the tree is not a binary tree.(True/False)
   [1987 : 1 Mark]
3. A binary tree T has n leaf nodes. The number of nodes of degree 2 in T is
   (a) $\log_2 n$ (b) n – 1
   (c) n (d) 2^n **[1995 : 1 Mark]**
4. Consider the following nested representation of binary trees: (X Y Z) indicates Y and Z are the left and right subtrees, respectively, of node X. Note that Y and Z may be NULL, or further nested. Which of the following represents a valid binary tree?
   (a) (1 2 (4 5 6 7)) (b) (1 ((234) 56)7)
   (c) (1(234) (567)) (d) (1(23NULL) (45))
   [2000 : 1 Mark]
5. The number of leaf nodes in a rooted tree of n nodes, with each node having 0 or 3 children is
   (a) n/2 (b) (n—1)/2
   (c) (n—1)/2 (d) [(2n + 1)/3]
   [2002 : 2 Marks]
6. Consider the following C program segment struct CellNode

```
{
struct CellNode *leftChild;
int element;
struct CellNode *rightChild ;
};
int DoSomething (struct CellNode *ptr)
{
int value = 0;
if (ptr ! = NULL)
{
if (ptr → leftChild ! = NULL)
value = 1 + DoSomething (ptr→ leftChild));
if (ptr → right Child ! = NULL)
value = max (value, 1 + DoSomething (ptr → rightChild));
}
return (value);
}
```

   The value returned by the function DoSomething when a pointer to the root of a non-empty tree is passed as argument is
   (a) The number of leaf nodes in the tree.
   (b) The number of nodes in the tree
   (c) The number of internal nodes in the tree
   (d) The height of the tree **[2004 : 2 Marks]**
7. In a binary tree, for every node the difference between the number of nodes in the left and right subtrees is at most 2. If the height of the tree is h > 0, then the minimum number of nodes in the tree is
   (a) 2^{h-1} (b) $2^{h-1} + 1$
   (c) $2^h - 1$ (d) 2^h
   [2005 : 2 Marks]
8. In a complete k-ary, every internal node has exactly k children. The number of leaves in such a tree with n internal nodes is
   (a) n k (b) (n – 1) k +1
   (c) n(k – 1) + 1 (d) n (k– 1)
   [2005 : 2 Marks]
9. In a binary tree, the number of internal nodes of degree 1 is 5, and the number of internal nodes of degree 2 is 10. The number of leaf nodes in the binary tree is
   (a) 10
   (b) 11
   (c) 12
   (d) 15 **[2006 : 1 Mark]**

Directions for Question 10 to 12:

An array X of n distinct integers is interpreted as a complete binary tree. The index of the first element of the array is 0.

10. The index of the parent of element X [i], i ≠ 0, is
   (a) $\lfloor i/2 \rfloor$
   (b) $\lceil (i-1)/2 \rceil$
   (c) $\lceil i/2 \rceil$
   (d) $\lceil i/2 \rceil - 1$

   [2006 : 2 Marks]

11. If only the root node does not satisfy the heap property, the algorithm to convert the complete binary tree into a heap has the best asymptotic time complexity of

(a) O(n) (b) O(log n)

(c) O(n log n) (d) O(n loglog n)

[2006 : 2 Marks]

12. If the root node is at level 0, the level of element X[i], $i \neq 0$, is

(a) $\lfloor \log_2 i \rfloor$ (b) $\lceil \log_2(i+1) \rceil$

(c) $\lfloor \log_2(i+1) \rfloor$ (d) $\lceil \log_2 i \rceil$

[2006 : 2 Marks]

13. The height of a binary tree is the maximum number of edges in any root to leaf path. The maximum number of nodes is a binary tree of height h is

(a) 2^h (b) $2h^{-1}$–1

(c) 2^{h+1}–1 (d) 2^{h+1} **[2007 :1 Mark]**

14. The maximum number of binary trees that can be formed with three unlabeled nodes is

(a) 1 (b) 5

(c) 4 (d) 3 **[2007 :1 Mark]**

15. Consider the following C program segment where CellNode represents a node in a binary tree

```
struct CellNode {
struct CelloNode * leftchild;
int element;
struct CellNode *rightchild;
};
int GetValue (struct CellNode-* ptr) {
int value = 0;
if (ptr! = NULL) {
if ((ptr → leftChild = = NULL) &&
(ptr → rightChild = = NULL))
Value =1;
else
value = value +
GetValue (ptr-+leftChild)
+ GetValue(ptr-4 rightChild);
}
return (value);
}
```

The value returned by Get Value when a pointer to the root of a binary tree is passed as its argument is

(a) the number of nodes

(b) the number of internal nodes in the tree

(c) the number of leaf nodes in the tree

(d) the height of the tree **[2007 : 2 Marks]**

Linked Questions 16 & 17:

A binary tree with n > 1 nodes has n1, n2 and n3 nodes of degree one, two and three respectively. The degree of a node is defined as the number of its neighbours.

16. n_3 can be expressed as:

(a) $n_1 + n_2 - 1$ (b) $n_1 - 2$

(c) $[((n_1 + n_2)/2)]$ (d) $n_2 - 1$

[2008 : 2 Marks]

17. Starting with the above tree, while there remains a node v of degree two in the tree, add an edge between the two neighbours of v and then remove v from the tree.

How many edges will remain at the end of the process?

(a) $2 * n_1 - 3$ (b) $n_2 + 2 * n_1 - 2$

(c) $n_3 - n_2$ (d) $n_2 + n_1 - 2$

[2008: 2 Marks]

18. We are given a set of n distinct elements and an unlabeled binary tree with n nodes. In how many ways can we populate the tree with the given set so that it becomes a binary search tree?

(a) 0 (b) 1

(c) n! (d) ${}^{2n}C_n/(n+1)$

[2011 : 2 Marks]

19. The height of a tree is defined as the number of edges on the longest path in the tree. The function shown in the pseudocode below is invoked as the height (root) to compute the height of a binary tree rooted at the tree pointer root.

```
int height(treeptr n) {
if(n=NULL)return –1;
if(n → left==NULL)
if(n → right=NULL)return();
else return [B1] ;//Box1
else {h1=height(n → left);
if(n → right=NULL) return(1+h1);
else {h2=height(n → right);
return [B2] ;//Box2 }
}
}
```

The appropriate expressions for the two boxes B1 and B2 are

(a) B1: (1 + height (n → right))
B2: (1 + max(h1, h2))

(b) B1: (height(n → right))
B2: (1 + max(h1, h2))

(c) Bl: height(n → right)

B2: max(h1, h2)

(d) Bl: (1 + height(n → right))

B2: max(h1, h2))

[2012 : 2 Marks]

20. Consider a rooted n node binary tree represented using pointers. The best upper bound on the time required to determine the number of subtrees having exactly 4 nodes is $O(n^a \log^b n)$. Then the value of a + 10b is ____.

[2014 (Set-1) : 1 Mark]

21. Consider the pseudocode given below. The function DoSomething() takes as argument a pointer to the root of an arbitrary tree represented by the leftMostChild-rightSibling representation. Each node of the tree is of type treeNode. typedef struct treeNode* treeptr; struct treeNode

```
{
treeptr leftMostChild, rightSibling;
};
int DoSomething (treeptr tree)
{
int value=0;
if (tree != NULL)
if (tree->leftMostChild = NULL)
value = 1;
else
value = DoSomething(tree->
leftMostChild); value=value+DoSomething(tree-
> rightSibling);
}
return(value);
}
```

When the pointer to the root of a tree is passed as the argument to DoSomething, the value returned by the function corresponds to the

(a) number of internal nodes in the tree.

(b) height of the tree.

(c) number of nodes without a right sibling in the tree.

(d) number of leaf nodes in the tree.

[2014 (Set-3) : 2 Marks]

22. Consider the C function given below. Assume that the array list A contains n (> 0) elements, sorted in ascending order.

```
int ProcessArray (int *listA, int x, int n)
{
int i, j, k;
i= 0;
j = n – 1;
do
{
k = (i +j )/2;
if (x <= listA[k])
j = k -1;
if (listA[k] <=x)
i = k+1;
} while (i <=j);
if (listA[k] == x)
return(k);
else
return -1;
}
```

Which one of the following statements about the function ProcessArray is CORRECT?

(a) It will run into an infinite loop when xis not in list A.

(b) It is an implementation of binary search

(c) It will always find the maximum element in list A

(d) It will return -1 even when x is present in list A.

[2014 (Set-3) : 2 Marks]

23. The height of a tree is the length of the longest root-to-leaf path in it. The maximum and minimum number of nodes in a binary tree of height 5 are

(a) 63 and 6, respectively

(b) 64 and 5, respectively

(c) 32 and 6, respectively

(d) 31 and 5, respectively

[2015 (Set-1) : 1 Mark]

24. A binary tree T has 20 leaves. The number of nodes in T having two children is

[2015 (Set-2) : 1 Mark]

TREE TRAVERSAL

25. It is possible to construct a binary tree uniquely whose pre-order and post-order traversals are given. (True/False)

[1987 : 1 Mark]

26. If the binary tree in figure is traversed in inorder, then the order in which the nodes will be visited is ________

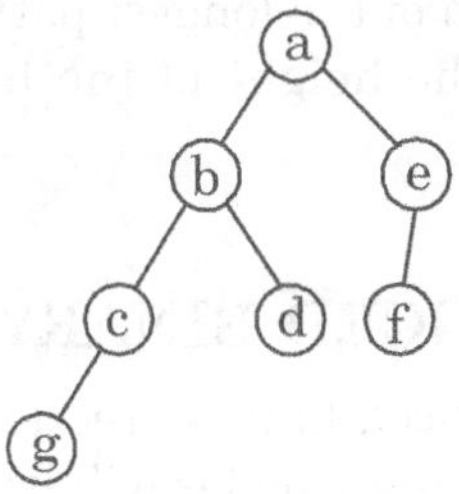

[1991 : 2 Marks]

27. Which of the following sequences denotes the post order traversal sequence of the tree of above question?

(a) fegcbdba (b) gcbdafe

(c) gcdbfea (d) fedgcba

[1996 : 1 Mark]

28. Which of the following statements is false?

(a) A tree with n nodes has (n –1) edges

(b) A labeled rooted binary tree can be uniquely constructed given its postorder and preorder traversal results.

(c) A complete binary tree with n internal nodes has (n + 1) leaves

(d) The maximum number of nodes in a binary tree of height h is $(2^{h+1} - 1)$

[1998 : 1 Mark]

29. Let LASTPOST, LASTIN and LASTPRE denote the last vertex visited in a postorder, inorder and preorder traversal. Respectively, of a complete binary tree. Which of the following is always true?

(a) LASTIN = LASTPOST

(b) LASTIN = LASTPRE

(c) LASTPRE = LASTPOST

(d) None of the above

[2000 : 2 Marks]

30. Level order traversal of a rooted tree can be done by starting from the root and performing

(a) preorder traversal (b) inorder traversal

(c) depth first search (d) breadth first search

[2004 : 1 Mark]

31. Consider the label sequences obtained by the following pairs of traversals on a labeled binary tree. Which of these pairs identify a tree uniquely?

1. preorder and postorder
2. inorder and postorder
3. preorder and inorder
4. level order and postorder

(a) 1 only (b) 2 and 3

(c) 3 only (d) 4 only

[2004 : 2 Marks]

32. Which one of the following binary trees has its inorder and preorder traversals as BCAD and ABCD, respectively?

(a) 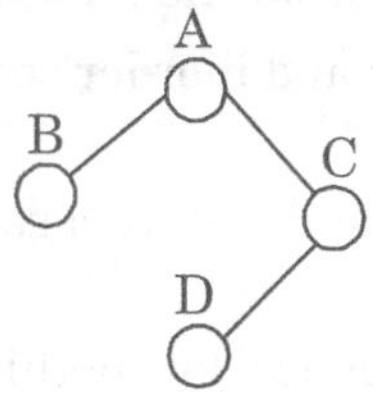

(b) 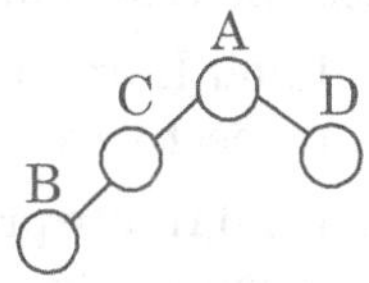

(c) 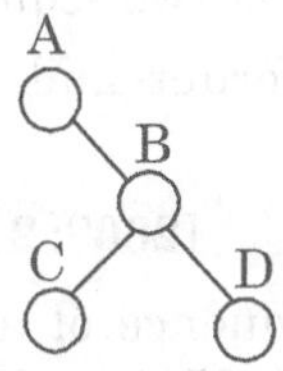

(d) 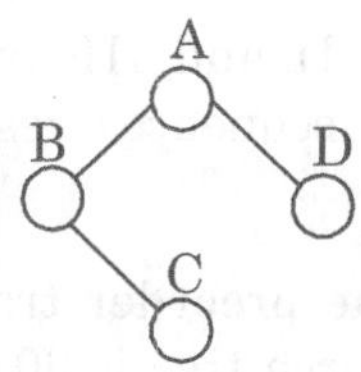

[2004 : 2 Mark]

33. Postorder traversal of a given binary search tree, T produces the following sequence of keys 10, 9, 23, 22, 27, 25, 15, 50, 95, 60, 40, 29

Which one of the following sequences of keys can be the result of an inorder traversal of the tree T?

(a) 9, 10, 15, 22, 23, 25, 27, 29, 40, 50, 60, 95

(b) 9, 10, 15, 22, 40, 50, 60, 95, 23, 25, 27, 29

(c) 29, 15, 9, 10, 25, 22, 23, 27, 40, 60, 50, 95

(d) 95, 50, 60, 40, 27, 23, 22, 25, 10, 0, 15, 29

[2005 : 2 Marks]

34. The inorder and preorder traversal of a binary tree are dbeafcg and abdecfg respectively. The postorder traversal of the binary tree is

(a) debfgca (b) edbgfca

(c) edbfgca (d) defgbca

[2007 : 2 Marks]

35. You are given the postorder traversal, P of a binary search tree on the n elements 1, 2, n. You have to determine the unique binary search tree that has P as its postorder traversal. What is the time complexity of the most efficient algorithm for doing this?

(a) Θ(log n)

(b) Θ(n)

(c) Θ(n log n)

(d) none of the above, as the tree cannot be uniquely determined.

[2008 : 2 Marks]

36. The following three are known to be the preorder, inorder and postorder sequences of a binary tree. But it is not known which is which.

I. MBCAFHPYK

II. KAMCBYPFH

III. MABCKYFPH

Pick the true statement from the following.

(a) I and II are preorder and inorder sequences, respectively

(b) I and III are preorder and postorder sequences, respectively

(c) II is the inorder sequence, but nothing more can be said about the other two sequences

(d) II and III are the preorder and inorder sequences, respectively

[2008: 2 Marks]

37. The preorder traversal sequence of a binary search tree is 30, 20, 10, 15, 25, 23, 39, 35, 42. Which one of the following is the postorder traversal sequence of the same tree?

(a) 10, 20, 15, 23, 25, 35, 42, 39, 30

(b) 15, 10, 25, 23, 20, 42, 35, 39, 30

(c) 15, 20, 10, 23, 25, 42, 35, 39, 30

(d) 15, 10, 23, 25, 20, 35, 42, 39, 30

[2013 : 2 Marks]

38. Consider the following rooted tree with the vertex labeled P as the root:

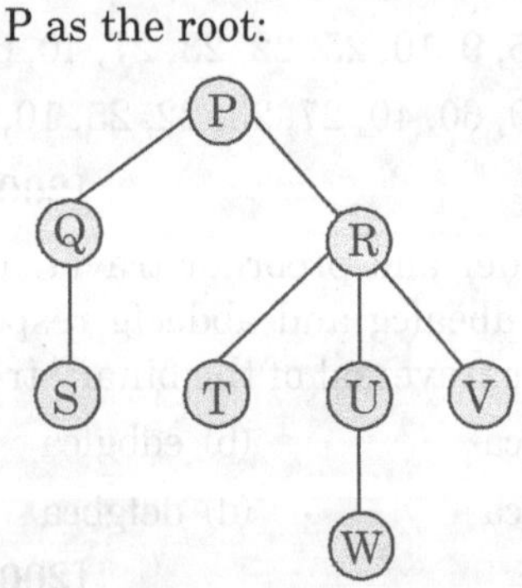

The order in which the nodes are visited during an in-order traversal of the tree is

(a) SQPTRWUV (b) SQPTUWRV

(c) SQPTWUVR (d) SQPTRUWV

[2014 (Set-3) : 1 Mark]

39. The pre-order traversal of a binary search tree is given by 12, 8, 6, 2, 7, 9, 10, 16, 15, 19, 17, 20. Then the post-order traversal of this tree is:

(a) 2, 6, 7, 8, 9, 10, 12, 15, 16, 17, 19, 20

(b) 2, 7, 6, 10, 9, 8, 15, 17, 20, 19, 16, 12

(c) 7, 2, 6, 8, 9, 10, 20, 17, 19, 15, 16, 12

(d) 7, 6, 2, 10, 9, 8, 15, 16, 17, 20, 19, 12

[2017 (Set-2) : 2 Marks]

40. The postorder traversal of a binary tree is 8, 9, 6, 7, 4, 5, 2, 3, 1. The inorder traversal of the same tree is 8, 6, 9, 4, 7, 2, 5, 1, 3. The height of a tree is the length of the longest path from the root to any leaf. The height of the binary tree above is________.

[2018 : 1 Mark]

BALANCED BINARY TREE

41. In the balanced binary tree in the figure given below, how many nodes will become unbalanced when a node is inserted as a child of the node "g"?

(a) 1 (b) 3

(c) 7 (d) 8

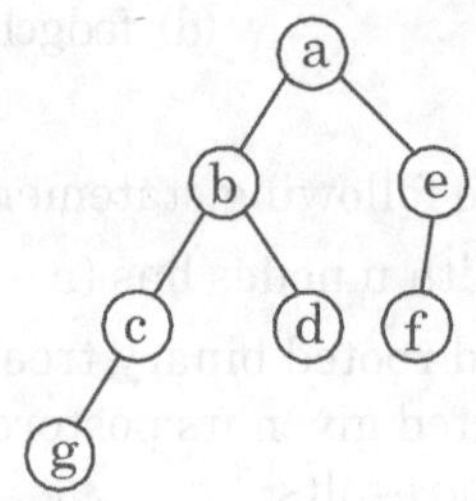

[1996 : 1 Mark]

BINARY SEARCH TREE

42. A binary search tree is generated by inserting in order of the following integers: 50, 15, 62, 5, 20, 58, 91, 3, 8, 37, 60, 24. The number of nodes in the left subtree and right subtree of the root respectively is

(a) (4, 7) (b) (7, 4)

(c) (8, 3) (d) (3, 8)

[1996 : 2 Marks]

43. A binary search tree is used to locate the number 43. Which of the following probe sequences are possible and which are not? Explain.

(a) 61 52 14 17 40 43 (b) 2 3 50 40 60 43

(c) 10 65 31 48 37 43 (d) 81 61 52 14 41 43

(e) 17 77 27 66 18 43

[1996 : 2 Marks]

44. A binary search tree is generated by inserting in order the following integers: 50, 15, 62, 5, 20, 58, 91, 3, 8, 37, 60, 24. The number of nodes in the left subtree and right subtree of the root respectively is

(a) (4, 7) (b) (7, 4)

(c) (8, 3) (d) (3, 8)

[1996 : 2 Marks]

45. A binary search tree contains the values 1, 2, 3, 4, 5, 6, 7, 8. The tree is traversed in pre-order and the values are printed out. Which of the following sequences is a valid output?

(a) 53124786 (b) 53126487
(c) 53241678 (d) None of these

[1997 : 2 Marks]

46. Let T(n) be the number of different binary search trees on n distinct elements.

Then $T(n) = \sum_{k=1}^{n} T(k-1)\ T(k—1)\ T(x)$, where x is

(a) n – k + 1 (b) n – k
(c) n – k – 1 (d) n – k – 2

[2003 : 1 Mark]

47. Suppose the numbers 7, 5, 1, 8, 3, 6, 0, 9, 4, 2 are inserted in that order into an initially empty binary search tree. The binary search tree uses the usual ordering on natural numbers. What is the inorder traversal sequence of the resultant tree?

(a) 7 5 1 0 3 2 4 6 8 9 (b) 0 2 4 3 1 6 5 9 8 7
(c) 0 1 2 3 4 5 6 7 8 9 (d) 9 8 6 4 2 3 0 1 5 7

[2003 : 1 Mark]

48. The following numbers are inserted into an empty binary search tree in the given order: 10, 1, 3, 5, 15, 12, 16. What is the height of the binary search tree (the height is the maximum distance of a leaf node from the root)?

(a) 2 (b) 3
(c) 4 (d) 6

[2004 : 1 Mark]

49. The numbers 1, 2,........ n are inserted in a binary search tree in some order. In the resulting tree, the right subtree of the root contains p nodes. The first number to be inserted in the tree must be

(a) p (b) p + 1
(c) n – p (d) n – p + 1

[2005 : 1 Mark]

50. A binary search tree contains the numbers 1, 2, 3, 4, 5, 6, 7, 8. When the tree is traversed in preorder and the values in each node printed out, the sequence of values obtained is 5, 3, 1, 2, 4, 6, 8, 7. If the tree is traversed in postorder, the sequence obtained would be

(a) 8, 7, 6, 5, 4, 3, 2, 1 (b) 1, 2, 3, 4, 8, 7, 6, 5
(c) 2, 1, 4, 3, 6, 7, 8, 5 (d) 2, 1, 4, 3, 7, 8, 6, 5

[2005 : 2 Marks]

51. How many distinct binary search trees can be created out of 4 distinct keys?

(a) 5 (b) 14
(c) 24 (d) 35 **[2005 : 2 Marks]**

52. Suppose that we have numbers between 1 and 100 in a binary search tree and want to search for the number 55. Which of the following sequences CANNOT be the sequence of nodes examined?

(a) {10, 75, 64, 43, 60, 57, 55}
(b) {90, 12, 68, 34, 62, 45, 55}
(c) {9, 85, 47, 68, 43, 57, 55}
(d) {79, 14, 72, 56, 16, 53, 55}

[2006 : 2 Marks]

53. When searching for the key value 60 in a binary search tree, nodes containing the key values 10, 20, 40, 50, 70 80, 90 are traversed, not necessarily in the order given. How many different orders are possible in which these key values can occur on the search path from the root to the node containing the value 60?

(a) 35 (b) 64
(c) 128 (d) 5040

[2007: 2 Marks]

Directions for Question 54 to 56:

A Binary Search Tree (BST) stores values in the range 37 to 573. Consider the following sequence of keys.

I. 81, 537, 102, 439, 285, 376, 305
II. 52, 97, 121, 195, 242, 381, 472
III. 142, 248, 520, 386, 345, 270, 307
IV. 550, 149, 507, 395, 463, 402, 270

54. Suppose the BST has been unsuccessfully searched for key 273. Which all of the above sequences list nodes in the order in which we could have encountered them in the search?

(a) II and III only (b) I and III only
(c) III and IV only (d) III only

[2008 : 2 Marks]

55. Which of the following statements is TRUE?

(a) I, II and IV are inorder sequences of three different BSTs
(b) I is a preorder sequence of some BST with 439 as the root
(c) II is an inorder sequence of some BST where 121 is the root and 52 is a leaf
(d) IV is a postorder sequence of some BST with 149 as the root

[2008: 2 Marks]

56. How many distinct BSTs can be constructed with 3 distinct keys?

(a) 4 (b) 5

(c) 6 (d) 9

[2008: 2 Marks]

57. Which of the following is/are correct inorder traversal sequence(s) of binary search tree(s)?

1. 3, 5, 7, 8, 15, 19, 25
2. 5, 8, 9, 12, 10, 15, 25
3. 2, 7, 10, 8, 14, 16, 20
4. 4, 6, 7, 9, 18, 20, 25

(a) 1 and 4 only (b) 2 and 3 only

(c) 2 and 4 only (d) 2 only

[2015 (Set-1) : 1 Mark]

58. While inserting the elements 71, 65, 84, 69, 67, 83 in an empty binary search tree (BST) in the sequence shown, the element in the lowest level is

(a) 65 (b) 67

(c) 69 (d) 83

[2015 (Set-3) :1 Mark]

59. The number of ways in which the numbers 1, 2, 3, 4, 5, 6,7 can be inserted in an empty binary search tree, such that the resulting tree has height 6, is . Note: The height of a tree with a single node is 0.

[2016 (Set-2) : 2 Marks]

60. Let The a binary search tree with 15 nodes. The minimum and maximum possible heights of T are:

Note: The height of a tree with a single node is 0.

(a) 4 and 15 respectively

(b) 3 and 14 respectively

(c) 4 and 14 respectively

(d) 3 and 15 respectively

[2017 (Set-1) :1 Mark]

COMPLETE BINARY TREE

61. A complete n-ary tree is one in which every node has 0 or n sons. If x is the number of internal nodes of a complete n-ary tree, the number of leaves in it is given by

(a) x (n – 1) +1 (b) xn – 1

(c) xn + 1 (d) x(n + 1)

[1998 : 2 Marks]

62. A complete n-ary tree is a tree in which each node has n children or no children. Let I be the number of internal nodes and L be the number of leaves in a complete n-ary tree. If L = 41, and I = 10, what is the value of n

(a) 3

(b) 4

(c) 5

(d) 6

[2007: 2 Marks]

ANSWERS

1. (c)	2. (flase)	3. (b)	4. (c)	5. (d)	6. (d)	7. (b)	8. (c)	9. (b)	10. (d)
11. (b)	12. (c)	13. (c)	14. (b)	15. (c)	16. (b)	17. (a)	18. (d)	19. (a)	20. (1)
21. (d)	22. (b)	23. (a)	24. (19)	25. (false)	26. (b)	27. (c)	28. (b)	29. (d)	30. (d)
31. (b)	32. (d)	33. (a)	34. (a)	35. (b)	36. (d)	37. (d)	38. (a)	39. (b)	40. (4)
41. (b)	42. (b)	43. (a,c,d)	44. (b)	45. (d)	46. (b)	47. (c)	48. (b)	49. (c)	50. (d)
51. (b)	52. (c)	53. (a)	54. (d)	55. (c)	56. (b)	57. (a)	58. (b)	59. (64)	60. (b)
61. (a)	62. (c)								

EXPLANATIONS

1.

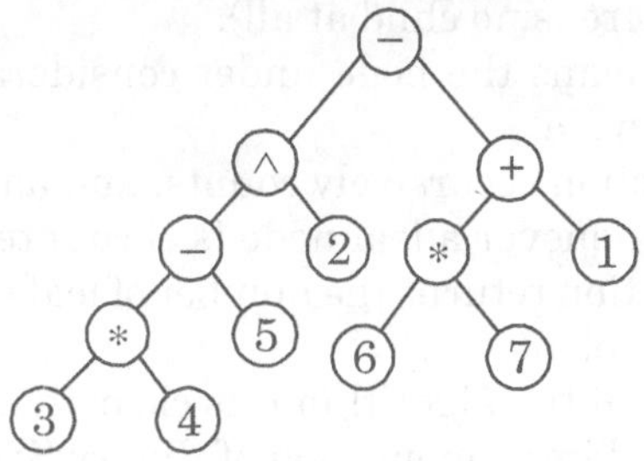

Given expression is 34 * 5 – 2 ∨ 6 7 * 1 + –

Now Converse it into preorder

1. Root
2. RST
3. LST

2. False Condition for binary tree is atmost two immediate child for every internal node.

3. If n leaf nodes then n-1 internal node.

4. In option (c), 2 is the root of subtree (2 3 4) and 5 is root of subtree (5 6 7). Now, in (1 (2 3 4) (5 6 7)) node 1 is the root of the binary tree, and subtree with root 2 is the left subtree and subtree with root 5 is the right subtree at root node 1. Hence it is giving valid binary tree.

5. Let a be the number of leaf nodes and b be the number of internal nodes, then following relation holds for above given tree.

$a = (3 - 1)b + 1 = 2b + 1$

Total number of nodes(n) is sum of leaf nodes and internal nodes

$n = a + b$

After solving above two, we get $a = (2n + 1)/3$.

6. This count the number of edge from the root node to the leaf which is height of the tree.

7. If the height of the tree is $h > 0$, then the minimum number of nodes in the tree is: $2^{h-1} + 1$.

8. For an k-ary tree where each node has k children or no children, following relation holds

$L = (k - 1) * n + 1$

Where L is the number of leaf nodes and n is the number of internal nodes.

9. Number of Leaf Nodes = Number of Internal nodes with 2 children + 1

Number of Leaf Nodes = 10 + 1 = 11.

10. left child of ith element will be at 2 * i + 1 and right child at 2(i + 1).

11. It takes O(logn) to heapify an element of heap.

12. Option C is correct.

13. Maximum nodes in binary tree of height 0 $= 1 = (2^{0+1} - 1)$

Maximum nodes in binary tree of height 1 $= 3 = (2^{1+1} - 1)$

$\therefore$ Maximum nodes in binary tree of height h $= (2^{h+1} - 1)$

14. 5 binary trees can be formed with three unlabeled nodes as shown below.

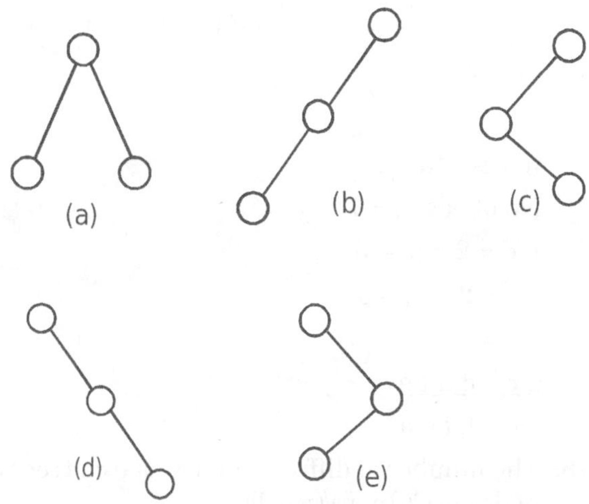

15. Since value = 1 only if nodes has no left as well as right node otherwise value = 0. Therefore it returns number of leg nodes in tree.

16. Definition of degree according to the question is no of neighbours of a node.

Total nodes(n) = n1 + n2 + n3

Apply handshaking Theorm:

Sum of degrees = 2 no of edges

1 * n1 + 2 * n2 + 3 * n3 = 2(n – 1)

Total number of edges in graph will always be (n1 + n2 + n3 – 1)

= 1 ? n1 + 2 ? n2 + 3 ? n3 = 2(n1 + n2 + n3 ? 1)

= n1 + 2n2 + 3n3 = 2n1 + 2n2 + 2n3 ? 2

then n3 = n1 ? 2

17. Consider the following tree.

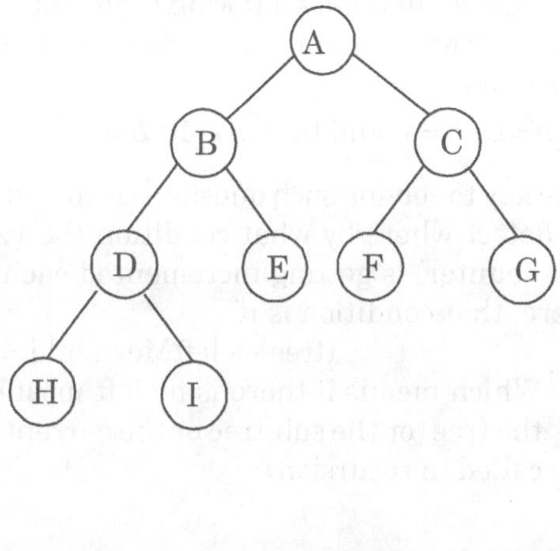

No of Node

with degree 2 = 1 (n_2)

No of degree 3 = 3 (n_2)

No of degree 1 = 5 (n_1)

degree of vertex A is 2. So after removing Node A connect an edge between B and C

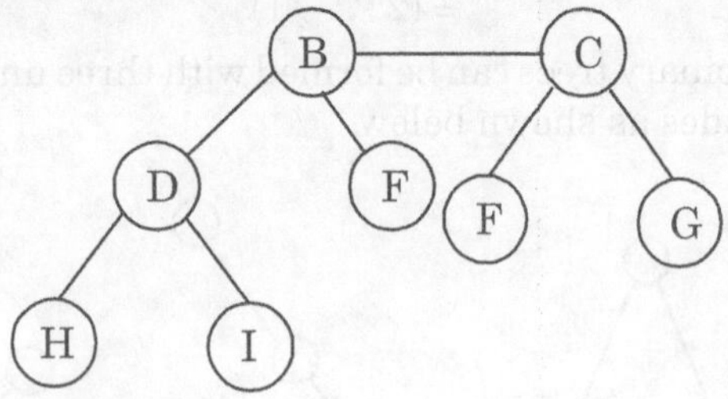

in resultant is

No of edges = 7

i. e = 2 * n, – 3

= 2 * n, – 3

= 7

gcbdafe

gcdbfea

18. The number of diffrent binary search tree with n nodes is C(2n, n)/(n + 1)

19. If right child is present

B1 = 1 + height ($n \to$ right)

Other if both are present

B2 = 1 + max (h_1, h_2)

20.
```
int print_subtrees_size_4(node *n)
{
int size=0;
if(node==null)
return 0;
size=print_subtrees_size_4 (node->left) +
        print_subtrees_size_4(node ->right) + 1;
if(size ==4)
printf("this is a subtree of size 4");
return size;
}
```

The above function on taking input the root of a binary tree prints all the subtrees of size 4 in O(n) time

so $a = 1$, $b = 0$ and then $a + 10\,b = 1$

21. The key to solving such questions is to understand or detect where/by what condition the value (or the counter) is getting incremented each time. Here, that condition is if

(tree → leftMostchild == Null)

⇒ Which means if there is no left most child of the tree (or the sub-tree or the current nodeas called in recursion)

⇒ Which means there is no child to that particular node (since if there is no left most child, there is no child at all).

⇒ Which means the node under consideration is a leaf node.

⇒ The function recursively counts, and adds to value, whenever a leaf node is encountered.

⇒ The function returns the number of leaf nodes in the tree.

22. By the logic of the algorithm it is clear that it is an attempted implementation of Binary Search. So option (*c*) is clearly eliminated. Let us now check for options (*a*) and (*d*).
A good way to do this is to create small dummy examples (arrays) and implement the algorithm as it is. One may make any array of choice. Running iterations of the algorithm would indicate that the loop exits when the x is not present. So option (*a*) is wrong. Also, when x is present, the correct index is indeed returned. (*d*) is also wrong.
Correct answer is (*b*). It is a correct implementation of Binary Search.

23. Maximum number of nodes with height $h \Rightarrow 2^{5+1} - 1 = 63$ nodes is $2^{h+1} - 1$
and minimum no. of nodes with height h is $h + 1$.

Hence 5 + 1 = 6 nodes.

24. Number of Leaf Nodes = Number of Internal nodes with 2 children + 1

20 = x + 1

x = 19

25. Unique tree is possible if we know inorder and preoder of tree or inoder and postoder of the tree but not possible if we dont know inorder.

26. Inorder traversal is gcbdafe

27. Postorder traversal is gcdbfea

28. Unique tree is possible if we know in order and preoder of tree or inoder and postoder of the tree but not possible if we don't know in order.

29. Option (a) is incorrect because the last node visited in Inorder traversal is right child and last node visited in Postorder traversal is root.

For option (b)

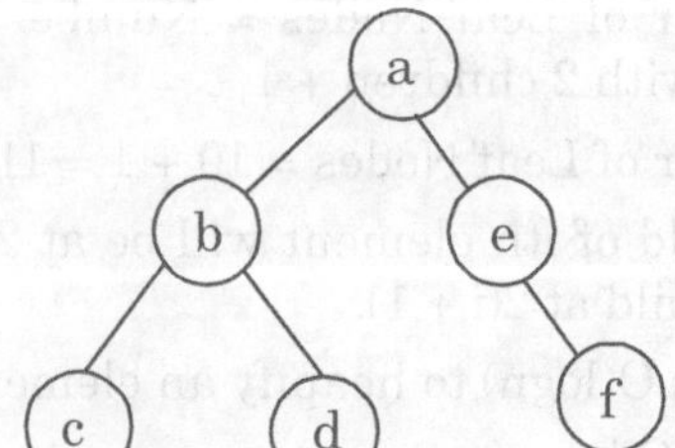

Inorder = c b d a f e

Preorder = a b c d e f

So Here last Node is different.

Option (c) is incorrect because the last node visited in Preorder traversal is right child and last node visited in Postorder traversal is root.

30. Level order traversal of a rooted tree can be done by starting from the root and performing DFS.

31. Unique tree is possible if we know in order and preoder of tree or inoder and postoder of the tree but not possible if we dont know inorder.

32. Inorder of option (d) is BCAD and preorder is ABCD

33. Inorder always have print in ascending order that why.

34. From given inorder and preorder traversal, the binary tree can be formed.

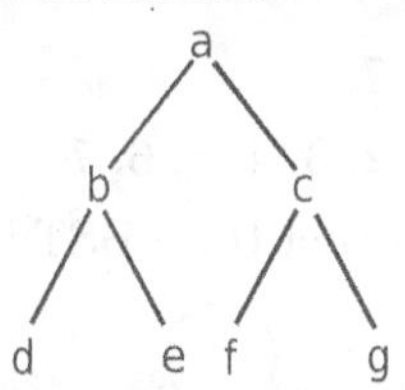

Since a is first node traversed in preorder, so it will be root of tree elements (nodes) left to a and right to a in inorder traversal will be left subtree and right subtree respectively of the tree.

In left subtree elements d, b, e since bcomes first in preorder, so b will be root of left subtree d is left to b in inorder, so it will be left child of d and e will be right child of d. Tree will be like

35. It is Binary Search Tree, not Binary Tree. In BST, in order traversal can always be obtained by sorting all keys.

So the time requierd is o(n).

36.

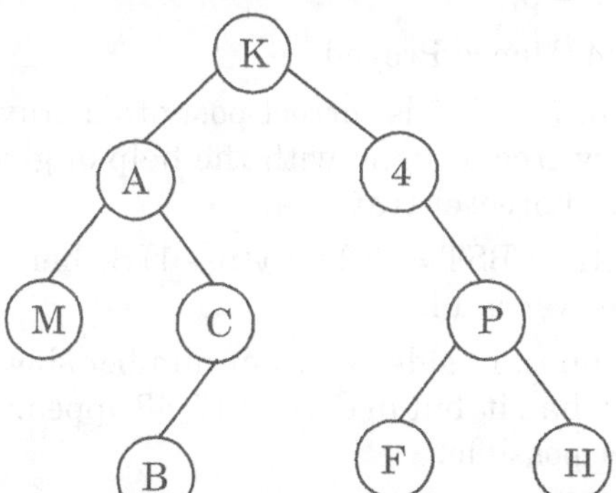

Pre order = KAMCBYPFH

Post order = MBCAFHPYK

37. Inorder = 10 15 20 23 25 30 35 39 42

Preorder = 30 20 10 15 25 23 39 35 42.

Unique tree is (construct with the help of given in 2 pe order)

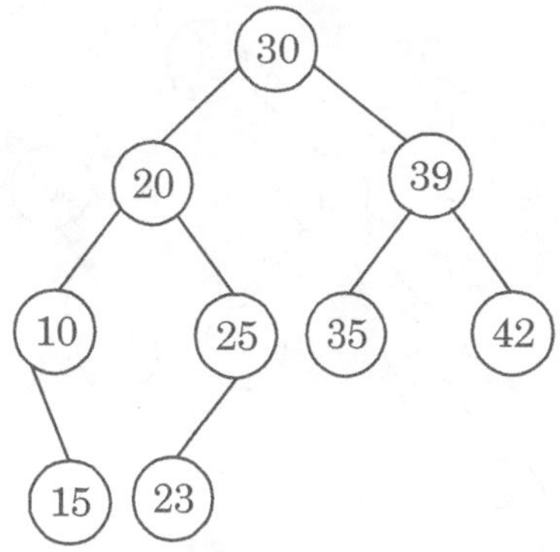

Postorder traversal of tree is

15, 10, 23, 25 20, 35 42 39 30

38. In order Traversal of Ternary Tree is done as follows:

Left → Root → Middle → Right

So the nodes are visited in SQPTRWUV order.

39. Given

Preorder : 12, 8, 6, 2, 7, 9, 10, 16, 15, 19, 17, 20

Inorder: 2, 6, 7, 8, 9, 10, 12, 15, 16, 17, 19, 20

Tree will be, formed as

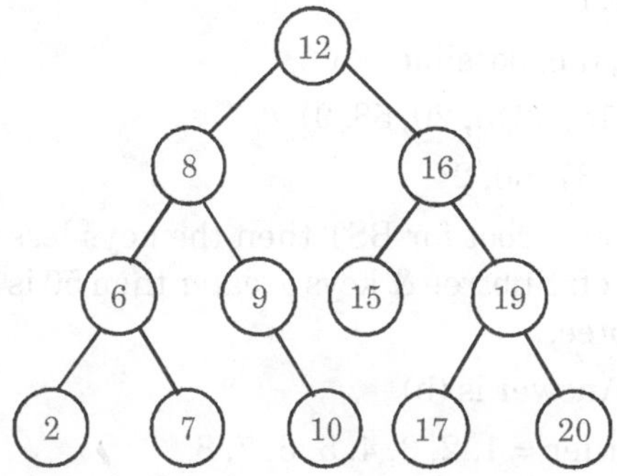

Postorder will be,

2, 7, 6, 10, 9, 8, 15, 17, 20, 19, 16, 12

40. Inorder = 8, 6, 9, 4, 7, 2, 5, 1, 3

Post order = 8, 9, 6, 7, 4, 5, 2, 3, 1

Primary tree is

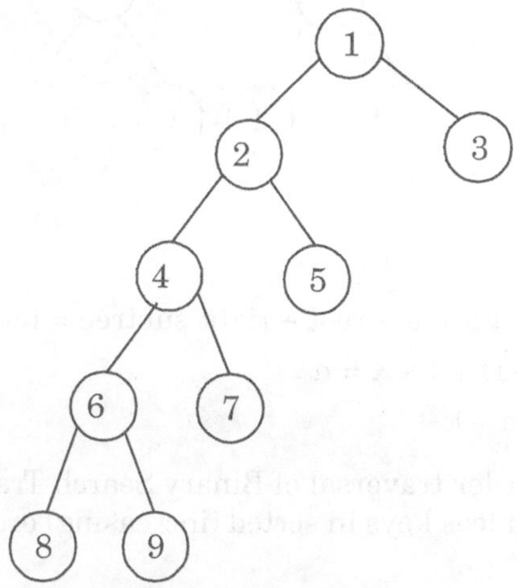

The height of binary tree is 4.

41.

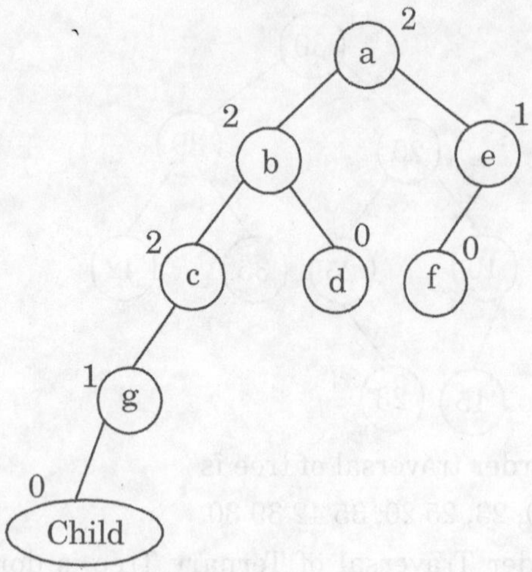

So three Nodes (a, b, c) are unbalanced

42. 50, 15, 62, 5, 20, 58, 9)
3, 8, 37, 60, 24.

So 50 is root for BST then the keys less than 50 in Left Subtree & keys greater then 50 is in Right Subtee.

So Answer is (b)

43. (a, c, d)

a, c, d is possible

44. 50, 15, 62, 5, 20, 58, 9)
3, 8, 37, 60, 24.

So 50 is root for BST then the keys less than 50 in Left Subtree & keys greater then 50 is in Right Subtee.

So Answer is (b)

45. Inorder = 1, 2, 3, 4, 5, 6, 7, 8

Preorder = A, B, C, are not valid Preorder the valid Preorder is 5 3 1 2 4 7 6 8 and tree is

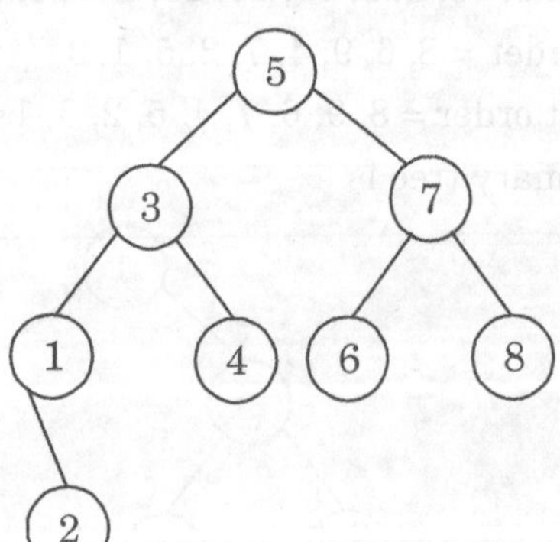

46. left subtree + root + right subtree = total node

(k – 1) + 1 + x = n

x = n – k

47. In order traversal of Binary Search Tree always produces keys in sorted (increasing) order.

48. Binary search tree formed affer inserting into empty binary search tree as

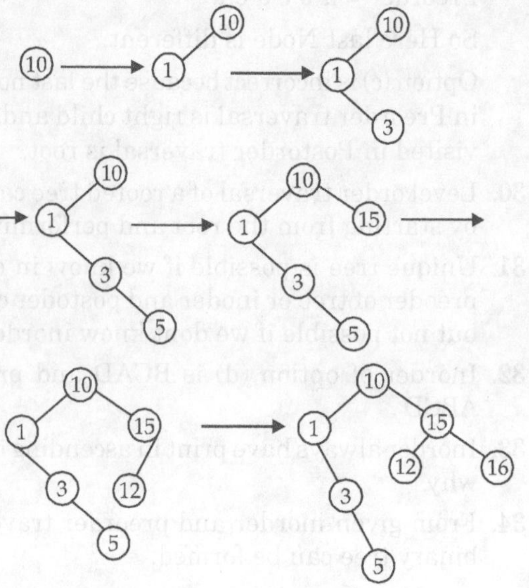

49. Assume n = 7

Keys one 1, 2, 3, 4, 5, 6, 7.

Suppose 4 is root than BST is

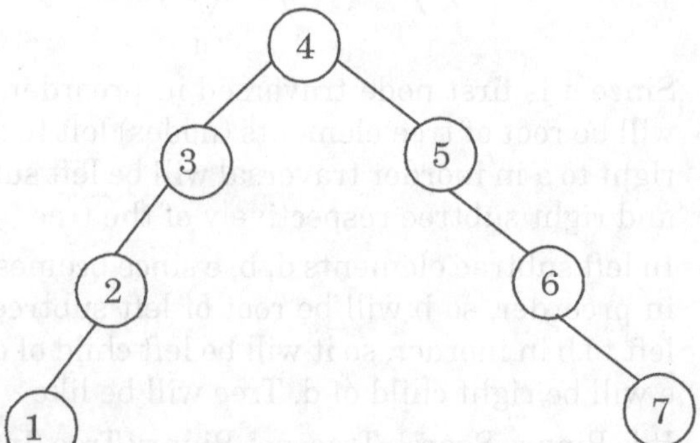

Here value of P = 3

The fist number to be inserted in tree must be

= n – p

7 – 3 = 4 (Hence Proved

50. 2, 1, 4, 3, 7, 8, 6, 5 is correct post order traversal of binary tree designe with the help of given in order and preorer traversal

51. No of istinct BST = C(2n, n)/(n + 1) So here n = 4 then answer is 14.

52. In BST on right side of parent number should be greater than it, but in C after 47, 43 appears that is never possible.

53. There are two set of values, smaller than 60 and greater than 60. Smaller values 10, 20, 40 and 50 are visited, means they are visited in order. Similarly, 90, 80 and 70 are visited in order.

= 7!/(4!3!)

= 35

54. Want to search key 273 :

(I) is wrong because we cannot go to 376 from 285 as 273 is smaller than 285.

(II) is wrong because we cannot go to 472 from 381 as 273 is smaller than 381.

(III) is correct sequence.

(IV) is wrong we cannot go to 463 from 395 in search of 273.

55. A : I and IV are not in ascending order

B : If 439 is root, It should be 1st element in preorder

D : If 149 is root, It should be last element in postorder

Hence only option (c) is correct

56. No of istinct BST = C(2n, n)/(n + 1) So here n = 3 then answer is 5.

57. 1. 3, 5, 7, 8, 15, 19, 25

4. 4, 6, 7, 9, 18, 20, 25

All nodes are in ascending order inorder traversal of a binary search tree.

58.

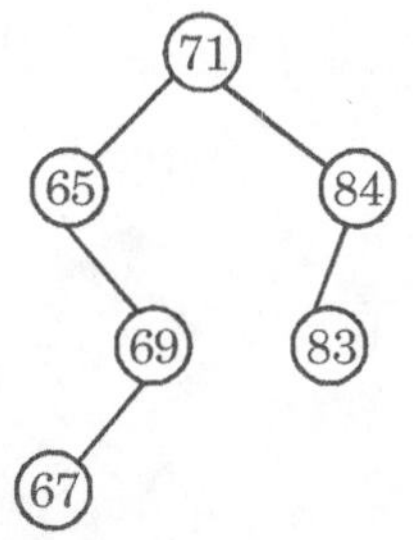

Lowest level element is 67.

59. To get height 6, we need to put either 1 or 7 at root.

Recursive relation to find total diffrent Bst of height 6 can be written as T(n) = 2 * T(n – 1) with T(1) = 1

So Answer is 26 = 64.

60. The minimum height of a binary search tree will be 3 if tree is full binary tree.

The maximum height of a binary search tree will be 14 if tree is either right skew or left skew tree.

61. For an n-ary tree where each node has n children or no children, following relation holds

$$y = (n - 1) * x + 1$$

Where y is the number of leaf nodes and x is the number of internal nodes.

62. For an n-ary tree where each node has n children or no children, following relation holds

$$y = (n - 1) * x + 1$$

Where y is the number of leaf nodes and x is the number of internal nodes.

So, y = 41, x = 10

$$41 = 10 * (n - 1) + 1$$

$$(n - 1) = 4$$

$$n = 5$$

6

CHAPTER

Graphs

Analysis of Previous GATE Papers											
Units	Year → Topics ↓		2019	2018	2017 Set 1	2017 Set 2	2016 Set 1	2016 Set 2	2015 Set 1	2015 Set 2	2015 Set 3
GRAPH	1 Mark	MCQ Type									
		Numerical Type									
	2 Marks	MCQ Type		1				1			
		Numerical Type									
	Total			2				2			
DEPTH FIRST TREE	1 Mark	MCQ Type									
		Numerical Type									
	2 Marks	MCQ Type									
		Numerical Type									
	Total										
BREADTH FIRST TREE	1 Mark	MCQ Type				1					
		Numerical Type						1			
	2 Marks	MCQ Type									
		Numerical Type									
	Total					1		1			
SHORTEST PATH	1 Mark	MCQ Type									
		Numerical Type									
	2 Marks	MCQ Type									
		Numerical Type									
	Total										

GRAPH

1. Consider the following directed graph:

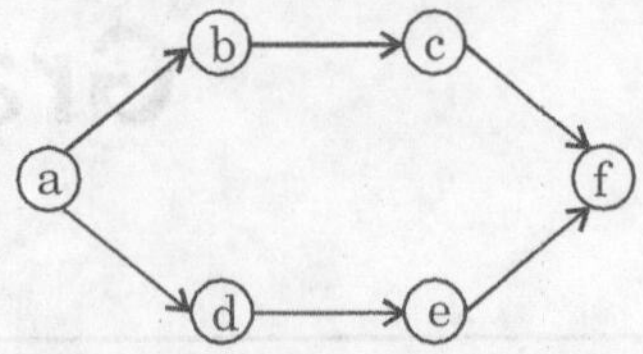

The number of different topological ordering of the vertices of the graph is

[2016 (Set-1) : 1 Mark]

2. Write the adjacency matrix representation of the graph given in figure.

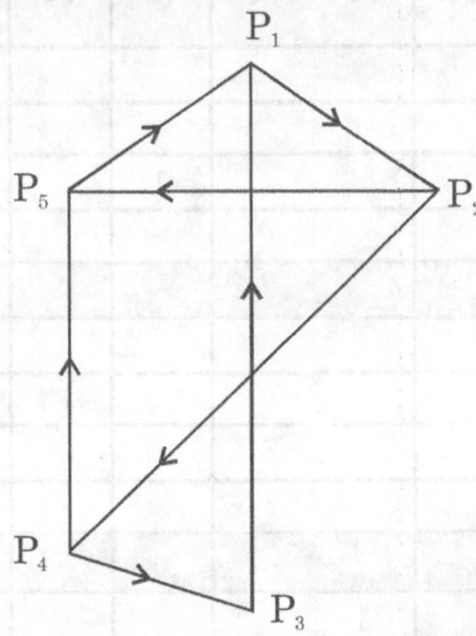

[1998 : 2 Marks]

3. Let G be a directed graph whose vertex set is the set of numbers from 1 to 100. There is an edge from a vertex i to a vertex j iff either j = i + 1 or j = 3i. The minimum number of edges in a path in G from vertex 1 to vertex 100 is

(a) 4 (b) 7

(c) 23 (d) 99

[2005 : 2 Marks]

4. The most efficient algorithm for finding the number of connected components in an undirected graph on n vertices and m edges has time complexity.

(a) $\Theta(n)$ (b) $\Theta(m)$

(c) $\Theta(m + n)$ (d) $\Theta(mn)$

[2008 : 1 Mark]

5. In an adjacency list representation of an undirected simple graph G = (V, E), each edge (u, v) has two adjacency list entries: [v] in the adjacency list of u, and [u] in the adjacency listof v. These are called twins of each other. A twin pointer is a pointer from an adjacency list entry to its twin. If $|E| = m$ and $|V| = n$, and the memory size is not a constraint, what is the time complexity of the most efficient algorithm to set the twin pointer in each entry in each adjacency list?

(a) $\Theta(n^2)$ (b) $\Theta(n + m)$

(c) $\Theta(m^2)$ (d) $\Theta(n^4)$

[2016 (Set-2) : 2 Marks]

6. Let G be a simple undirected graph. Let T_D be a depth first search tree of G. Let T_B be a breadth first search tree of G. Consider the following statements:

I. No edge of G is a cross edge with respect to T_D. (A cross edge in G is between two nodes neither of which is an ancestor of the other in T_D).

II. For every edge (u, v) of G, if u is at depth i and u is at depth j in T_B, then $|i - j| = 1$.

Which of the statements above must necessarily be true?

(a) I only (b) II only

(c) Both I and II (d) Neither I nor II

[2018 : 2 Marks]

DEPTH FIRST TREE

7. Lt G be an undirected graph. Consider a depth-first traversal of G, and let T be the resulting depth-first search tree. Let u be a vertex in G and let v be the first new (unvisited) vertex visited after visiting u in the traversal. Which of the following statements is always true?

(a) {u,v} must be an edge in G, and u is a descendant of v in T

(b) {u,v} must be an edge in G, and v is a descendant of u in T

(c) If {u,v} is not an edge in G then u is a leaf in T

(d) If {u,v} is not an edge in G then u and v must have the same parent in T

[2000 : 2 Marks]

8. Consider the following graph

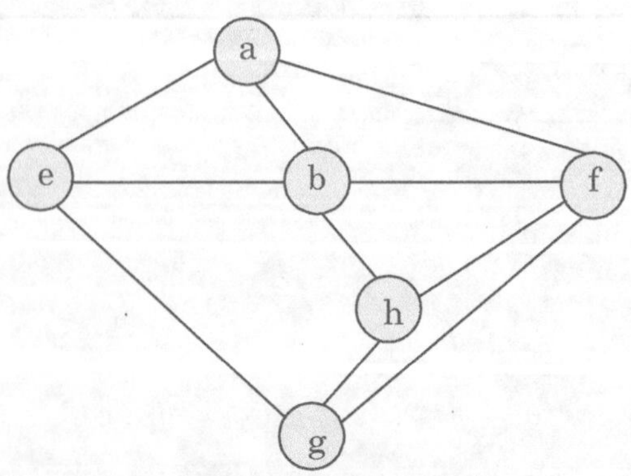

Among the following sequences

1. abeghf 3. abfhge

2. abfehg 4. afghbe

Which are depth first traversals of the above graph?

(a) 1, 2 and 4 only (b) 1 and 4 only

(c) 2, 3 and 4 only (d) 1, 3 and 4 only

[2003 : 1 Mark]

9. In a depth-first traversal of a graph G with n vertices, k edges are marked as tree edges. The number of connected components in G is

(a) k (b) k + 1

(c) n – k – 1 (d) n – k **[2005: 1 Mark]**

10. Let T be a depth first search tree in a undirected graph G. Vertices-u and v are leaves of this tree T. The degrees of both u and v in G are at least 2. Which one of the following statements is true?

(a) There must exist a vertex w adjacent to both u and v in G

(b) There must exist a vertex w whose removal disconnects u and v in G

(c) There must exist a cycle in G containing u and v

(d) There must exist a cycle in G containing u and all its neighbours in G

[2006 : 2 Marks]

11. Consider the depth-first-search of an undirected graph with 3 vertices P, Q, and R. Let discovery time d(u) represent the time instant when the vertex u is first visited, and finish time f(u) represent the time instant when the vertex u is last visited. Given that

d(P) = 5 units,f(P) = 12 units

d(Q) = 6 units,f(Q) = 10 units

d(R) = 14 unit,f(R) = 18 units

which one of the following statements is TRUE about the graph

(a) There is only one connected component

(b) There are two connected components, and P and R are connected

(c) There are two connected components, and Q and R are connected

(d) There are two connected components, and P and Q are connected **[2006 : 2 Marks]**

12. A depth-first search is performed on a directed acyclic graph. Let d[u] denote the time at which vertex u is visited for the first time and f[u] the time at which the dfs call to the vertex u terminates. Which of the following statements is always true for all edges (u, v) in the graph?

(a) d[u] < d[v] (b) d[u] < f[v]

(c) f[u] < f[v] (d) f[u] > f[v]

[2007 : 2 Marks]

13. Consider the following sequence of nodes for the undirected graph given below:

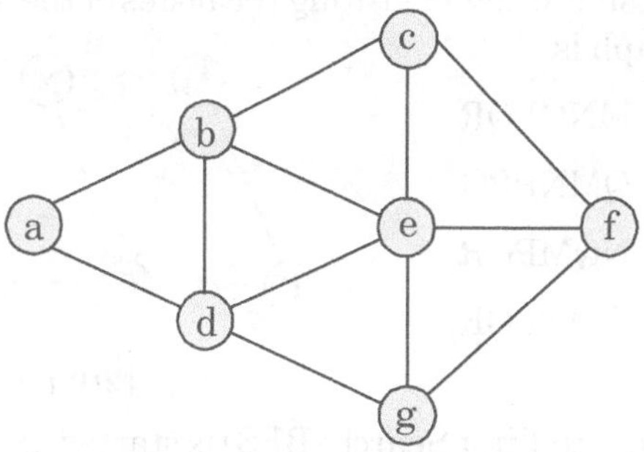

1. a b e f d g c 2. a b e f c g d

3. a d g e b c f 4. a d b c g e f

A Depth First Search (DFS) is started at node a. The nodes are listed in the order they are first visited. Which all of the above is (are) possible output(s)?

(a) 1 and 3 only (b) 2 and 3 only

(c) 2, 3 and 4 only (d) 1, 2 and 3 only

[2008 : 2 Marks]

14. Let G of be a graph with n vertices and m edges. What is the tightest upper bound on the running time of Depth First Search on G, when G is represented as an adjacency matrix ?

(a) Θ(n) (b) Θ(n + m)

(c) $\Theta(n)^2$ (d) $\Theta(m^2)$

[2014 (Set-1) :1 Mark]

15. Suppose depth first search is executed on the graph below starting at some unknown vertex. Assume that a recursive call to visit a vertex is made only after first checking that the vertex has not been visited earlier. Then the maximum possible recursion depth (including the initial call) is.

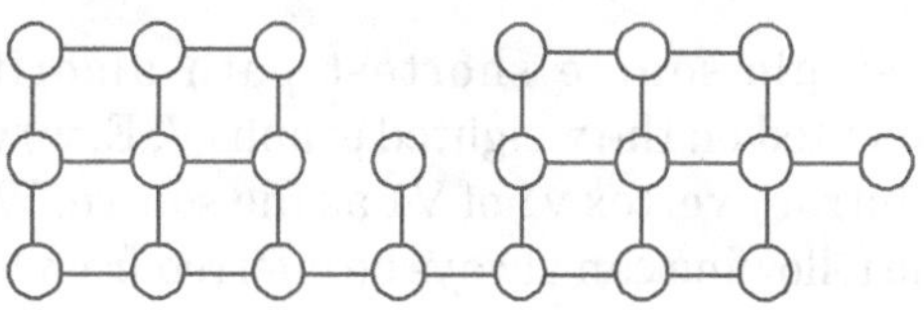

[2014 (Set-3) :1 Mark]

BREADTH FIRST TREE

16. Consider an undirected unweighted graph G. Let a breadth-first traversal of G be done starting from a node r. Let d(r, u) and d(r, v) be the lengths of the shortest paths from r to u and v respectively in G. If u is visited before v during the breadth-first traversal, which of the following statement is correct?

(a) d(r, u) < d(r, v) (b) d(r, u) > d(r, v)

(c) d(r, u) d(r, v) (d) None of these

[2001 : 2 Marks]

17. The Breadth First Search algorithm has been implemented using the queue data structure. One possible order of visiting the nodes of the following graph is

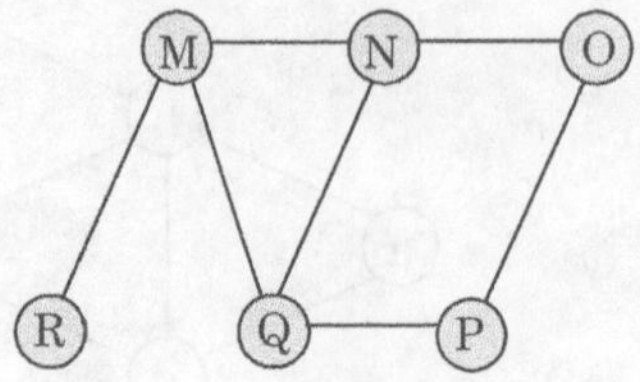

(a) MNOPQR

(c) QMNPRO

(b) NQMPOR

(d) QMNPOR

[2008 : 1 Mark]

18. Breadth First Search (BFS) is started on a binary tree beginning from the root vertex. There is a vertex t at a distance four from the root. If t is the n-th vertex in this BFS traversal, then the maximum possible value of n is

[2016 (Set-2) : 1 Mark]

19. The Breadth First Search (BFS) algorithm has been implemented using the queue data structure. Which one of the following is a possible order of visiting the nodes in the graph below?

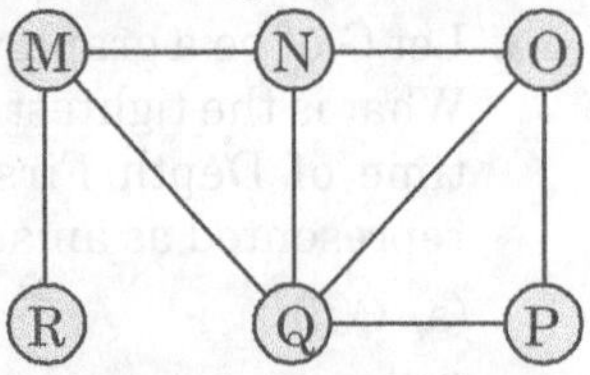

(a) MNOPQR

(c) QMNROP

(b) NQMPOR

(d) PO QNMR

[2017 (Set-2) : 1 Mark]

SHORTEST PATH

20. Let G = (V, E) be an undirected graph with a subgraph G1 = (V1, E1). Weights are assigned to edges of G as follows:

$$w(e) = \begin{cases} 0 \text{ if } e \in E_1 \\ 1 \text{ othrwise} \end{cases}$$

A single-source shortest path algorithm is executed on the weighted graph (V, E, w) with an arbitrary vertex v1 of V1 as the source. Which of the following can always be inferred from the path costs computed?

(a) The number of edges in the shortest paths from v1 to all vertices of G

(b) G1 is connected

(c) V1 forms a clique in G

(d) G1 is a tree

[2003 : 2 Marks]

21. Let G = (V, E) be a direction graph with n vertices. A path from vi to v in G is sequence of vertices (vi, 1, ..., such that (vk, vki)E E for all k in i through j — 1. A simple path is a path in which no vertex appears more than once. Let A be an n x n array initialized as follow:

$$A\,[j, k] = \begin{cases} 1 \text{ if } (j,k) \in E \\ 0 \text{ othrwise} \end{cases}$$

Consider the following algorithm for i = 1 to n for j = 1 to n for k = 1 to n A [j, k] = max (AU, k], (A[j, i] + A[i, k])); Which of the following statements is necessarily true for all j and k after terminal of the above algorithm?

(a) A[j, k] ≤ n

(b) If A [j, j] ≥ n – 1, then G has a Hamiltonian cycle

(c) If there exists a path from j to k, AU, k] contains the longest path lengths from j to k

(d) If there exists a path from j to k, every simple path from j to k contain most AU, k] edges

[2003 : 2 Marks]

22. What is the largest integer m such that every simple connected graph with n vertices and n edges contains at least m different spanning trees?

(a) 1

(b) 2

(c) 3

(d) n

[2007 : 2 Marks]

ANSWERS

1. (6)	**2.** (*)	**3.** (*b*)	**4.** (*c*)	**5.** (*b*)	**6.** (*a*)	**7.** (*c*)	**8.** (*d*)	**9.** (*d*)	**10.** (*d*)
11. (*d*)	**12.** (*d*)	**13.** (*d*)	**14.** (*c*)	**15.** (19)	**16.** (*c*)	**17.** (*c*)	**18.** (*c*)	**19.** (*d*)	**20.** (*b*)
21. (*d*)	**22.** (*c*)								

EXPLANATIONS

1.

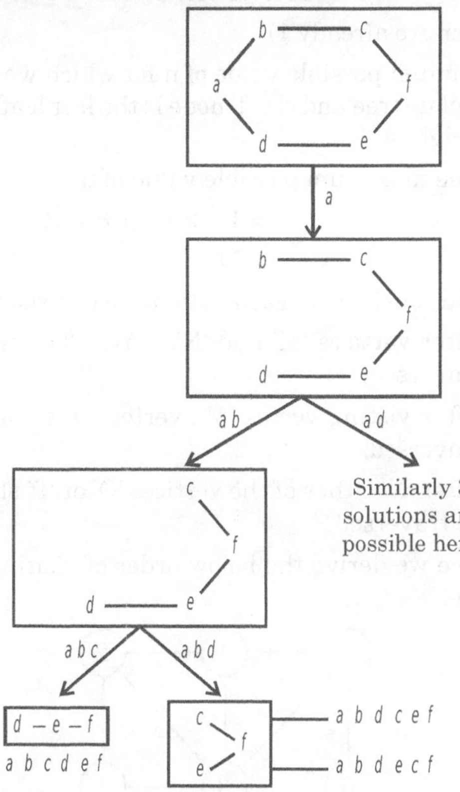

So total solution 6.

2. adjancey matrix is

$$\begin{array}{c} \\ P_1 \\ P_2 \\ P_3 \\ P_4 \\ P_5 \end{array} \begin{array}{c} \begin{array}{ccccc} P_1 & P_2 & P_3 & P_4 & P_5 \end{array} \\ \begin{bmatrix} 0 & 1 & 0 & 0 & 0 \\ 0 & 0 & 0 & 1 & 1 \\ 1 & 0 & 0 & 0 & 0 \\ 0 & 0 & 1 & 0 & 1 \\ 1 & 0 & 0 & 0 & 0 \end{bmatrix} \end{array}$$

3. Edge set consist edges it j = i + 1 or j = 3i

The edge sequence with minimum no of edges is
1 – 3 – 9 – 10 – 11
|
100 – 99 – 33

Which consist 7 edges.

4. The most efficient algorithm for finding the number of connected components (articulation point) in an undirected graph on *n* vertices and *n* edges using depth-first search takes O(*m* + *n*) time.Assume $n \leq m$.

5. Usinng BFS traversal we can set the twin pointer in each entry in each adjancey list. So it will take O(m + n) time.

6. Statement (i) is true.

(i) No edges of G is a cross edge with respect to T_D.

7. In DFS if 'v' is visited after 'u' then one of the following is true.

(i) if (u, v) is an edge

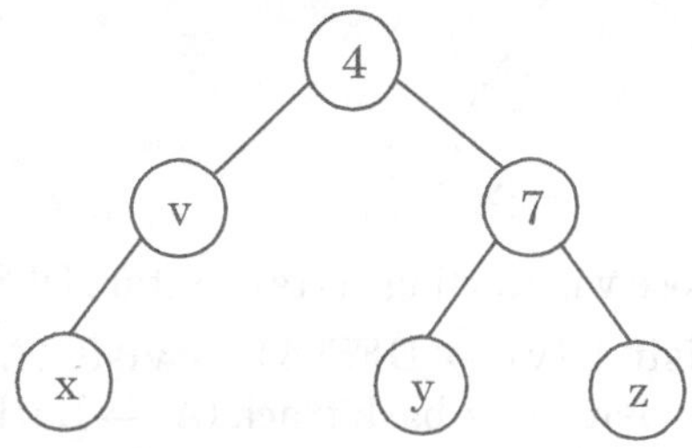

(ii) if 'u' is x leaf node

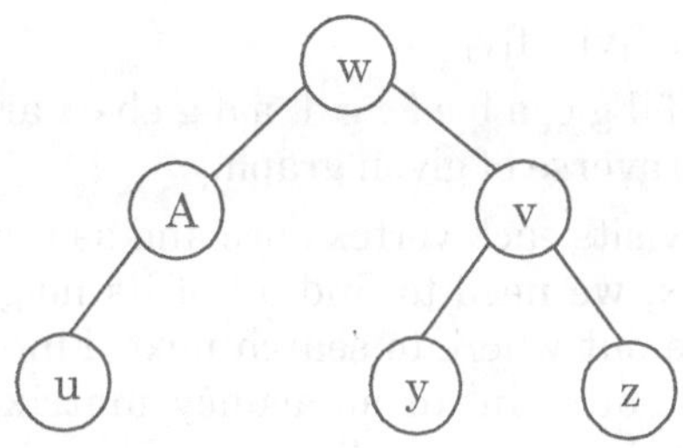

8. (1) a b e g h f

(3) a b f h g e

(4) a f g h b e is possible DFS of given graph.

9. If n vertex and K edges are there then the number of connected component in the graph is n – K.

10.

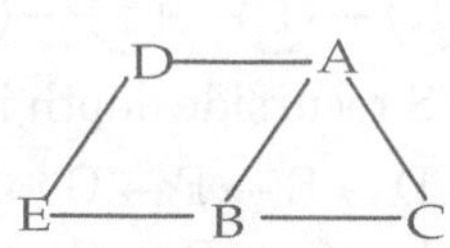

For the above graph, conducting depth First search:

Stack : A

Stack : DBC Tree : A

Stack : EBC Tree : A / D

Stack : BC Tree : A / D / E

Stack : BC

Stack : ϕ Tree :

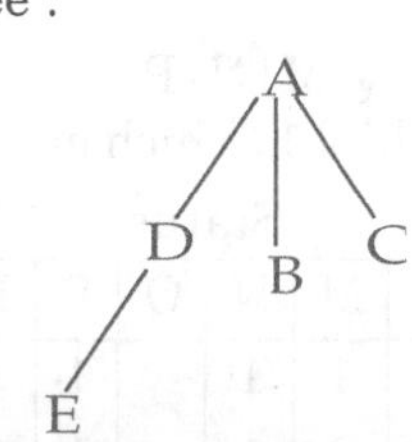

Considering leaf nodes E and C, the given condition is satisfied as their degrees are more than one. But none of (*a*), (*b*) or (*c*) hold.

But a cycle consisting of E and all its neighbour hold.

11. Since d(q) = d(p) + 1 and F(q) < f(P) which means p & q are connected and r is sperate so option (d) is correct answer.

12.

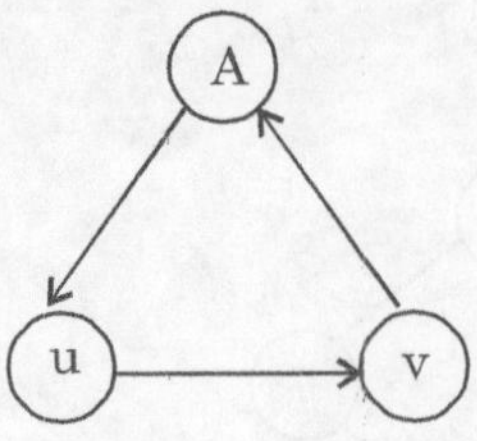

Suppose v is starting vertex so start DFS at node v

(i) visit t (v) → DFS(A) → visit (A) → DFS (v) → visit (u) → back track (A) → Back track (v) therefore d[v] > d[v], d[v] < f[v] f[v] < f[v]

But visiting order is just opposite of finishing order.

Hence f[v] > f[v]

13. a b e f d g c, a b e f c g d, a d g eb c f are possible dFs traverse of given graph.

14. DFS visits each vertex once and as it visits each vertex, we need to find all of its neighbours to figure out where to search next. Finding all its neighbours in an adjacency matrix requires O(V) time, so overall the running time will be $O(V^2)$.

15.

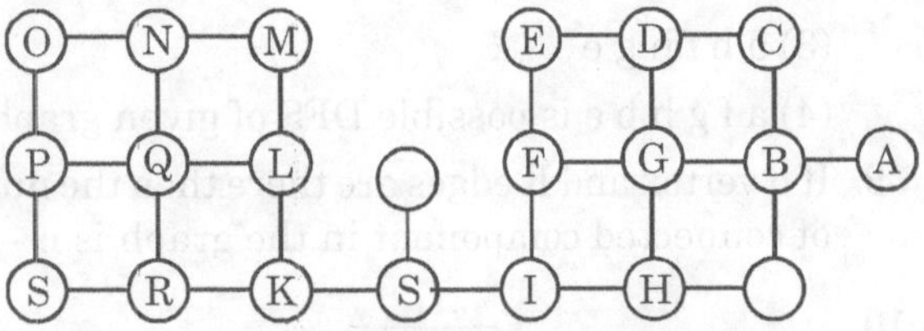

Maximum DFS recurside depth is 19

A → B → C → D → E → F → G → H → I → J → K → L → M → N → O → P → Q → R → S

16. d(r, v) and d(r, v) will be equal when u and v are at same level, otherwise d (r, v) will be less than d(r, v)

17. *Applying BFS Algorithms*

Starting from Q

Queue Q

Making Q's child's status 1.

Queue

Q | M | N | P

Making M's child 1 (which are not 1)

Status

Q	M	N	O	P	R
2	1	1		1	
2	2	1		1	1
2	2	2	1	1	1

Q | M | N | P | R

Making N's Child 1

Q | M | N | P | R | O

(other are already 1)

18. Maximum possible value of n for which we have complete tree and our 't' node is the last leaf node at height 4.

So, the maximum possible value of n

= 1 + 2 + 4 + 8 + 16

= 31

19. While considering each option, we can see that:

- After vertices 'M' and 'N', vertex 'O' can't be traversed.
- After visting vertex 'M', vertex 'O' should be traversed.
- After 'N' either of the vertices 'O' or 'P' should be traversed

Hence we derive the below order of visiting the nodes

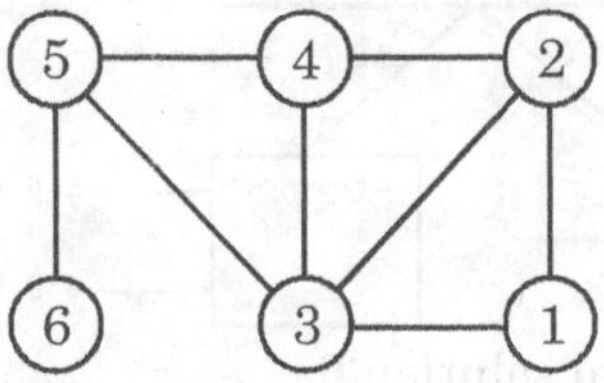

20. Suppose G = (v, E) and G_1 = (v, E_1) such that $E_1 \le E$ and $v_1 \le v$

Consider an example.

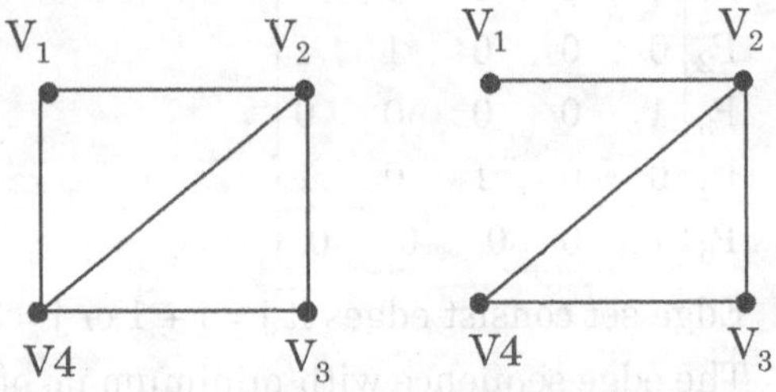

G $\qquad$ G_1

Consider the w(e) = 1 of e ∉ E_1 it means the cost of v_1 to v_4 is only 1 other edges having cost 0. It is noted that G_1 is connected (As shown in example).

21. for i = 1 ton

for j = 1 ton

for K = 1 ton

A[j, K] = max (j, K], A[j, i) + a(i, K)]

Anxn Matrix and A[j, K] = 1 if (j, K) ∈ E

so there exist a path from J to K and must contain A[j, K] edges

22. If E = V then graph is a simple cycle

∵ to create simple cycle minimum 3 vertex should be in graph so the number of spanning trees will be atleast 3.

7

CHAPTER

Searching & Hashing

Analysis of Previous GATE Papers											
Units	Year → Topics ↓		2019	2018	2017 Set 1	2017 Set 2	2016 Set 1	2016 Set 2	2015 Set 1	2015 Set 2	2015 Set 3
MEMORY	1 Mark	MCQ Type			1	1					
		Numerical Type									
	2 Marks	MCQ Type									
		Numerical Type									
	Total				1	1					
HEAP	1 Mark	MCQ Type									1
		Numerical Type									
	2 Marks	MCQ Type					1		1		
		Numerical Type		1				1			
	Total			2			2	2	2		1
AVL	1 Mark	MCQ Type		1							
		Numerical Type									
	2 Marks	MCQ Type									
		Numerical Type									
	Total			1							
LINEAR PROBING	1 Mark	MCQ Type									
		Numerical Type									
	2 Marks	MCQ Type									
		Numerical Type									
	Total										
HASHING CONCEPT	1 Mark	MCQ Type									
		Numerical Type								1	
	2 Marks	MCQ Type							1		
		Numerical Type									
	Total								2	1	

MEMORY

1. Match the pairs in the following

List-I	List-II
A. Pointer data type	P. Type conversion
B. Activation record	Q. Dynamic data structure
C. Repeat-until	R. Recursion
D. Coercion	S. Nondeterministic loop

[1990 : 2 Marks]

2. The correct matching for the following pairs is

List -I	List -II
A. Activation record	1. Linking loader
B. Location counter	2. Garbage collection
C. Reference counts	3. Subroutine call
D. Address relocation	4. Assembler

Codes:

(a) A - 3, B - 4, C - 1, D - 2

(b) A - 4, B - 3, C - 1, D - 2

(c) A - 4, B - 3, C - 2, D - 1

(d) A - 3, B - 4, C - 2, D - 1

[1996 : 2 Marks]

3. Heap allocation is required for languages

(a) that support recursion

(b) that support dynamic data structures

(c) that use dynamic scope rules

(d) None of the above

[1997 :1 Mark]

4. A certain processor supports only the immediate and the direct addressing modes. Which of the following programming language features cannot be implemented on this processor?

(a) Pointers

(b) Arrays

(c) Records

(d) Recursive procedures with local variable

[1999 : 2 Marks]

5. The most appropriate matching for the following pairs

List-I	List-II
X. Indirect addressing	1. Loops
Y. Immediate addressing	2. Pointers
Z. Auto decrement addressing	3. Constants

(a) X– 3 Y– 2 Z – 1

(b) X – 1 Y – 3 Z – 2

(c) X – 2 Y – 3 Z – 1

(d) X – 3 Y – 1 Z – 2

[2000 :1 Mark]

6. The most appropriate matching for the following pairs

List-I	List-II
X. m=malloc(5); m = NULL;	1. using dangling pointers
Y. free(n); n->value=5;	2. using uninitialized pointers
Z. char *p; *p='a';	3. lost memory

Codes:

(a) X – 1 Y – 3 Z – 2 (b) X – 2 Y – 1 Z – 3

(c) X – 3 Y – 2 Z – 1 (d) X – 3 Y – 1 Z – 2

[2000 :1 Mark]

7. The value of j at the end of the execution of the following C program is_____

```
int incr (int i) {
static int count = 0;
count = count + i;
return (count);
}
main ( ) {
int i,j;
for (i = 0; i <=4; i++)
j = incr(i);
}
```

(1) 10 (b) 4

(c) 6 (d) 7 **[2000 : 2 Marks]**

8. In the C language

(a) at most one activation record exists between the current activation record and the activation record for the main

(b) the number of activation records between the current activation record and the activation record for the main depends on the actual function calling sequence

(c) The visibility of global variables depends on the actual function calling sequence

(d) Recursion requires the activation record for the recursive function to be saved on a different stack before the recursive function can be called. **[2002 : 1 Mark]**

9. Consider the following declaration of a two-dimensional array in C

char a[100] [100];

Assuming that the main memory is byte-addressable and that the array is stored starting from memory address 0, the address of a [40] [50] is

(a) 4040 (b) 4050

(c) 5040 (d) 5050

[2002 : 2 Marks]

10. Consider the following C function

```
void swap (int a, int b)
{ int temp ;
temp = a ;
a = b ;
b = temp ;
}
```

In order to exchange the values of two variables x and y.

(a) call swap (x, y)

(b) call swap (&x, &y)

(c) swap (x, y) cannot be used as it does not return any value

(d) swap (x, y) cannot be used as the parameters are passed by value

[2004 :1 Mark]

11. An Abstract Data Type (ADT) is

(a) same as an abstract class

(b) a data type that cannot be instantiated

(c) a data type for which only the operations defined on it can be used, but none else

(d) all of the above

[2005 : 1 Mark]

12. Match the following:

List-I

(P) static char var;

(Q) m = malloc(10); m = NULL;

(R) char *ptr[10];

(S) register int varl;

List-II

(i) Sequence of memory locations to store addresses

(ii) A variable located in data section of memory

(iii) Request to allocate a CPU register to store data

(iv) A lost memory which cannot be freed

(a) P → (ii), Q → (iv), R → (i), S → (iii)

(b) P → (ii), Q → (i), R → (iv), S → (iii)

(c) P → (ii), Q → (iv), R → (iii), S → (i)

(d) P → (iii), **Q** → (iv), R → (i), S → (ii)

[2017 (Set-2) : 1 Mark]

13. Consider the following C code:

```
#include <stdio.h>
int *assignval (int *x, int val)
{ *x = val;
return x;
}
void main()
{ int *x = malloc (size of (int));
if (NULL == x) return;
x = assignval(x, 0);
if(x)
{ x = (int*) malloc (size of (int));
if (NULL = = x) return;
x = assignval (x, 10);
}
printf("%d"\n", *x);
free (x);
}
```

The code suffers from which one of the following problems:

(a) compiler error as the return of malloc is not typecast appropriately

(b) compiler error because the comparison should be made as x == NULL and not as shown

(c) compiles successfully but execution may result in dangling pointer

(d) compiles successfully but execution may result in memory leak

[2017 (Set-1) : 1 Mark]

HEAP

14. In a heap with n elements with the smallest element at the root, the 7th smallest element can be found in time

(a) $\Theta(n \log n)$ (b) $\Theta(n)$

(c) $\Theta(\log n)$ (d) $\Theta(1)$

[2003 : 1 Mark]

15. A data structure is required for storing a set of integers such that each of the following operations can be done in O(log n) time, where n is the number of elements in the set.

1. Deletion of the smallest element.
2. Insertion of an element if it is not already present in the set.

Which of the following data structures can be used for this purpose?

(a) A heap can be used but not a balanced binary search tree

(b) A balanced binary search tree can be used but not a heap

(c) Both balanced binary search tree and heap can be used

(d) Neither balanced binary search tree nor heap can be used

[2003 : 2 Marks]

16. The elements 32, 15, 20, 30, 12, 25, 16 are inserted one by one in the given order into a maxHeap. The resultant maxHeap is

(a) 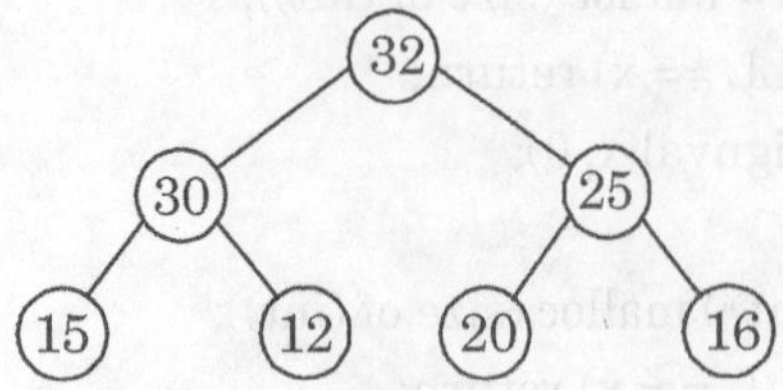

(b) 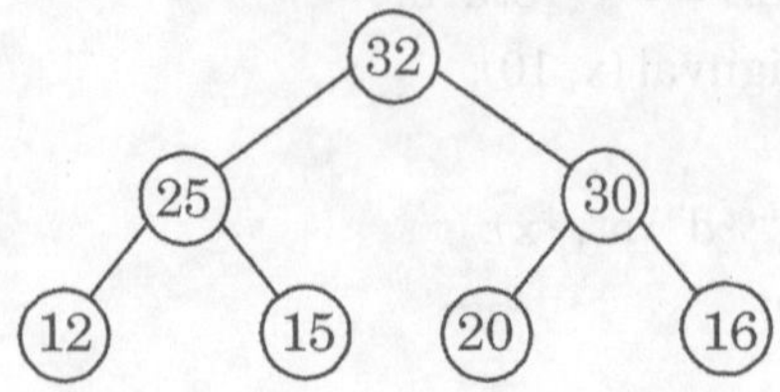

(c) 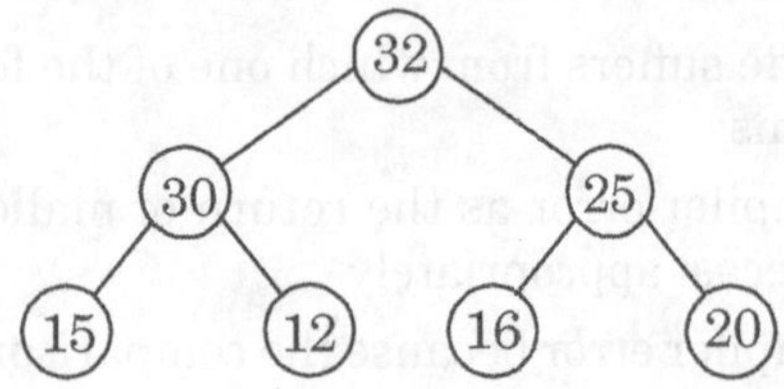

(d) 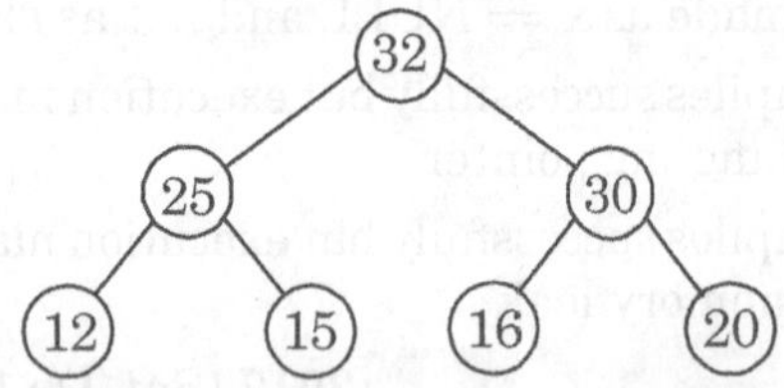

[2004 : 2 Marks]

17. In a binary max heap containing n numbers, the smallest element can be found in time

(a) θ (n) (b) θ (log n)

(c) θ (log log n) (d) θ (1)

[2006 : 1 Mark]

18. Which of the following sequences of array elements forms a heap?

(a) {23, 17, 14, 6, 13, 10, 1, 12, 7, 5}

(b) {23, 17, 14, 6, 13, 10, 1, 5, 7, 12}

(c) {23, 17, 14, 7, 13, 10, 1, 5, 6, 12}

(d) {23, 17, 14, 7, 13, 10, 1, 12, 5, 7}

[2006 : 2 Marks]

Common Data for Q. 19 & Q. 20:

A 3-ary max heap is like a binary max heap, but instead of 2 children, nodes have 3 children. A 3-ary heap can be represented by an array as follows: The root is stored in the first location, a [0], nodes in the next level, from left to right, is stored from a [1] to a [3]. The nodes from the second level of the tree from left to right are stored from a [4] location onward. An item x can be inserted into a 3-ary heap containing n items by placing x in the location a [n] and pushing it up the tree to satisfy the heap property.

19. Which one of the following is a valid sequence of elements in an array representing 3-ary max heap?

(a) 1, 3, 5, 6, 8, 9 (b) 9, 6, 3, 1, 8, 5

(c) 9, 3, 6, 8, 5, 1 (d) 9, 5, 6, 8, 3, 1

[2006 : 2 Marks]

20. Suppose the elements 7, 2, 10, and 4 are inserted, in that order, into the valid 3-ary max heap found in the above question. Which one of the following is the sequence of items in the array representing the resultant heap?

(a) 10, 7, 9, 8, 3, 1, 5, 2, 6, 4

(b) 10, 9, 8, 7, 6, 5, 4, 3, 2, 1

(c) 10, 9, 4, 5, 7, 6, 8, 2, 1, 3

(d) 10, 8, 6, 9, 7, 2, 3, 4, 1, 5 **[2006 : 2 Marks]**

21. Consider the process of inserting an element into a Max Heap, where the Max Heap is represented by an array. Suppose we perform a binary search on the path from the new leaf to the root to find the position for the newly inserted element, the number of comparisons performed is

(a) $\theta(\log_2 n)$ (b) $\theta(\log_2 \log_2 n)$

(c) $\theta(n)$ (d) $\theta(n \log_2 n)$

[2007 : 2 Marks]

22. We have a binary heap on n elements and wish to insert n more elements (not necessarily one after another) into this heap. The total time required for this is

(a) $\Theta(\log n)$ (b) $\Theta(n)$

(c) $\Theta(n \log n)$ (d) $\Theta(n^2)$

[2008 : 2 Marks]

Linked Answer Question 23 and 24:

Consider a binary max-heap implemented using an array

23. Which one of the following array represents a binary max-heap?

(a) {25, 12, 16, 13, 10, 8, 14}

(b) {25, 14, 13, 16, 10, 8, 12}

(c) {25, 14, 16, 13, 10, 8, 12}

(d) {25, 14, 12, 13, 10, 8, 16}

[2009 : 2 Marks]

24. What is the content of the array after two delete operations on the correct answer to the previous question?

(a) {14, 13, 12, 10, 8}

(b) {14, 12, 13, 8, 10}

(c) {14, 13, 8, 12, 10}

(d) {14, 13, 12, 8, 10}

[2009: 2 Marks]

25. A max-heap is a heap where the value of each parent is greater than or equal to the value of its children. Which of the following is a max-heap?

(a) 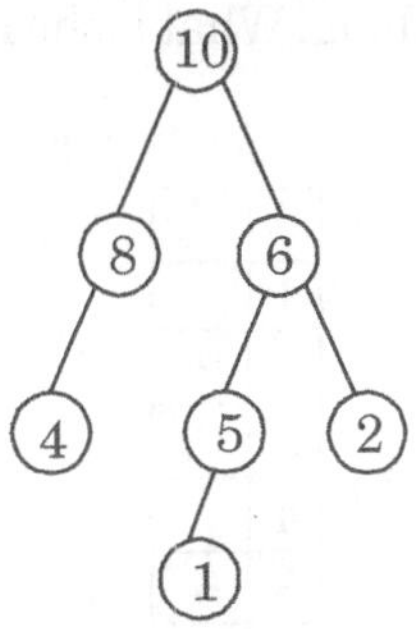

(b) 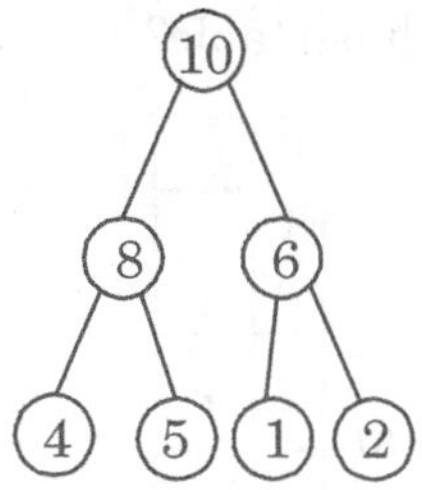

(c) 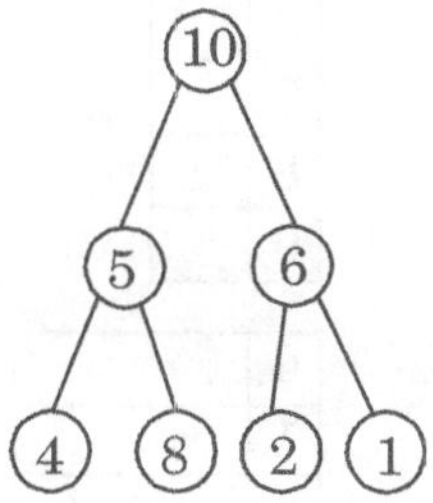

(d) 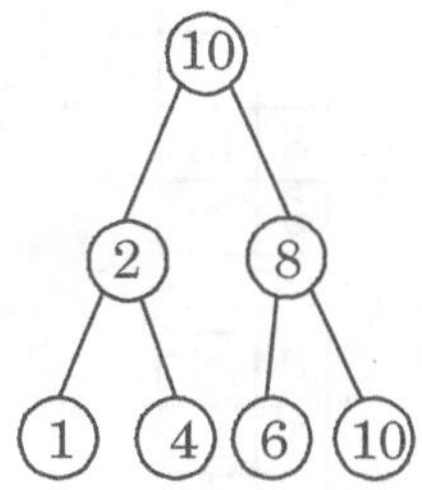

[2011: 1 Mark]

26. A priority queue is implemented as a Max-Heap. Initially, it has 5 elements. The level-order traversal of the heap is: 10, 8, 5, 3, 2. Two new elements 1 and 7 are inserted into the heap in that order. The level-order traversal of the heap after the insertion of the elements is:

(a) 10, 8, 7, 3, 2, 1, 5

(b) 10, 8, 7, 2, 3, 1, 5

(c) 10, 8, 7, 1, 2, 3, 5

(d) 10, 8, 7, 5, 3, 2, 1

[2014 (Set-2) : 1 Mark]

27. Consider a max heap, represented by the array: 40, 30, 20, 10, 15, 16, 17, 8, 4.

Array Index	1	2	3	4	5	6	7	8	9
Value	40	30	20	10	15	16	17	8	4

Now consider that a value 35 is inserted into this heap. After insertion, the new heap is

(a) 40, 30, 20, 10, 15, 16, 17, 8, 4, 35

(b) 40, 35, 20, 10, 30, 16, 17, 8, 4, 15

(c) 40, 30, 20, 10, 35, 16, 17, 8, 4, 15

(d) 40, 35, 20, 10, 15, 16, 17, 8, 4, 30

[2015 (Set-1) : 2 Marks]

28. Consider the following array of elements ('89, 19, 50, 17, 12, 15, 2, 5, 7, 11, 6, 9, 100). The minimum number of interchanges needed to convert it into a max-heap is

(a) 4 (b) 5

(c) 2 (d) 3

[2015 (Set-3) :1 Mark]

29. An operator delete (i) for a binary heap data structure is to be designed to delete the item in the i-th node. Assume that the heap is implemented in an array and i refers to the i-th index of the array. If the heap tree has depth d (number of edges on the path from the root to the farthest leaf), then what is the time complexity to re-fix the heap efficiently after the removal of the element?

(a) O(1)

(b) O(d) but not O(1)

(c) $O(2^d)$ but not O(d)

(d) $O(d2^d)$ but not O(2d)

[2016 (Set-1) : 2 Marks]

30. A complete binary min-heap is made by including each integer in [1, 1023] exactly once. The depth of a node in the heap is the length of the path from the root of the heap to that node. Thus, the root is at depth 0. The maximum depth at which integer 9 can appear is

[2016 (Set-2) : 2 Marks]

31. The number of possible min-heaps containing each value from {1, 2, 3, 4, 5, 6, 7} exactly once is ______

[2018: 2 Marks]

AVL

32. Which of the following is TRUE?

(a) The cost of searching an AVL tree is Θ(log n) but that of a binary search tree is O(n)

(b) The cost of searching an AVL tree is Θ(log n) but that of a complete binary tree is Θ(n log n)

(c) The cost of searching a binary search tree is O (log n) but that of an AVL tree is Θ(n)

(d) The cost of searching an AVL tree is Θ(n log n) but that of a binaiy search tree is O(n)

[20(18: 1 Mark]

33. What is the maximum height of any AVL-tree with 7 nodes? Assume that the height of a tree with a single node is 0.

(a) 2

(b) 3

(c) 4

(d) 5

[2009 : 2 Marks]

LINEAR PROBING

34. A Hash table with ten buckets with one slot per bucket is shown in the following figure with the symbols Si to S7 entered into it using some hashing function with linear probing. The worst case number of comparisons required when the symbol being searched is not in the table is

0	S_7
1	S_1
2	
3	S_4
4	S_2
5	
6	S_5
7	
8	S_6
9	S_3

[1989 : 2 Marks]

35. A hash table contains 10 buckets and uses linear probing to resolve collisions. The key values are integers and the hash function used is key % 10. If the values 43, 165, 62, 123, 142 are inserted in the table, in what location would the key value 142 be inserted?

(a) 2 (b) 3

(c) 4 (d) 6

[2005 : 1 Mark]

36. Consider a hash function that distributes keys uniformly. The hash table size is 20. After hashing of how many keys will the probability that any new key hashed collides with an existing one exceed 0.5.

(a) 5 (b) 6

(c) 7 (d) 10

[2007 : 2 Marks]

37. Consider a hash table of size 11 that uses open addressing with linear probing. Let h(k) = k mod 11 be the hash function used. A sequence of records with keys 43 36 92 87 11 4 71 13 14 is inserted into an initially empty hash table, the bins of which are indexed from zero to ten. What is the index of the bin into which the last record is inserted?

(a) 3 (c) 6

(b) 4 (d) 7

[2008 : 2 Marks]

38. The keys 12, 18, 13, 2, 3, 23, 5 and 15 are inserted into an initially empty hash table of length 10 using open addressing with hash function h(k) = k mod 10 and linear probing. What is the resultant hash table?

(a)

0	
1	
2	2
3	23
4	
5	15
6	
7	
8	18
9	

(b)

0	
1	
2	2
3	13
4	
5	5
6	
7	
8	18
9	

(c)

0	
1	
2	12
3	13
4	2
5	3
6	23
7	5
8	18
9	15

(d)

0	
1	
2	12, 2
3	13, 3, 23
4	
5	5, 15
6	
7	
8	18
9	

[2009 : 2 Marks]

Linked Answer Questions 39 and 40

A has table of length 10 uses open addressing with hash function h(k) = k mod 10, and linear probing. After inserting 6 values into an empty hash table, the table is as shown below.

0	
1	
2	42
3	23
4	34
5	52
6	46
7	33
8	
9	

39. Which one of the following choices gives a possible order in which the key values could have been inserted in the table?

(a) 46, 42, 34, 52, 23, 33

(b) 34, 42, 23, 52, 33, 46

(c) 46, 34, 42, 23, 52, 33

(d) 42, 46, 33, 23, 34, 52 **[2010 : 2 Marks]**

40. How many different insertion sequences of the key values using the same hash function and linear probing will result in the hash table shown above?

(a) 10 (b) 20

(c) 30 (d) 40

[2010 : 2 Marks]

41. Consider a hash table with 9 slots. The hash function is h(k) = k mod 9. The collisions are resolved by chaining. The following 9 keys are inserted in the order: 5, 28, 19, 15, 20, 33, 12, 17, 10. The maximum, minimum, and average chain lengths in the hash table, respectively, are

(a) 3, 0, and 1 (b) 3, 3, and 3

(c) 4, 0, and 1 (d) 3, 0, and 2

[2014 (Set-1) : 2 Marks]

42. Consider a hash table with 100 slots. Collisions are resolved using chaining. Assuming simple uniform hashing, what is the probability that the first 3 slots are unfilled after the first 3 insertions?

(a) $(97 \times 97 \times 97)/100^3$

(b) $(99 \times 98 \times 97)/100^3$

(c) $(97 \times 96 \times 95)/100^3$

(d) $(97 \times 96 \times 95)1(3! \times 100^3)$

[2014 (Set-3) : 2 Marks]

HASHING CONCEPT

43. An advantage of chained hash table (external hashing) over the open addressing scheme is

(a) worst case complekity of search operations is less

(b) space used is less

(c) deletion is easier

(d) None of the above

[1996 : 1 Mark]

44. Given the following input (4322, 1334, 1471, 9679, 1989, 6171, 6173, 4199) and the hash function x mod 10, which of the following statements are true?

1. 9679, 1989, 4199 hash to the same value
2. 1471, 6171 hash to the same value
3. All elements hash to the same value
4. Each element hashes to a different value

(a) 1 only (c) 1 and 2 only

(b) 2 only (d) 3 and 4 only

[2004 : 1 Mark]

45. Which of the following statement(s) is TRUE?

I. A hash function takes a message of arbitrary length and generates a fixed length code.

II. A hash function takes a message of fixed length and generates a code of variable length.

III. A hash function may give the same hash value for distinct messages.

(a) I only (b) II and III only

(c) I and III only (d) II only

[2006 : 1 Mark]

46. Consider the hash table of size seven, with starting index zero, and a hash function (3x + 4) mod 7. Assuming the has table is initially empty, which of the following is the contents of the table when the sequence 1, 3, 8,10 is inserted into the table using closed hashing? Note that -denotes an empty location in the table

(a) 8, -, -,-, 10 (b) 1, 8, 10, -, -, 3

(c) 1, -, 3 (d) 1, 10, 8, -, -, 3

[2007 : 2 Marks]

47. Which one of the following hash functions on integers will distribute keys most uniformly over 10 buckets numbered 0 to 9 for i ranging from 0 to 2020?

(a) $h(i) = i^2 \bmod 10$

(b) $h(i) = i^3 \bmod 10$

(c) $h(i) = (11 * i^2) \bmod 10$

(d) $h(i) = (12 * i) \bmod 10$

[2015 (Set-2) : 2 Marks]

48. Given a hash table T with 25 slots that stores 2000 elements, the load factor α for T is ____.

[2015 (Set-3) : 1 Mark]

ANSWERS

1. (*)	**2.** (*d*)	**3.** (*c*)	**4.** (*a,b,c,d*)	**5.** (*c*)	**6.** (*d*)	**7.** (*a*)	**8.** (*b*)	**9.** (*b*)	**10.** (*d*)
11. (*c*)	**12.** (*a*)	**13.** (*d*)	**14.** (*c*)	**15.** (*b*)	**16.** (*a*)	**17.** (*a*)	**18.** (*c*)	**19.** (*d*)	**20.** (*a*)
21. (*b*)	**22.** (*b*)	**23.** (*c*)	**24.** (*d*)	**25.** (*b*)	**26.** (*a*)	**27.** (*b*)	**28.** (*d*)	**29.** (*b*)	**30.** (8)
31. (80)	**32.** (*a*)	**33.** (*b*)	**34.** (5)	**35.** (*d*)	**36.** (*d*)	**37.** (*d*)	**38.** (*c*)	**39.** (*c*)	**40.** (*c*)
41. (*a*)	**42.** (*a*)	**43.** (*c*)	**44.** (*c*)	**45.** (*c*)	**46.** (*b*)	**47.** (*b*)	**48.** (80)		

EXPLANATIONS

1. A. Pointer data type — Q. Dynamic data structure
   B. Activation record — R. Recursion
   C. Repeat-until — S. Nondeterministic loop
   D. Coercion — P. Type Conversion
2. A - 3, B - 4, C - 2, D - 1
3. Heap allocation is needed for dynamic data structures like tree, linked list, etc.
4. All are true. The feature (Pointers, Arrays, Records, Recursive procedures with local variables) are not supported if procesor has only the immediate and the direct addressing modes.
5. X-2, Y-3, Z-1
6. X – 3, A pointer is assigned to NULL without freeing memory so it is example of memory leak

   Y – 1, Trying to retrieve value after freeing it so dangling pointer.

   Z – 2, Using uninitialized pointers
7. At i = 0, j = 0
   At i = 1, j = 1
   At i = 2, j = 3
   At i = 3, j = 6
   At i = 4, j = 10
8. (a) False.There is no such restriction in C language
   (b) True.
   (c) False. In C, variables are statically scoped, not dynamically.
   (d) False. The activation records are stored on the same stack.
9. By defalut we are assuming that array store in row major order.

   Address of a[40][50]

   = Base address + 40 * 100 * element_size + 50 * element_size

   = 0 + 4000*1 + 50*1

   = 4050
10. Since no print & instruction inside the body of the function and function will return nothing in the calling environment since (*x*, *y*) cannot be used as, the parameters are passed by value.
11. The abstract data type (ADT) refers to a programmer defined data type together with a set of operations that can be performed on that data so the choice (*c*) is correct.
12. P → (ii), Q → (iv), R → (i), S → (iii)
13. The output of code is 10.

    int * x = malloc (sizeof(int)); //assigns a memory to x.

    Now,

    (int*) malloc(sizeof(int)); // again assigns a memory to x. previous memory location is lost because now we have no reference to that location resulting in memory leak.
14. To find Kth smallest element the time Requierd is klogn.

    Here k is constant value so time complexity is O(logn).
15. Deletion of the smallest element or randomly any element is insertion or deletion.

    Complexity is O ($\log_2 n$).
16. Max Heap are those tree in which root node has larger value than that of the child and left sibling has larger value than right.

    Given numbers are 32, 15, 20, 30, 12, 25, 16 then Max Heap tree will be

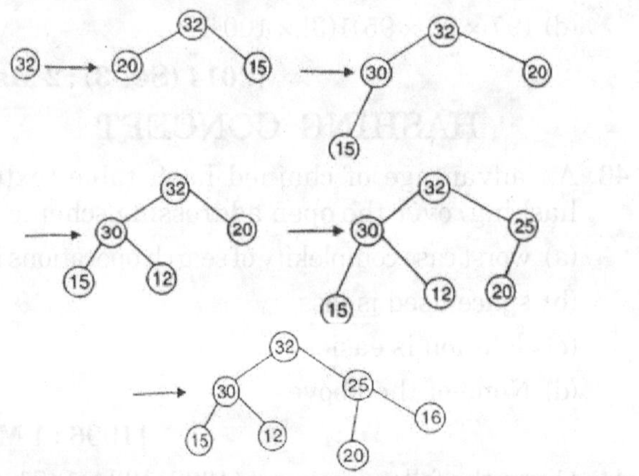

17. MAX Heap used to identity max element in O(1) time for to identity min element require O(*n*).
18. Option (c) is level order traversal so max heap.
19. For keys 9, 5, 6, 8, 3, 1

    3 - ary Max Heap is

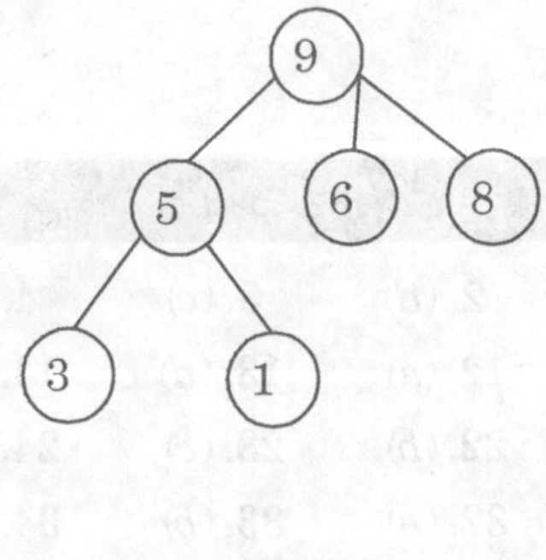

20. After insertion of 7.

Heap is :-

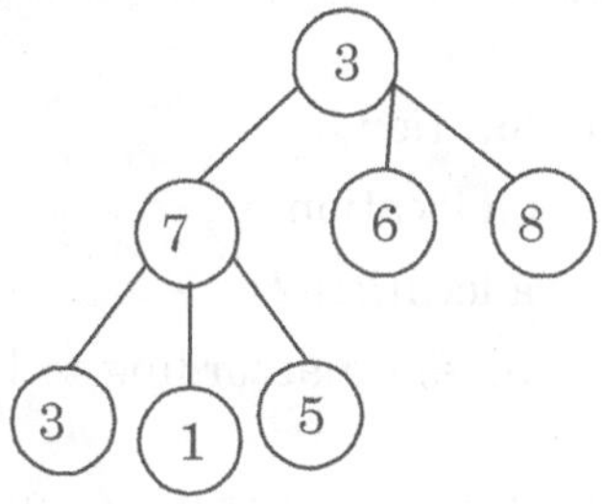

After inserting 2 &1024 resultant Head is {10, 7, 9, 8, 3, 1, 5 2, 6, 4 } is level order traversal.

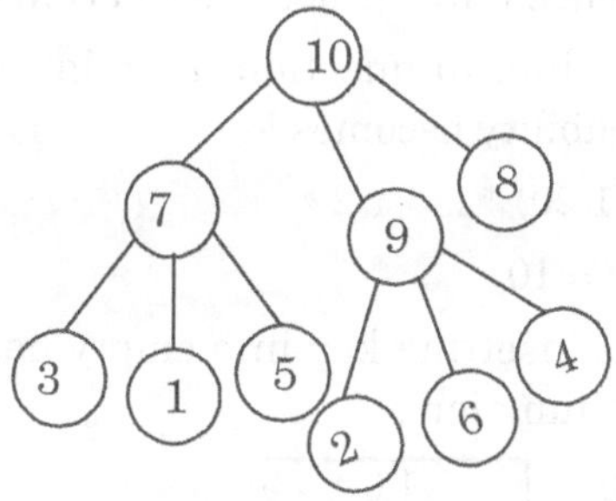

21. The height of a Max Heap is Θ(logn).

If we perform binary search for finding the correct position then we need to do Θ(Log Logn) comparisons.

22. Time complexity for build heap operation is O(n) for n elements. If there are 2n elements then still complexity is O(n).

23. Option (c) is level order traversal so max heap.

24.

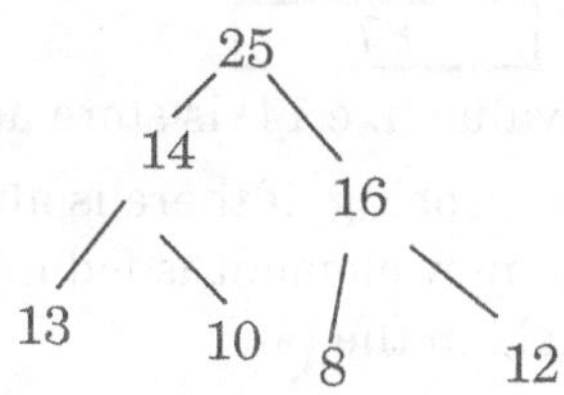

After deleting 25 the Resultant Heap is

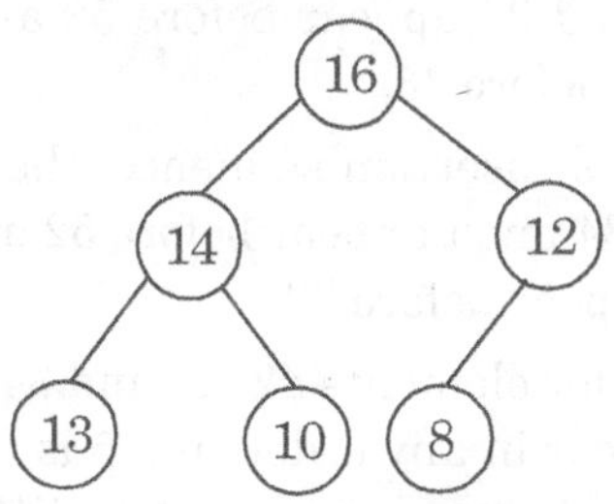

Now delete 16 then resultant Heap is

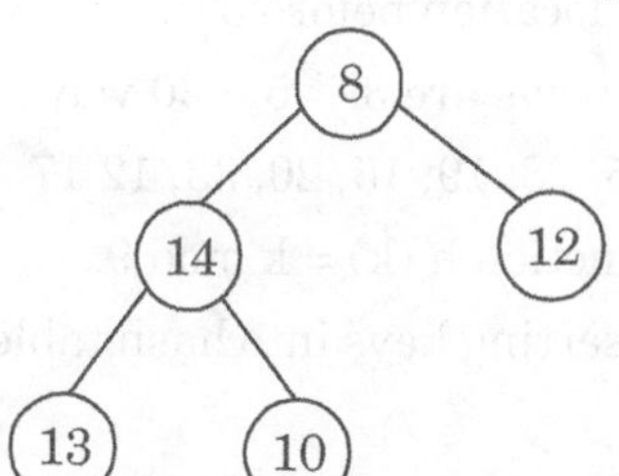

⇒ Heepify

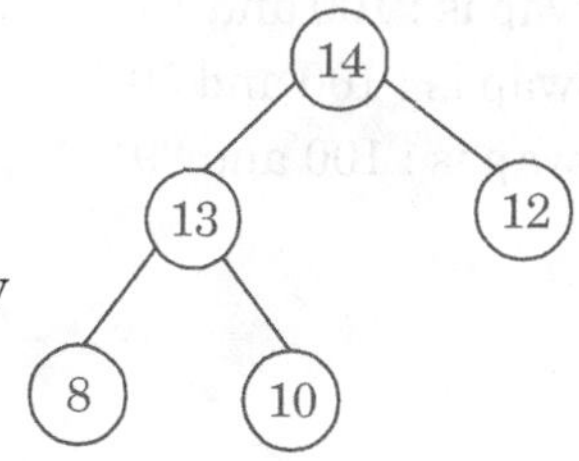

level order traversal of Max Heap is 14, 13, 12, 18, 10.

25. Heap is a complete binary tree.

26. Given level order traversal is 10, 8, 5, 3, 2

So Heap is

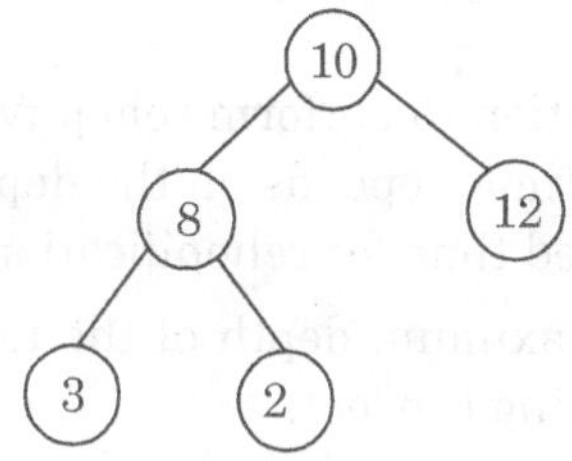

Now insert 1 & 7 after than the resultant Heap is

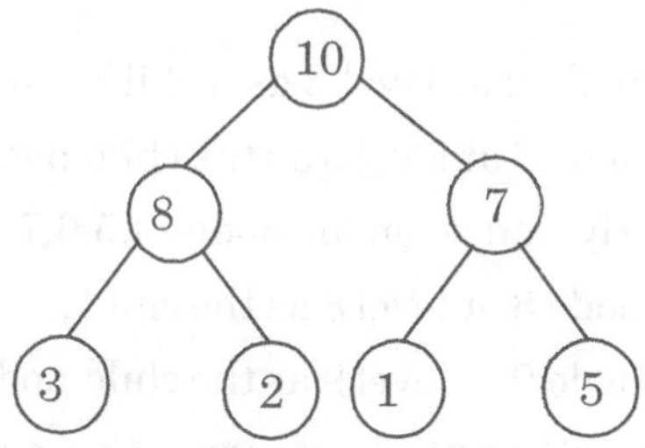

Now, Level order traversal is = 10, 8, 7, 3, 2, 1, 5

27. Given Heap is

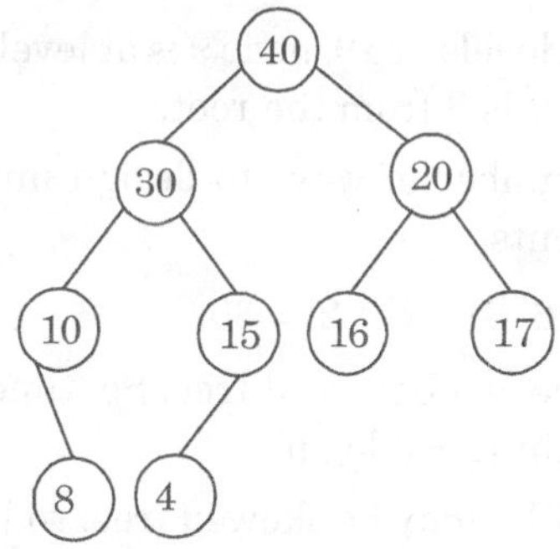

After inserting 35, find result is

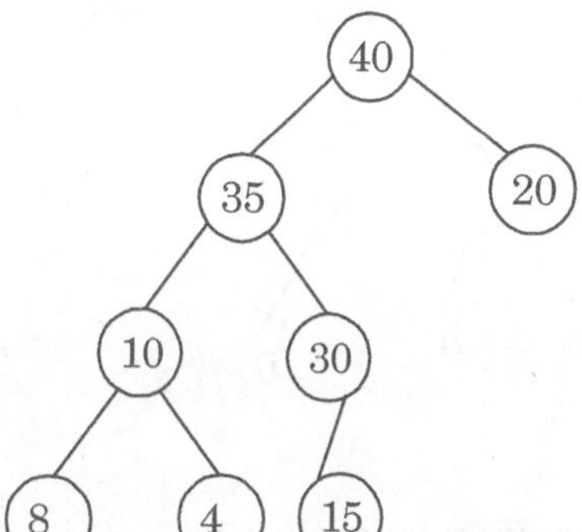

So Level order traversal is 40 35 20 10 30 8 4 15

28. 1st swap is : 100 and 15
2nd swap is : 100 and 50
3rd swap is : 100 and 89

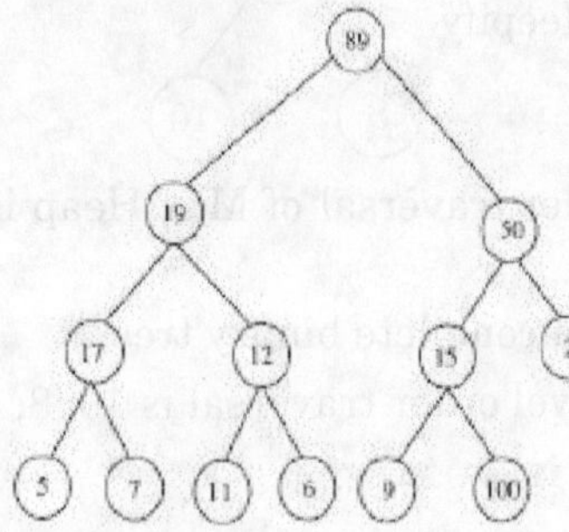

29. After deletion to perform rehepify operation the required time depends on the depth of the tree. So required time for rehepification is O(d).

30. To find maximum depth of the tree we can use the following concept.

Make integer 1 as a root node and take root as level 1.

Make node 2 at level 2 as a child node of node 1.

Make node 3 at level 3 as the child node of node 2.

Similarly and so on for nodes 4,5,6,7

Make node 8 at level 8 as the child node of node 7.

Make node 9 at level 9 as the child node of node 8.

Putting other nodes properly, this arrangement of the the complete binary tree will follow the property of min heap.

So total levels are 9. node 9 is at level 9 and depth of node 9 is 8 from the root.

31. Total number of ways to design min-heap with 7-elements

= C(6, 3) * 2! * 2! = 80.

32. AVL tree is a balanced tree. So, time complexity of searching = θ(log n)

But a BST, may be skewed tree, so in worst case BST searching time = θ(n)

33.

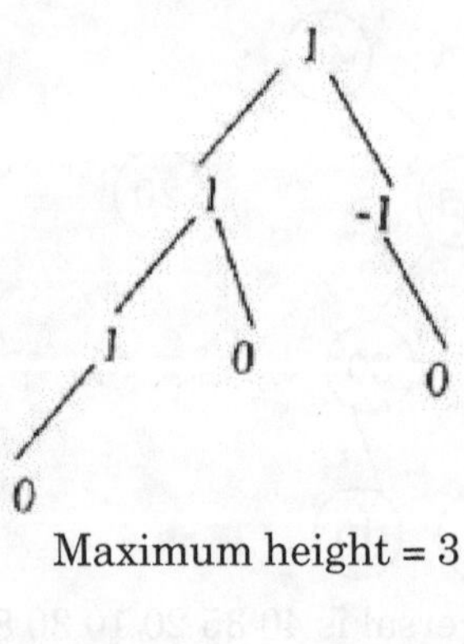

Maximum height = 3

34. If searching starts from index 8, so in that case the maximum number of comparision is required i.e. 5 comparisons will be made at index 8, 9, 0, 1 and 2.

35. 43 store at location 3

165 store at a location 5

62 store at a location 2

123 → 3(collide) So according to linear probing 3 + 1 = 4

142 → 2(collide), 3(collide), 4(collide), 5(collide) → = 6

36. For each entry probability of collision is 1/20.

According to question after inserting x values probability becomes ½

(1/20) * x = 1/2

so x = 10

37. After insetting key into empty hash table using hash function :-

0	11
1	
2	13
3	36
4	92
5	4
6	71
7	14
8	
9	43
10	87

So last value (i. e 14) is store at location 7.

38. In linear probing, if there is already an element then the new element is fed into the next blank value field in the table.

39. Sequencde in option (C) creates the hash table as 42, 23 and 34 appear before 52 and 33, and 46 appears before 33.

40. In a valid insertion sequence, the elements 42, 23 and 34 must appear before 52 and 33, and 46 must appear before 33.

So, 3! is for elements 42, 23 and 34 because they can appear in any order, and 5 is for element 46 because 46 can appear at 5 different places (i.e. any location before 33).

So total ways are 3! * 5 = 30 ways.

41. Keys :- 5, 28, 19, 15, 20, 33, 12 17, 10

Hash function h (k) = k mod 9.

After inserting keys into hash table the Status of table is

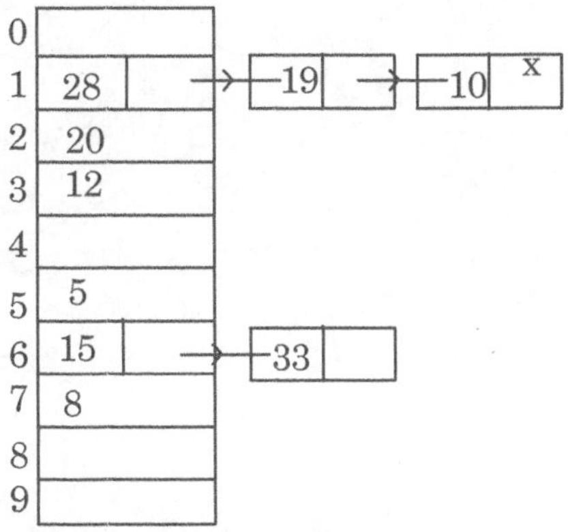

The Maximum chain length is 3.

The Minimum chain length is 0.

The average chain length is

$$\frac{(0+3+1+1+0+1+2+0+1)}{9} = 1$$

42. **A**

P(First insertion in such a way that first 3 slots are unfilled) $= \frac{97C_1}{100C_1} = \frac{97}{100}$

B

P(second insertion in such a way that first 3 slots are unfilled) $= \frac{97C_1}{100C_1} = \frac{97}{100}$

($\because$ chaining is used to resolve collision, so second insertion can be done at same index as first index]

C

P (Third insertion in such a way that first 3 slots are unfilled) $= \frac{97C_1}{100C_1} = \frac{97}{100}$

($\because$ Third insertion can be done at same index as first or second index]

So total prob. P (A) $\times$ P (B) $\times$P(C)

$$= \frac{97}{100} \times \frac{97}{100} \times \frac{97}{100} = \frac{(97 \times 97 \times 97)}{100^3}$$

43. Advantage is deletion is easier.

44. The given Hash function is h(key) = key mod(10).

(*) hash value for the keys 9679, 1989 and 4199 are same, i.e. 9.

(*) Hash value for the keys 1471 and 6171 are same i.e. 1

45. 1. True.

2. False.

3. True.

46. 1 will occupy location 0.

3 will occupy location 6.

8 hashed to location 0 which is already occupied, so it will be hashed to one location next to it (0) i.e. to location 1.

Since 10 also clashes, so it will be hashed to location 2.

47. $h(i) = i^3 \bmod 10$

$i = 1$	=	1^3	mod 10	=	1
2	=	2^3	mod 10	=	8
3	=	3^3	mod 10	=	7
4	=	4^3	mod 10	=	4
5	=	5^3	mod 10	=	5
6	=	6^3	mod 10	=	6
7	=	7^3	mod 10	=	3
8	=	8^3	mod 10	=	2
9	=	9^3	mod 10	=	9
10	=	10^3	mod 10	=	0

Hence the hash function will be $h(i) = i^3 \bmod 10$

48. The load factor = (no. of elements)/(no. of table slots)

= 2000/25 = 80

Unit - VI

Algorithms

Syllabus

Searching, sorting, hashing. Asymptotic worst case time and space complexity. Algorithm design techniques: greedy, dynamic programming and divide - and - conquer. Graph search, minimum spanning trees, shortest paths.

Contents

1 CHAPTER Algorithm Analysis & Sorting

Analysis of Previous GATE Papers											
Units	**Year →** **Topics ↓**		**2019**	**2018**	**2017 Set 1**	**2017 Set 2**	**2016 Set 1**	**2016 Set 2**	**2015 Set 1**	**2015 Set 2**	**2015 Set 3**
ASYMTOTIC NOTATION	**1 Mark**	MCQ Type			1	1	1	2		2	1
		Numerical Type									
	2 Marks	MCQ Type				2			2		1
		Numerical Type			1			2			
		Total			**3**	**5**	**1**	**6**	**4**	**2**	**3**
SORTING	**1 Mark**	MCQ Type									
		Numerical Type	1								
	2 Marks	MCQ Type									
		Numerical Type									
		Total	**1**								
QUICK SORT	**1 Mark**	MCQ Type							1		
		Numerical Type									
	2 Marks	MCQ Type								1	
		Numerical Type									
		Total							**1**	**2**	
INSERTION SORT	**1 Mark**	MCQ Type									
		Numerical Type									
	2 Marks	MCQ Type									
		Numerical Type									
		Total									
MERGE SORT	**1 Mark**	MCQ Type									
		Numerical Type									
	2 Marks	MCQ Type									1
		Numerical Type									
		Total									**2**
ALGO CONCEPT	**1 Mark**	MCQ Type			1			1	1		
		Numerical Type									
	2 Marks	MCQ Type								1	
		Numerical Type									
		Total			**1**			**1**	**1**	**2**	
LINEAR SEARCH	**1 Mark**	MCQ Type									
		Numerical Type									
	2 Marks	MCQ Type									
		Numerical Type									
		Total									

ASYMTOTIC NOTATION

1. Solve the recurrence equations

$T(n) = T(n-1) + n$

$T(1) = 1$

[1987 : 2 Marks]

2. What is the generating function G(z) for the sequence of Fibonacci numbers?

[1987:2 Marks]

3. $\sum_{1 \le k \le n} O(n)$, where O(n) stands for order n is

(a) O(n) (b) $O(n^2)$

(c) $O(m^3)$ (d) $O(3n^2)$

[1993 : 2 Marks]

4. Consider the following two functions:

$$g_1(n) = \begin{cases} n^3 \text{ for } 0 \le n \le 10{,}000 \\ n^2 \text{for } n \ge 10{,}000 \end{cases}$$

$$g_2(n) = \begin{cases} n \text{ for } 0 \le n \le 100 \\ n^3 \text{for } n > 100 \end{cases}$$

Which of the follovving is true?

(a) $g_1(n)$ is $O(g_2(n))$ (b) $g_1(n)$ is $O(n^3)$

(c) $g_2(n)$ is $O(g_1(n))$ (d) $g_2(n)$ is O(n)

5. Which of the following is false?

(a) $100n \log n = O\left(\frac{n \log n}{100}\right)$

(b) $\sqrt{\log n} = O(\log \log n)$

(c) If $0 < x < y$ then $n^x = O(n^y)$

(d) $2n \neq O(nk)$

[1996 : 1 Mark]

6. The concatenation of two lists is to be performed in O(1) time. Which of the follovving implementations of a list should be used?

(a) Singly linked list

(b) Doubly linked list

(c) Circular doubly linked list

(d) Arrayimplementationoflist

[1997 : 1 Mark]

7. Let $f(n) = n^2 \log n$ and $g(n) = n(\log n)^{10}$ be two positive functions of n. Which of the follovving statements is correct?

(a) $f(n) = O(g(n))$ and $g(n) \neq O(f(n))$

(b) $g(n) = O(f(n))$ and $f(n) \neq O(g(n))$

(c) $f(n) \neq O(g(n))$ and $g(n) \neq O(f(n))$

(d) $f(n) = O(g(n))$ and $g(n) = O(f(n))$

[2001 : 1 Mark]

8. In the worst case, the number of comparisons needed to search singly linked list of length n for a given element is

(a) $\log_2 n$ (b) n/2

(c) $\log_2 n-1$ (d) n

[2002 : 1 Mark]

9. Consider the follovving functions

$f(n) = 3n^{\sqrt{n}}$

$g(n) = 2^{\sqrt{n}\log_2 n}$

$h(n) = n!$

Which of the follovving is true?

(a) h(n) is O(f(n)) (b) h(n) is O(g(n))

(c) g(n)is not O(f(n)) (d) f(n) is O(g(n))

[2002 : 2 Marks]

10. Consider the follovving algorithm for searching for a given number x in an unsortedarray A[1 ....n] having n distinct values:

1. Choose an i uniformly at random from 1.. .n;
2. If A[i] = x then Stop else Goto 1;

Assuming that x is present on A, vvhat is the expected number of comparisons made by the algorithm before it terminates?

(a) n (b) n – 1

(c) 2n (d) n/2

[2002 : 2 Marks]

11. The running time of the follovving algorithm Procedure A(n)

If n < = 2 return (1) else return $\left(A\left(\lceil \sqrt{n} \rceil\right)\right)$; is best described by

(a) O(n) (b) O(logn)

(c) O(log logn) (d) O(1)

[2002:2 Marks]

12. Consider the foliowing three claims

1. $(n + k)m = \Theta(n^m)$, where k and m are constants
2. $2^{n+1} = O(2^n)$
3. $2^{2n+1} = O(2^n)$

Which of these claims are correct?

(a) 1 and 2

(b) 1 and 3

(c) 2 and 3

(d) 1, 2 and 3

[2003 : 1 Mark]

13. Consider the following C function.

```
float f (float x, int y)
{
    float p, s; int i;
    for (s = 1, p = 1, i = 1; i < y; i ++)
    {
        p* = x/i;
        s + = p;
    }
    return s;
}
```

For large values of y, the return value of the function f best approximates

(a) x^y (b) e^x

(c) ln (1 + x) (d) x^x

[2003 : 1 Mark]

14. The cube root of a natural number n is defined as the largest natural number m such that $m^3 \leq n$. The complexity of computing the cube root of n (n is represented in binary notation) is

(a) $O(n)$ but not $O(n^{0.5})$

(b) $O(n^{0.5})$ but not $O((\log n)^k)$ for any constant $k > 0$.

(c) $O((\log n)^k)$ for some constant $k > 0$, but not $O((\log \log n)^m)$ for any constant $m > 0$

(d) $O((\log \log n)^k)$ for some constant $k > 0.5$, but not$O((\log \log n)^{0.5})$

[2003 : 2 Marks]

15. The tightest lower bound on the number of comparisons, in the worst case, for comparison-based sorting is of the order of

(a) n (b) n^2

(c) n log n (d) n $\log^2$ n

[2004 : 1 Mark]

16. What does the following algorithm approximate? (Assume $m > 1, \in > 0$).

```
x = m ;
y = 1 ;
while (x - y > ∈)
{ x = (x + y) / 2 ;
  y = m / m ;
}
print (x) ;
```

(a) log *m*

(b) m^2

(c) $m^{1/2}$

(d) $m^{1/3}$

17. Let A [1,..., n] be an array storing a bit (1 or 0) at each location, and f(m) is a function whose time complexity is $\Theta(m)$. Consider the following program fragment written in a C like language:

```
counter = 0;
for(i = 1; i < n; i++)
{
    if (A[i] = = 1) counter ++;
    else
    {
    f(counter);
    counter = 0;
    }
}
```

The complexity of trris program fragment is

(a) $\Omega(n^2)$ (b) $\Omega(n \log n)$ and $O(n^2)$

(c) $\Theta(n)$ (d) O(n logn)

[2004 : 2 Marks]

18. The time complexity of the following C function is (assume n > 0)

```
int recursive (int n)
{
    if (n = = 1)
        return (1);
    else
        return(recursive(n-l)+ recursive(n-l));
}
```

(a) O(n) (b) O (n log n)

(c) $O(n^2)$ (d) $O(2^n)$

[2004 : 2 Marks]

19. The recurrence equation:

$T(1) = 1$

$T(n) = 2T(n-1) + n, n \geq 2$

evaluates to

(a) $2^{n+1} - n - 2$ (b) $2^n - n$

(c) $2^{n+1} - 2n - 2$ (d) $2^n + n$

[2004 : 2 Marks]

20. Let f (n), g(n) and h(n) be functions defined for positive integers such that f (n) = O(g(n), g(n)) ≠ O(f(n)), g(n) = O(h(n)), and h(n) = O(g(n)). Which one of the foliowing statements is FALSE?

(a) f(n) + g(n) = O(h(n)) + h(n))

(b) f(n) = O(h(n))

(c) h(n) ≠ O(f(n))

(d) f(n)h(n) ≠ O(g(n)h(n))

[Year : 2004] 2 Marks

21. The time complexity of computing the transitive closure of a binary relation on a set of n elements is known to be

(a) O(n) (b) O(nlogn)

(c) $O(n^{3/2})$ (d) $O(n^3)$

[2005 : 1 Mark]

22. Let T(n) be a function defined by the recurrence $T(n) = 2T(n/2) + \sqrt{n}$ for $n \geq 2$ and T(1) = 1. Which of the following statements is TRUE?

(a) $T(n) = \Theta(\log n)$ (b) $T(n) = \Theta(\sqrt{n})$

(c) $T(n) = \Theta(n)$ (d) $T(n) = \Theta(n \log n)$

[2005 : 2 Marks]

23. Suppose T(n) = 2T (n/2) + n, T(0) = T(l) = 1 Which one of the following is FALSE?

(a) $T(n) = O(n^2)$ (b) $T(n) = \Theta(n \log n)$

(c) $T(n) = \Omega(n^2)$ (d) $T(n) = O(n \log n)$

[2005 : 2 Marks]

Common Data for Q. 24 & Q. 25

Consider the following C function:

```
double foo(int n)
{
int i;
double sum;
if (n = = 0) return 1.0;
else
{
sum = 0.0;
for (i = 0; i < n ; i ++)
sum + = foo(i);
return sum;
}
}
```

24. The space complexity of the above function is

(a) O(1) (b) O(n)

(c) O(n!) (d) $O(n^n)$

[2005 : 2 Marks]

25. The space complexity of the above function is foo() and store the values of foo(i), 0 < = i < n, as and when they are computed. With this modification, the time complexity for function foo() is significantly reduced. The space complexity of the modified function would be

(a) O(1) (b) O(n)

(c) $O(n^2)$ (d) O(n!)

[2005 : 2 Marks]

26. Consider the following C-program fragment in which i, j, and n are integer variables.

```
for(i = n, j = 0; i > 0; i/ = 2, j + = i);
```

Let Val (j) = denote the value stored in the variable j after termination of the for loop. Which one of the follovving is true?

(a) val (j) = Θ (log n) (b) val (j) = $\Theta(\sqrt{n})$

(c) val (j) = Θ (n) (d) val (j) = Θ (n log n)

[2006 : 1 Mark]

27. Consider the following is true?

$$T(n) = 2T\left(\left\lceil \sqrt{n} \right\rceil\right) + 1, T(1) = 1$$

Which one of the follovving is true?

(a) T (n) = Θ (log log n)

(b) T (n) = Θ (log n)

(c) T (n) = $\Theta\left(\sqrt{n}\right)$

(d) T (n) = Θ (n)

[2006 : 2 Marks]

28. Consider the following segment of C code

```
int j, n;
j = i;
while (j < = n)
j = j*2;
```

The number of comparisons made in the execution of the loop for any n > 0 is

(a) $\lceil \log_2 n \rceil + 1$ (b) n

(c) $\lceil \log_2 n \rceil$ (d) $\lfloor \log_2 n \rfloor + 1$

[2007 : 1 Mark]

29. What is the time complexity of the following recursive function:

```
int DoSomething (int n)
{
    if (n < = 2)
        return 1;
    else
        return DoSomething (floor (sqrt (n)))+n;
}
```

(a) $\Theta(n^2)$

(b) $\Theta(n \log_2 n)$

(c) $\Theta(\log_2 n)$

(d) $\Theta(\log_2 \log_2 n)$

[2007 : 2 Marks]

30. An array of n numbers is given, where n is an even number. The maximum as well as the minimum of these n numbers needs to be determined. Which of the following is true about the number of comparisons needed?

(a) At least 2n – c comparisons, for some constant c, are needed.

(b) At most 1.5n – 2 comparisons are needed.

(c) At least n $\log_2$ n comparisons are needed.

(d) Noneoftheabove

[2007 : 2 Marks]

31. Consider the following C code segment:

```
int IsPrime(n)
{
  int i, n;
  for(i = 2; i < = sqrt(n); i ++)
 {
  if(n% i = = 0)
    printf ("Not Prime\n");
  return 0;
 }
return 1;
}
```

Let T(n) denote the number of times the for loop is executed by the program on input n. Which of the following is TRUE?

(a) $T(n) = O(\sqrt{n})$ and $T(n) = \Omega(\sqrt{n})$

(b) $T(n) = O(\sqrt{n})$ and $T(n) = \Omega(1)$

(c) $T(n) = O(n)$ and $T(n) = \Omega(\sqrt{n})$

(d) None of these

[2007 : 2 Marks]

32. Arrange the following functions in increasing asymptotic order:

A. $n^{1/3}$ B. e^n

C. $n^{7/4}$ D. $n \log^9 n$

E. 1.0000001^n

(a) A, D, C, E, B (b) D, A, C, E, B

(c) A, C, D, E, B (d) A, C, D, B, E

[2008 : 1 Mark]

33. When $n = 2^{2k}$ for some $k \geq 0$, the recurrence relation $T(n) = \sqrt{2}\, T(n/2) + \sqrt{n}$, $T(1) = 1$ evaluates to:

(a) $\sqrt{n}(\log n + 1)$ (b) $\sqrt{n} \log n$

(c) $\sqrt{n} \log \sqrt{n}$ (d) $n \log \sqrt{n}$

[2008 : 2 Marks]

34. Consider the follovving functions:

$f(n) = 2^n$

$g(n) = n!$

$h(n) = n^{\log n}$

which of the follovving statements about the asymptotic behaviour of f (n), g(n), and h (n) is true?

(a) $f(n) = O(g(n))$; $g(n) = O(h(n))$

(b) $f(n) = \Omega(g(n))$; $g(n) = O(h(n))$

(c) $g(n) = O(f(n))$; $h(n) = O(f(n))$

(d) $h(n) = O(f(n))$; $g(n) = \Omega(f(n))$

[2008 : 2 Marks]

35. The minimum number of comparison required to determine if an integer appears more than n/2 times in a sorted array of n integers is

(a) $\Theta(n)$ (b) $\Theta(\log n)$

(c) $\Theta(\log^2 n)$ (d) $\Theta(1)$

[2008 : 2 Marks]

Common Data Questions Q. 36 and Q. 37

Consider the following C functions:

```
int f l(int n)
{
if(n = = 0 | | n = = 1) return n;
else return (2* f1( n –1) + 3 * f1(n – 2));
}
intf2 (int n)
{ int i;
int X[N], Y[N], Z[N];
X[1] = 1; Y[1] = 2;Z[1] = 3;
for( i = 2; i < = n ; i ++ )
 {
  X[i]=Y[i-l] + Z[i-2];
  Y[i]=2*X[i];
  Z[i] = 3*X[i];
 }
return X[n] ;
 }
```

36. The running time of f 1 (n) and f2(n) are

(a) $\Theta(n)$ and $\Theta(n)$ (b) $\Theta(2^n)$ and $\Theta(n)$

(c) $\Theta(n)$ and $\Theta(2^n)$ (d) $\Theta(2^n)$ and $\Theta(2^n)$

[2008 : 2 Marks]

37. f1(8) and f2(8) return the values

(a) 1661 and 1640 (b) 59 and 59

(c) 1640 and 1640 (d) 1640 and 1661

[2008 : 2 Marks]

38. What is the number of swaps required to sort n elements using selection sort, in the worst case?

(a) $\Theta(n)$ (b) $\Theta(n \log n)$

(c) $\Theta(n^2)$ (d) $\Theta(n^2 \log n)$

[2009 : 1 Mark]

39. The running time of an algorithm is represented by the following recurrence relation:

$$T(n) = \begin{cases} n & n \le 3 \\ T\left(\frac{n}{3}\right) + cn & \text{otherwise} \end{cases}$$

Which one of the following represents the time complexity of the algorithm?

(a) $\Theta(n)$ (b) $\Theta(n \log n)$

(c) $\Theta(n^2)$ (d) $\Theta(n^2 \log n)$

[2009 : 2 Marks]

40. Two alternative packages A and B are available for processing a database having 10^k records. Package A requires $0.0001\ n^2$ time units and package B requires $10n\log_{10}n$ time units to process n records. What is the smallest value of k for which package B will be preferred over A?

(a) 12 (b) 10

(c) 6 (d) 5 **[2010 : 1 Mark]**

41. Let W(n) and A(n) denote respectively, the worst case and average case running time of an algorithm executed on an input of size n. Which of the following is ALWAYS TRUE?

(a) $A(n) = \Omega(W(n))$ (b) $A(n) = \Theta(W(n))$

(c) $A(n) = O(W(n))$ (d) $A(n) - o(W(n))$

[2012 : 1 Mark]

42. The recurrence relation capturing the optimal execution time of the Towers of Hanoi problem with n discs is

(a) $T(n) = 2T(n - 2) + 2$

(b) $T(n) = 2T(n - 1) + n$

(c) $T(n) = 2T(n/2) + 1$

(d) $T(n) = 2T(n - 1) + 1$ **[2012 : 1 Mark]**

43. Consider the following function:

```
int unknown (int n)
{
    int i, j, k = 0;
    for (i = n/2; i < = n; i++)
        for(j = 2; j< = n; j = j*2)
            k = k + n/2;
    return (k);
}
```

The return value of the function is

(a) $\Theta(n^2)$ (b) $\Theta(n^2 \log n)$

(c) $\Theta(n^3)$ (d) $\Theta(n^3 \log n)$

[2013 : 2 Marks]

44. Which one of the following correctly determines the solution of the recurrence relation with T(1)= 1?

$$T(n) = 2T\left(\frac{n}{2}\right) + \log n$$

(a) $\Theta(n)$ (b) $\Theta(n \log n)$

(c) $\Theta(n^2)$ (d) $\Theta(\log n)$

[2014 (Set-2) : 1 Mark]

45. Suppose we have a balanced binary search tree Tholding n-numbers. We are given two numbers L and H and wish to sum up all the numbers in Tthat lie between L and H. Suppose there are m such numbers in T.

If the tightest upper bound on the time to compute the sum is $0(n^a \log^b n + m^c \log^d n)$, the value of $\alpha + 10b + 100c + 1000d$ is ____.

[2014 (Set-3): 2 Marks]

46. Consider the following C function.

```
int fun 1 (int n)
{   int i, j, k, p, q = 0;
    for (i = 1; i<n; ++i)
    {    P = 0;
         for(j = n; j > 1; j = j/2)
         ++p;
         for (k=l; k<p; k=k*2)
         ++q;
    } return q;
}
```

Which one of the following most closely approximates the return value of the function fun1?

(a) n^3 (b) $n(\log n)^2$

(c) n log n (d) n log (log n)

[2015 (Set-1) : 2 Marks]

47. An algorithm performs $(\log N)^{1/2}$ find operations, N insert operations, $(\log N)^{1/2}$ delete operations, and $(\log N)^{1/2}$ decrease-key operations on a set of data items with keys drawn from a linearly ordered set. For a delete operation, a pointer is provided to the record that must be deleted. For the decrease-key operation, a pointer is provided to the record that has its key decreased. Which one of the foliowing data structures is the most suited for the algorithm to use, if the goal is to achieve the best total asymptotic complexity considering ali the operations?

(a) Unsorted array

(b) Min-heap

(c) Sorted array

(d) Sorted doubly linked list

[2015 (Set-1) : 2 Marks]

48. Consider a complete binary tree where the left and the right subtrees of the root are max-heaps. The lower bound for the number of operations to convert the tree to a heap is

(a) $\Omega(\log n)$ (b) $\Omega(n)$

(c) $\Omega(n\log n)$ (d) $\Omega(n^2)$

[2015 (Set-2) : 1 Mark]

49. An unordered list contains n distinct elements. The number of comparisons to find an element in this list that is neither maximum nor minimum is

(a) $\Theta(n \log n)$ (b) $\Theta(n)$

(c) $\Theta(\log n)$ (d) $\Theta(1)$

[2015 (Set-2) : 1 Mark]

50. Consider the equality $\sum_{i=0}^{n} i^3 = X$ andthe following choices for X

I. $\Theta(n^4)$ II. $\Theta(n^5)$

III. $O(n^5)$ IV. $\Omega(n^3)$

The equality above remains correct if X is replace by

(a) OnlyI

(b) OnlyII

(c) I or III or IV but not II

(d) II or III or IV but not I

[2015 (Set-3) : 1 Mark]

51. Let $f(n) = n$ and $g(n) = n^{(1+\sin n)}$, where n is a positive integer. Which of the following statements is/are correct?

I. $f(n) = O(g(n))$

II. $f(n) = \Omega(g(n))$

(a) Only I (c) Both I and II

(b) Only II (d) Neither I nor II

[2015 (Set-3): 2 Marks]

52. The given diagram shows the flow chart for a recursive function A(n). Assume that all statements, except for the recursive calls, have O(1) time complexity. If the worst case time complexity of this function is $O(n^\alpha)$, then the least possible value (accurate up to two decimal positions) of a is ________.

Flow chart for Recursive Function A(n)

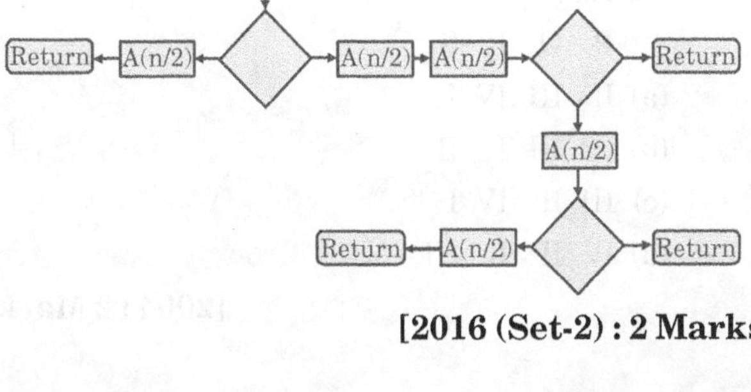

[2016 (Set-2) : 2 Marks]

53. N items are stored in a sorted doubly linked list. For a delete operation, apointer is provided to the record to be deleted. For a decrease-key operation, a pointer is provided to the record on which the operation is to be performed. An algorithm performs the following operations on the list in this order: $\Theta(N)$ delete, $O(\log N)$ insert, $O(\log N)$ find, and $\Theta(N)$ decrease-key. What is the time complexity of all these operations put together?

(a) $O(\log^2 N)$ (b) $O(N)$

(c) $O(N^2)$ (d) $\Theta(N^2 \log N)$

[2016 (Set-2) : 1 Mark]

54. Match the algorithms with their time complexities:

List-I (Algorithm)

(P) Towers of Hanoi with n disks

(Q) Binary search given n sorted numbers

(R) Heap sort given n numbers at the worst case

(S) Addition of two n × n matrices

List-II (Time complexity)

(i) $\Theta(n^2)$

(ii) $\Theta(n \log n)$

(iii) $\Theta(2^n)$

(iv) $\Theta(\log n)$

(a) P – (iii), Q – (iv), R – (i), S – (ii)

(b) P – (iv), Q – (iii), R – (i), S – (ii)

(c) P – (iii), Q – (iv), R – (ii), S – (i)

(d) P – (iv), Q – (iii), R – (ii), S – (i)

[2017 (Set-2) : 1 Mark]

55. Consider the recurrence function

$$T(n) = \begin{cases} 2T\left(\sqrt{n}\right)+1, & n > 2 \\ 2, & 0 < n \le 2 \end{cases}$$

Then T(n) in terms of Θ notation is

(a) $\Theta(\log\log n)$ (b) $\Theta(\log n)$

(c) $\Theta\left(\sqrt{n}\right)$ (d) $\Theta(n)$

[2017 (Set-2) : 2 Marks]

56. Consider the following C function.

```
int fun (int n)
{  int i, j;
   for (i = 1; i <= n; i++)
   {  for (j = 1; j < n; j + = i)
      {
           printf{"%d %d", i, j);
      }
   }
}
```

Time complexity of fun in terms of Θ notation is

(a) $\Theta\left(n\sqrt{n}\right)$ (b) $\Theta(n^2)$

(c) $\Theta(n \log n)$ (d) $\Theta(n^2 \log n)$

[2017 (Set-2) : 2 Marks]

57. Consider the following functions from positive integers to real numbers:

$$10, \sqrt{n}, n, \log_2 n, \frac{100}{n}$$

Tire CORRECT arrangement of the above functions in increasing order of asymptotic complexity is:

(a) $\log_2 n, \frac{100}{n}, 10, \sqrt{n}, n$

(b) $\frac{100}{n}, 10, \log_2 n, \sqrt{n}, n$

(c) $10, \frac{100}{n}, \sqrt{n}, \log_2 n, n$

(d) $\frac{100}{n}, \log_2 n, 10, \sqrt{n}, n$

[2017 (Set-l):l Mark]

58. Let A be an array of 31 numbers consisting of a sequence of 0's followed by a sequence of l's. The problem is to find the smallest index i such that A[i] is 1 by probing the minimum number of locations in A. The worst case number of probes performed by an optimal algorithm is ______.

[2017 (Set-1): 2 Marks]

59. Find a solution to the follovving recurrence equation

$$T(n) = T\left(\frac{n}{2}\right) + n$$

$$T(1) = 1$$

[1987 : 2 Marks]

60. The recurrence relation

$$T(1) = 2$$

$$T(n) = 3T\left(\frac{n}{4}\right) + n$$

Has the solution T(n) equal to

(a) O(n)

(b) O(log n)

(c) $O(n^{3/4})$

(d) None of these

[1996 : 2 Marks]

61. Let T(n) be the function defined by T(1) = 1, $T(n)\left(\left\lfloor\frac{n}{2}\right\rfloor\right) + \sqrt{n}$ for $n \geq 2$. Which of the foliowing statements is true?

(a) $T(n) = O(\sqrt{n})$ (b) T(n) = 0(n)

(c) T(n) = O(logn) (d) Noneofthese

[1997 : 2 Marks]

62. A sorting technique is called stable if

(a) it takes O(nlog n) time

(b) it maintains the relative order of occurrence of non-distinct elements

(c) it uses divide and conquer paradigm

(d) it takes O(n) space

[1999 : 1 Mark]

63. Randomized quicksort is an extension of quicksort where the pivot is chosen randomly. What is the worst case complexity of sorting n numbers using randomized quicksort?

(a) O(n) (b) (n log n)

(c) $O(n^2)$ (d) O(n!)

[2001 : 1 Mark]

64. Consider a list of recursive algorithms and a list of recurrence relations as shown below. Each recurrence relation corresponds to exactly one algorithm and is used to derive the time complexity of the algorithm.

List-I (Recursive Algorithm)

P. Binary search

Q. Merge sort

R. Quick sort

S. Tower of Hanoi

List-II (Recurrence Relation)

I. T(n) = T(n - k) + T(k) + cn

II. T(n) = 2T(n - 1) + 1

III. T(n) = 2T(n/2) + cn

IV. T(n) = T(n/2) + 1

Which of the following is the correct match between the algorithms and their recurrence relations?

Codes:

	P	Q	R	S
(a)	II	III	IV	I
(b)	IV	III	I	II
(c)	III	II	IV	I
(d)	IV	II	I	III

[2004 : 2 Marks]

65. Suppose there are log n sorted lists of n/log n elements each. The time complexity of producing a sorted list of all these elements is: (**Hint:** Use a heap data structure)

(a) $O(n \log\log n)$ (b) $\Theta(n \log n)$

(c) $\Omega(n \log n)$ (d) $\Omega(n^{3/2})$

[2005 : 2 Marks]

66. Which of the following sorting algorithms has the lowest worst-case complexity?

(a) Mergesort (b) Bubblesort

(c) Quicksort (d) Selectionsort

[2007 : 1 Mark]

67. A list of n strings, each of length n, is sorted into lexicographic order using the merge sort algorithm. The worst case running time of this computation is

(a) $O(n \log n)$ (b) $O(n^2 \log n)$

(c) $O(n^2 + \log n)$ (d) $O(n^2)$

[2012 : 2 Marks]

68. Which one of the foliowing is the tightest upper bound that represents the time complexity of inserting an object into a binary search tree of n nodes?

(a) $O(1)$ (b) $O(\log n)$

(c) $O(n)$ (d) $O(n \log n)$

[2013 : 1 Mark]

69. The worst case running times of Insertion sort, Merge sort and Quick sort, respectively, are:

(a) $\Theta(n \log n)$, $\Theta(n \log n)$, and $\Theta(n^2)$

(b) $\Theta(n^2)$, $\Theta(n^2)$, and $\Theta(n \log n)$

(c) $\Theta(n^2)$, $\Theta(n \log n)$, and $\Theta(n \log n)$

(d) $\Theta(n^2)$, $\Theta(n \log n)$, and $\Theta(n^2)$

[2016 (Set-1): 1 Mark]

70. Assume that the algorithms considered here sort the input sequences in ascending order. If the input is already in ascending order, which of the followingareTRUE?

I. Quicksort runs in $Q(n^2)$ time

II. Bubblesort runs in $Q(n^2)$ time

III. Mergesort runs in $Q(n)$ time

IV. Insertion sort runs in $Q(n)$ time

(a) I and II only

(b) I and III only

(c) II and IV only

(d) I and IV only

[2016 (Set-2): 1 Mark]

71. In the follovving table, the left column contains the names of standard graph algorithms and the right column contains the time complexities of the algorithms. Match each algorithm with its time complexity.

List-I

1. Bellman-Ford algorithm
2. Kruskal's algorithm
3. Floyd-Warshall algorithm
4. Topological sorting

List-II

A. $O(m \log n)$

B. $O(n^3)$

C. $O(nm)$

D. $O(n + m)$

(a) 1-C, 2-A, 3-B, 4-D

(b) 1-B, 2-D, 3-C, 4-A

(c) 1-C, 2-D, 3-A, 4-B

(d) 1-B, 2-A, 3-C, 4-D

[2005 : 1 Mark]

72. In an unweighted, undirected connected graph, the shortest path from a node S to every other node is computed most efficiently, in terms of time complexity, by

(a) Dijkstra's algorithm starting from S.

(b) Warshall's algorithm

(c) performing a DFS starting from S

(d) performing a BFS starting from S

[2007 : 2 Marks]

73. Consider n jobs $J_1, J_2, \ldots, J_n$ such that job J_i has execution time t_i and a non-negative integer weight w_i. The weighted mean completion time of the jobs is defined to be $\sum_{i=1}^{n} w_i T_i \Big/ \sum_{i=1}^{n} w_i$.

where T_i is the completion time of job J_i. Assuming that there is only one processor available, in what order must the jobs be executed in order to minimize the weighted mean completion time of thejobs?

(a) Non-decreasing order of t_i

(b) Non-increasing order of w_i

(c) Non-increasing order of $w_i t_i$

(d) Non-increasing order of w_i/t_i

[2007 : 2 Marks]

74. Suppose P, Q, R, S, T are sorted sequences havinglengths 20,24,30,35,50 respectively. They are to be merged into a single sequence by merging together two sequences at a time. The number of comparisons that will be needed in the worst case by the optimal algorithm for doing this is ______.

[2014 (Set-2) : 2 Marks]

75. Give the correct matching for the following pairs:

List-I	List-II
A. O(logn)	P. Selection
B. O(n)	Q. Insertion sort
C. O(n log n)	R. Binary search
D. $O(n^2)$	S. Merge sort

Codes:

(a) A – R B – P C – Q D – S
(b) A – R B – P C – S D – Q
(c) A – P B – R C – S D – Q
(d) A – P B – S C – R D – Q

[1998 : 1 Mark]

76. Suppose we want to arrange the n numbers stored in an array such that ali negative values occur before all positive ones. Minimum number of exchanges required in the worst case is

(a) n – 1 (b) n
(c) n + 1 (d) None of these

[1999 : 1 Mark]

77. If $T_1 = O(1)$, give the correct matching for the following pairs:

(m) $T_n = T_{n-1} + n$ (u) $T_n = O(n)$
(n) $T_n = T_{\frac{n}{2}} + n$ (v) $T_n = O(n \log n)$
(o) $T_n = T_{n/2} + n \log n$ (w) $T_n = O(n^2)$
(p) $T_n = T_{n-1} + \log n$ (x) $T_n = O(\log^2 n)$

(a) m – w, n – v, o – u, p – x
(b) m – w, n – u, o – x, p – v
(c) m – v, n – w, o – x, p – u
(d) m – w, n – u, o – v, p – x

[1999 : 2 Marks]

78. If all permutations are equally likely, what is the expected number of inversions in a randomly chosen permutation of l...n?

(a) n(n – 1)/2 (b) n(n – 1)/4
(c) n(n + 1)/4 (d) $2n[\log_2 n]$

[2003 : 2 Marks]

79. An element in an array X is called a leader if it is greater than all elements to the right of it in X. The best algorithm to find ali leaders in an array.

(a) Solves it in linear time using a left to right pass of the array
(b) Solves in linear time using a right to left pass
(c) Solves it is using divide and conquer in time $\Theta(n \log n)$
(d) Solves it in time $\Theta(n^2)$

[2006 : 1 Mark]

80. Given two arrays of numbers $a_1,..., a_n$ and $b_1,..., b_n$ where each number is 0 or 1, the fastest algorithm to find the largest span (i, j) such that $a_i + a_{i+i} +....+ a_j = b_i + b_{i+i} +....+ b_j$"or report that there is no such span,

(a) Takes $O(3^n)$ and $\Omega(2^n)$ time if hashing is permitted
(b) Takes $O(n^3)$ and $\Omega(n^{2.5})$ time in the key comparison model
(c) Takes $\Theta(n)$ time and space
(d) Takes $O(\sqrt{n})$ time only if the sum of the 2n

[2006 : 2 Marks]

SORTING

81. Find a solution to the follovving recurrence equation

$$T(n) = T\left(\frac{n}{2}\right) + n$$

$$T(1) = 1$$

[1987 : 2 Marks]

82. Following algorithm (s) can be used to sort n integers in the range $[1... n^3]$ in O(n) time?

(a) Heapsort (b) Quicksort
(c) Mergesort (d) Radixsort

[1992 : 2 Marks]

83. The minimum number of comparisons required to find the minimum and the maximum of 100 numbers is ______.

[2014 (Set-1) : 2 Marks]

84. Which one of the following is the tightest upper bound that represents the number of swaps required to sort n numbers using selection sort?

(a) O(log n) (b) O(n)
(c) O(n log n) (d) $O(n^2)$

[2013 : 1 Mark]

85. Which one the foll owing inplace sorting algorithms needs the minimum number of swaps?

(a) Quicksort (b) Insertion sort

(c) Selection sort (d) Heap sort

[2006 : 1 Mark]

86. If we use Radix Sort to sort n integers in the range $(n^{k/12}, n^k]$, for some k > 0 which is independent of n, the time taken would be

(a) $\Theta(n)$ (b) $\Theta(kn)$

(c) $\Theta(n \log n)$ (d) $\Theta(n^2)$

[2008 : 2 Marks]

87. The number of elements that can be stored in $\Theta(\log n)$ time using heap sort is

(a) $\Theta(1)$ (b) $\Theta\left(\sqrt{\log n}\right)$

(c) $\Theta\left(\frac{\sqrt{\log n}}{\log \log n}\right)$ (d) $\Theta(\log n)$

[2013 : 2 Marks]

88. An array of 25 distinct elements is to be sorted using quicksort. Assume that the pivot element is chosen uniformly at random. The probability that the pivot element gets placed in the worst possible location in the first round of partitioning (rounded off to 2 decimal places) is ________.

[2019 : 1 Mark]

QUICK SORT

89. Let P be a quicksort program to sort numbers in ascending order. Let t1 and t2 be the time taken by the program for the inputs [12 3 4] and [5 4 3 2 1], respectively. Which of the following holds?

(a) $t_1 = t_2$ (b) $t_1 > t_2$

(c) $t_1 < t_2$ (d) $t_1 = t_2 + 5 \log 5$

[1987:2 Marks]

90. Quicksort is run on two inputs shown below to sort in ascending order

(i) 1, 2, 3 .... n

(ii) n, n–l,n–2, ..., 2, 1

Let C_1 and C_2 be the number of comparisons made for the inputs (i) and (ii) respectively. Then,

(a) Cl < C2

(b) Cl > C2

(c) C1 = C2

(d) we cannot say anything for arbitrary n

91. The median of n elements can be found in O(n) time. Which one of the following is correct about the complexity of quick sort, in which remains is selected as pivot?

(a) $\Theta(n)$ (b) $\Theta(n \log n)$

(c) $\Theta(n^2)$ (d) $\Theta(n^3)$

[2006 : 2 Marks]

92. Consider the Quicksort algorithm. Suppose there is a procedure for finding a pivot element which splits the list into sub-lists each of which contains at least one-fifth of the elements. Let T(n) be the number of comparisons required to sort n elements. Then

(a) $T(n) \le 2T(n/5) + n$

(b) $T(n) \le T(n/5) + T(4n/5) + n$

(c) $T(n) \le 2T(4n/5) + n$

(d) $T(n) \le 2T(n/2) + n$ **[2008 : 2 Marks]**

93. In quick sort, for sorting n elements, the (n/4)th smallest element is selected as pivot using an O(n) time algorithm. What is the worst case time complexity of the quick sort?

(a) $\Theta(n)$ (b) $\Theta(n\log n)$

(c) $\Theta(n^2)$ (d) $\Theta(n^2 \log n)$

[2009 : 2 Marks]

94. Let P be a quicksort program to sort numbers in ascending order using the first element as the pivot. Let t_1 and t_2 be the number of comparisons made by Pfor the inputs [1 2 3 4 5] and [4 1 5 3 2] respectively. Which one of the following holds?

(a) $t_1 = 5$ (b) $t_1 < t_2$

(c) $t_1 > t_2$ (d) $t_1 = t_2$

[2014 (Set-1) : 1 Mark]

95. You have an array of n elements. Suppose you implement quicksort by always choosing the central element of the array as the pivot. Then the tightest upper bound for the worst case performance is

(a) $O(n^2)$ (b) $O(n\log n)$

(c) $\Theta(n\log n)$ (d) $O(n^3)$

[2014 (Set-3) : 1 Mark]

96. Which one of the following is the recurrence equation for the worst case time complexity of the Quicksort algorithm for sorting $n(\ge 2)$ numbers? In the recurrence equations given in the options below, c is a constant.

(a) $T(n) = 2T(n/2) + cn$

(b) $T(n) = T(n-1) + T(1) + cn$

(c) $T(n) = 2T(n-1) + cn$

(d) $T(n) = T(n/2) + cn$

[2015 (Set-1): 1 Mark]

97. Suppose you are provided with the following function declaration in the C programming language.

int partition (int a[ ], int n);

The function treats the first element of a[ ] as a pivot, and rearranges the array so that ali elements less than or equal to the pivot is in the left part of the array, and all elements greater than the pivot is in the right part. In addition, it moves the pivot so that the pivot is the last element of the left part. The return value is the number of elements in the left part. The following partially given function in the C programming language is used to find the kth smallest element in an array a[ ] of size n using the partition function. We assume k ≤ n. int kth_smallest (int a[ ], int n, int k)

```
{
    int left_end = partition (a, n);
    if(left_end+ 1==k)
    {
        return a [left_end];
    }
    if(left end+l>k)
    {
        return kth_smallest (________);
    }
    else
    {
        return kth_smallest (________);
    }
}
```

The missing argument lists are respectively

(a) (a, left_end, k) and (a+left_end+l, n-left_end-1, k-left_end-l)

(b) (a, left_end, k) and (a, n-left_end-l, k-left_end-l)

(c) (a+left_end+l, n-left_end-l, k-left_end-l) and(a, left_end, k)

(d) (a, n-left_end-l, k-left_end-l) and (a, left_end, k)

[2015 (Set-2) : 2 Marks]

INSERTION SORT

98. The usual $\Theta(n^2)$ implementation of Insertion Sort to sort an array uses linear search to identify the position where an element is to be inserted into the already sorted part of the array. If instead, we use binary search to identify the position, the worst case running time will

(a) remain $\Theta(n^2)$ (b) become $\Theta(n (\log n)^2)$

(c) become $\Theta(n \log n)$ (d) become $\Theta(n)$

[2003 : 1 Mark]

99. What would be the worst case time complexity of the insertion sort algorithm, if the inputs are restricted to permutations of l...n with at most n inversions?

(a) $\Theta(n^2)$ (b) $\Theta(n \log n)$

(c) $\Theta(n^{1.5})$ (d) $\Theta(n)$ **[2003 : 2 Marks]**

MERGE SORT

100. Merge sort uses

(a) Divide and conquer strategy

(b) Backtracking approach

(c) Heuristic search

(d) Greedy approach **[1995 : 1 Mark]**

101. For merging two sorted lists of sizes m and n into a sorted list of size m+n, we required comparisons of

(a) O(m) (b) O(n)

(c) O(m + n) (d) O(logm + logn)

[1995 : 1 Mark]

102. If one uses straight two-way merge sort algorithm to sort the following elements in ascending order:

20, 47, 15, 8, 9, 4, 40, 30, 12, 17

then the order of these elements after second pass of the algorithm is?

(a) 8, 9, 15, 20, 47, 4, 12, 17, 30, 40

(b) 8, 15, 20, 47, 4, 9, 30, 40, 12, 17

(c) 15, 20, 47, 4, 8, 9, 12, 30, 40, 17

(d) 4, 8, 9, 15, 20, 47, 12, 17, 30, 40

[1999 : 1 Mark]

103. Assume that a mergesort algorithm in the worst case takes 30 seconds for an input of size 64. Which of the following most closely approximates the maximum input size of a problem that can be solved in 6 minutes?

(a) 256 (b) 512

(c) 1024 (d) 2048

[2015 (Set-3): 2 Marks]

ALGO CONCEPT

104. Match the pairs in the following:

List-I

A. Straseen's matrix multiplication algorithm

B. Kruskal's minimum spanning tree algorithm

C. Biconnected components algorithm

D. Floyd's shortest path algorithm

List-II

P. Greedymethod

Q. Dynamic programming

R. Divide and Conquer

S. Depth first search

[1990 : 2 Marks]

105. The minimum number of comparisons required to sort 5 elements is

[1991 : 2 Marks]

106. The correct matching for the followir pairs is

List-I

A. All pairs shortest paths

B. Quick Sort

C. Minimum weight spanning tree

D. Connected Components

List-II

1. Greedy
2. Depth-First search
3. Dynamic Programming
4. Divide and Conquer

Codes:

(a) A – 2 B – 4 C – 1 D – 3

(b) A – 3 B – 4 C – 1 D – 2

(c) A – 3 B – 4 C – 2 D – 1

(d) A – 4 B – 1 C – 2 D – 3

[1997 : 1 Mark]

107. Suppose each set is represented as a linked list with elements in arbitrary order. Which of the operations among union, intersection, membership, cardinality will be the slowest?

(a) union only

(b) intersection, membership

(c) membership, cardinality

(d) union, intersection

[2004 : 2 Marks]

108. A set X can be represented by an array x[n] as follows

$$x[i] = \begin{cases} 1; & \text{if } i \in X \\ 0; & \text{otherwise} \end{cases}$$

Consider the following algorithm in which x, y, and z are boolean arrays of size n: algorithm zzz (x[ ], y[ ], z[ ])

```
{
   int i;
   for (i = 0; i < n; ++ i)
        z[i] = (x [i] ∧ ~ y[i]) ∨ (~x[i] ∧ y[i]);
}
```

The set Z computed by the algorithm is

(a) $(X \cup Y)$ (b) $(X \cap Y)$

(c) $(X - Y) \cap (Y - X)$ (d) $(X - Y) \cup (Y - X)$

[2006 : 2 Marks]

109. Suppose you want to move from 0 to 100 on the number line. In each step, you either move right by a unit distance or you take a shortcut. A shortcut is simply a pre-specified pair of integers i, j with i < j. Given a shortcut i, j if you are at position i on the number line, you may directly move to j. Suppose T(k) denotes the smallest number of steps needed to move from k to 100. Suppose further that there is at most 1 shortcut involving any number, and in particular from 9 there is a shortcut to 15.

Let y and z be such that T(9) = 1 + min (T(y), T(z)). Then the value of the product yz is_______.

[2014 (Set-3) : 2 Marks]

110. Match the follovving:

List-I

A. Prim's algorithm for minimum spanning tree

B. Floyd-Warshall algorithm for ali pairs shortest paths

C. Mergesort

D. Hamiltonian circuit

List-II

1. Backtracking
2. Greedy method
3. Dynamic programming
4. Divide and conquer

Codes:

	A	B	C	D
(a)	3	2	4	1
(b)	1	2	4	3
(c)	2	3	4	1
(d)	2	1	3	4

[2015 (Set-1) : 1 Mark]

111. Given below are some algorithms, and some algorithm design paradigms.

List-I

A. Dijkstra's Shortest Path

B. Floyd-Warshall algorithm to compute all pairs shortest path

C. Binary search on a sorted array

D. Backtracking search on a graph

List-II

1. Divide and Conquer
2. Dynamic Programming
3. Greedy design
4. Depth-first search
5. Breadth-first search

Match the above algorithms (List-I) to the corresponding design paradigm (List-II) they follow.

Codes:

	A	B	C	D
(a)	1	3	1	5
(b)	3	3	1	5
(c)	3	2	1	4
(d)	3	2	1	5

[2015 (Set-2): 2 Marks]

112. Consider the following table:

Algorithms	**Design Paradigms**
(P) Kruskal	(i) Divide and Conquer
(Q) Quicksort	(ii) Greedy
(R) Floyd-Warshall	(iii) Dynamic Programming

Match the algorithms to the design paradigms they are based on.

(a) (P)$\leftrightarrow$(ii), (Q)$\leftrightarrow$(iii), (R)$\leftrightarrow$(i)

(b) (P)$\leftrightarrow$(iii), (Q)$\leftrightarrow$(i), (R)$\leftrightarrow$(ii)

(c) (P)$\leftrightarrow$(ii), (Q)$\leftrightarrow$(i), (R)$\leftrightarrow$(iii)

(d) (P)$\leftrightarrow$(i), (Q)$\leftrightarrow$(ii), (R)$\leftrightarrow$(iii)

[2017 (Set-1) : 1 Mark]

113. The Floyd-Warshall algorithm for all-pair shortest paths computation is based on

(a) Greedy paradigm

(b) Divide-and-conquer paradigm

(c) Dynamic Programming paradigm

(d) Neither Greedy nor Divide-and-Conquer nor Dynamic Programming paradigm.

[2016 (Set-2): 1 Mark]

LINEAR SEARCH

114. The average number of key comparisons done on a successful sequential search in list of length n is

(a) log n

(b) $\frac{n-1}{2}$

(c) n/2

(d) $\frac{n+1}{2}$

[1996 : 2 Marks]

ANSWERS

1. (*)	**2.** (*)	**3.** (*b*)	**4.** (*a,b*)	**5.** (*b*)	**6.** (*c*)	**7.** (*b*)	**8.** (*d*)	**9.** (*d*)	**10.** (*a*)
11. (*c*)	**12.** (*a*)	**13.** (*b*)	**14.** (*c*)	**15.** (*c*)	**16.** (*c*)	**17.** (*c*)	**18.** (*d*)	**19.** (*a*)	**20.** (*d*)
21. (*d*)	**22.** (*c*)	**23.** (*c*)	**24.** (*b*)	**25.** (*b*)	**26.** (*c*)	**27.** (*b*)	**28.** (*d*)	**29.** (*d*)	**30.** (*b*)
31. (*b*)	**32.** (*a*)	**33.** (*a*)	**34.** (*d*)	**35.** (*b*)	**36.** (*b*)	**37.** (*c*)	**38.** (*a*)	**39.** (*a*)	**40.** (*c*)
41. (*c*)	**42.** (*d*)	**43.** (*b*)	**44.** (*a*)	**45.** (110)	**46.** (*d*)	**47.** (*a*)	**48.** (*a*)	**49.** (*d*)	**50.** (*c*)
51. (*d*)	**52.** (2.32)	**53.** (*c*)	**54.** (*c*)	**55.** (*b*)	**56.** (*c*)	**57.** (*b*)	**58.** (5)	**59.** (*)	**60.** (*a*)
61. (*a*)	**62.** (*b*)	**63.** (*c*)	**64.** (*b*)	**65.** (*a*)	**66.** (*a*)	**67.** (*b*)	**68.** (*b*)	**69.** (*d*)	**70.** (*d*)
71. (*a*)	**72.** (*d*)	**73.** (*d*)	**74.** (358 to 358)		**75.** (*)	**76.** (*d*)	**77.** (*d*)	**78.** (*b*)	**79.** (*b*)
80. (*c*)	**81.** (*)	**82.** (*d*)	**83.** (148)	**84.** (*b*)	**85.** (*c*)	**86.** (*c*)	**87.** (*c*)	**88.** (0.08)	**89.** (*a*)
90. (*c*)	**91.** (*d*)	**92.** (*b*)	**93.** (*b*)	**94.** (*c*)	**95.** (*a*)	**96.** (*b*)	**97.** (*a*)	**98.** (*a*)	**99.** (*d*)
100. (*a*)	**101.** (*c*)	**102.** (*b*)	**103.** (*b*)	**104.** (*)	**105.** (7)	**106.** (*b*)	**107.** (*d*)	**108.** (*d*)	**109.** (150)
110. (*c*)	**111.** (*c*)	**112.** (*c*)	**113.** (*c*)	**114.** (*d*)					

EXPLANATIONS

1. $T(n) = T(n-1) + n$

$= T(n-2) + (n-1) + n$

$= T(n-3) + (n-2) + \ldots.n$

$= T(n-k) + (n-(k-1) + \ldots.n$

let $n-k = 1$, so, $k = n-1$

$= T(1) + (n-(n-1-1) + \ldots\ldots.n$

$= 1 + 2 + \ldots\ldots.. n$

$= \frac{n(n+1)}{2}$

So complexity $[T(n) = Q(n^2)]$

2. Generating function for fibonacci series is

$$G(z) = \frac{Z}{(1 - Z - Z^2)}$$

3. $\sum_{1<k<n} O(n) = O(n) + O(n) + \ldots.$ ktins $= O(n*k)$

So for larger value of k it become $O(n^2)$.

4. The growth of $g_1(n) = n2$, $Vn \geq 10000$

The growth of $g_2(n) = n3$, $Vn > 100$

So $g_1(n) = O(g_2(n))$

or $g_1(n) = O(n^3)$

5. (a) $100n \log n = O\left(\frac{n \log n}{100}\right)$

Here 100 is constant so we can say both function are equal .

Hence it is true.

(b) $\sqrt{\log n} = O(\log \log n)$

growth rate of $\sqrt{\log n}$ is greater then loglogn so it is false.

(c) If $O < x < y$ then $n^x = O(n^y)$ is always true.

(d) $2n \neq O(nK)$

if k is constant then this statement is false but here nothing is mentioned about K.

6.

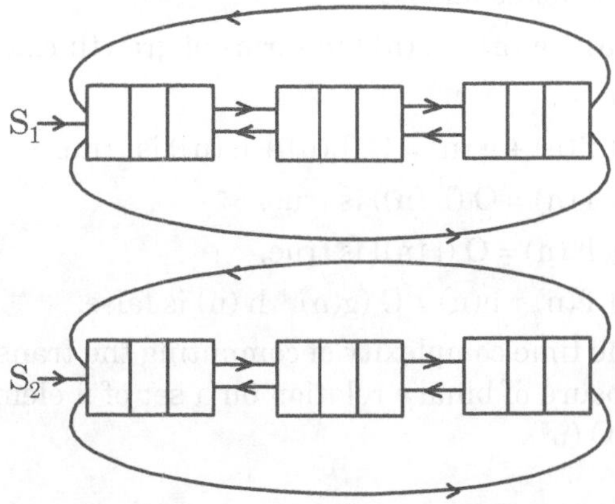

Algo for concatenation is ⇒

{

$t_1 = S_1 \rightarrow nxt$;

$t_2 = S_2 \rightarrow nxt$;

$t_1 \rightarrow nxt = S_2$

$t_2 \rightarrow nxt = S_1$

$S_1 \rightarrow nxt = t_2$

$S_2 \rightarrow nxt = t_1$

}

it is sequential alqoni them so complexity is O(1).

7. $f(n) = n^2 \log n$

$g(n) = n (\log n)^{10}$

Here we can remove common factor from both the function to simply the value of f (n) & g (n)

So $f(n) = n$

$g(n) = (\log n)^9$

Now choose the largest value of n to compare both the function.

if $n = 2^{100}$ then$f(n) = 2^{100}$

$g(n) = (100)^9$

$f(n) > g(n)$.

8. The worst case number of comparison is n. to search any element from singly link list.

9. $f(n) = 3n^{\sqrt{n}}$

$g(n) = 2^{\sqrt{n}\log_2 n} \Rightarrow 2^{\log 2n\sqrt{n}} \Rightarrow n^{\sqrt{n}}$

$h(n) = n! \cong h^n$

So, $f(n) \cong g(n) < h(n)$ (in terms of growth rate)

so $f(n) = O(g(n))$

10. The expected number of comparision is n.

11. Recurrance relation for procedure A (n) is

$T(n) = T\sqrt{n} + 1$ if $n > 2$

$T(n) = 1$ if $n \leq 2$

$T(n) = 1$

Now, $T(n) = T\sqrt{n} + 1$

Put $n = 2^k$, $T(2^k) = T(2^{k/2}) + 1$

Use S (K) for $T(2^K)$ then

$S(K) = S(k/2) + 1$

Apply masters method.

$K^{\log 21} \cong 1$

So $\theta(\log k)$

Now we know that

$n = 2^k$ so, $k = \log_2 n$

So, O (log logn).

12. Note:- In devotion place change first point by

1. $(n+k)^m = O(n^m)$, where k and m are constants.
1. $(n+k)m \cong O(nm)$ be cause k & m are constant then growth rate of both the function is same.
2. $2^{n+1} \Rightarrow 2.2^n$, Here 2 is constant So function is 2^n. Statement is true.
3. $2^{2n+1} \Rightarrow 2.2^{2n} \Rightarrow 2.4^n$ So $4^n > 2^n$ then $2^{2n+1} \neq O(2^n)$.

13. For large value of y

$$P = P * \frac{x}{i}$$

$$S = S + P$$

When i < y and i + +

$$S = 1 + \frac{x}{1} + \frac{x^2}{21} + \frac{x^3}{31} + ...$$

Hence $S = e^x$

14. Use binary search in the array of number from 1 .... n to check cube of the number matches n (i.e. a[i]* a [i]* a [i] = = n). option (c) is true.

15. The best complexity in worst case for any comparision based sorting technical cannot be less then nlogn.

16. Given program fragment in Pseudo language is

$x = m$;
$y = 1$;
while $(x - y > e)$
$x = (x + y) /2$;
$y = m/x$;
}
Print (x)

This program will find out the square root of m, suppose that m = 2

	X –	Y	X	Y
Ist looping		2	3/2 = 1.5	2/1.5 = 1.33
2nd looping	.16		$\frac{1.5+1.3}{2} = 1.415$	$\frac{2.0}{1.415} = 1.413$
3rd looping	0.02		1.414	1.414
4th looping	0			

as $x - y = 0$ exit from loop hence print 1.414 which is root of 2.

17. Case I :– if A = | 0 | 0 | 0 | 0 | 0 | 0 | 0 | ... |

then always else part is execute so f (wanter) where counter = 0

is executed n times. As given in clvestion complexity of f (o) is O (1) So O (1) + O (1)..... b times ⇒ O (n)

Case II : if A = [1, 1,................1]

the loop execute n time and only if statment is executed hence complexity is O (n).

Case III : if A = [1,0,1,0,1,0..........]

or A = [0,1,0,1,0,1..................]

or any other case.

Both if and else is executed but every time when else part is executed counter is again set to O. Hence complexity is O (n).

18. Recurrence relation for function is

$$T(n) = 2\,T(n-1) + 1$$
$$= 2\,[2T(n-2) + 1] + 1$$
$$= 4\,T(n-2) + 2 + 1$$
$$= 4\,[2T(n-3)+1] + 2 + 1$$
$$= 2^3\,T(n-3) + 2^2 + 2 + 1$$

$2k\,T(n-k) + 2^{K-1} + ---2+1$

put n–k = 1

So $2^{n-1}\,T(1) + 2^{h-2} + ----- 2 + 1$

$\Rightarrow 2^{n-1} + 2^{n-2} + --- 2 + 1$

$\Rightarrow 2^{n-1} \Rightarrow O(2^n)$.

19.
$$T(1) = 1$$
$$T(n) = 2\,T(n-1) + n\ ,\ n \geq 2$$

if n = 2 then

$$T(2) = 2\,T(1) + 2$$
$$= 2 \times 1 + 2 = 4$$

if n = 3 then $T(3) = 2\,T(2) + 3$
$= 2 * 4 + 3 = 11$

Put n = 3 in option (a)

$$2^4 - 3 - 2 = 16 - 3 - 2 = 11$$

so option (a) is true.

20. Given,

$f(n) = O(g(n))$
$g(n) \neq O(f(n))$
$g(n) = O(h(n))$
$h(n) = O(g(n))$

So conclusion is

$f(n) < g(n) = h(n)$ { in terms of growth rate}

So

(a) $f(n) + g(n) = O(h(n) + h(n))$ is true.

(b) $f(n) = O(h(n))$ is true.

(c) $h(n) \neq O(f(n))$ is true.

(d) $f(n) * h(n) \neq O(g(n) * h(n))$ is false.

21. The time complexity of computing the transitive closure of binary relation on a set of n elements is $O(n^3)$.

22. $T(n) = 2T\left(\frac{n}{2}\right) + \sqrt{n}$

Apply master's method

$n^{\log_2^2} \Rightarrow n > \sqrt{n}$

So $\boxed{T(n) = Q(n)}$

23. T (n) = 2 T (n/2) + n

Apply masters method.

$n^{\log_2^2} \Rightarrow n \cong n$

So T (n) = O (nlogn)

Now There growth rate of n^2 and hlogn is greater then and equal to nlogn theme (c) is flase T (n) = 52/ represent lower growth (n^2)

24. Here foo(1) is recursive function. Spare complexity is O (n) as there can be at most O (n) active function at a time.

25. Space complexity is O (n). The space we need array of size O (n). The space required for recursive call would be O (1) as the value would be taken from array again & again.

26. If n is a power of 2, then

$$j = n + \frac{n}{2} + \frac{n}{2} + \text{.............} + \log_2 n \text{ term}$$

If n is not a power of 2, then there will be minor differences of 1 at $\frac{n}{2^i}$ wherever $\frac{n}{2^{i-1}}$ is odd.

Hence val (j) computed on the basis of $n = 2^n$ will give a fair answer

$$j = n + \frac{n}{2} + \text{............}1 \text{ G.P.}$$

$$= \frac{n\left(\left(\frac{1}{2}\right)^{\log n} - 1\right)}{\frac{1}{2} - 1}$$

$$= 2n\left(1 - \frac{1}{2^{\log n}}\right) = 2n\left(1 - \frac{1}{n}\right)$$

$$= 2\,(n-1) = \theta\,(n)$$

27. $T(n) = 2T(\sqrt{n}) + 1$

Put n = 2^K

T (2^K) = 2T (n $^{k/2}$) + 1

replace T (2^k) by S (k)

S(k) = 2 S (k/2) + 1

Apply masters

$K^{\log_2^2} \Rightarrow K > 1$

So Q (k)

Now we know n=2^k, k = $\log_2$ (n)

Then Q (logn)

28. Since, j increases in power of 2's.

if statement $j = j * 2$ executes k times, then

$$2^k \le n$$

$$\Rightarrow \quad k \le \log_2 n$$

Since k will be integer,

total number of comparison

$$= \lfloor \log_2 n \rfloor + 1 \text{ (when loop exits)}$$

29. The given function is recursive so the equivalent recursion equation is

$$T(n) = 1 \quad n \le 2$$

$$T(n) = \lfloor \sqrt{n} \rfloor + n \quad n > 2$$

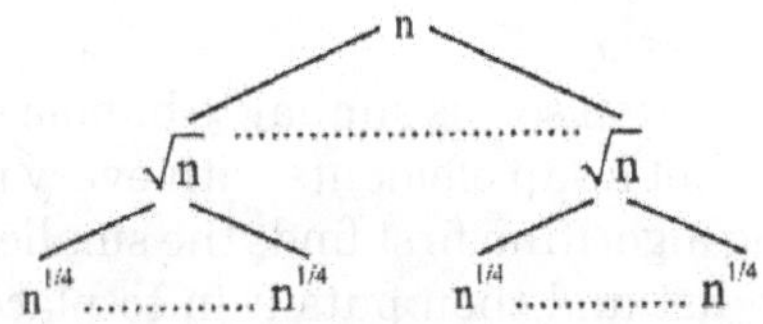

All the level sums are equal to n. The problem size at level k of the recursion tree is n^{2-k} and we stop recursing when this value is a constent. Setting $n^{2^{-k}} = 2$ and solving for k gives us

$$2^{-k} \log_2 n = 1$$

$$\Rightarrow \quad 2^k = \log_2 n$$

$$\Rightarrow \quad k = \log_2 \log_2 n$$

So $\quad T(n) = \theta(\log_2 \log_2 n)$

30. Since,

$2n - c$ = average number of comparison needed.

$1.5\,n - 2$ = number of comparison in case.

$n \log_2 n$ = also doesn't conform with number of comparison needed.

31. Upper bound may be $\sqrt{n}$ times it gets executed. Lower bound may be that if gets executed only once or twice.

32. B & E are exponential functional

so {B, E} > {A, C, D}

* for larger value of n E > B.

* A < C (clearly power is less)

* D < C for larger value of n

So A < D < C < E < B.

33. Given if n = 1 then T (1) = 1

So put n = 1 in all options only option (a) gives 1.

34. f (n) = 2^n

g (n) = n! ≅ n^n

h (n) = n ^{logn}

for larger value of n

g (n) > f (n) > h (n)

so we can conclude that

f (n) = O (g (n)) or g(n) = w(f(n))

and h (n)= Of(n).

35. The minimum number of comparison is logn.

36. Recurrence relation for $f_1()$is

T (n) = 2T (n–1) + 3 T (n–2)

After solving it would be O ((1.6)^n) so the largest value among the options is O(2^n).

f_2 () is simple loop executed n times.

So O (n).

37. Both function preform same operation so result is same 1640 & 1640

38. If there are n elements, then in worst case, total swaps will be (n-1) in selection sort. So the number of swaps is θ(n).

Alternately

The selection sort is similar to bubble sort except it does not swap elements with every move. The sorting algorithm first finds the smallest element in the list and then puts it in to place in single swap. So n swap required for n elements.

39. Applying Master's Theorem

$cn > n^{\ln_3 1}$

$cn > n^0$

Now checking af(n/b) ≤ kf(n) for some k < 1

1*cm/3 ≤ kcn

This is true for k > 1/3

Hence solution is θ(n).

40. B must be preferred on A as

$0.0001\, n^2 < 10\, n \log_{10} n$

$\Rightarrow \quad 10^{-5}\, n < \log_{10} n$

$\Rightarrow \quad 10^{-5} < \log_{10} n^{1/n}$

$\Rightarrow \quad n\, 10^{-5} < \log_{10} n$

We know $\log_{10} n = k$

$\Rightarrow \quad 10^k = t$

$\therefore \quad k > 10^{-5}\, 10k$

$\Rightarrow \quad k > 10^{k-5}$

$\Rightarrow \quad k - 5 > 0$

$\Rightarrow \quad k > 5$

Then min $k = 6$

41. If B(n), XXA(n) and W(n) denote best case , average case and worst case time complexities of an algorithm P respectively then B(n) = O(A(n)), A(n) = O(W(n))

42. Let the three pegs be A,B and C, the goal is to move n pegs from A to C usingpeg B

The following sequence of steps are executed recursively

1. move $n - 1$ discs from A to B. This leaves disc n alone on peg A ..... T(n – 1)
2. move disc n from A to C 1
3. move n – 1 discs from B to C so they sit on disc n T(n – 1)

So, T(n) = 2T(n – 1) + 1

43. So, this is in θ(log n)

Hence Answer is (c)

The outer for-loop goes for $\frac{n}{2}+1$ iterations. The inner for-loop runs independent of the otuer loop.

And for each inner iteration. $\frac{n}{2}$ gets added to k.

∴ Our answer = $\frac{n}{2}$ × # outer loops × #Inner loops per outer loop

Inner loops = θ(log n) $\quad [\because 2^{\theta(\log n)} = \theta(n)]$

$\therefore \quad$ Our answer $= \frac{n}{2} + \left[\frac{n}{2}+1\right] \cdot \theta(\log n) = \theta(n^2 \log n)$

$L_1 = \{0^p 1^q 0^r \mid p, q, r \geq 0\}$

$L_2 = \{0^p 1^q 0^r \mid p, q, r \geq 0, p \neq r\}$

44. Since $f(n) = \log n$

$a = 2, b = 2$

finding $\log_b a$ using master's method = $\log_2 2 = 1$

Hence, $f(n) = n'$

So, T(n) = O(n)

45. The time complexity is O (m+ logn)

So C = 1, d = 0, a = 0, b = 1

0 + 10 × 1 + 100 × 1 + 1000 × 0 = [110]

46. * Outer loop (for i) executed n times.

* Loop (for j) executed logn times so value of p = logn.

loop (for k) executed log p times.

So value of q = log p = log logn.

for every value of i loop (k) is executed so return value is n * log logn

47. Unsorted array

The algorithm perform

find operation (log N)^{½}

Insert operation N

delete operation (log N)^{½}

decrease key operations (log N)^{½}

Hence unsorted array is best data structure for all above operations.

48. The subtrees are already Max-heap, so to make it half, we have to heapify the root, which takes Ω(log n) time.

49. Suppose a list contains n elements, consider first three element and find middle element which will be neither maximum nor minimum.

Hence it is Θ(1) .

50. I or III or IV but not II

as $\sum_{i=0}^{n} i^3 \Rightarrow \frac{n^2(n+1)^2}{4}$,

this can be represent by Q(n^4), O(n^5) 4 Ω (n^3) but not Q(n^5).

51. As $-1 \le \sin x \le 1$, neither of them is true

52. The worst case recurrence reaction for flow chart is

$$T(n) = 5\,T(n/2) + 1$$

Apply master's method

$$n^{\log_2^5} \Rightarrow n^{2.32} > 1$$

$$T(n) = O(n^{2.32})$$

So $\propto = 2.32$

53. Delete operation require O (1) time total O (N) Delete so time is = O (n).

Insert require O (n) time in worst case total O (logn) insert so time is = O (Nlogn) to Search (logn) key time is = nlogn.

To perform decrease key we need O (n) time (because after decrease we need to arrange elements in sorted sequerce) so total O (N) decrease key So total time is O (N^2) All operations put together than worst time is O (N^2)

54. As per the given algorithms and time complexities we derive:

Towers of Hanoi with n disks

$$= 2T(n-1) + 1 = \Theta(2^n)$$

Binary search given n sorted numbers

$$= T(n/2) + 1 = \Theta(\log n)$$

Heap sort given n numbers at the worst case

$$= 2T(n/2) + n = \Theta(n \log n)$$

Addition of two $n \times n$ matrices

$$= 4T(n/2) + 1 = \Theta(n^2)$$

55. $T(n) = 2T\left(\sqrt{n}\right) + 1 \quad n > 2$ ...(*i*)

$$T(n) = 2T\left(\sqrt[2]{n}\right) + 1 \quad \text{...(ii)}$$

Put (*ii*) in (*i*)

$$T(n) = 2 * 2T\left(\sqrt[2]{n}\right) + 2$$

$$T(n) = 2^2 T\left(\sqrt[2]{n}\right) + 2 \quad \text{...(iii)}$$

$$T\left(\sqrt[2]{n}\right) = 2T\left(\sqrt[3]{n}\right) + 1 \quad \text{...(iv)}$$

Substituting (*iv*) in (*iii*)

$$T(n) = 2^3 T\left(\sqrt[3]{n}\right) + 3$$

Running the same till K times,

$$T(n) = 2^K T\left(\sqrt[K]{n}\right) + K$$

$$\sqrt[K]{n} = 2$$

$$K = \log_2 n$$

Solving this will give

$$T(n) = \Theta(\log n)$$

56. By the given C function

First loop will execute 'n' times and the inner loop will execute Θ ($n\log n$) times.

Hence the complexity will be Θ ($n\log n$)

57. 10 = growth is o because constant function

$\sqrt{n}$ = growth is slower but faster than logn.

n = growth is linear.

log n = logarithmic growth.

$\frac{100}{n}$ = growth rate decrease with n.

58. The worst number of probes perform by an best algorithm is $\log_2(31) \cong 5$.

59. T (n) = T (n/2) + n

Apply masters method.

$$n^{\log_2^1} \Rightarrow n^0$$

$$1 < n$$

$T(n) = Q(n)$

60. $T(n) = 3T(n/4) + n$

Apply master's method

$$n^{\log_4^3} < n$$

So Q (n)

61. $T(n) = T(n/2) + \sqrt{n}$

Apply master's method

$$n^{\log_2^1} = n^{\circ} = 1 < \sqrt{n}$$

So $O\left(\sqrt{n}\right)$.

62. A sorting technique is called stable if it maintainy the relative order of occurrale of non distinct elements.

63. The worst case time complexity is O (n^2).

64.

Algorithm	Recurrence Relation
P. Binary Search	IV. T (n) = T (n/2) + 1
Q. Merge Sort	III. T (n) = 2T (n/2) + cn
R. Quick Sort	I. T (n) = T (n-k) + T (K)
S. Tower of Hanoi	II T (n) = 2T (n-1)+1

65. $x = \frac{n}{\log n}$

y = logn

$$\text{we get } O\left(\frac{n}{109n} * \log n * \log\log n\right)$$

So O (n log logn)

66. Merge sort has lowest worst – case complexity, i.e. O(n log n), whereas all remaining three has O(n^2).

67. Recurrence relation for merge sort

T (n) = 2 T (n/2) + n

So T (n) = Q (n logn)

but instead of integers whose comparison take O (1) time, we are given n strings so to compare strings we need Q (n) time hence complexity is Q (n^2 logn)

68. Given: n numbers

To find: Tighest upper bound on number of swaps required to sort n numbers using selection sort.

Nalysis: In selection sort, in the unsorted part of the array, we find the minimum element and swap it with the value placed at the index where the unsorted array starts.

Hence, for each element to put it in its sorted position, we will do some swaps. In each itenation, when we find the minimum and place it in its sorted position, we do only one swap.

There are *n* such iterations, since maximum number of positions to sort is n.

Hence, there are n. 0(1) swaps

⇒ 0(n) swaps.

∴ The solution is (*b*)

69. Worst Case

Insertion sort	→	$O(n^2)$
Merge sort	→	$O(n \log n)$
Quick sort	→	$O(n^2)$

70. 1. Quicksort will take worst case, if the input is in ascending order i.e $\Theta(n^2)$

2. Insertion sort runs in Θ(n) time.

71. Bellman ford = O (n*m)

Kruskal's Alqo = O (m logn)

Floyd war shall = O (n^3)

Topological sort = O (n+m)

72. In case of unweighted, undirected graphs, BFS gives the most time efficient computation for shortest path. It is guaranteed to find first shortest path.

73. Non-increasing order of $\frac{w_i}{t_i}$

74. 20, 24, 30, 35, 50

Step 1 : We take

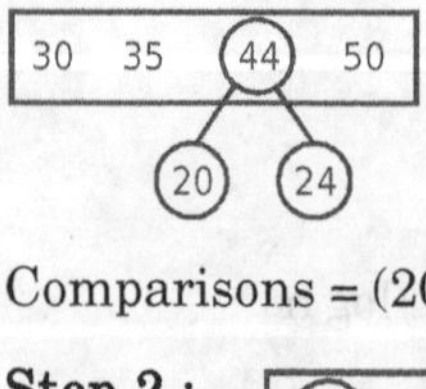

Comparisons = (20 + 24 – 1) Max = 43

Step 2 :

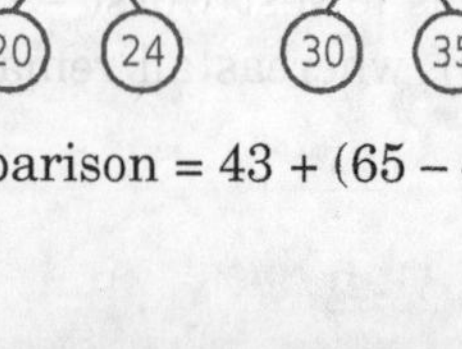

Total comparison = 43 + (65 – 44) = 64

Step 3 :

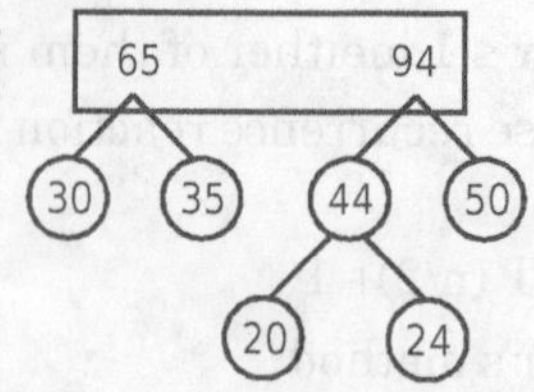

Total comparison = 64 + 19 = 83

Step 4 :

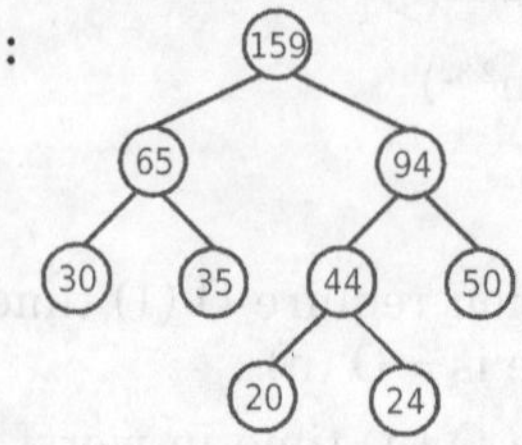

Total comparison = 93 + 65 = 158

= 158 + 93 + 64 + 43 = 358

75. Selection sort = O (n^2)

Insertion sort = O (n^2) or (O(n) in best case)

Binary Search = O (logn)

Merge Sort = O (n logn)

None of the option is true.

76. When we have 'n' numbers stored in an array, we have to swap all positive number with negative number so in worst case positive numbers will be n/2,

77. T (n) = T (n–1)+n ⇒ O (n^2)

T (n) = T (n/2) + n ⇒ O (n)

T (n) = T (n/2) + n logn ⇒ Q (n logn)

T (n) = T (n–1) + logn ⇒ Q ($\log^2$n)

78. There are $\frac{n(n-1)}{2}$ Pairs so average inversions are

$$\frac{n(n-1)}{2} * \frac{1}{2} = \frac{n(n-1)}{4}$$

79. The best algorithm is we can solve in linear time using right to left pass.

80. a_1, a_2 ....a_n

b_1, b_2 ....b_n

In order to find out the largest span, check the sums of

a_i +..........a_j and b_i +............b_j at each step.

If $a_1 + a_2 = b_1 + b_2$ go on, check $a_1 + a_2 + a_3$ and $b_1 + b_2 + b_3$.

If not, then check $a_2 + a_3$ and $b_2 + b_3$

Similarly a check is done at each of the *n* places during traversal. A separate variable has to be kept that contains the maximum span observed hitherto

Hence fastest algorithm computes with (~) (*n*) time and space.

81. T (n) = T (n/2) + n

Apply master's method

$n^{\log_2^1} \Rightarrow n^O \Rightarrow 1$

1 < n

So, Q (n) is value of T (n).

82. Radix sort is counting based sorting technical the time complexity is Q (n).

83. From the list of given n numbers [say n is even], Pick up first two elements, compare them

assign Current – min = min of two numbers

Current – max = max of two numbers

From the remaining n – 2 numbers, take pairs wise and follow this process given below.

1. Compare two elements

   Assign min = min of two numbers

   max = max of two numbers

2. Compare min and current – min

   Assign current – min

   = min{current–min,min}

3. Compare max and current – max

   Assign current – max

   = max{current – max, max}

Repeat above procedure for all the remaining pairs of numbers. We can observe that each of pair requires 3 comparisons

1. for finding min and max
2. For updating current – min
3. for updating current – max

But for initial pair we need only one comparison not 3.

$\therefore$ Total number of comparisons = $\dfrac{3(n-2)}{2}+1$

$$= \frac{3n}{2} - 3 + 1 = \frac{3n}{2} - 2$$

Here n =100, so number of comparisons = 148.

84. Given: n numbers

To find: Tighest upper bound on number of swaps required to sort n numbers using selection sort.

Nalysis: In selection sort, in the unsorted part of the array, we find the minimum element and swap it with the value placed at the index where the unsorted array starts.

Hence, for each element to put it in its sorted position, we will do some swaps. In each itenation, when we find the minimum and place it in its sorted position, we do only one swap.

There are n such iterations, since maximum number of positions to sort is n.

Hence, there are n. 0(1) swaps

$\Rightarrow$ 0(n) swaps.

$\therefore$ The solution is (*b*)

85. Minimum no of swap for selection sort is O when array is already sorted and maximum swap is Q(n).

86. Time complexity of radix sort is = O (nd)

Where n = keys, d = maximum digit in keys.

$$= d = \log(n^k)$$

$$O(nd) = O(n * k \log n)$$

$$= k \times O(n \log n)$$

$$= O(n\log n)$$

87. Let the number of element is "K", they can be sorted in θ(k log k) time.

We try the options in decreasing order of complexity since, we need a tight band i.e. θ

i.e. $\theta(\log n) \cdot \theta\left(\dfrac{(\log n)}{\log\log n}\right), \theta\left(\sqrt{\log n}\right), \ \theta(1)$

So if K ∈ θ(log n) time required for loop sort is. θ(k log k) i.e.

θ(log n × log log n), But this is not in θ(log n)

if $k \in \theta\left(\dfrac{\log n}{\log\log n}\right)$ time required for loop sort:

$$\theta\left(\frac{\log n}{\log\log n} \times \log\left(\frac{\log n}{\log\log n}\right)\right),$$

i.e. $$\theta\left(\log n \times \underbrace{\left[\frac{\log\left(\dfrac{\log n}{\log 1 > n}\right)}{\log\log n}\right]}_{\leq 1}\right)$$

89. It input is in either ascending order or in descending order both are worst case of quick sort Algorithms.

90. If Input is either in ascending order or in descending order both are worst case of quick sort algorithm.

91. T (n) = T (n/2) + T (n/2) + O (n) (for partition)

+ O (n) (for finding median)

On solving above using

Masters Method $\boxed{T(n)=O(n\log n)}$

92. In quicksort a set of number is reduced to sorting two smaller set. We take first element as key value and combine all other with this. A pivot element which splits list into two sublists each of which at least one fifth of element only (B), i.e.

T(n) ≤ T(n/5) + T(4n/5) + n the problem.

Alternately

If one sublist contains 1/5 elements other contains 4/5 elements.

If T(n) number of comparisons for sorting n elements.

So, for 1/5 elements = $T(1/5n)$

and for 4/5 elements = $T(4n/5)$

So, $T(n) \le T(n/5) + T(4n/5) + n$.

Here, n = time to spilt

93. Recurrance relation is

$T(n) = T(n/4) + T(3n/4) + n$

On solving using tree's method.

$\boxed{T(n) = O(n \log n)}$

94. Partition algorithm for quick sort

Partition (A, P, q)// A [P, ...q]

$x \leftarrow$ A [P] // pivot = A [P]

$i \leftarrow$ P

for j = P + 1 to q

do if A [j] $\le x$

then $i \leftarrow i + 1$

exchange A [i] $\leftrightarrow$ A [j]

exchange A [P] $\leftrightarrow$ A [i]

return i [returning where pivot element is there after partitioning]

Recursively call the above algorithm for the two sub arrays [elements before and after pivot element] to complete the sorting.

x = pivot

1 2 3 4 5 $2 \le 1$? NO
i j

1 2 3 4 5 $3 \le 1$? NO
i   j

1 2 3 4 5 $4 \le 1$? NO
i   j

1 2 3 4 5 $5 \le 1$? NO
i   j

exchange A [P] & A [i]

1 2 3 4 5
Pivot (1)   ≥ Pivot (2 3 4 5) — Call recursively for this subarray

↗ Pivot = x = A [B]

1 2 3 4 5 $3 \le 2$? NO
  i j

1 2 3 4 5 $4 \le 2$? NO
  i   j

1 2 3 4 5 $5 \le 2$? NO
  i   j

exchange A [P] & A [J]

1 2 3 4 5
Pivot (2)   ≥ Pivot (3 4 5) — Call recursively for this

↗ x = Pivot = A [P]

1 2 3 4 5 $4 \le 3$? NO
   i j

1 2 3 4 5 $5 \le 3$? NO
   i   j

exchange A [P] & A [i]

1 2 3 4 5
Pivot (3)   ≥ Pivot (4 5)

↗ x = Pivot

1 2 3 4 5 $5 \le 4$? NO
    i j

exchange A [P] & A[i]

1 2 3 4 5
Pivot (4)   ≥ Pivot (5)

$\therefore$ total 10 conparisons

↗ x = Pivot = A [P]

4 1 5 3 2

i j $\quad 1 \le 4$? Yes

$i \leftarrow i + 1$exchange A[i] & A[j] & increment j

4 1 5 3 2

i j $\quad 5 \le 4$? NO

4 1 5 3 2

i j $\quad 3 \le 4$? Yes

$i \leftarrow i + 1$ exchange A[i] & A[j] & increment j

4 1 3 5 2

i j $\quad 2 \le 4$? Yes

$i \leftarrow i + 1$

4 1 3 2 5

i j

exchange A[P] & A[i]

2 1 3 4 5

≤Pivot Pivot ≥Pivot

x = pivot = A (P)

2 1 3 |4| 5

i j $\quad 1 \le 2$? Yes

2 1 3 |4| 5

i j $\quad 3 \le 2$? NO

exchange A [P] & A[i]

1 (2) 3 4 5

Pivot

∴ 6 comparisons

95. The Worst case time complexity of quick sort is O (n^2). This will happen when the elements of the input array are already in order (ascending or descending), irrespective of position of pivot element in array.

96. The recurrence equation is

$$T(n) = T(n-1) + T(1) + cn$$

In quick sort, worst case divide the list into two list with 1 and $(n-1)$ elements each time.

97. When we put (a, left–End, K) and (a+ left – end + 1, n-- left – end –1, k– left–end –1)at the place of fill in the blank alqorithm work for partition.

98. Complexity is remain same because we had swap after finding to position of element so in worst case swapirg for each element requires Q (n) time hence complexihy is O (n^2).

99. If array of size n with n inversion then complexity of insation sort is Q (n)

Let us take an example.

(6 1 2 3 5 6 4)

total no. of comparision require to

Sort above array is 2 (n–1) = 2* 5 = 10

so complexity is Q (n).

100. If we take example, 40, 30, 10, 12, 85, 48, 9, 16

Next step : 30,40, 10, 12, 35, 48, 9, 16

Next step : 10, 12, 30, 40, 9, 16, 35, 48

101. We use merge sorting and finally we get comparison $O(m+n)$

102. Array is

20 , 47 , 15 , 8 , 9 , 4 , 40 , 30 , 12 , 17

After 1st pass

20 , 47 , 8 , 15 , 4 , 9 , 30 , 40 , 12 , 17

After 2nd pass

8 , 15 , 20 , 47 , 4 , 9 , 30 , 40 , 12 , 17

103. Time complexty is O (nlogn)

C * 64 log 64 = 30

(C = 5/14)

for 6 minuts

$$\frac{5}{64} * n \log n = 6 * 60 \Rightarrow [n = 512]$$

104. A – R, B–P, C–S, D–Q

105. $\text{Minimum Comparisons} = \lceil \log(n!) \rceil$

$$= \lceil \log(120) \rceil = 7$$

106. A – 3

B – 4

C – 1

D – 2

107. Union & intersection is Slowest opeeration among all.

108. The statement inside the for loop is similar to X–OR operation such that the set obtained is $(X \cap Y') \cup (X' \cap Y)$.

It is equivalent to $\quad (X - Y) \cup (Y - X)$.

109. By definition, T(9) = Dist. From 9 to 100

As given, T(9) = 1+min (T(y), T()(z) = 1 + min (Dist. from y to 100, Dist. From z to 100)

⇒ 1 = Dist. from 9 to y/Dist. From 9 to z

⇒ There are only two such values-one is the simple one step on number line i.e. 10, and the other is the shortcut associated with 9 i.e. 15.

⇒ Therefore, *y* and *z* are 10 and 15 (in any order)

⇒ Product $yz = 150$.

110. Prims algorithm is greedy method because it choose minimum distance node.

Floyd warshal's is dynamic because it changes the distance on each iteration.

Merge sort is divide and conquer because it divide the hole list is sublist and combine after sorting each sublist Hamiltonian cycle is based on backtracking.

111. Dijkstra use gready approach, warshals use dynamic programming approach, Binary search is based on divide and conquer and Back tracking is depth first search.

112. P – (ii)

Cl – (i)

R – (iii)

113. Dynamic programming

114. Suppose we want to search y.

No of comparision

= 1× Probability of 1st element being x

+ 2 * Probability of 2nd element beig x.

+ 3* Probability of 3rd element bing x.

+ n* Probability of nth element being x.

$$= \frac{1}{n} + \frac{2}{n} + \frac{3}{n} + \ldots\ldots\ldots\ldots \frac{h}{n}$$

$$= \frac{\frac{n(n+1)}{2}}{n}$$

$$\Rightarrow \frac{n+1}{2}$$

2

CHAPTER

Advance Data

Analysis of Previous GATE Papers

Units	Year → Topics ↓		2019	2018	2017 Set 1	2017 Set 2	2016 Set 1	2016 Set 2	2015 Set 1	2015 Set 2	2015 Set 3
BINARY SEARCH TREE	1 Mark	MCQ Type							1		
		Numerical Type									
	2 Marks	MCQ Type									
		Numerical Type									
	Total								1		
HASHING	1 Mark	MCQ Type									
		Numerical Type									
	2 Marks	MCQ Type									
		Numerical Type									
	Total										
RECURSIVE CALLING	1 Mark	MCQ Type									
		Numerical Type									
	2 Marks	MCQ Type									
		Numerical Type									
	Total										
AVL	1 Mark	MCQ Type									
		Numerical Type									
	2 Marks	MCQ Type									
		Numerical Type									
	Total										
BINARY TREE	1 Mark	MCQ Type									
		Numerical Type									
	2 Marks	MCQ Type									
		Numerical Type	1								
	Total		2								
BREADTH FIRST TRAVERSAL	1 Mark	MCQ Type									
		Numerical Type									
	2 Marks	MCQ Type									
		Numerical Type									
	Total										
B TREE	1 Mark	MCQ Type									
		Numerical Type									
	2 Marks	MCQ Type									
		Numerical Type									
	Total										
HEAP	1 Mark	MCQ Type									
		Numerical Type									
	2 Marks	MCQ Type	1								
		Numerical Type									
	Total		2								

BINARY SEARCH TREE

1. The recurrence relation that arises in relation with the complexity of binary search is

(a) $T(n) = T(n/2) + k$, k is a constant

(b) $T(n) = 2T(n/2) + k$, k is a constant

(c) $T(n) = T(n/2) + \log n$

(d) $T(n) = T(n/2) + n$

[1994 : 2 Marks]

2. What are the worst-case complexities of insertion and deletion of a key in a binary search tree?

(a) $\Theta(\log n)$ for both insertion and deletion

(b) $\Theta(n)$ for both insertion and deletion

(c) $\Theta(n)$ for insertion and $\Theta(\log n)$ for deletion

(d) $\Theta(\log n)$ for insertion and $\Theta(n)$ for deletion

[2015 (Set-1) : 1 Mark]

HASHING

3. Which of the folio wing statements is true?

I. As the number of entries in a hash table increases, the number of collisions increases.

II. Recursive programs are efficient

III. The worst case complexity for Quicksort is $O(n^2)$

IV. Binary search using a linear linked list is efficient.

(a) I and II

(b) II and III

(c) I and IV

(d) I and III

[1995 : 1 Mark]

RECURSIVE CALLING

4. In the following C function, let n > m. int gcd (n, m)

```
{  if (n%m = = 0} return m;
   n = n%m;
   return gcd (m, n);
}
```

How many recursive calls are made by this function?

(a) $\Theta(\log_2 n)$

(b) $\Omega(n)$

(c) $\Theta(\log_2 \log_2 n)$

(d) $\Theta\left(\sqrt{n}\right)$

[2007 : 2 Marks]

AVL

5. The worst case running time to search for an element in a balanced binary search tree with $n2^n$ elements is

(a) $\Theta(n \log n)$ (b) $\Theta(n2^n)$

(c) $\Theta(n)$ (d) $\Theta(\log n)$

[2012 : 1 Mark]

6. A program takes as input a balanced binary search tree with n leaf nodes and computes the value of a function g(x) for each node x. If the cost of computing g(x) is min(number of leaf-nodes in left-subtree of x, number of leaf-nodes in right-subtree of x) then the worst case time complexity of the program is

(a) $\Theta(n)$ (b) $O(n \log n)$

(c) $O(n)^2$ (d) $O(2^n)$

[2004 : 2 Marks]

BINARY TREE

7. The weighted external path length of the binary tree in figure is

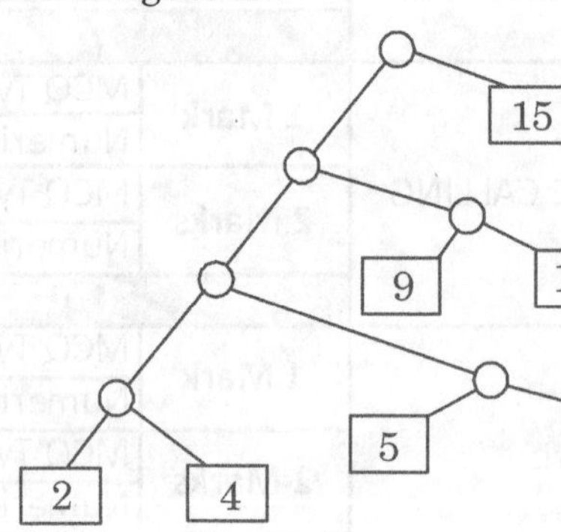

[1991 : 2 Marks]

8. A scheme for storing binary trees in an array X is as follows. Indexing of X starts at 1 instead of 0. The root is stored at X[1]. For a node stored at X[i], the left child, if any, is stored in X[2i] and the right child, if any, in X[2i + 1]. To be able to store any binary tree on n vertices, the minimum size of X should be

(a) $\log_2 n$ (b) n

(c) 2n + 1 (d) 2n

[2006 : 1 Mark]

9. Let T be a full binary tree with 8 leaves. (A full binary tree has every level full.) Suppose two leaves a and b of T are chosen uniformly and independently at random. The expected value of the distance between a and b in T(i.e., the number of edges in the unique path between a and b) is (rounded off to 2 decimal places) _______.

[2019 : 2 Marks]

BREADTH FIRST TRAVERSAL

10. Consider the tree arcs of a BFS traversal from a source node W in an unweighted, connected, undirected graph. The tree Tformed by the tree arcs is a data structure for computing

(a) the shortest path between every pair of vertices.

(b) the shortest path from Wto every vertex in the graph.

(c) the shortest paths from Wto only those nodes that are leaves of T.

(d) the longest path in the graph.

[2014 (Set-2) : 1 Mark]

B TREE

11. A B-tree of order 4 is built from scratch by 10 successive insertions. What is the maximum number of node splitting operations that may take place?

(a) 3 (b) 4

(c) 5 (d) 6

[2008 : 2 Marks]

HEAP

12. The minimum number of interchanges needed to convert the array

89,19,40,17,12,10,2, 5, 7,11,6,9, 70 into a heap with maximum element at the root is

(a) 0 (b) 1

(c) 2 (d) 3

[1996 : 2 Marks]

13. Consider any array representation of an n element binary heap where the elements are stored from index 1 to index n of the array. For the element stored at index i of the array ($i \le n$), the index of the parent is

(a) i - 1

(b) $\left\lfloor \frac{i}{2} \right\rfloor$

(c) $\left\lceil \frac{i}{2} \right\rceil$

(d) $\frac{(i+1)}{2}$

[2001 : 1 Mark]

14. Consider the following statements:

I. The smallest element in a max-heap is always at a leaf node

II. The second largest element in a max-heap is always a child of the root node

III. A max-heap can be constructed from a binary search tree in $\Theta(n)$ time

IV. A binary search tree can be constructed from a max-heap in $\Theta(n)$ time

Which of the above statements are true?

(a) I, II and III

(b) II, III and IV

(c) I, III and IV

(d) I, II and IV

[2019 : 12 Marks]

ANSWERS

1. (*a*) 2. (*b*) 3. (*d*) 4. (*a*) 5. (*c*) 6. (*a*) 7. (52) 8. (*d*) 9. (4.85) 10. (*b*)

11. (*a*) 12. (*c*) 13. (*b*) 14. (*a*)

EXPLANATIONS

1. In binary search once checked with middle value the list is break into two sublist so $T(n) = T\frac{n}{2}$ + constant time in comparing and finding mid element.
2. Both insertion and deletion of a key is a binary search tree is Q(n) in worst case as both are worst case of BST will take Q(n) for insertion and deletion.

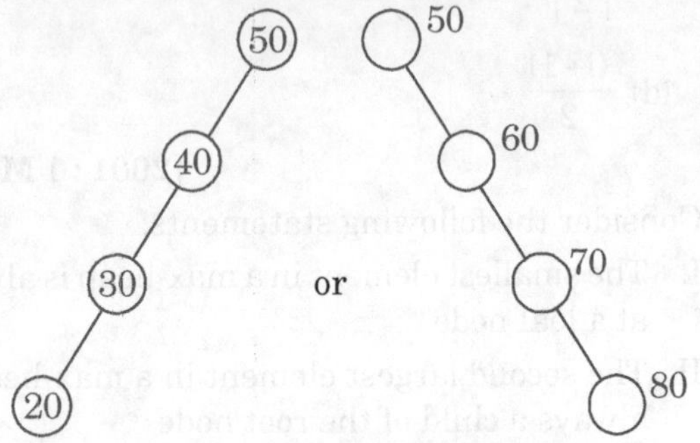

3. * In worst case complexity is O (n^2)
   * In best case complexity is O (n logn)
   In Hash table, = given value mode n
4. Let T (m, n) be the total number of steps.
   So T(m, 0) = 0 T(m, n) = 1 (n, m nod n) on average

$$T_n = \frac{1}{n}\sum_{0\le k\le n} T(k, n)$$

$$T_n \approx 1 + \frac{1}{n}(T_0\, T_1 + \ldots + T_{n-1})$$

$$T_n \approx S_n$$

$$S_n = 1 + \frac{1}{n}(S_0\, S_1 + \ldots + S_{n-1})$$

$$S_n = 1 + \frac{1}{n+1}(S_0\, S_1 + \ldots + S_n)$$

$$= 1 + \frac{1}{n+1}(n(S_{n-1}) + S_n)$$

$$= 1 + \frac{1}{n+1} = S_n + \frac{1}{n+1}$$

So $T_n \approx \theta(\log_2 n + 0(1)$
$T \approx \theta(\log_2 n)$

5. The worst case running time of search in BST is log n where n is total number of elements in the tree. The total number of elements are n. 2^n thus search R. T. will be long (n. 2^n).
6. g(x) is min {No. of leaf node in left subtree, of x No. of leaf node in right subtree of x}
   In balanced binary subtree worst case time complexity in O(n)
7.

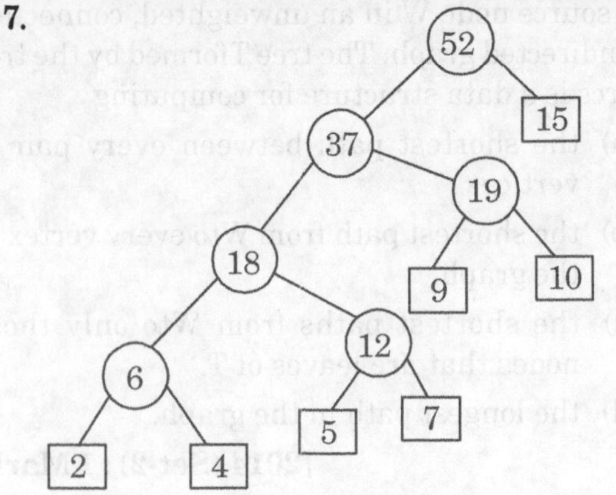

8. In case of complete binary tree total size = no. of element in tree.

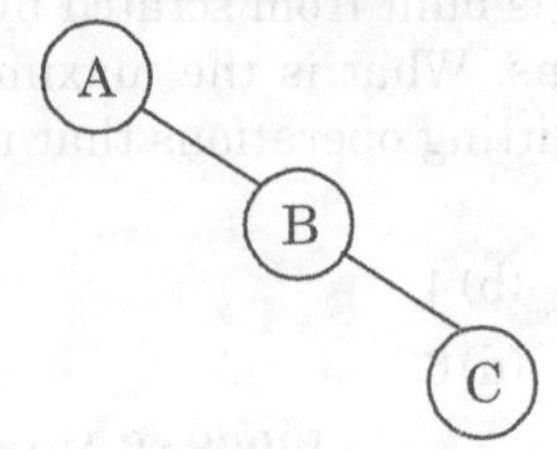

1	2	3	4	5	6	7
A	Null	B	Null	Null	Null	C

X[1] = A
X[3] = B
X[7] = C
So total size = $2^n - 1$

9. Two nodes can be selected in $^8C_2 = 28$ ways

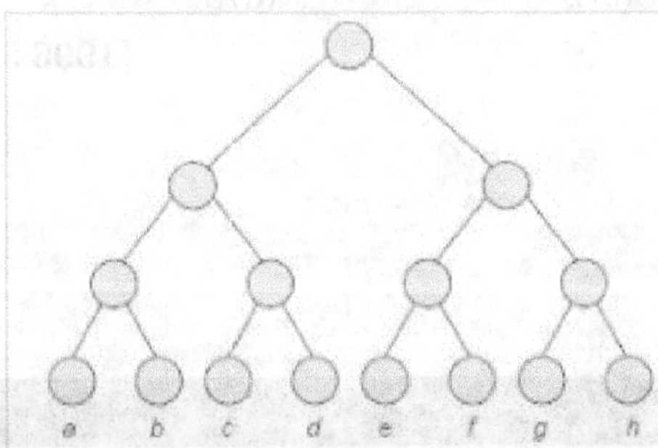

Where X is length between two nodes selected

X	2	4	6
P(x)	$\frac{4}{28}$	$\frac{8}{28}$	$\frac{16}{28}$

Expected length between a and b is given by

$$E[X] = 2\left(\frac{4}{28}\right) + 4\left(\frac{8}{28}\right) + 6\left(\frac{16}{28}\right)$$

$$= \frac{8+32+96}{28} = \frac{136}{28} = 4.857$$

10.

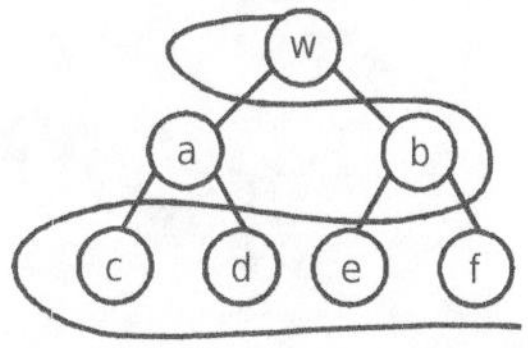

Shortest path from *w* to every vertex in graph.

11. A B-tree of order 4. All internal nodes except root have at most 4 children and at least 2 children. For 10 instruction, it will stake 3 node splitting operation.

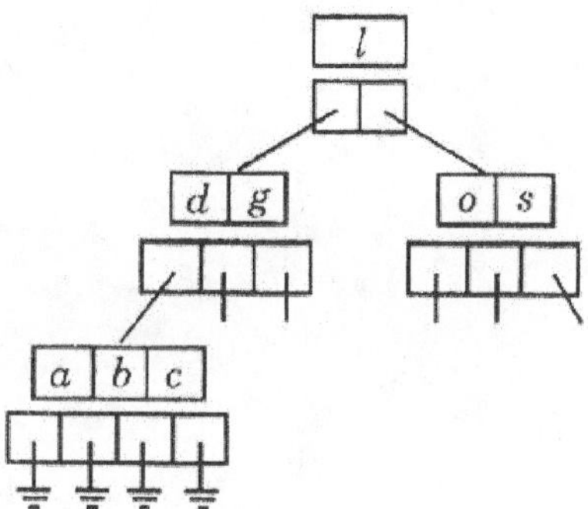

Alternately

Order 4-B tree can have maximum 3 keys in one node and each node have max 4 children so lets take values 84, 82, 29, 99, 65, 12, 50, 28, 58, 71

Inserting 84, 82, 29 | 29, 82, 84 |

Inserting 99

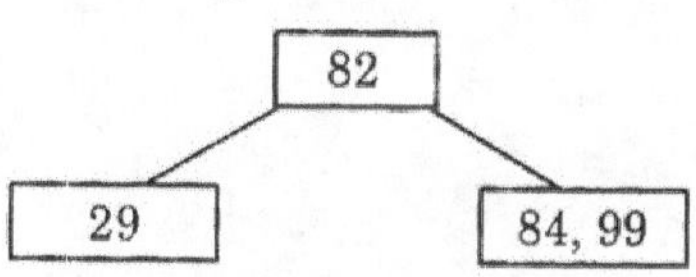

1st Splitting

Inserting 65, 12

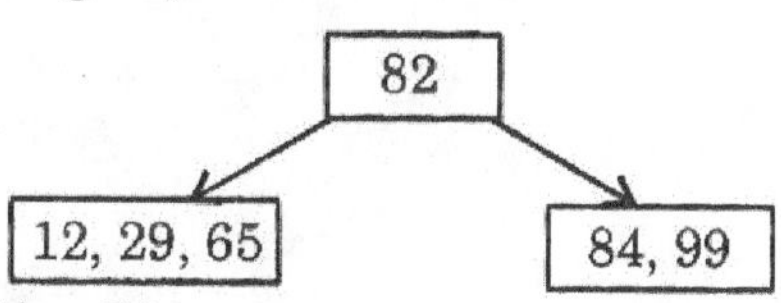

Inserting 50

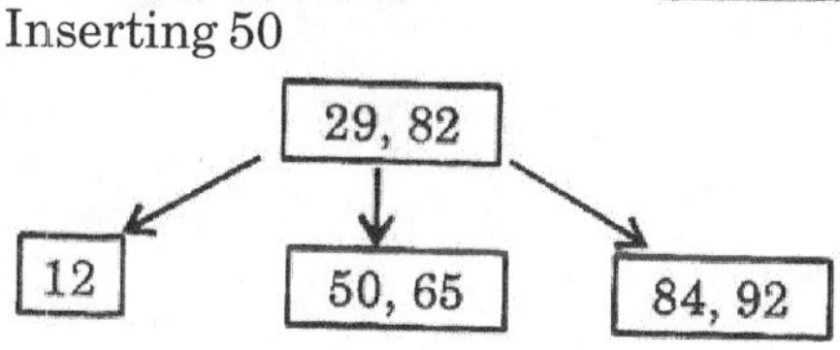

2nd Splitting

Inserting 28, 58

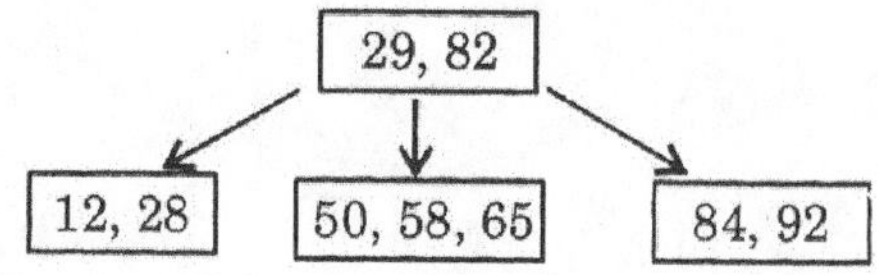

Inserting 71

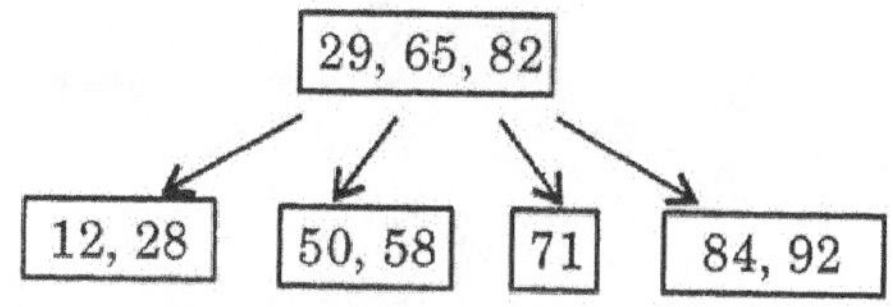

3rd Splitting

For any sequence of insertion, maximum spilliting is 3.

12. With heap sort,

⇒ 89, (19) 40, 17, 12, 10, 2, 5, 7, 11, 6, 9, (70)

⇒ 89, 70 40, 17, 12, 10, (2), 5, 7, 11, 6, 9, (19)

⇒ 89, 70 40, 17, 12, 10, 19, 5, 7, 11, 6, 9, 2

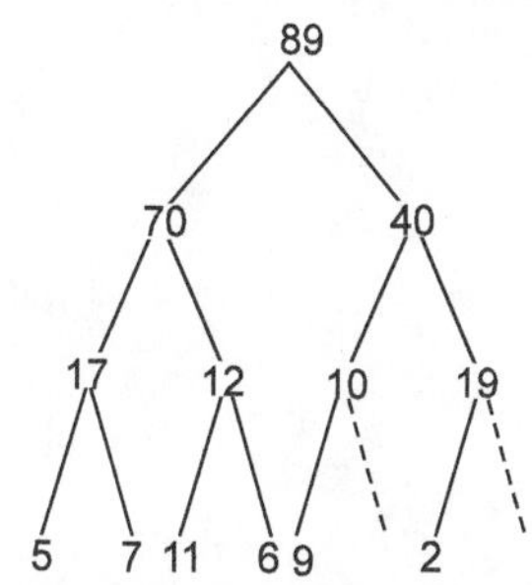

Minimum two interchanged.

13. Binary heap can be represented using arrays storing elements in an array and using their relative positions within the array to represent child-parent relationships.

For the binary heap element stored at index i of the array,

Parent Node will be at index floor $\left(\frac{i}{2}\right)$

Left Child will be at index: 2i

Right child will be at index: 2*i + i

3 CHAPTER

Divide & Conquer and Greedy Method

Analysis of Previous GATE Papers

Units	Year → Topics ↓		2019	2018	2017 Set 1	2017 Set 2	2016 Set 1	2016 Set 2	2015 Set 1	2015 Set 2	2015 Set 3
GRAPH	1 Mark	MCQ Type									
		Numerical Type									
	2 Marks	MCQ Type									
		Numerical Type					1				
	Total						2				
KRUSKAL	1 Mark	MCQ Type									
		Numerical Type									
	2 Marks	MCQ Type									
		Numerical Type									
	Total										
DI JKASTRA	1 Mark	MCQ Type									
		Numerical Type									
	2 Marks	MCQ Type									
		Numerical Type									
	Total										
MST	1 Mark	MCQ Type					2				
		Numerical Type	1								
	2 Marks	MCQ Type			1						
		Numerical Type		1			1		1		
	Total		1	2	2		4		2		
PRIME'S	1 Mark	MCQ Type									
		Numerical Type									
	2 Marks	MCQ Type									
		Numerical Type									
	Total										
GREEDY CONCEPT	1 Mark	MCQ Type									
		Numerical Type									
	2 Marks	MCQ Type									
		Numerical Type		1							
	Total			2							
POLYNOMIAL MULTI PLICATION	1 Mark	MCQ Type									
		Numerical Type									
	2 Marks	MCQ Type									
		Numerical Type									
	Total										
HUFFMANN CODING	1 Mark	MCQ Type									
		Numerical Type									
	2 Marks	MCQ Type									
		Numerical Type				1					
	Total					2					
BELLMAN FORD	1 Mark	MCQ Type									
		Numerical Type									
	2 Marks	MCQ Type									
		Numerical Type									
	Total										
MATRIX CHAIN MULTIPLICATION	1 Mark	MCQ Type									
		Numerical Type									
	2 Marks	MCQ Type		1							
		Numerical Type						1			
	Total			2				2			

GRAPH

1. Which one of the follovving statements is false?

(a) Optimal binary search tree construction can be performed efficiently using dynamic programming

(b) Breadth-first search cannot be used to find connected components of a graph

(c) Given the prefix and postfix walks over a binary tree, the binary tree cannot be uniquely constructed

(d) Depth-first search can be used to find connected components of a graph

[1994 : 2 Marks]

2. Consider the weighted undirected graph given by with 4 vertices, where the weight of edge {i, j} is the entry W_{ij} in the matrix W.

$$W = \begin{bmatrix} 0 & 2 & 8 & 5 \\ 2 & 0 & 5 & 8 \\ 8 & 5 & 0 & x \\ 5 & 8 & x & 0 \end{bmatrix}$$

The largest possible integer value of x, for which at least one shortest path betvveen some pair of vertices will contain the edge with weight x is ________ . **[2016 (Set-1): 2 Marks]**

3. The number of articulation points of the folio wing graph is

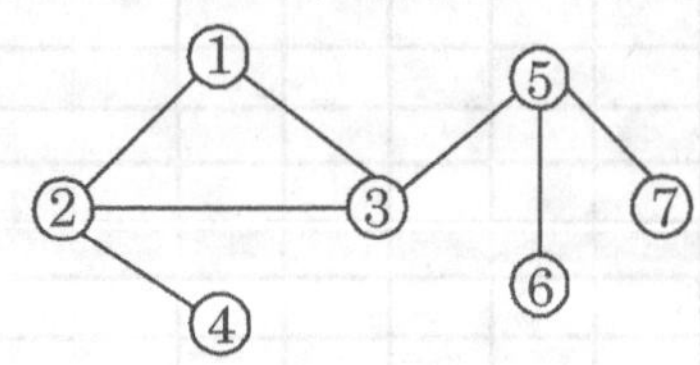

(a) 0 (b) 1

(c) 2 (d) 3

[1999 : 1 Mark]

4. Which of the following is the correct decomposition of the directed graph given below into its strongly connected components?

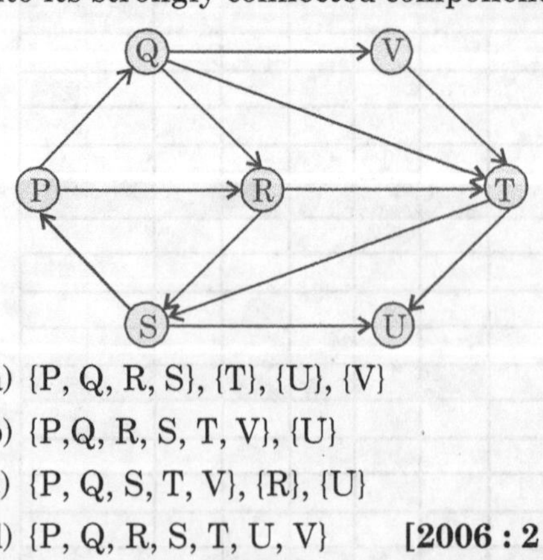

(a) {P, Q, R, S}, {T}, {U}, {V}

(b) {P,Q, R, S, T, V}, {U}

(c) {P, Q, S, T, V}, {R}, {U}

(d) {P, Q, R, S, T, U, V} **[2006 : 2 Marks]**

5. Consider the directed graph given below.

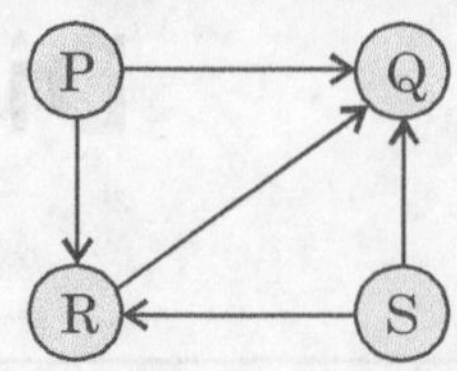

Which one of the following is TRUE?

(a) The graph does not have any topological ordering.

(b) Both PQRS and SRQP are topological orderings.

(c) Both PSRQ and SPRQ are topological orderings.

(d) PSRQ is the only topological ordering.

[2014 (Set-1) : 1 Mark]

KRUSKAL

6. Kruskal's algorithm for finding a minimum spanning tree of a weighted graph G with n vertices and m edges has the time complexity of

(a) $O(n^2)$ (b) O(mn)

(c) O(m + n) (d) O(mlogn)

(e) $O(m^2)$

[1991 : 2 Marks]

7. Complexity of Kruskal's algorithm for finding the minimum spanning tree of an undirected graph containing n vertices and m edges if the edges are sorted is ________.

[2002 : 2 Marks]

8. Consider the following graph:

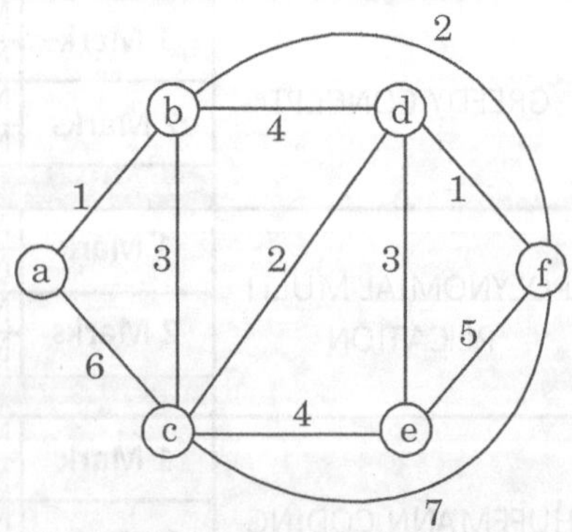

Which one of the following cannot be the sequence of edges added, in that order, to a minimum spanning tree using Kruskal's algorithm?

(a) (a-b),(d-f),(b-f),(d-c),(d-e)

(b) (a-b),(d-f),(d-c),(b-f),(d-e)

(c) (d-f),(a-b),(d-c),(b-f),(d-e)

(d) (d-f),(a-b),(b-f),(d-e),(d-c)

[2006 : 2 Marks]

9. Consider the following graph:

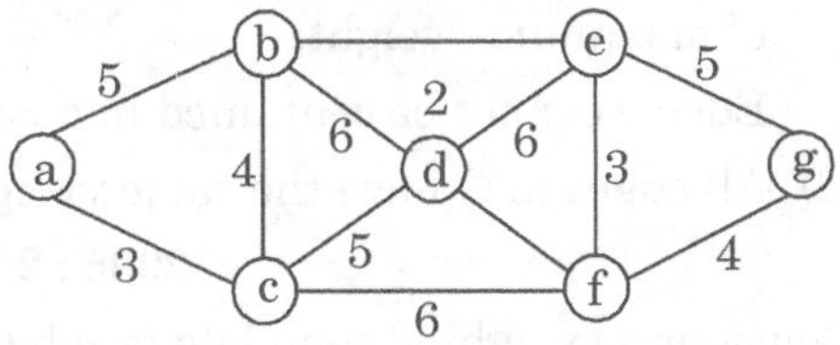

Which one of the following is NOT the sequence of edges added to the minimum spanning tree using Kruskal's algorithm?

(a) (b, e) (e, f) (a, c) (b, c) (f, g) (c, d)

(b) (b, e) (e, f) (a, c) (f, g) (b, c) (c, d)

(c) (b, e) (a, c) (e, f) (b, c) (f, g) (c, d)

(d) (b, e) (e, f) (b, c) (a, c) (f, g) (c, d)

[2009 : 2 Marks]

DIJKASTRA

10. Suppose we run Dijkstra's single source shortest-path algorithm on the following edge-weighted directed graph with vertex P as the source.

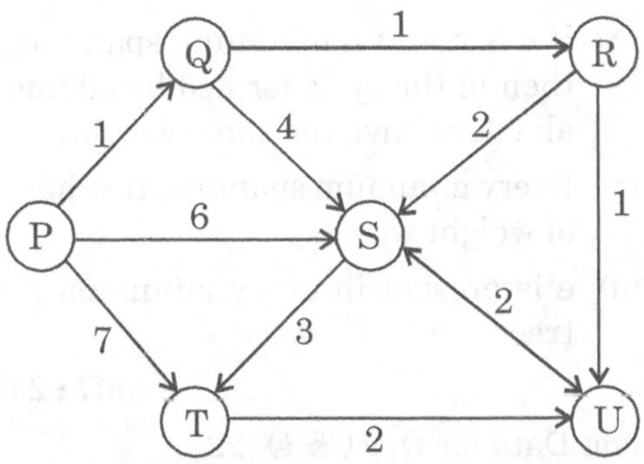

In what order do the nodes get included into the set of vertices for which the shortest path distances are finalized?

(a) P, Q, R, S, T, U

(b) P, Q, R, U, S, T

(c) P, Q, R, U, T, S

(d) P, Q, T, R, U, S

[2004 : 2 Marks]

11. Let G (V, E) an undirected graph with positive edge weights. Dijkstra's single source-shortest path algorithm can be implemented using the binary heap data structure vvith time complexity?

(a) $O(|V|^2)$

(b) $O(|E| + |V|\log|V|)$

(c) $O(|V|\log|V|)$

(d) $O((|E| + |V|)\log|V|)$

[2005 : 2 Marks]

Common Data for Q. 13 & Q. 14

We are given 9 tasks $T_1, T_2 \ldots T_9$. The execution of each task requires one unit of time. We can execute one task at a time. T_i has a profit P_i and a deadline d_i profit P_i is earned if the task is completed before the end of the d_i^{th} unit of time.

Task	T_1	T_2	T_3	T_4	T_5	T_6	T_7	T_8	T_9
Profit	15	20	30	18	18	10	23	16	25
Deadline	7	2	5	3	4	5	2	7	3

12. To implement Dijkstra's shortest path algorithm on unweighted graphs so that it runs in linear time, then data structure to be used is

(a) Queue (b) Stack

(c) Heap (d) B-Tree

[2006 : 1 Mark]

13. Dijkstra's single source shortest path algorithm when run from vertex a in the below graph, computes the corrects shortest path distance to

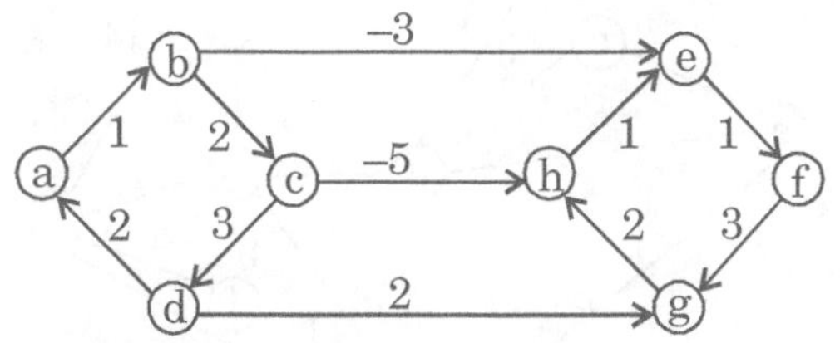

(a) only vertex a

(b) only vertices a, e, f, g, h

(c) only vertices, a, b, c, d

(d) ali the vertices **[2008 : 2 Marks]**

14. Consider the directed graph shown in the figure below. There are multiple shortest paths between vertices S and T. Which one will be reported by Dijkstra's shortest path algorithm? Assume that, in any iteration, the shortest path to a vertex v is updated only when a strictly shorter path to v is discovered.

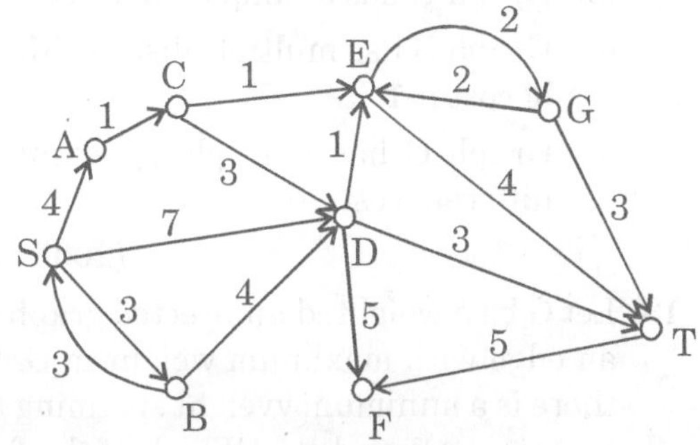

(a) SDT (c) SACDT

(b) SVDT (d) SACET

[2012 : 2 Marks]

MST

15. Let G be an undirected connected graph with distinct edge weights. Let e_{max} be the edge with maximum weight and e_{min} the edge with minimum weight. Which of the following statements is false?

(a) Every minimum spanning tree of G must contain e_{min}

(b) If e_{max} is in a minimum spanning tree, then its removal must disconnect G

(c) No minimum spanning tree contains e_{max}

(d) G has a unique minimum spanning tree

[2002 : 2 Marks]

16. What is the weight of a minimum spanning tree of the foliowing graph?

(a) 29 (b) 31

(c) 38 (d) 41

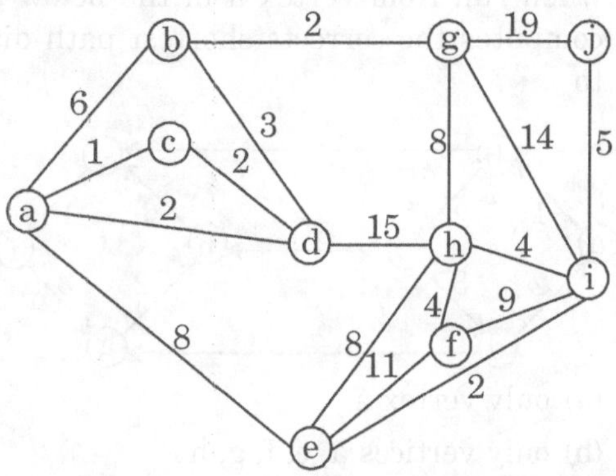

[2003 : 2 Marks]

17. A undirected graph G has n nodes. Its adj acency matrix is given by an n x n square matrix whose

1. diagonal elements are 0's, and
2. non-diagonal elements are l's.

Which one of the follovving is TRUE?

(a) Graph G has no minimum spanning tree (MST)

(b) Graph G has a unique MST of cost n-1

(c) Graph G has multiple distinct MST's, each of cost n-1

(d) Graph G has multiple spanning trees of different costs

[2005 : 1 Mark]

18. Let G be a weighted undirected graph and e be an edge with maximum weight in G. Suppose there is a minimum vveight spanning tree in G containing the edge e. Which of the follovving statements is always TRUE?

(a) There exists a cutset in G having all edges of maximum vveight.

(b) There exists a cycle in G having all edges of maximum vveight.

(c) Edge e cannot be contained in a cycle.

(d) All edges in G have the same vveight.

[2005 : 2 Marks]

19. Consider a vveighted complete graph G on the vertex set $\{v_1, v_2, ..., v_n\}$ such that the weight of the edge (v_i, v_j) is $2 \mid i - j \mid$. The weight of a minimum spanning tree of G is

(a) $n - 1$ (b) $2n - 2$

(c) $\binom{n}{2}$ (d) n^2

[2006 : 1 Mark]

20. Let w be the minimum weight among ali edge weights in an undirected connected graph. Let e be a specific edge of weight w. Which of the follovving is FALSE?

(a) There is a minimum spanning tree containing e.

(b) If e is not in a minimum spanning tree T, then in the cycle formed by adding e to T, ali edges have the same weight.

(c) Every minimum spanning tree has an edge of weight w;

(d) e is present in every minimum spanning tree

[2007 : 2 Marks]

Common Data for Q. 21 & Q. 22

Suppose the letters a, b, c, d, e have probabilities $\frac{1}{2}, \frac{1}{4}, \frac{1}{8}, \frac{1}{16}, \frac{1}{32}$ respectively.

21. For the undirected, weighted graph given below, which of the follovving sequences of edges represents a correct execution of Prim's algorithm to construct a Minimum Spanning Tree?

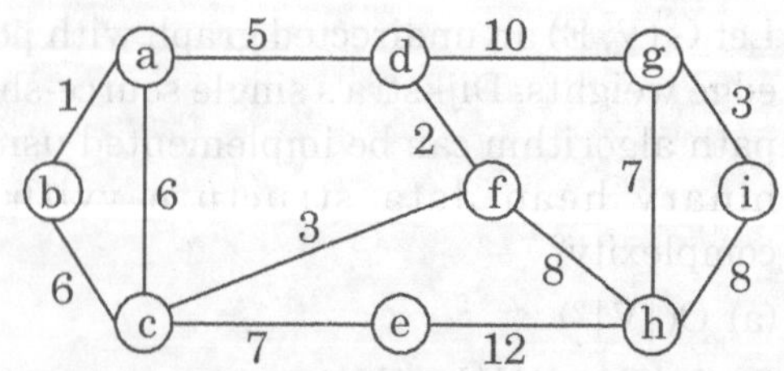

(a) (a, b), (d, f), (f, c), (g, i), (d, a), (g, h), (c, e), (f, h)

(b) (c, e), (c, f), (f, d), (d, a), (a, b), (g, h), (h, f), (g, i)

(c) (d, f), (f, c), (d, a), (a, b), (c, e), (f, h), (g, h), (g, i)

(d) (h, g), (g, i), (h, f), (f, c), (f, d), (d, a), (a, b), (c, e)

[2008 : 2 Marks]

22. G is a graph on n vertices and 2n - 2 edges. The edges of G can be partitioned into two edge-disjoint spanning trees. Which of the follovving is NOT true for G?

(a) For every subset of k vertices, the induced subgraph has a most 2k - 2 edges.

(b) The minimum cut in G has a least two edges

(c) There are two edges-disjoint paths between every pair of vertices

(d) There are two vertex-disjoint paths between every pair of vertices.

[2008 : 2 Marks]

23. The weight of a sequence a_0, a_1 ..., a_{n-1} of real numbers is defined as $a_0 + a_1/2 + ... a_{n-1}/2^{n-1}$. A subsequence of a sequence is obtained by deleting some elements from the sequence, keeping the order of the remaining elements the same. Let X denote the maximum possible weight of a subsequence of $a_0, a_1, \ldots, a_{n-1}$ and Y the maximum possible weight of a subsequence of a_1 a_2, ..., a_{n-1}. Then X is equal to

(a) $\max(Y, a_0 + Y)$

(b) $\max(Y, a_0 + Y/2)$

(c) $\max(Y, a_0 + 2Y)$

(d) $a_0 + Y/2$

[2010 : 2 Marks]

Common Data for Questions 24 and 25

Consider a complete undirected graph with vertex set {0, 1, 2, 3, 4}. Entry W_{ij} in the matrix W below is the weight of the edge {i, j}.

$$W = \begin{pmatrix} 0 & 1 & 8 & 1 & 4 \\ 1 & 0 & 12 & 4 & 9 \\ 8 & 12 & 0 & 7 & 3 \\ 1 & 4 & 7 & 0 & 2 \\ 4 & 9 & 3 & 2 & 0 \end{pmatrix}$$

24. What is the minimum possible weight of a spanning tree T in this graph such that vertex 0 is a leaf node in the tree T?

(a) 7 (b) 8

(c) 9 (d) 10

[2010 : 2 Marks]

25. What is the minimum possible weight of a path P from vertex 1 to vertex 2 in this graph such that P contains at most 3 edges?

(a) 7 (b) 8

(c) 9 (d) 10

[2010 : 2 Marks]

Linked Data Question 33 and 34

An undirected graph G(V, E) contains n(n > 2) nodes named $v_1, v_2, ..., v_n$. Two nodes v_i, v_j are connected if andonly if $0 < |i - j| \leq 2$. Each edge (v_i, v_j) is assigned a weight i + j. A sample graph with n = 4 is shown below.

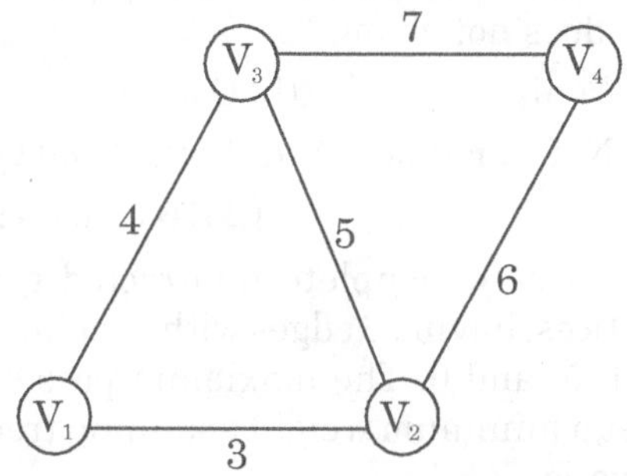

26. What will be the cost of the Minimum Spanning Tree (MST) of such a graph with n nodes?

(a) $\frac{1}{12}(11n^2 - 5n)$ (b) $n^2 - n + 1$

(c) 6n – 11 (d) 2n + 1

[2011 : 2 Marks]

27. The length of the path from v_5 to v_6 in the MST of previous question with n = 10 is

(a) 11 (b) 25

(c) 31 (d) 41 **[2011 : 2 Marks]**

28. Let G be a weighted graph with edge weights greater than one and G' be the graph constructed by squaring the weights of edge in G. Let T and T' be the minimum spanning trees of G and G' respectively, with total weights t and t'. Which of the following statements is TRUE?

(a) T' = T with total weight $t' = t^2$

(b) T' = T with total weight $t' < t^2$

(c) T' ≠ T but total weight $t' = t^2$

(d) None of the above

[2012 : 2 Marks]

29. The graph shown below has 8 edges with distinct integer edge weights. The minimum spanning tree (MST) is of weight 36 and contains the edges: {(A, C), (B, C), (B, E), (E, F), (D, F)}. The edge weights of only those edges which are in the MST are given in the figure shown below. The minimum possible sum of weights of all 8 edges of this graph is _______.

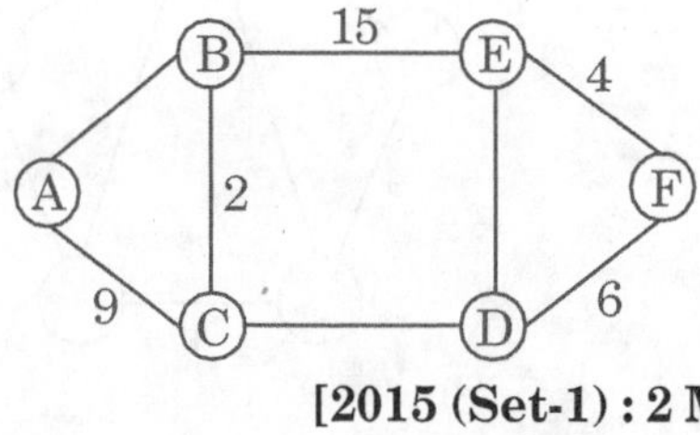

[2015 (Set-1) : 2 Marks]

30. Let G be a weighted connected undirected graph with distinct positive edge weights. If every edge weight is increased by the same value, then which of the following statements is/are TRUE?

P: Minimum spanning tree of G does not change

Q: Shortest path between any pair of vertices does not change

(a) Ponly (b) Q only

(c) Neither P nor Q (d) Both P and Q

[2016 (Set-1) : 1 Mark]

31. Let G be a complete undirected graph on 4 vertices, having 6 edges with weights being 1,2, 3, 4, 5, and 6. The maximum possible weight that a minimum weight spanning tree of G can have is ______.

[2016 (Set-1) : 2 Marks]

32. G = (V, E) is an undirected simple graph in which each edge has a distinct weight, and e is a particular edge of G. Which of the following statements about the minimum spanning trees (MSTS) of G is/are TRUE?

I. If e is the lightest edge of some cycle in G, then every MST of G includes e.

II. If e is the heaviest edge of some cycle in G, then every MST of G excludes e.

(a) I only (b) II only

(c) both I and II (d) neither I nor II

[2016 (Set-1) : 2 Marks]

33. Let G = (V,E) be any connected undirected edge-weighted graph. The weights of the edges in E are positive and distinct. Consider the following statements:

I. Minimum Spanning Tree of G is always unique.

II. Shortest path between any two vertices of G is always unique.

Which of the above statements is/are necessarily true?

(a) I only (b) II only

(c) Both I and II (d) Neither I nor II

[2017 (Set-1): 2 Marks]

34. Consider the following undirected graph G:

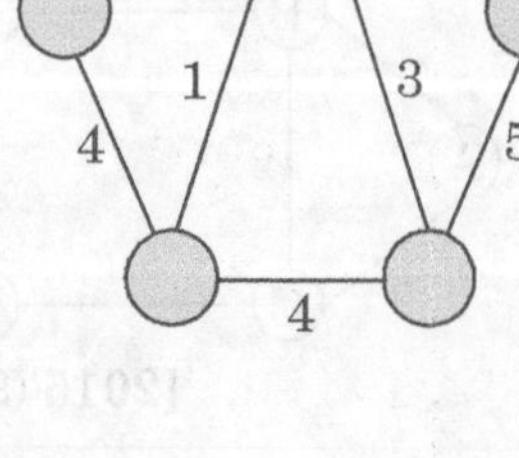

Choose a value of x that will maximize the number of minimum weight spanning trees (MWSTs) of G. The number of MWSTs of G for this value of x is ______.

[2018 : 2 Marks]

35. Consider a sequence of 14 elements: A = [–5, –10, 6, 3, –1, –2, 13, 4, –9, –1, 4, 12, –3, 0]. The subsequence sum $S(i, j) = \Sigma_{k=i}^{j} A[k]$. Determine the maximum of S(i, j), where $0 \le i \le j < 14$. (Divide and conquer approach may be used.)

[2019 : 1 Mark]

PRIME'S

36. Consider the undirected graph below:

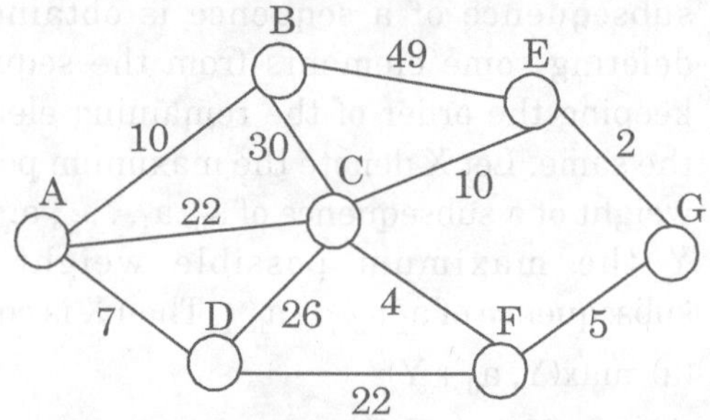

Using Prim's algorithm to construct a minimum spanning tree starting with node A, which one of the followving sequences of edges represents a possible order in which the edges would be added to construct the minimum spanning tree?

(a) (E,G), (C,F), (F,G), (A,D), (A,B), (A,C)

(b) (A,D), (A,B), (A,C), (CP), (G,E), (F,G)

(c) (A,B), (A,D), (D,F), (F,G), (G,E), (F,C)

(d) (A,D), (A,B), (D,F), (F,C), (F,G), (G,E)

[2004 : 2 Marks]

GREEDY CONCEPT

37. The following are the starting and ending times of activities A, B, C, D, E, F, G, and H respectively in chronological order: a_s b_s c_s a_e d_s c_e e_s f_s b_e d_e g_s e_e f_e h_s g_e h_e" Here, x_s denotes the starting time and x_e denotes the ending time of activity X. W need to schedule the activities in a set of rooms available to us. An activity can be scheduled in a room only if the room is reserved for the activity for its entire duration. What is the minimum number of rooms required?

(a) 3 (b) 4

(c) 5 (d) 6

[2003 : 2 Marks]

38. Are all tasks completed in the schedule that gives maximum profit?

(a) All tasks are completed

(b) T_1 and T_6 are left out

(c) T_1 and T_8 are left out

(d) T_4 and T_6 are left out **[2005 : 2 Marks]**

39. What is the maximum profit earned?

(a) 147 (b) 165

(c) 167 (d) 175 **[2005 : 2 Marks]**

40. Consider the weights and values of items listed below. Note that there is only one unit of each item.

Item Number	Weight in (Kgs)	Value in (Rupees)
1	10	60
2	7	28
3	4	20
4	2	24

The task is to pick a subset of these items such that their total weight is not more than 11 Kgs and their total value is maximized. Moreover, no item may be split. The total value of items picked by an optimal algorithm is denoted by V_{opt} t. A greedy algorithm sorts the items by their value-to-weight ratios in descending order and packs them greedily, starting from the first item in the ordered list. The total value of items picked by the greedy algorithm is denoted by V_{greedy}.

The value of $V_{opt} - V_{greedy}$ is ________.

[2018 : 2 Marks]

POLYNOMIAL MULTIPLICATION

41. Consider the polynominal $p(x) = a_0 + a_1x + a_2x^2 + a_3x^3$, where $a_i \neq 0, \forall i$. The minimum number of multiplcations needed to evaluate p on an input x is

(a) 3 (b) 4

(c) 6 (d) 9 **[2006 : 1 Mark]**

HUFFMANN CODING

42. The characters a to h have the set of frequencies based on the first 8 Fibonacci numbers as follows:

a : 1, b : 1, c : 2, d : 3, e : 5, f: 8, g : 13, h : 21

A Huffman code is used to represent the characters. What is the sequence of characters corresponding to the following code?

110111100111010

(a) fdheg (b) ecgdf

(c) dchfg (c) fehdg

[2006 : 2 Marks]

43. Which of the follovving is the Huffman code for the letters a, b, c, d, e?

(a) 0, 10, 110, 1110, 1111

(b) 11, 10, 011, 010, 001

(c) 11, 10, 01, 001, 0001

(d) 110, 100, 010, 000, 001

[2007 : 2 Marks]

44. What is the average length of the correct answer to above question?

(a) 3 (b) 2.1875

(c) 2.25 (d) 1.781

[2007 : 2 Marks]

45. A message is made up entirely of characters from the set X = {P, Q, R, S, T}. The table of probabilities for each of the characters is shown below:

Character	Probability
P	0.22
Q	0.34
R	0.17
S	0.19
T	0.08
Total	1.00

If a message of 100 characters over X is encoded using Huffman coding, then the expected length of the encoded message in bits is ________.

[2017 (Set-2) : 2 Marks]

BELLMAN FORD

46. Which of the follovving statement(s) is/are correct regarding Bellman-Ford shortest path algorithm?

P. Alvvays finds a negative vveighted cycle, if one exists.

Q. Finds vvhether any negative vveighted cycle is reachable from the source

(a) P only (b) Qonly

(c) both P and Q (d) neither P nor Q

[2009 : 1 Mark]

47. What is the time complexity of Bellman -Ford single-source shortest path algorithm on a complete graph of n vertices?

(a) $\Theta(n^2)$

(b) $\Theta(n^2 \log n)$

(c) $\Theta(n^3)$

(d) $\Theta(n^3 \log n)$

[2013 : 1 Mark]

MATRIX CHAIN MULTIPLICATION

48. Four matrices M_1, M_2, M_3 and M_4 of dimensions p x q, q x r, r x s and s x t respectively can be multiplied in several ways with different number of total scalar multiplications. For example when multiplied as $((M_1 \times M_2) \times (M_3 \times M_4))$, the total number of scalar multiplications is pqr + rst + prt. When multiplied as $(((M_1 \times M_2) \times M_3) \times M_4)$, the total number of scalar multiplications is pqr + prs + pst.

If p = 10, q = 100, r = 20, s = 5 and t = 80, then the minimum number of scalar multiplications needed is

(a) 248000 (b) 44000
(c) 19000 (d) 25000

[2011 : 2 Marks]

49. Two matrices M_1 and M_2 are to be stored in arrays A and B respectively. Each array can be stored either in row-major or column-major order in contiguous memory locations. The time complexity of an algorithm tocompute $M_1 \times M_2$ will be

(a) best if A is in row-major, and B is in column-major order
(b) best if both are in row-major order
(c) best if both are in column-major order
(d) independent of the Storage scheme

[2004 : 2 Marks]

50. Let A_1, A_2, A_3 and A_4 be four matrices of dimensions 10 × 5, 5 × 20, 20 × 10, and 10 × 5, respectively. The minimum number of scalar multiplications required to find the product $A_1 A_2 A_3 A_4$ using the basic matrix multiplication method is ________.

[2016 (Set-2) : 2 Marks]

51. Assume that multiplying a matrix G_1 of dimension p × q with another matrix G_2 of dimension q × r requires pqr scalar multiplications. Computing the product of n matrices $G_1 G_2 G_3 \ldots G_n$ can be done by parenthesizing in different ways. Define $G_i G_{i+1}$ as an explicitly computed pair for a given, paranthesization if they are directly multiplied. For example, in the matrix multiplication chain $G_1G_2G_3G_4G_5G_6$ using parenthesization $(G_1(G_2G_3))(G_4(G_5G_6))$. G_2G_3 and G_5G_6 are the only explicitly computed pairs.

Consider a matrix multiplication chain $F_1F_2F_3F_4$, where matrices F_1, F_2, F_3, F_4 and F_5 are of dimensions 2 × 25, 25 × 3, 3 × 16, 16 × 1 and 1 × 1000, respectively. In the parenthesization of $F_1F_2F_3F_4F_5$ that minimizes the total number of scalar multiplications, the explicitly computed pairs is/are

(a) F_1F_2, F_3F_4 only (b) F_2F_3 only
(c) F_3F_4 only (d) F_1F_2, F_4F_5 only

[2018 : 2 Marks]

ANSWERS

1. (b)	2. (12)	3. (d)	4. (b)	5. (c)	6. (d)	7. (*)	8. (d)	9. (d)	10. (b)
11. (d)	12. (c)	13. (d)	14. (d)	15. (c)	16. (b)	17. (c)	18. (a)	19. (b)	20. (d)
21. (c)	22. (d)	23. (b)	24. (d)	25. (b)	26. (b)	27. (c)	28. (d)	29. (69)	30. (a)
31. (7)	32. (c)	33. (a)	34. (4)	35. 29	36. (d)	37. (b)	38. (d)	39. (a)	40. (16)
41. (a)	42. (a)	43. (a)	44. (d)	45. (225)	46. (b)	47. (c)	48. (c)	49. (d)	50. (1500)
51. (c)									

EXPLANATIONS

1. BFS and DFS both algorithm are used to find connected component of graph in linear time.

2.

	A	B	C	D
A	0	2	8	5
B	2	0	5	8
C	8	5	0	x
D	5	8	x	0

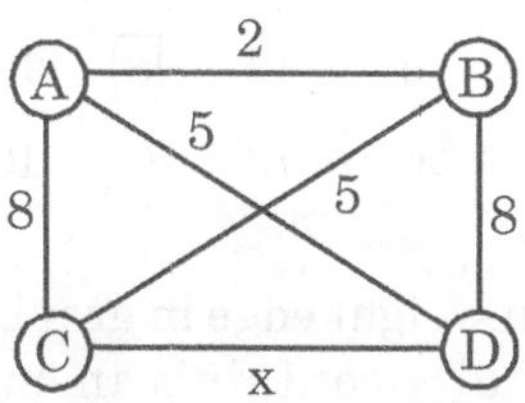

If we find shortestt path fram C to D then it is 13 currently. So we can use maximum 12 value for x so $\boxed{x = 12}$

3.

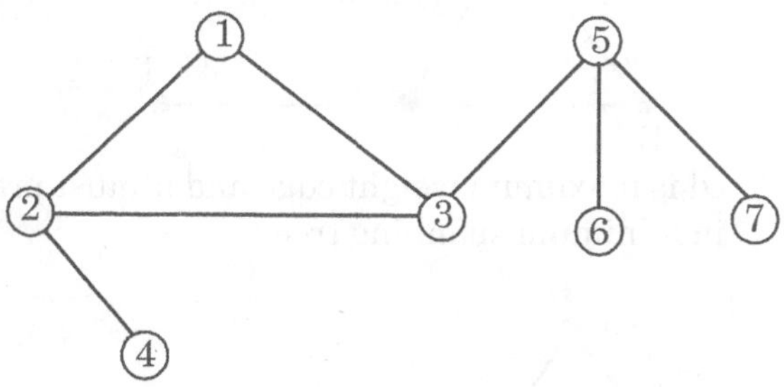

there are 3 aoticulation point in the given graph which break the graph in to component.

{2, 3, 5}

4. A graph is said to be strongly connected if there is path from each vertex of graph to every other vertex means every vertex is reachable from every other vertex. The strongly connected component is always maximal that is if A is strongly connected component there should not exist another strongly connected component which contains A.

5. Topological ordering of a directed graph is a linear ordering of its vertices such that for every directed edge uv from vertex u to vertex v, u comes before v in the ordering. Topological ordering is possible iff graph has no directed cycles.

   (*a*) As the given graph doesn't contain any directed cycles, it has at least one topological ordering. So option (A) is false

   (*b*) PQRS cannot be topological ordering because S should come before R in the ordering as there is a directed edge from S to R. SRQP cannot be topological ordering, because P should come before Q in the ordering as there is a directed edge from P to Q

   (*c*) PSRQ and SPRQ are topological orderings as both of then satisfy the above mentioned topological ordering conditions.

   (*d*) PSRQ is not the only one topological ordering as SPRQ is other possibility.

6. For krushkal's algorithm time complexity is O (log V)

   $\begin{cases} \because E \rightarrow \text{edges} \\ \because V \rightarrow \text{ventices)} \end{cases}$

   So O (m log n)

7. O(m + n) Because, edges are sorted so , no need to make min heap, so deletion from min heap time is saved.

8. Ordering the weights, the sequence obtained is 1, 1, 2, 2, 3, 3, 4, 4, 5, 6, 7

   Now, in order to obtain minimum spanning tree using Kruskal's algorithm, we have to add edges with weights in increasing order such that weight of the spanning tree is minimum.

   In option (*d*), weights of the edges are 1, 1, 2, 3, 2 which contradicts Kruskal's algorithm.

9. In Kruskal's Algorithm we choose on edge of G which has smallest weight among the edges of G.

   So (b, e) = 2, (e, f) = 3, (b, c) = 4, (a, c)= 8, (f,g) = 4 (c,d) = 5

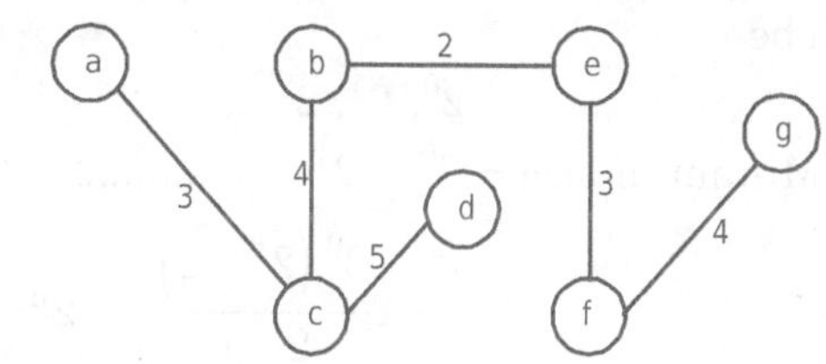

Alternately

Order the edges in non-decreasing order and pick edge one by one until all the nodes are completed with no edge making cycle on addition.

10.

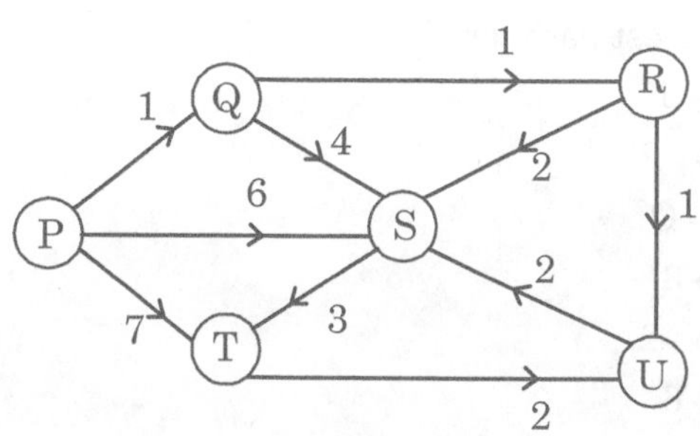

nodes are include in order

⇒ (P, O, R, U, S, T)

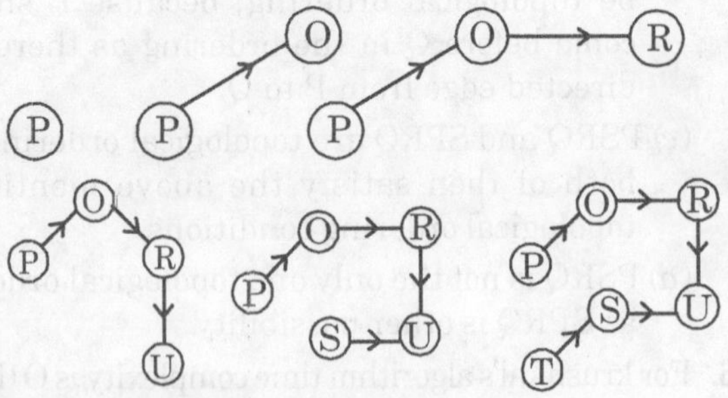

11. Using binary heap it requires

$$O((|E|+|V|)\log|V|)$$

12. In order to find minimum size of X capable of storing any kind of binary tree, the worst cose size of the tree has to be taken.

In the worst case size of the tree has to be taken.

In the worst case only a single node will contain the data at each level of the tree.

For example, for 4 data items, the worst case binary tree will be as follows

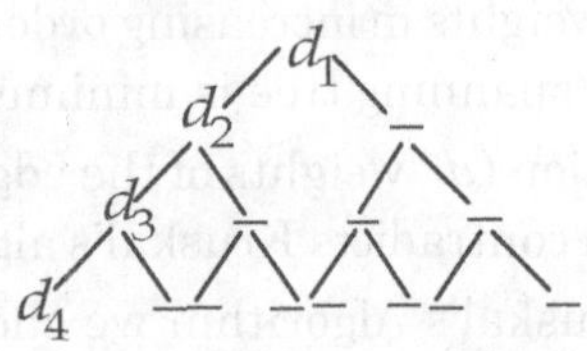

Generalizing the concept, for *n* vertices, the levels of tree that are required will be *n*.

Memory required at each level (starting from root) will be

$$2^0, 2^1, 2^2, \ldots\ldots 2^{n-1}$$

$$\therefore \text{ Minimum size} = 2^0 + 2^1 \ldots\ldots\ldots\ldots\ldots 2^{n-1}$$

$$= \frac{2^0(2^n - 1)}{2-1} = 2^{n-1}$$

13. Dijkstra's single source shortest path in not gives the guarantee to work on negative weight edges graph.

But in this graph it gives the correct shootest path for all vertex.

Shortest path for

B → 1

e → –2

F → O

g → 3

h → –2

d → 6

C → 3

14.

S	A	B	C	D	E	F	G	T
∞	∞	∞	∞	∞	∞	∞	∞	∞
4	[3]		7					
[4]	3		7					
4	3	[5]	7					
4	3	5	7	[6]				
4	3	5	7	6		8	10	
4	3	5	[7]	6	12	8	10	
4	3	5	7	6	12	[8]	10	
4	3	5	7	6	12	8	10	

SACET

15. If e_{max} is maximum weight edge in graph, them it is possible that e_{max} contain's in minimum spanning tree.

Example

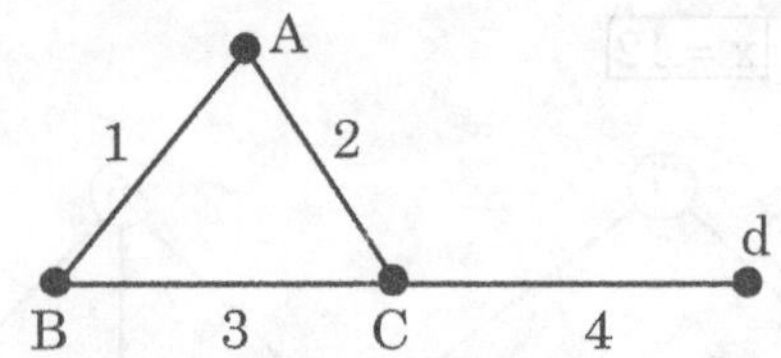

cd is maximum weight edge and it must present in minimum spanning tree

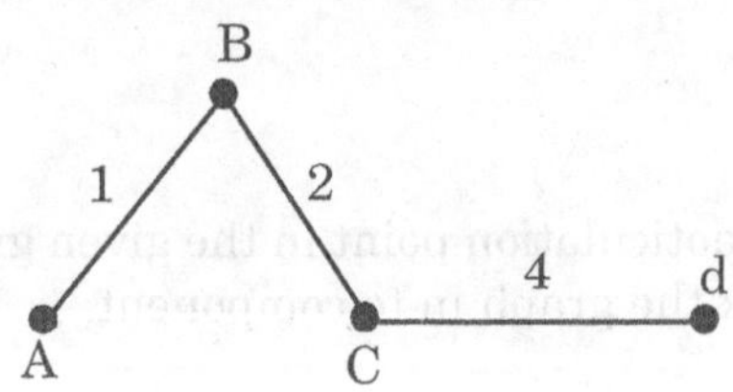

16. Minimum Spanning tree is

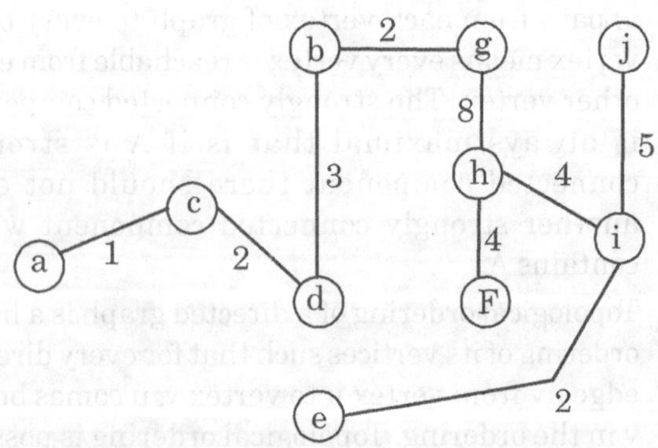

Total sum = 1 + 2 + 2 + 2 + 3 + 4 + 4 + 5 + 8 = 31

17. In adjacency matrix if diagonal elements are 0's and non-diagonal are 1's then it is complete graph and in complete graph of n vertices total n^{n-2} Spanning trees are possible and cost of each tree. is (n – 1) because for n vertex graph, (n – 1) edges required in a tree.

18. Option a is correct, there exists a cut set in G having all edges of maximum weight

19. Minimum spanning tree will be formed when $\forall$ $i. \in. \{1, 2, ... n\}$

V_i is connected to V_{i+1}, as in that case each edge will have the minimum weight of 2.

For example, for $n = 4$, the minimum spanning tree is as follows :

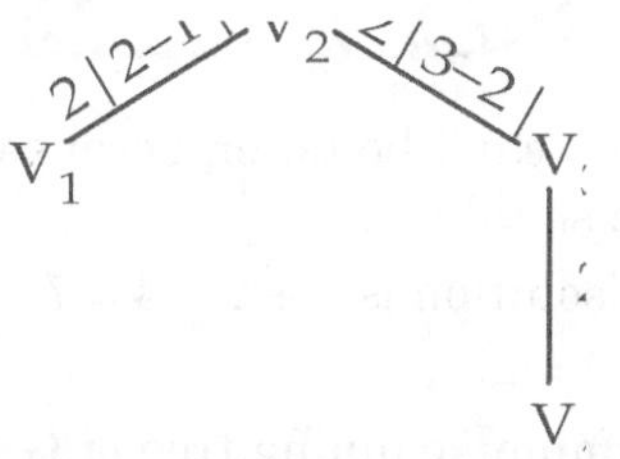

In such a tree, weight of tree consisting of $n-1$ edges each of weight 2 will be

$$2(n-1) = 2n-2$$

20. e is need not to be present in every spanning tree since there may be edges (in cycle formed by adding e), which has same weight as e has.

21.

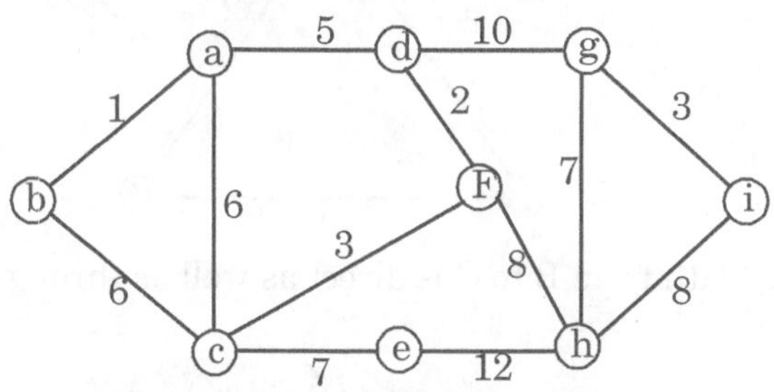

In prims algorithm we can select arbitary vertex and them, find all the edges that connect the tree to new vertex and find the minimum and add it to the tree. So option "C" is correct

(d, f), C), (d, a), (a, b), (c, e), (F, h), (g, h) (g, i).

22. Minimum number of edges for a connected graph = n

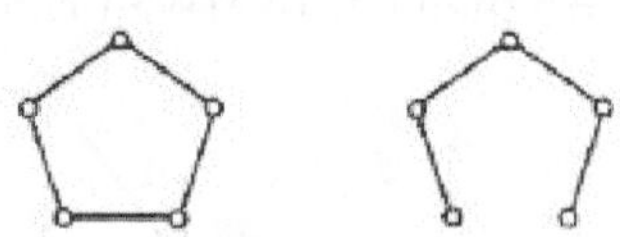

and for a connected tree = $n - 1$

Here given that $2n - 2$ edges and the edges of graph is partitioned into two edge disjoint trees. So there are two vertex disjoint paths between every pair of vertices.

23. Using concepts of Dynamic Programming to find the maximum possible weight of a subsequence of X, we will have two alternatives.

1. Do not include a0 in the subsequence: then the maximum possible weight will be equal to maximum possible weight of a subsequence of {a 1, a2....an} which is represented by Y.
2. Include a0: then maximum possible weight will be equal to a0 + (each number picked om Y will get divided by 2) a0 + Y/2. Here you can note that Y will itself pick optimal subsequence to maximum the weight.

Final answer will be Max (Case1, Case2) i.e. Max (Y, a0 + Y/2). Hence B.

24. Minimal possible spanning tree having vertex "0" is a leaf rode is :–

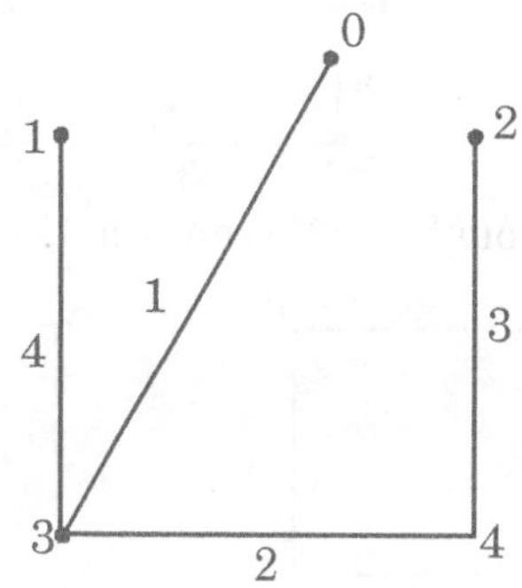

total weight = 4 + 1 + 2 + 3 = 10

25.

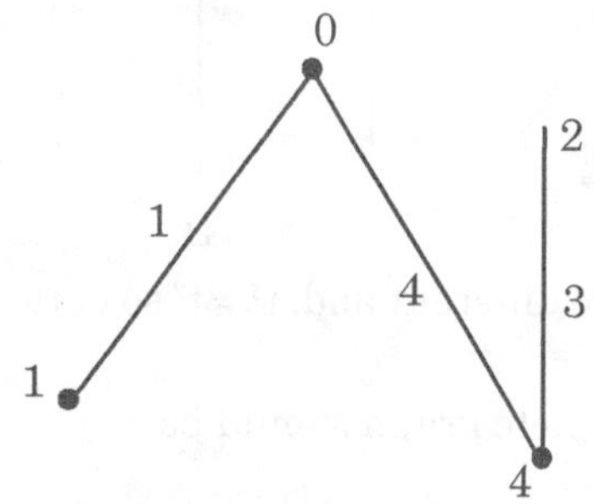

Path from vertex 1 to 2 is

(1 – 0) + (0 – 4) + (4 – 2)

1 + 4 + 3 = 8

26. If we construct graph for n = 6 vertices ($V_1, V_2, V_3, V_4, V_5, V_6$)

then minimum spanning tree for this graph is

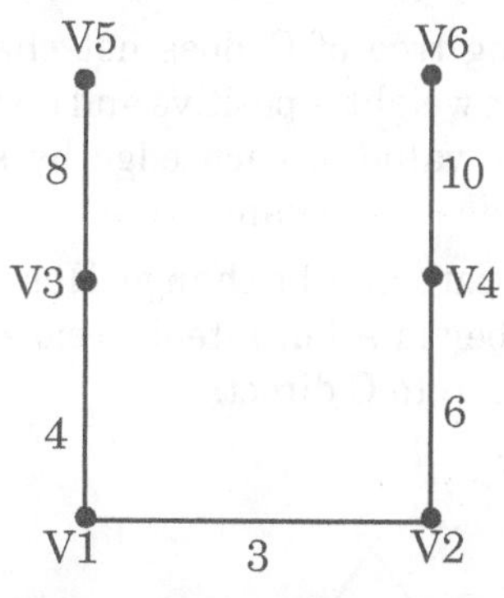

total weight = 31

so if we put n = 6 in option "b" then we get 31

i.e. $x^2 - n + 1$

$(6)^2 - 6 + 1 \Rightarrow 36 - 6 + 1 \Rightarrow 31.$

27. Length of path V_5 to V_6 in mst of n = 10 vertices is

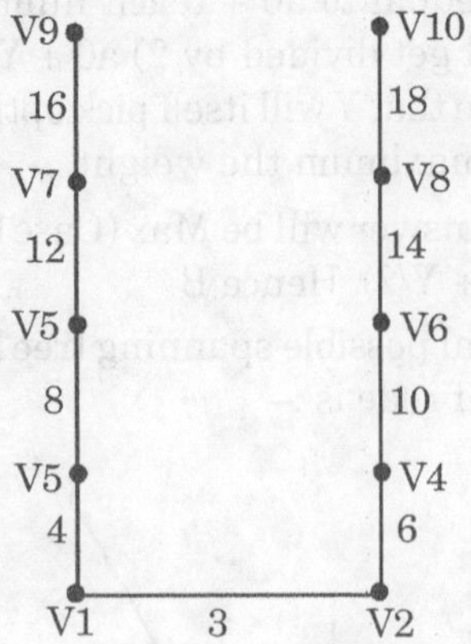

Path from V5 to V6 contain 8+4+3+6+10 = 31

28.

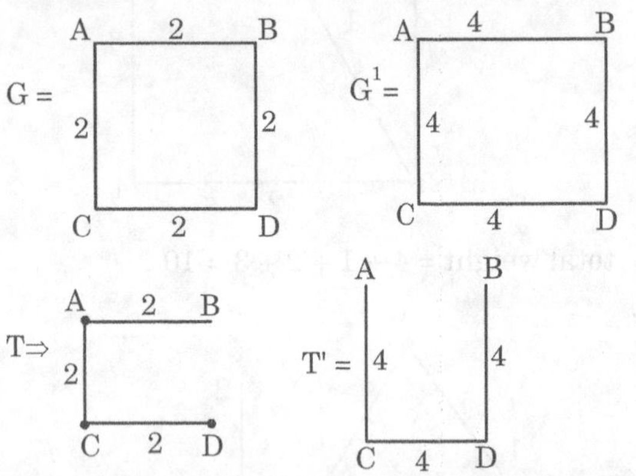

so both tree are different and. $t^1 \neq t^2$ so option "d" is correct

29. MST, The complete graph should be

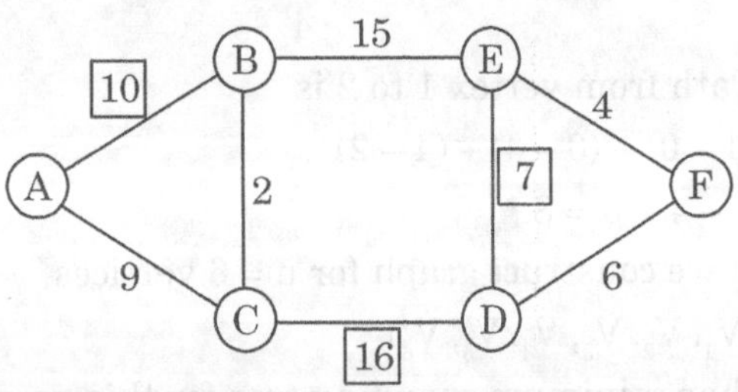

Total sum = 10 + 9 + 2 + 15 + 16 + 7 + 4 + 6 = 69.

30. Minimum sparring tree of G does not change, because every edge weight is positive and distinct, so to increase the value of each edge by same constant value it does not change tree.

Q is false because path may be change. Here path from B to C can. be via A but afteoincrease by 1 path must be from B to C direct.

Example

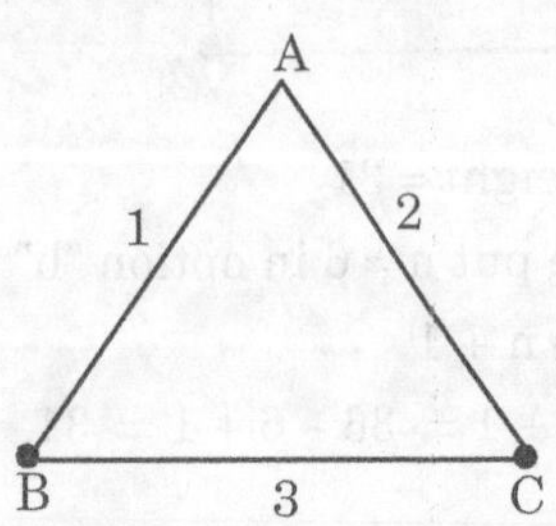

31.

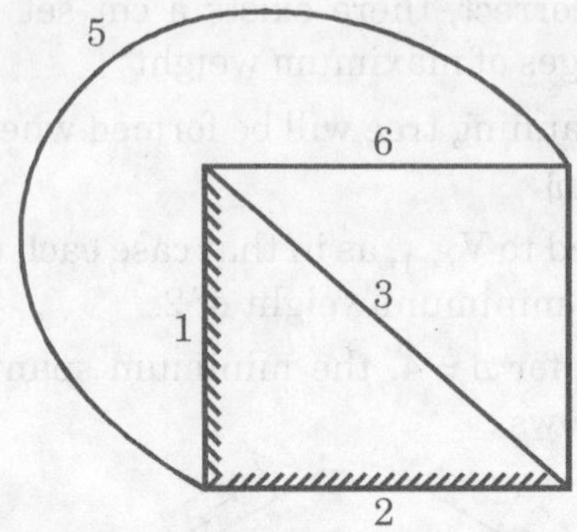

Here 3 can't be taken because it will produce a cycle so take 4.

This solution is 1 + 2 + 4 = 7

32. Both I and II

33. Minimum spanning tree of G is always unique, because weight's are distinct.

But shortest path between any two vertices of G is not always unique.

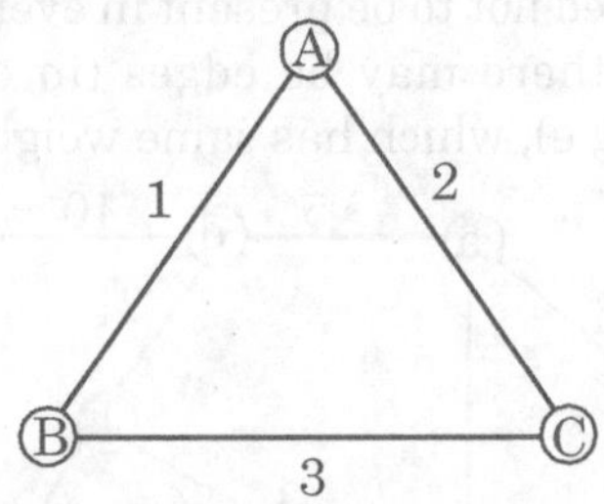

Path from B to C is direct as well as through "A"

34.

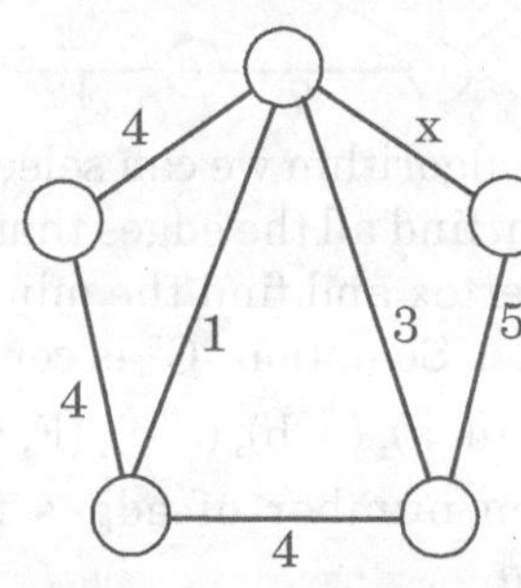

if we put x = 5 then total 4 MWST can be construct.

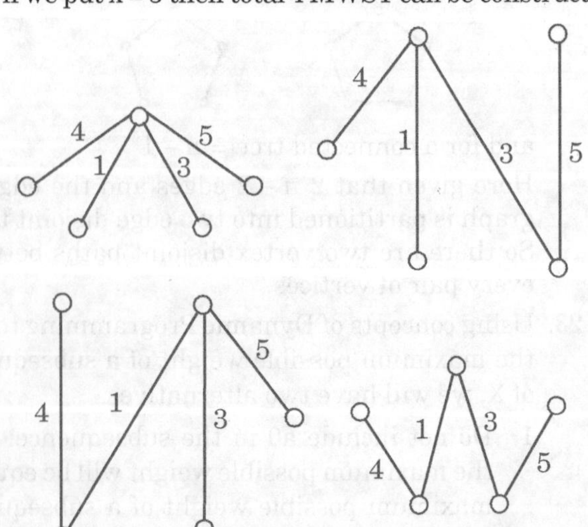

4 tree's

36. Option "a" and "b" produce disconnected components which is never allowed by primes algorithm

In option "C" if vertex "A" is randomly chosen, then first edge must be (A,D) so option "d" is correct.

37. So total 4 rooms are required.

38.

T_1	T_2	T_3	T_5	T_7	T_8	T_9

So T_4 and T_6 are Time out

39. Total profit = 15 + 20 + 30 + 18 + 26 + 16 + 25 = 147

40. By optimal we select 1 st object which gives maximum profit so

$\boxed{V_{opt} = 60}$

In greedy value/ weight ratio in sorted order,

Item No	Weight	Value	Value/ Weight
4	2	24	12
1	10	60	6
3	4	20	5
2	7	28	4

So we can select item 4 and 3 in that order

Vgreedy = 24 + 20 = 44

Vopt – Vgreedy = 60 – 44 = 16

41. $P(r) = a_0 + a_1x + a_2x^2 + a_3x^3$

$P(x) = a_0 + (Ca_3x + a_2)\,x + a_1)\,x$

$t = cl_3 * x$

$t = t + a_2$

$t = t * x$

$t = t + a_1$

$t = t * x$

$t = t + a_0$

So minimum 3 multiplication are needed to e valuate P.

42.

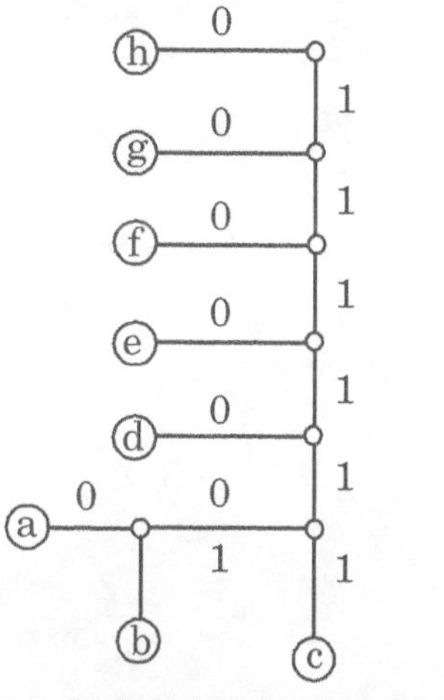

110 11110 0 1110 10

F d h e g

Fdheg

43.

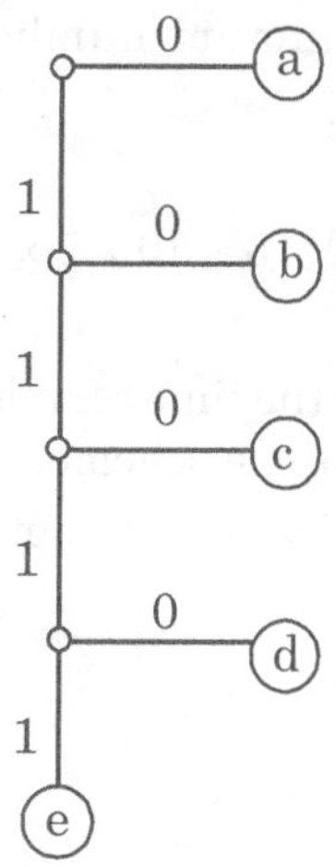

a, b, c, d, e

0, 10, 110, 1110, 1111

44. The average length is ⇒

$$= 1*\frac{1}{2} + 2*\frac{1}{4} + 3*\frac{1}{8} + 4*\frac{1}{16} + 5*\frac{1}{32}$$

⇒1.781

45.

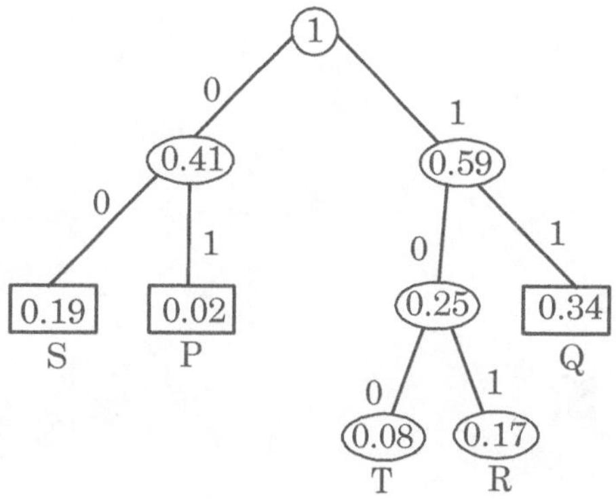

Expected length

= (22 * 2) + (34 * 2) + (17 * 3) + (19 * 2) + (8 * 3)

= 225 bits

46. In Bellman Ford shortest path algorithm, we choose a node first and then we find any negative weighted cycle is rechable from source.

47. Given: A complete graph on n vertices?

To find: Time complexity of Bellman-Ford Single source shortest path.

Analysis:

Time complexity of Bellman-ford algorithm on a graph with n vertices and m edges is $O(nm)$

For a complete graph, $m = {}^nC_2 = 0(n^2)$ (Since, there is an edge between all pair of vertices)

∴ Time Complexity = $0(n^2 \cdot n) = 0(n^3)$

∴ Solution is (c)

Note : Include vertex of degree zero in even degree vertices.

48. The problem can be solved using matrix chain multiplication. we get minimum number of multiplication using

$((M_1 \times (M_2 \times M_3) \times M_4)$

$= 100 \times 20 \times 5 + 10 \times 100 \times 5 + 10 \times 5 \times 80$

$= 19000.$

49. The question is asking about the time complexity so it does not depends on storage scheme.

50. Using matrix chain multiplication the optional way to multiply is

$A_1 \times (A_2 \times A_3) \times A_4$

$= (5 \times 20 \times 10) + (5 \times 10 \times 5) + (10 \times 5 \times 5)$

$= 1500.$

51. Matrix F_5 is of dimen side 1×1000, so multiplication cost of F_5 is very high. So Evaluating F_5 at last is optional

Using Matrix chain Multiplication the optimal way of multiplication is $((F_1 \times (F_2 \times (F_3 \times F_4))) X F_5)$

As concluded, F_3 and F_4 are explicitly computed pair.

4 CHAPTER

Dynamic Programming and P/NP Concept

Analysis of Previous GATE Papers

Topics ↓	Marks	Year →	2019	2018	2017 Set 1	2017 Set 2	2016 Set 1	2016 Set 2	2015 Set 1	2015 Set 2	2015 Set 3
DYNAMIC PROGRAMMING	1 Mark	MCQ Type									
		Numerical Type									
	2 Marks	MCQ Type									
		Numerical Type									
		Total									
SUBSET SUM PROBLEM	1 Mark	MCQ Type									
		Numerical Type									
	2 Marks	MCQ Type									
		Numerical Type									
		Total									
LCS	1 Mark	MCQ Type									
		Numerical Type									
	2 Marks	MCQ Type									
		Numerical Type									
		Total									
P & NP	1 Mark	MCQ Type								1	
		Numerical Type									
	2 Marks	MCQ Type									1
		Numerical Type									
		Total								1	2
VERTEX COLORING	1 Mark	MCQ Type									
		Numerical Type									
	2 Marks	MCQ Type									
		Numerical Type									
		Total									

DYNAMIC PROGRAMMING

1. Which one of the following algorithm design techniques is used in finding all pairs of shortest distances in a graph?
   (a) Dynamic programming
   (b) Backtracking
   (c) Greedy
   (d) Divide and Conquer

[1998 : 1 Mark]

2. The values of l(i,j) could be obtained by dynamic programming based on the correct recursive definition of l(i, j) of the form given above, using an array L[M, N], where M = m + 1 and N = n + 1, such that L[i, j] = l(i, j).

   Which one of the following statements would be TRUE regarding the dynamic programming solution for the recursive definition of l(i, j) ?
   (a) All elements of L should be initialized to 0 for the values of l(i,j) to be properly computed
   (b) The values of l(i, j) may be computed in a row major order or column major order of L [M, N]
   (c) The values of l(i, j) cannot be computed in either row major order or column major order ofL[M,N]
   (d) L [p, q] needs to be computed before L [r, s] if either p < r or q < s

[2009 : 2 Marks]

SUBSET SUM PROBLEM

3. The subset-sum problem is defined as follows: Given a set S of n positive integers and a positive integer W; determine whether there is a subset of S whose elements sum to W. An algorithm Q solves this problem in 0(nW) time. Which of the following statements is false?
   (a) Q solves the subset-sum problem in polynomial time when the input is encoded in unary
   (b) Q solves the subset-sum problem is polynominal time when the input is encoded in binary
   (c) The subset sum problem belongs to the class NP
   (d) The subset sum problem in NP-hard

[2008 : 2 Marks]

Linked Answers Questions 5 and 6

The subset-sum problem is defined as follows. Given a set of n positive integers, $S = \{a_1, a_2, a_3, \ldots\ldots, a_n\}$ and a positive integer W is there a subset S whose elements sum of W? A dynamic program for solving this problem uses a 2-dimensional Boolean array, X with n rows and W-1 columns X [i, j], $1 \le i \le n$, $0 \le j \le W$, is TRUE if and only if there is a subset of $\{a_1, a_2 \ldots\ldots\ldots, a_i\}$ whose elements sum to j.

4. Which of the following is valid for $2 < i < n$ and $a_i \le j \le W$?
   (a) $X[i, j] = X[i-1, j] \vee X[i, j-a_i]$
   (b) $X[i, j] = X[i-1, j] \vee X[i-1, j-a_j]$
   (c) $X[i, j] = X[i-1, j] \wedge X[i, j-a_i]$
   (d) $X[i, j] = X[i-1, j] \wedge X[i-1, j-a_i]$

[2008 : 2 Marks]

5. Which entry of the array X, if TRUE, implies that there is a subset whose elements sum to W?
   (a) X[1,W] (b) X[n, 0]
   (c) X[n,W] (d) X[n–1, n]

[2008 : 2 Marks]

LCS

6. We wish to find the length of the longest common subsequence (LCS) of X[m] and Y[n] as l(m, n), where an incomplete recursive definition for the function l(i, j) to compute the length of the LCS of X[m] and Y[n] is given below: l(i, j) = 0, if either i = 0 or j = 0
   = expr1, if i, j > 0 and x[i –1] = Y [j -1]
   = expr2, if i, j > 0 and x[i – 1] ≠ Y[j –1]

   Which one of the following options is correct?
   (a) expr1 ≡ l(i–1, j) + 1
   (b) expr1 ≡ l(i, j – 1)
   (c) expr2 ≡ max (l(i–1, j), l(i, j – 1))
   (d) expr2 ≡ max (l(i–1, j – 1), /(i, j))

[2009 : 2 Marks]

7. An algorithm to find the length of the longest monotonically increasing sequence of numbers in an array A[0: n-1] is givenbelow.

   Let L_i denotes the length of the longest monotonically increasing sequence starting at index i in the array

   Initialize $L_{n-1} = 1$

   For all i such that $0 \le i \le n-2$

$$L_i = \begin{cases} 1 + L_{i+1} & \text{If } A[i] < A[i+1] \\ 1 & \text{Otherwise} \end{cases}$$

Finally the length of the longest monotonically increasing sequence is Max(L_0, L_1, ..., L_{n+1}). Which of the foliowing statements is TRUE?

(a) The algorithm uses dynamic programming paradigm

(b) The algorithm has a linear complexity and uses branch and bound paradigm

(c) The algorithm has a non-linear polynomial complexity and uses branch and bound paradigm

(d) The algorithm uses divide and conquer paradigm

[2011 : 1 Mark]

8. Consider two strings A = "qpqrr" and B = "pqprqrp". Let x be the length of the longest common subsequence (not necessarily contiguous) between A and B and let y be the number of such longest common subsequences betvveen A and B.

Then x +10y = ________.

[2014 (Set-2): 2 Marks]

P & NP

9. A problem in NP is NP-complete if

(a) it can be reduced to the 3-SAT problem in polynomial time

(b) the 3-SAT problem can be reduced to it in polynomial time

(c) it can be reduced to any other problem in NP in polynomial time

(d) some problem in NP can be reduced to it in polynomial time

[2006 : 1 Mark]

10. For problems X and Y, Y is NP-complete and X reduces to Y in polynomial time. Which of the followingisTRUE?

(a) If X can be solved in polynomial time, then so can Y

(b) X is NP-complete

(c) XisNP-hard

(d) X is in NP, but not necessarily NP-complete

[2008 : 1 Mark]

11. Let π_A be a problem that belongs to the class NP.

Then which one of the following is TRUE?

(a) There is no polynomial time algorithm for π_A

(b) If π_A can be solved deterministically in polynomial time, then P = NP

(c) If π_A is NP-hard, then it is NP-complete

(d) π_A may be undecidable

[2009 : 1 Mark]

12. Which of the following statements are TRUE?

1. The problem of determining whether there exists a cycle in an undirected graph is in P.
2. The problem of determining whether there exists a cycle in an undirected graph is in NP.
3. If a problem A is NP-Complete, there exists a non-deterministic polynomial time algorithm to solve A.

(a) 1,2 and 3

(b) land3only

(c) 2only

(d) 3only

[2013 : 1 Mark]

13. Suppose a polynomial time algorithm is discovered that correctly computes the largest clique in a given graph. In this scenario, which one of the foliowing represents the correct Venn diagram of the complexity classes P, NP and NP Complete(NPC)?

(a)

(b)

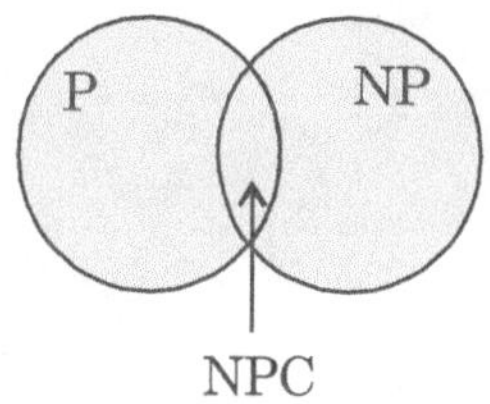

(c)

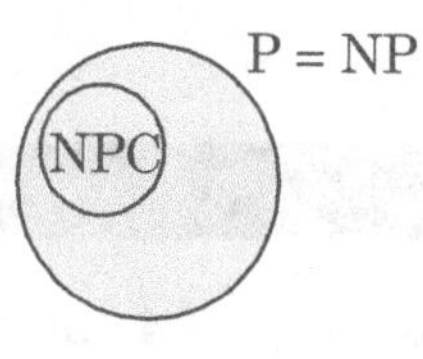

(d)

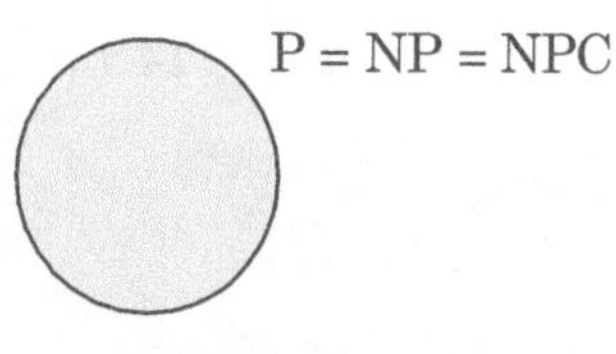

[2014 (Set-1) : 2 Marks]

14. Consider the decision problem 2CNFSAT defined as follows:

{Φ | Φ is a satisfiable propositional formula in CNF with at most two literals per clause}

For example, $\Phi = (x_1 \vee x_2) \wedge (x_1 \vee \overline{x_3}) \wedge (x_2 \vee x_4)$ is a Boolean formula and it is in 2CNFSAT. The decision problem 2CNFSATis

(a) NP-Complete.

(b) solvable in polynomial time by reduction to directed graph reachability.

(c) solvable in constant time since any input instance is satisfiable.

(d) NP-hard, but not NP-complete.

[2014 (Set-3): 2 Marks]

15. Consider two decision problems Q_1, Q_2 such that Q_1 reduces in polynomial time to 3-SAT and 3-SAT reduces in polynomial time to Q_2. Then which one of the following is consistent with the above statement?

(a) Q_1 is in NP, Q_2 is NP hard

(b) Q_2 is in NP, Q_1 is NP hard

(c) Both Q_1 and Q_2 are in NP

(d) Both Q_1 and Q_2 are NP hard

[2015 (Set-2) : 1 Mark]

16. Language L_1 is polynomial time reducible to language L_2. Language L_3 is polynomial time reducible to L_2, which in turn is polynomial time reducibel to language L_4. Which of the following is/are True?

I. If $L_4 \in P$, $L_2 \in P$

II. If $L_1 \in P$ or $L_3 \in P$, then $L_2 \in P$

III. $L_1 \in P$ or if and only if $L_3 \in P$

IV. If $L_4 \in P$ then $L_1 \in P$, then $L_3 \in P$

(a) II only (b) III only

(c) I and IV only (d) I only

[2015 (Set-3) : 2 Marks]

VERTEX COLORING

17. The minimum number of colours required to colour the vertices of a cycle with n nodes in such a way that no two adjacent nodes have the same colour is

(a) 2

(b) 3

(c) 4

(d) $n - 2\left\lfloor \frac{n}{2} \right\rfloor + 2$

[2002 : 1 Mark]

ANSWERS

1. (*a*)	**2.** (*b*)	**3.** (*b*)	**4.** (*b*)	**5.** (*c*)	**6.** (*c*)	**7.** (*a*)	**8.** (34 to 34)	**9.** (*b*)	**10.** (*d*)
11. (*d*)	**12.** (*a*)	**13.** (*d*)	**14.** (*b*)	**15.** (*a*)	**16.** (*c*)	**17.** (*d*)			

EXPLANATIONS

1. All pair shortest path Algorithm is Application of Dynamic Programming.
2. The value can be computed Either in row major or column major order. We can Swap the two 100 ps without effecting the output.
3. We can't solve in polynomial time if input is encoded in binary.
4. x[i, j] = x[i – 1] j] v x [i – 1, j – ai] x [i, j] is true if any one is true.

   or x[i – 1, j – ai] is true.
5. If we get the entry x[n, w] as true then there is a subset of $\{a_1, a_2 ...... a_n\}$ that has sum a_s. W.
6. Largest common subsequence is dynamic programming approach.

$$l(i,i)\begin{cases} l(i-1, j-1)+1 & \text{if } x[i-1]=y[j-1] \\ & \text{if } x[i1]\neq y[j-1] \\ \max\left[l[i-1], l[i-j-1]\right] & \text{if } x[i-1]\neq y[j-1] \\ 0 & \text{if } i=0 \text{ or } j=0 \end{cases}$$

7. The Algorithm uses dynamic programming approach.
8.

	•	p	q	p	r	q	r	p
	0	(0)	0	0	0	0	0	0
q	0	0↑	(↖1)	1 ←	1 ←	↖1	1 ←	1 ←
p	0	↖1	↑1	(↖2)	(2 ←)	2 ←	2 ←	↖2
q	0	↑1	↖2	↑2	↑2	(↖3)	3 ←	3 ←
r	0	↑1	↑2	↑2	↖3	(↑3)	↖4	4 ←
r	0	↑1	↑2	↑2	↖3	↑3	(↖4)	(4 ←)

Longest common subsequence : *qpqr*

$x + 10y = 4 + 10 \times 3 = 34$

9. A problem in NP becomes NP – C if all NP problems can be reduced to it in polynomial time. This is same as reducing any of the NPC to it. 3-SAT is an NP-C problem, reducing it to a NP Problem would means that NP Problem is NP – C.
10. By definition X is in NP, but not necessarily NP-Complete.
11. If π_A is NP-hard, then it is NP-complete

    Alternately

    π_A be a problem (given) in class NP. we say that π_A is NP complete if the following statements are true about L.

    (1) π_A is in NP

    (2) For every π_A' in NP there is polynomial time reduction of π_A' to π_A.
12. 1. We can use "Depth First Search" Algorithm, to check it there is a cycle is an undirected graph. It we encounter any "back edge" in "Depth first search" then given undirected graph has a cycle. Also, If there is a cycle in the Undirected graph, we must encounter a "back edge" in DFS. And, DFS can be done in O(|E| + |V|) time for graph G = (V, E). So, it can is in F.
    2. P ≤ NP, So, it is also in NP.
    3. NP - complete problem A ∈ NP. By, Definition Every problem in NP can be solved in polynomial time using non-deterministic turing machine.

    So, Answer is (*a*) i.e. 1, 2, and 3 are true.
13. The most important open question in complexity theory is whether the **P** = **NP** , which asks whether polynomial time algorithms actually exist for **NP**-complete and all **NP** problems (since a problem "C" is in NP-complete, iff C is in NP and every problem in NP is reducible to C in polynomial time). In the given question it is given that some polynomial time algorithm exists which computes the largest clique problem in the given graph which is known NP-complete problem. Hence P = NP = NP-Complete.
14. 2CNF SAT can be solvable in polynomial time by reduction to directed graph reach ability.
15. Q_1 is in NP and Q_2 is in NP-hard
16. $L_2 \leq pL_4$

    $L_1 \leq pL_2$

    If $L_4 \in P$

    then $L_2 \in P$

    $L_1 \in P,$

    Hence option (*c*).
17. 3-color if odd length cycle.

    2-color if even length cycle

Unit - VII

Compiler Design

Syllabus

Lexical analysis, parsing, syntax-directed translation. Runtime environments. Intermediate code generation.

Contents

1
CHAPTER

Lexical Analysis

Analysis of Previous GATE Papers											
	Year → Topics ↓		2019	2018	2017 Set 1	2017 Set 2	2016 Set 1	2016 Set 2	2015 Set 1	2015 Set 2	2015 Set 3
Lexical Analysis	1 Mark	MCQ Type				1		1			
		Numerical Type									
	2 Marks	MCQ Type		1							
		Numerical Type									
	Total			2		1		1			

1.2 Lexical Analysis

1. In a compiler the module that checks every character of the source text is called
   (a) The code generator
   (b) The code optimizer
   (c) The lexical analyzer
   (d) The syntax analyzer

[1988 :1 Mark]

2. Match the followings:

Group-I

A. Lexical analysis
B. Code optmization
C. Code generation
D. Abelian groups

Group-II

P. DAG's
Q. Syntax trees
R. Push down automation
S. Finite automaton

[1990 : 1 Mark]

3. Which of the foliowing strings can definitely be said to be token without looking at the next input character while compiling a Pascal program?

   I. begin   II. Program
   III. <>

   (a) I   (b) II
   (c) III   (d) All of these

[1995 : 1 Mark]

4. In some programming languages an identifier is permitted to be a letter followed by any number of letters or digits. If L and D denotes the sets of letters and digits respectively. Which of the following expression defines an identifier?
   (a) $(L + D)+$
   (b) $L(L + D)^*$
   (c) $(L.D)^*$
   (d) $L(L.D)^*$

[1995 : 1 Mark]

5. Type checking is normally done during
   (a) Lexical analysis
   (b) Syntax analysis
   (c) Syntax directed translation
   (d) Code optimization

[1998 : 1 Mark]

6. The number of tokens in the Fortran statement DO 10 I = 1.25 is

[1999 : 2 Marks]

7. The number of tokens in the following C statement printf("i = %d, &i = %x", i, &i); is
   (a) 3   (b) 26
   (c) 10   (d) 21

[2000 : 1 Mark]

8. Which of the following is NOT an advantage of using shared, dynamically linked libraries as opposed to using statically linked libraries?
   (a) Smallersizesofexecutable
   (b) Lesser overall page fault rate in the system
   (c) Faster program startup
   (d) Existing programs need not be re-linked to take advantage of newer versions of libraries

[2003 : 2 Marks]

9. Consider a program P that consists of two source modules M1 and M2 contained in two different files. If M1 contains a reference to a function defined in M2, the reference will be resolved at
   (a) Edit-time   (b) Compile-time
   (c) Link-time   (d) Load-time

[2004:1 Mark]

10. Consider line number 3 of the following C-program.

```
int main () {  /* Line 1 */
    int i, n;    /* Line 2 */
    fro (i = 0, i < n, i + +);    /* Line 3 */
}
```

   Identify the compiler's response about this line while creating the object - module
   (a) No compilation error
   (b) Only a lexical error
   (c) Only syntactic errors
   (d) Both lexical and syntactic errors

[2005 : 2 Marks]

11. Which of the following statements are TRUE?

   I. There exist parsing algorithms for some programming languages whose complexities are less than $\theta(n^3)$

   II. A programming language which allows recursion can be implemented with static storage allocation

   III. No L-attributed definition can be evaluated in the framework of bottom-up parsing

   IV. Code improving transformations can be performed at both source language and intermediate code level

   (a) I and II   (b) I and IV
   (c) III and IV   (d) I, III and IV

[2009 : 1 Mark]

12. Which data structure in a complier is used for managing information about variables and their attributes?

(a) Abstract syntax tree

(b) Symbol table

(c) Semantic stack

(d) Parse table

[2010 : 1 Mark]

13. In a compiler, keywords of a language are recognized during

(a) parsing of the program

(b) the code generation

(c) the lexical analysis of the program

(d) dataflow analysis

[2011 : 1 Mark]

14. Match the following

List-I

P: Lexical analysis

Q: Top down parsing

R: Semantic analysis

S: Runtime environments

List-II

(i) Leftmost derivation

(ii) Typechecking

(iii) Regular expressions

(iv) Activation records

Codes:

(a) P → (i), Q → (ii), R → (iv), S → (iii)

(b) P → (iii), Q → (i), R → (ii), S → (iv)

(c) P → (ii), Q → (iii), R → (i), S → (iv)

(d) P → (iv), Q → (i), R → (ii), S → (iii)

[2016 (Set-2) : 1 Mark]

15. Match the following according to input (from the left column) to the compiler phase (in the right column) that processes it:

List-I

(P) Syntax tree

(Q) Character stream

(R) Intermediate representation

(S) Token stream

List-II

(i) Code generator

(ii) Syntax analyzer

(iii) Semantic analyzer

(iv) Lexical analyzer

(a) P → (ii), Q → (iii), R → (iv), S → (i)

(b) P → (ii), Q → (i), R → (iii), S → (iv)

(c) P → (iii), Q → (iv), R → (i), S → (ii)

(d) P → (i), Q → (iv), R → (ii), S → (iii)

[2017 (Set-2) : 1 Mark]

16. A lexical analyzer uses the follovving patterns to recognize three tokens T_1, T_2 and T_3 over the alphabet {a, b, c}.

T_1 : a? (b | c)*a

T_2 : b? (a | c)*b

T_3 : c? (b | a)*c

Note that *x? means 0 or 1 occurrence of the symbol x. Note also that the analyzer outputs the token that matches the longest possible prefix. If the string bbaacabc is processed by the analyzer, which one of the following is the sequence of tokens it outputs?

(a) $T_1T_2T_3$ (b) $T_1T_1T_3$

(c) $T_2T_1T_3$ (d) T_3T_3

[2018 : 2 Marks]

ANSWERS

1. (*c*) **2.** (a-S, b-P, c-R, d-Q) **3.** (*c*) **4.** (*b*) **5.** (*c*) **6.** (5) **7.** (10) **8.** (*c*) **9.** (*c*)

10. (*c*) **11.** (*b*) **12.** (*b*) **13.** (*c*) **14.** (*b*) **15.** (*c*) **16.** (*d*)

EXPLANATIONS

1. Lexical analyser phase read the source code character by character and generate tokens for a particular lexeme (sequence of character that satisfy some pattern).
2. Finite automata, regular expressions are used for lexical analysis DAG are used in code optimization phase to improve the efficiency of intermediate code.
3. <> used in expression for using the token.
4. Identifier–Language use identifiers as names of variables, arrays, functions. A gramar for an language often treats an identifier as a token. Each time an identifier appears in the input.

   Example : Count = Count + increment :

   $id = id + id$ this token stream is used for parsing.
5. **Type checking.** A compiler must check that the source program follows both the syntactic and semantic conventions of the source language. This checking called static checking. Type checks is part of static checks. In type checking, a compiler should report an error if an operator is applied to an incompatible operand;

   e.g. An array variable and a function variable are added together.

   * A type checker verifies that the type of a construct mathes that expected by its content.

   * Type checker implements a type system. The type system are specified in a syntax-directed manner.

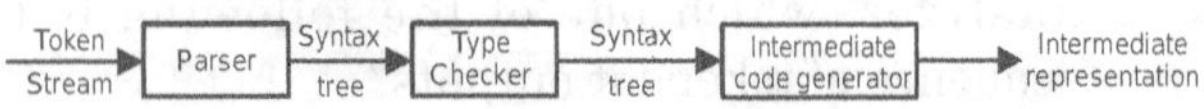

Position of type checker

6. No. of takens are ⇒ 5

Do	10	I	=	1.25
↓	↓	↓	↓	↓
1	2	3	4	5

   total 5 tokens.
7. $\underset{1}{\underline{\text{Print F}}}$ $\underset{3}{\underline{\text{"i = do d, \& i = \% x"}}}$

,	i	,	8	i	)	;
↓	↓	↓	↓	↓	↓	↓
4	5	0	7	8	9	10

   total 10 tokens
8. In Non-Shared (static) libraries, since library code is connected at compile time, the final executable has no dependencies on the library at run time i.e. no additional run-time loading costs, it means that you don't need to carry along a copy of the library that is being used and you have everything under your control and there is no dependency.
9. Linking between the different files during the compilation is done during the link time.
10. Consider 'fro' is also legel identifier, so loxical error is not generated.
11. Second option is false because recursion can not be implemented with static storage allocation.

    Third is false because L-attributed definition can be evaluated sin the framework of bottom-up parsing
12. Symbol table is a Data structure containing record for each identifier, with fields for the attribute of the identifier.

    The symbols entered into symbol table are nothing but identifier and operators. It contain information about variables and their attribute.
13. Any identifier is also a token so it is recognized in lexical Analysis
14. Lexical analysis uses Regular expression to recognize identifiers. Top down parsing uses Left Most Derivation to generate the string the of the language. Type checking is done at Semantic analysis phase of the compiler. Activation records of a function are loaded into stack memory at Run time.
15. According to the compiler phase process, we get the below structure:

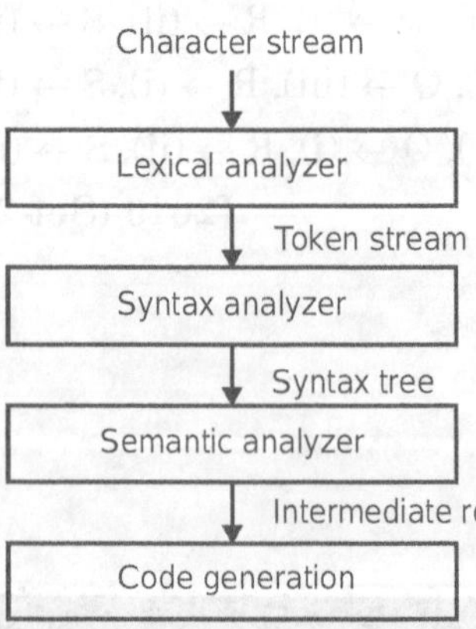

16. Ans is T_3T_3 because from first T_3 bbaac is taken from second T_3 abc is taken longest possible prefix.

    Hence T_3T_3 token output.

2
CHAPTER

Parsing Techniques

Analysis of Previous GATE Papers											
	Year → Topics ↓		2019	2018	2017 Set 1	2017 Set 2	2016 Set 1	2016 Set 2	2015 Set 1	2015 Set 2	2015 Set 3
PARSI NG	1 Mark	MCQ Type			1					1	
		Numerical Type									
	2 Marks	MCQ Type				1					
		Numerical Type									
	Total				1	2				1	
TOP DOWN PARSING	1 Mark	MCQ Type									
		Numerical Type	1								
	2 Marks	MCQ Type									
		Numerical Type									
	Total		1								
BOTTOM UP PARSING	1 Mark	MCQ Type				1			1		1
		Numerical Type									
	2 Marks	MCQ Type									1
		Numerical Type									
	Total					1			1		3
SHIFT REDUCE	1 Mark	MCQ Type	1								
		Numerical Type									
	2 Marks	MCQ Type									
		Numerical Type									
	Total		1								

PARSING

1. The pass numbers for each of the following activities

(i) object code generation

(ii) literals added to literal table

(iii) listing printed

(iv) address resolution of local symbols that occur in a two pass assembler respectively are

(a) 1, 2, 1, 2 (b) 2, 1, 2, 1

(c) 2, 1, l; 2 (d) 1, 2, 2, 2

[1996 : 1 Mark]

2. The process of assigning load addresses to the various parts of the program and adjusting the code and data in the program to reflect the assigned addresses is called

(a) Assembly

(b) Parsing

(c) Relocation

(d) Symbol resolution

[2001 : 1 Mark]

3. Which of the following statements is false?

(a) An unambiguous grammar has same leftmost and rightmost derivation

(b) An LL(1) parser is a top-down parser

(c) LALR is more powerful than SLR

(d) An ambiguous grammar can never be LR(k) for any k **[2001 : 1 Mark]**

4. Consider the context free grammar

$E \rightarrow E + E$

$E \rightarrow (E * E)$

$E \rightarrow id$

Where E is the starting symbol, the set of terminals is {id, (, + ,), *} and the set of non terminal is {E}. Which of the following terminal strings has more than one parse tree where parsed according to above grammar?

(a) id + id + id + id

(b) id + (id * (id * id))

(c) (id + id * id}} + id

(d) ((id * id + id) + id)

[2005 : 2 Marks]

5. For the terminal string with more than one parse tree obtained as solution to in above Question, how many parse trees are possible?

(a) 5 (b) 4

(c) 3 (d) 2

[2005 : 2 Marks]

6. Find the grammar that generates the language $L = (a^i b^j \mid i \neq j)$. In that grammar what is the length of the derivation (number of steps starring from S) to generate the string $a^l b^m$ with $l \neq m$

(a) max(l, m) +2

(b) l + m + 2

(c) l + m + 3

(d) max (l, m) + 3

[2006 : 2 Marks]

Common Data for Q. 23 & Q. 24

Consider the CFG with {S, A, B} as the non-terminal alphabet, {a, b} as the terminal alphabet, S as the start symbol and the foliowing set of production rules

$S \rightarrow bA$ $S \rightarrow aB$

$A \rightarrow a$ $B \rightarrow b$

$A \rightarrow aS$ $B \rightarrow bS$

$A \rightarrow bAA$ $B \rightarrow aBB$

7. Which of the follovving strings is generated by the grammar?

(a) aaaabb

(b) aabbbb

(c) aabbab

(d) abbbba

[2007 : 2 Marks]

8. For the correct answer string to above question how many derivation trees are there?

(a) 1

(b) 2

(c) 3

(d) 4

[2007 : 2 Marks]

Linked Data Questions 9 and 10

For the grammar below, a partial LL(1) parsing table is also presented along with the grammar. Entries that need to be filled are indicated as E1, E2, and E3. ε is the empty string, $ indicates end of input, and | separates alternate right hand sides of productions.

$S \rightarrow a\,A\,b\,B \mid b\,A\,a\,B \mid \varepsilon$

$A \rightarrow S$

$B \rightarrow S$

	a	b	$
S	E1	E2	$S \rightarrow \varepsilon$
A	$A \rightarrow S$	$A \rightarrow S$	error
B	$B \rightarrow S$	$B \rightarrow S$	E3

9. The FIRST and FOLLOW sets for the non-terminals A and B are

(a) FIRST (A) = {a, b, ε} = FIRST (B),
FOLLOW (A) = {a, b}
FOLLOW (B) = {a, b, $}

(b) FIRST (A) = {a, b, $}
FIRST (B) = {a, b, ε}
FOLLOW (A) = {a, b}
FOLLOW(B) = {$}

(c) FIRST (A) = {a, b, ε} = FIRST (B),
FOLLOW (A) = {a, b}
FOLLOW (B) = $

(d) FIRST (A) = {a, b} = FIRST (B)
FOLLOW (A) = {a, b}
FOLLOW (B) = {a, b}

[2012 : 2 Marks]

10. The appropriate entries for E1, E2 and E3 are

(a) E1 : S → aAbB, A → S
E2 : S → bAaB, B → S
E3 : B → S

(b) E1 : S → aAbB, S → ε
E2 : S → bAaB, B → ε
E3 : S → ε

(c) E1 : S → aAbB, S → ε
E2 : S → bAaB, S → E
E3 : B → S

(d) E1 : A → S, S → ε
E2 : B → S, S → ε
E3 : B → S

[2012 : 2 Marks]

11. Consider the grammar defined by the following production rules, with two operators * and +

S → T * P
T → U | T * U
P → Q + P | Q
Q → Id
U → Id

Which one of the following is TRUE?

(a) + is left associative, while * is right associative
(b) + is right associative, while * is left associative
(c) Both + and * are right associative
(d) Both + and * are left associative

[2014 (Set-2) : 1 Mark]

12. Match the following:

List-I
A. Lexical analysis
B. Parsing
C. Register allocation
D. Expression evaluation

List-II
1. Graph coloring
2. DFA minimization
3. Post-order traversal
4. Production tree

Codes:

	A	B	C	D
(a)	2	3	1	4
(b)	2	1	4	3
(c)	2	4	1	3
(d)	2	3	4	1

[2015 (Set-2) : 1 Mark]

13. Consider the following grammar:

- P → xQRx
- Q → yz|z
- R → w|ε
- S → y

What is FOLLOW (Q)?

(a) {R}
(b) {w}
(c) {w, y}
(d) {w, $}

[2017 (Set-1) : 1 Mark]

14. Consider the following expression grammar G:

E → E – T | T
T → T + F | F
F → (E) | id

Which of the following grammars is not left recursive, but is equivalent to G?

(a) E → E-T | T
T → T + F | F
F → (E) | id

(b) E → TE'
E' → TE' | ∊
T → T + F | F
F → (E) | id

(c) E → TX
X → –TX | ∊
T → FY
Y → +FY | ∊
F → (E) | id

(d) E → TX | (TX)
X → TX | +TX | ∊
T → id

[2017 (Set-2) : 2 Marks]

15. Consider the following expression grammar. The semantic rules for expression calculation are stated next to each grammar production.

E → numberE.val = number.val

| E '+' EE$^{(1)}$.val = E$^{(2)}$.val + E$^{(3)}$.val

| E '×' EE$^{(1)}$.val = E$^{(2)}$.val × E$^{(3)}$.val;

Assume the conflicts in Part (*a*) of this question are resolved and an LALR (1) parser is generated for parsing arithmetic expressions as per the given grammar. Consider an expression 3 × 2 + 1. What precedence and associativity properties does the generated parser realize?

(*a*) Equal precedence and left associativity; expression is evaluated to 7

(*b*) Equal precedence and right associativity; expression is evaluated to 9

(*c*) Precedence of '×' is higher than that of '+', and both operators are left associative; expression is evaluated to 7

(*d*) Precedence of '+' is higher than that of '×', and both operators are left associative; expression is evaluaterd to 9

[2005 : 2 Marks]

TOP DOWN PARSING

16. Which of the following suffices to convert an arbitrary CFG to an LL(1) grammar?

(a) Removing left recursion alone

(b) Factoring the grammar alone

(c) Removing left recursion and factoring the grammar

(d) None of the above

[2003 : 1 Mark]

17. The grammar A → AA | (A) | ε is not suitable for predictive-parsing because the grammar is

(a) ambiguous

(b) Left-recursive

(c) right-recursive

(d) an operator-grammar

[2005 : 1 Mark]

18. Which one of the following is a top-down parser?

(a) Recursive descent parser

(b) Operator precedence parser

(c) An LR(k) parser

(d) An LALR(k) parser

[2007 : 1 Mark]

19. Consider the grammar with non-terminals N = {S, C, S1}, terminals T = {a, b, i, t, e}, with S as the start symbol, and the following set of rules

$$S \rightarrow iCtSS_1 \mid a$$
$$S \rightarrow eS \mid \varepsilon$$
$$C \rightarrow b$$

The grammar is NOT LL(1) because:

(a) It is left recursive (b) It is right recursive

(c) It is ambiguous (d) It is not context-free

[2007 : 2 Marks]

20. Consider the following two statements:

P: Every regular grammar is LL (1)

Q: Every regular set has LR (1) grammar

Which of the following is TRUE?

(a) Both P and Q are true

(b) P is true and Q is false

(c) P is false and Q is true

(d) Both P and Q are false

[2007 : 2 Marks]

21. Consider the grammar given below:

S → Aa

A → BD

B → b | ∈

D → d | ∈

Let a, b, d, and $ be indexed as follows:

a	b	d	$
3	2	1	0

Compute the FOLLOW set of the non-terminal B and write the index values for the symbols in the FOLLOW set in the descendign order. (For example, if the FOLLOW set is {a, b, d, $}, then the answer should be 3210)

[2019 : 1 Mark]

BOTTOM UP PARSING

22. Consider the SLR(l) and LALR (1) parsing tables for a context free grammar. Which of the following statements is/are true?

(a) The goto part of both tables may be different.

(b) The shift entries are identical in both the tables.

(c) The reduce entries in the tables may be different.

(d) The error entries in the tables may be different.

[1992 : 2 Marks]

23. Which of the following statements is true?

(a) SLR parser is more powerful than LALR

(b) LALR parser is more powerful than Canonical LR parser

(c) Canonical LR parser is more powerful than LALR parser

(d) The parsers SLR, Canonical LR, and LALR have the same power

[1998 : 1 Mark]

24. Assume that the SLR parser for a grammar G has n_1 states and the LALR parser for G has n_2 states. The relationship between n_1 and n_2 is

(a) n_1 is necessarily less than n_2

(b) n_1 is necessarily equal to n_2

(c) n_1 is necessarily greater than n_2

(d) None of the above **[2003 : 1 Mark]**

25. Consider the grammar shown below

$S \rightarrow i\,E\,t\,S\,S' \mid \alpha$

$S' \rightarrow eS \mid \varepsilon$

$E \rightarrow b$

In the predictive parse table M, of this grammar, the entries M[S′, e] and M[S′, $] respectively are

(a) $\{S' \rightarrow e\,S\}$ and $\{S' \rightarrow \varepsilon\}$

(b) $\{S' \rightarrow e\,S\}$ and $\{\}$

(c) $\{S' \rightarrow \varepsilon\}$ and $\{S' \rightarrow e\}$

(d) $\{S' \rightarrow e\,S, S' \rightarrow \varepsilon\}$ and $\{S' \rightarrow \varepsilon\}$

[2003 : 2 Marks]

26. Which of the following grammar rules violate the requirements of an operator grammar? P, Q, R are not terminals and r, s, t are terminals.

(i) $P \rightarrow Q\,R$ (ii) $P \rightarrow Q\,s\,R$

(iii) $P \rightarrow \varepsilon$ (iv) $P \rightarrow Q\,t\,R\,r$

(a) (i) only (b) (i) and (iii) only

(c) (ii) and (iii) only (d) (iii) and (iv) only

[2004 : 1 Mark]

27. Consider the grammar

$S \rightarrow (S) \mid a$

Let the number of states in SLR (1), LR (1) and LALR(l) parsers for the grammar be n_1 n_2 and n_3 respectively. The following relationship holds good

(a) $n_1 < n_2 < n_3$

(b) $n_1 = n_3 < n_2$

(c) $n_1 = n_2 = n_3$

(d) $n_1 \geq n_3 \geq n_2$

[2005 : 2 Marks]

28. Consider the following grammar.

$$S \rightarrow S \times E$$
$$S \rightarrow E$$
$$E \rightarrow F + E$$
$$E \rightarrow F$$
$$F \rightarrow id$$

Consider the following LR(0) items corresponding to the grammar above.

(i) $S \rightarrow S \times .E$

(ii) $E \rightarrow F.+ E$

(iii) $E \rightarrow F + .E$

Given the items above, which two of them will appear in the same set in the canonical sets-of-items for the grammar?

(a) (i) and (ii)

(b) (ii) and (iii)

(c) (i) and (iii)

(d) None of these

[2006 : 1 Mark]

29. Consider the following grammar

$$S \rightarrow FR$$
$$R \rightarrow S^* \mid \varepsilon$$
$$F \rightarrow id$$

In the predictive parser table, M, of the grammar the entries M[S, id] andM[R, $] respectively

(a) $\{S \rightarrow FR\}$ and$\{R \rightarrow \varepsilon\}$

(b) $\{S \rightarrow FR\}$ and $\{\}$

(c) $\{S \rightarrow FR\}$ and $\{R \rightarrow {}^*S\}$

(d) $\{F \rightarrow id\}$ and $\{R \rightarrow \varepsilon\}$

[2006 : 2 Marks]

30. Which one of the following grammars generates the language $L = \{a^i b^j \mid i \neq j\}$?

(a) $S \rightarrow AC \mid CB$

$C \rightarrow aCb \mid a \mid b$

$A \rightarrow aA \mid \varepsilon$

$B \rightarrow Bb \mid \varepsilon$

(b) $S \rightarrow aS \mid Sb \mid a \mid b$

(c) $S \rightarrow AC \mid CB$

$C \rightarrow aCb \mid \varepsilon$

$A \rightarrow aA \mid \varepsilon$

$B \rightarrow Bb \mid \varepsilon$

(d) $S \rightarrow AClCB$

$C \rightarrow aCb \mid \varepsilon$

$A \rightarrow aA \mid a$

$B \rightarrow bB \mid b$ **[2006 : 2 Marks]**

31. Which of the following describes a handle (as applicable to LR-parsing) appropriately?

(a) It is the position in a sentential form where the next shift or reduce operation will occur

(b) It is a non-terminal whose production will be used for reduction in the next step

(c) It is a production that may be used for reduction in a future step along with a position in the sentential form where the next shift or reduce operation will occur.

(d) It is the production p that will be used for reduction in the next step along with a position in the sentential form where the right hand side of the production may be found

[2008 : 1 Mark]

32. An LALR(l) parser for a grammar G can have shift-reduce (S-R) conflicts if and only if

(a) the SLR(l) parser for G has S-R conflicts

(b) the LR(1) parser for G has S-R conflicts

(c) the LR(0) parser for G has S-R conflicts

(d) the LALR(l) parser for G has reduce-reduce conflicts **[2008 : 2 Marks]**

33. The grammar $S \rightarrow aSa \mid bS \mid c$ is

(a) LL(1) but not LR(1)

(b) LR(1) but not LL(1)

(c) Both LL(1) and LR (1)

(d) Neither LL(1) nor LR(1)

[2010 : 2 Marks]

34. What is the maximum number of reduces moves that can be taken by a bottom up parser for a grammar without epsilon and imit productions (i.e. of type $A \rightarrow \varepsilon$ and $A \rightarrow a$) to parse a string with n tokens?

(a) n/2 (b) n-1

(c) 2n-1 (d) 2^n

[2013 : 1 Mark]

35. Consider the following two sets of LR(1) items of LR(1) grammar.

$X \rightarrow c.X, c/d X \rightarrow c.X, \$$

$X \rightarrow .cX, c/d X \rightarrow .cX, \$$

$X \rightarrow .d, c/d \quad X \rightarrow .d, \$$

Which of the following statement related to merging of the two sets in the corresponding parser is/are FALSE?

1. Cannot be merged since look aheads are different.
2. Can be merged but will result in S-R conflict.
3. Can be merged but will result in R-R conflict.
4. Cannot be merged since goto on c will lead to two different sets.

(a) 1 only

(b) 2 only

(c) 1 and 4 only

(d) 1, 2, 3 and 4

[2013 : 2 Marks]

36. A canonical set of items is given below

$S \rightarrow L. > R$

$Q \rightarrow R.$

On input symbol > the set has

(a) a shift-reduce conflict and a reduce-reduce conflict.

(b) a shift-reduce conflict but not a reduce-reduce conflict.

(c) a reduce-reduce conflict but not a shift-reduce conflict.

(d) neither a shift-reduce nor a reduce-reduce conflict.

[2014 (Set-1) : 2 Marks]

37. Which one of the following is TRUE at any valid state in shift-reduce parsing?

(a) Viable prefixes appear only at the bottom of the stack and not inside

(b) Viable prefixes appear only at the top of the stack and not inside

(c) The stack contains only a set of viable prefixes

(d) The stack never contains viable prefixes

[2015 (Set-1) : 1 Mark]

38. Among simple LR (SLR), canonical LR, and look-ahead LR (LALR), which of the following pairs identify the method that is very easy to implement and the method that is the most powerful, in that order?

(a) SLR, LALR

(b) Canonical LR, LALR

(c) SLR, canonical LR

(d) LALR, canonical LR

[2015 (Set-3): 1 Mark]

39. Consider the following grammar G.

$S \rightarrow F \mid H$

$F \rightarrow p \mid c$

$H \rightarrow d \mid c$

Where S, F and H are non-terminal symbols, p, d and c are terminal symbols. Which of the following statement(s) is/are correct?

S1: LL(1) can parse all strings that are generated using grammar G.

S2: LR(1) can parse all strings that are generated using grammar G.

(a) Only S1 (b) Only S2

(c) Both S1 and S2 (d) Neither S1 and S2

[2015 (Set-3) : 2 Marks]

40. Which of the following statements about parser is/are CORRECT?

I. Canonical LR is more powerful than SLR.

II. SLR is more powerful than LALR.

III. SLR is more powerful than Canonical LR.

(a) I only

(b) II only

(c) III only

(d) II and III only

[2017 (Set-2) : 1 Mark]

SHIFT REDUCE

41. A shift reduce parser carries out the actions specified within braces immediately after reducing with the corresponding rule of grammar

S → xxW{print"1"}

S → y {print"2"}

W → Sz{print"3M}

What is the translation of xxxxyzz using the syntax directed translation scheme described by the above rules?

(a) 23131

(b) 11233

(c) 11231

(d) 33211

[1995 : 2 Marks]

42. Which one of the following kinds of derivation is used by LR parsers?

(a) Rightmost in reverse

(b) Rightmost

(c) Leftmost in reverse

(d) Leftmost

[2019 : 1 Mark]

ANSWERS

1. (b)	**2.** (c)	**3.** (a)	**4.** (a)	**5.** (a)	**6.** (a)	**7.** (c)	**8.** (b)	**9.** (a)	**10.** (c)
11. (b)	**12.** (c)	**13.** (c)	**14.** (c)	**15.** (c)	**16.** (c)	**17.** (a,b)	**18.** (a)	**19.** (c)	**20.** (c)
21. (31)	**22.** (b,c,d)	**23.** (c)	**24.** (b)	**25.** (a)	**26.** (b)	**27.** (b)	**28.** (d)	**29.** (a)	**30.** (d)
31. (d)	**32.** (b)	**33.** (c)	**34.** (b)	**35.** (d)	**36.** (d)	**37.** (c)	**38.** (c)	**39.** (d)	**40.** (a)
41. (a)	**42.** (a)								

EXPLANATIONS

1. In two pass assembler,

Purpose : Generate object program.

1. Substitute the corresponding address for each symbol.
2. Generate instruction, which are opcode are substituted for machine instruction.
3. Data is generated.
4. Some pseudo operations are also executed.

2. Relocation of code is the process done by the linker-loader when a program is copied from external storage into main memory.

3. A grammar is said to be ambiguous if there exixt more than one parse tree for a string.

4.

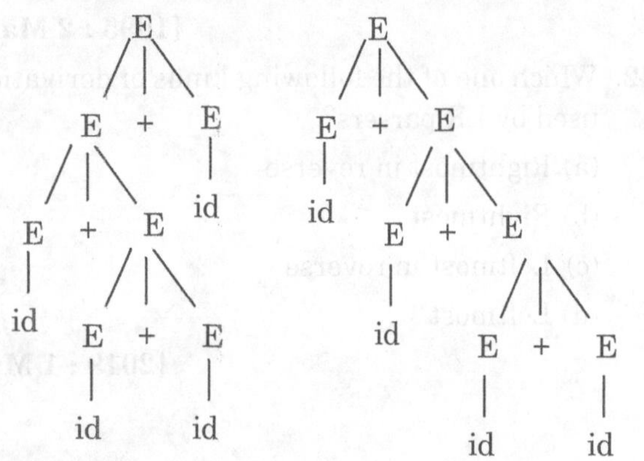

Has more than one parse tree.

5. Total 5 different parse trees are there.

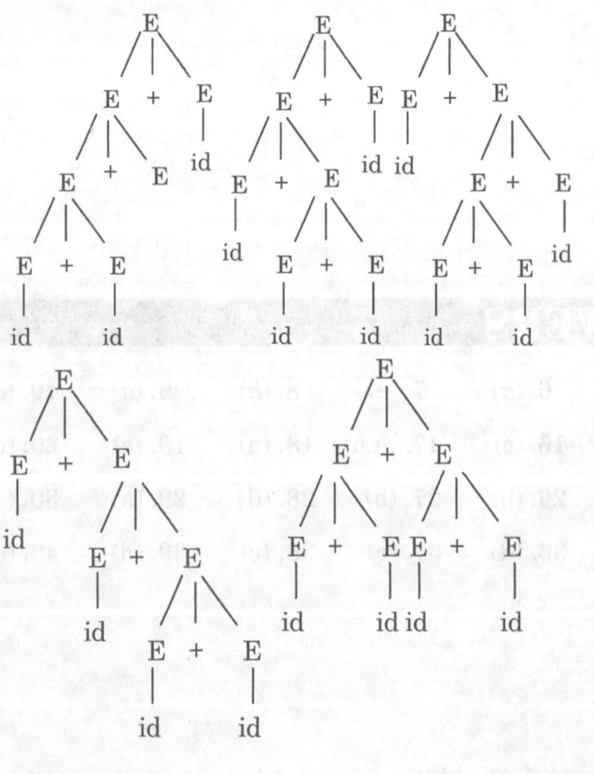

6. The grammar is

$S \to AC/CB$

$C \to aCb/\varepsilon$

$A \to aA/a$

$B \to Bb/b$

and number of derivation step is max(l, m) + 2

7. $S \to aB$

$\to aaBB$

$\to aabB$

$\to aabbS$

$\to aabbaB$

$\to aabbab$

8.

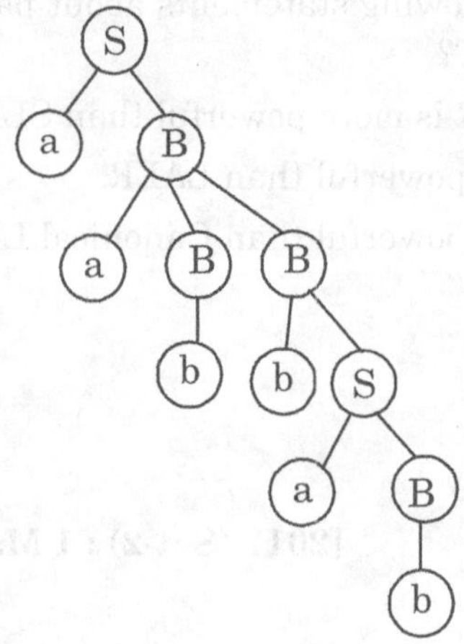

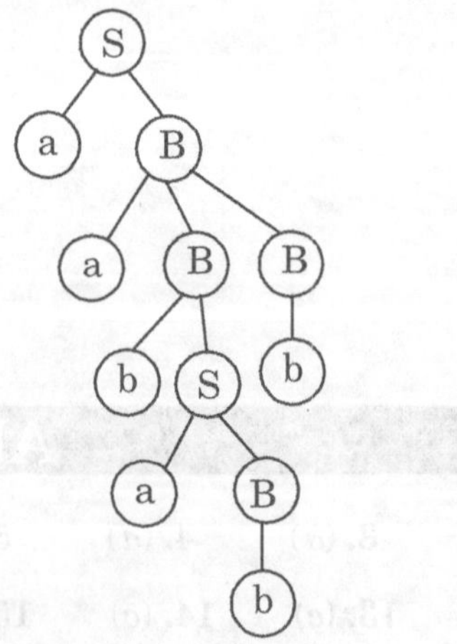

two parse tree.

9. FIRST(S) = {a, b, ε}

FIRST(A) = FIRST(S) = {a, b, ε}

FIRST(B) = FIRST(S) = {a, b, ε}

FOLLOW (A) = {b, a}

FOLLOW (S) = {$} U FOLLOW (A) = {b, a, $}

FOLLOW (B) = FOLLOW (S) = {b, a, $}

10. E1 : M[S, a] : S → aAbB, S → ε (because first of S contain a and ε)

E2 : M[S, b] : S → bAaB, S → ε (because first of S contain b and ε)

E3 : M[b, $] : B → S (because first of B contain ε)

11. 2nd production is

T → T * U (left recursive) so * is left associative.

Similarly

P → Q + P (Right recursion) so + is right associative.

12. The match are as follows

Lexical analysis – DFA minimization

Parsing – Production Tree

Register allocation – Graph coloring

expression evaluation – Post order traversal

13. FOLLOW(Q) = {w, y}

14. left recursion : A → Aα/β

After removing left recursion it can be written as

A→βA'

A' → αA'/ε

So apply above rule for Variable E and T resultant grammar is

E → TX

X → – TX | ε

T → FY

Y → +FY | ε

F → (E) → id

15. With look ahead, we would prefer to shift because the look ahead has higher precedence than X over + and both operation are left associative. So expression $3\times2+1=6+1=7$ will be evaluated.

16. LL (1) grammar is top down parsing. It is used in removing left recursion and factoring the grammar.

17. Grammar have multiple parse trees for string 'ε', so grammar is ambiguous, and also A → AA has left recusion.

18. Recursive descent parser is a kind of top – down parser.

19. It is ambiguous

20. Regular grammar may be ambigous and ambigous grammar is never LL(1).

Every regular set has a unambigous regular grammar so they are LL(1) and every LL(1) is LR(1)

21. S → Aa

A → BD

B → b | ∈

D → d | ∈

Follow (B) = {d, a}

Hence index value in descending order is 31.

22. (i) Goto part & shift entry must be same.

(ii) Reduce entry & error entry may b different due to conflicts.

23. LR is powerful than LALR parsers and LALR are powerful than SLR parsers.

24. Number of state in SLR is always same as number of state in LALR parser.

25. S → *i*E *t*SS¹*a*

S' ⇒ *e*S | *a*

E → *b*

This is left factor grammar

Thus we may expand S to ibtSS' on input *i* and wait untill ibtS has been seen to decide whether to expand S' → *e*S | ∈

26. P → QR and P → ε is not possible for operator grammmar.

27. Always the case SLR and LALR have same number of states.

while LR have more states than these two.

Because for any Bottom-up paring number of 'CORES' is always same while for LR() only other thing is lookahead is different.

28. Go to Graph is:-

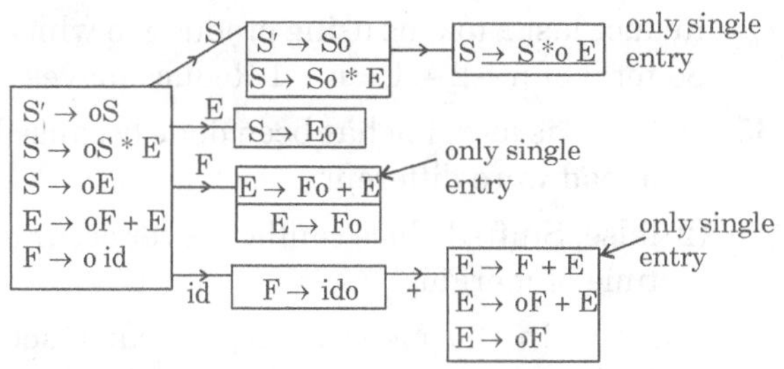

So all are in different set.

29.

	First	Follow
S	id	$
R	id, E	$
F	id	id, $

So table Entries are as follows

M [S, id] = {S → FR}

M[R, $] = {R → ∈}

30. The grammar is

S → AC/CB

C → aCb/null

A → aA/a

B → Bb/b

it generate set of all strings generated by above grammar

31. According to definition, handle is a production rule A → β and a position in the sentential form where string β may be found and replaced to produce the previous right sentiential form in a reightmost derivation of sentiential form.

32. An LALR(1) parser for a grammer G can have shift reduce S – R confilict if and only if the LR(1) parser for G has S – R conflicts.

33. It is LL(1) and LR(1)

because in S → *a*S*a*

S → *b*S

S → *c*

S	*a*	*b*	*c*
	s → *s*S*a*	*s* → *b*S	*s* → *c*

no multiple entries for 1 iteration, so it is LL(1) grammer mean by LR(1) that it is Left shift Reduced grammer and so it is also LR(1).

Hence it is both LL(1) and LR(1)

34. As per given question, a grammar with no epsilon- and unit-production (i.e., of type A → ε and A → a).

So To Reduce input string of n tokens, first Reduce n – 2 tokens using n – 2 reduce moves and then Reduce last 2 tokens using production which has. So total of n – 2 + 1 = n – 1 Reduce moves

35. (1) false, as merging has been done because look-ahead were different.

(2) false, Shift-Reduce conflict never occur at the time of merging.

(3) false, In the merged set, we can't see any Reduce-Reduce conflict (no reduction even possible, so no chances of R-R conflict)

(4) false, because goto is carried on Non-Terminals symbols, not on terminal symbols, and c is a terminal symbol.

36.

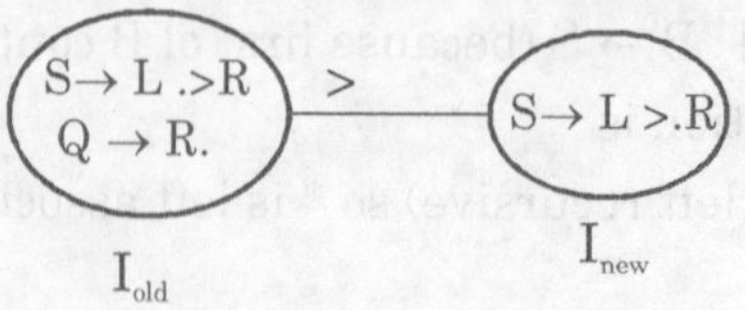

Form above diagram, we can see that there is no shift-reduce or reduce-reduce conflict.

37. In shift reduce parser, the stack contains only a set of variable prefix.

38. SLR and CLR are easy to implement. CLR is more powerful to any of the parsac.

39. The given grammar is ambiguous so neither LL(1) nor LR(1).

First Leftmost Derivation

S → F

F → c

Second Leftmost Derivation

S → H

H → c

34. LR parsers in term of power CLR > LALR > SLR > LR(0)

41. S → XXW{Print + 1}

S → Y {Print + 2}

W → SZ{Print + 3}

Translation of XXXXYZZ

S → XXW 1

→ XXSZ 3

→ XXXXWZ 1

→ XXXXSZZ 3

→ XXXXYZZ 2

Syntax directed translation scheme described by 23131

42. LR parser is a bottom up parser and so it uses right most derivation in reverse order.

∴ option (b) is the correct.

3 CHAPTER Syntax Directed Translation

Analysis of Previous GATE Papers											
	Year → Topics ↓		2019	2018	2017 Set 1	2017 Set 2	2016 Set 1	2016 Set 2	2015 Set 1	2015 Set 2	2015 Set 3
GRAMMARr	1 Mark	MCQ Type									
		Numerical Type									
	2 Marks	MCQ Type									
		Numerical Type									
	Total										
SYNTAX DIRECTED TRANSLATION	1 Mark	MCQ Type									
		Numerical Type									
	2 Marks	MCQ Type	1				1				
		Numerical Type									
	Total		2				2				
PARSER TREE & SYNTAX TREE	1 Mark	MCQ Type									
		Numerical Type									
	2 Marks	MCQ Type									
		Numerical Type									
	Total										
POST FIX NOTATION	1 Mark	MCQ Type									
		Numerical Type									
	2 Marks	MCQ Type									
		Numerical Type					1				
	Total						2				

INTERMEDIATE CODE

1. Generation of intermediate code based on an abstract machine model is useful in compilers because
(a) it makes implementation of lexical analysis and syntax analysis easier
(b) syntax-directed translations can be written for intermediate code generation
(c) it enhances the portability of the front end of the complier
(d) it is not possible to generate code for real machines directly from high level language programs

[1994 : 1 Mark]

2. A linker is given object modules for a set of programs that were compiled separately. What information need to be included in an object module?
(a) Object code
(b) Relocationbits
(c) Names and locations of ali external symbols defined in the object module
(d) Absolute addresses of internal symbols

[1995 : 1 Mark]

3. In a simplified computer the instructions are: OP R_j, R_i – Performs R_j OP R_i and stores the result in register R_i

OP m, R_i – Performs val OP R_i and stores the result in R_i. val denotes the content of memory location m.

MOV m, R_i – Moves the content of memory location m to register R_i.

MOV R_i, m – Moves the content of register R_i to memory location m.

The computer has only two registers, and OP is eitherADDorSUB.

Consider the following basic block:

$t_1 = a + b$

$t_2 = c + d$

$t_3 = e - t_2$

$t_4 - t_1 - t_3$

Assume that all operands are initially in memory. The final value of the computation should be in memory. What is the minimum number of MOV instructions in the code generated for this basic block?

(a) 2 (b) 3
(c) 5 (d) 6

[2007 : 2 Marks]

4. One of the purposes of using intermediate code in compilers is to
(a) make parsing and semantic analysis simpler.
(b) improve error recovery and error reporting.
(c) increase the chances of reusing the machine-independent code optimizer in other compilers.
(d) improve the register allocation.

[2014 (Set-3) : 1 Mark]

GRAMMAR

5. In the following grammar

X : : = X ⊕ Y/Y

Y : : = Z ◉ Y/Z

Z : : = id

Which of the follovving is true?
(a) '⊕' is left associative while '◉' is right associative
(b) Both '⊕' and'◉' is left associative
(c) '⊕' is the right associative while '◉' is left associative
(d) Noneoftheabove

[1997 : 1 Mark]

6. Consider the grammar rule $E \rightarrow E_1 - E_2$ for arithmetic expressions. The code generated is targeted to a CPU having a single user register. The subtraction operation requires the first operand to be in the register. If E_1 and E_2 do not have any common subexpression, in order to get the shortest possible code
(a) E_1 should be evaluated first
(b) E_2 should be evaluated first
(c) Evaluation of E_1 and E_2 should necessarily be interleaved
(d) Order of evaluation of E_1 and E_2 is of no consequence

[2004 : 1 Mark]

7. Consider the grammar with the following translation rules and E as the start symbol.

$E \rightarrow E_1$ # T{E.value = E_1.value * T.value}
  | T {E.value = T.value}
$T \rightarrow T_1$ & F{T.value = T_1.value + F.value}
  | F {T.value = F.value}
$F \rightarrow$ num{F.value = num.value}

Compute E. value for the root of the parse tree for the expression: 2 # 3 & 5 # 6 & 4.

(a) 200 (b) 180
(c) 160 (d) 40

[2004 : 2 Marks]

8. Consider the grammar E → E + n | Exn | n

For a sentence n + n x n, the handles in the right-sentential form of the reduction are

(a) n, E + n and E + n x n

(b) n, E + n and E + E x n

(c) n, n + n and n + n x n

(d) n, E + n and E x n **[2005 : 2 Marks]**

Data for Q. 10

Consider the following expression grammar. The semantic rules for expression calculation are stated next to each grammar production.

E → numberE.val = number.val

| E '+' EE$^{(1)}$.val = E$^{(2)}$.val + E$^{(3)}$.val

| E '×' EE$^{(1)}$.val = E$^{(2)}$.val × E$^{(3)}$.val;

9. The above grammar and the semantic rules are fed to a yacc tool (which is an LALR(l) parser generator) for parsing and evaluating arithmetic expressions. Which one of the following is true about the action of yacc for the given grammar?

(a) It detects recursion and eliminates recursion

(b) It detects reduce-reduce conflict, and resolves

(c) It detects shift-reduce conflict, and resolves the conflict in favor of a shift over a reduce action

(d) It detects shift-reduce conflict, and resolves the conflict in favor of a reduce over a shift action **[2005 : 2 Marks]**

10. Which one of the following statements is FALSE?

(a) Context-free grammar can be used to specify both lexical and syntax rules.

(b) Type checking is done before parsing.

(c) High-level language programs can be translated to different Intermediate Representations.

(d) Arguments to a function can be passed using the program stack.

[2018 : 1 Mark]

SYNTAX DIRECTED TRANSLATION

11. In a bottom-up evaluation of a syntax directed definition, inherited attributes can

(a) always be evaluated

(b) be evaluated only if the definition is L-attributed

(c) be evaluated only if the definition has synthesized attributes

(d) never be evaluated

[2003 : 1 Mark]

12. Consider the translation scheme shown below:

S → TR

R → + T {print ('+');} R | ε

T → num {print (num.val);}

Here num is a token that represents an integer and num.val represents the corresponding integer value. For an input string '9 + 5 + 2', this translation scheme will print

(a) 9 + 5 + 2 (b) 95 + 2 +

(c) 9 5 2 + + (d) + + 9 5 2

[2003 : 2 Marks]

13. Consider the syntax directed definition shown below:

S → id : = E {gen (id.place = E.place;);}

E → E_1 + E_2 {t = newtemp ();
gen (t = E_1. place + E_2. place;);
E.place = t}

E → id {E.place = id.place;}

Here, gen is a function that generates the output code, and newtemp is a function that returns the name of a new temporary variable on every call. Assume that t_1's are the temporary variable names generated by newtemp. For the statement 'X: = Y + Z', the 3-address code sequence generated by this definition is

(a) X = Y + Z

(b) t_1 = Y + Z; X = t_1

(c) t_1 = Y; t_2 = t_1 + Z; X = t_2

(d) t_1 = Y; t_2 = Z; t_3 = t_1 + t_2; X = t_3

[2003 : 2 Marks]

14. Consider the following translation scheme.

S → ER

R → *E{print('*');R | ε

E → F + E {print ('+'); | F

F → (S) | id {print (id. value);}

Here id is a token that represents an integer and id.value represents the corresponding integer value. For an input '2*3 + 4', this translation scheme prints

(a) 2*3 + 4 (b) 2* + 34

(c) 2 3 * 4 + (d) 2 3 4 + *

[2006 : 2 Marks]

15. Consider the following Syntax Directed Translation Scheme (SDTS), with non-terminals {S, A} and terminals {a, b}.

S → aA {print 1}

S → a {print 2}

A → Sb {print 3}

Using the above SDTS, the output printed by a bottom-up parser, for the input aab is:

(a) 1 3 2 (b) 2 2 3

(c) 2 3 1 (d) syntax error

[2016 (Set-1) : 2 Marks]

16. Consider the following grammar and the semantic actions to support the inherited type declaration attributes. Let X_1, X_2, X_3, X_4, X_5, and X_6 be the placeholders for the non-terminals D, T, L or L_1 in the following table:

Production rule	Semantic action
$D \rightarrow T\,L$	X_1.type = X_2.type
$T \rightarrow$ int	T.type = int
$T \rightarrow$ float	T.type = float
$L \rightarrow L_1$,id	X_3.type = X_4.type add Type(id.entry, X_5.type)
$L \rightarrow$ id	add Type(id.entry, X_6.type)

Which one of the following are the appropriate choices for X_1, X_2, X_3 and X_4?

(a) $X_1 = T, X_2 = L, X_3 = L_1, X_4 = T$

(b) $X_1 = T, X_2 = L, X_3 = T, X_4 = L_1$

(c) $X_1 = L, X_2 = L, X_3 = L_1, X_4 = T$

(d) $X_1 = L, X_2 = T, X_3 = L_1, X_4 = L$

[2019 : 2 Marks]

PARSER TREE & SYNTAX TREE

17. Consider two binary operators '↑' and '↓' with the precedence of operator ↓ being lower than that of the ↑ operator. Operator ↑ is right associative while operator ↓ is left associative. Which one of the following represents the parse tree for expression (7 ↓ 3 ↑ 4 ↑ 3 ↓ 2)?

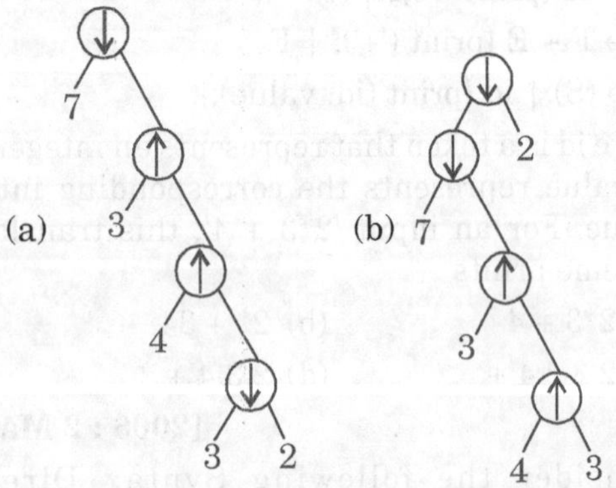

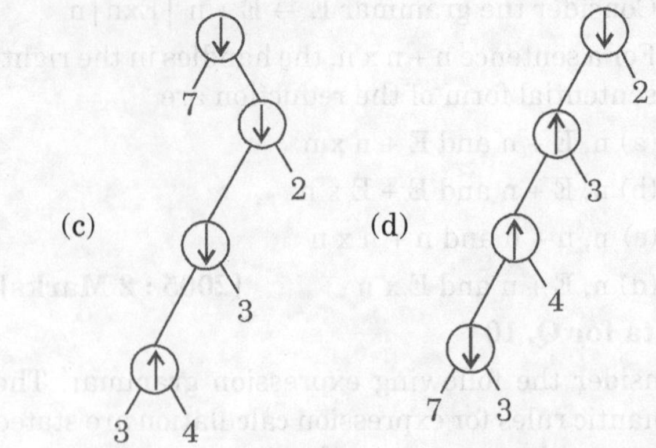

[2011 : 2 Marks]

18. Consider the expression tree shown. Each leaf represents a numerical value, which can either be 0 or 1. Over ali possible choices of the values at the leaves, the maximum possible value of the expression represented by the tree is ____.

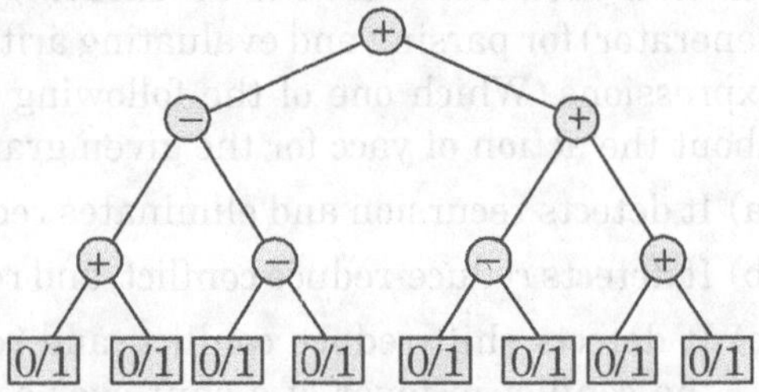

[2014 (Set-2) : 2 Marks]

POSTFIX NOTATION

19. The attributes of three arithmetic operators in some programming language are given below.

Operator	Precedence	Associativity	Arity
+	High	Left	Binary
–	Medium	Right	Binary
*	Low	Left	Binary

The value of the expression 2 – 5 + 1 – 7*3 in this language is ____.

[2016 (Set-1): 2 Marks]

ANSWERS

1. (a)	**2.** (d)	**3.** (b)	**4.** (c)	**5.** (a)	**6.** (b)	**7.** (c)	**8.** (d)	**9.** (c)	**10.** (b)
11. (c)	**12.** (b)	**13.** (b)	**14.** (d)	**15.** (c)	**16.** (*d*)	**17.** (b)	**18.** (6)	**19.** (9)	

EXPLANATIONS

1. Generation of intermediate code based on an abstract machine model is useful in compilers because, it makes implementation of lexical analysis and syntax analysis easier
2. Linker is a program in a system which helps to link a object modules of program into a single object file. It performs the process of linking. Linker are also called link editors. Linking is process of collecting and maintaining piece of code and data into a single file. Linker also link a particular module into system library. It takes object modules from assembler as input and forms an executable file as output for loader.
3. Instructions will be following :

MOV	b,	R_1
ADD	a,	R_1
MOV	d,	R_2
ADD	c,	R_2
SUB	e,	R_2
SUB	R_1,	R_2
MOV	R_2,	t_4

It takes 3 MOV instructions.

4. Intermediate code is machine independent code which makes it easy to retarget the compiler to generate code for newer and different processors.
5. "+" is left associative while '.' is right associative because in the productin X : : = X + Y there is a left recursion and in the production Y : : = Z . Y there is right recursion
6. To optimise the solution, evaluate the expression E_2. Then E_1 can calculated and finally E_1 will be one of operands that will be in register and subtraction can be performed directly. But if opposite is followed, then make move store operations.
7. The parse tree will be

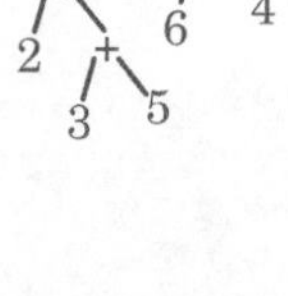

is multication

& is addition

so converting

This parse tree to multiplication and addition.

This will evaluated as

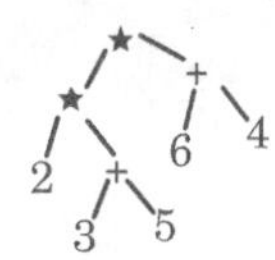

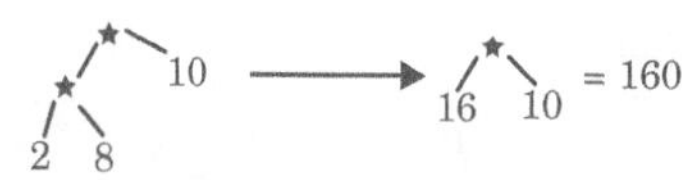

8. Derive the sentence

$E \rightarrow E * n \rightarrow E + n * n \rightarrow n + n * n$

Then handle is always substring, where reduction gives us previous right-sentential form.

$\underline{n} + n * n$,

Here, handle is underlined

If we reduce, we get $\underline{E + n} * n$

(consider this is same as previous right-sentential form)

$\underline{E * n}$

E

n , E + n , E * n

9. $E \rightarrow \text{number} \mid E' + E' \mid E' \times E'$

Then Y_{yacc} compiler detects shift-reduce conflict, and resolves the conflict in favor of a shift over a reduce action.

Consider following configuration where shift-reduce conflict occurs

Stack	Input
... E + Ex	E...$

10. Type checking is done before parsing is clearly false because in compiler type checking is done after parsing phase.

11. A syntax-directed definition is a generalization of a context free grammar in which each grammar or symbol has an associated into two subsets called the synthesized and inherited attributes of that grammar symbol.

12.

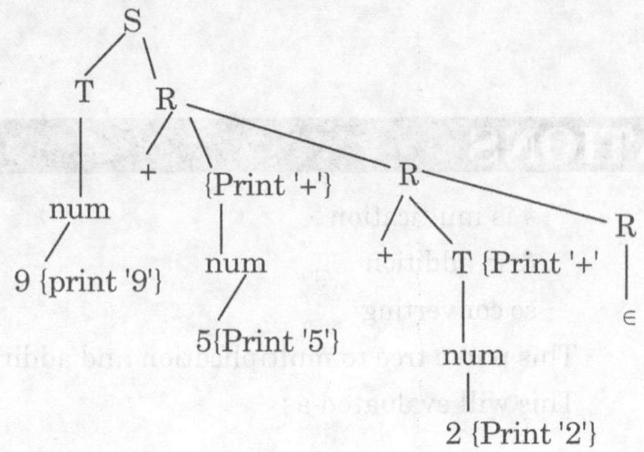

Output 95 + 2 +

13. x : = y + z;

$t_1 = y + z;$
$x = t_1$

3AC

14.

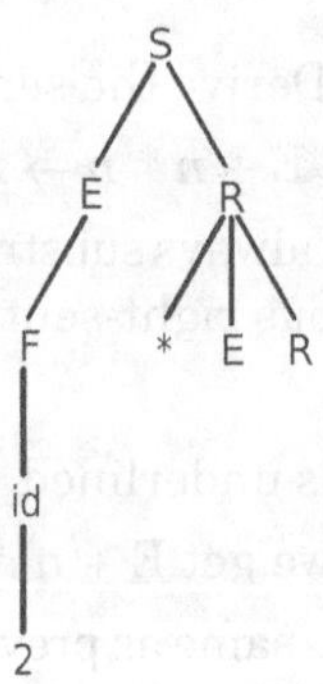

So an inoput 2 * 3 + 4 it prints

234+*

15.

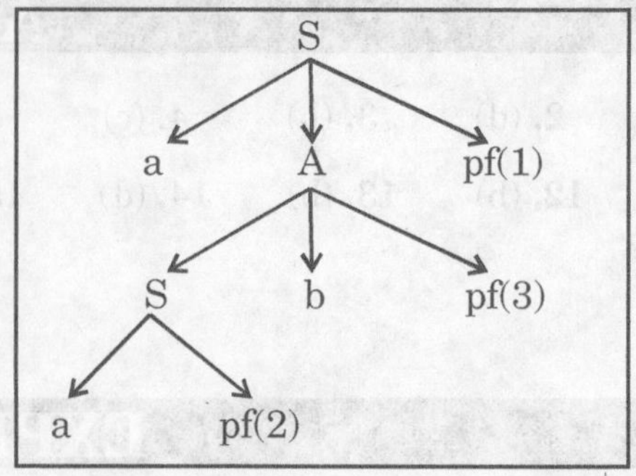

17. 7 ↓ 3 ↑ 4 ↑ 3 ↑ 2

Operator ↓ lower priority and left associative

operator ↑ Highest priority and right associative

7 ↓ 3 ↑ 4 ↑ 3 ↑ 2

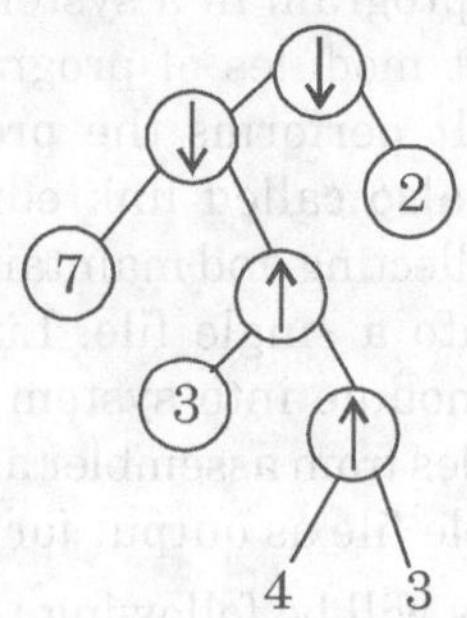

18.

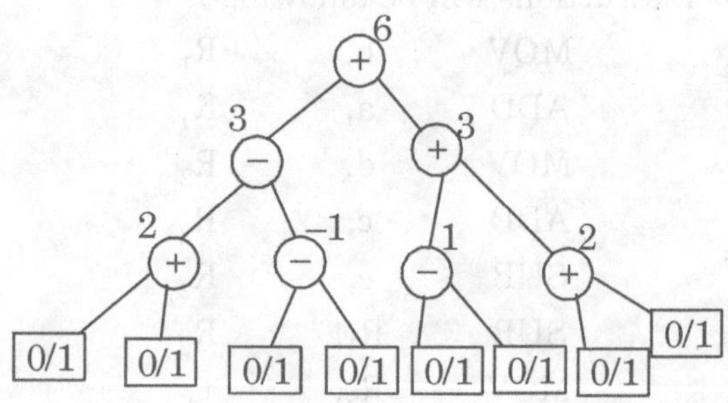

19. $2 - 5 + 1 - 7 * 3 = 2 - 6 - 7 * 3$

$= 2 - (-1) * 3$

$= 3 * 3 = 9$

4

CHAPTER

Code Generation & Optimization

Analysis of Previous GATE Papers											
	Year → Topics ↓		2019	2018	2017 Set 1	2017 Set 2	2016 Set 1	2016 Set 2	2015 Set 1	2015 Set 2	2015 Set 3
CODE GENERATION & OPTIMIZATION	1 Mark	MCQ Type			1					1	
		Numerical Type					1				
	2 Marks	MCQ Type						1	1	1	
		Numerical Type			2				1		
	Total				5		1	2	4	3	

1. Consider the following C code segment.

```
for (i = 0; i < n; i ++)
{
    for (j = 0; j < n; j ++)
    {
        if (i % 2)
    {   x+=(4 * j + 5*i);
        y+=(7 + 4 *j);
    }
  }
}
```

which one of the following is false?

(a) The code contains loop invariant computation

(b) There is scope of common sub-expression elimination in this code

(c) There is scope strength reduction in this code

(d) There is scope of dead code elimination in this code

[2006 : 2 Marks]

2. Some code optimizations are carried out on the intermediate code because

(a) They enhance the portability of the complier to other target processors

(b) Program analysis is more accurate on intermediate code than on machine code

(c) The information from data flow analysis cannot otherwise be used for optimization

(d) The information from the front end cannot otherwise be used for optimization

[2008 : 1 Mark]

3. Which languages necessarily need heap allocation in the runtime environment?

(a) Those that support recursion

(b) Those that use dynamic scoping

(c) Those that allow dynamic data structure

(d) Those that use global variables

[2010 : 1 Mark]

Common Data for Questions 4 and 5

The following code segment is executed on a processor which allows only register operands in its instructions. Each instruction can have almost two source operands and one destinations operand. Assume that all variables are dead after this code segment.

```
c = a + b;
d = c * a;
e = c + a;
x = c * c;
if (x > a) {
    y= a * a;
}
else {
    d = d * d;
    e = e * e;
}
```

4. Suppose the instruction set architecture of the processor has only two registers. The only allowed complier optimization is code motion, which moves statements from one place to another while preserving correctness. What is the minimum number of spills to memory in the compiled code?

(a) 0 (b) 1

(c) 2 (d) 3

[2013 : 2 Marks]

5. What is the minimum number of registers needed in the instruction set architecture of the processor to compile this code segment without any spill to memory? Do not apply any optimization other than optimizing register allocation?

(a) 3 (b) 4

(c) 5 (d) 6 **[2013 : 2 Marks]**

6. Which one of the following is FALSE?

(a) A basic block is a sequence of instructions where control enters the sequence at the beginning and exits at the end.

(b) Available expression analysis can be used for common subexpression elimination.

(c) Live variable analysis can be used for dead code elimination.

(d) $x = 4 \times 5 \Rightarrow 20$ is an example of common subexpression elimination.

[2014 (Set-1) :1 Mark]

7. Which one of the following is NOT performed during compilation?

(a) Dynamic memory allocation

(b) Type checking

(c) Symbol table management

(d) Inline expansion

[2014 (Set-2) : 1 Mark]

8. For a C program accessing X[i] [j] [k], the following intermediate code is generated by a compiler. Assume that the size of an integer is 32 bits and the size of a character is 8 bits.

```
t0 = i * 1024
t1 = j * 32
t2 = k * 4
t3 = t1 + t0
t4 = t3 + t2
t5 = X[t4]
```

Which one of the following statements about the source code for the C program is CORRECT?

(a) X is declared as "int X[32] [32] [8]".

(b) X is declared as "int X[4] [1024] [32]".

(c) X is declared as "char X[4] [32] [8]".

(d) X is declared as "char X[32] [16] [2]".

[2014 (Set-2) : 2 Marks]

9. Which of the following statements are CORRECT?

(1) Static allocation of ali data areas by a compiler makes it impossible to implement recursion.

(2) Automatic garbage collection is essential to implement recursion.

(3) Dynamic allocation of activation records is essential to implement recursion.

(4) Both heap and stack are essential to implement recursion.

(a) 1 and 2 only (b)2 and 3 only

(c) 3 and 4 only (d)1 and 3 only

[2014 (Set-3) : 1 Mark]

10. Consider the basic block given below.

a = b + c

c = a + d

d = b + c

e = d – b

a = e + b

The minimum number of nodes and edges present in the DAG representation of the above basic block respectively are

(a) 6 and 6 (b) 8 and 10

(c) 9 and 12 (d) 4 and 4

[2014 (Set-3) : 2 Marks]

11. A variable x is said to be live at a statement S- in a program if the follovving three conditions hold simultaneously:

1. There exists a statement S_j that uses x

2. There is a path from S_i to S_j in the flow graph corresponding to the program

3. The path has no intervening assignment to x including at S_i and S_j

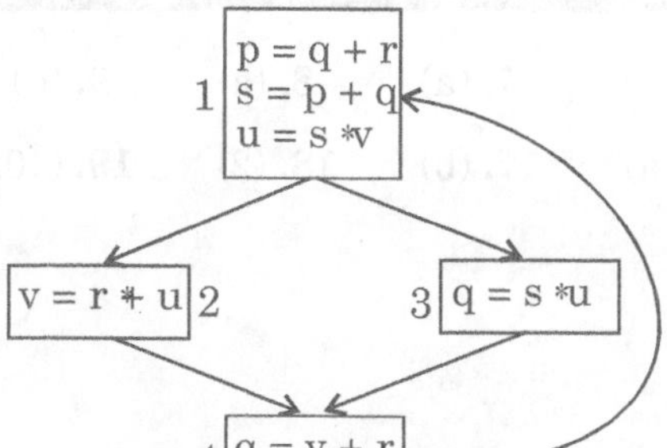

The variables which are live both at the statement in basic block 2 and at the statement in basic block 3 of the above control flow graph are

(a) p, s, u (b) r, s, u

(c) r, u (d) q, v

[2015 (Set-1): 2 Marks]

12. The least number of temporary variables required to create a three -address code in static single assignment form for the expression q+r/3 + s –t * 5+u * v/w is ________.

[2015 (Set-1): 2 Marks]

13. In the context of abstract-syntax-tree (AST) and control-flow-graph (CFG), which one of the follovving is True?

(a) In both AST and CFG, let node N_2 be the successor of node N_1. In the input program, the code corresponding to N_2 is present after the code corresponding to N_1

(b) For any input program, neither AST nor CFG will contain a cycle

(c) The maximum number of successors of a node in an AST and a CFG depends on the input program

(d) Each node in AST and CFG corresponds to at most one statement in the input program

[2015 (Set-2) : 1 Mark]

14. Consider the intermediate code given below:

1. i = 1 2. j = 1
3. t1 = 5 * i 4. t2 = t1 + j
5. t3 = 4 * t2 6. t4 = t3
7. a[t4] = –1 8. j = j + 1
9. if j < = 5 goto (3) 10. i = i + 1
11. if i < 5 goto (2)

The number of nodes and edges in the control-flow-graph constructed for the above code, respectively, are

(a) 5 and 7 (b) 6 and 7

(c) 5 and 5 (d) 7 and 8

[2015 (Set-2) : 2 Marks]

15. Consider the following code segment.

x = u – t;

y = x * v;

x = y + w;

y = t – z;

y = x * y;

The minimum number oftotal variables required to convert the above code segment to static single assignment form is ______.

[2016 (Set-1) : 1 Mark]

16. A student wrote two context-free grammars G1 and G2 for generating a single C-like array declaration. The dimension of the array is at least one. For example,

int a [10] [3];

The grammars use D as the start symbol, and use six terminal symbols int; id [ ] num.

Grammar GlGrammar G2

D → int L; D → int L;

L → id [E L → idE

E → num] E → E[num]

E → num] [E E → [num]

Which of the grammars correctly generate the declaration mentioned above?

(a) Both G1 and G2 (b) Only G1

(c) Only G2 (d) Neither G1 nor G2

[2016 (Set-2) : 2 Marks]

17. Consider the following intermediate program in three address code

p = a - b

q = p * c

p = u * v

q = p + q

Which one of the following corresponds to a static single assignment form of the above code?

(a) $p_1 = a - b$
$q_1 = p_1 * c$
$p_1 = u * v$
$q_1 = p_1 + q_1$

(b) $p_3 = a - b$
$q_4 = p_3 * c$
$p_4 = u * v$
$q_5 = p_4 + q_4$

(c) $p_1 = a - b$
$q_1 = p_2 * c$
$p_3 = u * v$
$q_2 = p_4 + q_3$

(d) $p_1 = a - b$
$q_1 = p * c$
$p_2 = u * v$
$q_2 = p + q$

[2017 (Set-1) : 1 Mark]

18. Consider the expression (a –1)* (((b + c) /3) + d)). Let X be the minimum number of registers required by an optimal code generation (without any register spill) algorithm for a load/store architecture, in which (i) only load and store instructions can have memory operands and (ii) arithmetic instructions can have only register or immediate operands. The value of X is ____.

[2017 (Set-1): 2 Marks]

19. Consider the following grammar:

stmt → if expr then expr else expr; stmt | 0 expr → term relop term | term

term → id | number

id → a | b c

number → [0-9]

where relop is a relational operator (e.g., <, >, ...), 0 refers to the empty statement, and if, then, else are terminals.

Consider a program P following the above grammar containing ten if terminals. The number of control flow paths in P is ______.

For example, the program

if e_1 then e_2 else e_3

has 2 control flow paths, $e_1 \rightarrow e_2$ and $e_1 \rightarrow e_3$.

[2017 (Set-1) : 2 Marks]

ANSWERS

1. (d)	**2.** (a)	**3.** (c)	**4.** (b)	**5.** (b)	**6.** (d)	**7.** (a)	**8.** (a)	**9.** (d)	**10.** (a)
11. (c)	**12.** (8)	**13.** (c)	**14.** (b)	**15.** (d)	**16.** (a)	**17.** (b)	**18.** (2)	**19.** (1024)	

EXPLANATIONS

1. 4 * j is comman subexpression so we can eleminate it. B is true.

5 * i can be moved out of inner loop so can be i % 2.

Means, A is true as we have loop invariant computation.

Now, 4 * j as well as 5*i can be replaced with a = – 4; before j loop then a = a + 4; where 4 * j is computed, likewise for 5 * i. So option C is true as there is scope of strength reduction.

2. Code optimizations are carried out on the intermediate code so that same source code can be converted to machine language of the target machine depending upon the back end tools. It also increases the probability of the compiler, i.e. compiler can generate machine code of different machine codes.

3. When dynamic data structure is used, heap should be used for runtime environment.

4. R1 R2

R1	R2	
a	b	c = a + b
a	c	x = c * c
a	x	but we will have to store c in memory as we don't know if x > a or not
y	x	y = a * a

The best case of x > a , min spills = 1

5. 4 register Requierd

Statement	Registers used
c = a + b;	R2 ← R1 + R2
d = c * a;	R3 ← R2 * R1
e = c + a;	R4 ← R2 + R1
x = c * c;	R2 ← R2 * R2
if(x > a){	Here Wd Compare R2 and R1
y = a * a;	R1 ← R1 * R1
}	
else{	
d = d * d;	R3 ← R3 * R3
e = e * e;	R4 ← R4 * R4
}	

6. X = 4 * 5 ⇒ x = 20 is an example of Constant folding.

7. At compilation time dynamic memory allocation is not feasible.

8. The expression correspoint to t5 to calculate address of array is

$$\begin{aligned} t5 &= X[t4] \\ &= X[t3 + t2] \\ &= X[t1 + t0 + t2] \\ &= X[i * 1024 + j * 32 + k * 4] \\ &= X + i * 1024 + j * 32 + k * 4 \end{aligned}$$

So, X is declared as "int X[32][32][8]".

9. Statement 1 and 3 is true.

10. The given basic block can be rewritten as

$a = b + c$	$a = b + c$
$c = a + d$	$c = b + c + d$
$d = b + c \Rightarrow$	$d = b + b + c + d = 2b + c + d$
$e = d - b$	$e = b + b + c + d - b = b + c + d$
$a = e + b$	$a = b + b + c + d = 2b + c + d$

From above simplification it is visible that e is same as c and final value of a is same as *d*. So the final basic block can be written as follows:

$a = b + c$

$c = a + d$

$d = 2b + c + d$

$e = c$

$a = d$

The DAG generated for the above basic block in as

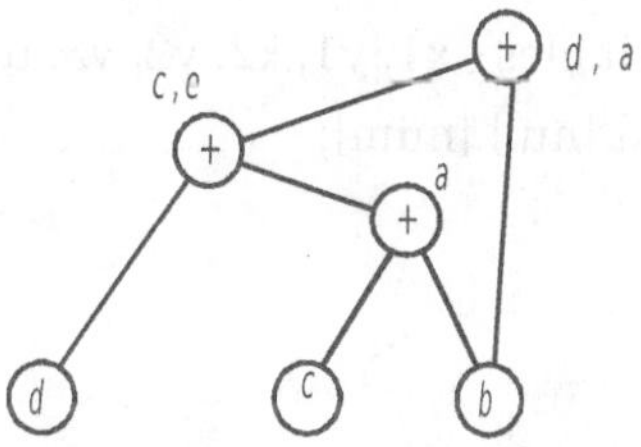

Maximum number of modes and edges in above DAG is (6,6)

11. According to question, a variable is live if it holds a value that may be needed in the future i.e. it is used in future before any new assignment.

So r and u is live variable.

12. The three address code is as follows

t1 = r/3;

t2 = t * 5;

t3 = u * v;

t4 = t3/w;

t5 = q + t1;

t6 = t5 + s;

t7 = t6 – t2;

t8 = t7 + t4;

13. (A) false, In CFG, code of N2 may be present before N1 when there is a loop or goto.

(B) false,CFG has cycle when input program has loop.

(C) true, successors in AST and CFG depedend on input program.

(D) false, a single statement may belong to a block of statements.

14.

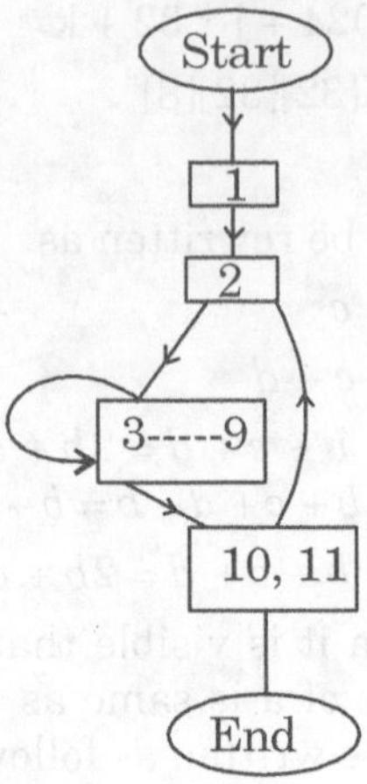

15. In static single assignment the code is

x1 = u – t;

y1 = x1 * v;

x2 = y1 + w;

y2 = t – z;

y3 = x2 * y2;

total 10 variables (x1, y1, x2, y2, y3, u, t, v, w, z)

16. String int id [nu,] [num];

Using G_1:-

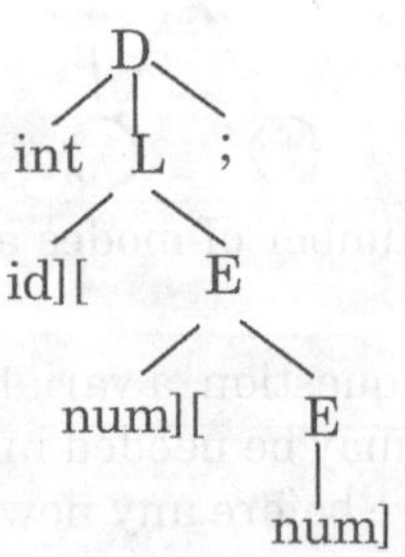

Using G_2:-

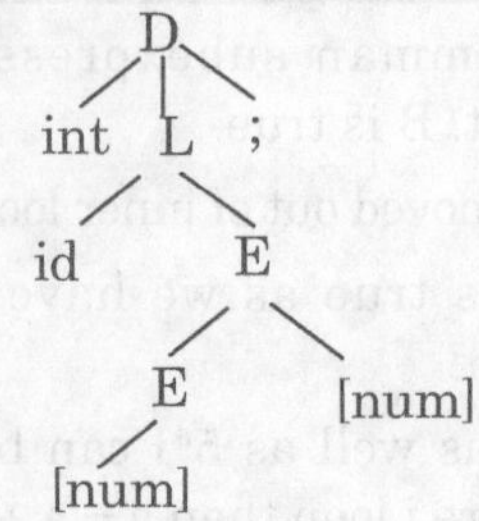

17. Static single assignment is

p3 = a – b

q4 = p3 * c

p4 = u * v

q5 = $p_4 + q_4$

18. The Code for the expression is as follows :

Load R1, b

Load R2, c

ADD R1, R2

Div R1, 3

Load R2, d

Add R1, R2

Load R2, a

Sub R2, 1

Mul R2, R1

Hence two register is requierd.

19. Every if structure has 2 control flows.

For 10 if structure number of control flow paths

= 2 * 2 * 2 * 2 * 2 ... 10 times = 2^10 = 1024

Unit - VIII

Operating System

Syllabus

Processes, threads, inter-process communication, concurrency and synchronization. Deadlock. CPU scheduling. Memory management and virtual memory. File systems.

Contents

1 CHAPTER

Process Management

Analysis of Previous GATE Papers											
	Year → Topics ↓		2019	2018	2017 Set 1	2017 Set 2	2016 Set 1	2016 Set 2	2015 Set 1	2015 Set 2	2015 Set 3
SCHEDULING & CONCEPT	1 Mark	MCQ Type									
		Numerical Type									
	2 Marks	MCQ Type									
		Numerical Type									
	Total										
SCHEDULING ALGO	1 Mark	MCQ Type					1				
		Numerical Type			1						
	2 Marks	MCQ Type									1
		Numerical Type	1			1		1	1		
	Total		2		1	2	1	2	2		2
PROCESS TRANSITION DIAGRAM	1 Mark	MCQ Type									1
		Numerical Type									
	2 Marks	MCQ Type									
		Numerical Type									
	Total										1
MULTIPROCESSOR SYSTEM	1 Mark	MCQ Type									
		Numerical Type									
	2 Marks	MCQ Type									
		Numerical Type									
	Total										

SCHEDULING & CONCEPT

1. State an undesirable characteristic of each of the following criteria for measuring performance of an operating system:
(a) Turn around time
(b) Waitingtime **[1988 : 2 Marks]**

2. The highest-response ratio next scheduling policy favours ....jobs, but it also limits the waiting time of .... jobs.
[1990 : 2 Marks]

3. Which of the following is an example of spooled device?
(a) A line printer used to print the output of a number of jobs
(b) A terminal used to enter input data to a running program
(c) A secondary Storage device in a virtual memory system
(d) A graphic display device **[1996 : 1 Mark]**

4. Four jobs are waiting to be run. Their expected run times are 6,3,5 and x in what order should they be run to minimize the average response time?
[1998 : 2 Marks]

5. **List-I** contains some CPU scheduling algorithms and **List-II** contains some applications. Match entries in **List-I** entries in **List-II**

List-I
A. Gang Scheduling
B. Rate Monotonic Scheduling
C. Fair Share Scheduling

List-II
1. Guaranteed Scheduling
2. Real-time Scheduling
3. Thread Scheduling

Code:

	A	B	C
(a)	3	2	1
(b)	1	2	3
(c)	2	3	1
(d)	1	3	2

[2007 : 1 Mark]

SCHEDULING ALGO

6. Assume that the following jobs are to be executed on a single processor system

Job Id	CPU Brust time
P	4
q	1
r	8
s	1
t	2

The jobs are assumed to have arrived at time 0^+ and in the order p, q, r, s, t. Calculate the departure time (completion time) for job p if scheduling is round robin with time slice 1.
(a) 4 (b) 10
(c) 11 (d) 12 **[1993 : 2 Marks]**

7. Which scheduling policy is most suitable for a time-shared operating systems?
(a) Shortest Job First
(b) Round Robin
(c) First come first serve
(d) Elevator **[1995 : 1 Mark]**

8. The sequence .... is an optimal non-preemptive scheduling sequence for the following jobs which leaves the CPU idle for........ unit(s) of time.

Job	Arrival time	Burst time
1	0.0	9
2	0.6	5
3	1.0	1

(a) {3, 2, 1} 1 (b) {2, 1, 3}, 0
(c) {3, 2, 1}, 0 (d) {1, 2, 3}, 5

9. Four jobs to be executed on a single processor system arrive at time 0^+ in the order A, B, C, D. Their burst CPU time requirements are 4,1, 8, 1 time units respectively. The completion time of A under round robin scheduling with time slice of one time unit is
(a) 10 (b) 4
(c) 8 (d) 9 **[1996 : 2 Marks]**

10. Consider n processes sharing the CPU in a round-robin fashion. Assuming that each process switch takes s seconds, what must be the quantum size q such that the overhead resulting from process switching is minimizedbut at the same time each process is guaranteed to get its turn at the CPU at least every t seconds?
(a) $q \le \frac{t-ns}{n-1}$ (b) $q \le \frac{t-ns}{n+1}$
(c) $q \ge \frac{t-ns}{n-1}$ (d) $q \ge \frac{t-ns}{n+1}$
[1998 : 1 Mark]

11. Consider a set of n tasks with known runtimes r_1, r_2,...,r_n to be run on a uniprocessor machine. Which of the following processor scheduling algorithms will result in the maximum throughput?
(a) Round-Robin
(b) Shortest-Job-First
(c) Highest-Response-Ratio-Next
(d) First-Come-First-Served **[2001 : 1 Mark]**

12. Which of the following scheduling algorithms is non-preemptive?

(a) Round Robin
(b) First-in-First-out
(c) Multilevel Queue Scheduling
(d) Multilevel Queue Scheduling with Feedback

[2001 : 1 Mark]

13. A uni-processor computer system only has two processes, both of which alternate 10 ms CPU bursts with 90 ms I/O bursts. Both the processes were created at nearly the same time. The I/O of both processes can proceed in parallel. Which of the following scheduling Strategies will result in the least CPU utilization (over a long period of time) for this system?

(a) First come first served scheduling
(b) Shortest remaining time first scheduling
(c) Static priority scheduling with different priorities for the two processes
(d) Round robin scheduling with a time quantum of 5 ms.

[2003 : 2 Marks]

14. Consider the following set of processes, vvith the arrival times and the CPU-burst times given in milliseconds

Pr ocess	Arrival time	Burst time
P1	0	5
P2	1	3
P3	2	3
P4	4	1

What is the average turnaround time for these processes vvith the preemptive Shortest Remaining Processing Time first (SRPT) algorithm?

(a) 5.50 (b) 5.75
(c) 6.00 (d) 6.25

[2004 : 2 Marks]

15. We wish to schedule three processes P1, P2 and P3 on a uniprocessor system. The priorities, CPU time requirements and arrival times of the processes are as shown below.

Process	Priority	CPU time required	Arrival time (hh : mm:ss)
P1	10 (highest)	20 sec	00:00:05
P2	9	10 sec	00:00:03
P3	8 (lowest)	15 sec	00:00:00

We have a choice of preemptive or non-preemptive scheduling. In preemptive scheduling, a late-arriving higher priority process can preempt a currently running process with lower priority. In non-preemptive scheduling, a late-arriving higher priority process must wait for the currently executing process to complete before it can be scheduled on the processor. What are the turnaround times (time from arrival tili completion) of P2 using preemptive and non-preemptive scheduling respectively?

(a) 30 sec, 30 sec (b) 30 sec, 10 sec
(c) 42 sec, 42 sec (d) 30 sec, 42 sec

[2005 : 2 Marks]

16. The arrival time, priority, and durations of the CPU and I/O bursts for each of three processes P_1, P_2 and P_3 are given in the table below. Each process has a CPU burst followed by an I/O burst followed by another CPU burst. Assume that each process has its own I/O resource.

Process	Arrival time	Priority	Burst durations CPU, I/O CPU
P_1	0	2	1, 5, 3
P_2	2	3 (lowest)	3, 3, 1
P_3	3	1 (highest)	2, 3, 1

The multi-programmed operating system uses preemptive priority scheduling. What are the finish times of the processes P1, P2 and P3?

(a) 11, 15, 9 (b) 10, 15, 9
(c) 11, 16, 10 (d) 12, 17, 11

[2006 : 2 Marks]

17. Consider three processes, all arriving at time zero, with total execution time of 10, 20 and 30 units, respectively. Each process spends the first 20% of execution time doing I/O, the next 70% of time doing computation, and the last 10% of time doing I/O again. The operating system uses a shortest remaining compute time first scheduling algorithm and schedules a new process either when the running process get blocked on I/O or when the running process finishes its compute burst. Assume that ali I/O operations can be overlapped as much as possible. For what percentage of time does the CPU remain idle?

(a) 0% (b) 10.6%
(c) 30.0% (d) 89.4%

[2006 : 2 Marks]

18. Consider three processes (process id 0, 1, 2, respectively) with compute time bursts 2, 4, and 8 time units. All processes arrive at time zero. Consider the longest remaining time first (LRTF) scheduling algorithm. In LRTF ties are broken by giving priority to the process with the lowest process id. The average turn around time is

(a) 13 units (b) 14 units

(c) 15 units (d) 16 units

[2006 : 2 Marks]

19. Let a memory have four free blocks of sizes 4k, 8k, 20k, 2k. These blocks are allocated following the best-fit strategy. The allocation requests are stored in a queue as shown below.

Request No.	Request sizes	Usage Time
J1	2k	4
J2	14k	10
J3	3k	2
J4	6k	8
J5	6k	4
J6	10k	1
J7	7k	8
J8	20k	6

The time at which the request for J7 will be completed will be

(a) 16 (b) 19

(c) 20 (d) 37 **[2007 : 1 Mark]**

20. An operating system uses Shortest Remaining Time first (SRT) process scheduling algorithm. Consider the arrival times and execution times for the following processes

Process	Execution time	Arrival time
Pl	20	0
P2	25	15
P3	10	30
P4	15	45

What is the total waiting time for process P2?

(a) 5 (b) 15

(c) 40 (d) 55 **[2007 : 2 Marks]**

21. If the time-slice used in the round-robin scheduling policy is more than the maximum time required to execute any process, then the policy will

(a) degenerate to shortest job first

(b) degenerate to priority scheduling

(c) degenerate to first come first serve

(d) None of the above

[2008 : 2 Marks]

22. Which of the following statements are true?

I. Shortest remaining time first scheduling may cause starvation

II. Preemptive scheduling may cause starvation

III. Round robin is better than FCFS in terms of response time

(a) I only

(b) I and III only

(c) II and III only

(d) I, II and III

[2010 : 1 Mark]

23. Consider the following table of arrival time and burst time for three processes P0, Pl and P2.

Process	Arrival time	Burst time
PO	0 ms	9 ms
Pl	1 ms	4 ms
P2	2 ms	9 ms

The pre-emptive shortest job first scheduling algorithm is used. Scheduling is carried out only at arrival or completion of processes. What is the average waiting time for the three processes?

(a) 5.0 ms

(b) 4.33 ms

(c) 6.33 ms

(d) 7.33 ms

[2011 : 2 Marks]

24. Consider the 3 processes, Pl, P2 and P3 shown in the table.

Process Name	Arrival Time	Time Unit Required
Pl	0	5
P2	1	7
P3	3	4

The completion order of the 3 processes under the policies FCFS and RR2 (round robin scheduling with CPU quantum of 2 time units) are:

(a) FCFS: Pl, P2, P3 RR2: Pl, P2, P3

(b) FCFS: Pl, P3, P2 RR2: Pl, P3, P2

(c) FCFS: Pl, P2, P3 RR2: Pl, P3, P2

(d) FCFS: Pl, P3, P2 RR2: Pl, P2, P3

[2012 : 2 Marks]

25. A scheduling algorithm assigns priority proportional to the waiting time of a process. Every process starts with priority zero (the lowest priority). The schedule reevaluates the process priorities every T time units and decides the next process to schedule. Which one of the following is TRUE if the processes have no I/O operations and ali arrive at time zero?

(a) This algorithm is equivalent to the first come first serve algorithm

(b) This algorithm is equivalent to the round-round algorithm

(c) This algorithm is equivalent to the shortest-job-first algorithm

(d) This algorithm is equivalent to the shortest-remaining-time-first algorithm

[2013 : 1 Mark]

26. Consider the following set of processes that need to be scheduled on a single CPU. All the times are given in milliseconds.

Process Name	Arrival Time	Execution Time
A	0	6
B	3	2
C	5	4
D	7	6
E	10	3

Using the shortest remaining time first scheduling algorithm, the average process turnaround time (in msec) is _____. **[2014 (Set-1) : 2 Marks]**

27. Three processes A, B and C each execute a loop of 100 iterations. In each iteration of the loop, a process performs a single computation that requires t_c CPU milliseconds and then initiates a single I/O operation that lasts for t_{io} milliseconds. It is assumed that the computer where the processes execute has sufficient number of I/O devices and the OS of the computer assigns different I/O devices to each process. Also, the scheduling overhead of the OS is negligible. The processes have the following characteristics:

Process id	t_c	t_{io}
A	100 ms	500 ms
B	350 ms	500 ms
C	200 ms	500 ms

The processes A, B, and C are started at times 0, 5 and 10 milliseconds respectively, in a pure time sharing system (round robin scheduling) that uses a time slice of 50 milliseconds. The time in milliseconds at which process C would complete its first I/O operation is _______.

[2014 (Set-2) : 2 Marks]

28. An operating system uses shortest remaining time first scheduling algorithm for pre-emptive scheduling of processes. Consider the following set of processes with their arrival times and CPU burst times (in milliseconds):

Process	Arrival Time	Burst Time
Pl	0	12
P2	2	4
P3	3	6
P4	8	5

The average waiting time (in milliseconds) of the processes is _____.

[2014 (Set-3) : 2 Marks]

29. Consider a uniprocessor system executing three tasks T_1 T_2 and T_3, each of which is composed of an infinite sequence of jobs (or instances) which arrive periodically at intervals of 3, 7 and 20 milliseconds, respectively. The priority of each task is the inverse of its period, and the available tasks are scheduled in order of priority, with the highest priority task scheduled first. Each instance of T_1 T_2 and T_3 requires an execution time of 1, 2 and 4 milliseconds, respectively. Given that ali tasks initially arrive at the beginning of the lst millisecond and task preemptions are allowed, the first instance of T_3 completes its execution at the end of ____ milliseconds. **[2015 (Set-1) : 2 Marks]**

30. For the processes listed in the following table, which of the following scheduling schemes will give the lowest average turnaround time?

Process	Arrival Time	Processing Time
A	0	3
B	1	6
C	4	4
D	6	2

(a) First Come First Serve

(b) Non-preemptive Shortest Job First

(c) Shortest Remaining Time

(d) Round Robin with Quantum value two

[2015 (Set-3): 2 Marks]

31. Consider an arbitrary set of CPU-bound processes with unequal CPU burst lengths submitted at the same time to a computer system. Which one of the following process scheduling algorithms would minimize the average waiting time in the ready queue?

(a) Shortest remaining time first

(b) Round-robin with time quantum less than the shortest CPU burst

(c) Uniform random

(d) Highest priority first with priority proportional to CPU burst length

[2016 (Set-1) : 1 Mark]

32. Consider the following processes, with the arrival time and the length of the CPU burst given in milliseconds. The scheduling algorithm used is preemptive shortest remaining-time first.

Process	Arrival Time	Burst Time
P1	0	10
P2	3	6
P3	7	1
P4	8	3

The average turn around time of these processes is _____milliseconds. **[2016 (Set-2): 2 Marks]**

33. Consider the following CPU processes with arrival times (in milliseconds) and length of CPU bursts (in milliseconds) as given below:

Process	Arrival time	Burst time
P1	0	7
P2	3	3
P3	5	5
P4	6	2

If the pre-emptive shortest remaining time first scheduling algorithm is used to schedule the processes, then the average waiting time across all processes is _____________ milliseconds.

[2017 (Set-1) : 1 Mark]

34. Consider the set of processes with arrival time (in milliseconds), CPU burst time (in milliseconds), and priority (0 is the highest priority) shown below. None of the processes have I/O burst time.

Process	Arrival Time	Burst Time	Priority
P1	0	11	2
P2	5	28	0
P3	12	2	3
P4	2	10	1
P5	9	16	4

The average waiting time (in milliseconds) of ali the processes using preemptive priority scheduling algorithm is________.

[2017 (Set-2): 2 Marks]

35. Consider an operating system capable of loading and executing a single sequential user process at a time. The disk head scheduling algorithm used is First Come First Served (FCFS). If FCFS is replaced by Shortest Seek Time First (SSTF), claimed by the vendor to given 50% better benchmark results, what is the expected improvement in the I/O performance of user programs?

(a) 50% (b) 40%

(c) 25% (d) 0%

[2004 : 1 Mark]

36. The head of a hard disk serves requests following the shortest seek time first (SSTF) policy. The head is initially positioned at track number 180. Which of the request sets will cause the head to change its direction after servicing every request assuming that the head does not change direction if there is a tie in SSTF and all the requests arrive before the servicing starts?

(a) 11, 139, 170, 178, 181, 184, 201, 265

(b) 10, 138, 170, 178, 181, 185, 201, 265

(c) 10, 139, 169, 178, 181, 184, 201, 265

(d) 10, 138, 170, 178, 181, 185, 200, 265

[2007 : 2 Marks]

37. Consider the following four processes with arrival times (in milliseconds) and their length of CPU bursts (in milliseconds) as shown below:

Process	P1	P2	P3	P4
Arrival time	0	1	3	4
CPU burst time	3	1	3	Z

These processes are run on a single processor using preemptive Shortest Remaining Time First scheduling algorithm. If the average waiting time of the processes is 1 milliseconds, then value of Z is ______. **[2019 : 2 Marks]**

PROCESS TRANSITION DIAGRAM

38. The process state transition diagram in figure is representative of

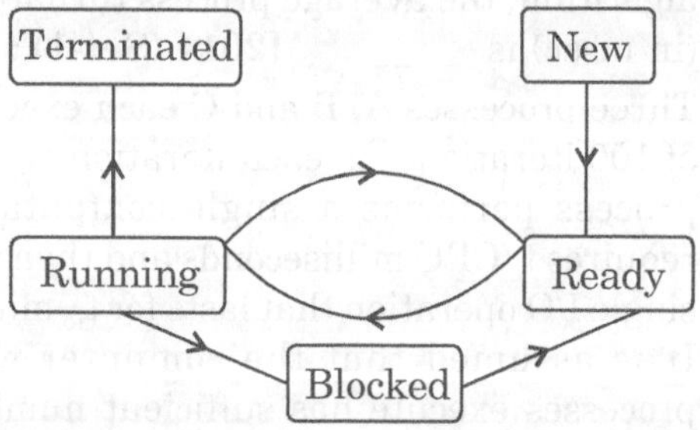

(a) a batch operating system

(b) an operating system with a preemptive scheduler

(c) an operating system with a non-preemptive scheduler

(d) a uni-programmed operating system

[1996 : 1 Mark]

39. Draw the process state transition diagram of an OS in which (i) each process is in one of the five states: created, ready, running, blocked (i.e. sleep or wait), or terminated, and (ii) only non-preemptive scheduling is used by the OS. Label the transitions appropriately.

[2002 : 2 Marks]

40. In the following process state transition diagram for a uniprocessor system, assume that there are always some processes in the ready state:

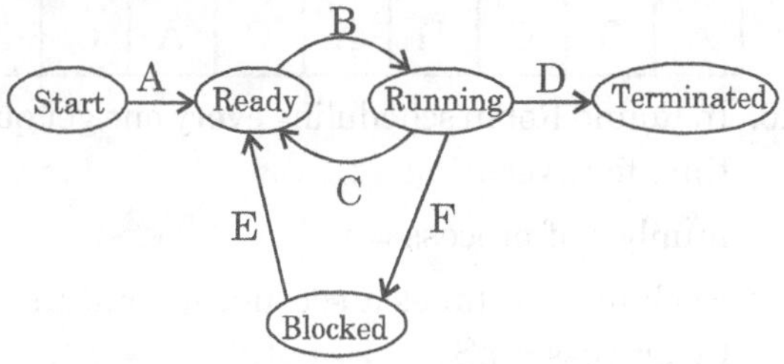

Now consider the following statements:

I. If a process makes a transition D, it would result in another process making transition A immediately

II. A process P2 in blocked state can make transition E while another process P1 is in running state

III. The OS uses preemptive scheduling

IV. The OS uses non-preemptive scheduling

Which of the above statements are TRUE?

(a) I and II (b) I and III

(c) IIandIII (d) II and IV

[2009 : 2 Marks]

41. The maximum number of processes that can be in Ready state for a computer system with n CPUs is

(a) n

(b) n^2

(c) 2^n

(d) Independent of n

[2015 (Set-3) : 1 Mark]

MULTIPROCESSOR SYSTEM

42. A multi-user, multi-processing operating system cannot be implemented on hardware that does not support

(a) Address translation

(b) DMA for disk transfer

(c) At least two modes of CPU execution (privileged and non-privileged)

(d) Demandpaging

[1999 : 2 Marks]

ANSWERS

1. (*)	**2.** (*)	**3.** (*a*)	**4.** (*)	**5.** (*a*)	**6.** (*c*)	**7.** (*b*)	**8.** (*a*)	**9.** (*d*)	**10.** (*b*)
11. (*b*)	**12.** (*b*)	**13.** (*d*)	**14.** (*a*)	**15.** (*d*)	**16.** (*b*)	**17.** (*b*)	**18.** (*a*)	**19.** (*b*)	**20.** (*b*)
21. (*c*)	**22.** (*d*)	**23.** (*a*)	**24.** (*c*)	**25.** (*b*)	**26.** (7.2)	**27.** (1000)	**28.** (5.5)	**29.** (*)	**30.** (*c*)
31. (*a*)	**32.** (8.25)	**33.** (3)	**34.** (*)	**35.** (*d*)	**36.** (*b*)	**37.** (2)	**38.** (*b*)	**39.** (*)	**40.** (*c*)
41. (*d*)	**42.** (*a,b,c*)								

EXPLANATIONS

1. (a) Turn around time :- (TAT) :- Burst time of process should not be too long.

   (b) Waiting time :- Arrival time of the process should be different.

2. The highest response ratio next Scheduling policy favours shorter jobs, but it is also limits the waiting time of longer jobs.

3. Spool device. Spooling is a process in which high speed hardware can be used to temporarily store the data transferred by processor to the Input/ Output device. When Input/Output device is free, the transferred data is send to the device, thus spooling can keep both the **CPU** and Input Output devices working at much higher rates.

4. The average response time depends on the value of x.

   Case I If x < 3

   then order is x, 3, 5, 6

   Case II if x > 3 & x < 5

   then order is 3, x, 5, 6

   Case III if x > 5 & x < 6

   then order is 3, 5, x, 6

   Case IV if x > 6 then order is 3, 5, 6, x

5. | Group I | Group 2 |
   |---|---|
   | P. Gang Scheduling | 3. Thread Scheduling |
   | Q. Rate Monotonic Scheduling | 2. Real-time Scheduling |
   | R. Fair Show Scheduling | 1. Guaranteed Scheduling |

6. Gantt chart for RR1

p	q	r	s	t	p	r	t	p	r	p	r	r	r	r	r

   0 1 2 3 4 5 6 7 8 9 10 11 12 13 14 15 16

   Completion time of process is 11.

7. Round Robin–A small unit of time, quantum is selected. Each process in the ready queue is allotted the CPU for this quantum.

8. For option non-preemptive Scheduling Sequence if CPU is idle for 1 time unit then smaller process execute first. So the sequence of execution is {3, 2, 1}.

9. | Jobs | Burst time |
   |---|---|
   | A | 4 |
   | B | 1 |
   | C | 8 |
   | D | 1 |

1	2	3	4	5	6	7	8	9
A	B	C	D	A	C	A	C	A

10. In Round Robin scheduling every one get quantum time for executing.

    number of process = n

    Each process takes S second, so total time taken by process = nS

    For process switching is minimized.

    For quantum size $q \geq t$-total time taken by process number of process –1.

    So, $$q \geq = \frac{t - nS}{n-1}$$

    where, t = total time.

11. **Throughput.** If the CPU is busy executing processor, then work is being done. One measure of work is the number of process that are coupleted per time unit called throughput. By increasing the number of processors, we hope to get more work done in shorter period of time.

    * For uniprocessor first come first served gives maximum throughput, but in case of known runtime shortest job first is used.

    * If multiprocess then round robin scheduling is the best.

    * In the case of turnaround shortest job first is the best.

12. First in first out is non preemptive CPU schduling

13. CPU = 10 ms

    I/o = 90 ms

    FCFS Gantt chart

P_1	P_2	idle	P_1	P_2	idle	–

    0 10 20 100 110 120 200

    CPU idle time is 80 + 20 + - -

    RR5 Gantt chart

P_1	P_2	P_1	P_2	idle	P_1	P_2	P_1	P_2	idle	- - -

    0 5 10 15 20 105 110 115 120 125 210 - -

    CPU idle time 25 + 85 + --

    So RR5 has least CPU utilization

14.

Process	Arrival Time	Burst Time
P1	0	5
P2	1	3
P3	2	3
P4	4	1

P_1	P_2	P_2	P_2	P_4	P_3	P_3	P_3	P_1	P_1	P_1	P_1

1 2 3 4 5 6 7 8 9 10 11 12

Gantt chart for scheduling.

Turn arround time for

$P_1 = 12$

$P_2 = 4 - 1$

$= 3$

$P_3 = 6$

$P_4 = 1$

Average turn around time

$$= \frac{P_1 + P_2 + P_3 + P_4}{4}$$

$$= \frac{12 + 3 + 6 + 1}{4}$$

$$= 5.5$$

15. Gantt chart for non preemptive process

P_3	P_1	P_2

0 15 35 45

TAT = Completion time - Arrival time.

TAT (P_1) = 35 – 5 = 30

TAT (P_2) = 45 – 3 = 42

TAT (P_3) = 15 – 0 = 15

Gantt chart for preemptive process.

P_3	P_2	P_1	P_2	P_3

0 3 5 25 33 45

So TAT (P_1) = 25 – 5 = 20

TAT (P_2) = 33 – 3 = 30

TAT (P_3) = 45 – 0 = 45

So TAT for P_2 is 30, 42 respectively.

16. Gantt chart is

P_1	idle	P_2	P_3	P_2	P_1	P_3	P_1	P_2	idle	P_2

0 1 2 3 5 6 8 9 10 11 14 15

So completion time for P_1, P_2, P_3 one 10, 15, 9.

17.

Process	Total burst time	I/o time	CPU time	I/o time
P_1	10	2	7	1
P_2	20	4	14	2
P_3	30	6	21	3

Gantt chart is

idle	P_1	P_2	P_3	idle

0 2 9 23 44 47

Total idle time = 2 + 3 = 5

total time = 47

$$\text{\% of idle} = \frac{5}{47} \times 100 = 10.6\%.$$

18.

Process	id	Arrival time	CPU Burst
P_0	0	0	2
P_1	1	0	4
P_2	2	0	8

Remaining Time

P_0 2

P_1 4

P_2 8

The Gannt chart for LRTF scheduling algorithm

P_0	P_1	P_2	P_2	P_2	P_2	P_2	P_1	P_2	P_1	P_2	P_0	P_1	P_2

0 12 3 4 5 6 7 8 9 10 11 12 13 14

Turn around time for P_0 = 12 – 0

= 12

Turn around time for P_1 = 13 – 1

= 12

Turn around time for P_2 = 14 – 2

= 12

Average Turn around Time = 36/3

$= 12 \approx 13$

19. At time t = o

Memory block	Size	Job
M_1	4k	J_3 (fiish at t = 2)
M_2	8k	J_4 (finish at t = 8)
M_3	20k	J_2 (finish at t = 10
M_4	2k	J_1 (finish at t = 4

according to the remaining jobs execution time at time t = 8

Memory block	Size	Job
M_1	4k	
M_2	8k	J_5 (finishes at t = 14)
M_3	20k	J_2 (finishes at t = 10
M_4	2k	

Similarly at time t = 10

M. b.	Size	Job
M_1	4k	
M_2	8k	J_5 (finish at t = 14)
M_3	20k	J_6 (finish at t = 11
M_4	2k	

at t = 11

M. b.	Size	Job
M_1	4k	
M_2	8k	J_5 (finishes at t = 14)
M_3	20k	J_7 (finishes at t = 19
M_4	2k	

So Answer is 19.

20. Gant chart of scheduling can be given as

P_1	P_2	P_3	P_2	P_4

0 20 30 40 55 70

Waiting time of process, $P_2 = (20 - 15) + 10 = 15$

21. If time since in RR is more than the highest burst time of process. than RR is like FCFS.

22. SRTF (Shortest Remaining Time First)

Preemptive may cause of starvation and RR (Round Robin) is better than FCFS in response time because in RR if some process comes letter, then after some time it brings in process but in FCFS it is not upto finishing of First process.

Alternately

I. In SRTF case, if processes with small processing time keep on coming, then processes with higher processing time has to wait and may starve.

II. In preemptive scheduling, if processes of high priority keep on coming, then processes with low priority may starve.

III.In RR, every process is served for a quantam time period but it is not in FCFS.

Thus all I, II and III are true.

23. Gantt chart is

P_0	P_1	P_0	P_2

0 1 5 13 22

$$\text{Average waiting time} = \frac{w_1 + w_2 + w_3}{3}$$

$$= \frac{(5-1) + 0 + (13-2)}{3} = 5.0$$

24. FCFS will complete in

P_1 P_2 P_3

and Round Robin

P_1 P_3 P_2

P_1	P_2	P_1	P_3	P_2	P_1	P_3

0 2 4 6 8 10 11 13

25. The Scheduling algorithm is equivalent to the round. Robin algorithm with quantum time equal to T.

26.

Process	Arrival Time	Execution Time
A	0	6
B	3	2
C	5	4
D	7	6
E	10	3

By SRTF Gantt chart

A	B	A	C	E	D

0 3 5 8 12 15 21

Turn Around time of

A = (8 – 0) = 8

B = (5 – 3) = 2

C = (12 – 5) = 7

D = (21 – 7) = 14

E = (15 – 10) = 5

$$\text{Average} = \frac{8+2+7+14+5}{5} = 7.2$$

27.

Process id	t_c	t_{io}
A	100ms	500ms
B	350ms	500ms
C	200ms	500ms

Time slice = 50 ms

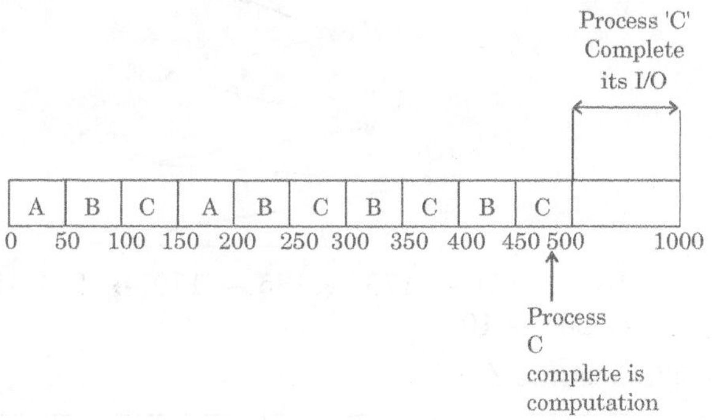

28. Gantt chart of SRTF

P_1	P_2	P_3	P_4	P_1

0 2 6 12 17 27

Average waiting time

$$= \frac{P_1 + P_2 + P_3 + P_4}{4}$$

$$= \frac{(17-2)+(2-2)+(6-3)+(12-8)}{4}$$

$$= \frac{15+0+3+4}{4} = 5.5$$

29. Gantt chart is

T_1^1	T_2^1	T_1^2	T_3^1	T_1^3	T_2^2	T_1^4	T_3^1	T_1^5

0 1 3 4 6 7 9 10 12

all tasks are arriving at beginning of 1 ms means at 0. T_1 has highest priority, then T_2 and the T_3. Hence first instance of T_1 by end of 12.

30.

Process	AT	BT
A	0	3
B	1	6
C	4	4
D	6	2

} Given Snapshot

(*i*) FcFs

Process	AT	BT	LT	TAT
A	0	3	3	3
B	1	6	9	8
C	4	4	13	9
D	6	2	15	9

$$\frac{29}{4} = 7.25$$

Gantt chart

A	B	C	D

0 3 9 13 15

(*ii*) SJF

Process	AT	BT	LT	TAT
A	0	3	3	3
B	1	6	9	8
C	4	4	15	11
D	6	2	11	5

$$\frac{27}{4} = 6.75$$

Gantt chart

A	B	D	C

0 3 9 11 15

B – 6 C – 9

D – 2

(*iii*) SRTF

Process	AT	BT	CT	TAT
A	0	3	3	3
B	1	6	15	14
C	4	4	8	4
D	6	2	10	4

$$\frac{25}{4} = 6.25$$

Gantt chart

A	A	B	C	C	D	B

0 1 3 4 6 8 10 15

A – 2 B – 5 C – 2 B – 5 B – 5

B – 6 C – 4 B – 5 D – 2

D – 2

(*iv*) R.Q (Q = 2)

Process	AT	BT	CT	TAT
A	0	3	5	5
B	1	6	15	14
C	4	4	13	9
D	6	2	11	5

$$\frac{33}{4} = 8.25$$

Gantt Chart

R. Q

A	B	A	C	B	D	C	B

0 2 4 5 7 9 11 13 15

31. Shortest remaining time first minimizes the average waiting time in the ready queue.

32. Gantt chart is

P_1	P_2	P_3	P_2	P_4	P_1

0 3 7 8 10 13 20

TAT = Completion time – Arrival time

TAT (P_1) = 20 – 0 = 20

TAT (P_2) = 10 – 3 = 7

TAT (P_3) = 8 – 7 = 1

TAT (P_4) = 13 – 8 = 5

So Average TAT $= \frac{20+7+1+5}{4} = 8.25$

33. Gantt chart is

P_1	P_2	P_4	P_1	P_3

0 3 6 8 12 17

TAT for process is

$P_1 = 12 - 0 = 12$

$P_2 = 6 - 3 = 3$

$P_3 = 7 - 5 = 12$

$P_4 = 8 - 2 = 2$

Waiting time for Processes is

WT = TAT – BT

$P_1 = 12 - 7 = 5$

$P_2 = 3 - 3 = 0$

$P_3 = 12 - 5 = 7$

$P_4 = 2 - 2 = 0$

So AWT $= \frac{7+0+5+0}{4} = 3$

34. As given in the table

Process	Arrival Time	Burst Time	Priority	C.T.	T.A.T.	W.T.
P_1	0	11	2	49	49	38
P_2	5	28	0 (high)	33	28	0
P_3	12	2	3	51	39	37
P_4	2	10	1	40	38	28
P_5	9	16	4	67	58	42
					Total	145

P_1	P_4	P_2	P_4	P_1	P_3	P_5

0 2 5 33 40 49 51 67

Hence

Average waiting time $= \frac{145}{5}$

= 29 Ms

35. Note:- Question belongs to Disk scheduling topic.

Since os can execute a single Sequential user process at a time so disk is always accessed in FCFS manner. So the improvement in the I/o performance is 0 %

36.

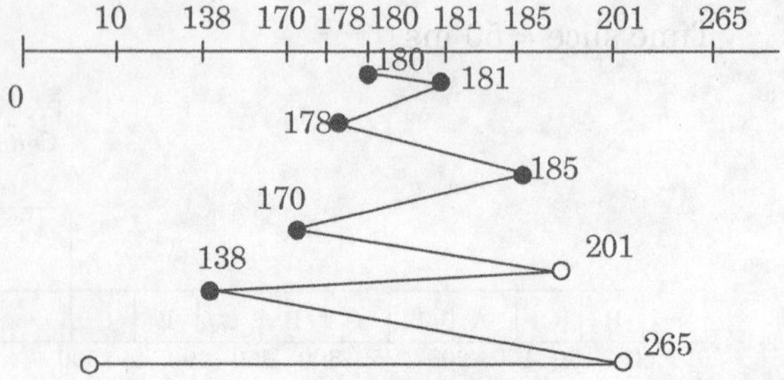

180 → 181 → 178 → 185 → 170 → 201 → 138 → 265 → 10

37. Assume Z = 2

	Arrival time	CPU burst time	Completion time	Waiting time
P_1	0	3	4	1
P_2	1	1	2	0
P_3	3	3	9	3
P_4	4	Z = 2	6	0

Average waiting time $= \frac{1+0+3+0}{4} = \frac{4}{4} = 1$ ms

Hence, Z = 2

38. Preemptive Scheduling. In pre-emptive scheduling, the process which is allocated the CPU keeps it and releases it only when it switching to a waiting state.

39.

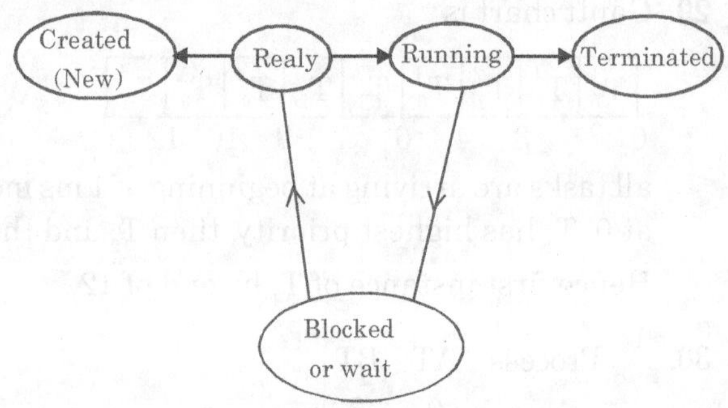

40. In premptive sheduling the process which allocated the CPU keeps it and release it only whne it switching to wating state. Also a process P_2 in blocked state can make transition E while other process P_1 in running.

Alternately

A process P_2 in blocked state can make transition E while another P_1 is in running state.

OS uses preemptive Scheduling.

41. The maximum number of processor is not dependent upon number of CPU's.

42. Should support if we want to implement a multi user, multi Processing os.

2 CHAPTER

Synchronization

Analysis of Previous GATE Papers

Topics ↓		Year →	2019	2018	2017 Set 1	2017 Set 2	2016 Set 1	2016 Set 2	2015 Set 1	2015 Set 2	2015 Set 3
CONTEXT SWITCHING	1 Mark	MCQ Type									
		Numerical Type									
	2 Marks	MCQ Type	1								
		Numerical Type									
	Total		2								
INTERRUPT	1 Mark	MCQ Type									1
		Numerical Type									
	2 Marks	MCQ Type					1	1			
		Numerical Type									
	Total						2	2			1
MUTUAL EXCLUSION	1 Mark	MCQ Type									
		Numerical Type									
	2 Marks	MCQ Type									
		Numerical Type									
	Total										
SYNCHRONIZATION	1 Mark	MCQ Type									
		Numerical Type	1								
	2 Marks	MCQ Type		1							
		Numerical Type						1			
	Total		1	2				2			
CONCURRENCY	1 Mark	MCQ Type									
		Numerical Type							1		
	2 Marks	MCQ Type									
		Numerical Type									
	Total								1		

CONTEXT SWITCHING

1. System calls are usually invoked by using
   (a) a software interrupt
   (b) polling
   (c) an indirect jump
   (d) a privileged instruction **[1999 : 1 Mark]**

2. Which of the following actions is/are typically not performed by the operating system when switching context from process A to process B?
   (a) Saving current register values and restoring saved register values for process B.
   (b) Changing address translation tables.
   (c) Swapping out the memory image of process A to the disk.
   (d) Invalidating the translation look-aside buffer.
   [1999 : 2 Marks]

3. A processor needs software interrupt to
   (a) Test the interrupt system of the processor
   (b) Implement co-routines
   (c) Obtain system services which need execution of privileged instructions
   (d) Return from subroutine
   [2001 : 1 Mark]

4. A CPU has two modes-privileged and non-privileged. In order to change the mode from privileged to non-privileged
   (a) a hardware interrupt is needed
   (b) a software interrupt is needed
   (c) a privileged instruction (which does not generate an interrupt) is needed
   (d) a non-privileged instruction (which does not generate an interrupt) is needed
   [2001 : 1 Mark]

5. Which of the following does not interrupt a running process?
   (a) A device (b) Timer
   (c) Scheduler process (d) Powerfailure
   [2001 : 2 Marks]

6. Consider three CPU-intensive processes, which require 10, 20 and 30 time units and arrive at times 0,2, and 6, respectively. How many context switches are needed if the operating system implements a shortest remaining time first scheduling algorithm? Do not count the context switches at time zero and at the end
   (a) 1 (b) 2
   (c) 3 (d) 4 **[2006 : 1 Mark]**

7. Consider the following snapshot of a system running n concurrent processes. Process i is holding Xi instances of a resource R. $1 \leq i \leq n$. Assume that all instances of R are currently in use Further, for all i, process i can place a request for at most Yi additional instances of R while holding the Xi instances it already has. Of the n processes, there are exactly two processes p and q such, that $Y_p = Y_q = 0$. Which one of the following conditions guarantees that no other process apart from p and q can complete execution?
   (a) $\text{Min}(X_p, X_q) \geq \text{Min}\{Y_k \mid 1 \leq k \leq n, k \neq p, 1 \neq q\}$
   (b) $X_p + X_q < \text{Min}\{Y_k \mid 1 \leq k \leq n, k \neq p, k \neq q\}$
   (c) $\text{Min}(X_p, X_q) \leq \text{Max}\{Y_k \mid 1 \leq k \leq n, k \neq p, k \neq q\}$
   (d) $X_p + X_q < \text{Max}\{Y_k \mid 1 \leq k \leq n, k \neq p, k \neq q\}$
   [2019 : 2 Marks]

INTERRUPT

8. A computer handles several interrupt sources of which the following are relevant for this question.
   - Interrupt frorn CPU temperature sensor (raises interrupt if CPU temperature is too high)
   - Interrupt from Mouse (raises interrupt if the mouse is moved or a button is pressed)
   - Interrupt from Keyboard (raises interrupt when a key is pressed or released)
   - Interrupt from Hard Disk (raises interrupt when a disk read is completed)

   Which one of these will be handled at the HIGHESTpriority?
   (a) Interrupt from Hard Disk
   (b) Interrupt from Mouse
   (c) Interrupt from Keyboard
   (d) Interrupt from CPU temperature sensor
   [2011 : 1 Mark]

9. Suppose a processor does not have any stack pointer register. Which of the following statement is true?
   (a) It cannot have subroutine call instruction
   (b) It can have subroutine call instruction, but no nested subroutine calls
   (c) Nested subroutine calls are possible, but interrupts are not
   (d) All sequences of subroutine calls and also interrupts are possible
   [2001 : 1 Mark]

10. The correct matching for the following pairs is

List-I	List-II
A. DMA I/O	1. High speed RAM
B. Cache	2. Disk
C. Interrupt I/O	3. Printer
D. Condition Code Register	4. ALU

Codes:

(a) A-4 B-3 C-1 D-2 (b) A-2 B-1 C-3 D-4
(c) A-4 B-3 C-2 D-1 (d) A-2 B-3 C-4 D-1

[1997 : 1 Mark]

11. When an interrupt occurs, an operating system
(a) ignores the interrupt
(b) always changes state of interrupted process after processing the interrupt
(c) always resumes execution of interrupted process after processing the interrupt
(d) may change state of interrupted process to `blocked' and schedule another process

[1997 :1 Mark]

12. Which of the following devices should get higher priority in assigning interrupts?
(a) Hard disk (b) Printer
(c) Keyboard (d) Floppy disk

[1998 :1 Mark]

13. Which of the following is true?
(a) Unless enabled, a CPU will not be able to process interrupts.
(b) Loop instructions cannot be interrupted till they complete.
(c) A processor checks for interrupts before executing a new instruction.
(d) Only level triggered interrupts are possible on microprocessors

[1998 :1 Mark]

MUTUAL EXCLUSION

14. A critical region is
(a) One which is enclosed by a pair of P and V operations on semaphores.
(b) A program segment that has not been proved bug-free
(c) A program segment that often causes unexpected system crashes
(d) A program segment where shared resources are accessed.

[1987 : 2 Marks]

15. A critical section is a program segment.
(a) Which should run in certain specified amount of time
(b) Which avoids deadlocks
(c) Where shared resources are accessed
(d) Which must be enclosed by a pair of semaphore operations, P and V

[1996 : 1 Mark]

16. Each process Pi, i = 1... 9 is coded as follows repeat

P(mutex)
{critical section}
V(mutex)

forever

The code for P_{10} is identical except that it uses V(mutex) in place of P(mutex). What is the largest number of processes that can be inside the critical section at any moment?
(a) 1 (b) 2
(c) 3 (d) Noneofthese

[1997 : 2 Marks]

17. Let m [0]... m [4] be mutexes (binary semaphores) and P[0] ...P[4] be processes. Suppose each process P[i] executes the following; wait (m[i]);wait (m[(i+l) mode 4]); .... release (m[i]); release (m[(i+l)mod 4]); This could cause
(a) Thrashing
(b) Deadlock
(c) Starvation, but not deadlock
(d) None of the above **[2000 : 1 Mark]**

18. Consider Peterson's algorithm for mutual exclusion between two concurrent processes i and j. The program executed by process is shown below.

repeat
flag[i]=true;
turn-j;
while (P) do no-op;
Enter critical section, perform actions, then exit critical section
flag[i]=false;
Perform other non-critical section actions.
Until false;

For the program to guarantee mutual exclusion, the predicate P in the while loop should be
(a) flag[j] = true and turn = i
(b) flag [j] = true and turn = j
(c) flag [i] = true and turn = j
(d) flag [i] = true and turn = i **[2001 : 2 Marks]**

19. Processes Pl and P2 use critical_flag in the following routine to achieve mutual exclusion. Assume that critical_flag is initialized to FALSE in the main program.

```
get_exclusive_access ()
{
    if (critical _flag = = FALSE)
    {
        critical_flag = TRUE;
        critical_region ();
        critical_flag = FALSE;
    }
}
```

Consider the follovving statements.

(i) It is possible for both Pl and P2 to access critical_region concurrently.

(ii) This may lead to a deadlock. Which of the follovving holds?

(a) (i) is false and (ii) is true
(b) Both (i) and (ii) are false
(c) (i) is true and (ii) is false
(d) Both (i) and (ii) are true

[2007 : 1 Mark]

20. Two processes, Pl and P2, need to access a critical section of code. Consider the following synchronization construct used by the processes:

```
/*P1*/
    while (true) {
    wantsl = true;
    while (wants2 = = true);
    /* Critical
        Section * /
    wants 1 = false;
}
/* Remainder secti
/*P2*/
    while (true) {
    wants2 = true;
    while (wantsl = = true);
    /* Critical
        Section * /
    wants 2 = false;
}
/* Remainder section */
```

Here, wantsl and wants2 are shared variables, Which are initialized to false. Which one of the following statements is TRUE about the above construct?

(a) It does not ensure mutual exclusion.
(b) It does not ensure bounded waiting.
(c) It requires that processes enter the critical section in strict alternation.
(d) It does not prevent deadlocks, but ensures mutual exclusion.

[2007 : 2 Marks]

21. The enter_CS () and leave_CS () functions to implement critical section of a process are realized using test-and-set instruction as follows:

```
Void enter_CS(X)
{
    while (test-and-set (X));
}
Void leave_CS(X)
{
    X = 0;
}
```

In the above solution, X is a memory location associated with the CS and is initialized to 0. Now consider the following statements

I. The above solution to CS problem is deadlock-free.
II. The solution is starvation free.
III. The processes enter CS in FIFO order.
IV. More than one process can enter CS at the same time.

Which of the above statements are TRUE?

(a) I only
(b) I and II
(c) II and III
(d) IV only

[2009 : 2 Marks]

22. Consider the methods used by processes Pl and P2 for accessing their critical sections whenever needed, as given below. The initial values of shared boolean variables Sl and S2 are randomly assigned.

Method used by P1	Method used by P2
while (S1==S2);	while (S1!=S2);
Critical Section	Critical Section
S1=S2;	S2=not (S1);

Which one of the following statements describes the properties achieved?

(a) Mutual exclusion but not progress
(b) Progress but not mutual exclusion
(c) Neither mutual exclusion nor progress
(d) Both mutual exclusion and progress

[2010 : 1 Mark]

23. Two processes Xand Yneed to access a critical section. Consider the following synchronization construct used by both the processes

Process X

```
I* other code for process X*/
while (true)
{  varP = true;
   while (varQ = = true)
   { */* Critical Section */
   varP = false;
   }
}
/* other code for process X*/
```

Process Y

```
I* other code for process Y*l
while (true)
{ varQ = true;
  while (varP = = true)
  { /* Critical Section */
     varQ = false;
  }
}
/* other code for process Y*l
```

Here, varP and varQ are shared variables and both are initialized to false. Which one of the following statements is true?

(a) The proposed solution prevents deadlock but fails to guarantee mutual exclusion

(b) The proposed solution guarantees mutual exclusion but fails to prevent deadlock

(c) The proposed solution guarantees mutual exclusion and prevents deadlock

(d) The proposed solution fails to prevent deadlock and fails to guarantee mutual exclusion

[2015 (Set-3) : 1 Mark]

24. Consider the following proposed solution for the critical section problem. There are n processes: P_0 .... P_{n-1}. In the code function pmax returns an integer not smaller than any of its arguments. For all i, t[i] is initialized to zero. Code for P_i:

```
do
{
   c[i]=1; t[i] = pmax (t[0],..., t[n – 1]) +1; c[i] = 0;
   for every j ≠ i in {0,..., n – 1}
   {    while (c[j]);
   while (t[j] != 0 && t[j] <= t[i]);
   }
   Critical Section; t[i] = 0;
   Remainder Section;
} while (true);
```

Which one of the following is TRUE about the above solution?

(a) At most one process can be in the critical section at any time

(b) The bounded wait condition is satisfied

(c) The progress condition is satisfied

(d) It cannot cause a deadlock

[2016 (Set-1) : 2 Marks]

25. Consider the following two-process synchronization solution

Process 0

```
    Entry: loop while (turn == 1);
    (critical section)
    Exit: turn = 1;
```

Process 1

```
    Entry : loop while (turn == 0);
    (critical section)
    Exit: turn = 0;
```

The shared variable turn in initialized to zero. Which one of the following is TRUE?

(a) This is a correct two-process synchronization solution

(b) This solution violates mutual exclusion requirement

(c) This solution violates progress requirement

(d) This solution violates bounded wait requirement

[2016 (Set-2) : 2 Marks]

26. The following is a code with two threads, producer and consumer, that can run in parallel. Further, S and Q are binary semaphores equipped with the standard P and V operations.

```
semaphore S = 1, Q = 0;
integer x ;
producer :      consumer :
while (true) doWhile (true) do
P(S) ;                P(Q) ;
x = produce( ) ;consume (x);
V(Q) ;              V(S) ;
done                 done
```

Which of the following is TRUE about the program above?

(a) The process can deadlock

(b) One of the threads can starve

(c) Some of the items produced by the producer may be lost

(d) Values generated and stored in 'x' by the producer will always be consumed before the producer can generate a new value

[2008 : 2 Marks]

27. Match the pairs in the following Questions.

(a) Critical region	(p) Hoare's monitor
(b) Wait/Signal	(q) Mutual exclusion
(c) Working set	(r) Principle of locality
(d) Deadlock	(s) Circular wait

[1990 : 2 Marks]

SYNCHRONIZATION

28. Semaphore operations are atomic because they are implemented within the OS

[1990 : 2 Marks]

29. At a particular time of computation the value of a counting semaphore is 7. Then 20 P operations and 15 V operations were completed on this semaphore. The resulting value of the semaphore is:

(a) 42 (b) 2
(c) 7 (d) 12 **[1992 : 2 Marks]**

30. A counting semaphore was initialized to 10. Then 6 P (wait) operations and 4V (signal) operations were completed on this semaphore. The resulting value of the semaphore is

(a) 0 (b) 8
(c) 10 (d) 12 **[1998 : 1 Mark]**

Common Data for Q. 31 & 32

Suppose we want to synchronize two concurrent processes P and Q using binary semaphores S and T. The code for the processes P and Q is shown below.

```
Process P:        Process Q:
while(1){         while(1){
   W:                Y:
   print '0';        print '1' ;
   print '0';        print '1' ;
   X:                Z:
}                 }
```

Synchronization statements can be inserted only at points W, X, Y and Z.

31. Which of the following will always lead to an output string with '001100110011'?

(a) P(S) at W, V(S) at X, P(T) at Y, V(T) at Z, S and T initially 1
(b) P(S) at W, V(T) at X, P(T) at Y, V(S) at Z, S initially 1, and T initially 0
(c) P(S) at W, V(T) at X, P(T) at Y, V(S) at Z, S and T initially 1
(d) P(S) at W, V(T) at X, P(T) at Y, V(T) at Z, S initially 1, and T initially 0

[2003 : 2 Marks]

32. Which of the following will ensure that the output string never contains a substring of the form 01^n0 or 10^n1 where n is odd?

(a) P(S) at W, V(S) at X, P(T) at Y, V(T) at Z, S and T initially 1
(b) P(S) at W, V(T) at X, P(T) at Y, V(S) at Z, S and T initially 1
(c) P(S) at W, V(S) at X, P(S) at Y, V(S) at Z, S initially 1
(d) V(S) at W, V(T) at X, P(S) at Y, P(T) at Z, S and T initially 1

[2003 : 2 Marks]

33. Consider two processes P_1 and P_2 accessing the shared variables X and Y protected by two binary semaphores S_X and S_Y respectively, both initialized to 1. P and V denote the usual semaphore operators, where P decrements the semaphore value, and V increments the semaphore value. The pseudocode of P_1 and P_2 is as follows:

```
P1:                 P2:
while true do {     while true do {
L1 :                L3:
L2 :                L4:
X = X+1;            Y = Y + 1;
Y = Y–1;            X = X – 1;
V(SX);              V(SY);
V(SY) }             V(SX)}
```

In order to avoid deadlock, the correct operators at L_1, L_2, L_3 and L_4 are respectively

(a) $P(S_Y), P(S_X), P(S_X), P(S_Y)$
(b) $P(S_X), P(S_Y), P(S_Y), P(S_X)$
(c) $P(S_X), P(S_X), P(S_Y), P(S_Y)$
(d) $P(S_X), P(S_Y), P(S_X), P(S_Y)$

[2004 : 2 Marks]

34. The semaphore variables full, empty and mutex are initialized to 0, n and 1, respectively. Process P_1 repeatedly adds one item at a time to a buffer of size n, and process P_2 repeatedly removes one item at a time from the same buffer using the programs given below. In the programs, K, L, M and N are unspecified statements.

```
P1: while (1)
{
    K;
    P(mutex);
```

```
    Add an item to the buffer;
    V(mutex);
    L;
}
P2: while(l)
{
    M;
    P(mutex);
    Remove an item from the buffer;
    V(mutex);
    N;
}
```

The statements K, L, M and N are respectively

(a) P(full), V(empty), P(full), V(empty)

(b) P(full), V(empty), P(empty), V(full)

(c) P(empty), V(full), P(empty), V(full)

(d) P(empty), V(full), P(full), V(empty)

[2004 : 2 Marks]

35. Given below is a program which when executed pawns two concurrent processes:

semaphore X : = 0 ;

/* Process now forks into concurrent processes P_1 & P_2 */

P_1: repeat forever	P_2: repeat forever
V(X) ;	P(X) ;
Compute;	Compute;
P(X) ;	V(X);

Consider the following statements about processes P1 and P2:

I: It is possible for process P1 to starve.

II: It is possible for process P2 to starve. Which of the following holds?

(a) Both I and II are true.

(b) I is true but II is false.

(c) II is true but I is false

(d) Both I and II are false.

[2005 : 2 Marks]

36. Two concurrent processes Pl and P2 use four shared resources Rl, R2, R3 and R4, as shown below. Pl:

Compute:	Compute;
Use Rl;	Use Rl;
Use R2;	Use R2;
Use R3;	Use R3;
Use R4;	Use R4;

Both processes are started at the same time, and each resource can be accessed by only one process at a time. The following scheduling constraints exist between the access of resources by the processes:

- P2 must complete use of R1 before P1 gets access to Rl.
- P1 must complete use of R2 before P2 gets access to R2.
- P2 must complete use of R3 before P1 gets access to R3.
- P1 must complete use of R4 before P2 gets access to R4.

There are no other scheduling constraints between the processes. If only binary semaphores are used to enforce the above scheduling constraints, what is the minimum number of binary semaphores needed?

(a) 1 (b) 2

(c) 3 (d) 4

[2005 : 2 Marks]

37. The atomic fetch-and-set x, y instruction unconditionally sets the memory location x to 1 and fetches the old value of x in y without allowing any intervening access to the memory location x. Consider the following implementation of P and V functions on a binary semaphore S.

```
void P(binary_semaphore *S) {
    unsigned y;
unsigned *x = & (S -> value);
    do{
        fetch-and-set x, y;
    } while (y);
}
void V (binary_semphore *S) {
    S → value = 0;
}
```

Which one of the following is true?

(a) The implementation may not work if context switching is disabled in P

(b) Instead of using fetch-and-set, a pair ofnormal load/store can be used

(c) The implementation of V is wrong

(d) The code does not implement a binary semaphore

[2006 : 2 Marks]

Common Data for Q. 38 & Q. 39:

Barrier is a synchronization construct where a set of processes synchronizes globally i.e. each process in the set arrives at the barrier and waits for all others to arrive and then ali processes leave the barrier. Let the number of processes in the set be three and S be a binary semaphore with the usual P and V functions. Consider the following C implementation of a barrier with line numbers shown on the left.

```
void barrier (void) {
1  :  P(S);
2  :  process_arrived + +;
3  :  V(S);
4  :  while (process_arrived! = 3);
5  :  P(S);
6  :  process_left + +;
7  :  if (process_left = = 3){
o  :  process_arrived = 0;
9  :     process_left = 0;
10 :  }
11 :  V(S);
12 :  }
```

The variables process_arrived and process_left are shared among ali processes and are initialized to zero. In a concurrent program ali the three processes call the barrier function when they need to synchronize globally.

38. The above implementation of barrier is incorrect. Which one of the following is true?

(a) The barrier implementation is wrong due to the use of binary semaphore S

(b) The barrier implementation may lead to a deadlock if two barrier invocations are used in immediate succession

(c) Lines 6 to 10 need not be inside a critical section

(d) The barrier implementation is correct if there are only two processes instead of three

[2006 : 2 Marks]

39. Which one of the following rectifies the problem in the implementation?

(a) Lines 6 to 10 are simply replaced by process_arrived

(b) At the beginning of the barrier the first process to enter the barrier waits until process_arrived becomes zero before proceeding to execute P(S)

(c) Context switch is disabled at the beginning of the barrier and re-enabled at the end

(d) The variable process_left is made private instead of shared

[2006 : 2 Marks]

40. Synchronization in the classical readers and writers problem can be achieved through use of semaphores. In the following incomplete code for readers-writers problem, two binary semaphores mutex and wrt are used to obtain synchronization

```
wait (wrt)
writing is performed
signal (wrt)
wait (mutex)
readcount = readcount + 1
if readcount = 1 then Sl
S2
reading is performed
S3
readcount = readcount - 1
if readcount = 0 then S4
Signal (mutex)
```

The values of SI, S2, S3, S4, (in that order) are

(a) signal (mutex), wait (wrt), signal (wrt), wait (mutex)

(b) signal (wrt), signal (mutex), wait (mutex), wait (wrt)

(c) wait (wrt), signal (mutex), wait (mutex), signal (wrt)

(d) signal (mutex), wait (mutex), signal (mutex), wait (mutex)

[2007 : 2 Marks]

41. The P and V operations on counting semaphores, where s is a counting semaphore, are defined as followvs:

```
P(s): s = s - 1;
      if s < 0 then wait;
V(s): s = s + 1;
      if s < 0 then wakeup a process waiting on s;
```

Assume that P_b and V_b, the wait and signal operations on binary semaphores are provided. Two binary semaphores X_b and Y_b are used to implement the semaphore operations P(s) and V(s) as follows:

```
P(s): Pb(Xb);
      s = s – 1;
      if(s < 0) {
      Vb(Xb);
      Pb(Yb);
      }
      elseVb.(Xb);
V(s): Pb(Xb);
      s = s + 1;
      if(s ≤ 0)Vb(Yb);
      Vb(Xb);
```

The initial values of Xb and Yb are respectively

(a) 0 and 0

(b) 0 and 1

(c) 1 and 0

(d) 1 and 1

[2008 : 2 Marks]

42. The following program consists of 3 concurrent processes and 3 binary semaphores. The semaphores are initialized as S0 = 1, S1 = 0, S2 = 0.

Process P0	Process P1	Process P2

while (true) {
wait (S0);
print '0'
release (S1);
release (S2);
}
	wait (S1);
	release (S0);
		wait (S2);
		release (S0);

How many times will process P0 print '0'?

(a) At least twice

(b) Exactly twice

(c) Exactly thrice

(d) Exactly once

[2010 : 2 Marks]

43. A shared variable x, initialized to zero, is operated on by four concurrent process W, X, Y, Z as follows. Each of the processes W and X reads x from memory, increments by one, stores it to memory, and then terminates. Each of the processes Y and Z reads x from memory, decrements by two, stores it to memory and then terminates. Each process before reading x invokes the P operations (i.e., wait) on a counting semaphore S and invokes the V operation (i.e., signal) on the semaphore S after storing x to memory. Semaphore S is initialized to two. What is the maximum possible value of x after all processes complete execution?

(a) –2

(b) –1

(c) 1

(d) 2

[2013 : 2 Marks]

44. A certain computation generates two arrays a and b such that a[i] = f for $0 \le i \le n$ and b[i] = g(a[i]) for $0 \le i < n$. Suppose this computation is decomposed into two concurrent processes X and Y such that X computes the array a and Y computes the array b. The processes employ two binary semaphores R and S, both initialized to zero. The array a is shared by the two processes. The structure of the processes are shown below.

Process X	Process Y
private i;	private i;
for (i = 0; i < n; i++)	for (i = 0; i < n; i++)
{	{
a[i]=f(i);	EntryY(R,S);
ExitsX(R,S);	b[i] = g(a[i]);
}	}

Which one of the following represents the CORRECT implementations of ExitsX and EntryY?

(a)
```
ExitsX (R, S) {
  P(R);
  V(S)
}
EntryY(R, S) {
  P(S);
  V(R);
}
```

(b)
```
ExitsX (R, S) {
  V(R);
  V(S);
}
EntryY(R, S) {
  P(R);
  P(S);
}
```

(c)
```
ExitsX (R, S) {
  P(S);
  V(R);
}
EntryY(R, S) {
  V(S);
  P(R);
}
```

(d)
```
ExitsX (R, S) {
  V(R);
  P(S);
}
EntryY(R, S) {
  V(S);
  P(R);
}
```

[2013 : 2 Marks]

45. Consider the procedure below for the Producer-Consumer problem which uses semaphores:

```
semaphore n = 0;
semaphore s = 1;
```

```
void consumer()         void producer()
{                       {
  while (true)            while (true)
  {                       {
    produce();              semWait (s);
    semWait(s);             semWait (n);
    addToBuffer();          removeFromBuffer ();
    semSignal(s);           semSignal (s);
    semSignal(n);           consume();
  }                       }
}                       }
```

Which one of the following is TRUE?

(a) The producer will be able to add an item to the buffer, but the consumer can never consume it.

(b) The consumer will remove no more than one item from the buffer.

(c) Deadlock occurs if the consumer succeeds in acquiring semaphore s when the buffer is empty.

(d) The starting value for the semaphore n must be 1 and not 0 for deadlock-free operation.

[2014 (Set-2) : 2 Marks]

46. Consider a non-negative counting semaphore S. The operation P(S) decrements S, and V(S) increments S. During an execution, 20 P(S) operations and 12 V(S) operations are issued in some order. The largest initial value of S for which at lest one P(S) operation will remain blocked is ________.

[2016 (Set-2) : 2 Marks]

47. Consider the following solution to the producer-consumer synchronization problem. The shared buffer size is N. Three semaphores empty, full and mutex are defined with respective initial values of 0, N and 1. Semaphore empty denotes the number of available slots in the buffer, for the consumer to read from. Semaphore full denotes the number of available slots in the buffer, for the producer to write to. The placeholder variables, denoted by P, Q, R and S, in the code below can be assigned either empty or full. The valid semaphore operations are: wait () and signal ().

Producer:	Consumer

do {
wait (P);
wait (mutex);
//Add item to buffer
signal (mutex);
signal (Q);
} while (1);
	do {
	wait (R);
	wait (mutex);
	//Consume item from buffer
	signal (mutex);
	signal (S);
	} while (1);

Which one of the following assignment to P, Q, R and S will yield the correct solution?

(a) P: full, Q: full, R: empty, S; empty

(b) P: empty, Q: empty, R: full, S: full

(c) P: full, Q: empty, R: empty, S: full

(d) P: empty, Q: full, R: full, S: empty

[2018 : 2 Marks]

48. Consider the solution to the bounded buffer producer/consumer problem by using general semaphores S, F, and E. The semaphore S is the mutual exclusion semaphore initialized to 1. The semaphore F corresponds to the number of free slots in the buffer and is initialized to N. The semaphore E corresponds to the number of elements in the buffer and is initialized to 0.

Producer Process	Consumer Process
Produce an item;	Wait (E);
Wait (F);	Wait (S);
Wait (S);	Remove an item from the buffer;
Append the item to the buffer;	Signal (S);
Signal (S);	Signal (F);
Signal (E);	Consumer the item;

Which of the following interchange operations may result in a deadlock?

I. Interchanging Wait (F) and Wait (S) in the Producer process.

II. Interchanging Signal (S) and Signal (F) in the Consumer process.

(a) I only

(b) II only

(c) Neither I nor II

(d) Both I and II

[2006 : 2 Marks]

49. Consider three concurrent processes P1, P2 and P3 as shown below, which access a shared variable D that has been initialized to 100.

P1	P2	P3
⋮	⋮	⋮
⋮	⋮	⋮
D = D + 20	D = D − 50	D = D + 10
⋮	⋮	⋮
⋮	⋮	⋮

The processes are executed on a uniprocessor system running a time-shared operating system. If the minimum and maximum possible values of D after the three processes have completed execution are X and Y respectively, then the value of Y − X is ______.

[2019 : 1 Mark]

CONCURRENCY

50. A solution to the Dining Philosophers Problem which avoids deadlock is
   (a) ensure that ali philosophers pick up the left fork before the right fork
   (b) ensure that all philosophers pick up the right fork before the left fork
   (c) ensure that one particular philosophers picks up the left fork before the right fork, and that ali other philosophers pick up the right fork before the left fork
   (d) None of the above

[1996 : 2 Marks]

51. When the result of a computation depends on the speed of the processes involved there is said to be
   (a) cycle stealing (b) race condition
   (c) a time lock (d) a deadlock

[1998 : 1 Mark]

52. The following two functions Pl and P2 that share a variable B with an initial value of 2 execute concurrently.

```
PK)              P2()
{                {
  C = B-1;         D = 2*B;
  B = 2*C;         B = D-1;
}                }
```

The number of distinct values that B can possibly take after the execution is ______.

[2015 (Set-1) : 1 Mark]

ANSWERS

1. (a)	**2.** (c, d)	**3.** (*c*)	**4.** (*b*)	**5.** (*c*)	**6.** (b)	**7.** (*b*)	**8.** (*d*)	**9.** (a)	**10.** (b)
11. (d)	**12.** (c)	**13.** (a)	**14.** (d)	**15.** (c)	**16.** (d)	**17.** (b)	**18.** (b)	**19.** (c)	**20.** (d)
21. (a)	**22.** (a)	**23.** (a)	**24.** (a)	**25.** (c)	**26.** (d)	**27.** (*)	**28.** (*)	**29.** (b)	**30.** (b)
31. (b)	**32.** (b)	**33.** (d)	**34.** (d)	**35.** (a)	**36.** (b)	**37.** (a)	**38.** (b)	**39.** (b)	**40.** (c)
41. (c)	**42.** (a)	**43.** (d)	**44.** (c)	**45.** (c)	**46.** (7)	**47.** (c)	**48.** (a)	**49.** 80	**50.** (b)
51. (b)	**52.** (3)								

EXPLANATIONS

1. **System calls,** State changes can be caused by program commands, which are referred to as system calls and are implemented using softwere interrupts or automatically following certain events.
2. Context switch does involve saving current register values and restoring saved register values for process B.
   Address translation tables are changed and new ones for the incoming process are loaded.
   C and D are typically not done on a context switch.
3. Obtain system services which need execution of privileged instructions
   Software interrupts are required by CPU to obtain System services which need execution of privileged instructions. A software interrupt is caused either by an exceptional condition in the processor itself, or a special instruction in the instruction set which causes an interrupt when it is executed. The former is often called a trap or exception and is used for errors or events occurring during program execution that are exceptional enough that they cannot be handled within the program itself. An interrupt alerts the processor to a high-priority condition requiring the interruption of the current code the processor is executing. The processor responds by suspending its current activities, saving its state, and executing a function called an *interrupt handler* (or an interrupt service routine, ISR) to deal with the event. This interruption is temporary, and, after the interrupt handler finishes, the processor resumes normal activities.
4. A software interrupt is needed
   Software interrupt occurs when a program terminates or a program invokes some system calls to request for some services like I/O request etc. This type of interrupt is caused by the program in user mode.
   Thus, a software interrupt is required to switch from kernel (privilege) mode to user (non-privilege) mode.
5. Scheduler process
   Scheduler process doesn't interrupt any process, it's Job is to select the processes for following three purposes.
   Long-term scheduler(or job scheduler) –selects which processes should be brought into the ready queue
   Short-term scheduler(or CPU scheduler) –selects which process should be executed next and allocates CPU.
   Mid-term Scheduler (Swapper)- present in all systems with virtual memory, temporarily removes processes from main memory and places them on secondary memory (such as a disk drive) or vice versa. The mid-term scheduler may decide to swap out a process which has not been active for some time, or a process which has a low priority, or a process which is page faulting frequently, or a process which is taking up a large amount of memory in order to free up main memory for other processes, swapping the process back in later when more memory is available, or when the process has been unblocked and is no longer waiting for a resource.
6. Context-Switches will be needed only at the time of switching over to some other process. Following table shows **time remaining** for three processes at different instants of time.

Time/Processes →	I	II	III	Process continued
0	10	-	-	I
2	8	20	-	I
6	4	20	30	I
10	0	20	30	II
30	0	0	30	III
60	0	0	0	-

Hence context-witches are needed only at times 10 and 30.

8. Interrupt from CPU temperature sensor
   Higher priority interrupt levels are assigned to requests which, if delayed or interrupted, could have serious consequences. Devices with high speed transfer such as magnetic disks are given high priority, and slow devices such as keyboard receive low priority
9. It cannot have subroutine call instruction
   Stack pointer register hold the address of top of stack, which is the location of memory at which CPU should resume its execution after servicing some interrupt or subroutine call.
   So if SP register is not available then no subroutine call instructions are possible. So (A) is correct option.
10. A-2 B-1 C-3 D-4

11. When an interrupt occurs, an operating system changed their state and process have goto, wait or blocked or in ready queue.

12. Keyboard

13. In system programming, an interrupt is a signal to the processor emitted by hardware or software indicating an event that needs immediate attention. An interrupt alerts the processor to a high-priority condition requiring the interruption of the current code the processor is executing. The processor responds by suspending its current activities, saving its state, and executing a function called an interrupt handler (or an interrupt service routine, ISR) to deal with the event. This interruption is temporary, and, after the interrupt handler finishes, the processor resumes normal activities. There are two types of interrupts: hardware interrupts and software interrupts.

14. A program segment where shared resources are accessed.

In simple terms a critical section is group of instructions/statements or region of code that need to be executed atomically (read this post for atomicity), such as accessing a resource (file, input or output port, global data, etc.).

In concurrent programming, if one thread tries to change the value of shared data at the same time as another thread tries to read the value (i.e. data race across threads), the result is unpredictable.

The access to such shared variable (shared memory, shared files, shared port, etc.).to be synchronized. Few programming languages have built in support for synchronization.

15. Critical section. A critical section is a segment of code in which a process may be reading common variables, updating a table etc.

16. A process must execute wait (mutex) before entering the monitor and must execute signal (mutex) after leaving the monitor.

Since a signaling process must wait until the resumed process either leaves or waits, an additional semaphore next is introduced, initialized to 0. On which the signaling process may suspended themselves.

P = 1 to 9.

If P = 9 (for max)

then P (mutex) = 8

then V (mutex) = 8 + 1 = 9

18. flag [j] = true and turn = j

Basically, Peterson's algorithm provides guaranteed mutual exclusion by using the two following constructs – *flag[]* and *turn*. *flag[]* controls that the willingness of a process to be entered in critical section. While *turn* controls the process that is allowed to be entered in critical section. So by replacing P with the following,

flag [j] = true and turn = j

process i will not enter critical section if process j wants to enter critical section and it is process j's *turn* to enter critical section. The same concept can be extended for more than two processes. For details, refer the following.

19. (i) is true and (ii) is false

Say P1 starts first and executes statement 1, after that system context switches to P2 (before executing statement 2), and it enters inside if statement, since the flag is still false.

So now both processes are in critical section!! so (i) is true.. (ii) is false

By no way it happens that flag is true and no process' are inside the if clause, if someone enters the critical section, it will definitely make flag = false. So no deadlock.

20. Since there is no way to synchronize two statementwants 1 = true (in P_1) and wants 2 = true (in P_2).

So both of them may get executed one after other. In this situation there will be a dead lock.

But if only of the two is true, other will not go beyond cuhile loop, hence ensure nutual exclusion.

21. In given program the process test-and-set in critical section and in function leaves _CS initialise memory location *x* to zero. So this process is dead lock free.

22. Both process can't be in critical section simulteneously, so they should be in mutual exclusion.

23. The proposed solution prevents deadlock but fails to guarantee mutual exclusion.

When both processes try to enter critical section simultaneously,both are allowed to do so since both shared variables varP and varQ are true.So, clearly there is NO mutual exclusion. Also, deadlock is prevented because mutual exclusion is one of the four conditions to be satisfied for deadlock to happen. Hence, answer is A.

26. Values generated and stored in 'x' by the producer will always be consumed before the producer can generate a new value

A semaphore is hardware or a software tag variable whose value indicates the status of a common resource. Its purpose is to lock the resource being used. A process which needs the resource will check the semaphore for determining the status of the resource followed by the decision for proceeding. In multitasking operating systems, the activities are synchronized by using the semaphore techniques. Wait and signal are defined on the semaphore. Entry to the critical section is controlled by the wait operation and exit from a critical region is taken care by signal operation. The wait, signal operations are also called P and V operations. The manipulation of semaphore (S) takes place as following:

1. The wait command P(S) decrements the semaphore value by 1. If the resulting value becomes negative then P command is delayed until the condition is satisfied.
2. The V(S) i.e. signals operation increments the semaphore value by 1.

Consumer can consume only once the producer has produced the item, and producer can produce(except the first time) only once the consumer has consumed the item.

Let's explain the working of this code.

It is mentioned that Producer and Consumer execute parallely.

Producer:

st1 – S value is 1, P(S) on S makes it 0 and

st2 – and then x item is produced.

st3 – Q value is 0. V(Q) on Q makes it 1.

this being an infinite while loop should infinitely iterate. In the next iteration of while loop, S is already 0 ,further P(S) on 0 sends P to blocked list of S. So producer is blocked.

Consumer:

P(Q) on Q makes Q =0 and then consumes the item.

V(S) on S, now instead of changing the value of S to 1,consumer wakes up the blocked process on Q 's queue. Hence process P is awaken. P resumes from st2,since it was blocked at statement 1. So P now produces the next item. So consumer consumes an item before producer produces the next item.

Correct Option is (D).

Choice of this question:

(a) deadlock cannot happen has both producer and consumer are operating on different semaphores (no hold and wait)

(b) No starvation happen because there is alteration between P and Consumer Which also makes them have bounded waiting.

(c) Some of the items produced by the producer may be lost but it can't.

27. a-q,b-p,c-r,d-s

A. Circular Wait is one of the conditions for deadlock.

B. To avoid race conditions, the execution of critical sections must be mutually exclusive (e.g., at most one process can be in its critical section at any time).

C. Monitors using blocking condition variables are often called Hoare-style monitors or signal-and-urgent-wait monitors.

D. locality is commonly used to determine the number of assigned pages. The number of pages that meet the requirement of locality is called a working set.

28. The concept of semaphores is used for synchronization.

Semaphore is an integer with a difference. Well, actually a few differences.

You set the value of the integer when you create it, but can never access the value directly after that; you must use one of the semaphore functions to adjust it, and you cannot ask for the current value.

There are semaphore functions to increment or decrement the value of the integer by one.

Decrementing is a (possibly) blocking function. If the resulting semaphore value is negative, the calling thread or process is blocked, and cannot continue until some other thread or process increments it.

Incrementing the semaphore when it is negative causes one (and only one) of the threads blocked by this semaphore to become unblocked and runnable.

Therefore, all semaphore operations are atomic. Implemented in kernel,

29. Value of a counting semaphore = 7

After 20 P operations value of semaphore

$$= 7 - 20 = -13$$

After 15 V operations value of semaphore

$$= -13 + 15 = 2$$

So, option (B) is correct.

30. 6P (Wait) operations will change the value to 4 and 4V (signal) operations will make it to 8.

31. To get the expected output, The sequence of process is P, Q, P, Q, P, Q and so on we must initialize S = 1 and T = 0.

32. If the output string never contains a substring of the from 01^n0 or 10^n1 where n is odd then the procedures becomes.

S = 1

```
Process P:          Process Q:
While (1){          While (1){
W : P(S)             Y : P(S)
print '0';           print '1';
print '0';           print '1';
X : V (S)            Z : V(S)
  }                    }
```

33. S_x and S_y are two binary semaphore if assume P means wait or V means signal then for two process P_1 and P_2 we take alternate then there in no chance of dead lock.

The code is as follows :

P_1	P_2
while true do {	while true do {
$L_1 : P(S_x)$	$L_3 : P(S_x)$
$L_2 : P(S_y)$	$L_4 : P(S_y)$
$x = x + 1;$	$y = y + 1;$
$y = y - 1;$	$x = y - 1;$
$V(S_x);$	$V(S_y);$
$V(S_y);\}$	$V(S_x);\}$

34. P(empty), V(full), P(full), V(empty)

Process P1 is the producer and process P2 is the consumer.

Semaphore 'full' is initialized to '0'. This means there is no item in the buffer.

Semaphore 'empty' is initialized to 'n'. This means there is space for n items in the buffer.

In process P1, wait on semaphore 'empty' signifies that if there is no space in buffer then P1 can not produce more items. Signal on semaphore 'full' is to signify that one item has been added to the buffer.

In process P2, wait on semaphore 'full' signifies that if the buffer is empty then consumer can't not consume any item. Signal on semaphore 'empty' increments a space in the buffer after consumption of an item

35. Both I and II are true.

P1 can get stuck on its P, while P2 loops forever. The dual is also possible: P2 gets stuck on its P while P1 loops forever.

Both statements are correct. Option (A).

36. We use two semaphores : A and B.

A is initialized to 0 and B is initialized to 1

```
P1:
Compute;
Wait(A);
Use R1;
Use R2;
Signal(B);
Wait(A);
Use R3;
Use R4;
Signal(B);
P2:
Compute;
Wait(B);
User1;
Signal(A);
Wait(B);
Use R2;
Use R3;
Signal(A);
Wait(B);
Use R4;
Signal(B);
```

In process p1, initially control will be stuck in while loop of Wait(A) because A = 0.

In process p2, Wait(B) decrements the value of B to 0 . Now, P2 uses the resource R1 and increments the value to A to 1 so that process P1 can enter its critical section and use resource R1.

Thus, P2 will complete use of R1 before P1 gets access to R1.

Now, in P2 values of B = 0. So, P2 can not use resource R2 till P1 uses R2 and calls function Signal(B) to increment the value of B to 1.

Thus, P1 will complete use of R2 before P2 gets access to R2.

Now, semaphore A = 0. So, P1 can not execute further and gets stuck in while loop of function Wait(A).

Process P2 uses R3 and increments the value of semaphore A to 1.Now, P1 can enter its critical section to use R3.

Thus, P2 will complete use of R3 before P1 gets access to R3.

Now, P1 will use R4 and increments the value of B to 1 so that P2 can enter is critical section to use R4.

Thus, P1 will complete use of R4 before P2 gets access to R4.

37. The P and V function is as follows :

1. void P (binary-semaphore * S) {
2. unsigned *y*;
3. unsigned * *x* = & (S → value);}
4. do {
5. fetch-and-set *x*, *y*;
6. } while (*y*);
7. }
8. void V (binary-semaphore *S) {
9. {S → value = 0;}
10. }

fetch-and-set instruction always sets the memory location $x = 1$ and fetches the old value of x into y. The binary-semphore * S takes only two values either 0 and 1. When we initiliaze S = 0 then in statement 3 this value will be start at location x and fetch-and-set instruction charge the value of $x = 0$ to $x = 1$ and y becomes 0. If there are more than two processes and context switching between processes is disabled in P then this implementation doesn't work properly and can't synchronize the processes.

38. The barrier implementation may lead to a deadlock if two barrier invocations are used in immediate succession

It is possible that process_arrived becomes greater than 3. It will not be possible for process arrived to become 3 again, hence deadlock.

39. At the beginning of the barrier the first process to enter the barrier waits until process_arrived becomes zero before proceeding to execute P(S)

Step '2' should not be executed when the process enters the barrier second time till other two processes have not completed their 7th step. This is to prevent variable process_arrived becoming greater than 3.

So, when variable process_arrived becomes zero and variable process_left also becomes zero then the problem of deadlock will be resolved.

Thus, at the beginning of the barrier the first process to enter the barrier waits until process_arrived becomes zero before proceeding to execute P(S).

40. wait (wrt), signal (mutex), wait (mutex), signal(wrt)

For S1: if readcount =1 ⇒ reader is reading now, so no writer must execute. Hence, S1 has to be wait(wrt)

For S2: After readcount has been updated, is made to 1, so other readers can enter into entry section. Multiple readings are allowed. (Only 1 at a time can be in entry section) hence signal(mutex)

For S3: Now at a time only one process can be in Exit section and semaphore mutex is used to implement it (only 1 at a time can be in exit section).Hence wait(mutex)

For S4: If readcount is zero i.e no reader is reading, means last reader has completed reading, it should unlock resources so that any writer waiting for it can use it .hence signal(wrt).The above values of S1, S2, S3, and S4 are all nothing but implementing first reader writer problem.

41. I and O

Suppose Xb = 0, then because of P(s): Pb(Xb) operation, Xb will be -1 and processs will get blocked as it will enter into waiting section.

So, Xb will be one.

Suppose s = 2(means 2 process are accessing shared resource), taking Xb as 1,

first P(s): Pb(Xb) operation will make Xb as zero. s will be 1 and Then Vb(Xb) operation will be executed which will increase the count of Xb as one. Then same process will be repeated making Xb as one and s as zero.

Now suppose one more process comes, then Xb will be 1 but s will be -1 which will make this process go into loop (s < 0) and will result into calling Vb(Xb) and Pb(Yb) operations. Vb(Xb) will result into Xb as 2 and Pb(Yb) will result into decrementing the value of Yb.

case 1: if Yb has value as 0, it will be -1 and it will go into waiting and will be blocked.total 2 process will access shared resource (according to counting semaphore, max 3 process can access shared resource) and value of s is -1 means only 1 process will be waiting for resources and just now, one process got blocked. So it is still true.

case 2: if Yb has value as 1, it will be 0. Total 3 process will access shared resource (according to counting semaphore, max 3 process can access shared resource) and value of s is -1 means only 1 process will be waiting for resources and but there is no process waiting for resources.So it is false.

42. Initial P1 and P2 does not go because they are not using semaphore initially. P0 uses semaphore whose value S0 = 1, and P1 and P2 uses S1 = S2 = 0, So initially P0 executes so it prints '0'.

Now, it release S1 and S2 means value of these now 1 = S1 = S2. Then process P1 & P2 executes after that they Release. So and it is S0 = 1 again. Then this prints '0' again means at least twice **0** print.

Alternately

- Initially P1 and P2 can't proceed because S1 and S2 are 0.
- P0 will proceed and print '0' then it release S1 and S2.
- Either of S1 and S2 will release so it prints '0' again.

43. A shared variable x_1 initialized to zero, is opereated on by four concurrent processes W, X, Y, Z as follows. Each of the processes W and X reads X from memory, increments by one. Stores it to memory and the terminates. Each of processes Y and z reads x from memory, decrements by two, stores it to memory and then terminates. Each process before reading x invokes the P operation (i.e. wait) on a counting semaphore S and invokes the V operation (i.e. signal) on the semaphore s after storing x to memory. Semaphore S is initalized to two. What is the maximum possible value of x after all processes complete execution?

⇒ x, w reads x and increment x by 1.

y, z reads x and decrement by 2.

Start with x. will perform P(s) then s = 1. read $x = 0$ $x = x + 1 = 1$

then y will perform P(s) then s = 0. read $x = 0$

$x = x - 2 = -2$, then store $x \cdot v(s)$, $s = 1$

then z will perform P(s) there s = 0, read $x = -2$

$x = x - 2 = -4$, then store x, $v(s)$, $s = 1$

then x will store $x \cdot v(s)$, $s = 2$, $x = 1$

then w will perform P(s), $s = 1$, read $x = 1$

$x = x + 1 = 2$, store x, $v(s)$, $s = 2$, $\boxed{x = 2}$

44. The purpose here is neither the deadlock should occur nor the binary semaphores be assigned value greater than one.

A leads to deadlock

B can increase value of semaphores b/w 1 to n

D may increase the value of semaphore R and S to 2 in some cases

45. Deadlock occurs if the consumer succeeds in acquiring semaphore s when the buffer is empty.

Initially, there is no element in the buffer.

Semaphore $s = 1$ and semaphore $n = 0$.

We assume that initially control goes to the consumer when buffer is empty.

semWait(s) decrements the value of semaphore 's'. Now, s = 0 and *semWait(n)* decrements the value of semaphore 'n'.

Since, the value of semaphore 'n' becomes less than 0, the control stucks in while loop of function semWait() and a deadlock arises.

Thus, deadlock occurs if the consumer succeeds in acquiring semaphore s when the buffer is empty.

46. 20 – 7 → 13 will be in blocked state, when we perform 12 V(S) operation makes 12 more process to get chance for execution from blocked state. So one process will be left in the queue (blocked state) here i have considered that if a process is in under CS then it not get blocked by other process.

47. Full = N, empty = 0, mutex = 1

- Initially buffer will be empty, so consumer should not start first, so option b, D are eliminated.
- With option A consumer will never consume the item, so it is wrong.
- Option 'c' is correct answer which proper functionality of produce and consumer.

48. I only

Suppose F = 0. Now, if Wait(F) and Wait(S) are interchanged and Wait(S) in producer succeeds, the producer will wait for Wait(F) which is signalled in Consumer, which is never going to succeed as it is waiting for Wait(S) to be signal by producer. So, deadlock can happen.

50. Dining Philosophers Problem.

Representation of the need to allocate several processes in a dead lock and startvation free manner. Its simple solution by *semaphore.*

Solution to the Dining - Philosophers problem that ensures freedom from dead lock.

* Allow at most four philosophies to be sitting simultaneously at the table.
* Allow a philospher to pickup her chopstics only if both chopstics are available.
* Use an asymmetric solution, that is, an odd philospher picks up first her left chopstick, where as an even philospher picks up her right chop stick and then her left chopstick.

51. A situation like this, where several processes access and manipulate the same data conveniently and the outcome of the execution depends on the particular order in which the access take place is called a race condition.

52. There are following ways that concurrent processes can follow.

C = B – 1; // C = 1
B = 2 × C; // B = 2
D = 2 × B; // D = 4
B = D – 1; // B = 3

C = B – 1; // C = 1
D = 2 × B; // D = 4
B = D – 1; // B = 3
B = 2 × C; // B = 2

C = B – 1; // C = 1
D = 2 × B; // D = 4
B = 2 × C; // B = 2
B = D – 1; // B = 3

D = 2 × B; // D = 4
C = B – 1; // C = 1
B = 2 × C; // B = 2
B = D – 1; // B = 3

D = 2 × B; // D = 4
B = D – 1; // B = 3
C = B – 1; // C = 2
B = 2 × C; // B = 4

There are 3 different possible values of B: 2, 3 and 4

3
CHAPTER

CPU Scheduling

Analysis of Previous GATE Papers												
	Year → Topics ↓		2019	2018	2017 Set 1	2017 Set 2	2016 Set 1	2016 Set 2	2015 Set 1	2015 Set 2	2015 Set 3
MULTI USER	1 Mark	MCQ Type									
		Numerical Type									
	2 Marks	MCQ Type									
		Numerical Type									
	Total										
THREAD & THEIR MANAGEMENT	1 Mark	MCQ Type			1	1					
		Numerical Type									
	2 Marks	MCQ Type			1						
		Numerical Type									
	Total				3	1					
KERNAL	1 Mark	MCQ Type									
		Numerical Type									
	2 Marks	MCQ Type									
		Numerical Type									
	Total										
COMPILER ORGANIZATION	1 Mark	MCQ Type									
		Numerical Type									
	2 Marks	MCQ Type									
		Numerical Type									
	Total										

MULTIUSER

1. Which combination of the following features will suffice to characterize an OS as a multi-programmed OS? (i) more than one program may be loaded into main memory at the same time for execution. (ii) If a program waits for certain events such as I/O, another program is immediately scheduled for execution. (iii) If the execution of a program terminates, another program is immediately scheduled for execution

   (a) (i) (b) (i) and (ii)

   (c) (i) and (iii) (d) (i), (ii) and (iii)

[2002 : 2 Marks]

THREAD & THEIR MANAGEMENT

2. Consider the following statements with respect to user-level threads and kernel-supported threads

   (i) Context switch is faster with kernel-supported threads

   (ii) For user-level threads, a system call can block the entire process

   (iii) Kernel-supported threads can be scheduled independently

   (iv) User-level threads are transparent to the kernel

   Which of the above statements are true?

   (a) (ii), (iii) and (iv) only

   (b) (ii) and (iii) only

   (c) (i), and (iii) only

   (d) (i) and (ii) only

[2004 : 1 Mark]

3. Which one of the following is NOT shared by the threads of the same process?

   (a) Stack

   (b) Address Space

   (c) File Descriptor Table

   (d) Message Queue **[2004 : 1 Mark]**

4. A process executes the follovving segment of code:

```
for(i = 1; i < = n; i++)
fork();
```

   The number of new processes created is

   (a) n (b) ((n(n + 1))/2)

   (c) $2^n - 1$ (d) $3^n - 1$

[2004 : 2 Marks]

5. Consider the following code fragment:

```
if(fork() = = 0)
{a = a + 5; printf("%d, %d\n", a, &a);}
else{a = a - 5; printf("%d, %d\n", a, &a);}
```

   Let u, v be the values printed by the parent process, and x, y be the values printed by the child process. Which one of the foliowing is TRUE?

   (a) u = x + 10 and v = y

   (b) u = x + 10 and v $\neq$ y

   (c) u + 10 = x and v = y

   (d) u + 10 = x and v $\neq$ y

[2005 : 2 Marks]

6. The process state transition diagram of an operating system is as given below.

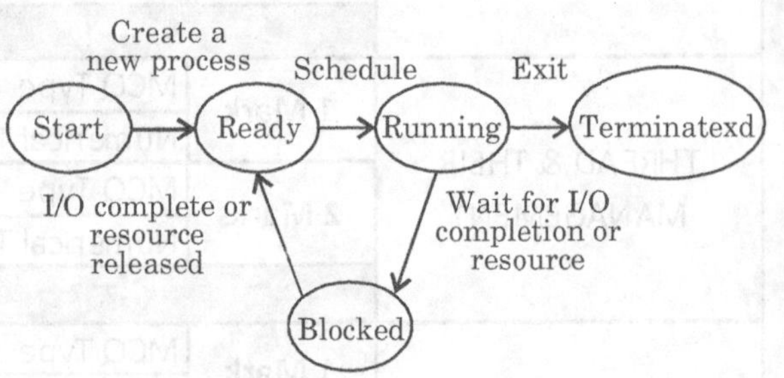

   Which of the following must be FALSE about the above operating system?

   (a) It is a multiprogrammed operating system

   (b) It uses preemptive scheduling

   (c) It uses non-preemptive scheduling

   (d) It is a multi-user operating system

[2006 : 1 Mark]

7. Consider the following statements about user level threads and kernel level threads. Which one of the following statements is FALSE?

   (a) Context switch time is longer for kernel level threads than for user level threads

   (b) User level threads do not need any hardware support

   (c) Related kernel level threads can be scheduled on different processors in a multiprocessor system

   (d) Blocking one kernel level thread blocks ali related threads

[2007 : 1 Mark]

8. A process executes the following code for (i = 0; i < n; i ++) fork ();

The total number of child processes created is

(a) n (b) $2^n - 1$

(c) 2^n (d) $2^{n+1} - 1$

[2008 : 2 Marks]

9. A thread is usually defined as a "light weight process" because an Operating System (OS) maintains smaller data structures for a thread than for a process. In relation to this, which of the followingisTRUE?

(a) On per-thread basis, the OS maintains only CPU register state

(b) The OS does not maintain a separate stack for each thread

(c) On per-thread basis, the OS does not maintain virtual memory state

(d) On per-thread basis, the OS maintains only scheduling and accounting information

[2011 : 1 Mark]

10. A process executes the code

fork();

fork();

fork();

The total number of child processes created is

(a) 3 (b) 4

(c) 7 (d) 8

[2012 : 1 Mark]

11. Which one of the following is FALSE?

(a) User level threads are not scheduled by the kernel.

(b) When a user level thread is blocked, ali other threads of its process are blocked.

(c) Context switching between user level threads is faster than context switching between kernel level threads.

(d) Kernel level threads cannot share the code segment.

[2014 (Set-1): 1 Mark]

12. Threads of a process share

(a) global variables but not heap

(b) heap but not global variables

(c) neither global variables nor heap

(d) both heap and global variables

[2017 (Set-1) : 1 Mark]

13. Which of the following is/are shared by all the threads in a process?

I. Program counter

II. Stack

III. Address space

IV. Registers

(a) I and II only (c) IV only

(b) III only (d) III and IV only

[2017 (Set-2) : 1 Mark]

14. A multithreaded program P executes with x number of threads and uses y number of locks for ensuring mutual exclusion while operating on shared memory locations. Ali locks in the program are non-reentrant, i.e., if a thread holds a lock l. then it cannot re-acquire lock l vvithout releasing it. If a thread is unable to acquire a lock, it blocks until the lock becomes available. The minimum value of x and the minimum value of y together for which execution of P can result in a deadlock are:

(a) x = 1, y = 2 (b) x = 2, y = 1

(c) x – 2, y = 2 (d) x = 1, y = 1

[2017 (Set-1): 2 Marks]

KERNAL

15. A user level process in Unix traps the signal sent on a Ctrl-C input, and has a signal handling routine that saves appropriate files before terminating the process. When a Ctrl-C input is given to this process, what is the mode in which the signal handling routine executes?

(a) kernel mode

(b) super user mode

(c) privileged mode

(d) user mode

[2005 : 1 Mark]

16. Let the time taken to switch between user and kernel modes of execution be t_1 while the time taken to switch between two processes be t_2. Which of the following is TRUE?

(a) $t_1 > t_2$

(b) $t_1 = t_2$

(c) $t_1 < t_2$

(d) nothing can be said about the relation between t_1 and t_2

[2011 : 1 Mark]

COMPILER ORGANIZATION

17. State whether the following statements are TRUE or FALSE with reason. The Link-load-and-go loading scheme required less storage space than the Link-and-go loading scheme.

[1990 : 2 Marks]

18. Match the pairs in the following question by writing the corresponding letters only.

(a) Buddy system	(p) Run-time type specification
(b) Interpretation	(q) Segmentation
(c) Pointer type	(r) Memory allocation
(d) Virtual memory	(s) Garbage collection

[1991 : 2 Marks]

19. A "link editor" is a program that:

(a) Matches the parameters of the macro definition with locations of the parameters of the macro call.

(b) Matches external names of one program with their location in other programs.

(c) Matches the parameters of subroutine definition with the location of parameters of subroutine call.

(d) Acts as link between text editor and the user.

(e) Acts as a link between compiler and user program.

[1991 : 2 Marks]

20. A simple two-pass assembler does the following in the first pass:

(a) it allocates space for the literals

(b) it computes the total length of the program

(c) it builds the symbol table for the symbols and their values

(d) it generates code for all the load and store register instructions.

[1993 : 2 Marks]

21. A linker is given object modules for a set of programs that were compiled separately. What information need to be included in an object module?

(a) Object code

(b) Relocationbits

(c) Names and locations of ali external symbols defined in the object module

(d) Absolute addresses of internal symbols

[1995 : 1 Mark]

ANSWERS

1. (*b*)	**2.** (b)	**3.** (*a*)	**4.** (*c*)	**5.** (b)	**6.** (*b*)	**7.** (d)	**8.** (b)	**9.** (a)	**10.** (c)
11. (d)	**12.** (*d*)	**13.** (*)	**14.** (d)	**15.** (*a*)	**16.** (*c*)	**17.** (*)	**18.** (*)	**19.** (b)	**20.** (a, b, v)
21. (d)									

EXPLANATIONS

1. (i) and (ii)

(a) More than one program may be loaded into main memory at the same time for execution.

True: Only done in a multiprogrammed OS, not in single programmed OS

(b) If a program waits for certain events such as I/O, another program is immediately scheduled for execution.

True: Only done in a multiprogrammed OS, not in single programmed OS

(c) If the execution of program terminates, another program is immediately scheduled for execution.

False: Done in both Multiprogrammed and single programmed Oss

2. Consider the each statement

(*i*) Statement is false because there is no connection between kernel-supported threads and context switch.

(*ii*) Statement is true because it is the drawback of user-level threads blocking system call can block the entire process.

(*iii*) Statement is true because kernel-supported threads having own memory area and scheduled independently by the operating system.

(*iv*) Statement is false because kernel is unware about user level threads and there is no kernel support to user-level threads.

3. Stack

Threads can not share stack (used for maintaining function calls) as they may have their individual function call sequence.

4. $2^n - 1$

```
fork ();   // Line 1
fork ();   // Line 2
fork ();   // Line 3
.....till n
```

With n fork statements, there are always $2^n - 1$ child processes

5. Here, we follow concept of copy on write

So, we have two different pages one for child and one for parent.

Because value of *v* and *y* are different, so they read (assume value 10), then child increases to '15' and parent decrement to '5'.

6. It uses preemptive scheduling

A–It is **Correct** – In a multiprogramming environment, multiple processes can be in ready state

B–It is **Incorrect** because once in running state there is no provision to go back to ready state

C–It is **Correct** because once in running state there is no provision to go back to ready state

D–It is **Correct** In a multi User environment, multiple processes can be in ready state

7. Blocking one kernel level thread doesn't block all related threads.

8. Number of child processes $2^n - 1$

10. If fork is called n times, there will be total 2^n running processes including the parent process. So, there will be $2^n - 1$ child processes.

11. User threads are supported above the kernel and a managed without kernel support. The thread function library to implement user level threads usually runs on top of the system in user mode. Thus these threads with in a process are invisible to the operating system. Since the kernel is unaware of the existence of such threads; when one user level thread is blocked in the kernel all other threads of its process are blocked. So options (*a*) and (*b*) are true. (*c*) The OS is aware of kernel level threads. Kernel threads are scheduled by the OS's scheduling algorithms and require a "lightweight" context switch to switch between (that is, registers, PC and SP must be changed, but the memory context remains the same among kernel threads in the (same process). User level threads are much faster to switch between as there is not context switch.(*d*) False Kernel level threads within the same process share code section, data section and other operating system resources such as open files and signals.

12. both heap and global variables

Thread share all other resources of process **except** local data like – register, stack.

13. Only address space is shared by all the threads in a process, the other entities such as stack, PC, resisters are not shared as each thread has its own.

14. In ques option c is x = 2.

x = 1, y = 1

Reentrant (Recursive) locks allow a thread to reacquire the lock. That means same process can claim the lock multiple times without blocking on itself. This prevents the thread from deadlocking itself. This is main advantage of reentrant locks over non-reentrant locks.

Non-reentrant (Non- recursive) locks not allow a thread to reacquire the lock. That means same process can not claim the lock multiple times without releasing it. So, if a thread/process is unable to acquire a lock, it blocks until the lock becomes available. This situation is deadlocked.

15. kernel mode

16. t1 < t2

Process switches or Context switches can occur in only kernel mode . So for process switches first we have to move from user to kernel mode. Then we have to save the PCB of the process from which we are taking off CPU and then we have to load PCB of the required process . At switching from kernel to user mode is done. But switching from user to kernel mode is a very fast operation(OS has to just change single bit at hardware level)

Thus T1 < T2

17. TRUE

In link and go scheme the linkage editor coexists with program in main memory while performing linking task whereas link, load and go scheme the linkage editor does not coexists with program in main memory while performing linking task

18. a-r, b-p, c-s, d-q

Buddy system - The buddy memory allocation technique is a memory allocation algorithm that divides memory into partitions to try to satisfy a memory request as suitably as possible. This system makes use of splitting memory into halves to try to give a best fit.

Interpretation - Run-time (pretty obvious)

Pointer type - Garbage collector dereference the dangling pointers

Virtual memory – Segmentation

19. Matches external names of one program with their location in other programs.

Link editor or (linker) performs

external symbol resolution , relocation

20. scan the code twice. The first time, just count how long the machine code instructions will be, just to find out the addresses of all the labels. Also, create a table that has a list of all the addresses and where they will be in the program. This table is known as the symbol table. On the second scan, generate the machine code, and use the symbol table to determine how far away jump labels are, and to generate the most efficient instruction.

21. Absolute addresses of internal symbols

Absolute addresses of internal symbols have to be mapped with an object module.

4 CHAPTER

Deadlock

Analysis of Previous GATE Papers

Year → Topics ↓			2019	2018	2017 Set 1	2017 Set 2	2016 Set 1	2016 Set 2	2015 Set 1	2015 Set 2	2015 Set 3
DEADLOCK (SYSTEM MODEL)	1 Mark	MCQ Type									
		Numerical Type									
	2 Marks	MCQ Type									
		Numerical Type									
	Total										
DEADLOCK CHARACTERI ZATION	1 Mark	MCQ Type								1	
		Numerical Type									
	2 Marks	MCQ Type				1					
		Numerical Type									
	Total					2				1	
DEADLOCK PREVENTION	1 Mark	MCQ Type									
		Numerical Type									
	2 Marks	MCQ Type									1
		Numerical Type									
	Total										2
DEADLOCK AVOIDANCE & DETECTION	1 Mark	MCQ Type									
		Numerical Type		1							
	2 Marks	MCQ Type		1							
		Numerical Type									
	Total			3							

DEADLOCK (SYSTEM MODEL)

1. Two shared resources R_1 and R_2 are used by processes P_1 and P_2. Each process has a certain priority for accessing each resource. Let T_{ij} denote the priority of P_i for accessing R_j. A process P_i can snatch a resource R_k from process P_j, if T_{ik} is greater than T_{jk}.

Given the following:

I. $T_{11} > T_{21}$ II. $T_{12} > T_{22}$

III. $T_{11} < T_{21}$ IV. $T_{12} < T_{22}$

Which of the following conditions ensures that P_1 and P_2 can never deadlock?

(a) (I) and (IV)

(b) (II) and (III)

(c) (I) and (II)

(d) None of these

[2005 : 2 Marks]

2. Fetch_And_Add(X, i) is an atomic Read-Modify-Write instruction that reads the value of memory location X, increments it by the value i, and returns the old value of X, it is used in the pseudocode shown below to implement a busy-wait lock. L is unsigned integer shared variable initialized to 0. The value of 0 corresponds to lock being available, while any non-zero value corresponds to the lock being not available.

```
AcquireLock (L){
    while (Fetch_And_Add( L, 1))
    L = 1;
}
ReleaseLock (L){
    L = 0;
}
```

This implementation

(a) fails as L can overflow

(b) fails as L can take on a non-zero value when the lock is actually available

(c) works correctly but may starve some processes

(d) works correctly vvithout starvation

[2012 : 2 Marks]

3. Three concurrent processes X, Y and Z execute three different code segments that access and update ceratin shared variables. Process X execute the P operation (i.e., wait) on semaphores a, b and c; process Y executes the P operation on semaphores b, c and d; process Z executes the P operation on semaphores c, d and a before entering the respective code segments. After completing the execution of its code segments, each process invokes the V operation (i.e., signal) on its three semaphores. All semaphores are binary semaphores initialized to one. Which one of the following represents a deadlock-free order of invoking the P operations by the processes?

(a) X: P(a)P(b)P(c)
Y:P(b)P(c)P(d)
Z: P(c)P(d)P(a)

(b) X: P(b)P(a)P(c)
Y:P(b)P(c)P(d)
Z: P(a)P(c)P(d)

(c) X:P(b)P(a)P(c)
Y:P(c)P(b)P(d)
Z: P(a)P(c)P(d)

(d) X:P(a)P(b)P(c)
Y:P(b)P(c)P(d)
Z: P(c)P(d)P(a)

[2013 : 1 Mark]

4. Which of the following is NOT a valid deadlock prevention scheme?

(a) Release all resources before requesting a new resource.

(b) Number the resources uniquely and never request a lower numbered resource than the last one requested.

(c) Never request a resource after releasing any resource

(d) Request and ali required resources be allocated before execution.

[2000 : 2 Marks]

DEADLOCK CHARACTERIZATION

5. A computer system has 6 tape drives, with n process completing for them. Each process may need 3 tape drives. The maximum value of n for which the system is guaranteed to be deadlock free is

(a) 2 (b) 3

(c) 4 (d) 1 **[1992 : 2 Marks]**

6. Consider a system having m resources of the same type. These resources are sharedby 3 processes A, B and C, which have peak demands of 3, 4 and 6 respectively. For what value of m deadlock will not occur?

(a) 7 (b) 9

(c) 10 (d) 13

[1993 : 2 Marks]

7. An operating system contains 3 user processes each requiring 2 units of resource R. the minimum number of units of r such that no deadlocks will ever arise is

(a) 3 (b) 5

(c) 4 (d) 6 **[1997 : 2 Marks]**

8. A computer has six tape drives, with n processes competing for them. Each process may need two drives. What is the maximum value of n for the system to be deadlock free?

(a) 6 (b) 5

(c) 4 (d) 3 **[1998 : 1 Mark]**

9. Suppose n processes, $P_1 ..., P_n$ share m identical resource units, which can be reserved and released one at a time. The maximum resource requirement of process P_i is s_p where $s_i > 0$. Which one of the following is a sufficient condition for ensuring that deadlock does not occur?

(a) $\forall i, s_i < m$ (b) $\forall i, s_i < n$

(c) $\sum_{i=1}^{n} s_i < (m+n)$ (d) $\sum_{i=1}^{n} s_i < (m*n)$

[2005 : 2 Marks]

10. Consider the following snapshot of a system running n processes. Process i is holding x_i instances of a resource R, for $1 \leq i \leq n$. Currently, all instances of R are occupied. Further, for all i, process i has placed a request for an additional yi instances while holding the xi instances it already has. There are exactlytwo processes p and q such that $y_p = y_q = 0$. Which one of the following can serve as a necessary condition to guarantee that the system is not approaching a deadlock?

(a) $\min(x_p, x_q) < \max_{k \neq p, q} y_k$

(b) $x_p + x_q \geq \max_{k \neq p, q} y_k$

(c) $\min(x_p, x_q) < 1$

(d) $\min(x_p, x_q) > 1$ **[2006 : 2 Marks]**

11. A single processor system has three resource types X, Y, and Z, which are shared by three processes. There are 5 units of each resource type. Consider the following scenario, where the column alloc denotes the number of units of each resource type allocated to each process, and the column request denotes the number of units of each resource type requested by a process in order to complete execution. Which of these processes will finish LAST?

	alloc	request
	X Y Z	X Y Z
P0	1 2 1	1 0 3
P1	2 0 1	0 1 2
P2	2 2 1	1 2 0

(a) P0

(b) P1

(c) P2

(d) None of the above, since the system is in a deadlock **[2007 : 2 Marks]**

12. Consider a system with 4 types of resources Rl (3 units), R2 (2 units), R3 (3 units), R4 (2 units). A non-preemptive resource allocation policy is used. At any given instance, a request is not entertained if it cannot be completely satisfied. Three processes Pl, P2, P3 request the resources as follows if executed independently.

Process Pl:	Process P2:	Process P3:
t = 0 : requests 2 units of R2	t = 0 : requests 2 units of R3	t = 0 : requests 1 unit of R4
t = 1: requests 1 unit of R3 t = 3 : requests 2 units of Rl	t = 2 : requests 1 unit of R4 t = 4 : requests 1 unit of Rl	t = 2 : requests 2 units of R1 t = 5 : Releases 2 units of R1
t = 5 : releases 1 unit of R2 and 1 unit of Rl t = 7 : releases 1 unit of R3	t = 6 : releases 1 unit of R3 t = 8 : Finishes	t = 7 : requests 1 unit of R2 t = 8 : requests 1 unit of R3
t = 8 : requests 2 units of R4		t = 9 : Finishes
t = 10 : Finishes		

Which one of the following statements is TRUE if all three processes run concurrently starting at time t = 0?

(a) All processes will finish without any deadlock

(b) Only Pl and P2 will be in deadlock

(c) Only Pl and P3 will be in deadlock

(d) All three processes will be in deadlock

[2009 : 2 Marks]

13. A system has n resources $R_0, R_1 ..., R_{n-1}$? and k processes $P_0, P_1 ..., P_{k-1}$. The implementation of the resource request logic of each process P_i is as follows:

```
if(i%2 = = 0){
    if (i < n) request R_i;
    if (i+2 < n) request R_{i + 2};
}
else {
    if (i < n) request R_{n - i};
    if (i+2 < n) request R_{n - i - 2};
}
```

In which one of the following situations is a deadlock possible?

(a) n = 40, k = 26 (b) n = 21, k =12

(c) n = 20, k = 10 (d) n = 41, k = 19

[2010 : 2 Marks]

14. A system contains three programs and each requires three tape units for its operation. The minimum number of tape units Which the system must have such that deadlocks never arise is ______.

[2014 (Set-3) : 2 Marks]

15. A system has 6 identical resources and N processes competing for them. Each process can request atmost 2 resources. Which one of the following values of N could lead to a deadlock?

(a) 1 (b) 2

(c) 3 (d) 4

[2015 (Set-2) : 1 Mark]

16. A system shares 9 tape drives. The current allocation and maximum requirement of tape drives for three processes are shown below:

Process	Current Allocation	Maximum Requirement
P1	3	7
P2	1	6
P3	3	5

Which of the following best describes current state of the system?

(a) Safe, Deadlocked

(b) Safe, Not Deadlocked

(c) Not Safe, Deadlocked

(d) Not Safe, Not Deadlocked

[2017 (Set-2): 2 Marks]

DEADLOCK PREVENTION

17. In a certain operating system, deadlock prevention is attempted using the following scheme. Each process is assigned a unique timestamp, and is restarted with the same timestamp if killed. Let P_h be the process holding a resource R, P_r be a process requesting for the same resource R, and $T(P_h)$ and $T(P_r)$ be their timestamps respectively. The decision to wait or preempt one of the processes is based on the following algorithm.

if$T(P_r) < T(P_h)$ then

kill P_r

else

wait

Which one of the following is TRUE?

(a) The scheme is deadlock-free, but not starvation-free

(b) The scheme is not deadlock-free, but starvation-free

(c) The scheme is neither deadlock-free nor starvation-free

(d) The scheme is both deadlock-free and starvation-free

[2004 : 2 Marks]

18. An operating system implements a policy that requires a process to release all resources before making a request for another resource.

Select the TRUE statement from the following:

(a) Both starvation and deadlock can occur

(b) Starvation can occur but deadlock cannot occur

(c) Starvation cannot occur but deadlock can occur

(d) Neither starvation nor deadlock can occur

[2008 : 2 Marks]

19. An operating system uses the Banker's algorithm for deadlock avoidance when managing the allocation of three resource types X, Y, and Z to three processes PO, Pl, and P2. The table given below presents the current system state. Here, the Allocation matrix shows the current number of resources of each type allocated to each process and the Max matrix shows the maximum number of resources of each type required by each process during its execution.

	Allocation			Max		
	X	Y	Z	X	Y	Z
P0	0	0	1	8	4	3
Pl	3	2	0	6	2	0
P2	2	1	1	3	3	3

There are 3 units of type X, 2 units of type Y and 2 units of type Z still available. The system is currently in a safe state. Consider the following independent requests for additional resources in the current state:

REQ1: P0 requests 0 units of X, 0 units of Yand 2 units of Z

REQ2: P1 requests 2 units of X, 0 units of Yand 0 units of Z

Which one of the following is TRUE?

(a) Only REQ1 can be permitted.

(b) Only REQ2 can be permitted.

(c) Both REQ1 and REQ2 can be permitted.

(d) Neither REQ1 nor REQ2 can be permitted.

[2014 (Set-1) : 2 Marks]

20. Consider the following policies for preventing deadlock in a system with mutually exclusive resources.

I. Processes should acquire ali their resources at the beginning of execution. If any resource is not available, ali resources acquired so far are released.

II. The resources are numbered uniquely, and processes are allowed to request for resources only in increasing resource numbers.

III. The resources are numbered uniquely, and processes are allowed to request for resources only in decreasing resource numbers.

IV. The resources are numbered uniquely. A process is allowed to request only for a resource with resource number larger than its currently held resources.

Which of the above policies can be used for preventing deadlock?

(a) Any one of I and III but not II or IV

(b) Any one of I, III and IV but not II

(c) Any one of II and III but not I or IV

(d) Any one of I, II, III and IV

[2015 (Set-3) : 2 Marks]

DEADLOCK AVOIDANCE & DETECTION

21. Which of the following is NOT true of deadlock prevention and deadlock avoidance schemes?

(a) In deadlock prevention, the request for resources is always granted if the resulting state is safe

(b) In deadlock avoidance, the request for resources is always granted if the resulting state is safe

(c) Deadlock avoidance is less restrictive than deadlock prevention

(d) Deadlock avoidance requires knowledge of resource requirements a priori

[2008 : 2 Marks]

22. Consider a system with 3 processes that share 4 instances of the same resource type. Each process can request a maximum of K instances. Resource instances can be requested and released only one at a time. The largest value of K that will always avoid deadlock is ______.

[2018 : 1 Mark]

23. In a system, there are three types of resources: E, F and G. Four processes P_0, P_1 P_2 and P_3 execute concurrently. At the outset, the processes have declared their maximum resource requirements using a matrix named Max as given below. For example Max[P_2, F] is the maximum number of instances of F that P_2 would require. The number of instances of the resources allocated to the various processes at any given state is given by a matrix named

Allocation.

Consider a state of the system with the Allocation matrix as shown below and in which 3 instances of E and 3 instances of F are the only resources available.

Allocation			
	E	F	G
P_0	1	0	1
P_1	1	1	2
P_2	1	0	3
P_3	2	0	0

Max			
	E	F	G
P_0	4	3	1
P_1	2	1	4
P_2	1	3	3
P_3	5	4	1

From the perspective of deadlock avoidance, which one of the foliowing is true?

(a) The system is in safe state.

(b) The system is not in safe state, but would be safe if one more instance of E were available.

(c) The system is not in safe state, but would be safe if one more instance of F were available.

(d) The system is not in safe state, but would be safe if one more instance of G were available.

[2018 : 2 Marks]

ANSWERS

1. (*c*)	**2.** (b)	**3.** (b)	**4.** (c)	**5.** (a)	**6.** (d)	**7.** (c)	**8.** (b)	**9.** (c)	**10.** (a)
11. (c)	**12.** (a)	**13.** (b)	**14.** (*)	**15.** (d)	**16.** (b)	**17.** (a)	**18.** (b)	**19.** (b)	**20.** (d)
21. (a)	**22.** (2)	**23.** (a)							

EXPLANATIONS

1. (I) and (II)

If all the resources are allocated to one process then deadlock will never occur.

So, if we allocate both R1 and R2 to process P1 or both R1 and R2 to process P2 then deadlock can be prevented.

When one process completes its execution then both the resources are allocated to the other process.

So, either condition (I) and (II) or condition (III) and (IV) ensures that deadlock never occurs.

2. fails as L can take on a non-zero value when the lock is actually available

Consider a situation where a process has just released the lock and made L = 0. Let there be one more process waiting for the lock, means executing the AcquireLock() function. Just after the L was made 0, let the waiting processes executed the line L = 1. Now, the lock is available and L = 1. Since L is 1, the waiting process (and any other future coming processes) can not come out of the while loop.

3. (*b*) Correct

(*a*)

X	Y	Z
P(*a*)	P(*b*)	P(*c*)
P(*b*)	P(*c*)	P(*d*)
P(*c*)	P(*d*)	P(*a*)

wrong answer because:

suppose X execute first & executed P(*a*) & P(*b*) then process switches to Z, then Z executed P(*c*), P(*d*) & wait for P(*a*) then again process switches to X & X then wait for P(*c*).

so, X is waiting for C which is occupied by Z & Z is waiting for X so no one can execute & deadlock occur.

(*b*) Correct

X	Y	Z
P(*b*)	P(*b*)	P(*a*)
P(*a*)	P(*c*)	P(*c*)
P(*c*)	P(*d*)	P(*d*)

Correct because all process does not have reverse call for wait on any variable.

(*c*)

X	Y	Z
P(*b*)	P(*c*)	P(*a*)
P(*a*)	P(*b*)	P(*c*)
P(*c*)	P(*d*)	P(*d*)

wrong answer because sequence of P(*b*) & P(*c*) are reverse or opposite in X & Y respectively so deadlock may occur.

(*d*)

X	Y	Z
P(*a*)	P(*c*)	P(*c*)
P(*b*)	P(*b*)	P(*d*)
P(*c*)	P(*d*)	P(*a*)

wrong answer because sequence of P(*c*) & P(*a*) are opposite in Z & X. so deadlock may occur.

4. Never request a resource after releasing any resource

A deadlock situation on a resource can arise if and only if all of the following conditions hold simultaneously in a system

Mutual exclusion: At least one resource must be held in a non-shareable mode. Otherwise, the processes would not be prevented from using the resource when necessary. Only one process can use the resource at any given instant of time.

Hold and wait or resource holding: a process is currently holding at least one resource and requesting additional resources which are being held by other processes.

No preemption: a resource can be released only voluntarily by the process holding it.

Circular wait: each process must be waiting for a resource which is being held by another process, which in turn is waiting for the first process to release the resource. In general, there is a set of waiting processes, P = {P1, P2, ., PN}, such that P1 is waiting for a resource held by P2, P2 is waiting for a resource held by P3 and so on until PN is waiting for a resource held by P1.

5. For a system to be deadlock free, Sum of max need of processes < No. of processes + No. of resources

$3n < n + 6$

$\Rightarrow 2n < 6$

$\Rightarrow n < 3$

so the maximum value of n for which the system is guaranteed to be deadlock free is 2 [n is less than 3 means max value for n is 2]

6. Formula-

Total of max needs < (no. of resource instances + no. of processes)

$(3 + 4 + 6) < m + 3.$

m > 10. hence m should be eleven or above.

Only 13 qualify the criteria.

7. Number of users = 3

Energy one need of resources = 2.

So, minimum number of resources for no dead lock is = 4

because Ist user = 2

2nd user = 1

3rd user = 1

Ist user used the resource, then transfer the next process.

8. Tape drive = 6

Each process needs = 2

There are n number of process.

For deedlock free, $n = 6 - 1 = 5$.

9. There are n process $P_1, P_2, ..., P_n$.

Number of identical resources = m

The maximum resource requirement for a process P_2 is S_P where $S_i > 0$

If all processes is in safe state or system can allocate resources to each process P_i in some order and still avoid a dead lock. We can avoid the dead lock if each P_i can still request can be satisfied by the current avialable resources plus the resources held by process P_j such that $j < i$ The maximum resource requirement of n processes

is $\sum_{i=1}^{n} S_i$ and this amout must less than $m + n$ so

$$\sum_{i=1}^{n} S_i < (m+n)$$

10. Total number of processes = n

Process i is holding x_i instances of a resource R for $1 \le i \le n$

Process i holding resource x_i and additional required y_i

There are two processes p and q such that $y_p = y_q = 0$

For no dead lock can occur

$\min(x_p, x_q) < (\max_{k \neq p,q} yk)$

11. In present situation free resources are 0.12, so P_1 can be processed, after this resources will be 213 so P_0 can be processed therefore P_2 will be last to be processed.

12. *At resource use*

t = 0 R2 - 2units R3 - 2 units R4 - 1units

t = 2 R2 - 2units R3 - 3 units R4 - 2 units R1- 1units

t = 3 R2 - 2units R3 - 3 units R4 -2 units<u>R1- 4 units</u>

t = 4 R2 - 2units R3 - 3 units R4 - 2units<u>R1- 5 units</u>

t = 5 R2 - 1 units R3 - 3units R4 - 2unitsR 1 - 2units

t = 6 R2 - 1units R3 - 2 units R4 - 2units R1-2units

t = 7 R2- 2 units R3 - 1 units R4 - 2unitsR 1- 2units

t = 8 R2 - 2 units R3- 1 units <u>R4- 3 units</u> R1- 1units

t = 9

Underline show that at that time requirement of resource is less than avaiability but it does not cause dead lock. All process finsh without any dead lock.

13. If $n = 21$, $k = 12$

(if (i%2 = = 0) {if ($i < n$) Request Ri;

if ($i + 2 < n$) Request R_{i+2};

else (if (i<n) Request R_{n-i}, if (i+2<n) Request (R_{n-i-2i})

We seen that if value of k = 11, 12.

Now first $k = 11$ means $p_{11-1} = p_{10} = p_i \Rightarrow i = 10$

then according to logic

initially it goes if block because (i%2 = 0)

(10%2 = = 0)

then it Request R_{10}, R_{10+2} (R_{12})

$\Rightarrow R_{10}, R_{12}$ Resources

if now next $k = 12$ then $i = 11$

Now it goes in else block and

Request R_{n-i}, R_{n-i-2}

$\Rightarrow R_{21-11}, R_{21-11-2}$

$\Rightarrow R_{10}, R_8$

then it also Request R_{10} then

both $k = 11$, $k = 12$ request R_{10}.

It is problem of dead lock.

14. If 6 resources are there then it may be possible that all three process have 2 resources and waiting for 1 more resource. Therefore, all of them will have to wait indefinitely. If 7 resources are there, then atleast one must have 3 resources so deadlock can never occur.

16. Safe, Not Deadlocked

Given there are total 9 tape drives,

so, according to the above table we can see we have currently allocated (7 tape drive), so currently Available tape drive = 2

So, P3 can use it and after using it will release it 3 resources New Available = 5

then P1 can use it and will release it 3 resources so New Available = 8

and lastly P2 so, all the process are in SAFE STATE and there will be NO DEADLOCK

Safe Sequence will be P3 → P2 → P1 or P3 → P1 → P2.

Answer will be (B) only.

17. The scheme is deadlock-free, but not starvation-free

1. This scheme is making sure that the timestamp of requesting process is always lesser than holding process
2. The process is restarted with same timestamp if killed and that timestamp can NOT be greater than the existing time stamp

From 1 and 2, it is clear that any new process coming having LESSER timestamp will be KILLED. So, NO DEADLOCK possible

However, a new process will lower timestamp may have to wait infinitely because of its LOWER timestamp(as killed process will also have same timestamp, as it was killed earlier). STARVATION IS Definitely POSSIBLE

18. Starvation can occur but deadlock cannot occur

Starvation can occur as each time a process requests a resource it has to release all its resources. Now, maybe the process has not used the resources properly yet. This will happen again when the process requests another resource. So, the process starves for proper utilisation of resources.

Deadlock will not occur as it is similar to a deadlock prevention scheme.

19. Only REQ2 can be permitted.

Available: X = 3, Y = 2, Z = 0

Now we can satisfy P12 s requirement completely. So Available becomes : X = 6, Y = 4, Z = 0.

Since, Z is not available now, neither P02 s nor P22 s requirement can be satisfied. So. it is an unsafe state.

20. For deadlock prevention we need to dissatisfy any of the necessary condition for deadlock

1. For hold and wait if we are disatisfy it can be hold or wait for hold ... before process start os assign all resources. While executing if process making new resource request it has to release all its assign resources that is waiting for release resources.

21. In deadlock avoidance, the request for resources is granted if only the state guarantees deadlock would never occur (safe state)

Deadlock prevention provides a set of methods that ensures that at least one of the necessary condition cannot hold – (mutual exclusion, hold & wait, no preemption & circular wait). These methods prevents deadlock by constraining how request can be made.

22. Number of processes = 3

Number of Resources = 4

Let's distribute each process one less than maximum demand (K – 1) resources. i.e. 3(K – 1)

Provide an additional resource to any of three processes for deadlock avoidance.

Total resources = 3(K – 1) + 1 = 3K – 2

Now, this 3K – 2 should be less than or equal to the number of resources we have right now.

$3K - 2 \le 4$

$3K \le 6$

$K \le 2$

So, largest value of K = 2

23.

Max need			
	E	F	G
P_0	4	3	1
P_1	2	1	4
P_2	1	3	3
P_3	5	4	1

Current allocation			
	E	F	G
P_0	1	0	1
P_1	1	1	2
P_2	1	0	3
P_3	2	0	0

Current available			
	E(3)	F(3)	G(0)
P_0	4	3	1
P_1	5	3	4
P_2	6	4	6
P_3	8	4	6

Remaining need			
	E	F	G
P_0	3	3	0
P_1	1	0	2
P_2	0	3	0
P_3	3	4	1

Safe sequence: P_0, P_2, P_1, P_3

Safe state

5
CHAPTER

Memory Management & Virtual Memory

Analysis of Previous GATE Papers

	Year → Topics ↓		2019	2018	2017 Set 1	2017 Set 2	2016 Set 1	2016 Set 2	2015 Set 1	2015 Set 2	2015 Set 3
VITUAL MEMORY	1 Mark	MCQ Type									
		Numerical Type								1	
	2 Marks	MCQ Type									
		Numerical Type					1			1	
	Total						2			3	
MEMORY MANAGEMENT	1 Mark	MCQ Type									
		Numerical Type									
	2 Marks	MCQ Type									
		Numerical Type									
	Total										
PAGING	1 Mark	MCQ Type							1		
		Numerical Type									
	2 Marks	MCQ Type	1								
		Numerical Type									
	Total		2						1		
DEAMAND PAGING	1 Mark	MCQ Type									
		Numerical Type									
	2 Marks	MCQ Type									
		Numerical Type									
	Total										
PAGE SEGMENTATION	1 Mark	MCQ Type						1			
		Numerical Type									
	2 Marks	MCQ Type			1				1	1	
		Numerical Type					1				
	Total				2		2	1	2	2	
PAGE REPLACEMENT	1 Mark	MCQ Type									
		Numerical Type									
	2 Marks	MCQ Type									
		Numerical Type									
	Total										
MULTI PROGRAMMING WITH VARIABLIE PARTITION	1 Mark	MCQ Type									
		Numerical Type									
	2 Marks	MCQ Type									
		Numerical Type									
	Total										
CACHE MEMORY ORGANIZATION	1 Mark	MCQ Type									
		Numerical Type									
	2 Marks	MCQ Type									
		Numerical Type									
	Total										

VITUAL MEMORY

1. In a virtual memory system the address space specified by the address Iines of the CPU must be than the physical memory size and than the secondary storage size.

(a) smaller, smaller

(b) smaller, larger

(c) larger, smaller

(d) larger, larger

[1995 : 2 Marks]

2. Thrashing

(a) Reduces page I/O

(b) Decreases the degree of multipro-gramming

(c) Implies excessive page I/O

(d) Improve the system performance

[1997 : 1 Mark]

3. If an instruction takes i microseconds and a page fault takes an additional j microseconds, the effective instruction time if on the average a page fault occurs every k instruction is

(a) $i + \frac{j}{k}$

(b) $i + j*k$

(c) $\frac{i + j}{k}$

(d) $(i + j) * k$

[1998 : 2 Marks]

4. Which of the following is/are advantage of virtual memory?

(a) Faster access to memory on an average.

(b) Processes can be given protected address spaces.

(c) Linker can assign addresses independent of where the program will be loaded in physical memory.

(d) Programs larger than the physical memory size can be run.

[1999 : 2 Marks]

5. Suppose the time to service a page fault is on the average 10 milliseconds, while a memory access takes 1 microsecond. Then a 99.99% hit ratio results in average memory access time of

(a) 1.9999 milliseconds

(b) 1 millisecond

(c) 9.999 microseconds

(d) 1.9999 microseconds

[2000 : 2 Marks]

6. Which of the following statements is/are false?

(a) Virtual memory implements the translation of a program's address space in to physical memory address space.

(b) Virtual memory allows each program to exceed the size of the primary memory.

(c) Virtual memory increases the degree of multiprogramming.

(d) Virtual memory reduces the context switching overhead.

[2001 : 1 Mark]

7. In a system with 32 bit virtual addresses and 1 KB page size, use of one-level page tables for virtual to physical address translation is not practical because of

(a) the large amount of internal fragmentation

(b) the large amount of external fragmentation

(c) the large memory overhead in maintaining page tables

(d) the large computation overhead in the translation process

[2003 : 1 Mark]

Common Data for Q. 8 & 9

A processor uses 2-level page tables for virtual to physical address translation. Page tables for both levels are stored in the main memory. Virtual and physical addresses are both 32 bits wide. The memory is byte addressable. For virtual to physical address translation, the 10 most significant bits of the virtual address are used as index into the first level page table while the next 10 bits are used as index into the second level page table. The 12 least significant bits of the virtual address are used as offset within the page. Assume that the page table entries in both levels of page tables are 4 bytes wide. Further, the processor has a translation look-aside buffer (TLB), with a hit rate of 96%. The TLB caches recently used virtual page numbers and the corresponding physical page numbers. The processor also has a physically addressed cache with a hit ratio of 90%. Main memory access time is 10 ns, cache access time is 1 ns, and TLB access time is also 1 ns.

8. Assuming that no page faults occur, the average time taken to access a virtual address is approximately (to the nearest 0.5 ns)

(a) 1.5 ns (b) 2 ns

(c) 3 ns (d) 4 ns

[2003 : 2 Marks]

9. Suppose a process has only the following pages in its virtual address space: two contiguous code pages starting at virtual address 0 × 00000000, two contiguous data pages starting at virtual address 0 × 00400000, and a stack page starting at virtual address 0 × FFFFF000. The amount of memory required for storing the page tables of this process is

(a) 8KB (b) 12KB
(c) 16KB (d) 20KB

[2003 : 2 Marks]

10. The minimum number of page frames that must be allocated to a running process in a virtual memory environment is determined by

(a) the instruction set architecture
(b) page size
(c) physical memory size
(d) number ofprocesses in memory

[2004 : 1 Mark]

11. In a virtual memory system, size of virtual address is 32-bit, size of physical address is 30-bit, page size is 4 Kbyte and size of each page table entry is 32-bit. The main memory is byte addressable. Which one of the following is the maximum number of bits that can be used for storing protection and other information in each page table entry?

(a) 2 (b) 10
(c) 12 (d) 14 **[2004 : 2 Marks]**

12. A CPU generates 32-bit virtual addresses. The page size is 4 KB. The processor has a translation look-aside buffer (TLB) which can hold a total of 128 page table entries and is 4-way set associative. The minimum size of the TLB tag is

(a) 11 bits (b) 13 bits
(c) 15 bits (d) 20 bits

[2006 : 2 Marks]

13. A computer system supports 32-bit virtual addresses as well as 32-bit physical addresses. Since the virtual address space is of the same size as the physical address space, the operating system designers decide to get rid of the virtual memory entirely. Which one of the following is true?

(a) Efficient implementation of multi-user support is no longer possible
(b) The processor cache organization can be made more efficient now
(c) Hardware support for memory management is no longer needed
(d) CPU scheduling can be made more efficient now

[2006 : 2 Marks]

14. Match the following flag bits used in the context of virtual memory management on the List-I (Name of the bit) with the different purposes on the List-II (Purpose) of the table below.

List-I	**List-II**
I. Dirty	a. Page initialization
II. R/W	b. Write-back policy
III. Reference	c. Page protection
IV. Valid	d. Page replacement policy

Codes:

(a) I-d, II-a, III-b, IV-c
(b) I-b, II-c, III-a, IV-d
(c) I-c, II-d, III-a, IV-b
(d) I-b, II-c, III-d, IV-a

[2008 : 2 Marks]

15. The essential content(s) in each entry of a page table is/are

(a) virtual page number
(b) page frame number
(c) both virtual page number and page frame number
(d) access right information

[2009 : 1 Mark]

16. Let the page fault service time be 10 ms in a computer with average memory access time being 20 ns. If one page fault is generated for every 10^6 memory accesses, what is the effective access time for the memory?

(a) 21ns (b) 30 ns
(c) 23 ns (d) 35 ns

[2011 : 1 Mark]

17. A system uses 3 page frames for storing process pages in main memory. It uses the Least Recently Used (LRU) page replacement policy. Assume that all the page frames are initially empty. What is the total number of page faults that will occur while processing the page reference string given below?

4, 7, 6, 1, 7, 6, 1, 2, 7, 2

[2014 (Set-3) : 1 Mark]

18. Consider a paging hardware with a TLB. Assume that the entire page table and all the pages are in the physical memory. It takes 10 milliseconds to search the TLB and 80 milliseconds to access the physical memory. If the TLB hit ratio is 0.6, the effective memory access time (in milliseconds) is_______.

[2014 (Set-3) : 2 Marks]

19. A computer system implements a 40 bit virtual address, page size of 8 kilobytes, and a 128-entry translation look-aside buffer (TLB) organized into 32 sets each having four ways. Assume that the TLB tag does not store any process id. The minimum length of the TLB tag in bits is______.

[2015 (Set-2): 1 Mark]

20. A Computer system implements 8 kilobyte pages and a 32-bit physical address space. Each page table entry contains a valid bit, a dirty bit, three permission bits, and the translation. If the maximum size of the page table of a process is 24 megabytes, the length of the virtual address supported by the system is____________bits.

[2015 (Set-2) : 2 Marks]

21. Consider a computer system with 40-bit virtual addressing and page size of sixteen kilobytes. If the computer system has a one-level page table per process and each page table entry requires 48 bits, then the size of the per-process page table is_______megabytes. **[2016 (Set-1) : 2 Marks]**

22. In the working-set strategy, which of the following is done by the operating system to prevent thrashing?

1. It initiates another process if there are enough extra frames.
2. It selects a process to suspend if the sum of the sizes of the working-sets exceeds the total number of available frames.

(a) I only (b) II only

(c) Neither I nor II (d) Both I and II

[2006 : 1 Mark]

23. A multilevel page table is preferred in comparison to a single level page table for translating virtual address to physical address because

(a) it reduces the memory access time to read or write a memory location

(b) it helps to reduce the size of page table needed to implement the virtual address space of a process

(c) it is required by the translation look a side buffer

(d) it helps to reduce the number of page faults in page replacement algorithms.

[2009 : 2 Marks]

MEMORY MANAGEMENT

24. Where does the swap space reside?

(a) RAM (b) Disk

(c) ROM (d) On-chip cache

[2001 : 1 Mark]

25. Match the pairs in the following questions.

Pair-I	Pair-II
A. Virtual Memory	P. Temporal locality
B. Shared memory	Q. Spatial locality
C. Look-ahead buffer	R. Address translation
D. Look-aside buffer	S. Mutual exclusion

[1989 : 2 Marks]

26. Indicate all the false statements from the statements given below:

(a) The amount of virtual memory available is limited by the availability of the secondary memory

(b) Any implementation of a critical section requires the use of an indivisible machine-instruction ,such as test-and-set.

(c) The use of monitors ensure that no dead-locks will be caused .

(d) The LRU page-replacement policy may cause thrashing for some type of programs.

(e) The best fit techniques for memory allocation ensures that memory will never be fragmented. **[1991 : 2 Marks]**

27. The capacity of a memory unit is defined by the number of words multiplied by the number of bits/word. How many separate address and data lines are needed for a memory of 4 K × 16?

(a) 10 address, 16 data Iines

(b) 11 address, 8 data Iines

(c) 12 address, 16 data Iines

(d) 12 address, 12 data Iines **[1995 : 2 Marks]**

28. A ROM is used to store the table for multiplication of two 8-bit unsigned integers. The size of ROM required is

(a) 256 × 16 (b) 64K × 8

(c) 4K × 16 (d) 64K × 16

[1996 : 1 Mark]

29. A1000 Kbyte memory is managed using variable partitions but no compaction. It currently has two partitions of sizes 200 Kbytes and 260 Kbytes respectively. The smallest allocation request in Kbytes that could be denied is for

(a) 151 (b) 181

(c) 231 (d) 541

[1996 : 2 Marks]

30. In a resident-OS computer, which of the following system software must reside in the main memory under all situations?

(a) Assembler (b) Linker

(c) Loader (d) Compiler

[1998 : 1 Mark]

31. The overlay tree for a program is as shown below:

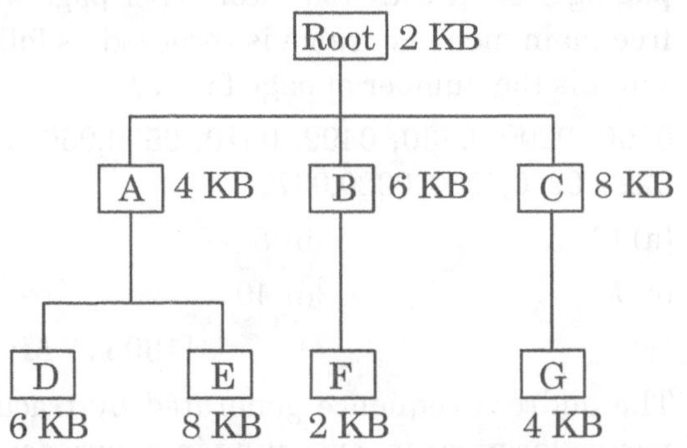

What will be the size of the partition (in physical memory) required to load (and run) this program?

(a) 12KB (b) 14KB

(c) 10KB (d) 8KB

[1998 : 2 Marks]

32. The process of assigning load addresses to the various parts of the program and adjusting the code and data in the program to reflect the assigned addresses is called

(a) assembly

(b) parsing

(c) relocation

(d) symbol resolution

[2001 : 1 Mark]

33. Which of the following is not a form of memory?

(a) Instruction cache

(b) Instruction register

(c) Instruction opcode

(d) Translation look a side buffer

[2002 : 1 Mark]

34. Dynamic linking can cause security concerns because

(a) Security is dynamic

(b) The path for searching dynamic libraries is not known tili runtime

(c) Linking is insecure

(d) Cryptographic procedures are not available for dynamic linking

[2002 : 2 Marks]

PAGING

35. Under paged memory management scheme simple lock and key memory protection arrangement may still be required if the ______ processors do not have address mapping hardware.

[1990 : 2 Marks]

36. A memory page containing a heavily used variable that was initialized very early and is in constant use is removed when

(a) LRU page replacement algorithm is used

(b) FIFO page replacement algorithm is used

(c) LFU page replacement algorithm is used

(d) None of these above

[1994 : 2 Marks]

37. Locality of reference implies that the page reference being made by a process

(a) will always be to the page used in the previous page reference

(b) is likely to be to one of the pages used in the last few page references

(c) will always be to one of the pages existing in memory

(d) will always lead to a page fault

[1997 : 1 Mark]

38. Consider a machine with 64 MB physical memory and a 32-bit virtual address space. If the page size of 4 KB, what is the approximate size of the page table?

(a) 16 MB

(b) 8 MB

(c) 2 MB

(d) 24 MB

[2001 : 2 Marks]

39. Consider a virtual memory system with FIFO page replacement policy. For an arbitrary page access pattern, increasing the number of page frames in main memory will

(a) always decrease the number of page faults

(b) always increase the number of page faults

(c) sometimes increase the number of page faults

(d) never affect the number of page faults

[2001 : 1 Mark]

40. Consider a system with a two-level paging scheme in which a regular memory access takes 150 nanoseconds, and servicing a page fault takes 8 milliseconds. An average instruction takes 100 nanoseconds of CPU time, and two memory accesses. The TLB hit ratio is 90%, and the page fault rate is one in every 10,000 instructions. What is the effective average instruction execution time?

(a) 645 nanoseconds (b) 1050 nanoseconds

(c) 1215 nanoseconds (d) 1230 nanoseconds

[2004 : 2 Marks]

Linked Answer Questions 41 and 42:

A computer uses 46-bit virtual address, 32-bit physical address, and a three-level paged page table organization. The page table base register stores the base address of the first-level (T_1), which occupies exactly one page. Each entry of T_1 stores the base address of a page of the second-level table (T_2). Each entry of T_2 stores the base address of a page of the third-level table (T_3). Each entry of T_3 stores a page table entry (PTE). The PTE is 32 it in size. The processor used in the computer has a 1 MB 16-way-set associative virtually indexed physical tagged cache the cache block size is 64 bytes.

41. What is the size of a page in KB in this computer?

(a) 2 (b) 4

(c) 8 (d) 16 **[2013 : 2 Marks]**

42. What is the minimum number of page colours needed to guarantee that no two synonyms map to different sets in the processor cache of this computer?

(a) 2 (b) 4

(c) 8 (d) 16

[2013 : 2 Marks]

43. Consider a system with byte-addressable memory, 32 bit logical addresses, 4 kilobyte page size and page table entries of 4 bytes each. The size of the page table in the system in megabytes is

[2015 (Set-1) : 1 Mark]

44. Assume that in a certain computer, the virtual addresses are 64 bits long and the physical addresses are 48 bits long. The memory is word addressible. The page size is 8kB and the word size is 4 bytes. The Translation Look-aside Buffer (TLB) in theaddress translation path has 128 valid entries. At most how many distinct virtual addresses can be translated without any TLB miss?

(a) 8×2^{20} (b) 256×2^{10}

(c) 4×2^{20} (d) 16×2^{10}

[2019 : 2 Marks]

DEMAND PAGING

45. The address sequence generated by tracing a particular program executing in a pure demand paging system with 100 records per page with 1 free main memory frame is recorded as follows. What is the number of page faults?

0100, 0200, 0430, 0499, 0510, 0530,0560,0120, 0220, 0240,0260, 0320,0370

(a) 13 (b) 8

(c) 7 (d) 10

[1995 : 2 Marks]

46. The address sequence generated by tracing a particular program executing in a pure demand paging system with 100 bytes per page is 0100, 0200, 0430,0499, 0510,0530, 0560,0120, 0220, 0240,0260, 0320, 0410.

Suppose that the memory can store only one page and if x is the address which causes a page fault then the bytes from addresses x to x + 99 are loaded on to the memory. How many page faults will occur?

(a) 0 (b) 4

(c) 7 (d) 8

[2007 : 1 Mark]

47. A demand paging system takes 100 time units to service a page fault and 300 time units to replace a dirty page. Memory access time is 1 time unit. The probability of a page fault is p. In case of a page fault, the probability of page being dirty is also p. It is observed that the average access time is 3 time units. Then the value of p is

(a) 0.194

(b) 0.233

(c) 0.514

(d) 0.981

[2007 : 2 Marks]

48. Consider a process executing on an operating system that uses demand paging. The average time for a memory access in the system is M units if the corresponding memory page is available in memory and D units if the memory access causes a page fault. It has been experimentally measured that the average time taken for a memory access in the process is X units.

Which one of the following is the correct expression for the page fault rate experienced by the process?

(a) (D–M)/(X–M) (b) (X–M)/(D–M)
(c) (D–X)/(D–M) (d) (X–M)/(D–X)

[2018 : 1 Marks]

PAGE SEGMENTATION

49. In a paged segmented scheme of memory management, the segment table itself must have a page table because

(a) the segment table is often too large to fit in one page
(b) each segment is spread over a number of pages
(c) segment tables point to page table and not to the physical locations of the segment
(d) the processor's description base register points to a page table **[1995 : 1 Mark]**

50. For each of the four processes P_1, P_2, P_3 and P_4. The total size in kilobytes (KB) and the number of segments are given below.

Process	Total size (in KB)	Number of segments
P_1	195	4
P_2	254	5
P_3	45	3
P_4	364	8

The page size is 1 KB. The size of an entry in the page table is 4 bytes. The size of an entry in the segment table is 8 bytes. The maximum size of a segment is 256 KB. The paging method for memory management uses two-level paging, and its storage overhead is P. The storage overhead for the segmentation method is S. The storage overhead for the segmentation and paging method is T. What is the relation among the overheads for the different methods of memory management in the concurrent execution of the above four processes?

(a) P < S < T (b) S < P < T
(c) S < T < P (d) T < S < P

[2006 : 2 Marks]

PAGE REPLACEMENT

51. Which page replacement policy sometimes leads to more page faults when size of memory is increased?

(a) Optimal (c) FIFO
(b) LRU (d) None of these

[1992 :1 Mark]

52. Dirty bit for a page in a page table

(a) Helps avoid unnecessary writes on paging device
(b) Helps maintain LRU information
(c) Allows only read on a page
(d) None of the above **[1997 : 1 Mark]**

53. The optimal page replacement algorithm will, select the page that

(a) Has not been used for the longest time in the past
(b) Will not be used for the longest time in the future
(c) Has been used least number of times
(d) Has been used most number of times

[2002 : 1 Mark]

Common Data for Q. 54 & Q. 55:

A process has been allocated 3 page frames. Assume that none of the pages of the process are available in the memory initially. The process makes the following sequence of page references (reference string): 1, 2,1, 3, 7, 4, 5, 6, 3, 1.

54. If optimal page replacement policy is used, how many page faults occur for the above reference string?

(a) 7 (b) 8
(c) 9 (d) 10 **[2007 : 2 Marks]**

55. Least Recently Used (LRU) page replacement policy is a practical approximation to optimal page replacement. For the above reference string, how many more page faults occur with LRU than with the optimal page replacement policy?

(a) 0 (b) 1
(c) 2 (d) 3 **[2007 : 2 Marks]**

56. A processor uses 36 bit physical addresses and 32 bit virtual addresses, with a page frame size of 4 Kbytes. Each page table entry is of size 4 bytes. A three level page table is used for virtual-to-physical address translation, where the virtual address is used as follows:

- bits 30- 31 are used to index into the first level page table,

- bits 21-29 are used to index into the second level page table
- bits 12 - 20 are used to index into the third level page table
- bits 0-11 are used as offset within the page

The number of bits required for addressing the next level page table (or page frame) in the page table entry of the first, second and third level page tables are respectively.

(a) 20, 20 and 20 (b) 24, 24, and 24
(c) 24, 24 and 20 (d) 25, 25 and 24

[2008 : 2 Marks]

57. Assume that a main memory with only 4 pages, each of 16 bytes, is initially empty. The CPU generates the following sequence of virtual addresses and uses the Least Recently Used (LRU) page replacement policy.

0, 4, 8, 20, 24, 36, 44, 12, 68, 72, 80, 84, 28, 32, 88, 92

How many page faults does this sequence cause? What are the page numbers of the pages present in the main memory at the end of the sequence?

(a) 6 and 1, 2, 3, 4 (b) 7 and 1, 2, 4, 5
(c) 8 and 1, 2, 4, 5 (d) 9 and 1, 2, 3, 5

[2008 : 2 Marks]

58. In which one of the following page replacement policies, Bleady's anomaly may occur?

(a) FIFO (b) Optimal
(c) LRU (d) MRU

[2009 : 1 Mark]

59. A system uses FIFO policy for page replacement. It has 4 page frames with no pages loaded to begin with. The system first accesses 100 distinct pages in some order and then accesses the same 100 pages but now in the reverse order. How many page faults will occur?

(a) 196 (b) 192
(c) 197 (d) 195 **[2010 : 1 Mark]**

60. Consider the virtual page reference string 1, 2, 3, 2, 4, 1, 3, 2, 4, 1

on a demand paged virtual memory system running on computer system that has main memory size of 3 page frames which are initially empty. Let LRU, FIFO and OPTIMAL denote the number of page faults under the corresponding page replacement policy. Then

(a) OPTIMAL < LRU < FIFO
(b) OPTIMAL < FIFO < LRU
(c) OPTIMAL = LRU
(d) OPTIMAL = FIFO **[2012 : 2 Marks]**

61. Assume that there are 3 page frames which are initially empty. If the page reference string is 1, 2, 3, 4, 2, 1, 5, 3, 2, 4, 6, the number of page faults using the optimal replacement policy is______.

[2014 (Set-1): 2 Marks]

62. A computer has twenty physical page frames which contain pages numbered 101 through 120. Now a program accesses the pages numbered 1, 2,..., 100 in that order, and repeats the access sequence THRICE. Which one of the following page replacement policies experiences the same number of page faults as the optimal page replacement policy for this program?

(a) Least-recently-used
(b) First-in-first-out
(c) Last-in-first-out
(d) Most-recently-used **[2014 (Set-2): 2 Marks]**

63. Consider a main memory with five page frames and the following sequence of page references: 3, 8, 2, 3, 9, 1, 6, 3, 8, 9, 3, 6, 2, 1, 3 Which one of the following is true with respect to page replacement policies First-In-First Out (FIFO) and Least Recently Used (LRU)?

(a) Both incur the same number of page faults
(b) FIFO incurs 2 more page faults than LRU
(c) LRU incurs 2 more page faults than FIFO
(d) FIFO incurs 1 more page faults than LRU

[2015 (Set-1): 2 Marks]

64. Consider six memory partitions of size 200 KB, 400 KB, 600 KB, 500 KB, 300 KB, and 250 KB, where KB refers to kilobyte. These partitions need to be allotted to four processes of sizes 357 KB, 210 KB, 468 KB and 491 KB in that order. If the best fit algorithm is used, which partitions are NOT allotted to any process?

(a) 200 KB and 300 KB
(b) 200 KB and 250 KB
(c) 250 KB and 300 KB
(d) 300 KB and 400 KB

[2015 (Set-2): 2 Marks]

65. Consider a computer system with ten physical page frames. The system is provided with an access sequence (a_1, a_2, ..., a_{20}, a_1 a_2, . . ., a_{20}), where each at is a distinct virtual page number. The difference in the number of page faults between the last-in-first-out page replacement policy and the optimal page replacement policy is_______. **[2016 (Set-1) : 2 Marks]**

66. In which one of the following page replacement algorithms it is possible for the page fault rate to increase even when the number of allocated frames increases?

(a) LRU (Least Recently Used)

(b) OPT (Optimal Page Replacement)

(c) MRU (Most Recently Used)

(d) FIFO (First In First Out)

[2016 (Set-2) : 1 Mark]

67. Recall that Belady's anomaly is that the page-fault rate may increase as the number of allocated frames increases. Now, consider the following statements:

SI: Random page replacement algorithm (where a page chosen at random is replaced) suffers from Belady's anomaly

S2: LRU page replacement algorithm suffers from Belady's anomaly

Which of the following is CORRECT?

(a) S1 is true, S2 is true

(b) S1 is true, S2 is false

(c) S1 is false, S2 is true

(d) S1 is false, S2 is false

[2017 (Set-1) : 2 Marks]

68. A virtual memory system uses First In First Out (FIFO) page replacement policy and allocates a fixed number of frames to a process. Consider the following statements:

P : Increasing the number of page frames allocated to a process sometimes increases the page fault rate.

Q : Some programs do not exhibit locality of reference.

Which one of the following is TRUE?

(a) Both P and Q are true, and Q is the reason for P

(b) Both P and Q are true, but Q is not the reason for P

(c) P is false, but Q is true

(d) Both P and Q are false

[2007 : 2 Marks]

MULTI PROGRAMMING WITH VARIABLIE PARTITION

69. Consider the following heap (figure) in which blank regions are not in use and hatched regions are in use.

The sequence of requests for blocks of size 300, 25,125, 50 can be satisfied if we use

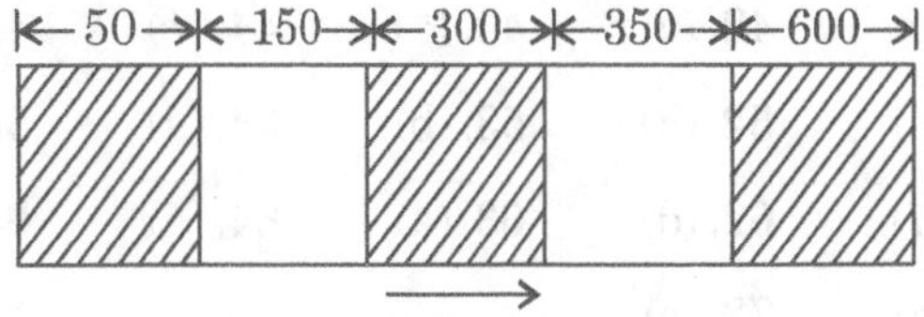

Increasing addresses

Increasing addresses

(a) either first fit or best fit policy (any one)

(b) first fit but not best fit policy

(c) best fit but not first fit policy

(d) none of the above **[1994 : 2 Marks]**

CACHE MEMORY ORGANIZATION

70. Consider a fully associative cache with 8 cache blocks (numbered 0-7) and the following sequence of memory block requests: 4, 3, 25, 8, 19, 6, 25, 8, 16, 35, 45, 22, 8, 3, 16, 25, 7.

If LRU replacement policy is used, which cache block will have memory block 7?

(a) 4 (b) 5

(c) 6 (d) 7 **[2004 : 2 Marks]**

71. Consider a 2-way set associative cache memory with 4 sets and total 8 cache blocks (0-7) and a main memory with 128 blocks (0-127). What memory blocks will be present in the cache after the following sequence of memory block references if LRU policy is used for cache block replacement. Assuming that initially the cache did not have any memory block from the current job?

05 3 9 7016 55

(a) 0 3 5 7 16 55 (b) 0 3 5 7 9 16 55

(c) 0 5 7 9 16 55 (d) 3 5 7 9 16 55

[2005 : 2 Marks]

72. A paging scheme uses a Translation Look- aside Buffer (TLB). A TLB-access takes 10 ns and a main memory access takes 50 ns. What is the effective access time(in ns) if the TLB hit ratio is 90% and there is no page-fault? (a) 54

(a) 54 (b) 60

(c) 65 (d) 75

[2008 : 1 Mark]

ANSWERS

1. (c)	**2.** (c)	**3.** (a)	**4.** (b and d)	**5.** (d)	**6.** (d)	**7.** (a)	**8.** (c)	**9.** (c)	**10.** (a)
11. (d)	**12.** (a)	**13.** (c)	**14.** (d)	**15.** (b)	**16.** (b)	**17.** (6)	**18.** (122)	**19.** (22)	**20.** (36)
21. (384)	**22.** (d)	**23.** (b)	**24.** (b)	**25.** (*)	**26.** (*)	**27.** (c)	**28.** (d)	**29.** (b)	**30.** (c)
31. (b)	**32.** (c)	**33.** (c)	**34.** (b)	**35.** (*)	**36.** (b)	**37.** (b)	**38.** (c)	**39.** (c)	**40.** (d)
41. (c)	**42.** (c)	**43.** (*)	**44.** (*b*)	**45.** (c)	**46.** (c)	**47.** (a)	**48.** (b)	**49.** (a)	**50.** (c)
51. (c)	**52.** (a)	**53.** (b)	**54.** (a)	**55.** (c)	**56.** (b)	**57.** (b)	**58.** (a)	**59.** (a)	**60.** (b)
61. (7)	**62.** (d)	**63.** (a)	**64.** (a)	**65.** (1)	**66.** (d)	**67.** (b)	**68.** (b)	**69.** (b)	**70.** (b)
71. (c)	**72.** (c)								

EXPLANATIONS

1. larger, smaller

Primary memory < virtual memory < secondary memory

We can extend VM upto the size of disk(secondary memory).

2. In thrashing, paging activity is more comparegion to executing high paging activity is called thrashing.

3. Effective instruction for k instructions

$$= i \times k + j$$

Effective instruction for 1 instruction

$$= \frac{i \times k + j}{k} = i + \frac{j}{k}$$

4. Virtual memory provides an interface through which processes access the physical memory. So,

A. Swapping of pages increases time while virtual memory concept is there and it slower the execution as compared to Direct access from physical memory. So, it is false.

B. Without virtual memory, it is difficult to give protected address space to processes as they will be accessing physical memory directly. So, it is true

C. Some other method can be used to assign addresses independent of where the program. so it is false.

D. Virtual memory allows a process to run using a virtual address space which is larger in size then the address of physical memory and pages are swapped in between physical memory and virtual memory when physical memory gets full. So, it is True.

6. Virtual memory reduces the context switching overhead.

VM requires switching of page tables (this is done very fast via switching of pointers) for the new process and thus it is theoretically slower than without VM. In anyway VM doesn't directly decrease the context switching overhead.

7. Number of page $= \dfrac{2^{32}}{2^{12}} = 2^{20}$

Hence, number of pages is much in number, thus, chances to internal fragmentation due to size of pages is larger, then overhead is reduced.

8. TLB hit ratio = 96 %

TLB access time = 1 ns

Virtual page hit ratio = 90 %

Main memory access time = 10 ns

For no page faults Average time

= hit ratio × cache acess time

+ (1 – hit ratio) × memory access time

$= 0.9 \times 1 + 0.1 \times 10$

$= 1.9$ ns

$\cong 2$ns

9. Total amount of memory required for starting the page tables of this process

$= 4 \times 2^{12}$ byte

$= 4 \times 4 \times 2^{10}$ byte

$= 16$ kB

10. If the processes are in the memory, page frames is created in the virtual memory to minimize the system load and to improve the preformance.

11. Page table entry must contain bits for representing frames and other bits for storing information like dirty bit,reference bit etc

No. of frames (no. of possible pages) = Physical memory size/ Page size = 230/212 = 218

18 + x = 32 (PT entry size = 32 bit)

x = 14 bits

12. *Number of bits required for various purposes in the 32 bit address is as follows :*

To find memory cell out of 4-way associative memory – 2 bits are needed.

To find page out of 128 page table entries - 7 bits are needed.

To find required byte in the page of size 4 kB – 12 bits are needed.

Total bits consumed in this way = 21

TLB tag's minimum size = 32 – 21 = 11 bits

13. Hardware support for memory management is no longer needed

For supporting virtual memory, special hardware support is needed from Memory Management Unit. Since operating system designers decide to get rid of the virtual memory entirely, hardware support for memory management is no longer needed

14. I-b, II-c, III-d, IV-a

Dirty bit : The dirty bit is set when the processor writes to (modifies) this memory. The bit indicates that its associated block of memory has been modified and has not been saved to storage yet. Dirty bits are used by the CPU cache and in the page replacement algorithms of an operating system.

R/W bit : If the bit is set, the page is read/write. Otherwise when it is not set, the page is read-only.

Reference bit is used in a version of FIFO called second chance (SC) policy, in order to avoid replacement of heavily used page.. It is set to one when a page is used heavily and periodically set to 0. Since it is used in a version FIFO which is a page replacement policy, this bit is come under category of page replacement.

Valid bit is not used for page replacement. It is not used in any page replacement policy. It tells the page in the memory is valid or not. If it is valid it is directly used and if it is not then a fresh page is loaded.

15. Page frame number is essential content in each entry of the page table.

Alternately

The page table has the ability to mark on entry invalid through a valid invalid bit or special value of protection bit, which is often called page frame number.

16. P = page fault rate

EA = $p \times$ page fault service time
+ $(1 - p) \times$ Memory access time

$$= \frac{1}{10^6} \times 10 \times 10^6 + \left(1 - \frac{1}{10^6}\right) \times 20$$

$\cong 29.9$ ns

17. What is a Page fault ? An interrupt that occurs when a program requests data that is not currently in real memory. The interrupt triggers the operating system to fetch the data from a virtual memory and load it into RAM.

Now, 4, 7, 6, 1, 7, 6, 1, 2, 7, 2 is the reference string, you can think of it as data requests made by a program.

Now the system uses 3 page frames for storing process pages in main memory. It uses the Least Recently Used (LRU) page replacement policy.

[ ] - Initially page frames are empty. i.e. no process pages in main memory.

[4] - Now 4 is brought into 1st frame (1st page fault)

Process page 4 was requested by the program, but it was not in the main memory (in form of page frames),which resulted in a page fault, after that process page 4 was brought in the main memory by the operating system.

[47] - Now 7 is brought into 2nd frame (2nd page fault) - Same explanation.

[476] - Now 6 is brought into 3rd frame (3rd page fault)

[176] - Now 1 is brought into 1st frame, as 1st frame was least recently used (4th page fault).

After this 7, 6 and 1 are were already present in the frames hence no replacements in pages.

[126] - Now 2 is brought into 2nd frame, as 2nd frame was least recently used (5th page fault).

[127] - Now 7 is brought into 3rd frame, as 3rd frame was least recently used (6th page fault).

Hence, total number of page faults (also called pf) are 6.

18. EMAT = TLB hit × (TLB access time + memory access time) + TLB miss (TLB access time + page table access time + memory access time)

=0.6(10 + 80) + 0.4(10 + 80 + 80)

=54 + 68

=122 msec

19. Total virtual address size = 40

Since there are 32 sets, set offset = 5

Since page size is 8kilobytes, word offset = 13

Minimum tag size = 40 – 5 – 13 = 22

20. Assume Virtual Address = x bits

entry size in page table = 19(frame bits) + 5(permission bits) = 24 bits = 3 Bytes

$2^{(x-13)} \times 3 = 24 \times 2^{(20)}$

solving we get x = 36 bits

21. 40 bit address system. So total Address Space $=2^{40}$ Bytes

16 Kbytes Page size = 2^{14}bytes

Total Frames(Number of pages of page table) $= (2^{40})/(2^{16}) = 2^{26}$

As Table entry is 48 bits, so each page = 6 bytes

Total = $2^{26} \times 6 = 2^{20} \times 2^{6} \times 6$ = 384MB

22. Both I and II

I is true because to prevent thrashing we must provide processes with as many frames as they really need "right now". If there are enough extra frames, another process can be initiated.

II is true because The total demand, D, is the sum of the sizes of the working sets for all processes. If D exceeds the total number of available frames, then at least one process is thrashing, because there are not enough frames available to satisfy its minimum working set. If D is significantly less than the currently available frames, then additional processes can be launched.

23. Most computer system support a large logical address space (2^{32} to 2^{64}). The page table become excessively large for example.

Consider a system with a 32 bit logical address space. If page size 4K(2^{12}), then page table may consist 1 million page. For this we use multilevels page table.

24. Disk

Swap space is an area on disk that temporarily holds a process memory image. When physical memory demand is sufficiently low, process memory images are brought back into physical memory from the swap area. Having sufficient swap space enables the system to keep some physical memory free at all times.

25. A-R,B-S,C-Q,D-P

Look Aside Buffer - TLB - Most recently used page addresses translation present in it, Why? Because of the high probability that they are going to use again in future. Temporal Locality.

Look Ahead Buffer - I relate it to look ahead compiler which looks one or more symbol forward from the position where it is currently in, means scanning a nearby area or in COA similar happen when we refer a data at some address and a block of nearby data comes with it. So Spatial locality.

27. 12 address, 16 data lines

ROM memory size = 2m × n

m = no. of address lines n = no. of data lines

Given, 4K × 16

=22 × 210 × 16

=212 × 16

Address lines =12

Data lines=16

28. 64K × 16

When we multiply two 8 bit numbers result can go up to 16 bits. So, we need 16 bits for each of the multiplication result. Number of results possible = 28 × 28 = 216 = 64 K as we need to store all possible results of multiplying two 8 bit numbers. So, 64 K × 16is the answer.

29. Memory size of variable partition are 200 K bytes and 260 K bytes.

So, total memory left = 1000 (200 + 260) = 540.

So, 541 Kbytes could denied for reqeust.

30. Loader

In many operating systems the loader is permanently resident in memory, although some operating systems that support virtual memory may allow the loader to be located in a region of memory that is pageable.

31. Required physical memory for run the program is maximum load of any overlay tree

= size of D + size of E

= 6 KB + 8KB = 14 KB

32. Relocation is the process of assigning load addresses to position-dependent code of a program and adjusting the code and data in the program to reflect the assigned addresses.

33. Instruction opcode

The instruction opcode is a part of the instruction which tells the processor what operation is to be performed so it is not a form of memory.

34. The path for searching dynamic libraries is not known till runtime

Dynamic linking is type of linking in which libraries required by the program are linked during run time.

35. i/o processors

37. Locality of references implies to cache memory, in which condition we get that are of the pages used in last few page references.

38. Number of pages = 232/4KB = 220 as we need to map every possible virtual address.

So, we need 220 entries in the page table. Physical memory being 64 MB, a physical address must be 26 bits and a page (of size 4KB) address needs 26 – 12 = 14 address bits. So, each page table entry must be at least 14 bits.

So, total size of page table = 220 × 14 bits ≈ 2 MB (assuming PTE is 2 bytes)

39. sometimes increase the number of page faults

Belady anomaly is the name given to the phenomenon in which increasing the number of page frames results in an increase in the number of page faults for certain memory access patterns. This phenomenon is commonly experienced when using the First in First Out (FIFO) page replacement algorithm

40. First P_1 issue signal wait(x) at that time process P_2 issue wait(y) and when P_1 issue wait(y) then process P_2 issue wait (x); so correct sequence is

$$P(S_x), P(S_y) ; P(S_x), P(S_y)$$

41. Let size of the page be x.

Total number of entries in T1 = x/4.

Total number of entries in T2 = x/4 × x/4

Total number of entries in T3 = x/4 × x/4 × x/4 which is also total number of pages

Total virtual address space = (x/4 × x/4 × x/4) × x = 2^{46}

$\therefore x^4/2^6 = 2^{46}$

4" x = 2^{13} bytes = 8Kb

42. PA bits - (cache indexing + cache offset + page offset) = page color bits

32 – (10 + 6 + 13) = 3

Thus 23 = 8 colors

43. 4MB

LA = 32 bits

Page size or offset = 4KB ⇒ 12 bits

pages = 32 – 12 = 20 bits so there are 220 pages For each page there would be an entry in the page table and PTE = 4 bytes

page table size = 220 × 4 B ⇒ 4MB

44. 1 word = 4 bytes

Page size = 8 kB = 2^{13} B

Now, Number of words in 1 page = $\frac{2^{13}}{2^2} = 2^{11}$

TLB can hold 128 valid entries so, at most 128×2^{11} memory address can be addressed

$128 \times 2^{11} = 128 \times 2 \times 2^{10} = 256 \times 2^{10}$

So option (d) is correct.

45. Since no of record in each page is 100 try to normalize the given value.

normalized value for each record is given by floor (given value /100)

so you will get 01, 02, 04, 04, 05, 05, 05, 01, 02, 02, 02, 03, 03

you can remove 0 from prefix if you love to remove.

now easily we can get 7 as total page fault.

46.

Address	Page faults	last byte in memory
0100	page fault,	199
0200	page fault,	299
0430	page fault,	529
0499	no page fault	
0510	no page fault	
0530	page fault,	629
0560	no page fault	
0120	page fault,	219
0220	page fault,	319
0240	no page fault	
0260	no page fault	
0320	page fault,	419
0410	no page fault	

So, 7 is the answer- (C)

47. Page fault service time = 100

page fault service time = 300 (if there is dirty page)

probability of page fault = p

probability of being dirty is = p

so total page fault service time(ps) = p(300) + (1 – p)(100) = 200p + 100 now given EAT = 3 so

EAT = p(page fault service time +memory access time) + (1 – p) memory access time

3 = p × page fault service time + memory access time

3 = p(200p + 100) + 1 = 200p2 + 100p + 1

p = 0.0194

48. EMAT = P * S + (1 – P) * M

X = P * D + (1 – P) * M

X = P * D + M – P * M

X – M = P (D – M)

$P = \frac{X - M}{D - M}$

49. Segmentation may be cause of external fragmentation. a segment table kept in register and used quickly. In segment table, the addition to the base and compression with the limit can be done simultaneously to same time.

50. S < T < P

Here we segment first and then page. So, we need the page table size. We are given maximum size of a segment is 256 KB and page size is 1KB and thus we require 256 entries in the page table. So, total size of page table =256 × 4 = 1024 bytes (exactly 1 page size).

So, now for P1 we require 1 segment table of size 32 bytes plus 4 page table of size 1KB for the 4 segments. Similarly,

P2 - 40 bytes and 5KB

P3 - 24 bytes and 3KB

P4 - 64 bytes and 8KB.

Thus total overhead =160 bytes 4KB + 5KB + 3KB + 8KB = 20480 + 160 = 20640 bytes.

So, T = 20640B.

51. FIFO\

Belady's anomaly proves that in case of First in First Out (FIFO) page replacement algorithm it is possible to have more page faults when increasing the no of page frames.

52. Dirty bit. If no free frames, then two page transfers one page out and one page in are required. In this situation effectively doubles the page fault service time, which will increase the effective access time accordingly.

This overhead can be reduced by the use of a modify (dirty) bit. Each page or frame may have a modify bit associated with it in the hardware. The modify bit or dirty bit for a page is set by the hardware whenever anyword or byte in the page is written into indicating that page has been modified.

53. Will not be used for the longest time in the future

Optimal page replacement algorithm will always select the page that will not be used for the longest time in the future for replacement, and that is why the it is called optimal page replacement algorithm.

54. 1 2 1 3 7 4 5 6 3 1

In optimal scheduling we schedule page in place of that page which is not used for scheduling in future ....

If initially memory is empty so 3 page faults

1,2 , (1) ,3 so initially 3 pages are there now - 3 faults

7 in place of (2) because 2 is not in future - 1 fault

4 in place of 7 - 1 fault

5 in place of 4 - 1 fault

6 in place of 5 - 1 fault

so total faults = 3 + 1 + 1 + 1 + 1 = 7

55. Optimal replacement policy

1 1 1 1 1

2 7 4 5 6

3 3 3 3 3

For Pages 1 2 3 6 4 5 6, page faults occur

LRU replacement policy

9 page faults occur page fault occurs for pages 1 2 3 7 4 5 6 3 1

So 2 more page faults than optimal algorithm

56. Number of bits required for first lent = 24

Number of bits required for second lent = 24

Number of bits required for third lent = 24

57. We have 4 spaces for a page and there will be a replacement only when a 5th distinct page comes. Lets see what happens for the sequence of memory accesses:

(Each page is of 16 bytes, so say for page 0, it contains virtual addresses from 0"15)

0: Page fault - 1, Pages in memory - 0

4: Page faults - 1, Pages in memory - 0

8: Page faults - 1, Pages in memory - 0

20: Page faults - 2, Pages in memory - 0,1

24: Page faults - 2, Pages in memory - 0,1

36: Page faults - 3, Pages in memory - 0,1,2

44: Page faults - 3, Pages in memory - 0,1,2

12: Page faults - 3, Pages in memory - 1,2,0

68: Page faults - 4, Pages in memory - 1,2,0,4

72: Page faults - 4, Pages in memory - 1,2,0,4

80: Page faults - 5, Pages in memory - 2,0,4,5

84: Page faults - 5, Pages in memory - 2,0,4,5
28: Page faults - 6, Pages in memory - 0,4,5,1
32: Page faults - 7, Pages in memory - 4,5,1,2
88: Page faults - 7, Pages in memory - 4,1,2,5
92: Page faults - 7, Pages in memory - 4,1,2,5

58. FIFO may have Belady's Anamoly

e.g. in FIFO for three frames the reference string

1, 2, 3, 4, 1, 2, 5, 1, 2, 3, 4, 5

There are 9 page faults and for four frames for the reference string there will be 10 faults.

59. Initially all pages are bring in physical memory and all are different, so that all time page fault occur.

So, 100 page fault after that in reverse order pages required.

So we see that 4 pages at last already in memory.

So there is no page fault for these.

So only 100 – 4 = 96 page faults occur.

∴ Total page faults = 100 + 96 = 196

60. 1, 2, 3, 2, 4, 1, 3, 2, 4, 1

LRU	1	1	1	1	3	2	4	1	3	2	
		2	2	3	2	4	1	3	2	4	
			3	2	4	1	3	2	4	1	
	F	F	F		F	F	F	F	F		F = 9
FIFO	1	1	1	1	2	3	3	4	4	4	
		2	2	2	3	4	4	1	1	1	
			3	3	4	1	1	2	2	2	
	F	F	F		F	F		F			= 6
OPTIMAL	1	1	1	1	4	4	4	2	2	2	
		2	2	2	1	1	1	1	1	1	
			3	3	3	3	3	4	4	4	
	F	F	F	NF	F			F			= 5

Optimal < FIFO < LRU

5 < 6 < 9

61. initially all empty frames fill by 1, 2, 3 so all time page fault which is 3 .

Then next 4 was not available in frame set so, we look at ahead of request which was coming last we replace 4 with that so, 3 will be replace by 4 and like wise next 2 and 1 is present already, so no. page fault and then next 5 is not present so, replace with 1 and then 3 was not present and replace with 5 and then 2 and 4 are present already so no page fault and then last 6th was not already there so, page fault.

So, total page fault at : 1, 2, 3, 4, 5, 3, 6 . so, total 7 page fault occur.

62. Physical page frames are 20 contain pages numbered 101 to 120.

Program accessed page numbered 1, 2, - - - - 100 in that order and repeat thrice.

63.

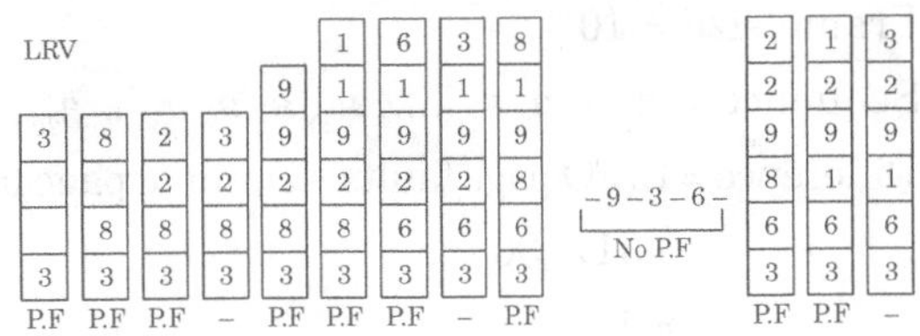

Total page fault = 9

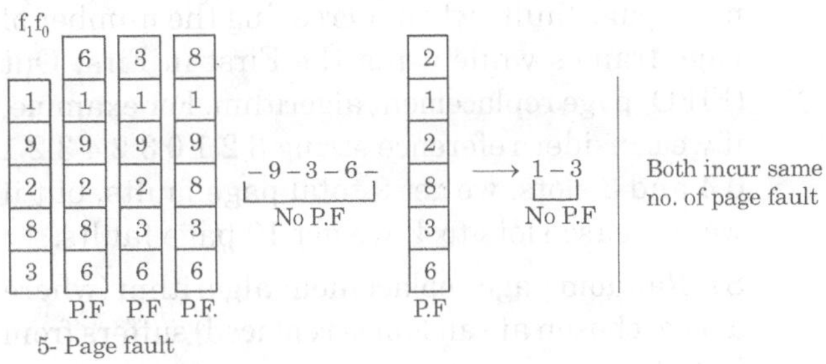

Total page fault = 9.

64. Consider the memory partition and using best fit algorithm

200	400	600	500	300	250
	357	491	468		201

Hence 200 and 300 are not alloted to any process.

65. Frame size = 10

Sequence $\{a_1, a_2, ..., a_{20}, a_1, a_2, ..., a_{20}\}$

⇒ Find difference of page fault of LIFO & optimal page replacement policy.

Consider a small case :

Frame size = 2

Sequence = $a_1\,a_2\,a_3\,a_4\,a_1\,a_2\,a_3\,a_4$

LIFO :

a_1	a_2	a_3	a_4	a_1	a_2	a_3	a_4	
	~~a_2~~	~~a_3~~	a_4	~~a_4~~	~~a_2~~	~~a_3~~	a_4	⇒ 7 faults
a_1	a_1	a_1	a_1	a_1	a_1	a_1	a_1	
F	F	F	F	H	F	F	F	

Optional :

a_1	a_2	a_3	a_4	a_1	a_2	a_3	a_4	
	~~a_2~~	~~a_3~~	a_4	a_4	a_4	a_4	a_4	⇒ 6 faults
a_1	a_1	a_1	a_1	~~a_1~~	~~a_2~~	a_3	a_3	
F	F	F	F	H	F	F	H	

Difference = LIFO page faults – Optimal page faults

= 7 – 6

= 1

Similarly for :

Frame size = 10

Sequence = $a_1\ a_2\ a_3\ a_4\ ......\ a_{20}\ a_1\ a_2\ a_3\ ...\ a_{20}$

Difference = LIFO page faults – Optimal page faults

= 31 – 30

= 1

67. S1 is true, S2 is false

Belady's anomaly proves that it is possible to have more page faults when increasing the number of page frames while using the First in First Out (FIFO) page replacement algorithm. For example, if we consider reference string 3 2 1 0 3 2 4 3 2 1 0 4 and 3 slots, we get 9 total page faults, but if we increase slots to 4, we get 10 page faults.

S1: Random page replacement algorithm (where a page chosen at random is replaced) suffers from Belady's anomaly.

→ Random page replacement algorithm can be any including FIFO so its true

S2: LRU page replacement algorithm suffers from Belady's anomaly .

→ LRU doesn't suffer from Belady's anomaly.

68. Both P and Q are true But Q is not the reason for P because page fault is concerned with pages present in frame not with pages nearly the page accessed recently.

69. first fit but not best fit policy

In first fit, block request will be satisfied from the first free block that fits it.

So, request for 300 will be satisfied by 350 size block reducing the free size to 50.

Request for 25, satisfied by 125 size block, reducing it to 125.

Request for 125 satisfied by 125 size block.

And request for 50 satisfied by the 50 size block.

So, all requests can be satisfied.

In best fit strategy, a block request is satisfied by the smallest block in that can fit it.

So, request for 300 will be satisfied by 350 size block reducing the free size to 50.

Request for 25, satisfied by 50 size block as its the smallest size that fits 25, reducing it to 25.

Request for 125, satisfied by 150 size block, reducing it to 25.

Now, request for 50 cannot be satisfied as the two 25 size blocks are not contiguous.

70. Block size is =8

Given 4, 3, 25, 8, 19, 6, 25, 8, 16, 35, 45, 22, 8, 3, 16, 25, 7

So from 0 to 7 ,we have

4 3 25 8 19 6 16 35 //25,8 LRU so next 16,35 come in the block.

45 3 25 8 19 6 16 35

45 22 25 8 19 6 16 35

45 22 25 8 19 6 16 35

45 22 25 8 3 6 16 35 //16 and 25 already there

45 22 25 8 3 7 16 35 //7 in 5th block

71. 128 main memory blocks are mapped to 4 sets in cache. So, each set maps 32 blocks each. And in each set there is place for two blocks (2-way set).

Now, we have 4 sets meaning 2 index bits. Also, 32 blocks going to one set means 5 tag bits.

Now, these 7 bits identify a memory block and tag bits are placed before index bits. (otherwise adjacent memory references- spatial locality- will hamper cache performance)

So, based on the two index bits (lower 2 bits) blocks will be going to sets as follows:

Set Number	Block Numbers
0	0,16
1	5,9
2	
3	3, 7,55

Since, each set has only 2 places, 3 will be throw out as its the least recently used block. So, final content of cache will be

0 5 7 9 16 55

72. Effective access time = hit ratio × time during hit + miss ratio × time during miss

TLB time = 10ns,

Memory time = 50ns

Hit Ratio = 90%

E.A.T. = (0.90) × (60) + 0.10 × 110

= 65

6 CHAPTER

IO Sheduling & Disk Management

Analysis of Previous GATE Papers

Topics ↓		Year →	2019	2018	2017 Set 1	2017 Set 2	2016 Set 1	2016 Set 2	2015 Set 1	2015 Set 2	2015 Set 3
IO MANAGEMENT	1 Mark	MCQ Type									
		Numerical Type									
	2 Marks	MCQ Type									
		Numerical Type		1			1				
	Total			**2**			**2**				
DISK SCHEDULING	1 Mark	MCQ Type									
		Numerical Type									
	2 Marks	MCQ Type							1		
		Numerical Type									
	Total								**2**		
IO DEVICES & MANAGEMENT	1 Mark	MCQ Type									
		Numerical Type									
	2 Marks	MCQ Type									
		Numerical Type									
	Total										
FI LE SYSTEM	1 Mark	MCQ Type									
		Numerical Type									
	2 Marks	MCQ Type				1					
		Numerical Type	1								
	Total		**2**			**2**					

IO MANAGEMENT

1. Which of the following statements about synchronous and asynchronous I/O is NOT true?
   (a) An ISR is invoked on completion of I/O in synchronous I/O but not in asynchronous I/O
   (b) In both synchronous and asynchronous I/O an ISR (Interrupt Service Routine) is invoked after completion of the I/O
   (c) A process making a synchronous I/O call waits until I/O is complete, but a process making an asynchronous I/O call does not wait for completion of the I/O
   (d) In the case of synchronous I/O, the process waiting for the completion of I/O is woken up by the ISR that is invoked after the completion of I/O

   [2008 : 2 Marks]

DISK SCHEDULING

2. Disk requests come to disk driver for cylinders 10, 22, 20, 2, 40, 56 and 38 in that order at a time when the disk drive is reading from cylinder 20. The seek time is 6 msec per cylinder. Compute the total seek time if the disk arm scheduling algorithm is
   (a) First come first served
   (b) Closest cylinder next **[1989 : 2 Marks]**

3. The root directory of a disk should be placed
   (a) at a fixed address in main memory
   (b) at a fixed location on the disk
   (c) any where on the disk
   (d) at a fixed location on the system disk

   [1993 : 2 Marks]

4. The correct matching for the following pairs is

List-I	List-I
A. Disk scheduling	1. Round robin
B. Batch processing	2. SCAN
C. Time sharing	3. LIFO
D. Interrupt processing	4. FIFO

   Codes:
   (a) A-3, B-4, C-2, D-1
   (b) A-4, B-3, C-2, D-1
   (c) A-2, B-4, C-1, D-3
   (d) A-3, B-4, C-3, D-2 **[1997 : 1 Mark]**

5. Which of the following disk scheduling strategies is likely to give the best throughput?
   (a) Farthest cylinder next
   (b) Nearest cylinder next
   (c) First come first served
   (d) Elevator algorithm **[1999 :1 Mark]**

6. A disk has 200 tracks (numbered 0 through 199). At a given time, it was servicing the request of reading data from track 120, and at the previous request, service was for track 90. The pending requests (in order of their arrival) are for track numbers.

   30 70 115 130 110 80 20 25.

   How many times will the head change its direction for the disk scheduling policies SSTF (Shortest Seek Time First) and FCFS (First Come Fist Serve)?
   (a) 2 and 3 (b) 3 and 3
   (c) 3 and 4 (d) 4 and 4

   [2004 : 2 Marks]

7. The head of a hard disk serves requests following the shortest seek time first (SSTF) policy. The head is initially positioned at track number 180. What is the maximum cardinality of the request set, so that the head changes its direction after servicing every request if the total number of tracks are 2048 and the head can start from any track?
   (a) 9 (b) 10
   (c) 11 (d) 12 **[2007 : 2 Marks]**

8. Consider a disk system with 100 cylinders. The requests to access the cylinders occur in following sequence:

   4, 34, 10, 7, 19, 73, 2, 15, 6, 20

   Assuming that the head is currently at cylinder 50, what is the time taken to satisfy all requests if it takes 1 ms to move from one cylinder to adjacent one and shortest seek time first policy is used?
   (a) 95 ms (b) 119 ms
   (c) 233 ms (d) 276 ms

   [2009 : 2 Marks]

9. Suppose a disk has 201 cylinders, numbered from 0 to 200. At some time the disk arm is at cylinder 100, and there is a queue of disk access requests for cylinders 30, 85, 90, 100, 105, 110, 135 and 145. If Shortest-Seek Time First (SSTF) is being used for scheduling the disk access, the request for cylinder 90 is serviced after servicing ____ number of requests. **[2014 (Set-1) : 1 Mark]**

10. Suppose the following disk request sequence (track numbers) for a disk with 100 tracks is given: 45, 20, 90, 10, 50, 60, 80, 25, 70. Assume that the initial position of the RIW head is on track 50. The additional distance that will be traversed by the R/W head when the Shortest Seek Time First (SSTF) algorithm is used compared to the SCAN (Elevator) algorithm (assuming that SCAN algorithm moves towards 100 when it starts execution) is tracks.

    [2015 (Set-1) : 2 Marks]

11. Consider a disk queue with requests for I/O to blocks on cylinders 47, 38, 121, 191, 87, 11, 92, 10. The C-LOOK scheduling algorithm is used. The head is initially at cylinder number 63, moving towards larger cylinder numbers on its servicing pass. The cylinders are numbered from 0 to 199. The total head movement (in number of cylinders) incurred while servicing these requests is

[2016 (Set-1) : 2 Marks]

12. Consider a storage disk with 4 platters (numbered as 0, 1, 2 and 3), 200 cylinders (numbered as 0, 1, ..., 199) and 256 sectors per track (numbered as 0, 1, ..., 255). The following 6 disk requests of the form [sector number, cylinder number, platter number] are received by the disk controller at the same time:

[120, 72, 2], [180, 134, 1], [60, 20, 0],
[212, 86, 3], [56, 116, 2], [118, 16, 1]

Currently the head is positioned at sector number 100 of cylinder 80 and is moving towards higher cylinder numbers. The average power dissipation in moving the head over 100 cylinders is 20 milliwatts and for reversing the direction of the head movement once is 15 milliwatts. Power dissipation associated with rotational latency and switching of head between different platters is negligible. The total power consumption in milliwatts to satisfy all of the above disk requests using the Shortest Seek Time First disk scheduling algorithm is ________ .

[2018: 2 Marks]

IO DEVICES & MANAGEMENT

13. State whether the following statements are TRUE or FALSE with reason. The data transfer between memory and I/O devices using programmed I/O is faster than interrupt-driven I/O.

[1990 : 2 Marks]

14. I/O redirection
(a) implies changing the name of a file
(b) can be employed to use an existing file as input file for a program
(c) implies connecting 2 programs through a pipe
(d) None of the above **[1997 : 1 Mark]**

15. Listed below are some operating system abstractions (in the left column) and the hardware components (in the right column)?

A. Thread	1. Interrupt
B. Virtual address space	2. Memory
C. File system	3. CPU
D. Signal	4. Disk

[1999 : 1 Mark]

16. Which of the following requires a device driver?
(a) Register (b) Cache
(c) Main memory (d) Disk **[2001 : 1 Mark]**

FILE SYSTEM

17. In the index allocation scheme of blocks to a file, the maximum possible size of the file depends on
(a) the size of the blocks, and the size of the address of the blocks.
(b) the number of blocks used for the index, and the size of the blocks
(c) the size of the blocks, the number of blocks used for the index, and the size of the address of the blocks
(d) None of the above **[2002 : 2 Marks]**

18. Using a larger block size in a fixed block size file system leads to
(a) better disk throughput but poorer disk space utilization
(b) better disk throughput and better disk space utilization
(c) poorer disk throughput but better disk space utilization
(d) poorer disk throughput and poorer disk space utilization **[2003 : 1 Mark]**

19. A Unix-style I-node has 10 direct pointers and one single, one double and one triple indirect pointers. Disk block size is 1 Kbyte, disk block address is 32 bits, and 48-bit integers are used. What is the maximum possible file size?
(a) 2^{24} bytes (b) 2^{32} bytes
(c) 2^{34} bytes (d) 2^{48} bytes

[2004 : 2 Marks]

20. In a particular Unix OS, each data block is of size 1024 bytes, each node has 10 direct data block addresses and three additional addresses: one for single indirect block, one for double indirect block and one for triple indirect block. Also, each block can contain addresses for 128 blocks. Which one of the following is approximately the maximum size of a file in the file system?
(a) 512 MB (b) 2 GB
(c) 8 GB (d) 16 GB

[2004 : 2 Marks]

21. A student wishes to create symbolic links in a computer system running Unix. Three text files named "file 1", "file2" and "file3" exist in her current working directory, and the student has read and write permissions for all three files. Assume that file 1 contains information about her hobbies, file2 contains information about her friends and file3 contains information about her courses. The student executes the following sequence of commands from her current working directory

In -s file1 file2

In -s file2 file3

Which of the following types of information would be lost from her file system?

I. Hobbies II. Friends

III. Courses

(a) I and II only (b) II and III only

(c) II only (d) I and III only

[2005 : 1 Mark]

22. The shell command

find -name password -print

is executed in /etc directory of a computer system running Unix. Which of the following shell commands will give the same information as the above command when executed in the same directory?

(a) is passwd

(b) cat passwd

(c) grep name passwd

(d) grep print passwd **[2005 : 1 Mark]**

23. In a computer system, four files of size 11050 bytes, 4990 bytes, 5170 bytes and 12640 bytes need to be stored. For storing these files on disk, we can use either 100 byte disk blocks or 200 byte disk blocks (but can't mix block sizes). For each block used to store a file, 4 bytes of bookkeeping information also needs to be stored on the disk. Thus, the total space used to store a file is the sum of the space taken to store the file and the space taken to store the book keeping information for the blocks allocated for storing the file. A disk block can store either bookkeeping information for a file or data from a file, but not both.

What is the total space required for storing the files using 100 byte disk blocks and 200 byte disk blocks respectively?

(a) 35400 and 35800 bytes

(b) 35800 and 35400 bytes

(c) 35600 and 35400 bytes

(d) 35400 and 35600 bytes **[2005 : 2 Marks]**

24. The data block of a very large file in the Unix file system are allocated using

(a) Contiguous allocation

(b) Linked allocation

(c) indexed allocation

(d) an extension of indexed allocation

[2008 :1 Mark]

25. A file system with'300 GByte disk uses a file descriptor with 8 direct block addresses, I indirect block address and 1 doubly indirect block address. The size of each disk block is 128 Bytes and the size of each disk block address is 8 Bytes. The maximum possible file size in this file system is

(a) 3 KBytes

(b) 35 KBytes

(c) 280 KBytes

(d) dependent on the size of the disk

[2012 : 2 Marks]

26. A FAT (file allocation table) based file system is being used and the total overhead of each entry in the FAT is 4 bytes in size. Given a 100×10^6 bytes disk on which the file system is stored and data block size is 10^3 bytes, the maximum size of a file that can be stored on this disk in units of 10^6 bytes is **[2014 (Set-2) :1 Mark]**

27. In a file allocation system, which of the following allocation scheme(s) can be used if no external fragmentation is allowed?

I. Contiguous II. Linked

III. Indexed

(a) I and III only (b) II only

(c) III only (d) II and III only

[2017 (Set-2) :1 Mark]

28. The index node (inode) of a Unix-like file system has 12 direct, one single-indirect and one double -indirect pointers. The disk block size is 4 kB, and the disk block address is 32-bits long. The maximum possible file size is (rounded off to 1 decimal place)______ GB

[2019 : 2 Marks]

ANSWERS

1. (b) **2.** (a) **3.** (b) **4.** (c) **5.** (b) **6.** (c) **7.** (c) **8.** (b) **9.** (3) **10.** (10)

11. (346) **12.** (85) **13.** (false) **14.** (b) **15.** (c) **16.** (d) **17.** (c) **18.** (d) **19.** (b) **20.** (b)

21. (b) **22.** (c) **23.** (c) **24.** (d) **25.** (b) **26.** (*) **27.** (d) **28.** 4.0

EXPLANATIONS

1. ISR is invoked after completion of I/O irrespective of the type of I/O.

2. First come first served

Total seek time

$= 10 \times 6 + 12 \times 6 + 2 \times 6 + 18 \times 6 + 38 \times 6 + 34 \times 6 + 32 \times 6$

$= 146 \times 6$

$= 876$ ms

(b) Closest cylinder next

Here the service order will be

20 22 10 6 2 38 40

So, total seek time

$= (0 + 2 + 12 + 4 + 4 + 36 + 2) \times 6$

$= 60 \times 6 = 360$

3. at a fixed location on the disk

The top directory in a file system. The root directory is provided by the operating system and has a special name; for example, in DOS systems the root directory is called \. The root directory is sometimes referred to simply as the root.

4. (*a*) SCAN is case of disk scheduling in which disk arm starts at one end of the disk and moves towards the other end, servicing request as it reaches each cylinder, until it gets to the other end of the disk. At the other end, the direction of head movement is reversed and servicing continues. The head continuously scans back and forth across the disk. SCAN algorithm is sometimes called *elevator algorithm.*

(*b*) **Batch processing** : Batch processing look like queus. It works like first in first out.

(*c*) **Time sharing.** In the case of Round Robin, it works like time sharing processing. It takes quantum of time for each process.

(*d*) **LIFO** is used like a interrupt processes. In the case of interrupt processing, last in first out method is used.

5. Nearest cylinder nect gives the best through put because: First nearest cylinder gives first ouput.

6. SSTF: (90) 120 115 110 130 80 70 30 25 20

Direction changes at 120, 110, 130

FCFS: (90) 120 30 70 115 130 110 80 20 25

direction changes at 120, 30, 130, 20

7. Here Head is changing it's direction after servicing every request.

Now, we can see distance of SSTF changing like 1, 3, 7, 15, 31, 63, 127, 255, 511, 1023, 2047

So, maximum cardinality will be 11

8. Requests : 4, 34, 10, 7, 19, 73, 2, 15, 6, 20

Current Position of head is 50.

Current	50	34	20	19	15	10	7	6	4	2
Next Access	34	20	19	15	10	7	6	4	2	73
Difference	16	14	1	4	5	5	1	2	2	71

Total time = 16 + 14 + 1 + 4 + 5 + 3 + 1 + 2 + 2 + 71

= 119 ms

9. Requests are serviced in following order

100 105 110 90 85 135 145 30

So, request of 90 is serviced after 3 requests.

10. for SSTF it takes 130 head movements and for SCAN it takes 140 head movements.

Hence, not additional but 140 – 130 = 10 less head movements SSTF takes.

11. $63 \rightarrow 191 = 128$

$191 \rightarrow 10 = 181$

$10 \rightarrow 47 = 37$

Total = 346

12. Total head movements in SSTF = (86 – 80) + (86 – 72) + (134 – 72) + (134 – 16) = 200

Power dissipated in moving 100 cylinder = 20mW

Power dissipated by 200 movements(say P1) $= 0.2 \times 200 = 40$mW

Power dissipated in reversing head direction once = 15mW

Number of times head changes its direction= 3

Power dissipated in reversing head direction(say P2) $= 3 \times 15 = 45$mW

Total Power Consumption is P1 + P2 = 85mW

Hence, 85mW is the correct answer.

13. False because in programmed I/O, CPU will check the I/O devices' status according to written program. Suppose CPU requested 5 I/O devices and the program is written to check sequentially and 5th device is ready before 2nd device, then also CPU will come to check at its turn.

So, programmed I/O doesn't care about availability status of devices. it blindly works according to written program. That's why it is slow.

Interrupt driven IO/ : Here, if any device is ready then it won't wait for CPU, it will say to CPU that "I am ready" by sending interrupt request and the delay here will be only "time taken in servicing the interrupt" which is less than programmed I/O.

14. I/O redirection. The common shells have a simple syntax for changing what files are open for standard I/O streams of a process. Changing a standard file is called *I/O redirection*. The subsequent command forces all output and all error messages to be redirected to a file without the ampers and error message appear on the terminals.

15. Threads refer to the execution of different processes simultaneously in the CPU. Virtual address space is implemented in memory. The file-system in the way in which data in a disk is organized. A signal is acted upon using the mechanism of interrupts.

16. A disk driver is software which enables communication between internal hard disk (or drive) and computer.

It allows a specific disk drive to interact with the remainder of the computer.

17. the size of the blocks, the number of blocks used for the index, and the size of the address of the blocks

In Index allocation size of maximum file can be derived like following:

No of addressable blocks using one Index block (A) = Size of block / Size of block address

No of block addresses available for addressing one file (B) = No of Maximum blocks we can use for the Index × No of addressable blocks using one Index block (A)

Size of File = B × Size of Block

18. Throughput → one measure of work is the number of processes that are completed per time unit, called throughput.

CPU Utilization : We want to keep CPU as busy as possible. In case of larger block size and fixed block size file system, CPU utilization is poorer and throughput is also decresead.

19. Disk block address = 32 bit

It can address 2^{32} location, i.e. 2^{32} byte, so size of file is 2^{32}. Hence correct answer is 2^{32}.

20. 2 GB

Maximum file size = 10 × 1024 Bytes + 1 × 128 × 1024 Bytes + 1 × 128 × 128 × 1024 Bytes +1 × 128 × 128 × 128 × 1024 Bytes = approx 2 GB.

21. II and III only

As ln -s is symbolic link. In this case

File3 ⇒ File2 ⇒ File1 ⇒ Hobbies(actual data).

So File2 and File3 content are lost.

22. grep name password

Find is a Unix (or Linux) command used for searching the files in a directory hierarchy. The syntax of find command is :

find –name "filename" –print

Grep is a unix command which can be used to find file names with a watching string. The syntax of grep command is :

grep name "filename"

23. 35600 and 35400 bytes

for 100 bytes block:

11050 = 111 blocks requiring 111 × 4 = 444 bytes of bookkeeping info which requires another 5 disk blocks. So, totally 111 + 5 = 116 disk blocks. Similarly,

4990 = 50 + (50 × 4)/100 = 52

5170 = 52 + (52 × 4)/100 = 55

12640 =1 27 + (127 × 4/100) = 133

356 × 100 = 35600 bytes

For 200 bytes block:

56 + (56 × 4/200) = 58

25 + (25 × 4/200) = 26

26 + (26 × 4/200) = 27

64 + (64 × 4/200) = 66

177 × 200 = 35400

24. Index allocation cannot allocate very large file.

25. 35 Kbytes

Direct block addressing will point to 8 disk blocks = 8 × 128 B = 1 KB

Singly Indirect block addressing will point to 1 disk block which has 128/8 disc block addresses =(128/8) × 128 B = 2 KB

Doubly indirect block addressing will point to 1 disk block which has 128/8 addresses to disk blocks which in turn has 128/8 addresses to disk blocks = 16 × 16 × 128 B = 32 KB

Total = 35 KB

26. 99.55 to 99.65

Here block size is 10^3 B.

No. of entries in the FAT = Disk capacity/ Block size

$= 10^8/10^3$

$= 10^5$

Total space consumed by FAT = $10^5 \times 4B$

$= 0.4 \times 10^6 B$

Max. size of file that can be stored

$= 100 \times 10^6 - 0.4 \times 10^6$

$= 99.6 \times 10^6 B.$

So answer 99.6.

27. Only as linked and indexed allocations are non cantagious, they will not suffer from external fragmentation.

Unit - IX

Databases

Syllabus

ER-model. Relational model: relational algebra, tuple calculus, SQL. Integrity constraints, normal forms. File organization, indexing (e.g., B and B+ trees). Transactions and concurrency control.

Contents

1 CHAPTER

Introduction & Database Modelling

Analysis of Previous GATE Papers											
	Year → Topics ↓		2019	2018	2017 Set 1	2017 Set 2	2016 Set 1	2016 Set 2	2015 Set 1	2015 Set 2	2015 Set 3
ENTITY RELATIONSHIP	1 Mark	MCQ Type		1			1				
		Numerical Type				1					
	2 Marks	MCQ Type									
		Numerical Type							1		
	Total			1		1	1		2		
KEY CONTRAINTS	1 Mark	MCQ Type									
		Numerical Type									
	2 Marks	MCQ Type									
		Numerical Type									
	Total										

ENTITY RELATIONSHIP

1. It is desired to design an object-oriented employee record system for a company. Each employee has a name, unique id and salary. Employees belong to different categories and their salary is determined by their category. The functions getName, getId and computeSalary are required. Given the class hierarchy below, possible locations for these functions are:
   - (i) getId is implemented in the superclass
   - (ii) getId is implemented in the subclass
   - (iii) getName is an abstract function in the superclass
   - (iv) getName is implemented in the superclass
   - (v) getName is implemented in the subclass
   - (vi) getSalary is an abstract function in the superclass
   - (vii) getSalary is implemented in the superclass
   - (viii) getSalary is implemented in the subclass

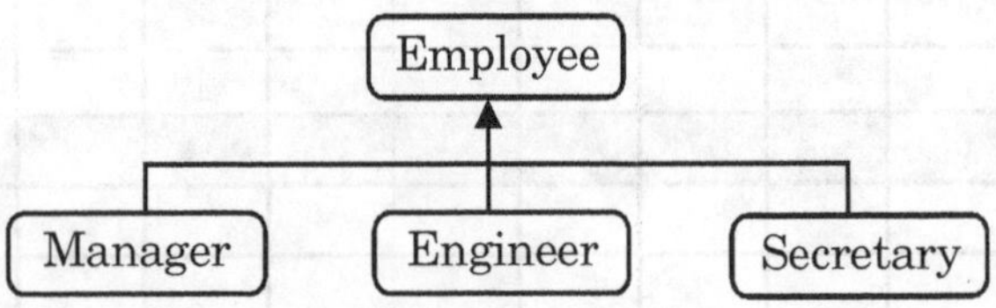

Choose the best design
(a) (i), (iv), (vi), (viii)
(b) (i), (iv), (vii)
(c) (i), (iii), (v), (vi), (viii)
(d) (ii), (v), (viii)

[2004 : 2 Marks]

2. Consinder the following entity relationship diagram (ERD), where two entities E1 and E2 have a relation R of cardinality 1 : m

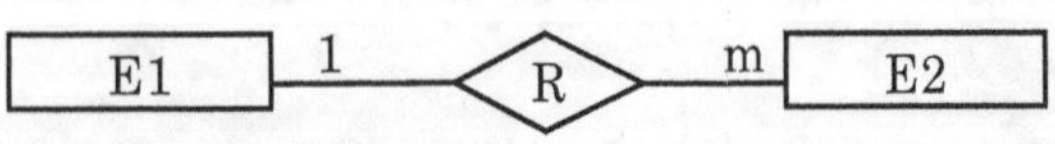

The attributes of E1 are A11, A12 and A13 where A11 is the key attribute. The attributes of E2 are A21, A22 and A23 where A21 is the key attribute and A23 is a multi-valued attribute. Relation R does not have any attribute. A relational database containing minimum number of tables with each table satisfying the requirements of the third normal form (3NF) is designed from the above ERD. The number of tables in the database is

(a) 2 (b) 3
(c) 5 (d) 4

[2004 : 2 Marks]

3. Consider the entities 'hotel room', and 'person' with a many to many relationship 'lodging' as shown below:

If we wish to storre information about the rent payment to be made by person (s) occupying different hotel rooms, then this information should appear as an attribute of

(a) Person (b) Hotel Room
(c) Lodging (d) None of these

[2005 : 1 Mark]

4. Let E_1 and E_2 be two entities in an E/R diagram with simple single-valued attributes. R_1 and R_2 are two relationships between E_1 and E_2, where R_1 is one-to-many and R_2 is many-to-many. R_1 and R_2 do not have any attributes of their own. What is the minimum number of tables required to represent this situation in the relationship model?

(a) 2 (b) 3
(c) 4 (d) 5 **[2005 : 2 Marks]**

Common Data for Q. 5 & Q. 6

Consider the following ER diagram

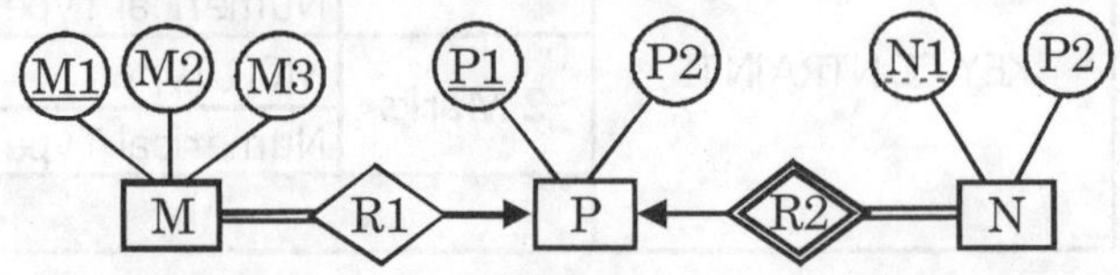

5. The minimum number of tables needed to represent M, N, P, R1, R2 is

(a) 2 (b) 3
(c) 4 (d) 5 **2008 : 2 Marks]**

6. Which of the following is a correct attribute set for one of the tables for the correct answer to the above questions?

(a) {M1, M2, M3, P1} (b) {M1, P1, N1, N2}
(c) {M1, P1, N1} (d) {M1, P1}

[2008 : 2 Marks]

7. Given the basic ER and relational models, which of the following is INCORRECT?

(a) An attribute of an entity can have more than one value
(b) An attribute of an entity can be composite
(c) In a row of a relational table, an attribute can have more than one value
(d) In a row of a relational table, an attribute can have exactly one value or a NULL value

[2012 : 1 Mark]

8. Consider an Entity-Relationship (ER) model in which entity sets E_1 and E_2 are connected by an m : n relationship R_{12}. E_1 and E_3 are connected by a 1 : n (1 on the side of E_1 and n on the side of E_3 relationship R_{13}.

E_1 has two single-valued attributes a_{11} and a_{12} of which a_{11} is the key attribute. E_2 has two single-valued attributes a_{21} and a_{22} of which a_{21} is the key attribute. E_3 has two single-vallued attribtes a_{31} and a_{32} of which a_{31} is the key attribute. The relationships do not have any attributes.

If a relational model is derived from the above ER model, then the minimum number of relations that would be generated if all the relations are in 3NF is ______.

[2015 (Set-1) : 2 Marks]

9. An ER model of a database consists of entity types A and B. These are connected by a relationship R which does not have its own attribute. Under which one of the following conditions, can the relational table for R be merged with that of A?

(a) Relationship R is one-to-many and the participation of A in R is total.

(b) Relationship R is one-to-many and he participation of A in R is partial.

(c) Relationship R is many-toone and the participation of A in R is total.

(d) Relationship R is many-to-one and the participation of A in R is partial.

[2017 (Set-2): 1 Mark]

10. In an Entity-Relationship (ER) model, suppose R is a many-to-one relationship from entity set E1 to entity set E2. Assume that E1 and E2 participate totally in R and that the cardinality of E1 is greater than the cardinality of E2. Which one of the following is true about R?

(a) Every entity in E1 is associated with exactly one entity in E2.

(b) Sone entity in E1 is associated with more than one entity in E2.

(c) Every entity in E2 is associated with exactly one entity in E1.

(d) Every entity in E2 is associated with at most one entity in E1.

[2018 : 1 Mark]

KEY CONTRAINTS

11. Consider a relational table with a single record from each registered student with the following attributes.

1. Registration_Num: Unique registration number of each registered student
2. UID: Unique identity number, unique at the national level for each citizen
3. BankAccount_Num: Unique account number at the bank. A student can have multiple accounts or joint accounts. This attribute stores the primary account number
4. Name: Name of the student
5. Hostel_Room: Room number of the hostel

Which of the following options in INCORRECT?

(a) BankAccount_Num is a candidate key

(b) Registration_Num can be a primary key

(c) UID is a candidate key if all students are from the same country

(d) If S is a superkey suchh that $S \cap$ UID is NULL then $S \cup$ UID is also a superkey

12. Consider the relation scheme $R = (E, F, G H, I, J, K, L, M, N)$ and the set of functional dependencies $\{\{E,F\} \rightarrow \{G\}, \{F\} \rightarrow \{I,J\}, \{E, H\} \rightarrow \{K, L\}, \{K\} \rightarrow \{M\}, \{L\} \rightarrow \{N\}\}$ on R. What is the key for R?

(a) $\{E, F\}$ (b) $\{E, F, H\}$

(c) $\{E, F, H, K, L\}$ (d) $\{E\}$

[2014 (Set-1): 1 Mark]

13 Given the following statements:

S1: A foreign key declaration can always be replaced by an equivalent check assertion in SQL.

S2: Given the table R(a, b, c) where a and b together form the primary key, the following is a valid table definition.

CREATE TABLES(

a INTEGER,

d INTEGER,

e INTEGER,

PRIMARY KEY (d),

FOREIGN KEY (a)references R)

Which one of the following statements is **CORRECT**?

(a) S1 is TRUE and S2 is FALSE.

(b) Both S1 and S2 are TRUE.

(c) S1 is FALSE and S2 is TRUE.

(d) Both S1 and S2 are FALSE.

[2014 (Set-1): 1 Mark]

14. The maximum number of superkeys for the relation schema R(E,F,G,H) with E as the key is _______.

[2014 (Set-2): 1 Mark]

15. Given an instance of the STUDENTS relation as shown below:

Student ID	Student Name	Student Email	Student Age	CPI
2345	Shankar	shankar@math	X	9.4
1287	Swati	swati@ee	19	9.5
7853	Shankar	shankar@cse	19	9.4
9876	Swati	swati@mech	18	9.3
8765	Ganesh	ganesh@civil	19	8.7

For **(StudentName, StudentAge)** to be a key for this instance, the vlaue *X* should NOT be equal to _______. **[2014 (Set-2) : 1 Mark]**

16. A prime attribute of a relation scheme *R* is an attribute that appears

(a) in all candidate keys of *R*.

(b) in some candidate keys of *R*.

(c) in a foreign key of R.

(d) only in the primary key of *R*.

[2014 (Set-3) : 1 Mark]

17. Which of the following is NOT a superkey in a relational schema with attributes *V, W, X, Y, Z* and primary key *V Y*?

(a) *V X Y Z*

(b) *V W X Z*

(c) *V W X Y*

(d) *V W X Y Z*

[2016 (Set-1) : 1 Mark]

18. An instance of a relational scheme R(A, B, C) has distinct values for attributes A. Can you conclude that A is a candidate key for R?

[1994 : 1 Mark]

19. An index is clustered, if

(a) it is on a set of fields that form a candidate key.

(b) it is on a set of fields that include the primary key.

(c) the data record of the file are organized in the same order as the date entries of the index

(d) the data records of the file are organized not in the same order as the data entries of the index.

[2013 : 1 Mark]

ANSWERS

1. (*c*)	**2.** (*b*)	**3.** (*c*)	**4.** (*b*)	**5.** (*b*)	**6.** (*a*)	**7.** (*c*)	**8.** (4)	**9.** (*c,d*)	**10.** (*a*)
11. (*a*)	**12.** (*b*)	**13.** (*d*)	**14.** (8 to 8)	**15.** (19 to 19)	**16.** (*b*)	**17.** (*b*)	**18.** (No)	**19.** (*c*)	

EXPLANATIONS

1. It should not be visible to outside world and should be extracted through super class. Name can be duplicate should be implemented in sub class. Salary is dependent on category should be implemented in subclass.
2. Total 3 tables are there.
   1. $E_1 (A_{11}, A_{12}, A_{13})$
   2. $E_2 (A_{11}, A_{12}, A_{13})$
   2 $E_{23} (A_{21}, A_{23})$ Multivalued Attribute
3. Since it is many, rent cannot be an attribute of room or person entities alone. If depending on number of persons sharing a room the rent for each person for the room will be different Otherwise rent can be attribute of room. here attribute id Lodging.
4. One table for E_1;
   One table for E_2;
   One table for R_2
   * Remember that only one to many relationship can be represented with entity set from one's side, because each entity in this entity set can be associated with at most one entity of another set.
5. Total 13 tables
   1. $M (M_1, M_2, M_3, P_1)$
   2. $P (P_1, P_2)$
   3. $N (P, N_1, N_2)$
6. $\{M_1, M_2, M_3, P_1\}$ is the atribute set of table M.
7. Row cannot have attribute more than one value.
8. The E–R diagram is

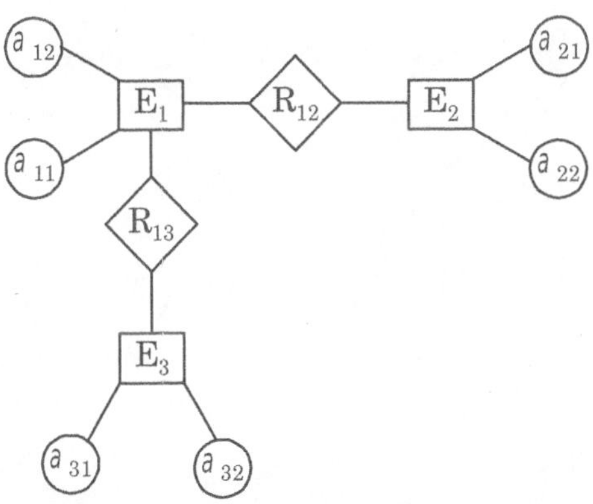

9. There are 2 entities sets A, B
   1 relationship set R
   As relation R merges with that of A

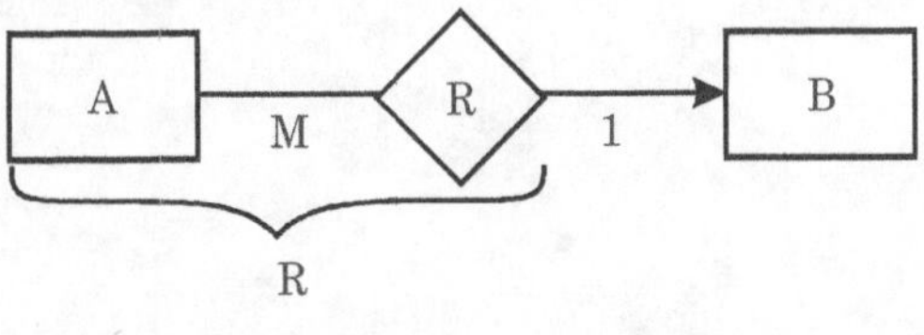

As many to one relationship set can merge towards entity set 'A'

The partipation towards A side can be total/partial

10.

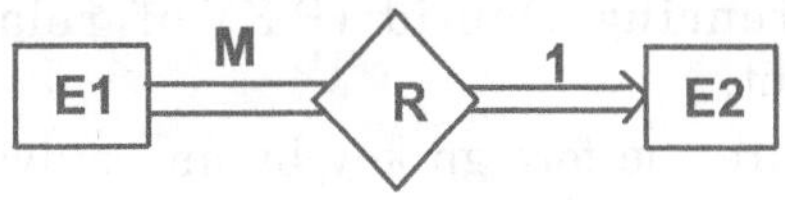

E1 entries > E2 entities

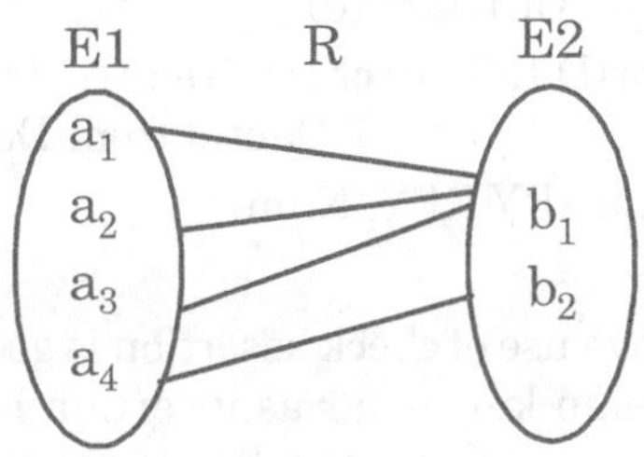

Every entity in E1 associated with exactly one entity in E2.

11. A Candidate key value must uniquely identify the corresponding row in table. Bank Account Number is not a candidate key. as per the question " A student can have multiple accounts or joint accounts This attributes stores the primary account number". If two students have a joint account and if the joint account is their primary account then Bank Account Number value cannot uniquely identify a row.
12. R (EFGHI, JKLMN)
    F = {
    $EF \to G$
    $F \to IJ$
    $EH \to KL$
    $K \to M$
    $L \to N$
    }

$(EF)^+$ = EFGIJ, E & F

Together functionally derive GIJ and if we observe given FDs, H can't be determined by any other attributes. So H must be part of all the (candidate) keys. H along with E determines K and L, K & L functionally determine M and N respectively.

$\therefore$ $(EFH)^+$ = EFGIJHKLMN

$\therefore$ EFH is the only candidate for key.

13. S_1 : Manger (<u>Name</u>, Dept ID)

Department (DeptName, <u>Deptid</u>)

In given relation Manager DeptID is a foreign key referencing Deptid (P.K) of relation Department.

Let's declare the foreign key by an equivalent check assertion as follows:-

```
CREATE TABLE Manager (
    Name Varchar (10)
    DeptID INT (6) check (DeptID IN (select
                        Deptid from Department)),
    PRIMARY KEY (Name)
    );
```

The above use of check assertion is good to declare the foreign key as far as insertion is considered for relation manager (will not insert any tuple in Manager containing such DeptID value which is not present in any tuple of Department).

But the above declaration will fail to implement changes done in Department relation in terms of deletion & updation. For an instance if a deptid present in Department gets deleted, then respective reference in Manager should also be deleted.

∴ S_1 is false

S_2 : The given table definition is not valid due to invalid foreign key declaration. Attribute a is declared as foreign key which is a single valued attribute and it is referencing the primary key (<u>ab</u>) of relation R (<u>a, b</u>, c), which is a composite key.

A single value attribute cannot refer a composite key.

S_2 is false.

14. Since the number of super keys is given by 2^{n-1} where n is number of attributes.

Hence, total number of super keys with n attributes are = $2^{n-1} = 2^{4-1} = 2^8$

15. If we put value of student age to be 19, then student name, student age will not be key, that's why value of x should not be equal to 19 because it may be same for another student.

16. A prime attribute or key attribute of a relation scheme R is an attribute that appears in any of the candidate key of R, remaining attributes are known as non-prime or non-key tribute.

17. Super key

= Candidate key + Other Attribute of set

= Primary key + Other Attribute of set.

Given, Primary key = VY

So, VXYZ, VWXY, VWXYZ are super keys except VWXZ.

18. No, for given instance "A" Value Unique doesn't mean candidate key Because candidate key identification based on constraints of D B design not based on Perticulor instance.

19. An index is clustered, if the data records of the file are organized in the same order as the data entires of the index.

2 CHAPTER

Relational Data Model & Structured Query Language

Analysis of Previous GATE Papers											
	Year → Topics ↓		2019	2018	2017 Set 1	2017 Set 2	2016 Set 1	2016 Set 2	2015 Set 1	2015 Set 2	2015 Set 3
INTEGRI TY CONTRAINT	1 Mark	MCQ Type							1		
		Numerical Type									
	2 Marks	MCQ Type									
		Numerical Type									
	Total								1		
VIEWS & INDEXES	1 Mark	MCQ Type									
		Numerical Type									
	2 Marks	MCQ Type									
		Numerical Type									
	Total										
JOINS	1 Mark	MCQ Type								1	
		Numerical Type									
	2 Marks	MCQ Type		1							
		Numerical Type									
	Total			2						1	
QUERIES & SUB QUERIES	1 Mark	MCQ Type		1					1		1
		Numerical Type			1	1					
	2 Marks	MCQ Type						1			
		Numerical Type	1			1			1		
	Total		2	1	1	3		2	3		1
SQL	1 Mark	MCQ Type									
		Numerical Type									
	2 Marks	MCQ Type									
		Numerical Type									
	Total										
RELATIONAL ALGEBRA	1 Mark	MCQ Type									
		Numerical Type									
	2 Marks	MCQ Type									
		Numerical Type	1		1						
	Total		2		2						
RELATIONAL CALCULAS	1 Mark	MCQ Type			1						
		Numerical Type									
	2 Marks	MCQ Type									
		Numerical Type									
	Total				1						

INTEGRITY CONTRAINT

1. The following table has two attributes A and C where A is the primary key and C is the foreign key referencing A with on-delete cascade.

A	C
2	4
3	4
4	3
5	2
7	2
9	5
6	4

The set of all tuples that must be additionally deleted to preserve referential integrity when the tuple (2, 4) is deleted is:

(a) (3, 4) and (6, 4)

(b) (5, 2) and (7, 2)

(c) (5, 2) and (7, 2) and (9, 5)

(d) 1

[2005 : 2 Marks]

2. Let R (a, b, c) and S(d, e, f) be two relations in which d is the foreign key of S that refers to the primary key of R. Consider the following four operations on R and S

(i) Insert into R

(ii) Insert into S

(iii) Delete from R

(iv) Delete from S

Which of the follolwing is true about the referential integrity constraint above?

(a) None of (i), (ii), (iii) or (iv) can cause its violation

(b) All of (i), (ii), (iii) and (iv) can cause its violation

(c) Both (i) and (iv) can cause its violation

(d) Both (ii) and (iii) can cause its violation

[1997 : 2 Marks]

3. Suppose R_1 (A, B) and R_2(C, D) are two relation schemes. Let rl and r2 be the corresponding relation instances. B is a foreign key that refers to C in R2. If data in rl and r2 satisfy referential integrity constraints, which of the following is ALWAYS TRUE?

(a) $\Pi_B(r_1) - \Pi_C(r_2) = \phi$

(b) $\Pi_C(r_2) - \Pi_B(r_1) = \phi$

(c) $\Pi_B(r_1) = \Pi_C(r_2)$

(d) $\Pi_B(r_1) - \Pi_C(r_2) \neq \phi$

[2012 : 2 Marks]

VIEWS & INDEXES

4. There are five records in a database.

Name	Age	Occupation	Category
Rama	27	CON	A
Abdul	22	ENG	A
Jeniffer	28	DOC	B
Maya	32	SER	D
Dev	24	MUS	C

There is an index file associated with this and it contains the values 1, 3, 2, 5 and 4. Which one of the fields is the index built from?

(a) Age

(b) Name

(c) Occupation

(d) Category

[1998 : 1 Mark]

5. A clustering index is defined on the fields which are of type

(a) Non-key and ordering

(b) Non-key and non-ordering

(c) Key and ordering

(d) key and non-ordering

[2008 : 1 Mark]

6. Consider a file of 16384 records. Each record is 32 bytes long and its key field is of size 6 bytes. The file is ordered on a non-key field, and the file organization is unspanned. The file is stored in a file system with block size 1024 bytes, and the size of a block pointer is 10 bytes. If the secondary index is built on the key field of the file, and a multilevel index scheme is used to store the secondary index, the number of first level and second blocks in the multilevel index are respectively

(a) 8 and 0

(b) 128 and 6

(c) 256 and 4

(d) 512 and 5

[2008: 2 Marks]

7. A file is organized so that the ordering of data records is the same as or close to the ordering of data entries in some index. Then that index is called

(a) Dense

(b) Sparse

(c) Clustered

(d) Unclustered

[2015 (Set-1) : 1 Mark]

JOINS

8. Consider the following relation schema pertaining to a students database:

Student (rollno, name, address)

Enroll (rollno, courseno, coursename)

where thte primary keys are shown underlined. The number of tuples in the student and Enroll tables are 120 and 8 respectively. What are the maximum and minimum number of tuples that can be present in (Student * Enroll), where '*' denotes natural join?

(a) 8, 8 (b) 120, 8

(b) 960, 8 (d) 960, 120

[2004 : 1 Mark]

9. Consider the relations r1(P,Q,R) and r2 (R,S,T) with primary keys P and R respectively. The relation r_1 contains 2000 truples and r_2 contains 2500 truples. The maximum Size of the join $r_1 \bowtie r_2$ $r_1$and r_2 is:

(a) 2000 (b) 2500

(c) 4500 (d) 5000 **[2006 : 1 Mark]**

10. Let R(A, B, C, D) be a relational schema with the following functional dependencies:

$A \to B, B \to C, C \to D$ and $D \to B$.

The decomposition of R into (A, B), (B, C), (B, D)

(a) Gives a lossless join, and is dependency preserving

(b) Gives a lossless join, but is not dependency preserving

(c) Does not give a lossless join, but is dependency preserving

(d) Does not give a lossless join, and is not dependency preserving **[2008 : 2 Marks]**

11. The following functional dependencies hold for relations R(A, B, C) and S(B, D, E):

$B \to A$

$A \to C$

The relatioln R contains 200 tuples and the relation S contains 100 tuples. What is the maximum number of tuples possible in the natural join R $\bowtie$ S ?

(a) 100 (b) 200

(b) 300 (d) 2000

[2010 : 2 Marks]

12. Consider the join of a relation R with a relation S. If R has m tuples and S has n tuples then the maximum and minimum sizes of the join respectively are

(a) m + n and 0 (b) mn and 0

(c) m + n and | m – n | (d) mn and m + n

[1999 : 1 Mark]

13. Let r be a relation instance with schema R = (A, B, C, D). We define $r_1 = \Pi_{A,B,C}(r)$ and $r_2 = \Pi_{A,D}(r)$. let $S = r_1 * r_2$ where * denotes natural join. Given that the decomposition of r into r_1 and r_2 is lossy, which one of the following is TRUE?

(a) $s \subset r$ (b) $r \cup s = r$

(c) $r \subset s$ (d) $r * s = s$

[2005 : 1 Mark]

14. Consider two relations R_1, (A, B) with the tuples (1, 5) (3, 7) and (R_2) (A, C) = (1, 7) (4, 9).

Assume that R(A, B, C) is the full natural outer join of R_1 and R_2. Consider the following tuples of the form (A, B, C): a = (1, 5, null), b = (1, null, 7), c = (3, null, 9), d = (4, 7, null), e = (1, 5, 7), f = (3, 7, null), g = (4, null, 9). Which one of the following statements is correct?

(a) R contains a, b, e, f, g but not c, d

(b) R contains all of a, b, c, d, e, f, g

(c) R contains e, f, g but not a, b

(d) R contains e but not f, g

[2015 (Set-2): 1 Mark]

15. Consider the relations *r(A, B)* and *s(B, C),* where *s.B* is a primary key and *r.B* is a foreign key referencing *s.B*. Consider the query

$$Q: r \bowtie (\sigma_{B<5}(s))$$

Let LOJ denote the natural left outer-join operation. Assume that *r* and *s* contain no null values.

Which one of the following queries is NOT equivalent to Q?

(a) $\sigma_{B<5}(r \bowtie s)$ (b) $\sigma_{B<5}(r\text{LOJ } s)$

(c) $r\text{LOJ}(\sigma_{B<5}(s))$ (d) $\sigma_{B<5}(r)\text{LOJ } s$

[2018(Set-1) : 2 Mark]

Linked Answer Questions 16 and 17:

A database table T1 has 2000 records and occupies 80 disk blocks. Another table T2 has 400 records and occupies 20 disk blocks. These two tables have to be joined as per specified join condition that needs to be evaluated for every pair of records form these two tables. The memory buffer space available can hold exactly one block of records for T1 and one block of records for T2 simultaneously at any point in time. No index is available on either table.

16. If Nested-loop join algorithm is employed to perform the join, with the most appropriate choice of table to be used in outer loop, the number of block accesses required for reading the data are

(a) 80000 (b) 40080

(c) 32020 (d) 100 **[2005 : 2 Marks]**

17. If, instead of Nested-loop join, Block nested-loop join is used, again with the most appropriate choice of table in the outer loop, the reduction in number of block accesses required for reading the data will be

(a) 0

(b) 30400

(c) 38400

(d) 798400

[2005 : 2 Marks]

QUERIES & SUB QUERIES

18. Consider the following tables T_1 and T_2.

T_1	
P	Q
2	2
3	8
7	3
5	8
6	9
8	5
9	8

T_2	
R	S
2	2
8	3
3	2
9	7
5	7
7	2

In table T_1, ***P*** is the primary key and ***Q*** is the foreign key referencing ***R*** in table T_2 with on-delete cascade and on-update cascade. In table T_2, ***R*** is the primary key and ***S*** is the foreign key referencing ***P*** in table T_1 with on-delete set NULL and on-update cascade. In order to delee record ⟨3,8⟩ from table T_1, the number of additional records that need to be deleted from table T_1 is ______.

[2017 (Set-2) : 1 Mark]

19. Suppose we hve a database consisting of the following three relations.

FREQUENTS (student, parlor) giving the parlors each student visits.

SERVES (parlor, ice-cream) indicating what kind of ice-creams each parlor serves.

LIKES (student, ice-cream) indicating what ice-creams each student likes.

(Assume that each student likes at least one ice-cream and frequents at least one parlor)

Express the following in SQL:

Print the students the frequent at least one parlor that serves some icecream that they like.

[1998 : 2 Marks]

20. Consider the set of relations

EMP (Employee-no, Dept-no, Employee-name, Salary)

DEPT (Dept-no, Dept-name, Location)

Write an SQL query to:

(a) Find all employee names who work in departments located at 'Calcutta' and whose salary is greater than Rs. 50,000.

(b) Calculate, for each department number, the number of employees with a salary greater than Rs. 1,00,000.

[1999 : 2 Marks]

21. Given relations r(w, x) and s(y, z), the result of select distinct w, x from r, s is guaranteed to be same as r, provided

(a) r has no duplicates and s is non-empty

(b) r and s have no duplicates

(c) s has no duplicates and r is non-empty

(d) r and s have the same number of truples

[2000 : 2 Marks]

22. Consider the set of relations shown below and the SQL query that follow:

Students:

(Roll_number, Name, Date_of_birth)

Courses:

(Course_number, Course_name, Instructor)

Grades:

(Roll_number, Course_number, Grade)

select distinct Name

from Students, Courses, Grades

where

Students.Roll_number=Grades.Roll_number

and

Courses.Instructor=Korth and

Courses.Course_number=

Grades. Course_number and

Grades. grade=A

Which of the following sets is computed by the above query?

(a) Names of students who have got an A grade in all courses taught by Korth

(b) Names of students who have got an A grade in all courses

(c) Name of students who have got an A grade in at least one of the courses taught by Korth

(d) None of the above

[2003 : 2 Marks]

23. The employee information in a company is stored in the relation

Employee (name, sex, salary, deptName)

Consider the following SQL query

select deptName

from Employee

where sex = 'M'

group by deptName

having avg (salary)>

(select avg (salary) from Employee)

It returns the names of the department in which

(a) the average salary is more than the average salary in the company

(b) the average salary of male employees is more than the average salary of all male employees in the company

(c) the average salary of male employees is more than the average salary of employees in the same department

(d) the average salary of male employees is more than the average salary in the company

[2004 : 2 Marks]

24. A relational database contains two tables student and department in which student table has columns roll_no, name and dept_id and department table has columns dept_id and dept_name. The following insert statements were executed successfully to populate the empty tables:

Insert into department values 1,'Mathematics')

Insert into department values (2, 'Physics')

Insert into student values (1, 'Navin', 1)

Insert into student values (2, 'Mukesh', 2)

Insert into student values (3, 'Gita', 1)

How many rows and columns will be retrieved by the following SQL statement? Select * from student, department

(a) 0 row and 4 columns

(b) 3 rows and 4 columns

(c) 3 rows and 5 columns

(d) 6 rows and 5 columns **[2004 : 2 Marks]**

25. A table T1 in a relational database has the following rows and columns:

roll no.	marks
1	10
2	20
3	30
4	Null

The following sequence of SQL statements was successfully excuted on table T1.

Update T1 set marks = marks +5

Select avg(marks) from T1

What is the output of the select statement?

(a) 18.75 (b) 20

(c) 25 (d) Null **[2004 : 2 Marks]**

26. Consider two tables in a relational database with columns and rows as follows:

Table : Student

Roll_no	Name	Dept_id
1	ABC	1
2	DEF	1
3	GHI	2
4	JKL	3

Table : Department

Dept_id	Dept_name
1	A
2	B
3	C

Roll_no is the primary key of the Student table, Dept_id is the primary key of the Department table and Student.Dept_id is a foreign key from Department.Dept_id

What will hapen if we try to execute the following two SQL statements?

(i) update Student set Dept_id = Null where Roll_no = 1

(ii) update Department set Dept_id=Null where Dept_id = 1

(a) Both (i) and (ii) will fail

(b) (i) will fail but (ii) will succeed

(c) (i) will succeed but (ii) will fail

(d) Both (i) and (ii) will succeed **[2004 : 2 Marks]**

27. In an inventory management system implemented at a trading corporation, there are several tables designed to hold all information. Amongst these, the following two tables hold information on which items are supplied by which suppliers, and which warehouse keeps which items along with the stock-level of these items.

Supply = (supplierid, itemcode)

Inventory = (itemcode, warehouse, stocklevel)

For a specific information required by the management, following SQL query has been written

Select distinct STMP.supplierid

From Supply as STMP

Where Supply as STMP
Where not unique (Select ITMP.supplierid
From Inventory, Supply as ITMP
Where STMP.supplierid = ITMP.supplierid
And ITMP.itemcode = Inventory.itemcode
And Inventory.warehouse = 'Nagpur');

For the warehouse at Nagpur, this query will find all suppliers who

(a) do not supply any item
(b) supply exactly one item
(c) supply one or more items
(d) supply two or more items

[2005 : 2 Marks]

28. The relation book (tittle, price) contains the titles and prices of different books. Assuming that no two books have the same price, what does the following SQL

select title
from book as B
where (select count (*)
from book as T
where T. price > B. Price) < 5

(a) Titles of the four most expensive books
(b) Title of the fifth most inexpensive book
(c) Title of the fifth most expensive book
(d) Title of the five most expensive books

[2005 : 2 Marks]

Directions for Question 29 to 30:

Consider a database with three relation instances shown below. The primary keys for the Drivers and Cars relation are *did* and *cid* respectively and the records are stored in ascending order of these primary key as given in the tables. No indexing is available in the database.

D: Drivers relation

did	dname	rating	age
22	Karthikeyan	7	25
29	Salman	1	33
31	Boris	8	55
32	Amoldt	8	25
58	Schumacher	10	35
64	Sachin	7	35
71	Senna	10	16
74	Sachin	9	35
85	Rahul	3	25
95	Ralph	3	53

R : Reserves relation

did	cid	day
22	101	10/10/06
22	102	10/10/06
22	103	08/10/06
22	104	07/10/06
31	102	10/11/06
31	103	06/11/06
31	104	12/11/06
64	101	05/09/06
64	102	08/09/06
74	103	08/09/06

C: Cars relation

cid	cname	colour
101	Renault	blue
102	Renault	red
103	Ferrari	green
104	Jaguar	red

29. What is the output of the following SQL query?

select D. dname
from Drivers D
where D. did in (
select R.did
from Cars C, Reserves R
Where R.cid=C.cid and C.colour = 'red'
intersect
select R.did
from Cars C, Reserves R
where R.cid=C.cid and C. colour= 'green'
)

(a) Karthikeyan, Boris
(b) Sachin, Salman
(c) Karthikeyan, Boris, Sachin
(d) Schumacher, Senna

[2006 : 2 Marks]

30. Let n be the number of comarisons performed when the above SQL query is optimally executed. If linear search is used to locate a tuple in a relation using primary key, then n lies in the range

(a) 36 – 40
(b) 44 – 48
(c) 60 – 64
(d) 100 – 104

[2006 : 2 Mar ks]

31. Consider the relation account (customer, balance) where customer is a primary key and there are no null values. We would like to rank customers according to decreasing balance. The customer with the largest balance gets rank 1. Ties are not broken but ranks are skipped: if exactly two customers have the largest balance they each get rank 1 and rank 2 is not assigned.

Query 1: Select A.customer, count (B.customer) from account A, account B where A.balance < = B.balance Group by A.customer

Query 2: Select A. customer, 1 + count (B.customer) from account A, account B where A.balance < B.balance group by A.customer Consider these statements about Query 1 and Query 2.

1. Query 1 will produce the same row set as Query 2 for some but not all databases
2. Both Query 1 Query 2 are correct implementations of the specification
3. Query 1 is a correct implementation of the specification but Query 2 is not
4. Neither Query 1 nor Query 2 is a correct implementation of the specification
5. Assigning rank with a pure relational Query takes less time than scanning in decreasing balance order and assigning ranks using ODBC

Which two of the above statements are correct?

(a) 2 and 5 (b) 1 and 3

(c) 1 and 4 (d) 3 and 5

[2006 : 2 Marks]

32. Consider the relation enrolled (student, course) in which (student, course) is the primary key, and the relation paid (student, amount) where student is the primary key. Assume no null values and no foreign keys or integrity constraints. Given the following four queries:

Query 1: Select student from enrolled where student in (select student form paid)

Query 2: Select student from paid where student in (select from enrolled)

Query 3: Select E.student from enrolled E, paid P where E.student = P.student

Query 4: Select student from paid where exists (select * from enrolled where enrolled.student = paid.student)

which one of the following statements is correct?

(a) All queries return identical row sets for any database

(b) Query 2 and Query 4 return identical row sets for all databases but there exist databases for which Query 1 and Query 2 return different row sets

(c) There exist databases for which Query 3 returns strictly fewer rows than Query 2

(d) There exist databases for which Query 4 will encounter an intergrity violation at runtime

[2006 : 2 Marks]

33. Consider the table employee (empId, name, department, salary) and the two queries Q_1, Q_2 below. Assuming that department 5 has more than one employee, and we want to find the employees who get higher salary than anyone in the department 5, which one of the statements is TRUE for any arbitrary employee table?

Q_1 : Select e.empId
From employee e
Where not exists
(Select * From employee s Where s.department= "5" and s.salary >= e.salary)

Q_2: Select e. empId
From employee e
Where e.salary > Any
(Select distinct salary From employee s Where s.department = "5")

(a) Q_1 is the correct query

(b) Q_2 is the correct query

(c) Both Q_1 and Q_2 produce the same answer

(d) Neither Q_1 nor Q_2 is the correct query

[2007 : 2 Marks]

Directions for Question 34 to 35:

Consider the following relational schema:

Student (school-id, sch-roll-no, sname, saddress)

School (school-id, sch-name, sch-address, sch-phone)

Enrolment(school-id sch-roll-no, erollno, examname)

ExamResult (erollno, examname, marks)

34. What does the following SQL query output?

```
SELECTsuch-name, COUNT (*)
FROMSchool C, Enrolment E, ExamResult R
WHEREE.school-id C.school-id
                AND
    E.examname = R.examname AND
    E.Erollno = R.erollno
                AND
    R.marks = 100 AND S.school-id IN
      (SELECT school-id
         FROM student
    GROUP BY school-id
    HAVING COUNT (*) > 200)
GROUP By school-id
```

(a) for each school with more than 200 students appearing in exams, the name of the school and the number of 100s scored by its students

(b) for each school with more than 200 students in it, the name of the school and the number of 100s scored by its students

(c) for each school with more than 200 students in it, the name of the schol and the number of its students scoring 100 in at least one exam

(d) nothing; the query has a syntax error

[2008 : 2 Marks]

35. Consider the following tuple relational calculus query.

{t | ∃E ∈ Enrolment t = E.school-id ∧ | {x | x Enrolment ∧ x.school-id= t ∧ (∃B ExamResult B.erollno = x.erollno ∧ B.examname = x.examname ∧ B.marks > 35)} | ÷ | {x | x Enrolment ∧ x.school-ied = t} | * 100 > 35}

If a student needs to score more than 35 marks to pass an exam, what does the query return?

(a) The empty set

(b) schools with more than 35% of its students enrolled in some exam or the other

(c) schools with a pass percentage above 35% over all exams taken together

(d) schools with a pass percentage above 35% over each exam

[2008 : 2 Marks]

36. Consider a database table T containing two columns X and Y each of type integer. After the creation of the table, one record (X = 1, Y = 1) is inserted in the table.

Let MX and MY denote the respective maximum values of X and Y among all records in the table at any point in time. Using MX and MY, new records are interested in the table 128 times with X and Y values being MX + 1, 2*MY + 1 respectively. It may be noted that each time after the insertion, values of MX and MY change.

What will be the output of the following SQL query after the steps mentioned above are carried out?

SELECT Y FROM T WHERE X = 7;

(a) 127 (b) 255

(c) 129 (d) 257

[2011 : 2 Marks]

37. Database table by name Loan_Records is given below:

Borrower	Bank_Manager	Loan_Amount
Ramesh	Sunderajan	10000.00
Suresh	Ramgopal	5000.00
Mahesh	Sunderajan	7000.00

What is the output of the following SQL query?

SELECT count(*)
FROM (
(SELECT Borrower, Bank_Manager FROM Loan_Records) AS S NATURAL JOIN
(SELECT Bank-Manager, Loan_Amount
FROM Loan_Records) AS T
);

(a) 3 (b) 9

(c) 5 (d) 6

[2011 : 2 Marks]

38. Which of the following statements are TRUE about an SQL query?

P : An SQL query can contain a HAVING clause even if it does not have a GROUP BY clause

Q : An SQL query can contain a HAVING clause only if it has a GROUP BY clause

R : All attributes used in the GROUP BY clause must appear in the SELECT clause

S : Not all atributes used in the GROUP BY clause need to appear in the SELECT clause

(a) P and R (b) P and S

(c) Q and R (d) Q and S

[2012 : 1 Mark]

Common Data for Questions 39 and 40

A.

Id	Name	Age
12	Arun	60
15	Shreya	24
99	Rohit	11

B.

Id	Name	Age
15	Shreya	24
25	Hari	40
98	Rohit	20
99	Rohit	11

C.

Id	Phone	Age
10	2200	02
99	2100	01

39. Consider the relation enrolled (student, course) in which (student, course) is the primary key, and the relation paid (student, amount) where student is the primary key. Assume no null values and no foreign keys or integrity constraints. Assume that amounts 6000, 7000, 8000, 9000 and 10000 were each paid by 20% of the students. Consider these query plans (Plan 1 on left, Plan 2 on right) to "list all courses taken by students who have paid more than x."

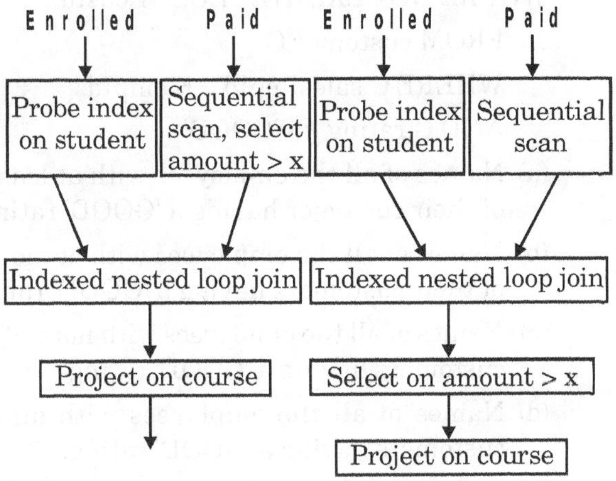

A disk seek takes 4 ms.disk data transfer bandwidth is 300 MB/s and checking a tuple to see if amount is greater than x takes 10 μs. Which of the following statements is correct?

(a) Plan 1 and Plan 2 will not output identical row sets for all databases

(b) A course may be listed more than once in the output of Plan 1 for some databases

(c) For x = 5000, Plan 1 executes faster than Plan 2 for all databases

(d) For x = 9000, Plan 1 executes slower than Plan 2 for all databases

[2006 : 2 Marks]

40. Consider the following relational schema:

Suppliers(sid: integer, sname: string, city: string, street: string)

Parts(pid:integer, pname:string, color:string)

Catalog(sid:integer, pid:integer, cost:real)

Consider the following relational query on the above database:

```
SELECT S. sname
FROM Suppliers S
WHERE S. sid NOT IN (SELECT C.sid
FROM Catalog C
WHERE C.pid NOT IN (SELECT P.pid
FROM Parts P
WHERE P.color <> 'blue'))
```

Assume that relations corresponding to the above schema are not empty. Which one of the following is the correct interpretation of the above query?

(a) Find the names of all suppliers who have supplied a non-blue part

(b) Find the names of all suppliers who have not supplied a non-blue part

(c) Find the names of all suppliers who have supplied only blue parts

(d) Find the names of all suppliers who have not supplied only blue parts

[2009 : 2 Marks]

SQL

41. Which of the following is/are correct?

(a) An SQL query automatically eliminates duplicates

(b) An SQL query will not work if there are no indexes on the relations

(c) SQL permits attribute names to be repeated in the same relation

(d) None of the above

[1999 : 2 Marks]

42. In SQL, relations can contain null values, and comparisons with null values are treated as unknown. Suppose all comparisons with a null value are treated as false. Which of the following pairs is not equivalent?

(a) x = 5, not (not (x = 5))

(b) x = 5, x > 4 and x < 6, where x is an integer

(c) $x \neq 5$, not (x = 5)

(d) None of the above

[2000 : 2 Marks]

43. How many tuples does the result of the following SQL query contain?

```
SELECT A.Id
FROM A
WHERE A.Age > All (SELECT B.Age
                   FROM B
WHERE B.Name='Arun')
```

Consider the following relations A, B and C :

A

ID	Name	Age
12	Arun	60
15	Shreya	24
99	Rohit	11

B

ID	Name	Age
15	Shreya	24
25	Hari	40
98	Rohit	20
99	Rohit	11

C

ID	Phone	Area
10	2200	02
99	2100	01

(a) 4 (b) 3

(c) 0 (d) 1

[2012 : 2 Marks]

44. Given the following schema:

employees(emp-id, first-name, last-name, hire-date, dept-id, salary)

departments(dept-id, dept-name manager-id, location-id)

You want to display the last names and hire dates of all latest hires in their respective departments in the location ID 1700. You issue the following query:

SQL > SELECT last-name, hire-date
FROM employees
WHERE (dept-id, hire-date) IN
(SELECT dept-id, MAX(hire-date) FROM employees JOIN departments USING(dept-id)
WHERE location-id = 1700
GROUP BY dept-id);

What is the outcome?

(a) It executes but does not give the correct result.
(b) It executes and gives the correct result.
(c) It generates an error because of pairwise comparision.
(d) It generates an error because the GROUP BY clause cannot be used with table joins in a subquery.

[2014 (Set-1) : 2 Marks]

45. SQL allows duplicate tuples in relations, and correspondingly defines the multiplicity of tuples in result of joins. Which one of the following queries always gives the same answer as the nessted query shown below:

select * from R where a in (select S.a from S)

(a) select R.* from R, S where R.a = S.a
(b) select distinct R. * from R,S where R.a = S.a
(c) select R. * from R, (select distinct a from S as S1 where R.a = S1.a
(d) slect R.* from R,S where R.a = S.a and is unique R

[2014 (Set-2) : 2 Marks]

46. Consider the following relational schema:

employee (**empId**, empName, empDept)
customer(**custId**,custName,salesRepId,rating)

salesRepId is a foreign key referring to **emId** of the employee relation. Assume that each employee makes a sale to at least one customer. What does the following query return?

SELECT empName
FROM employee E
WHERE NOT EXISTS (SELECT cusId
FROM customer C
WHERE C.salesRepId = E.empId
AND C.rating <> 'GOOD');

(a) Names of all the employees with at least one of their customer having a 'GOOD' rating.
(b) Names of all the employees with at most one of their customers having a 'GOOD' rating.
(c) Names of all the employees with none of their customers having a 'GOOD' rating.
(d) Names of all the employees with all their customers having a 'GOOD' rating.

[2014 (Set-3) : 2 Marks]

47. Consider the following relations:

Student

Roll_No	Student_Name
1	Raj
2	Rohit
3	Raj

Performance

Roll_No	Course	Marks
1	Math	80
1	English	70
2	Math	75
3	English	80
2	Physics	65
3	Math	80

Consider the following SQL query.

SELECTS. Student_Name, sum (P.Marks)
FROM Student S, Performance P
WHERES. Roll_No =P.Roll_No
GROUP BY S.Student_Name

The number of rows that will be returned by the SQL query is ______.

[2015 (Set-1) : 2 Marks]

48. SELECT operation in SQL is equivalent to

(a) the selection operation in relational algebra
(b) the selection operation in relational algebra, exept that SELECT in SQL retains deplicates
(c) the projection operation in relational algebra
(d) the projection operation in relational algebra, except that SELECT in SQL retains duplicates

[2015 (Set-1) : 1 Mark]

49. Consider the following relation

Cinema (*theater, address, capacity*)

Which of the following options will be needed at the end of the SQL query

SELECT Pl.address

FROM Cinema P1

such that it always finds the addresses of theaters with maximum capacity?

(a) WHERE P1.*capacity* > =All (select P2. *capacity* from Cinema P2)

(b) WHERE P1.*capacity* > = Any (select P2. *capacity* from Cinema P2)

(c) WHERE P1 .*capacity* > All (select max (P2. *capacity*) from Cinema P2)

(d) WHERE P1 .*capacity* > Any (select max (P2.*capacity*) from Cinema P2)

[2015 (Set-3) : 1 Mark]

50. Consider the following database table named water_schemes:

water_schemes		
Scheme_no	**district_name**	**capacity**
1	Ajmer	20
1	Bikaner	10
2	Bikaner	10
3	Bikaner	20
1	Churu	10
2	Churu	20
1	Dungargarh	10

the number of tuples returned by the following SQL query is:

with total (name, capacity) **as**
select district_name, **sum** (capacity)
from water_schemes
group by district_name
with total_avg (capacity) **as**
select avg (capacity)
from total
select name
from total, total_avg
where total.capacity $\geq$ total_avg. capacity

[2016 (Set-2): 2 Marks]

51. Consider a database that has the relation schema EMP (Empld, EmpName, and DeptName). An instance of the schema EMP and a SQL query on it are given below:

EMP

EmpId	EmpName	DeptName
1	XYA	AA
2	XYB	AA
3	XYC	AA
4	XYD	AA
5	XYE	AB
6	XYF	AB
7	XYG	AB
8	XYH	AC
9	XYI	AC
10	XYJ	AC
11	XYK	AD
12	XYL	AD
13	XYM	AE

SELECT AVG(EC.Num)
FROM EC
WHERE (DeptName, Num) IN
(SELECT DeptName, COUNT(EmpId) AS EC(DeptName, Num)
FROM EMP
GROUP BY DeptName)

The output of executing the SQL query is __.

[2017 (Set-1) : 1 Mark]

52. Consider the following database table named *top_scorer.*

top_score

player	country	goals
Klose	Germany	16
Ronaldo	Brazil	15
G Muller	Germany	14
Fontaine	France	13
Pele	Brazil	12
Klinsmann	Germany	11
Kocsis	Hungary	11
Batistuta	Argentina	10
Cubillas	Peru	10
Lato	Poland	10
Lineker	England	10
T Muller	Germany	10
Rahn	Germany	10

Consider the following SQL query:

SELECT ta.player FROM top_scorer AS ta

WHERE ta.goals > ALL (SELECT tb.goals
FROM top_scorer AS tb
WHERE tb.country = 'Spain')
AND ta.goals > ANY (SELECT tc.goals
FROM top_scorer AS tc
WHERE tc.country =
'Germany')

The number of tuples returned by the above SQL query is ______. **[2017 (Set-2) : 2 Marks]**

53. Consider the following two tables and four queries in SQL.

Book (isbn, bname), Stock (isbn, copies)

Query 1: SELECT B.isbn, S.copies
FROM Book B INNER JOIN Stock S
ON B.isbn = S.isbn;

Query 2: SELECT B.isbn, S.copies
FROM Book B LEFT OUTER JOIN Stock S
ON B.isbn = S.isbn;

Query 3: SELECT B.isbn, S.copies
FROM Book B RIGHT OUTER JOIN Stock S
ON B.isbn = S.isbn;

Query 4: SELECT B.isbn, S.copies
FROM Book B FULL OUTER JOIN Stock S
ON B.isbn = S.isbn;

Which one of the queries above is certain to have an output that is superset of the outputs of the other three queries?

(a) Query 1 (b) Query 2
(c) Query 3 (d) Query 4

[2018 : 1 Mark]

54. A relational database contains two tables Student and Performance as shown below:

Student

Roll_no.	Student_name
1	Amit
2	Priya
3	Vinit
4	Rohan
5	Smita

Performance

Roll_no	Subject_code	Marks
1	A	86
1	B	95
1	C	90
2	A	89
2	C	92
3	C	80

The primary key of the Student table is Roll_no. For the Performance table, the columns Roll_no. and Subject_code together form the primary key. Consider the SQL query given below:

SELECT S. Student name, sum(P. Marks)
FROM Student S, Performance P
WHERE P. Marks > 84
GROUP BY S. Student_name;

The number of rows returned by the above SQL query is ______.

[2019 : 2 Marks]

RELATIONAL ALGEBRA

55. Consider the following SQL query

select distinct $a_1, a_2, ..., a_n$
from $r_1, r_2, ..., r_m$
where ρ

For an arbitrary predicate ρ, this query is equivalent to which of the following relational algebra expressions?

(a) $\Pi_{a_1,a_2,...,a_n} \sigma_\rho (r_1 \times r_2 \times ... \times r_m)$

(b) $\Pi_{a_1,a_2,...,a_n}$ sr $(r_1 \bowtie r_2 \bowtie ... \bowtie r_m)$

(c) $\Pi_{a_1,a_2,...,a_n} \sigma_\rho (r_1 \cup r_2 \cup ... \cup r_m)$

(d) $\Pi_{a_1,a_2,...,a_n} \sigma_\rho (r_1 \cap r_2 \cap ... \cap r_m)$

[2003 : 1 Mark]

56. How many tuples does the result of the following relational algebra expression contain? Assume that the schema of $A \cup B$ is the same as that of A.

$$(A \cup B) \bowtie_{A.Id>40 \vee C.Id<15} C$$

Consider the following relations A, B and C :

A

ID	Name	Age
12	Arun	60
15	Shreya	24
99	Rohit	11

B

ID	Name	Age
15	Shreya	24
25	Hari	40
98	Rohit	20
99	Rohit	11

C

ID	Phone	Area
10	2200	02
99	2100	01

(a) 7 (b) 4
(c) 5 (d) 9

[2012 : 2 Marks]

57. What is the optimized version of the relation algebra expression $\pi_{A1}(\pi_{A_2}(\sigma_{F1}(\sigma_{F2}(r))))$, where $A1$, $A2$ are sets of attributes in r with $A1 \subset A2$ and $F1$,$F2$ are Boolean expressions based on the attributes in r?

(a) $\pi_{A1}(\sigma_{(F1 \wedge F2)}(r))$ (b) $\pi_{A1}(\sigma_{(F1 \vee F2)}(r))$

(c) $\pi_{A2}(\sigma_{(F1 \wedge F2)}(r))$ (d) $\pi_{A2}(\sigma_{(F1 \vee F2)}(r))$

[2014 (Set-3) : 1 Mark]

58. Give a relational algebra expression using only the minimum number of operators from $\{\cup, -\}$ is equivalent to $R \cap S$.

[1994 : 1 Mark]

59. A library relational database system uses the following schema

USERS (User#, UserName, HomeTown)

BOOK (Book#, BookTitle, AuthorName)

ISSUED (Book#, User#, Date)

Explain in one English sentence, what each of the following relational algebra queries is designed to determine.

(a) $\sigma_{\text{User\#=6}}(\pi_{\text{USER\#,BookTitle}}((\text{USERS} \bowtie \text{ISSUED} \bowtie \text{BOOK}))$

(b) $\sigma_{\text{AuthorName}}(\text{BOOK} \bowtie (\sigma_{\text{HomeTown=Delhi}}(\text{USERS} \bowtie \text{ISSUED})))$

[1996 : 2 Marks]

60. Which of the following query transformations (i.e. replacing the LHS Expression by the RHS expression) is incorrect? R_1 and R_2 are relations, C_1, C_2 are selection conditions and A_1, A_2 are attributes of R_1?

(a) $\sigma_{c1}(\sigma_{c2}(R_1)) \rightarrow \sigma_{c2}(\sigma_{c1}(R_1))$

(b) $\sigma_{c1}(\pi_{A1}(R_1)) \rightarrow \pi_{A1}(\sigma_{c1}(R_1))$

(c) $\sigma_{c1}(R_1 \cup R_2) \rightarrow \sigma_{c1}(R_1) \cup \sigma_{c1}(R_2)$

(d) $\pi_{A1}(\sigma_{c1}(R_1)) \rightarrow \sigma_{c1}(\pi_{A1}(R_1))$

[1998 : 2 Marks]

61. The relational algebra expression equivalent to the following tuple calculus expression:

$\{t \mid t \in r \wedge (t[A] = 10 \wedge t[B] = 20)\}$ is

(a) $\sigma_{(A=10 \vee B=20)}(r)$

(b) $\sigma_{(A=10)}(r) \cup \sigma_{(B=20)}(r)$

(C) $\sigma_{(A=10)}(r) \cap \sigma_{(B=20)}(r)$

(d) $\sigma_{(A=10)}(r) - \sigma_{(B=20)}(r)$

[1999 : 1 Mark]

62. Given the relations

employee (name, salary, deptno), and department (deptno, deptname, address)

Which of the following queries cannot be expressed using the basic relational algebra operations (σ, π, $\times$, $\bowtie$, $\cup$, $\cap$, $-$)?

(a) Department address of every employee

(b) Employees whose name is the same as their department name

(c) The sum of all employees salaries

(d) All employees of a given department

[2000 : 1 Mark]

63. With regard to the expressive power of the formal relational query languages, which of the following statements is true?

(a) Relational algebra is more powerful than relational calculus

(b) Relational algebra has the same power as relational calculus

(c) Relational algebra has the same power as safe relational calculus

(d) None of the above **[2002 : 1 Mark]**

64. Let R_1(A, B, C) and R_2(D, E) be two relation schema, where the primary keys are shown underlined, and let C be a foreign key in R_1 referring to R_2. Suppose there is no violation of the above referential integrity constraint in the corresponding relation instances r_1 and r_2. Which one of the following relational algebra expressions would necessarily produce an empty relation?

(a) $\Pi_D(r_2) - \Pi_C(r_1)$

(b) $\Pi_C(r_1) - \Pi_D(r_2)$

(c) $\Pi_D(r_1 \bowtie_{C \neq D} R_2) - \Pi_C(r_1)$

(d) $\Pi_C(r_1 \bowtie_{C=D} R_2)$ **[2004 : 1 Mark]**

65. Consider the relation Student (name, sex, marks), where the primary key is shown underlined, pertaining to students in a class that has at least one boy and one girl. What does the following relational algebra expression produce? (Note: ρ is rename operator)

$$\Pi_{\text{name}}\left(\sigma_{\text{sex=female}}(\text{Student})\right) - \Pi_{\text{name}}\left(\text{Student} \bowtie_{(\text{sex = female} \wedge \text{x = male} \wedge \text{marks} \le \text{m})} \rho_{n,x,m}(\text{Student})\right)$$

(a) names of girl students with the highest marks

(b) names of girl students with more marks than some boy student

(c) names of girl students with marks not less than some boy student

(d) names of girl students with more marks than all the boy students **[2004 : 2 Marks]**

66. A table 'student' with schema (roll, name, hostel, marks), and another table 'hobby' with schema (roll, hobbyname) contains records as shown below:

Table Student

Roll	Name	Hostel	Marks
1798	Manoj rathor	7	95
2154	Soumic Banerjee	5	68
2369	Gumma Reddy	7	86
2581	Pradeep Pendse	6	92
2643	Suhas Kulkarni	5	78
2711	Nitin kadam	8	72
2872	Kiran Vora	5	92
2926	Manoj Kunkalikar	5	94
2959	Hemant Karkhanis	7	88
3125	Rajesh karkhanis	5	82

Table Hobby

Roll	Hobbyname
1798	chess
1798	music
2154	music
2369	swimming
2581	cricket
2643	chess
2643	hockey
2711	volleyball
2872	football
2926	cricket
2959	photography
3125	music
3125	chess

The following SQL query is executed on the above tables:

```
select hostel
from student natural join hobby
where marks > = 75 and roll between 2000 and 3000;
```

Relations S and H with the same schema as those of these two tables respectively contain the same information as tuples. A new relation S' is obtained by the following relational algebra operation:

$$S' = \Pi_{hostel}((\sigma_{s.roll=H.roll}(\sigma_{marks>75 and roll>2000 and roll<3000}(S)) \times (H))$$

The difference between the number of rows output by the SQL statement and the number of tuples in S' is

(a) 6 (b) 4
(c) 2 (d) 0 **[2005 : 2 Marks]**

67. Which of the following relational query languages have the same expressive power?

I. Relational algebra.

II. Tuple relational calculus restricted to safe expressions.

III. Domain relational calculus restricted to safe expressions.

(a) II and III only (b) I and II only
(c) I and III only (d) I, II and III

[2006 : 1 Mark]

68. Consider a selection of the form $\sigma_{A \le 100}(r)$, where r is a relation with 1000 tuples. Assume that the attribute values for A among the tuples are uniformly distributed in the interval [0, 500].

Which one of the following options is the best estimate of the number of tuples returned by the given selection query?

(a) 50 (b) 100
(c) 150 (d) 200

[2007 : 2 Marks]

69. Consider the following relation schemas:

b-Schema = (b-name, b-city, assets)

a-Schema = (a-num, b-name, bal)

d-Schema = (c-name, a-number)

Let branch, account and depositor be respectively instances of the above schemas. Assume that account and depositor relations are much bigger than the branch relation.

Consider the following query:

$\Pi_{c\text{-name}}\left(\sigma_{b\text{-city}=\text{"Agra"} \wedge bal<0}\left(branch \text{--} (account \bowtie depositor)\right)\right)$

Which one of the following queries is the most efficient version of the above query?

(a) $\Pi_{c\text{-name}}\left(\sigma_{bal<0}\left(\sigma_{b\text{-city}=\text{"Agra"}}\, branch \bowtie account\right) \bowtie depositor\right)$

(b) $\Pi_{c\text{-name}}\left(\sigma_{b\text{-city}=\text{"Agra"}}\, branch \bowtie \left(\sigma_{bal<0}\, account \bowtie depositor\right)\right.$

(c) $\Pi_{c\text{-name}}\left(\sigma_{b\text{-city}=\text{"Agra"}}\, branch \bowtie \left(\sigma_{b\text{-city}=\text{"Agra"} \wedge bal<0}\, account \bowtie depositor\right)\right.$

(d) $\Pi_{c\text{-name}}\left(\sigma_{b\text{-city}=\text{"Agra"}}\, branch \bowtie \left(\sigma_{b\text{-city}=\text{"Agra"} \wedge bal<0}\, account \bowtie depositor\right)\right)$

[2007 : 2 Marks]

70. Information about a collection of students is given by the relation studInfo (studId, name, sex). The relation enroll (studId, CourseId) gives which student has enrolled for (or taken) what course(s). Assume that every course is taken by at least one male and at least one female student. What does the following relational algebra expression represent?

$\Pi_{courseId}((\Pi_{studId}(\sigma_{sex="female"}(studInfo)) \times \Pi_{courseId}(enroll)) - enroll)$

(a) Courses in which all the female students are enrolled

(b) Courses in which a proper subset of female students are enrolled

(c) Courses in which only male students are enrolled

(d) None of the above **[2007 : 2 Marks]**

71. Let R and S be two relations with the following schema

R(P, Q, R1, R2, R3)

S(P, Q, S1, S2)

where {P, Q} is the key for both schemas. Which of the following queries are equivalent?

I. $\Pi_P(R \bowtie S)$

II. $\Pi_P(R) \bowtie \Pi_P(S)$

III. $\Pi_P(\Pi_{P,Q}(R) \cap \Pi_{P,Q}(S))$

IV. $\Pi_P(\Pi_{P,Q}(R) - (\Pi_{P,Q}(R) - \Pi_{P,Q}(S)))$

(a) Only I and II (b) Only I and III

(c) Only I, II and III (d) Only I, III and IV

[2008 : 2 Marks]

72. Let R and S be relational schemes such that R = {a, b, c} and S = {c}. Now consider the following queries on the database :

I. $\pi_{R-S}(r) - r_{R-S}(\pi_{R-S}(r) \times S - \pi_{R-S,S}(r))$

II. $\{t \mid t \in \pi_{R-S}(r) \wedge \forall u \in s(\exists v \in r(u = v[s] \wedge t = v[R-S]))\}$

III. $\{t \mid t \in \pi_{R-S}(r) \wedge \forall v \in r(\exists u \in s(u = v[s] \wedge t = v[R-S]))\}$

IV. Select R.a, R.b

from R, S where R.c = S.c

Which of the above queries are equivalent?

(a) I and II (b) I and III

(c) II and IV (d) III and IV

[2009 : 2 Marks]

73. Consider the following relational schema.

Student (rollno: integer: sname string)

Courses (courseno: integer, cname: string)

Registration (rollno: integer, courseno: integer, percent: real)

Which of the following queries are equivalent to this query in English?

"Find the distinct names of all students who score more than 90% in the course numbered 107"

I. SELECT DISTINCT S.sname
FROM Students as S, Registration as R
WHERE R.rollno=S.roll.no AND
R.courseno=107 and R.percent>90

II. $\Pi_{sname}\left(\sigma_{courseno=107 \wedge persent>90}\left(\text{Regis-tration} \bowtie \text{Student}\right)\right)$

III. {T | ∃S ∈Students, ∃R ∈Registration (S.rollno=R.rollno ∧ R.courseno=107 ∧ R.percent>90 ∧ T.sname=S.sname)}

IV. $\{<S_N> \mid \exists S_R \exists R_P(<S_R, S_N> \in Student \wedge <S_R, 107, R_P> \in Registration \wedge R_P > 90)\}$

(a) I, II, III and IV (b) I, II and III only

(c) I, II and IV only (d) I, III and IV only

[2013 : 2 Marks]

74. Consider a join (relation algebra) between relations *r*(R) and *s*(S) using the nested loop method. There are 3 buffers each of size equal to disk block size, out of which one buffer is reserved for intermediate results.

Assuming size(*r*(R)) < size(*s*(S)), the join will have fewer number of disk block accesses if

(a) relation *r*(R) is in the outer loop.

(b) relation *s*(S)is in the outer loop.

(c) join selection factor between *r*(R) and *s*(S) is more than 0.5.

(d) join selection factor between *r*(R) and *s*(S) is less than 0.5. **[2014 (Set-2) : 2 Marks]**

75. Consider the relational schema given below, where **eId** of the **dependent** is a foreign key referring to **empId** of the relation **employee.**

Assume that every employee has at least one associated dependent in the **dependent** relation.

employee (empId, empName, empAge)

dependent(depId, eId, depName, depAge)

Consider the following relational algebra query:

$\Pi_{empId}(employee - \Pi_{empId}(employee \bowtie_{(empId = eId) \wedge (empAge \leq depAge)} dependent)$

The above query evaluates to the set or empIds of employees whose age is greater than that of

(a) some dependent.

(b) all dependents.

(c) some of his/her dependents.

(d) all of his/her dependents.

[2014 (Set-3) : 2 Marks]

76. Consider a database that has the relation schema CR (StudentName, CourseName). An instance of the schema CR is as given below:

CR	
Student Name	Course Name
SA	CA
SA	CB
SA	CC
SB	CB
SB	CC
SC	CA
SC	CB
SC	CC
SD	CA
SD	CB
SD	CC
SD	CD
SE	CD
SE	CA
SE	CB
SF	CA
SF	CB
SF	CC

The following query is made on the database.

$$T_1 \leftarrow \pi_{CourseName}(\sigma_{StudentName} = 'SA'(CR))$$

$$T_2 \leftarrow CR \div T_1$$

The number of rows in T_2 is __________.

[2017(Set-1) : 2 Mark]

77. Consider the following relations P(X, Y, Z), Q(X, Y, T) and R(Y, V).

P			Q			R	
X	Y	Z	X	Y	T	Y	V
X1	Y1	Z1	X2	Y1	2	Y1	V1
X1	Y1	Z2	X1	Y2	5	Y3	V2
X2	Y2	Z2	X1	Y1	6	Y2	V3
X2	Y4	Z4	X3	Y3	1	Y2	V2

How many tuples will be returned by the following relational algebra query?

$$\prod_x(\sigma_{P.Y=R.Y \wedge R.V=V2})(P \times R) - \prod_x(\sigma_{Q.Y=R.Y \wedge Q.T>2})(Q \times R)$$

[2019 : 2 Marks]

RELATIONAL CALCULAS

78. Which of the following relational calculus expressions is not safe?

(a) $\{t \mid \exists u \in R_1(t[A] = u[A] \wedge \neg \exists s \in R_2(t[A] = s[A])\}$

(b) $\{t \mid \forall u \in R_1(u[A] = "x" \Rightarrow \exists s \in R_2(t[A] = s[A] \wedge s[A] = u[A]))\}$

(c) $\{t \mid \neg(t \in R_1)\}$

(d) $\{t \mid \exists u \in R_1(t[A] = u[A]) \wedge \exists s \in R_2(t[A] = s[A])\}$

[2001 : 2 Marks]

79. Consider the relation employee (name, sex, supervisorName) with name as the key. supervisor Name gives the name of the supervisor of the employee under consideration. What does the following Tuple Relational Calculus query produce?

$$\{e.name \mid employee(e) \wedge$$
$$(\forall x)[\neg\, employee(x) \vee x.supervisorName$$
$$\neq e.name \vee x.sex = "male"]\}$$

(a) Names of employees with a male supervisor

(b) Names of employees with no immediate male subordinates

(c) Names of employees with no immediate female subordinates

(d) Names of employees with a female supervisor

[2007 : 2 Marks]

80. Consider a database that has the relation schemas EMP (EmpId, EmpName, Deptid) and DEPT(DeptName, Deptid). Note that the Deptid can be permitted to be NULL in the relation EMP. Consider the following queries on the database expressed in tuple relational calculus.

I. $\{t\{\exists u \in EMP(t[EmpName] = u[EmpName] \wedge \forall v \in DEPT(t[DeptId] \neq v[DeptId))]\}$

II. $\{t\{\exists u \in EMP(t[EmpName] = u[EmpName] \wedge \exists v \in DEPT(t[DeptId] \neq v[DeptId))]\}$

III. $\{t\{\exists u \in EMP(t[EmpName] = u[EmpName] \wedge \exists v \in DEPT(t[DeptId] \neq v[DeptId))]\}$

Which of the above queries are safe?

(a) I and II only
(b) I and III only
(c) II and III only
(d) I, II and III

[2017 (Set-1) : 1 Mark]

ANSWERS

1. (c)	2. (d)	3. (a)	4. (c)	5. (a)	6. (c)	7. (c)	8. (a)	9. (a)	10. (a)
11. (a)	12. (b)	13. (c)	14. (c)	15. (c)	16. (c)	17. (b)	18. (0)	19. (*)	20. (*)
21. (a)	22. (c)	23. (d)	24. (d)	25. (c)	26. (c)	27. (d)	28. (d)	29. (a)	30. (b)
31. (c)	32. (b)	33. (b)	34. (d)	35. (b)	36. (a)	37. (c)	38. (c)	39. (c)	40. (a)
41. (d)	42. (c)	43. (b)	44. (b)	45. (c)	46. (d)	47. (2)	48. (d)	49. (a)	50. (2)
51. (2.6)	52. (7)	53. (d)	54. (5)	55. (a)	56. (a)	57. (a)	58. (*)	59. (*)	60. (a)
61. (c)	62. (c)	63. (c)	64. (b)	65. (d)	66. (b)	67. (d)	68. (d)	69. (a)	70. (a)
71. (d)	72. (a)	73. (a)	74. (a)	75. (d)	76. (c)	77. (1)	78. (c)	79. (c)	80. (d)

EXPLANATIONS

1. When (2, 4) is deleted any record that have '2' in the foreign key must have to be deleted.

   Here, records are < 5, 2 >, <7, 2>

   Then because of cascade any record that have 5 or 7 as foreign key must be deleted. There is no record that have 7 as foreign key (9, 5) is gone to delete. Now, any record that have 9 has an foreign key have to delete but there is no one.

2. For referential integrity constraint

   (*b*) Insert Into S (*c*) Deletes from R

   because R (*a*, *b*, *c*) is primary key. If we insert into S, not change value of R (*a*, *b*, *c*) and when delete from R, then we have need to delete from S also.

3. As per question, B is a foreign key in r1 that refers to C in r2.

   r1 and r2 satisfy referential integrity constraints.

   So every value that exists in column B of r1 must also exist in column C of r2.

   Hence B is subset of C.

4. We find from question, index file associated and contains the values of 1, 3, 2, 5, 4, we get **Index filed from occupation.** One to this conflicting never occur.

5. Clustering index in unique and is created automatically when primary key is declared it is ordered.

6. Block size is given 1024 so first level and second level multiplication must be 2^{10}, so only (c) satisfy $2^8 \times 22 = 2^{10}$.

7. A file is organized so that the ordering of data records is the same as or close to the ordering of data entries in some index. Such type of index is called Clustered Index

8. In both the cases it gives same number of tuple i.e. 8

9. r1 natural join r2 is a join operation done on the common attribute R. And we know that R is the primary key of R2.The value of common attribute (i.e. R2) should match. The value of R in r2 is matched with corresponding R in r1 . So it will have 2000 tuples.

10. Note that A, B, C and D are all key attributes. We can derive all attributes from every attribute.

    Since Intersection of all relations is B and B derives all other attributes, relation is lossless.

    The relation is dependency preserving (directly or indirectly). Note that $C \rightarrow D$ is also preserved with following two $C \rightarrow B$(is derived when we find closure of relation R2) and $B \rightarrow D$.

11. CLOSURE(B) = {A,B,C}. i.e. B is a candidate key of R.

    So B must be unique in R i.e. all 200 values are unique.

    Now, All 100 values of S is present in B (beacuse of foreign key constraint) So in any possibility only 100 tuples are selected when we take natural join.

12. If there is no foreign key constraint between two tables then

    The max number of tuples = m * n

    and min number of tuples = 0.

13. If the decomposition is lossy then after joining such type of decomposed relation the total number of tuples in the relation is increased. So r is subset of S.

14. R_1

A	B
1	5
3	7

R_2

A	B
1	7
4	9

R_1 full outer join R_2

A	B	C
1	5	7
3	7	NULL
4	NULL	9

So e, f, g is in Result.

15.

R

A	(B)
a_1	2
a_2	4
a_3	4
a_4	6
a_5	6

S

<u>B</u>	C
2	c_1
4	c_2
4	c_2
8	c_2

⇑ Foreign key ⇑ Primary key

Given query: $r \bowtie (\sigma_{B<5}(s))$

A	B	C
a_1	2	c_1
a_2	4	c_1
a_3	4	c_1

A : $\sigma_{B<5}(r \bowtie s)$

A	B	C
a_1	2	c_1
a_2	4	c_1
a_3	4	c_1

B : $\sigma_{B<5}(r ⟕ s)$

A	B	C
a_1	2	c_1
a_2	4	c_1
a_3	4	c_1

C : $r ⟕ (\sigma_{B<5}(s))$

A	B	C
a_1	2	c_1
a_2	4	c_1
a_3	4	c_1
a_4	6	Null
a_5	6	Null

D : $\sigma_{B<5}(r) ⟗ s$

A	B	C
a_1	2	c_1
a_2	4	c_1
a_3	4	c_1

Option "C" query result not equal to given query.

16. Nested loop Alqorithm will involve $n_r * b_s + b_r$ block trasfer.

Either T_1 can be R or T_2.

If R is T1 then total block access is

2000 * 20 + 80 = 40080

If R Ps to T2 then total block access is

400 * 80 + 20 = 32020

No then Minimum block access is 32020.

17. Number of block access = $n_r * b_s + b_r$

where br and bs are number of blocks in relations R and S respectively, and n_r is the number of tuples in relation R.

We select the relation with small number of tuples as outer relation R. So, R is T2.

Number of block access = 400 * 80 + 20 = 32020

The memory buffer space holds one block of records for T1 and one block of records for T2 simultaneously.

So, number of block accesses is 80 * 20 + 20 = 1620

So, Total number of block access = 32020 – 1620 = 30400

18. Given that

Q → R(Primary Key)

S → P (Primary Key)

(3,8) is deleted from relation T1.

So, Q can be deleted directly. Now, S → P but the relationship given is on delete set NULL, Therefore when we delete 3 from T1 ,the entry in T2 having 3 will be NULL.

So no additional record is deleted.

19. SQL query is :

SELECT DISTINCT A. student FROM FREQUENTS A, SERVES B, LIKES C WHERE A.parlor = B.parlor AND B.ice-cream = C.ice-cream AND A.student = C.student;

20. Sql query is :

(a) Select Employee-name from EMP, DEPT where Salary>50000 and EMP.Dept-no=DEPT.Dept-no and Location="Calcutta".

(b) Select Dept-no, count(*) from EMP where salary > 100000 group by Dept-no.

21. The given query selects all attributes of r.

As distinct keyword used in query so result is equal to r iff r doesn't have duplicates.

Now if no common attribute between the tables then join is equivalent to cartesian product. Cartisian product of two sets will be empty if any of the two sets is empty. So, s should have atleast one record to get all rows of r.

22. There are three relations

Select distinct name, select the name of students and then there are three predicates

Courses. instructor = korth specify the courses taught by korth.

The other two predicate specify that student can earn a grade at least A from causes so the SQL query compute.

Name of students who have got an A grade in at least one of the courses taught by korth.

23. Given relation is

Employee (<u>Name</u>, Sex, Salary, deptName)

SQL query is

Select deptName,

from Employee

Where Sex = 'M'

group by deptName

having avg (Salary) > (Select avg (Salary) from Employee)

This will retrieve the department in which average salary of male employee is more than the average salary in the company.

24. After inserting tuples in the table

Department table has two rows and Employee table has three rows.

Since, there is no specific joining condition specified, it will retrieve Cartesian product of the table

Number of rows = product of number of rows in each relation = 3 × 2 = 6

Number of columns = sum of number of columns = 3 + 2 = 5

25. According to query the updated marks will be

10 + 5 = 15

20 + 5 = 25

30 + 5 = 35

Null + 5 = Null(Update on null gives null).

Now, avg function ignores null values. So, here avg will be (15 + 25 + 35)/3 = 25.

26. (i) when we update in STUDENT table dept id =NULL then it will not cause any problem to referenced table.

(ii) if we set in DEPARTMENT table dept id = NULL then it will produce inconsistency (because of refrential integrity constraint) in STUDENT table we still have the tuples containing the dept id.

27. Here [not unique] in nested query ensures that only for those suppliers it return True which supplies more than 1 item in which case supplier id in inner query will be repeated for that supplier.

28. The given SQL query compute "Titles of the five most expensive books".

29. if color = "Red"

then did = {22, 22, 31, 31,64}

if color = "Green"

then did = {22, 31, 74}

intersection of Red and Green will give = {22, 31} which is Karthikeyan and Boris

30. If linear search is used to locate a tuple in a relation using primary key, then n lies in the range of 44 to 48.

31. Query 1 and Query 2 will give the same result if all the customers have distinct balance. So, for some databases, the result of query 1 and query 2 will be same. But the output of query 1 and 2 is not requierd output as question says "We would like to rank customers according to decreasing balance."

32. Query2 and Query4 return identical row sets for all databases but there exist databases for which Query1 and Query2 return different row sets.

33. Query Q_1 doesn't give correct result because it contain not exists clause which lead to wrong answer. Q_2 is correct.

34. Query gives error because Sch-name is selected in SQL query while grouping is performed on school-id.

35. The query returns the tuples where 35% students enrolled and all of them got >35 marks in some exam.

36.

X	Y
1	1
2	3
3	7
4	15
5	31
6	63
7	127

37. S

Borrower	Bank_Manager
Ramesh	Sunderajan
Suresh	Ramgopal
Mahesh	Sunderjan

T

Bank_Manager	Loan_Amount
Sunderajan	10000.00
Ramgopal	5000.00
Sunderjan	7000.00

After executing the given query, the output would be

Borrower	Bank_Manager	Loan_Amount
Ramesh	Sunderajan	10000.00
Ramesh	Sunderajan	7000.00
Suresh	Ramgopal	5000.00
Mahesh	Sunderajan	10000.00
Mahesh	Sunderajan	7000.00

38. Following statments are true

Q : An SQL query can contain a HAVING clause only if it has a GROUP BY clause.

R : All attributes used in the GROUP BY clause must appear in the SELECT clause.

39. In all cases plan 1 is faster than plan 2 because in plan 1 we are reducing the load by doing select amount >x and then the loop.

But, in case of plan 2 its in the nested loop so it need to check every time and will take more time to execute.

40. The innermost query

"SELECT P.pid FROM Parts P WHERE P.color<> 'blue'" returns pids of parts which are not blue.

The subquery "SELECT C.sid FROM Catalog C WHERE C.pid NOT IN (SELECT P.pid FROM Parts P WHERE P.color<> 'blue')" returns sids of all those suppliers who have supplied some blue parts.

So, the complete query gives the names of all suppliers who have not supplied any blue parts.

41. An SQL query automatically not eliminates duplicates.

* An sql query will work if index are not given on the relation.
* SQL not permit attribute n axes for fepetition

42. For all values smaller than 5, x < 5 will always be true but x = 5 will be false.

43. The subquery return Null beacuse no entry with name "arun".

The meaning of "ALL" is the A.Age should be greater than all the values returned by the subquery.

Then the condition becomes true for all rows of A. So all rows of table A are selected.

44. In the inner sub query, "employees" and "departments" tables are joined by "using" clause (first Cartesian product of those two tables will be done and then and wherever these is a match on the dept-ids that tuple will be filtered). After this, the tuples of the resultant table will be filtered by using the condition "location-id=1700" and then will grouped on deptid(all the tuples having equal values under dept-id will come into one group). After grouping, the columns dept-id in location-id 1700 and maximum of hire dates in that respective dept-id will be selected. Format of the tuples in the resultant table will be dept-id in location-id 1700 along with the latest hire date in the respective dept (two columns). Outer query takes each tuple from "employees" table and it will check whether dept-id and hire-date pair for this tuple is contained in the table given by inner sub query. If this is the case it will display the last-name of respective employee

IN operator compares one or multiple expressions on the left side of the operator to a set of one or more values on the right side of the operator. When using multiple expressions (like 2 columns - pair wise comparison), the number and data types of expressions in the list must match on both sides of the operator.

45. When we execute query R * from (select distinct from S) as S_1 where $R \cdot a = S_1 \cdot a$, it will give the same results.

46. The subquery gives " All customer that did not gave a good rating"

Outer query says that the result of inner query is not exist. Hence it returns "Names of all the employees with all their customers having a 'GOOD' rating."

47. The output is

Raj	310
Rohit	140

Hence no of rows returned are 2

48. SELECT operation in SQL is equivalent to the projection operation in relational algebra, except that SELECT in SQL retains duplicates

49. Inner query collects capacities of all the theatres and in outer query we are filtering the tuples with the condition "capacity>=All". So the theatres which are having maximum capacity will be satisfy the conductivity and they will.

50. The result of the query is:

name
Bikaner
churu

Total	
District name	**Capacity**
Ajmeer	20
Bikaner	40
Churu	30
Dungargarh	10

$$\text{Total} - \text{Average} = \frac{\text{Capacity of (Ajmer + Bikaner + Churu + Dungargarh)}}{4}$$

$$= \frac{20+40+30+10}{4}$$

$$= \frac{110}{4} = 25$$

Total – avg capacity
25

So, the number of tables returned by the given SQL query is 2.

51. Output of given query is

Dept Name	Number
AA	4
AB	3
AC	3
AD	2
AE	1

Average is (4 + 3 + 3 + 2 + 1)/5 = 13 / 5 = 2.6

52. The subquery " SELECT tb.goals FROM top_scorer AS tb WHERE tb.country = 'Spain' " returns Null because country spain is not in the table.

The Subquery " SELECT tc.goals FROM top_scorer AS tc
WHERE tc.country = 'Germany' " returns all the goals of country germany i.e. (16, 14, 11, 10, 10)

Note the Complete query is like

SELECT ta.player FROM top_scorer AS ta

WHERE ta.goals > ALL (NULL) AND ta.goals > ANY (16,14,11,10,10)

So the above query gives the name of all players whose goal is greater than 10.

Hence total 7 tuples are returend.

53.

Book (isbn, bname)

isbn	bname
2	A
4	B
6	C
8	D
10	E

Stock (isbn, copies)

isbn	copies
4	100
6	200
10	200
12	400

Query 1:

isbn	copies
4	100
6	200
10	200

Query 2:

isbn	copies
4	100
6	200
10	200
2	Null
8	Null

Query 3:

isbn	copies
4	100
6	200
10	200
12	400

Query 4:

isbn	copies
4	100
6	200
10	200
2	Null
8	Null
12	400

Query 4 is full outer join so that full order join record set superset of records compare to inner join, left outer join & right outer join.

54.

Student	
Roll_no.	**Student_name**
1	Amit
2	Priya
3	Vinit
4	Rohan
5	Smita

Performance		
Roll_no.	**Student_code**	**Marks**
1	A	86
1	B	95
1	C	90
2	A	89
2	C	92
3	C	80

Hence total 5 rows are returned by above SQL query.

55. SQL form the cartesian product of the relation named in the form cluase, perform a relational algebra selection using the where clause predicate and then projects the result onto the attributes of the select clause.

56. Result of A U B gives 5 tuples
Now when we perform join between(A U B) and C using theta condition A.id >40 and C.id < 15.
Then the total number of tuple returned is 7.

57. Query is equvivalent to option (a).

58. R-(R-S) is minimal expression that is equal to $R \cap S$.

59. (a) Select the user# and titles of the books issued to User# 6.
(b) Select author names of the books issued to users whose home town is Delhi.

60. Condition C_1 may be different from C_2.

61. We have to select tuples having A = 10 and tuples having B = 20. So option (c) is true only.

62. We cannot generate relational algebra of aggregate functions using basic operations. We need extended operations here.

63. Relational algebra has the same power as safe relational calculus. Unsafe query is possible in relational calculus but not possible in relational algebra.

64. – empty table is generated by the query

$$\pi_C(r_1) - \pi_D(r_2)$$

65. Relation is
Student (name, sex, marks)
expression for query is

$$\pi_{name}(\sigma_{six=female}(student)) - \pi_{name}(student \bowtie_{(sex = female \wedge X = male \wedge marks \leq m)} \rho_{n,x,m}(student))$$

this will retrience the name of girl student with more marks than all the boy student.

66. Output of SQL Query is

Roll No	Hostel
2369	7
2581	6
2643	5
2643	5
2572	5
2926	5
2959	7

Total row by SQL is 7 rows. SQL and RA is equivalent but RA eliminated duplicate value so unique Hotel is {5, 6,7} only 3 rows
so 7 – 3 = 4

67. Relational algebra has the same power as safe relational calculus. Unsafe query is possible in relational calculus but not possible in relational algebra.

68. σA <= 100 means "selects all the tuples which has attribute A's value less than or equal to 100."
Now as per question, Attribute A's values in the range [0,500] are uniformaly distributed among 1000 tuples.

So firstly arrange all 1000 tuples in the ascending order of attribute A's value, then first 200 tuples will have attribute A's values in the range [0,99] and next 200 tuples will have attribute A's values in the range [100, 199] and so on .So number of tuples returned by the given selection query is 200.

69. Only A is correct.

70. The given relational algebra query returns "Courses in which a proper subset of female students are enrolled."

71. Query i, iii and iv is equivalent.

72. I and II describe the division operator in relational algebra and tuple relational calculus respectively.

73. Find the distinct names of all students who score more than 90% in the course no. 107.

1. SQL query

Condition would give all S. name having score > 90 and attending course no. 107 and DISTINCT S.sname will give distinct student names.
TRUE

2. Relational Algebra

πsname gives projection of all students meeting the condition and 'π' gives DISTINCT value.
TRUE

3. Tuple Calculus

gives DISTINCT student name having score > 90 and course no. is 107. TRUE

4. Domain Calculus

domain calculus is equivalent to relational algebra and provide distinct value for the query.
TRUE

74. A join between r(R) and s (S) using nested loop method will be as follows.

For each tuple r in R do
For each tuple s in S do
If r and s satisfy the join condition then output the tuple <r, s>

This algorithm will involve $n_r * b_s + b_r$ block transfers and $n_r + b_r$ seeks, where b_r and b_s are number of blocks in relations R and S respectively and n_r is number of tuple in relation R. Now to have less block accesses, n_r should be less and it is already given that |R|<|S|. Relation r(R) should be in the outer loop to have fewer number of disk block accesses.

75.

$$\Pi_{empId}(employee) - \Pi_{empId}(employee \bowtie_{(empId = eID) \wedge (empAge \leq depAge)} dependent)$$

(A: $\Pi_{empId}(employee \bowtie_{(empId = eID) \wedge (empAge \leq depAge)} dependent)$; B: the whole expression)

Part A of the above given relational algebra query will give the set of empIds of those employees whose age is less than or equal to the age of some of his/her dependents. Now when set of empIds of all employees minus set of empIds obtained from part A is done, then we get the set of empIds of employees whose age is greater than that of all of his/her dependents.

76. Result of T1:

CA

CB

CC

Result of T2 = CR/T1

SA

SC

SD

SF

Total = 4

47.

P

X	Y	Z
X1	Y1	Z1
X1	Y1	Z2
X2	Y2	Z2
X2	Y4	Z4

R

Y	V
Y1	V1
Y2	V2
Y2	V3
Y2	V2

$$\Pi_X\left(\sigma_{(P.Y=R.Y \wedge R.V=V2)}(P \times R)\right) \Rightarrow \begin{array}{|c|}\hline X \\ \hline X2 \\ \hline\end{array} \quad \ldots (I)$$

Q

X	Y	Z
X2	Y1	2
X1	Y2	5
X1	Y1	6
X3	Y4	1

R

Y	V
Y1	V1
Y3	V2
Y2	V3
Y2	V2

$$\Pi_X\left(\sigma_{(Q.Y=R.Y \wedge Q.T > 2)}(Q \times R)\right) \Rightarrow \begin{array}{|c|}\hline X \\ \hline X1 \\ \hline\end{array} \quad \ldots (II)$$

$$I - II \Rightarrow \begin{array}{|c|}\hline X \\ \hline X2 \\ \hline\end{array}$$ one record in result.

78. OPTION (C) is unsafe because it represent " select the tuples that are not present in table."

79. The query

{e· name | employee (e) ∧ (∀x) [¬employee (x)] vx· supervisor Name ≠ e · name v xssex = "male"]} computes the names of employees with no immediate female subordinates.

80. A SAFE EXPRESSION is one that is guaranteed to yield a finite number of tuples as its results. Otherwise, it is called UNSAFE here all are safe query.

3 CHAPTER

Database Design and Normalization

Analysis of Previous GATE Papers											
	Year → Topics ↓		2019	2018	2017 Set 1	2017 Set 2	2016 Set 1	2016 Set 2	2015 Set 1	2015 Set 2	2015 Set 3
BCNF	1 Mark	MCQ Type									
		Numerical Type									
	2 Marks	MCQ Type	1								
		Numerical Type									
	Total		2								
FUNCTIONAL DEPENDENCY	1 Mark	MCQ Type			1						1
		Numerical Type									
	2 Marks	MCQ Type									
		Numerical Type									
	Total				1						1
NORMAL FORMS	1 Mark	MCQ Type					1				
		Numerical Type									
	2 Marks	MCQ Type		1							
		Numerical Type									
	Total			2			1				

BCNF

1. State True or False with reason

There is always a decomposition into Boyce-Codd normal form (BCNF) that is lossless and dependency preserving.

[1994 : 1 Mark]

2. R(A, B, C, D) is a relation. Which of the following does not have a lossless join, dependency preserving BCNF decomposition?

(a) $A \to B, B \to CD$ (b) $A \to B, B \to C, C \to D$

(c) $AB \to C, C \to AD$ (d) $A \to BCD$

[2001 : 2 Marks]

3. Relation R with an associated set of functional dependencies, F, is decomposed into BCNF. The redundancy (arising out of functional dependencies) in the resulting set of relation is

(a) Zero

(b) More than zero but less than that of an equivalent 3NF cocomposition

(c) Proportional to the size of F^+

(d) Indeterminate

[2002 : 1 Mark]

4. Let the set of functional dependencies F = {QR → S, R → P, S → Q} hold on a relation schema X = (PQRS). X is not a BCNF. Suppose X is decomposed into two schemas Y and Z, where Y = (PR) and Z = (QRS).

Consider the two statements given below.

I. Both Y and Z are in BCNF

II. Decomposition of X into Y and Z is dependency preserving and lossless

Which of the above statements is/are correct?

(a) Both I and II (b) II only

(c) Neither I nor II (d) I only

[2019 : 2 Marks]

FUNCTIONAL DEPENDENCY

5. (a) Consider the relation scheme R(A, B, C) with the following functional dependencies:

$AB \to C$

$C \to A$

Show that the scheme R is the Third Normal Form (3NF) but not in Boyce-Code Normal Form (BCNF).

(b) Determine the minimal keys of relation R.

[1995 : 2 Marks]

6. For a database relation R(a, b, c, d), where the domains of a, b, c, d include only atomic values, only the following functilonal dependencies and those that can be inferred from them hold:

$a \to c$

$b \to d$

This relation is

(a) in first normal form but not in second normal form

(b) in second normal form but not in third normal form

(c) in third normal form

(d) none of the above

[1997 : 2 Marks]

7. Let R = (A, B, C, D, E, F) be a relation scheme with the following dependencies $C \to F$, $E \to A$, $EC \to D$, $A \to B$. Which of the following is a key for R?

(a) CD (b) EC

(b) AE (d) AC

[1999 : 1 Mark]

8. Give the folllowing relation instance

X	Y	Z
1	4	2
1	5	3
1	6	3
3	2	2

Which of the following functional dependencies are satisfied by the instance?

(a) $XY \to Z$ and $Z \to Y$

(b) $YZ \to X$ and $Y \to Z$

(c) $YZ \to X$ and $X \to Z$

(d) $XZ \to Y$ and $Y \to X$

[2000 : 2 Marks]

9. Consider a schema R(A,B,C,D) and functional dependencies $A \to B$ and $C \to D$. Then the decomposition of R into R_1 (AB) and R_2 (CD) is

(a) dependency preservinig and lossless join

(b) lossless join but not dependency preserving

(c) dependency preserving but not lossless join

(d) not dependency preserving and not lossless join

[2001 : 1 Mark]

10. From the following instance of a relation scheme R(A, B, C), we can conclude that:

A	B	C
1	1	1
1	1	0
2	3	2
2	3	2

(a) A functionally determines B and B functionally determines C
(b) A functionally determines B and B does not functionally determines C
(c) B does not functionally determines C
(d) A does not functionally determines B and B does not functionally determines C

[2002 : 2 Marks]

11. Consider the following functional dependencies in a database:

Data_of_Birth $\rightarrow$ Age
Age $\rightarrow$ Eligibility
Name $\rightarrow$ Roll_number
Roll_number $\rightarrow$ Name
Course_number $\rightarrow$ Course_name
Cource_number $\rightarrow$ Instructor
(Roll_number; Course_number) $\rightarrow$ Grade

The relation (Roll_number; Name, Date_of_birth, Age) is
(a) in second normal form but not in third normal form
(b) in third normal form but not in BCNF
(c) in BCNF
(d) in none of the above **[2003 : 2 Marks]**

12. Consider a relation scheme R = (A, B, C, D, E, H) on which the following funcional dependencies hold:

$\{A \rightarrow B, BC \rightarrow D, E \rightarrow C, D \rightarrow A\}$

What are the candidate keys of R?
(a) AE, BE (b) AE, BE, DE
(b) AEH, BEH, BCH (d) AEH, BEH, DEH

[2005 : 2 Marks]

13. In a schema with attributes A, B, C, D and E following set of functional dependencies are given

$A \rightarrow B$
$A \rightarrow C$
$CD \rightarrow E$
$B \rightarrow D$
$E \rightarrow A$

Which of the following functional dependencies is NOT implied by the above set
(a) $CD \rightarrow AC$ (b) $BD \rightarrow CD$
(d) $BC \rightarrow CD$ (d) $AC \rightarrow BC$

[2005 : 2 Marks]

14. Consider a relation R with five attributes V, W, X, Y, and Z. The following functional dependencies hold : $VY \rightarrow W, WX \rightarrow Z$, and $ZY \rightarrow V$. Which of the following is a candidate key for R?
(a) VXZ (b) VXY
(c) VWXY (d) VWXYZ

[2006 : 2 Marks]

15. The following functional dependencies are given:
$AB \rightarrow CD$, $AF \rightarrow D$, $DE \rightarrow F$, $C \rightarrow G$, $F \rightarrow E$, $G \rightarrow A$.
Which one of the following options is false?
(a) $\{CF\}^+ = \{ACDEFG\}$ (b) $\{BG\}^+ = \{ABCDG\}$
(c) $\{AF\}^+ = \{ACDEFG\}$ (d) $\{AB\}^+ = \{ACDFG\}$

[2006 : 2 Marks]

16. Consider the following implications relating to functional and multivalued dependencies given below, which may or may not be correct.
(i) If $A \rightarrow\rightarrow B$ and $A \rightarrow\rightarrow C$ then $A \rightarrow BC$
(ii) If $A \rightarrow B$ and $A \rightarrow C$ then $A \rightarrow\rightarrow BC$
(iii) If $A \rightarrow\rightarrow BC$ and $A \rightarrow B$ then $A \rightarrow C$
(iv) If $A \rightarrow BC$ and $A \rightarrow B$ then $A \rightarrow\rightarrow C$

Exactly how many of the above implications are valid?
(a) 0 (b) 1
(c) 2 (d) 3

[2007 : 2 Marks]

Linked Answer Questions 17 and 18

Relation R has eight attributes ABCDEFGH. Fields of R contain only atomic values.

$F = \{CH \rightarrow G, A \rightarrow BC, B \rightarrow CFH, E \rightarrow A, F \rightarrow EG\}$ is a set of functional dependencies (FDs) so that F is exactly the set of FDs that hold for R.

17. How many candidate keys does the relation R have?
(a) 3 (b) 4
(c) 5 (d) 6 **[2013 : 2 Marks]**

18. The relation R is

(a) in 1NF, but not in 2NF.

(b) in 2NF, but not in 3NF.

(c) in 3NF, but not in BCNF.

(d) in BCNF.

[2013 : 2 Marks]

19. Given the following two statements:

S1: Every table with two single-valued attributes is in 1NF, 2NF, 3NF and BCNF.

S2: $AB \to C, D \to E, E \to C$ is a minimal cover for the set of functional dependencies $AB \to C, D \to E, AB \to E, E \to C$.

Which one of the following is **CORRECT**?

(a) S1 is TRUE and S2 is FALSE.

(b) Both S1 and S2 are TRUE.

(c) S1 is FALSE and S2 is TRUE.

(d) Both S1 and S2 are FALSE.

[2014 (Set-1) : 2 Marks]

20. Consider the relation $X(P, Q, R, S, T, U)$ with the following set of functional dependencies

F = {

$\{P, R\} \to \{S, T\}$

$\{P, S, U\} \to \{Q, R\}$

}

Which of the following is the trivial functional dependency in F^+ is closue of F?

(a) $\{P, R\} \to \{S, T\}$ (b) $\{P, R\} \to \{R, T\}$

(c) $\{P, S\} \to \{S\}$ (d) $\{P, S, U\} \to \{Q\}$

[2015 (Set-3) : 1 Mark]

21. The following functional dependencies hold true for the relational schema $R\{V, W, X, Y, Z\}$:

$V \to W$

$VW \to X$

$Y \to VX$

$Y \to Z$

Which of the following is irreducible equivalent for this set of functional dependencies?

(a)	(b)	(c)	(d)
$V \to W$	$V \to W$	$V \to W$	$V \to W$
$V \to X$	$W \to X$	$V \to X$	$W \to X$
$Y \to V$	$Y \to V$	$Y \to V$	$Y \to V$
$Y \to Z$	$Y \to Z$	$Y \to X$	$Y \to X$
		$Y \to Z$	$Y \to Z$

[2017 (Set-1): 1 Mark]

NORMAL FORMS

22. Which normal form is considered adequate for normal relational database design?

(a) 2 NF

(b) 5 NF

(c) 4 NF

(d) 3 NF

[1998 : 1 Mark]

23. Consider the following database relations containing the attributes

Book_id

Subject_Category_of_book

Name_of_Author

Nationality_of_Author

With book_id as the primary key.

(a) What is the highest normal form satisfied by this relation?

(b) Suppose the attributes Book_title and Author_address are added to the relation, and the primary key is changed to {Name_of_Author, Book_title}, what will be the highest normal form satisfied by the relation?

[1998 : 2 Marks]

24. Consider the schema R = (S T U V) and the dependencies $S \to T, T \to U, U \to V$ and $V \to S$. Let R = (R1 and R2) be a decomposition such that $R1 \cap R2 = \phi$. The decomposition is

(a) not is 2NF

(b) in 2 NF but not 3NF

(c) in 3NF but not in 2NF

(d) in both 2NF and 3NF

[1999 : 2 Marks]

25. Relation R is decomposed using a set of functional dependencies, F, and relation S is decomposed using another set of functional dependencies, G. One decomposition is definitely BCNF, the other is definitely 3 NF, but it is not know which is which. To make a guaranteed indentification, which one of the following tests should be used on the docompositions? (Assume that the closures of F and G are available).

(a) Dependency-preservation

(b) Lossless-join

(c) BCNF definition

(d) 3 NF definition

[2002 : 2 Marks]

26. The relation scheme student Performance (name, courseNo, rollNo, grade) has the following functional dependencies:

name, courseNo $\rightarrow$ grade

RollNo, courseNo $\rightarrow$ grade

name $\rightarrow$ rollNo

rollNo $\rightarrow$ name

The highest normal form of this relation scheme is

(a) 2 NF (b) 3 NF

(c) BCNF (d) 4 NF

[2004 : 2 Marks]

27. A relation Empdtl is defined with attributes empcode (unique), name, street, city, state and pincode. For any pincode, there is only one city and state. Also for any given street, city and state, there is just one pincode. In normalization terms, Empdtl is a relation in

(a) 1 NF only

(b) 2 NF and hence also in 1NF

(c) 3NF and hence also in 2NF and 1NF

(d) BCNF and hence also in 3NF, 2NF an 1NF

[2004 : 2 Marks]

28. A table has fields F1, F2, F3, F4, F5 with the following functional dependencies

$$F1 \rightarrow F3, F2 \rightarrow F4, (F1, F2) \rightarrow F5$$

In terms of Normalization, this table is in

(a) 1 NF (b) 2 NF

(b) 3 NF (d) None of these

[2005: 1 Mark]

29. Which-one of the following statements about normal forms in FALSE?

(a) BCNF is stricter than 3 NF

(b) Loss less, dependency-preserving decomposition into 3 NF is always possible

(c) Loss less, dependency-preserving decomposition into BCNF is always possible

(d) Any relation with two attributes is BCNF

[2005 : 1 Mark]

30. Which one of the following statements is FALSE?

(a) Any relation with two attributes is in BCNF

(b) A relation in which every key has only one attribute is in 2NF

(c) A prime attribute can be transitively dependent on a key in 3NF relation

(d) A prime attribute can be transitively dependent on a key in a BCNF relation.

[2007 : 2 Marks]

31. Let R(A, B, C, D, E, P, G) be a relational schema in which the following functional dependencies are known to hold:

$$AB \rightarrow CB, DE \rightarrow P, C \rightarrow E, P \rightarrow C \text{ and } B \rightarrow G.$$

The relational schema R is

(a) in BCNF

(b) in 3NF, but not in BCNF

(c) in 2NF, but not in 3NF

(d) not in 2NF

[2008 : 2 Marks]

32. Consider the following relational schemes for a library database:

Book (Title, Author, Catalog_no, Publisher, Year, price)

Collection (Title, Author, Catalog_no)

which the following functional dependencies:

I. Title Author $\rightarrow$ Catalog_no

II. Catalog_no $\rightarrow$ Title Author Publisher Year

III. Publisher Title Year $\rightarrow$ Price

Assume {Author, Title} is the key for both schemes: which of the following statements is true?

(a) Both Book and Collectioln are in BCNF

(b) Both Book and Collectioln are in 3NF only

(c) Book is in 2NF and Collection is in 3NF

(d) Both Book and Collection are in 2NF only

[2008 : 2 Marks]

33. Which of the following is TRUE?

(a) Every relation in 3NF is also in BCNF

(b) A relation R is in 3NF if every non-prime attribute of R is fully functionally dependent on every key of R

(c) Every relation in BCNF is also in 3NF

(d) No relation can be in both BCNF and 3NF

[2012 : 1 Mark]

34. A database of research articles in a journal uses the following schema.

(VOLUME, NUMBER, STARTPAGE, ENDPAGE, TITLE, YEAR, PRICE)

The primary key is (VOLUME, NUMBER, STARTPAGE, ENDPAGE) and the following functional dependencies exist in the schema.

(VOLUME, NUMBER, STARTPAGE, ENDPAGE) → TITLE

(VOLUME, NUMBER) → YEAR

(VOLUME, NUMBER, STARTPAGE, ENDPAGE) → PRICE

The database is redesigned to use the following schemas.

(VOLUME, NUMBER, STARTPAGE, ENDPAGE, TITLE, PRICE)

(VOLUME, NUMBER, YEAR)

Which is the weakest normal form that the new database satisfies, but the old one does not?

(a) 1 NF (b) 2 NF

(c) 3 NF (d) BCNF

[2016 (Set-1) : 1 Mark]

35. Consider the following four relational schemas. For each schema, all non-trivial functional dependencies are listed. The underlined attributes are the respectie primary keys.

Schema I:

Registration (rollno, courses) Field 'courses' is a set-valuedattribute containing the set of courses a student has registered for. Non-trivial functions dependency: rollno → courses

Schema II:

Registration (rollno, courseid, email) Non-trivial functional dependencies: rollno, courseid → email email → rollno

Schema III:

Registration (rollno, courseid, marks, grade) Non-trivial functional dependencies: rollno, courseid → marks, grade marks → grade

Schema IV:

Registration (rollno, courseid, credit) Non-trivial functional dependencies: rollno, courseid → credit courseid → credit

Which one of the relational schemas above is in 3NF but not in BCNF?

(a) Schema I

(b) Schema II

(c) Schema III

(d) Schema IV

[2018 : 2 Marks]

36. Consider the following relational schema:

Suppliers(sid: integer, sname: string, city: string, street: string)

Parts(pid:integer, pname:string, color:string)

Catalog(sid:integer, pid:integer, cost:real)

Assume that, in the suppliers relation above, each supplier and each street within a city has a unique name, and (sname, city) forms a candidate key. No other functional dependencies are implied other than those implied by primary and candidate keys. Which one of the following is TRUE about the above schema?

(a) The schema is in BCNF

(b) The schema is in 3NF but not in BCNF

(c) The schema is in 2NF but not in 3 NF

(d) The schema is not in 2NF

[2009 : 2 Marks]

ANSWERS

1. (False)	2. (*c*)	3. (*a*)	4. (*b*)	5. (*a*)	6. (*a*)	7. (*b*)	8. (*b*)	9. (*c*)	10. (*b*)
11. (*d*)	12. (*d*)	13. (*b*)	14. (*b*)	15. (*c,d*)	16. (*c*)	17. (*b*)	18. (*a*)	19. (*a*)	20. (*c*)
21. (*a*)	22. (*d*)	23. (*)	24. (*a*)	25. (*c*)	26. (*b*)	27. (*b*)	28. (*a*)	29. (*c*)	30. (*d*)
31. (*)	32. (*c*)	33. (*c*)	34. (2NF)	35. (*b*)	36. (*d*)				

EXPLANATIONS

1. False. BCNF decomposition may or may not be dependancy Presening.

2. R (A, B, C, D) is relation, and R(A), R(B), R(C), and R(D) is decomposition, then

   $R_1 \cap R_2 \to R_1$ $\quad R_1 \cup R_2 \cup R_3 \cup R_4 = R$

   $R_1 \cap R_2 \to R_2$

   $A \to B$, $B \to C$, so $A \to C$

   $B \to C$, $C \to D$, so $B \to D$

   $A \to B, A \to C, A \to BC$

   $B \to C, B \to D$, $B \to CD$, so, its multivalued dependency so it is in BC at E].

3. Relation R with an associated set of functional dependencies, F, is decomposed into BCNF. The redundancy in the resulting set of relation is zero.

4. X(PQRS) {QR → S, R → P, S → Q} decomposed into

Y(PR)	Z(QRS)
{R → P}	{QR → S, S → Q}
Candidate key: R	Candidate key: QR, RS
Relation Y in BCNF	Relation Z in 3NF but not BCNF

   Common attribute between Y and Z relations is R which is key for relation Y. So that given decomposition is lossless join decomposition.

   R → P in Y

   $\left.\begin{array}{l} QR \to S \\ S \to Q \end{array}\right\}$ are in Z

   and dependency preserving decomposition.

5. RCA, B, C)

   AB → C

   C → A

   Candidate key of R is A B, and BC

   AB → C is allowed in Both BCNF & 3 N F

   but F. D. C → is in 3 N F but not in BCNF because " A " is prime Attribute and " C " is non-key.

   (b) Minimal key's = { A B, B C }

6. A relation R is in first normal form (1NF) if the domains of all attributes of R are atomic. A domain is atomic if elements of the domain are considered to be indivisible units.

   Given, $a \to c$ $\quad a^+ = \{a, c\}$ $\quad b^+ = \{b, d\}$

   $b \to d$ It is Ist normal form (It have no key] so, it is not in 2 NF.

7. EC is the key as

   E → A →B, so EC → B

   C → F, so EC → F

   Also, EC → D and EC → EC

   Hence, taking all the above, EC → ABCDE

8. YZ → X and Y → Z both satisfied.

YZ → X	Y→ Z
42 → 1	4 → 2
53 → 1	5 → 3
63 → 1	6 → 3
22 → 3	2 → 2
↑	↑
All different	All different

9. R (A, B, C D)

$R_1(A, B)$ | $R_2(C, D$

$A \rightarrow B$ | $C \rightarrow D$

All functional dependancy Hold So it is dependancy presenving

But it is not lossless because the intersection of R_1 and R_2 is empty.

10. For each value of A there is execting and value in B, so "A" functionally determines "B"

But when B = 1 then C is 1 and 0 both so A is not functioanally detemines C.

11. Relation (Roll - number, Name, Date-of-Birth, Age)

F. D. used for Relation is :-

Date-of-Birth → Age

Name → Roll - number

Roll - number → Name

Candidate key is :- { Name, date-of Birth } and { Roll number, date-of-Birth }

So Date-of-Birth → Age generate

Partial functional dependancy so it is not in 2NF.

12. When we consider

$A = \{A, B\}$

$B = \{B\}$

and $H = \{H\}$

$\{A, B, H\} = \{A, B, C, D, E, H\}$

$\{B, E, H\} = \{A, B, C, D, F, H\}$

$\{D, E, H\} = \{A, B, C, D, E, H\}$

13. B D → C D is not implied

if we find closure of B C then CD is not derived in that closure.

(BD) = { B D }

14. R (V, W, X, Y, Z)

fd's V Y → W

WX → Z

ZY → Y

in R. H. S. of fd's X, Y ,must be.

present

$(XY)^+ = \{ XY \}$

$(VXY)^+ = \{ V X Y W Z \}$

So VXY is Candidate key.

15. AB → CD

AF → D

DE → F

C → G

G → A

$(AF)^+ = \{ A F D R \}$

$(AB)^+ = \{ A B C D G \}$

So both option c & d are false

16. Every functional dependancy is also multivalued dependancy but reverse is not true so ii and iv implications are correct.

(ii) A → B and A → C then A → BC which can be A →→ BC

(iv) gf A → BC and A → B then A → C which can be A →→ C

17. R (A B C D E F G H)

F = { CH → G

A → BC

B → CFH

E → A

F → EG

in every candidate key Attribute "D" must present because D is not is right - hand of fd's

so key is AD, ED, BD, FD

18. Relation is in 1NF but not in 2 NF because there exists partial functional dependencies.

19. S :True

Consider any table R with two attributes R (A.B)

The possible FD sets are

F_1 {

A → B

}

Key :A and is in BCNF

F_2 {

B → A

}

Key : B and is in BCNF

F_3 = {

A → B

B → A

}

Key : A & B it is in BCNF

F_4 = {

}

Key : AB and is in BCNF

If a table is in BCNF it is also in 1NF, 2NF and 3NF also

S_2 : False

First FD set cannot cover second FD set because in second FD set AB can functionally derive E but that is not happing in first FD set.

20. {P, S} → {S}

On finding closure of F^+, we can define {P, S} → {S} is trival functional dependency.

21. R (V, W, X, Y, Z)

fd's = { V → W

VW → X

Y → VX

Y → Z }

minimal cover of given fd's is

V → W

V → X { Here we can remove extra Attribute "W"}

Y → V { Y → X can be evaluate indirectly }

Y → Z

22. **NF.** A relation R is third normal form (3NF) if and only if it is 2NF and every non key attribute is non transitively dependent on the primary key.

Main Functions of 3NF

(1) A relation R is in 3NF with respect to F of functional dependency if all function at dependencies in F^+ of the form $\alpha \to \beta$, where $\alpha \le R$ and $\beta \le R$ atleast one of the following folds.

* $\alpha \to \beta$ is trial functional dependency.
* α is superkey of R.

(2) In 3NF, we find lossless join, dependency per serving decomposition.

23. (*a*) Following diagram shows the functional dependencies in the relation :

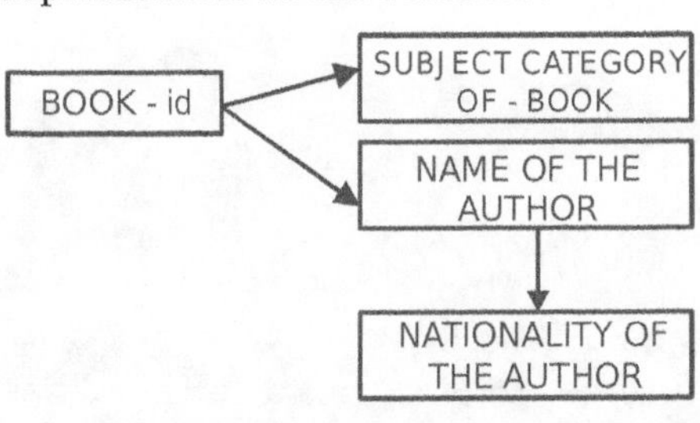

Nationality of the Author transitively depends on Book -id, primary key. So it can't be in the 3NF but is in the 2NF.

(*b*) Following diagrams shows the functional dependencies in the relation :

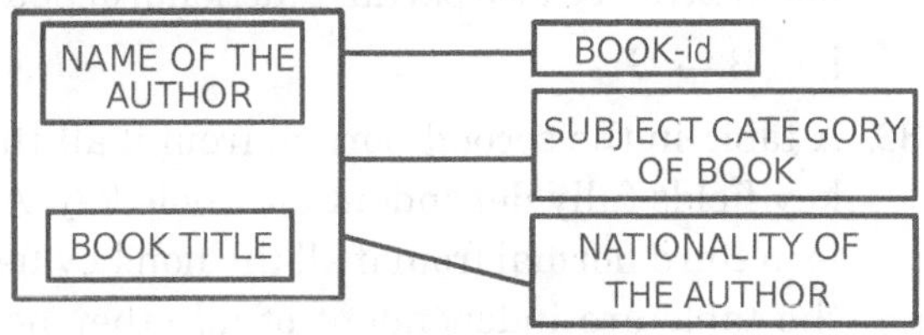

The above relation is in 3NF.

24. R (S T U V)

S → T

T → U

U → V

V → S

R decomposed into R_1 & R^2

and $R_1 \cap R_2 = \phi$, so it is not in 2 NF_1 3 NF and BCNF.

25. Every BCNF relation is also in 3NF , but reverse is not true, so to make a guaranteed identification we use BCNF defination.

26. Condidate key's are ⇒ { name, course No }

⇒ { Roll no, course No }

so Relation is in 3NF because there is not any partial functional dependencies.

27. Relation is in 2NF because key contain only one attribute (empcode), so there does not exists any partial functional dependency. But there is a transitive dependency so not in 3 NF.

28. R (F, F_2, F_3,F_4,F_5)

fd's = $F_1 \to F_3$

$F_2 \to F_4$

$(F_1, F_2) \to F_5$

key is (F_1, F_2) so not in 2NF because there is a partial functional dependencies in 1_{st} fd's.

29. Note that B.C.N.F. is not dependency-preserving in all cases.

30. In BCNF, a prime attribute cannot be transitively dependent on a key.

31. R (A, B, C, D, E, P, G)

AB → CD

DE → P

C → E

P → C

B → G

(a, b)

not in 2NF because partial functional dependancy

i. e. B → G

32. A table in the second normal from if all the non key fields fully dependent on whole key. A table is in third normal from if all the non key fields of the table are independent of all other non key field of table.

Alternately

If we have a function dependency of kind

{A, B} → {C, D}

C → B

then Tables are not in BCNF, so Book is not in BCNF.

If a non key value is depndent on other non key, then table is not in 3NF, of Book is also not in 3NF and collection is in 3NF.

33. Option A is false since BCNF is stricter than 3NF

Option B is false since the definition given here is of 2NF

Option C is true, since BCNF is stricter than 3NF, every relation in BCNF satisfies all the properties of 3NF.

34. It is 2NF because initially it contains partial dependency.

35. Schema II : Registration (<u>rollno, courseid</u>, email)

Primary key [<u>rollno, courseid</u>]

Non-trivial functional dependencies:

{rollno, courseid → email

email → rollno}

candidate keys {<u>rollno, courseid,</u>}

<u>email courseid</u>}

Given relation is in 3NF but not in BCNF.

36. Suppliers (Sid, Sname, City, Street)

Sid Street City → Sname

Sname City → Sid Street

Sid → Sname City Street

4 CHAPTER

Transaction Processing Concept

Analysis of Previous GATE Papers

Topics ↓	Year →		2019	2018	2017 Set 1	2017 Set 2	2016 Set 1	2016 Set 2	2015 Set 1	2015 Set 2	2015 Set 3
TRANSACTION SYSTEM	1 Mark	MCQ Type					1			1	
		Numerical Type									
	2 Marks	MCQ Type									
		Numerical Type									
	Total						1			1	
SERIALIZABILITY & SCHEDULE	1 Mark	MCQ Type						1			
		Numerical Type									
	2 Marks	MCQ Type									
		Numerical Type									
	Total							1			
RECOVERABILITY	1 Mark	MCQ Type									
		Numerical Type									
	2 Marks	MCQ Type						1			
		Numerical Type									
	Total							2			
TESTING OF SERIALIZABILITY	1 Mark	MCQ Type									
		Numerical Type									
	2 Marks	MCQ Type									
		Numerical Type									
	Total										
LOCKING TEC FOR CONCURRENCY CONTROL	1 Mark	MCQ Type									
		Numerical Type									
	2 Marks	MCQ Type					1				
		Numerical Type									
	Total						2				
CONFLICT & VIEW SERIALIZABILITY	1 Mark	MCQ Type									
		Numerical Type									
	2 Marks	MCQ Type									
		Numerical Type				1					
	Total					2					
RECOVERY FROM TRANSACTION FAILURE	1 Mark	MCQ Type								1	
		Numerical Type									
	2 Marks	MCQ Type			1						1
		Numerical Type									
	Total				2					1	2

TRANSACTION SYSTEM

1. A company maintains records of sales made by its salespersons and pays them commission based on each individual's total sales made in a year. This data is maintained in a table with following schema:

   salesinfo = (salespersonid, totalsales, commission)

   In a certain year, due to better business results, the company decides to further reward its salespersons by enhancing the commission paid to them as per the following formula:

   If commission < = 50000, enhance it by 2%

   If 50000 < commission < = 100000, enhance it by 4%

   If commission > 100000, enhance it by 6%

   The IT staff has written three different SQL scripts to calculate enhancement for each slab, each of these scripts is to run as a separate transaction as follows:

   T1 Update salesinfo

   Set commission = commission * 1.02

   Where commission < = 50000;

   T2 Update salesinfo

   Set commission = commission * 1.04

   Where commission > 50000 and commission is < = 100000;

   T3 Update salesinfo

   Set commission = commission * 1.06

   Where commission > 100000;

   Which of the following options of running these transactions will update the commission of all salespersons correctly?

   (a) Execute T1 followed by T2 followed by T3 (b) Execute T2, followed by T3; T1 running concurrently throughout

   (c) Execute T3 followed by T2; T1 running concurrently throughout

   (d) Execute T3 followed by T2 followed by T1

   [2005 : 2 Marks]

2. Amongst the ACID properties of a transaction, the 'Durability' property requires that the changes made to the database by a successful transaction persist

   (a) Except in case of an Operation System crash

   (b) Except in case of a Disk crash

   (c) Except in case of a power failure

   (d) Always, even if there is a failure of any kind

   [2005 : 1 Mark]

3. Consider the following transaction involving two bank accounts x and y.

   Read (x); $x: = x - 50$; write (x); read (y); $y: = y + 50$; write (y)

   The constant that the sum of the accounts x and y should remain constant is that of

   (a) Atomicity

   (b) Consistency

   (c) Isolation

   (d) Durability

   [2015 (Set-2): 1 Mark]

4. Which one of the following is NOT a part of the ACID properties of database transactions?

   (a) Atomic

   (b) Consistency

   (c) Isolation

   (d) Deadlock-freedom

   [2016 (Set-1) : 1 Mark]

SERIALIZABILITY & SCHEDULE

5. For the schedule given below, which of the following is correct?

1. Read A	2. Read B
3. Write A	4. Read A
5. Write A	6. Write B
7. Read B	8. Write B

   (a) This schedule is serializable and can occur in a scheme using 2PL protocol.

   (b) This schedule is serializable but cannot occur in a scheme using 2PL protocol.

   (c) This schedule is not serializable but can occur in a scheme using 2PL protocol.

   (d) This schedule is serializable and cannot occur in a scheme using 2PL protocol.

   [1999 : 2 Marks]

6. Suppose a database schedule S involves transactions $T_1, \ldots T_n$. Construct the precedence graph of S with vertices representing the transactions and edges representing the conflicts. If S is serializable, which one of the following orderings of the vertices of the precedence graph is guaranteed to yield a serial schedule?

   (a) Topological order

   (b) Depth-first order

   (c) Breadth-first order

   (d) Ascending order of transaction indices

   [2016 (Set-2) : 1 Mark]

RECOVERABILITY

7. Which of the following scenarios may lead to an irrecoverable error in a database system?

(a) A transaction writes a data item after it is read by an uncommitted transaction

(b) A transaction reads a data item after it is read by an uncommitted transaction

(c) A transaction reads a data item after it is written by a committed transaction

(d) A transaction reads a data item after it is written by an uncommitted transaction

[2003 : Mark]

8. Consider the following log sequence of two transactions on a bank account, with initial balance 12000, that transfer 2000 to a mortgage payment and, then apply a 5% interest.

1. T1: start
2. T1: B old = 12000, new = 10000
3. T1: M old = 0, new = 2000
4. T1: commit
5. T2: start
6. T2: B old = 10000, new = 10500
7. T2: commit

Suppose the database system crashed just before log record 7 is written. When the system is restarted, which one statement is true of the recovery procedure?

(a) We must redo log record 6 to set B to 10500

(b) We must undo log record 6 to set B to 10000 and then redo log records 2 and 3

(c) We need not redo log records 2 and 3 because transaction T1 has committed

(d) We can apply redo and undo operations in arbitrary order because they are idempotent

[2006 : 1 Mark]

9. Consider the following database schedule with two transactions, T_1 and T_2.

$S = r_2(X); r_1(X); r_2(Y); w_1(X); r_1(Y); w_2(X); a_1; a_2$

where $r_i(Z)$ denoted a *read* operation by transaction T_i on a variable Z, $w_i(Z)$ denotes a *write* operation by T_i on a variable Z and a_i denotes an *abort* by transation T_i.

Which one of the following statements about the above schedule is **TRUE**?

(a) S is non-recoverable

(b) S is recoverable, but has a cascading abort

(c) S does not have a cascading abort

(d) S is strict

[2016 (Set-2): 2 Marks]

TESTING OF SERIALIZABILITY

10. Consider three data item D1, D2, and D3, and the following execution schedule of transactions T1, T2, and T3. In the diagram, R(D) and W(D) denote the actions reading and writing the data item D respectively.

T1	T2	T3
	R(D3);	
	R(D2);	
	W(D2);	
		R(D2);
		R(D3);
R(D1);		
W(D1);		
		W(D2);
		W(D3);
	R(D1);	
R(D2);		
W(D2);		
	W(D1);	

(a) The schedule is serializable as T2; T3; T1;

(b) The schedule is serializable as T2; T1; T3;

(c) The schedule is serializable as T3; T2; T1;

(d) The schedule is not serializable

[2003 : 2 Marks]

11. Consider the following schedule S of transactions T1 and T2:

T1	T2
Read(A)	
A=A-10	
	Read(A)
	Temp = 0.2*A
	Write(A)
	Read(B)
Write(A)	
Read(B)	
B = B + 10	
Write(B)	
	B = B + Temp
	Write(B)

Which of the following is TRUE about the schedule S?

(a) S is serializable only as T1, T2

(b) S is serializable only as T2, T1

(c) S is serializable both as T1, T2 and T2, T1

(d) S is not serializable either as T1 or as T2

[2004 : 2 Marks]

12. Consider the following schedule for transactions T1, T2 and T3:

T1	**T2**	**T3**
Read (X)		
	Read (Y)	
		Read (Y)
	Write (Y)	
Write (X)		
		Write (X)
	Read (X)	
	Write (X)	

Which one of the schedules below is the correct serialization of the above?

(a) T1 → T3 → T2 (b) T2 → T1 → T3

(c) T2 → T3 → T1 (d) T3 → T1 → T2

[2010 : 2 Marks]

13. Consider the following two statements about database transaction schedules:

I. Strict two-phase locking protocol generates conflict serializable schedules that are also recoverable.

II. Timestamp-ordering concurrency control protocol with Thomas' Write Rule can generate view serializable schedules that are not conflict serializable.

Which of the above statements is/are TRUE?

(a) Both I and II

(b) II only

(c) I only

(d) Neither I nor II

LOCKING TEC FOR CONCURRENCY CONTROL

14. Which level of locking provides the highest degree of concurrency in a relation database?

(a) Page

(b) Table

(c) Row

(d) Page, table and row level locking allow the same degree of concurrency **[2004 : 1 Mark]**

15. Consider the following two transactions : T_1 and T2.

T_1:	T_2:
read(A); read(B) If A = 0 then B → B +1; write (B);	read(B); read(A) If B ≠ 0 than A → A − 1; write (A);

Which of the following schemes, using shared and exclusive locks, satisfy the requirements for strict two phase locking for the above transactions?

(a)

S1 :	**S2 :**
lock S(A);	lock S(B);
read (A);	read (B);
lock S(B);	lock S(A);
read (B);	read (A);
if A = 0	if B ≠ 0
then B ← B + 1;	then A ← A − 1;
write (B);	write (A);
commit;	commit;
unlock (B);	unlock (A);

(b)

S1 :	**S2 :**
lock X(A);	lock X(B);
read(A);	read(B);
lock X(B);	lock X(A);
read (B);	read (A);
if A = 0	if B ≠ 0
then B ← B + 1	then A ← A − 1
write (B);	write (A);
unlock (A);	unlock (A);
commit;	commit;
unlock (B);	unlock (A);

(c)

S1 :	**S2 :**
lock S(A);	lock S(B);
read(A);	read(B);
lock X(B);	lock X(A);
read (B);	read (A);
if A = 0	if B ≠ 0
then B ← B + 1;	then A ← A − 1;
write (B);	write (A);
unlock (A);	unlock (A);
commit;	commit;
unlock (B);	unlock (A);

(d)

S1 :	**S2 :**
lock S(A);	lock S(B);
read(A);	read(B);
lock X(B);	lock X(A);
read (B);	read (A);
if A = 0	if B ≠ 0
then B ← B + 1;	then A ← A − 1;
write (B);	write (A);
unlock (A);	unlock (A);
unlock (B);	unlock (B);
commit;	commit;

[2007 : 2 marks]

16. Which of the following concurrency control protocols ensure both conflict serializablity and freedom from deadlock?

I. 2-phase locking

II. Time-stamp ordering

(a) I only

(b) II only

(c) Both I and II

(d) Neither I nor II

[2010 : 1 Mark]

17. Consider the following two phase locking protocol. Suppose a transaction T accesses (for read or write operations), a certain set of objects $\{O_1,..,O_k\}$. This is done in the following manner:

Step 1. T a acquires exclusive locks to $O_1,..,O_k$ in increasing order of their addresses.

Step 2. The required operations are performed.

Step 3. All locks are released.

This protocol will

(a) guarantee serializability and deadlock-freedom

(b) guarantee neither serializability nor deadlock-freedom

(c) guarantee serializability but not deadlock-freedom

(d) guarantee deadlock-freedom but not serializability **[2016 (Set-1): 2 Marks]**

CONFLICT & VIEW SERIALIZABILITY

18. Consider the following schedules involving two transactions. Which one of the following statements is TRUE?

$S_1 : r_1(X);r_1(Y);r_2(X);r_2(Y); w_2(Y); w_1(X)$

$S_2 : r_1(X);r_2(X);r_2(Y); W_2(Y); R_1(Y); w_1(X)$

(a) Both S_1 and S_2 are conflict serializable

(b) S_1 is conflict serializable and S_2 is not conflict serializable

(c) S_1 is not conflict serializable and S_2 is conflict serializable

(d) Both S_1 and S_2 are not conflict serializable

[2007 : 2 Marks]

19. Consider the following three schedules of transactions T1, T2 and T3. [Notation: In the following NYO represents the action Y (R for read W for write) performed by transaction N on object O].

S1: 2RA 2WA 3RC 2WB 3WA 3WC 1RA 1RB 1WA 1WB

S2: 3RC 2RA 2WA 2WB 3WA 1RA 1RB 1WA 1WB 3WC

S3: 2RA 3RC 3WA 2WA 2WB 3WC 1RA 1RB 1WA WB

Which of the following statements is TRUE?

(a) S1, S2 and S3 are all conflict equivalent to each other

(b) No two of S1, and S2 and S3 are conflict equivalent to each other

(c) S2 is conflict equivalent to S3, but not to S1

(d) S1 is conflict equivalent to S2, but not to S3

[2008 : 2 Marks]

20. Consider two transactions T_1 and T_2, and four schedules S_1, S_2, S_3, S_4 of T_1 and T_2 as given below:

$T_1 : R_1[x]\ W_1\ [x]\ W_1[y]$

$T_2 : R_2[x]\ R_2\ [y]\ W_2[y]$

$S_1 : R_1[x]\ R_2[x]\ R_2[x]\ W_1[x]\ W_1[y]\ W_2[y]$

$S_2 : R_1[x]\ R_2[x]\ R_2[y]\ W_1[x]\ W_2[y]\ W_1[y]$

$S_3 : R_1[x]\ W_1[x]\ R_2[x]\ W_1[y]\ R_2[y]\ W_2[y]$

$S_4 : R_2[x]\ R_2[y]\ R_1[x]\ W_1[x]\ W_1[y]\ W_2[y]$

Which of the above schedules are conflict serialazable?

(a) S_1 and S_2 (b) S_2 and S_3

(c) S_3 only (d) S_4 only

[2009 : 2 Marks]

21. Consider the following transactions with data items P and Q initialized to zero:

T_1 : read (P);
Read (Q);
if P = 0 then Q: = Q + 1;
write (Q);

T_2 : read (Q);
read (P);
if Q = 0 then P: = P + 1;
write (P);

Any non-serial interleaving of T_1 and T_2 for concurrent execution leads to

(a) a serializable schedule

(b) a schedule that is not conflict serializable

(c) a conflict serializable schedule

(d) a schedule for which a precedence graph cannot be drawn **[2012 : 2 Marks]**

22. Consider the following four schedules dues to three transactions (indicated by the subscript) using *read* and *write* on a data item x, denoted by r(x) and w(x) respectively. Which one of them is conflict serializable?

(a) $r_1(x); r_2(x); w_1(x); r_3(x); w_2(x)$

(b) $r_2(x); r_1(x); w_2(x); r_3(x); w_1(x)$

(c) $r_3(x); r_2(x); r_1(x); w_2(x); w_1(x)$

(d) $r_2(x); w_2(x); r_3(x); r_1(x); w_1(x)$

[2014 (Set-1) : 2 Marks]

23. Consider the following schedule S of transactions T1, T2, T3 and T4:

T1	T2	T3	T4
	Reads (X)		
		Writes (X)	
		Commit	
Writes (X)			
Commit	Writes (Y)		
	Reads (Z)		
	Commit		
			Reads (X)
			Reads (Y)
			Commit

Which one of the following statements is correct?

(a) **S** is conflict-serializable but not recoverable

(b) **S** is conflict-serializable but is recoverable

(c) **S** is both conflict-serializable and recoverable

(d) **S** is neither conflict-serializable nor is it recoverable

[2014 (Set-2) : 2 Marks]

24. Consider the transactions *T*1, *T*2, and *T*3 and the schedules *S*1 and *S*2 given below.

*T*1: *r*1 (*X*); *r*1 (*Z*); *w*1 (*X*); *w*1 (*Z*)

*T*2: *r*2 (*Y*); *r*2 (*Z*); *w*2 (*Z*)

*T*3; *r*3 (*Y*); *r*3 (*X*); *w*3 (*Y*)

S1 : *r*1(*X*); *r*3 (*Y*); *r*3 (*X*); *r*2 (*Y*); *r*2 (*Z*); *w*3 (*Y*); *w*2 (*Z*); *r*1(*Z*); *w*1 (*X*); *w*1 (*Z*)

S2 : *r*1(*X*); *r*3 (*Y*); *r*2 (*Y*); *r*3 (*X*); *r*1 (*Z*); *r*2(*Z*); *w*3 (*Y*); *w*1 (*X*); *w*2 (*Z*); *w*1 (*Z*)

Which one of the following statements about the schedules is **TRUE**?

(a) Only S1 is conflict-serializable.

(b) Only S2 is conflict-serializable.

(c) Both S1 and S2 are conflict-serializable.

(d) Neither S1 nor S2 is conflict-serializable.

[2014 (Set-3) : 2 Marks]

25. Twp transactions T_1 and T_2 are given as

T_1: $r_1(X)\ w_1(X)\ r_1(Y)\ w_1(Y)$

T_2: $r_1(Y)\ w_2(Y)\ r_2(Z)\ w_2(Z)$

where r_i(V) denotes a read operation by transaction T_i on a variable V and $w_i(V)$ denotes a write operation by transaction T_i on a variable V. The total number of conflict serializable schedules that can be formed by T_1 and T_2 is ________.

[2017 (Set-2) : 2 Marks]

RECOVERY FROM TRANSACTION FAILURE

26. Consider a simple checkpointing protocol and the following set of operations in the log.

(start, T4; (write, T4, y, 2, 3); (start, T1); (commit, T4); (write, T1, z, 5, 7);

(checkpoint);

(start, T2; (write, T2, x, 1, 9); (commit, T2); (start, T3); (write, T3, z, 7, 2);

If a crash happens now and the system tries to recover using both undo and redo operations, what are the contents of the undo list and the redo list.

(a) Undo: T3, T1; Redo: T2

(b) Undo: T3, T1; Redo: T2, T4

(c) Undo: none; Redo: T2, T4, T3, T1

(d) Undo: T3, T1; T4; Redo: T2

[2015 (Set-2): 1 Mark]

27. Consider the following partial Schedule *S* involving two transactions *T*1 and *T*2. Only the *read* and the *write* operations have been shown. The *read* operation on data item P is denoted by *read*(*P*) and the *write* operation on data item *P* is denoted by *write* (*P*).

Time instanc	Transacation-id *T*1	*T*2
1	*Read(A)*	
2	*write(A)*	
3		*read (C)*
4		*write(C)*
5		*read (B)*
6		*write (B)*
7		*read (A)*
8		*commit*
9	*read (B)*	

Suppose that the transaction $T1$ fails immediately after time instance 9. Which one of the following statements is correct?

(a) $T2$ must be aborted and then both $T1$ and $T2$ must be restarted to ensure transaction atomicity

(b) Schedule S is nonrecoverable and cannot ensure transaction atomicity

(c) Only $T2$ must be aborted and then restarted to ensure transaction atomicity

(d) Schedule S is recoverable and can ensure atomicity and nothing else needs to be done

[2015 (Set-3) : 2 Marks]

28. In a database system, unique timestamps are assigned to each transaction using Lamport's logical clock. Let $TS(T_1)$ and $TS(T_2)$ be the timestamps of transactions T_1 and T_2 respectively. Besides, T_1 holds a lock on the resource R and T_2 has requested a conflicting lock on the same resource R. The following algorithm is used to prevent deadlocks in the database system assuming that a killed transaction is restarted with the same timestamp.

if $TS(T_2) < TS(T_1)$ then
    T_1 is killed
Else T_2 waits

Assume any transaction that is not killed terminates eventually. Which of the following is TRUE about the database system that uses the above algorithm to prevent deadlocks?

(a) The database system is both deadlock-free and starvation-free.

(b) The database system is deadlock-free but not starvation-free.

(c) The database system is starvation-free, but not deadlock-free.

(d) The database system is neither deadlock-free nor starvation-free.

[2017 (Set-1) : 2 Marks]

ANSWERS

1. (*d*)	**2.** (*d*)	**3.** (*b*)	**4.** (*d*)	**5.** (*d*)	**6.** (*a*)	**7.** (*d*)	**8.** (*c*)	**9.** (*c*)	**10.** (*c*)
11. (*d*)	**12.** (*a*)	**13.** (*a*)	**14.** (*c*)	**15.** (*c*)	**16.** (*b*)	**17.** (*a*)	**18.** (*c*)	**19.** (*d*)	**20.** (*b*)
21. (*b*)	**22.** (*d*)	**23.** (*c*)	**24.** (*a*)	**25.** (54)	**26.** (*a*)	**27.** (*b*)	**28.** (*a*)		

EXPLANATIONS

1. T_3 followed by T_2 followed by T_1 gives correct execution sequence
2. The Result of transaction should persist always, even if there is a failure of any kind
3. Consistency : Consistancy properly ensure that any transaction will bring the database from one valid state to another

read (x);	
x : = x – 50;	
write (x) ;	
	read (y);
	y : = y + 50;
	write (y)

4. 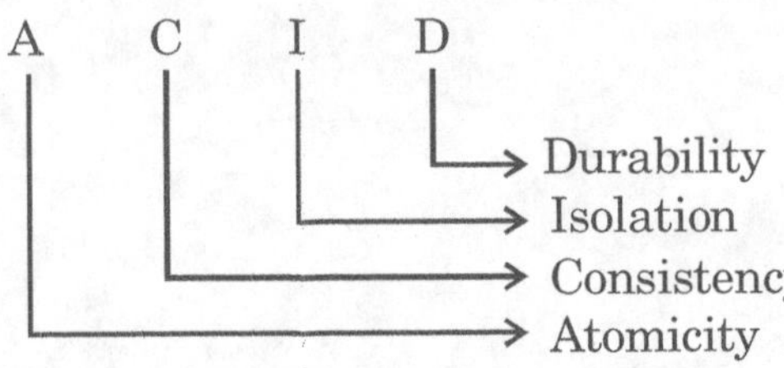

5. 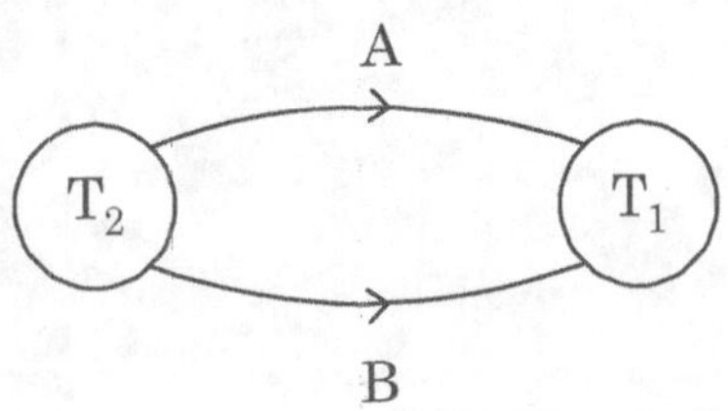

* not conflict serializable and not view serializable schedule and cannot occur is a scheme of 2 PL.

6. If a schedule(s) is serializable, the topological order of a graph (also called precedence graph) yields a serial schedule.
7. If data is uncommitted, then transactions reads a data after write always give error.
8. Once a transaction commits, the changes made by it to the database get permanent and there is no effect of system failure over the data. Since T_2 is not allowed to commit, we must undo log record 6.
9. As there is no dirty-read in the given schedule, the schedule is both recoverable and cascadeless.

10.

T_1	T_2	T_3
	R (D3);	
	R (D2);	
	W (D2);	
		R (D2);
		W (D1);
R (D1);		
W (D1);		
R (D2);	R (D1);	W (D2);
W (D2);	W (D1);	W (D3);

In transation T_3 R(D2) is conflict with original R (D2), because R (D2) is read W (D2).
Again an transaction T_2, R (D1) is conflict with R (D1) in T_1 because it read (D1) as W (D1)
In transaction T_1, R(D2) conflicts with R(D2) in T_2, because it is W(D2) in T_2.
So, finally transaction is conflict serialization schedule as T_3 ; T_2; T_1.

11. In question option d is wrong correct option is S is not serializable either as T_1 or as T_2
There is a cycle in Precedance graph of transaction so it is and conflict
i. e. $W_2(D_2) \rightarrow W_1(D_1)\{T_2 \rightarrow T_1\}$
$W1(D_1)\ R2(D_1)\{T_1 \rightarrow T_2\}$
so schedule is not serializable.

12. By using the precedence graph we can solve this problem

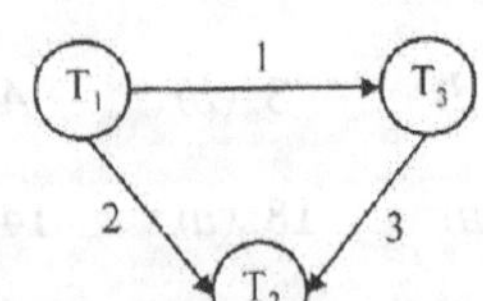

1. Read (x) in T_1 is followed by write (x) in T_2
2. Read (x) in T_1 is followed by write (x) in T_3
3. Read (y) in T_3 is followed by write (y) in T_2

So it in clear from precedence graph

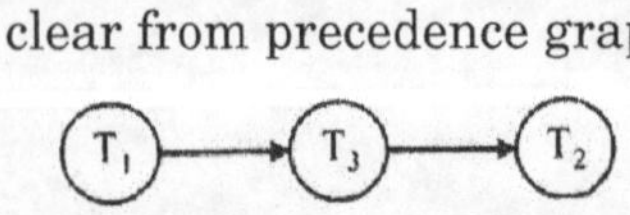

13. I. Strict 2PL guaranteed conflict serializable because of 2PL condition and also strict recoverable.
II. Timestamp-ordering concurrency control protocol with Thomas' Write Rule can generate view serializable schedules that are not conflict serializable.

14. Row Level locking provides more concurrency, because different transation can access different rows, in table

15. In strict 2PL :- exclusive locks should be released before the commit and it must be in 2PL

In option C if both execute serial order without concurrency then that is perfectly valid and yes it follows strict 2PL.

16. Only Time - stamp protocol gives freedom from delock and ensure comflict serializable schedule.

17. The given step's define the consenvative 2PL. In concentrative 2PL protect, a transaction has Lock all the item it access before the transection begins execution. So it used to avoid deadlock. Also 2PL gives guarantees of serviceability.

18. HereS_1 is not conflict serializable whereas S_2 is conflict serializable.

19.

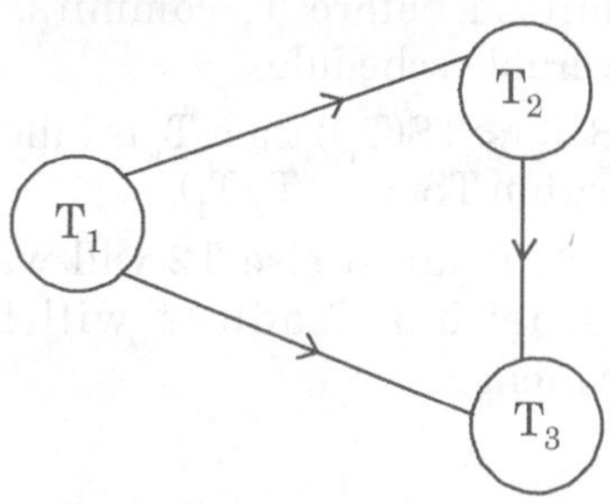

S_1 is :-
conflict serializable

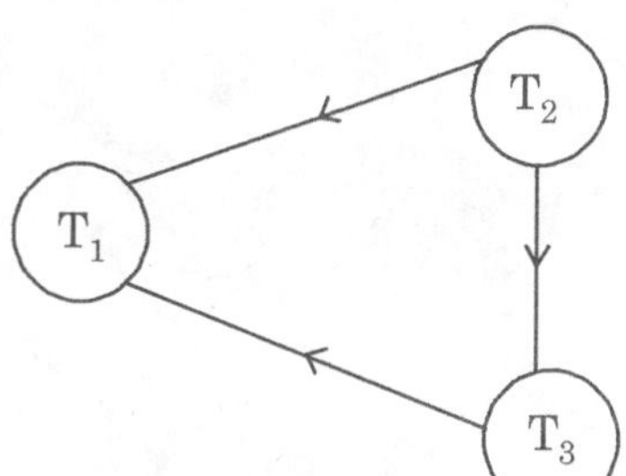

$S_2$is
confililct serializable

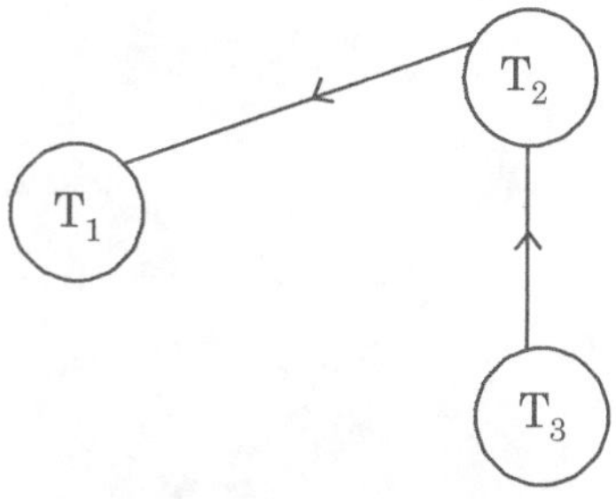

S_3 is not
conflict serializable

So S_1 and S_2 are conflict equivalent but S_3 is not

20.

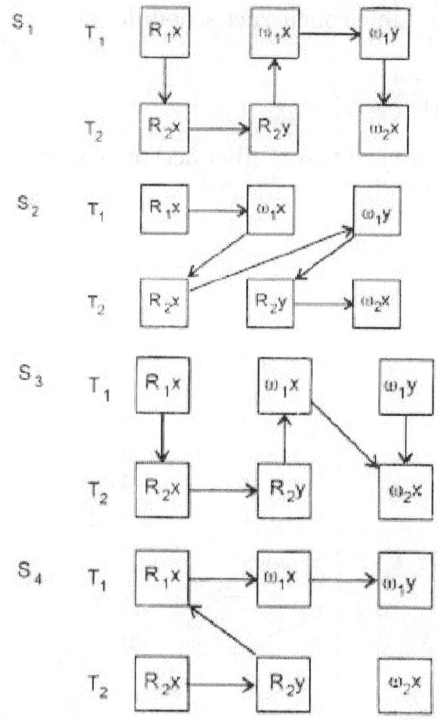

Clearly S_2 and S_3 are conflict - serializable.

21.

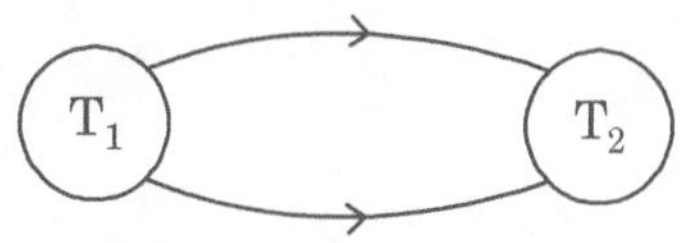

not conflict serializable s

22.

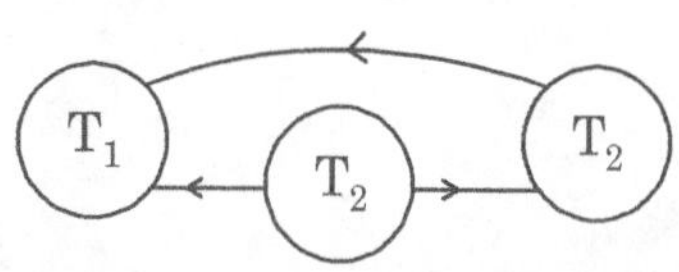

not only cycle so conflict serializable

23. Since, the graph contains no cycle, that's why it is called conflict serializable.

Since, in this schedule, transaction reads data item previously written by committed transactions. The commit operation of former transactions occur before later transactions, hence it is recoverable also. That's why 'S' is both conflict serializable and recoverable.

24. Precedence graph for S_1 & S_2 are as follows

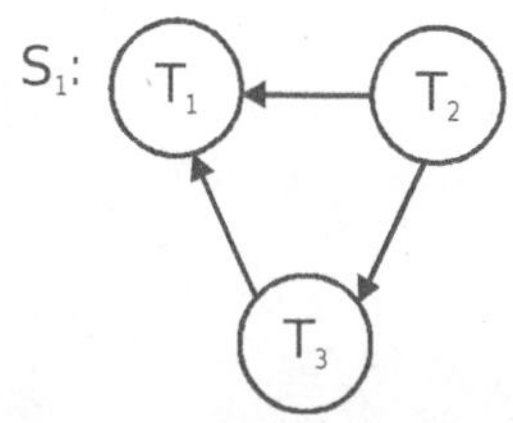

No cycle

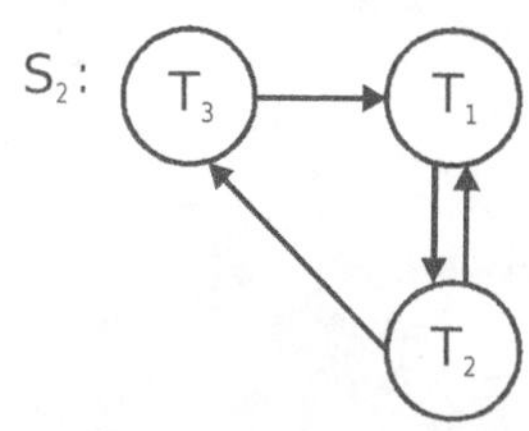

Cycle

∴ Only S_1 is conflict serializable.

25. Total possible concurrect schedule

is $\Rightarrow \dfrac{(4+4)!}{4!*4!} = 70$

Now there are two conflict actions possible

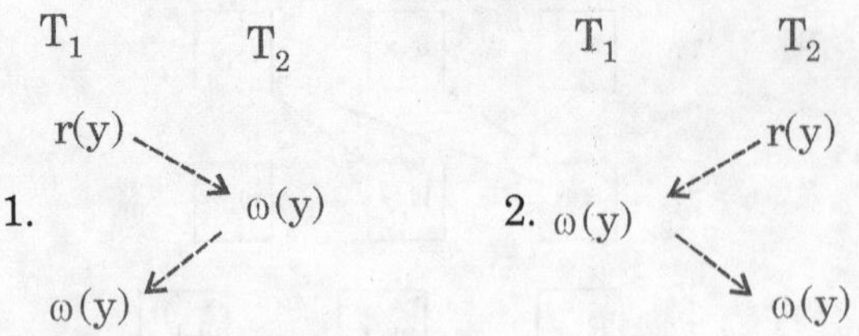

Case 2

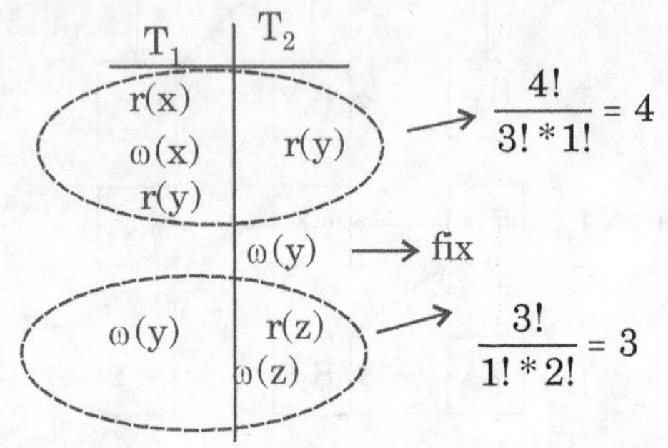

Total no of permutations

Case 2

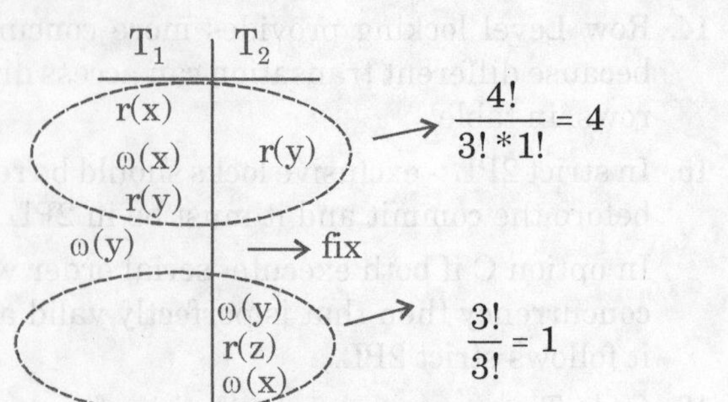

Total no. of permutations = 4 ×1 = 4

Total no. of conflict serial schdules are = 79 – 12 – 4 = 54

26. Undo T_3, T_{ij} Redo T_2

T_1 and T_3 will be undo, the transaction after checkpoint is T_2 which must be redo.

27. T_2 is reading the value written by T_1 and getting committed before T_1 commits. So it is non-recoverable schedule.

28. if ($TS(T_2) < TS(T_1)$) then T_1 is killed According to Algorithm $TS(T_2) < T_2(T_1)$

then T1 is killed else T2 will wait. So in both cases neither deadlock will happen nor - starration.

5

CHAPTER

File Structures

Analysis of Previous GATE Papers											
	Year → Topics ↓		2019	2018	2017 Set 1	2017 Set 2	2016 Set 1	2016 Set 2	2015 Set 1	2015 Set 2	2015 Set 3
FI LE STRUCTURES (B+ TREE)	1 Mark	MCQ Type	1					1			
		Numerical Type					1			1	
	2 Marks	MCQ Type									
		Numerical Type				1					1
	Total		1			2	1	1		1	2

FILE STRUCTURES (B+ TREE)

1. Consider the following directed graph:

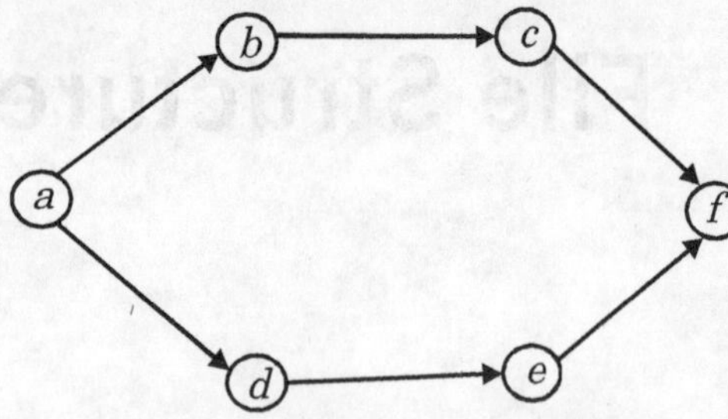

The number of different topological ordering of the vertices of the graph is ___________.

[2016 (Set-1): 1 Mark]

2. Which of the following is correct?
   (a) B-trees are for storing data on disk and B^+ trees are for main memory.
   (b) Range queries are faster on B^+ trees.
   (c) B-trees are for primary indexes and B^+ trees are for secondary indexes.
   (d) The height of a B^+ tree is independent of the number of records.

[1999: 1 Mark]

3. B^+ –trees are preferred to binary trees in database because
   (a) Disk capacities are greater than memory capacities
   (b) Disk access is much slower than memory access
   (c) Disk data transfer rates are much less than memory data transfer rates
   (d) Disks are more reliable than memory

[2000 : 1 Mark]

4. AB^+ tree index is to be built on the Name attribute of the relation STUDENT. Assume that all student names are of length 8 bytes, disk blocks are of size 512 bytes, and index pointers are of size 4 bytes. Given this scenario, what would be the best choice of the degree (i.e. the number of pointers pernode) of the B^+ - tree?
   (a) 16 (b) 42
   (c) 43 (d) 44

[2002 : 2 Marks]

5. The order of an internal node in a B^+ tree index is the maximum number of children it can have. Suppose that a child pointer takes 6 bytes, the search field value takes 14 bytes, and the block size is 512 bytes. What is the order of the internal node?
   (a) 24 (b) 25
   (c) 26 (d) 27 **[2004 : 2 Marks]**

6. Consider a table T in a relational database with a key field K. A B-tree of order p is used as an access structure on K, where p denotes the maximum number of tree pointers in a B-tree index node. Assume that K is 10 bytes long; disk block size is 512 bytes; each data pointer P_D is 8 bytes long and each block pointer P_B is 5 bytes long. In order for each B-tree node to fit in a single disk block, the maximum value is p is
   (a) 20 (b) 22
   (c) 23 (d) 32

[2004 : 2 Marks]

7. Which one of the following is a key factor for preferring B^+-trees to binary search trees for indexing database relations?
   (a) Database relations have a large number of record
   (b) Database relations are sorted on the primary key
   (c) B^+-trees require less memory than binary search trees
   (d) Data transfer from disks is in blocks

[2005 : 1 Mark]

8. A B-Tree used as an index for a large database table has four levels including the root node. If a new key is inserted in this index, then the maximum number of nodes that could be newly created in the process are
   (a) 5 (b) 4
   (c) 3 (d) 2

[2005: 1 Mark]

9. In a database file structure, the search key field is 9 bytes long, the block size is 512 bytes, a record pointer is 7 bytes and a block pointer is 6 bytes. The largest possible order of a non-leaf node in a B^+ tree implementing this file structure is
   (a) 23 (b) 24
   (c) 34 (d) 44

[2006 : 2 Marks]

10. The order of a leaf node in B^+–tree is the maximum number of (value, data record pointer) pairs it can hold. Given that the block size is 1K bytes data record pointer is 7 bytes long, the value field is 9 bytes long and a block pointer is 6 bytes long, what is the order of the leaf node?
   (a) 63 (b) 64
   (c) 67 (d) 68

[2007: 2 Marks]

Directions for questions 11 to 12:
Consider the B+ tree in the adjoining figure, where each node has at most two keys and three links.

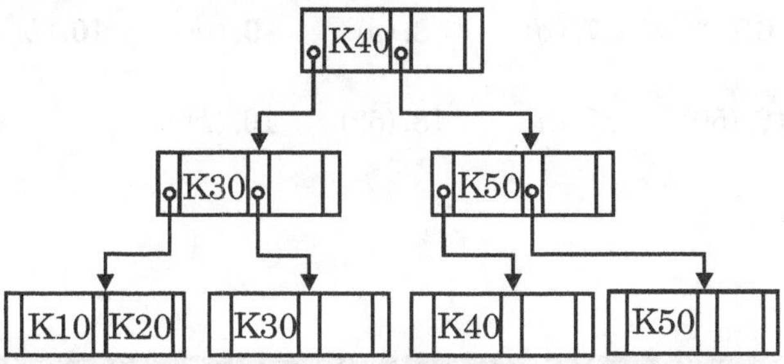

11. Keys K15 and then K25 are inserted into this tree in that order. Exactly how many of the following nodes (disregarding the links) will be present in the tree after the two insertions?

| K30 | K50 | | K25 | K30 | | K20 | K25 | | K50 | K20 |

(a) 1 (b) 2
(c) 3 (d) 4 **[2007: 2 Marks]**

12. Now the key K50 is deleted from the B+ trees resulting after the two insertions made earlier. Consider the following statements about the B+ tree resulting after this deletion.

(i) The height of the tree remains the same
(ii) The node | k20 | (disregarding the links) is present in the tree.
(iii) The root node remains unchanged (disregarding the links).

Which one of the following options is true?

(a) Statements (i) and (ii) are true
(b) Statements (i) and (iii) are true
(c) Statements (iii) and (i) are true
(d) All the statements are false

[2007 : 2 Marks]

13. The following key values are inserted into a B+-tree in which order of the internal nodes is 3, and that of the leaf nodes is 2, in the sequence given below. The order of internal nodes is the maximum number of data items that can be stored in it.

The B+- tree is initially empty.

10, 3, 6, 8, 4, 2, 1

The maximum number of times leaf nodes would get split up as a result of these insertions is

(a) 2 (b) 3
(c) 4 (d) 5 **[2009: 2 Marks]**

14. Consider a B+-tree in which the maximum number of keys in a node is 5. What is the minimum number of keys in any non-root node?

(a) 1 (b) 2
(c) 3 (d) 4

[2010: 1 Mark]

15. With reference to the B+ tree index of order 1 shown below, the minimum number of nodes (including the Root node) that must be fetched in order to satisfy the following query: "Get all records with a search key greater than or equal to 7 and less than 15" is ________.

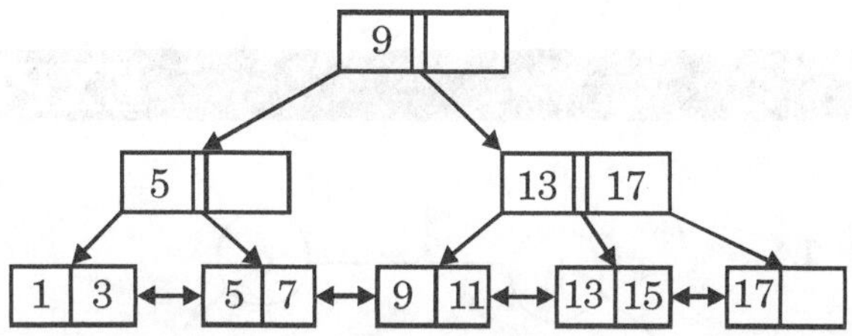

[2015 (Set-2) : 1 Mark]

16. Consider a B+ tree in which the search key is 12 bytes long, block size is 1024 bytes, record pointer is 10 bytes long and block pointer is 8 bytes long. The maximum number of keys that can be accommodated in each non-leaf node of the tree is____________.

[2015 (Set-3) : 2 Marks]

17. B+ Trees are considered BALANCED because

(a) the lengths of the paths from the root to all leaf nodes are all equal.
(b) the lengths of the paths from the root to all leaf nodes differ from each other by at most 1.
(c) the number of children of any two non-leaf sibling nodes differ by at most 1.
(d) the number of records in any two leaf nodes differ by at most 1.

[2016 (Set-2): 1 Mark]

18. In a B+ tree, if the search-key value is 8 bytes long, the block size is 512 bytes and the block pointer size is 2 bytes, then the maximum order of the B+ tree is __________.

[2017 (Set-2): 2 Marks]

19. Which one of the following statement is NOT correct about the B+ tree data structure used for creating an index of a relational database table?

(a) B+ Tree is a height-balanced tree
(b) Non-leaf nodes have pointers to data records
(c) Each leaf node has a pointer to the next leaf node
(d) Key values in each node are kept in sorted order

[2019 : 1 Mark]

ANSWERS

1. (6)	**2.** (*b*)	**3.** (*b*)	**4.** (*c*)	**5.** (*c*)	**6.** (*c*)	**7.** (*d*)	**8.** (*a*)	**9.** (*c*)	**10.** (*b*)
11. (*a*)	**12.** (*a*)	**13.** (*b*)	**14.** (*b*)	**15.** (5)	**16.** (50)	**17.** (*a*)	**18.** (52)	**19.** (*b*)	

EXPLANATIONS

1.

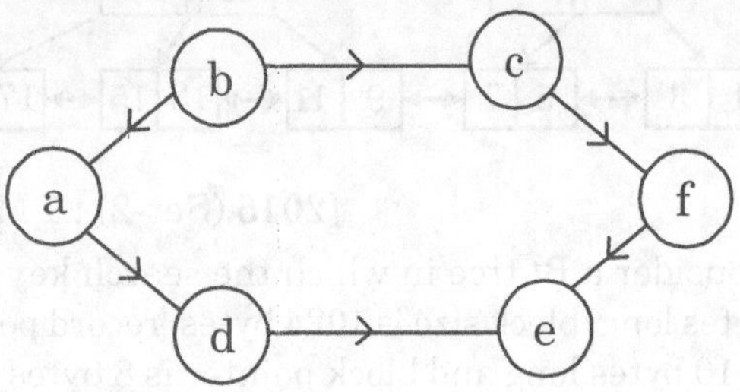

(1) a b c d e f

(2) a b d c e f

(3) a d e b c f

(4) a d b c e f

(5) a b d e c f

(6) a d b e c f

2. In a B⁺ tree, the leaf nodes are linked together to provide ordered access- hence, range queries are faster for B⁺ tress.

3. B_+ tree provides search in less number of disk hits. So disk access in faster by B_+ tree.

4. $(n - 1) * k + n * b = \text{block}$

$\{\because$ n is degree $\}$

$\Rightarrow (n - 1) * 8 + n * 4 = 512$

$12n = 520$

$n = \frac{520}{12} = 43$

5. Child pointer takes b byte

Search field= 14 byte

block size= 512 byte

The order of internal node is 9 + 14 + 3 = 26

6. B tree node contain

$n \rightarrow$ child pointer

$(n - 1) \rightarrow$ key

$(n - 1) \rightarrow$ Record. pointer

$n * 5 + (n-1) * 10 + (n - 1) * 8 \leq s\ 12$

$\boxed{n = 23}$

7. Because data transfer take place in the form of block's frame disk, so, any data structure which store as large as can, information in a single block is more efficient.

8. In case of complete full tree. if we insert a new key them at every level new node will be created. There are 4 level in worst case when root node is broken into two parts., tree will be increased with one more level.

So answer should be 5.

9. In B+ tree, non-leaf node contain

$(n - 1) \rightarrow$ key

$n \rightarrow$ block pointer

$o \rightarrow$ Record pointer

So $9 * (n - 1) + 6 * n \leq 512$

$\boxed{n = 34}$

10. Let the order be n

So, $n \times 7 + (n - 1) 9 = 1024$

$\Rightarrow 16n = 1033$

$\Rightarrow \quad n = \left\lceil \frac{1033}{16} \right\rceil = 64$

11. After inserting K_{15} tree is :-

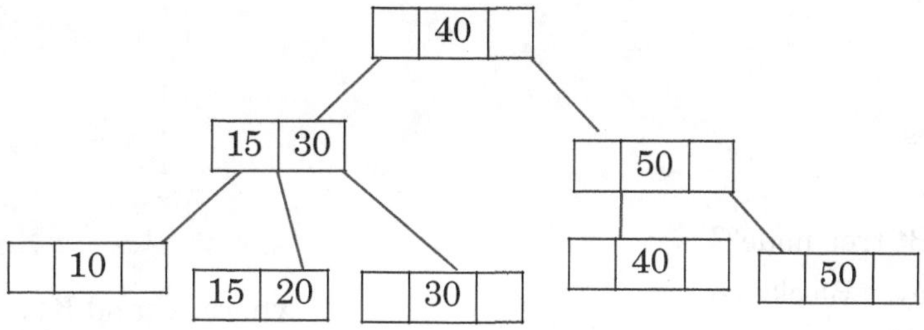

Now after inserting k_{25} tree is

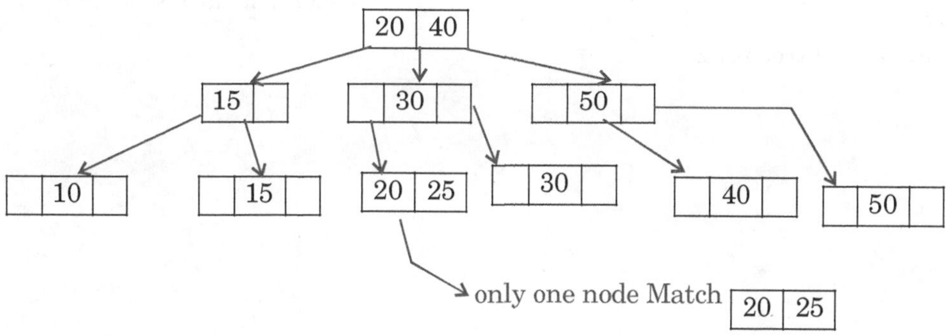

12. The root is 20 and height is remains the same.

final tree is

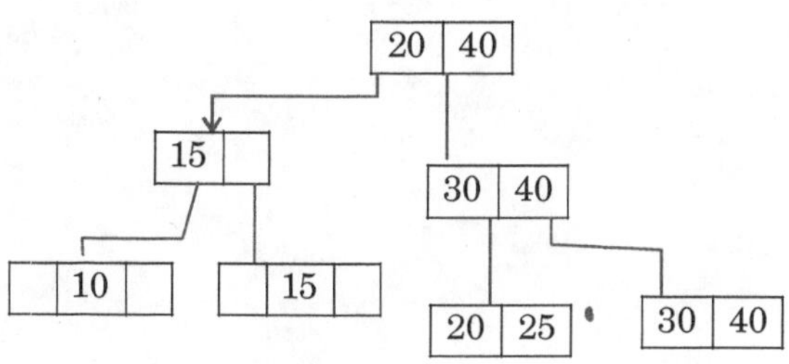

13.

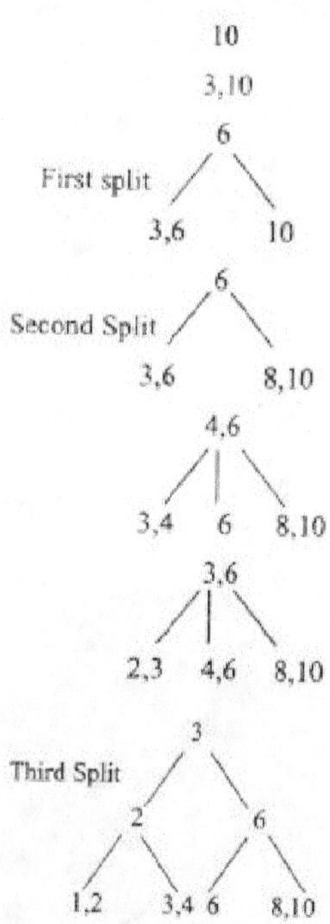

14. Minimum number of keys = $\left\lfloor \frac{n}{2} \right\rfloor = \left\lfloor \frac{5}{2} \right\rfloor = 2$

15. In given B^+ tree

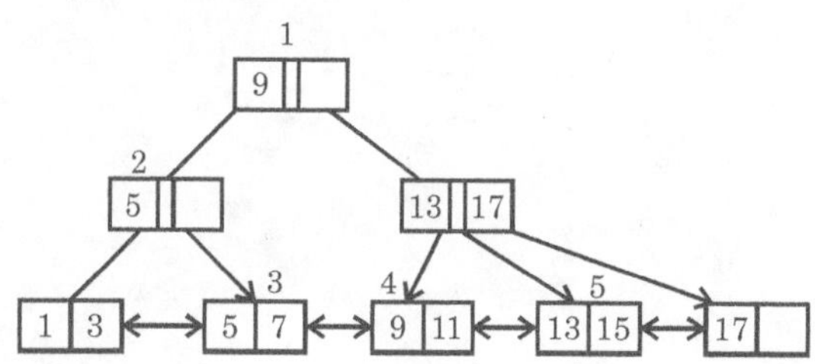

So to find greater than or equal to 7 and less than 15. It will fatch 5 nodes.

As shown in above diagram it may be

1 – 2 – 3 – 4 – 5

or

1 – 6 – 5 – 4– 3

Ans = 5

16. At B^+ tree non- leaf node of order n

→ (n –1) key

→ (n) child pointer

→ O Record point 8

So n * 8 + (n – 1) * 12 ≤ 024

n = 51

So No. of key = (n – 1)

= (51 – 1)

= 50

17. B^+ tree are balanced because, the length of path from the root to all leaf nodes are all equal.

18. B^+ tree

Search key : 8 bytes

Block size : 512 bytes

Block pointer : 2 bytes

Maximum order of B^+ tree node??

$P \times B_P + (P - 1) \times \text{Key} \le \text{Block size}$

$$P \times 2 + (P - 1)8 \le 512$$

$$10P \le 520$$

$$P = \left\lceil \frac{520}{10} \right\rceil = 52$$

Maximum order of B^+ tree is 52

19. • Below is the structure of B^+ tree non leaf node.

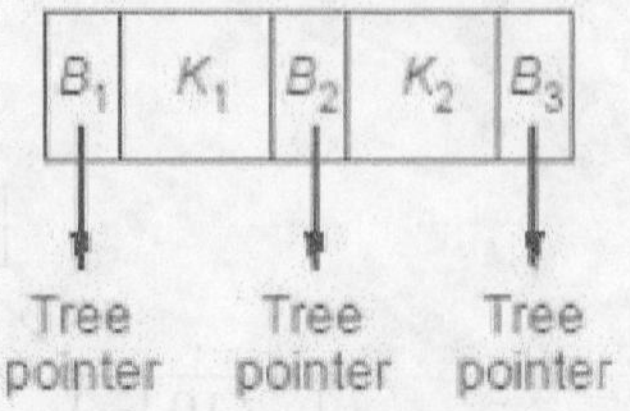

where K_1 and K_2 are keys

- B^+ tree non leaf node consists of only keys and tree pointers (node pointers).
- B^+ tree non leaf node have pointer to data records is false statement.

Unit - X

Computer Networks

Syllabus

Concept of layering. LAN technologies (Ethernet). Flow and error control techniques, switching. IPv4/IPv6, routers and routing algorithms (distance vector, link state). TCP/UDP and sockets, congestion control. Application layer protocols (DNS, SMTP, POP, FTP, HTTP). Basics of Wi-Fi. Network security: authentication, basics of public key and private key cryptography, digital signatures and certificates, firewalls.

Contents

1 CHAPTER

Instruction of CN & Physical Layer

Analysis of Previous GATE Papers

Topics ↓		Year →	2019	2018	2017 Set 1	2017 Set 2	2016 Set 1	2016 Set 2	2015 Set 1	2015 Set 2	2015 Set 3
BANDWIDTH	1 Mark	MCQ Type									
		Numerical Type									
	2 Marks	MCQ Type				1					
		Numerical Type						1	1		2
		Total				2		2	2		4
INTRODUCTION	1 Mark	MCQ Type									
		Numerical Type									
	2 Marks	MCQ Type									
		Numerical Type									
		Total									
ISDN	1 Mark	MCQ Type									
		Numerical Type									
	2 Marks	MCQ Type									
		Numerical Type									
		Total									

BANDWIDTH

1. Host A is sending data to host B over a full duplex link. A and B are using the sliding window protocol for flow control. The send and receive window sizes are 5 packets each. Data packets (sent only from A to B) are all 1000 bytes long and the transmission time for such a packet is 50 μs. Acknowledgment packets (sent only from B to A) are very small and require negligible transmission time. The propagation delay over the link is 200 μs. What is the maximum achievable throughput in this communication?

   (a) 7.69×10^6 bps (b) 11.11×10^6 bps
   (c) 12.33×10^6 bps (d) 15.00×10^6 bps

   [2003 : 2 Marks]

2. How many 8-bit characters can be transmitted per second over a 9600 baud serial communication link using asynchronous mode of transmission with one start bit, eight data bits, and one parity bit and two stop bits?

   (a) 600 (b) 800
   (c) 876 (d) 1200

   [2004 : 1 Mark]

3. A serial transmission T1 uses 8 information bits, 2 start bits, 1 stop bit and 1 parity bit for each character. A synchronous transmission T2 uses 3 eight-bit sync characters followed by 30 eight-bit information characters. If the bit rate is 1200 bits/second in both cases, what are the transfer rates of T1 and T2?

   (a) 100 characters/sec, 153 characters/sec
   (b) 80 characters/sec, 136 characters/sec
   (c) 100 characters/sec, 136 characters/sec
   (d) 80 characters/sec, 153 characters/sec

   [2004 : 2 Marks]

4. How many bytes of data can be sent in 15 seconds over a serial link with baud rate of 9600 in asynchronous mode with odd parity and two stop bits in the frame?

   (a) 10,000 bytes
   (b) 12,000 bytes
   (c) 15,000 bytes
   (d) 27,000 bytes

   [2008 : 1 Mark]

5. Suppose that the stop-and-wait protocol is used on a link with a bit rate of 64 kilobits per second and 20 milliseconds propagation delay. Assume that the transmission time for the acknowledgment and the processing time at nodes are negligible. Then the minimum frame size in bytes to achieve a link utilization of at least 50% is _______.

   [2015 (Set-1) : 2 Marks]

6. Consider a network connecting two systems located 8000 kilometers apart. The bandwidth of the network is 500×10^6 bits per second. The propagation speed of the media is 4×10^6 meters per second. It is needed to design a Go-Back-N sliding window protocol for this network. The average packet size is 10^7 bits. The network is to be used to its full capacity.

   Assume that processing delays at nodes are negligible. Then, the minimum size in bits of the sequence number field has to be ______.

   [2015 (Set-3) : 2 Marks]

7. Two hosts are connected via a packet switch with 10^7 bits per second links. Each link has a propagation delay of 20 microseconds. The switch begins forwarding a packet 35 microseconds after it receives the same. If 10000 bits of data are to be transmitted between the two hosts using a packet size of 5000 bits, the time elapsed between the transmission of the first bit of data and the reception of the last bit of the data in microseconds is______.

   [2015 (Set-3) : 2 Marks]

8. Consider two hosts *X* and *Y* connected by a single direct link of rate 10^6 bits/sec. The distance between the two hosts is 10,000 km and the propagation speed along the link is 2×10^8 m/sec. Host *X* sends a file of 50,000 bytes as one large message to host *Y* continuously. Let the transmission and propagation delays be *p* milliseconds and *q* milliseconds, respectively. Then the values of *p* and *q* are

   (a) $p = 50$ and $q = 100$
   (b) $p = 50$ and $q = 400$
   (c) $p = 100$ and $q = 50$
   (d) $p = 400$ and $q = 50$

   [2017 (Set-2) : 2 Marks]

9. A broadcast channel has 10 nodes and total capacity of 10 Mbps. It uses polling for medium access. Once a node finishes transmission, there is a polling delay of 80 μs to poll the next node. Whenever a node is polled, it is allowed to transmit a maximum of 1000 bytes. The maximum throughput of the broadcast channel is

(a) 1 Mbps (b) 100/11 Mbps
(c) 10 Mbps (d) 100 Mbps

[2007 : 2 Marks]

10. Consider a source computer (S) transmitting a file of size 10^6 bits to a destination computer (D) over a network of two routers (R_1 and R_2) and three links (L_1, L_2 and L_3). L_1 connects S to R_1; L_2 connects R_1 to R_2; and L_3 connects R_2 to D. Let each link be of length 100 km. Assume signals travel over each link at a speed of 10^8 meters per second. Assume that the link bandwidth on each link is 1 Mbps. Let the file be broken down into 1000 packets each of size 1000 bits. Find the total sum of transmission and propagation delays in transmitting the file from S to D?

(a) 1005 ms (b) 1010 ms
(c) 3000 ms (d) 3003 ms

[2012 : 2 Marks]

11. Consider a 128×10^3 bits/second satellite communication link with one way propagation delay of 150 milliseconds. Selective retransmission (repeat) protocol is used on this link to send data with a frame size of 1 kilobyte. Neglect the transmission time of acknowledgement. The minimum number of bits required for the sequence number field to achieve 100% utilization is ______.

[2016 (Set-2) : 2 Marks]

12. Suppose the round trip propagation delay for a 10 Mbps Ethernet having 48-bit jamming signal is 46.4 ms. The minimum frame size is:

(a) 94 (b) 416
(c) 464 (d) 512

[2005 : 2 Marks]

13. A link of capacity 100 Mbps is carrying traffic from a number of sources. Each source generates an on-off traffic stream; when the source is on, the rate of traffic is 10 Mbps, and when the source is off, the rate of traffic is zero. The duty cycle, which is the ratio of on-time to off-time, is 1 : 2. When there is no buffer at the link, the minimum number of sources that can be multiplexed on the link so that link capacity is not wasted and no data loss occurs is S_1. Assuming that all sources are synchronized and that the link is provided with a large buffer, the maximum number of sources that can be multiplexed so that no data loss occurs is S_2. The values of S_1 and S_2 are, respectively,

(a) 10 and 30 (b) 12 and 25
(c) 5 and 33 (d) 15 and 22

[2006 : 2 Marks]

14. A layer-4 firewall (a device that can look at all protocol headers up to the transport layer) CANNOT

(a) block entire HTTP traffic during 9:00 pm and 5:00 am
(b) block all ICMP traffic
(c) stop incoming traffic from a specific IP address but allow outgoing traffic to the same IP address
(d) block TCP traffic from a specific user on a multi-user system during 9:00 pm and 5:00 am

[2011 : 1 Mark]

INTRODUCTION

15. Choose the best matching between **List-I** and **List-II.**

List-I
P. Data link layer
Q. Network layer
R. Transport layer

List-II
1. Ensures reliable transport of data over a physical point-to-point link
2. Encodes / decodes data for physical transmission
3. Allow end-to-end communication between two processes
4. Routes data from one network node to the next

	P	Q	R
(a)	1	4	3
(b)	2	4	1
(c)	2	3	1
(d)	1	3	2

[2004 : 1 Mark]

ISDN

16. In the diagram shown below, L1 is an Ethernet LAN and L2 is a Token-Ring LAN. An IP packet originates from sender S and traverses to R, as shown. The links within each ISP and across the two ISPs, are all point-to-point optical links. The initial value of the TTL field is 32. The maximum possible value of the TTL field when R receives the datagram is ________.

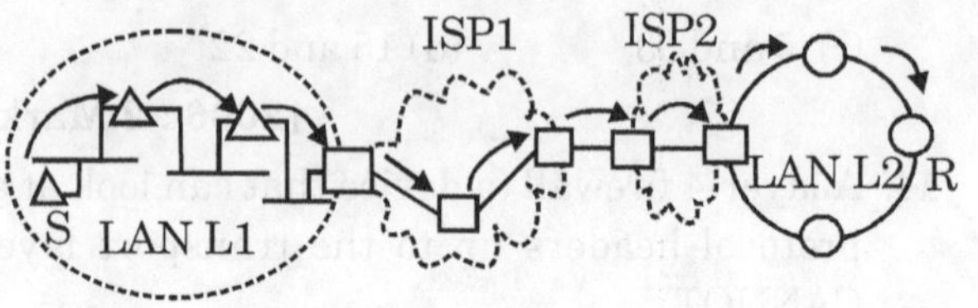

[2014 (Set-2) : 1 Mark]

Linked Data for Q.17 and Q.18

Consider the diagram shown below where a number of LANs are connected by (transparent) bridges. In order to avoid packets looping through circuits in the graph, the bridges organize themselves in a spanning tree. First, the root bridge is identified as the bridge with the least serial number. Next, the root sends out (one or more) data units to enable the setting up of the spanning tree of shortest paths from the root bridge to each bridge.

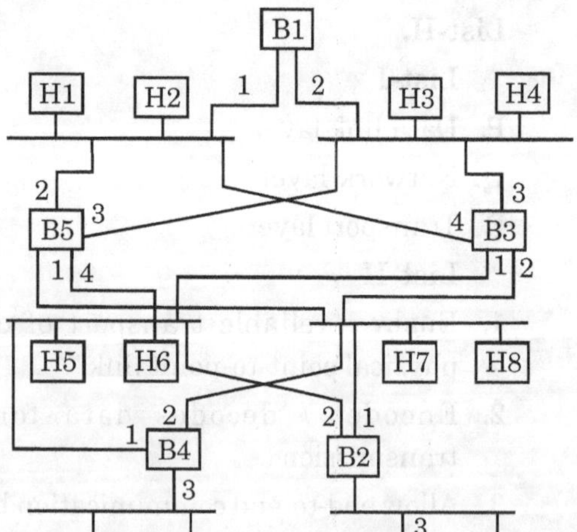

Each bridge identifies a port (the root port) through which it will forward frames to the root bridge. Port conflicts are always resolved in favour of the port with the lower index value. When there is a possibility of multiple bridges forwarding to the same LAN (but not through the root port), ties are broken as follows : bridges closest to the root get preference and between such bridges, the one with the lowest serial number is preferred.

17. For the given connection of LANs by bridges, which one of the following choices represents the depth first traversal of the spanning tree of bridges?

(a) B1, B5, B3, B4, B2

(b) B1, B3, B5, B2, B4

(c) B1, B5, B2, B3, B4

(d) B1, B3, B4, B5, B2 **[2006 : 2 Marks]**

18. Consider the correct spanning tree for the previous question. Let host H1 send out a broadcast ping packet. Which of the following options represents the correct forwarding table on B3?

(a)

Hosts	Port
H1, H2, H3, H4	3
H5, H6, H9, H10	1
H7, H8, H11, H12	2

(b)

Hosts	Port
H1, H2	4
H3, H4	3
H5, H6	1
H7, H8, H9, H10, H11, H12	2

(c)

Hosts	Port
H3, H4	3
H5, H6, H9, H10	1
H1, H2	4
H7, H8, H11, H12	2

(d)

Hosts	Port
H1, H2, H3, H4	3
H5, H7, H9, H10	1
H7, H8, H11, H12	4

[2006 : 2 Marks]

ANSWERS

1. (*b*) **2.** (b) **3.** (c) **4.** (b) **5.** (320) **6.** (8) **7.** (1575) **8.** (d) **9.** (b) **10.** (a)
11. (a) **12.** (c,d) **13.** (c) **14.** (d) **15.** (a) **16.** (26 to 26) **17.** (a) **18.** (a)

EXPLANATIONS

1. Given :

Window size = 5 packet
Packet size = 1000 bytes
= 2^{10} (approx. 10 bits)
Window size = 5000 byte (13 bits approx.)
Transmission time = $5 \times 50 = 250\ \mu$ sec
Propagation delay = $200\ \mu$ sec
Total time = $250 + 200\ \mu$ sec
= $450\ \mu$ sec

Maximum achievable throughput

$$= \frac{5000}{450} \times 10^6 \text{ bps}$$
$$= 11.11 \times 10^6 \text{ bps}$$

2. 8-bits characters

$$= \frac{9600}{\text{(start bit + data bit + end bit + parity bit)}}$$
$$= \frac{9600}{12} = 800$$

3. In T_1 :⇒

1 character = (8 + 2 + 1 + 1) = 12 bit

$$\text{So transfer rute} = \frac{\text{bit rate}}{\text{No. of bits in character}}$$
$$= \frac{1200}{12} \text{char / sec}$$
= 100 char / sec.

In T_2 :- Transfer character

= (3 * 8 + 30 * 8) bits
= 264 bits

If 264 bits for 30 char then 1200 bits is

$$\frac{26Y}{30} = \frac{1200}{X}$$
X = 136.3 character/sec

4. The serial port is capable of transferring a maximum of 9600 bits per second because there are 9600 baud.

So in 1 sec it send 9600 bits

So in 15 sec = 9600 * 15 bits

Data in 1 frame

= 1 bit(start) + 2 bits(Stop) + 8 bits(char size) + 1 bit(Parity)

= 12 bits.

Number of 8-bit characters that can be transmitted per second

= (9600 * 15)/12 = 12000 bytes.

5. Utilization is at least 50%, minimum possible total time for one packet is twice of transmission delay so Minimum frame size

= 64 kbps * 40ms
= 2560bits = 320 byte

6. Propagation delay = (8000 * 1000)/ (4 * 10^6)
= 2 seconds

Total round trip propagation time = 4 seconds

Transmission delay = (packet size)/(bandwidth)
= (10^7)/(500 * 10^6)
= 0.02 second

Efficiency = N/(1 + 2a)

1 = N/(1 + 2 * 100) {a = Propagation delay/ Transmission delay}

N = 201

So total 201 sequence numbers are needed. 201 different sequence numbers can be represented using 8 bits.

7. Sender host transmits first packet to switch, the transmission time = 5000/107 = 500 microseconds.

The first packet reaches destination in 500 + 35 + 20 + 20 + 500 = 1075 microseconds.

While the first packet is traveling to destination, the second packet starts its journey after 500 microseconds and rest of the time taken by second packet overlaps with first packet. So overall time is 1075 + 500 = 1575.

$$\therefore \quad a = \frac{T_p}{T_n}$$
$$= \frac{2}{0.02} = 100$$

8. Transmission time is ratio of Data size to Bandwidth

$$\text{Transmission time} = \frac{\text{Data size}}{\text{Bandwidth}}$$

$$= \frac{50000\times 8 \text{ bits}}{10^6 \text{ bits/sec}}$$

$$= 400 \text{ m sec}$$

Also

$$\text{Propagation time} = \frac{\text{Distance}}{\text{Velocity}}$$

$$= \frac{10000\times 10^3 \text{ m}}{2\times 10^8 \text{ m/sec}}$$

$$= \frac{10^3\times 10^{-4}}{2}$$

$$= 50 \text{ msec}$$

9. Efficiency = transmission time/(transmission time + polling delay time)

Tt =1000 bytes/10Mbps =800?s.

Polling delay is = 80 ?s

Efficiency = 800/(800 + 80) = 10/11

Maximum throughput is = (10/11) * 10 Mbps

= 100/11 Mbps

10. Propogation Delay to travel from S to R1

= (Distance)/(Link Speed) = 10^5/10^8 = 1ms

Total prorogation delay to travel from S to D

= 3*1 ms = 3ms

Total Transmission rate for 1 packet = 3 * (Number of Bits) / Bandwidth = 3*(1000/10^6) = 3ms. The first packet will take 6ms to reach D. While first packet was reaching D, other packets must have been processing in parallel. So D will receive remaining packets 1 packet per 1 ms from R2. So remaining 999 packets will take 999 ms. And total time will be 999 + 6 = 1005 ms

11. 10 Mbps * n stations <= 100 Mbps

n = 10 if n is very large:

a station transmits with probability 1/(1 + 2 = 1/3, with a capacity of 10Mbps so, for n stations:

(1/3) * 10 + (1/3) * 10 + (1/3) * 10 + ..+ n times <= 100 Mbps

(1/3) * 10[1 + 1 + 1 + 1 +...+ n times] <= 100

(1/3) * 10 * n< = 100

n = 30

12. Transmission Speed = 10Mbps.

Round trip propagation delay = 46.4 ms

The minimum frame size

= (Round Trip Propagation Delay) * (Transmission Speed)

= 10 * (10^6) * 46.4 * (10^–3)

= 464 * 10^3 = 464 Kbit

14. Since it is a layer 4 firewall it cannot block application layer protocol like HTTP.

15. P — 1; Q — 4; R — 3

By the definition and function of data link layer, Network layer and Transport layer.

16. From S to R_1, there are 10 nodes but only 6 of them will decrement the TTL value. That's why, the maximum value of TTL field when R receives datagram is 32 – 6 = 26.

17.

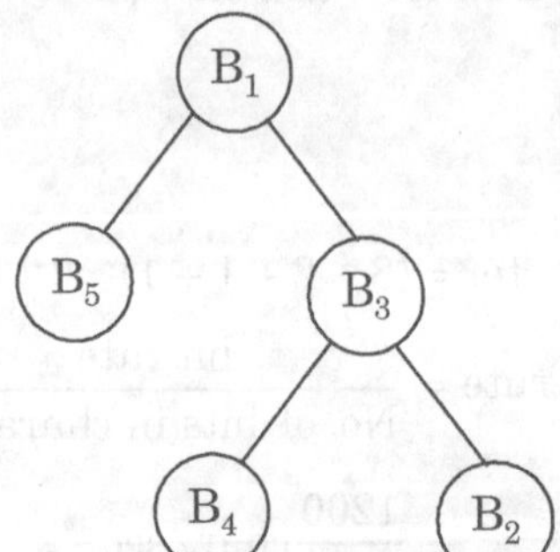

DFS transfer of tree is B_1 B_5 B_3 B_4 B_2J

18. Only option A match with given picture.

2
CHAPTER

Data Link Layer

Analysis of Previous GATE Papers

Topics ↓		Year →	2019	2018	2017 Set 1	2017 Set 2	2016 Set 1	2016 Set 2	2015 Set 1	2015 Set 2	2015 Set 3
ERROR CONTROL	1 Mark	MCQ Type							1		
		Numerical Type									
	2 Marks	MCQ Type			1	1					
		Numerical Type			1		1				
		Total			4	2	2		1		
ENCODING	1 Mark	MCQ Type									
		Numerical Type									
	2 Marks	MCQ Type									
		Numerical Type									
		Total									
CHANNEL ALLOCATION	1 Mark	MCQ Type									
		Numerical Type									1
	2 Marks	MCQ Type									
		Numerical Type		1				2	1		
		Total		2				4	2		1
DLL	1 Mark	MCQ Type									
		Numerical Type									
	2 Marks	MCQ Type					1	1			
		Numerical Type	1								
		Total	2				2	2			

ERROR CONTROL

1. In a sliding window ARQ scheme, the transmitter's window size is N and the receiver's window size is M. The minimum number of distinct sequence numbers required to ensure correct operation of the ARQ scheme is
(a) min (M, N) (b) max (M, N)
(c) M + N (d) MN
[2004 : 2 Marks]

2. A 20 Kbps satellite link has a propagation delay of 400 ms. The transmitter employs the "go back n ARQ" scheme with n set to 10. Assuming that each frame is 100 bytes long, what is the maximum data rate possible?
(a) 5 Kbps (b) 10 Kbps
(c) 15 Kbps (d) 20 Kbps
[2004 : 2 Marks]

3. Consider a parity check code with three data bits and four parity check bits. Three of the code words are 0101011,1001101 and 1110001.
Which of the following are also code words?
I. 0010111 II. 0110110
III. 1011010 IV. 0111010
(a) I and III (b) I, II and III
(c) II and IV (d) I, II, III and IV
[2004 : 2 Marks]

4. The maximum window size for data transmission using the selective reject protocol with n-bit frame sequence numbers is
(a) 2^n (b) 2^{n-1}
(c) $2^n - 1$ (d) 2^{n-2}
[2005 : 1 Mark]

5. Consider the following message M = 1010001101. The cyclic redundancy check (CRC) for this message using the divisor polynomial $x^5 + x^4 + x^2 + 1$ is :
(a) 01110 (b) 01011
(c) 10101 (d) 10110
[2005 : 2 Marks]

6. A channel has a bit rate of 4 kbps and one-way propagation delay of 20 ms. The channel uses stop and wait protocol. The transmission time of the acknowledgement frame is negligible. To get a channel efficiency of at least 50%, the minimum frame size should be
(a) 80 bytes (b) 80 bits
(c) 160 bytes (d) 160 bits
[2005 : 2 Marks]

7. On a wireless link, the probability of packet error is 0.2. A stop-and-wait protocol is used to transfer data across the link. The channel condition is assumed to be independent from transmission to transmission. What is the average number of transmission attempts required to transfer 100 packets?
(a) 100 (b) 125
(c) 150 (d) 200 **[2006 : 2 Marks]**

8. Station A uses 32 byte packets to transmit messages to Station B using a sliding window protocol. The round trip delay between A and B is 80 milliseconds and the bottleneck bandwidth on the path between A and B is 128 kbps. What is the optimal window size that A should use?
(a) 20 (b) 40
(c) 160 (d) 320 **[2006 : 2 Marks]**

9. Station A needs to send a message consisting of 9 packets to Station B using a siding window (window size 3) and go-back-n error control strategy. All packets are ready and immediately available for transmission. If every 5th packet that A transmits gets lost (but no acks from B ever get lost), then what is the number of packets that A will transmit for sending the message to B?
(a) 12 (b) 14
(c) 16 (d) 18 **[2006 : 2 Marks]**

10. The message 11001001 is to be transmitted using the CRC polynomial $x^3 + 1$ to protect it from errors. The message that should be transmitted is:
(a) 11001001000 (b) 11001001011
(c) 11001010 (d) 110010010011
[2007 : 2 Marks]

11. An error correcting code has the following code words: 00000000, 00001111, 01010101, 10101010, 11110000. What is the maximum number of bit errors that can be corrected?
(a) 0 (b) 1
(c) 2 (d) 3 **[2007 : 2 Marks]**

12. A 1 Mbps satellite link connects two ground stations. The altitude of the satellite is 36,504 km and speed of the signal is 3×10^8 m/s. What should be the packet size for a channel utilization of 25% for a satellite link using go-back-127 sliding window protocol?
Assume that the acknowledgment packets are negligible in size and that there are no errors during communication.
(a) 120 bytes (b) 60 bytes
(c) 240 bytes (d) 90 bytes
[2008 : 2 Marks]

13. Data transmitted on a link uses the following 2D parity scheme for error detection:

Each sequence of 28 bits is arranged in a 4 × 7 matrix (rows r_0 through r_3, and columns d_7 through d_1) and is padded with a column d_0 and row r_4 of parity bits computed using the Even parity scheme. Each bit of column d_0 (respectively, row r_4) gives the parity of the corresponding row (respectively, column). These 40 bits are transmitted over the data link.

	d_7	d_6	d_5	d_4	d_3	d_2	d_1	d_0
r_0	0	1	0	1	0	1	1	1
r_1	1	1	0	0	1	1	0	0
r_2	0	0	0	1	1	0	0	0
r_3	0	1	1	0	0	1	0	0
r_4	1	1	0	0	1	1	0	0

The table shows data received by a receiver and has n corrupted bits. What is the minimum possible value of n?

(a) 1 (b) 2
(c) 3 (d) 4 **[2008 : 2 Marks]**

14. Let G(x) be the generator polynomial used for CRC checking. What is the condition that should be satisfied by G(x) to detect odd number of bits in error?

(a) G(x) contains more than two terms
(b) G(x) does not divide $1 + x^k$, for any k not exceeding the frame length
(c) 1 + x is a factor of G(x)
(d) G(x) has an odd number of terms

[2009 : 2 Marks]

Linked Answer for Q.15 and Q. 16

Frames of 1000 bits are sent over a 10^6 bps duplex link between two hosts. The propagation time is 25 ms. Frames are to be transmitted into this link to maximally pack them in transit (within the link).

15. What is the minimum number of bits (*l*) that will be required to represent the sequence numbers distinctly? Assume that no time gap needs to be given between transmission of two frames.

(a) $l = 2$ (b) $l = 3$
(c) $l = 4$ (d) $l = 5$

[2009 : 2 Marks]

16. Suppose that the sliding window protocol is used with the sender window size of 2^l, where *l* is the number of bits identified in the earlier part and acknowledgments are always piggy backed. After sending 2^l frames, what is the minimum time the sender will have to wait before starting transmission of the next frame? (Identify the closest choice ignoring the frame processing time).

(a) 16 ms (b) 18 ms
(c) 20 ms (d) 22 ms

[2009 : 2 Marks]

17. How many 8-bit characters can be transmitted per second over a 9600 baud serial communication link using asynchronous mode of transmission with one start bit, eight data bits, and one parity bit and two stop bits?

(a) 600 (b) 800
(c) 876 (d) 1200 **[2004 : 1 Mark]**

18. The distance between two stations M and N is L kilometres. All frames are K bits long. The propagation delay per kilometre is t seconds. Let R bits/second be the channel capacity. Assuming that processing delay is negligible, the minimum number of bits for the sequence number field in a frame for maximum utilization, when the sliding window protocol is used, is:

(a) $\left\lceil \log_2 \frac{2LtR + 2K}{K} \right\rceil$ (b) $\left\lceil \log_2 \frac{2LtR}{K} \right\rceil$

(c) $\left\lceil \log_2 \frac{2LtR + K}{K} \right\rceil$ (d) $\left\lceil \log_2 \frac{2LtR + K}{2K} \right\rceil$

[2007 : 2 Marks]

19. A sender uses the Stop-and-Wait ARQ protocol for reliable transmission of frames. Frames are of size 1000 bytes and the transmission rate at the sender is 80 Kbps (1 Kbps = 1000 bits/second). Size of an acknowledgment is 100 bytes and the transmission rate at the receiver is 8 Kbps. The one-way propagation delay is 100 milliseconds. Assuming no frame is lost, the sender throughput is ________ bytes/second.

[2016 (Set-1) : 2 Marks]

20. The values of parameters for the Stop-and-Wait ARQ protocol are as given below:

- Bit rate of the transmission channel = 1 Mbps.
- Propagation delay from sender to receiver = 0.75 ms.
- Time to process a frame = 0.25 ms.
- Number of bytes in the information frame = 1980.
- Number of bytes in the acknowledge frame = 20.
- Number of overhead bytes in the information frame = 20.

Assume that there are no transmission errors. Then, the transmission efficiency (expressed in percentage) of the Stop-and-Wait ARQ protocol for the above parameters is ______ (correct to 2 decimal places).

[2017 (Set-1) : 2 Marks]

21. A computer network uses polynomials over *GF(2)* for error checking with 8 bits as information bits and uses $x^3 + x + 1$ as the generator polynomial to generate the check bits. In this network, the message 01011011 is transmitted as

(a) 01011011010 (b) 01011011011
(c) 01011011101 (d) 01011011100

[2017 (Set-1) : 2 Marks]

22. Consider a binary code that consists of only four valid codewords as given below:

00000, 01011, 10101, 11110

Let the minimum Hamming distance of the code be *p* and the maximum number of erroneous bits that can be corrected by the code be *q*. Then the values of *p* and *q* are

(a) $p = 3$ and $q = 1$ (b) $p = 3$ and $q = 2$
(c) $p = 4$ and $q = 1$ (d) $p = 4$ and $q = 2$

[2017 (Set-2) : 2 Marks]

23. On a TCP connection, current congestion window size is Congestion Window = 4 KB. The window size advertised by the receiver is Advertise Window = 6 KB. The last byte sent by the sender is LastByteSent = 10240 and the last byte acknowledged by the receiver is LastByteAcked = 8192. The current window size at the sender is

(a) 2048 bytes (b) 4096 bytes
(c) 6144 bytes (d) 8192 bytes

[2005 : 2 Marks]

24. In a communication network, a packet of length L bits takes link L_1 with a probability of p_1 or link L2 with a probability of p_2. Link L1 and L2 have bit error probability of b_1 and b_2 respectively. The probability that the packet will be received without error via either L1 or L2 is

(a) $(1-b_1)^L p_1 + (1-b_2)^L p_2$

(b) $[1-(b_1+b_2)^L]p_1p_2$

(c) $(1-b_1)^L(1-b_2)^L p_1p_2$

(d) $1-(b_1^L p_1 + b_2^L p_2)$

[2005 : 2 Marks]

25. Which of the following statements is TRUE?

(a) Both Ethernet frame and IP packet include checksum fields
(b) Ethernet frame includes a checksum field and IP packet includes a CRC field
(c) Ethernet frame includes a CRC field and IP packet includes a checksum field
(d) Both Ethernet frame and IP packet include CRC fields

[2006 : 1 Mark]

26. Consider a selective repeat sliding window protocol that uses a frame size of 1 KB to send data on a 1.5 Mbps link with a one-way latency of 50 msec. To achieve a link utilization of 60%, the minimum number of bits required to represent the sequence number field is ______.

[2014 (Set-1) : 2 Marks]

27. Host A (on TCP/IP v4 network A) sends an IP datagram D to host B (also on TCP/IP v4 network B). Assume that no error occurred during the transmission of D. When D reaches B, which of the following IP header field(s) may be different from that of the original datagram D?

(*i*) TTL
(*ii*) Checksum
(*iii*) Fragment Offset

(a) (*i*) only
(b) (*i*) and (*ii*) only
(c) (*ii*) and (*iii*) only
(d) (*i*), (ii) and (*iii*)

[2014 (Set-3) : 1 Mark]

28. Which one of the following fields of an IP header is NOT modified by a typical IP router?

(a) Checksum
(b) Source address
(c) Time to Live (TTL)
(d) Length

[2015 (Set-1) : 1 Mark]

29. A subnet has been assigned a subnet mask of 255.255.255.192. What is the maximum number of hosts that can belong to this subnet?

(a) 14
(b) 30
(c) 62
(d) 126

[2004 : 1 Mark]

ENCODING

30. In the 4B/5B encoding scheme, every 4 bits of data are encoded in a 5-bit codeword. It is required that the codewords have at most 1 leading and at most 1 trailing zero. How many such codewords are possible?

(a) 14
(b) 16
(c) 18
(d) 20

[2006 : 2 Marks]

31. In the waveform (a) given below, a bit stream is encoded by Manchester encoding scheme. The same bit stream is encoded in a different coding scheme in wave form (b). The bit stream and the coding scheme are

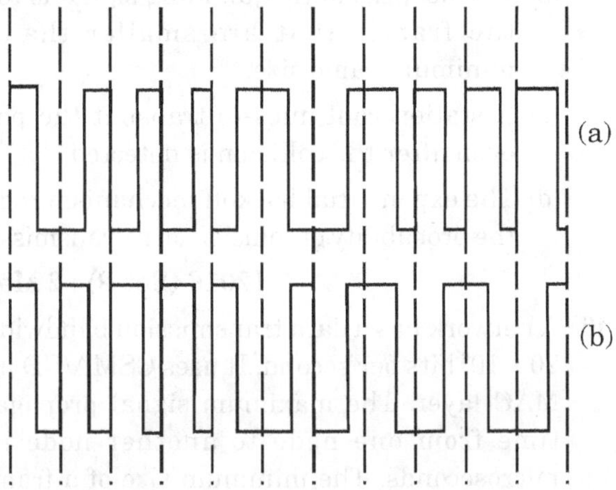

(a) 1000010111 and Differential Manchester respectively

(b) 0111101000 and Differential Manchester respectively

(c) 1000010111 and Integral Manchester respectively

(d) 0111101000 and Integral Manchester respectively **[2007 : 2 Marks]**

32. Your are given the following four bytes :

10100011 00110111 11101001 10101011

Which of the following are substrings of the base 64 encoding of the above four bytes?

(a) zdp (b) fpq

(c) qwA (d) oze **[2007 : 2 Marks]**

33. In Ehernet when Manchester encoding is used, the bit rate is

(a) Half the baud rate

(b) Twice the baud rate

(c) Same as the baud rate

(d) None of these **[2007:1 Mark]**

CHANNEL ALLOCATION

34. Let us consider a statistical time division multiplexing of packets. The number of sources is 10. In a time unit, a source transmits a packet of 1000 bits. The number of sources sending data for the first 20 time units is 6, 9, 3, 7, 2, 2, 2, 3, 4, 6, 1, 10, 7, 5, 8, 3, 6, 2, 9, 5 respectively. The output capacity of multiplexer is 5000 bits per time unit. Then the average number of backlogged of packets per time unit during the given period is

(a) 5 (b) 4.45

(c) 3.45 (d) 0 **[2007 : 2 Marks]**

35. A 2 km long broadcast LAN has 10^7 bps bandwidth and uses CSMA/CD. The signal travels along the wire at 2×10^8 m/s. What is the minimum packet size that can be used on this network?

(a) 50 bytes (b) 100 bytes

(c) 200 bytes (d) None of these

[2003 : 2 Marks]

36. Consider a simplified time slotted MAC protocol, where each host always has data to send and transmits with probability p = 0.2 in every slot. There is no backoff and one frame can be transmitted in one slot. If more than one host transmits in the same slot, then the transmissions are unsuccessful due to collision. What is the maximum number of hosts which this protocol can support, if each host has to be provided a minimum through put of 0.16 frames per time slot?

(a) 1 (b) 2

(c) 3 (d) 4

[2004 : 2 Marks]

37. A and B are the only two stations on an Ethernet. Each has a steady queue of frames to send. Both A and B attempt to transmit a frame, collide, and A wins the first backoff race. At the end of this successful transmission by A, both A and B attempt to transmit and collide. The probability that A wins the second backoff race is

(a) 0.5 (b) 0.625

(c) 0.75 (d) 1.0

[2004 : 2 Marks]

38. Which of the following statements is TRUE about CSMA/CD

(a) IEEE 802.11 wireless LAN runs CSMA/CD protocol

(b) Ethernet is not based on CSMA/CD protocol

(c) CSMA/CD is not suitable for a high propagation delay network like satellite network

(d) There is no contention in a CSMA/CD network

[2005 : 1 Mark]

39. A network with CSMA/CD protocol in the MAC layer is running at 1 Gbps over a 1 km cable with no repeaters. The signal speed in the cable is 2×10^8 m/sec. The minimum frame size for this network should be

(a) 10000 bits

(b) 10000 bytes

(c) 5000 bits

(d) 5000 bytes

[2005 : 2 Marks]

40. In a TDM medium access control bus LAN, each station is assigned one time slot per cycle for transmission. Assume that the length of each time slot is the time to transmit 100 bits plus the end-to-end propagation delay. Assume a propagation speed of 2×10^8 m/sec. The length of the LAN is 1 km with a bandwidth of 10 Mbps. The maximum number of stations that can be allowed in the LAN so that the throughput of each station can be 2/3 Mbps is

(a) 3 (b) 5
(c) 10 (d) 20

[2005 : 2 Marks]

41. There are n stations in a slotted LAN. Each station attempts to transmit with a probability p in each time slot. What is the probability that ONLY one station transmits in a given time slot?

(a) $np(1-p)^{n-1}$ (b) $(1-p)^{n-1}$

(c) $p(1-p)^{n-1}$ (d) $1-(1-p)^{n-1}$

[2007 : 2 Marks]

42. The minimum frame size required for a CSMA/CD based computer network running at 1 Gbps on a 200 m cable with a link speed of 2×10^8 m/s is

(a) 125 bytes (b) 250 bytes
(c) 500 bytes (d) None of these

[2008 : 2 Marks]

43. Consider a LAN with four nodes S_1, S_2, S_3 and S_4. Time is divided into fixed-size slots, and a node can begin its transmission only at the beginning of a slot. A collision is said to have occurred if more than one node transmit in the same slot. The probabilities of generation of a frame in a time slot by S_1, S_2, S_3 and S_4 are 0.1, 0.2, 0.3 and 0.4, respectively. The probability of sending a frame in the first slot without any collision by any of these four stations is ________.

[2015 (Set-1) : 2 Marks]

44. Consider a CSMA/CD network that transmits data at a rate of 100 Mbps (10^8 bits per second) over a 1 km (kilometer) cable with no repeaters. If the minimum frame size required for this network is 1250 bytes, what is the signal speed (km/sec) in the cable?

(a) 8000
(b) 10000
(c) 16000
(d) 20000

[2015 (Set-3) : 1 Mark]

45. In an Ethernet local area network, which one of the following statements is **TRUE?**

(a) A station stops to sense the channel once it starts transmitting a frame.
(b) The purpose of the jamming signal is to pad the frames that are smaller than the minimumframe size.
(c) A station continues to transmit the packet even after the collision is detected.
(d) The exponential backoff mechanism reduces the probability of collision on retransmissions.

[2016 (Set-2) : 2 Marks]

46. A network has a data transmission bandwidth of 20×10^6 bits per second. It uses CSMA/CD in the MAC layer. The maximum signal propagation time from one node to another node is 40 microseconds. The minimum size of a frame in the network is ________ bytes.

[2016 (Set-2) : 2 Marks]

47. Consider a simple communication system where multiple nodes are connected by a shared broadcast medium (like Ethernet or wireless). The nodes in the system use the following carrier-sense based medium access protocol. A node that receives a packet to transmit will carrier-sense the medium for 5 units of time. If the node does not detect any other transmission in this duration, it starts transmitting its packet in the next time unit. If the node detects another transmission, it waits until this other transmission finishes, and then begins to carrier-sense for 5 time units again. Once they start to transmit, nodes do not perform any collision detection and continue transmission even if a collision occurs. All transmissions last for 20 units of time. Assume that the transmission signal travels at the speed of 10 meters per unit time in the medium.

Assume that the system has two nodes P and Q, located at a distance d meters from each other. P starts transmitting a packet at time $t = 0$ after successfully completing its carrier-sense phase. Node Q has a packet to transmit at time $t = 0$ and begins to carrier-sense the medium.

The maximum distance d (in meters, rounded to the closest integer) that allows Q to successfully avoid a collision between its proposed transmission and P's ongoing transmission is ________.

[2018 : 2 Marks]

DLL

48. In the following pairs of OSI protocol layer/sub-layer and its functionality, the **INCORRECT** pair is

(a) Network layer and Routing

(b) Data Link Layer and Bit synchronization

(c) Transport layer and End-to-end process communication

(d) Medium Access Control sub-layer and Channel sharing

[2014 (Set-3) : 1 Mark]

49. In a network of LANs connected by bridges, packets are sent from one LAN to another through intermediate bridges. Since more than one path may exist between two LANs, packets may have to be routed through multiple bridges. Why is the spanning tree algorithm used for bridge-routing?

(a) For shortest path routing between LANs

(b) For avoiding loops in the routing paths

(c) For fault tolerance

(d) For minimizing collisions

[2005 : 1 Mark]

50. Which of the following statements is FALSE regarding a bridge

(a) Bridge is a layer 2 device

(b) Bridge reduces collision domain

(c) Bridge is used to connect two or more LAN segments

(d) Bridge reduces broadcast domain

[2005 : 1 Mark]

51. Determine the maximum length of the cable (in km) for transmitting data at a rate of 500 Mbps in an Ethernet LAN with frames of size 10,000 bits. Assume the signal speed in the cable to be 2,00,000 km/s.

(a) 1 (b) 2

(c) 2.5 (d) 5

[2013 : 2 Marks]

52. Which one of the following protocols is NOT used to resolve one form of address to another one?

(a) DNS (b) ARP

(c) DHCP (d) RARP

[2016 (Set-1) : 2 Marks]

53. For the IEEE 802.11 MAC protocol for wireless communication, which of th following statements is/are **TRUE?**

I. At least three non-overlapping channels are available for transmission.

II. The RTS-CTS mechanism is used for collision detection.

III. Unicast frames are ACKed

(a) All I, II, and III

(b) I and III only

(c) II and III only

(d) II only

[2016 (Set-2) : 2 Marks]

54. Consider that 15 machines need to be connected in a LAN using 8-port Ethernet switches.

Assume that these switches do not have any separate uplink points. The minimum number of switches needed is______________.

[2019) : 2 Marks]

ANSWERS

1. (c)	**2.** (b)	**3.** (a)	**4.** (b)	**5.** (a)	**6.** (d)	**7.** (b)	**8.** (b)	**9.** (c)	**10.** (b)
11. (d)	**12.** (a)	**13.** (c)	**14.** (c)	**15.** (d)	**16.** (b)	**17.** (b)	**18.** (c)	**19.** (2500)	**20.** (a)
21. (c)	**22.** (a)	**23.** (b)	**24.** (a)	**25.** (c)	**26.** (5)	**27.** (d)	**28.** (b)	**29.** (c)	**30.** (c)
31. (a)	**32.** (b)	**33.** (a)	**34.** (b)	**35.** (d)	**36.** (b)	**37.** (b)	**38.** (c)	**39.** (a)	**40.** (b)
41. (a)	**42.** (b)	**43.** (0.44)	**44.** (d)	**45.** (d)	**46.** (200)	**47.** (a)	**48.** (b)	**49.** (b)	**50.** (d)
51. (b)	**52.** (c)	**53.** (b)	**54.** (3)						

EXPLANATIONS

1. The minimum number of distinct sequence numbers required to ensure correct operation of the ARQ scheme is M + N.

2. Given Data is

   Bandwidth = 20 Kbps

   Propogation dealy(PD) = 400 ms

   window size = 10

   frame size = 100 bytes or 800 bits

   Now, RTT = 2 * PD = 800 ms

   Even though bandwidth is 20kbps, we are restricted with window size here

   In 1 RTT we are sending 10 * 800 bits i.e. in 800 ms we are sending 10 * 800 bits.

   So, in 1 ms we are sending 10 bits i.e. in 1 sec we are sending 10 * 1000 bits

   So effective bandwidth = 10 Kb/sec.

3. Assume

   x = 0101011

   y = 1001101

   z = 1110001

   We know that XOR of two codewords is itself a codeword.

   x XOR z = 1011010

   So, III is a codeword.

   w = 1011010

   y XOR w = 0010111

   So, I is a codeword.

4. Stalling networks assume here window size of 8, i.e., (0 – 7)

   1. Station A under frame 0 through 6 to station B
   2. Station B receives all seven frames, and ack with R R 7 (Receive Ready 7)
   3. R R 7 is lost
   4. A times out and retransmit frame O.
   5. B has already advanced its receive window to accept frames 7, 0, 1, 2, 3, 4 and 5 thus it assume that 7 has been lost and this is a new frame O.

   To overcome this problem, the maximum windows size is 2^{n-1}

5. ****

6. One way propagation delay (PD) = 20 ms

   Bit rate = 4 kbps

   Efficiency = Transmission time of packet/(Transmission time of packet + 2 * PD)

   $0.5 = a/(a + 2 * 20 * 10^{-3})$

   $a = 20 * 10^{-3}$

   $a = 40 * 10^{-3}$

   Minimum frame size / Bit rate = $40 * 10^{-3}$

   Therefore, Minimum frame size

   $= 40 * 10^{-3} * 4 * 10^{3} = 160$ bits

7. Probability of success = 0.8

   E = 0.8 * 1 + 0.8 * 1 +..n times

   = 100 {for 100 packets}

   $\Rightarrow$ 0.8 * 1 * n = 100

   $\Rightarrow$ n = 125

   To receive 100 packets we have to transmit 125 packets.

8. Band width delay product

   = Round trip delay × bottle neck bind width

   $= 80 \times 128 \times 10^{-3} \times 1024$ bits

   $= \dfrac{80 \times 128 \times 10^{-3} \times 1024}{8}$ bytes

   $\therefore$ Optimal size window

   $= \dfrac{80 \times 128 \times 10^{-3} \times 1024}{8 \times 32} = 40$

9. 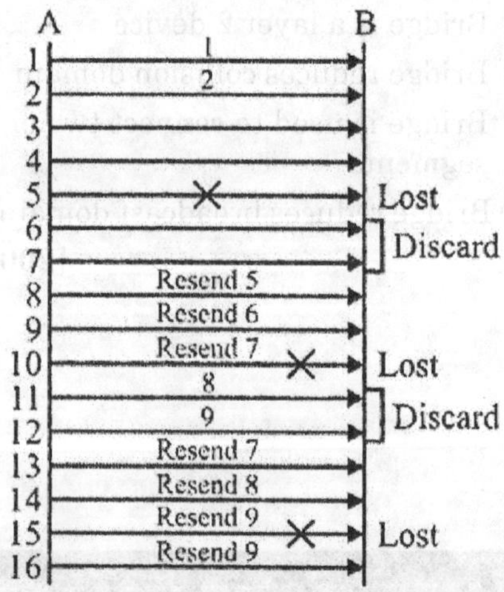

10. P(x) = 11001001

    divisor D(x) = 1001 and CRC remainder is 011 so the transmitted message is 11001001011.

11. We can use the formula d = (2t + 1)

    Where d = maximum hamming distance

    t = number of bits could be corrected maximum hamming distance between 01010101 and 10101010 code is 8

    so 8 = 2t + 1

    t = 3.5

    integer value of t is 3.

12. Time to reach satellite = 36504000 / 300000000

= 0.12168s

RTT (for a bit) = 4 × Time to reach satellite

Efficiency = Transmitted Data Size / (PacketSize + RTTbit × Bandwidth)

0.25 = (127 × a)/(a + 4 × 0.12168 × B)

0.25a + 0.25 × 4 × 0.12168 × B = 127a

0.25 × a + 0.12168 × 106 = 127a

121680 = 126.75a

a = 9.6 × 10 – 4 × 106 = 960

Packet Size = 960 bits i.e. 120 Bytes

13. Answer is (c)

(r1, d5) should be 1.

(r4, d2) should be 0.

(r4, d0) should be 1.

14. When polynomial code method is employed, the sender and receiver must agree upon a generator polynomial G(*x*). Both high and low order bit of the generator must be 1 .

So $1 + x$ is a factor of G(*x*).

Alternately

For odd number of bits error, error function will be having a factor of $(1 + x^2 + x^4 + ...)$ which can not be divided by the generator having $(1 + x)$ as a factor.

15. Transmission delay for 1 frame = $1000/(10^6)$ = 1 ms

Propagation time = 25 ms

The sender can transfer at most 25 frames before the first frame reaches the destination.

The number of bits needed for representing 25 different frames = 5.

16. Given Data

Size of sliding window = $2^5 = 32$

Transmission time for a frame = 1ms

Total time taken for 32 frames = 32ms

The sender receive acknoledgement after RTT i.e. after 50ms

So, After sending 32 frames, the sender must wait for 18ms(50 – 32) before starting transmission of the next frame.

17. 8-bits characters

$$= \frac{9600}{(\text{start bit} + \text{data bit} + \text{end bit} + \text{parity bit})}$$

$$= \frac{9600}{12} = 800$$

18. Total propagation delay = Lt sec.

Roundtrip time = 2 Lt = 2 Lt sec

Number of bits transmitted in roundtrip

= 2 LtR bits

$$\text{Number of frames} = \frac{2\text{LtR}}{\text{K}}$$

Let number of bits in sequent numbers be b.

$$\therefore \quad 2^b = \frac{2\text{LtR}}{\text{K}}$$

$$\Rightarrow b = \left\lceil \log_2 \frac{2\text{LtR}}{\text{K}} \right\rceil$$

19. $$\text{Throughput} = \frac{\text{output}}{\text{time}} = \frac{L}{T_{data} + T_{ack} + 2P_d}$$

$$T_d = \frac{1000 \times 8}{80 \times 1000} = \frac{1}{10} \text{ sec} = 100 \text{ ms}$$

$$T_{ack} = \frac{100 \times 8}{8 \times 1000}$$

$$= \frac{1}{10} \text{ sec} = 100 \text{ ms}$$

$$= \frac{1000}{100 + 100 + 2 \times 100} = 2500$$

20. Given data is

Information frame = 1980bytes

Acknowledge frame = 20bytes

Number of overhead bytes in the information frame = 20bytes

Useful Data = Total Data – Overhead

= 1980 – 20 = 1960bytes

Transmission time for Data(TD)

= (1960 * 8)/10^6

= 15.68 millisecond

Transmission time for ACK(TA)

= 20*8 / 10^6

= 0.16 millisecond

RTT = 2 * Tp

= 2*0.75 = 1.5 millisecond

T(process) = 0.25(for info) + 0.25(for ack)

= 0.5 millisecond

Efficiency = Useful Time / (TD+ + TA + RTT + Tprocess)

= 15.68 / (15.84 + 0.16 + 2*0.75+ 0.5)

= 0.87 i.e. 87%

21. Message = 01011011

divisor D(x) = 1011 and CRC remainder is 101 so the transmitted message is 01011011101.

22. By question, codewords are

00000
01011
10101
11110

Minimum hamming distance = min (hamming distance between every 2 pair) = 3

for correcting errors, we know that

$2d + 1 = 3$

$\Rightarrow \quad d = 1$

23. Current window size = min(congestion window, receiver advertised window)

= min(4KB,6KB)
= 4KB
= 4 * 1024 bytes
= 4096bytes

24. Given data

L = Number of bits in a packet.

P1 = Probability of link 'l1'.

B1 = Bit error probability for link 'l1'

So, no bit error probability for link 'l1' is (1 – b1)

p2 = Probability of link 'l2'

b2 = Bit error probability for link 'l2'

So, no bit error probability for link 'l2' is (1 – b2)

Link 'l1' and 'l2' are mutually exclusive.

So, Probability that the packet will be received without error

$= (1 - b1)^L p1 + (1 - b2)^L p2$

25. Ethernet frame includes a CRC field and IP packet includes a checksum field.

26. Given L = 1KB

B = 1.5Mbps

T = 50ms

$\eta = 60\%$

Efficiency formula for SR protocol is

$$\eta = \frac{W}{1+2a}$$

$$\Rightarrow \frac{60}{100} = \frac{W}{1+2a} \quad \left(\because a = \frac{T_p}{T_x}\right)$$

$$T_x = \frac{L}{B} = \frac{8\times10^3}{1.5\times10^6} = 5.3 \text{ ms}$$

$$a = \frac{T_p}{T_x} = \frac{50}{5.3} = \frac{500}{53} = 9.43$$

$$\Rightarrow \frac{60}{100} = \frac{W}{19.86} \Rightarrow W = 11.9 \approx 12$$

$$\Rightarrow W = 2^{n-1} = 12$$

$$\Rightarrow 2^n = 24$$

$$\Rightarrow 2^n = 24 \approx 2^5 \Rightarrow n = 5$$

27. All are changed.

(i) TTL is decremented at every hop.

(ii) If TTL change that means the Checksum of the packet also change.

(iii) A packet is fragmented if it has a size greater than the Maximum Transmission Unit (MTU) of the network. There may be intermediate networks that may change fragment offset by fragmenting the packet.

28. Length and checksum can be modified when IP fragmentation happens and TTL is reduced by every router on the route to destination But source address is never changed.

29. Subnet mask is 255.255.255.192,

Binary is : 11111111.11111111.11111111.1100000

Network bits are = 8 + 8 + 8 + 2 = 26

Number of bits avaiable for hosts is = 32 – 26 = 6

Number of Host addresses available = 26 – 2 = 64

30. It is given that we have 5bit codeword such that "it can't have two consecutive zeros in first and second bit" and also "can't have two consecutive zeros in last two bits."

Code word with first two bits zero

= 00xxx = 2^3 = 8 {x can be 0 or 1}

Code word with last two bits zero

= xxx00 = 23 = 8 {x can be 0 or 1}

Code word with first and last two bits zero

= 00 x 00 = 21 {x can be 0 or 1}

Code word with first OR last two bits zero

= 8 + 8 – 2 = 14

Therefore possible codewords = 32 – 14 = 18.

31. 1000010111 and Differential Manchester respectively.

32. Convert the given code in multiple of 6 so append 4 zero's at the end.

101000	110011	011111	101001	101010	110000
40	51	31	41	42	48
o	z	f	p	q	w{using base-64 table}.

So the logest substring of ozfpqw is fpq.

33. In Manchester encoding bit rate is half the baud rate.

34. We can send at max 5(5000/1000) packets per Time unit.

So, whatever which is not sent is backlog.

First Time Unit is 6.

Backlog in First time unit is 6 – 5 ⇒ 1 { Now this one gets added to next Time units load }

So, Second time unit ⇒ 9 + 1 (One from Previous Time Unit)

Backlog in Second time Unit is 10 – 5 = 5 (This result gets added to next Time Units load.)

Simlilarly Total Backlog is

= 1 + 5 + 3 + 5 + 2 + 0 + 0 + 0 + 0 + 1 + 0 + 5 + 7 + 7 + 10 + 8 + 9 + 6 + 10 + 10

= 89

Average Backlog is 89/20 = 4.45

35. Given

RTT = Transmission Time

Transmission Time

= Length of packet / Bandwidth

RTT = 2 (d/v) = 2(2000/2 × 108)

To find minimum size of the packet.

RTT = Length of packet/Bandwidth

Length of packet

= RTT × Bandwith

= 2(2000/2 × 108) × 107 = 200bits = 25bytes

So, minimum size of the packet = 25bytes

36. Let there be N such hosts.

Then when one host is transmitting then others must be silent for successful transmission.

So the throughput per host

$0.16 = 0.2 \times (0.8)^{N-1}$

$\rightarrow 0.8 = (0.8)^{N-1}$

Compare the cofficent, Hence,

$N - 1 = 1 \rightarrow N = 2.$

37. There are two condition when A will win the first back-off (0, 1). In second back-off there are four condition (0, 1, 2, 3) [22 – 1 = 4 – 1 = 3]. If A choose 10 in first then required probability

$$= \frac{1}{2}\cdot\frac{3}{4}+\frac{1}{2}\cdot\frac{1}{2} = \frac{3}{8}+\frac{1}{4} = \frac{5}{8} = 0.625$$

38. CSMA/CD is not suitable for a high propagation delay network like satellite network.

39. Frame Size (FS) > = 2BL/P

Where, Cable Length L = 1KM = 1000M

Propogation Speed P = 2 × 10^8 m/sec

Bandwidth = 1 Gbps = 10^9 bps

FS >= (2 * 10^9 * 1000)/(2 × 10^8)

>= 10000 bits

40. Tt = 10 microseconds

Tp = 5 microseconds

Efficiency of the network

= Tt/(Tt + Tp) = 10/15 = 0.67.

Total throughput available for the entire network

= Efficiency × Bandwidth

= 0.67 × 10 Mbps = 6.7 Mbps

Let, No. of stations = N (each wants a Throughput of 0.67 Mbps).

N × 0.67Mbps = 6.7 Mbps

⇒ N = 10.

41. Let 1 : event when station 1 transmits

2 : event when station 2 transmits

N : event when station N transmits

Given : $P(i) = P \quad 1 \le i \le N$

$P(\bar{i}) = (1 - p) \quad (\le i \le N)$

Probability that only one station transmits is given as

$$P(1\,\bar{2}\,\bar{3} \ldots \bar{N} \cup \bar{1}\,2\,\bar{3}\,\bar{4} \ldots \bar{N} \cup \bar{1}\,\bar{2}\,3\,\bar{4}\,\bar{5} \ldots \bar{N} \cup \ldots)$$

$$= P(1\,\bar{2}\,\bar{3} \ldots \bar{N}) + P(\bar{1}\,2\,\bar{3}\,\bar{4} \ldots \bar{N}) + P(\bar{1}\,\bar{2}\,3\,\bar{4}\,\bar{5} \ldots \bar{N}) + \ldots$$

Since all events are mutually exclusive, hence probability

$$= P(1)\,P(\bar{2})\,P(\bar{3}) \ldots P(\bar{N}) + P(\bar{1})\,P(2)\,P(\bar{3})\,P(\bar{4}) \ldots P(\bar{N}) + P(\bar{1})P(\bar{2})P(3)P(\bar{4})P(\bar{5}) \ldots P(\bar{N}) + \ldots$$

Since all events are independent, hence probability

$$= p(1-p)(1-p) \ldots (1-p) + (1-p)\,p\,(1-p) \ldots (1-p) + (1-p)(1-p)\,p\,(1-p) \ldots (1-p) + \ldots$$

$$= n\,p\,(1-p)^{n-1}$$

42. S > = 2 × bandwidth × Td

$>= 2 \times 10^9 \times 200 / (2 \times 10^8)$

>= 2000 bits

>= 2000 / 8 bytes >= 250 byte

43. The probability of sending a frame in the first slot without any collision by any of these four stations is sum of following 4 probabilities

Probability that S1 sends a frame and no one else does +

Probability thatS2 sends a frame and no one else does +

Probability thatS3 sends a frame and no one else does +

Probability thatS4 sends a frame and no one else does

$$= 0.1 * (1 - 0.2) * (1 - 0.3) * (1 - 0.4)$$
$$+ (1 - 0.1) * 0.2 * (1 - 0.3) * (1 - 0.4)$$
$$+ (1 - 0.1) * (1 - 0.2) * 0.3 * (1 - 0.4)$$
$$+ (1 - 0.1) * (1 - 0.2) * (1 - 0.3) * 0.4$$
$$= 0.4404$$

44. Given data

Length of Frame L = 1250 Bytes

Data Transmission Rate B = 100 mbps

Distance d = 1km

Let Signal Speed (km/sec) in cable is V.

In CSMA/CD, L = 2 * dB/V

1250 = 2 * 1Km * 100mbps / V

So, V = 20,000 km/sec

45. According to the concept of binary exponential backoff algorithm the exponential backoff mechanism reduces the probability of collision on retransmissions.

46. From the given data

The size of a frame(L) = ?

Transmission bandwidth (B) = 20 Mbps

Propagation time (T_p) = 40 microse conds

T_x = L/B = 100 ms

$T_x = 2T_p$

The minimum size of a frame

$$(L_{min}) = 2T_p B = 2(40)(20)/8 = 200 \text{ Bytes}$$

47. Given that Signal speed is 10 meter/time.

Which means in 5 unit of time packet can travel 50 meters in max, that allow Q to successfully avoid the collision.

48. (*a*) One of the main functionality of Network Layer is Routing. So Option (a) is CORRECT.

(*b*) Bit Synchronization is always handled by Physical Layer of OSI model but not Data Link Layer. So Option (*b*) is INCORRECT.

(*c*) End – to – End Process Communication is handled by Transport Layer. So Option (c) is CORRECT.

(*d*) MAC sub layer have 3 types of protocols (Random, Controlled and Channelized Access).

49. The main idea for using Spanning Trees is to avoid loops.

50. False. Bridge reduces broadcast domain.

51. Data should be transmitted at the rate of 500 Mbps.

Transmission Time >= 2*Propagation Time

→ 10000bits/(500Mbps) >= (2*d)/(2*105 Kmpersec)

d =< 2km

52. DHCP is used to assign IP dynamically which means- it doesn't resolve addresses.

53. In case of IEEE 802.11 MAC protocol for wireless communication RTS and CTS mechanism is used for collision avoidance, not for collision detection.

54. 3 switches of ethernet are required to connect 15 computers.

3
CHAPTER

Network Layer

Analysis of Previous GATE Papers

Topics ↓		Year →	2019	2018	2017 Set 1	2017 Set 2	2016 Set 1	2016 Set 2	2015 Set 1	2015 Set 2	2015 Set 3
SYNCHORONOUS TRANSMISSION	1 Mark	MCQ Type									
		Numerical Type									
	2 Marks	MCQ Type									
		Numerical Type									
		Total									
NL	1 Mark	MCQ Type		1							
		Numerical Type									
	2 Marks	MCQ Type									
		Numerical Type									
		Total		1							
IP ADDRESS	1 Mark	MCQ Type				1					
		Numerical Type				1					
	2 Marks	MCQ Type	1							1	
		Numerical Type					1				1
		Total	2			2	2			2	2
ROUTING	1 Mark	MCQ Type			1				1		1
		Numerical Type		1							
	2 Marks	MCQ Type								2	
		Numerical Type		1							
		Total		3	1				1	4	1
TCP/IP	1 Mark	MCQ Type									
		Numerical Type									
	2 Marks	MCQ Type									
		Numerical Type									
		Total									

SYNCHORONOUS TRANSMISSION

1. In a data link protocol, the frame delimiter flag is given by 0111. Assuming that bit stuffing is employed, the transmitter sends the data sequence 01110110 as
   (a) 01101011 (b) 011010110
   (c) 011101100 (d) 0110101100
   [2004 : 2 Marks]

2. A bit-stuffing based framing protocol uses an 8-bit delimiter pattern of 01111110. If the output bit-string after stuffing is 01111100101, then the input bit-string is
   (a) 0111110100 (b) 0111110101
   (c) 0111111101 (d) 0111111111
   [2014 (Set-3) : 1 Mark]

3. A computer on a 10 Mbps network is regulated by a token bucket. The token bucket is filled at a rate of 2 Mbps. It is initially filled to capacity with 16 Megabits. What is the maximum duration for which the computer can transmit at the full 10 Mbps?
   (a) 1.6 seconds (b) 2 seconds
   (c) 5 seconds (d) 8 seconds
   [2008 : 2 Marks]

NL

4. A host is connected to a Department network which is part of a University network. The University network, in turn, is part of the Internet. The largest network in which the Ethernet address of the host is unique is
   (a) the subnet to which the host belongs
   (b) the Department network
   (c) the University network
   (d) the Internet **[2004 : 1 Mark]**

5. A router has two full-duplex Ethernet interfaces each operating at 100 Mb/s. Ethernet frames are at least 84 bytes long (including the Preamble and the Inter-Packet-Gap).
   The maximum packet processing time at the router for wirespeed forwarding to be possible is (in micro-seconds)
   (a) 0.01 (b) 3.36
   (c) 6.72 (d) 8 **[2006 : 2 Marks]**

6. Which of the following assertions is FALSE about the Internet Protocol (IP)?
   (a) It is possible for a computer to have multiple IP addresses
   (b) IP packets from the same source to the same destination can take different routes in the network
   (c) IP ensures that a packet is farwarded if it is unable to reach its destination within a given number of hopes
   (d) The packet source cannot set the route of an outgoing packets; the route is determined only by the routing tables in the routers on the way
   [2003 : 1 Mark]

7. Packets of the same session may be routed through different paths in
   (a) TCP, but not UDP
   (b) TCP and UDP
   (c) UDP, but not TCP
   (d) Neither TCP, nor UDP
   [2005 : 1 Mark]

8. The address resolution protocol (ARP) is used for
   (a) Finding the IP address from the DNS
   (b) Finding the IP address of the default gateway
   (c) Finding the IP address that corresponds to a MAC address
   (d) Finding the MAC address that corresponds to an IP address
   [2005 : 1 Mark]

9. Consider the store and forward packet switched network given below. Assume that the bandwidth of each link is 10^6 bytes/sec. A user on host A sends a file of size 10^3 bytes to host B through routers $R1$ and $R2$ in three different ways. In the first case a single packet containing the complete file is transmitted from A to B. In the second case, the file is split into 10 equal parts, and these packets are transmitted from A to B. In the third case, the file is split into 20 equal parts and these packets are sent from A to B. Each packet contains 100 bytes of header information along with the user data. Consider only transmission time and ignore processing, queuing and propagation delays. Also assume that there are no errors during transmission. Let $T1$, $T2$ and $T3$ be the times taken to transmit the file in the first, second and third case respectively. Which one of the following is CORRECT?

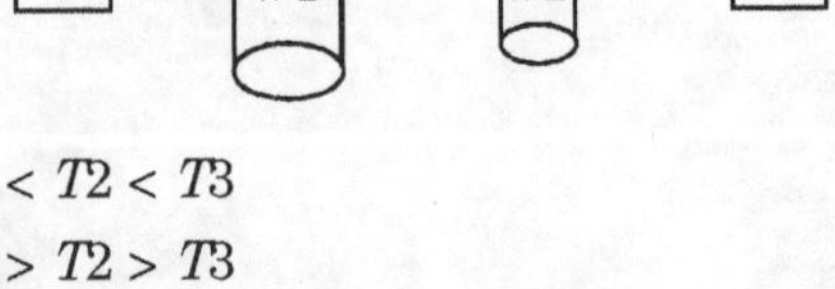

   (a) $T1 < T2 < T3$
   (b) $T1 > T2 > T3$
   (c) $T2 = T3$, $T3 < T1$
   (d) $T1 = T3$, $T3 > T2$ **[2014 (Set-2) : 2 Marks]**

10. Match the following:

Field	Length in bits
P. UDP Header's Port Number	**I.** 48
Q. Ethernet MAC Address	**II.** 8
R. IPv6 Next Header	**III.** 32
S. TCP Header's Sequence Number	**IV.** 16

(a) P-III, Q-IV, R-II, S-I (b) P-II, Q-I, R-IV, S-III

(c) P-IV, Q-I, R-II, S-III (d) P-IV, Q-I, R-III,S-II

[2018 : 1 Mark]

11. Which one of the following statements is FALSE?

(a) Packet switching leads to better utilization of bandwidth resources than circuit switching

(b) Packet switching results in less variation in delay than circuit switching

(c) Packet switching requires more per-packet processing than circuit switching

(d) Packet switching can lead to reordering unlike in circuit switching

[2004 : 1 Mark]

IP ADDRESS

12. The subnet mask for a particular network is 255.255.31.0 Which of the following pairs of IP addresses could belong to this network?

(a) 172.57.88.62 and 172.56.87.23.2

(b) 10.35.28.2 and 10.35.29.4

(c) 191.203.31.87 and 191.234.31.88

(d) 128.8.129.43 and 128.8.161.55

[2003 : 2 Marks]

13. A subnet has been assigned a subnet mask of 255.255.255.192. What is the maximum number of hosts that can belong to this subnet?

(a) 14 (b) 30

(c) 62 (d) 126 **[2004 : 1 Mark]**

14. The routing table of a router is shown below:

Destination	*Subnet Mask*	*Interface*
128.72.43.0	255.255.255.0	Eth0
128.72.43.0	255.255.255.128	Eth1
128.72.43.5	255.255.255.255	Eth3
defualt		Eth2

On which interfaces will the router farward packets addressed to destinations 128.75.43.16 and 192.12.17.10 respectively?

(a) Eth1 and Eth2 (b) Eth0 and Eth2

(c) Eth0 and Eth3 (d) Eth1 and Eth3

[2004 : 2 Marks]

15. An organization has a class B network and wishes to form subnets for 64 departments. The subnet mask would be

(a) 255.255.0.0 (b) 255.255.64.0

(c) 255.255.128.0 (d) 255.255.252.0

[2005 : 1 Mark]

16. A company has a class C network address of 204.204.204.0. It wishes to have three subnets, one with 100 hosts and two with 50 hosts each. Which one of the following options represents a feasible set of subnet address/subnet mask pairs?

(a) 204.204.204.128/255.255.255.192
204.204.204.0/255.255.255.128
204.204.204.64/250.255.255.128

(b) 204.204.204.0/255.255.255.192
204.204.204.192/255.255.255.128
204.204.204.64/255.255.255.128

(c) 204.204.204.128/255.255.255.128
204.204.204.192/255.255.255.192
204.204.204.224/255.255.255.192

(d) 204.204.204.128/255.255.255.128
204.204.204.64/255.255.255.192
204.204.204.0/255.255.255.192

[2005 : 2 Marks]

17. A router uses the following routing table:

Destination	Mask	Interface
144.16.0.0	255.255.0.0	eth0
144.16.64.0	255.255.224.0	eth1
144.16.68.0	255.255.255.0	eth2
144.16.68.64	255.255.255.224	eth3

A packet bearing a destination address 144.16.68.117 arrives at the router. On which interface will it be forwarded?

(a) eth0

(b) ethl

(c) eth2

(d) eth3

[2006 : 2 Marks]

18. A subnetted Class B network has the following broadcast address : 144.16.95.255. Its subnet mask

(a) is necessarily 255.255.224.0

(b) is necessarily 255.255.240.0

(c) is necessarily 255.255.248.0.

(d) could be any one of
255.255.224.0, 255.255.240.0,255.255.248.0

[2006 : 2 Marks]

19. Two computers C1 and C2 are configured as follows. C1 has IP address 203. 197.2.53 and netmask 255.255.128.0. C2 has IP address 203.197.75.201 and netmask 255.255.192.0. Which one of the following statements is true?

(a) C1 and C2 both assume they are on the same network

(b) C2 assumes C1 is on same network, but C1 assumes C2 is on a different network

(c) Cl assumes C2 is on same network, but C2 assumes C1 is on a different network

(d) C1 and C2 both assume they are on different networks

[2006 : 2 Marks]

20. The address of a class B host is to be split into subnets with a 6-bit subnet number. What is the maximum number of subnets and the maximum number of hosts in each subnet?

(a) 62 subnets and 262142 hosts

(b) 64 subnets and 262142 hosts

(c) 62 subnets and 1022 hosts

(d) 64 subnets and 1024 hosts

[2007 : 2 Marks]

21. Host X has IP address 192.168.1.97 and is connected through two routers R1 and R2 to another host Y with IP address 192.168.1.80. Router R1 has IP addresses 192.168.1.135 and 192.168.1.110. R2 has IP addresses 192.168.1.67 and 192.168.1.155. The netmask used in the network is 255.255.255.224.

Giventhe information above, how many distinct subnets are guaranteed to already exist in the network ?

(a) 1 (b) 2

(c) 3 (d) 6 **[2008 : 2 Marks]**

22. Host X has IP address 192.168.1.97 and is connected through two routers R1 and R2 to another host Y with IP address 192.168.1.80. Router R1 has IP addresses 192.168.1.135 and 192.168.1.110. R2 has IP addresses 192.168.1.67 and 192.168.1.155. The netmask used in the network is 255.255.255.224.

Which IP address should X configure its gateway as?

(a) 192.168.1.67 (b) 192.168.1.110

(c) 192.168.1.135 (d) 192.168.1.155

[2008 : 2 Marks]

23. If a class B network on the Internet has a subnet mask of 255.255.248.0, what is the maximum number of hosts per subnet?

(a) 1022 (b) 1023

(c) 2046 (d) 2047 **[2008 : 2 Marks]**

24. Suppose computers A and B have IP addresses 10.105.1.113 and 10.105.1.91 respectively and they both use the same netmask N. Which of the values of N given below should not be used if A and B should belong to the same network?

(a) 255.255.255.0 (b) 255.255.255.128

(c) 255.255.255.192 (d) 255.255.255.224

[2010 : 2 Marks]

25. In the IPv4 addressing format, the number of networks allowed under Class C addresses is

(a) 2^{14} (b) 2^{7}

(c) 2^{21} (d) 2^{24} **[2012 : 1 Mark]**

26. An Internet Service Provider (ISP) has the following chunk of CIDR-based IP addresses available with it: 245.248.128.0/20. The ISP wants to give half of this chunk of addresses to Organization A, and a quarter of Organization B, while retaining the remaining with itself. Which of the following is a valid allocation of addresses to A and B?

(a) 245.248.136.0/21 and 245.248.128.0/22

(b) 245.248.128.0/21 and 245.248.128.0/22

(c) 245.248.132.0/22 and 245.248.132.0/21

(d) 245.248.136.0/24 and 245.248.132.0/21

[2012 : 2 Marks]

27. In an IPv4 datagram, the M bit is 0, the value of HLEN is 10, the value of total length is 400 and the fragment offset value if 300. The position of the datagram, the sequence numbers of the first and the last bytes of the payload, respectively are

(a) Last fragment, 2400 and 2789

(b) First fragment, 2400 and 2759

(c) Last fragment, 2400 and 2759

(d) Middle fragment, 300 and 689 **[2013 : 2 Marks]**

28. An IP router implementing Classless Interdomain Routing (CIDR) receives a packet with address 131.23.151.76. The router's routing table has the following entries:

Prefix	Output Interface Identifier
131.16.0.0 / 12	3
131.28.0.0 / 14	5
131.19.0.0 / 16	2
131.22.0.0 /15	1

The identifier of the output interface on which this packet will be forwarded is______.

[2014 (Set-3) : 2 Marks]

29. Every host in an IPv4 network has a 1-second resolution real-time clock with battery backup. Each host needs to generate up to 1000 unique identifiers per second. Assume that each host has a globally unique IPv4 address. Design a 50-bit globally unique ID for this purpose. After what period (in seconds) will the identifiers generated by a host wrap around?

[2014 (Set-3) : 2 Marks]

30. An IP router with a Maximum Transmission Unit (MTU) of 1500 bytes has received an IP packet of size 4404 bytes with an IP header of length 20 bytes. The values of the relevant fields in the header of the third IP fragment generated by the router for this packet are

(a) MF bit: 0, Datagram Length: 1444; Offset: 370
(b) MF bit: 1, Datagram Length: 1424; Offset: 185
(c) MF bit: 1, Datagram Length: 1500; Offset: 370
(d) MF bit: 0, Datagram Length: 1424; Offset: 2960

[2014 (Set-3) : 2 Marks]

31. Consider the following routing table at an IP

Network No.	Net Mask	Next Hop
128.96.170.0	255.255.254.0	Interface 0
128.96.168.0	255.255.254.0	Interface 1
128.96.166.0	255.255.254.0	R2
128.96.164.0	255.255.252.0	R3
0.0.0.0	Default	R4

For each IP address in Group-I identify the correct choice of the next hop from Group-II using the entries from the routing table above.

List-I	**List-II**
A. 128.96.171.92	**1.** Interface 0
B. 128.96.167.151	**2.** Interface 1
C. 128.96.163.121	**3.** R2
D. 128.96.165.121	**4.** R3
	5. R4

Codes:

	A	B	C	D
(a)	1	3	5	4
(b)	1	4	2	5
(c)	2	3	4	5
(d)	2	3	5	4

2015 (Set-2) : 2 Marks]

32. In the network 200.10.11.144/27, the fourth octet (in decimal) of the last IP address of the network which can be assigned to a host is________.

[2015 (Set-3) : 2 Marks]

33. An IP datagram of size 1000 bytes arrives at a router. The router has to forward this packet on a link whose MTU (maximum transmission unit) is 100 bytes. Assume that the size of the IP header is 20 bytes. The number of fragments that the IP datagram will be divided into for transmission is ______.

[2016 (Set-1) : 2 Marks]

34. The maximum number of IPv4 router addresses that can be listed in the record route (RR) option field of an IPv4 header is ___________.

[2017 (Set-2) : 1 Mark]

35. Consider the following statements about the routing protocols, Routing Information Protocol (RIP) and Open Shortest Path First (OSPF) in an IPv4 network.

I: RIP uses distance vector routing
II: RIP packets are sent using UDP
III: OSPF packets are sent using TCP
IV: OSPF operation is based on link-state routing

Which of the statements above are CORRECT?

(a) I and IV only (b) I, II and III only
(c) I, II and IV only (d) II, III and IV only

[2017 (Set-2) : 1 Mark]

36. Assume that "hostl.mydomain.dom" has an IP address of 145.128.16.8. Which of the following options would be most appropriate as a subsequence of steps in performing the reverse lookup of 145.128.16.8? In the following options "NS" is an abbreviation of "nameserver".

(a) Query a NS for the root domain and then NS for the "dom" domains
(b) Directly query a NS for "dom" and then a NS for "mydomain.dom" domains
(c) Query a NS for in-addr.arpa and then a NS for 128.145.in-addr.arpa domains
(d) Directly query a NS for 145.in-addr.arpa and then a NS for 128.145.in-addr.arpa domains

[2005 : 2 Marks]

37. Consider three machine M, N, and P with IP addresses 100.10.5.2, 100.10.5.5, and 100.10.5.6 respectively. The subnet mask is set to 255.255.255.252 for all the three machines. Which one of the following is true?

(a) M, N, and P belong to three different subnets
(b) M, N, and P all belong to the same subnet
(c) Only N and P belong to the same subnet
(d) Only M and N belong to the same subnet

[2019 : 2 Marks]

ROUTING

38. Which of the following is NOT true with respect to a transparent bridge and a router?

(a) Both bridge and router selectively farward data packets

(b) A bridge uses IP addresses while a router uses MAC addresses

(c) A bridge builds up its routing table by inspecting incoming packets

(d) A router can connect between a LAN and a WAN

[2004 : 1 Mark]

Common Data Questions Q. 39 & Q. 40

Consider three IP networks A, B and C. Host H_A in network A sends messages each containing 180 bytes of application data to a host H_C in network C. The TCP layer prefixes a 20 byte header to the message. This passes through an intermediate network B. The maximum packet size, including 20 byte IP header, in each network is

A : 1000 bytes

B : 100 bytes

C : 1000 bytes

The network A and B are connected through a 1 Mbps link, while B and C are connected by a 512 Kbps link (bps = bits per second).

39. Assuming that the packets are correctly delivered, how many bytes, including headers, are delivered to the IP layer at the destination for one application message, in the best case? Consider only data packets.

(a) 200 (b) 220

(a) 240 (b) 260

[2004 : 2 Marks]

40. What is the rate at which application data is transferred to host H_c? Ignore errors, acknowledgments, and other overheads.

(a) 325.5 Kbps (b) 354.5 Kbps

(c) 409.6 Kbps (d) 512.0 Kbps

[2004 : 2 Marks]

41. In a packet switching network, packets are routed from source to destination along a single path having two intermediate nodes. If the message size is 24 bytes and each packet contains a header of 3 bytes, then the optimum packet size is

(a) 4 (b) 6

(c) 7 (d) 9

[2005 : 2 Marks]

42. Suppose that it takes 1 unit of time to transmit a packet (of fixed size) on a communication link. The link layer uses a window flow control protocol with a window size of N packets. Each packet causes an ack or a nak to be generated by the receiver, and ack/nak transmission times are negligible. Further, the round trip time on the link is equal to N units. Consider time i > N. If only acks have been received till time i(no naks), then the goodput evaluated at the transmitter at time i(in packets per unit time) is

(a) 1 – N/i (b) i/(N + i)

(c) 1 (d) $1 - e^{(i/N)}$

[200s6 : 2 Marks]

43. Count to infinity is a problem associated with

(a) link state routing protocol.

(b) distance vector routing protocol.

(c) DNS while resolving host name.

(d) TCP for congestion control.

[2005 : 1 Mark]

44. For the network given in the figure below, the routing tables of the four nodes A, E, D and G are shown. Suppose that F has estimated its delay to its neighbors, A, E, D and G as 8, 10, 12 and 6 msecs respectively and updates its routing table using distance vector routing technique.

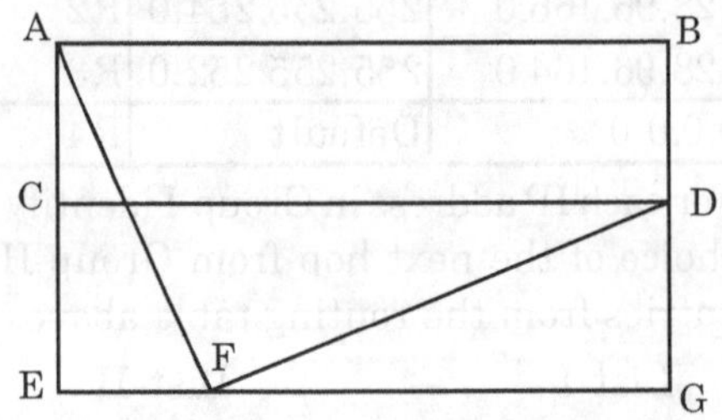

Routing Table of A	
A	0
B	40
C	14
D	17
E	21
F	9
G	24

Routing Table of E	
A	24
B	27
C	7
D	20
E	0
F	11
G	22

Routing Table of D	
A	20
B	8
C	30
D	0
E	14
F	7
G	22

Routing Table of G	
A	21
B	24
C	22
D	19
E	22
F	10
G	0

(a)

A	8
B	20
C	17
D	12
E	10
F	0
G	6

(b)

A	21
B	8
C	7
D	19
E	14
F	0
G	22

(c)

A	8
B	20
C	17
D	12
E	10
F	16
G	6

(d)

A	8
B	8
C	7
D	12
E	10
F	0
G	6

[2007 : 2 Marks]

45. A group of 15 routers are interconnected in a centralized complete binary tree with a router at each tree node. Router i communicates with router j by sending a message to the root of the tree. The root then sends the message back down to router j. The mean number of hops per message, assuming all possible router pairs are equally likely is

(a) 3 (b) 4.26

(c) 4.53 (d) 5.26

[2007 : 2 Marks]

46. A sender is employing public key cryptography to send a secret message to a receiver. Which one of the following statements is TRUE?

(a) Sender encrypts using receiver's public key

(b) Sender encrypts using his own public key

(c) Receiver decrypts using sender's public key

(d) Receiver decrypts using his own public key

[2004 : 1 Mark]

Common data for question 47 and 48

Consider a simple graph with unit edge costs. Each node in the graph represents a router. Each node maintains a routing table indicating the next hop router to be used to relay a packet to its destination and the cost of the path to theh destinationthrough that router. Initially, the routing table is empty. The routing table is synchronously updated as follows. In each updated interval, three tasks are performed.

i. A node determines whether it sneighbours in the graph are accessible. If so, it sets the tentative cost to each accessible neighbour as 1. otherwise, the cost is set to ∞.

ii. From each accessible neighbour, it gets the costs to relay to other nodes via that neighbour (as the next hop).

iii. Each node updates its routing table based on the information received in the previous two steps by choosing the minimum cost.

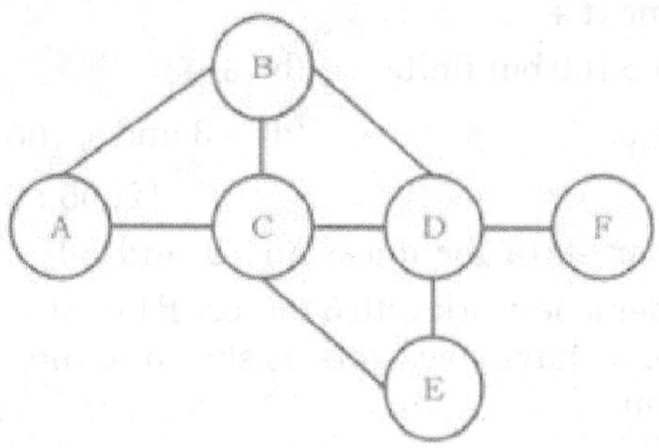

For the graph given above, possible routing tables for various nodes after they have stabilized, are shown in the following options. Identify the correct table.

47. For the graph given above, possible routing tables for various nodes after they have stabilized, are shown in the following options. Identify the correct table.

(a)

Table for node A		
A	-	-
B	B	1
C	C	1
D	B	3
E	C	3
F	C	4

(b)

Table for node C		
A	A	1
B	B	1
C	-	-
D	D	1
E	E	1
F	E	3

(c)

Table for node B		
A	A	1
B	-	-
C	C	1
D	D	1
E	C	2
F	D	2

(d)

Table for node D		
A	B	3
B	B	1
C	C	1
D	-	-
E	E	1
F	F	1

[2005 : 2 Marks]

48. Continuing from the earlier problem, suppose at some time t, when the costs have stabilized, node A goes down. The cost from node F to node A at time (t + 100) is :

(a) >100 but finite (b) ∞

(c) 3 (d) > 3 and $\leq$ 100

[2005 : 2 Marks]

Common data for question 49 and 50

Consider a network with 6 routers R1 to R6 connected with links having weights as shown in the following diagram.

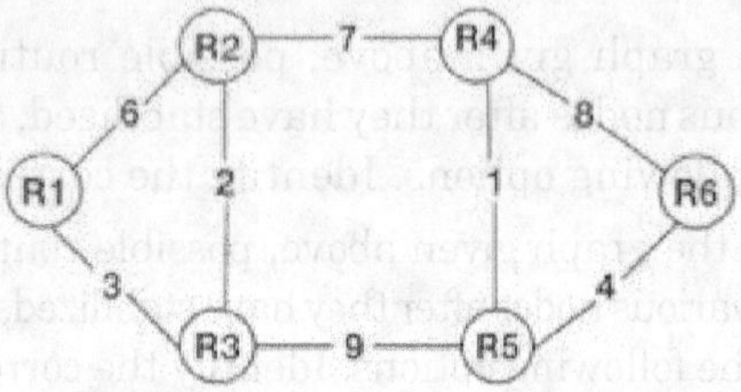

49. All the routers use the distance vector based routing algorithm to update their routing tables. Each router starts with its routing table initialized to contain an entry for each neighbour with the weight of the respective connecting link. After all the routing tables stabilize, how many links in the network will never be used for carrying any data?

(a) 4 (b) 3

(c) 2 (d) 1 **[2010 : 2 Marks]**

50. Suppose the weights of all unused links in the previous question are changed to 2 and the distance vector algorithm is used again until all routing tables stabilize. How many links will now remain unused?

(a) 0 (b) 1

(c) 2 (d) 3 **[2010 : 2 Marks]**

Common data for question 51 and 52

Consider a network with five nodes, N1 to N5, as shown as below.

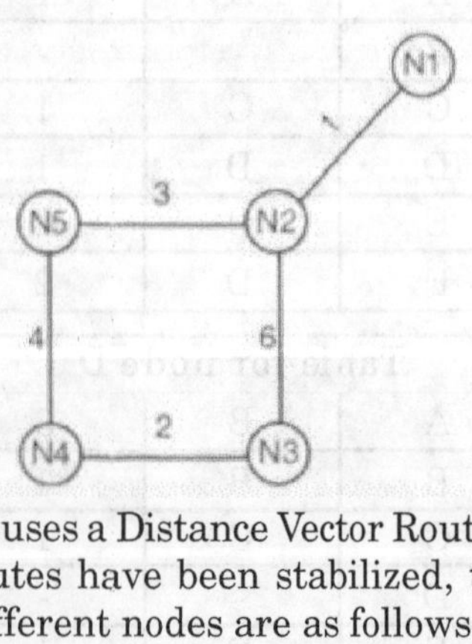

The network uses a Distance Vector Routing protocol. Once the routes have been stabilized, the distance vecotrs at different nodes are as follows.

N1 : (0, 1, 7, 8, 4) **N2** : (1, 0, 6, 7, 3)

N3 : (7, 6, 0, 2, 6) **N4** : (8, 7, 2, 0, 4)

N5 : (4, 3, 6, 4, 0)

Each distane vector is the distance of the best known path at that instance to nodes, N1 to N5, where the distance to itself is 0. Also, all links are symmetric and the cost is identical inboth directions. In each round, all nodes exchange their distance vectors with their respective neighbors. Then all nodes update their distance vectors. In between two rounds, any change in cost of a link will cause the two incident nodes to change only that entry in their distance vectors.

51. The cost of link N2-N3 reduces to 2(in both directions). After the next round of updates, what will be the new distance vector at node, N3?

(a) (3, 2, 0, 2, 5) (b) (3, 2, 0, 2, 6)

(c) (7, 2, 0, 2, 5) (d) (7, 2, 0, 2, 6)

[2011 : 2 Marks]

52. After the update in the previous question, the link N1-N2 goes down. N2 will reflect this change immediately in its distance vector as cost ∞. After the NEXT ROUND of update, what will be the cost to N1 in the distance vector of N3?

(a) 3 (b) 9

(c) 10 (d) ∞ **[2011 : 2 Marks]**

53. Assume that source S and destination D are connected through two intermediate routers labels R. Determine how many times each packet has to visit the network layer and the data link layer during a transmission form S to D.

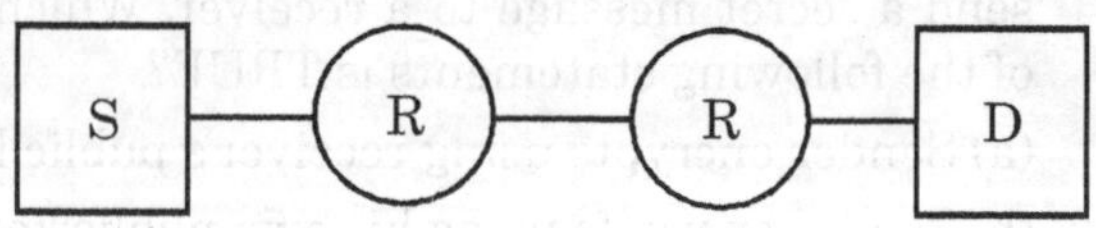

(a) Network layer - 4 times and Data link layer - 4 times

(b) Network layer - 4 times and Data link layer - 3 times

(c) Network layer - 4 times and Data link layer - 6 times

(d) Network layer - 2 times and Data link layer - 6 times **[2013 : 1 Mark]**

54. Consider the following three statements about link state and distance vector routing protocols, for a large network with 500 network nodes and 4000 links.

S1: The computational overhead in link state protocols is higher than in distance vector protocols.

S2: A distance vector protocol (with split horizon) avoids persistent routing loops, but not a link state protocol.

S3: After a topology change, a link state protocol will converge faster than a distance vector protocol.

Which one of the following is correct about S1, S2, and S3?

(a) S1, S2, and S3 are all true.

(b) S1, S2, and S3 are all false.

(c) S1 and S2 are true, but S3 is false.

(d) S1 and S3 are true, but S2 is false.

[2014 (Set-1) : 1 Mark]

55. Which one of the following is TRUE about the interior gateway routing protocols - Routing Information Protocol (RIP) and Open Shortest Path First (OSPF)

(a) RIP uses distance vector routing and OSPF uses link state routing

(b) OSPF uses distance vector routing and RIP uses link state routing

(c) Both RIP and OSPF use link state routing

(d) Both RIP and OSPF use distance vector routing

[2014 (Set-2) : 1 Mark]

56. An IP machine Q has a path to another IP machine H via three IP routers $R1$, $R2$, and $R3$.

$Q — R1— R2 — R3 — H$

H acts as an HTTP server, and Q connects to H via HTTP and downloads a file. Session layer encryption is used, with DES as the shared key encryption protocol. Consider the following four pieces of information:

[I1] The URL of the file downloaded by Q

[I2] The TCP port numbers at Q and H

[I3] The IP addresses of Q and H

[I4] The link layer addresses of Q and H

Which of I1, I2, I3, and I4 can an intruder learn through sniffing at $R2$ alone?

(a) Only I1 and I2

(b) Only I1

(c) Only I2 and I3

(d) Only I3 and I4

[2014 (Set-2) : 2 Marks]

57. Consider an IP packet with a length of 4500 bytes that includes a 20-byte IPv4 header and a 40-byte TCP header. The packet is forwarded to an IPv4 router that supports a Maximum Transmission Unit (MTU) of 600 bytes. Assume that the length of the IP header in all the outgoing fragments of this packet is 20 bytes. Assume that the fragmentation offset value stored in the first fragment is 0.

The fragmentation offset value stored in the third fragment is ________.

[2018 : 2 Marks]

TCP/IP

58. Which one of the following statements is FALSE?

(a) TCP guarantees a minimum communication rate

(b) TCP ensures in-order delivery

(c) TCP reacts to congestion by reducing sender window size

(d) TCP employs retransmission to compensate for packet loss **[2004 : 1 Mark]**

59. In TCP, a unique sequence number assigned to each

(a) byte (b) word

(c) segment (d) message

[2004 : 1 Mark]

60. In the TCP/IP protocol suite, which one of the following is NOT part of the IP header?

(a) Fragment Offset

(b) Source IP address

(c) Destination IP address

(d) Destination port number **[2004 : 2 Marks]**

61. A TCP message consisting of 2100 bytes is passed to IP for delivery across two networks. The first network can carry a maximum payload of 1200 bytes per frame and the second network can carry a maximum payload of 400 bytes per frame, excluding network overhead. Assume that IP overhead per packet is 20 bytes. What is the total IP overhead in the second network for this transmission?

(a) 40 bytes (b) 80 bytes

(c) 120 bytes (d) 160 bytes

[2004 : 2 Marks]

62. Suppose that the maximum transmit window size for a TCP connection is 12000 bytes. Each packet consists of 2000 bytes. At some point of time, the connection is in slow-start phase with a current transmit window of 4000 bytes. Subsequently, the transmitter receives two acknowledgement. Assume that no packets are lost and there are no time-outs. What is the maximum possible value of the current transmit window?

(a) 4000 bytes (b) 8000 bytes

(c) 10000 bytes (d) 12000 bytes

[2004 : 2 Marks]

63. For which one of the following reasons does Internet Protocol (IP) use the time-to-live (TTL) field in the IP datagram header?

(a) Ensure packets reach destination within that time

(b) Discard packets that reach later than that time

(c) Prevent packets from looping indefinitely

(d) Limit the time for which a packet gets queued in intermediate routers **[2006 : 1 Mark]**

64. Consider the following statements about the timeout value used in TCP.

(i) The timeout value is set to the RTT (Round Trip Time) measured during TCP connection establishment for the entire duration of the connection.

(ii) Appropriate RTT estimation algorithm is used to set the timeout value of a TCP connection.

(iii) Timeout value is set to twice the propagation delay from the sender to the receiver.

Which of the following choices hold?

(a) (i) is false, but (ii) and (iii) are true
(b) (i) and (iii) are false, but (ii) is true
(c) (i) and (ii) are false, but (iii) is true
(d) (i), (ii) and (iii) are false

[2007 : 1 Mark]

65. Consider a TCP connection in a state where there are no outstanding ACKs. The sender sends two segments back to back. The sequence numbers of the first and second segments are 230 and 290 respectively. The first segment was lost, but the second segment was received correctly by the receiver.

Let X be the amount of data carried in the first segment (in bytes), and Y be the ACK number sent by the receiver. The values of X and Y (in that order) are

(a) 60 and 290 (b) 230 and 291
(c) 60 and 231 (d) 60 and 230

[2007 : 1 Mark]

66. Which of the following system calls results in the sending of SYN packets?

(a) socket (b) bind
(c) listen (d) connect

[2008 : 1 Mark]

67. The three way handshake for TCP connection establishment is shown below.

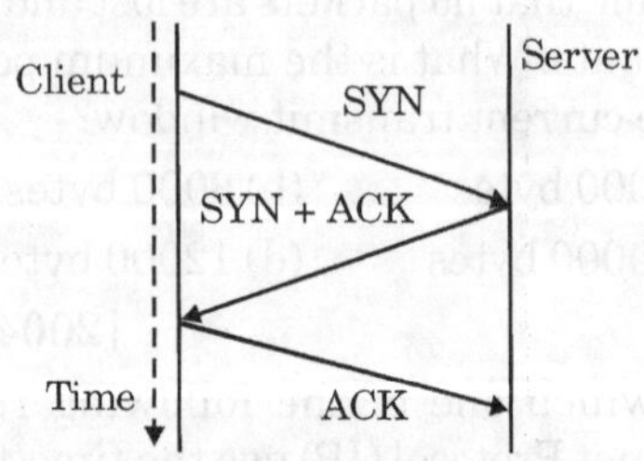

Which of the following statements are TRUE?

S1: Loss of SYN + ACK from the server will not establish a connection

S2: Loss of ACK from the client cannot establish the connection

S3: The server moves LISTEN → SYN_RCVD → SYN_SENT → ESTABLISHED in the state machine on no packet loss

S4: The server moves LISTEN → SYN_RCVD → ESTABLISHED in the state machine on packet loss.

(a) S2 and S3 only (b) S1 and S4 only
(c) S1 and S3 only (d) S2 and S4 only

[2008 : 2 Marks]

68. In the slow start phase of the TCP congesting control algorithm, the size of the congestion window

(a) Does not increase
(b) Increases linearly
(c) Increases quadratically
(d) Increases exponentially **[2008 : 2 Marks]**

69. A client process P needs to make a TCP connection to a server process S. Consider the following situation: the server process S executes a socket ( ), a bind ( ) and a listen ( ) system call in that order, following which it is preempted. Subsequently, the client process P executes a socket ( ) system call followed by connect ( ) system call to connect to the server process S. The server process has not executed any accept ( ) system call. Which one of the following events could take place?

(a) connect( ) system call returns successfully
(b) connect( ) system call blocks
(c) connect( ) system call returns an error
(d) connect( ) system call results in a core dump

[2008 : 2 Marks]

70. While opening a TCP connection, the initial sequence number is to be derived using a time-of-day (ToD) clock that keeps running even when the host is down. The low order 32 bits of the counter of the ToD clock is to be used for the initial sequence numbers. The clock counter increments once per millisecond. The maximum packet lifetime is given to be 64s.

Which one of the choices given below is closest to the minimum permissible rate at which sequence numbers used for packets of a connection can increase?

(a) 0.015/s (b) 0.064/s
(c) 0.135/s (d) 0.327/s

[2009 : 2 Marks]

71. One of the header fields in an IP datagram is the Time-to-Live (TTL) field. Which of the following statements best explains the need for this field?

(a) It can be used to prioritize packets
(b) It can be used to reduce delays
(c) It can be used to optimize throughput
(d) It can be used to prevent packet looping

[2010 : 1 Mark]

72. Consider an instance of TCP's Additive Increase Multiplicative Decrease (AIMD) algorithm where the windows size at the start of the slow start phase is 2 MSS and the threshold at the start of the first transmission is 8 MSS. Assume that a time-out occurs during the fifth transmission. Find the congestion window size at the end of the tenth transmission.

(a) 8 MSS (b) 14 MSS

(c) 7 MSS (d) 12 MSS

[2012 : 2 Marks]

73. Let the size of congestion window of a TCP connection be 32 KB when a timeout occurs. The round trip time of the connection is 100 msec and the maximum segment size used is 2 KB. The time taken (in msec) by the TCP connection to get back to 32 KB congestion window is ________.

[2014 (Set-1) : 2 Marks]

74. Suppose two hosts use a TCP connection to transfer a large file. Which of the following statements is/are FALSE with respect to the TCP connection?

1. If the sequence number of a segment is m, then the sequence number of the subsequent segment is always m+1.
2. If the estimated round trip time at any given point of time is t sec, the value of the retransmission timeout is always set to greater than or equal to t sec.
3. The size of the advertised window never changes during the course of the TCP connection.
4. The number of unacknowledged bytes at the sender is always less than or equal to the advertised window.

(a) 3 only

(b) 1 and 3 only

(c) 1 and 4 only

(d) 2 and 4 only

[2015 (Set-1) : 1 Mark]

75. Assume that the bandwidth for a TCP connection is 1048560 bits/sec. Let α be the value of RTT in milliseconds (rounded off to the nearest integer) after which the TCP window scale option is needed. Let β be the maximum possible window size with window scale option. Then the values of α and β are

(a) 63 milliseconds 65535×2^{14}

(b) 63 milliseconds 65535×2^{16}

(c) 500 milliseconds 65535×2^{14}

(d) 500 milliseconds 65535×2^{16}

[2015 (Set-2) : 2 Marks]

76. Host A sends a UDP datagram containing 8880 bytes of user data to host B over an Ethernet LAN. Ethernet frames may carry data up to 1500 bytes (i.e. MTU = 1500 bytes). Size of UDP header is 8 bytes and size of IP header is 20 bytes. There is no option field in IP header. How may total number of IP fragments will be transmitted and what will be the contents of offset field in the last fragment?

(a) 6 and 925 (b) 6 and 7400

(c) 7 and 1110 (d) 7 and 8880

[2015 (Set-2) : 2 Marks]

77. Consider the following statements.

I. TCP connections are full duplex.

II. TCP has no option for selective acknowledgment

III. TCP connections are message streams.

(a) Only I is correct

(b) Only I and II are correct

(c) Only II and III are correct

(d) All of I, II and III are correct

[2015 (Set-3) : 1 Mark]

78. Consider a TCP client and a TCP server running on two different machines. After completing data transfer, the TCP client calls **close** to terminate the connection and a FIN segment is sent to the TCP server. Server-side TCP responds by sending an ACK. which is received by the client-side TCP. As per the TCP connection state diagram (RFC 793). In which state does the client-side TCP connection wait for the FIN from the server- side TCP?

(a) LAST-ACK (b) TIME-WAIT

(c) FIN-WAIT-1 (d) FIN-WAIT-2

[2017 (Set-1) : 1 Mark]

79. Consider a long-lived TCP session with an end-to-end bandwidth of 1 Gbps (= 10^9 bits-per- second). The session starts with a sequence number of 1234. The minimum time (in seconds, rounded to the closest integer) before this sequence number can be used again is ________.

[2018 : 1 Mark]

ANSWERS

1. (d)	2. (b)	3. (b)	4. (d)	5. (b)	6. (d)	7. (a)	8. (d)	9. (d)	10. (c)
11. (b)	12. (d)	13. (c)	14. (a)	15. (d)	16. (d)	17. (c)	18. (d)	19. (c)	20. (c)
21. (c)	22. (b)	23. (c)	24. (d)	25. (c)	26. (a)	27. (c)	28. (1)	29. (256)	30. (a)
31. (a)	32. (158)	33. (13)	34. (9)	35. (c)	36. (c)	37. (c)	38. (b)	39. (d)	40. (b)
41. (d)	42. (a)	43. (b)	44. (a)	45. (c)	46. (a)	47. (*)	48. (a)	49. (c)	50. (b)
51. (a)	52. (c)	53. (c)	54. (d)	55. (a)	56. (c)	57. (144)	58. (a)	59. (a)	60. (d)
61. (c)	62. (b)	63. (c)	64. (b)	65. (d)	66. (d)	67. (b)	68. (d)	69. (c)	70. (a)
71. (d)	72. (c)	73. (1100)	74. (b)	75. (c)	76. (c)	77. (a)	78. (d)	79. (34)	

EXPLANATIONS

1. Delimiter flag: 0111

   Data sequence: 01110110

   So, for a flag of 4 bits we will compare data sequence with pattern of 3 bits i.e. 011.

   Data sequence : 0 1 1 1 0 1 1 0

   The underlined bits are found matched, hence, 0 is stuffed.

   Thus resulting in the data sequence as 0110101100 which is option (d).

2. The given 8-bit delimiter pattern is 01111110.

   The output bit-string after stuffing is 01111100101.

   The above bold underline bit is stuffed bit.

   So input bit-string must be 0111110101.

3. Let duration is t sec.

   $\therefore \quad 16 + 2t = 10 \times t$

   $\Rightarrow \quad t = 2$ sec

4. Ethernet address is basically the MAC address, which is supposed to be unique to a NIC. Thus it is unique over the Internet.

5. Minimum transmission time

   = (84 bytes) / (2*100 bps)

   = (84 * 8 bits) / (2*100 bps)

   = 3.36 seconds

6. The packet source cannot set the route of an outgoing packets; the route is determined only by the routing tables in the routers on the way.

7. TCP and UDP are Transport layer protocols. Packets of same session may be routed through different routes.

8. The Address Resolution Protocol (ARP), allows a host to find the MAC (Physical) address of a target host on the same physical network, given only the targets IP address.

9. The following data is given

   File Size = 1000 bytes

   Header Size = 100 bytes

   Transmission Speed of all links = 10^6 bytes/sec

   Case (1) :

   Transmission time for one link

   = packetsize/bandwidth

   = (1000 + 100)/10^6

   = 1100 microsecond.

   So, Total time(T1) is 3*1100

   = 3300 microsecond

   Case (2) :

   Transmission time for one link and one part

   = (100 + 100)/10^6

   = 200 microseccond

   Note : While a packet is being transmitted from R1 to R2, at the same time other packet is being transmitted from A to R1.

   So, Total time(T2) = 3 * 200 + 9 * 200

   = 2400 microsecond

   Case (3) :

   Transmission time for one link and one part

   = (50 + 100)/10^6

   = 150 microsecond

   Total time (T3) = 3 * 150 + 19 * 150

   = 3300 microsecond

   hence T1 = T3, T3 > T2

10. UDP Header's Port Number ⇒ 16 bit

    Ethernet MAC Address ⇒ 48 bit

    IPv6 Next Header ⇒ 8 bit

    TCP Header's Sequence Number ⇒ 32 bit

11. False. Packet switching results in less variation in delay than circuit switching.

12. Subnet mask 255.255.31.0 shows class C network
So, class C network. IP address is
191.203.31.87 and 191.234.31.88

13. Network Address = IP address BITWISE AND Subnet Mask
128.8.129.43 BITWISE-AND 255.255.31.0
= 128.8.1.0
128.8.161.55 BITWISE-AND 255.255.31.0
= 128.8.1.0.

14. For 1st packet,
128.75.43.16 BITWISE-AND 255.255.255.0
= 128.75.43.0
128.75.43.16 BITWISE-AND 255.255.255.128
= 128.75.43.0
Now, since both these subnet masks are producing the same Network ID, hence The one with greater number of ones will be selected, and the packet will be forwarded there. Hence packet 1 will be forwarded to Eth1.
For 2nd packet,
192.12.17.10 BITWISE-AND 255.255.255.0
= 192.12.17.0
{Does not match with any of the network addresses}
192.12.17.10 BITWISE-AND 255.255.255.128
= 192.12.17.0
{Does not match with any of the network addresses}
192.12.17.10 BITWISE-AND 255.255.255.255
=192.12.17.10
{Does not match with any of the network addresses}
Hence, default interface must be selected for packet 2, i.e Interface Eth2.

15. Since, we have to support 64 department so our first
1 1 1 1 1 1 0 0
= 252

16. MSB in last 8 bits helps us to get two subnets
10000000 → subnet1
00000000 → subnet2
subnet2 is divided into 2 more subnets using 7th bit
00000000 → subnet2(0)
01000000 → subnet2(1)

17. Subnet address of interface = 144. 16 . 68 .0
Subnet address of incoming IP
= 144. 16. 68. 117 BITWISE AND 255.255.255.0
= 144. 16. 68.0
Both subnetwork addresses are same, so packet is forwarded to interface eth2

18. For broadcast address of a subnet, all the host bits are set to 1.
Broadcast address for subnet is
.95.255 ---> .0101 1111. 1111 1111
So, Possible host bits can be 13 to 0
Hence could be any one of 255.255.224.0, 255.255.240.0, 255.255.248.0

19. The two computer C1 and C2 are configured as follows :

	C1	C2
IP Address	203.197.2.53	203.197.75.201
AND		AND
Netmask	255.255.128.0	255.255.192.0
	203.197.0.0	203.197.64.0
	Network Address	Network Address

203.197.2.53 → 203.197.00000010.00111001
255.255.192.0 →255.255.11000000.00000000
203.197.0.0 203.197.0.0
203.197.75.201
255.255.128.0
203.192.0.0

∴ C1 assumes C2 is on same network but C2 assumes C1 is on different network.

20. Maximum number of subnets
$= 2^6 - 2 = 62$
Maximum number of host in each subnet
$= 2^{10} - 2 = 1022$

21. Given IP addresses are of Class C
default Mask for class C = 24
The given mask is 11 bits 11111111 11111111 11111111 11100000
subnet ID: 3 bits
existing subnets: 011, 010 and 100

22. For ip address 192.168.1.110/28
For network address keep Network bits as it is and put host bits =0 in any given IP address.
Network address
= 192.168.1.01100000 → 192.168.1.96
For: 192.168.1.97/28
Network address
= 192.168.1.01100000 →192.168.1.96

23. Starting address : 255. 255. 248. 0
End address : 255. 255. 255. 254.

24. Given : 10.105.1.113 and 10.105.1.91

When these are in same network, then AND with netmask give the address of same ID otherwise these are in different class in these only AND with 255.255.255.224 are in different class

This is 96 and 64. Then these are different ID means 10.105.1.96 and 10.105.1.64 are different ID. So this is not in same network.

Alternately

10.105.1.113	→ 00001010	01101001	00000001	01110001
	→ 11111111	11111111	11111111	11100000
	00001010	01101001	00000001	01100000
	10 .	105	1 .	96

When we do the similar operation with 2nd IP, it gives 10.105.1.64

Here, it gives different IP

but for the rest it gives same IP.

25. For class C address, size of network field is 24 bits. But first 3 bits are fixed as 110; hence total number of networks possible is 2^{21}

26.

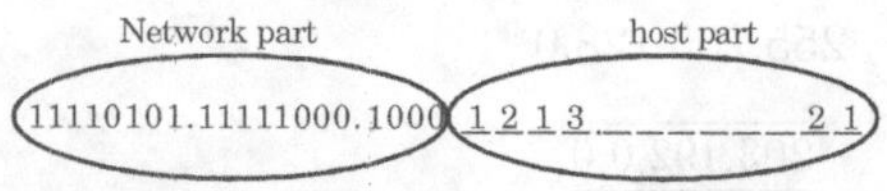

Since half of 4096 host addresses must be given to organization A, we can set 12th bit to 1 and include that bit into network part of organization A, so the valid allocation of addresses to A is 245.248.136.0/21

Now for organization B, 12th bit is set to '0' but since we need only half of 2048 addresses, 13th bit can be set to '0' and include that bit into network part of organization B so the valid allocation of addresses to B is 245.248.128.0/2.

27. Since M bit is 0, so there is no fragments after this fragment. Hence this <u>fragment is the "last fragment"</u> Tow, H LEN defines the length of Header in datagram. Since H LEN is 10 so size of header is 10 * 4 = 40B.

Length of data = Total length – Leader length
= 400 – 40 = 360 B.

Few, fragment offset of data in original datagram is measured in units of 8B. So to find first Byte of this fragment,

$$\frac{\text{first Byte}}{\text{B}} = \text{fragment offset}$$

⇒ <u>first Byte</u> = 300 * 8 = <u>"2400"</u> B

since length of data is 360B

so last Byte on this datagram will be <u>"2759"</u> B

i.e. "first last"
2400 – 2759
(360B length)

28. Given address 131.23. 151.76. coming to the first field of given routing table

⇒ 131.16. 0.0/12

131.0001 0111.151.76

131.0001 0000.0.0 (∵ given mask bits = 12)

⇒ 131.16.0.0 Matched

Coming to the 2nd field of given Routing table

⇒ 131.28.0.0/14

131.0001 0111. 151. 76

131.0001 0100.0.0 (∵ given mask bits = 14)

⇒ 131.20.0.0 not matched

Coming to the 3rd field of given Routing table

Error ! Not a valid link 131.19.0.0/16

131.0001 0111.151.76

131.0001 0111.0.0 (∵ given mask bits = 16)

⇒ 131.23.0.0 Not matched

Coming to the 4th field of given Routing table

⇒ 131.22.0.0/15

131.0001 0111.151.76

131.0001 0110.0.0 (∵ given mask bits = 15)

⇒ 131.22.0.0 Matched

We are getting 1st and 4th entries are matched so among them we have to picked up the longest mask bit, so output interface identifier is 1.

29. Given that each host has a globally unique IPv4 Address and we have to design 50 – bit unique Id. So, 50 – bit in the sense (32 + 18). So, It is clearly showing that IP Address (32 – bit) followed by 18 bits.

1000 unique Ids => 1Sec

2^{18} unique Ids => 2^{18} / 1000 = 2^8 = 256

30.

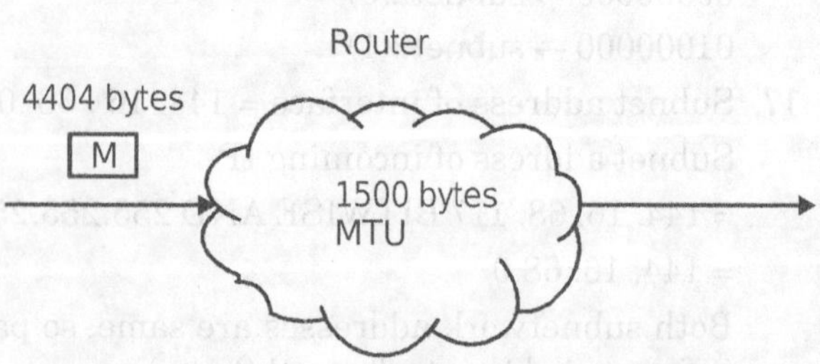

Data length	1480	1480	1444
	+	+	
Header length	20	20	
MF	1	1	0

31. Do the BITWISE AND operation of group 1 with netmask given in the table.

32. Fourth octet of network address is 144 i.e. 10010000.

The first three bits of this octal is subnet bit (100), remaining bits can get maximum value as 11111.

So the maximum possible last octal IP address is 10011111 which is 159.

But the address with all 1s in host part is broadcast address and can't be assigned to a host. So the maximum possible host is 158.

33. IP datagram = 1000 bytes.

MTU = 100 bytes

IP header = 20 bytes.

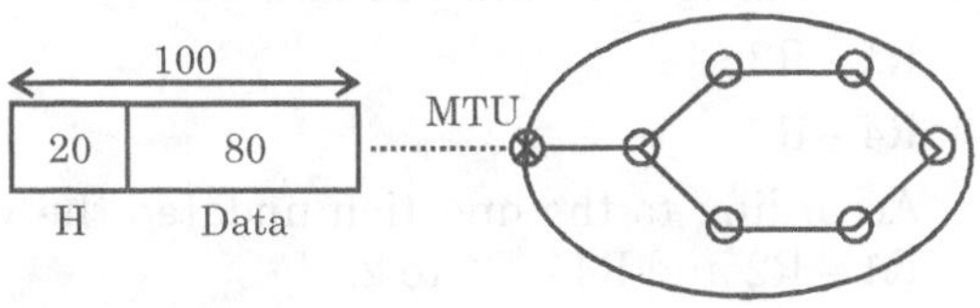

Number of fragments $\Rightarrow \left\lceil \frac{1000}{80} \right\rceil$

$\Rightarrow [12.4] \Rightarrow 13$

34. In IPv4, 40 bytes are alloted for options and padding.

and maximum nine routers addresses are allowed.

Each IPv4 address is 32 bits or 4 bytes

Hence $4 \times 9 = 36$ bytes

The remaining byte are used for the option.

35. As we know:

- RIP uses distance vector routing.
- OSPF uses link-state routing protocols.
- RIP uses UDP as transport protocol.
- OSPF neither uses TCP nor UDP.

[Link state packet should be given to all routers in subnet so it's not possible with TCP. These link state packets should be reliable at that same time which is not possible with UDP.]

36. We need to get NS for in-addr.arpa before doing query to 8.16.128.145.in-addr.arpa

37.

	100.10.5.2	2	00000010
M→	255.255.255.252	252	11111100
	194.56.10.0	0	00000000
	100.10.5.5	2	00000101
N→	255.255.255.252	252	11111100
	194.56.10.4	4	00000100
	100.10.5.6	6	00000110
P→	255.255.255.252	252	11111100
	194.56.10.4	4	00000100

N and P belongs to same subnet.

38. Choice (*b*) is not true.

A bridge operates at layer 2 (Data Link Layer) so it uses MAC address while routes operates at layer 3 (Network Layer) so it uses IP addresses.

39. Packet A sends an IP packet of 180 bytes of data +20 bytes of TCP header +20 bytes of IP header to B.

Ip layer of B now removes 20 bytes of IP header and has 200 bytes of data.

So, it makes 3 IP packets – (80 + 20, 80 + 20, 40 + 20) and sends to C as the Ip packet size of B is 100. So, C receives 260 bytes of data which includes 60 bytes of Ip headers and 20 bytes of TCP header.

40. Ignoring errors, i.e. noise, we have

$$B = 2H \text{ (Nyquist theorem)}$$
$$= 354.5 \text{ kbps}$$

41. Consider optimum packet size which required minimum number of packet and does not waste any space.

Here consider each packet header because they are all work on packet switching network.

3 bytes is header size;

9 – 3 = 6 is data size

24/6 = 4 are the required packet

For case 1 : 24 packets are required

For case 2 : 8 packets are required

For case 3 : 6 packets are required

42. Goodput (is the application level throughput) = Successfully delivered data/ Time = (i-N)/i = 1- N/i.

43. This Problems can happen in distance vector routing protocol when a link or a router fails.

44. Distance from F to F is 0 So option C is flase.

Using Distance Vector routing protocol, F → D → B distance is 20

So option B and D is alse false.

45. As per question, we have to count average hops per message.

Steps used:

1) Message goes up from sender to root.

2) Message comes down from root to destination

1) Average hops message goes to root – $((3 \times 8) + (2 \times 4) + (1 \times 2) + (0 \times 1))/15 = 2.267$

// 3×8 means represents 3 hops & 8 routers for Bottom most level & So on.

2) Similarly average hops when message comes down -

$((3 \times 8) + (2 \times 4) + (1 \times 2) + (0 \times 1))/15 = 2.267$

So, Total Hops = 2.267 + 2.267 = 4.53.

46. Sender encrypts using receiver's public key.

47. After statizing every node the updated table as follows :-

(1) Table for node A

A	–	
B	B	1
C	C	1
D	B	2
E	C	2
F	C	3

(2) Table for Node B

A	A	1
B	–	–
C	C	1
D	D	1
E	C	2
F	D	2

(3) Table for node C

A	A	1
B	–	1
C	C	–
D	D	1
E	C	1
F	D	2

(4) Table for Node D

A	B	2
B	B	1
C	C	1
D	–	
E	E	1
F	F	1

48. Count to infinity problem.

49. Following will be distance vectors of all nodes.

Shortest Distances from R1 to other nodes (i.e. R2, R3, R4, R5, R6) is represented by vector R1(5, 3, 12, 12, 16).

Used links are R1 – R3, R3 – R2, R2 – R4, R3 – R5, R5 – R6

Shortest Distances from R2 to other nodes (i.e. R3, R4, R5, R6) is R2(2, 7, 8, 12) used links are R2 – R3, R2 – R4, R4 – R5, R5 – R6.

Shortest Distances from R3 to other nodes (i.e. R4, R5, R6) is R3(9, 9, 13) used links are R3 – R2, R2 – R4, R3 – R5, R5 – R6

Shortest Distances from R4 to R5 and R6 is R4(1, 5) used links are R4 – R5, R5 – R6

Shortest Distance from R5 to R6 is R5(4) Used links are R5 – R6

If we mark, all the used links one by one, we can see that following links are never used.

R1 – R2

R4 – R6

50. Following two links are unused

R1 – R2

R4 – R6

According to the question updated the value of R1 – R2 and R4 – R6 to 2.

Now apply Distance vector routing algorithm

Hence, R1 (2, 3, 9, 10, 11)

Links used: R1 – R2, R1 – R3, R2 – R4, R4 – R5, R4 – R6

R2 (2, 7, 8, 9)

Links used: R2 – R3, R2 – R4, R4 – R5, R4 – R6

R3 (9, 9, 11)

Links used: R3 – R2, R2 – R4, R3 – R5, R4 – R6

R4 (1, 2)

Links used: R4 – R5, R4 – R6

R5 (3)

Links Used: R5 – R4, R4 – R6

As we can see all links are used except R5-R6.

51. In the next round, every node will send and receive distance vectors to and from neighbors, and update its dostance vector.

N3 will recieve (1, 0, 2, 7, 3) from N2 and it will update distances to N1 and N5 as 3 and 5 respectively.

52. In the next round, N3 will receive distance from N2 to N1 as infinite. It will receive distance from N4 to N1 as 8. So it will update distance to N1 as 8 + 2 = 10.

53. Assume the source S & destination D are connected through two intermediate routers labled R. Determine how many times each packet has to visit the network layer and data link layer during a transmission from S to D.

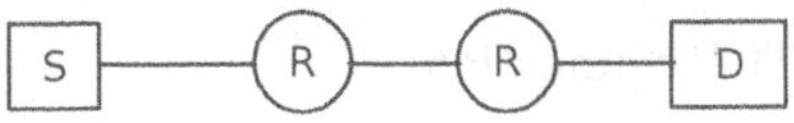

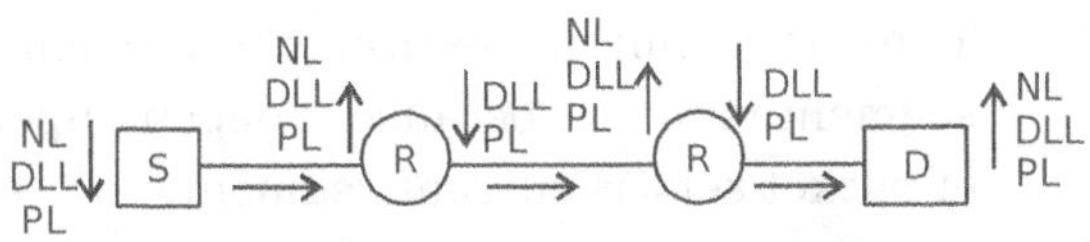

⇒ Network Layer 4 times

⇒ Data link layer 6 times

54. Statement S1

The Distance Vector routing protocols rely on the information from their directly connected neighbours in order to calculate and accumulate route information. Distance Vector routing protocols require very little overhead as compared to Link State routing protocols as measured by memory and processor power while the Link State routing protocols do not rely solely on the information from the neighbours or adjacent router in order to calculate route information. Instead, Link State routing protocols have a system of databases that they use in order to calculate the best route to destinations in the network. This is TRUE

Statement S3

Distance Vector exchanges the routing updates periodically whether the topology is change or not, this will maximize the convergence time which increases the chance of routing loops while the Link State routing protocols send triggered change based updates when there is a topology change. After initial flood, pass small event based triggered link state updates to all other routers. This will minimize the convergence time that's why there is no chance of routing loops. This is TRUE.

55. We know that RIP uses distance vector routing and QSPF uses link state routing.

56. $Q - R_1 - R_2 - R_3 - H$

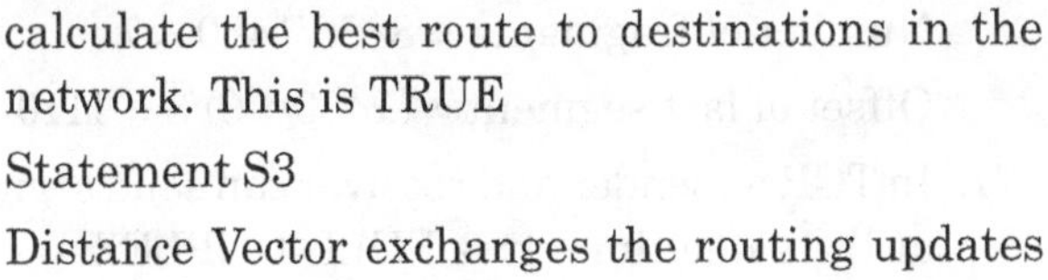

P-Physical Layer, d-data link layer, N-Network layer

Since, the router R_1 contains TCP part numbers of Q and R_2 contains the TCP part numbers of H at Data link layer, and with both routers contains IP addresses of Q and H at Network layer. So, only statement I_2 and I_3 will be true.

57.

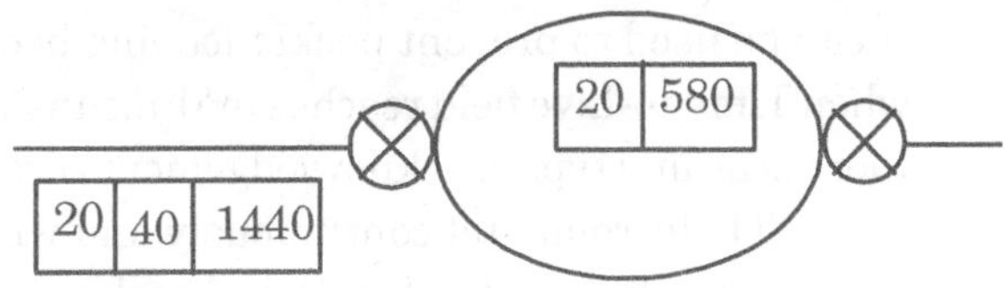

Fragment Bytes

1st		2nd		3rd		4th	
20	576	20	576	20	576	20	576

Fragment Offset

(0 – 71) (72 – 143) (144 – 215) (216 – 287)

58. TCP guarantees a minimum communication rate.

59. In TCP, a unique sequence number is assigned to each byte.

60. In IPv4 header format Destination port filed is not available.

61. Total IP overhead is 120bytes.

62. In slow-start phase, for each ACK, the sender increases the current transmit window by Maximum Segment Size (MSS).

As per question, a packet consists of 2000 bytes and that can be taken as MSS. So, after two ACKs, current transmit window

$= 4000 + 2000 + 2000$

$= 8000$

63. TTL field is used to Prevent packets from looping indefinitely.

64. (i) and (iii) are false, but (ii) is true.

65. Data in 1st segment is from 230 to 289 (byte number) i.e. 60 bytes data.

As given 1st segment is lost so, TCP will send ACK for the next in-order segment receiver is expecting. So it will be for 230.

66. Connect() is used on the client side, and assigns a free local port number to a socket. In case of a TCP socket, it causes an attempt to establish a new TCP connection.

67. S1 and S4 is true.

68. Congestion window increases exponentially.

69. As there is no accept() at server side, the connect() at client could not get anything that can respond to its requests, so error occurs.

70. The maximum packet lifetime = 64 seconds i.e. a sequence number increments after every 64 seconds.

So, minimum permissible rate = 1/64 = 0.015 per second

71. It can be used to prevent packet looping because when Time-to-Live field reaches to '0' means when there is no any type of acknowledgement received, then TTL decrementet continuously and when it reaches '0', then it stop looping of packet.

72. Window size for 1st transmission = 2 MSS

Window size for 2nd transmission = 4 MSS

Window size for 3rd transmission = 8 MSS

Threshold reached, increase linearly (according to AIMD)

Window size for 4th transmission = 9 MSS

Window size for 5th transmission = 10 MSS

Time out occurs, resend 5th with window size starts with as slow start.

Window size for 6th transmission = 2 MSS

Window size for 7th transmission = 4 MSS

Threshold reached, now increase linearly (according to AIMD)

Additive Increase: 5 MSS (since 8 MSS isn't permissible anymore)

Window size for 8th transmission = 5 MSS

Window size for 9th transmission = 6 MSS

Window size for 10th transmission = 7 MSS

73. Given that at the time of Time Out, Congestion Window Size is 32KB and RTT = 100 ms,

When Time Out occurs, for the next round of Slow Start,

Threshold = (size of congestion window) / 2 = 16KB

Suppose we have a slow start

$\Rightarrow$ 2KB – 4KB – 8KB – 16KB

(As the threshold is reached, Additive increase starts)

– 18KB – 20KB – 22KB – 24KB – 26KB – 28KB – 30KB – 32KB

Here - (dash line) is representing RTT so the total number of dash lines is 11 × 100ms = 1100msec

74. In a TCP connection

- If the sequence number of a segments is *m*. Then it is not necessary the subsequent segment is *m* + 1, because it depend upon no of packet sent is current segment.
- Advertise window can not be fixed it may change on changing the capacity of receiver window.

75. (1) we have bandwidth delay product

= (1048560/8) B * α = 64 K

α = (64 K * 8)/1048560

= 0.5 s = 500 milliseconds.

(2) If window scaling happens, a 14 bit shift count is used in TCP header. So, the maximum possible window size gets increased from $2^{16} - 1$ to $(2^{16} - 1) * 2^{14}$ or from 65535 to $65535 * 2^{14}$.

76. UDP data = 8880 bytes

UDP header = 8 bytes

IP Header = 20 bytes

Total Size(excluding IP Header) = 8888 bytes.

Number of fragments = 8888/1480 = 7

Offset of last segment = (1480 * 6)/8 = 1110

77. In TCP, as sender and receiver can send segments at the same time, It is FULL-DUPLEX.

78. FIN-WAIT-2

79. 1 sec = 10^9 bits

$$\frac{2^{32} \times 8}{10^9} = 2^{32} \text{ bytes}$$

$\Rightarrow$ 34.35 sec

4

CHAPTER

Transport Layer

Analysis of Previous GATE Papers

	Year → Topics ↓		2019	2018	2017 Set 1	2017 Set 2	2016 Set 1	2016 Set 2	2015 Set 1	2015 Set 2	2015 Set 3
TL	1 Mark	MCQ Type									
		Numerical Type									
	2 Marks	MCQ Type									
		Numerical Type									
	Total										
UDP	1 Mark	MCQ Type				1					
		Numerical Type									
	2 Marks	MCQ Type									
		Numerical Type									
	Total					1					
PORT ADDRESSING	1 Mark	MCQ Type								1	
		Numerical Type									
	2 Marks	MCQ Type									
		Numerical Type	1								
	Total		2							1	
CONGESTION CONTROL	1 Mark	MCQ Type									
		Numerical Type									
	2 Marks	MCQ Type									
		Numerical Type									
	Total										

TL

1. Which of the following functionalities must be implemented by a transport protocol over and above the network protocol?

(a) Recovery from packet losses

(b) Detection of duplicate packets

(c) Packet delivery in the correct order

(d) End to end connectivity

[2003 : 1 Mark]

2. Which of the following transport layer protocols is used to support electronic mail?

(a) SMTP (b) IP

(c) TCP (d) UDP

[2012 : 1 Mark]

UDP

3. Consider socket API on a Linux machine that supports connected UDP sockets. A connected UDP socket is a UDP socket on which **connect** function has already been called. Which of the following statements is/are CORRECT?

I. A connected UDP socket can be used to communicate with multiple peers simultaneously.

II. A process can successfully call **connect** function again for an already connected UDP socket.

(a) I only (b) II only

(c) Both I and II (d) Neither I nor II

[2017 (Set-2) : 1 Mark]

4. Which one of the following uses UDP as the transport protocol? 1

(a) HTTP (b) Telnet

(c) DNS (d) SMTP

[2007 : 1 Mark]

PORT ADDRESSING

5. Which of the following functionalities must be implemented by a transport protocol over and above the network protocol?

(a) Recovery from packet losses

(b) Detection of duplicate packets

(c) Packet delivery in the correct order

(d) End to end connectivity

[2003 : 1 Mark]

6. Which one of the following socket API functions converts an unconnected active TCP socket into a passive socket?

(a) connect

(b) bind

(c) listen

(d) accept

[2014 (Set-2) : 1 Mark]

7. Identify the correct order in which a server process must invoke the function calls **accept, bind, listen,** and **recv** according to UNIX socket API.

(a) listen, accept, bind recv

(b) bind, listen, accept, recv

(c) bind, accept, listen, recv

(d) accept, listen, bind, recv

[2015 (Set-2) : 1 Mark]

8. Consider the augmented grammar given below:

$S' \to S$

$S \to \langle L \rangle \mid id$

$L \to L, S \mid S$

Let I_0 = CLOSURE ({[$S' \to \bullet S$]}). The number of items in the set GOTO(I_0, ⟨) is: ______.

[2019 : 2 Marks]

CONGESTION CONTROL

9. Which of the following statements are TRUE?

S1: TCP handles both congestion and flow control

S2: UDP handles congestion but not flow control

S3: Fast retransmit deals with congestion but not flow control

S4: Slow start mechanism deals with both congestion and flow control

(a) S1, S2 and S3 only

(b) S1 and S3 only

(c) S3 and S4 only

(d) S1, S3 and S4 only

[2008 : 2 Marks]

10. While an IP Datagram is transferring from one host to another host, TTL, Checksum and Fragmentation Offset will be changed.

ANSWERS

1. (d)	**2.** (c)	**3.** (b)	**4.** (c)	**5.** (d)	**6.** (c)	**7.** (b)	**8.** (5)	**9.** (b)	**10.** (c)

EXPLANATIONS

1. Transport protocol is called end to end connecting layer.
2. E-mail uses SMTP, application layer protocol which intern uses TCP transport layer protocol.
3. Frist statement is WRONG : Even if UDP is connectionless, every UDP socket has a single specified IP number and port number to connect to. Therefore we can not use same socket to connect to multiple peers simultaneously.

   Second statement is RIGHT : We can call connect again to connect to a new peer and disconnect previous peer if implementation allows.
4. DNS uses UDP as the transport protocal.
5. Transport protocol is called end to end connecting layer.
6. Listen() convert an unconnected active socket into passive socket, that is, as a socket that will be used to accept incoming connection requests using accept().
7. Bind() associates a socket with a socket address structure, i.e. a specified local port number and IP address.

   Listen() causes a bound TCP socket to enter listening state.

   Accept() accepts a received incoming attempt to create a new

   TCP connection from the remote client, recv() is used to receive data from a remote socket.
8. 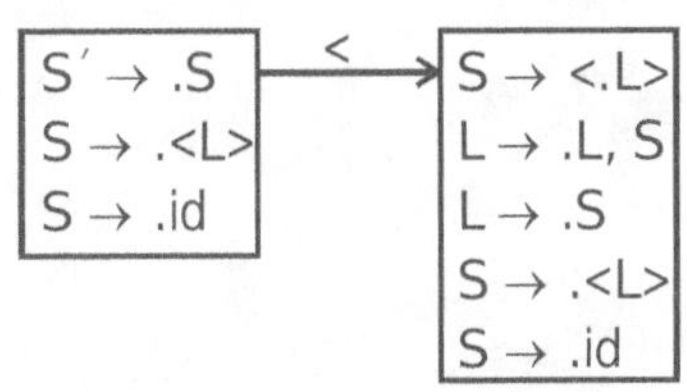

   Hence total number of items in the set GOTO (I_0, ⟨) is 5.
9. TCP handles both congestion and flow control.

   Fast retransmit and fast recovery are part of TCP congestion control. No field are there in UDP header to control flow or congestion.
10. While an IP Datagram is transferring from one host to another host, TTL, Checksum and Fragmentation Offset will be changed.

5
CHAPTER

Application, Authentication & Security

Analysis of Previous GATE Papers											
	Year → Topics ↓		2019	2018	2017 Set 1	2017 Set 2	2016 Set 1	2016 Set 2	2015 Set 1	2015 Set 2	2015 Set 3
AL	1 Mark	MCQ Type	1					1	1		
		Numerical Type									
	2 Marks	MCQ Type					1				
		Numerical Type									
	Total		1				2	1	1		
AUTHENTICATION & SECURITY	1 Mark	MCQ Type			1			1	1		
		Numerical Type									
	2 Marks	MCQ Type	1				1				
		Numerical Type	1		1			1			
	Total		4		3		2	3	1		

AL

1. Which of the following is/are example(s) of statefull application layer protocols?

   (i) HTTP *(ii)* FTP
   (iii) TCP *(iv)* POP3

   (a) *(i)* and *(ii)* only (b) *(ii)* and *(iii)* only
   (c) *(ii)* and *(iv)* only (d) *(iv)* only

   [2016 (Set-1) : 2 Marks]

2. What is the maximum size of data that the application layer can pass on to the TCP layer below?
   (a) Any size
   (b) 2^{16} bytes – size of TCP header
   (c) 2^{16} bytes
   (d) 1500 bytes

   [2008 : 1 Mark]

3. Consider the three commands: PROMPT, HEAD and RCPT. Which of the following options indicate a correct association of these commands with protocols where these are used?
   (a) HTTP, SMTP, FTP
   (b) FTP, HTTP, SMTP
   (c) HTTP, FTP, SMTP
   (d) SMTP, HTTP, FTP

   [2005 : 1 Mark]

4. Traceroute reports a possible route that is taken by packets moving from some host A to some other host B. Which of the following options represents the technique used by traceroute to identify these hosts
   (a) By progressively querying routers about the next router on the path to B using ICMP packets, starting with the first router
   (b) By requiring each router to append the address to the ICMP packet as it is forwarded to B. The list of all routers en-route to B is returned by B in an ICMP reply packet
   (c) By ensuring that an ICMP reply packet is returned to A by each router en-route to B, in the ascending order of their hop distance from A
   (d) By locally computing the shortest path from A to B

   [2005 : 1 Mark]

5. HELO and PORT, respectively, are commands from the protocols
   (a) FTP and HTTP
   (b) TELNET and POP3
   (c) HTTP and TELNET
   (d) SMTP and FTP

   [2006 : 2 Marks]

6. Match the following:

P. SMTP	**1.** Application layer
Q. BGP	**2.** Transport layer
R. TCP	**3.** Data link layer
S. PPP	**4.** Network layer
	5. Physical layer

   Codes:
   (a) P-2, Q-1, R-3, S-5
   (b) P-1, Q-4, R-2, S-3
   (c) P-1, Q-4, R-2, S-5
   (d) P-2, Q-4, R-1, S-3

   [2007 : 2 Marks]

7. Which one of the following is not a client-server application?
   (a) Internet chat (b) Web browsing
   (c) E-mail (d) Ping

   [2010 : 1 Mark]

8. Consider different activities related to email
   ml: Send an email from a mail client to a mail server
   m2: Download an email from mailbox server to a mail client
   m3: Checking email in a web browser
   (a) m1:HTTP m2:SMTP m3:P0P
   (b) m1:SMTP m2:FTP m3:HTTP
   (c) m1:SMTP m2:P0P m3:HTTP
   (d) m1:POP m2:SMTP m3:IMAP

   [2011 : 1 Mark]

9. The Protocol Data Unit (PDU) for the application layer in the Internet stack is
   (a) Segment
   (b) Datagram
   (c) Message
   (d) Frame

   [2012 : 1 Mark]

10. The transport layer protocols used for real time multimedia, file transfer, DNS and email respectively are
(a) TCP, UDP, UDP and TCP
(b) UDP, TCP, TCP and UDP
(c) UDP, TCP, UDP and TCP
(d) TCP, UDP, TCP and UDP
[2013 : 1 Mark]

11. In one of the pairs of protocols given below, both the protocols can use multiple TCP connections between the same client and the server. Which one is that?
(a) HTTP, FTP (b) HTTP, TELNET
(c) FTP, SMTP (d) HTTP, SMTP
[2015 (Set-1) : 1 Mark]

12. Identify the correct sequence in which the following packets are transmitted on the network by a host when a browser requests a webpage from a remote server, assuming that the host has just been restarted.
(a) HTTP GET request, DNS query, TCP SYN
(b) DNS query, HTTP GET request, TCP SYN
(c) DNS query, TCP SYN, HTTP GET request
(d) TCP SYN, DNS query, HTTP GET request
[2016 (Set-2) : 1 Mark]

13. Which of the following protocol pairs can be used to send and retrieve e-mails (in that order)?
(a) IMAP, SMTP (b) IMAP, POP3
(c) SMTP, POP3 (d) SMTP, MIME
[2019 : 1 Mark]

AUTHENTICATION & SECURITY

14. A sender is employing public key cryptography to send a secret message to a receiver. Which one of the following statements is TRUE?
(a) Sender encrypts using receiver's public key
(b) Sender encrypts using his own public key
(c) Receiver decrypts using sender's public key
(d) Receiver decrypts using his own public key
[2004 : 1 Mark]

15. Suppose that two parties A and B wish to setup a common secret key (D-H key) between themselves using the Diffie-Hellman key exchange technique. They agree on 7 as the modulus and 3 as the primitive root. Party A chooses 2 and party B chooses 5 as their respective secrets. Their D-H key is
(a) 3 (b) 4
(c) 5 (d) 6
[2005 : 2 Marks]

16. Consider the following two statements:
(i) A hash function (these are often used for computing digital signatures) is an injective function.
(ii) An encryption technique such as DES performs a permutation on the elements of its input alphabet.

Which one of the following options is valid for the above two statements?
(a) Both are false
(b) Statement (i) is true and the other is false
(c) Statement (ii) is true and the other is false
(d) Both are true
[2007 : 1 Mark]

17. The minimum positive integer p such that 3^p modulo 17 = 1 is
(a) 5 (b) 8
(c) 12 (d) 16 **[2007 : 1 Mark]**

18. Exponentiation is a heavily used operation in public key cryptography. Which of the following options is the tightest upper bound on the number of multiplications required to compute b^n modulo $m, \ 0 \le b, \ n \le m$?
(a) O(log n)
(b) $O(\sqrt{n})$
(c) O(n/log n)
(d) O(n)
[2007 : 1 Mark]

19. A firewall is to be configured to allow hosts in a private network to freely open TCP connections and send packets on open connections. However, it will only allow external hosts to send packets on existing open TCP connections or connections that are being opened (by internal hosts) but not allow them to open TCP connections to hosts in the private network. To achieve this the minimum capability of the firewall should be that of
(a) A combinational circuit
(b) A finite automaton
(c) A pushdown automaton with one stack
(d) A pushdown automaton with two stacks
[2007 : 1 Mark]

20. Consider the following clauses:

(i) Not inherently suitable for client authentication.

(ii) Not a state sensitive protocol.

(iii) Must be operated with more than one server.

(iv) Suitable for structured message organization.

(v) May need two ports on the serve side for proper operation.

The option that has the maximum number of correct matches is

(a) IMAP-(i), FTP-(ii), HTTP-(iii), DNS- (iv), POP3-(v)

(b) FTP-(i), POP3-(ii), SMTP-(iii), HTTP- (iv), IMAP-(v)

(c) POP3-(i), SMTP-(ii), DNS-(iii), IMAP- (iv), HTTP-(v)

(d) SMTP-(i), HTTP-(ii), IMAP-(iii), DNS-(iv), FTP-(v)

[2007 : 2 Marks]

21. The total number of keys required for a set of n individuals to be able to communicate with each other using secret key and public key cryptosystems, respectively are:

(a) $n(n-1)$ and $2n$

(b) $2n$ and $((n(n-1))/2)$

(c) $((n(n-1))/2)$ and $2n$

(d) $((n(n-1))/2)$ and n

[2008 : 2 Marks]

22. In the RSA public key cryptosystem, the private and public keys are (e, n) and (d, n) respectively, where $n = p*q$ and p and q are large primes. Besides, n is public and p and q are private. Let M be an integer such that $0 < M < n$ and $\phi(n) = (p-1)(q-1)$. Now consider the following equations.

I. $M' = M^e \bmod n$

$M = (M')^d \bmod n$

II. $ed \equiv 1 \bmod n$

III. $ed \equiv 1 \bmod \phi(n)$

IV. $M' = M^e \bmod \phi(n)$

$M = (M')^d \bmod \phi(n)$

Which of the above equations correctly represent RSA cryptosystem?

(a) I and II (b) I and III

(c) II and IV (d) III and IV

[2009 : 2 Marks]

23. Using public key cryptography, X adds a digital signature σ to message M, encrypts $<M, \sigma>$, and sends it to Y, where it is decrypted. Which one of the following sequence of keys is used for the operations?

(a) Encryption : X's private key followed by Y's private key; Decryption : X's public key followed by Y's public key

(b) Encryption : X's private key followed by Y's private key; Decryption : X's public key followed by Y's private key

(c) Encryption : X's public key followed by Y's private key; Decryption : Y's public key followed by X's private key

(d) Encryption: X's private key followed by Y's public key; Decryption : Y's private key followed by X's public key

[2013 : 1 Mark]

24. Which of the following are used to generate a message digest by the network security protocols?

(P) RSA (Q) SHA-1

(R) DES (S) MD5

(a) P and R only

(b) Q are R only

(c) Q and S only

(d) R and S only

[2014 (Set-1) : 1 Mark]

25. Suppose that everyone in a group of N people wants to communicate secretly with the N – 1 others using symmetric key cryptographic system. The communication between any two persons should not be decodable by the others in the group. The number of keys required in the system as a whole to satisfy the confidentiality requirement is

(a) 2N

(b) N(N – 1)

(c) N(N – 1) / 2

(d) $(N-1)^2$

[2015 (Set-1) : 1 Mark]

26. Consider that B wants to send a message m that is digitally signed to A. Let the pair of private and public keys for A and B be denoted by K_x^- and K_x^+ for $x = A, B$, respectively. Let $K_x(m)$ represent the operation of encrypting m with a key K_x and $H(m)$ represent the message digest. Which one of the following indicates the CORRECT way of sending the message m along with the digital signature to A?

(a) $\{m, K_B^+(H(m))\}$

(b) $\{m, K_B^-(H(m))\}$

(c) $\{m, K_A^-(H(m))\}$

(d) $\{m, K_A^+(m)\}$

[2016 (Set-1) : 2 Marks]

27. Anarkali digitally signs a message and sends it to Salim. Verification of the signature by Salim requires

(a) Anarkali's public key

(b) Salim's public key

(c) Salim's private key

(d) Anarkali's private key

[2016 (Set-2) : 1 Mark]

28. The value of the expression 13^{99}(mod 17), in the range 0 to 16, is _______.

[2016 (Set-2) : 2 Marks]

29. In a RSA cryptosystem, a participant A uses two prime numbers $p = 13$ and $q = 17$ to generate her public and private keys. If the public key of A is 35, then the private key of A is _______.

[2017 (Set-1) : 2 Marks]

30. A sender S sends a message m to receiver R. which is digitally signed by S with its private key. In this scenario, one or more of the following security violations can take place.

I. S can launch a birthday attack to replace m with a fraudulent message.

II. A third party attacker can launch a birthday attack to replace m with a fraudulent message.

III. R can launch a birthday attack to replace m with a fraudulent message.

Which of the following are possible security violations?

(a) I and II only
(b) I only
(c) II only
(d) II and III only

[2017 (Set-1) : 1 Mark]

31. In an RSA cryptosystem, the value of the public modulus parameter n is 3007. If it is also known that φ (n) = 2880, where φ () denotes Euler's Totient Function, then the prime factor of n which is greater than 50 is_______.

[2019 : 2 Marks]

32. Suppose that in an IP-over-Ethernet network, a machine X wishes to find the MAC address of another machine Y in its subnet. Which one of the following techniques can be used for this?

(a) X sends an ARP request packet to the local gateway's IP address which then finds the MAC address of Y and sends to X

(b) X sends an ARP request packet with broadcast IP address in its local subnet

(c) X sends an ARP request packet to the local gateway's MAC address which then finds the MAC address of Y and sends to X

(d) X sends an ARP request packet with broadcast MAC address in its local subnet

[2019 : 2 Marks]

ANSWERS

1. (c)	2. (a)	3. (b)	4. (a)	5. (d)	6. (b)	7. (d)	8. (c)	9. (c)	10. (c)
11. (a)	12. (c)	13. (c)	14. (13)	15. (b)	16. (c)	17. (d)	18. (a)	19. (d)	20. (d)
21. (c)	22. (b)	23. (d)	24. (c)	25. (*)	26. (b)	27. (a)	28. (4)	29. (11)	30. (b)
31. 97	32. (d)								

EXPLANATIONS

1. FTP and POP3 are non-HTTP protocols

   These are stateful application layer protocols.

2. Application layer just takes the data from user, pass it on the TCP layers below. It is the work of other TCP layer to actually disintegrate the data into packets accroding to network parameters to transmit in the network and assemble different packets on receiving them and handling it to the application layer. So, application layer doesnot bother about size.

3. PROMPT- Used for FTP transfers, Ftp prompts during multiple file transfers to allow you to selectively retrieve or store files.

   HEAD-This is used in HTTP to get meta data information ,to decide the category of packet.

   RCPT-Used in SMTP ,with the help of this you tell the mail server who the recipient of your message is by using the RCPT command.

4. Traceroute tracks the route packets taken from an IP network on their way to a given host. It utilizes the IP protocol's time to live (TTL) field and attempts to elicit an ICMP TIME_EXCEEDED response from each gateway along the path to the host.

5. SMTP : The client sends 'HELO' command to the SMTP server to identify itself and initiate the SMTP conversation. It is an Internet standard used for transmitting email. Electronic mail servers and other mail transfer agents use SMTP to send and receive mail messages.

   File Transfer Protocol (FTP) : The PORT command is sent by an FTP client to establish a secondary connection (address and port) for data to travel over.

6. TCP protocol works on Transport layer.

   SMTP protocol works on Application layer.

   PPP Protol works on Data link layer.

   BGP protol works on Physical layer.

7. Internet chat, web browsing and E-mail all are client-server application. Ping is a utility. It is mainly used to check the connection between two computer, there is a chance both are client or one is client and another server. In chat system first user authentication required and it requires server.

8. Sending an email will be done through user agent and message transfer agent by SMTP, downloading an email from mail box is done through POP, checking email in a web browser is done through HTTP

9. The PDU for Datalink layer, Network layer, Transport layer and Application layer are frame, datagram, segment and message respectively.

10. 1. **Real Time Multimedia:** Can be unreliable but have to be fast so UDP
    2. **File Transfer:** Has to be secure & reliable so uses TCP
    3. **DNS:** Work or part 953, can be both TCP and UDP
    4. **Email:** uses TCP, for reliability

    ∴ UDP, TCP, TCP/UDP, TCP

11. HTTP and FTP may use multiple TCP connection. HTTP may use different TCP connection for different objects of a webpage if non-persistent connections are used. FTP uses two TCP connections, one for data and another control. TELNET and FTP can only use ONE connection at a time.

12. Theere are following steps in which packets are transmitted on the network by a host when a browser requests a webpage from a remote server :

    Step 1 : The client(browser) initiates a DNS query for remote server. It may be that they already have this server in their DNS cache, in which case the client may simply send a TCP SYN directly to the application server.

    Step 2 : The client will next send a connection request to the application server. This will be a TCP SYN packet, the first in the TCP three-way handshake.

    Step 3 : Next, after the TCP connection has been established, the client will request data from the server. In the web-based application, the client performs an HTTP GET.

13. SMTP is push protocol and is used to send email and while POP3 is pull protocol and is used to retrieve email.

14. Sender encrypts using receiver's public key so decryptions of massage is possible only by using private key of receiver.

15. Primitive root g = 3

    We assume D-H key to be K.

    K = gAB mod n

    K = 32 * 5mod 7 = 4

16. In DES encryption scheme, it performs P-Box permutation.

So hash function is many to one.

17. By Fermat's Theorem, 3^{17-1} modulo 17 = 1

So p = 16.

18. Recurrence Relation for computing the time complexity of the given problem using Divide And Conquer technique

$T(n) = T(n/2) + \text{constant} = O(\log n)$.

19. A pushdown automaton with two stacks is TM. It can do everything our normal computer can do so a firewall can be created out of TM.

20. FTP need to open two ports at server, 1 for control information at 21 and another for data. SMTP-Not suitable for client authentication, SMTP AUTH an extension is provided for authentication now.

HTTP-It doesn't depend on the state of the device or OS.

IMAP-It includes a central server ,hence must have more than one server

DNS-Suitable for structured message organization.

FTP-needs port 20 and 21 for control and data.

21. If there are n individuals then total number of distinct keys for communication will be n – 1 So, total number of keys will be 1 + 2 + 3 +..n – 1 = (n(n – 1)/2) Now for a public key encryption scheme every individual will have two keys one public key and one private key.

Therefore, for n individuals to communicate we will have 2 * n keys

Hence, the correct answer will be ((n(n – 1))/2) and 2n.

22. In RSA public key cryptography, a public key provide for every one but they have their seprate private key.

According to formula of public key cryptography

I. $M' = M^e$ mod, $M = (M')^d \bmod n$

IV. $M' = M^e \bmod \phi(n)$, $M = (M')^d \bmod \phi(n)$

represent RSA cryptosystem.

23. **Given:** X encrypts a message and send it to Y.

To find: Correction encryption - decryption order

Analysis: To make sure that Y receives the message & is able to decrypt it and no one else is able to X. The message over the network should be encrypted by Y's public key.

So, order of encryption is X's private key, Y's public key. On receiving the encrypted message, Y will have to decrypt it using its private key & then use X's public key for signature. So, order of decryption is Y's private key followed by X's public key.

So, the answer is (*d*)

24. RSA and DES are for Encryption where MD5 and SHA – 1 are used to generate Message Digest.

25. ****

26. So Option B is correct as it is encrypting digest of message H(m) using its private key K-B

27. To achieve verification or authentication Sender uses its private key to digitally sign a document and Receiver uses public key of sender to verify.

28. 13^{99}(mod 17)

$= (13^3 \bmod 17)^{33}$

$= (4 \bmod 17)^{33}$

$= (4^3 \bmod 17)11$

$= (4^{11} \bmod 17) = 4$

29. In an RSA cryptosystem, for public key:

GCD(□(n), e) = 1

And, for private key: (e * d) mod □ (n) = 1

30. Instead of intended message, Sender can take some fraudulent message and encrypt it with own private key and then receiver's public key.

Using Birthday Attack, some fraudulent message can be generated which has same hash value and digital signature as the original message. So 1st statement is true.

31. $n = p \times q = 3007$

$\phi(n) = (p-1)(q-1) = 2880$

Using RSA algorithm, $n = 31 \times 97$ in which 97 is prime factor which is greater than 50.

32. ****

Unit - XI

General Aptitude

Syllabus

Verbal Ability: English grammar, sentence completion, verbal analogies, word groups, instructions, critical reasoning and verbal deduction.

Numerical Ability: Numerical computation, numerical estimation, numerical reasoning and data interpretation.

Contents

1
CHAPTER

General Aptitude

Analysis of Previous GATE Papers

Topics ↓		Year →	2019	2018	2017 Set 1	2017 Set 2	2016 Set 1	2016 Set 2	2015 Set 1	2015 Set 2	2015 Set 3
Verbal Ability	1 Mark	MCQ Type	2	2	2	2	3	2	3	3	1
		Numerical Type									
	2 Marks	MCQ Type	1		1	1	1	2	1	1	2
		Numerical Type									
		Total	**4**	**2**	**4**	**4**	**5**	**6**	**5**	**5**	**5**
Reasoning Ability	1 Mark	MCQ Type		1	1	2	1	2	1	1	2
		Numerical Type									
	2 Marks	MCQ Type	1		1	1	1		1	2	1
		Numerical Type									
		Total	**2**	**1**	**3**	**4**	**3**	**2**	**3**	**5**	**4**
Numerical Ability	1 Mark	MCQ Type	3	2	2	1	1	1	1	1	1
		Numerical Type									
	2 Marks	MCQ Type	3	5	2	3	3	3	3	2	2
		Numerical Type									
		Total	**9**	**12**	**6**	**7**	**7**	**7**	**7**	**5**	**5**

VERBAL ABILITY

1. Which of the following options is the closest in meaning to the word below?

Circuitous

(a) Cyclic (b) Indirect
(c) Confusing (d) Crooked

[2010:1 Mark]

2. The question below consists of a pair of related words followed by four pairs of words. Select the pair that best expresses the relation in the original pair.

Unemployed: Worker

(a) Fallow:Land (b) Unaware: Sleeper
(c) Wit: Jester (d) Renovated: House

[2010:1 Mark]

3. Choose the most appropriate word from the options given below to complete the following sentence:

If we manage to .... our natural resources, we would leave a better planet for our children.

(a) uphold (b) restrain
(c) cherish (d) conserve

[2010:1 Mark]

4. Choose the most appropriate word from the options given below to complete the following sentence:

His rather casual remarks on politics .... his lack of seriousness about the subject.

(a) masked (b) belied
(c) betrayed (d) suppressed

[2010:1 Mark]

5. Modern warfare has changed from large scale clashes of armies to suppression of civilian populations. Chemical agents that do their work silently appear to be suited to such warfare; and regretfully, there exist people in military establishments who think that chemical agents are usefull fools for their cause.

Which of the following statements best sums up the meaning of the above passage?

(a) Modern warfare has resulted in civil strife.
(b) Chemical agents are useful in modern warfare.
(c) Use of chemical agents in warfare would be undesirable.
(d) People in military establishments like to use chemical agents in war.

[2010:2 Marks]

6. Which of the following options is the closest in the meaning to the word below:

Inexplicable

(a) Incomprehensible (b) Indelible
(c) Inextricable (d) Infallible

[2011:1 Mark]

7. Choose the most appropriate word(s) from the options given below to complete the following sentence.

In contemplated ________ Singapore for my vacation but decided against it.

(a) to visit (b) having to visit
(c) visiting (d) for a visit

[2011:1 Mark]

8. Choose the most appropriate word from the options given below to complete the following sentence.

If you are trying to make a strong impression on your audience, you cannot do so by being understated, tentative or

(a) hyperbolic (b) restrained
(c) argumentative (d) indifferent

[2011:1 Mark]

9. Choose the word from the options given below that is most nearly opposite in meaning to the given word:

Amalgamate

(a) merge (b) split
(c) collect (d) separate

[2011:1 Mark]

10. Few school curricula include a unit on how to deal with bereavement and grief, and yet all students at some point in their lives suffer from losses through death and parting.

Based on the above passage which topic would not be included in a unit on bereavement?

(a) how to write a letter of condolence
(b) what emotional stages are passed through in the healing process
(c) what the leading causes of death are
(d) how to give support to a grieving friend

[2011: 2 Marks]

11. Choose the most appropriate alternative from the options given below to complete the following sentence:

Despite several _____ the mission succeeded in its attempt to resolve the conflict.

(a) attempts (b) setbacks
(c) meetings (d) delegations

[2012:1 Mark]

12. Which one of the following options is the closest in meaning to the word given below?

Mitigate

(a) Diminish (b) Divulge

(c) Dedicate (d) Denote

[2012:1 Mark]

13. Choose the grammatically INCORRECT sentence:

(a) They gave us the money back less the service charges to Three Hundred rupees.

(b) This country's expenditure is not less than that of Bangladesh.

(c) The committee initially asked for a funding of Fifty Lakh rupees, but later settled for a lesser sum.

(d) This country's expenditure on educational reforms is very less. **[2012:1 Mark]**

14. Choose the most appropriate alternative from the options given below to complete the following sentence:

Suresh's dog is the one ______ was hurt in the stampede.

(a) that (b) which

(c) who (d) whom

[2012:1 Mark]

15. Wanted Temporary, Part-time persons for the post of Field Interviewer to conduct personal interviews to collect and collate economic data. Requirements: High School-pass, must be available for Day, Evening and Saturday work. Transportation paid, expenses reimbursed. Which one of the following is the best inference from the above advertisement?

(a) Gender-discriminatory

(b) Xenophobic

(c) Not designed to make the post attractive

(d) Not gender-discriminatory

[2012:2 Marks]

16. Which one of the following options is the closest in meaning to the word given below?

Nadir

(a) Highest (b) Lowest

(c) Medium (d) Integration

[2013:1 Mark]

17. Complete the sentence:

Universalism is to particularism as diffuseness is to ______.

(a) specificity (b) neutrality

(c) generality (d) adaptation

[2013:1 Mark]

18. Were you a bird, you ______ in the sky.

(a) would fly (b) shall fly

(c) should fly (d) shall have flown

[2013:1 Mark]

19. Choose the grammatically INCORRECT sentence:

(a) He is of Asian origin.

(b) They belonged to Africa

(c) She is an European.

(d) They migrated from India to Australia.

[2013:1 Mark]

20. After several defeats in wars, Robert Bruce went in exile and wanted to commit suicide. Just before committing suicide, the came across a spider attempting tirelessly to have its net. Time and again, the spider failed but the did not deter it to refrain from making attempts. Such attempts by the spider made Bruce curious. Thus, Bruce started observing the near-impossible goal of the spider to have the net. Ultimately, the spider succeeded in having its net despite several failures. Such act of the spider encouraged Bruce not to commit suicide. And then, Bruce went back again and won many a battle, and the rest is history.

Which one of the following assertions is best supported by the above information?

(a) Failure is the pillar of success

(b) Honesty is the best policy

(c) Life begins and ends with adventures

(d) No adversity justifies giving up hope

[2013:2 Marks]

21. Which of the following options is the closest in meaning to the phrase underlined in the sentence below?

It is fascinating to see life forms **cope with** varied environmental conditions,

(a) adopt to (b) adapt to

(c) adept in (d) accept with

[2014 (Set-1) : 1 Mark]

22. Choose the most appropriate word from the options given below to complete the following sentence.

He could not understand the judges awarding her the first prize, because he thought that her performance was quite______.

(a) superb (b) medium

(c) mediocre (d) exhilarating

[2014 (Set-1) : 1 Mark]

23. In a press meet on the recent scam, the minister said, "The buck stops here". What did the minister convey by the statement?

(a) He wants all the money

(b) He will return the money

(c) He will assume final responsibility

(d) He will resist all enquiries

[2014 (Set-1) : 1 Mark]

24. The Palghat Gap (or Palakkad Gap), a region about 30 km wide in the southern part of the Western Ghats in India, is lower than the hilly terrain to its north and south. The exact reasons for the formation of this gap are not clear. It results in the neighbouring regions of Tamil Nadu getting more rainfall from the South West monsoon and the neighbouring regions of Kerala having higher summer temperatures.

What can be inferred from this passage?

(a) The Palghat gap is caused by high rainfall and high temperatures in southern Tamil Nadu and Kerala

(b) The regions in Tamil Nadu and Kerala that are near the Palghat Gap are low-lying

(c) The low terrain of the Palghat Gap has a significant impact on weather patterns in neighbouring parts of Tamil Nadu and Kerala

(d) Higher summer temperatures result in higher rainfall near the Palghat Gap area

[2014 (Set-1): 2 Marks]

25. Geneticists say that they are very close to confirming the genetic roots of psychiatric illnesses such as depression and schizophrenia, and consequently, that doctors will be able to eradicate these diseases through early identification and gene therapy.

On which of the following assumptions does the statement above rely?

(a) Strategies are now available for eliminating psychiatric illnesses

(b) Certain psychiatric illnesses have a genetic basis

(c) All human diseases can be traced back to genes and how they are expressed

(d) In the future, genetics will become the only relevant field for identifying psychiatric illnesses

[2014 (Set-1): 2 Marks]

26. Choose the most appropriate phrase from the options given below to complete the following sentence. India is a post-colonial country because

(a) it was a former British colony

(b) Indian Information Technology professionals have colonized the world

(c) India does not follow any colonial practices

(d) India has helped other countries gain freedom

[2014 (Set-2):1 Mark]

27. Who _______ was coming to see us this evening?

(a) you said (b) did you say

(c) did you say that (d) had you said

[2014 (Set-2) : 1 Mark]

28. Match the columns.

Column 1	Column 2
(1) eradicate	(P) misrepresent
(2) distort	(Q) soak completely
(3) saturate	(R) use
(4) utilize	(S) destroy utterly

Codes:

(a) 1:S, 2:P, 3:Q, 4:R

(b) 1:P, 2:Q, 3:R, 4:S

(c) 1:Q, 2:R, 3:S, 4:P

(d) 1:S, 2:P, 3:R, 4:Q

[2014 (Set-2) :1 Mark]

29. The old city of Koenigsberg, which had a German majority population before World War 2, is now called Kaliningrad. After the events of the war, Kaliningrad is now a Russian territory and has a predominantly Russian population. It is bordered by the Baltic Sea on the north and the countries of Poland to the south and west and Lithuania to the east respectively. Which of the statements below can be inferred from this passage?

(a) Kaliningrad was historically Russian in its ethnic make up

(b) Kaliningrad is a part of Russia despite it not being contiguous with the rest of Russia

(c) Koenigsberg was renamed Kaliningrad, as that was its original Russian name

(d) Poland and Lithuania are on the route from Kaliningrad to the rest of Russia

[2014 (Set-2) : 2 Marks]

30. The number of people diagnosed with dengue fever (contracted from the bite of a mosquito) in north India is twice the number diagnosed last year. Municipal authorities have concluded that measures to control the mosquito population have failed in this region.

Which one of the following statements, if true, does not contradict this conclusion?

(a) A high proportion of the affected population has returned from neighbouring countries where dengue is prevalent

(b) More cases of dengue are now reported because of an increase in the Municipal Office's administrative efficiency

(c) Many more cases of dengue are being diagnosed this year since the introduction of a new and effective diagnostic test

(d) The number of people with malarial fever (also contracted from mosquito bites) has increased this year

[2014 (Set-2): 2 Marks]

31. <u>While trying to collect</u> an envelope
(I)
<u>from under the table</u>, <u>Mr. X fell down</u> and
(II) (III)
<u>was losing consciousness</u>.
(IV)

Which one of the above underlined parts of the sentence is NOT appropriate?

(a) I (b) II

(c) III (d) IV

[2014 (Set-3) : 1 Mark]

32. If she ______ how to calibrate the instrument, she ______done the experiment.

(a) knows, will have

(b) knew, had

(c) had known, could have

(d) should have known, would have

[2014 (Set-3) : 1 Mark]

33. Choose the word that is opposite in meaning to the word "coherent".

(a) sticky

(b) well-connected

(c) rambling

(d) friendly

[2014 (Set-3) : 1 Mark]

34. A dance programme is scheduled for 10.00 a.m. Some students are participating in the programme and they need to come an hour earlier than the start of the event. These students should be accompanied by a parent. Other students and parents should come in time for the programme. The instruction you think that is appropriate for this is

(a) Students should come at 9.00 a.m. and parents should come at 10.00 a.m.

(b) Participating students should come at 9.00 a.m. accompanied by a parent, and other parents and students should come by 10.00 a.m.

(c) Students who are not participating should come by 10.00 a.m. and they should not bring their parents. Participating students should come at 9.00 a.m.

(d) Participating students should come before 9.00 a.m. Parents who accompany them should come at 9.00 a.m. All others should come at 10.00 a.m.

[2014 (Set-3): 2 Marks]

35. By the beginning of the 20th century, several hypotheses were being proposed, suggesting a paradigm shift in our understanding of the universe. However, the clinching evidence was provided by experimental measurements of the position of a star which was directly behind our sun. Which of the following inference(s) may be drawn from the above passage?

(i) Our understanding of the universe changes based on the positions of stars

(ii) Paradigm shifts usually occur at the beginning of centuries

(iii) Stars are important objects in the universe

(iv) Experimental evidence was important in confirming this paradigm shift

(a) (i), (ii) and (iv) (b) (iii) only

(c) (i) and (iv) (d) (iv) only

[2014 (Set-3) : 2 Marks]

36. Didn't you buy _____ when you went shopping?

(a) any paper

(b) much paper

(c) no paper

(d) a few paper

[2015 (Set-1) : 1 Mark]

37. Which of the following options is the closet in meaning to the sentence below?

She enjoyed herself immensely at the party.

(a) She had a terrible time at the party

(b) She had a horrible time at the party

(c) She had a terrific time at the party

(d) She had a terrifying time at the party

[2015 (Set-1) : 1 Mark]

38. Which one of the following combinations is incorrect?

(a) Acquiescence - Submission

(b) Wheedle - Roundabout

(c) Flippancy - Lightness

(d) Profligate - Extravagant

[2015 (Set-1) : 1 Mark]

39. Select the alternative meaning of the underlined part of the sentence.

The chain snatchers **took to their heels** when the police party arrived.

(a) took shelter in a thick jungle

(b) open indiscriminate fire

(c) took to flight

(d) unconditionally surrendered

[2015 (Set-1): 2 Marks]

40. We _____ our friend's birthday and we _____ how to make it up to him.

(a) completely forgot — don't just know

(b) forgot completely — don't just know

(c) completely forgot — just don't know

(d) forgot completely — just don't know

[2015 (Set-2): 1 Mark]

41. Choose the statement where underlined word is used correctly.

(a) The industrialist had a personnel jet

(b) I write my experience in my personnel diary

(c) All personnel are being given the day off

(d) Being religious is a personnel aspect

[2015 (Set-2): 1 Mark]

42. A generic term that includes various items of clothing such as a skirt, a pair of trousers and a shirt is

(a) fabric (b) textile

(c) fibre (d) apparel

[2015 (Set-2) : 1 Mark]

43. Out of the following four sentences, select the most suitable sentence with respect to grammar and usage:

(a) Since the report lacked needed information, it was of no use to them

(b) The report was useless to them because there were no needed information in it

(c) Since the report did not contain the needed information, it was not real useful to them

(d) Since the report lacked needed information, it would not had been useful to them

[2015 (Set-2):2Marks]

44. The Tamil version of _____ John Abraham-starrer *Madras Cafe* _____ cleared by the Censor Board with no cuts last week, but the film's distributors _____ no takers among the exhibitors for a release in Tamil Nadu _____ this Friday.

(a) Mr., was, found, on(b) a, was, found, at

(c) the, was, found, on(d) a, being, find at

[2015 (Set-3) : 1 Mark]

45. Extreme focus on syllabus and studying for tests has become such a dominant concern of Indian students that they close their minds to anything _____ to the requirements of the exam.

(a) related

(b) extraneous

(c) outside

(d) useful

[2015 (Set-3): 1 Mark]

46. Alexander turned his attention towards India, since he had conquered Persia. Which one of the statements below is logically valid and can be inferred from the above sentence?

(a) Alexander would not have turned his attention towards India had he not conquered Persia

(b) Alexander was not ready to rest on his laurels, and wanted to march to India

(c) Alexander was completely in control of his army and could command it to move towards India.

(d) Since Alexander's kingdom extended to Indian borders after the conquest of Persia, he was keen to move further.

[2015 (Set-3): 2 Marks]

47. Most experts feel that in spite of possessing all the technical skills required to be a batsman of the highest order, he is unlikely to be so due to lack of requisite temperament. He was guilty of throwing away his wicket several times after working hard to lay a strong foundation. His critics pointed out that until he addressed this problem, success at the highest level will continue to elude him. Which of the statement(s) below is/are logically valid and can be inferred from the above passage?

(i) He was already a successful batsman at the highest level,

(ii) He has to improve his temperament in order to become a great batsman.

(iii) He failed to make many of his good starts count,

(iv) Improving his technical skills will guarantee success.

(a) (iii) and (iv) (b) (ii) and (iii)

(c) (i), (ii) and (iii) (d) (ii)only

[2015 (Set-3) : 2 Marks]

48. Out of the following four sentences, select the most suitable sentence with respect to grammar and usage.

(a) I will not leave the place until the minister does not meet me.

(b) I will not leave the place until the minister doesn't meet me.

(c) I will not leave the place until the minister meet me.

(d) I will not leave the place until the minister meets me.

[2016 (Set-1): 1 Mark]

49. A rewording of something written or spoken is a ________.

(a) paraphrase (b) paradox

(c) paradigm (d) paraffin

[2016 (Set-1): 1 Mark]

50. Archimedes said, "Give me a lever long enough and a fulcrum on which to place it, and I will move the world." The sentence above is an example of a ______ statement.

(a) figurative

(b) collateral

(c) literal

(d) figurine

[2016 (Set-1): 1 Mark]

51. Indian currency notes show the denomination indicated in at least seventeen languages. If this is not an indication of the nation's diversity, nothing else is. Which of the following can be logically inferred from the above sentences?

(a) India is a country of exactly seventeen languages.

(b) Linguistic pluralism is the only indicator of a nation's diversity.

(c) Indian currency notes have sufficient space for all the Indian languages.

(d) Linguistic pluralism is strong evidence of India s diversity.

[2016 (Set-1): 2 Marks]

52. The man who is now Municipal Commissioner worked as________.

(a) the security guard at a university

(b) a security guard at the university

(c) a security guard at university

(d) the security guard at the university

[2016 (Set-2) : 1 Mark]

53. Nobody knows how the Indian cricket team is going to cope with the difficult and seamer-friendly wickets in Australia. Choose the option which is closest in meaning to the underlined phrase in the above sentence.

(a) put up with (b) put in with

(c) put down to (d) put up against

[2016 (Set-2) : 1 Mark]

54. Computers were invented for performing only high-end useful computations. However, it is no understatement that they have taken over our world today. The internet, for example, is ubiquitous. Many believe that the internet itself is an unintended consequence of the original invention. With the advent of mobile computing on our phones, a whole new dimension is now enabled. One is left wondering if all these developments are good or, more importantly, required.

Which of the statement(s) below is/are logically valid and can be inferred from the above paragraph?

(i) The author believes that computers are not good for us.

(ii) Mobile computers and the internet are both intended inventions

(a) (i) only (b) (ii) only

(c) both (i) and (ii) (d) neither (i) nor (ii)

[2016 (Set-2): 2 Marks]

55. All hill-stations have a lake. Ooty has two lakes. Which of the statement(s) below is/are logically valid and can be inferred from the above sentences?

(i) Ooty is not a hill-station.

(ii) No hill-station can have more than one lake.

(a) (i)only

(b) (ii)only

(c) both (i) and (ii)

(d) neither (i) nor (ii)

[2016 (Set-2): 2 Marks]

56. After Rajendra Chola returned from his voyage to Indonesia, he ______ to visit the temple in Thanjavur.

(a) was wishing (b) is wishing

(c) wished (d) had wished

[2017 (Set-1): 1 Mark]

57. Research in the workplace reveal that people work for many reasons________.

(a) money beside (b) beside money

(c) money besides (d) besides money

[2017 (Set-1) : 1 Mark]

58. "The hold of the nationalist imagination on our colonial past is such that anything inadequately or improperly nationalist is just not history." Which of the following statements best reflects the author's opinion?

(a) Nationalists are highly imaginative

(b) History is viewed through the filter of nationalism

(c) Our colonial past never happened

(d) Nationalism has to be both adequately and properly imagined.

[2017 (Set-1):2Marks]

59. Saturn is ______ to be seen on a clear night with the naked eye.

(a) enough bright (b) bright enough

(c) as enough bright (d) bright as enough

[2017 (Set-2): 1 Mark]

60. Choose the option with words that are not synonyms.

(a) aversion, dislike (b) luminous, radiant

(c) plunder, loot (d) yielding, resistant

[2017 (Set-2) : 1 Mark]

61. "We lived in a culture that denied any merit to literary works, considering them important only when they were handmaidens to something seemingly more urgent-namely ideology. This was a country where all gestures, even the most private, were interpreted in political terms,".

The author's belief that ideology is not as important as literature is revealed by the word:

(a) 'culture' (b) 'seemingly'

(c) 'urgent' (d) 'political'

[2017 (Set-2): 2 Marks]

62. "From where are they bringing their books? ______ bringing ______ books from ______."

The words that best fill the blanks in the above sentence are

(a) Their, they're, there

(b) They're, their, there

(c) There, their, they're

(d) They're, there, there **[2018:1 Mark]**

63. "A _____ investigation can sometimes yield new facts, but typically organized ones are more successful."

The word that best fills the blank in the above sentence is

(a) meandering (b) timely

(c) consistent (d) systematic

[2018:1 Mark]

64. A court is to a judge as ________ is to a teacher.

(1) a student (2) a syllabus

(3) a school (4) a punishment

[2019 : 1 Mark]

65. The search engine's business model ________ around the fulcrum of trust.

(1) bursts (2) revolves

(3) plays (4) sinks

[2019 : 1 Mark]

66. "A recent High Court judgement has sought to dispel the idea of begging as a disease — which leads to its stigmatization and criminalization — and to regard it as a symptom. The underlying disease is the failure of the state to protect citizens who fall through the social security net."

Which one of the following statements can be inferred from the given passage?

(1) Begging is an offence that has to be dealt with firmly

(2) Beggars are lazy people who beg because they are unwilling to work

(3) Beggars are created because of the lack of social welfare schemes

(4) Beggings has to be banned because it adversely affects the welfare of the state

[2019 : 2 Marks]

REASONING ABILITY

67. Hari (H), Gita (G), Irfan (I) and Saira (S) are siblings (i.e. brothers and sisters). All were born on I[st] January. The age difference between any two successive siblings (that is born one after another) is less than 3 years. Given the following facts:

1. Hari's age + Gita's age > Irfan's age + Saira's age.
2. The age difference between Gita and Saira is 1 year. However, Gita is not the oldest and Saira is not the youngest.
3. There are no twins.

In what order were they born (oldest first)?

(a) HSIG (b) SGHI
(c) IGSH (d) IHSG

[2010: 2 Marks]

68. Given the sequence of terms, AD CG FK JP, the next time is

(a) OV (b) OW
(c) PV (d) PW **[2012:2 Marks]**

69. Which number does not belong in the series below?

2, 5, 10, 17, 26, 37, 50, **64**

(a) 17 (b) 37
(c) 64 (d) 26

[2014 (Set-3) : 1 Mark]

70. Based on the given statements, select the most appropriate option to solve the given question. If two floors in a certain building are 9 feet apart, how many steps are there in a set of stairs that extends from the first floor to the second floor of the building?

Statements:

1. Each step is 3/4 foot high.
2. Each step is 1 foot wide.

(a) Statement 1 alone is sufficient, but statement 2 alone is not sufficient
(b) Statement 2 alone is sufficient, but statement 1 alone is not sufficient
(c) Both statement together are sufficient, but neither statement alone is sufficient
(d) Statement 1 and 2 together are not sufficient

[2015 (Set-1): 1 Mark]

71. The given statement is following by some courses of action. Assuming the statement to be true, decide the correct option.

Statement: There has been a significant drop in the water level in the lakes supplying water to the city.

Course of action:

1. The water supply authority should impose a partial cut in supply to tackle the situation.
2. The government should appeal to all the residents through mass media for minimal use of water.
3. The government should ban the water supply in lower areas.

(a) Statement 1 and 2 follow
(b) Statement 1 and 3 follow
(c) Statement 2 and 3 follow
(d) All statements follow

[2015 (Set-1): 2 Marks]

72. Based on the given statements, select the most appropriate option to solve the given question. What will be the total weight of 10 poles each of same weight?

Statements:

1. One fourth of the weight of a pole is 5 Kg.
2. The total weight of these poles is 160 Kg more than the total weight of two poles.

(a) Statement 1 alone is sufficient, but Statement 2 alone is not sufficient
(b) Statement 2 alone is sufficient, but Statement 1 alone is not sufficient
(c) Either of the Statements 1 or 2 alone is sufficient.
(d) Both statements 1 and 2 are not sufficient

[2015 (Set-2) : 1 Mark]

73. If the list of letters, P, R, S, T, U is an arithmetic sequence, which of the following are also in arithmetic sequence?

1. 2P, 2R, 2S, 2T, 2U
2. P-3, R-3, S-3, T-3, U-3
3. P^2, R^2, S^2, T^2, U^2

(a) 1 only (b) 1 and 2
(c) 2 and 3 (d) 1 and 3

[2015 (Set-2) : 2 Marks]

74. Four branches of a company are located at M, N, O and P. M is north of N at a distance of 4 km; P is south of O at a distance of 2 km; N is southeast of O by 1 km. What is the distance between M and P in km?

(a) 5.34
(b) 6.74
(c) 28.5
(d) 45.49

[2015 (Set-2): 2 Marks]

75. If ROAD is written as URDG, then SWAN should be written as:

(a) VXDQ (b) VZDQ
(c) VZDP (d) UXDQ

[2015 (Set-3): 1 Mark]

76. Select the pair that best expresses a relationship similar to that expressed in the pair:

Children: Pediatrician

(a) Adult: Orthopaedist
(b) Females : Gynaecologist
(c) Kidney: Nephrologist
(d) Skin : Dermatologist

[2015 (Set-3) : 1 Mark]

77. The head of a newly formed government desires to appoint five of the six selected members P, Q, R, S, T and U to portfolios of Home, Power, Defense, Telecom, and Finance. U does not want any portfolio if S gets one of the five. R wants either Home or Finance or no portfolio. Q says that if S gets either Power of Telecom, then she must get the other one. T insists on a portfolio if P gets one.

Which is the valid distribution of portfolios?

(a) P-Home, Q-Power, R-Defense, S-Telecom, T- Finance
(b) R-Home, S-Power, P-Defense, Q-Telecom, T- Finance
(c) P-Home, Q-Power, T-Defense, S-Telecom, U-Finance
(d) Q-Home, U-Power, T-Defense, R-Telecom, P-Finance

[2015 (Set-3) : 2Marks]

78. If 'relftaga' means carefree, 'otaga' means careful and 'fertaga' means careless, which of the following could mean 'aftercare'?

(a) zentaga (b) tagafer
(c) tagazen (d) relffer

[2016 (Set-1): 1 Mark]

79. Consider the following statements relating to the level of poker play of four players P, Q, R and S. I. P always beats Q II. R always beats S III. S loses to P only sometimes IV. R always loses to Q. Which of the following can be logically inferred from the above statements?

(i) Pis likely to beat all the three other players
(ii) S is the absolute worst player in the set

(a) (i)only (b) (ii)only
(c) (i)and(ii) (d) neither (i) nor (ii)

[2016 (Set-1): 2 Marks]

80. Find the odd one in the following group of words.

mock, deride, praise, jeer

(a) mock (b) deride
(c) praise (d) jeer

[2016 (Set-2) : 1 Mark]

81. Pick the odd one from the following options,

(a) CADBE (b) JHKIL
(c) XVYWZ (d) ONPMQ

[2016 (Set-2): 1 Mark]

82. Rahul, Murali, Srinivas and Arul are seated around a square table. Rahul is sitting to the left of Murali. Srinivas is sitting to the right of Arul. Which of the following pairs are seated opposite each other?

(a) Rahul and Murali
(b) Srinivas and Arul
(c) Srinivas and Murali
(d) Srinivas and Rahul

[2017 (Set-1): 1 Mark]

83. Arun, Gulab, Neel and Shweta must choose one shirt each from a pile of four shirts coloured red, pink, blue and white respectively. Arun dislikes the colour red and Shweta dislikes the colour white. Gulab and Neel like all the colours. In how many different ways can they choose the shirts so that no one has a shirt with a colour he or she dislikes?

(a) 21 (b) 18
(c) 16 (d) 14

[2017 (Set-1): 2 Marks]

84. Six people are seated around a circular table. There are at least two men and two women. There are at least three right-handed persons. Every woman has a left-handed person to her immediate right. None of the women are right-handed. The number of women at the table is

(a) 2 (b) 3
(c) 4 (d) Cannot be determined

[2017 (Set-2) : 1 Mark]

85. There are five buildings called V, W. X, Y and Z in a row (not necessarily in that order). V is to the West of W. Z is to the East of X and the West of V. W is to the West of Y. Which is the building in the middle?

(a) V
(b) W
(c) X
(d) Y

[2017 (Set-2) : 1 Mark]

86. There are three boxes. One contains apples, another contains oranges and the last one contains both apples and oranges. All three are known to be incorrectly labelled. If you are permitted to open just one box and then pull out and inspect only one fruit, which box would you open to determine the contents of all three boxes?

(a) The box labelled'Apples'

(b) The box labelled 'Apples and Oranges'

(c) The box labelled 'Oranges'

(d) Cannot be determined

[2017 (Set-2): 2 Marks]

87. What is the missing number in the following sequence?

2, 12, 60, 240, 720, 1440,_______, 0

(a) 2880 (b) 1440

(c) 720 (d) 0 **[2018:1 Mark]**

88. The police arrested four criminals – P, Q, R and S. The criminals knew each other. They made the following statements :

P says "Q committed the crime."

Q says "S committed the crime."

R says "I did not do it."

S says "What Q said about me is false."

Assume only one of the arrested four committed the crime and only one of the statements made above is true. Who committed the crime?

(1) R (2) P

(3) Q (4) S

[2019 : 2 Marks]

NUMERICAL ABILITY

89. 25 persons are in a room. 15 of them play hockey, 17 of them play football and 10 of them play both hockey and football. Then the number of persons playing neither hockey nor football is

(a) 2 (b) 17

(c) 13 (d) 3

[2010:1 Mark]

90. If 137 + 276 = 435 how much is 731 + 672?

(a) 534 (b) 1403

(c) 1623 (d) 1531

[2010:2 Marks]

91. 5 skilled workers can build a wall in 20 days; 8 semi-skilled workers can build a wall in 25 days; 10 unskilled workers can build a wall in 30 days. If a team has 2 skilled, 6 semi-skilled and 5 unskilled workers, how long will it take to build the wall?

(a) 20 days (b) 18 days

(c) 16 days (d) 15 days

[2010:2 Marks]

92. Given digits 2, 2, 3, 3, 3, 4, 4, 4, 4 how many distinct 4 digit numbers greater than 3000 can be formed?

(a) 50 (b) 51

(c) 52 (d) 54

[2010:2 Marks]

93. If Log(P) = (1/2)Log(Q) = (1/3)Log(R), then which of the following options is TRUE?

(a) $P^2 = Q^3R^2$ (b) $Q^2 = PR$

(c) $Q^2 = R^3P$ (d) $R = P^2Q^2$

[2011:1 Mark]

94. P, Q, R and S are four types of dangerous microbes recently found in a human habitat. The area of each circle with its diameter printed in brackets represents the growth of a single microbe surviving human immunity system within 24 hours of entering the body. The danger to human beings varies proportionately with the toxicity, potency and growth attributed to a microbe shown in the figure below:

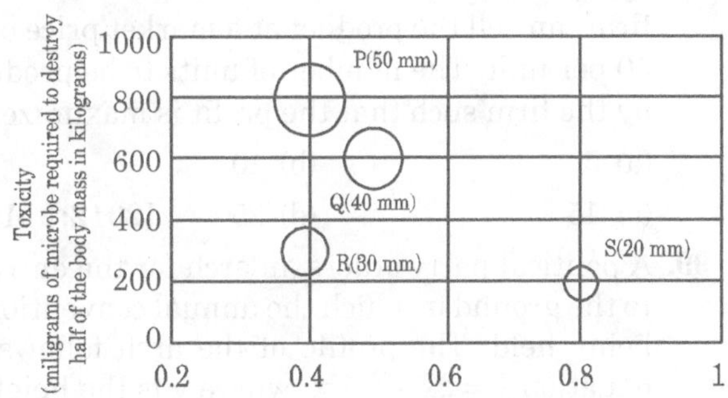

(Probability that microbe will overcome human immunity system)

A pharmaceutical company is contemplating the development of a vaccine against the most dangerous microbe. Which microbe should the company target in its first attempt?

(a) P (b) Q

(c) R (d) S

[2011:2 Marks]

95. The variable cost (V) of manufacturing a product varies according to the equation V = 4q, where q is the quantity produced. The fixed cost (F) of production of same product reduces with q according to the equation F = 100/q. How many units should be produced to minimize the total cost (V + F)?

(a) 5 (b) 4

(c) 7 (d) 6

[2011:2 Marks]

96. A transporter receives the same number of orders each day. Currently, he has some pending orders (backlog) to be shipped. If he uses 7 trucks, then at the end of the 4th day he can clear all the orders. Alternatively, if he uses only 3 trucks, then all the orders are cleared at the end of the 10th day. What is the minimum number of trucks required so that there will be no pending order at the end of the 5th day?

(a) 4 (b) 5
(c) 6 (d) 7

[2011:2 Marks]

97. A container originally contains 10 litres of pure spirit. From this container 1 litre of spirit is replaced with 1 litre of water. Subsequently, 1 litre of the mixture is again replaced with 1 litre of water and this processes is repeated one more time. How much spirit is now left in the container?

(a) 7.58 litres (b) 7.84 litres
(c) 7 litres (d) 7.29 litres

[2011: 2 Marks]

98. The cost function for a product in a firm is given by $5q^2$, where q is the amount of production. The firm can sell the product at a market price of Rs. 50 per unit. The number of units to be produced by the firm such that the profit is maximized is

(a) 5 (b) 10
(c) 15 (d) 25 **[2012:1 Mark]**

99. A political party orders an arch for the entrance to the ground in which the annual conventions is being held. The profile of the arch follows the equation $y = 2x - 0.1\,x^2$ where y is the height of the arch in meters. The maximum possible height of the arch is

(a) 8 meters (b) 10 meters
(c) 12 meters (d) 14 meters

[2012:2 Marks]

100. An automobile plant contracted to buy shock absorbers from two supplies X and Y. X supplies 60% and Y supplies 40% of the shock absorbers. All shock absorbers are subjected to a quality test. The ones that pass the quality test are considered reliable. Of X's shock absorbers, 96% are reliable. OF Ys shock absorbers, 72% are reliable. The probability that a randomly chosen shock absorber, which is found to be reliable, is made by Y is

(a) 0.288 (b) 0.334
(c) 0.667 (d) 0.720

[2012:2 Marks]

101. Which of the following assertions are CORRECT?

P : Adding 7 to each entry in a list adds 7 to the mean of the list

Q : Adding 7 to each entry in a list adds 7 to the standard deviation of the list

R : Doubling each entry n a list doubles the mean of the list

S : Doubling each entry in a list leaves the standard deviation of the list unchanged

(a) P,Q (b) Q,R
(c) P,R (d) R,S

[2012:2 Marks]

102. What will be the maximum sum of 44, 42, 40, ______?

(a) 502 (b) 504
(c) 506 (d) 500

[2013:1 Mark]

103. Find the sum of the expression

$$\frac{1}{\sqrt{1}+\sqrt{2}}+\frac{1}{\sqrt{2}+\sqrt{3}}+\frac{1}{\sqrt{3}+\sqrt{4}}+\ldots+\frac{1}{\sqrt{80}+\sqrt{81}}$$

(a) 7 (b) 8
(c) 9 (d) 10

[2013:2 Marks]

104. Out of all the 2-digit integers between 1 and 100, a 2-digit number has to be selected at random. What is the probability that the selected number is not divisible by 7?

(a) 13/90 (b) 12/90
(c) 78/90 (d) 77/90

[2013:2 Marks]

105. A tourist covers half of this journey by train at 60 km/h, half of the remainder by bus at 30 km/ h and the rest by cycle at 10 km/h. The average speed of the tourist in km/h during his entire journey is

(a) 36 (b) 30
(c) 24 (d) 18

[2013:2 Marks]

106. The current erection cost of a structure is Rs. 13,200. If the labour wages per day increase by 1/5 of the current wages and the working hours decrease by 1/24 of the current period, then the new cost of erection in Rs., is

(a) 16,500 (b) 15,180
(c) 11,000 (d) 10,120

[2013:2 Marks]

107. If $(z + 1/z)^2 = 98$, compute $(z^2 + 1/z^2)$.

[2014 (Set-1) : 1 Mark]

108. The roots of $ax^2 + bx + c = 0$ are real and positive. a, b and c are real. Then $ax^2 + b\,|x| + c = 0$ has

(a) no roots (b) 2 real roots

(c) 3 real roots (d) 4 real roots

[2014 (Set-1) : 1 Mark]

109. Round-trip tickets to a tourist destination are eligible for a discount of 10% on the total fare. In addition, groups of 4 or more get a discount of 5% on the total fare. If the one way single person fare is Rs 100, a group of 5 tourists purchasing round-trip tickets will be charged Rs_______.

[2014 (Set-1) : 2 Marks]

110. In a survey, 300 respondents were asked whether they own a vehicle or not. If yes, they were further asked to mention whether they own a car or scooter or both. Their responses are tabulated below. What percent of respondents do not own a scooter?

		Men	Women
Own vehicle	Car	40	34
	Scooter	30	40
	Both	60	46
Do not won vehicle		20	50

[2014 (Set-1) : 2 Marks]

111. When a point inside of a tetrahedron (a solid with four triangular surfaces) is connected by straight lines to its corners, how many (new) internal planes are created with these lines?_______.

[2014 (Set-1): 2 Marks]

112. What is the average of all multiples of 10 from 2 to 198?

(a) 90 (b) 100

(c) 110 (d) 120

[2014 (Set-2) : 1 Mark]

113. The value of $\sqrt{12+\sqrt{12+\sqrt{12+...}}}$ is

(a) 3.464 (b) 3.932

(c) 4.000 (d) 4.444

[2014 (Set-2) : 1 Mark]

114. If x is real and $|x^2 - 2x + 3| = 11$, then possible values of $|-x^3 + x^2 - x|$ include

(a) 2,4

(b) 2,14

(c) 4,52

(d) 14,52

[2014 (Set-2): 2 Marks]

115. The ratio of male to female students in a college for five years is plotted in the following line graph. If the number of female students doubled in 2009, by what percent did the number of male students increase in 2009?

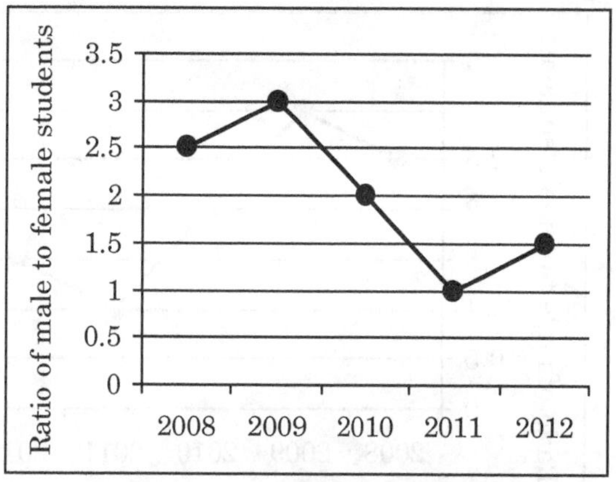

[2014 (Set-2) : 2 Marks]

116. At what time between 6 a.m. and 7 a.m. will the minute hand and hour hand of a clock make an angle closest to 60°?

(a) 6 : 22 a.m. (b) 6 : 27 a.m.

(c) 6 : 38 a.m. (d) 6 : 45 a.m.

[2014 (Set-2): 2 Marks]

117. The table below has question-wise data on the performance of students in an examination. The marks for each question are also listed. There is no negative or partial marking in the examination.

Q. No.	Marks	Answered Correctly	Answered Wrongly	Not Attempted
1	2	21	17	6
2	3	15	27	2
3	2	23	18	3

What is the average of the marks obtained by the class in the examination?

(a) 1.34 (b) 1.74

(c) 3.02 (d) 3.91

[2014 (Set-3) : 1 Mark]

118. The Gross Domestic Product (GDP) in Rupees grew at 7% during 2012-2013. For international comparison, the GDP is compared in US Dollars (USD) after conversion based on the market exchange rate. During the period 2012-2013 the exchange rate for the USD increased from Rs. 50/ USD to Rs. 60/ USD. India's GDP in USD during the period 2012-2013

(a) increased by 5 % (b) decreased by 13%

(c) decreased by 20% (d) decreased by 11%

[2014 (Set-3) : 2 Marks]

119. The ratio of male to female students in a college for five years is plotted in the following line graph. If the number of female students in 2011 and 2012 is equal, what is the ratio of male students in 2012 to male students in 2011?

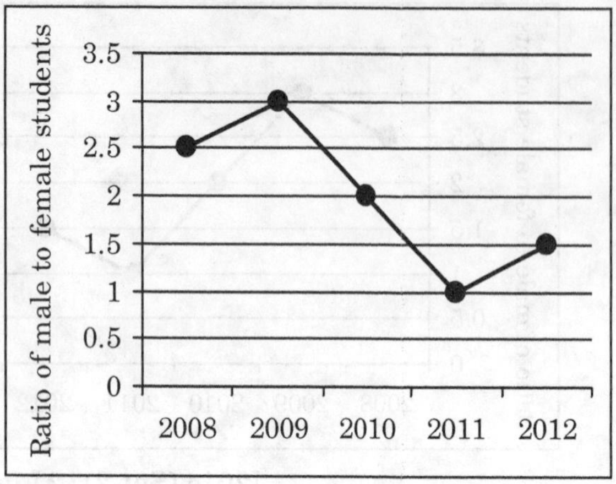

(a) 1:1 (b) 2:1
(c) 1.5:1 (d) 2.5:1

[2014 (Set-3) : 2 Marks]

120. Consider the equation: $(7526)_8 - (Y)_8 = (4364)_8$, where $(X)_N$ stands for X to the base N. Find Y.

(a) 1634 (b) 1737
(c) 3142 (d) 3162

[2014 (Set-3): 2 Marks]

121. Given Set A = {2, 3, 4, 5} and Set B = {11,12,13, 14,15}, two numbers are randomly selected, one from each set. What is the probability that the sum of the two numbers equals 16?

(a) 0.20 (b) 0.25
(c) 0.30 (d) 0.33

[2015 (Set-1) : 1 Mark]

122. The number of students in a class who have answered correctly, wrongly, or not attempted each question in an exam, are listed in the table below. The marks for each question are also listed. There is no negative or partial marking.

Q. No.	Marks	Answered Correctly	Answered Wrongly	Not Attempted
1	2	21	17	6
2	3	15	27	2
3	1	11	29	4
4	2	23	18	3
5	5	31	12	1

What is the average of the marks obtained by the class in the examination?

(a) 2.290 (b) 2.970
(c) 6.795 (d) 8.795

[2015 (Set-1): 2 Marks]

123. The pie chart below has the breakup of the number of students, from different departments in an engineering college for the year 2012. The proportion of male to female students in each department is 5 : 4. There are 40 males in Electrical Engineering. What is the different between the numbers of female students in the Civil department and the female students in the Mechanical department?

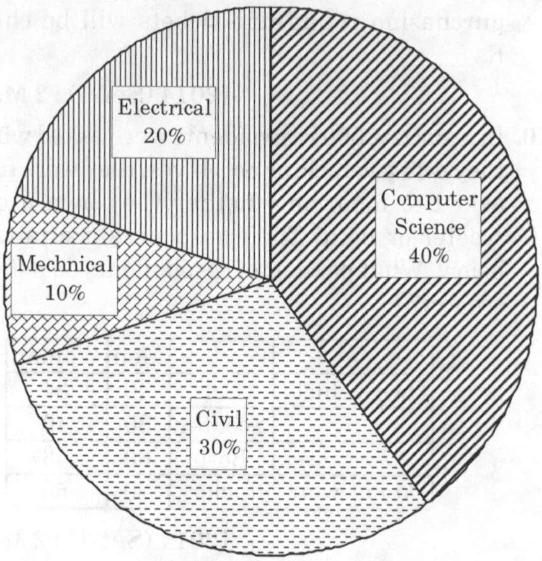

[2015 (Set-1): 2 Marks]

124. The probabilities that a student passes in Mathematics, Physics and Chemistry are m, p, and c respectively. Of these subjects, the student has 75% chance of passing in at least one, a 50% chance of passing in at least two and a 40% chance of passing in exactly two. Following relations are drawn in m, p and c:

1. $p + m + c = 27 / 20$
2. $p + m + c = 13 / 20$
3. $(p) \times (m) \times (c) = 1 / 10$

(a) Only relation 1 is true
(b) Only relation 2 is true
(c) Relations 2 and 3 are true
(d) Relations 1 and 3 are true.

[2015 (Set-1): 2 Marks]

125. Consider a function $f(x) = 1 - |x|$ on $-1 \le x \le 1$. The value of x at which the function attains a maximum, and the maximum value of the function are:

(a) 0, –1 (b) –1, 0
(c) 0, 1 (d) –1, 2

[2015 (Set-2) : 1 Mark]

126. In a triangle PQR, PS is the angle bisector of $\angle QPR$ and $\angle QPS = 60°$. What is the length of PS?

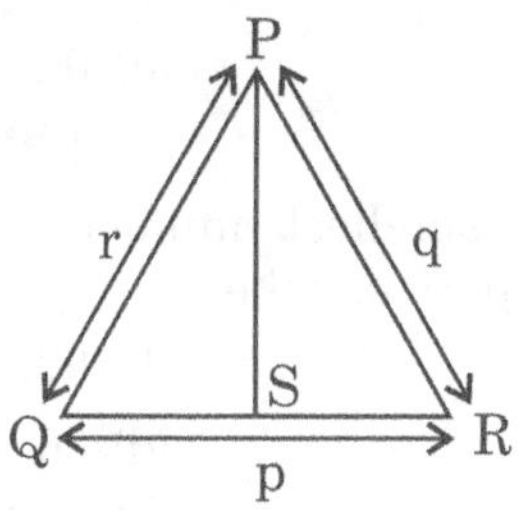

(a) $\frac{(q+r)}{qr}$ (b) $\frac{qr}{(q+r)}$

(c) $\sqrt{(q^2+r^2)}$ (d) $\frac{(q+r)^2}{qr}$

[2015 (Set-2) : 2 Marks]

127. If p, q, r, s are distinct integers such that:

f(p, q, r, s) = max (p, q, r, s)

g(p, q, r, s) = min (p, q, r, s)

h(p, q, r, s) = remainder of (p × q) /(r × s) if (p × q) > (r × s) or remainder of (r × s)/ (p × q) if (r × s) > (p × q)

Also a function fgh (p, q, r, s) = f(p, q, r, s) × g(p, q, r, s) × h(p, q, r, s).

Also the same operation are valid with two variable functions of the form f(p, q).

What is the value of fg(h(2, 5, 7, 3), 4, 6, 8)?

[2015 (Set-2): 2 Marks]

128. A function f(x) is linear and has a value of 29 at x = –2 and 39 at x = 3. Find its value at x = 5.

(a) 59 (b) 45

(c) 43 (d) 35

[2015 (Set-3) : 1 Mark]

129. Choose the most appropriate equation for the function drawn as a thick line, in the plot below.

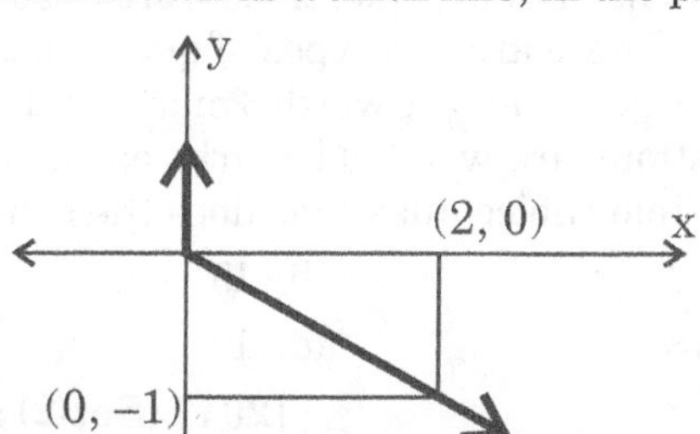

(a) $x = y - |y|$

(b) $x = -(y - |y|)$

(c) $x = y + |y|$

(d) $x = -(y + |y|)$

[2015 (Set-3) : 2 Marks]

130. The exports and imports (in crores of Rs.) of a country from the year 2000 to 2007 are given in the following bar chart. In which year is the combined percentage increase in imports and exports the highest?

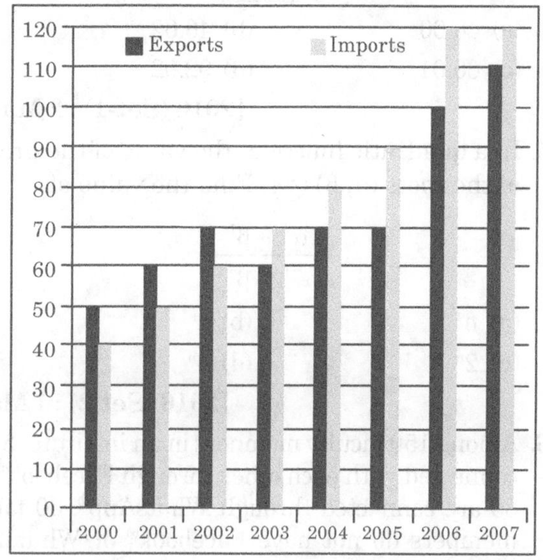

[2015 (Set-3) : 2 Marks]

131. A cube is built using 64 cubic blocks of side one unit. After it is built, one cubic block is removed from every corner of the cube. The resulting surface area of the body (in square units) after the removal is____.

(a) 56 (b) 64

(c) 72 (d) 96

[2016 (Set-1) : 1 Mark]

132. A shaving set company sells 4 different types of razors, Elegance, Smooth, Soft and Executive. Elegance sells at Rs. 48, Smooth at Rs. 63, Soft at Rs. 78 and Executive at Rs. 173 per piece. The table below shows the numbers of each razor sold in each quarter of a year.

Quarter/ Product	Elegance	Smooth	Soft	Executive
Q1	27300	20009	17602	9999
Q2	25222	19392	18445	8942
Q3	28976	22429	19544	10234
Q4	21012	18229	16595	10109

Which product contributes the greatest fraction to the revenue of the company in that year?

(a) Elegance (b) Executive

(c) Smooth (d) Soft

[2016 (Set-1): 2 Marks]

133. If $f(x) = 2x^7 + 3x - 5$, which of the following is a factor f(x)?

(a) $(x^3 + 8)$ (b) $(x - 1)$

(c) $(2x - 5)$ (d) $(x + 1)$

[2016 (Set-1) : 2 Marks]

134. In a process, the number of cycles to failure decreases exponentially with an increase in load. At a load of 80 units, it takes 100 cycles for failure. When the load is halved, it takes 10000 cycles for failure. The load for which the failure will happen in 5000 cycles is________.

(a) 40.00 (b) 46.02

(c) 60.01 (d) 92.02

[2016 (Set-1) : 2 Marks]

135. In a quadratic function, the value of the product of the roots (α, β) is 4. Find the value of

$$\frac{\alpha^n + \beta^n}{\alpha^{-n} + \beta^{-n}}$$

(a) n^4 (b) 4^n

(c) 2^{n-1} (d) 4^{n-1}

[2016 (Set-2) : 1 Mark]

136. Among 150 faculty members in an institute, 55 are connected with each other through Facebook® and 85 are connected through WhatsApp®. 30 faculty members do not have Facebook® or WhatsApp® accounts. The number of faculty members connected only through Facebook® accounts is________.

(a) 35 (b) 45

(c) 65 (d) 90

[2016 (Set-2) : 2 Marks]

137. In a 2 × 4 rectangle grid shown below, each cell is a rectangle. How many rectangles can be observed in the grid?

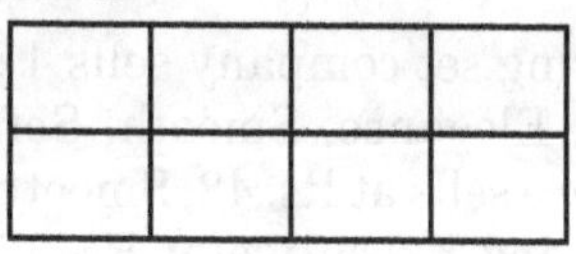

(a) 21 (b) 27

(c) 30 (d) 36

[2016 (Set-2) : 2 Marks]

138. Choose the correct expression for f(x) given in the graph.

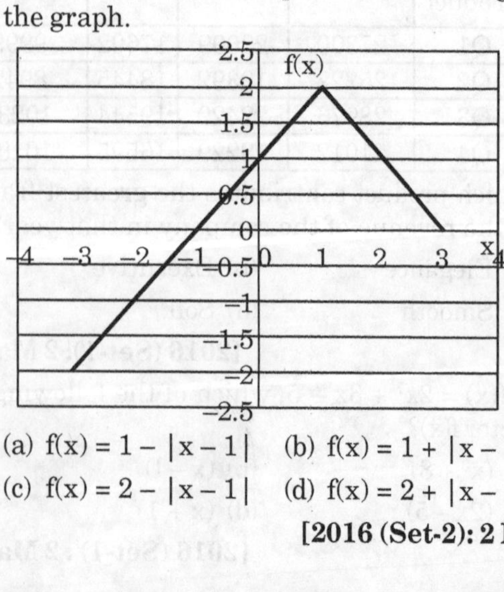

(a) f(x) = 1 − |x − 1| (b) f(x) = 1 + |x − 1|

(c) f(x) = 2 − |x − 1| (d) f(x) = 2 + |x − 1|

[2016 (Set-2): 2 Marks]

139. The probability that a k-digit number does NOT contain the digits 0, 5 or 9 is

(a) 0.3^k (b) 0.6^k

(c) 0.7^k (d) 0.9^k

[2017 (Set-l):l Mark]

140. Find the smallest number y such that that y x 162 is a perfect cube.

(a) 24 (b) 27

(c) 32 (d) 36

[2017 (Set-1) : 1 Mark]

141. A contour line joins locations having the same height above the mean sea level. The following is a contour plot of a geographical region. Contour lines are shown at 25 m intervals in this plot. If in a flood, the water level rises to 525 m, which of the villages P, Q, R, S, T get submerged?

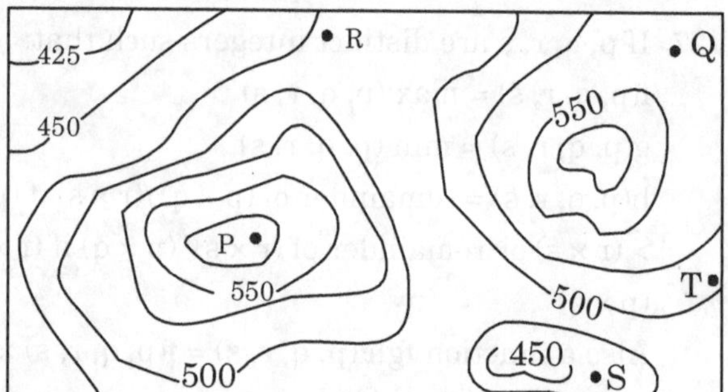

(a) P, Q (b) P, Q, T

(c) R, S, T (d) Q, R, S

[2017 (Set-1): 2 Marks]

142. The expression $\frac{(x+y)-|(x-y)|}{2}$ is equal to

(a) the maximum of x and y

(b) the minimum of JC and y

(c) 1

(d) None of the above

[2017 (Set-1): 2 Marks]

143. A test has twenty questions worth 100 marks in total. There are two types of questions. Multiple choice questions are worth 3 marks each and essay questions are worth 11 marks each. How many multiple choice questions does the exam have?

(a) 12 (b) 15

(c) 18 (d) 19

[2017 (Set-2) : 1 Mark]

144. There are 3 red socks. 4 green socks and 3 blue socks. You choose 2 socks. The probability that they are of the same colour is

(a) 1/5 (b) 7/30

(c) 1/4 (d) 4/15

[2017 (Set-2): 1 Mark]

145. X is a 30 digit number starting with the digit 4 followed by the digit 7. Then the number X^3 will have

(a) 90 digits (b) 91 digits

(c) 92 digits (d) 93 digits

[2017 (Set-2): 2 Marks]

146. The number of roots of $e^x + 0.5x^2 - 2 = 0$ in the range [–5, 5] is

(a) 0 (b) 1

(c) 2 (d) 3

[2017 (Set-2): 2 Marks]

147. An air pressure contour line joins locations in a region having the same atmospheric pressure. The following is an air pressure contour plot is a geographical region. Contour lines are shown at 0.05 bar intervals in this plot.

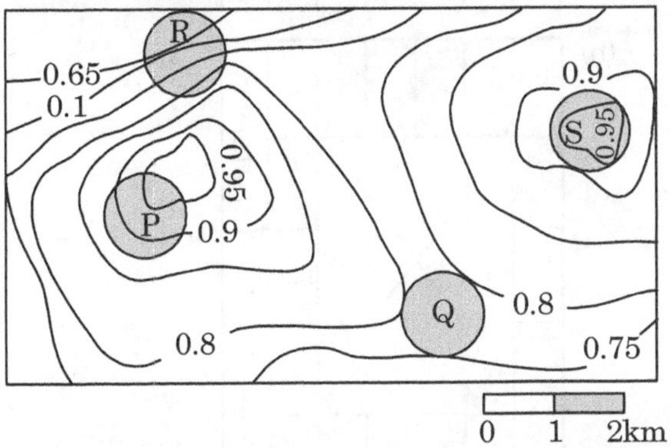

If the possibility of a thunderstorm is given by how fast air pressure rises or drops over a region, which of the following regions is most likely to have a thunderstorm?

(a) P (b) Q

(c) R (d) S

[2017 (Set-2) : 2 Marks]

148. What would be the smallest natural number which when divided either by 20 or by 42 or by 76 leaves a remainder of 7 in each case?

(a) 3047 (b) 6047

(c) 7987 (d) 63847 **[2018:1 Mark]**

149. The area of a square is d. What is the area of the circle which has the diagonal of the square as its diameter?

(a) πd (b) πd^2

(c) $\frac{1}{4}\pi d^2$ (d) $\frac{1}{2}\pi d$ **[2018:1 Mark]**

150. In $pqr \neq 0$ and $p^{-x} = \frac{1}{q}, q^{-y} = \frac{1}{r}, r^{-z} = \frac{1}{p}$, what is the value of the product xyz

(a) –1 (b) $\frac{1}{pqr}$

(c) 1 (d) pqr **[2018:2 Marks]**

151. In appreciation of the social improvements completed in a town, a wealthy philanthropist decided to gift Rs 750 to each male senior citizen in the town and Rs 1000 to each female senior citizen. Altogether, there were 300 senior citizens eligible for this gift. However, only 8/9th of the eligible men and 2/3rd of the eligible women claimed the gift. How much money (in Rupees) did the philanthropist give away in total?

(a) 1,50,000 (b) 2,00,000

(c) 1,75,000 (d) 1,51,000

[2018:2 Marks]

152. In the figure below, $\angle DEC + \angle BFC$ is equal to _____

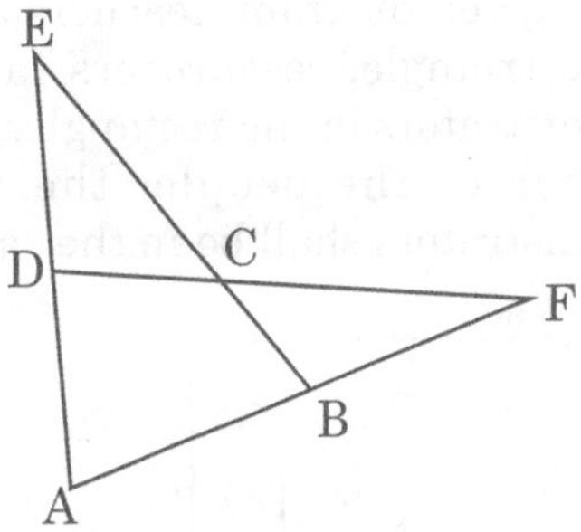

(a) $\angle BCD - \angle BAD$ (b) $\angle BAD + \angle BCF$

(c) $\angle BAD + \angle BCD$ (d) $\angle CBA + \angle ADC$

[2018:2 Marks]

153. A six sided unbiased die with four green faces and two red faces is rolled seven times. Which of the following combinations is the most likely outcome of the experiment?

(a) Three green faces and four red faces.

(b) Four green faces and three red faces.

(c) Five green faces and two red faces.

(d) Six green faces and one red face.

[2018:2 Marks]

154. In a party, 60% of the invited guests are male and 40% are female. If 80% of the invited guests attended the party and if all the invited female guests attended, what would be the ratio of males to females among the attendees in the party?

(a) 2 : 3 (b) 1 : 1

(c) 3 : 2 (d) 2 : 1

[2018: 2 Marks]

155. Ten friends planned to share equally the cost of buying a gift for their teacher. When two of them decided not to contribute, each of the other friends had to pay Rs. 150 more. The cost of the gift was Rs. _______.

(a) 666 (b) 6000

(c) 3000 (d) 12000

[2019 : 1 Mark]

156. Two cars start at the same time from the same location and go in the same direction. The speed of the first car is 50 km/h and the speed of the second car is 60 km/h. The number of hours it takes for the distance between the two cars to be 20 km is ______.

(a) 2 (b) 1

(c) 6 (d) 3 **[2019 : 1 Mark]**

157. The expenditure on the project ________ as follows: equipment Rs. 20 lakhs, salaries Rs. 12 lakhs, and contingency Rs. 3 lakhs.

(a) break (b) break down

(c) breaks down (d) breaks

[2019 : 1 Mark]

158. In the given diagram, teachers are represented in the triangle, researchers in the circle and administrators in the rectangle. Out of the total number of the people, the percentage of administrators shall be in the range of _______.

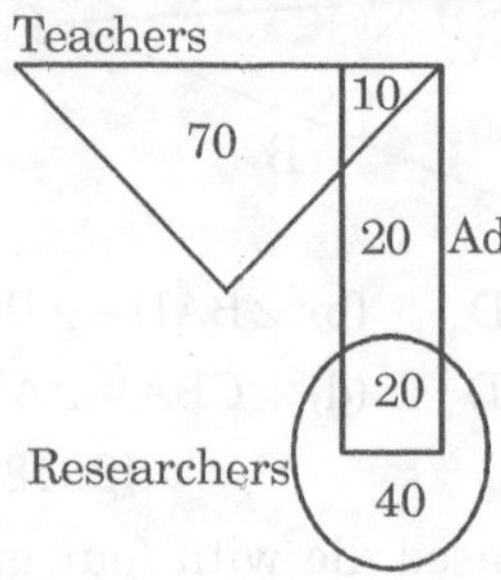

(a) 0 to 15 (b) 31 to 45

(c) 46 to 60 (d) 16 to 30

[2019 : 2 Marks]

159. In a college, there are three student clubs. Sixty students are only in the Drama club, 80 students are only in the Dance club, 30 students are only in the Maths club, 40 students are in both Drama and Dance clubs, 12 students are in both Dance and Maths clubs, 7 students are in both Drama and Maths clubs, and 2 students are in all the clubs. If 75% of the students in the college are not in any of these clubs, then the total number of students in the college is _____.

(a) 975 (b) 1000

(c) 225 (d) 900

[2019 : 2 Marks]

160. Three of the five students allocated to a hostel put in special requests to the warden. Given the floor plan of the vacant rooms, select the allocation plan that will accommodate all their requests.

Request by X : Due to pollen allergy, I want to avoid a wing next to the garden.

Request by Y : I want to live as far from the washrooms as possible, since I am very sensitive to smell.

Request by Z : I believe in Vaastu and so want to stay in the South-west wing.

The shaded room are already occupied. WR is washroom.

(a)

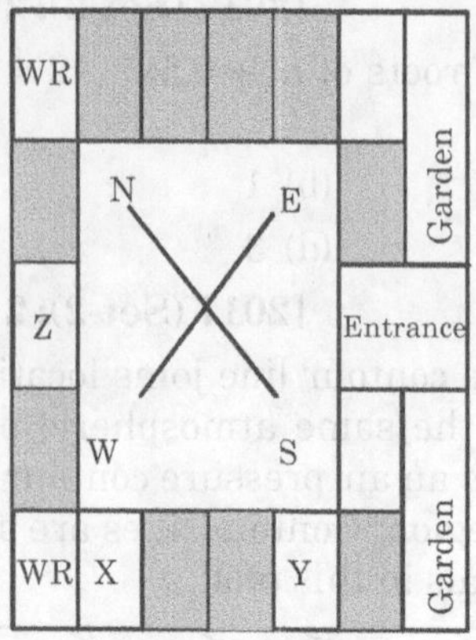

(b)

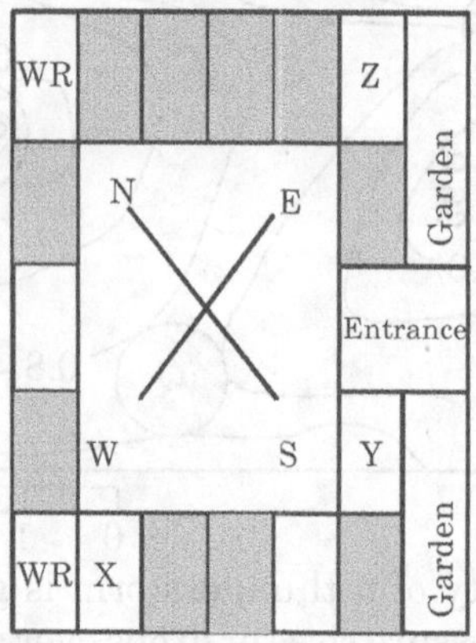

(c)

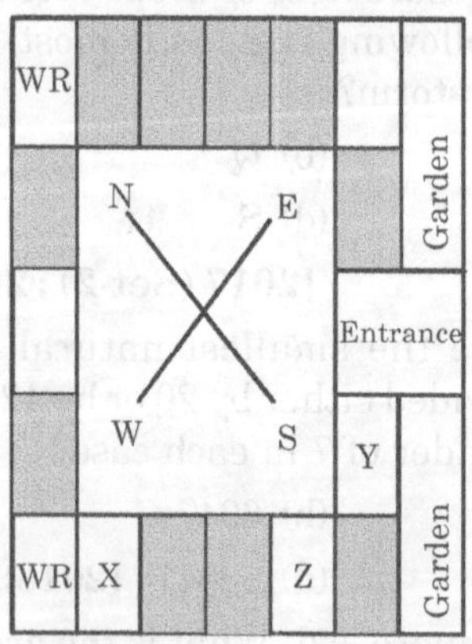

(d)

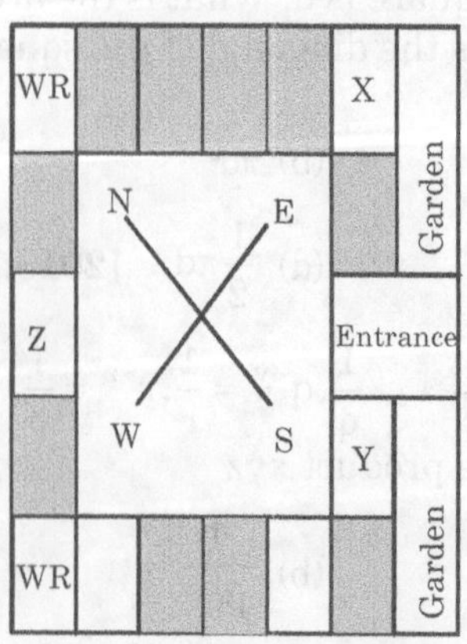

[2019 : 2 Marks]

ANSWERS

1. (b) 2. (a) 3. (d) 4. (c) 5. (c) 6. (a) 7. (c) 8. (b) 9. (b) 10. (c)
11. (b) 12. (a) 13. (a) 14. (a) 15. (d) 16. (b) 17. (a) 18. (a) 19. (c) 20. (a)
21. (b) 22. (c) 23. (c) 24. (c) 25. (b) 26. (a) 27. (b) 28. (a) 29. (b) 30. (d)
31. (d) 32. (c) 33. (c) 34. (b) 35. (c) 36. (a) 37. (c) 38. (b) 39. (c) 40. (c)
41. (c) 42. (d) 43. (c) 44. (c) 45. (b) 46. (a) 47. (b) 48. (d) 49. (a) 50. (a)
51. (d) 52. (b) 53. (a) 54. (d) 55. (d) 56. (c) 57. (d) 58. (b) 59. (b) 60. (d)
61. (c) 62. (b) 63. (a) 64. (c) 65. (b) 66. (c) 67. (b) 68. (a) 69. (c) 70. (a)
71. (a) 72. (c) 73. (b) 74. (a) 75. (b) 76. (b) 77. (b) 78. (c) 79. (d) 80. (c)
81. (d) 82. (c) 83. (d) 84. (a) 85. (a) 86. (b) 87. (b) 88. (a) 89. (d) 90. (c)
91. (d) 92. (b) 93. (b) 94. (d) 95. (a) 96. (c) 97. (d) 98. (a) 99. (b) 100. (b)
101. (c) 102. (c) 103. (b) 104. (d) 105. (c) 106. (a) 107. (96) 108. (d) 109. (*) 110. (48)
111. (6) 112. (b) 113. (c) 114. (d) 115. (140 to 140) 116. (a) 117. (c) 118. (d) 119. (c)
120. (c) 121. (a) 122. (c) 123. (32) 124. (d) 125. (c) 126. (b) 127. (8) 128. (c) 129. (b)
130. (2006) 131. (c) 132. (b) 133. (b) 134. (b) 135. (b) 136. (a) 137. (c) 138. (c)
139. (c) 140. (d) 141. (c) 142. (b) 143. (b) 144. (d) 145. (a) 146. (c) 147. (c) 148. (c)
149. (d) 150. (c) 151. (b) 152. (a) 153. (c) 154. (b) 155. (b) 156. (a) 157. (c) 158. (b)
159. (d) 160. (c)

EXPLANATIONS

1. **Circuitous** means round about or not direct
   So circuitous : indirect.
2. A worker is one who has skills but can be without work or unemployed. Similarly, fallow land is land that is ploughed but but left without being sown.
3. Since the sentence is about natural resources, 'conserve' would be the best word, especially since the sentence says that by doing so, we would leave a better planet for our children. Cherish comes close, but since it means to feel love for, conserve is the better word to apply to resources.
4. Betrayed, **means** 'showed' or revealed.
5. Use of chemical agents in warfare would be undesirable.
6. Inexplicable means not explicable; that cannot be explained, understood, or accounted for. So the best synonym here is incomprehensible.
7. Contemplate is a transitive verb and hence is followed by a gerund Hence the correct usage of contemplate is verb + ing form.
8. Tone of the sentence clearly indicates a word that is similar to understated is needed for the blank. Alternatively, word should be antonym of strong (fail to make strong impression). Therefore, best choice is restrained which means controlled / reserved / timid.
9. Amalgamate means combine or unite to form one organization or structure. So the best option here is split. Separate on the other hand, although a close synonym, it is too general to be the best antonym in the given question while Merge is the synonym; Collect is not related.
10. The given passage clearly deals with how to deal with bereavement and grief and so after the tragedy occurs and not about precautions. Therefore, irrespective of the causes of death, a school student rarely gets into details of causes—which is beyond the scope of the context. Rest all are important in dealing with grief.
11. The word despite tells us that mission succeeded even though there were problems. Hence the correct answer is Setbacks.
12. 'Mitigate' means to make something less harmful, serious, intense etc. Hence correct answer is 'Diminis'
13. There is an unnecessary 'to' in the sentence.
14. The relative pronouns 'that' or 'which' can be used to refer to a dog. However, in this sentence, the last part of the sentence is a description of the dog and therefore a necessary clause, so, the relative pronoun 'that' should be used. The relative pronoun 'which' is generally preceded by a comma and indicates unnecessary or additional information.
15. The post mentions "persons" meaning any gender hence option (d) is the correct option.
    Xenophobic means having or showing an intense or irrational dislike or fear of people from other countries, so option (b) can be ruled out.
    Options (a) and (c) are clearly out of scope.

16. Given: A word "Nadir"

To find: Closest meaning word to 'Nadir' in the given options.

Analysis: The dictionary meaning of 'Nadir' is 'Lowest' which is potion (*b*)

Source: Google

Given: A sequence 44, 42, 40,......

To find: Maximum sum of the sequence

Analysis: To find the maximum sum, we have to ignore all the negative terms (they will only decrease the sum). Hence, we terminate the sequence at 0.

Now, the sequence is 44, 42,......,2, 0.

This sequence is an Arithmetic progression with common difference –2. Now, the problem reduces to finding the sum of this A.P.

To find the sum of A.P., we have to find the number of terms in A.P.

Let n be the number of terms

a be the first term

l be the last term

d be the common difference.

$n = ?$

$a = 44, \quad l = 0, \quad d = -2$

Now, $l = a + (n-1)d$

17. The relationship between 'universalism' and 'particularism' is that of opposites. 'Specificity' is the closest antonym for 'diffuseness', which means to be spread out.

18. The sentence is a conditional sentence, which has a fixed structure. The first part of the sentence should have the verb in the past tense (were) and the second part of the sentence should have would+verb in the simple present tense (fly).

19. The word 'European' is pronounced with a consonant sound, so, it should be preceded by 'a' and not 'an'.

20. The story mentions success and failure on the part of the spider and Bruce. It also ends by stating that Bruce went back and won his war. While the overall story also contains a message about not losing hope, Option d states that 'no' adversity justifies giving up hope, which may be an extreme statement. Option a is better supported by the story.

21. The phrase 'cope with' means to deal with. 'Adapt to' means to adjust to, so the closest in meaning would be Option b. Adept means skilled, so it is irrelevant here. So are Options a and d.

22. The word in the blank ought to be a negative one, since the sentence states that he could not understand the judges awarding her the first prize. If so, he must have thought that her performance was not great. 'Mediocre', which means not satisfactory, or inferior, suits the blank. Options a and d are positive, so, they do not fit into the blank. 'Medium' cannot be used to describe a performance.

23. The phrase means that responsibility will not be passed on. So, Option c is right.

24. The passage gives us information about the Palghat Gap and the regions around it and the impact of the Gap on those regions. Option a reverses the information in the passage by stating that the Gap is caused by the weather conditions in the neighbouring regions. Option b also contradicts the passage by stating that the neighbouring regions are low-lying, when the passage states that there is hilly terrain to the north and south of the Gap. Option d connects two separate points from the passage. So, option c is correct.

25. The conclusion in the passage is that the geneticists think that they will be able to eradicate these diseases through identification and gene therapy. This is based on the premise that they can identify the genetic roots of certain psychiatric illnesses. So, the assumption here is that certain psychiatric illnesses have a genetic basis. Options c and d are extreme. Option a does not mention the specific strategy, which is gene therapy.

26. The phrase 'post-colonial' means of or relating to the period following a state of colonialism. So, Option a is correct.

27. Option a is grammatically incorrect. The interrogative pronoun (who) must be followed by the helping verb (did) + subject (you)+ main verb (say). Option c has an unnecessary 'that'. Option d has the wrong tense (past perfect tense).

28. Option a has the right combinations.

29. The passage provides us with information about Kaliningrad's earlier name and population and the present name and population. It also tells us about the boundaries. It doesn't give us information about the ethnic history, so Option a cannot be inferred. Nor is there any information about whether the name was originally Russian, so Option c is also incorrect. The passage tells us about another boundary of Kaliningrad, so, the route to Russia could also be via that. So, Option b is correct, because the passage tells us that Kaliningrad is now Russian territory.

30. Among given option, option (*d*) *i.e.* the number of people with malarial fever has increased this year do not contradic the conclusion.

31. The correct version of 'd' is 'lost consciousness'. The past continuous tense is unnecessary, since it was not a continuous process. The other verb in the sentence (fell) is in the simple past, so this verb should also be in the simple past tense.

32. The sentence is a past conditional one, which has a fixed structure. The conditional part of the sentence has the verb in the past perfect tense (had known) and the main part of the sentence has could/would + verb in the present perfect tense (have done).

33. The word coherent means logically connected or consistent. So, rambling, which means wandering aimlessly, will be the one most opposite in meaning. Well-connected would be close in meaning. Options a and d are irrelevant.

34. Option (a) is not the appropriate instruction as only the participating students and their parents have to come at 9.00 a.m. and other students along with their parents have to come at 10.00 a.m., while the statement in (a) says that all students should come at 9.00 a.m. and all the parents should come at 10.00 a.m.

(b) is the most appropriate instruction and covers all the aspects of the information to be conveyed.

(c) is not the appropriate instruction as the non participating students have to come at 10.00 a.m. with their parents, while the statement in (b) says that these students have to come without their parents.

(d) also is not the appropriate instruction as it states that the participating students have to come before 9.00 a.m. whereas they have to come at 9.00 a.m.

35. The words 'paradigm shift' and 'clinching evidence' point to Options i and iv. ii cannot be inferred, since the passage only states that by the beginning of the 20th century, several hypotheses were being proposed. We cannot generalize about all centuries. The position of a star provided important information in this case, but we cannot generalize from this information that stars are important objects in the universe, so Statement iii cannot be inferred.

36. The correct phrase is 'any paper'. 'Paper' is an uncountable noun, so we cannot use 'a few' with it. The sentence seems to refer to a newspaper, so 'much paper' would be incorrect. There is already a negative at the beginning of the sentence (didn't), so 'no paper' is also incorrect.

37. Options a, b and d are negative. Since the sentence states that she enjoyed herself immensely, Option c is correct.

38. Acquiescence and Submission both mean agreement. Flippancy and lightness are also synonymous. So are Profligate and Extravagant, which mean wasteful. Roundabout means circuitous or indirect, as a road, journey, method, statement or person. Wheedle means to endeavor to influence (a person) by smooth, flattering, or beguiling words or acts.

39. To take to one's heels means to run away. So, Option c is correct.

40. Options b and d are incorrect because 'forgot completely' is incorrect usage. Option a is incorrect because the adverb 'just' should come before the verb, not in between.

41. The word 'personnel' means a body of persons employed in an organization or place of work. In Options a, b and d, the word should have been personal, which means individual or private.

42. This is the correct term for clothing. Textile and fabric refer to cloth.

43. All the other sentences are incorrect because the word 'needed' should be preceded by 'the' to refer to 'necessary' or 'required' information. (This option is also incorrect because the word 'real' is incorrect. It should be 'really').

44. John-Abraham starrer Madras Cafe talks about the movie not the person, so Mr. is ruled out.

'Find no takers' is not the correct phrase. At this Friday is incorrect.

So, option (*c*) is correct.

45. Extraneous -irrelevant or unrelated to the subject being dealt with.

46. Options c and d cannot be inferred since there isn't enough information. Option b seems likely but the tone of the option is different from that of the passage. The phrase 'not willing to rest on his laurels' means that he was ambitious and wanted to achieve more. But the tone of the passage is practical. Option a is directly related to the cause-effect relationship brought about by the the word 'since' in the passage. The word is significant because it conveys the idea that Alexander turned his attention to India because he had conquered Persia implying that he would not have done so otherwise. Option a conveys that.

47. Statement iv is extreme. There is no information in the passage to show that success is guaranteed. Statement i clearly contradicts the passage, which states that unless he worked on his problem, he would not achieve success at the highest level.

48. Options a and b have a double negative (will not and doesn't meet). Option c has a subject-verb agreement error in the form of 'meet'.

49. Paradox means a self-contradictory and false proposition. Paradigm means an example serving as a model; pattern. Paraffin means a white or colorless, tasteless, odorless, water-insoluble, solid substance used in candles.

50. A figurative sentence is of the nature of or involves a figure of speech, especially a metaphor or comparison. Archimedes does not mean that he will actually move the world but is making a point by using that example. A figurine is a small statue. Collateral means subordinate or additional. Literal means the opposite of figurative.

51. Options a and b are extreme. The passage states that there is space on the notes for at least seventeen languages, so Option c is extereme.

52. Options a and d are incorrect because the usage of the definite article makes it seem as if there were only one security guard. Option c is wrong because 'university' should be preceded by an article.

53. From the given underlined phrase <u>copewith</u> means put up with.

54. Statement ii is very clearly contradicted by the passage, which says that the internet is believed to be an unintended consequence of the original invention. Statement i is extreme. The author only says that one is left wondering whether all these developments are good or required.

55. The given statement – "All hill-stations have a lake" – doesn't say that any place having a lake is surely a hill station. Thus, Ooty may or may not be a hill station and Hence (i) is false.

Statement (ii) is false because it is not a compulsion that a place needs to have exactly one lake to be a hill station.

Therefore, neither (i) nor (ii) follows.

56. The first verb (returned) in the sentence is in the simple past tense, so, the other verb must also be in the past tense or the past perfect tense. The past perfect tense is used only if the action conveyed by it is the earlier action in the sequence. In this sentence, the action conveyed by the verb in the blank happens after the action conveyed by the first verb, so, the simple past tense is correct.

57. Options a and c are incorrect because the word 'besides' should be placed before the word 'money'. Beside means next to and besides means apart from. The sentence states that people work for many reasons . Money is one of the reasons. So, besides fits into the blank.

58. Option a goes beyond the scope of the passage. Option c is extreme. Option d leaves out information from the passage and twists the passage. The author establishes a connection between nationalism and history. So, Option b is correct.

59. Saturn is bright enough to be seen on a clear night with the naked eye.

$\therefore$ Option (*b*) is correct

60. Yielding and resistant are antonyms.

61. The author's belief that ideology is not as important as literature is revealed by the word 'urgent' in above paragraph.

$\therefore$ Option (*c*) is correct.

62. They're used for pointing group.

Their is pointing people.

There is used for place.

63. Meandering : wandering aimlessly/indirect.

64. Court is a place where a judge works.

Similarly, school is a place where a teacher works.

65. Fulcrum is any thing that plays a central or an essential role in an activity, event, or situation.

Hence among the given options, 'revolves' is the most appropriate.

66. The passage states that the underlying disease behind begging is the failure of the state to protect citizens who fall through the social security net.

Only option (b) can be inferred from this.

67. $H + G > I + S$ ...(1)

and $G - S = 1$ ...(2)

G is not oldest, S is not youngest

$\therefore$ $H + 1 > I$

Irfan older than Hari

Gita older than Sarita

From given option SGHI

68.

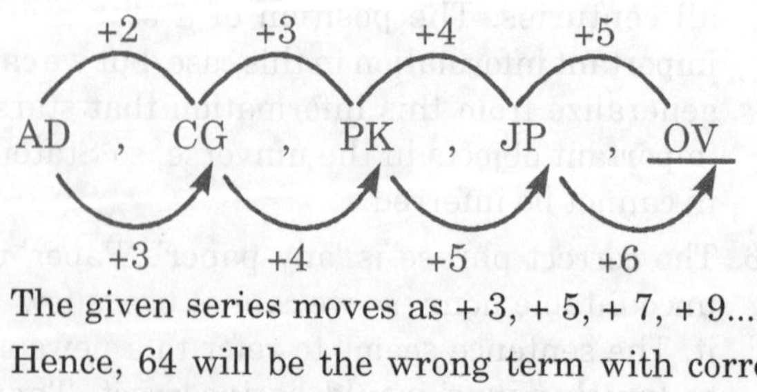

69. The given series moves as + 3, + 5, + 7, + 9....

Hence, 64 will be the wrong term with correct term as 50 + 15 = 65.

70. When we climb from one floor to other, it is the height that matters and not the width of the staircase. Therefore, from statement (I) alone, we can determine that 9/ (0.75) = 12 steps are required.

71. Option (a) is the correct asnwer because 3rd course of action is in-correct. Banning water supply in the lower areas only can not solve the problem.

72. Either of the two statements is sufficient to answer the question alone.

73. Take the values of P, R, S, T and U as 2, 4, 6, 8 and 10. Accordingly, 1 and 2 will become an AP while 3 will be ruled out.

74.

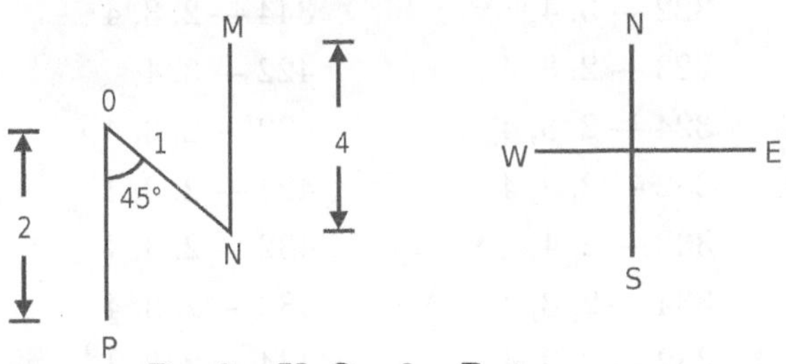

75. R + 3 = U, O + 3 = R,

A + 3 = D, D + 3 = G;

S + 3 = V, W + 3 = Z,

A + 3 = D, N + 3 = Q

76. Community of people : Doctor

77. Since U does not want any portfolio, (*c*) and (*d*) are ruled out. R wants Home, or Finance or No portfolio, (*a*) is not valid.

Hence option (*b*) is correct.

78. From the words given, 'taga' seems to mean 'care'. In all the words given, care appears first but taga appears towards the end of the word. So, for 'aftercare', 'taga' should appear first. That leaves us with options b and c. 'Fer' appears in the word for careless, so Option c is correct.

79. All three can Beat S, but S loses to P only sometimes. So, (ii) can not be inferred from the given statements.

Defeating in Poker is not transitive. P beats Q, Q beats R and R beats S. Yet S loses to P only sometimes, meaning that S mostly wins against P. So we can not logically infer that P is likely to beat R.

80. Given words 'mock, deride and jeer' are synonyms which means mockery. So, the given word praise is odd one.

81. C A D B E, J H K I L

+1 +1 +1 +1 +1 +1

X V Y W Z, O N P M Q

+1 +1 +1 +1 +1 −1

So, option (d) is odd one from the given group.

82. Srinivas and Murali will be seated opposite to each other.

83. Arun can wear one among Pink, Blue and White shirts and Shweta can wear one among Red, Pink and Blue shirts. Gulab and Neil can wear remaining of the two shirts in two ways by interchanging for every unique set of combination of Arun and Shweta.

Therefore, total number of ways

$= (1 \times 2 + 1 \times 2 + 1 \times 3) \times 2 = 14$ combinations.

84. There are atleast Two Men and Two Women and atleast 3 Right Handed persons with no women being right handed. Which means the number of women can be either 2 or 3.

Now, if there are 3 women and 3 men then the 3 women will have to sit together but the person to the immediate right of the 3rd woman will have to be left handed which contradicts the given condition.

Hence, the number of woman will be 2.

85. From the given condition of sequence we get following order of building in

X, Z, V, W, Y

Hence 'V' building is in the middle

∴ Option (*a*) is correct.

86. The box labelled 'Apples and Oranges' will be the correct option because it can't have both apples and oranges as all the three labels are wrong.

Thus, if I pick up an apple then it means that the mixed fruits are labelled as orange and oranges are labelled as apple.

Same will be the case when I will pick up an orange.

87. 2, 12, 60, 240, 720, 1440, 1440, 0

(2×6), (12×5), (60×4), (240×3), (720×2), (1440×1), (1440×0)

−1 −1 −1 −1 −1 −1

So, 1440 must be answer.

88. Suffix C as criminal, NC as not criminal.

Case I :

Criminals	P	Q	R	S
Assumption	T	F	F	F
Result	Q_C	S_{NC}	R_C	S_C

Q and R are criminal in the result is impossible because only one person committed the crime.

Case II :

Criminals	P	Q	R	S
Assumption	F	F	T	F
Result	Q_{NC}	S_{NC}	R_{NC}	S_C

S_{NC} and S_C in the result which is contradiction. [S committed crime and same time not committed crime which is contradiction]

Case III :

Criminals	P	Q	R	S
Assumption	F	T	F	F
Result	Q_{NC}	S_C	R_C	S_C

S and R are criminal in the result is impossible because only one person committed the crime.

Case IV :

Criminals	P	Q	R	S
Assumption	F	F	F	T
Result	Q_{NC}	S_{NC}	R_C	S_{NC}

R is criminal in the result.

Hence this case satisfies only one person committed the crime.

So option (a) is correct.

89. The number of persons playing neither hockey nor football

$$= 25 - (15 + 17 - 10) = 3.$$

90.

$$\begin{array}{rl} 137 - & \overline{001}\ \overline{011}\ \overline{111} \\ +276 - & 010\ \ 111\ \ 110 \\ \hline & 100\ \ 011\ \ 101 = 435 \end{array}$$

Octal number system

$$\begin{array}{rl} \therefore\ 731 - & 111\ \ 011\ \ 001 \\ 672 - & 110\ \ 111\ \ 110 \\ \hline & 100\ \ 010\ \ 011 \end{array}$$

Hence 1623

91. 5 skilled workers build wall in 20 days

1 skilled worker build wall in 20 × 5 days

Hence in 1 day, part of work done by skilled work

$$= \frac{1}{100}$$

Similarly in 1 day part of work done by semi-skilled workers

$$= \frac{1}{25 \times 8}$$

and in 1 day part of work done by un-skilled worker

$$= \frac{1}{30 \times 10}$$

So part of work done in 1 day by 2 skilled, 6 semi-skilled and 5 unskilled

$$= \frac{2}{100} + \frac{6}{200} + \frac{5}{300} = \frac{1}{15}$$

So work done by given workers in days = 15

92. 2, 2, 3, 3, 4, 4, 4, 4 $x > 3000$

322 — 3, 4	344 — 2, 3, 4
323 — 2, 3, 4	422 — 3, 4
324 — 2, 3, 4	423 — 2, 3, 4
332 — 2, 3, 4	424 — 2, 3, 4
333 — 2, 4	432 — 2, 3, 4
334 — 2, 3, 4	433 — 2, 3, 4
342 — 2, 3, 4	434 — 2, 3, 4
343 — 2, 3, 4	442 — 2, 3, 4
	443 — 2, 3, 4
	444 — 2, 3, 4

93. $\log P = \frac{1}{2} \log Q = \frac{1}{3} \log (R) = k$

$\therefore\ P = b^k, Q = b^{2k}, R = b^{3k}$

Hence, $Q^2 = b^{4k} = b^{3k}\, b^k = PR$

94. By observation of the table, we can say S

	P	Q	R	S
Requirement	800	600	300	200
Potency	0.4	0.5	0.4	0.8

95. In such questions the best method is to check the options. In this case at q = 5 we get V = F = 20 thereby getting the minimum value of V + F.

96. Let each truck can take at most x units. Let the daily order be y and the backlog be z units.

$\Rightarrow\quad 7 \times 4 \times x = 4y + z \quad$ ...(i)

and $\quad 3 \times 10 \times x = 10y + z \quad$ ...(ii)

Now, we need the value of $\frac{5y + z}{5x}$ in terms of x.

Subtracting (i) from (ii) we get:

$$y = \frac{x}{3}$$

Now substituting the value of y in (i) we get:

$$\frac{4x}{3} + z = 28x$$

$\Rightarrow z = \frac{80x}{3}$

Hence, the value of $\frac{5y+z}{5x} = \frac{\frac{5x+80x}{3}}{5} = \frac{85x}{15x} \approx 6$

Therefore, 6 days will be required.

97. $10\left(\frac{10-1}{10}\right)^3 = 10\left(\frac{9}{10}\right)^3 = \frac{729}{1000}$

$\therefore \frac{729}{1000} \times 1 = 7.29$ litres

98. $P = 50q - 5q^2$

$\frac{dp}{dq} = 50 - 10q;\ \frac{d^2p}{dq^2} < 0$

$\therefore$ p is maximum at $50 - 10q = 0$ or, $q = 5$

Else check with options

99. $y = 2x - 0.1x^2;\ \frac{dy}{dx} = 2 - 0.2x;\ \frac{d^2y}{dx^2} < 0$

$\therefore$ y maximises at $2 - 0.2x = 0$

$\Rightarrow x = 10$

$\therefore$ $y = 20 - 10 = 10$m

100.

	X	Y
Supply	60%	40%
Reliable	96%	72%
Overall	0.576	0.288

$\therefore \quad P(x) = \frac{0.288}{0.576 + 0.288} = 0.334$

101. P and R always holds true

Else consider a sample set {1, 2, 3, 4} and check accordingly

102. $0 = 44 + (n-1)(-2)$

$n - 1 = 22$

$n = 23$

Sum $= \frac{n}{2}(a + l)$

$= \frac{23}{2}(44 + 0)$

$= 23 \times 22 = 506$

Hence (c) is the answer

103. Given: The expression

$$S = \frac{1}{\sqrt{1}+\sqrt{2}} + \frac{1}{\sqrt{2}+\sqrt{3}} + \ldots\ldots + \frac{1}{\sqrt{80}+\sqrt{81}}$$

To find: Sum of the expression.

Analysis: Each term of the expression is having irrational denominator. One can also see, that both the elements in the denominator of a term differ by only 1.

This gives an idea that on rationalising the denominator, each denominator will become 1, so the sum will be easier than earlier.

Rationalising the denominator,

$$S = \frac{\sqrt{2}-\sqrt{1}}{(\sqrt{2})^2-(\sqrt{1})^2} + \frac{\sqrt{3}-\sqrt{2}}{(\sqrt{3})^2-(\sqrt{2})^2} + \ldots + \frac{\sqrt{81}-\sqrt{80}}{(\sqrt{81})^2-(\sqrt{80})^2}$$

$$= \frac{\sqrt{2}-\sqrt{1}}{1} + \frac{\sqrt{3}-\sqrt{2}}{3-2} + \ldots. + \frac{\sqrt{81}-\sqrt{80}}{81-80}$$

$$= \sqrt{2}-\sqrt{1}+\sqrt{3}-\sqrt{2}+\ldots.+81-\sqrt{80}$$

Now, one can see that the terms will cancel out.

Each term except $\sqrt{1}$ & $\sqrt{81}$

Occurs twice, once as positive and once a negative. So, after cancelling out, we are left with the following:

$$S = \sqrt{81} - \sqrt{1} = 9 - 1 = 8$$

So, the answer is (b).

104. Given: All the 2-digit numbers

To find: Probability of selecting a number at random not divisible by 7

Analysis: Total number of 2-digit numbers

10, 11, ..., 99 → 90 numbers

Unfavourable numbers *i.e.* numbers divisible by

7 : 14, 21, ..., 98

Number of unfavourable numbers = 13

This can be hand counted or we can use the following properties:

Last term = First time + (no. – 1) Diff

98 = 14 + (no. – 1) 7

$\Rightarrow$ no. = 13

$\Rightarrow$ Probability $= \frac{\text{Total} - \text{unfavourable}}{\text{Total}}$

$= \frac{90-13}{90} = 77/90$

Hence, the solution is (d)

105. Given: A tourist covers half the journey at 60 km/h, one fourth at 30 km/h and the remaining one fourth at 10 km/h

To find: Avearge speed of the whole journey.

Analysis: One approach to this is to find individual time consumed in each of the three parts and use that value to get total time, and find average speed.

So,

Lets assume total length of journey = x km

$\therefore$ First phase at 60 km/h

$$\text{Time } t_1 = \frac{\text{Distance}}{\text{Speed}} = \frac{x}{2}\frac{1}{60} = \frac{x}{120}\,h$$

Second phase at 30 km/h

$$\text{Distance} = \frac{x}{4}\text{ km}$$

$$\text{Time } t_2 = \frac{x}{4.30} = \frac{x}{120}$$

Third phase at 10 km/h

$$\text{Distance} = \frac{x}{4}\text{ km}$$

$$\text{Time } t_3 = \frac{x}{4.10} = \frac{x}{40}h$$

$$\therefore \quad \text{Total time} = \frac{x}{120}+\frac{x}{120}+\frac{x}{40} = \frac{x}{40}\left(\frac{1}{3}+\frac{1}{3}+1\right)$$

$$= \frac{x}{40}\frac{(1+1+3)}{3} = \frac{5x}{120}$$

$$\therefore \text{Average speed} = \frac{\text{Total Distance}}{\text{Total time}}$$

$$= \frac{x\cdot 120}{5x} = 24 \text{ km}/h$$

Hence, the answer is (c)

106. Let 'd' be the # of days required

Let 'h' be the daily working hours.

$\therefore$ dh can be taken as a measure of the total work be done in order to erect the structure.

Now working hours per day $h' = \frac{23}{24}h$

$$\therefore \text{ \# of days} \quad d' = \frac{dh}{h'} = \frac{dh}{\left(\frac{23}{24}h\right)} = \frac{24}{23}d$$

Let $\quad c$ = daily wages earlier

$$\therefore \quad c = \frac{13,200}{d}$$

Now daily wages $c' = \frac{6}{5}c$

$\therefore$ Total new cost = $c' \times d'$

$$= \frac{6}{5}\times\frac{13200}{d}\times\frac{24}{23}d \approx 16,500$$

107. Expanding

$$\left(z+\frac{1}{z}\right)^2 = 98$$

$$\therefore \quad z^2+\frac{1}{z^2}+2(z)\left(\frac{1}{z}\right) = 98$$

$$\therefore \quad z^2+\frac{1}{z^2} = 96$$

108. $ax^2 + bx + c = 0$

Roots are real and positive

$$\therefore \quad b^2 - 4ac > 0$$

By the above condition we get two positive real roots

Now, $ax^2 + b|x| + c = 0$

This can be written as;

$ax^2 + bx + c$

$$\Delta = b^2 - 4ac > 0$$

Now for $ax^2 - bx + c$

$$(-b)^2 - 4ac$$

$$\Rightarrow \quad b^2 - 4ac$$

Again $b^2 - 4ac > 0$

So again we get real roots

Thus we have 4 real roots of $ax^2 + b|x| + c = 0$

109. Round-trip tickets' fare for one person = Rs. 200 and that of 5 persons = Rs. 1000.

Hence, net discount percent = 15% and thus the required amount to be charged = Rs. 850.

110. Total respondents = 300

Now men respondents who do not have scooter

$$= 40 + 20 = 60$$

And women respondents who do not have scooter

$$= 34 + 50 = 84$$

$\therefore$ Total respondents who do not have scooter

$$= 60 + 84 = 144$$

$$\therefore \text{Required percent} = \left(\frac{144}{300}\times 100\right)\% = 48\%$$

111. A tetrahedron has 4 triangular surfaces with 4 vertices or corners – let's say A, B, C and D.

If we take a point inside the tetrahedron as O and connect it with any two of its corners A and B we will get 1 internal plane as OAB.

Similarly, we can take any other 2 corners like (A, C) or (A, D) or (B, C) or (B, D) or (C, D).

Hence, six new internal planes will be formed.

112. All multiples of 10 from 2 to 198

$$= 10, 20, \ldots\ldots\ldots\ldots 190$$

Now $\quad a_n = a + (n-1)d$

$$190 = 10 + (n-1)\times 10$$

$$180 = (n-1)\times 10$$

$$18 = n - 1$$

$$\therefore \quad n = 19$$

Hence total number of multiples are 19.

Now $\quad S_n = \frac{n}{2}[2a+(n-1)d]$

$$= \frac{19}{2}[20+(18)(10)]$$

$$= \frac{19}{2}[20+180] = 1900$$

Now average of all multiples of 10 from 2 to198

$$= \frac{10+20+...+190}{19}$$

$$\therefore \quad = \frac{1900}{19} = 100$$

113. $\sqrt{12+\sqrt{12+\sqrt{12+...}}}$

For a particular type of question

i.e. $\sqrt{a+\sqrt{a+\sqrt{a+...}}}$ we find a two consecutive number whose product is *a*. The greater number among the two consecutive number is the answer.

Here $a = 12$

i.e. $12 = 3 \times 4$
↓
greater number

Hence $\sqrt{12+\sqrt{12+\sqrt{12+...}}} = 4$

114. Here it is given that x is real

Now $|x^2 - 2x + 3| = 11$

$\Rightarrow x^2 - 2x + 3 = 11$ or $x^2 - 2x + 3 = -11$

For $x^2 - 2x + 3 = 11 \Rightarrow x^2 - 2x - 8 = 0$

$b^2 - 4ac = 4 - 4(1)(-8) = 36 > 0$

Hence roots are real.

and for $x^2 - 2x + 14 = 0$

$b^2 - 4ac = 4 - 4(1)(14) < 0$

Hence roots are imaginary

$\therefore$ The value of x is the root of $x^2 - 2x - 8 = 0$

Now $x = \frac{+2 \pm \sqrt{4 - 4(1)(-8)}}{2}$

$= \frac{2 \pm \sqrt{36}}{2} = \frac{2 \pm 6}{2}$

$\therefore \quad x = 4, -2.$

Now for $x = 4$,

$|-x^3 + x^2 - x| = |-64 + 16 - 4| = 52.$

and for $x = -2$

$|-x^3 + x^2 - x| = |+8 + 4 + 2| = 14$

Hence possible values of $|-x^3 + x^2 - x| = 14, 52$

115. In the question the monthly average rainfall chart for 50 years has been given.

Let us check the options.

(*i*) On average, it rains more in July than in December ⇒ correct.

(*ii*) Every year, the amount of rainfall in August is more than that in January.

⇒ may not be correct because average rainfall is given in the question.

(*iii*) July rainfall can be estimated with better confidence than February rainfall.

⇒ From chart it is clear the gap between 5 percentile and 95 percentile from average is higher in February than that in July ⇒ correct.

(*iv*) In August at least 500 mm rainfall

⇒ May not be correct, because its 50 year average.

So correct option (*b*) (*i*) and (*iii*).

116.

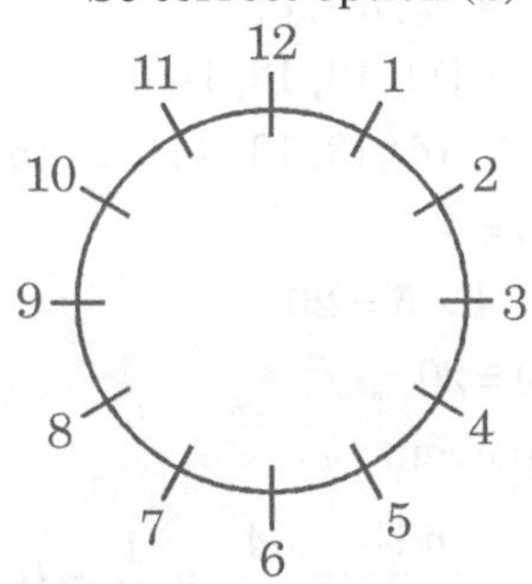

From option

At 6 a.m.

Both hand – 180° aparts,

At 6 : 20 a.m. – both hand apart

⇒ $180° + 10° - 120° = 70°$

At 6 : 22 a.m. – both hand apart

⇒ $180° + 12° - 132° = 60°$ (closest)

117. Total question

$44 \times 2 = 88$

$44 \times 3 = 132$

$\frac{144}{132} = \frac{88}{308}$

Total marks obtained = $(21\times2) + (15\times3) + (23\times2)$

$= 133$

Total Number of students = 44

Average $= \frac{133}{44} = 3.02$

118. Per ₹ 100 final value ₹ 107

⇒ per $\frac{100}{50}$ Dollars final value $\frac{107}{60}$

for 100 dollars ____?

$= \frac{100 \times 50}{100} \times \frac{107}{60} = 89.16$

Descreased by 11%

119. Take number of female students in 2011 = 100

$\therefore$ Number of male in 2011 = 100

No. of female in 2012 = 100

No. of male in 2012 = 150

Ratio $= \frac{150}{100}$

120. $(7526)_8 - (y)_8 = (4364)_8$

$\Rightarrow y_8 = (7526)_8 - (4364)_8$

$$\begin{array}{cccc} & 4 & (8+2=10) & \\ 7 & \not{5} & 2 & 6 \\ 4 & 3 & 6 & 4 \\ \hline 3 & 1 & 4 & 2 \\ \hline \end{array}$$

When we have base 8, we borrow 8 instead of 10 as done in normal subtraction.

121. Here the given sets are

$$A = \{2, 3, 4, 5\}$$

and $$B = \{11, 12, 13, 14, 15\}$$

desired outcome = {(2, 14), (3, 13), (4, 12), (5, 11)}

$\therefore$ $n(E) = 4$

and total outcome = 4 × 5 = 20

$\therefore$ $n(s) = 20$

$\therefore$ Probability of an event

$$= \frac{n(E)}{n(s)} = \frac{4}{20} = \frac{1}{5} = 0.2$$

122. Total number of students in class = 44

Average of marks,

$$= \frac{(2\times 21)+(3\times 15)+(1\times 11)+(2\times 23)+(5\times 31)}{42}$$

$$= \frac{42+45+11+46+155}{44} = \frac{299}{44} = 6.795$$

$\therefore$ Option (*c*) is correct.

123. According to question,

There are 40 males in Electrical Engg.

$\therefore$ Total number of females in Electrical Engg.

$$= 72 - 40 = 32$$

$\therefore$ Total number of students in Electrical Engg. = 72

$\Rightarrow$ 20% = 72

$\therefore$ 30% = Total number of students in Civil Engg.

$\therefore$ Total number of students in Civil Engg.

$$= \frac{30 \times 72}{20} = 36 \times 3 = 108$$

$\therefore$ Number of female students in Civil Engg.

$$= \frac{4 \times 108}{9} = 4 \times 12 = 48$$

Now, total number of students in Mechanical Engg.

$$= \frac{10 \times 72}{20} = 36$$

$\therefore$ Number of female students in Mechanical Engg.

$$= \frac{4 \times 36}{9} = 16$$

$\therefore$ Difference between female students in Civil and Mechanical departments = 48 − 16 = 32

124. Given that:

$1 - [(1 - m)(1 - p)(1 - c)] = 0.75$ ...(i)

and $(1 - m)pc + (1 - p)mc + (1 - c)mp + mpc = 0.5$ ...(ii)

and $(1 - m)pc + (1 - p)mc + (1 - c)mp = 0.4$ ...(iii)

From (ii) and (iii) we get: **mpc = 0.1**

Simplifying equation (i), we get:

$p + c + m - (mp + mc + pc) + mpc = 0.75$

or $p + c + m - (mp + mc + pc) = 0.65$ ...(iv)

Similarly, simplifying equation (iii) we get:

$pc + mc + mp - 3mpc = 0.4$

$\Rightarrow pc + mc + mp = 0.7$

Now, putting this value in (iv) we get:

$p + c + m - 0.7 = 0.65$

$\Rightarrow$ **p + c + m = 27/20.**

Hence, both relations 1 and 3 are true.

125. The given function is

$$f(x) = 1 - |x| \text{ on } -1 \le x \le 1$$

In order to find maximum and minimum value of function in interval [−1, 1]

At $x = -1$, $f(-1) = 1 - |-1| = 1 - 1 = 0$

At $x = -0.5$, $f(-0.5) = 1 - |-0.5| = 1 - 0.5 = 0.5$

At $x = 0$, $f(0) = 1 - |0| = 1$

At $x = 0.5$, $f(0.5) = 1 - |0.5| = 0.5$

At $x = 1$, $f(1) = 1 - |1| = 1 - 1 = 0$

$\therefore$ Hence, maximum value occurs at $x = 0$ and its maximum value is 1.

$\therefore$ Option (*c*) is correct.

126. Area of triangle PQR

= Area of triangle PQS + Area of triangle PRS

$\Rightarrow 0.5 \times rq \times \sin 120° = 0.5 \times rs \times \sin 60° + 0.5 \times qs \times \sin 60°$

$\Rightarrow 0.5 \times rq \times \mathbf{\cos 30°}$

$= 0.5 \times rs \times \sin 60° + 0.5 \times qs \times \sin 60°$

Hence, PS or $s = \dfrac{rq}{r+q}$

127. From the given graph function $f(x)$ must be equals to zero at $x = 3$.

From Option A :

$f(x) = 1 - |x - 1|$

at $x = 3$

$f(x) = 1 - |3 - 1| = 1 - 2 = -1$

So, it is false

From Option B :

$f(x) = 1 + |x - 1|$

at $x = 3$

$f(x) = 1 + |3 - 1| = 1 + 2 = 3$

So, it is false

From Option C :

$$f(x) = 2 - |x - 1|$$

at $x = 3$

$$f(x) = 2 - |3 - 1| = 2 - 2 = 0$$

So, it is true.

From Option D :

$$f(x) = 2 + |x - 1|$$

at $x = 3$

$$f(x) = 2 - |3 - 1| = 2 + 2 = 4$$

So, it is false.

Hence the correct expression for $f(x)$ given in the graph is $2 - |x - 1|$.

128. $f(x) = 2x + 33 = 2(5) + 33 = 43$

129. Taking x = 2 and y = – 1 and then putting in each of the four options, we get the correct option as

$$x = -(y - |y|).$$

130. Given, $|9y - 6| = 3$

It has two values either

$$(9y - 6) = 3 \quad ...(i)$$

Or $-(9y - 6) = 3$

$$9y - 6 = -3 \quad ...(ii)$$

From equation (*i*),

$$9y = 9$$

$$\therefore \quad y = 1$$

Or from equation (*ii*),

$$9y = 3$$

$$\therefore \quad y = \frac{1}{3}$$

Now $\quad y^2 = \frac{4y}{3}$

put $\quad y = 1,$

we get $\quad = 1 - \frac{4}{3} = -\frac{1}{3}$

and also put $\quad y = \frac{1}{3}$

we get, $\quad \frac{1}{9} - \frac{4}{9} = \frac{-3}{9} = \frac{-1}{3}$

So, the required value is $\frac{-1}{3}$.

131. Resultant surface area

$$= 4 \times 4 \times 6 - (1 \times 1 \times 3 \times 8)$$

$$= 72.$$

132. Revenue from Elegance

= (27300 + 25222 + 28976 + 21012) × Rs. 48

= Rs. 4920480

Revenue from Smooth

= (20009 + 19392 + 22429 + 18229) × Rs. 63

= Rs. 5043717

Revenue from Soft

= (17602 + 18445 + 19544 + 16595) × Rs. 78

= Rs. 5630508

Revenue from Executive

= (9999 + 8942 + 10234 + 10109) × Rs. 173

= Rs. 6796132

Thus, total Revenue = Rs. 22390837

Fraction of Revenue for Elegance = 0.219

Fraction of Revenue for Smooth = 0.225

Fraction of Revenue for Soft = 0.251

Fraction of Revenue for Executive = 0.303

Hence, option (b) i.e. Executive is the correct answer.

133. In the given equation i.e. $f(x) = 2x^7 + 3x - 5$

If we check each of the four options then we get that f(1) = 0 and thus we get the correct factor of f(x) as (x – 1).

134. For exponential dependence we must have functions of the form:

$f(x) = a \times k^x$: a and k are constants and f(0) = a

Let us assume: C = cycles for failure ; L = Load

According to the question C is an inverse exponential function of L

Hence we have:

$C = \frac{a}{k^L}$ (in case if C decreases exponentially

Now applying log to both sides of equation (ii) we get:

$$\log C + L(\log k) = \log a \quad ...(i)$$

Putting (C = 100 for L = 80) and (C = 10000 for L = 40) in equation (i) we get:

$$\log a = \log 100 + 80 \log k \quad ...(ii)$$

$$\log a = \log 10000 + 40 \log k \quad ...(iii)$$

Solving (ii) and (iii) we get:

$$\log a = 6 \text{ and } \log k = 1/20$$

Hence, $L = \frac{\log a - \log C}{\log k}$ for C = 5000 cycles

$$\Rightarrow \quad L = (6 - \log 5000) \times 20 = 46.0206$$

135. $\frac{\alpha^n + \beta^n}{\alpha^{-n} + \beta^{-n}} = \frac{\alpha^n + \beta^n}{\frac{1}{\alpha^n} + \frac{1}{\beta^n}} = \frac{\alpha^n + \beta^n}{\frac{\beta^n + \alpha^n}{\alpha^n \times \beta^n}} = \alpha^n \times \beta^n$

$$\alpha^n \times \beta^n = (\alpha \times \beta)^n = (4)^n$$

So, the value of $\frac{\alpha^n + \beta^n}{\alpha^{-n} + \beta^{-n}}$ is 4^n.

136. From question

Total number of faculty members = 150

The number of faculty members having facebook account = (FB) = 55

The number of faculty members having whatsapp = (W) = 85

The number of faculty members do not have face book or Whats App accounts = 30

The number of faculty members having any account = 150 – 30 = 120

The number of faculty members having both the accounts = (FB + W) – 120 = (55 + 85) – 120 = 20

$\therefore$ The number of faculty members connected only through Facebook accounts = 55 – 20 = 35

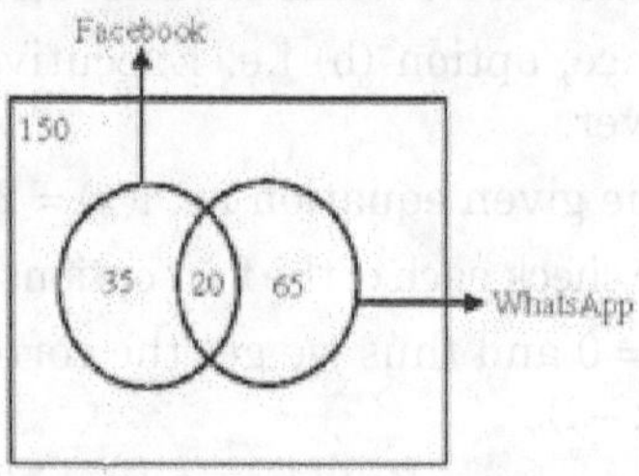

So the number of faculty members connected only through facebook accounts is 35.

137. In the given 2 × 4 rectangle grid, the following type of rectangles are present.

One figured rectangles = 8

Two figured rectangles = 10

Three figured rectangles = 4

Four figured rectangles = 5

Six figured rectangles = 2

Eight figured rectangles = 1

$\therefore$ Total number of rectangles

= 8 + 10 + 4 + 5 + 2 + 1 = 30

So the number of rectangles observed in the given grid is 30.

138. From the given graph function $f(x)$ must be equals to zero at $x = 3$.

From Option A :

$$f(x) = 1 - |x - 1|$$

at $x = 3$

$$f(x) = 1 - |3 - 1| = 1 - 2 = -1$$

So, it is false

From Option B :

$$f(x) = 1 + |x - 1|$$

at $x = 3$

$$f(x) = 1 + |3 - 1| = 1 + 2 = 3$$

So, it is false

From Option C :

$$f(x) = 2 - |x - 1|$$

at $x = 3$

$$f(x) = 2 - |3 - 1| = 2 - 2 = 0$$

So, it is true.

From Option D :

$$f(x) = 2 + |x - 1|$$

at $x = 3$

$$f(x) = 2 - |3 - 1| = 2 + 2 = 4$$

So, it is false.

Hence the correct expression for $f(x)$ given in the graph is $2 - |x - 1|$.

139. For k = 1, we have sample space = 10 and favorable digits excluding 0, 5, 9 will be 1, 2, 3, 4, 6, 7, 8.

Hence, required probability = 7/10 = 0.7.

140. $162 = 81 \times 2 = 27 \times 3 \times 2$

Hence, required number will be 6 × 6 = 36.

141. The following data gives the height of all the villages:

P = 575, Q = 525, R = 475, S = 425 and T = 500

Hence, the villages which will fall below the flood level will be R, S and T.

142. Take any value of (x, y) for example (5, 3), (4, –2), (–3, –2) and put it in the given expression

$$\frac{(x + y) - |(x - y)|}{2}$$

The answer will always be the minimum of x and y.

143. Let number of multiple choice question be 'x'

$\therefore$ Total number of essay type question = $20 - x$

Now according to question

$$x \times 3 + (20 - x)11 = 100$$

$$\therefore \quad 3x + 220 - 11x = 100$$

$$\therefore \quad 220 - 100 = 8x$$

$$\therefore \quad x = \frac{120}{8}$$

$$\therefore \quad x = 15$$

$\therefore$ Opation (b) is correct

144. $n(R) = 3$

$n(G) = 4$

$n(B) = 3$

Probability that 2 socks choosen are of both Red or Both Green or Both blue

$$\text{Same colour} = \frac{3}{10} \times \frac{2}{9} + \frac{4}{10} \times \frac{3}{9} + \frac{3}{10} \times \frac{2}{9}$$

$$= \frac{6}{90} + \frac{12}{90} + \frac{6}{10} = \frac{24}{90} = \frac{4}{15}$$

$\therefore$ Option (d) is correct.

145. $X = 4777....777$ (till 30 digits)

$\Rightarrow X = 4.777....777 \times 10^{29}$

$\Rightarrow X^3 = (4.777....777 \times 10^{29})^3$

$= (4.777....777)^3 \times 10^{87}$

Hence, X^3 will have 3 + 87(zeroes) = 90 digits.

146. $e^x + 0.5x^2 - 2 = 0$

Differention w.r.t to 'x' we get

$e^x + x = 0$

$\therefore$ Hence 'x' has total number of root which lies in the range [– 5,5] is '2'.

147. Since the air pressure variation is the main factor for the thunderstorm to occur, hence the region which has maximum number of lines crossing will depict the required region with a larger variance of air pressure. Therefore, as per the contour figure number of lines crossing region R is maximum, so R will be the answer.

148. Number is divided by either by 20 or 42 or by 76

K × LCM (20, 42, 76) + constant difference

= 7890 K + 7 (K is natural number)

Least number will be 7890 + 7 = 7897.

149.

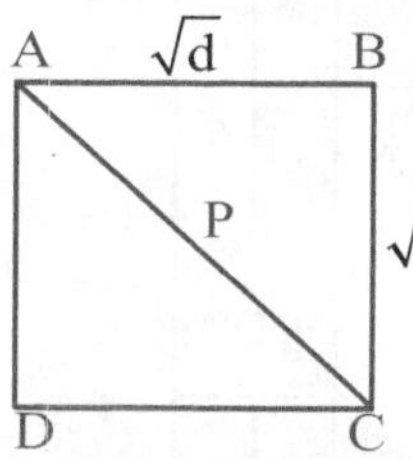

Area of square = d

Side one side of square = $\sqrt{d}$

Now Diagonal of square (AC) = $\sqrt{d+d} = \sqrt{2d}$

Now, Area of circle = πr^2

$$= \pi\left(\frac{\sqrt{2d}}{2}\right)^2 \quad \left(\because r = \frac{\text{diameter}}{2}\right)$$

$$= \pi\frac{d}{2}$$

$$= \frac{1}{2}\pi d$$

150. $p^x = q \Rightarrow x\log p = \log q$

and $q^y = r \Rightarrow y\log q = \log r$

and $z^2 = p \Rightarrow z\log r = \log p$

$$\therefore \quad xyz = \frac{\log q}{\log p}\times\frac{\log r}{\log q}\times\frac{\log p}{\log r} = 1$$

151. Male (M) + Female (F) = 300

$$\text{Total money} = \frac{8}{9}\text{M}\times 750 + \frac{2}{3}\text{F}\times 1000 \quad ...(i)$$

$$= \frac{6000}{9}\text{M} + \frac{6000}{9}\text{F} = \frac{6000}{9}(\text{M}+\text{F})$$

From equation (i) we get,

$$\text{Total money} = \frac{6000\times 300}{9} = 2,00,000$$

152.

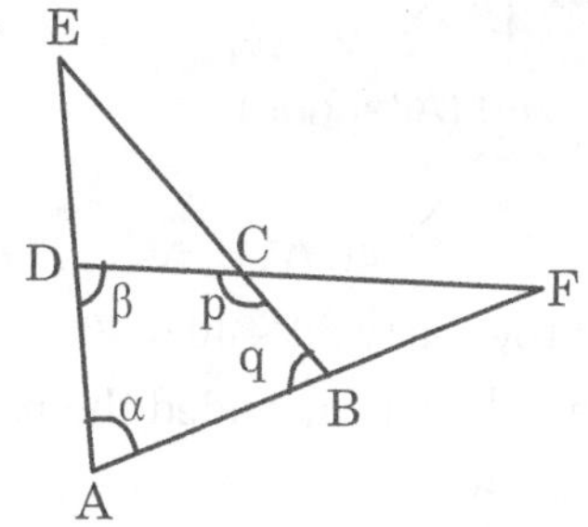

$\angle E + \angle F = ?$

$\alpha + q + E = 180$ ....(i)

and $\alpha + \beta + F = 180$ ....(ii)

and $\alpha + \beta + p + q = 360$ ....(iii)

Adding equations (i) and (ii) and equating it to (iii) we get

$\alpha + q + E + \alpha + \beta + F = \alpha + \beta + p + q$

$\therefore \quad E + F = p - \alpha$

153. Four green, two red face

$$P(G) = \frac{4}{6} = \frac{2}{3}$$

$$q(R) = 1 - P(G) = \frac{1}{3}$$

n = 7

Now from options

From option (a), $P(G=3) = {}^7C_3\left(\frac{2}{3}\right)^3\left(\frac{1}{4}\right)^4$

$$\frac{35\times 2^3}{(3)^7} = \frac{35\times 2^3}{(3)^7}$$

From option (b), $P(G=4) = {}^7C_4\left(\frac{2}{3}\right)^4\left(\frac{1}{3}\right)^3$

$$\frac{35\times 2^4}{(3)^7} = \frac{35\times 2^4}{(3)^7}$$

From option (c), $P(G=5) = {}^7C_5\left(\frac{2}{3}\right)^5\left(\frac{1}{3}\right)^2$

$$\frac{21\times 2^5}{(3)^7} = \frac{42\times 2^4}{(3)^7}$$

From option (d), $P(G=6) = {}^7C_6\left(\frac{2}{3}\right)^6\times\left(\frac{1}{3}\right)$

$$\frac{7\times 2^6}{(3)^7} = \frac{28\times 2^4}{(3)^7}$$

Option c is maximum value.

154. Let total number of people are 100.

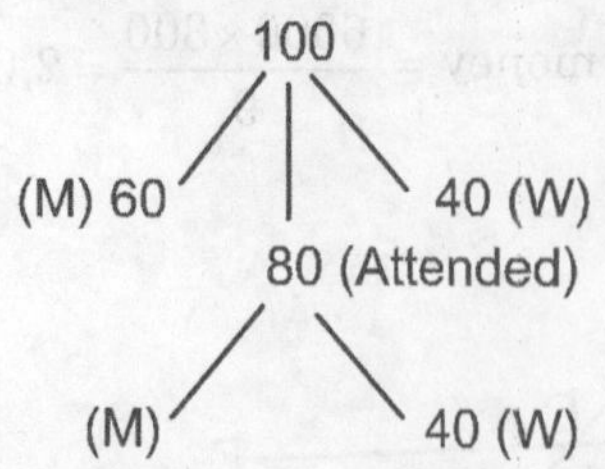

So, male attended the party 80 – 40 = 40

Ratio of male to female who attended the party

$$M : W = 40 : 40$$
$$= 1 : 1$$

155. Let share of each student be Rs. x

Now, cost of gift = $10 \times x$

According to question

$$x = 8(x + 150)$$
$$x = 600$$

$\therefore$ cost of gift = $10 \times 600 = (6000)$

156. Speed of 1st car = 50 km/hr

Speed of 2nd car = 60 km/hr

Since, both cars A and B are moving in same direction, the relative speed = (60 – 50) = 10 km/hr

Distance to be covered = 20 km

$$\therefore \text{ Time} = \frac{\text{Distance}}{\text{Speed}} = \frac{20}{10} = 2 \text{ hrs}$$

157. 'Breaks down' means to divide something such as a total amount into separate parts.

158. Percentage of Administrators

$$= \left[\frac{\text{Administrators}}{\text{Total number of people}} \times 100\right]\%$$

$$= \left[\frac{50}{160} \times 100\right]\% = 31.25\%$$

159. According to question, following venn diagram is formed

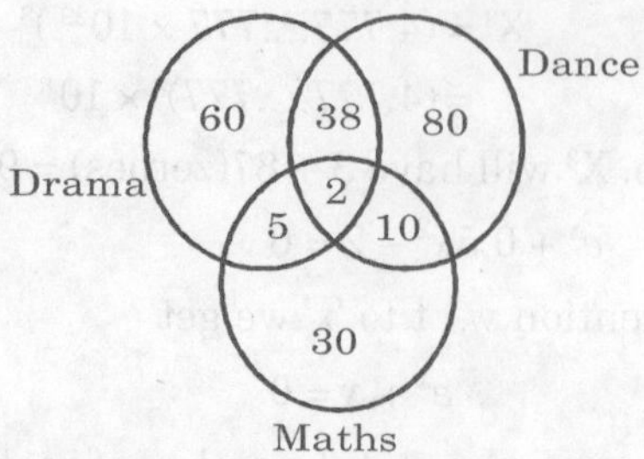

Total number of students = 60 + 80 + 30 + 38 + 5 + 10 + 2 = 225

$$25\% = 225$$

If $$25\% = 225$$

$$\therefore \quad 100\% = \frac{225}{25} \times 100 = 900$$

160. Request by Z : I believe in Vaastu and so want to stay in the South-west wing.

Among the given figures, only (c) is the one where Z get south-west wing.

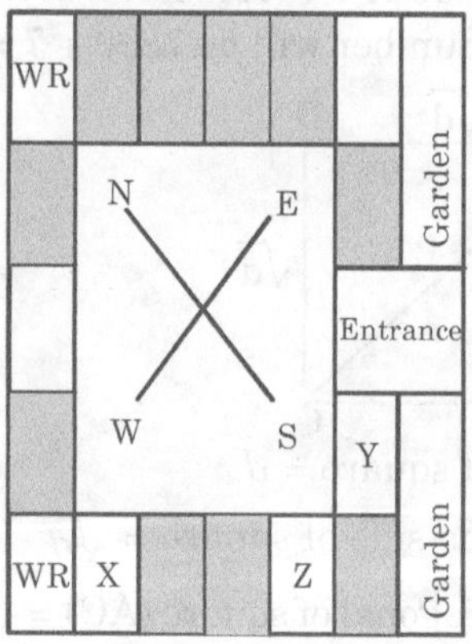